A Reader's
Hebrew-English Lexicon
of the Old Testament

A Reader's Hebrew-English Lexicon of the Old Testament

Four Volumes in One

Terry A. Armstrong

Douglas L. Busby

Cyril F. Carr

Regency
Reference Library
Zondervan Publishing House
Grand Rapids, Michigan

A Reader's Hebrew-English Lexicon of the Old Testament
Copyright © 1989 by the Zondervan Corporation Grand Rapids, Michigan

Regency Reference Library is an imprint of Zondervan Publishing House,
1415 Lake Drive, SE, Grand Rapids, Michigan 49506.

Library of Congress Cataloging in Publication Data

Armstrong, Terry A., 1944–
   A reader's Hebrew-English lexicon of the Old Testament : complete
  in one volume / Terry A. Armstrong, Douglas L. Busby, Cyril F. Carr.
     p.   cm.
   ISBN 0-310-36980-0
   1. Hebrew language—Dictionaries—English.   2. Hebrew language-
-Word Frequency.   3. Aramaic language—Dictionaries—English.
4. Aramaic language—Word frequency.   5. Bible.   O.T.   Hebrew-
-Glossaries, vocabularies, etc.   I. Busby, Douglas L., 1946–
II. Carr, Cyril F., 1949–82.   III. Title.
PJ4833.A69   1989

        221.4′4—dc20 89-10217
                CIP

Printed in the United States of America

89 90 91 92 93 94 95 / DH / 10 9 8 7 6 5 4 3 2 1

CONTENTS

PREFACE

A Reader's Hebrew-English Lexicon of the Old Testament is an attempt to meet the need for an Old Testament translation tool on the level of Sakae Kubo's *Reader's Greek-English Lexicon of the New Testament*. With the student and pastor in view, it has been developed as a means to a more rapid reading of the Hebrew text. The *Reader's Lexicon* should not, therefore, be considered a replacement to a standard lexicon.

The format of the *Reader's Lexicon,* then, serves the purpose of eliminating most of the time-consuming lexical work from basic translation. The appendix contains words occurring over fifty times in the Old Testament. For speed and convenience the reader is encouraged to master this list. In the body of the book, words that occur fifty or fewer times in the Old Testament are listed verse by verse in the order of their occurrence. Nouns and adjectives appear in their vocabulary form. Verbs appear in the perfect third person masculine singular form of the stem used at that point in the text (e.g., וַיַּבְדֵּל appears in Genesis 1:4; in the *Reader's Lexicon* it is listed as הִבְדִּיל). This allows the reader to identify both the root (בדל)and the stem (hiphil). When these verb forms are not pointed, it simply means that the specific form is not extant.

In rare situations, forms other than those described will appear in the *Reader's Lexicon*. In each case clarity is the governing principle. This lexicon does not include numerals or proper nouns.

Along with the definition of the Hebrew words, their respective frequencies are given. For words other than verbs, the first number indicates the frequency of that word in the entire Old Testament. In the case of verbs the first number indicates the frequency of the given stem in the Bible book in which it is being studied. The second number gives the number of occurrences of that stem in the entire Old Testament. The third number gives the frequency of all the stems of a given verb in the entire Old Testament.

Example: Genesis 1:22 פרה (10-22-29)

> 10—The Qal stem occurs ten times in Genesis.
>
> 22—The Qal stem occurs twenty-two times in the Old Testament.
>
> 29—The cumulative occurrence of all stems in the Old Testament is twenty-nine.

Konkordanz zum Hebräischen Alten Testament by Gerhard Lisowsky has been relied on for verb, noun, and adjective frequencies. Frequencies for words in other categories come from *Veteris Testamenti Concordantiae Hebraicae Atque Chaldaicae* by Solomon Mandelkern. Occasionally Lisowsky departs from *A Hebrew and English Lexicon of the Old Testament* by Francis Brown, S. R. Driver, and Charles A. Briggs (hereafter designated BDB) in accepting one root, whereas BDB sees two roots (or vice versa). An example of this is Genesis 3:15. Lisowsky assumes the two occurrences of שׁוּף to be two different words, while BDB lists but one root. When a question mark follows the frequency, it indicates this disharmony.

For the sake of ease in rapid reading, the compound form of particles appears in the *Reader's Lexicon* even when the simple form exists in excess of fifty times (e.g., מִלְמַעְלָה, Genesis 6:16, which occurs only twenty-four times, though its basic part, מַעְלָה, occurs more than fifty times). Thus each compound is treated on its own and the numbers appearing with it indicate the frequency of that particle or compound only.

Definitions have been taken from BDB and checked against the text for meaning in context. Question marks following definitions indicate the interrogative. Suggested meanings are indicated by "perh.," while questionable definitions are designated as [dub.]. The number at the end of the entry gives the page number in BDB carrying a discussion of the word.

As an exegetical tool, this work allows the user to (1) estimate the work involved in any given word study he might wish to pursue, (2) appraise the degree of certainty of a given definition, and (3) go directly to the correct page of a standard lexicon for further investigation. As a translational tool, this lexicon has the primary function of making rapid reading of the Hebrew text possible. Students of Hebrew will be enabled to examine the syntax of the language and, by extensive reading of the text, acquire an understanding of the contexts in which a given word occurs.

It is our prayer that this tool will make Hebrew reading and Hebrew exegesis more delightful and more common among students and pastors who have a high regard for the Word of God as given in the Old Testament.

GENESIS

Chapter 1

תֹהוּ 2 formlessness (1·20) 1062

בֹהוּ emptiness (1·3) 96

תְּהוֹם deep (4·36) 1062

רחף to hover (1·2·3) 934

הִבְדִּיל 4 to divide (5·31·41) 95

רָקִיעַ 6 expanse (9·17) 956

הִבְדִּיל to divide (5·31·41) 95

רָקִיעַ 7 expanse (9·17) 956

הִבְדִּיל to divide (5·31·41) 95

רָקִיעַ 8 expanse (9·17) 956

נקוה 9 to be collected (1·2·2) 876

יַבָּשָׁה dry land (2·14) 387

יַבָּשָׁה 10 dry land (2·14) 387

מִקְוֶה collection (1·7) 876

הדשיא 11 to cause to sprout (1·1·2) 205

דֶּשֶׁא grass (2·14) 206

עֵשֶׂב herb (7·33) 793

מִין species (11·22) 568

דֶּשֶׁא 12 grass (2·14) 206

עֵשֶׂב herb (7·33) 793

מִין species (11·22) 568

מָאוֹר 14 luminary (5·19) 22

רָקִיעַ expanse (9·17) 956

הִבְדִּיל to divide (5·31·41) 95

מָאוֹר 15 luminary (5·19) 22

רָקִיעַ expanse (9·17) 956

הֵאִיר to cause to shine (2·34·40) 21

מָאוֹר 16 luminary (5·19) 22

מֶמְשָׁלָה dominion (5·17) 606

כּוֹכָב star (5·37) 456

רָקִיעַ 17 expanse (9·17) 956

הֵאִיר to cause to shine (2·34·40) 21

הִבְדִּיל 18 to divide (5·31·41) 95

שָׁרַץ 20 to swarm (5·14·14) 1056

שֶׁרֶץ coll. swarming things, swarm (2·15) 1056

עוֹפֵף to fly about (1·5·25) 733

רָקִיעַ expanse (9·17) 956

תַּנִּין 21 sea monster (1·15) 1072

רמש to move about, to glide about (10·16·16) 942

שָׁרַץ to swarm (5·14·14) 1056

מִין species (11·22) 568

פרה 22 to be fruitful (10·22·29) 826

מִין 24 species (11·22) 568

רֶמֶשׂ creeping things (9·16) 943

מִין 25 species (11·22) 568

רֶמֶשׂ creeping things (9·16) 943

צֶלֶם 26 image (5·17) 873

דְּמוּת likeness (3·25) 198

רדה to rule (2·22·23) 921

דָּגָה fish (2·15) 185

רֶמֶשׂ creeping things (9·16) 943

רמש to creep (10·16·16) 942

צֶלֶם 27 image (5·17) 853

נְקֵבָה female (6·22) 666

פרה 28 to be fruitful (10·22·29) 826

כבש to subdue (1·8·14) 461

רדה to rule (2·22·23) 921

דָּגָה fish (2·15) 185

רמש to creep (10·16·16) 942

עֵשֶׂב 29 herb (7·33) 793

אָכְלָה food (4·18) 38

רמש 30 to creep (10·16·16) 942

יֶרֶק green (1·8) 438

עֵשֶׂב herb (7·33) 793

אָכְלָה food (4·18) 38

Chapter 2

תּוֹלְדוֹת 4 account of, generations (13·39) 410

שִׂיחַ 5 shrub (2·4) 967

טֶרֶם not yet (5·16) 382

1

עֵשֶׂב	herb (7·33) 793		נָחָשׁ	4 serpent (6·31) 638
צָמַח	to sprout (3·15·33) 855		נפקח	5 to be opened (2·3·20) 824
הִמְטִיר	to make rain fall (3·16·17) 565		מַאֲכָל	6 food (4·30) 38
אֵד	6 mist (1·2) 15		תַּאֲוָה	desirable (2·21) 16
יָצַר	7 to form, fashion (3·41·44) 427		נחמד	to be desirable (2·4·21) 326
נפח	to blow (1·9·12) 655		נפקה	7 to be opened (2·3·20) 824
נְשָׁמָה	breath (2·24) 675		עֵירֹם	naked (3·10) 735
גַּן	8 garden (14·41) 171		תפר	to sew together (1·3·4) 1074
יָצַר	to form, fashion (3·41·44) 427		עָלֶה	leaves (2·17) 750
הִצְמִיחַ	9 to cause to grow, sprout (1·14·33) 855		תְּאֵנָה	fig [tree] (1·38) 1061
נחמד	to be desirable (2·4·21) 326		חֲגוֹרָה	loin covering, girdle (1·5) 292
מַאֲכָל	food (4·30) 38		גַּן	8 garden (14·41) 171
גַּן	garden (14·41) 171		התחבא	to hide oneself (1·10·34) 285
גַּן	10 garden (14·41) 171		אֵי	9 where? (3·39) 32
נפרד	to divide (7·12·26) 825		גַּן	10 garden (14·41) 171
בְּדֹלַח	12 bdellium (1·2) 95		עֵירֹם	naked (3·10) 735
שֹׁהַם	onyx (1·11) 995		נֶחְבָּא	to hide oneself (2·16·34) 285
קִדְמָה	14 in front of (2·4) 870		עֵירֹם	11 naked (3·10) 735
גַּן	15 garden (14·41) 171		נָחָשׁ	13 serpent (6·31) 638
גַּן	16 garden (14·41) 171		נשא	to deceive (1·14·15) 674
עֵזֶר	18 helper (2·21) 740		נָחָשׁ	14 serpent (6·31) 638
כְּנֶגֶד	corresponding to (2·2) 617		גָּחוֹן	belly (1·2) 161
יָצַר	19 to form, fashion (3·41·44) 427		אֵיבָה	15 enmity, personal hostility (1·5) 33
עֵזֶר	20 helper (2·21) 740		שׁוּף	to bruise (1·1·1[?]) 1003
כְּנֶגֶד	corresponding to (2·2) 617		שׁוּף	to bruise (1·3·3[?]) 1003
תַּרְדֵּמָה	21 deep sleep (2·7) 922		עָקֵב	heel (3·14) 784
ישן	to sleep (2·24·25) 445		עִצָּבוֹן	16 pain (3·3) 781
צֵלָע	rib (2·39) 854		הֵרוֹן	pregnancy, conception (1·1) 248
צֵלָע	22 rib (2·39) 854		עֶצֶב	pain (1·6) 780
לְזֹאת	23 this one (1·2) 260		תְּשׁוּקָה	longing (2·3) 1003
עָרוֹם	25 naked (1·16) 736		בַּעֲבוּר	17 because of (15·46) 721
Chapter 3			עִצָּבוֹן	pain (3·3) 781
נָחָשׁ	1 serpent (6·31) 638		קוֹץ	18 thorn [bush] (1·11) 881
עָרוּם	crafty (1·11) 791		דַּרְדַּר	thistles (1·2) 205
גַּן	garden (14·41) 171		הִצְמִיחַ	to cause to grow, sprout (2·14·33) 855
נָחָשׁ	2 serpent (6·31) 638		עֵשֶׂב	herb (7·33) 793
גַּן	garden (14·41) 171		זֵעָה	19 sweat (1·1) 402
גַּן	3 garden (14·41) 171		כֻּתֹּנֶת	21 tunic (9·30) 509

גַּן 23 garden (14·41) 171

גרש 24 to drive out (3·35·48) 176

גַּן garden (14·41) 171

לַהַט flame (1·1) 529

Chapter 4

הָרָה 1 to conceive, become pregnant
(20·38·40) 247

שָׁעָה 4 to regard, gaze (2·12·15) 1043

שָׁעָה 5 to regard, gaze (2·12·15) 1043

שְׂאֵת 7 acceptance, forgiveness, uplifting
[dub.] (2·7) 673

רָבַץ to lie down, lie, make its lair
(5·24·30) 918

תְּשׁוּקָה longing (2·3) 1003

אֵי 9 where? (3·9) 32

פצה 11 to open wide (1·15·15) 822

נוע 12 to totter (2·22·38) 631

נוד to wander (2·19·26) 626

גרש 14 to drive out, drive away (3·33·48)
176

נוע to totter (2·22·38) 631

נוד to wander (2·19·26) 626

נקם 15 to take vengeance (2·3·34) 667

קִדְמָה 16 in front of (2·4) 870

הָרָה 17 to conceive, become pregnant
(20·38·40) 247

כִּנּוֹר 21 lyre (2·41) 490

עוּגָב flute (1·4) 721

לטש 22 to hammer (1·4·5) 538

הַאֲזִין 23 to listen (1·41·41) 24

אִמְרָה word, utterance (1·30) 57

פֶּצַע wound (1·8) 822

חַבּוּרָה stripe, blow (1·8) 289

נקם 24 to take vengeance (2·3·34) 667

Chapter 5

תּוֹלְדוֹת 1 generations (13·39) 410

דְּמוּת likeness (3·25) 198

נְקֵבָה 2 female (6·22) 666

דְּמוּת 3 likeness (3·25) 198

צֶלֶם image (5·17) 853

עִצָּבוֹן 29 pain (3·3) 781

Chapter 6

רבב 1 to be many (2·23·24) 912

דון 3 to contend [dub.] (1·1·1) 192

שגג to go astray (1·5·5) 992

נְפִילִים 4 giants (1·3) 658

יֵצֶר 5 imagination (2·9) 428

התעצב 6 to grieve (2·2·15) 780

מחה 7 to blot out (3·22·35) 562

רֶמֶשׂ creeping things (9·16) 943

תּוֹלְדוֹת 9 generations (13·39) 410

תֵּבָה 14 ark (26·28) 1061

גֹּפֶר gopher [dub.] (1·1) 172

קֵן cell (1·13) 890

כֹּפֶר pitch (1·1) 498

תֵּבָה 15 ark (26·28) 1061

קוֹמָה height (1·45) 879

צֹהַר 16 roof (1·1) 844

תֵּבָה ark (26·28) 1061

מִלְמַעְלָה above (2·24) 751

צַד side (1·32) 841

תַּחְתִּי lower (1·18) 1066

מַבּוּל 17 flood (12·13) 550

גָּוַע to perish (6·24·24) 157

תֵּבָה 18 ark (26·28) 1061

תֵּבָה 19 ark (26·28) 1061

נְקֵבָה female (6·22) 666

מִין 20 species (11·22) 568

רֶמֶשׂ creeping thing (9·16) 943

מַאֲכָל 21 food (4·30) 38

אָכְלָה food (4·18) 38

Chapter 7

תֵּבָה 1 ark (26·28) 1061

3

נְקֵבָה	3 female (6·22) 666		רֶמֶשׂ	creeping thing (9·16) 943
הַמְטִיר	4 to make rain fall (3·16·17) 565		תֵּבָה	ark (26·28) 1061
מחה	to blot out (3·22·35) 562		גָּבַר	24 to prevail (5·17·25) 149
יְקוּם	substance, existance (2·3) 879			
מַבּוּל	6 flood (12·13) 550		**Chapter 8**	
תֵּבָה	7 ark (26·28) 1061		תֵּבָה	1 ark (26·28) 1061
מַבּוּל	flood (12·13) 550		שׁכך	to abate, decrease (1·4·5) 1013
רמשׂ	8 to creep (10·16·16) 942		נסכר	2 to be stopped (1·2·4) 698
תֵּבָה	9 ark (26·28) 1061		מַעְיָן	spring (2·23) 745
נְקֵבָה	female (6·22) 666		תְּהוֹם	deep (4·36) 1062
מַבּוּל	10 flood (12·13) 550		אֲרֻבָּה	opening, window (2·8) 70
מַעְיָן	11 spring (2·23) 745		נכלא	to restrain (1·3·17) 476
תְּהוֹם	deep (4·36) 1062		גֶּשֶׁם	rain (2·36) 177
אֲרֻבָּה	lattice, window (2·8) 70		חָסֵר	3 to lack, decrease (3·20·24) 341
גֶּשֶׁם	12 rain (2·36) 177		תֵּבָה	4 ark (26·28) 1061
תֵּבָה	13 ark (26·28) 1061		חָסֵר	5 to lack, decrease (3·20·24) 341
מִין	14 species (11·22) 568		חַלּוֹן	6 window (2·30) 319
רֶמֶשׂ	creeping thing (9·16) 943		תֵּבָה	ark (26·28) 1061
רמשׂ	to creep (10·16·16) 942		עֹרֵב	7 raven (1·12) 788
צִפּוֹר	bird[s] (2·40) 861		יוֹנָה	8 dove (5·35) 401
תֵּבָה	15 ark (26·28) 1061		יוֹנָה	9 dove (5·35) 401
נְקֵבָה	16 female (6·22) 666		מָנוֹחַ	resting place (1·7) 629
מַבּוּל	17 flood (12·13) 550		תֵּבָה	ark (26·28) 1061
תֵּבָה	ark (26·28) 1061		חול	10 to twist or writhe in anxious
גָּבַר	18 to prevail (5·17·25) 149			longing, i.e., to wait with extreme
תֵּבָה	ark (26·28) 1061			anxiety (1·5) 296
גָּבַר	19 to prevail (5·17·25) 149		יוֹנָה	dove (5·35) 401
גָּבֹהַ	high (1·41) 147		תֵּבָה	ark (26·28) 1061
מִלְמַעְלָה	20 above (2·24) 751		יוֹנָה	11 dove (5·35) 401
גָּבַר	to prevail (5·17·25) 149		עָלֶה	leaf (2·17) 750
גָּוַע	21 to perish (6·24·24) 157		זַיִת	olive tree (1·38) 268
רמשׂ	to creep (10·16·16) 942		טָרָף	fresh plucked (1·2) 383
שֶׁרֶץ	swarming thing (2·15) 1056		נוחל	12 to wait (1·2·42) 403
שָׁרַץ	to swarm (5·14·14) 1056		יוֹנָה	dove (5·35) 401
נְשָׁמָה	22 breath (2·24) 675		חרב	13 to be dry (2·17·37[?]) 351
חָרָבָה	dry ground (1·8) 351		מִכְסֶה	covering (1·16) 492
מחה	23 to blot out (3·22·35) 562		תֵּבָה	ark (26·28) 1061
יְקוּם	substance, existance (2·3) 879		תֵּבָה	16 ark (26·28) 1061

רֶמֶשׁ	17 creeping thing (9·16) 943	
רמשׂ	to creep (10·16·16) 942	
שָׁרַץ	to swarm (5·14·14) 1056	
פרה	to be fruitful (10·22·29) 826	
רֶמֶשׂ	19 creeping thing (9·16) 943	
רמשׂ	to move about (10·16·16) 942	
תֵּבָה	ark (26·28) 1061	
הריח	21 to smell (2·11·14) 926	
נִיחוֹחַ	soothing, tranquillizing (1·43) 629	
בַּעֲבוּר	for the sake of (15·46) 721	
יֵצֶר	imagination (2·9) 428	
נְעוּרִים	youth (2·46) 655	
קָצִיר	22 crop, harvest (3·49) 894	
קֹר	cold (1·1) 903	
חֹם	heat (1·4) 328	
קַיִץ	summer (1·20) 884	
חֹרֶף	autumn (1·7) 358	

Chapter 9

פרה	1 to be fruitful (10·22·29) 826	
מוֹרָא	2 fear (1·12) 432	
חַת	terror, fear (1·4) 369	
רמשׂ	to creep (10·16·16) 942	
דָּג	fish (1·19) 185	
רֶמֶשׂ	3 moving things (9·16) 943	
אָכְלָה	food (4·18) 38	
יֶרֶק	green (2·8) 438	
עֵשֶׂב	herb (7·33) 793	
צֶלֶם	6 image (5·17) 853	
פרה	7 to be fruitful (10·22·29) 826	
שָׁרַץ	to swarm (5·14·14) 1056	
תֵּבָה	10 ark (26·28) 1061	
מַבּוּל	11 flood (12·13) 550	
ענן	14 to bring clouds (1·1·11) 778	
מַבּוּל	15 flood (12·13) 550	
תֵּבָה	18 ark (26·28) 1061	
נָפַץ	19 to be scattered (1·5·21[?]) 659	

שׁכר	21 to become drunk (2·9·20) 1016	
שִׂמְלָה	23 garment (7·29) 971	
שְׁכֶם	shoulder (6·22) 1014	
אֲחֹרַנִּית	backwards (2·7) 30	
יקץ	24 to awake (5·11·11) 429	
קָטָן	young (6·47) 881	
פתה	27 to make wide (1·1·1) 834	
מַבּוּל	28 flood (12·13) 550	

Chapter 10

תּוֹלְדוֹת	1 generations (13·39) 410	
מַבּוּל	flood (12·13) 550	
נפרד	5 to divide (7·12·26) 825	
אִי	coast, region (1·36) 15	
צַיִד	9 hunting, game (12·14) 844	
נפלג	25 to divide (1·2·4) 811	
מוֹשָׁב	30 dwelling place (3·43) 444	
תּוֹלְדוֹת	32 generations (13·39) 410	
נפרד	to divide (7·12·26) 825	
מַבּוּל	flood (12·13) 550	

Chapter 11

בִּקְעָה	2 plain, broad valley (1·19) 132	
יהב	3 to come now (8·27·27) 396	
לבן	to make brick (1·3·3) 527	
לְבֵנָה	brick (2·12) 527	
שְׂרֵפָה	[place of] burning (1·13) 977	
חֵמָר	asphalt (2·3) 330	
חֹמֶר	mortar, cement (1·17) 330	
יהב	4 to come now (8·27·27) 396	
מִגְדָּל	tower (2·49) 154	
מִגְדָּל	5 tower (2·49) 154	
נבצר	6 to be withheld (1·2·4) 130	
זָמַם	to purpose, divise (1·13·13) 273	
יהב	7 to come now (8·27·27) 396	
בָּלַל	to confuse, confound (2·41·42) 117	
בָּלַל	9 to confuse, confound (2·41·42) 117	
תּוֹלְדוֹת	10 generations (13·39) 410	

5

מַבּוּל   flood (12·13) 550

תּוֹלְדוֹת   27 generations (13·39) 410

מוֹלֶדֶת   28 kindred (9·22) 409

עָקָר   30 barren (3·11) 785

וָלָד   offspring, child (1·1) 409

כַּלָּה   31 daughter-in-law (4·34) 483

Chapter 12

מוֹלֶדֶת   1 kindred (9·22) 409

רְכוּשׁ   5 property (11·28) 940

רָכַשׁ   to gather [property], acquire (5·5·5) 940

אֵלוֹן   6 terebinth, tall tree (4·10) 18

הַעְתִּיק   8 to move forward (2·5·9) 801

כָּבֵד   10 grievous (9·39) 458

יָפֶה   11 beautiful (9·40) 421

בַּעֲבוּר   13 on account of (15·46) 721

בִּגְלַל   on account of, for the sake of (3·10) 164

יָפֶה   14 beautiful (9·40) 421

בַּעֲבוּר   16 for the sake of (15·46) 721

אָתוֹן   she-ass (4·35) 87

Chapter 13

כָּבֵד   2 rich (9·39) 458

מַסַּע   3 journey (1·12) 652

תְּחִלָּה   beginning (4·22) 321

רְכוּשׁ   6 property (11·28) 940

מְרִיבָה   8 strife, contention (1·2) 937

נפרד   9 to divide, separate (7·12·26) 825

הֵימִין   to go to the right (1·5·5) 412

הִשְׂמְאִיל   to go to the left (1·5·5) 970

מַשְׁקֶה   10 well-irrigated (11[?]·19[?]) 1052

גַּן   garden (14·41) 171

נפרד   11 to divide, separate (7·12·26) 825

אהל   12 to pitch one's tent (2·2·3) 14

חַטָּא   13 sinner, sinful (1·19) 308

נפרד   14 to divide, separate (7·12·26) 825

קֶדֶם   eastward (3·26) 870

מנה   16 to count (1·12·28) 584

נמנה   to be counted (1·6·28) 584

אהל   18 to move one's tent (2·2·3) 14

אֵלוֹן   terebinth, tall tree (4·10) 18

Chapter 14

חבר   3 to come as allies, unite (1·11·28) 287

מֶלַח   salt (2·28) 571

מרד   4 to rebel (1·25·25) 597

שָׁוֵה   5 plain (1·1) 1001

בְּאֵר   10 pit (24·38) 91

חֵמָר   asphalt (2·3) 330

רְכוּשׁ   11 property (11·28) 940

אֹכֶל   food (16·44) 38

רְכוּשׁ   12 property (11·28) 940

פָּלִיט   13 fugitive (1·19) 812

אֵלוֹן   terebinth, tall tree (4·10) 18

נִשְׁבָּה   14 to be taken captive (1·8·37) 985

הֵרִיק   to lead forth, i.e., muster (2·17·19) 937

חָנִיךְ   trained, experienced (1·1) 335

יָלִיד   born (4·12) 409

רְכוּשׁ   16 property (11·28) 940

קָנָה   19 to get, acquire, i.e., to create (2·5·5[?]) 888

מִגֵּן   20 to deliver (1·3·3) 171

מַעֲשֵׂר   tithe (1·31) 78

רְכוּשׁ   21 property (11·28) 940

קָנָה   22 to get, acquire, i.e., to create (2·5·5[?]) 888

חוּט   23 thread, cord (1·7) 296

שְׂרוֹךְ   thong (1·2) 976

נַעַל   sandal (1·22) 653

הֶעֱשִׁיר   23 to make rich (1·14·17) 799

בִּלְעָדֵי   24 not to me!, i.e., not at all! (3·5) 116

6

Chapter 15

מַחֲזֶה 1 vision (1·4) 303

שָׂכָר reward (7·28) 969

עֲרִירִי 2 childless (1·4) 792

מֶשֶׁק acquisition (1·1) 606

מֵעֶה 4 inward parts (2·31) 588

כּוֹכָב 5 star (5·37) 456

בַּמָּה 8 whereby (1·29) 552

עֶגְלָה 9 heifer (1·12) 722

שִׁלֵּשׁ to divide into three parts; here=three-years old (3·5·9·) 1026

תּוֹר turtledove (1·14) 1076

גּוֹזָל young |of a bird| (1·2) 160

בתר 10 to cut in two (1·1·2) 144

בֶּתֶר half, piece (1·3) 144

צִפּוֹר bird|s| (2·4) 861

בתר to cut in two (1·1·2) 144

עַיְט 11 birds of prey (1·8) 743

פֶּגֶר corpse (1·22) 803

הנשב to drive away (1·2·3) 674

תַּרְדֵּמָה 12 deep sleep (2·7) 922

אֵימָה terror, dread (1·17) 33

חֲשֵׁכָה darkness (1·6) 365

דִּין 14 to judge (4·23·24) 192

רְכוּשׁ property (11·28) 940

שֵׂיבָה 15 old age (5·20[?]) 966

הֵנָּה 16 hither (8·49) 244

שָׁלֵם full (3·28) 1023

עֲלָטָה 17 thick darkness (1·4) 759

תַּנּוּר firepot (1·15) 1072

עָשָׁן smoke (1·25) 798

לַפִּיד torch (1·13) 542

גֶּזֶר half, part (1·2) 160

Chapter 16

עָצַר 2 to restrain (3·36·46) 783

אוּלַי perhaps (12·45) 19

הָרָה 4 to conceive (20·38·40) 247

גְּבֶרֶת mistress (3·15) 150

חֵיק 5 bosom (1·38) 300

הָרָה to conceive (20·38·40) 247

אֵי 8 where? (3·29) 32

אָנָה whither? where? (3·39) 33

גְּבֶרֶת mistress (3·15) 150

גְּבֶרֶת 9 mistress (3·15) 150

הָרָה 11 to conceive (20·38·40) 247

עֳנִי affliction (4·36) 777

פֶּרֶא 12 wild ass (1·10) 825

רָאִי 13 seeing (1·4) 909

הֲלֹם here (1·11) 240

בְּאֵר 14 well, pit (24·38) 91

Chapter 17

שַׁדַּי 1 Almighty (6·48) 994

הפרה 6 to make fruitful (5·7·29) 826

מְגוּרִים 8 sojourning (6·11) 158

נָמוֹל 10 to be circumcised (13·17·29) 557

מלל 11 to be circumcised (1·3|?|·4|?|) 576

עָרְלָה foreskin (6·16) 790

נָמוֹל 12 to be circumcised (13·17·29) 557

יָלִיד born (4·12) 409

מִקְנָה possession (5·15) 889

נֵכָר that which is foreign, foreigner (4·36) 648

נָמוֹל 13 to be circumcised (13·17·29) 557

יָלִיד born (4·12) 409

מִקְנָה possession (5·15) 889

עָרֵל 14 uncircumcised (1·35) 790

נָמוֹל to be circumcised (13·17·29) 557

עָרְלָה foreskin (6·16) 790

עַם kinsman (6·34) 769

הֵפֵר to break (1·41·44) 830

צחק 17 to laugh (6·6·13) 850

לוּ 18 if only (4·19) 530

אֲבָל 19 nay, but (2·11) 6

הַפְרֵה 20 to make fruitful (5·7·29) 826

יָלִיד 23 born (4·12) 409

מִקְנָה possession (5·15) 889

מוֹל to circumcise (2·12·29) 557

עָרְלָה foreskin (6·16) 790

נִמּוֹל 24 to be circumcised (13·17·29) 557

עָרְלָה foreskin (6·16) 790

נִמּוֹל 25 to be circumcised (13·17·29) 557

עָרְלָה foreskin (6·16) 790

נִמּוֹל 26 to be circumcised (13·17·29) 557

יָלִיד 27 born (4·12) 409

מִקְנָה possession (5·15) 889

נֵכָר that which is foreign = foreigner (4·36) 648

נִמּוֹל to be circumcised (13·17·29) 557

Chapter 18

אֵלוֹן 1 terebinth, tall tree (4·10) 18

חֹם heat (1·1[?]) 328

נִשְׁעַן 4 to support oneself (1·22·22) 1043

פַּת 5 bit (1·14) 837

סָעַד to sustain (1·12·12) 703

סְאָה 6 measure of grain (1·9) 684

קֶמַח flour (1·14) 887

לוּשׁ to knead (1·5·5) 534

עֻגָה bread cake (1·7) 728

רַךְ 7 tender (3·16) 940

חֶמְאָה 8 curd (1·10) 326

חָלָב milk (2·44) 316

אַיֵּה 9 where? (4·44) 32

צָחַק 12 to laugh (6·6·13) 850

בָּלָה to become old and worn out (1·11·16) 115

עֶדְנָה delight (1·1) 726

זָקֵן to be old (6·25·27) 278

צָחַק 13 to laugh (6·6·13) 850

אָמְנָם truly, verily, indeed (1·5) 53

זָקֵן to be old (6·25·27) 278

נִפְלָא 14 to be beyond one's power (1·13·24) 810

כָּחַשׁ 15 to deceive (1·19·22) 471

צָחַק to laugh (6·6·13) 850

הִשְׁקִיף 16 to look down (3·12·22) 1054

עָצוּם 18 mighty (1·31) 783

זְעָקָה 20 outcry against (1·18) 277

רָבַב to be great (2·23·24) 912

צְעָקָה 21 outcry (3·21) 858

כָּלָה completely, altogether (1·22) 478

סָפָה 23 to sweep away (2·8·18) 705

אוּלַי 24 if perhaps (12·45) 19

סָפָה to sweep away (2·8·18) 705

חָלִילָה 25 far be it (4·21) 321

בַּעֲבוּר 26 on account of (15·46) 721

הוֹאֵל 27 to undertake to do (2·18·18) 383

אֵפֶר ashes (1·22) 68

אוּלַי 28 if perhaps (12·45) 19

חָסֵר to lack, be lacking (3·20·24) 341

אוּלַי 29 if perhaps (12·45) 19

בַּעֲבוּר on account of (15·46) 721

אוּלַי 30 if perhaps (12·45) 19

הוֹאֵל 31 to undertake to do (2·18·18) 383

אוּלַי if perhaps (12·45) 19

בַּעֲבוּר on account of (15·46) 721

אוּלַי 32 if perhaps (12·45) 19

בַּעֲבוּר on account of (15·46) 721

Chapter 19

רְחוֹב 2 broad open place, plaza (1·43) 932

פָּצַר 3 to urge (3·6·7) 823

מִשְׁתֶּה feast (5·45) 1059

אָפָה to bake (1·9·12) 66

טֶרֶם 4 not yet (5·16) 382

אַיֵּה 5 where? (4·44) 32

אֵל 8 these (4·10[?]) 41

קוֹרָה roof (1·5) 900

הָלְאָה 9 out there, onward (1·13) 229

פָּצַר	to press (3·6·7) 823	
סַנְוֵרִים	11 sudden blindness (1·3) 703	
לָאָה	to be weary (1·3·19) 521	
פֹּה	12 here (3·44) 805	
חָתָן	son-in-law (3·20) 368	
צְעָקָה	13 outcry (3·21) 858	
חָתָן	14 son-in-law (3·20) 368	
צחק	to jest (5·7·13) 850	
שַׁחַר	15 dawn (3·23) 1007	
האוץ	to hasten (1·2·10) 21	
נספה	to be swept away (2·9·18) 705	
התמהמה	16 to linger (2·9·9) 554	
חֶמְלָה	compassion, mercy (1·2) 328	
נספה	17 to be swept away (2·9·18) 705	
מִצְעָר	20 small thing (2·6) 859	
הִמְטִיר	24 to rain (3·16·17) 565	
גָּפְרִית	brimstone (1·7) 172	
אֵל	25 these (4·10) 41	
צֶמַח	growth (1·12) 855	
נְצִיב	26 pillar (1·11) 662	
מֶלַח	salt (2·28) 571	
הִשְׁקִיף	28 to look down (3·12·22) 1054	
קִיטוֹר	thick smoke (2·4) 882	
כִּבְשָׁן	kiln (1·4) 461	
מְעָרָה	30 cave (11·40) 792	
בְּכִירָה	31 firstborn (5·6) 114	
צָעִיר	young (8·22) 859	
זָקֵן	to be old (6·25·27) 278	
בְּכִירָה	33 firstborn (5·6) 114	
מָחֳרָת	34 the morrow (1·32) 564	
בְּכִירָה	firstborn (5·6) 114	
צָעִיר	young (8·22) 859	
אֶמֶשׁ	yesterday (3·5) 57	
צָעִיר	35 young (8·22) 859	
הָרָה	36 to conceive (20·28·40) 247	
בְּכִירָה	37 firstborn (5·6) 114	
צָעִיר	38 young (8·22) 859	

Chapter 20

בָּעַל	3 to marry (1·1·13) 127	
תֹּם	5 integrity (2·23) 1070	
נִקָּיוֹן	innocency (1·5) 667	
תֹּם	6 integrity (2·23) 1070	
חָשַׂךְ	to withhold (4·26·28) 362	
יִרְאָה	11 fear, reverence (1·45) 432	
אָמְנָה	12 truly, indeed (1·2[?]) 53	
התעה	13 to cause to wander about (1·21·49) 1073	
כְּסוּת	16 covering (1·8) 492	
עָצַר	18 to shut up (3·36·46) 783	
רֶחֶם	womb (4·33) 933	

Chapter 21

הָרָה	2 to conceive (20·38·40) 247	
זְקֻנִים	old age (4·4) 279	
מול	4 to circumcise (2·12·29) 557	
צְחֹק	6 laughter (1·2) 850	
צחק	to laugh (6·6·13) 850	
מִלֵּל	7 to speak (1·4·5[?]) 576	
היניק	to nurse (2·10·18) 413	
זְקֻנִים	old age (4·4) 279	
נגמל	8 to be weaned (2·3·37) 168	
מִשְׁתֶּה	feast (5·45) 1059	
צחק	9 to play, sport (5·7·13) 850	
גרשׁ	10 to drive out (3·35·48) 176	
אוֹדֹת	11 cause; 'א-עַל=because of (3·11) 15	
חֵמֶת	14 waterskin (3·3) 332	
שְׁכֶם	shoulder (6·22) 1014	
תָּעָה	to wander about (2·26·49) 1073	
חֵמֶת	15 waterskin (3·3) 332	
שִׂיחַ	bush (2·4) 967	
מִנֶּגֶד	16 opposite (2·26) 617	
טחה	to shoot (1·1) 377	
בַּאֲשֶׁר	17 in where (3·19) 84	
פָּקַח	19 to open (1·17·20) 824	

9

בְּאֵר	well, pit (24·38) 91	

בְּאֵר well, pit (24·38) 91
חֵמֶת waterskin (3·3) 332
רבה 20 to shoot, ptc.=a shooter (1·1·1) 916
קַשָּׁת bowman (1·1) 906
הֵנָּה 23 here (8·49) 244
שקר to do falsely (1·1·6) 1055
נִין offspring (1·4) 630
נֶכֶד posterity (1·3) 645
אוֹדֹת 25 cause; 'על-א=because of (3·11) 15
בְּאֵר well, pit (24·38) 91
גָּזַל to seize (2·29·30) 159
בִּלְתִּי 26 except (4·24) 116
כִּבְשָׂה 28 ewe lamb (3·8) 461
כִּבְשָׂה 29 ewe lamb (3·8) 461
כִּבְשָׂה 30 ewe lamb (3·8) 461
בַּעֲבוּר in order that (15·46) 721
עֵדָה witness (2·3) 729
חָפַר to dig (7·22·22) 343
בְּאֵר well, pit (24·38) 91
אֵשֶׁל 33 tamarisk tree (1·3) 79

Chapter 22

נִסָּה 1 to test (9·36·36) 650
יָחִיד 2 only (3·12) 402
חבש 3 to bind, bind on, i.e., to saddle (1·27·31) 289
פֹּה 5 here (3·44) 805
מַאֲכֶלֶת 6 knife (2·4) 38
אַיֵּה 7 where? (4·44) 32
שֶׂה a sheep (4·44) 961
שֶׂה 8 a sheep (4·44) 961
עקד 9 to bind (1·1·1) 785
מִמַּעַל on top of (1·29) 751
מַאֲכֶלֶת 10 knife (2·4) 38
מְאוּמָה 12 anything (6·32) 548
יָרֵא fearing (1·46) 431
חָשַׂךְ to withhold (4·26·28) 362
יָחִיד only (3·12) 402

סְבַךְ 13 thicket (1·3) 687
חָשַׂךְ 16 to withhold (4·26·28) 362
יָחִיד only (3·12) 402
כּוֹכָב 17 star (5·37) 456
חוֹל sand (3·22) 297
עֵקֶב 18 because (2·15) 784
פִּילֶגֶשׁ 24 concubine (4·37) 811

Chapter 23

ספד 2 to lament (2·27·29) 704
תּוֹשָׁב 4 sojourner (1·14) 444
מִבְחָר 6 choicest (1·12) 104
פָּגַע 8 to entreat (3·40·46) 803
מְעָרָה 9 cave (11·40) 792
מְעָרָה 11 cave (11·40) 792
לוּ 13 if only (4·19) 530
שָׁקַל 16 to weigh out (1·19·22) 1053
סֹחֵר trader, merchant (2·16[?]) 695
מְעָרָה 17 cave (11·40) 792
מִקְנָה 18 possession (5·15) 889
מְעָרָה 19 cave (11·40) 792
מְעָרָה 20 cave (11·40) 792

Chapter 24

זָקֵן 1 to be old (6·25·27) 278
יָרֵךְ 2 thigh, loins (9·34) 437
מוֹלֶדֶת 4 kindred (9·22) 409
אוּלַי 5 perhaps (12·45) 19
מוֹלֶדֶת 7 kindred (9·22) 409
נקה 8 to be free (2·23·36) 667
שְׁבוּעָה oath (2·30) 989
יָרֵךְ 9 thigh, loins (9·34) 437
טוּב 10 goods (4·32) 375
הברך 11 to cause to kneel (1·1·3) 138
בְּאֵר well (24·38) 91
שֹׁאֵב water drawer (1·5) 980
הִקְרָה 12 to cause to occur, i.e., grant success (2·3·27) 899

שָׁאַב	13 to draw (7·14·14) 980	שָׁאַב	44 to draw (7·14·14) 980
כַּד	14 jar (9·18) 461	טֶרֶם	45 not yet (5·16) 382
טֶרֶם	15 not yet (5·16) 382	כַּד	jar (9·18) 461
כַּד	jar (9·18) 461	שְׁכֶם	shoulder (6·22) 1014
שְׁכֶם	shoulder (6·22) 1014	שָׁאַב	to draw (7·14·14) 980
בְּתוּלָה	16 virgin (1·50) 143	כַּד	46 jar (9·18) 461
כַּד	jar (9·18) 461	נֶזֶם	47 ring (4·17) 633
הַגְמִיא	17 to let [one] drink (1·1·2) 167	צָמִיד	bracelet (3·6) 855
כַּד	jar (9·18) 461	קָדַד	48 to bow down (3·15·15) 869
כַּד	18 jar (9·18) 461	הנחה	to lead (1·26·40) 634
שָׁאַב	19 to draw (7·14·14) 980	מִגְדָּנָה	53 choice thing (1·4) 550
עָרָה	20 to empty (1·8·14) 788	עָשׂוֹר	55 period of ten days (1·15) 797
כַּד	jar (9·18) 461	אחר	56 to keep back (2·15·17) 29
שֹׁקֶת	watering trough (2·2) 1052	מֵינֶקֶת	59 nurse (2·5[?]) 413
בְּאֵר	well (24·38) 91	רְבָבָה	60 myriad (1·16) 914
שָׁאַב	to draw (7·14·14) 980	שֹׂנֵא	enemy (1·41) 971
הִשְׁתָּאָה	21 to gaze (1·1·1) 981	שׁוּחַ	63 to rove about (1·1·1) 962
הֶחֱרִישׁ	to be silent (2·38·46) 361	הַלָּזֶה	65 this (2·3) 229
נֶזֶם	22 ring (4·17) 633	צָעִיף	veil (3·3) 858
בֶּקַע	half [shekel] (1·2) 132		
מִשְׁקָל	weight (3·48) 1054		
צָמִיד	bracelet (3·6) 855		**Chapter 25**
תֶּבֶן	25 straw (2·17) 1061	פִּילֶגֶשׁ	6 concubine (4·37) 811
מִסְפּוֹא	fodder (4·5) 704	מַתָּנֹת	gifts (1·17) 682
קָדַד	26 to bow down (3·15·15) 869	בְּעוֹד	while yet (4·20) 728
נחה	27 to lead (1·14·40) 634	קֶדֶם	eastward (3·26) 870
נֶזֶם	30 ring (4·17) 633	גָּוַע	8 to expire, die (6·24·24) 157
צָמִיד	bracelet (3·6) 855	שֵׂיבָה	old age (5·20[?]) 966
תֶּבֶן	32 straw (2·17) 1061	עַם	kinsman (6·34) 769
מִסְפּוֹא	fodder (4·5) 704	מְעָרָה	9 cave (11·40) 792
זְקֻנָה	36 old age (1·6) 279	תּוֹלְדֹת	12 generations (13·39) 410
אוּלַי	39 perhaps (12·45) 19	תּוֹלְדֹת	13 generations (13·39) 410
נָקָה	41 to be free (2·23·36) 667	טִירָה	16 encampment (1·7) 377
אָלָה	oath (3·36) 46	אֻמָּה	tribe (1·3) 52
נָקִי	free from (2·43) 667	גָּוַע	17 to expire, die (6·24·24) 157
עַלְמָה	43 young woman (1·9) 761	עַם	kinsman (6·34) 769
שָׁאַב	to draw (7·14·14) 980	תּוֹלְדֹת	19 generations (13·39) 410
כַּד	jar (9·18) 461	עתר	21 to pray (1·5·20) 801
		לְנֹכַח	on behalf of (2·3) 647

עָקָר	barren (3·11) 785	
נעתר	to be moved by entreaties (1·8·20 801	
הָרָה	to conceive (20·38·40) 247	
הִתְרֹצֵץ	22 to crush one another (1·1·19) 954	
לְאֹם	23 people (4·35) 522	
מֵעֶה	womb (2·31) 588	
נפרד	to divide (7·12·26) 825	
אמץ	to be strong (1·16·41) 54	
צָעִיר	young (8·22) 859	
תוֹמִם	24 twins (2·6) 1060	
אַדְמוֹנִי	25 red, ruddy (1·3) 10	
אַדֶּרֶת	cloak (1·12) 12	
שֵׂעָר	hair (1·28) 972	
עָקֵב	26 heel (3·14) 784	
צַיִד	27 hunting (12·14) 844	
תָּם	wholesome (1·15) 1070	
צַיִד	28 game (12·14) 844	
הֵזִיד	29 to boil (1·8·10) 267	
נָזִיד	boiled leguminous food (2·6) 268	
עָיֵף	weary (2·17) 746	
הַלְעִיט	30 to swallow (1·1·1) 542	
אָדֹם	red (2·9) 10	
עָיֵף	weary (2·17) 746	
בְּכֹרָה	31 right of first born (6·10) 114	
בְּכֹרָה	32 right of first born (6·10) 114	
בְּכֹרָה	33 right of first born (6·10) 114	
נָזִיד	34 boiled leguminous food (2·6) 268	
עֲדָשָׁה	lentile (1·4) 727	
בזה	to despise (1·31·42) 102	
בְּכֹרָה	right of first born (6·10) 114	

Chapter 26

מִלְּבַד	1 besides (2·33) 94
אֵל	3 these (4·10[?]) 41
שְׁבוּעָה	oath (2·30) 989
כּוֹכָב	4 star (5·37) 456
אֵל	these (4·10[?]) 41

עֵקֶב	5 because (2·15) 784
אָרֵךְ	8 to be long (1·3·34) 73
הִשְׁקִיף	to look down (3·12·22) 1054
חַלּוֹן	window (2·30) 319
צחק	to toy with, to caress (5·7·13) 850
אָשָׁם	10 guilt (1·46) 79
שַׁעַר	12 measure (1·1) 1045
עֲבֻדָּה	14 service [referring to body of household servants] (1·2) 850
קִנֵּא	to be envious of (3·30·34) 888
בְּאֵר	15 well (24·38) 91
חָפַר	to dig (8·23·23) 343
סתם	to stop up (2·2·13) 711
עָצַם	16 to be mighty (1·16·18) 782
חָפַר	18 to dig (8·23·23) 343
בְּאֵר	well (24·38) 91
סתם	to stop up (2·2·13) 711
חָפַר	19 to dig (8·23·23) 343
בְּאֵר	well (24·38) 91
בְּאֵר	20 well (24·38) 91
הִתְעַשֵּׂק	to contend (1·1·1) 796
חָפַר	21 to dig (8·23·23) 343
בְּאֵר	well (24·38) 91
הֶעְתִּיק	22 to move forward (2·5·9) 801
חָפַר	to dig (8·23·23) 343
בְּאֵר	well (24·38) 91
הִרְחִיב	to enlarge (1·21·25) 931
פרה	to be fruitful (10·22·29) 826
בַּעֲבוּר	24 for the sake of (15·46) 721
כָּרָה	25 to dig (2·13·14) 500
בְּאֵר	well (24·38) 91
מֵרֵעַ	26 companion (1·7) 946
אָלָה	28 oath (3·36) 46
מִשְׁתֶּה	30 feast (5·45) 1059
אֹדוֹת	32 cause; עַל־א׳=because of (3·11) 15
בְּאֵר	well (24·38) 91
חָפַר	to dig (8·23·23) 343
מֹרָה	35 bitterness (1·2[?]) 601

Chapter 27

זָקֵן	1 to be old (6·25·27) 278	
כהה	to grow dim (1·5·8) 462	
זָקֵן	2 to be old (6·25·27) 278	
תְּלִי	3 quiver (1·1) 1068	
צוד	to hunt (3·12·16) 844	
צַיִד	game (12·14) 844	
מַטְעַמִּים	4 savory food (6·8) 381	
בַּעֲבוּר	in order that (15·46) 721	
בְּטֶרֶם	before (5·39) 382	
צוד	5 to hunt (3·12·16) 844	
צַיִד	game (12·14) 844	
צַיִד	7 game (12·14) 844	
מַטְעַמִּים	savory food (6·8) 381	
לַאֲשֶׁר	8 to that which (4·38) 81	
גְּדִי	9 kid (5·16) 152	
מַטְעַמִּים	savory food (6·8) 381	
בַּעֲבוּר	10 in order that (15·46) 721	
שָׂעִר	11 hairy (2·2) 972	
חָלָק	smooth (1·12) 325	
אוּלַי	12 perhaps (12·45) 19	
משש	to feel (2·2·8) 606	
מְתַעְתֵּעַ	ptc. of תעע, a mocker (1·1·2) 1073	
קְלָלָה	curse (2·33) 887	
קְלָלָה	13 curse (2·33) 887	
מַטְעַמִּים	14 savory food (6·8) 381	
חֲמוּדָה	15 desirable choice (1·9) 326	
קָטָן	young (6·47) 881	
גְּדִי	16 kid (5·16) 152	
חֶלְקָה	smooth part (1·2) 325	
צַוָּאר	neck (8·41) 848	
מַטְעַמִּים	17 savory food (6·8) 381	
צַיִד	19 game (12·14) 844	
בַּעֲבוּר	in order that (15·46) 721	
הִקְרָה	20 to cause to occur (2·3·27) 899	
מוש	21 to feel (1–1·4[?]) 559	
משש	22 to feel (2·6·8) 606	
הִכִּיר	23 to recognize (6·37·40) 647	

שָׂעִר	hairy (2·2) 972	
צַיִד	25 game (12·14) 844	
נשק	26 to kiss (7·26·32) 676	
נשק	27 to kiss (7·26·32) 676	
הֵרִיח	to smell (2·11·14) 926	
טַל	28 dew (2·31) 378	
שָׁמָן	fat, fertile place (2·2) 1032	
דָּגָן	grain (2·40) 186	
תִּירוֹשׁ	new wine (2·38) 440	
לְאֹם	29 people (4·35) 522	
גְּבִיר	lord (2·2) 150	
צַיִד	30 hunting (12·14) 844	
מַטְעַמִּים	31 savory food (6·8) 381	
צַיִד	game (12·14) 844	
בַּעֲבוּר	in order that (15·46) 721	
חָרַד	33 to tremble (2·23·39) 353	
חֲרָדָה	trembling, fear (1·9[?]) 353	
אֵפוֹא	then (3·15) 66	
צוד	to hunt (3·12·16) 844	
צַיִד	game (12·14) 844	
בְּטֶרֶם	before (5·39) 382	
צְעָקָה	34 cry of distress (3·21) 858	
מַר	bitter (1·38) 600	
מִרְמָה	35 deceit (2·39) 941	
עָקַב	36 to overreach, i.e., to supplant (1·3·3) 784	
בְּכֹרָה	right of firstborn (6·10) 114	
אצל	to reserve, withdraw (1·4·5) 69	
גְּבִיר	37 lord (2·2) 150	
דָּגָן	grain (2·40) 186	
תִּירוֹשׁ	new wine (2·38) 440	
סָמַךְ	to support, sustain (1·41·48) 701	
אֵפוֹא	then (3·15) 66	
שָׁמָן	39 fat, fertile place (2·2) 1032	
מוֹשָׁב	dwelling place (3·43) 444	
טַל	dew (2·31) 378	
עַל	above (2·7) 752	
הֵרִיד	40 to show restlessness (1·2·4) 923	

13

פרק	to tear away (1·4·10)	830
עֹל	yoke (1·40)	760
צַוָּאר	neck (8·41)	848
שׂטם 41	to bear a grudge against (3·6)	966
אָבֵל	mourning (4·24)	5
קָטָן 42	young (6·47)	881
שׁכל 45	to be bereaved (3·4·24)	1013
קוץ 46	to feel a loathing (1·8·8)	880

Chapter 28

שַׁדַּי 3	Almighty (6·48)	994
הפרה	to make fruitful (5·7·29)	826
פָּגַע 11	to meet, light upon (3·40·46)	803
מְרַאֲשׁוֹת	head place (2·10)	912
חלם 12	to dream (14·26·28)	321
סֻלָּם	ladder (1·1)	700
פָּרַץ 14	to break over, increase (4·46·49)	829
קֶדֶם	eastward (3·26)	870
יקץ 16	to awake (5·11·11)	429
שְׁנָת	sleep (2·23)	446
אָכֵן	surely, truly (1·18)	38
נוֹרָא 17	awe-inspiring (1·44)	431
מְרַאֲשׁוֹת 18	head place (2·10)	912
מַצֵּבָה	pillar (10·35)	663
אוּלָם 19	but (2·19)	19
נָדַר 20	to vow (2·30·30)	623
מַצֵּבָה 22	pillar (10·35)	663
עשׂר	to give tithe (2·5·9)	797

Chapter 29

בְּאֵר 2	well (24·38)	91
עֵדֶר	flock (10·39)	727
רָבַץ	to lie down (5·24·30)	918
עֵדֶר 3	flock (10·39)	727
גלל	to roll away (3·10·17)	164
בְּאֵר	well (24·38)	91
מֵאַיִן 4	where? whence? (2·48)	32

עֵדֶר 8	flock (10·39)	727
גלל	to roll away (3·10·17)	164
בְּאֵר	well (24·38)	91
גלל 10	to roll away (3·10·17)	164
בְּאֵר	well (24·38)	91
נָשַׁק 11	to kiss (7·26·32)	676
שָׁמַע 13	report (1·17)	1034
חבק	to embrace (3·10·13)	287
נָשַׁק	to kiss (4·5·32)	676
חִנָּם 15	gratuitously, for nothing (1·32)	336
מַשְׂכֹּרֶת	wages (3·4)	969
קָטָן 16	young (6·47)	881
רַךְ 17	weak (3·16)	940
יָפֶה	beautiful (9·40)	421
תֹּאַר	form (4·15)	1061
קָטָן 18	young (6·47)	881
יהב 21	to give (8·27·27)	396
מִשְׁתֶּה 22	feast (5·45)	1059
רָמָה 25	to deceive (1·8·8)	941
צָעִיר 26	young (8·22)	859
בְּכִירָה	firstborn (5·6)	114
שָׁבוּעַ 27	week (2·20)	988
שָׁבוּעַ 28	week (2·20)	988
רֶחֶם 31	womb (4·33)	933
עָקָר	barren (3·11)	785
הָרָה 32	to conceive (20·38·40)	247
עֳנִי	affliction (4·36)	777
הָרָה 33	to conceive (20·38·40)	247
הָרָה 34	to conceive (20·38·40)	247
נִלְוָה	to be joined (1·11·12)	530
הָרָה 35	to conceive (20·38·40)	247

Chapter 30

קָנָא 1	to be envious of (3·30·34)	888
יהב	to give (8·27·27)	396
מָנַע 2	to withhold (1·25·29)	586
בֶּרֶךְ 3	knee (3·25)	139
הָרָה 5	to conceive (20·38·40)	247

דִּין	6	to execute vindication (4·23·24[?]) 192	טָלוּא		spotted (6·7) 378
הָרָה	7	to conceive (20·38·40) 247	חוּם		dark brown, black (4·4) 299
נַפְתּוּלִים	8	wrestlings (1·1) 836	כֶּשֶׂב		lamb (4·13) 461
נפתל		to wrestle (1·3·5) 836	גנב		to steal (9·30·38) 170
גָּד	11	good fortune (1·2) 151	לוּ	34	if only (4·19) 530
אֹשֶׁר	13	happiness (1·1) 81	תַּיִשׁ	35	he-goat (2·4) 1066
אשר		to call blessed (1·7·9) 80	עָקֹד		striped (7·7) 758
קָצִיר	14	time of harvest (3·49) 894	טָלוּא		spotted (6·7) 378
חִטָּה		wheat (1·30) 334	נָקֹד		speckled (8·8) 666
דּוּדַי		mandrake (5·6) 188	לָבָן		white (3·28) 526
דּוּדַי	15	mandrake (5·6) 188	חוּם		dark brown, black (4·4) 299
שָׂכַר	16	to hire (2·17·20) 968	כֶּשֶׂב		lamb (4·13) 461
דּוּדַי		mandrake (5·6) 188	מַקֵּל	37	rod (7·18) 596
הָרָה	17	to conceive (20·38·40) 247	לִבְנֶה		poplar (1·2) 527
שָׂכָר	18	wages (7·28) 969	לַח		fresh (1·6) 535
הָרָה	19	to conceive (20·38·40) 247	לוּז		almond wood (1·1) 531
זבד	20	to endow (1·1·1) 256	עַרְמוֹן		plane-tree (1·2) 790
זֶבֶד		gift (1·1) 256	פָּצֵל		to peel (2·2·2) 822
זבל		prob. to exalt, honor (1·1·1) 259	פְּצָלוֹת		peeled spot, stripe (1·1) 822
רֶחֶם	22	womb (4·33) 933	לָבָן		white (3·28) 526
הָרָה	23	to conceive (20·38·40) 247	מַחְשֹׂף		a laying-bare (1·1) 362
נָחַשׁ	27	to observe signs (3·9·9) 638	הַצִּיג	38	to set (4·15·16) 426
בִּגְלַל		on account of (3·10) 164	מַקֵּל		rod (7·18) 596
נקב	28	to designate (1·13·19[?]) 666	פָּצֵל		to peel (2·2·2) 822
שָׂכָר		wages (7·28) 969	רַהַט		trough (2·4) 923
פָּרַץ	30	to break over, increase (4·46·49) 829	שֹׁקֶת		watering trough (2·2) 1052
מָתַי		when? (1·42) 607	לְנֹכַח		in front of (2·3) 647
מְאוּמָה	31	anything (6·32) 548	יחם		to be ruttish (2·2·6) 404
שֶׂה	32	a sheep (4·44) 961	יחם	39	to be ruttish (2·2·6) 404
נָקֹד		speckled (8·8) 666	מַקֵּל		rod (7·18) 596
טָלוּא		spotted (6·7) 378	עָקֹד		striped (7·7) 758
חוּם		dark brown, black (4·4) 299	נָקֹד		speckled (8·8) 666
כֶּשֶׂב		lamb (4·13) 461	טָלוּא		spotted (6·7) 378
שָׂכָר		wages (7·28) 969	כֶּשֶׂב	40	lamb (4·13) 461
שָׂכָר	33	wages (7·28) 969	הִפְרִיד		to divide (1·7·26) 825
נָקֹד		speckled (8·8) 666	עָקֹד		striped (7·7) 758
			חוּם		dark brown, black (4·4) 299
			עֵדֶר		flock (10·39) 727

יחם	41 to be ruttish (3·4·6) 404	
מְקֻשָּׁרוֹת	Pu. ptc. of קשׁר, vigorous (1·1·44) 905	
מַקֵּל	rod (7·18) 596	
רַהַט	trough (2·4) 923	
יחם	to be ruttish (3·4·6) 404	
הַעֲטֻף	42 to show feebleness (1·1·11) 742	
עָטוּף	feeble (1·2) 742	
קָשׁוּר	vigorous (1·1[?]) 905	
פָּרַץ	43 to increase (4·46·49) 829	

Chapter 31

מֵאֲשֶׁר	1 from that which (1·17) 84	
תְּמוֹל	2 yesterday; ת׳ שׁלשׁום=formerly (2·22) 1069	
שִׁלְשׁוֹם	three days ago (2·25) 1026	
מוֹלֶדֶת	3 kindred (9·22) 409	
תְּמֹל	5 yesterday; ת׳ שׁלשׁום=formerly (2·22) 1069	
שִׁלְשׁוֹם	three days ago (2·25) 1026	
הֵתֶל	7 to mock, trifle with (1·7·8) 1068	
הֶחֱלִיף	to change (1·2·26) 322	
מַשְׂכֹּרֶת	wages (3·4) 969	
מֹנֶה	time, counted number (2·2) 584	
נָקֹד	8 speckled (8·8) 666	
שָׂכָר	wages (7·28) 969	
עָקֹד	striped (7·7) 758	
יחם	10 to be ruttish (3·4·6) 404	
עַתּוּד	he-goat (2·29) 800	
עָקֹד	striped (7·7) 758	
נָקֹד	speckled (8·8) 666	
בָּרֹד	spotted (2·4) 136	
עַתּוּד	12 he-goat (2·29) 800	
עָקֹד	striped (7·7) 758	
נָקֹד	speckled (8·8) 666	
בָּרֹד	spotted (2·4) 136	

מַצֵּבָה	13 pillar (10·35) 663	
נָדַר	to vow (2·30·30) 623	
מוֹלֶדֶת	kindred (9·22) 409	
נָכְרִי	15 foreign (1·45) 648	
עֹשֶׁר	16 riches (1·37) 799	
נָהַג	18 to drive (1·20·30) 624	
רְכוּשׁ	property (11·28) 940	
רָכַשׁ	to gather [property] (5·5·5) 940	
קִנְיָן	thing acquired (3·9) 889	
גזז	19 to shear (3·14·15) 159	
גנב	to steal (9·30·38) 170	
תְּרָפִים	idols (3·15) 1076	
גנב	20 to steal (9·30·38) 170	
בְּלִי	not (1·23) 115	
הִשִּׂיג	25 to overtake (4·49·49) 673	
גנב	26 to steal (9·30·38) 170	
נָהַג	to drive away (1·10·30) 624	
שָׁבָה	to take captive (2·29·37) 985	
נֶחְבָּא	27 to be hidden (2·16·34) 285	
גנב	to steal (9·30·38) 170	
תֹּף	timbrel (1·17) 1074	
כִּנּוֹר	lyre (2·41) 490	
נָטַשׁ	28 to let (1·33·40) 643	
נשׁק	to kiss (4·5·32) 676	
הִסְכִּיל	to do foolishly (1·2·8) 698	
אֵל	29 power (1·5) 43	
אֶמֶשׁ	yesterday (3·5) 57	
נכסף	30 to long for (2·4·6) 493	
גנב	to steal (9·30·38) 170	
גָּזַל	31 to seize, rob (2·29·30) 159	
הִכִּיר	32 to identify (8·37·40) 647	
גנב	to steal (9·30·38) 170	
תְּרָפִים	34 idols (3·15) 1076	
כַּר	basket saddle (1·1) 468	
משׁשׁ	to feel (2·6·8[?]) 606	
חפשׂ	35 to search (2·8·23) 344	
תְּרָפִים	idols (3·15) 1076	
דלק	36 to hotly pursue (1·7·9) 196	

16

מֹשֵׁשׁ 37 to feel (2·6·8[?]) 606

רָחֵל 38 ewe (2·4) 932

שָׁכֹל to miscarry (2·18·24) 1013

טְרֵפָה 39 animal torn (1·9) 383

גנב to steal (9·30·38) 170

חֹרֶב 40 parching heat (1·16) 351

קֶרַח frost (1·7) 901

נדד to flee (1·20·24) 622

שְׁנָת sleep (2·23) 446

הֶחֱלִיף 41 to change (1·2·26) 322

מַשְׂכֹּרֶת wages (3·4) 969

מֹנֶה time, counted number (2·2) 584

לוּלֵי 42 unless (1·10) 530

פַּחַד dread (2·49) 808

רֵיקָם empty [handed] (1·16) 938

עֳנִי affliction (4·36) 777

יְגִיעַ toil (1·16) 388

אֶמֶשׁ yesterday (3·5) 57

מַצֵּבָה 45 pillar (10·35) 663

לקט 46 to gather (1·14·36) 544

גַּל heap (9·20) 164

יְגַר 47 Aram. [stone] heap (1·1) 1094

שָׂהֲדוּ Aram. testimony (1·1) 1113

גַּל, גַּלְעֵד heap; גַּלְעֵד=heap of witness (9·20) 164

גַּל 48 heap (9·20) 164

צפה 49 to keep watch (1·9·18) 859

גַּל 51 heap (9·20) 164

מַצֵּבָה pillar (10·35) 663

גַּל 52 heap (9·20) 164

עֵדָה witness (2·3) 729

מַצֵּבָה pillar (10·35) 663

פַּחַד 53 dread (2·49) 808

Chapter 32

נשק 1 to kiss (4·5·32) 676

פָּגַע 2 to meet (3·40·46) 803

אחר 5 to tarry (1·1·17) 29

חצה 8 to divide (2·11·15) 345

פְּלֵיטָה 9 escaped remnant (2·28) 812

מוֹלֶדֶת 10 kindred (9·22) 409

קטן 11 to be insignificant (1·3·4) 881

מַקֵּל staff (7·11) 596

חוֹל 13 sand (3·22) 297

תַּיִשׁ 15 he-goat (2·4) 1066

רָחֵל ewe (2·4) 932

הֵינִיק 16 to give suck to (2·10·18) 413

פָּרָה cow (12·26) 831

אָתוֹן she-ass (4·35) 87

עַיִר male ass (2·9) 747

עֵדֶר 17 herd (10·39) 727

רֶוַח space, interval (1·2) 926

פגש 18 to meet (2·10·14) 803

לְמִי to whom, whose (3·20) 566

אָנָה whither? where? (3·39) 33

עֵדֶר 20 herd (10·39) 727

אוּלַי 21 perhaps (12·45) 19

מַעֲבַר 23 ford (1·3) 721

נאבק 25 to wrestle (2·2·2) 7

שַׁחַר dawn (3·23) 1007

יָרֵךְ 26 thigh (9·34) 437

יקע to be dislocated (1·4·8) 429

נאבק to wrestle (2·2·2) 7

שַׁחַר 27 dawn (3·23) 1007

שָׂרָה 29 to persist, exert onesel (1·2) 975

זרח 32 to rise, come forth (1·18·18) 280

צלע to limp (1·4) 854

יָרֵךְ thigh (9·34) 437

גִּיד 33 sinew (2·7) 161

נָשֶׁה thigh-vein (2·2) 674

יָרֵךְ thigh (9·34) 437

Chapter 33

חצה 1 to divide (2·11·15) 345

חבק 4 to embrace (3·10·13) 287

צַוָּאר neck (8·41) 848

17

נָשַׁק   to kiss (7·26·32) 676

פָּגַשׁ   8 to meet (2·10·14) 803

פָּצַר   11 to urge (3·6·7) 823

לְנֶגֶד   12 before (1·32) 617

רַךְ   13 tender (3·16) 940

עוּל   to nurse (1·5·5) 732

דפק   to beat (1·2·3) 200

הִתְנַהֵל   14 to journey by stages (1·1·10) 624

אַט   gently (1·5) 31

הִצִּיג   15 to place (4·15·16) 426

סֻכָּה   17 booth (1·31) 697

שָׁלֵם   18 safe (3·28) 1023

חֶלְקָה   19 portion [of ground] (1·24) 324

קְשִׂיטָה   unit of weight [dub.] (1·3) 903

Chapter 34

הֶחֱרִישׁ   5 to be silent (2·38·46) 361

הִתְעַצֵּב   7 to be vexed, grieved (2·2·15) 780

נְבָלָה   disgraceful folly (1·13) 615

חָשַׁק   8 to love (1·8·11) 365

הִתְחַתֵּן   9 to form a marriage alliance with (1·11·11) 368

רחס   10 to go about (3·4·5) 695

מֹהַר   12 purchase price (1·3) 555

מַתָּן   gift[s] (1·5) 682

מִרְמָה   13 deceit (2·39) 941

עָרְלָה   14 foreskin (6·16) 790

בְּזֹאת   15 with this = on these conditions (4·15) 260

נֵאוֹת   to consent (3·4·4) 22

נִמּוֹל   to be circumcised (13·17·29) 557

נִמּוֹל   17 to be circumcised (13·17·29) 557

אֵחַר   19 to delay, tarry (2·15·17) 29

שָׁלֵם   21 at peace (3·28) 1023

סָחַר   to go about (3·4·5) 695

רָחָב   wide, broad (1·21) 932

בְּזֹאת   22 with this = on these conditions (4·15) 260

נֵאוֹת   to consent (3·4·4) 22

נִמּוֹל   to be circumcised (13·17·29) 557

קִנְיָן   23 acquired thing (3·9) 889

נֵאוֹת   to consent (3·4·4) 22

נִמּוֹל   24 to be circumcised (13·17·29) 557

כָּאַב   25 to be in pain (1·4·8) 456

בֶּטַח   securely (1·43) 105

בזז   27 to plunder (2·37·40) 102

טַף   29 children (8·41) 381

שָׁבָה   to take captive (2·29·37) 985

בזז   to plunder (2·37·40) 102

עָכַר   30 to trouble (1·12·14) 747

הִבְאִישׁ   to cause to stink (1·7·16) 92

מַת   man (1·21) 607

זוֹנָה   31 harlot (2·33[?]) 275

Chapter 35

נֵכָר   2 foreignness (4·36) 648

הֶחֱלִיף   to change (1·2·26) 322

שִׂמְלָה   mantle, garment (7·29) 971

נֵכָר   4 foreignness (4·36) 648

נֶזֶם   ring (4·17) 633

טָמַן   to hide (1·28·31) 380

אֵלָה   terebinth [tree] (1·17) 18

חִתָּה   5 terror (1·1) 369

מֵינֶקֶת   8 nurse (2·5) 413

אַלּוֹן   oak [tree] (2·9) 47

בָּכוּת   weeping (1·1) 113

שַׁדַּי   11 Almighty (6·48) 994

פרה   to be fruitful (10·22·29) 826

חָלָץ   loins (1·10) 323

מַצֵּבָה   14 pillar (10·35) 663

הִסִּיךְ   to pour out (1·13·24) 650

כִּבְרָה   16 distance (2·3) 460

קָשָׁה to make hard, severe (1·1·28) 904

הִקְשָׁה 17 to make difficult (1·21·28) 904

מְיַלֶּדֶת midwife (2·9) 408

מַצֵּבָה 20 pillar (10·35) 663

קְבוּרָה grave (3·14) 869

מֵהָלְאָה 21 beyond (1·3) 229

פִּילֶגֶשׁ 22 concubine (4·37) 811

גָּוַע 29 to die, expire (6·24·24) 157

עַם kinsman (6·34) 769

שָׂבֵעַ satisified (2·10) 960

Chapter 36

תּוֹלְדוֹת 1 generations (13·39) 410

קִנְיָן 6 acquired thing (3·9) 889

רָכַשׁ to gather [property] (5·5·5) 940

רְכוּשׁ 7 property (11·28) 940

תּוֹלְדוֹת 9 generations (13·39) 410

פִּילֶגֶשׁ 12 concubine (4·37) 811

יֵמִם 24 hot springs (1·1) 411

מוֹשָׁב 43 dwelling place (3·44) 444

Chapter 37

מְגוּרִים 1 sojourning (6·11) 158

תּוֹלְדוֹת 2 generations (13·39) 410

דִּבָּה evil report (1·9) 179

זְקֻנִים 3 old age (4·4) 279

כֻּתֹּנֶת tunic (9·30) 509

פַּס flat of hand or foot; כְּתֹנֶת פַּסִּים
= floor length, long sleeved tunic
(3·5) 821

חָלַם 5 to dream (14·26·28[?]) 321

חָלַם 6 to dream (14·26·28[?]) 321

אָלַם 7 to bind (1·1·9) 47

אֲלֻמָּה sheaf (4·5) 48

חָלַם 9 to dream (14·26·28[?]) 321

יָרֵחַ moon (1·27) 437

כּוֹכָב star (5·37) 456

גָּעַר 10 to rebuke (1·14·14) 172

חָלַם to dream (14·26·28[?]) 321

קָנָא 11 to be envious of (3·30·34) 888

תָּעָה 15 to wander about (2·26·49) 1073

אֵיפֹה 16 where? (1·10) 33

בְּטֶרֶם 18 before (5·39) 382

התנכל to deal knavishly (1·2·4) 647

הַלָּזֶה 19 this (2·3) 229

הִפְשִׁיט 23 to strip (1·15·43) 832

כֻּתֹּנֶת tunic (9·30) 509

פַּס flat of hand or foot, cf. v.3 (3·5) 821

רֵיק 24 empty (2·14) 938

אֹרְחָה 25 caravan (1·3[?]) 73

נְכֹאת spice (2·2) 644

צֳרִי a kind of balsam (2·6) 863

לֹט myrrh (2·2) 538

בֶּצַע 26 [selfish] profit (1·23) 130

סֹחֵר 28 trader (2·16) 695

מָשַׁךְ to draw out (1·30·36) 604

אָנָה 30 whither? where? (3·39) 33

כֻּתֹּנֶת 31 tunic (9·30) 509

טָבַל to dip (1·15·16) 371

כֻּתֹּנֶת 32 tunic (9·30) 509

פַּס flat of hand or foot, cf. v.3
(3·5) 821

הִכִּיר to observe (8·37·40) 647

הִכִּיר 33 to observe (8·37·40) 647

כֻּתֹּנֶת tunic (9·30) 509

טָרַף to tear (3·13·24) 382

טרף to be torn (2·2·24) 382

שִׂמְלָה 34 clothes (7·29) 971

שַׂק sack cloth (5·48) 974

מָתְנַיִם loins (1·50) 608

הִתְאַבֵּל to mourn (1·19·38) 5

מֵאֵן 35 to refuse (3·45·45) 549

אָבֵל mourning (1·8) 5

סָרִיס 36 eunuch (4·45) 710

טַבָּח guardsman (6·32) 371

19

Chapter 38

הָרָה 3 to conceive (20·38·40) 247

הָרָה 4 to conceive (20·38·40) 247

יִבֵּם 8 to do the duty of a husband's brother (2·3·3) 386

כַּלָּה 11 daughter-in-law (4·34) 483

גָזַז 12 to shear (3·14·15) 159

חָם 13 father-in-law (2·4) 327

גָזַז to shear (3·14·15) 159

אַלְמָנוּת 14 widowhood (2·4) 48

צָעִיף shawl, veil (3·3) 858

הִתְעַלֵּף to enwrap oneself (1·3·5) 763

זוֹנָה 15 harlot (2·33[?]) 275

יָהַב 16 to come now (8·23·27) 396

כַּלָּה daughter-in-law (4·34) 483

גְּדִי 17 kid (5·16) 152

עֵרָבוֹן pledge (3·3) 786

עֵרָבוֹן 18 pledge (3·3) 786

חֹתָם signet ring (1·13) 368

פָּתִיל cord (2·11) 836

הָרָה to conceive (20·38·40) 247

צָעִיף 19 wrapper, veil (3·3) 858

אַלְמָנוּת widowhood (2·4) 48

גְּדִי 20 kid (5·16) 152

עֵרָבוֹן pledge (3·3) 786

אַיֵּה 21 where? (4·44) 32

קָדֵשׁ temple prostitute (3·11) 873

בָּזֶה in this [place], here (3·19) 260

בָּזֶה 22 in this [place], here (3·19) 260

קָדֵשׁ temple prostitute (3·11) 873

בּוּז 23 object of contempt (1·11) 100

גְּדִי kid (5·16) 152

כַּלָּה 24 daughter-in-law (4·34) 483

הָרָה to conceive (20·38·40) 247

זְנוּנִים fornication (1·11) 276

חָם 25 father-in-law (2·4) 327

הָרָה to conceive (20·38·40) 247

הִכִּיר to regard, observe (8·37·40) 647

לְמִי to whom, whose (3·20) 566

חֹתֶמֶת signet ring (1·1) 368

פָּתִיל cord (2·11) 836

הִכִּיר 26 to regard, observe (8·37·40) 647

צָדַק to be in the right (1·22·41) 842

תְּאוֹמִים 27 twins (2·6) 1060

מְיַלֶּדֶת 28 midwife (2·9) 408

קָשַׁר to bind (3·35·44) 905

שָׁנִי scarlet [thread] (2·42) 1040

פָּרַץ 29 to break out (4·46·49) 829

פֶּרֶץ a bursting forth (1·18) 829

שָׁנִי 30 scarlet [thread] (2·42) 1040

Chapter 39

סָרִיס 1 eunuch (4·45) 710

טַבָּח guardsman (6·32) 371

מֵאָז 5 since (1·18) 23

בִּגְלַל on account of (3·10) 164

מְאוּמָה 6 anything (6·32) 548

יָפֶה beautiful (9·40) 421

תֹּאַר form (4·15) 1061

מָאֵן 8 to refuse (3·45·45) 549

חָשַׂךְ 9 to withhold (4·26·28) 362

מְאוּמָה anything (6·32) 548

בַּאֲשֶׁר inasmuch as (3·19) 84

צָחַק 14 to make a toy of (5·7·13) 850

צָחַק 17 to make a toy of (5·7·13) 850

סֹהַר 20 roundness (8·8) 690

אָסִיר prisoner (3·18) 64

סֹהַר 21 roundness (8·8) 690

סֹהַר 22 roundness (8·8) 690

אָסִיר prisoner (3·18) 64

סֹהַר 23 roundness (8·8) 690

מְאוּמָה anything (6·32) 548

בַּאֲשֶׁר inasmuch as (3·19) 84

Chapter 40

מַשְׁקֶה	1 cupbearer (11[?]·19[?])	1052
אֹפֶה	baker (8·12[?])	66
קָצַף	2 to be wroth (2·28·34)	893
סָרִיס	eunuch (4·45)	710
מַשְׁקֶה	cupbearer (11[?]·19[?])	1052
אֹפֶה	baker (8·12[?])	66
מִשְׁמָר	3 prison (6·20)	1038
טַבָּח	guardsman (6·32)	371
סֹהַר	roundness (8·8)	690
טַבָּח	4 guardsman (6·32)	371
מִשְׁמָר	prison (6·20)	1038
חָלַם	5 to dream (14·26·28[?])	321
פִּתְרוֹן	interpretation (5·5)	837
מַשְׁקֶה	cupbearer (11[?]·19[?])	1052
אפה	baker (8·12[?])	66
סֹהַר	roundness (8·8)	690
זָעֵף	6 to be out of humor (1·1·4)	277
סָרִיס	7 eunuch (4·45)	710
מִשְׁמָר	prison (6·20)	1038
חָלַם	8 to dream (14·26·28[?])	321
פָּתַר	to interpret (9·9·9)	837
פִּתְרוֹן	interpretation (5·5)	837
מַשְׁקֶה	9 cupbearer (11[?]·19[?])	1052
שָׂרִיג	10 twig (2·3)	974
פָּרַח	to bud (1·29·34)	827
נִצָּה	blossom (1·4)	665
הבשיל	to be ripened (1·1·27)	143
אֶשְׁכּוֹל	cluster (1·9)	79
עֵנָב	grape[s] (3·19)	772
כּוֹס	11 cup (5·31)	468
עֵנָב	grape[s] (3·19)	772
שׁחט	to squeeze out (1·1·1)	965
פִּתְרוֹן	12 interpretation (5·5)	837
שָׂרִיג	twig (2·3)	974
בְּעוֹד	13 within yet (4·20)	728
כֵּן	office (2·7)	487

כּוֹס	cup (5·31)	468
מַשְׁקֶה	cupbearer (11[?]·19[?])	1052
גנב	15 to be stolen away (2·4·39)	170
פֹּה	here, hither (3·44)	805
מְאוּמָה	anything (6·32)	548
אֹפֶה	16 baker (8·12[?])	66
פָּתַר	to interpret (9·9·9)	837
סַל	basket (4·15)	700
חֹרִי	white bread (1·1)	301
סַל	17 basket (4·15)	700
מַאֲכָל	food (4·30)	38
אֹפֶה	baker (8·12[?])	66
פִּתְרוֹן	18 interpretation (5·5)	837
סַל	basket (4·15)	700
בְּעוֹד	19 within yet (4·20)	728
תָּלָה	to hang (3·23·27)	1067
מִשְׁתֶּה	20 feast (5·45)	1059
מַשְׁקֶה	cupbearer (11[?]·19[?])	1052
אֹפֶה	baker (8·12[?])	66
מַשְׁקֶה	21 cupbearer (11[?]·19[?])	1052
כּוֹס	cup (5·31)	468
אֹפֶה	22 baker (8·12[?])	66
תָּלָה	to hang (3·23·27)	1067
פָּתַר	to interpret (9·9·9)	837
מַשְׁקֶה	23 cupbearer (11[?]·19[?])	1052

Chapter 41

חָלַם	1 to dream (14·26·28)	321
פָּרָה	2 cow (12·26)	831
יָפֶה	fair (9·40)	421
בָּרִיא	fat (6·14)	135
אָחוּ	reeds (2·3)	28
פָּרָה	3 cow (12·26)	831
דַּק	thin (6·14)	201
פָּרָה	4 cow (12·26)	831
דַּק	thin (6·14)	201
יָפֶה	fair (9·40)	421
בָּרִיא	fat (6·14)	135

21

יקץ	to awake (5·11·11) 429	
יָשֵׁן	5 to sleep (2·24·25) 445	
חָלַם	to dream (14·26·28) 321	
שִׁבֹּלֶת	ear of grain (10·20[?]) 987	
בָּרִיא	fat (6·14) 135	
שִׁבֹּלֶת	6 ear of grain (10·20[?]) 987	
דַּק	thin (6·14) 201	
שָׁדַף	to scorch (3·3·3) 995	
צָמַח	to sprout (3·15·33) 855	
שִׁבֹּלֶת	7 ear of grain (10·20[?]) 987	
דַּק	thin (6·14) 201	
בָּרִיא	fat (6·14) 135	
יקץ	to awake (5·11·11) 429	
נפעם	8 to be disturbed (1·3·5) 821	
חַרְטֹם	magician (2·11) 355	
פָּתַר	to interpret (9·9·9) 837	
מַשְׁקֶה	9 cupbearer (11[?]·19[?]) 1052	
חֵטְא	sin (1·33) 307	
קָצַף	10 to be wroth (2·28·34) 893	
מִשְׁמָר	prison (6·20) 1038	
טַבָּח	guardsman (6·32) 371	
אֹפֶה	baker (8·12[?]) 66	
חָלַם	11 to dream (14·26·28) 321	
פִּתְרוֹן	interpretation (5·5) 837	
טַבָּח	12 guardsman (6·32) 371	
פָּתַר	to interpret (9·9·9) 837	
פָּתַר	13 to interpret (9·9·9) 837	
כֵּן	office (2·7) 487	
תָּלָה	to hang (3·23·27) 1067	
גלח	14 to shave oneself (1·18·23) 164	
חלף	to change (1·2·26) 322	
שִׂמְלָה	clothes (7·29) 971	
חָלַם	15 to dream (14·26·28) 321	
פָּתַר	to interpret (9·9·9) 837	
בִּלְעָדַי	16 not to me! i.e., not at all! (3·5) 116	
פָּרָה	18 cow (12·26) 831	
בָּרִיא	fat (6·14) 135	
יָפֶה	fair, beautiful (9·40) 421	

תֹּאַר	form (4·15) 1061	
אָחוּ	reeds (2·3) 28	
פָּרָה	19 cow (12·26) 831	
דַּל	weak, thin (1·48) 195	
תֹּאַר	form (4·15) 1061	
רַק	thin (3·3) 956	
רֹעַ	badness (1·19) 947	
פָּרָה	20 cow (12·26) 831	
רַק	thin (3·3) 956	
בָּרִיא	fat (6·14) 135	
תְּחִלָּה	21 beginning (4·22) 321	
יקץ	to awake (5·11·11) 429	
שִׁבֹּלֶת	22 ear of grain (10·20[?]) 987	
שִׁבֹּלֶת	23 ear of grain (10·20[?]) 987	
צְנֻמוֹת	Qal ptc. pass. = dried up, hardened (1·1·1) 856	
דַּק	thin (6·14) 201	
שָׁדַף	to scorch (3·3·3) 995	
צָמַח	to sprout (3·15·33) 855	
שִׁבֹּלֶת	24 ear of grain (10·20[?]) 987	
דַּק	thin (6·14) 201	
חַרְטֹם	magician (2·11) 355	
פָּרָה	26 cow (12·26) 831	
שִׁבֹּלֶת	ear of grain (10·20[?]) 987	
פָּרָה	27 cow (12·26) 831	
רַק	thin (3·3) 956	
שִׁבֹּלֶת	ear of grain (10·20[?]) 987	
רֵיק	empty (2·14) 938	
שָׁדַף	to scorch (3·3·3) 995	
שָׂבָע	29 plenty (6·8) 960	
שָׂבָע	30 plenty (6·8) 960	
שָׂבָע	31 plenty (6·8) 960	
כָּבֵד	grievous (9·39) 458	
נשנה	32 to be repeated (1·1·26[?]) 1040	
פָּקִיד	34 overseer (1·13) 824	
חמש	to take a fifth part of (1·1·5[?]) 332	
שָׂבָע	plenty (6·8) 960	
אֹכֶל	35 food (16·44) 38	

צבר	to heap up (2·7·7) 840	שבר	5 to buy grain (13·16·21) 991
בָּר	grain (5·14) 141	שַׁלִּיט	6 ruler (1·4) 1020
אֹכֶל	36 food (16·44) 38	השבר	to sell grain (1·5·21) 991
פִּקָּדוֹן	store (1·2) 824	הִכִּיר	7 to recognize (8·37·40) 647
כָּזֶה	38 such (1·6) 262	התנכר	to disguise oneself (1·2·40) 647
נָשַׁק	40 to kiss (7·26·32) 676	קָשֶׁה	hard, severe (2·36) 904
טַבַּעַת	42 signet ring (1·44) 371	מֵאַיִן	where? whence? (2·48) 32
שֵׁשׁ	linen (1·38) 1058	שבר	to buy grain (13·16·21) 991
רָבִיד	ornament for neck, necklace (1·2) 914	אֹכֶל	food (16·44) 38
צַוָּאר	neck (8·41) 848	הִכִּיר	8 to recognize (8·37·40) 647
מֶרְכָּבָה	43 chariot (2·44) 939	חָלַם	9 to dream (14·26·28) 321
מִשְׁנֶה	second (3·35) 1041	מְרַגְּלִים	spies (6·10) 920
אַבְרֵךְ	prostrate yourself! bow down! [dub.] (1·1) 7	שבר	10 to buy grain (13·16·21) 991
		אֹכֶל	food (16·44) 38
בִּלְעָדֵי	44 apart from, without (3·5) 116	כֵּן	11 honest (5·23) 467
שָׂבָע	47 plenty (6·8) 960	מְרַגְּלִים	spies (6·10) 920
קֹמֶץ	handfuls (1·4) 888	מְרַגְּלִים	14 spies (6·10) 920
אֹכֶל	48 food (16·44) 38	בְּזֹאת	15 by, through this (4·15) 260
צבר	49 to heap up (2·7·7) 840	נבחן	to be tried, proved (2·3·28) 103
בָּר	grain (5·14) 141	הֵנָּה	hither (8·49) 244
חוֹל	sand (3·22) 292	נבחן	16 to be tried, proved (2·3·28) 103
בְּטֶרֶם	50 before (5·39) 382	מְרַגְּלִים	spies (6·10) 920
נשׁה	51 to make to forget (1·1·5) 674	מִשְׁמָר	17 prison (6·20) 1038
הפרה	52 to make fruitful (5·7·29) 826	כֵּן	19 honest (5·23) 467
עֳנִי	affliction (4·36) 777	מִשְׁמָר	prison (6·20) 1038
שָׂבָע	53 plenty (6·8) 960	שֶׁבֶר	grain (7·9) 991
רָעֵב	55 to be hungry (1·12·14) 944	רְעָבוֹן	famine (2·3) 944
שבר	56 to buy grain (13·16·21) 991	אֲבָל	21 of a truth, verily (2·11) 6
שבר	57 to buy grain (13·16·21) 991	אָשֵׁם	guilty (1·3) 79
		הֵלִיץ	23 ptc.=interpreter (1·9·12) 539
		בָּר	25 grain (5·14) 141
Chapter 42		שַׂק	sack (5·48) 974
		צֵידָה	provision (2·9) 845
שֶׁבֶר	1 grain (7·9) 991	שֶׁבֶר	26 grain (7·9) 991
שֶׁבֶר	2 grain (7·9) 991	שַׂק	27 sack (5·48) 974
שבר	to buy grain (13·16·21) 991	מִסְפּוֹא	fodder (4·5) 704
שבר	3 to buy grain (13·16·21) 991	מָלוֹן	lodging-place (2·8) 533
בָּר	grain (5·14) 141	אַמְתַּחַת	sack (15·15) 607
אָסוֹן	4 mischief, evil (3·5) 62		

אַמְתַּחַת	28 sack (15·15) 607
חָרַד	to tremble (2·23·39) 353
קרה	29 to befall (2·13·27) 899
קָשֶׁה	30 hard, severe (2·36) 904
רגל	to go about as a spy (1·14·16) 920
כֵּן	31 honest (5·23) 467
מְרַגְּלִים	spies (6·10) 920
בְּזֹאת	33 by, through this (4·15) 260
כֵּן	honest (5·23) 467
רְעָבוֹן	famine (2·3) 944
מְרַגְּלִים	34 spies (6·10) 920
כֵּן	honest (5·23) 467
סחר	to go about (3·4·5) 695
הריק	35 to empty out (2·17·19) 937
שַׂק	sack (5·48) 974
צְרוֹר	bundle (2·7) 865
שכל	36 to make childless (2·18·24) 1013
אָסוֹן	38 mischief, evil (3·5) 62
שֵׂיבָה	grey hair (5·20[?]) 966
יָגוֹן	sorrow (2·14) 387

Chapter 43

כָּבֵד	1 grievous (9·39) 458
שֶׁבֶר	2 grain (7·9) 991
שבר	to buy grain (13·16·21) 991
אֹכֶל	food (16·44) 38
הֵעִיד	3 to warn (2·40·45) 729
בִּלְתִּי	except (4·24) 116
שבר	4 to buy grain (13·16·21) 991
אֹכֶל	food (16·44) 38
בִּלְתִּי	5 except (4·24) 116
מוֹלֶדֶת	7 kindred (9·22) 409
טַף	8 children (8·41) 381
ערב	9 to be surety (2·15·17) 786
הַצִּיג	to set (4·15·16) 426
לוּלֵא	10 unless (1·4) 530
התמהמה	to linger (2·9·9) 554
אֵפוֹא	11 then (3·15) 66

זִמְרָה	choice products (1·4[?]) 275
צֳרִי	a kind of balsam (2·6) 863
נְכֹאת	a spice (2·2) 644
לֹט	myrrh (2·2) 538
בָּטְנִים	pistachio nuts (1·1) 106
שָׁקֵד	almond (1·4) 1052
מִשְׁנֶה	12 double (3·35) 1041
אַמְתַּחַת	sack (15·15) 607
אוּלַי	perhaps (12·45) 19
מִשְׁגֶּה	mistake (1·1) 993
שַׁדַּי	14 Almighty (6·48) 994
רַחֲמִים	compassion (2·38) 933
שכל	to be bereaved (3·4·24) 1013
מִשְׁנֶה	15 double (3·35) 1041
לַאֲשֶׁר	16 to him who (4·38) 81
טבח	to slaughter (1·11·11) 370
טֶבַח	slaughter (1·12) 370
צָהֳרַיִם	midday, noon (2·23) 843
אַמְתַּחַת	18 sack (15·15) 607
תְּחִלָּה	beginning (4·22) 321
התגלל	to roll oneself (1·2·17) 164
בִּי	20 I pray, excuse me (2·12) 106
תְּחִלָּה	beginning (4·22) 321
שבר	to buy grain (13·16·21) 991
אֹכֶל	food (16·44) 38
מָלוֹן	21 lodging-place (2·8) 533
אַמְתַּחַת	sack (15·15) 607
מִשְׁקָל	weight (3·49) 1054
שבר	22 to buy grain (13·16·21) 991
אֹכֶל	food (16·44) 38
אַמְתַּחַת	sack (15·15) 607
מַטְמוֹן	23 treasure (1·5) 380
אַמְתַּחַת	sack (15·15) 607
מִסְפּוֹא	24 fodder (4·5) 704
צָהֳרַיִם	25 midday, noon (2·23) 843
קדד	28 to bow down (3·15·15) 869
נכמר	30 to grow tender (1·4·4) 485

רַחֲמִים compassion (2·38) 933

חֶדֶר chamber, room (1·34) 293

הִתְאַפֵּק 31 to restrain oneself (2·7·7) 67

בְּכֹרָה 33 right of first-born (6·10) 114

צָעִיר young (8·22) 859

צְעִירָה youth (1·2) 859

תמה to look in astonishment (1·8·9) 1069

מַשְׂאֵת 34 portion (3·16) 673

שכר to become drunken (2·9·20) 1016

Chapter 44

אַמְתַּחַת 1 sack (15·15) 607

אֹכֶל food (16·44) 38

גָּבִיעַ 2 cup (5·14) 149

אַמְתַּחַת sack (15·15) 607

שֶׁבֶר grain (7·9) 991

לַאֲשֶׁר 4 to him who (4·38) 81

הִשִּׂיג to overtake (4·49·49) 673

נָחֵשׁ 5 to practice divination (3·9·9) 638

הִשִּׂיג 6 to overtake (4·49·49) 673

חָלִיל 7 far be it [for] (4·21) 321

אַמְתַּחַת 8 sack (15·15) 607

גנב to steal (9·30·39) 170

נָקִי 10 free from, exempt (2·43) 667

אַמְתַּחַת 11 sack (15·15) 607

חפשׂ 12 to search for (2·8·23) 344

גָּבִיעַ cup (5·14) 149

אַמְתַּחַת sack (15·15) 607

שִׂמְלָה 13 clothes (7·29) 971

עמס to load (1·7·9) 770

נָחֵשׁ 15 to practice divination (3·9·9) 638

נִצְטַדָּק 16 Hithp. צדק, to justify oneself (1·1·41) 842

גָּבִיעַ cup (5·14) 149

חָלִיל 17 far be it [for] (4·21) 321

גָּבִיעַ cup (5·14) 149

בִּי 18 I pray, excuse me (2·12) 106

זְקֻנִים 20 old age (4·4) 279

קָטָן young (6·47) 881

שבר 25 to buy grain (13·16·21) 991

אֹכֶל food (16·44) 38

טָרַף 28 to tear (3·13·24) 382

טרף to be torn (2·2·24) 382

הֵנָּה hither (8·49) 244

קרה 29 to befall (2·13·27) 899

אָסוֹן mischief, evil (3·5) 62

שֵׂיבָה gray hair (5·20[?]) 966

קָשַׁר 30 to bind (2·35·43) 905

שֵׂיבָה 31 gray hair (5·20[?]) 966

יָגוֹן sorrow (2·14) 387

עָרַב 32 to be surety (2·15·17) 786

Chapter 45

הִתְאַפֵּק 1 to restrain oneself (2·7·7) 67

בְּכִי 2 weeping (1·30) 113

נִבְהַל 3 to be disturbed, dismayed (1·24·39) 96

נֶעְצַב 5 to be grieved (1·7·15) 780

הֵנָּה hither (8·49) 244

מִחְיָה preservation of life (1·8) 313

חָרִישׁ 6 ploughing (1·3) 361

קָצִיר harvesting (3·49) 894

פְּלֵיטָה 7 escape, deliverance (2·28) 812

הֵנָּה 8 hither (8·49) 244

מֹשֵׁל ruler (2·24) 605

כִּלְכֵּל 11 to sustain (3·23·36) 465

הֵנָּה 13 hither (8·49) 244

צַוָּאר 14 neck (8·41) 848

נשׁק 15 to kiss (4·5·32) 676

טען 17 to load (1·1·1) 381

בְּעִיר beast (1·6) 129

טוּב 18 good things (4·32) 375

עֲגָלָה 19 cart (4·25) 722

טַף children (8·41) 381

חוס 20 to pity (1·24·24) 299

טוּב good things (4·32) 375

עֶגְלָה 21 cart (4·25) 722

צֵידָה provision (2·9) 845

חֲלִיפָה 22 change [of raiment] (2·12) 322

שִׂמְלָה garment (7·29) 971

כָּזֹאת 23 the like of this = as follows (1·1) 260

טוּב good things (4·32) 375

אָתוֹן she-ass (4·35) 87

בָּר grain (5·14) 141

מָזוֹן sustenance (1·2) 266

רָגַז 24 to quarrel (1·30·41) 919

מֹשֵׁל 26 ruler (2·24) 605

פוּג to grow numb (1·3·4) 806

עֲגָלָה 27 cart (4·25) 722

בְּטֶרֶם 28 before (5·39) 382

Chapter 46

מַרְאָה 2 vision (1·12) 909

טַף 5 children (8·41) 381

עֲגָלָה cart (4·25) 722

רְכוּשׁ 6 property (11·28) 940

רכש to gather [property] (5·5·5) 940

יָרֵךְ 26 thigh, loins (9·34) 437

מִלְּבַד besides (2·33) 94

הורה 28 to teach (1·45[?]·45[?]) 434

מֶרְכָּבָה 29 chariot (2·44) 939

צַוָּאר neck (8·41) 848

נְעוּרִים 34 youth (2·46) 655

בַּעֲבוּר in order that (15·46) 721

Chapter 47

הִצִּיג 2 to set (4·15·16) 426

מִרְעֶה 4 pasture (1·13) 945

כָּבֵד grievous (9·39) 458

מֵיטָב 6 best (2·5) 406

כַּמָּה 8 how much? how many? (1·13) 552

מְגוּרִים 9 sojourning (6·11) 158

הִשִּׂיג to reach (4·49·49) 673

מֵיטָב 11 best (2·5) 406

כִּלְכֵּל 12 to sustain (3·23·36) 465

טַף children (8·41) 381

כָּבֵד 13 grievous (9·39) 458

להה to faint, languish (1·1·2) 529

לקט 14 to gather (1·21·36) 544

שֶׁבֶר grain (7·9) 991

שבר to buy grain (13·16·21) 991

יהב 15 to give (8·27·27) 396

אָפֵס to cease, fail (2·5) 67

יהב 16 to give (8·27·27) 396

אָפֵס to cease, fail (2·5) 67

נהל 17 to refresh with food (1·9·10) 624

כָּחֵד 18 to hide (1·15·30) 470

בִּלְתִּי except (4·24) 116

גְּוִיָּה body (1·12) 156

הֵא 23 behold (1·2) 210

תְּבוּאָה 24 product, yield (1·43) 100

אֹכֶל food (16·44) 38

לַאֲשֶׁר to those who (4·38) 81

טַף children (8·41) 381

פרה 27 to be fruitful (10·22·29) 826

יָרֵךְ 29 thigh, loins (9·34) 437

קְבוּרָה 30 grave (3·14) 869

מִטָּה 31 bed (3·29) 641

Chapter 48

מִטָּה 2 bed (3·29) 641

שַׁדַּי 3 Almighty (6·48) 994

הִפְרָה 4 to make fruitful (5·7·29) 826

מוֹלֶדֶת 6 kindred (9·22) 409

בְּעוֹד 7 within yet (4·20) 728

כִּבְרָה a distance (2·3) 460

בָּזֶה 9 in this [place], here (3·19) 260

זָקֵן 10 old age (1·1) 279

נשק to kiss (4·5·32) 676

חבק to embrace (3·10·13) 287

פלל 11 to judge (1·4·5) 813

בֶּרֶךְ 12 knee (3·25) 139

צָעִיר 14 young (8·22) 859

שָׂכֵל to lay crosswise (1·1·1) 968

מֵעוֹד 15 ever since (1·2) 728

דגה 16 to multiply (1·1·1) 185

תמך 17 to grasp (1·20·21) 1069

מאן 19 to refuse (3·45·45) 549

אוּלָם but, indeed (2·19) 19

מְלֹא multitude (1·38) 571

שְׁכֶם 22 shoulder (6·22) 1014

Chapter 49

אוֹן 3 manly vigor (1·10) 20

שְׂאֵת dignity (2·7) 673

עַז strong (1·22) 738

פַּחַז 4 wantonness, recklessness (1·1) 808

מִשְׁכָּב bed (1·46) 1012

יָצוּעַ couch, bed (1·5) 426

מְכֵרָה 5 name of a weapon (1·1) 468

סוֹד 6 council (1·21) 691

יחד to be united (1·2·3) 402

עקר to hamstring (1·5·7) 785

עֶבְרָה 7 overflowing rage (1·34) 720

קשה to be hard, severe (1·5·28) 904

עֹרֶף 8 back of neck (1·33) 791

גּוּר 9 whelp, young (1·7) 158

טֶרֶף prey (1·17) 383

כָּרַע to bow down (1·29·35) 502

רָבַץ to lie down (5·24·30) 918

לָבִיא lion (1·11) 522

מְחֹקֵק 10 commander's staff (1·7) 349

מִבֵּין from between (1·21) 107

שִׁילֹה he whose it is (1·1) 1010

יְקָהָה obedience (1·2) 429

עַיִר 11 male ass (2·9) 747

שֹׂרֵקָה choice vine (1·1) 977

אָתוֹן she-ass (4·35) 87

לְבוּשׁ garment (1·31) 528

עֵנָב grape[s] (3·19) 772

סוּת vesture (1·1) 691

חַכְלִילִי 12 dull (1·1) 314

לָבָן white (3·28) 526

חָלָב milk (2·44) 316

חוֹף 13 shore, coast (2·7) 342

אֳנִיָּה ship (1·31) 58

יַרְכָּה further side (1·28) 438

גֶּרֶם 14 strength (1·5) 175

רָבַץ to lie down (5·24·30) 918

מִשְׁפְּתַיִם fireplaces, ash heaps (1·2) 1046

מְנוּחָה 15 resting-place (1·21) 629

נעם to be pleasant (1·8·8) 653

שְׁכֶם shoulder (6·22) 1014

סבל to bear a heavy load (1·7·9) 687

מַס labor band (1·23) 586

דין 16 to judge (4·23·24[?]) 192

נָחָשׁ 17 serpent (6·31) 638

שְׁפִיפֹן horned snake, viper (1·1) 1051

נָשַׁךְ to bite (1·10·12) 675

עָקֵב heel (3·14) 784

אָחוֹר backwards (1·41) 30

קוה 18 to look eagerly for (1·40·45) 875

גְּדוּד 19 marauding band (1·33) 151

גוד to attack (2·3[?]) 156

עָקֵב rear, heel (3·14) 784

שָׁמֵן 20 fat, rich (1·10) 1032

מַעֲדָן dainty food (1·3) 726

אַיָּלָה 21 doe (1·11) 19

אמר rd.'אָמִיר; אמר=top, summit (1·1) 57

שֶׁפֶר beauty (1·1) 1051

פרה 22 to be fruitful; pct. = fruit bearer, fruitful bough (10·22·29) 826

צעד to climb [dub.] (1·7·8) 857

שׁוּר wall (1·3) 1004

מרר 23 to show bitterness (1·3·14) 600

רבב to shoot (1·1·1) 914

שֹׂטֵם	to bear a grudge against (3·3·6) 966

Chapter 50

אֵיתָן 24 enduring, firm (1·14) 450

פֹּזז to be agile (1·1·2) 808

אָבִיר strong (1·6) 7

שַׁדַּי 25 Almighty (6·48) 994

עַל above (2·7) 752

תְּהוֹם deep (4·36) 1062

רָבַץ to lie down (5·24·30) 918

שַׁד [female] breast (1·21) 994

רַחַם womb (4·33) 933

גָּבַר 26 to be strong, prevail (5·17·25) 149

הֹרָה ptc. of הָרָה = parents, ancestors (1·3) 223

תַּאֲוָה boundary (2·21[?]) 1063

קָדְקֹד hairy crown, scalp (1·11) 869

נָזִיר one devoted (1·15) 634

זְאֵב 27 wolf (1·8) 255

טָרַף to tear (3·19·24) 382

עַד booty, prey (1·3) 723

עַם 29 kinsman (6·34) 769

מְעָרָה cave (11·40) 792

מְעָרָה 30 cave (11·40) 792

מְעָרָה 32 cave (11·40) 792

מִטָּה 33 bed (3·29) 641

גוע to die (6·24·24) 157

עַם kinsman (6·34) 769

נָשַׁק 1 to kiss (7·26·32) 676

אֹפֵר 2 physician (2·5[?]) 950

חנט to embalm (3·4·4) 334

חֲנֻטִים 3 embalming (1·1) 334

בְּכִית 4 weeping (1·1) 114

כָּרָה 5 to dig (2·13·14) 500

טַף 8 children (8·41) 381

כָּבֵד 9 numerous (9·39) 458

ספד 10 to lament (2·27·29) 704

מִסְפֵּד wailing (1·16) 704

כָּבֵד grievous (9·39) 458

אֵבֶל mourning (4·24) 5

אֵבֶל 11 mourning (4·24) 5

כָּבֵד vehement, sore (9·39) 458

מְעָרָה 13 cave (11·40) 792

לוּ 15 if (4·19) 530

שֹׂטֵם to bear a grudge against (3·3·6) 966

גָּמַל to deal out, to repay (2·34·37) 168

אָנָּא 17 we beseech thee (1·7) 58

גָּמַל to deal out, to repay (2·34·37) 168

כִּלְכֵּל 21 to sustain (3·23·36) 465

טַף children (8·41) 381

שִׁלֵּשִׁים 23 those of the third generation (1·5) 1026

בֶּרֶךְ knee (3·25) 139

חנט 26 to embalm (3·4·4) 334

EXODUS

Chapter 1

יָרֵךְ	5	thigh, loins (7·34) 437
פרה	7	to be fruitful (2·22·29) 826
שָׁרַץ		to swarm (2·14·14) 1056
עָצַם		to be numerous (2·16·18) 782
עָצוּם	9	mighty (1·31) 783
יהב	10	to come now (1·27·27) 396
התחכם		to deal wisely (1·2·26) 314
שֹׂנֵא		enemy (3·41) 971
מַס	11	slave gang (1·23) 586
סבלה		burden (6·6) 688
מִסְכְּנוֹת		storage (1·7) 698
פָּרַץ	12	to break over; increase (3·46·49) 829
קוץ		to feel a sickening dread (1·8·8) 880
פֶּרֶךְ	13	harshness; severity (2·6) 827
מרר	14	to make bitter (1·3·14) 600
קָשֶׁה		severe (7·36) 904
חֹמֶר		mortar (1·17) 330
לְבֵנָה		brick (8·12) 527
פֶּרֶךְ		harshness; severity (2·6) 827
מְיַלֶּדֶת	15	midwife (7·9) 408
אֹבֶן	16	midwife's stool (1·2) 7
מְיַלֶּדֶת	17	midwife (7·9) 408
מְיַלֶּדֶת	18	midwife (7·9) 408
מְיַלֶּדֶת	19	midwife (7·9) 408
חָיֶה		lively; bearing quickly (1·1) 313
בְּטֶרֶם	19	before (1·39) 382
מְיַלֶּדֶת	20	midwife (7·9) 408
עָצַם		to be numerous (2·16·18) 782
מְיַלֶּדֶת	21	midwife (7·9) 408
ילוד	22	born (1·5) 409

Chapter 2

הָרָה	2	to conceive (1·38·40) 247
צָפַן		to hide (1·23·28) 860
יֶרַח		month (1·12) 437
הצפן	3	to hide (1·2·28) 860
תֵּבָה		ark (2·28) 1061
גֹּמֶא		rush; reed; papyrus (1·4) 167
חמר		to cover; smear (1·5·5[?]) 330
חֵמָר		bitumen; asphalt (1·3) 330
זֶפֶת		pitch (1·3) 278
סוּף		reeds (2·4) 693
הִתִיצֵב	4	to station oneself (6·48·48) 426
תֵּבָה	5	ark (2·28) 1061
סוּף		reeds (2·4) 693
חָמַל	6	to spare (1·40·40) 328
היניק	7	to nurse (4·10·18) 413
עַלְמָה	8	young woman (1·9) 761
היניק	9	to nurse (4·10·18) 413
שָׂכָר		hire; wages (2·29) 969
משה	10	to draw (1·1·3) 602
סבלה	11	burden (6·6) 688
טָמַן	12	to hide (1·28·31) 380
חוֹל		sand (1·22) 297
נצה	13	to struggle with each other (2·5·8) 663
אָכֵן	14	surely; truly (1·18) 38
בְּאֵר	15	well (1·36) 91
דָּלָה	16	to draw [water] (2·4·5) 194
רהט		trough (1·4) 923
גרש	17	to drive out (1·7·46) 176
דָּלָה	19	to draw [water] (2·4·5) 194
אִי	20	where (1·39) 32
הוֹאִיל	21	to show willingness (1·18·18) 383
נָכְרִי	22	foreign (3·45) 648
נאנח	23	to sigh (1·12·12) 58
שַׁוְעָה		cry for help (1·11) 1003
נאקה	24	groaning (2·4) 611

Chapter 3

חֹתֵן	1	wife's father (15·21) 368
נָהַג		to drive (1·20·30) 624
לַבַּה	2	flame (1·1[?]) 529
סְנֶה		blackberry bush[?] (5·6) 702
סְנֶה	3	blackberry bush[?] (5·6) 702
סְנֶה	4	blackberry bush[?] (5·6) 702
הֲלֹם	5	hither; here (1·11) 240
נָשַׁל		to draw off (1·6·7) 675
נַעַל		sandle (2·22) 653
עֳנִי	7	affliction (3·36) 777
צְעָקָה	7	cry of distress (5·21) 858
נֹגֵשׂ		taskmaster (5·15) 620
מַכְאֹוב		pain (1·16) 456
רָחָב	8	wide; broad (1·21) 932
זוּב		to flow (4·29·29) 264
חָלָב		milk (6·44) 316
צְעָקָה	9	cry of distress (5·21) 858
לַחַץ		oppression (1·11) 537
לָחַץ		to oppress (3·14·15) 537
זֵכֶר	15	memorial (2·33) 271
עֳנִי	17	affliction (3·36) 777
זוּב		to flow (4·29·29) 264
חָלָב		milk (6·44) 316
נִקְרָה	18	to encounter; meet (1·6·27) 899
נִפְלָאֹות	20	wonderful acts (2·43) 810
רֵיקָם	21	in empty condition; emptily (3·16) 938
שָׁכֵן	22	neighbor (2·20) 1015
שִׂמְלָה		clothes (6·29) 971

Chapter 4

נָחָשׁ	3	serpent (2·31) 638
זָנָב	4	tail (1·11) 275
חֵיק	6	fold of the garment at the breast (5·38) 300
מְצֹרָע		leprous (1·15) 863

שֶׁלֶג		snow (1·20) 1017
חֵיק	7	fold of the garment at the breast (5·38) 300
יַבָּשָׁה	9	dry ground (5·14) 387
בִּי	10	I pray!; excuse me (2·12) 106
תְּמֹול		yesterday; afore-time (7·23) 1069
שִׁלְשֹׁם		three days ago; specif. = the day before yesterday (6·25) 1026
מֵאָז		since (3·18) 23
כָּבֵד		heavy (9·39) 458
אִלֵּם	11	dumb; unable to speak (1·6) 48
חֵרֵשׁ		deaf (1·9) 361
פִּקֵּחַ		seeing (2·2) 824
עִוֵּר		blind (1·25) 734
הֹורָה	12	to teach (5·45·45[?]) 434
בִּי	13	I pray!; excuse me (2·12) 106
הֹורָה	15	to teach (5·45·45[?]) 434
חֹתֵן	18	wife's father (15·21) 368
מֹופֵת	21	wonder (5·36) 68
מֵאֵן	23	to refuse (8·45·45) 549
מָלֹון	24	lodging-place (1·8) 533
פגשׁ		to meet; encounter (2·10·14) 803
צֹר	25	flint [used as a knife] (1·6) 866
עָרְלָה		foreskin (1·16) 790
חָתָן		daughter's husband; bridegroom (2·20) 368
רָפָה	26	to relax; withdraw (1·14·44) 951
חָתָן		bridegroom; daughter's husband (2·20) 368
מוּלָה		circumcision (1·1) 558
פגשׁ	27	to meet; encounter (2·10·14) 803
נָשַׁק		to kiss (2·26·32) 676
עֳנִי	31	affliction (3·36) 777 ·
קדד		to bow down (3·15·15) 869

Chapter 5

חגג	1	to keep a pilgrim feast (4·16·16) 290

פָּגַע 3 to fall upon (3·40·46) 803

דֶּבֶר plague (3·46) 184

הִפְרִיעַ 4 to cause to refrain (1·2·16) 828

סבלה burden (6·6) 688

סבלה 5 burden (6·6) 688

נֹגֵשׂ 6 taskmaster (5·15) 620

שֹׁטֵר official; officer (5·25) 1009

תֶּבֶן 7 straw (8·17) 1061

לבן to make brick (2·3·3) 527

לְבֵנָה brick (8·12) 527

תְּמוֹל yesterday; formerly (7·23) 1069

שִׁלְשֹׁם three days ago; specif. = the day before yesterday (6·25) 1026

קֹשֵׁשׁ to gather stubble (2·6·8) 905

מַתְכֹּנֶת 8 proportion (3·5) 1067

לְבֵנָה brick (8·12) 527

תְּמוֹל yesterday; formerly (7·23) 1069

שִׁלְשֹׁם three days ago; specif. = the day before yesterday (6·25) 1026

גרע to diminish (3·14·22) 175

נרפה to be idle (2·2·44) 951

שָׁעָה 9 to gaze (1·12·15) 1043

נֹגֵשׂ 10 taskmaster (5·15) 620

שֹׁטֵר official; officer (5·25) 1009

תֶּבֶן straw (8·17) 1061

תֶּבֶן 11 straw (8·17) 1061

מֵאֲשֶׁר from that which (3·17) 84

נגרע to be withdrawn (1·7·22) 175

קֹשֵׁשׁ 12 to gather stubble (2·6·8) 905

קַשׁ stubble, chaff (2·16) 905

תֶּבֶן straw (8·17) 1061

נֹגֵשׂ 13 taskmaster (5·15) 620

אוץ to press; hasten (1·8·10) 21

תֶּבֶן straw (8·17) 1061

שֹׁטֵר 14 official; officer (5·25) 1009

נֹגֵשׂ taskmaster (5·15) 620

לבן to make brick (2·3·3) 527

תְּמוֹל yesterday; formerly (7·23) 1069

שִׁלְשֹׁם three days ago; specif. = the day before yesterday (6·25) 1026

שֹׁטֵר 15 official; officer (5·25) 1009

תֶּבֶן 16 straw (8·17) 1061

לְבֵנָה brick (8·12) 527

נרפה 17 to be idle (2·2·44) 951

תֶּבֶן 18 straw (8·17) 1061

תֹּכֶן measurement (1·2) 1067

לְבֵנָה brick (8·12) 527

שֹׁטֵר 19 official; officer (5·25) 1009

גרע to diminish (3·14·22) 175

לְבֵנָה brick (8·12) 527

פָּגַע 20 to meet; light upon (3·40·46) 803

הִבְאִישׁ 21 to cause to stink (2·7·16) 92

מֵאָז 23 since (3·18) 23

Chapter 6

גרש 1 to drive out (1·7·46) 176

מָגוּר 4 sojourning (1·11) 158

נאקה 5 groaning (2·4) 611

סבלה 6 burden (6·6) 688

שפט judgement (3·16) 1048

סבלה 7 burden (6·6) 688

מוֹרָשָׁה 8 possession (1·9) 440

קֹצֶר 9 shortness (1·1) 894

קָשֶׁה severe (7·36) 904

עָרֵל 12 uncircumcised (3·35) 790

תּוֹלְדוֹת 16 generations (3·39) 410

תּוֹלְדוֹת 19 generations (3·39) 410

דֹּדָה 20 aunt (1·3) 187

עָרֵל 30 uncircumcised (3·35) 790

Chapter 7

הִקְשָׁה 3 to make stiff; stubborn (2·21·28) 904

מוֹפֵת wonder (5·36) 68

שפט 4 judgment (3·16) 1048

מוֹפֵת 9 wonder (5·36) 68

תַּנִּין serpent (3·15) 1072

תַּנִּין 10 serpent (3·15) 1072

31

כָּשַׁף	11 to practice sorcery (2·6·6) 506
חרטם	magician (7·11) 355
לְהָטִים	mysteries (1·1[?]) 532
תַּנִּין	12 serpent (3·15) 1072
בָּלַע	to swallow down (2·20·41[?]) 118
כָּבֵד	14 heavy, hard (9·39) 458
מֵאֵן	to refuse (8·45·45) 549
נָחָשׁ	15 serpent (2·31) 638
בְּזֹאת	17 by; through this (1·15) 260
דָּגָה	18 fish [collective] (2·15) 185
בָּאַשׁ	to stink (4·5·16) 92
נִלְאָה	to be weary (1·10·19) 521
אֲגַם	19 pool; pond (2·8) 8
דָּגָה	21 fish [collective] (2·15) 185
בָּאַשׁ	to stink (4·5·16) 92
חרטם	22 magician (7·11) 355
לָט	mystery (3·7) 532
לָזֹאת	23 for this (1·3) 260
חָפַר	24 to dig; search for (1·22·22) 343
מֵאֵן	27 to refuse (8·45·45) 549
נָגַף	to strike (7·24·48) 619
צְפַרְדֵּעַ	frog (11·13) 862
שָׁרַץ	28 to swarm (2·14·14) 1056
צְפַרְדֵּעַ	frog (11·13) 862
חֶדֶר	room; chamber (1·34) 293
מִשְׁכָּב	lying down (2·46) 1012
מִטָּה	bed (1·29) 641
תַּנּוּר	stove; firepot (1·15) 1072
משארת	kneading trough (2·4) 602
צְפַרְדֵּעַ	29 frog (11·13) 862

Chapter 8

אֲגַם	1 pool; pond (2·8) 8
צְפַרְדֵּעַ	frog (11·13) 862
צְפַרְדֵּעַ	2 frog (11·13) 862
חרטם	3 magician (7·11) 355
לָט	mystery (3·7) 532
צְפַרְדֵּעַ	frog (11·13) 862
הַעְתִּיר	4 to make supplication (6·7·20) 801
צְפַרְדֵּעַ	frog (11·13) 862

הִתְפָּאֵר	5 to glorify oneself (1·7·13) 802
לְמָתַי	against when (1·1) 607
הַעְתִּיר	to make supplication (6·7·20) 801
צְפַרְדֵּעַ	frog (11·13) 862
צְפַרְדֵּעַ	7 frog (11·13) 862
צְפַרְדֵּעַ	8 frog (11·13) 862
צְפַרְדֵּעַ	9 frog (11·13) 862
צבר	10 to heap up (1·7·7) 840
חֹמֶר	heap (2·12) 330
בָּאַשׁ	to stink (4·5·16) 92
רְוָחָה	11 respite; relief (1·2) 926
כֵּן	12 gnat (3·5) 487
כִּנָּם	13 gnats (2·2) 487
כֵּן	gnat (3·5) 487
חרטם	14 magician (7·11) 355
לָט	mystery (3·7) 532
כֵּן	gnat (3·5) 487
כִּנָּם	14 gnats (2·2) 487
חרטם	15 magician (7·11) 355
אֶצְבַּע	finger (3·31) 840
הִתְיַצֵּב	16 to set oneself (6·48·48) 426
עָרֹב	17 a swarm (7·9) 786
הִפְלָה	18 to make separate; set apart (3·3·4) 811
עָרֹב	a swarm (7·9) 786
פְּדוּת	19 ransom (1·4) 804
עָרֹב	20 a swarm (7·9) 786
כָּבֵד	heavy (9·39) 458
סָקַל	22 to stone (4·12·22) 709
הַעְתִּיר	24 to make supplication (6·7·20) 801
הַעְתִּיר	25 to make supplication (6·7·20) 801
עָרֹב	a swarm (7·9) 786
הֵתֵל	to mock; trifle with (1·1·1[?]) 1068
עתר	26 to pray; supplicate (2·5·20) 801
עָרֹב	a swarm (7·9) 786

Chapter 9

מֵאֵן	2 to refuse (8·45·45) 549
דֶּבֶר	3 plague (3·46) 184

32

כָּבֵד grievous (9·39) 458

הִפְלָה 4 to make separate; to set apart (3·3·4) 811

מָחֳרָת 6 the morrow (4·32) 564

חֹפֶן 8 hollow of hand (1·6) 342

פִּיחַ soot (2·2) 806

כִּבְשָׁן kiln (3·4) 461

זָרַק to toss (6·32·34) 284

אָבָק 9 dust (1·6) 7

שְׁחִין boil (4·13) 1006

פָּרַח to break out (2·29·34) 827

אֲבַעְבֻּעֹת blisters; boils (2·2) 101

פִּיחַ 10 soot (2·2) 806

כִּבְשָׁן kiln (3·4) 461

זָרַק to toss (6·32·34) 284

שְׁחִין boil (4·13) 1006

אֲבַעְבֻּעֹת blisters; boils (2·2) 101

פָּרַח to break out (2·29·34) 827

חרטם 11 magician (7·11) 355

שְׁחִין boil (4·13) 1006

הִתְיַצֵּב 13 to set oneself (6·48·48) 426

מַגֵּפָה 14 plague (1·26) 620

בַּעֲבוּר for the sake of (6·46) 21

דֶּבֶר 15 plague (3·46) 184

נִכְחַד to be destroyed (1·9·30) 470

אוּלָם 16 but; but indeed (1·19) 19

בַּעֲבוּר for the sake of (6·46) 721

הִסְתּוֹלֵל 17 to exalt oneself (1·1·10) 699

הִמְטִיר 18 to rain (3·16·17) 565

בָּרָד hail (17·24) 135

כָּבֵד grievous (9·39) 458

לְמִן from (1·14) 583

נוסד to be founded (1·2·42) 413

הֵעִיז 19 to bring into safety (1·4·5) 731

בָּרָד 19 hail (17·29) 135

בָּרָד 22 hail (17·29) 135

עֵשֶׂב herb (5·33) 793

בָּרָד 23 hail (17·29) 135

הִמְטִיר to rain (3·16·17) 565

בָּרָד 24 hail (17·29) 135

כָּבֵד grievous (9·39) 458

מֵאָז since (3·18) 23

בָּרָד 25 hail (17·29) 135

עֵשֶׂב herb (5·33) 793

בָּרָד 26 hail (17·29) 135

הֶעְתִּיר 28 to make supplication (6·7·20) 801

בָּרָד hail (17·29) 135

בָּרָד 29 hail (17·29) 135

טֶרֶם 30 not yet (3·16) 382

פִּשְׁתָּה 31 flax (2·4) 834

שְׂעֹרָה barley (2·34) 972

אָבִיב young ears (5·8) 1

גִּבְעֹל bud (1·1) 149

כֻּסֶּמֶת 32 spelt (1·3) 493

אפיל late [of crops] (1·1) 66

בָּרָד 33 hail (17·29) 135

מָטָר rain (2·37) 564

נִתַּךְ to be poured (1·8·21) 677

מָטָר 34 rain (2·37) 564

בָּרָד hail (17·29) 135

Chapter 10

הִתְעַלֵּל 2 to make a toy of (1·7·17) 759

מָתַי 3 when? (2·42) 607

מֵאָן to refuse (8·45·45) 549

מֵאָן 4 to refuse (8·45·45) 549

אַרְבֶּה locust (7·24) 916

פְּלֵיטָה 5 escaped remnant (1·28) 812

בָּרָד hail (17·29) 135

צָמַח to sprout (1·15·33) 855

מָתַי 7 when? (2·42) 607

מוֹקֵשׁ snare (3·27) 430

טֶרֶם not yet (3·16) 382

טַף 10 children (3·41) 381

גרש 11 to drive away (9·33·33[?]) 176

אַרְבֶּה 12 locust (7·24) 916

עֵשֶׂב herb (5·33) 793

בָּרָד hail (17·29) 135

נָהַג 13 to drive away (2·10·30) 624

אַרְבֶּה locust (7·24) 916

אַרְבֶּה 14 locust (7·24) 916

כָּבֵד numerous (9·39) 458

חָשַׁךְ 15 to have a dark color; to be dark (1·11·17) 364

עֵשֶׂב herb (5·33) 793

בָּרָד hail (17·29) 135

יֶרֶק green (1·8) 438

הֶעְתִּיר 17 to make supplication (6·7·20) 801

עתר 18 to pray; supplicate (2·5·20) 801

אַרְבֶּה 19 locust (7·24) 916

המשׁ 21 to feel (1·3·4[?]) 606

אֲפֵלָה 22 darkness (1·10) 66

מוֹשָׁב 23 dwelling place (4·43) 444

הצג 24 to be detained (1·1·16) 426

טַף children (3·41) 381

פַּרְסָה 26 hoof (1·21) 828

Chapter 11

כָּלָה 1 complete destruction (1·22) 478

גרשׁ to drive out (9·33·46) 176

רְעוּת 2 fellow [woman] (1·6) 946

רחה 5 [hand] mill (1·5) 932

צְעָקָה 6 cry of distress (5·21) 858

חָרַץ 7 to sharpen; to sharpen tongue = to utter a sound (1·5·10) 358

כֶּלֶב dog (2·32) 476

הִפְלָה to make separate; to set apart (3·3·4) 811

חֳרִי 8 burning (1·6) 354

מוֹפֵת 9 wonder (5·36) 68

מוֹפֵת 10 wonder (5·36) 68

Chapter 12

עָשׂוֹר 3 tenth day (1·15) 797

שֶׂה one of a flock; sheep; goat (13·44) 961

מעט 4 to be small (1·8·22) 589

שֶׂה one of a flock; sheep; goat (13·44) 961

שָׁכֵן neighbor (2·20) 1015

מִכְסָה number (1·2) 493

כסס to compute (1·1·1) 493

שֶׂה 5 one of a flock; sheep; goat (13·44) 961

מְזוּזָה 7 doorpost (4·20) 265

מַשְׁקוֹף lintel[?] (3·3) 1054

צָלִי 8 roasted (2·3) 852

מרר bitter herb (1·5[?]) 601

נָא 9 raw (1·1) 644

בשׁל boiled (1·2·27) 143

בשׁל to be boiled (1·4·27) 143

צָלִי roasted (2·3) 852

כרע leg (2·9) 502

כָּכָה 11 thus (2·34) 462

מָתְנַיִם loins (2·50) 608

חגר to gird on (2·44·44) 291

נַעַל sandal (2·22) 653

מַקֵּל staff (1·18) 596

חִפָּזוֹן hurried flight (1·3) 342

פֶּסַח passover (6·49) 820

שׁפט 12 judgment (3·16) 1048

פָּסַח 13 to pass over (3·5·7) 820

נֶגֶף blow; plague (2·7) 620

מַשְׁחִית destruction (2·19) 1008

זִכָּרוֹן 14 memorial day; memorial (8·24) 272

חגג to keep a pilgrim feast (4·16·16) 290

שְׂאֹר 15 leaven (3·5) 959

חָמֵץ that which is leavened (5·11) 329

מִקְרָא 16 convocation (2·22) 896

לְבַדּוֹ alone (3·35) 94

בְּעֶצֶם 17 selfsame; itself (3·17) 783

שְׂאֹר 19 leaven (3·5) 959
מַחְמֶצֶת anything leavened (2·2) 330
אֶזְרָח native (3·17) 280
מַחְמֶצֶת 20 anything leavened (2·2) 330
מוֹשָׁב dwelling place (4·43) 444
מָשַׁךְ 21 to proceed (2·30·36) 604
פֶּסַח passover (6·49) 820
אֲגֻדָּה 22 bunch; band (1·4) 8
אֵזוֹב hyssop (1·10) 23
טָבַל to dip (1·15·16) 371
סַף basin (1·6) 706
מַשְׁקוֹף lintel[?] (3·3) 1054
מְזוּזָה doorpost (4·20) 265
נָגַף 23 to strike (7·24·48) 619
מַשְׁקוֹף lintel[?] (3·3) 1054
מְזוּזָה doorpost (4·20) 265
פָּסַח to pass over (3·5·7) 820
מַשְׁחִית destroyer (2·19) 1008
פֶּסַח 27 passover (6·49) 820
פָּסַח to pass over (3·5·7) 820
נָגַף to strike (7·24·48) 619
קדד 27 to bow down (3·15·15) 869
שְׁבִי 29 captive (1·46) 985
צְעָקָה 30 cry of distress (5·21) 858
בָּצֵק 34 dough (2·5) 130
טֶרֶם ere; before that (3·16) 382
חָמֵץ to be leavened (2·3·4) 329
משארת kneading trough (2·4) 602
שִׂמְלָה wrapper; mantle (6·29) 971
שְׁכֶם shoulder (1·22) 1014
שִׂמְלָה 35 clothes (5·29) 971
רַגְלִי 37 on foot (1·12) 920
טַף children (3·41) 381
עֵרֶב 38 mixture; mixed company (1·5) 786
כָּבֵד heavy (9·39) 458
אָפָה 39 to bake (2·9·12) 66
בָּצֵק dough (2·5) 130
עֻגָה cake of bread (1·7) 728
חָמֵץ to be leavened (2·3·4) 329
גרש to drive out (1·7·46) 176
התמהמה to tarry (1·9·9) 554
צֵידָה provision (1·9) 845
מוֹשָׁב 40 time of dwelling (4·43) 444
בְּעֶצֶם 41 selfsame; itself (3·17) 783
פֶּסַח 43 passover (6·49) 820
נֵכָר foreignness (1·36) 648
מול 44 to circumcise (1·12·29) 557
תּוֹשָׁב 45 sojourner (1·14) 444
שָׂכִיר 45 hired laborer (2·18) 969
פֶּסַח 48 passover (6·49) 820
נִמּוֹל to be circumcised (1·17·29) 557
אֶזְרָח native (3·17) 280
עָרֵל uncircumcised (3·35) 790
אֶזְרָח 49 native (3·17) 280
בְּעֶצֶם 51 selfsame; itself (3·17) 783

Chapter 13

פֶּטֶר 2 firstborn (8·11) 809
רֶחֶם womb (4·32) 933
חֹזֶק 3 strength (3·5) 305
חָמֵץ that which is leavened (5·11) 329
זוב 5 to flow (4·29·29) 264
חָלָב milk (6·44) 316
חָמֵץ 7 that which is leavened (5·11) 329
שְׂאֹר leaven (3·5) 959
בַּעֲבוּר 8 for the sake of (6·46) 721
זִכָּרוֹן 9 memorial (8·24) 272
פֶּטֶר 12 firstborn (8·11) 809
רֶחֶם womb (4·32) 933
שֶׁגֶר offspring; young [of beasts] (1·5) 993
פֶּטֶר 13 firstborn (8·11) 809
שֶׂה one of a flock; sheep, goat (13·44) 961
ערף to break the neck (2·6·6) 791
חֹזֶק 14 strength (3·5) 305

הַקְשָׁה 15 to make stiff; stubborn (2·21·28) 904

פֶּטֶר firstborn (8·11) 809

רֶחֶם womb (4·32) 933

טוֹטָפוֹת 16 bands (1·3) 377

חֹזֶק strength (3·5) 305

נחה 17 to lead (4·14·40) 634

חֲמֻשִׁים 18 in battle array (1·4·5[?]) 332

נחה 21 to lead (4·14·40) 634

הֵאִיר to light up; shine (3·34·40) 21

הֵמִישׁ 22 to remove (2·20[?]·20) 559

Chapter 14

נֹכַח 2 in front of (3·22) 647

נבוך 3 to be confused; perplexed (1·3·3) 100

בָּחוּר 7 chosen (1·19[?]) 103

שָׁלִישׁ adjutant; officer (2·16) 1026

רָם 8 high; exalted (1·31)[?] 926

הִשִּׂיג 9 to overtake (2·48·48) 673

מִבְּלִי 11 from want of (1·25) 115

הִתְיַצֵּב 13 to take one's stand (6·48·48) 426

הֶחֱרִישׁ 14 to be silent (2·38·46) 361

יַבָּשָׁה 16 dry ground (5·14) 387

הֵאִיר 20 to light up; shine (3·34·40) 21

עָז 21 strong; mighty (1·22) 738

חָרָבָה dry ground (1·8) 351

יַבָּשָׁה 22 dry ground (5·14) 387

תָּוֶךְ 23 midst; middle (1·33) 1063

אַשְׁמֹרֶת 24 watch (1·7) 1038

הִשְׁקִיף to look down (1·12·22) 1054

הָמַם to confuse; discomfit (2·13·13) 243

אוֹפָן 25 wheel (1·34) 66

מֶרְכָּבָה chariot (2·44) 939

נָהַג to drive away (2·10·30) 624

כְּבֵדֻת heaviness (1·1) 459

אֵיתָן 27 steady flow (1·14) 450

נער to shake off (1·3·10) 654

יַבָּשָׁה 29 dry ground (5·14) 387

Chapter 15

שִׁירָה 1 song (1·13) 1010

גָּאָה to be lifted up; exalted (2·5·5) 144

רָמָה to cast (2·4·4) 941

זִמְרָה 2 melody; song (1·4) 274

הנוה to adorn (1·1·1[?]) 627

מֶרְכָּבָה 4 chariot (2·44) 939

ירה to throw (2·13·25[?]) 434

מבחר choicest (1·12) 104

שָׁלִישׁ adjutant; officer (2·16) 1026

טבע to be sunk (1·1·10) 371

תְּהוֹם 5 sea; abyss (2·36) 1062

מְצוּלָה depth (1·12) 846

נֶאְדָּר 6 majestic (2·2) 12

רעץ to shatter (1·2·2) 950

גָּאוֹן 7 exaltation (1·49) 144

הָרַס to throw down (3·40·43) 248

קם adversary (2·12) 878

חָרוֹן [burning of] anger (2·41) 354

קַשׁ stubble; chaff (2·16) 905

נערם 8 to be heaped up (1·1·1) 790

נֵד heap of waters (1·6) 622

נֹזֵל flood (1·5) 633

קפא to condense (1·2·3) 891

תְּהוֹם sea; abyss (2·36) 1062

הִשִּׂיג 9 to overtake (2·48·48) 673

הריק to make empty (1·17·19) 937

נָשַׁף 10 to blow (1·2·2) 676

צלל to sink (1·1·1) 853

עֹפֶרֶת lead (metal) (1·9) 780

אַדִּיר majestic (1·27) 12

נֶאְדָּר 11 majestic (2·2) 12

נוֹרָא fearful (2·44) 431

פֶּלֶא wonder (1·13) 810

בָּלַע 12 to swallow down (2·20·41[?]) 118

נחה 13 to lead (4·14·40) 634

36

זוּ which (2·16) 262

נהל to lead to a station (1·9·10) 624

נָוֶה habitation (1·45) 627

רָגַז 14 to quake (1·30·41) 919

חִיל writhing (1·6) 297

נִבְהַל 15 to be dismayed (1·1·39) 96

רַעַד trembling (1·2) 944

נָמוֹג to melt (1·8·17) 556

אֵימָה 16 terror; dread (2·17) 33

פַּחַד dread (1·49) 808

דמם to be struck dumb; astonished (1·23·30) 198

זוּ which (2·16) 262

מָכוֹן 17 fixed place (1·17) 467

עַד 18 forever (1·48) 723

יַבָּשָׁה 19 dry ground (5·14) 387

נְבִיאָה 20 prophetess (1·6) 612

תֹף timbrel; tamborine (2·17) 1074

מחולה dance (2·8) 298

ענה 21 to sing (3·13·16) 777

גָּאָה to be lifted up; exalted (2·5·5) 144

רָמָה to cast (2·4·4) 941

מַר 23 bitter (1·37) 600

נלון 24 to murmur (3·8·18) 534

הורה 25 to teach (5·45·45[?]) 434

מתק to be sweet (1·4·6) 608

נָסָה to test (5·36·36) 650

הֶאֱזִין 26 to listen (1·41·41) 24

מַחֲלָה sickness (2·4) 318

רֹפֵא physician (1·5)[?] 950

תָּמָר 25 palm tree; date palm (1·12) 1041

Chapter 16

נלון 2 to murmur (3·8·18) 534

סִיר 3 pot (3·29) 696

שֹׂבַע satiety; abundance (1·8) 959

הִמְטִיר 4 to rain (3·16·17) 565

לקט to gather (9·14·36) 544

נִסָּה to test (5·36·36) 650

מִשְׁנֶה 5 double (2·35) 1041

לקט to gather (9·14·36) 544

תלנה 7 murmuring (5·8) 534

הלין to murmur (4·10·18) 534

תלנה 8 murmuring (5·8) 534

הלין to murmur (4·10·18) 534

תלנה 9 murmuring (5·8) 534

תלנה 12 murmuring (5·8) 534

שְׂלָו 13 quail (1·4) 969

שכבה layer [of dew] (2·9) 1012

טַל dew (2·31) 378

שכבה 14 layer [of dew] (2·9) 1012

טַל dew (2·31) 378

דַּק small; fine (2·14) 201

חספס to be scalelike (1·1·1) 341

כְּפוֹר hoar frost (1·3) 499

מָן 15 what (1·1) 577

לקט 16 to gather (9·14·36) 544

אֹכֶל food; food supply (4·44) 38

עֹמֶר omer (6·6) 771

גֻּלְגֹּלֶת head [in counting]="for each man" (2·12) 166

לַאֲשֶׁר to whom (1·38) 81

לקט 17 to gather (9·14·36) 544

הִמְעִיט to make small (3·13·22) 589

עֹמֶר 18 omer (6·6) 771

הֶעְדִּיף to have a surplus (1·1·9) 727

הִמְעִיט to make small (3·13·22) 589

הֶחְסִיר to cause to lack (1·2·24) 341

אֹכֶל food; food supply (4·44) 38

לקט to gather (9·14·36) 544

רמם 20 to be wormy (1·1·1) 942

תּוֹלֵעָה worm, grub (27·41) 1069

בָּאַשׁ to stink (4·5·16) 92

קָצַף to be wroth (1·28·34) 893

לקט 21 to gather (9·14·36) 544

כְּפִי in proportion to (3·16) 804

אֹכֶל	food; food supply (4·44) 38		גָּבַר	11 to prevail (2·17·25) 149
חמם	to be or grow warm (1·23·26) 328		כָּבֵד	12 heavy (9·39) 458
נָמֵס	to melt (1·19·21) 587		תמך	to hold up; support (1·20·21) 1069
לקט	22 to gather (9·14·36) 544		חלש	13 to disable (1·3·3) 325
מִשְׁנֶה	double (2·35) 1041		זִכָּרוֹן	14 memorial; reminder (8·24) 272
עֹמֶר	omer (6·6) 771		מָחָה	to exterminate (3·22·35) 562
שַׁבָּתוֹן	23 Sabbath observance (3·11) 992		זֵכֶר	remembrance; memory (2·23) 271
אָפָה	to bake (2·9·12) 66		נֵס	15 standard (1·21) 651
בשל	to boil; cook (4·20·27) 143		כֵּס	16 throne (1·1) 490
עדף	to remain over; be in excess (4·8·9) 727			

Chapter 18

הִבְאִישׁ	24 to emit a stinking odor (2·7·16) 92		חֹתֵן	1 wife's father (15·21) 368
רִמָּה	worm (1·7) 942		חֹתֵן	2 wife's father (15·21) 368
לקט	26 to gather (9·14·36) 544		שִׁלּוּחִים	a sending away (1·3) 1019
לקט	27 to gather (9·14·36) 544		נָכְרִי	3 foreign (3·45) 648
אָנָה	28 whither? where? (1·39) 33		עֵזֶר	4 help; one who helps (1·21) 740
מֵאַן	to refuse (8·45·45) 549		חֹתֵן	5 wife's father (15·21) 368
מָן	31 manna (5·14) 577		חֹתֵן	6 wife's father (15·21) 368
גַּד	coriander (1·2) 151		חֹתֵן	7 wife's father (15·21) 368
לָבָן	white (1·28) 526		נָשַׁק	to kiss (2·26·32) 676
טַעַם	taste (1·13) 381		חֹתֵן	8 wife's father (15·21) 368
צַפִּיחִת	flat cake; wafer (1·1) 860		אוֹדָה	cause (1·11) 15
עֹמֶר	32 omer (6·6) 771		תְּלָאָה	weariness; hardship (1·15) 521
צִנְצֶנֶת	33 jar (1·1) 857		חדה	9 to rejoice (1·2·3) 292
עֹמֶר	omer (6·6) 771		זוד	11 to act presumptuously; rebelliously (1·2·10) 267
מָן	manna (5·14) 577			
מָן	manna (5·14) 577		חֹתֵן	12 wife's father (15·21) 368
עֹמֶר	36 omer (6·6) 771		מָחֳרָת	13 the morrow (4·32) 564
אֵיפָה	ephah (1·38) 35		יָרָה	to throw (2·13·25[?]) 434
			חֹתֵן	14 wife's father (15·21) 368

Chapter 17

			חֹתֵן	15 wife's father (15·21) 368
מַסַּע	1 journey by stages (3·12) 652		חֹתֵן	17 wife's father (15·21) 368
נסה	2 to test (5·36·36) 650		נָבֵל	18 to sink down (2·20·24[?]) 615
צָמֵא	3 to be thirsty (1·10·10) 854		כָּבֵד	heavy (9·39) 458
הלין	to murmur (4·10·18) 534		מוּל	19 in front of (6·25) 557
צָמָא	thirst (1·17) 854		הִזְהִיר	20 to teach; warn (1·13·21) 264
סקל	4 to stone (4·12·22) 709		יָרֵא	21 fear (1·45) 431
נסה	7 to test (5·36·36) 650		בֶּצַע	unjust gain (1·23) 130

38

חֹתֵן 24 wife's father (15·21) 368

קָשָׁה 26 hard; difficult (7·36) 904

חֹתֵן 27 wife's father (15·21) 368

Chapter 19

נֶשֶׁר 4 eagle (1·26) 676

סְגֻלָּה 5 possession (1·8) 688

עָב 9 thickness (1·30) 716

בַּעֲבוּר in order that (6·46) 721

שִׂמְלָה 10 clothes (6·29) 971

הִגְבִּיל 12 to set bounds (2·2·5) 148

סָקַל 13 to stone (4·12·22) 709

נִסְקַל to be stoned (4·4·22) 709

יָרָה to shoot (2·13·25[?]) 434

נוֹרָה to be shot through (1·1·25[?]) 434

מָשַׁךְ to draw out (2·30·36) 604

יוֹבֵל ram's horn (1·27) 385

שִׂמְלָה 14 clothes (6·29) 971

בָּרָק 16 lightning (1·20) 140

כָּבֵד heavy (9·39) 458

חָרַד 16 to tremble (2·23·39) 353

הִתְיַצֵּב 17 to station oneself (6·48·48) 426

תַּחְתִּי lower; lowest (1·19) 1066

עָשַׁן 18 to smoke (1·6·6) 798

עָשָׁן smoke (2·25) 798

כִּבְשָׁן kiln (3·4) 461

חָרַד to tremble (2·23·39) 353

חָזֵק 19 strong (1·2) 304

הֵעִיד 21 to affirm solemnly; warn (2·40·45) 729

הָרַס to break through (3·20·43) 248

פָּרַץ 22 to break out upon (3·46·49) 829

הֵעִיד 23 to exhort solemnly; admonish (2·40·45) 729

הִגְבִּיל to set bounds (2·2·5) 148

הָרַס 24 to break through (3·30·43) 248

פָּרַץ to break out upon (3·46·49) 829

Chapter 20

פֶּסֶל 4 idol; image (1·31) 820

תְּמוּנָה likeness; representation (1·10) 568

מִמַּעַל above; on top of (3·29) 751

קַנָּא 5 jealous (3·6) 888

שִׁלֵּשׁ those of the third generation; i.e., grandsons (2·5) 1026

רִבֵּעַ pertaining to the fourth (2·4) 918

שֹׂנֵא enemy (3·41) 971

אֹהֵב 6 lover; friend (1·36[?]) 12

נִקָּה 7 to leave unpunished (2·12·36) 667

רָצַח 13 to murder; slay (1·38·43) 953

נָאַף 14 to commit adultery (1·16·30) 610

גָּנַב 15 to steal (4·30·39) 170

חָמַד 17 to desire (3·16·21) 326

לַפִּיד 18 torch (1·13) 542

עָשֵׁן smoking (1·2) 798

נוּעַ to tremble (1·22·38) 631

לְבַעֲבוּר 20 in order to (1·3) 721

נִסָּה to test (5·36·36) 650

בַּעֲבוּר in order that (6·46) 721

יִרְאָה fear (1·45) 432

עֲרָפֶל 21 heavy cloud (1·15) 791

גָּזִית 25 a hewing; cutting (1·11) 159

הֵנִיף to wield (4·32·34[?]) 631

מַעֲלָה 26 step (1·45[?]) 752

Chapter 21

חָפְשִׁי 2 free (4·17) 344

חִנָּם · freely (2·32) 336

גַּף 3 body; self (2·2) 172

גַּף 4 body; self (2·2) 172

חָפְשִׁי 5 free (4·17) 344

מְזוּזָה 6 doorpost (4·20) 265

רָצַע to bore; pierce (1·1·1) 954

מַרְצֵעַ awl (1·2) 954

יָעַד 8 to designate (2·5·28) 416

נָכְרִי	foreign (3·45) 648	
בגד	to act or deal treacherously (1·42·42) 93	
יָעַד	9 to designate (2·5·28) 416	
שְׁאֵר	10 flesh (1·17) 984	
כְּסוּת	covering (2·8) 492	
ענה	cohabitation (1·1) 773	
גרע	to diminish (3·14·22) 175	
חִנָּם	11 freely (2·32) 336	
צָדָה	13 to lie in wait (1·2·2) 841	
אָנָה	to cause [or allow] to meet (1·4·4) 58	
הֵזִיד	14 to act insolently (2·10·12) 267	
עָרְמָה	craftily (1·5) 791	
גנב	16 to steal (4·30·39) 120	
אֶגְרֹף	18 fist (1·2) 175	
מִשְׁכָּב	bed (2·46) 1012	
מִשְׁעֶנֶת	19 staff (1·12) 1044	
נָקָה	to be exempt from punishment (1·23·36) 667	
שֶׁבֶת	cessation (1·7)[?] 992	
נקם	20 to avenge (1·13·34) 667	
נקם	to be avenged (1·12·34) 667	
הקם	21 to be avenged (1·3·34) 667	
נצה	22 to struggle with each other (2·5·8) 663	
נָגַף	to strike (7·24·48) 619	
הָרָה	pregnant (1·15[?]) 247	
אָסוֹן	mischief; evil; harm (2·5) 62	
ענש	to fine; punish (1·6·9) 778	
נענש	to be fined; punished (1·3·9) 778	
פְּלִיל	judge (1·3) 813	
אָסוֹן	23 mischief; evil; harm (2·5) 62	
כְּוִיָּה	25 burning (2·2) 465	
פֶּצַע	bruise; wound (2·8) 822	
חַבּוּרָה	stripe; blow (2·7) 289	
חָפְשִׁי	26 free (4·17) 344	
חָפְשִׁי	27 free (4·17) 344	

נָגַח	28 to gore (4·4·11) 618	
סקל	to stone (4·12·22) 709	
נסקל	to be stoned (4·4·22) 709	
נָקִי	free from punishment (2·43) 667	
נַגָּח	29 addicted to goring (2·2) 618	
תְּמוֹל	yesterday; aforetime (7·23) 1069	
שִׁלְשֹׁם	three days ago; specif. = the day before yesterday (6·25) 1026	
הוּעַד	"and protest be entered" (1·1·45) 729	
נסקל	to be stoned (4·4·22) 709	
כֹּפֶר	30 ransom (2·13) 497	
פִּדְיוֹן	ransom (1·3) 804	
נָגַח	31 to gore (4·4·11) 618	
נָגַח	32 to gore (4·4·11) 618	
נסקל	to be stoned (4·4·22) 709	
כָּרָה	33 to dig (1·13·14) 500	
נָגַף	35 to strike (7·24·48) 619	
חָצָה	to divide (2·11·15) 345	
נַגָּח	36 addicted to goring (2·2) 618	
תְּמוֹל	yesterday (7·23) 1069	
שִׁלְשֹׁם	three days ago; specif. = the day before yesterday (6·25) 1026	
גנב	37 to steal (4·30·37) 170	
שֶׂה	one of a flock; sheep; goat (13·44) 961	
טבח	37 to slaughter (1·11·11) 370	

Chapter 22

מַחְתֶּרֶת	1 burglary (1·2) 369	
גַּנָּב	thief (3·17) 170	
זָרַח	2 to rise (1·18·18) 280	
גְּנֵבָה	thing stolen (2·2) 170	
גְּנֵבָה	3 thing stolen (2·2) 170	
שֶׂה	one of a flock; sheep; goat (13·44) 961	
בְּעִיר	4 beast (1·6) 129	
בָּעַר	to consume (1·26·28[?]) 129	

מֵיטָב   the best (2·6) 406

קוֹץ   5 thornbush (1·11) 881

גָּדִישׁ   heap; stack [of sheaves] (1·4) 155

קָמָה   standing grain (1·10) 879

בְּעֵרָה   burning (1·1) 129

גָּנַב   6 to be stolen away (1·4·39) 170

גַּנָּב   thief (3·17) 170

גַּנָּב   7 thief (3·17) 170

שֶׂה   8 one of a flock; sheep; goat (13·44) 961

שַׂלְמָה   outer garment (2·16) 971

אֲבֵדָה   a lost thing (1·4) 2

הִרְשִׁיעַ   to condemn as guilty (1·25·34) 957

שֶׂה   9 one of a flock; sheep; goat (13·44) 961

נִשְׁבָּה   to be taken captive (1·8·37) 985

שְׁבוּעָה   10 oath; curse (1·30) 989

גנב   11 to steal (4·30·39) 170

נגנב   to be stolen (1·1·39) 170

טָרַף   12 to tear (1·19·24) 382

נטרף   to be torn (1·2·24) 382

טְרֵפָה   animal torn (2·9) 383

שָׂכִיר   14 hired (2·18) 969

שָׂכָר   hire; wages (2·29) 969

פִּתָּה   15 to seduce (1·17·27) 834

בְּתוּלָה   virgin (2·50) 143

ארשׂ   to be betrothed (1·5·11) 76

מהר   to acquire by paying a purchase price (2·3·3) 555

מֵאֵן   16 to refuse (8·45·45) 549

שָׁקַל   to weigh out (1·19·22) 1053

מֹהַר   purchase price (1·3) 555

בְּתוּלָה   virgin (2·50) 143

כַּשֵּׁף   17 to practice sorcery (2·6·6) 506

החרם   19 to be put under the ban (1·3·49) 355

בִּלְתִּי   except (1·24) 116

לְבַדּוֹ   alone (3·35) 94

הוֹנָה   20 to maltreat (1·14·18) 413

לָחַץ   to oppress (3·14·15) 537

יָתוֹם   21 orphan (2·42) 450

צְעָקָה   22 cry of distress (5·21) 858

יָתוֹם   23 orphan (2·42) 450

הלוה   24 to lend (1·9·14) 531

נשׁה   creditor (1·4[?]) 674

נֶשֶׁךְ   interest (1·12) 675

חבל   25 to bind by pledge (1·11·12) 286

שַׂלְמָה   outer garment (2·16) 971

כְּסוּת   26 covering (2·8) 492

שִׂמְלָה   wrapper; mantle (6·29) 971

בַּמֶּה   wherein (2·29) 552

חַנּוּן   gracious (2·13) 337

מְלֵאָה   28 full produce (1·3) 571

דמע   juice (1·1) 199

אָחַר   to keep back (1·15·17) 29

טְרֵפָה   30 animal torn (2·9) 383

כֶּלֶב   dog (2·32) 476

Chapter 23

שֵׁמַע   1 hearing; report (1·17) 1034

דַּל   3 the poor (2·48) 195

הדר   to pay honor to (1·4·6) 213

פָּגַע   4 to meet; light upon (3·40·46) 803

תָּעָה   to wander about (1·26·49) 1073

שׂנֵא   5 enemy (3·41) 971

רָבַץ   to lie down (1·24·30) 918

מַשָּׂא   load (1·43) 672

נָקִי   7 clean (2·43) 667

הצדיק   to declare righteous; to justify (1·12·41) 842

שֹׁחַד   8 bribe (2·23) 1005

עִוֵּר   to blind (1·5·5) 734

פִּקֵּחַ   seeing (2·2) 824

סִלֵּף   to subvert (1·7·7) 701

לָחַץ   9 to oppress (3·14·15) 537

תְּבוּאָה   10 product; yield (1·43) 100

שָׁמַט 11 to let drop; let fall (1·7·9) 1030
נָטַשׁ to let alone (1·33·40) 643
זַיִת olives; olive tree (3·38) 268
נפשׁ 12 to refresh oneself (2·3·3) 661
חגג 14 to keep a pilgrim feast (4·16·16) 290
רֵיקָם 15 in empty condition; emptily (3·16) 938
קָצִיר 16 harvest (3·49) 894
בִּכּוּרִים first fruits (4·17) 114
אָסִיף ingathering; harvest (2·2) 63
זכור 17 male (2·4) 271
חָמֵץ 18 that which is leavened (5·11) 329
בִּכּוּרִים 19 firstfruits (4·17) 114
בשׁל to boil (4·20·27) 143
גְּדִי kid (2·16) 152
חָלָב milk (6·44) 316
הֵמַר 21 to show bitterness (1·3·14) 600
איב 22 to be hostile to (1·2·2) 33
צור to show hostility to; to treat as foe (1·5·5) 849
צֹרֵר vexer, harasser (1·17) 865
הכחיד 23 to annihilate (1·6·30) 470
הרס 24 to overthrow; to tear down (2·3·43) 248
מַצֵּבָה pillar (3·35) 663
מַחֲלָה 25 sickness (2·4) 318
שׁכל 26 to show abortion; to miscarry (1·18·24) 1013
עָקָר barren (1·11) 785
אֵימָה 27 terror; dread (2·17) 33
עֹרֶף back of neck (5·33) 791
צִרְעָה 28 hornets (1·3) 864
גרשׁ to drive out (9·33·46) 176
גרשׁ 29 to drive out (9·33·46) 176
רבב to be; become many (1·23·24) 912
גרשׁ 30 to drive out (9·33·46) 176
פרה to be fruitful (2·22·29) 826

גרשׁ 31 to drive out (9·33·46) 176
מוֹקֵשׁ lure (3·27) 430

Chapter 24

לְבַדּוֹ 2 alone (3·35) 94
מַצֵּבָה 4 pillar (3·35) 663
אַגָּן 6 basin (1·3) 8
זָרַק to throw; scatter abundantly (6·32·34) 284
זָרַק 8 to throw; scatter abundantly (6·32·34) 284
לְבֵנָה 10 tile, pavement (8·12) 527
סַפִּיר sapphire (3·11) 705
טֹהַר purity (1·3) 372
אָצִיל 11 noble (1·1[?]) 69
לוּחַ 12 tablet (14·40) 531
הורה to teach (5·45·45[?]) 434
מְשָׁרֵת 13 servant (2·20) 1058
בָּזֶה 14 in this [place]; here (1·19) 261

Chapter 25

נָדַב 2 to incite (3·3·17) 621
תְּכֵלֶת 4 violet (34·49) 1067
אַרְגָּמָן purple thread (26·39) 71
תּוֹלֵעָה coccus ilicis [yielding scarlet color] (27·41) 1069
שָׁנִי scarlet (26·42) 1040
שֵׁשׁ linen (33·37) 1058
אדם 5 to be reddened; dyed red (6·7·10) 10
תַּחַשׁ dugong[?] (6·14) 1065
שִׁטָּה acacia (wood) (26·28) 1008
מָאוֹר 6 light (7·19) 22
בֶּשֶׂם balsam (6·30) 141
מִשְׁחָה ointment (13·21) 603
סם spice (11·16) 702
שֹׁהַם 7 onyx (7·11) 995
מִלוּא setting (8·15) 571

אֵפוֹד	ephod; a priestly garment (29·49) 65
חֹשֶׁן	breast piece (23·25) 365
תַּבְנִית	9 pattern (3·20) 125
שִׁטָּה	10 acacia [wood] (26·28) 1008
קוֹמָה	height (10·45) 879
צִפָּה	11 to overlay (25·42·46) 860
זֵר	border (10·10) 267
טַבַּעַת	12 ring (35·44) 371
צֵלָע	side (19·39) 854
בַּד	13 pole; stave (27·41) 94
שִׁטָּה	acacia [wood] (26·28) 1008
צִפָּה	to overlay (25·42·46) 860
בַּד	14 pole; stave (27·41) 94
טַבַּעַת	ring (35·44) 371
צֵלָע	side (19·39) 854
טַבַּעַת	15 ring (35·44) 371
בַּד	pole; stave (27·41) 94
כַּפֹּרֶת	17 propitiatory (18·27) 498
מִקְשָׁה	18 hammered work[?] (6·9) 904
קָצָה	end (21·28) 892
כַּפֹּרֶת	propitiatory (18·27) 498
קָצָה	19 end (21·28) 892
כַּפֹּרֶת	propitiatory (18·27) 498
לְמַעְלָה	20 upward (2·34) 751
סכך	to cover (3·12·18[?]) 696
כַּפֹּרֶת	propitiatory (18·27) 498
כַּפֹּרֶת	21 propitiatory (18·27) 498
מִלְמַעְלָה	above (6·24) 751
נועד	22 to meet at an appointed place (4·18·28) 416
כַּפֹּרֶת	propitiatory (18·27) 498
מִבֵּין	from between (1·21) 107
שִׁטָּה	23 acacia [wood] (26·28) 1008
קוֹמָה	height (10·45) 879
צִפָּה	24 to overlay (25·42·46) 860
זֵר	border (10·10) 267
מִסְגֶּרֶת	25 rim (6·17) 689

טֶפַח	handbreadth (2·9) 381
זֵר	border (10·10) 267
טַבַּעַת	26 ring (35·44) 371
לְעֻמַּת	27 close by; side by side with (5·31) 769
מִסְגֶּרֶת	rim (6·17) 689
טַבַּעַת	ring (35·44) 371
בַּד	pole; stave (27·41) 94
בַּד	28 pole; stave (27·41) 94
שִׁטָּה	acacia [wood] (26·28) 1008
צִפָּה	to overlay (25·42·46) 860
קְעָרָה	29 dish; platter (2·17) 891
קַשְׂוָה	jug; jar (2·4) 903
מנקיה	sacrificial bowl (2·4) 667
הסך	to be poured out (2·2·24) 650
מְנוֹרָה	31 lampstand (18·39) 633
מְקֻשָׁה	hammered work[?] (6·9) 904
יָרֵךְ	base (7·34) 437
גָּבִיעַ	cup (8·14) 149
כַּפְתּוֹר	knob (14·16) 499
פֶּרַח	bud; sprout (8·17) 827
צַד	32 side (9·31) 841
מְנוֹרָה	lampstand (18·39) 633
גָּבִיעַ	33 cup (8·14) 149
שׁקד	pu. ptc. = shaped as almond [blossoms] (6·6·17) 1052
כַּפְתּוֹר	knob (14·16) 499
פֶּרַח	bud; sprout (8·17) 827
מְנוֹרָה	lampstand (18·39) 633
מְנוֹרָה	34 lampstand (18·39) 633
גָּבִיעַ	cup (8·14) 149
שׁקד	pu. ptc. = shaped as almond [blossoms] (6·6·17) 1052
כַּפְתּוֹר	knob (14·16) 499
פֶּרַח	bud; sprout (8·17) 827
כַּפְתּוֹר	35 knob (14·16) 499
מְנוֹרָה	lampstand (18·39) 633
כַּפְתּוֹר	36 knob (14·16) 499

מִקְשָׁה hammered work[?] (6·9) 904

נֵר 37 lamp (11·44) 632

הֵאִיר to shine (3·34·40) 21

מֶלְקָחַיִם 38 snuffers (2·6) 544

מַחְתָּה snuff holder (4·21) 367

תַּבְנִית 40 pattern (3·20) 125

Chapter 26

שֵׁשׁ 1 linen (33·37) 1058

השזר to be twisted (21·21·21) 1004

תְּכֵלֶת violet (34·49) 1067

אַרְגָּמָן purple thread (26·39) 71

תּוֹלֵעָה coccus ilicis [yielding scarlet color] (27·41) 1069

שָׁנִי scarlet (26·42) 1040

חֹשֵׁב workman (11·12) 362

חבר 3 to unite; be joined (4·11·28) 287

לולי 4 loop (13·13) 533

תְּכֵלֶת violet (34·49) 1067

קָצָה end (21·28) 892

חֹבֶרֶת a thing that joins or is joined; curtain pieces (4·4) 289

קִיצוֹן at the end; outermost (4·4) 894

מַחְבֶּרֶת thing joined (8·8) 289

לולי 5 loop (13·13) 533

מַחְבֶּרֶת thing joined (8·8) 289

הקביל to show oppositeness in corresponding to one another (2·2·13) 867

קרס 6 hook (10·10) 902

חִבַּר 9 to unite; join (8·9·29) 287

חִבַּר to unite; join (8·9·29) 287

כָּפַל to double over (3·3·4) 495

מוּל the forefront of (6·25) 557

לולי 10 loop (13·13) 533

קִיצוֹן at the end of; outermost (4·4) 894

חֹבֶרֶת a thing that joins or is joined; curtain pieces (4·4) 289

קרס 11 hook (10·10) 902

לולי loop (13·13) 533

חִבַּר to unite; join (8·9·29) 287

סֶרַח 12 excess (1·1) 710

עדף to remain over; be in excess (4·8·9) 727

סרח to overrun (1·3·4[?]) 710

עדף 13 to remain over; be in excess (4·8·9) 727

סָרוּחַ overhang (1·3[?]) 710

צַד side (9·31) 841

מִכְסֶה 14 covering (8·16) 492

אדם to be reddened; dyed red (6·7·10) 10

תַּחַשׁ dugong[?] (6·14) 1065

מִלְמַעְלָה above (6·24) 751

קֶרֶשׁ 15 board (43·46) 903

שִׁטָּה acacia [wood] (26·28) 1008

קֶרֶשׁ 16 board (43·46) 903

קֶרֶשׁ 17 board (43·46) 903

שׁלב to be bound; joined (2·2·2) 1016

קֶרֶשׁ 18 board (43·46) 903

תֵּימָן [toward] the south (5·24) 412

קֶרֶשׁ 19 board (43·46) 903

צֶלָע 20 side (19·39) 854

קֶרֶשׁ board (43·46) 903

קֶרֶשׁ 21 board (43·46) 903

ירכה 22 extreme parts (6·28) 438

קֶרֶשׁ board (43·46) 903

קֶרֶשׁ 23 board (43·46) 903

קצע[?] pu. ptc. = corner post (2·2·3) 893

ירכה extreme parts (6·28) 438

תֹּאֲמִים 24 double (2·6)[?] 1060

מִלְמַטָּה beneath (6·6) 641

תָּם complete (2·15) 1070

טַבַּעַת ring (35·44) 371

מִקְצֹעַ corner-buttress (2·11) 893

קֶרֶשׁ	25 board (43·46) 903
בְּרִיחַ	26 bar (15·41) 138
שִׁטָּה	acacia [wood] (26·28) 1008
קֶרֶשׁ	board (43·46) 903
צֶלָע	side (19·39) 854
בְּרִיחַ	27 bar (15·41) 138
קֶרֶשׁ	board (43·46) 903
צֶלָע	side (19·39) 854
ירכה	extreme parts (6·28) 438
בְּרִיחַ	28 bar (15·41) 138
תִּיכוֹן	middle (2·12) 1064
קֶרֶשׁ	board (43·46) 903
קֶרֶשׁ	29 board (43·46) 903
צִפָּה	to overlay (25·42·46) 860
טַבַּעַת	ring (35·44) 371
בְּרִיחַ	bar (15·41) 138
פָּרֹכֶת	31 curtain (15·25) 827
תְּכֵלֶת	violet (34·49) 1067
אַרְגָּמָן	purple thread (26·39) 71
תּוֹלָעָה	coccus ilicis [yielding scarlet color] (27·41) 1069
שָׁנִי	scarlet (26·42) 1040
שֵׁשׁ	linen (33·37) 1058
השזר	to be twisted (21·21·21) 1004
חֹשֵׁב	workman (11·12[?]) 362
שִׁטָּה	32 acacia [wood] (26·28) 1008
צפה	to be overlaid (1·2·46) 860
וו	hook; pin; peg (13·13) 255
פָּרֹכֶת	33 curtain (15·25) 827
קרס	hook (10·10) 902
הִבְדִּיל	to divide (1·32·42) 95
כַּפֹּרֶת	34 propitiatory (18·27) 498
פָּרֹכֶת	35 curtain (15·25) 827
מְנוֹרָה	lampstand (18·39) 633
נוֹכַח	in front of (3·22) 647
צֶלָע	side (19·39) 854
תֵּימָן	[toward] the south (5·24) 412
מָסָךְ	36 screen (16·25) 697

תְּכֵלֶת	violet (34·49) 1067
אַרְגָּמָן	purple thread (26·39) 71
תּוֹלָעָה	coccus ilicis [yielding scarlet color] (27·41) 1069
שָׁנִי	scarlet (26·42) 1040
שֵׁשׁ	linen (33·37) 1058
השזר	to be twisted (21·21·21) 1004
רקם	to variegate; weave (8·8·9) 955
מָסָךְ	37 screen (16·25) 697
שִׁטָּה	acacia [wood] (26·28) 1008
צִפָּה	to overlay (25·42·46) 860
וו	hook; pin; peg (13·13) 255

Chapter 27

שִׁטָּה	1 acacia [wood] (26·28) 1008
רבע	to be squared (6·9·12) 917
קוֹמָה	height (10·45) 879
פִּנָּה	2 corner (2·30) 819
צִפָּה	to overlay (25·42·46) 860
סִיר	3 pot (3·29) 696
דִּשֵּׁן	to take away the fat ashes (1·5·11) 206
יע	shovel (2·9) 418
מִזְרָק	basin (2·32) 284
מזלגה	three-pronged fork (2·5) 272
מַחְתָּה	fire pan (4·21) 367
מִכְבָּר	4 grating (6·6) 460
רֶשֶׁת	network (4·22) 440
טַבַּעַת	ring (35·44) 371
קָצָה	end (21·28) 892
כַּרְכֹּב	5 rim (2·2) 501
מִלְמַטָּה	beneath (6·6) 641
רֶשֶׁת	network (4·22) 440
בַּד	6 poles; staves (27·41[?]) 94
שִׁטָּה	acacia [wood] (26·28) 1008
צִפָּה	to overlay (25·42·46) 860
בַּד	7 poles; staves (27·41[?]) 94
טַבַּעַת	ring (35·44) 371

45

צֶלָע	side (19 · 39) 854		**Chapter 28**	

נבב	8 to hollow out (2 · 4 · 4) 612
לוּחַ	board (14 · 40) 531
תֵּימָן	9 [toward] the south (5 · 24) 412
קֶלַע	curtain; hanging (13 · 16) 887
שֵׁשׁ	linen (33 · 37) 1058
השׁזר	to be twisted (21 · 21 · 21) 1004
וו	10 hook; pin; peg (13 · 13) 255
חֲשׁוּק	fillet; ring (8 · 8) 366
קֶלַע	11 curtain; hanging (13 · 16) 887
וו	hook; pin; peg (13 · 13) 255
חֲשׁוּק	fillet; ring (8 · 8) 366
קֶלַע	12 curtain; hanging (13 · 16) 887
קֵדְם	13 eastward (2 · 26) 870
קֶלַע	14 curtain; hanging (13 · 16) 887
קֶלַע	15 curtain; hanging (13 · 16) 887
מָסָךְ	16 screen (16 · 25) 697
תְּכֵלֶת	violet (34 · 49) 1067
אַרְגָּמָן	purple thread (26 · 39) 71
תּוֹלֵעָה	coccus ilicis [yielding scarlet color] (27 · 41) 1069
שָׁנִי	scarlet (26 · 42) 1040
שֵׁשׁ	linen (33 · 37) 1058
השׁזר	to be twisted (21 · 21 · 21) 1004
רקם	to variegate; weave (8 · 8 · 9) 955
חשׁק	17 to be furnished with fillets or rings (2 · 2 · 11) 366
וו	hook; pin; peg (13 · 13) 255
קוֹמָה	18 height (10 · 45) 879
שֵׁשׁ	linen (33 · 37) 1058
השׁזר	to be twisted (21 · 21 · 21) 1004
יָתֵד	19 peg; pin (8 · 24) 450
זַיִת	20 olives (3 · 38) 268
זַךְ	pure; unmixed (2 · 11) 269
כָּתִית	beaten (2 · 5) 510
מָאוֹר	light (7 · 19) 22
נֵר	lamp (11 · 44) 632
פָּרֹכֶת	21 curtain (15 · 25) 827

כֹּהֵן	1 to act as priest (12 · 23 · 23) 464
כֹּהֵן	3 to act as priest (12 · 23 · 23) 464
חֹשֶׁן	4 breast piece (23 · 25) 365
אֵפוֹד	ephod; priestly garment (29 · 49) 65
מְעִיל	robe (9 · 28) 591
כְּתֹנֶת	tunic (8 · 30) 509
תַּשְׁבֵּץ	checkered; plaited (1 · 1) 990
מִצְנֶפֶת	turban (8 · 12) 857
אַבְנֵט	girdle (5 · 9) 126
כֹּהֵן	to act as priest (12 · 23 · 23) 464
תְּכֵלֶת	5 violet (34 · 49) 1067
אַרְגָּמָן	purple thread (26 · 39) 71
תּוֹלֵעָה	coccus ilicis [yielding scarlet color] (27 · 41) 1069
שָׁנִי	scarlet (26 · 42) 1040
שֵׁשׁ	linen (33 · 37) 1058
אֵפוֹד	6 ephod; priestly garment (29 · 49) 65
תְּכֵלֶת	violet (34 · 49) 1067
אַרְגָּמָן	purple thread (26 · 39) 71
תּוֹלֵעָה	coccus ilicis [yielding scarlet color] (27 · 41) 1069
שָׁנִי	scarlet (26 · 42) 1040
שֵׁשׁ	linen (33 · 37) 1058
השׁזר	to be twisted (21 · 21 · 21) 1004
חֹשֵׁב	workman (11 · 12[?]) 362
חבר	7 to unite; be joined (4 · 11 · 28) 287
קָצָה	end (21 · 28) 892
חבר	to be united; joined (2 · 4 · 28) 287
חֵשֶׁב	8 girdle; ingenious work (7 · 8) 363
אֲפֻדָּה	ephod; high priestly garment (2 · 3) 65
תְּכֵלֶת	violet (34 · 49) 1067
אַרְגָּמָן	purple thread (26 · 39) 71
תּוֹלֵעָה	coccus ilicis [yielding scarlet color] (27 · 41) 1069
שָׁנִי	scarlet (26 · 42) 1040

שֵׁשׁ	linen (33 · 37) 1058
הֻשְׁזָר	to be twisted (21 · 21 · 21) 1004
שֹׁהַם	9 onyx (7 · 11) 995
פִּתַּח	to engrave (3 · 8 · 9) 836
תּוֹלְדוֹת	10 generations (3 · 39) 410
חָרָשׁ	11 graver, artificer (3 · 38) 360
פִּתּוּחַ	engraving (6 · 11) 836
חֹתָם	engraving of a seal (6 · 13) 368
פִּתַּח	to engrave (3 · 8 · 9) 836
מִשְׁבְּצוֹת	checkered work (8 · 9) 990
אֵפוֹד	12 ephod; priestly garment (29 · 49) 65
זִכָּרוֹן	memorial (8 · 24) 272
מִשְׁבְּצוֹת	13 checkered work (8 · 9) 990
שַׁרְשְׁרָה	14 chain (4 · 8) 1057
מִגְבָּלֹת	the twisted (1 · 1) 148
עֲבֹת	cordage; cord (8 · 24) 721
מִשְׁבְּצֹת	checkered work (8 · 9) 990
חֹשֶׁן	15 breast piece (23 · 25) 365
חֹשֵׁב	workman (11 · 12[?]) 362
אֵפוֹד	ephod; priestly garment (29 · 49) 65
תְּכֵלֶת	violet (34 · 49) 1067
אַרְגָּמָן	purple thread (26 · 39) 71
תּוֹלַעַה	coccus ilicis [yielding scarlet color] (27 · 41) 1069
שָׁנִי	scarlet (26 · 42) 1040
שֵׁשׁ	linen (33 · 37) 1058
הֻשְׁזָר	to be twisted (21 · 21 · 21) 1004
רבע	16 ptc. pass. = to be squared (6 · 9 · 12) 917
כָּפַל	to double (3 · 3 · 4) 495
זֶרֶת	span (4 · 7) 284
מלאה	17 setting of jewel (3 · 3) 571
טוּר	row (12 · 26) 377
אֹדֶם	carnelian [ruby] (2 · 3) 10
פִּטְדָה	topaz (2 · 4) 809
בָּרֶקֶת	emerald (2 · 3) 140
טוּר	18 row (12 · 26) 377
נֹפֶךְ	ruby[?] (2 · 4) 656
סַפִּיר	sapphire (3 · 11) 705
יַהֲלֹם	jasper[?] (2 · 3) 240
טוּר	19 row (12 · 26) 377
לֶשֶׁם	precious stone (2 · 2) 545
שְׁבוֹ	precious stone (2 · 2) 986
אַחְלָמָה	amethyst[?] (2 · 2) 21
טוּר	20 row (12 · 26) 377
תַּרְשִׁישׁ	yellow jasper[?] (2 · 7) 1076
שֹׁהַם	onyx (7 · 11) 995
יָשְׁפֶה	jasper (2 · 3) 448
שֻׁבָּץ	pu. ptc. = inwoven (1 · 1 · 2) 990
מלאה	setting of jewel (3 · 3) 571
פִּתּוּחַ	21 engraving (6 · 11) 836
חוֹתָם	engraving of a seal (6 · 13) 368
חֹשֶׁן	22 breast piece (23 · 25) 365
שַׁרְשְׁרָה	chain (4 · 8) 1057
גַּבְלֻת	twisting (2 · 2) 148
עֲבֹת	cordage; cord (8 · 24) 721
חֹשֶׁן	23 breast piece (23 · 25) 365
טַבַּעַת	ring (35 · 44) 371
קָצֶה	end (21 · 28) 892
עֲבֹת	24 cordage; cord (8 · 24) 721
טַבַּעַת	ring (35 · 44) 371
קָצֶה	end (21 · 28) 892
חֹשֶׁן	breast piece (23 · 25) 365
קָצֶה	25 end (21 · 28) 892
עֲבֹת	cordage; cord (8 · 24) 721
מִשְׁבְּצוֹת	checkered work (8 · 9) 990
אֵפוֹד	ephod; priestly garment (29 · 49) 65
מוּל	the forefront of (6 · 25) 557
טַבַּעַת	26 ring (35 · 44) 371
קָצֶה	end (21 · 28) 892
חֹשֶׁן	breast piece (23 · 25) 365
אֵפוֹד	ephod; priestly garment (29 · 49) 65
טַבַּעַת	27 ring (35 · 44) 371
אֵפוֹד	ephod; priestly garment (29 · 49) 65
מִלְמַטָּה	beneath (6 · 6) 641
מִמּוּל	on the forefront of (2 · 9) 557

לְעֻמַּת	close by; side by side with (5·31) 769	פִּתַּח	to engrave (3·8·9) 836
מַחְבֶּרֶת	place of joining (8·8) 289	פִּתּוּחַ	engraving (6·11) 836
מִמַּעַל	above; on top of (3·29) 751	חוֹתָם	engraving of a seal (6·13) 368
חֵשֶׁב	girdle; ingenious work (7·8) 363	פָּתִיל	37 cord (5·11) 836
רכס	28 to bind (2·2·2) 940	תְּכֵלֶת	violet (34·49) 1067
חֹשֶׁן	breast piece (23·25) 365	מִצְנֶפֶת	turban of high priest (8·12) 857
טַבַּעַת	ring (35·44) 371	מוּל	the forefront (6·25) 557
אֵפוֹד	ephod; priestly garment (29·49) 65	מֵצַח	38 forehead (2·13) 594
פָּתִיל	cord (5·11) 836	מַתָּנָה	gift (1·17) 682
תְּכֵלֶת	violet (34·49) 1067	שׁבץ	39 to weave in checker[?] (1·1·2) 990
חֵשֶׁב	girdle; ingenious work (7·8) 363	כְּתֹנֶת	tunic (8·30) 509
נזחח	to be displaced (2·2·2) 267	שֵׁשׁ	linen (33·37) 1058
חֹשֶׁן	29 breast piece (23·25) 365	מִצְנֶפֶת	turban of high priest (8·12) 857
זִכָּרֹן	memorial (8·24) 272	אַבְנֵט	girdle (5·9) 126
חֹשֶׁן	30 breast piece (23·25) 365	רקם	to variegate; weave (8·8·9) 955
אוּרִים	Urim (1·7) 22	כְּתֹנֶת	40 tunic (8·30) 509
תֻּמִּים	Thummim[?] (1·5) 1070	אַבְנֵט	girdle (5·9) 126
מְעִיל	31 robe (9·28) 591	מִגְבָּעוֹת	turban of common priest (3·4) 149
אֵפוֹד	ephod; priestly garment (29·49) 65	כָּהֵן	41 to act as priest (12·23·23) 464
כָּלִיל	entirety (2·15) 483	מכנס	42 drawers (2·5) 488
תְּכֵלֶת	violet (34·49) 1067	בַּד	white linen (2·23) 94
אֹרֵג	32 weaver (4·10[?]) 70	מָתְנַיִם	loins (2·50) 608
כְּפִי	in proportion to (3·16) 804	יָרֵךְ	thigh (7·34) 437
תַּחְרָא	corselet? (2·2) 1065		
שׁוּל	33 skirt [of robe] (6·11) 1002		Chapter 29
רִמּוֹן	pomegranate (8·32) 941	כָּהֵן	1 to act as priest (12·23·23) 464
תְּכֵלֶת	violet (34·49) 1067	חַלָּה	2 a kind of cake (2·14) 319
אַרְגָּמָן	purple thread (26·39) 71	בָּלַל	to mix (2·42·42[?]) 117
תּוֹלֵעָה	coccus ilicis [yielding scarlet color] (27·41) 1069	רָקִיק	a thin cake; wafer (2·8) 956
שָׁנִי	scarlet (26·42) 1040	סַל	3 basket (4·15) 700
פַּעֲמֹון	bell (7·7) 822	כְּתֹנֶת	5 tunic (8·30) 509
פַּעֲמֹון	34 bell (7·7) 822	מְעִיל	robe (9·28) 591
רִמּוֹן	pomegranate (8·32) 941	אֵפוֹד	ephod; priestly garment (29·49) 65
שׁוּל	skirt [of robe] (6·11) 1002	חֹשֶׁן	breast piece (23·25) 365
מְעִיל	robe (9·28) 591	אפד	to gird on [an ephod] (1·2·2) 65
צִיץ	36 shining plate [of gold] (2·15) 847	חֵשֶׁב	girdle; ingenious work (7·8) 363
		מִצְנֶפֶת	6 turban of high priest (8·12) 857
		נֵזֶר	crown (2·24) 634

מִשְׁחָה 7 ointment (13·21) 603

כְּתֹנֶת 8 tunic (8·30) 509

חגר 9 to gird on (2·44·44) 291

אַבְנֵט girdle (5·9) 126

חבש to bind; bind on (1·27·31) 289

מִגְבָּעוֹת turban of a common priest (3·4) 149

כְּהֻנָּה priesthood (2·13) 464

סָמַךְ 10 to lay (3·41·48) 701

אֶצְבַּע 12 finger (3·31) 840

יְסוֹד base (1·19) 414

יֹתֶרֶת 13 appendage (2·11) 452

כָּבֵד liver (2·14) 458

כִּלְיָה kidney (2·30) 480

פֶּרֶשׁ 14 offal [contents of stomach] (1·7) 831

סָמַךְ 15 to lay (3·41·48) 701

זָרַק 16 to toss; scatter abundantly (6·32·34) 284

נִתַּח 17 to cut in pieces (1·9·9) 677

נֵתַח piece of a divided carcass (2·12) 677

כְּרָעַיִם leg (2·9) 502

נִיחוֹחַ 18 soothing (3·43) 629

סָמַךְ 19 to lay (3·41·48) 701

תְּנוּךְ 20 tip, i.e., lobe of ear (2·8) 1072

יְמָנִי right (3·33) 412

בֹּהֶן thumb; great toe (2·14) 97

זָרַק to toss; scatter abundantly (6·32·34) 284

מִשְׁחָה 21 ointment (13·21) 603

הִזָּה to sprinkle (1·20·24) 633

אַלְיָה 22 fat tail (1·5) 46

יֹתֶרֶת appendage (2·11) 452

כָּבֵד liver (2·14) 458

כִּלְיָה kidney (2·30) 480

שׁוֹק leg (2·19) 1003

מִלּוּא installation (8·15) 571

חַלָּה 23 a kind of cake (2·3) 319

רָקִיק thin cake; wafer (2·8) 956

סַל basket (4·15) 700

הֵנִיף 24 to wave (4·32·34[?]) 631

תְּנוּפָה wave offering; wave breast (6·30) 632

נִיחוֹחַ 25 soothing (3·43) 629

חָזֶה 26 breast (2·13) 303

מִלּוּא installation (8·15) 571

הֵנִיף to wave (4·32·34[?]) 631

תְּנוּפָה wave offering; wave breast (6·30) 632

מָנָה portion (1·12) 584

חָזֶה 27 breast (2·13) 303

תְּנוּפָה wave offering; wave breast (6·30) 632

שׁוֹק leg (2·19) 1003

הוּנַף to be waved (1·1·34[?]) 631

מִלּוּא installation (8·15) 571

מֵאֲשֶׁר from that which (3·17) 84

מִלּוּא 31 installation (8·15) 571

בִּשֵּׁל to cook (4·20·27) 143

סַל 32 basket (4·15) 700

מִלּוּא 34 installation (8·15) 571

כָּכָה 35 thus (2·34) 462

כִּפֻּרִים 36 atonement (3·8) 498

עִשָּׂרוֹן 40 tenth part (1·28) 798

בָּלַל to mix (2·41·42) 117

כָּתִית beaten (2·5) 510

רֶבַע fourth part (1·7) 917

הִין hin; liquid measure (3·22) 228

נִיחוֹחַ 41 soothing (3·43) 629

נוֹעַד 42 to meet at an appointed place (4·18·28) 416

נוֹעַד 43 to meet at an appointed place (4·18·28) 416

כָּהֵן 44 to act as priest (12·23·23) 464

Chapter 30

מֻקְטָר 1 place of sacrificial smoke (1·1) 883

שָׁטָּה		acacia [wood] (26·28) 1008	מוֹר		myrrh (1·12) 600
רבע	2	ptc. pass. = to be squared (6·9·12) 917	דְּרוֹר		fine-flowing (1·1[?]) 204
קוֹמָה		height (10·45) 879	קִנָּמוֹן		cinnamon (1·3) 890
צָפָה	3	to overlay (25·42·46) 860	מַחֲצִית		half (5·16) 345
גַּג		top; roof (2·29) 150	קִדָּה	24	cassia [a spice] (1·2) 869
זֵר		circlet; border (10·10) 267	זַיִת		olive[s] (3·38) 268
טַבַּעַת	4	ring (35·44) 371	הִין		hin; liquid measure (3·22) 228
זֵר		circlet; border (10·10) 267	מִשְׁחָה	25	ointment (13·21) 603
צֵלָע		side (19·39) 854	רֹקַח		spice mixture; perfume (2·2) 955
צַד		side (9·31) 841	מִרְקַחַת		ointment mixture (1·3) 955
בַּד		pole; stave (27·41) 94	רקח		to mix; compound (4·6·8) 955
בַּד	5	pole; stave (27·41) 94	מְנוֹרָה	27	lampstand (18·39) 633
שָׁטָּה		acacia [wood] (26·28) 1008	כִּיּוֹר	28	basin (9·23) 468
צָפָה		to overlay (25·42·46) 860	כֵּן		base (7·17) 487
פָּרֹכֶת	6	curtain (15·25) 827	כִּהֵן	30	to act as priest (12·23·23) 464
כַּפֹּרֶת		propitiatory (18·27) 498	מִשְׁחָה	31	ointment (13·21) 603
נועד		to meet at an appointed place (4·18·28) 416	סוּךְ	32	to be poured (1[?]·1[?]·9) 691
			מַתְכֹּנֶת		proportion (3·5) 1067
סַם	7	spice (11·16) 702	רקח	33	to mix; compound (4·6·8) 955
נֵר		lamp (11·44) 632	עַם		kinsman (3·34) 769
נֵר	8	lamp (11·44) 632	סַם	34	spice (11·16) 702
נָסַךְ	9	to pour out (1·7·24) 650	נָטָף		an odoriferous gum (1·1) 643
כִּפֻּרִים	10	atonement (3·8) 498	שְׁחֵלֶת		an ingredient of the holy incense (1·1) 1006
כֹּפֶר	12	ransom (2·13) 497	חֶלְבְּנָה		a kind of gum (1·1) 317
נֶגֶף		plague (2·7) 620	לְבֹנָה		frankincense (1·21) 526
מַחֲצִית	13	half (5·16) 345	זַךְ		pure; unmixed (2·11) 269
גֵּרָה		a gerah; one-twentieth of a shekel (1·5) 176	בַּד		part (1·3[?]) 94
עָשִׁיר	15	rich (1·23) 799	רֹקַח	35	spice mixture; perfume (2·2) 955
דַּל		low; weak; poor (2·48) 195	רקח		to mix; compound (4·6·8) 955
הִמְעִיט		to make small (3·13·22) 589	מלח		to be salted (1·1·3) 572
מַחֲצִית		half (5·16) 345	שָׁחַק	36	to beat fine; pulverize (1·4·4) 1007
כִּפֻּרִים	16	atonement (3·8) 498	הֵדַק		to pulverize (1·8·13) 200
זִכָּרוֹן		memorial (8·24) 272	נועד		to meet at an appointed place (4·18·28) 416
כִּיּוֹר	18	basin (9·23) 468	מַתְכֹּנֶת	37	proportion (3·5) 1067
כֵּן		base (7·17) 487	הֵרִיחַ	38	to smell (1·11·14) 926
בֶּשֶׂם	23	spice; balsam (6·30) 141	עַם		kinsman (3·34) 769

Chapter 31

תְּבוּנָה	3	understanding (3·42) 108
חָרֹשֶׁת	5	carving; skillful working (4·4) 360
כַּפֹּרֶת	7	propitiatory (18·27) 498
מְנוֹרָה	8	lampstand (18·39) 633
כִּיוֹר	9	basin (9·23) 468
כֵּן		base (7·17) 487
שְׂרָד	10	plaited; braided work[?] (4·4) 975
כֹּהֵן		to act as priest (12·23·23) 464
מִשְׁחָה	11	ointment (13·21) 603
סַם		spice (11·16) 702
עַם		kinsman (3·34) 769
שַׁבָּתוֹן	15	Sabbath observance (3·11) 992
נפשׁ	17	to refresh oneself (2·3·3) 661
לוּחַ	18	tablet (14·40) 531
אֶצְבַּע		finger (3·31) 840

Chapter 32

נקהל	1	to assemble (1·19·39) 874
פרק	2	to tear off (1·3·10) 830
נֶזֶם		ring (3·17) 633
התפרק	3	to tear off (2·3·10) 830
נֶזֶם		ring (3·17) 633
צור	4	to fashion; delineate (1·2·2) 849
חֶרֶט		graving tool; stylus (1·2) 354
עֵגֶל		calf (6·35) 722
מַסֵּכָה		molten metal (3·25) 651
מָחֳרָת	6	the morrow (4·32) 564
צחק		sport; to play (1·7·13) 850
עֵגֶל	8	calf (6·35) 722
מַסֵּכָה		molten metal (3·25) 651
קָשֶׁה	9	stiff; stubborn (7·36) 904
עֹרֶף		neck (5·33) 791
חָרוֹן	12	[burning of] anger (2·41) 354
כּוֹכָב	13	star (1·37) 456
לוּחַ	15	tablet (14·40) 531
לוּחַ	16	tablet (14·40) 531

מִכְתָּב		handwriting (3·9) 508
חרת		to engrave (1·1·1) 362
רֵעַ	17	shouting (1·3) 929
עָנָה	18	to sing (3·13·16) 777
חֲלוּשָׁה		weakness; prostration (1·1) 325
עֵגֶל	19	calf (6·35) 722
מְחוֹלָה		dancing (2·8) 298
לוּחַ		tablet (14·40) 531
עֵגֶל	20	calf (6·35) 722
טחן		to grind (1·7·7) 377
דַּק		to be fine (1·4·13) 200
זרה		to scatter (1·9·38) 279
התפרק	24	to tear off (2·3·10) 830
עֵגֶל		calf (6·35) 722
פָּרַע	25	to let loose, i.e., remove restraint (2·13·16) 828
שִׁמְצָה		whisper; derision (1·1) 1036
יָרֵךְ	27	thigh (7·34) 437
מָחֳרָת	30	the morrow (4·32) 564
חֲטָאָה		sin (3·8) 308
אוּלַי		perhaps (1·45) 19
אָנָּא	31	ah, now! (1·13) 58
חֲטָאָה		sin (3·8) 308
מָחָה	32	to wipe (3·22·35) 562
מָחָה	33	to wipe (3·22·35) 562
נחה	34	to lead (4·14·40) 634
נָגַף	35	to smite (7·24·48) 619
עֵגֶל		calf (6·35) 722

Chapter 33

גרש	2	to drive out (9·33·46) 176
זוב	3	to flow (4·29·29) 264
חָלָב		milk (6·44) 316
קָשֶׁה		stiff; stubborn (7·36) 904
עֹרֶף		neck (5·33) 791
הִתְאַבֵּל	4	to mourn (1·19·38) 5
עֲדִי		ornaments (3·13) 725
קָשֶׁה	5	stiff; stubborn (7·36) 904

עֹרֶף	neck (5 · 33) 791	
רֶגַע	moment (1 · 22) 921	
עֲדִי	ornaments (3 · 13) 725	
עֲדִי	6 ornaments (3 · 13) 725	
מְשָׁרֵת	11 servant (2 · 20) 1058	
הֵמִישׁ	to depart (2 · 20[?] · 20) 559	
בַּמֶּה	16 whereby (2 · 29) 552	
אֵפוֹא	then (1 · 15) 66	
נפלה	to be distinct (1 · 1 · 4) 811	
טוּב	19 goodness (1 · 32) 375	
רָחַם	to have compassion (2 · 41 · 46) 933	
נקרה	22 crevice (1 · 2) 669	
שׂכך	to cover (1 · 1 · 1) 967	
אָחוֹר	23 hinder parts (2 · 41) 30	

Chapter 34

פָּסַל	1 to hew out (2 · 6 · 6) 820	
לוּחַ	tablet (14 · 40) 531	
מוּל	3 in front of (8 · 33) 557	
פָּסַל	4 to hew out (2 · 6 · 6) 20	
לוּחַ	tablet (14 · 40) 531	
רַחוּם	6 compassionate (1 · 13) 933	
חַנּוּן	gracious (2 · 13) 337	
חַטָּאָה	7 sinful thing (1 · 2) 308	
נקה	to leave unpunished (2 · 12 · 36) 667	
שִׁלֵּשִׁים	those of the third generation, i.e., grandsons (2 · 5) 1026	
רִבֵּעַ	pertaining to the fourth (2 · 4) 918	
קדד	8 to bow down (3 · 15 · 15) 869	
קָשֶׁה	9 stiff; stubborn (7 · 36) 904	
עֹרֶף	neck (5 · 33) 791	
סלח	to pardon (1 · 33 · 46) 699	
נִפְלָאוֹת	10 wonderful acts (2 · 43) 810	
נברא	to be created (1 · 10 · 48) 135	
גרש	11 to drive out (1 · 7 · 46) 176	
מוֹקֵשׁ	12 bait (3 · 27) 430	
נָתַץ	13 to pull down (1 · 31 · 42) 683	
מַצֵּבָה	pillar (3 · 35) 663	

אֲשֵׁרָה	a sacred pole (1 · 40) 81	
קַנָּא	14 jealous (3 · 6) 888	
מַסֵּכָה	17 molten metal (3 · 25) 651	
פֶּטֶר	19 firstborn (8 · 11) 809	
רֶחֶם	womb (4 · 32) 933	
שֶׂה	one of flock; sheep; goat (13 · 44) 961	
פֶּטֶר	20 firstborn (8 · 11) 809	
שֶׂה	one of flock; sheep; goat (13 · 44) 961	
ערף	to break the neck (2 · 6 · 6) 791	
רֵיקָם	in empty condition; emptily (3 · 16) 938	
חָרִישׁ	21 ploughing (1 · 3) 361	
קָצִיר	harvest (3 · 49) 894	
שָׁבוּעַ	22 week; period (1 · 20) 988	
בִּכּוּרִים	firstfruits (4 · 17) 114	
קָצִיר	harvest (3 · 49) 894	
אָסִיף	ingathering; harvest (2 · 2) 63	
תקופה	circuit (1 · 4) 880	
הִרְחִיב	24 to enlarge (1 · 21 · 25) 931	
חָמַד	to desire (3 · 16 · 21) 326	
חָמֵץ	25 that which is leavened (5 · 11) 329	
בִּכּוּרִים	26 firstfruits (4 · 17) 114	
בשל	to boil (4 · 20 · 27) 143	
גְּדִי	kid (2 · 16) 152	
חָלָב	milk (6 · 44) 316	
לוּחַ	28 tablet (14 · 40) 531	
לוּחַ	29 tablet (14 · 40) 531	
קָרַן	to send out rays (3 · 3 · 4) 902	
קָרַן	30 to send out rays (3 · 3 · 4) 902	
מַסְוֶה	33 veil (3 · 3) 691	
מַסְוֶה	34 veil (3 · 3) 691	
קָרַן	35 to sent out rays (3 · 3 · 4) 902	
מַסְוֶה	veil (3 · 3) 691	

Chapter 35

הקהל	1 to summon an assembly (1 · 20 · 39) 874	

שַׁבָּתוֹן	2	Sabbath observance (3·11) 992		כִּיּוֹר		basin (9·23) 468
מוֹשָׁב	3	dwelling place (4·43) 444		כֵּן		base (7·17) 487
נָדִיב	5	willing (2·27) 622		קֶלַע	17	curtain; hanging (13·16) 887
תְּכֵלֶת	6	violet (34·49) 1067		מָסָךְ		screen (16·25) 697
אַרְגָּמָן		purple thread (26·39) 71		יָתֵד	18	peg (8·24) 450
תּוֹלֵעָה		coccus ilicis [yielding scarlet color] (27·41) 1069		מֵיתָר		cord (2·9) 452
שָׁנִי		scarlet (26·42) 1040		שְׂרָד	19	plaited; braided work (4·4) 975
שֵׁשׁ		linen (33·37) 1058		כָּהֵן		to act as priest (12·23·23) 464
אדם	7	to be red (6·7·10) 10		נָדַב	21	to incite (3·3·17) 621
תַּחַשׁ		dugong[?] (6·14) 1065		נָדִיב	22	willing (2·27) 622
שִׁטָּה		acacia [wood] (26·28) 1008		חָח		hook (1·7) 296
מָאוֹר	8	light (7·19) 22		נֶזֶם		ring (3·17) 633
בֶּשֶׂם		spice; balsam (6·30) 141		טַבַּעַת		ring (35·44) 371
מִשְׁחָה		ointment (13·21) 603		כּוּמָז		name of a golden ornament (1·2) 484
סם		spice (11·16) 702		הֵנִיף		to wave (4·32·34[?]) 631
שֹׁהַם	9	onyx (7·11) 995		תְּנוּפָה		offering; wave offering (6·30) 632
מִלֻּוא		setting (8·15) 571		תְּכֵלֶת	23	violet (34·49) 1067
אֵפוֹד		ephod; priestly garment (29·49) 65		אַרְגָּמָן		purple thread (26·39) 71
חֹשֶׁן		breast piece (23·25) 365		תּוֹלֵעָה		coccus ilicis [yielding scarlet color] (27·41) 1069
מִכְסֶה	11	covering (8·16) 492		שָׁנִי		scarlet (26·42) 1040
קֶרֶס		hook (10·10) 902		שֵׁשׁ		linen (33·37) 1058
קֶרֶשׁ		board (43·46) 903		אדם		to be red (6·7·10) 10
בְּרִיחַ		bar (15·41) 138		תַּחַשׁ		dugong[?] (6·14) 1065
בַּד	12	pole; stave (27·41) 94		שִׁטָּה	24	acacia [wood] (26·28) 1008
כַּפֹּרֶת		propitiatory (18·27) 498		טוה	25	to spin (2·2·2) 376
פָּרֹכֶת		curtain (15·25) 827		מַטְוֶה		yarn (1·1) 376
מָסָךְ		screen (16·25) 697		תְּכֵלֶת		violet (34·49) 1067
בַּד	13	pole; stave (27·41) 94		אַרְגָּמָן		purple thread (26·29) 71
מְנוֹרָה	14	lampstand (18·39) 633		תּוֹלֵעָה		coccus ilicis [yielding scarlet color] (27·41) 1069
מָאוֹר		light (7·19) 22		שָׁנִי		scarlet (26·42) 1040
נֵר		lamp (11·44) 632		שֵׁשׁ		linen (33·37) 1058
בַּד	15	pole; stave (27·41) 94		טוה	26	to spin (2·2·2) 376
מִשְׁחָה		ointment (13·21) 603		שֹׁהַם	27	onyx (7·11) 995
סם		spice (11·16) 702		מִלֻּוא		setting (8·15) 571
מָסָךְ		screen (16·25) 697		אֵפוֹד		ephod; priestly garment (29·49) 65
מִכְבָּר	16	grating (6·6) 460				
בַּד		pole; stave (27·41) 94				

חֹשֶׁן   breast piece (23·25) 365

בֶּשֶׂם   28 spice; balsam (6·30) 141

מָאוֹר   light (7·19) 22

מִשְׁחָה   ointment (13·21) 603

סם   spice (11·16) 702

נָדַב   29 to incite (3·3·17) 621

נְדָבָה   freewill offering (2·27) 621

תְּבוּנָה   31 understanding (3·42) 108

חָרֹשֶׁת   33 carving; skillful working (4·4) 360

מִלוּא   setting (8·15) 571

הוֹרָה   34 to instruct (5·45·45[?]) 434

חָרָשׁ   35 graver; artificer (3·38) 360

חֹשֵׁב   workman (11·12[?]) 362

רקם   to variegate; weave (8·8·9) 955

תְּכֵלֶת   violet (34·49) 1067

אַרְגָּמָן   purple thread (26·39) 71

תּוֹלֵעָה   coccus ilicis [yielding scarlet color]
   (27·41) 1069

שָׁנִי   scarlet (26·42) 1040

שֵׁשׁ   linen (33·37) 1058

אֹרֵג   weaver (4·10[?]) 70

Chapter 36

תְּבוּנָה   1 understanding (3·42) 108

נְדָבָה   3 freewill offering (2·27) 621

דַּי   5 enough (2·39[?]) 191

נכלא   6 to be restrained (1·3·17) 476

דַּי   7 enough (2·39[?]) 191

שֵׁשׁ   8 linen (33·37) 1058

השׁזר   to be twisted (21·21·21) 1004

תְּכֵלֶת   violet (34·49) 1067

אַרְגָּמָן   purple thread (26·39) 71

תּוֹלֵעָה   coccus ilicis [yielding scarlet color]
   (27·41) 1069

שָׁנִי   scarlet (26·42) 1040

חֹשֵׁב   workman (11·12[?]) 362

חִבַּר   10 to unite; join (8·9·28) 287

לוּלִי   11 loop (13·13) 533

תְּכֵלֶת   violet (34·49) 1067

קָצָה   end (21·28) 892

מַחְבֶּרֶת   thing joined (8·8) 289

קִיצוֹן   at the end; outermost (4·4) 894

לוּלִי   12 loop (13·13) 533

מַחְבֶּרֶת   thing joined (8·8) 289

הקביל   to show oppositeness in;
   corresponding to one another
   (2·2·13) 867

קרס   13 hook (10·10) 902

חִבַּר   to unite; join (8·9·28) 287

חִבַּר   16 to unite; join (8·9·28) 287

לוּלִי   17 loop (13·13) 533

קִיצוֹן   at the end; outermost (4·4) 894

מַחְבֶּרֶת   place of joining (8·8) 289

חֹבֶרֶת   a thing that joins; curtain piece
   (4·4) 289

קרס   18 hook (10·10) 902

חִבַּר   to unite; join (8·9·28) 287

מִכְסֶה   19 covering (8·16) 492

אדם   to be red (6·7·10) 10

תַּחַשׁ   dugong[?] (6·14) 1065

מִלְמַעְלָה   above (6·24) 751

קֶרֶשׁ   20 board (43·46) 903

שִׁטָּה   acacia [wood] (26·28) 1008

קֶרֶשׁ   21 board (43·46) 903

קֶרֶשׁ   22 board (43·46) 903

שׁלב   to be bound; joined (2·2·2) 1016

קֶרֶשׁ   23 board (43·46) 903

תֵּימָן   [toward] the south (5·24) 412

קֶרֶשׁ   24 board (43·46) 903

צֶלָע   25 side (19·39) 854

קֶרֶשׁ   board (43·46) 903

קֶרֶשׁ   26 board (43·46) 903

ירכה   27 extreme parts (6·28) 438

קֶרֶשׁ   board (43·46) 903

קֶרֶשׁ   28 board (43·46) 903

קצע[?]   pu. ptc. = corner post (2·2·3) 893

ירכה extreme parts (6·28) 438
תּוֹאֲמִים 29 double (2·6)[?] 1060
מִלְמַטָּה beneath (6·6) 641
טַבַּעַת ring (35·44) 371
מִקְצֹעַ corner buttress (2·11) 893
קֶרֶשׁ 30 board (43·46) 903
בְּרִיחַ 31 bar (15·41) 138
שִׁטָּה acacia [wood] (26·28) 1008
קֶרֶשׁ board (43·46) 903
צֶלָע side (19·39) 854
בְּרִיחַ 32 bar (15·41) 138
קֶרֶשׁ board (43·46) 903
צֶלָע side (19·39) 854
ירכה extreme parts (6·28) 438
בְּרִיחַ 33 bar (15·41) 138
תּיכן middle (2·12) 1064
קֶרֶשׁ board (43·46) 903
קֶרֶשׁ 34 board (43·46) 903
צִפָּה to overlay (25·42·46) 860
טַבַּעַת ring (35·44) 371
בְּרִיחַ bar (15·41) 138
פָּרֹכֶת 35 curtain (15·25) 827
תְּכֵלֶת violet (34·49) 1067
אַרְגָּמָן purple thread (26·39) 71
תּוֹלָעָה coccus ilicis [yielding scarlet color] (27·41) 1069
שָׁנִי scarlet (26·42) 1040
שֵׁשׁ linen (33·37) 1058
השזר to be twisted (21·21·21) 1004
חֹשֵׁב workman (11·12[?]) 362
שִׁטָּה 36 acacia [wood] (26·28) 1008
צִפָּה to overlay (25·42·46) 860
וו hook; pin; peg (13·13) 255
מָסָךְ 37 screen (16·25) 697
תְּכֵלֶת violet (34·49) 1067
אַרְגָּמָן purple thread (26·39) 71
תּוֹלָעָה coccus ilicis [yielding scarlet color] (27·41) 1069

שָׁנִי scarlet (26·42) 1040
שֵׁשׁ linen (33·37) 1058
השזר to be twisted (21·21·21) 1004
רקם to variegate; weave (8·8·9) 955
וו 38 hook; pin; peg (13·13) 255
צִפָּה to overlay (25·42·46) 860
חשוק fillet; ring (8·8) 366

Chapter 37

שִׁטָּה 1 acacia [wood] (26·28) 1008
קוֹמָה height (10·45) 879
צִפָּה 2 to overlay (25·42·46) 860
זֵר border (10·10) 267
טַבַּעַת 3 ring (35·44) 371
צֶלָע side (19·39) 854
בַּד 4 pole; stave (27·41) 94
שִׁטָּה acacia [wood] (26·28) 1008
צִפָּה to overlay (25·42·46) 860
בַּד 5 pole; stave (27·41) 94
טַבַּעַת ring (35·44) 371
צֶלָע side (19·39) 854
כַּפֹּרֶת 6 propitiatory (18·27) 498
מִקְשָׁה 7 hammered work? (6·9) 904
קָצָה end (21·28) 892
כַּפֹּרֶת propitiatory (18·27) 498
קָצָה 8 end (21·28) 892
כַּפֹּרֶת propitiatory (18·27) 498
קָצָה end (3·9) 892
לְמַעְלָה 9 upward (2·34) 751
סכך to cover (3·12·18[?]) 696
כַּפֹּרֶת propitiatory (18·27) 498
שִׁטָּה 10 acacia [wood] (26·28) 1008
קוֹמָה height (10·45) 879
צִפָּה 11 to overlay (25·42·46) 860
זֵר border (10·10) 267
מִסְגֶּרֶת 12 border (6·17) 689
טֶפַח handbreadth (2·9) 381
זֵר border (10·10) 267

טַבַּעַת 13 ring (35·44) 371

לְעֻמַּת 14 close by; side by side with (5·31) 769

מִסְגֶּרֶת border (6·17) 689

טַבַּעַת ring (35·44) 371

בַּד pole; stave (27·41) 94

בַּד 15 pole; stave (27·41) 94

שִׁטָּה acacia [wood] (26·28) 1008

צָפָה to overlay (25·42·46) 860

קְעָרָה 16 dish; platter (2·17) 891

מְנַקִּית sacrificial bowl (2·4) 667

קַשְׂוָה jug; jar (2·4) 903

הֻסַּךְ to be poured out (2·2·24) 650

מְנוֹרָה 17 lampstand (18·39) 633

מִקְשָׁה hammered work[?] (6·9) 904

יָרֵךְ base (7·34) 437

גָּבִיעַ cup (7·13) 149

כַּפְתּוֹר bulb (14·16) 499

פֶּרַח bud; sprout (8·17) 827

צָד 18 side (9·31) 841

מְנוֹרָה lampstand (18·39) 633

גָּבִיעַ 19 cup (7·13) 149

שֻׁקַּד to be shaped as almond [blossoms] (6·6·17) 1052

כַּפְתּוֹר bulb (14·16) 499

פֶּרַח bud; sprout (8·17) 827

מְנוֹרָה lampstand (18·39) 633

מְנוֹרָה 20 lampstand (18·39) 633

גָּבִיעַ cup (7·13) 149

שֻׁקַּד to be shaped as almond [blossoms] (6·6·17) 1052

כַּפְתּוֹר bulb (14·16) 499

פֶּרַח bud; sprout (8·17) 827

כַּפְתּוֹר 21 bulb (14·16) 499

כַּפְתּוֹר 22 bulb (14·16) 499

מִקְשָׁה hammered work[?] (6·9) 904

נֵר 23 lamp (11·44) 632

מֶלְקָחַיִם snuffers (2·6) 544

מַחְתָּה snuff holder (4·21) 367

שִׁטָּה 25 acacia [wood] (26·28) 1008

רבע ptc. pass. = to be squared (6·9·12) 917

קוֹמָה height (10·45) 879

צָפָה 26 to overlay (25·42·46) 860

גָּג top; roof (2·29) 150

זֵר border (10·10) 267

טַבַּעַת 27 ring (35·44) 371

זֵר border (10·10) 267

צֵלָע side (19·39) 854

צַד side (9·31) 841

בַּד pole; stave (27·41) 94

בַּד 28 pole; stave (27·41) 94

שִׁטָּה acacia [wood] (26·28) 1008

צָפָה to overlay (25·42·46) 860

מִשְׁחָה 29 ointment (13·21) 603

סם spice (11·16) 702

רקח to mix; compound (4·6·8) 955

Chapter 38

שִׁטָּה 1 acacia [wood] (26·28) 1008

רבע ptc. pass. = to be squared (6·9·12) 917

קוֹמָה height (10·45) 879

פִּנָּה 2 corner (2·30) 819

צָפָה to overlay (25·42·46) 860

סִיר 3 pot (3·27) 696

יע shovel (2·9) 418

מִזְרָק basin (2·32) 284

מזלגה three-pronged fork (2·5) 272

מַחְתָּה fire pan (4·21) 367

מִכְבָּר 4 grating (6·6) 460

רֶשֶׁת network (4·22) 440

כַּרְכֹּב rim (2·2) 501

מִלְמַטָּה beneath (6·6) 641

טַבַּעַת 5 ring (35·44) 371

קָצֶה end (3·9) 892

מִכְבָּר grating (6·6) 460

בַּד pole; stave (27·41) 94

בַּד 6 pole; stave (27·41) 94

שִׁטָּה acacia [wood] (26·28) 1008

צָפָה to overlay (25·42·46) 860

בַּד 7 pole; stave (27·41) 94

טַבַּעַת ring (35·44) 371

צֶלַע side (19·39) 854

נבב to hollow out (2·4·4) 612

לוּחַ plank (14·40) 531

כִּיּוֹר 8 basin (9·23) 468

כֵּן base (7·17) 487

מַרְאָה mirror (1·12) 909

צבא to serve (2·12·14) 838

תֵּימָן 9 [toward] the south (5·24) 412

קלע curtain; hanging (13·16) 887

שֵׁשׁ linen (33·37) 1058

השזר to be twisted (21·21·21) 1004

וו 10 hook; pin; peg (13·13) 255

חשוק fillet; ring (8·8) 366

וו 11 hook; pin; peg (13·13) 255

חשוק fillet; ring (8·8) 366

קלע 12 curtain; hanging (13·16) 887

וו hook; pin; peg (13·13) 255

חשוק fillet; ring (8·8) 366

קלע 14 curtain; hanging (13·16) 887

קלע 15 curtain; hanging (13·16) 887

קלע 16 curtain; hanging (13·16) 887

שֵׁשׁ linen (33·37) 1058

השזר to be twisted (21·21·21) 1004

וו 17 hook; pin; peg (13·13) 255

חשוק fillet; ring (8·8) 366

צפוי metal plating (2·5) 860

חשק to be furnished with fillets or rings (2·2·11) 366

מָסָךְ 18 screen (16·25) 697

רקם to variegate; weave (8·8·9) 955

תְּכֵלֶת violet (34·49) 1067

אַרְגָּמָן purple thread (26·39) 71

תּוֹלֵעָה coccus ilicis [yielding scarlet color] (27·41) 1069

שָׁנִי scarlet (26·42) 1040

שֵׁשׁ linen (33·37) 1058

השזר to be twisted (21·21·21) 1004

קוֹמָה height (10·45) 879

לְעֻמַּת close by; side by side with (5·31) 769

קלע curtain; hanging (13·16) 887

וו 19 hook; pin; peg (13·13) 255

צפוי metal plating (2·5) 860

חשוק fillet; ring (8·8) 366

יָתֵד 20 peg (8·24) 450

פקודים 21 musterings, i.e., expenses (1·3)[?] 824

חָרָשׁ 23 graver; artificer (3·38) 360

חֹשֵׁב workman (11·12[?]) 362

רקם to variegate; weave (8·8·9) 955

תְּכֵלֶת violet (34·49) 1067

אַרְגָּמָן purple thread (26·39) 71

תּוֹלֵעָה coccus ilicis [yielding scarlet color] (27·41) 1069

שָׁנִי scarlet (26·42) 1040

שֵׁשׁ linen (33·37) 1058

תְּנוּפָה 24 offering; wave offering (6·30) 632

בֶּקַע 26 half; half shekel (1·2) 132

גֻּלְגֹּלֶת for each man; head; skull (2·12) 166

מַחֲצִית half (5·16) 345

פָּרֹכֶת 27 curtain (15·25) 827

וו 28 hook; pin; peg (13·13) 255

צָפָה to overlay (25·42·46) 860

חָשַׁק to furnish with fillets or rings (1·1·11) 365

תְּנוּפָה 29 offering; wave offering (6·30) 632

מִכְבָּר 30 grating (6·6) 460

יָתֵד 31 peg (8·24) 450

Chapter 39

תְּכֵלֶת	1 violet (34·49) 1067
אַרְגָּמָן	purple thread (26·39) 71
תּוֹלֵעָה	coccus ilicis [yielding scarlet color] (27·41) 1069
שָׁנִי	scarlet (26·42) 1040
שְׂרָד	plaited; braided work (4·4) 975
אֵפוֹד	2 ephod; priestly garment (29·49) 65
תְּכֵלֶת	violet (34·49) 1067
אַרְגָּמָן	purple thread (26·39) 71
תּוֹלֵעָה	coccus ilicis [yielding scarlet color] (27·41) 1069
שָׁנִי	scarlet (26·42) 1040
שֵׁשׁ	linen (33·37) 1058
השזר	to be twisted (21·21·21) 1004
רקע	3 to hammer out (1·3·11) 955
פַּח	plate [of metal] (1·2) 809
קָצֵץ	to cut in two (1·9·14) 893
פָּתִיל	thread (5·11) 836
תְּכֵלֶת	violet (34·49) 1067
אַרְגָּמָן	purple thread (26·39) 71
תּוֹלֵעָה	coccus ilicis [yielding scarlet color] (27·41) 1069
שָׁנִי	scarlet (26·42) 1040
שֵׁשׁ	linen (33·37) 1058
חֹשֵׁב	workman (11·12[?]) 362
חבר	4 to unite (4·11·28) 287
קָצָה	end (3·9) 892
חֻבַּר	to be joined together (2·4·28) 287
חֵשֶׁב	5 girdle; ingenious work (7·8) 363
אֲפֻדָּה	high priest's ephod (2·3) 65
תְּכֵלֶת	violet (34·49) 1067
אַרְגָּמָן	purple thread (26·39) 71
תּוֹלֵעָה	coccus ilicis [yielding scarlet color] (27·41) 1069
שָׁנִי	scarlet (26·42) 1040
שֵׁשׁ	linen (33·37) 1058
השזר	to be twisted (21·21·21) 1004
שֹׁהַם	6 onyx (7·11) 995
מְשֻׁבָּצֹת	checkered work (8·9) 990
פתח	to engrave (1·1·9) 836
פִּתּוּחַ	engraving (6·11) 836
חוֹתָם	seal; signet ring (6·13) 368
אֵפוֹד	7 ephod; priestly garment (29·49) 65
זִכָּרוֹן	memorial; reminder (8·24) 272
חֹשֶׁן	8 breast piece (23·25) 365
חֹשֵׁב	workman (11·12[?]) 362
אֵפוֹד	ephod; priestly garment (29·49) 65
תְּכֵלֶת	violet (34·49) 1067
אַרְגָּמָן	purple thread (26·39) 71
תּוֹלֵעָה	coccus ilicis [yielding scarlet color] (27·41) 1069
שָׁנִי	scarlet (26·42) 1040
שֵׁשׁ	linen (33·37) 1058
השזר	to be twisted (21·21·21) 1004
רבע	9 ptc. pass. = to be squared (6·9·12) 917
כָּפַל	to double over (3·3·4) 495
חֹשֶׁן	breast piece (23·25) 365
זֶרֶת	span (4·7) 284
טוּר	10 row (12·26) 377
אֹדֶם	carnelian (2·3) 10
פִּטְדָה	topaz (2·4) 809
בָּרֶקֶת	a precious stone; emerald (2·3) 140
טוּר	11 row (12·26) 377
נֹפֶךְ	ruby[?] (2·4) 656
סַפִּיר	sapphire (3·11) 705
יַהֲלֹם	jasper[?] (2·3) 240
טוּר	12 row (12·26) 377
לֶשֶׁם	precious stone (2·2) 545
שְׁבוֹ	precious stone (2·2) 986
אַחְלָמָה	amethyst[?] (2·2) 21
טוּר	13 row (12·26) 377
תַּרְשִׁישׁ	yellow jasper[?] (2·7) 1076
שֹׁהַם	onyx (7·11) 995

58

יָשְׁפֵה	jasper (2·3) 448	
מְשֻׁבְּצוֹת	checkered work (8·9) 990	
מִלֻּאָה	setting of jewel (3·3) 571	
פִּתּוּחַ	14 engraving (6·11) 836	
חֹתָם	seal; signet ring (6·13) 368	
חֹשֶׁן	15 breast piece (23·25) 365	
שרשרה	chain (4·8) 1057	
גַּבְלֻת	twisting (2·2) 148	
עֲבֹת	cordage; cord (8·24) 721	
מְשֻׁבְּצוֹת	16 checkered work (8·9) 990	
טַבַּעַת	ring (35·44) 371	
קָצָה	end (21·28) 892	
חֹשֶׁן	breast piece (23·25) 365	
עֲבֹת	17 cordage; cord (8·24) 721	
טַבַּעַת	ring (35·44) 371	
קָצָה	end (21·28) 892	
חֹשֶׁן	breast piece (23·25) 365	
קָצָה	18 end (21·28) 892	
עֲבֹת	cordage; cord (8·24) 721	
מְשֻׁבְּצוֹת	checkered work (8·9) 990	
אֵפוֹד	ephod; priestly garment (29·49) 65	
מוּל	the forefront of (6·25) 557	
טַבַּעַת	19 ring (35·44) 371	
קָצָה	end (21·28) 892	
חֹשֶׁן	breast piece (23·25) 365	
אֵפוֹד	ephod; priestly garment (29·49) 65	
טַבַּעַת	20 ring (35·44) 371	
אֵפוֹד	ephod; priestly garment (29·49) 65	
מִלְמַטָּה	beneath (6·6) 641	
מִמּוּל	on the front of (2·9) 557	
לְעֻמָּה	close by; side by side with (5·31) 789	
מַחְבֶּרֶת	thing joined (8·8) 289	
חֵשֶׁב	girdle; ingenious work (7·8) 363	
רכס	21 to bind (2·2·2) 940	
חֹשֶׁן	breast piece (23·25) 365	
טַבַּעַת	ring (35·44) 371	
אֵפוֹד	ephod; priestly garment (29·49) 65	

פָּתִיל	cord (5·11) 836	
תְּכֵלֶת	violet (34·49) 1067	
חֵשֶׁב	girdle; ingenious work (7·8) 363	
נזחח	to remove; displace (2·2·2) 267	
מְעִיל	22 robe (9·28) 591	
אֵפוֹד	ephod; priestly garment (29·49) 65	
אֹרֵג	weaver (4·16[?]) 70	
כָּלִיל	entirety (2·15) 483	
תְּכֵלֶת	violet (34·49) 1067	
מְעִיל	23 robe (9·28) 591	
כְּפִי	in proportion to (3·16) 804	
תַּחְרָא	corselet (2·2) 1065	
שׁוּל	24 skirt [of robe] (6·11) 1002	
מְעִיל	robe (9·28) 591	
רִמּוֹן	pomegranate (8·32) 941	
תְּכֵלֶת	violet (34·49) 1067	
אַרְגָּמָן	purple thread (26·39) 71	
תּוֹלֵעָה	coccus ilicis [yielding scarlet color] (27·41) 1069	
שָׁנִי	scarlet (26·42) 1040	
השזר	to be twisted (21·21·21) 1004	
פַּעֲמוֹן	25 bell (7·7) 822	
רִמּוֹן	pomegranate (8·32) 941	
שׁוּל	skirt [of robe] (6·11) 1002	
מְעִיל	robe (9·28) 591	
פַּעֲמוֹן	26 bell (7·7) 822	
רִמּוֹן	pomegranate (8·32) 941	
שׁוּל	skirt [of robe] (6·11) 1002	
מְעִיל	robe (9·28) 591	
כֻּתֹּנֶת	27 tunic (9·30) 509	
שֵׁשׁ	linen (33·37) 1058	
אֹרֵג	weaver (4·10[?]) 70	
מִצְנֶפֶת	28 turban of high priest (8·12) 857	
שֵׁשׁ	linen (33·37) 1058	
פְּאֵר	headdress; turban (1·7) 802	
מִגְבָּעוֹת	turban of common priest (3·4) 149	
מכנס	drawers (2·5) 488	
בַּד	white linen (2·23) 94	

הֻשְׁזַר	to be twisted (21·21·21) 1004	
אַבְנֵט	29 girdle (5·9) 126	
שֵׁשׁ	linen (33·37) 1058	
הֻשְׁזַר	to be twisted (21·21·21) 1004	
תְּכֵלֶת	violet (34·49) 1067	
אַרְגָּמָן	purple thread (26·39) 71	
תּוֹלֵעָה	coccus ilicis [yielding scarlet color] (27·41) 1069	
שָׁנִי	scarlet (26·42) 1040	
רקם	to variegate; weave (8·8·9) 955	
צִיץ	30 shining plate [of gold] (2·15) 847	
נֵזֶר	crown (2·24) 634	
מִכְתָּב	writing (3·9) 508	
פִּתּוּחַ	engraving (6·11) 836	
חוֹתָם	seal; signet ring (6·13) 368	
פְּתִיל	31 cord (5·11) 836	
תְּכֵלֶת	violet (34·49) 1067	
מִצְנֶפֶת	turban of high priest (8·12) 857	
מִלְמַעְלָה	above (6·24) 751	
קרס	33 hook (10·10) 902	
קֶרֶשׁ	board (43·46) 903	
בְּרִיחַ	bar (15·41) 138	
מִכְסֶה	34 covering (8·16) 492	
אדם	to be reddened (6·7·10) 10	
תַּחַשׁ	dugong[?] (6·14) 1065	
פָּרֹכֶת	curtain (15·25) 827	
מָסָךְ	screen (16·25) 697	
בַּד	35 pole; stave (27·41) 94	
כַּפֹּרֶת	propitiatory (18·27) 498	
מְנוֹרָה	37 lampstand (18·39) 633	
נֵר	lamp (11·44) 632	
מַעֲרָכָה	row (1·18) 790	
מָאוֹר	light (7·19) 22	
מִשְׁחָה	38 ointment (13·21) 603	
סם	spice (11·16) 702	
מָסָךְ	screen (16·25) 697	
מִכְבָּר	39 grating (6·6) 460	
בַּד	pole; stave (27·41) 94	

כִּיּוֹר	basin (9·23) 468	
כֵּן	base (7·17) 487	
קֶלַע	40 curtain; hanging (13·16) 887	
מָסָךְ	screen (16·25) 697	
מֵיתָר	cord (2·9) 452	
יָתֵד	peg (8·24) 450	
שָׂרָד	41 plaited; braided work (4·4) 975	
כָּהֵן	to act as priest (12·23·23) 464	

Chapter 40

סכך	3 to cover (3·12·18[?]) 696	
פָּרֹכֶת	curtain (15·25) 827	
עֶרֶךְ	4 order; row (2·33) 789	
מְנוֹרָה	lampstand (18·39) 633	
נֵר	lamp (11·44) 632	
מָסָךְ	5 screen (16·25) 697	
כִּיּוֹר	7 basin (9·23) 468	
מָסָךְ	8 screen (16·25) 697	
מִשְׁחָה	9 ointment (13·21) 603	
כִּיּוֹר	11 basin (9·23) 468	
כֵּן	base (7·17) 487	
כָּהֵן	13 to act as priest (12·23·23) 464	
כֻּתֹּנֶת	14 tunic (9·30) 509	
כָּהֵן	15 to act as priest (12·23·23) 464	
כְּהֻנָּה	priesthood (2·13) 464	
קֶרֶשׁ	18 board (43·46) 903	
בְּרִיחַ	bar (15·41) 138	
מִכְסֶה	19 covering (8·16) 492	
מִלְמַעְלָה	above (6·24) 751	
בַּד	20 pole; stave (27·41) 94	
כַּפֹּרֶת	propitiatory (18·27) 498	
מִלְמַעְלָה	above (6·24) 751	
פָּרֹכֶת	21 curtain (15·25) 827	
מָסָךְ	screen (16·25) 697	
סכך	to screen out (1·5·18[?]) 696	
יָרֵךְ	22 side (7·34) 437	
פָּרֹכֶת	curtain (15·25) 827	
עֶרֶךְ	23 order; row (2·33) 789	

60

מְנוֹרָה 24 lampstand (18·39) 633

נֹכַח opposite to (4·27) 647

יָרֵךְ side (7·34) 437

נֵר 25 lamp (11·44) 632

פָּרֹכֶת 26 curtain (15·25) 827

סם 27 spice (11·16) 702

מָסָךְ 28 screen (16·25) 697

כִּיּוֹר 30 basin (9·23) 468

מָסָךְ 33 screen (16·25) 697

מַסַּע 36 journey (3·12) 652

מַסַּע 38 journey (3·12) 652

LEVITICUS

Chapter 1

סָמַךְ 4 to lay (14·41·48) 701

זָרַק 5 to throw, scatter abundantly (12·32·34) 284

הִפְשִׁיט 6 to flay, skin (1·15·43) 832

נִתַּח to cut up (3·9·9) 677

נֵתַח piece of a divided carcass (6·12) 677

נֵתַח 8 piece of a divided carcass (6·12) 677

פֶּדֶר suet (3·3) 804

כְּרַע 9 leg (6·9) 502

נִיחוֹחַ soothing (17·43) 629

כֶּשֶׂב 10 lamb (7·13) 461

יָרֵךְ 11 side (1·34) 437

זָרַק to throw, scatter abundantly (12·32·34) 284

נִתַּח 12 to cut up (3·9·9) 677

נֵתַח piece of a divided carcass (6·12) 677

פֶּדֶר suet (3·3) 804

כְּרַע 13 leg (6·9) 502

נִיחוֹחַ soothing (12·43) 629

תּוֹר 14 turtle dove (9·14) 1076

יוֹנָה dove (10·35) 401

מָלַק 15 to nip off (2·2·2) 577

נִמְצָה to be drained (2·3·7) 594

מֻרְאָה 16 crop (1·1) 597

נוֹצָה plumage (1·1) 663

קֶדֶם eastward (2·26) 870

דֶּשֶׁן fat ashes (5·15) 206

שִׁסַּע 17 to tear in two (1·3·8) 1042

הִבְדִּיל to separate, divide (8·32·42) 95

נִיחוֹחַ soothing (17·43) 629

Chapter 2

לְבֹנָה 1 frankincense (7·21) 526

קָמַץ 2 to enclose with hand, grasp (2·3·3) 888

קֹמֶץ closed hand, fist (3·4) 888

לְבֹנָה frankincense (7·21) 526

אַזְכָּרָה memorial offering (6·7) 272

נִיחוֹחַ soothing (17·43) 629

מַאֲפֶה 4 a thing baked (1·1) 66

תַּנּוּר stove, firepot (4·15) 1072

חַלָּה a kind of cake (7·13) 319

בָּלַל to mix (9·42·42[?]) 117

רָקִיק thin cake, wafer (3·8) 956

מַחֲבַת 5 griddle (3·5) 290

בָּלַל to mix (9·42·42[?]) 117

פָּתַת 6 to break up, crumble (1·1) 837

פַּת fragment, bit, morsel (2·14) 839

מַרְחֶשֶׁת 7 stewpan (2·2) 935

אַזְכָּרָה 9 memorial offering (6·7) 272

נִיחוֹחַ soothing (17·43) 629

חָמֵץ 11 that which is leavened (4·11) 329

שְׂאֹר leaven (1·5) 959

נִיחוֹחַ 12 soothing (17·43) 629

מֶלַח 13 salt (3·28) 571

מלח to salt (1·1·3) 572

בִּכּוּרִים 14 first fruits (4·17) 114

אָבִיב fresh young ears (1·8) 1

קָלָה to roast, parch (1·3·4) 885

גֶּרֶשׂ grits (2·2) 176

כַּרְמֶל fruit, garden growth (2·3[?]) 502

לְבֹנָה 15 frankincense (7·21) 526

אַזְכָּרָה 16 memorial offering (6·7) 272

גֶּרֶשׂ grits (2·2) 176

לְבֹנָה frankincense (7·21) 526

Chapter 3

נְקֵבָה 1 female (12·22) 666

סָמַךְ 2 to lay (14·41·48) 701

זָרַק to throw, scatter abundantly (12·32·34) 284

כִּלְיָה 4 kidney (13·30) 480

כֶּסֶל loin (4·5[?]) 492

62

יֹתֶרֶת	appendage (9·11) 452
כָּבֵד	liver (9·14) 458
נִיחוֹחַ	5 soothing (17·43) 629
נְקֵבָה	6 female (12·22) 666
כֶּשֶׂב	7 lamb (7·13) 461
סָמַךְ	8 to lay (14·41·48) 701
זָרַק	to throw, scatter abundantly (12·32·34) 284
אַלְיָה	9 fat tail (4·5) 46
לְעֻמָּה	close by, side by side with (1·32) 769
עָצֶה	spine, or as sacrum [bone close to fat tail] (1·1) 782
כִּלְיָה	10 kidney (13·30) 480
כֶּסֶל	loin (4·5[?]) 492
יֹתֶרֶת	appendage (9·11) 452
כָּבֵד	liver (9·14) 458
סָמַךְ	13 to lay (14·41·48) 701
זָרַק	to throw, scatter abundantly (12·32·34) 284
כִּלְיָה	15 kidney (13·30) 480
כֶּסֶל	loin (4·5[?]) 492
יֹתֶרֶת	appendage (9·11) 452
כָּבֵד	liver (9·14) 458
נִיחוֹחַ	16 soothing (17·43) 629
מוֹשָׁב	17 dwelling place (8·43) 444

Chapter 4

שְׁגָגָה	2 sin of error, inadvertence (6·19) 993
מָשִׁיחַ	3 anointed (4·40) 603
אַשְׁמָה	guiltiness (4·19) 80
סָמַךְ	4 to lay (14·41·48) 701
מָשִׁיחַ	5 anointed (4·40) 603
טָבַל	6 to dip (6·15·16) 371
אֶצְבַּע	finger (13·31) 840
הִזָּה	to sprinkle (13·20·24) 633
פָּרֹכֶת	curtain (7·25) 827
סַם	7 spice (2·16) 702

יְסוֹד	base (8·19) 414
כִּלְיָה	9 kidney (3·13) 480
כֶּסֶל	loin (4·5[?]) 492
יֹתֶרֶת	appendage (9·11) 452
כָּבֵד	liver (9·14) 458
כְּרַע	11 leg (6·9) 502
פֶּרֶשׁ	offal [as ripped out in preparing victim] (3·7) 831
שֶׁפֶךְ	12 [place of] pouring (2·2) 1050
דֶּשֶׁן	fat ashes (5·15) 206
שׁגה	13 to commit a sin of ignorance (1·7·21) 993
נֶעְלַם	to be concealed (4·11·29) 761
אָשֵׁם	to be guilty (10·31·33) 79
סָמַךְ	15 to lay (14·41·48) 701
מָשִׁיחַ	16 anointed (4·40) 603
טָבַל	17 to dip (6·15·16) 371
אֶצְבַּע	finger (13·31) 840
הִזָּה	to sprinkle (13·20·24) 633
פָּרֹכֶת	curtain (7·25) 827
יְסוֹד	18 base (8·19) 414
נִסְלַח	20 to be forgiven (10·13·46) 699
שְׁגָגָה	22 sin of error, inadvertence (6·19) 993
אָשֵׁם	to be guilty (10·31·33) 79
סָמַךְ	24 to lay (14·41·48) 701
אֶצְבַּע	25 finger (13·31) 840
יְסוֹד	base (8·19) 414
נִסְלַח	26 to be forgiven (10·13·46) 699
שְׁגָגָה	27 sin of error, inadvertence (6·19) 993
אָשֵׁם	to be guilty (10·31·33) 79
שְׂעִירָה	28 she-goat (2·2) 972
נְקֵבָה	female (12·22) 666
סָמַךְ	29 to lay (14·41·48) 701
אֶצְבַּע	30 finger (13·31) 840
יְסוֹד	base (8·19) 414
נִיחוֹחַ	31 soothing (17·43) 629
נִסְלַח	to be forgiven (10·13·46) 699
נְקֵבָה	32 female (12·22) 666

סָמַךְ	33 to lay (14·41·48) 701		תּוֹר	turtle dove (9·14) 1076

סָמַךְ 33 to lay (14·41·48) 701

אֶצְבַּע 34 finger (13·31) 840

יְסוֹד base (8·19) 414

כֶּשֶׂב 35 lamb (7·13) 461

נִסְלַח to be forgiven (10·13·46) 699

Chapter 5

אָלָה 1 oath (1·36) 46

נְבֵלָה 2 corpse (19·48) 615

שֶׁרֶץ swarmers, swarming things (2·15) 1056

נֶעְלַם to be concealed (4·11·29) 761

אָשֵׁם to be guilty (10·31·33) 79

טֻמְאָה 3 uncleanness (18·37) 380

נֶעְלַם to be concealed (4·11·29) 761

אָשֵׁם to be guilty (10·31·33) 79

בטא 4 to speak rashly (2·3·4) 104

שְׁבֻעָה oath (1·30) 989

נֶעְלַם to be concealed (4·11·29) 761

אָשֵׁם to be guilty (10·31·33) 79

אָשֵׁם 5 to be guilty (10·31·33) 79

אָשָׁם 6 trespass offering (27·46) 79

נְקֵבָה female (12·22) 666

כִּשְׂבָּה ewe lamb (1·1) 461

דֵּי 7 sufficiency, enough (3·12) 191

שֶׂה sheep, goat (5·44) 961

אָשָׁם trespass offering (27·46) 79

תּוֹר turtle dove (9·14) 1076

יוֹנָה dove (10·35) 401

מָלַק 8 to nip off (2·2·2) 577

מִמּוּל off the front of (1·9) 557

עֹרֶף neck (1·33) 791

הִבְדִּיל to divide (8·32·42) 95

הִזָּה 9 to sprinkle (13·20·24) 633

נִמְצָה to be drained (2·3·7) 594

יְסוֹד base (8·19) 414

נִסְלַח 10 to be forgiven (10·13·46) 699

הִשִּׂיג 11 to reach (12·48·48) 673

תּוֹר turtle dove (9·14) 1076

יוֹנָה dove (10·35) 401

אֵפָה ephah, a measure (3·38) 35

לְבֹנָה frankincense (7·21) 526

קָמַץ 12 to enclose with hand, grasp (2·3·3) 888

קֹמֶץ fist (3·4) 888

אַזְכָּרָה memorial offering (6·7) 272

נִסְלַח 13 to be forgiven (10·13·46) 699

מָעַל 15 to act unfaithfully (3·35·35) 591

מַעַל unfaithful act (3·29) 591

שְׁגָגָה sin of error, inadvertence (6·19) 993

אָשָׁם trespass offering (27·46) 79

עֵרֶךְ valuation, estimate (24·33) 789

אָשָׁם 16 trespass offering (27·46) 79

נִסְלַח to be forgiven (10·13·46) 699

אָשֵׁם 17 to be guilty (10·31·33) 79

עֵרֶךְ 18 valuation, estimate (24·33) 789

אָשָׁם trespass offering (27·46) 79

שְׁגָגָה sin of error, inadvertence (6·19) 993

שָׁגַג to sin, go astray (1·5·5) 992

נִסְלַח to be forgiven (10·13·46) 699

אָשָׁם 19 trespass offering (27·46) 79

אָשֵׁם to commit an offence (10·31·33) 79

מָעַל 21 to act unfaithfully (10·13·42) 591

מַעַל unfaithful act (3·35·35) 591

כִּחֵשׁ to deceive (3·19·22) 471

עֲמִית associate, fellow, relation (11·12) 765

פִּקָּדוֹן deposit, store (2·3) 824

תְּשׂוּמֶת pledge, security (1·1) 965

גָּזֵל robbery (1·4) 160

עָשַׁק to oppress, wrong (3·36·37) 798

אֲבֵדָה 22 a lost thing (2·4) 2

כִּחֵשׁ to deceive (3·19·22) 471

אָשֵׁם 23 to be guilty (10·31·33) 79

גְּזֵלָה plunder, spoil (1·6) 160

גזל to tear away, seize (2·29·30) 159

עֹשֶׁק   gain from extortion (1·15) 799

עָשַׁק   to oppress, wrong (3·36·37) 798

פִּקָּדוֹן   deposit, store (2·3) 824

אֲבֵדָה   a lost thing (2·4) 2

לַאֲשֶׁר   24 to (one whom) (3·38) 82

אַשְׁמָה   guiltiness (4·19) 80

אָשָׁם   25 tresspass offering (27·46) 79

עֵרֶךְ   estimate, valuation (24·33) 789

נִסְלַח   26 to be forgiven (10·13·46) 699

אַשְׁמָה   guiltiness (4·19) 80

Chapter 6

מוֹקֵד   2 hearth (1·3) 428

הוּקַד   to be burning (3·5·8) 428

מַד   3 garment (1·12) 551

בַּד   white linen (8·23) 94

מִכְנָס   drawers (2·5) 488

דֶּשֶׁן   fat ashes (5·15) 206

פָּשַׁט   4 to strip off, put off (2·24·43) 833

דֶּשֶׁן   fat ashes (5·15) 206

הוּקַד   5 to be burning (3·5·8) 428

כבה   to be extinguished (2·14·24) 459

הוּקַד   6 to be burning (3·5·8) 428

כבה   to be extinguished (2·14·24) 459

קֹמֶץ   8 fist (3·4) 888

לְבֹנָה   frankincense (7·21) 526

נִיחוֹחַ   soothing (17·43) 629

אַזְכָּרָה   memorial offering (6·7) 272

נאפה   10 to be baked (3·3·12) 66

חָמֵץ   that which is leavened (4·11) 329

אָשָׁם   trespass offering (27·46) 79

אֵפָה   13 ephah, a measure (3·38) 35

מַחֲצִית   half (2·16) 345

מַחֲבַת   14 griddle (3·5) 290

הרבך   to be well mixed (2·3·3) 916

תֻּפִינִים   [dub.] baken pieces (1·1) 1074

פַּת   fragment, bit, morsel (2·14) 837

נִיחוֹחַ   soothing (17·43) 629

מָשִׁיחַ   15 anointed (4·40) 603

כָּלִיל   whole offering (2·15) 483

כָּלִיל   16 whole offering (2·15) 483

נזה   20 to spatter (2·4·24) 633

חֶרֶשׂ   21 earthen vessel (5·16) 360

בֻּשַּׁל   to be boiled (2·4·27) 143

מֹרַק   to be well scoured (1·1·14) 599

שֻׁטַּף   to be rinsed (1·1·31) 1009

Chapter 7

אָשָׁם   1 trespass offering (27·46) 79

אָשָׁם   2 trespass offering (27·46) 79

זָרַק   to throw, scatter abundantly (12·32·34) 284

אַלְיָה   3 fat tail (4·5) 46

כִּלְיָה   4 kidney (13·30) 480

כֶּסֶל   loin (4·5[?]) 492

יוֹתֶרֶת   appendage (9·11) 452

כָּבֵד   liver (9·14) 458

אָשָׁם   5 trespass offering (27·46) 79

אָשָׁם   7 trespass offering (27·46) 79

נאפה   9 to be baked (3·3·12) 66

תַּנּוּר   stove, firepot (4·15) 1092

מַרְחֶשֶׁת   stewpan (2·2) 935

מַחֲבַת   griddle (3·5) 290

בָּלַל   10 to mix (9·42·42[?]) 117

חָרֵב   dry, unmoistened (1·10?) 351

תּוֹדָה   12 thank offering (5·32) 392

חַלָּה   a kind of cake (8·14) 319

בָּלַל   to mix (9·42·42[?]) 117

רָקִיק   thin cake, wafer (3·8) 956

הרבך   to be well mixed (2·3·3) 916

חַלָּה   13 a kind of cake (8·14) 319

חָמֵץ   that which is leavened (4·11) 329

תּוֹדָה   thank offering (5·32) 392

זָרַק   14 to throw, scatter abundantly (12·32·34) 284

תּוֹדָה   15 thank offering (5·32) 392

נְדָבָה   16 freewill offering (5·27) 621

65

מָחֳרָת — on the morrow of, after (5·32) 564

פִּגּוּל — 18 foul thing, refuse (2·4) 803

טֻמְאָה — 20 uncleanness (18·37) 380

עַם — kinsman (12·34) 769

טֻמְאָה — 21 uncleanness (18·37) 380

שֶׁקֶץ — detestable thing (9·11) 1054

עַם — kinsman (12·34) 769

כֶּשֶׂב — 23 lamb (7·13) 461

נְבֵלָה — 24 carcass (19·48) 615

טְרֵפָה — animal torn (3·9) 383

עַם — 25 kinsman (12·34) 769

מוֹשָׁב — 26 dwelling place (8·43) 444

עַם — 27 kinsman (12·34) 769

חָזֶה — 30 breast (9·13) 303

הֵנִיף — to wave (11·32·34[?]) 631

תְּנוּפָה — waving, wave offering (14·30) 632

חָזֶה — 31 breast (9·13) 303

שׁוֹק — 32 leg (8·19) 1003

שׁוֹק — 33 leg (8·19) 1003

מָנָה — portion (2·12) 584

חָזֶה — 34 breast (9·13) 303

תְּנוּפָה — waving, wave offering (14·30) 632

שׁוֹק — leg (8·19) 1003

מִשְׁחָה — 35 consecrated portion (2·2[?]) 603

כֹּהֵן — to minister as a priest (12·23·23) 464

אָשָׁם — 37 trespass offering (27·46) 79

מִלּוּא — installation (6·15) 571

Chapter 8

מִשְׁחָה — 2 ointment (7·21[?]) 603

סַל — basket (3·15) 700

הִקְהִיל — 3 to summon an assembly (1·20·39) 874

נִקְהַל — 4 to assemble (1·19·39) 874

כֻּתֹּנֶת — 7 tunic (4·30) 509

חָגַר — to gird on (4·4·44) 291

אַבְנֵט — girdle (5·9) 126

מְעִיל — robe (1·28) 591

אֵפוֹד — priestly garment (2·49) 65

חֵשֶׁב — ingenious work, girdle (1·8) 363

אפד — to gird on an ephod (1·2·2) 65

חֹשֶׁן — 8 breast piece (2·25) 365

אוּרִים — Urim (1·7) 22

תֻּמִּים — [dub.] Thummin (1·5) 1070

מִצְנֶפֶת — 9 turban of high priest (3·12) 857

מוּל — the forefront of (1·23) 557

צִיץ — shining thing (1·15) 847

נֵזֶר — crown (2·24) 634

מִשְׁחָה — 10 ointment (7·21) 603

נזה — 11 to spatter (2·4·24) 633

כִּיּוֹר — basin (1·23) 468

כֵּן — base (1·17) 487

מִשְׁחָה — 12 ointment (7·21) 603

כֻּתֹּנֶת — 13 tunic (4·30) 509

חגר — to gird on (4·4·44) 291

אַבְנֵט — girdle (5·9) 126

חבש — to bind (on) (1·27·31) 289

מִגְבָּעוֹת — headgear (1·4) 149

סָמַךְ — 14 to lay (14·41·48) 701

אֶצְבַּע — 15 finger (13·31) 840

יְסוֹד — base (8·19) 414

יוֹתֶרֶת — 16 appendage (9·11) 452

כָּבֵד — liver (9·14) 458

כִּלְיָה — kidney (13·30) 480

פֶּרֶשׁ — 17 offal |as ripped out in preparing a victim| (3·7) 831

סָמַךְ — 18 to lay (14·41·48) 701

זָרַק — 19 to throw, scatter abundantly (12·32·34) 284

נִתַּח — 20 to cut up (3·9·9) 677

נֵתַח — piece of a divided carcass (6·12) 677

פֶּדֶר — suet (3·3) 804

כְּרַע — 21 leg (6·9) 502

נִיחוֹחַ — soothing (17·43) 629

מִלּוּא — 22 installation (6·15) 571

סָמַךְ — to lay (14·41·48) 701

תְּנוּךְ 23 tip, lobe of ear (6·8) 1072

יְמָנִי right (20·33) 412

בֹּהֶן thumb, great toe (12·14[?]) 97

תְּנוּךְ 24 tip, lobe of ear (6·8) 1072

יְמָנִי right (20·33) 412

בֹּהֶן thumb, great toe (12·14[?]) 97

זָרַק to throw, scatter abundantly (12·32·34) 284

אַלְיָה 25 fat tail (4·5) 46

יוֹתֶרֶת appendage (9·11) 452

כָּבֵד liver (9·14) 458

כִּלְיָה kidney (13·30) 480

שׁוֹק leg (8·19) 1003

סַל 26 basket (3·15) 700

חַלָּה kind of cake (8·14) 319

רָקִיק thin cake, wafer (3·8) 956

שׁוֹק leg (8·19) 1003

הֵנִיף 27 to wave (11·32·34[?]) 631

תְּנוּפָה waving, wave offering (14·30) 632

מִלּוּא 28 installation (6·15) 571

נִיחוֹחַ soothing (17·43) 629

חָזֶה 29 breast (9·13) 303

הֵנִיף to wave (11·32·34[?]) 631

תְּנוּפָה waving, wave offering (14·30) 632

מִלּוּא installation (6·15) 571

מָנָה portion (2·12) 584

מִשְׁחָה 30 ointment (7·21) 603

נזה to spatter (2·4·24) 633

בשל 31 to cook, boil (1·20·27) 143

סַל basket (3·15) 700

מִלּוּא installation (6·15) 571

מִלּוּא 33 installation (6·15) 571

Chapter 9

עֵגֶל 2 calf (3·35) 722

עֵגֶל 3 calf (3·35) 722

בָּלַל 4 to mix (9·42·42[?]) 117

עֵגֶל 8 calf (3·35) 722

טָבַל 9 to dip (6·15·16) 371

אֶצְבַּע finger (13·31) 840

יְסוֹד base (8·19) 414

כִּלְיָה 10 kidney (13·30) 480

יוֹתֶרֶת appendage (9·11) 452

כָּבֵד liver (9·14) 458

זָרַק 12 to throw, scatter abundantly (12·32·34) 284

נֵתַח 13 piece of a divided carcass (6·12) 677

כֶּרַע 14 leg (6·9) 502

מִלְּבַד 17 besides (5·33) 94

זָרַק 18 to throw, scatter abundantly (12·32·34) 284

אַלְיָה 19 fat tail (4·5) 46

מְכַסֶּה covering (1·4) 492

כִּלְיָה kidney (13·30) 480

יוֹתֶרֶת 19 appendage (9·11) 452

כָּבֵד liver (9·14) 458

חָזֶה 20 breast (9·13) 303

חָזֶה 21 breast (9·13) 303

שׁוֹק leg (8·19) 1003

הֵנִיף to wave (11·32·34[?]) 631

תְּנוּפָה waving, wave offering (14·30) 632

Chapter 10

מַחְתָּה 1 censer (2·21) 367

דמם 3 to be silent (1·23·30) 198

כֻּתֹּנֶת 5 tunic (4·30) 509

פָּרַע 6 to let loose, remove restraint (3·13·16) 828

פרם to tear a garment (3·3·3) 827

קָצַף to be wroth (2·28·34) 893

שְׂרֵפָה burning (1·13) 977

מִשְׁחָה 7 ointment (7·21) 603

שֵׁכָר 9 intoxicating drink (1·23) 1016

הַבְדִּיל 10 to make a distinction (8·32·42) 95

חֹל profaneness (1·7) 320

הורה 11 to teach (2·45[?]·45[?]) 434

חָזֶה 14 breast (9·13) 303

תְּנוּפָה waving, wave offering (14·30) 632

שׁוֹק leg (8·19) 1003

שׁוֹק 15 leg (8·19) 1003

חָזֶה breast (9·13) 303

תְּנוּפָה waving, wave offering (14·30) 632

הֵנִיף to wave (11·32·34[?]) 631

קָצַף 16 to be wroth (2·28·34) 893

פְּנִימָה 18 towards the [in]side (1·5) 819

Chapter 11

הִפְרִיס 3 to divide [the hoof] (7·12·14) 828

פַּרְסָה hoof (9·21) 828

שָׁסַע to divide, cleave (3·5·8) 1042

שֶׁסַע cleft (3·4) 1043

גֵּרָה cud (7·11) 176

מִמַּעַל 4 above, on the top of (7·29) 751

גֵּרָה cud (7·11) 176

הִפְרִיס to divide [the hoof] (7·12·14) 828

פַּרְסָה hoof (9·21) 828

שָׁפָן 5 rock badger (1·4) 1050

גֵּרָה cud (7·11) 176

פַּרְסָה hoof (9·21) 828

הִפְרִיס to divide [the hoof] (7·12·14) 828

אַרְנֶבֶת 6 hare (1·2) 58

גֵּרָה cud (7·11) 176

פַּרְסָה hoof (9·21) 828

הִפְרִיס to divide [the hoof] (7·12·14) 828

חֲזִיר 7 swine (1·7) 306

הִפְרִיס to divide [the hoof] (7·12·14) 828

פַּרְסָה hoof (9·21) 828

שָׁסַע to divide, cleave (3·5·8) 1042

שֶׁסַע cleft (3·4) 1043

גֵּרָה cud (7·11) 176

נגרר to chew (1·3·4) 176

נְבֵלָה 8 carcass (19·48) 615

סְנַפִּיר 9 fin (3·5) 703

קַשְׂקֶשֶׂת scale [of fish] (3·8) 903

סְנַפִּיר 10 fin (3·5) 703

קַשְׂקֶשֶׂת scale [of fish] (3·8) 903

שֶׁרֶץ swarmers, swarming things (12·15) 1056

שֶׁקֶץ detestable thing (9·11) 1054

שֶׁקֶץ 11 detestable thing (9·11) 1054

נְבֵלָה carcass (19·48) 615

שִׁקֵּץ to detest (4·6·6) 1055

סְנַפִּיר 12 fin (3·5) 703

קַשְׂקֶשֶׂת scale [of fish] (3·8) 903

שֶׁקֶץ detestable thing (9·11) 1054

שִׁקֵּץ 13 to detest (4·6·6) 1055

שֶׁקֶץ detestable thing (9·11) 1054

נֶשֶׁר eagle (1·26) 676

פֶּרֶס bearded vulture (1·2) 828

עָזְנִיָּה unclean bird of prey, apparently akin to vulture (1·2) 740

דָּאָה 14 bird of prey, kite (1·1) 178

אַיָּה hawk, falcon (1·3) 17

מִין species (9·31) 568

עֹרֵב 15 raven (1·12) 788

מִין species (9·31) 568

יַעֲנָה 16 ostrich (1·8) 419

תַּחְמָס male ostrich (1·2) 329

שַׁחַף sea mew, gull (1·2) 1006

נֵץ bird of prey (1·3) 665

מִין species (9·31) 568

כּוֹס 17 a kind of owl (1·3) 468

שָׁלָךְ cormorant (1·2) 1021

יַנְשׁוּף a bird (1·3) 676

תִּנְשֶׁמֶת 18 unclean bird (1·2) 675

קָאָת bird, usually a pelican (1·5) 866

רָחָם carrion vulture (1·2) 934

חֲסִידָה 19 stork (1·6) 339

אֲנָפָה an unclean bird (1·2) 60

מִין species (9·31) 568

דּוּכִיפַת unclean bird, hoopoe[?] (1·2) 189

עֲטַלֵּף bat (1·3) 742

שֶׁרֶץ 20 swarmers, swarming things (12·15) 1056

שֶׁקֶץ detestable thing (9·11) 1054

שֶׁרֶץ 21 swarmers, swarming things (12·15) 1056

כְּרַע leg (6·9) 502

מִמַּעַל above, on the top of (7·29) 751

נתר to leap (1·1·5) 684

אַרְבֶּה 22 a locust (1·24) 916

מִין species (9·31) 568

סָלְעָם locust (1·1) 701

חַרְגֹּל a kind of locust (1·1) 353

חָגָב locust (1·5) 290

שֶׁרֶץ 23 swarmers, swarming things (12·15) 1056

שֶׁקֶץ detestable thing (9·11) 1054

נְבֵלָה 24 carcass (19·48) 615

נְבֵלָה 25 carcass (19·48) 615

הִפְרִיס 26 to divide [the hoof] (7·12·14) 828

פַּרְסָה the hoof (9·21) 828

שֶׁסַע cleft (3·4) 1043

שסע to divide, cleave (3·5·8) 1042

גֵּרָה cud (7·11) 176

נְבֵלָה 27 carcass (19·48) 615

נְבֵלָה 28 carcass (19·48) 615

שֶׁרֶץ 29 swarmers, swarming things (12·15) 1056

שָׁרַץ to swarm (5·14·14) 1056

חֹלֶד weasel (1·1) 317

עַכְבָּר mouse (1·6) 747

צָב lizard (1·1) 839

מִין species (9·31) 568

אֲנָקָה 30 ferret, shrew mouse (1·1) 60

כֹּחַ a kind of lizard (1·1) 470

לְטָאָה lizard (1·1) 538

חֹמֶט a kind of lizard (1·1) 328

תִּנְשֶׁמֶת lizard, chameleon (1·1) 675

שֶׁרֶץ 31 swarmers, swarming things

(12·15) 1056

שַׂק 32 sack (1·48) 974

חֶרֶשׂ 33 earthenware (5·16) 360

אֹכֶל 34 food (2·44) 38

מַשְׁקֶה drink (1·19) 1052

נְבֵלָה 35 carcass (19·48) 615

תַּנּוּר stove, firepot (4·15) 1072

כִּיר cooking furnace (1·1) 468

התץ to be broken down (1·1·42) 683

מַעְיָן 36 spring (1·23) 475

מִקְוֶה collection, collected mass (1·7) 876

נְבֵלָה carcass (19·48) 615

נְבֵלָה 37 carcass (19·48) 615

זֵרוּעַ thing sown (1·2) 283

נְבֵלָה 38 carcass (19·48) 615

אָכְלָה 39 food, eating (2·18) 38

נְבֵלָה carcass (19·48) 615

נְבֵלָה 40 carcass (19·48) 615

שֶׁרֶץ 41 swarmers, swarming things (12·15) 1056

שָׁרַץ to swarm, teem (5·14·14) 1056

שֶׁקֶץ detestable thing (9·11) 1054

גָּחוֹן 42 belly (1·2) 161

שֶׁרֶץ swarmers, swarming things (12·15) 1056

שָׁרַץ to swarm, teem (5·14·14) 1056

שֶׁקֶץ detestable thing (9·11) 1054

שִׁקֵּץ 43 to make detestable (4·6·6) 1055

שֶׁרֶץ swarmers, swarming things (12·15) 1056

שָׁרַץ to swarm, teem (5·14·14) 1056

שֶׁרֶץ 44 swarmers, swarming things (12·15) 1056

רמשׂ to creep, move about (3·16·16) 942

רמשׂ 46 to creep, move about (3·16·16) 942

שָׁרַץ to swarm, teem (5·14·14) 1056

הִבְדִּיל 47 to make a distinction (8·32·42) 95

Chapter 12

נִדָּה	2 impurity (13·30)	622
דּוֹת	to be ill (1·1·1)	188
נִמּוֹל	3 to be circumcised (1·12·29)	557
עָרְלָה	foreskin (2·16)	790
נְקֵבָה	5 female (12·22)	666
שָׁבוּעַ	week (1·20)	988
נִדָּה	impurity (13·30)	622
יוֹנָה	6 dove (10·35)	401
תּוֹר	turtle dove (9·14)	1076
מָקוֹר	7 flow (3·18)	881
נְקֵבָה	female (12·22)	666
דֵּי	8 sufficiency, enough (3·12)	191
שֶׂה	sheep, goat (5·44)	961
תּוֹר	turtle dove (9·14)	1076
יוֹנָה	dove (10·35)	401

Chapter 13

שְׂאֵת	2 swelling (7·7)	673
סַפַּחַת	eruption (2·2)	705
בַּהֶרֶת	bright spot (12·12)	97
צָרַעַת	leprosy (29·35)	863
שֵׂעָר	3 hair (15·28)	972
לָבָן	white (20·28)	526
עָמֹק	deep (7·17)	771
צָרַעַת	leprosy (29·35)	863
בַּהֶרֶת	4 bright spot (12·12)	97
לָבָן	white (20·28)	526
עָמֹק	deep (7·17)	771
שֵׂעָר	hair (15·28)	972
פָּשָׂה	5 to spread (18·18·18)	832
כֵּהָה	6 to grow faint (2·3·9[?])	462
פָּשָׂה	to spread (18·18·18)	832
מִסְפַּחַת	eruption (3·3)	705
פָּשָׂה	7 to spread (18·18·18)	832
מִסְפַּחַת	eruption (3·3)	705
פָּשָׂה	8 to spread (18·18·18)	832

מִסְפַּחַת	eruption (3·3)	705
צָרַעַת	leprosy (29·35)	863
צָרַעַת	9 leprosy (29·35)	863
שְׂאֵת	10 swelling (7·7)	673
לָבָן	white (20·28)	526
שֵׂעָר	hair (15·28)	972
מִחְיָה	10 the quick (2·8)	313
צָרַעַת	11 leprosy (29·35)	863
נושן	to be old (2·3·3[?])	445
פָּרַח	12 to break out (8·29·34)	827
צָרַעַת	leprosy (29·35)	863
צָרַעַת	13 leprosy (29·35)	863
לָבָן	white (20·28)	526
צָרַעַת	15 leprosy (29·35)	863
לָבָן	16 white (20·28)	526
לָבָן	17 white (20·28)	526
שְׁחִין	18 a boil (4·13)	1006
שְׁחִין	19 a boil (4·13)	1006
שְׂאֵת	swelling (7·7)	673
לָבָן	white (20·28)	526
בַּהֶרֶת	bright spot (12·12)	97
אֲדַמְדָּם	reddish (6·6)	10
שָׁפָל	20 low (4·18)	1050
שֵׂעָר	hair (15·28)	972
לָבָן	white (20·28)	526
צָרַעַת	leprosy (29·35)	863
שְׁחִין	a boil (4·13)	1006
פָּרַח	to break out (8·29·34)	827
שֵׂעָר	21 hair (15·28)	972
לָבָן	white (20·28)	526
שָׁפָל	low (9·18)	1050
כֵּהָה	faint (4·7)	462
פָּשָׂה	22 to spread (18·18·18)	832
בַּהֶרֶת	23 bright spot (12·12)	97
פָּשָׂה	to spread (18·18·18)	832
צָרֶבֶת	scab/scar of a sore (2·2)	863
שְׁחִין	a boil (4·13)	1006
מִכְוָה	24 burn spot (5·5)	465

מְחִיָה	the quick (2·8) 313
בַּהֶרֶת	bright spot (12·12) 97
לָבָן	white (20·28) 526
אֲדַמְדַּם	reddish (6·6) 10
שֵׂעָר	25 hair (15·28) 972
לָבָן	white (20·28) 526
בַּהֶרֶת	bright spot (12·12) 97
עָמֹק	deep (7·17) 771
צָרַעַת	leprosy (29·35) 863
מִכְוָה	burn spot (5·5) 465
פָּרַח	to break out (8·29·34) 827
בַּהֶרֶת	26 bright spot (12·12) 97
שֵׂעָר	hair (15·28) 972
לָבָן	white (20·28) 526
שָׁפָל	low (4·18) 1050
כֵּהֶה	faint (4·7) 462
פָּשָׂה	27 to spread (18·18·18) 832
צָרַעַת	leprosy (29·35) 863
בַּהֶרֶת	28 bright spot (12·12) 97
פָּשָׂה	to spread (18·18·18) 832
כֵּהֶה	faint (4·7) 462
שְׂאֵת	swelling (7·7) 673
מִכְוָה	burn spot (5·5) 465
צָרֶבֶת	scab/scar of a sore (2·2) 863
זָקָן	29 chin, beard (5·18) 278
עָמֹק	30 deep (7·17) 771
שֵׂעָר	hair (15·28) 972
צָהֹב	gleeming, yellow (3·3) 843
דַּק	thin, small, fine (3·14) 201
נֶתֶק	scab (14·14) 683
צָרַעַת	leprosy (29·35) 863
זָקָן	chin, beard (5·18) 278
נֶתֶק	31 scab (14·14) 683
עָמֹק	deep (7·17) 771
שֵׂעָר	hair (15·28) 972
שָׁחֹר	black (2·6) 1007
פָּשָׂה	32 to spread (18·18·18) 832
נֶתֶק	scab (14·14) 683

שֵׂעָר	hair (15·28) 972
צָהֹב	gleaming, yellow (3·3) 843
עָמֹק	deep (7·17) 771
הִתְגַּלָּח	33 to shave oneself (1·2·23) 164
נֶתֶק	scab (14·14) 683
גִּלַּח	to shave off (5·18·23) 164
נֶתֶק	34 scab (14·14) 683
פָּשָׂה	to spread (18·18·18) 832
עָמֹק	deep (7·17) 771
פָּשָׂה	35 to spread (18·18·18) 832
נֶתֶק	scab (14·14) 683
פָּשָׂה	36 to spread (18·18·18) 832
נֶתֶק	scab (14·14) 683
בִּקֵּר	to seek, look for (2·7·7) 133
שֵׂעָר	hair (15·28) 972
צָהֹב	gleaming, yellow (3·3) 843
נֶתֶק	37 scab (14·14) 683
שֵׂעָר	hair (15·28) 972
שָׁחֹר	black (2·6) 1007
צָמַח	to sprout, spring up (1·15·33) 855
בַּהֶרֶת	38 bright spot (12·12) 97
לָבָן	white (20·28) 526
בַּהֶרֶת	39 bright spot (12·12) 97
כֵּהֶה	faint (4·7) 462
לָבָן	white (20·28) 526
בֹּהַק	harmless eruption on the skin (1·1) 97
פָּרַח	to break out (8·29·34) 827
נמרט	40 to be made bald (2·2·14) 598
קֵרֵחַ	bald (1·3) 901
נמרט	41 to be made bald (2·2·14) 598
גִּבֵּחַ	having a bald forehead (1·1) 147
קָרַחַת	42 baldness of head (4·4) 901
גַּבַּחַת	bald forehead (4·4) 147
לָבָן	white (20·28) 526
אֲדַמְדָּם	reddish (6·6) 10
צָרַעַת	leprosy (29·35) 863
פָּרַח	to break out (8·29·34) 827

קָרַחַת	baldness of head (4·4) 901	
שְׂאֵת	43 swelling (7·7) 673	
לָבָן	white (20·28) 526	
אֲדַמְדָּם	reddish (6·6) 10	
קָרַחַת	baldness of head (4·4) 901	
גַּבַּחַת	bald forehead (4·4) 147	
צָרַעַת	leprosy (29·35) 863	
צָרוּעַ	44 leper (4·5) 863	
צָרוּעַ	45 leper (4·5) 863	
פָּרַם	to tear/rend garment (3·3·3) 827	
פָּרַע	to let loose, to remove restraint (3·13·16) 828	
שָׂפָם	moustache (1·5) 974	
עָטָה	to wrap, envelop [oneself] (1·11·14) 741	
בָּדָד	46 isolation, separation (1·11) 94	
מוֹשָׁב	dwelling place (8·43) 444	
צָרַעַת	47 leprosy (29·35) 863	
צֶמֶר	wool (4·16) 856	
פֵּשֶׁת	flax, linen (4·16) 833	
שְׁתִי	48 warp (9·9) 1059	
עֵרֶב	woof (9·9) 786	
פֵּשֶׁת	flax, linen (4·16) 833	
צֶמֶר	wool (4·16) 856	
יְרַקְרַק	49 greenish (2·3) 439	
אֲדַמְדָּם	reddish (6·6) 10	
שְׁתִי	warp (9·9) 1059	
עֵרֶב	woof (9·9) 786	
צָרַעַת	leprosy (29·35) 863	
פָּשָׂה	51 to spread (18·18·18) 832	
שְׁתִי	warp (9·9) 1059	
עֵרֶב	woof (9·9) 786	
צָרַעַת	leprosy (29·35) 863	
הַמְאִיר	to pain (3·4·4) 549	
שְׁתִי	52 warp (9·9) 1059	
עֵרֶב	woof (9·9) 786	
צֶמֶר	wool (4·16) 856	
פֵּשֶׁת	flax, linen (4·16) 833	
צָרַעַת	leprosy (29·35) 863	
הַמְאִיר	to pain (3·4·4) 549	
פָּשָׂה	53 to spread (18·18·18) 832	
שְׁתִי	warp (9·9) 1059	
עֵרֶב	woof (9·9) 786	
פָּשָׂה	55 to spread (18·18·18) 832	
פְּחֶתֶת	a boring, eating out (1·1) 809	
קָרַחַת	baldness of head (4·4) 901	
גַּבַּחַת	bald forehead (4·4) 147	
כֵּהָה	56 to grow faint (2·3·9[?]) 462	
שְׁתִי	warp (9·9) 1059	
עֵרֶב	woof (9·9) 786	
שְׁתִי	57 warp (9·9) 1059	
עֵרֶב	woof (9·9) 786	
פָּרַח	to break out (8·29·34) 827	
שְׁתִי	58 warp (9·9) 1059	
עֵרֶב	woof (9·9) 786	
צָרַעַת	59 leprosy (29·35) 863	
צֶמֶר	wool (4·16) 856	
פֵּשֶׁת	flax, linen (4·16) 833	
שְׁתִי	warp (9·9) 1059	
עֵרֶב	woof (9·9) 786	

Chapter 14

מְצֹרָע	2 leprous (1·15) 863
צָרַעַת	3 leprosy (29·35) 863
צָרוּעַ	leper (4·5) 863
צִפּוֹר	4 bird|s| (13·40) 861
שָׁנִי	scarlet (5·42) 1040
תּוֹלַעָה	coccus ilicis |yielding scarlet color| (5·41) 1069
אֵזוֹב	hyssop (5·10) 23
צִפּוֹר	5 bird|s| (13·40) 861
חֶרֶשׂ	earthenware (5·16) 360
צִפּוֹר	6 bird|s| (13·40) 861
שָׁנִי	scarlet (5·42) 1040
תּוֹלַעָה	coccus ilicis |yielding scarlet color| (5·41) 1069

אֵזוֹב	hyssop (5·10) 23		תְּנוּפָה	waving, wave offering (14·30) 632
טָבַל	to dip (6·15·16) 371		עִשָּׂרוֹן	tenth part (5·28) 798
הִזָּה	7 to sprinkle (13·20·24) 633		בָּלַל	to mix (9·42·42[?]) 117
צָרַעַת	leprosy (29·35) 863		לֹג	a liquid measure (5·5) 528
צִפּוֹר	bird[s] (3·40) 861		תּוֹר	22 turtle dove (9·14) 1076
גִּלַּח	8 to shave off (5·18·23) 164		יוֹנָה	dove (10·35) 401
שֵׂעָר	hair (15·28) 972		הִשִּׂיג	to reach (12·48·48) 673
גִּלַּח	9 to shave off (5·18·23) 164		אָשָׁם	24 trespass offering (27·46) 79
שֵׂעָר	hair (15·28) 972		לֹג	a liquid measure (5·5) 528
זָקָן	chin, beard (5·18) 278		הֵנִיף	to wave (11·32·34[?]) 631
גַּב	brow, anything curved (1·13) 146		תְּנוּפָה	waving, wave offering (14·30) 632
כִּבְשָׂה	10 ewe lamb (1·7) 461		אָשָׁם	25 trespass offering (27·46) 79
בָּלַל	to mix (9·42·42[?]) 117		תְּנוּךְ	tip, lobe of ear (6·8) 1072
לֹג	a liquid measure (5·5) 528		יְמָנִי	right (20·33) 412
אָשָׁם	12 trespass offering (27·46) 79		בֹּהֶן	thumb, great toe (12·14[?]) 97
לֹג	a liquid measure (5·5) 528		שְׂמָאלִי	26 left, on the left (4·9) 970
הֵנִיף	to wave (11·32·34[?]) 631		הִזָּה	27 to sprinkle (13·20·24) 633
תְּנוּפָה	waving, wave offering (14·30) 632		אֶצְבַּע	finger (13·31) 840
אָשָׁם	13 trespass offering (27·46) 79		יְמָנִי	right (20·33) 412
אָשָׁם	14 trespass offering (27·46) 79		שְׂמָאלִי	left, on the left (4·9) 970
תְּנוּךְ	tip, lobe of ear (6·8) 1072		תְּנוּךְ	28 tip, lobe of ear (6·8) 1072
יְמָנִי	right (20·33) 412		יְמָנִי	right (20·33) 412
בֹּהֶן	thumb, great toe (12·14[?]) 97		בֹּהֶן	thumb, great toe (12·14[?]) 97
לֹג	15 a liquid measure (5·5) 528		אָשָׁם	trespass offering (27·46) 79
שְׂמָאלִי	left, on the left (4·9) 970		תּוֹר	30 turtle dove (9·14) 1076
טָבַל	16 to dip (6·15·16) 371		יוֹנָה	dove (10·35) 401
אֶצְבַּע	finger (13·31) 840		הִשִּׂיג	to reach (12·48·48) 673
יְמָנִי	right (20·33) 412		הִשִּׂיג	31 to reach (12·48·48) 673
שְׂמָאלִי	left, on the left (4·9) 970		צָרַעַת	32 leprosy (29·35) 863
הִזָּה	to sprinkle (13·20·24) 633		צָרַעַת	34 leprosy (29·35) 863
תְּנוּךְ	17 tip, lobe of ear (6·8) 1072		בְּטֶרֶם	36 before (1·39) 382
יְמָנִי	right (20·33) 412		שְׁקַעֲרוּרֹת	37 depression, hollow (1·1) 891
בֹּהֶן	thumb, great toe (12·14[?]) 97		יְרַקְרַק	greenish (2·3) 439
אָשָׁם	trespass offering (27·46) 79		אֲדַמְדָּם	reddish (6·6) 10
טֻמְאָה	19 uncleanness (18·37) 380		שָׁפָל	low (4·18) 1050
דַּל	21 poor (2·48) 195		פָּשָׂה	39 to spread (18·18·18) 832
הִשִּׂיג	to reach (12·48·48) 673		חָלַץ	to pull out, tear out (2·14·27) 322
אָשָׁם	trespass offering (27·46) 79		הִקְצִיעַ	41 to scrape, scrape off (1·1·1) 892

הִקְצָה	to scrape, scrape off (2·2·5) 891
טוּחַ	42 to coat (1·9·11) 376
פָּרַח	43 to break out (8·29·34) 827
חִלֵּץ	to pull out, tear out (2·14·27) 322
הִקְצָה	to scrape, scrape off (2·2·5) 891
נָטוֹחַ	to be coated (2·2·11) 376
פָּשָׂה	44 to spread (18·18·18) 832
צָרַעַת	leprosy (29·35) 863
הַמְאִיר	to pain, prick (3·4·4) 549
נָתַץ	45 to pull down (1·31·42) 683
פָּשָׂה	48 to spread (18·18·18) 832
נָטוֹחַ	to be coated (2·2·11) 376
צִפּוֹר	49 bird[s] (13·40) 861
שָׁנִי	scarlet (5·42) 1040
תּוֹלֵעָה	coccus ilicis [yielding scarlet color] (5·41) 1069
אֵזוֹב	hyssop (5·10) 23
צִפּוֹר	50 bird[s] (13·40) 861
חֶרֶשׂ	earthenware (5·16) 360
אֵזוֹב	51 hyssop (5·10) 23
שָׁנִי	scarlet (5·42) 1040
תּוֹלֵעָה	coccus ilicis [yielding scarlet color] (5·41) 1069
צִפּוֹר	bird[s] (13·40) 861
טָבַל	to dip (6·15·16) 371
הִזָּה	to sprinkle (13·20·24) 633
צִפּוֹר	52 bird[s] (13·40) 861
אֵזוֹב	hyssop (5·10) 23
שָׁנִי	scarlet (5·42) 1040
תּוֹלֵעָה	coccus ilicis [yielding scarlet color] (5·41) 1069
צִפּוֹר	53 bird[s] (13·40) 861
צָרַעַת	54 leprosy (29·35) 863
נֶתֶק	scab (14·14) 683
צָרַעַת	55 leprosy (29·35) 863
שְׂאֵת	56 swelling (7·7) 673
סַפַּחַת	eruption (2·2) 705
בַּהֶרֶת	bright spot (12·12) 97
הוֹרָה	57 to teach (2·45[?]·45[?]) 434

צָרַעַת	leprosy (29·35) 863

Chapter 15

זָב	2 to flow (5·29·29) 264
זוֹב	issue, flux (13·13) 264
טֻמְאָה	3 uncleanness (18·37) 380
זוֹב	issue, flux (13·13) 264
רָר	to flow [like slime] (1·1·1) 938
הֶחְתִּים	to show stoppage (1·1·27) 367
מִשְׁכָּב	4 bed (9·46) 1012
זָב	to flow (5·29·29[?]) 264
מִשְׁכָּב	5 bed (9·46) 1012
זָב	6 one who has an issue (11·13[?]) 264
זָב	7 one who has an issue (11·13[?]) 264
רקק	8 to spit (1·1·1) 956
זָב	one who has an issue (11·13[?]) 264
מֶרְכָּב	9 saddle (1·3) 939
זָב	one who has an issue (11·13[?]) 264
זָב	11 one who has an issue (11·13[?]) 264
שָׁטַף	to rinse off (1·28·31) 1009
חֶרֶשׂ	12 earthenware (5·16) 360
זָב	one who has an issue (11·13[?]) 264
נשטף	to be rinsed out, off (1·21·31) 1009
זָב	13 one who has an issue (11·13[?]) 264
זוֹב	issue, flux (13·13) 264
תּוֹר	14 turtle dove (9·14) 1076
יוֹנָה	dove (10·35) 401
זוֹב	15 issue, flux (13·13) 264
שִׁכְבָה	16 act of lying, sexual intercourse (6·9) 1012
שִׁכְבָה	17 act of lying, secual intercourse (6·9) 1012
שִׁכְבָה	18 act of lying, sexual intercourse (6·9) 1012
זָב	19 one who has an issue (11·13[?]) 264
זוֹב	issue, flux (13·13) 264
נִדָּה	impurity (13·30) 622
נִדָּה	20 impurity (13·30) 622
מִשְׁכָּב	21 bed (9·46) 1012

74

מִשְׁכָּב 23 bed (9·46) 1012
נִדָּה 24 impurity (13·30) 622
מִשְׁכָּב bed (9·46) 1012
זָב 25 to flow (5·29·29[?]) 264
זוֹב issue, flux (13·13) 264
בְּלֹא outside of (1·29) 520
נִדָּה impurity (13·30) 622
טֻמְאָה uncleanness (18·37) 380
מִשְׁכָּב 26 bed (9·46) 1012
זוֹב issue, flux (13·13) 264
נִדָּה impurity (13·30) 622
טֻמְאָה uncleanness (18·37) 380
זוֹב 28 issue, flux (13·13) 264
תּוֹר 29 turtle dove (9·14) 1076
יוֹנָה dove (10·35) 401
זוֹב 30 issue, flux (13·13) 264
טֻמְאָה uncleanness (18·37) 380
הִזִּיר 31 to sacredly separate (1·6·10) 634
טֻמְאָה uncleanness (18·37) 380
זָב 32 one who has an issue (11·13[?]) 264
שְׁכָבָה act of lying, sexual intercourse (6·9) 1012
דָּוֶה 33 menstruous faint, unwell (2·5) 188
נִדָּה impurity (13·30) 622
זָב to flow (5·29·29[?]) 264
זוֹב issue, flux (13·13) 264
נְקֵבָה female (12·22) 666

Chapter 16

פָּרֹכֶת 2 curtain (7·25) 827
כַּפֹּרֶת propitiatory (7·27) 498
כֻּתֹּנֶת 4 tunic (4·30) 509
בַּד white linen (8·23) 94
מִכְנָס drawers (2·5) 488
אַבְנֵט girdle (3·9) 126
חגר to gird on (4·4·44) 291
מִצְנֶפֶת turban of high priest (3·12) 857
צנף to wrap, windup together (1·2·2) 857

מַחְתָּה 12 censer (2·21) 367
גַּחֶלֶת coal (1·18) 160
חֹפֶן hollow of hand (1·6) 342
סַם 12 spice (2·15) 702
דַּק small, fine (3·14) 201
פָּרֹכֶת curtain (7·25) 827
כַּפֹּרֶת 13 propitiatory (7·27) 498
הִזָּה 14 to sprinkle (13·20·24) 633
אֶצְבַּע finger (13·31) 840
כַּפֹּרֶת propitiatory (7·27) 498
קֶדֶם eastward (2·26) 870
פָּרֹכֶת 15 curtain (7·25) 827
הִזָּה to sprinkle (13·20·24) 633
כַּפֹּרֶת propitiatory (7·27) 498
טֻמְאָה 16 uncleanness (18·37) 380
הִזָּה 19 to sprinkle (13·20·24) 633
אֶצְבַּע finger (13·31) 840
טֻמְאָה uncleanness (18·37) 380
סָמַךְ 21 to lay (14·41·48) 701
עִתִּי timely, ready (1·1) 774
גְּזֵרָה 22 separation (1·1) 160
פָּשַׁט 23 to strip off, put off (2·24·43) 833
בַּד white linen (8·23) 94
פֶּרֶשׁ 27 offal [as ripped out in preparing victim] (3·7) 831
אֶזְרָח 29 native (7·17) 280
שַׁבָּתוֹן 31 sabbath observance (8·11) 992
כֹּהֵן 32 to minister as priests (2·23·23) 464
בַּד white linen (8·23) 94

Chapter 17

כֶּשֶׂב 3 lamb (7·13) 461
זָרַק 6 to throw, scatter abundantly (12·32·34[?]) 284
נִיחוֹחַ soothing (17·43) 629
צוּד 13 to hunt (1·12·16) 844
צַיִד game (1·14) 844
נְבֵלָה 15 carcass (19·48) 615

טְרֵפָה   animal torn (3·9) 383

אֶזְרָח   native (7·17) 280

Chapter 18

שְׁאֵר 6 flesh relation, kinsman (7·17) 984

מוֹלֶדֶת 9 offspring (3·22) 409

מוֹלֶדֶת 11 begotten, offspring (3·22) 409

שְׁאֵר 12 flesh relation, kinsman (7·17) 984

שְׁאֵר 13 flesh relation, kinsman (7·17) 984

דּוֹדָה 14 aunt (2·3) 187

כַּלָּה 15 daughter-in-law (2·34) 483

שְׁאֵר 17 flesh relation, kinsman (7·17) 984

זִמָּה wickedness, device (5·28[?]) 273

צרר 18 to show hostility toward (1·10·10) 865

נִדָּה 19 impurity (13·30) 622

טֻמְאָה uncleanness (18·37) 380

עָמִית 20 associate, fellow (11·12) 765

שְׁכֹבֶת copulation (3·4) 1012

מִשְׁכָּב 22 bed (9·46) 1012

שְׁכֹבֶת 23 copulation (3·4) 1012

רבע to lie down (2·3·4) 918

תֶּבֶל confusion (2·2) 117

הֵקִיא 25 to vomit up, spue out, disgorge (3·7·8) 883

אֶזְרָח 26 native (7·17) 280

אֵל 27 these (1·10) 41

הֵקִיא 28 to vomit up, spue out, disgorge (3·7·8) 883

קִיא to vomit up, spue out, disgorge (1·1·8) 883

Chapter 19

אֱלִיל 4 worthless idols (2·20) 47

מַסֵּכָה molten metal (1·25) 651

מָחֳרָת 6 on the morrow, after (5·32) 564

פִּגּוּל 7 foul thing, refuse (2·4) 803

עָם 8 kinsman (12·34) 769

קצר 9 to reap, harvest (7·24·24) 894

קָצִיר harvest (7·49) 894

לֶקֶט gleaning (2·2) 545

לקט to gather (3·21·36) 544

עוֹלֵל 10 to glean (1·8·17) 760

פֶּרֶט broken off [ones], fallen grapes (1·1) 827

לקט to gather (3·21·36) 544

גנב 11 to steal (1·30·39) 170

כָּחַשׁ to deceive (3·19·22) 471

שׁקר to deal falsely (1·5·6) 1055

עָמִית associate, fellow relation (11·12) 765

עָשַׁק 13 to oppress, wrong (3·36·37) 798

גָּזַל to tear away, rob (2·29·30) 159

פְּעֻלָּה wages (1·14) 821

שָׂכִיר hired laborer (6·18) 969

חֵרֵשׁ 14 deaf (1·9) 361

עִוֵּר blind (2·25) 734

מִכְשׁוֹל stumbling block (1·14) 506

עָוֶל 15 injustice, unrighteousness (2·21) 732

דַּל low, poor (2·48) 195

הדר to honor (2·4·6) 213

עָמִית associate, fellow, relation (11·12) 765

רָכִיל 16 slanderer (1·6) 940

עַם kinsman (12·34) 769

עָמִית 17 associate, fellow, relation (11·12) 765

חֵטְא punishment for sin (4·33) 307

נקם 18 to take vengeance (2·13·34) 667

נטר to maintain (1·5·5[?]) 643

הרביע 19 to cause to lie down (1·1·4) 918

כִּלְאַיִם two kinds (3·4) 476

שַׁעַטְנֵז mixed stuff (1·2) 1043

שְׁכָבָה 20 act of lying, sexual intercourse (6·9) 1012

נחרף to remain in harvest time (1·1·2[?]) 358

חֻפְשָׁה freedom (1·1) 344

בְּקֹרֶת punishment [after examination] (1·1) 134

אָשָׁם 21 trespass offering (27·46) 79

אָשָׁם 22 trespass offering (27·46) 79

נִסְלַח to be forgiven (10·13·46) 699

מַאֲכָל 23 food (1·30) 38

ערל to regard as uncircumcised (1·1·2) 790

עָרְלָה foreskin (2·16) 790

עָרֵל uncircumcised (2·35) 790

הִלּוּלִים 24 rejoicing praise (1·2) 239

תְּבוּאָה 25 product yield (11·43) 100

נִחֵשׁ 26 to practice divination (1·9·9) 638

עוֹנֵן to practice sooth-saying, divine (1·10·11) 778

הִקִּיף 27 to round off (1·16·17) 668

זָקָן beard (5·18) 278

שֶׂרֶט 28 incision (2·2) 976

קַעֲקַע incision, imprintment, tatoo (1·1) 891

זִמָּה 29 wickedness (5·28[?]) 273

אוֹב 31 necromancer (3·16) 15

יִדְּעֹנִי familiar spirit (3·11) 396

שֵׂיבָה 32 gray hair (1·20) 966

הדר to honor (2·4·6) 213

הוֹנָה 33 to oppress (3·14·18) 413

אֶזְרָח 34 native (7·17) 280

עָוֶל 35 injustice, unrighteousness (2·21) 732

מִשְׁקָל weight (2·48) 1054

מְשׂוּרָה measure (1·4) 601

מאזן 36 scales (1·15) 24

אֵיפָה ephah, quantity of wheat or barley (3·38) 35

הִין hin, a liquid measure (2·22) 228

Chapter 20

רגם 2 to kill by stoning, to stone (5·15·15) 920

הֶעְלִים 4 to conceal, hide (1·11·29) 761

אוֹב 6 necromancer (3·16) 15

יִדְּעֹנִי familiar spirit (3·11) 396

נאף 10 to commit adultery (3·16·30) 610

כַּלָּה 12 daughter-in-law (2·34) 483

תֶּבֶל confusion (2·2) 117

מִשְׁכָּב 13 bed (9·46) 1012

זִמָּה 14 wickedness (5·28[?]) 273

שִׁכְבַת 15 copulation (3·4) 1012

רבע 16 to lie down [for copulation] (2·3·4) 918

חֶסֶד 17 shame, reproach (1·2) 340

דָּוֶה 18 menstruous, unwell (2·5) 188

מָקוֹר source (3·18) 881

הֶעֱרָה to make naked (2·3·14) 788

שְׁאֵר 19 flesh relation, kinsman (7·17) 984

הֶעֱרָה to make naked (2·3·14) 788

דּוֹדָה 20 aunt (2·3) 187

עֲרִירִי stripped, i.e., childless (2·4) 792

נִדָּה 21 impurity (13·30) 622

עֲרִירִי stripped, i.e., childless (2·4) 792

הֵקִיא 22 to vomit up, spue out, disgorge (3·7·8) 883

קוּץ 23 to abhor (1·8·8) 880

זָב 24 to flow, issue (5·29·29[?]) 264

חָלָב milk (1·44) 316

הִבְדִּיל to make a distinction (between) (8·32·42) 95

הִבְדִּיל 25 to make a distinction (between) (8·32·42) 95

שִׁקֵּץ to make detestable (4·6·6) 1055

רמש to creep, move about (3·16·16) 942

הִבְדִּיל 26 to make a distinction (between) (8·32·42) 95

אוֹב 27 necromancer (3·16) 15

יִדְּעֹנִי familiar spirit (3·11) 396

רגם to kill by stoning, to stone (5·15· 920

Chapter 21

שְׁאָר	2 flesh relation, kinsman (7·17) 984
בְּתוּלָה	3 virgin (2·50) 143
עַם	4 kinsman (12·34) 769
קרח	5 to make bald (1·2·5) 901
קָרְחָה	baldness, bald spot |made in mourning| (1·11) 901
זָקָן	beard (5·18) 278
גָּלַח	to shave off (5·18·23) 164
שׂרט	to make incision (1·2·3) 976
שֶׂרֶט	incision (2·2) 976
זוֹנָה	7 harlot (2·33|?|) 275
גרש	to drive out, cast out (3·8·47) 176
מִשְׁחָה	10 ointment (13·21) 603
פָּרַע	to let loose, remove restraint (3·13·16) 828
פרם	to tear/rend garment (3·3·3) 827
נֵזֶר	12 consecration (2·24) 634
מִשְׁחָה	ointment (13·21) 603
בְּתוּלִים	13 virginity, tokens of virginity (1·10) 144
גרש	14 to drive out, cast out (3·8·47) 176
זוֹנָה	harlot (2·33|?|) 275
בְּתוּלָה	virgin (2·50) 143
עַם	kinsman (12·34) 769
עַם	15 kinsman (12·34) 769
מוּם	17 blemish (10·21) 548
מוּם	18 blemish (10·21) 548
עִוֵּר	blind (2·25) 734
פִּסֵּחַ	lame (1·14) 820
חָרֻם	mutilated (1·1) 356
שׂרע	to extend (2·2·3) 976
שֶׁבֶר	19 breaking, shattering (4·45) 991
גִּבֵּן	20 crook-backed (1·1) 148
דַּק	withered, thin (3·14) 201
תְּבַלֻּל	confusion, obscurity (1·1) 117
גָּרָב	itch, scab (2·3) 173

יַלֶּפֶת	an eruptive disease (2·2) 410
מָרוֹחַ	dubious (1·1) 598
אֶשֶׁךְ	testicle (1·1) 79
מוּם	21 blemish (10·21) 548
פָּרֹכֶת	23 curtain (7·25) 827
מוּם	blemish (10·21) 548

Chapter 22

נזר	2 to hold sacredly aloof (1·4·10) 634
טֻמְאָה	3 uncleanness (18·37) 380
צָרוּעַ	4 leper (4·5) 863
זָב	one that has as issue, flow (11·13|?|) 264
שְׁכָבָה	act of lying, sexual intercourse (6·9) 1072
שֶׁרֶץ	5 swarmers, swarming things (12·15) 1056
טֻמְאָה	uncleanness (18·37) 380
נְבֵלָה	8 carcass (19·48) 615
טְרֵפָה	animal torn (3·9) 383
חֵטְא	9 punishment for sin (4·33) 307
תּוֹשָׁב	10 sojourner (8·14) 444
שָׂכִיר	hired laborer (6·18) 969
קִנְיָן	11 acquisition (1·9) 889
יָלִיד	born (1·12) 409
גרש	13 to drive out, cast out (3·8·47) 176
נְעוּרִים	youth (1·46) 655
שְׁגָגָה	14 sin of error, inadvertence (6·19) 993
אַשְׁמָה	16 trespass offering (4·19) 80
נֵזֶר	18 crown (2·24) 634
נְדָבָה	freewill offering (5·27) 621
כֶּשֶׂב	19 lamb (7·13) 461
מוּם	20 blemish (10·21) 548
פלא	21 to make a special votive offering (1·3·5) 810
נְדָבָה	freewill offering (5·27) 621
מוּם	blemish (10·21) 548
עַוֶּרֶת	22 blindness (1·1) 734

שָׁבוּר	broken (1·1) 991		נִיחוֹחַ	soothing (17·43) 629	
חָרוּץ	cut, mutilated (1·4[?]) 358		הִין	hin, a liquid measure (2·22) 228	
יַבָּל	running (1·1) 385		קָלִי	14 parched grain (1·6) 885	
גָּרָב	itch, scab (2·3) 173		כַּרְמֶל	fruit, garden growth (2·3[?]) 502	
יַלֶּפֶת	an eruptive disease (2·2) 410		מוֹשָׁב	dwelling place (8·43) 444	
שֶׂה	23 sheep, goat (5·44) 961		מָחֳרָת	15 on the morrow, after (5·32) 564	
שׂרע	to extend (2·2·3) 976		עֹמֶר	sheaf (4·8) 771	
קלט	to be stunted (1·1·1) 886		תְּנוּפָה	waving, wave offering (14·30) 632	
נְדָבָה	freewill offering (5·27) 621		מָחֳרָת	16 on the morrow, after (5·32) 564	
מעך	24 to press (1·2·3) 590		מוֹשָׁב	17 dwelling place (8·43) 444	
כתת	to crush (1·15·17) 510		תְּנוּפָה	waving, wave offering (14·30) 632	
נתק	to pull away (1·3·27) 683		חָמֵץ	that which is leavened (4·11) 329	
נֵכָר	25 foreignness (1·36) 648		נאפה	17 to be baked (3·3·12) 66	
מָשְׁחָת	corruption (1·1) 1008		בִּכּוּרִים	firstfruits (4·17) 114	
מוּם	blemish (10·21) 548		נִיחוֹחַ	18 soothing (17·43) 629	
כֶּשֶׂב	lamb (7·13) 461		הֵנִיף	20 to wave (11·32·34[?]) 631	
הָלְאָה	27 onwards (1·13) 229		בִּכּוּרִים	firstfruits (4·17) 114	
שֶׂה	28 sheep, goat (5·44) 961		תְּנוּפָה	waving, wave offering (14·30) 632	
תּוֹדָה	29 thank offering (5·32) 392		בְּעֶצֶם	21 selfsame (4·17) 782	
			מִקְרָא	convocation (11·22) 896	
Chapter 23			מוֹשָׁב	dwelling place (8·43) 444	
מִקְרָא	2 convocation (11·23) 896		קצר	22 to reap, harvest (7·24·24) 894	
שַׁבָּתוֹן	3 sabbath observance (8·11) 992		קָצִיר	harvest (7·49) 894	
מִקְרָא	convocation (11·23) 896		לֶקֶט	gleaning (2·2) 545	
מוֹשָׁב	dwelling place (8·43) 444		לקט	to gather (3·21·36) 544	
מִקְרָא	4 convocation (11·23) 896		שַׁבָּתוֹן	24 sabbath observance (8·11) 992	
פֶּסַח	5 passover [festival of] (1·49) 820		זִכָּרוֹן	memorial, reminder (1·24) 272	
מִקְרָא	7 convocation (11·23) 896		תְּרוּעָה	blast [for march] (2·36) 929	
מִקְרָא	8 convocation (11·23) 896		מִקְרָא	convocation (11·22) 896	
קצר	10 to reap, harvest (7·24·24) 894		מִקְרָא	27 convocation (11·22) 896	
קָצִיר	harvest (7·49) 894		עָשׂוֹר	tenth day [of month] (3·15) 797	
עֹמֶר	sheaf (4·8) 771		כִּפֻּרִים	atonement (3·8) 498	
הֵנִיף	11 to wave (11·32·34[?]) 631		בְּעֶצֶם	28 selfsame (4·17) 782	
עֹמֶר	sheaf (4·8) 771		כִּפֻּרִים	atonement (3·8) 498	
מָחֳרָת	on the morrow, after (5·32) 564		בְּעֶצֶם	29 selfsame (4·17) 782	
עֹמֶר	12 sheaf (4·8) 771		עַם	kinsman (12·34) 769	
עִשָּׂרוֹן	13 tenth part (5·28) 798		בְּעֶצֶם	30 selfsame (4·17) 782	
בָּלַל	to mix (9·42·42[?]) 117		מוֹשָׁב	31 dwelling place (8·43) 444	

שַׁבָּתוֹן	32 sabbath observance (8·11) 992	
סֻכָּה	34 booth (4·31) 697	
מִקְרָא	35 convocation (11·23) 896	
מִקְרָא	36 convocation (11·23) 896	
עֲצָרָה	assembly (1·11) 783	
מִקְרָא	37 convocation (11·23) 896	
מִלְּבַד	38 besides (5·33) 94	
נְדָבָה	freewill offering (5·27) 621	
תְּבוּאָה	39 product, yield (11·43) 100	
חגג	to keep a pilgrim feast (3·16·16) 290	
שַׁבָּתוֹן	sabbath observance (8·11) 992	
הָדָר	40 ornament, honor (1·30) 214	
כַּפָּה	branch (1·4) 497	
תָּמָר	palm branches (1·12) 1071	
עָנָף	branches, boughs (1·7) 778	
עָבוֹת	leafy (1·4) 721	
עֲרָבָה	poplar (1·5) 788	
חגג	41 to keep a pilgrim feast (3·16·16) 290	
סֻכָּה	42 booth (4·31) 697	
אֶזְרָח	native (7·17) 280	
סֻכָּה	43 booth (4·31) 697	

Chapter 24

זַיִת	2 olives, olive tree (1·38) 268	
זַךְ	pure, unmixed (2·11) 269	
כָּתִית	beaten (1·5) 510	
מָאוֹר	light (1·19) 22	
נֵר	lamp (2·45) 632	
פָּרֹכֶת	3 curtain (7·25) 827	
מְנֹרָה	4 lampstand (1·39) 633	
נֵר	lamp (2·45) 632	
אָפָה	5 to bake (2·9·12) 66	
חַלָּה	a kind of cake (8·14) 319	
מַעֲרֶכֶת	6 row (2·9) 790	
מַעֲרֶכֶת	7 row (2·9) 790	
לְבֹנָה	frankincense (7·21) 526	
זַךְ	pure, unmixed (2·11) 269	
אַזְכָּרָה	memorial offering (6·7) 272	

נצה	10 to struggle with each other (1·5·8) 663	
נקב	11 to pierce (3·3·19) 666	
מִשְׁמָר	12 prison (1·20) 1038	
פרש	to declare distinctly (1·1·5) 831	
סָמַךְ	14 to lay (14·41·48) 701	
רגם	to kill by stoning, to stone (5·15·15) 920	
חֵטְא	15 punishment for sin (4·33) 307	
נקב	16 to pierce (3·13·19) 666	
רגם	to kill by stoning, to stone (5·15·15) 920	
אֶזְרָח	native (7·17) 280	
מוּם	19 blemish (10·21) 548	
עָמִית	associate, fellow, relation (11·12) 765	
שֶׁבֶר	20 breaking, shattering (5·45) 991	
מוּם	blemish (10·21) 548	
אֶזְרָח	22 native (7·17) 280	
רגם	23 to kill by stoning, to stone (5·15·15) 920	

Chapter 25

זמר	3 to trim, prune (2·3·3) 274	
תְּבוּאָה	product, yield (11·43) 100	
שַׁבָּתוֹן	4 sabbath observance (8·11) 992	
זמר	to trim, prune (2·3·3) 274	
סָפִיחַ	5 growth from spilled kernels (2·4) 705	
קצר	to reap, harvest (7·24·24) 894	
קָצִיר	harvest (7·49) 894	
עֵנָב	grapes (1·19) 772	
נָזִיר	untrimmed vine (2·15) 634	
בצר	to cut off (2·7·7) 130	
שַׁבָּתוֹן	sabbath observance (8·11) 992	
אָכְלָה	6 food, eating (2·18) 38	
שָׂכִיר	hired laborer (6·18) 969	
תּוֹשָׁב	sojourner (8·14) 444	
תְּבוּאָה	7 product, yield (11·43) 100	
תְּרוּעָה	9 blast [for march] (2·36) 929	

כְּפֻּרִים atonement (3·8) 498

דְּרוֹר 10 liberty, free run (1·7) 204

יוֹבֵל ram's horn (20·27) 385

יוֹבֵל 11 ram's horn (20·27) 385

קָצַר to reap, harvest (7·24·24) 894

סָפִיחַ growth from spilled kernels (2·4) 705

בָּצַר to cut off (2·7·7) 130

נָזִיר untrimmed vine (2·15) 634

יוֹבֵל 12 ram's horn (20·27) 385

תְּבוּאָה product, yield (11·43) 100

יוֹבֵל 13 ram's horn (20·27) 385

מִמְכָּר 14 sale (7·10) 569

עֲמִית associate, fellow, relation (11·12) 765

הוֹנָה to oppress (3·14·18) 413

יוֹבֵל 15 ram's horn (20·27) 385

עֲמִית associate, fellow, relation (11·12) 765

תְּבוּאָה product, yield (11·43) 100

מִקְנָה 16 purchase (4·15) 889

מָעַט to become small (1·8·22) 589

הַמְעִיט to make small (2·13·22) 589

תְּבוּאָה product, yield (11·43) 100

הוֹנָה 17 to oppress (3·14·18) 413

עֲמִית associate, fellow, relation (11·12) 765

בֶּטַח 18 securely (3·43) 105

שֹׂבַע 19 satiety, fill (2·8) 959

בֶּטַח securely (3·43) 105

תְּבוּאָה 20 product, yield (11·43) 100

תְּבוּאָה 21 product, yield (11·43) 100

תְּבוּאָה 22 product, yield (11·43) 100

יָשָׁן old (4·8) 445

צְמִתֻת 23 completion, finality (2·2) 856

תּוֹשָׁב sojourner (8·14) 444

גְּאֻלָּה 24 redemption (9·14) 145

מָךְ 25 to grow poor (5·5·5) 557

גָּאַל kinsman, redeemer (2·44[?]) 145

מִמְכָּר sale (7·10) 569

גֹּאֵל 26 kinsman, redeemer (2·44[?]) 145

הִשִּׂיג to reach (12·48·48) 673

כְּדֵי according to the sufficiency of, i.e.
as much as it demands (1·5) 191

גְּאֻלָּה right of redemption, redemption
(9·14) 145

מִמְכָּר 27 sale (7·10) 569

עָדַף to remain over, be in excess (1·8·9)
727

דֵּי 28 sufficiency, enough (3·12) 191

מִמְכָּר sale (7·10) 569

קֹנֶה owner [as purchaser] (2·7) 888

יוֹבֵל ram's horn (20·27) 385

מוֹשָׁב 29 dwelling place (8·43) 444

גְּאֻלָּה right of redemption, redemption
(9·14) 145

מִמְכָּר sale (7·10) 569

צְמִתֻת 30 completion, finality (2·2) 856

יוֹבֵל ram's horn (20·27) 385

גְּאֻלָּה 31 right of redemption, redemption
(9·14) 145

יוֹבֵל ram's horn (20·27) 385

גְּאֻלָּה 32 right of redemption, redemption
(9·14) 145

מִמְכָּר 33 sale (7·10) 569

יוֹבֵל ram's horn (20·27) 385

מָךְ 35 to grow poor (5·5·5) 557

מוֹט to totter (1·15·39) 556

תּוֹשָׁב sojourner (8·14) 444

נֶשֶׁךְ 36 interest (2·12) 675

תַּרְבִּית increment, interest (1·6) 916

נֶשֶׁךְ 37 interest (2·12) 675

מַרְבִּית increment (1·5) 916

אֹכֶל food (2·44) 38

מָךְ 39 to grow poor (5·5·5) 557

שָׂכִיר 40 hired laborer (6·18) 969

תּוֹשָׁב sojourner (8·14) 444

יוֹבֵל ram's horn (20·27) 385

מִמְכֶּרֶת 42 sale (1·1) 569

רָדָה 43 to have dominion, rule,

81

	dominate (4·22·23) 921
פֶּרֶךְ	harshness, severity (3·6) 827
תּוֹשָׁב	45 sojourner (8·14) 444
רדה	46 to have dominion, rule, dominate (4·22·23) 921
פֶּרֶךְ	harshness, severity (3·6) 827
הִשִּׂיג	47 to reach (12·48·48) 673
תּוֹשָׁב	sojourner (8·14) 444
מָךְ	to grow poor (5·5·5) 557
עֵקֶר	offshoot, member (1·1) 785
גְּאֻלָּה	48 right of redemption, redemption (9·14) 145
שְׁאֵר	49 flesh relation, kinsman (7·17) 984
הִשִּׂיג	to reach (12·48·48) 673
קָנָה	50 owner [as purchaser] (2·7) 888
יוֹבֵל	ram's horn (20·27) 385
מִמְכָּר	sale (7·10) 569
שָׂכִיר	hired laborer (6·18) 969
גְּאֻלָּה	51 price of redemption, redemption (9·14) 145
מִקְנָה	purchase (4·15) 889
יוֹבֵל	52 ram's horn (20·27) 385
כְּפִי	according to (1·16) 804
גְּאֻלָּה	price of redemption, redemption (9·14) 145
שָׂכִיר	53 hired laborer (6·18) 969
רדה	to have dominion, rule, dominate (4·22·23) 921
פֶּרֶךְ	harshness, severity (3·6) 827
יוֹבֵל	54 ram's horn (20·27) 385

Chapter 26

אֱלִיל	1 worthless idol (2·20) 47
פֶּסֶל	idol, image (1·31) 820
מַצֵּבָה	pillar (1·35) 663
מַשְׂכִּית	carved figure (1·6) 967
גֶּשֶׁם	4 rain, shower (1·36) 177
יְבוּל	produce (2·13) 385

הִשִּׂיג	5 to reach (12·48·48) 673
דַּיִשׁ	threshing (1·1) 190
בָּצִיר	vintage (2·7) 131
שֹׂבַע	satiety, fill (2·8) 959
בֶּטַח	securely (3·43) 105
הֶחֱרִיד	6 drive in terror, terrify (1·16·39) 353
רְבָבָה	8 hundred (1·16) 914
הפרה	9 to make fruitful (1·27·29) 826
יָשָׁן	10 old (4·8) 445
נושן	to be old (2·3·3[?]) 445
געל	11 to abhor, loathe (5·8·10) 171
מוֹטָה	13 bar (1·10) 557
עֹל	yoke (1·40) 760
קוֹמְמִיּוּת	uprightness, upright (1·1) 879
געל	15 to abhor, loathe (5·8·10) 171
הֵפֵר	to break, frustrate (2·41·44) 830
בֶּהָלָה	16 dismay, sudden terror (1·4) 96
שַׁחֶפֶת	consumption (1·2) 1006
קַדַּחַת	fever (1·2) 869
הדיב	to cause to pine away (1·1·1) 187
רִיק	emptiness, vanity (2·12) 938
נִגַּף	17 to be smitten (1·23·48) 619
רדה	to have dominion, rule, dominate (4·22·23) 921
שֹׂנֵא	enemy (1·41) 971
יִסַּר	18 to chastise (2·26·37) 415
גָּאוֹן	19 exaltation (1·49) 144
רִיק	20 emptiness, vanity (2·12) 938
יְבוּל	produce (2·13) 385
קֳרִי	21 opposition, contrariness, (7·7) 899
מַכָּה	plague (1·48) 646
שׁכל	22 to make childless (1·18·24) 1013
המעיט	to make small (2·13·22) 589
נוסר	23 to let oneself be chastened (1·5·41) 415
קֳרִי	opposition, contrariness (7·7) 899
קֳרִי	24 opposition, contrariness (7·7) 899
נקם	25 to take vengeance (2·13·34) 667

דֶּבֶר	pestilence, plague (1·46) 184	
אָפָה	26 to bake (2·9·12) 66	
תַּנּוּר	stove, firepot (4·15) 1072	
מִשְׁקָל	weight (2·48) 1054	
קְרִי	27 opposition, contrariness (7·7) 899	
קְרִי	28 opposition, contrariness (7·7) 899	
יִסַּר	to chastise (2·26·37) 415	
חַמָּן	30 sun pillar (1·8) 329	
פֶּגֶר	corpse, carcass (2·22) 803	
גִּלּוּל	idol (1·48) 165	
גָעַל	to abhor, loathe (5·8·10) 171	
חָרְבָּה	31 waste, desolation (2·42) 352	
הריח	to smell (1·11·14) 926	
ניחוח	soothing (17·43) 629	
זרה	32 to scatter, disperse (1·25·38) 279	
הריק	to make empty, empty out (1·17·19) 937	
חָרְבָּה	33 waste, desolation (2·42) 352	
רָצָה	34 to make acceptable (4·4·5) 953	
הרצה	to pay off (1·1·5) 953	
מֹרֶךְ	36 weakness (1·1) 940	
עָלֶה	leaf, leafage (1·17) 750	
נִדַּף	to be driven about (1·6·9) 623	
מְנוּסָה	flight, fleeing (1·2) 631	
כְּמִפְּנֵי	37 as from, as from before (1·1) 816	
תְּקוּמָה	standing, power to stand (1·1) 879	
נמקק	39 to pine away (2·9·10) 596	
מַעַל	40 unfaithful act (3·29) 591	
מָעַל	to act unfaithfully (3·35·35) 591	
קְרִי	opposition, contrariness (7·7) 899	
קְרִי	41 opposition, contrariness (7·7) 899	
נִכְנַע	to humble oneself (1·25·36) 488	
עָרֵל	uncircumcised (2·35) 790	
רָצָה	to make acceptable (4·4·5) 953	
רָצָה	43 to make acceptable (4·4·5) 953	
בְּיַעַן	by the cause (1·3) 774	
גָעַל	to abhor, loathe (5·8·10) 171	
גָעַל	44 to abhor, to loathe (5·8·10) 171	

הֵפֵר	to break, to frustrate (2·41·44) 830	

Chapter 27

הפליא	2 to be a hard or difficult thing (1·2·5[?]) 810	
עֵרֶךְ	estimate, valuation (24·33) 789	
עֵרֶךְ	3 estimate, valuation (24·33) 789	
נְקֵבָה	4 female (12·22) 666	
עֵרֶךְ	estimate, valuation (24·33) 789	
עֵרֶךְ	5 estimate, valuation (24·33) 789	
נְקֵבָה	female (12·22) 666	
עֵרֶךְ	6 estimate, valuation (24·33) 789	
נְקֵבָה	female (12·22) 666	
עֵרֶךְ	7 estimate, valuation (24·33) 789	
נְקֵבָה	female (12·22) 666	
מָךְ	8 to grow poor (5·5·5) 557	
עֵרֶךְ	estimate, valuation (24·33) 789	
הִשִּׂיג	to reach (12·48·48) 673	
נָדַר	to make a vow (1·30·30) 623	
הֶחֱלִיף	10 to change (1·10·26) 322	
הֵמִיר	to exchange (4·12·13) 558	
תְּמוּרָה	exchange, recompense (2·6) 558	
עֵרֶךְ	12 estimate, valuation (24·33) 789	
עֵרֶךְ	13 estimate, valuation (24·33) 789	
עֵרֶךְ	15 estimate, valuation (24·33) 789	
עֵרֶךְ	16 estimate, valuation (24·33) 789	
חֹמֶר	a dry measure (1·12) 330	
שְׂעֹרָה	barley (1·34) 972	
יוֹבֵל	17 ram's horn (20·27) 385	
עֵרֶךְ	estimate, valuation (24·33) 789	
יוֹבֵל	18 ram's horn (20·27) 385	
נִגְרַע	to be withdrawn (1·7·22) 175	
עֵרֶךְ	estimate, valuation (24·33) 789	
עֵרֶךְ	19 estimation, valuation (24·33) 789	
יוֹבֵל	21 ram's horn (20·27) 385	
חֵרֶם	devoted [to sanctuary] (4·29) 356	
מִכְסָה	23 valuation (1·2) 493	
עֵרֶךְ	estimation, valuation (24·33) 789	

יוֹבֵל   ram's horn (20·27) 385

יוֹבֵל 24 ram's horn (20·27) 385

לַאֲשֶׁר   to him, one who (3·38) 82 para.

עֵרֶךְ 25 estimate, valuation (24·33) 789

גֵּרָה   a weight, one-twentieth of a shekel
       (1·5) 176

בכר 26 to be made a firstborn (1·1·4) 114

שֶׂה   sheep, goat (5·44) 961

עֵרֶךְ   estimate, valuation (24·33) 789

חֵרֶם 28 devoted [to sanctuary] (4·29) 356

הֶחֱרִים   to devote for sacred use (1·46·49)
       355

חֵרֶם 29 devoted [to sanctuary] (4·29) 356

החרם   to be devoted (1·3·49) 355

מַעֲשֵׂר 30 tithe (3·31) 798

מַעֲשֵׂר 31 tithe (3·31) 798

מַעֲשֵׂר 32 tithe (3·31) 798

בקר 33 to seek to distinguish (2·7·7) 133

הֵמִיר   to exchange (4·12·13) 558

תְּמוּרָה   exchange, recompense (2·6) 558

NUMBERS

Chapter 1

גֻּלְגֹּלֶת 2 each man, head (5·12) 166

אֶלֶף 16 thousand (4·12[?]) 48

נקב 17 to be designated (1·6·19) 666

הקהיל 18 to summon an assembly (6·20·39) 874

גֻּלְגֹּלֶת each man, head (5·12) 166

תּוֹלְדֹת 20 generations (13·39) 410

גֻּלְגֹּלֶת each man, head (5·12) 166

תּוֹלְדֹת 22 generations (13·39) 410

גֻּלְגֹּלֶת each man, head (5·12) 166

תּוֹלְדֹת 24 generations (13·39) 410

תּוֹלְדֹת 26 generations (13·39) 410

תּוֹלְדֹת 28 generations (13·39) 410

תּוֹלְדֹת 30 generations (13·39) 410

תּוֹלְדֹת 32 generations (13·39) 410

תּוֹלְדֹת 34 generations (13·39) 410

תּוֹלְדֹת 36 generations (13·39) 410

תּוֹלְדֹת 38 generations (13·39) 410

תּוֹלְדֹת 40 generations (13·39) 410

תּוֹלְדֹת 42 generations (13·39) 410

קָרֵב 51 approaching (5·11) 898

דֶּגֶל 52 standard, banner (13·14) 186

קֶצֶף 53 wrath (3·29) 893

Chapter 2

דֶּגֶל 2 standard, banner (13·14) 186

מִנֶּגֶד some way off from, at a distance (1·26) 617

קָדֶם 3 eastward (8·26) 870

דֶּגֶל standard, banner (13·14) 186

דֶּגֶל 10 standard, banner (13·14) 186

תֵּימָן toward the south (3·24) 412

דֶּגֶל 17 standard, banner (13·14) 186

דֶּגֶל 18 standard, banner (13·14) 186

דֶּגֶל 25 standard, banner (13·14) 186

דֶּגֶל 31 standard, banner (13·14) 186

דֶּגֶל 34 standard, banner (13·14) 186

Chapter 3

תּוֹלְדֹת 1 generations (13·39) 410

כהן 3 to minister as a priest (2·23·23) 464

כהן 4 to minister as a priest (2·23·23) 464

כְּהֻנָּה 10 priesthood (6·13) 464

קָרֵב approaching (5·11) 898

פֶּטֶר 12 "first opens" i.e., firstborn (2·11) 809

רֶחֶם womb (4·33) 933

מִכְסֶה 25 covering (7·16) 492

מָסָךְ screen (6·25) 697

קֶלַע 26 curtain, hanging (2·16) 887

מָסָךְ screen (6·25) 697

מֵיתָר cord (4·9) 452

יָרֵךְ 29 side (6·34) 437

תֵּימָן toward the south (3·24) 412

מְנוֹרָה 31 lampstand (6·39) 633

מָסָךְ screen (6·25) 697

פְּקֻדָּה 32 overseer (5·32) 824

יָרֵךְ 35 side (6·34) 437

פְּקֻדָּה 36 oversight, charge (5·32) 824

בְּרִיחַ bar (2·41) 138

יָתֵד 37 peg (2·24) 450

מֵיתָר cord (4·9) 452

קֶדֶם 38 eastward (8·26) 870

קָרֵב approaching (5·11) 898

פְּדוּיִם 46 ransom (5·5) 804

עדף to remain over, be in excess (3·8·9) 727

גֻּלְגֹּלֶת 47 each man, head (5·12) 166

גֵּרָה a weight, one-twentieth of a shekel (2·5) 176

פְּדוּיִם 48 ransom (5·5) 804

עֹדֵף	to remain over, be in excess (3·8·9) 727	
פְּדוּיִם	49 ransom (1·3) 804	
עֹדֵף	to remain over, be in excess (3·8·9) 727	
פְּדוּיִם	ransom (5·5) 804	
פְּדוּיִם	51 ransom (5·5) 804	

Chapter 4

פָּרֹכֶת	5 curtain (2·25) 827	
מָסָךְ	screen (6·25) 697	
כָּלִיל	6 entirely (1·15) 483	
תְּכֵלֶת	violet stuff, fabric (6·49) 1067	
מִלְמָעְלָה	above (2·24) 751	
בַּד	pole, stave (4·41) 94	
תְּכֵלֶת	7 violet stuff, fabric (6·49) 1067	
קְעָרָה	dish, platter (15·17) 891	
מְנַקִּיָּה	sacrificial bowl (1·4) 667	
קַשְׂוָה	jug, jar (1·4) 903	
תּוֹלַעַה	8 coccus ilocus [yielding scarlet color] (2·41) 1069	
שָׁנִי	scarlet (2·42) 1040	
מִכְסֶה	covering (7·16) 492	
תַּחַשׁ	a kind of leather or skin, and perhaps the animal yielding it (7·14) 1065	
בַּד	pole, stave (4·41) 94	
תְּכֵלֶת	9 violet stuff, fabric (6·49) 1067	
מְנוֹרָה	lampstand (6·39) 633	
מָאוֹר	light (2·19) 22	
נֵר	lamp (4·44) 632	
מֶלְקָחַיִם	snuffers (1·6) 544	
מַחְתָּה	fire pan (11·21) 367	
מִכְסֶה	10 covering (7·16) 492	
תַּחַשׁ	leather or skin, and perhaps the animal yielding it (7·14) 1065	
מוֹט	pole (3·4) 557	
תְּכֵלֶת	11 violet stuff, fabric (6·49) 1067	
מִכְסֶה	covering (7·16) 492	

תַּחַשׁ	leather or skin, and perhaps the animal yielding it (7·14) 1065	
בַּד	pole, stave (4·41) 94	
שָׁרֵת	12 vessels (1·2) 1058	
תְּכֵלֶת	violet stuff, fabric (6·49) 1067	
מִכְסֶה	covering (7·16) 492	
תַּחַשׁ	leather or skin, and perhaps the animal yielding it (7·14) 1065	
מוֹט	pole (3·4) 557	
דִּשֵּׁן	13 to clear away the fat ashes (1·5·11) 206	
אַרְגָּמֶן	purple cloth (1·39) 71	
מַחְתָּה	14 censer (11·21) 367	
מִזְלָגָה	three-pronged fork (1·5) 272	
יָע	shovel (1·9) 418	
מִזְרָק	basin (15·32) 284	
תַּחַשׁ	leather or skin, and perhaps the animal yielding it (7·14) 1065	
בַּד	pole, stave (4·41) 94	
פְּקֻדָּה	16 oversight, charge (5·32) 824	
מָאוֹר	light (2·19) 22	
סַם	spice (1·16) 702	
מִשְׁחָה	ointment (1·21) 603	
בֶּלַע	20 inf. = a swallowing, i.e., an instant (1·20·41) 118	
צבא	23 to serve (4·12·14) 838	
מִכְסֶה	25 covering (7·16) 492	
תַּחַשׁ	leather or skin, and perhaps the animal yielding it (7·14) 1065	
מִלְמָעְלָה	above (2·24) 751	
מָסָךְ	screen (6·25) 697	
קֶלַע	26 curtain, hanging (2·16) 887	
מָסָךְ	screen (6·25) 697	
מֵיתָר	cord (4·9) 452	
בְּרִיחַ	31 bar (2·41) 138	
יָתֵד	32 peg (2·24) 450	
מֵיתָר	cord (4·9) 452	

Chapter 5

צָרוּעַ	2 leper (1·5) 863	
זָב	one that has had an issue, flux (1·13[?]) 264	
נְקֵבָה	3 female (2·22) 666	
מָעַל	6 to act unfaithfully (3·35·35) 591	
אָשַׁם	to be, become guilty (2·31·33) 79	
אָשָׁם	7 compensation for trespass (4·46) 79	
לַאֲשֶׁר	to him who (1·38) 81	
אָשַׁם	to commit an offence (2·31·33) 79	
גֹּאֵל	8 kinsman, redeemer (8·44[?]) 145	
אָשָׁם	compensation for trespass (4·46) 79	
מִלְּבַד	besides (15·33) 94	
כִּפֻּרִים	atonement (2·8) 498	
שֹׂטֶה	12 to turn aside (4·6·6) 966	
מָעַל	to act unfaithfully (3·35·35) 591	
שְׁכָבָה	13 a lying (1·9) 1012	
נעלם	to be concealed (1·1·29) 761	
קִנְאָה	14 jealousy (9·43) 888	
קִנֵּא	to be jealous of (6·30·34) 888	
אֵיפָה	15 ephah, a certain quantity of wheat, barley (2·38) 35	
קֶמַח	flour, meal (1·14) 887	
שְׂעֹרָה	barley (1·34) 972	
לְבֹנָה	frankincense (1·21) 526	
קִנְאָה	jealousy (9·43) 888	
זִכָּרוֹן	memorial (5·24) 272	
חֶרֶשׂ	17 earthenware (1·16) 360	
קַרְקַע	floor (1·8) 903	
פָּרַע	18 to let go, let loose, i.e., remove restraint (1·13·16) 828	
זִכָּרוֹן	memorial (5·24) 272	
קִנְאָה	jealousy (9·43) 888	
מַר	bitterness (6·37) 600	
שֹׂטֶה	19 to turn aside (4·6·6) 966	
טֻמְאָה	uncleanness (2·37) 380	
נִקָּה	to be exempt from (3·23·36) 667	

מַר	bitterness (6·37) 600	
שטה	20 to turn aside (4·6·6) 966	
שְׁכֹבֶת	copulation (1·4) 1012	
מִבַּלְעֲדֵי	apart from, without (1·12) 116	
שְׁבוּעָה	21 curse (5·30) 989	
אָלָה	oath, curse (4·36) 46	
יָרֵךְ	thigh (6·34) 437	
צָבֶה	swelling, swollen (1·1) 839	
מֵעֶה	22 belly (1·31) 588	
הצבה	to swell, swell up (1·1·2) 839	
יָרֵךְ	thigh (6·34) 437	
אָמֵן	verily, truly (2·26) 53	
אָלָה	23 curse (4·36) 46	
מָחָה	to wipe (1·21·33) 562	
מַר	bitterness (6·37) 600	
מַר	24 bitterness (6·37) 600	
קִנְאָה	25 jealousy (9·43) 888	
הֵנִיף	to wave (6·32·34[?]) 631	
קָמַץ	26 to enclose with hand, grasp (1·3·3) 888	
אַזְכָּרָה	memorial offering (1·7) 272	
מָעַל	27 to act unfaithfully (3·35·35) 591	
מַר	bitterness (6·37) 600	
צבה	to swell, swell up (1·1·2) 839	
יָרֵךְ	thigh (6·34) 437	
אָלָה	execration, curse, oath (4·36) 46	
נִקָּה	28 to be exempt from (3·23·36) 667	
קִנְאָה	29 jealousy (9·43) 888	
שטה	to turn aside (4·6·6) 966	
קִנְאָה	30 jealousy (9·43) 888	
קִנֵּא	to be jealous of (6·30·34) 888	
נִקָּה	31 to be free from guilt (3·23·36) 667	

Chapter 6

הִפְלִיא	2 to do a hard or difficult thing (1·2·5) 810	
נָדַר	to vow (7·30·30) 623	
נָזִיר	one consecrated, devoted (6·16) 634	

הַזִּיר	to live as a Nazarite (5·6·10[?]) 634
שֵׁכָר	3 intoxicating drink, strong drink (3·23) 1016
הַזִּיר	to live as a Nazarite (5·6·10[?]) 634
חֹמֶץ	vinegar (2·6) 330
מִשְׁרָה	juice (1·1) 1056
עֵנָב	grape[s] (4·19) 772
לַח	moist (1·6) 535
יָבֵשׁ	dried (2·9) 386
גֶּזֶר	4 consecration (12·24) 634
חַרְצָן	grape-stones (1·1) 359
זָג	name of some comparitively insignificant product of the vine, perh. skin of grape (1·1) 260
גֶּזֶר	5 consecration (12·24) 634
תַּעַר	razor (2·13) 789
הַזִּיר	to live as a Nazarite (5·6·10[?]) 634
פֶּרַע	long hair [of head], locks (1·2) 828
שֵׂעָר	hair (2·28) 972
הַזִּיר	6 to live as a Nazarite (5·6·10[?]) 634
גֶּזֶר	7 consecration (12·24) 634
גֶּזֶר	8 consecration (12·24) 634
פֶּתַע	9 suddenness (2·7) 837
פִּתְאֹם	suddenly (2·25) 837
גֶּזֶר	consecration (12·24) 634
גַּלַּח	to shave (3·18·23) 164
תּוֹר	10 turtle dove (1·14) 1076
יוֹנָה	dove (1·35) 401
מֵאֲשֶׁר	11 from [or than] that which (1·17) 84
הַזִּיר	12 to live as a Nazarite (5·6·10[?]) 634
גֶּזֶר	consecration (12·24) 634
אָשָׁם	trespass offering (4·46) 79
נָזִיר	13 one consecrated, devoted (6·16) 634
גֶּזֶר	consecration (12·24) 634
סַל	15 basket (3·15) 700
חַלָּה	a kind of cake (3·14) 319
בָּלַל	to mix (26·42·42[?]) 117
רָקִיק	thin cake, wafer (2·8) 956
סַל	17 basket (3·15) 700
גַּלַּח	18 to shave (3·18·23) 164
נָזִיר	one consecrated, devoted (6·16) 634
נֵזֶר	consecration (12·24) 634
שֵׂעָר	hair (2·28) 972
בָּשֵׁל	19 cooked, boiled (1·2) 143
חַלָּה	a kind of cake (3·14) 319
סַל	basket (3·15) 700
רָקִיק	thin cake, wafer (2·8) 956
נָזִיר	one consecrated, devoted (6·16) 634
הִתְגַּלַּח	to shave oneself (1·2·23) 164
נֵזֶר	hair (12·24) 634
הֵנִיף	20 to wave (6·32·34[?]) 631
תְּנוּפָה	wave offering, wave breast (8·30) 632
חָזֶה	breast (2·13) 303
שׁוֹק	leg (2·19) 1003
נָזִיר	one consecrated, devoted (6·16) 634
נָזִיר	21 one consecrated, devoted (6·16) 634
נָדַר	to vow (7·30·30) 623
נֵזֶר	consecration (12·24) 634
מִלְּבַד	besides (15·33) 94
הִשִּׂיג	to reach, overtake (1·49) 673
כְּפִי	according to (5·16) 804
הֵאִיר	25 to make shine (2·34·40) 21

Chapter 7

פְּקוּדִים	2 musterings (2·3) 823
עֲגָלָה	3 cart (5·25) 722
צָב	litter (1·2) 839
כְּפִי	5 according to (5·16) 804
עֲגָלָה	6 cart (5·25) 722
עֲגָלָה	7 cart (5·25) 722
כְּפִי	according to (5·16) 804
עֲגָלָה	8 cart (5·25) 722
כְּפִי	according to (5·16) 804
חֲנֻכָּה	10 dedication, consecration (4·8) 335
חֲנֻכָּה	11 dedication, consecration (4·8) 335

קְעָרָה	13	dish, platter (15·17) 891
מִשְׁקָל		weight (12·49) 1054
מִזְרָק		basin (15·32) 284
בָּלַל		to mix (26·42·42[?]) 117
עַתּוּד	17	he-goat (13·29) 800
קְעָרָה	19	dish, platter (15·17) 891
מִשְׁקָל		weight (12·49) 1054
מִזְרָק		basin (15·32) 284
בָּלַל		to mix (26·42·42[?]) 117
עַתּוּד	23	he-goat (13·29) 800
קְעָרָה	25	dish, platter (15·17) 891
מִשְׁקָל		weight (12·49) 1054
מִזְרָק		basin (15·32) 284
בָּלַל		to mix (26·42·42[?]) 117
עַתּוּד	29	he-goat (13·29) 800
קְעָרָה	31	dish, platter (15·17) 891
מִשְׁקָל		weight (12·49) 1054
מִזְרָק		basin (15·32) 284
בָּלַל		to mix (26·42·42[?]) 117
עַתּוּד	35	he-goat (13 29) 800
קְעָרָה	37	dish, platter (15·17) 891
מִשְׁקָל		weight (12·49) 1054
מִזְרָק		basin (15·32) 284
בָּלַל		to mix (26·42·42[?]) 117
עַתּוּד	41	he-goat (13·29) 800
קְעָרָה	43	dish, platter (15·17) 891
מִשְׁקָל		weight (12·49) 1054
מִזְרָק		basin (15·32) 284
בָּלַל		to mix (26·42·42[?]) 117
עַתּוּד	47	he-goat (13·29) 800
קְעָרָה	49	dish, platter (15·17) 891
מִשְׁקָל		weight (12·49) 1054
מִזְרָק		basin (15·32) 284
בָּלַל		to mix (26·42·42[?]) 117
עַתּוּד	53	he-goat (13·29) 800
קְעָרָה	55	dish, platter (15·17) 891
מִשְׁקָל		weight (12·49) 1054

מִזְרָק		basin (15·32) 284
בָּלַל		to mix (26·42·42[?]) 117
עַתּוּד	59	he-goat (13·29) 800
קְעָרָה	61	dish, platter (15·17) 891
מִשְׁקָל		weight (12·49) 1054
מִזְרָק		basin (15·32) 284
בָּלַל		to mix (26·42·42[?]) 117
עַתּוּד	65	he-goat (13·29) 800
קְעָרָה	67	dish, platter (15·17) 891
מִשְׁקָל		weight (12·49) 1054
מִזְרָק		basin (15·32) 284
בָּלַל		to mix (26·42·42[?]) 117
עַתּוּד	71	he-goat (13·29) 800
קְעָרָה	73	dish, platter (15·17) 891
מִשְׁקָל		weight (12·49) 1054
מִזְרָק		basin (15·32) 284
בָּלַל		to mix (26·42·42[?]) 117
עַתּוּד	77	he-goat (13·29) 800
קְעָרָה	79	dish, platter (15·17) 891
מִשְׁקָל		weight (12·49) 1054
מִזְרָק		basin (15·32) 284
בָּלַל		to mix (26·42·42[?]) 117
עַתּוּד	83	he-goat (13·29) 800
חֲנֻכָּה	84	dedication, consecration (4·8) 335
קְעָרָה		dish, platter (15·17) 891
מִזְרָק		basin (15·32) 284
קְעָרָה	85	dish, platter (15·17) 891
מִזְרָק		basin (15·32) 284
עַתּוּד	88	he-goat (13·29) 800
חֲנֻכָּה		dedication, consecration (4·8) 335
כַּפֹּרֶת	89	propitiatory (1·27) 498
מִבֵּין		from between (2·21) 107

Chapter 8

נֵר	2	lamp (4·44) 632
מוּל		the forefront of (2·25) 557
מְנוֹרָה		lampstand (6·39) 633

הָאִיר	to light (2·34·40) 21	
מוּל	3 the forefront of (2·25) 557	
מְנוֹרָה	lampstand (6·39) 633	
נֵר	lamp (4·44) 632	
מְנוֹרָה	4 lampstand (6·39) 633	
מִקְשָׁה	perh. hammered work (3·9) 904	
יָרֵךְ	base (6·34) 437	
פֶּרַח	bud, sprout (2·17) 827	
הִזָּה	7 to sprinkle (5·20·24) 633	
תַּעַר	razor (2·13) 789	
בָּלַל	8 to mix (26·42·42[?]) 117	
הִקְהִיל	9 to summon an assembly (6·20·39) 874	
סָמַךְ	10 to lay (4·41·48) 701	
הֵנִיף	11 to wave (6·32·34[?]) 631	
תְּנוּפָה	waving, wave offering (8·30) 632	
סָמַךְ	12 to lay (4·41·48) 701	
הֵנִיף	13 to wave (6·32·34[?]) 631	
תְּנוּפָה	waving, wave offering (8·30) 632	
הִבְדִּיל	14 to separate (2·32·42) 95	
הֵנִיף	15 to wave (6·32·34[?]) 631	
תְּנוּפָה	waving, wave offering (8·30) 632	
פִּטְרָה	16 that which separates, first opens, i.e., firstborn (1·1) 809	
רֶחֶם	womb (4·33) 933	
נֶגֶף	19 plague (3·7) 620	
הֵנִיף	21 to wave (6·32·34[?]) 631	
תְּנוּפָה	waving, wave offering (8·30) 632	
צבא	24 to serve (4·12·14) 838	
כָּכָה	26 thus (5·34) 462	

Chapter 9

פֶּסַח	2 festival of the passover (11·49) 820
פֶּסַח	4 festival of the passover (11·49) 820
פֶּסַח	5 festival of the passover (11·49) 820
פֶּסַח	6 festival of the passover (11·49) 820
נִגְרַע	7 to be restrained (5·7·22) 175

פֶּסַח	10 festival of the passover (11·49) 820
מָרֹר	11 bitter herb (1·5) 601
פֶּסַח	12 festival of the passover (11·49) 820
פֶּסַח	13 festival of the passover (11·49) 820
עַם	kinsman (4·34) 769
חֵטְא	punishment for sin (4·33) 307
פֶּסַח	14 festival of the passover (11·49) 820
אֶזְרָח	native (4·17) 280
הֶאֱרִיךְ	19 to tarry long, be long (2·31·34) 73
הֶאֱרִיךְ	22 to tarry long, be long (2·31·34) 73

Chapter 10

חֲצֹצְרָה	2 clarion (5·29) 348
מִקְשָׁה	perh. hammered work (3·9) 904
מִקְרָא	convocation (7·22) 896
מַסַּע	breaking camp (7·12) 652
נוֹעַד	3 to assemble by appointment (6·18·28) 416
אֶלֶף	4 thousand (4·12[?]) 48
תְּרוּעָה	5 blast [for march] (6·36) 929
קֶדֶם	eastward (8·26) 870
תְּרוּעָה	6 blast [for march] (6·36) 929
תֵּימָן	toward the south (3·24) 412
מַסַּע	setting out (7·12) 652
הִקְהִיל	7 to summon an assembly (6·20·39) 874
הֵרִיעַ	sound signal for war, march (2·40·44) 929
חֲצֹצְרָה	8 clarion (5·29) 348
צָרַר	9 to show hostility towards, vex (4·10·10) 865
הֵרִיעַ	to sound signal for war, march (2·40·44) 929
חֲצֹצְרָה	clarion (5·29) 348
חֲצֹצְרָה	10 clarion (5·29) 348
זִכָּרוֹן	memorial (5·24) 272
מַסַּע	12 journey (7·12) 652
דֶּגֶל	14 standard, banner (13·14) 186

דֶּגֶל	18 standard, banner (13·14) 186	עֻגָה	disk or cake of bread (1·7) 728
דֶּגֶל	22 standard, banner (13·14) 186	טַעַם	taste (2·13) 381
דֶּגֶל	25 standard, banner (13·14) 186	לָשָׁד	dainty bit (1·2) 545
מַסַּע	28 setting out (7·12) 652	טַל	9 dew (1·31) 378
חֹתֵן	29 wife's father (1·21) 368	מָן	manna (3·14) 577
מוֹלֶדֶת	30 kindred (1·22) 409	הָרָה	12 to conceive (1·38·40) 247
תּוּר	33 to seek out, select (14·19·22) 1064	חֵיק	bosom (1·38) 300
מְנוּחָה	resting-place (1·21) 629	אֹמֵן	foster father (1·7[?]) 52
רְבָבָה	36 multitude, myriad (1·16) 914	יוֹנֵק	suckling (1·11) 413
אֶלֶף	thousand (4·12[?]) 12	מֵאַיִן	13 whence? (1·48) 32
		כָּבֵד	14 heavy (2·39) 458
Chapter 11		כָּכָה	15 thus (5·34) 462
		שֹׁטֵר	16 official, officer (1·25) 1009
הִתְאֹנֵן	1 to complain, murmer (1·2·2) 59	הִתְיַצֵּב	to station oneself, take one's stand (4·48·48) 426
שָׁקַע	2 to sink, sink down (1·3·6) 1054		
אֲסַפְסֻף	4 collection, rabble (1·1) 63	אָצַל	17 to set apart (2·4·5) 69
הִתְאַוָּה	to desire, lust after (3·16·27) 16	טוֹב	18 to be well, good (3·18·21) 373
תַּאֲוָה	desire (1·21) 16	זָרָא	20 loathsome thing (1·1) 266
דָּגָה	5 fish [coll.] (1·15) 185	רַגְלִי	21 on foot (1·12) 920
חִנָּם	for naught (1·32) 336	דָּג	22 fish (1·19) 185
קִשֻּׁאָה	cucumber (1·1) 903	קָצַר	23 to be short (2·11·13) 894
אֲבַטִּחִים	watermelons (1·1) 105	קָרָה	to befall (1·13·27) 889
חָצִיר	green grass, herbage (1·1[?]) 348	אָצַל	25 to set apart (2·4·5[?]) 69
בָּצָל	onion (1·1) 130	מְשָׁרֵת	28 servant (1·20) 1058
שׁוּם	garlic (1·1) 1002	בְּחוּרִים	youth (1·3) 104
בִּלְתִּי	6 except (3·24) 116	כָּלָא	to withhold (1·14·17) 476
מָן	manna (3·14) 577	קִנֵּא	29 to be jealous of (6·30·34) 888
מָן	7 manna (3·14) 577	גּוּז	31 to bring over (1·2·2) 156
גַּד	coriander (1·2) 151	שְׂלָו	quail (2·4) 969
בְּדֹלַח	bdellium (1·2) 95	נָטַשׁ	to leave alone (1·33·40) 643
שׁוּט	8 to go, rove about (1·7·13) 1001	מָחֳרָת	32 the morrow (4·32) 564
לָקַט	to gather (1·14·36) 544	שְׂלָו	quail (2·4) 969
טָחַן	to grind (1·7·7) 377	הִמְעִיט	to make small (4·13·22) 589
רֵחַיִם	[hand] mill (1·5) 932	חֹמֶר	heap (1·12) 330
דּוּךְ	to pound, beat (1·1) 188	שָׁטַח	to spread, spread abroad (1·4·5) 1008
מְדֹכָה	mortar (1·1) 189		
בָּשַׁל	to boil, cook (1·20·27) 143	טֶרֶם	33 not yet (1·16) 382
פָּרוּר	pot (1·3) 807		

91

הִתְאַוָּה 34 to desire, lust after (3·16·27) 16

Chapter 12

אֹדֹת 1 cause; 'על־א = because of (2·11) 15

עָנָו 3 humble, lowly, meek (1·21) 776

פִּתְאֹם 4 suddenly (2·25) 837

חִידָה 8 riddle, enigmatic saying (1·17) 295

תְּמוּנָה form, semblance (1·10) 568

מְצֹרָע 10 leprous (2·15) 863

שֶׁלֶג snow (1·20) 1017

בִּי 11 I pray, excuse me (1·12) 106

נוֹאַל to be foolish (1·4·4) 383

רֶחֶם 12 womb (4·33) 933

יָרַק 14 to spit (1·2·2) 439

בְּפָנֵי in the face of (1·17) 816

Chapter 13

תּוּר 2 to spy out, explore (14·19·22) 1064

תּוּר 16 to spy out, explore (14·19·22) 1064

תּוּר 17 to spy out, explore (14·19·22) 1064

רָפֶה 18 slack (1·4) 952

מִבְצָר 19 fortification (3·37) 131

שָׁמֵן 20 fertile (1·10) 1032

רָזֶה lean [as in barren] (1·2) 931

בִּכּוּרִים firstfruits (3·17) 114

עֵנָב grape[s] (4·19) 772

תּוּר 21 to spy out, explore (14·19·22) 1064

יָלִיד 22 born (2·12) 409

אֶשְׁכּוֹל 23 cluster (2·9) 79

זְמוֹרָה branch (1·5) 274

עֵנָב grape[s] (4·19) 772

מוֹט pole (3·4) 557

רִמּוֹן pomegranate (2·32) 941

תְּאֵנָה fig tree, fig (2·25·39) 1061

אֶשְׁכּוֹל 24 cluster (2·9) 79

אֹדֹת cause; 'על־א = because of (2·11) 15

תּוּר 25 to spy out, explore (14·19·22) 1064

זוּב 27 to flow (4·29·29[?]) 264

חָלָב milk (4·44) 316

אֶפֶס 28 כי א = save that, howbeit (3·43) 67

עַז strong, mighty, fierce (2·22) 738

בָּצוּר fortified (1·25[?]) 130

יָלִיד born (2·12) 409

ההסה 30 to still (1·1·1[?]) 245

דִּבָּה 32 evil report (3·9) 179

תּוּר to spy out, explore (14·19·22) 1064

נְפִילִים 33 giants (1·3) 658

חָגָב locust, grasshopper (1·5) 290

Chapter 14

נלון 2 to murmur (4·8·18) 534

לוּ if only! O that! (4·19) 530

טַף 3 children (10·41) 381

בַּז spoil, plunder (3·27) 103

תּוּר 6 to spy out, explore (14·19·22) 1064

תּוּר 7 to spy out, explore (14·19·22) 1064

זוּב 8 to flow (4·29·29[?]) 264

חָלָב milk (4·44) 316

מרד 9 to rebel (1·25·25) 597

רגם 10 to kill by stoning, to stone (3·15·15) 920

אָנָה 11 with עד = to what point, how long? (2·39) 33

נָאֵץ perh. to abhor, spurn (3·15·24) 611

דֶּבֶר 12 plague, pestilence (1·46) 184

עָצוּם mighty [strong] (3·31) 783

שֵׁמַע 15 hearing, report (1·17) 1034

מִבִּלְתִּי 16 on account of not (1·2) 116

אֶרֶךְ 18 long; אַפַּיִם א = slow to anger (1·15) 74

נקה to leave unpunished (2·13·37) 667

שִׁלֵּשִׁים those of the third generation (1·5) 1026

רִבֵּעַ pertaining to the fourth (1·4) 918

סלח 19 to pardon (5·33·46) 699

גֹּדֶל greatness (1·14) 152

הֵנָּה hither (1·49) 244

סְלַח 20 to pardon (5·33·46) 699

אוּלָם 21 but, but indeed (1·19) 19

נִסָּה 22 to test (1·36·36) 650

נָאֵץ 23 perh. to abhor, spurn (3·15·24) 611

עֵקֶב 24 because of (1·15) 784

מָתַי 27 when? (1·42) 607

נלין to murmur (4·8·18) 534

תְּלֻנָּה murmuring (3·8) 534

פֶּגֶר 29 corpse, carcass (3·22) 803

הלין to murmur (6·10·18) 534

טַף 31 children (10·41) 381

בַּז spoil, plunder (3·27) 103

פֶּגֶר 32 corpse, carcass (3·22) 803

זְנוּת 33 fornication (1·9) 276

פֶּגֶר corpse, carcass (3·22) 803

תּוּר 34 to spy out, explore (14·19·22) 1064

תְּנוּאָה opposition (1·2) 626

נועד 35 to assemble by appointment (6·18·28) 416

תּוּר 36 to spy out, explore (14·19·22) 1064

נלין to murmur (4·8·18) 534

דִּבָּה evil report (3·9) 179

דִּבָּה 37 evil report (3·9) 179

מַגֵּפָה plague (9·26) 620

תּוּר 38 to spy out, explore (14·19·22) 1064

הִתְאַבֵּל 39 to mourn (1·19·38) 5

נָגַּף 42 to be struck (1·23·48) 619

הֶעְפִּיל 44 to be needless (1·1·2) 779

מוּשׁ to depart (1·20[?]·20) 559

הַכְתִּית 45 to beat in pieces (1·2·17) 510

Chapter 15

מוֹשָׁב 2 dwelling place (4·43) 444

פלא 3 inf. only; to make a special votive offering (2·3·5) 810

נְדָבָה freewill offering (3·27) 621

נִיחֹחַ soothing (18·43) 629

עִשָּׂרוֹן 4 tenth part (27·33) 798

בָּלַל to mix (26·42·42[?]) 117

הִין hin, a liquid measure (11·22) 228

הִין 5 hin, a liquid measure (11·22) 228

עִשָּׂרוֹן 6 tenth part (27·33) 798

בָּלַל to mix (26·42·42[?]) 117

הִין hin, a liquid measure (11·22) 228

הִין 7 hin, a liquid measure (11·22) 228

נִיחֹחַ soothing (18·43) 629

פלא 8 to make a special votive offering (2·3·5) 810

עִשָּׂרוֹן 9 tenth part (27·33) 798

בָּלַל to mix (26·42·42[?]) 117

הִין hin, a liquid measure (11·22) 228

הִין 10 hin, a liquid measure (11·22) 228

נִיחֹחַ soothing (18·43) 629

כָּכָה 11 thus (5·34) 462

שֶׂה sheep, goat (1·44) 961

כָּכָה 12 thus (5·34) 462

אֶזְרָח 13 native (4·17) 280

כָּכָה thus (5·34) 462

נִיחֹחַ soothing (18·43) 629

נִיחֹחַ 14 soothing (18·43) 629

עֲרִיסָה 20 coarse meal [dub.] (2·4) 791

חַלָּה a kind of cake (3·14) 319

גֹּרֶן treshing floor (3·34) 175

עֲרִיסָה 21 coarse meal [dub.] (2·4) 791

שׁגה 22 to commit sin of ignorance (1·17·21) 993

הָלְאָה 23 onwards (3·13) 229

שְׁגָגָה 24 sin of error, inadvertence (9·19) 993

נִיחֹחַ soothing (18·43) 629

נִסְלַח 25 to be forgiven (3·13·46) 699

שְׁגָגָה sin of error, inadvertence (9·19) 993

נִסְלַח 26 to be forgiven (3·13·46) 699

שְׁגָגָה sin of error, inadvertence (9·19) 993

שְׁגָגָה 27 sin of error, inadvertence (9·19) 993

שָׁגַג	28	to sin, go astray (1·5·5) 992
חֲטָאָה		fault, sin (1·1[?]) 306
שְׁגָגָה		sin of error, inadvertence (9·19) 993
נִסְלַח		to be forgiven (3·13·46) 699
אֶזְרָח	29	native (4·17) 280
שְׁגָגָה		sin of error, inadvertence (9·19) 993
רָם	30	high, lifted, exalted (2·31[?]) 926
אֶזְרָח		native (4·17) 280
גָדַף		to revile, blaspheme (1·7·7) 154
בָּזָה	31	to despise (6·31·42) 102
הֵפֵר		to break, frustrate (6·41·44) 830
קֹשֵׁשׁ	32	to gather stubble (2·6·8) 905
קֹשֵׁשׁ	33	to gather stubble (2·6·8) 905
מִשְׁמָר	34	prison (1·20) 1038
פרש		to be declared distinctly, made distinct (1·2·5) 831
רגם	35	to kill by stoning, to stone (3·15·15) 920
רגם	36	to kill by stoning, to stone (3·15·15) 920
צִיצַת	38	tassel (3·4) 851
פָּתִיל		cord, thread (2·11) 836
תְּכֵלֶת		violet thread (6·49) 1067
צִיצַת	39	tassel (3·4) 851
תּוּר		to go about (14·19·22) 1064

Chapter 16

קָרִיא	2	called, summoned (2·2) 896
נקהל	3	to assemble (3·19·39) 874
מַחְתָּה	6	censer (11·21) 367
הִבְדִּיל	9	separate (2·32·42) 95
כְּהֻנָּה	10	priesthood (6·13) 464
נועד	11	to assemble by appointment (6·18·28) 416
הלין		to murmur (6·10·18) 534
זוב	13	to flow (4·29·29) 264
חָלָב		milk (4·44) 316

הִשְׂתָּרֵר		to play the prince over one (1·1·7) 979
זוב	14	to flow (4·29·29) 264
חָלָב		milk (4·44) 316
נקר		to bore out (1·3·6) 669
מַחְתָּה	17	censer (11·21) 367
מַחְתָּה	18	censer (11·21) 367
הִקְהִיל	19	to summon an assembly 6·20·39) 874
נבדל	21	to be separated (1·10·42) 95
רֶגַע		moment (2·22) 921
קָצַף	22	to be wroth (2·28·34) 893
נִסְפָּה	26	to be swept away (1·9·18) 705
טַף	27	children (10·41) 381
פְּקֻדָּה	29	visitation (5·32) 824
בְּרִיאָה	30	a creation, thing created (1·1) 135
בָּרָא		to create, fashion (1·38·48) 135
פצה		to part, open (1·15·15) 822
בָּלַע		to swallow up (4·20·41) 118
נָאֵץ		perh. to abhor, spurn (3·15·24) 611
בָּלַע	32	to swallow up (4·20·41) 118
רְכוּשׁ		property, goods (2·28) 940
בָּלַע	34	to swallow up (4·20·41) 118

Chapter 17

מַחְתָּה	2	censer (11·21) 367
מִבֵּין		out of the midst of (2·21) 107
שְׂרֵפָה		burning (3·13) 977
זרה		to scatter (1·9·38) 279
הָלְאָה		yonder, out there (3·13) 229
מַחְתָּה	3	censer (11·21) 367
חַטָּא		sinner, sinful (2·19) 308
רִקּוּעַ		expansion (1·1) 956
פַּח		plate [of metal] (1·2) 809
צִפּוּי		metal plating (2·5) 860
מַחְתָּה	4	censer (11·21) 367
רקע		to beat out (1·3·11) 955
צִפּוּי		metal plating (2·5) 860

זְכָּרוֹן 5 memorial (5·24) 272

נלין 6 to murmur (4·8·18) 534

מָחֳרָת the morrow (4·32) 564

נקהל 7 to assemble (3·19·39) 874

נרמם 10 to arise (1·4·5) 942

רֶגַע moment (2·22) 921

מַחְתָּה 11 censer (11·21) 367

קֶצֶף wrath (3·29) 893

נֶגֶף plague (3·7) 620

נֶגֶף 12 plague (3·7) 620

נעצר 13 to be restrained, be retained
(3·10·46) 783

מַגֵּפָה pestilence (9·26) 620

מַגֵּפָה 14 pestilence (9·26) 620

מִלְּבַד besides (15·33) 94

מַגֵּפָה 15 pestilence (9·26) 620

נעצר to be restrained, be retained
(3·10·46) 783

נועד 19 to meet at an appointed place
(6·18·28) 416

פָּרַח 20 to bud, sprout, shoot (2·29·34) 827

שכה to allay, cause to abate (1·1·5)
1013

תְּלֻנָּה murmuring (3·8) 534

הלין to murmur (6·10·18) 534

מָחֳרָת 23 the morrow (4·32) 564

פָּרַח to bud, sprout, shoot (2·29·34) 827

פֶּרַח bud, sprout (2·17) 827

צִיץ to put forth blossoms (1·7·8) 847

צִיץ blossom, flower (1·15) 847

גָּמַל to ripen, bear ripe [fruits] (1·34·37)
168

שָׁקֵד almond [tree] (1·4) 1052

מְרִי 25 rebellion (1·22) 598

תְּלֻנָּה murmuring (3·8) 534

גוע 27 to expire, perish (4·23·23) 157

קָרֵב 28 approaching (5·11) 898

גוע to expire, perish (4·23·23) 157

Chapter 18

כְּהֻנָּה 1 priesthood (6·13) 464

נִלְוָה 2 to be joined (2·11·12) 530

נִלְוָה 4 to be joined (2·11·12) 530

קֶצֶף 5 wrath (3·29) 893

מַתָּנָה 6 gift (4·18) 682

כְּהֻנָּה 7 priesthood (6·13) 464

פָּרֹכֶת curtain (2·25) 827

מַתָּנָה gift (4·18) 682

קָרֵב approaching (5·11) 898

מָשְׁחָה 8 consecrated portion (1·1) 603

אָשָׁם 9 trespass offering (4·42) 79

מַתָּנָה 11 gift (4·18) 682

תְּנוּפָה wave offering, wave breast (8·30)
632

יִצְהָר 12 fresh oil (1·23) 844

תִּירוֹשׁ must, fresh or new wine (1·38) 440

דָּגָן grain (2·40) 186

בכורים 13 firstfruits (3·17) 114

חֵרֶם 14 devoted (1·29) 356

פֶּטֶר 15 "first opens", i.e., firstborn (2·11)
809

רֶחֶם womb (4·33) 933

פְּדוּיִם 16 ransom (5·5) 804

עֵרֶךְ estimate, valuation (1·33) 789

גֵּרָה gerah, one-twentieth of a shekel
(2·5) 176

זָרַק 17 to throw or scatter abundantly
(1·32·34[?]) 284

נִיחֹחַ soothing (18·43) 629

חָזֶה 18 breast (2·13) 303

תְּנוּפָה wave offering, wave breast (8·30)
632

שׁוֹק leg (2·19) 1003

מֶלַח 19 salt (3·28) 571

מַעֲשֵׂר 21 tithe (5·31) 798

חֵלֶף exchange = in return for (2·2) 322

חֵטְא	22	punishment for sin (4·33) 307
מַעֲשֵׂר	24	tithe (5·31) 798
מַעֲשֵׂר	26	tithe (5·31) 798
דָּגָן	27	grain (2·40) 186
גֹּרֶן		treshing floor (3·34) 175
יֶקֶב		wine vat (2·16) 428
מַעֲשֵׂר	28	tithe (5·31) 798
מַתָּנָה	29	gift (4·18) 682
תְּבוּאָה	30	product, yield (2·43) 100
גֹּרֶן		treshing floor (3·34) 175
יֶקֶב		wine vat (2·16) 428
שָׂכָר	31	hire, wages (1·29) 969
חֵלֶף		exchange =in return for (2·2) 322
חֵטְא	32	punishment for sin (4·33) 307

Chapter 19

פָּרָה	2	heifer (5·26) 831
אָדֹם		red (1·9) 10
מוּם		defect (1·21) 548
עֹל		yoke (1·40) 760
אֶצְבַּע	4	finger (1·31) 840
הִזָּה		to sprinkle (5·20·24) 633
נֹכַח		front of (1·22) 647
פָּרָה	5	heifer (5·26) 831
פֶּרֶשׁ		offal, refuse (1·7) 831
אֵזוֹב	6	hyssop (2·10) 23
שָׁנִי		scarlet (2·42) 1040
תּוֹלֵעָה		coccus ilicius |yielding scarlet color| (2·41) 1069
שְׂרֵפָה		burning (3·13) 977
פָּרָה		heifer (5·26) 831
אֵפֶר	9	ashes (2·22) 68
פָּרָה		heifer (5·26) 831
נִדָּה		impurity (6·30) 622
אֵפֶר	10	ashes (2·22) 68
פָּרָה		heifer (5·26) 831
נִדָּה	13	impurity (6·30) 622
זרק		to be poured (2·2·34[?]) 284

טֻמְאָה		uncleanness (2·37) 380
צָמִיד	15	cover (1·1) 855
פָּתִיל		cord, thread (2·11) 836
שְׂרֵפָה	17	burning (3·13) 977
אֵזוֹב	18	hyssop (2·10) 23
טָבַל		to dip (1·15·16) 371
הִזָּה		to sprinkle (5·20·24) 633
הִזָּה	19	to sprinkle (5·20·24) 633
נִדָּה	20	impurity (6·30) 622
זרק		to be poured (2·2·34[?]) 284
הִזָּה	21	to sprinkle (5·20·24) 633
נִדָּה		impurity (6·30) 622

Chapter 20

נקהל	2	to assemble (3·19·39) 874
לוּ	3	if only! O that! (3·19) 530
גָּוַע		to perish, die (4·23·23) 157
בְּעִיר	4	beasts, cattle (3·6) 129
תְּאֵנָה	5	fig tree, fig (2·25·39) 1061
הִקְהִיל	8	to summon an assembly (6·20·39) 874
בְּעִיר		beasts, cattle (3·6) 129
הִקְהִיל	10	to summon an assembly (6·20·39) 874
מָרָה		to be stubborn (3·21·43) 598
בְּעִיר	11	beasts, cattle (3·6) 129
מְרִיבָה	13	strife, contention (1·2) 937
תְּלָאָה	14	weariness, hardship (1·5) 521
בְּאֵר	17	well (5·36) 91
מְסִלָּה	19	highway (1·27) 700
כָּבֵד	20	heavy (2·39) 458
מֵאֵן	21	to refuse (3·45·45) 549
עַם	24	kinsman (4·34) 769
מָרָה		to be stubborn (3·21·43) 598
הִפְשִׁיט	26	to strip (2·15·43) 832
הִפְשִׁיט	28	to strip (2·15·43) 832
גָּוַע	29	to perish, die (4·23·23) 157

Chapter 21

שׁבה 1 to take captive (3·29·37) 985

שְׁבִי captivity, captives (4·46) 985

נָדַר 2 to vow (7·30·30) 623

הֶחֱרִים to devote to destruction (2·46·49) 355

הֶחֱרִים 3 to devote to destruction (2·46·49) 355

קָצַר 4 to be short (2·11·13) 894

קוּץ 5 to feel a loathing, abhor (2·8·8) 880

קְלֹקֵל contemptible, worthless (1·1) 887

נָחָשׁ 6 serpent (5·31) 638

שָׂרָף fiery serpent (2·7) 977

נשׁךּ to bite fatally (1·2·12) 675

נָחָשׁ 7 serpent (5·31) 638

שָׂרָף 8 fiery serpent (2·7) 977

נֵס standard (3·21) 651

נָשַׁךּ to bite (2·10·12) 675

נָחָשׁ 9 serpent (5·31) 638

נֵס standard (3·21) 651

נָשַׁךּ to bite (2·10·12) 675

אֶשֶׁד 15 lower part, bottom (1·7) 78

נִשְׁעַן to lean, support oneself (1·22·22) 1043

בְּאֵר 16 well (5·36) 91

שִׁירָה 17 song (1·13) 1010

בְּאֵר well (5·36) 91

ענה to sing (1·13·16) 777

בְּאֵר 18 well (5·36) 91

חָפַר to dig, search for (1·22·22) 343

כָּרָה to dig (1·13·14) 500

נָדִיב noble (1·27) 622

מְחֹקֵק commander's staff (1·7) 349

מִשְׁעֶנֶת staff (1·12) 1044

גַּיְא 20 valley (1·47) 161

נשׁקף to overhang, look out and down (2·10·22) 1054

יְשִׁימוֹן wilderness (2·13) 445

בְּאֵר 22 well (5·36) 91

עַז 24 strong, mighty, fierce (2·22) 738

מֹשֵׁל 27 one who uses a proverb (1·2[?]) 605

לֶהָבָה 28 flame (1·19) 529

קִרְיָה town, city (1·30) 900

אוֹי 29 Woe! Alas! (2·24) 17

פָּלִיט escaped one, fugitive (1·5) 812

שְׁבִית captivity, captives (1·6) 986

יָרָה 30 to throw (1·13·25[?]) 434

רגל 32 go about as explorer, spy (1·14·16) 920

בִּלְתִּי 35 not, except (3·24) 116

שָׂרִיד survivor (2·28) 975

Chapter 22

גוּר 3 to be afraid of (1·10·10) 158

קוּץ to feel a sickening dread (2·8·8) 880

לחךּ 4 Pi. = to lick up (1·5·6) 535

לחךּ Qal = to lick (1·1·6) 535

יֶרֶק green (1·8) 438

מִמּוּל 5 close in front of (1·9) 660

עָצוּם 6 mighty [strong] (3·31) 783

אוּלַי perhaps (5·45) 19

גרשׁ to drive out (2·33·47) 176

קֶסֶם 7 divination (2·11) 890

פֹּה 8 here, hither (3·44) 805

קבב 11 to utter a curse against, curse (10·14·14) 866

אוּלַי perhaps (5·45) 19

גרשׁ to drive out (2·33·47) 176

מֵאֵן 13 to be recusant (3·45·45) 549

מֵאֵן 14 to refuse (3·45·45) 549

נִמְנַע 16 to be withheld (1·4·29) 586

קבב 17 to utter a curse against, curse (10·14·14) 866

מְלֹא 18 fulness (2·38) 571

קָטֹן small (1·47) 881

בָּזֶה 19 in this [place], here (5·19) 261

חבש 21 to bind up, i.e., equip for riding (1·27·31) 289

אָתוֹן she-ass (15·35) 87

הִתְיַצֵב 22 to station oneself, take one's stand (4·48·48) 426

שָׂטָן adversary (2·27) 966

אָתוֹן she-ass (15·35) 87

שָׁלַף 23 to draw out (2·25·25) 1025

אָתוֹן she-ass (15·35) 87

מִשְׁעוֹל 24 hollow way (1·1) 1043

גָּדֵר wall, fence (1·13) 154

אָתוֹן 25 she-ass (15·35) 87

נלחץ to squeeze oneself (1·1·15) 537

לָחַץ to squeeze (1·14·15) 537

צַר 26 narrow, tight (1·20) 865

אָתוֹן 27 she-ass (15·35) 87

רָבַץ to lie down, lie (1·24·30) 918

מַקֵּל staff (1·18) 596

אָתוֹן 28 she-ass (15·35) 87

אָתוֹן 29 she-ass (15·35) 87

הִתְעַלֵּל to deal wantonly, ruthlessly (1·7·17) 759

לוּ If only! O that! (4·19) 530

אָתוֹן 30 she-ass (15·35) 87

מֵעוֹד ever since (1·2) 728

הַסְכֵּן to exhibit use or habit (2·4·11) 698

שָׁלַף 31 to draw out (2·25·25) 1025

קדד to bow down (1·15·15) 869

אָתוֹן 32 she-ass (15·35) 87

שָׂטָן adversary (2·27) 966

יָרַט to precipitate (1·2·2) 437

לְנֶגֶד in front of, before (1·32) 617

אָתוֹן 33 she-ass (15·35) 87

אוּלַי perhaps (5·45) 19

אֶפֶס 35 only (3·43) 67

אֻמְנָם 37 truly, indeed (1·5) 53

מְאוּמָה 38 anything (1·32) 548

Chapter 23

בָּזֶה 1 in this [place], here (5·19) 261

הִתְיַצֵב 3 to station oneself, take one's stand (4·48·48) 426

אוּלַי perhaps (5·45) 19

נִקְרָה to encounter, meet (4·6·27) 899

שְׁפִי bare place, height (1·10) 1046

נִקְרָה 4 to encounter, meet (4·6·27) 899

מָשָׁל 7 proverb (7·39) 605

הַנְחָיָה to lead (1·26·40) 634

זָעַם to denounce (2·10·11) 276

קבב 8 to utter a cruse against, curse (10·14·14) 866

זָעַם to denounce (2·10·11) 276

שׁוּר 9 to behold (2·16·16) 1003

בָּדָד isolation (1·11) 94

מָנָה 10 to count (1·12·28) 584

רֹבַע fourth part (1·1) 917

קבב 11 to utter a curse against, curse (10·14·14) 866

אֶפֶס 13 only (3·43) 67

קבב to utter a cruse against, curse (10·14·14) 866

צֹפֶה 14 watchman (1·19) 859

הִתְיַצֵב 15 to station oneself, take one's stand (4·48·48) 426

נִקְרָה to encounter, meet (4·6·27) 899

נִקְרָה 16 to encounter, meet (4·6·27) 899

מָשָׁל 18 proverb (7·39) 605

הַאֲזֵין to listen (1·41·41) 24

כזב 19 to lie (1·12·16) 469

תְּרוּעָה 21 battle cry (6·36) 929

תּוֹעָפָה 22 eminence (2·4) 419

רְאֵם wild ox (2·9) 910

נַחַשׁ 23 divination (2·2) 638

קֶסֶם divination (2·11) 890

לָבִיא 24 lioness (2·11) 522

98

אֲרִי lion (2·35) 71

טֶרֶף prey (1·17) 383

קבב 25 to utter a curse against, curse
(10·14·14) 866

אוּלַי 27 perhaps (5·45) 19

יָשַׁר to be pleasing, right, agreeable
(1·13·25) 448

קבב to utter a curse against, curse
(10·14·14) 866

נשקף 28 to overhang, look out and down
(2·10·22) 1054

יְשִׁימוֹן wilderness (2·13) 445

בָּזֶה 29 in this [place], here (5·19) 261

Chapter 24

טוֹב 1 to be pleasing (3·18·21) 373

נַחַשׁ divination (2·2) 638

מָשָׁל 3 proverb (7·39) 605

שׁתם to open [dub.] (2·2·2) 1060

אֱמֶר 4 word (2·48) 56

מַחֲזֶה vision (2·4) 303

שַׁדַּי name of God (2·48) 994

טוֹב 5 to be pleasant, delightful (3·18·21)
373

גַּנָּה 6 garden (1·16) 171

אֲהָלִים odoriferous trees, perh. aloes (1·4) 14

נזל 7 to flow (1·8·9) 633

דְּלִי bucket (1·2) 194

תּוֹעָפָה 8 eminence (2·4) 419

רְאֵם wild ox (2·9) 910

גרם to break bones, break (1·2·3[?]) 175

מָחַץ to shatter (2·14·14) 563

כָּרַע 9 to bow down (1·29·35) 502

אֲרִי lion (2·35) 71

לָבִיא lioness (2·11) 522

סָפַק 10 to clap (1·6·6[?]) 706

קבב to utter a curse against, curse
(10·14·14) 866

מָנַע 11 to hold back (1·25·29) 586

מָלֵא 13 fulness (2·38) 571

מָשָׁל 15 proverb (7·39) 605

שׁתם to open [dub.] (2·2·2) 1060

אֱמֶר 16 word (2·48) 56

מַחֲזֶה vision (2·4) 303

שַׁדַּי name of God (2·48) 994

שׁור 17 to behold (2·16·16) 1003

כּוֹכָב star (1·37) 456

מָחַץ to shatter (2·14·14) 563

קַרְקַר hairy crown, scalp (1·1) 903

שֵׁת [battle] din (1·1) 981

יְרֵשָׁה 18 possession (2·2) 440

רדה 19 to have dominion, rule, dominate
(1·22·23) 921

שָׂרִיד survivor (2·28) 975

מָשָׁל 20 proverb (7·39) 605

אֹבֵד destruction (2·2) 2

עֲדֵי even to (2·11) 723

מָשָׁל 21 proverb (7·39) 605

עֲדֵי even to (2·11) 723

אֵיתָן enduring, firm (1·14) 450

מוֹשָׁב dwelling place (4·43) 444

קֵן nest (1·13) 890

בָּעַר 22 to devour, burn (1·26·28[?]) 129

שבה to take captive (3·29·37) 985

מָשָׁל 23 proverb (7·39) 605

אוֹי Woe! Alas! (2·24) 17

אֵל these (1·10[?]) 41

צִי 24 ship (1·4) 850

עֲדֵי even to (2·11) 723

אֹבֵד destruction (2·2) 2

Chapter 25

צמד 3 to join or attach oneself (2·3·5) 855

הוֹקִיעַ 4 to crucify [dub.]; some solemn form
of execution (1·3·8) 429

חָרוֹן [burning of] anger (2·41) 354

צָמַד 5 to join or attach oneself (2·3·5) 855

רֹמַח 7 spear, lance (1·15) 942

קֻבָּה 8 large vaulted tent (1·1) 866

דָּקַר to pierce, pierce through (1·7·11) 201

קֵבָה stomach, belly (1·2) 867

נֶעְצַר to be restrained, be retained (3·10·46) 783

מַגֵּפָה plague (9·26) 620

מַגֵּפָה 9 plague (9·26) 620

קִנֵּא 11 to be jealous of (6·30·34) 888

קִנְאָה jealousy (9·43) 888

כְּהֻנָּה 13 priesthood (6·13) 464

קִנֵּא to be jealous of (6·30·34) 888

אֻמָּה 15 tribe, people (1·3) 52

צָרַר 17 to show hostility towards, vex (4·10·10) 865

צָרַר 18 to show hostility towards, vex (4·10·10) 865

נֵכֶל knavery (1·1) 647

נִכֵּל to beguile (1·1·4) 647

מַגֵּפָה plague (9·26) 620

מַגֵּפָה 19 plague (9·26) 620

Chapter 26

קָרִיא 9 called, summoned (2·2) 896

הִצָּיה to engage in a struggle (2·3·8) 663

בָּלַע 10 to swallow up (4·20·41) 118

נֵס warning (3·21) 651

הַמְעִיט 54 to make small (4·13·22) 589

Chapter 27

נוֹעַד 3 to assemble by appointment (6·18·18) 416

חֵטְא guilt of sin, sin (4·33) 307

נִגְרַע 4 to be withdrawn (5·7·22) 175

שְׁאֵר 11 flesh relation (1·17) 984

עַם 13 kinsman (4·34) 769

מָרָה 14 to be stubborn (3·21·43) 598

מְרִיבָה strife, contention (1·2) 937

סָמַךְ 18 to lay (4·41·48) 701

הוֹד 20 majesty, splendor (1·24) 217

אוּר 21 Urim (1·7) 22

סָמַךְ 23 to lay (4·41·48) 701

Chapter 28

נִיחֹחַ 2 soothing (18·43) 629

אֵיפָה 5 ephah, quantity of wheat, barley = 10 omers (2·38) 35

בָּלַל to mix (26·42·42[?]) 117

כָּתִית beaten (1·5) 510

הִין hin, a liquid measure (11·22) 228

נִיחֹחַ 6 soothing (18·43) 629

הִין 7 hin, a liquid measure (11·22) 228

הִסִּיךְ to pour out (1·13·24) 650

שֵׁכָר intoxicating drink, strong drink (3·23) 1016

נִיחֹחַ 8 soothing (18·43) 629

עִשָּׂרוֹן 9 tenth part (27·33) 798

בָּלַל to mix (26·42·42[?]) 117

עִשָּׂרוֹן 12 tenth part (27·33) 798

בָּלַל to mix (26·42·42[?]) 117

עִשָּׂרוֹן 13 tenth part (27·33) 798

בָּלַל to mix (26·42·42[?]) 117

נִיחֹחַ soothing (18·43) 629

הִין 14 hin, a liquid measure (11·22) 228

פֶּסַח 16 festival of the passover (11·49) 820

מִקְרָא 18 convocation (7·22) 896

בָּלַל 20 to mix (26·42·42[?]) 117

עִשָּׂרוֹן tenth part (27·33) 798

עִשָּׂרוֹן 21 tenth part (27·33) 798

מִלְּבַד 23 besides (15·33) 94

נִיחֹחַ 24 soothing (18·43) 629

מִקְרָא 25 convocation (7·22) 896

בִּכּוּרִים 26 firstfruits (3·17) 114

שָׁבוּעַ week (1·20) 988

מִקְרָא convocation (7·22) 896
נִיחֹחַ 27 soothing (18·43) 629
בָּלַל 28 to mix (26·42·42[?]) 117
עִשָּׂרוֹן tenth part (27·33) 798
עִשָּׂרוֹן 29 tenth part (27·33) 798
מִלְּבַד 31 besides (15·33) 94

Chapter 29

מִקְרָא 1 convocation (7·22) 896
תְּרוּעָה blast [for march] (6·36) 929
נִיחֹחַ 2 soothing (18·43) 629
בָּלַל 3 to mix (26·42·42[?]) 117
עִשָּׂרוֹן tenth part (27·33) 798
עִשָּׂרוֹן 4 tenth part (27·33) 798
מִלְּבַד 6 besides (15·33) 94
נִיחֹחַ soothing (18·43) 629
עָשׂוֹר 7 tenth day (1·15) 797
מִקְרָא convocation (7·22) 896
נִיחֹחַ 8 soothing (18·43) 629
בָּלַל 9 to mix (26·42·42[?]) 117
עִשָּׂרוֹן tenth part (27·33) 798
עִשָּׂרוֹן 10 tenth part (27·33) 798
מִלְּבַד 11 besides (15·33) 94
כִּפֻּרִים atonement (2·8) 498
מִקְרָא 12 convocation (7·22) 896
חגג to keep a pilgrim feast (1·16·16) 290
נִיחֹחַ 13 soothing (18·43) 629
בָּלַל 14 to mix (26·42·42[?]) 117
עִשָּׂרוֹן tenth part (27·33) 798
עִשָּׂרוֹן 15 tenth part (27·33) 798
מִלְּבַד 16 besides (15·33) 94
מִלְּבַד 19 besides (15·33) 94
מִלְּבַד 22 besides (15·33) 94
מִלְּבַד 25 besides (15·33) 94
מִלְּבַד 28 besides (15·33) 94
מִלְּבַד 31 besides (15·33) 94
מִלְּבַד 34 besides (15·33) 94

עֲצֶרֶת 35 assembly (1·11) 783
נִיחֹחַ 36 soothing (18·43) 629
מִלְּבַד 38 besides (15·33) 94
נְדָבָה 39 freewill offering (3·27) 621

Chapter 30

נדר 3 to vow (7·30·30) 623
שְׁבוּעָה oath (5·30) 989
אִסָּר binding obligation (11·11) 64
נדר 4 to vow (7·30·30) 623
אִסָּר binding obligation (11·11) 64
נְעוּרִים youth (2·46) 655
הֶחֱרִישׁ 5 to be silent (6·38·46) 361
אִסָּר binding obligation (11·11) 64
הֵנִיא 6 to restrain (6·8·8) 626
אִסָּר binding obligation (11·11) 64
סלח to forgive (5·33·46) 699
מִבְטָא 7 rash utterance (2·2) 105
הֶחֱרִישׁ 8 to be silent (6·38·46) 361
אִסָּר binding obligation (11·11) 64
הֵנִיא 9 to restrain (6·8·8) 626
הֵפֵר to make ineffectual, annul (6·41·44) 830
מִבְטָא rash utterance (2·2) 105
סלח to forgive (5·33·46) 699
גרש 10 to drive out (1·8·47) 176
נָדַר 11 to vow (7·30·30) 623
אִסָּר binding obligation (11·11) 64
שְׁבוּעָה oath (5·30) 989
הֶחֱרִישׁ 12 to be silent (6·38·46) 361
הֵנִיא to restrain (6·8·8) 626
אִסָּר binding obligation (11·11) 64
הֵפֵר 13 to make ineffectual, annul (6·41·44) 830
מוֹצָא that which goes forth (3·37) 425
אִסָּר binding obligation (11·11) 64
סלח to forgive (5·33·46) 699
שְׁבוּעָה 14 oath (5·30) 989

אָסָּר binding obligation (11·11) 64

הֵפֵר to make ineffectual, annul (6·41·44) 830

הֶחֱרִישׁ 15 to be silent (5·38·46) 361

אִסָּר binding obligation (11·11) 64

הֵפֵר 16 to make ineffectual, annul (6·41·44) 830

נְעוּרִים 17 youth (2·46) 655

Chapter 31

נקם 2 to avenge (1·13·34) 667

נְקָמָה vengence (2·27) 668

עַם kinsman (4·34) 769

נֶחֱלַץ 3 to be equipped (3·7·27) 323

נְקָמָה vengence (2·27) 668

נמסר 5 to be delivered over (1·1·2) 588

אֶלֶף thousand (4·12[?]) 48

חָלוּץ equipped (6·17[?]) 323

חֲצֹצְרָה 6 clarion (5·29) 348

תְּרוּעָה blast [for march] (6·36) 929

צבא 7 to wage war, fight (4·12·14) 838

שׁבה 9 to take captive (3·29·37) 985

טַף children (10·41) 381

בָּזַז to spoil, plunder (3·37·40) 102

מוֹשָׁב 10 dwelling place (4·43) 444

טִירָה encampment (1·7) 377

מַלְקוֹחַ 11 booty (5·7) 544

שְׁבִי 12 captivity, captives (4·46) 985

מַלְקוֹחַ booty (5·7) 544

קָצַף 14 to be wroth (2·28·34) 893

נְקֵבָה 15 female (2·22) 666

מסר 16 to offer (1·1·2) 588

מַגֵּפָה plague (9·26) 620

טַף 17 children (10·41) 381

מִשְׁכָּב act of lying [sexually] (3·46) 1012

טַף 18 children (10·41) 381

מִשְׁכָּב act of lying [sexually] (3·46) 1012

שְׁבִי 19 captivity, captives (4·46) 985

בְּדִיל 22 tin, alloy (1·5) 95

עֹפֶרֶת lead (1·9) 780

נִדָּה 23 impurity (6·30) 622

מַלְקוֹחַ 26 booty (5·7) 544

שְׁבִי captivity, captives (4·46) 985

חָצָה 27 to divide (2·11·15) 345

מַלְקוֹחַ booty (5·7) 544

מֶכֶס 28 tax (6·6) 493

מַחֲצִית 29 half (4·16) 345

מַחֲצִית 30 half (4·16) 345

מַלְקוֹחַ 32 booty (5·7) 544

בַּז spoil, plunder (3·27) 103

בָּזַז to spoil, plunder (3·37·40) 102

מִשְׁכָּב 35 act of lying [sexually] (3·46) 1012

מֶחֱצָה 36 half (2·2) 345

מֶכֶס 37 tax (6·6) 493

מֶכֶס 38 tax (6·6) 493

מֶכֶס 39 tax (6·6) 493

מֶכֶס 40 tax (6·6) 493

מֶכֶס 41 tax (6·6) 493

מַחֲצִית 42 half (4·16) 345

חָצָה to divide (2·11·15) 345

צבא to wage war, fight (4·12·14) 838

מֶחֱצָה 43 half (2·2) 345

מֶחֱצִית 47 half (4·16) 345

אֶצְעָדָה 50 armlet band clasping upper arm (1·2) 858

צָמִיד bracelet (1·6) 855

טַבַּעַת ring (1·44) 371

עָגִיל hoop, ring (1·2) 722

כּוּמָז name of a golden ornament (1·2) 484

בָּזַז 53 to spoil, plunder (3·37·40) 102

זִכָּרוֹן 54 memorial, reminder (5·24) 272

Chapter 32

עָצוּם 1 mighty [strong] (3·31) 783

פֹּה 6 here, hither (3·44) 805

הֵנִיא	7 to restrain (6·8·8) 626	
הֵנִיא	9 to restrain (6·8·8) 626	
בִּלְתִּי	12 except (3·24) 116	
הֵנִיע	13 to cause to wander (1·14·36) 631	
תַּרְבּוּת	14 increase, brood (1·1) 916	
חַטָּא	sinner; sinful (3·19) 308	
ספה	to add (1·8·18) 705	
חָרוֹן	anger (2·41) 354	
גְּדֵרָה	16 wall, hedge (3·8) 155	
פֹּה	here, hither (3·44) 805	
טַף	children (10·41) 381	
נֶחֱלַץ	17 to be equipped (3·7·22) 323	
חוש	to make haste (1·15·21) 301	
טַף	children (10·41) 381	
מִבְצָר	fortification (3·37) 131	
הָלְאָה	19 forwards (3·13) 229	
נֶחֱלַץ	20 to be equipped (3·7·27) 323	
חָלוּץ	21 warrior, equipped one (6·17[?]) 323	
נכבש	22 to be subdued (2·5·14) 461	
נָקִי	exempt (1·43) 667	
טַף	24 children (10·41) 381	
גְּדֵרָה	wall, hedge (3·8) 155	
צֹנֶה	flocks, sf. צנאכם (1·2) 856	
טַף	26 children (10·41) 381	
חָלוּץ	27 warrior, equipped one (6·17[?]) 323	
חָלוּץ	29 warrior, equipped one (6·17[?]) 323	
נכבש	to be subdued (2·5·14) 461	
חָלוּץ	30 warrior, equipped one (6·17[?]) 323	
חָלוּץ	32 warrior, equipped one (6·17[?]) 323	
גְּבוּלָה	33 border, boundary (3·10) 148	
מִבְצָר	36 fortification (3·37) 131	
גְּדֵרָה	wall, hedge (3·8) 155	
חַוָּה	41 tent village (2·7) 295	

Chapter 33

מַסַּע	1 journey (7·12) 652	
מַסַּע	2 journey (7·12) 652	
מוֹצָא	place of going forth (3·27) 425	

מָחֳרָת	3 the morrow (4·32) 564	
פֶּסַח	festival of the passover (11·49) 820	
רָם	high, lifted, exalted (2·31[?]) 926	
שֶׁפֶט	4 judgement (1·16) 1048	
תָּמָר	9 palm tree, date palm (1·12) 1071	
מַשְׂכִּית	52 carved figure (1·6) 967	
צֶלֶם	image (1·17) 853	
מַסֵּכָה	molten image (1·25) 651	
הֶמְעִיט	54 to make diminish (4·13·22) 589	
שֵׂךְ	55 thorn (1·1) 968	
צָנִין	thorn, prick (1·2) 856	
צַד	side (1·31) 841	
צרר	to show hostility towards, vex (4·10·10) 865	
דמה	56 to intend, think (1·13·27) 197	

Chapter 34

גְּבוּלָה	2 border, boundary (3·10) 148	
מֶלַח	3 salt (3·28) 571	
קֶדֶם	eastward (8·26) 870	
מַעֲלֵה	4 ascent (1·19) 751	
עַקְרָב	scorpion (1·9) 785	
תּוֹצָאָה	outgoing, extremity (5·23) 426	
תּוֹצָאָה	5 outgoing, extremity (5·23) 426	
תאה	7 to mark out (2·2·2) 1060	
תאה	8 to mark out (2·2·2) 1060	
תּוֹצָאָה	outgoing, extremity (5·23) 426	
תּוֹצָאָה	9 outgoing, extremity (5·23) 426	
הִתְאַוָּה	10 to desire (3·16·27) 16	
קֶדֶם	eastward (8·26) 870	
מָחָה	11 to strike (1·1·1) 562	
קֶדֶם	eastward (8·26) 870	
תּוֹצָאָה	12 outgoing, extremity (5·23) 426	
מֶלַח	salt (3·28) 571	
גְּבוּלָה	border, boundary (3·10) 148	
קֶדֶם	15 eastward (8·26) 870	

Chapter 35

רְכוּשׁ	3 property, goods (2·28) 940
קֵדֶם	5 eastward (8·26) 870
מִקְלָט	6 refuge (11·20) 886
רָצַח	to murder, slay (18·38·43) 953
הַמְעִיט	8 to make diminish (4·13·22) 589
כְּפִי	according to (5·16) 804
הִקְרָה	11 to select as suitable (1·3·27) 899
מִקְלָט	refuge (11·20) 886
רָצַח	to murder, slay (18·38·43) 953
שְׁגָגָה	sin of error, inadvertence (9·19) 993
מִקְלָט	12 refuge (11·20) 886
גֹּאֵל	kinsman (8·44[?]) 145
רָצַח	to murder, slay (18·38·43) 953
מִקְלָט	13 refuge (11·20) 886
מִקְלָט	14 refuge (11·20) 886
תּוֹשָׁב	15 sojourner (1·14) 444
מִקְלָט	refuge (11·20) 886
שְׁגָגָה	sin of error, inadvertence (9·19) 993
רָצַח	16 to murder, slay (18·38·43) 953
רָצַח	17 to murder, slay (18·38·43) 953
רָצַח	18 to murder, slay (18·38·43) 953
גֹּאֵל	19 kinsman (8·44[?]) 145
רָצַח	to murder, slay (18·38·43) 953
פָּגַע	to meet, light upon (2·40·46) 803
שֹׂנְאָה	20 hating, hatred (1·17) 971
הֲדָף	to push, thrust (2·11·11) 213
צְדִיָּה	lying-in-wait (2·2) 841
אֵיבָה	21 personal hostility (2·5) 33
רָצַח	to murder, slay (18·38·43) 953
גֹּאֵל	kinsman (8·44[?]) 145

פָּגַע	to meet, light upon (2·40·46) 803
פֶּתַע	22 suddenness (2·7) 837
בְּלֹא	without (3·29) 518
אֵיבָה	personal hostility (2·5) 33
הֲדָף	to push, thrust (2·11·11) 213
צְדִיָּה	lying-in-wait (2·2) 841
בְּלֹא	23 without (3·29) 518
גֹּאֵל	24 kinsman (8·44[?]) 145
רָצַח	25 to murder, slay (18·38·43) 953
גֹּאֵל	kinsman (8·44[?]) 145
מִקְלָט	refuge (11·20) 886
רָצַח	26 to murder, slay (18·38·43) 953
מִקְלָט	refuge (11·20) 886
גֹּאֵל	27 kinsman (8·44[?]) 145
מִקְלָט	refuge (11·20) 886
רָצַח	to murder, slay (18·38·43) 953
מִקְלָט	28 refuge (11·20) 886
רָצַח	to murder, slay (18·38·43) 953
מוֹשָׁב	29 dwelling place (4·43) 444
רָצַח	30 to murder, slay (18·38·43) 953
כֹּפֶר	31 ransom (2·13) 497
רָצַח	to murder, slay (18·38·43) 953
כֹּפֶר	32 ransom (2·13) 497
מִקְלָט	refuge (11·20) 886
הֶחֱנִיף	33 to pollute (2·4·10) 337

Chapter 36

נִגְרַע	3 to be withdrawn (5·7·22) 175
יֹבֵל	4 ram (1·27) 385
נִגְרַע	to be withdrawn (5·7·22) 175

DEUTERONOMY

Chapter 1

מוֹל 1 in front of (1·1) 557

הוֹאִיל 5 to undertake to do (1·18·18) 383

בֵּאֵר   to make plain (2·3·3) 91

שָׁכֵן 7 neighbor (1·20) 1015

שְׁפֵלָה   lowland (1·20) 1050

חוֹף   shore, coast (1·7) 342

כּוֹכָב 10 star (4·37) 456

אֵיכָה 12 in what manner (5·18) 32

טֹרַח   burden (1·2) 382

יהב 13 to give, provide (2·31·31) 396

נָבוֹן   discerning (2·21) 106

שֹׁטֵר 15 official, officer (7·25) 1009

הִכִּיר 17 to regard (4·37·40) 647

גּוּר   to dread, be afraid of (3·10·10) 158

קשׁה   to be hard, difficult (2·5·28) 904

נוֹרָא 19 dreadful (6·44) 431

חָפַר 22 to search out (2·22·22) 343

רגל 24 to go about as explorer, spy (1·14·16) 920

המרה 26 to show rebelliousness (6·22·43) 598

נרגן 27 to murmur (1·2·3) 920

שְׂנְאָה   hating, hatred (2·17) 971

אָנָה 28 whence? whither? (1·39) 33

המסיס   to cause to melt (1·1·20) 587

רָם   high, i.e., tall (7·31[?]) 926

בָּצוּר   made inaccessible, fortified (4·25) 130

ערץ 29 to tremble (4·11·14) 792

תּוּר 33 to seek out, select (1·19·22) 1064

קָצַף 34 to be wroth (2·28·34) 893

זוּלָה 36 with the exception of (2·16) 265

הִתְאַנַּף 37 be angry (4·6·14) 60

בִּגְלַל   on account of (3·10) 164

טַף 39 children (7·41) 381

בַּז   spoil, plunder (1·27) 103

חָגַר 41 to gird on (1·44·44) 291

ההין   to be easy (1·1·1) 223

נִגַּף 42 to be smitten (3·23·48) 619

המרה 43 to show rebelliousness (6·22·43) 598

הזיד   to act presumptuously (3·8·10) 267

דְּבוֹרָה 44 bee (1·4) 184

הכתית   to beat in pieces (1·2·17) 510

הֶאֱזִין 45 to give ear, listen (2·41·41) 24

Chapter 2

התגרה 5 to excite oneself, engage in strife with (4·11·14) 173

יְרֵשָׁה   possession, inheritance (7·14) 440

אֹכֶל 6 food (3·44) 38

שׁבר   to buy grain (1·16·21) 991

כרה   to get by trade (1·4·4) 500

חָסֵר 7 to lack, decrease (3·20·24) 341

צור 9 to show hostility, to treat as foe (2·5·5) 849

התגרה   to excite oneself, engage in strife with (4·11·14) 173

יְרֵשָׁה   possession, inheritance (7·14) 440

רָם 10 high, i.e., tall (7·31[?]) 926

יְרֵשָׁה 12 possession, inheritance (7·14) 440

הָמַם 15 to confuse, discomfit (1·13·13) 243

מוּל 19 in front of (5·25) 557

צור   to show hostility to, to treat as foe (2·5·5) 849

התגרה   to excite oneself, engage in strife with (4·11·14) 173

יְרֵשָׁה   possession, inheritance (7·14) 440

התגרה 24 to excite oneself, engage in strife with (4·11·14) 173

פַּחַד 25 dread (3·49) 808

שֵׁמַע   hearing, report (1·17) 1034

רָגַז	to quake (1·30·41) 919		אָשֵׁד	mountain slope (2·7) 78
חִיל	to writhe (1·29·46) 296		חָלוּץ	18 equipped (1·17[?]) 323
הִשְׁבִּיר	28 to sell grain (1·5·21) 991		טַף	19 children (7·41) 381
הִקְשָׁה	30 to make stiff, stubborn (2·21·28) 904		יְרֻשָּׁה	20 possession, inheritance (7·14) 440
אמץ	to harden, make obstinate (3·19·41) 54		גֹּדֶל	24 greatness, magnificence (6·14) 152
הֶחֱרִים	34 to devote to destruction (6·46·49) 355		הִתְעַבֵּר	26 to put oneself in a fury, become furious (1·8·8) 720
מַת	man (6·21) 607		תֵּימָן	27 south, southern quarter (1·24) 412
טַף	children (7·41) 381		אמץ	28 to make firm, strengthen, harden (3·19·41) 54
שָׂרִיד	survivor (2·28) 975		גַּיְא	29 valley (3·47) 161
בָּזַז	35 to plunder (3·37·40) 102		מוּל	in front of (5·25) 557
קִרְיָה	36 town, city (2·30) 900			
שָׂגַב	to be high (1·2·20) 960			
אֹכֶל	38 food (3·44) 38			

Chapter 4

גרע	2 to diminish (2·14·22) 175
דָּבֵק	4 clinging (1·3) 180
בִּינָה	6 understanding (1·37) 108
נָבוֹן	discerning (2·21) 106

Chapter 3

בִּלְתִּי	3 except, besides that[?] (1·24) 116
שָׂרִיד	survivor (2·28) 975
קִרְיָה	4 town, city (2·30) 900
חֶבֶל	lot, region (4·49) 286
בָּצוּר	5 made inaccessible, fortified (4·25) 130
גָּבֹהַּ	high (2·41) 147
בְּרִיחַ	bar (1·41) 138
פְּרָזִי	hamlet dweller (1·3) 826
הֶחֱרִים	6 to devote to destruction (6·46·49) 355
מַת	man (6·21) 607
טַף	children (7·41) 381
בָּזַז	7 to plunder (3·37·40) 102
מִישׁוֹר	10 tableland (2·23) 449
עֶרֶשׂ	11 couch, divan (2·10) 793
חֶבֶל	13 region, lot (4·49) 286
חֶבֶל	14 region, lot (4·49) 286
חַוָּה	tent village (1·7) 295
מֶלַח	17 salt (2·28) 571

הִקְהִיל	10 to summon an assembly (3·20·39) 874
עֲרָפֶל	11 heavy cloud (2·15) 791
תְּמוּנָה	12 form, semblance (6·10) 568
זוּלָה	except, only (2·16) 265
לוּחַ	13 tablet (16·40) 531
תְּמוּנָה	15 form, semblance (6·10) 568
פֶּסֶל	16 idol, image (5·31) 820
תְּמוּנָה	form, semblance (6·10) 568
סֶמֶל	image (1·5) 702
תַּבְנִית	figure, image (5·20) 125
נְקֵבָה	female (1·22) 666
תַּבְנִית	17 figure, image (5·20) 125
צִפּוֹר	bird[s] (3·40) 861
עוּף	to fly (1·18·25) 733
תַּבְנִית	18 figure, image (5·20) 125
רמשׂ	to creep (1·16·16) 942
דָּגָה	fish [coll.] (1·15) 185
יָרֵחַ	19 moon (2·27) 437
כּוֹכָב	star (4·37) 456

נדח to be thrust aside (4·13·43) 623

כּוּר 20 furnace (1·8) 468

הִתְאַנַּף 21 to be angry (4·6·14) 60

פֶּסֶל 23 idol, image (5·31) 820

תְּמוּנָה likeness, representation (6·10) 568

קַנָּא 24 jealous (3·6) 888

נוֹשַׁן 25 to be old (1·3·3[?]) 445

פֶּסֶל idol, image (5·31) 820

תְּמוּנָה likeness, representation (6·10) 568

הֵעִיד 26 to call as witness (5·39·44) 729

הֶאֱרִיךְ to prolong (11·31·34) 73

מַת 27 man (6·21) 607

נָהַג to lead off (2·10·30) 624

הֵרִיחַ 28 to smell (1·11·14) 926

רַחוּם 31 compassionate (1·13) 933

הרפה to abandon, forsake (4·21·44) 951

לְמִן 32 from (2·14) 583

בָּרָא to create (1·38·48) 135

נִסָּה 34 to try (8·36·36) 650

מַסָּה trial (3·3) 650

מוֹפֵת sign (9·36) 68

מוֹרָא awe-inspiring spectacular deed (4·12) 432

מִלְּבַד 35 besides (2·33) 94

יִסַּר 36 to discipline (5·30·41) 415

בִּפְנֵי 37 in the face of (4·17) 816

עָצוּם 38 mighty [strong] (6·31) 783

מִמַּעַל 39 above, on the top of (2·29) 751

הֶאֱרִיךְ 40 to prolong (11·31·34) 73

הִבְדִּיל 41 to separate, make a division between (6·32·42) 95

רָצַח 42 to murder, slay (7·38·43) 953

בִּבְלִי without (2·5) 115

שֹׂנֵא enemy (9·41) 971

תְּמוֹל aforetime (3·23) 1069

שִׁלְשׁוֹם aforetime, previously (3·25) 1026

אֵל these (3·10) 41

מִישׁוֹר 43 tableland (2·23) 449

עֵדָה 45 testimony (3·32) 730

גַּיְא 46 valley (3·47) 161

מוּל in front of (5·25) 557

אַשֵּׁד 49 mountain slope (2·7) 78

Chapter 5

פֹּה 3 here, hither (4·44) 805

בִּפְנֵי 4 in the face of (5·17) 816

פֶּסֶל 8 idol, image (5·31) 820

תְּמוּנָה likeness, representation (6·10) 568

מִמַּעַל 8 above, on the top of (2·29) 751

קַנָּא 9 jealous (3·6) 888

שִׁלֵּשִׁים pertaining to the third (1·5) 1026

רִבֵּעַ pertaining to the fourth (1·4) 918

אֹהֵב 10 friend (2·36[?]) 12

נִקָּה 11 to leave unpunished (1·12·36) 667

הֶאֱרִיךְ 16 to prolong (11·31·34) 73

רָצַח 17 to murder, slay (7·38·43) 953

נָאַף 18 to commit adultery (1·16·30) 610

גָּנַב 19 to steal, take by stealth (2·30·39) 170

חָמַד 21 to desire (2·16·21) 326

הִתְאַוָּה to desire, long for (1·16·27) 16

עֲרָפֶל 22 heavy cloud (2·15) 791

לוּחַ tablet (16·40) 531

גֹּדֶל 24 greatness (6·24) 152

פֹּה 31 here, hither (4·44) 805

הֶאֱרִיךְ 33 to prolong (11·31·34) 73

Chapter 6

הֶאֱרִיךְ 2 to prolong (11·31·34) 73

זָב 3 to flow (6·29·29) 264

חָלָב milk (8·44) 316

שִׁנֵּן 7 to teach incisively (1·1·9) 1041

קָשַׁר 8 to bind, confine (2·36·44) 905

טוֹטָפוֹת bands (2·3) 377

מְזוּזָה 9 doorpost (2·20) 265

107

טוֹב 11 good things, goods, property (2·32) 375

חָצֵב to hew out, dig (3·14·17) 345

זַיִת olive, olive tree (5·38) 268

קַנָּא 15 jealous (3·6) 888

נִסָּה 16 to test (8·36·36) 650

עֵדָה 17 testimony (3·32) 730

הָדַף 19 to thrust out (2·11·11) 213

עֵדָה 20 testimony (3·32) 730

מוֹפֵת 22 sign (9·36) 68

פֹּה 28 here, hither (4·44) 805

Chapter 7

נָשַׁל 1 to clear away (4·6·7) 675

עָצוּם mighty [strong] (6·31) 783

הֶחֱרִים 2 to devote to destruction (6·46·49) 355

הִתְחַתֵּן 3 to form a marriage alliance with (1·11·11) 368

נָתַץ 5 to tear down (1·31·42) 683

מַצֵּבָה pillar (3·35) 663

אֲשֵׁירָה a sacred pole, symbol of Canaanite goddess (3·40) 81

גִּדֵּעַ to hew down (2·9·22) 154

פָּסִיל idol, image (3·23) 820

סְגֻלָּה 6 property (3·8) 688

רבב 7 to be, become many (1·23·24) 912

חָשַׁק to love (3·8·11) 365

שְׁבוּעָה 8 oath (1·30) 989

אֹהֵב 9 friend (2·36[?]) 36

שֹׂנֵא 10 enemy (9·41) 971

אֵחַר keep back, bring late (2·15·17) 29

עֵקֶב 12 because of (2·15) 784

דָּגָן 13 grain (7·40) 186

תִּירוֹשׁ fresh or new wine (7·38) 440

יִצְהָר fresh oil (6·23) 844

שֶׁגֶר offspring, young [of beasts] (4·5) 993

אֶלֶף cattle (4·8) 48

עַשְׁתְּרוֹת ewes, young (4·4) 300

עָקָר 14 barren (1·11) 785

חֲלִי 15 sickness (3·24) 318

מַדְוֶה sickness (2·2) 188

שֹׂנֵא enemy (9·41) 971

חוס 16 to pity (5·24·24) 299

מוֹקֵשׁ lure (1·27) 430

אֵיכָה 17 in what manner (5·18) 32

מַסָּה 19 trial (3·3) 650

מוֹפֵת sign (9·36) 68

צִרְעָה 20 hornets (1·3) 864

ערץ 21 to tremble (4·11·14) 792

נוֹרָא dreadful (6·44) 431

נָשַׁל 22 to clear away (4·6·7) 675

אֵל these (3·10) 41

הום to discomfit (1·1·6) 223

מְהוּמָה 23 discomfiture (2·12) 223

הִתְיַצֵּב 24 to hold one's ground, to take one's stand (5·48·48) 426

בִּפְנֵי in the face of (5·17) 816

פָּסִיל 25 idol, image (3·23) 820

חמד to desire (2·16·21) 326

נוקש to be ensnared (1·4·8) 430

חֵרֶם 26 ban, devoted thing (3·29) 356

שִׁקֵּץ to detest (1·6·6) 1055

תעב to regard as an abomination, abhor (3·14·21) 1073

Chapter 8

נִסָּה 2 to test (8·36·36) 650

הִרְעִיב 3 to allow to be hungry (1·2·14) 944

מָן manna (2·14) 577

מוֹצָא that which goes forth [of mouth, i.e., utterance] (2·27) 425

שִׂמְלָה 4 wrapper, mantle (6·29) 971

בלה become old and worn out (3·11·16) 115

בָּצֵק to swell, blister (1·2·2) 130

יִסַּר 5 to discipline (5·30·41) 415

תְּהוֹם 7 deep, sea, abyss (2·36) 1062

בִּקְעָה valley, plain (3·19) 132

חִטָּה 8 wheat (2·30) 334

שְׂעֹרָה barley (1·34) 972

תְּאֵנָה fig tree, fig (1·39) 1061

רִמּוֹן pomegranate (1·32) 941

זַיִת olive, olive tree (5·38) 268

מִסְכֵּנוּת 9 poverty (1·1) 587

חָסֵר to lack, decrease (3·20·24) 341

חָצֵב to hew out, dig (3·14·17) 345

נוֹרָא 15 dreadful (6·44) 431

נָחָשׁ serpent (1·31) 638

שָׂרָף fiery serpent (1·7) 977

עַקְרָב scorpion (1·9) 785

צִמָּאוֹן thirsty ground (1·3) 855

חַלָּמִישׁ flint (2·5) 321

מָן 16 manna (2·14) 577

נִסָּה to test (8·36·36) 650

עֹצֶם might (1·4) 782

הֵעִיד 19 to testify (5·39·44) 729

עֵקֶב 20 because of (2·15) 784

Chapter 9

עָצוּם 1 mighty [strong] (6·31) 783

בָּצוּר made inaccessible, fortified (4·25) 130

רָם 2 high, i.e., tall (7·31[?]) 926

הִתְיַצֵּב to hold one's ground, take one's stand (3·48·48) 426

הִכְנִיעַ 3 to subdue (1·11·36) 488

הָדַף 4 to thrust out (2·11·11) 213

רִשְׁעָה wickedness (3·15) 958

יֹשֶׁר rightness, uprightness (1·14) 449

רִשְׁעָה wickedness (3·15) 958

קָשֶׁה 6 stiff, stubborn (4·36) 904

עֹרֶף neck (4·33) 791

הִקְצִיף 7 to provoke to wrath (3·5·34) 893

לְמִן from (2·14) 583

הִמְרָה to show rebelliousness (6·22·43) 598

הִקְצִיף 8 to provoke to wrath (3·5·34) 893

הִתְאַנַּף to be angry (4·6·14) 60

לוּחַ 9 tablet (16·40) 531

לוּחַ 10 tablet (16·40) 531

אֶצְבַּע finger (1·31) 840

לוּחַ 11 tablet (16·40) 531

מַסֵּכָה 12 molten image (3·25) 651

קָשֶׁה 13 stiff, stubborn (4·36) 904

עֹרֶף neck (4·33) 791

הִרְפָּה 14 to refrain, let alone (4·21·44) 951

מָחָה to blot out (3·22·25) 562

עָצוּם mighty [strong] (6·31) 783

לוּחַ 15 tablet (16·40) 531

עֵגֶל 16 calf (2·35) 722

מַסֵּכָה molten metal (3·25) 651

לוּחַ 17 tablet (16·40) 531

יָגֹר 19 to be afraid (2·5·5) 388

קָצַף to be wroth (2·28·34) 893

הִתְאַנַּף 20 be angry (4·6·14) 60

עֵגֶל 21 calf (2·35) 722

כָּתַת to crush (1·5·17) 510

טָחַן to grind (1·7·7) 377

דָּקַק to crush, thresh (1·4·13) 200

הִקְצִיף 22 to provoke to wrath (3·5·34) 893

הִמְרָה 23 to show rebelliousness (6·22·43) 598

הִמְרָה 24 to show rebelliousness (6·22·43) 598

גֹּדֶל 26 greatness (6·14) 152

קְשִׁי 27 stubborness (1·1) 904

רֶשַׁע wickedness (1·30) 957

מִבְּלִי 28 from want of (2·25) 115

שִׂנְאָה hating, hatred (2·17) 971

109

Chapter 10

פֶּסֶל	1 to hew out (2·6·6) 820
לוּחַ	tablet (16·40) 531
לוּחַ	2 tablet (16·40) 531
שִׁטִּים	3 acacia (1·28) 1008
פֶּסֶל	to hew out (2·6·6) 820
לוּחַ	tablet (16·40) 531
לוּחַ	4 tablet (16·40) 531
מִכְתָּב	writing (3·9) 508
לוּחַ	5 tablet (16·40) 531
כֹּהֵן	6 to act as priest (1·23·23) 464
הִבְדִּיל	8 to separate, make a distinction between (6·32·42) 95
מַסַּע	11 journey (1·12) 652
הִנֵּה = הֵן	14
חָשַׁק	15 to love (3·8·11) 365
מוּל	16 to circumcise (2·12·29) 557
עָרְלָה	foreskin (1·16) 790
עֹרֶף	16 neck (4·33) 791
הִקְשָׁה	to make stiff, stubborn (2·21·28) 904
נוֹרָא	17 dreadful (6·44) 431
שֹׁחַד	bribe (4·23) 1005
יָתוֹם	18 orphan (11·42) 450
שִׂמְלָה	wrapper, mantle (6·29) 971
נוֹרָא	21 dreadful, wonderful thing (6·44) 431
כּוֹכָב	22 star (4·37) 456

Chapter 11

מוּסָר	2 correction (1·50) 416
גֹּדֶל	greatness (6·14) 152
הֵצִיף	4 to cause to overflow (1·2·3) 847
פָּצָה	6 to part, open (1·15·15) 822
בָּלַע	to swallow up, engulf (1·20·41) 118
יְקוּם	substance (1·3) 879
הֶאֱרִיךְ	9 to prolong (11·31·34) 73

זָב	to flow (6·29·29) 264
חָלָב	milk (8·44) 316
גַּן	10 garden, enclosure (1·41) 171
יָרָק	herbage (1·3) 438
בִּקְעָה	11 valley, plain (3·19) 132
מָטָר	rain (6·37) 564
מָטָר	14 rain (6·37) 564
יוֹרֶה	early rain (1·2) 435
מַלְקוֹשׁ	later rain (1·8) 545
דָּגָן	grain (7·40) 186
תִּירוֹשׁ	fresh or new wine (7·38) 440
יִצְהָר	fresh oil (6·23) 844
עֵשֶׂב	15 herb, herbage (3·33) 793
פָּתָה	16 to be enticed, deceived (1·5·27) 834
עָצַר	17 to restrain, refrain (2·36·46) 783
מָטָר	rain (6·37) 564
יְבוּל	produce (2·13) 385
מְהֵרָה	quickly, hastily (1·20) 555
קָשַׁר	18 to bind, confine (2·36·44) 905
טוֹטָפֹת	bands (2·3) 377
מְזוּזָה	20 doorpost (2·20) 265
עָצוּם	23 mighty [strong] (6·31) 783
הִתְיַצֵּב	25 to hold one's ground, take one's stand (5·48·48) 426
בִּפְנֵי	in the face of (5·17) 816
פַּחַד	dread (3·49) 808
מוֹרָא	fear (4·12) 432
קְלָלָה	26 curse (11·33) 887
קְלָלָה	28 curse (11·33) 887
קְלָלָה	29 curse (11·33) 887
מוּל	30 in front of (5·25) 557
אֵלוֹן	terebinth, tall tree (1·10) 18
מוֹרֶה	teacher (1·9) 435

Chapter 12

רָם	2 high, lifted, exalted (7·31[?]) 926
רַעֲנָן	luxuriant, fresh (1·19) 947

110

<table>
<tr><td>

נָתַץ 3 to tear down (1·6·42) 683

מַצֵּבָה pillar (3·35) 663

אֲשֵׁרָה a tree, symbol of Canaanite goddess (3·40) 81

פָּסִיל idol, image (3·23) 820

גִּדֵּעַ to hew down (2·9·22) 154

מַעֲשֵׂר 6 tithe (7·31) 798

נְדָבָה freewill offering (4·27) 621

מִשְׁלַח 7 outstretching (6·7) 1020

פֹּה 8 here, hither (4·44) 805

מְנוּחָה 9 resting-place (1·21) 629

בֶּטַח 10 securely (3·43) 105

מַעֲשֵׂר 11 tithe (7·31) 798

מִבְחָר choicest, best (1·12) 104

נָדַר to vow (5·30·30) 623

אַוָּה 15 desire, will (4·7) 16

צְבִי gazelle (4·11) 840

אַיָּל hart, deer (4·11) 19

מַעֲשֵׂר 17 tithe (7·31) 798

דָּגָן grain (7 40) 186

תִּירוֹשׁ fresh or new wine (7·38) 440

יִצְהָר fresh oil (6·23) 844

נָדַר to vow (5·30·30) 623

נְדָבָה freewill offering (4·27) 621

מִשְׁלַח 18 outstretching (6·7) 1020

הִרְחִיב 20 to enlarge (3·21·25) 931

אִוָּה to desire (2·11·27) 16

אַוָּה desire, will (4·7) 16

אַוָּה 21 desire, will (4·7) 16

צְבִי 22 gazelle (4·11) 840

אַיָּל hart, deer (4·11) 19

נָקַשׁ 30 to be thrust (1·1·5) 669

אֵיכָה in what manner (5·18) 32

Chapter 13

גרע 1 to diminish (2·14·22) 175

חלם 2 to dream (3·26·28) 321

מוֹפֵת sign (9·36) 68

</td><td>

מוֹפֵת 3 sign (9·36) 68

חלם 4 to dream (3·26·28) 321

נִסָּה to test (8·36·36) 650

חלם 6 to dream (3·26·28) 321

סָרָה apostasy (2·7) 694

הִדִּיחַ to thrust away (4·27·43) 623

הֵסִית 7 to instigate (1·18·18) 694

בִּעֵר to consume (12·26·28[?]) 129

חֵיק fold of garment at breast (5·38) 300

סֵתֶר 7 secrecy (4·35) 712

חוס 9 to pity (5·24·24) 299

חָמַל to spare (1·40·40) 328

בִּגְלַל 10 on account of (3·10) 164

סָקַל 11 to stone (4·12·22) 709

הִדִּיחַ to thrust away (4·27·43) 623

בְּלִיַּעַל 14 worthlessness (2·27) 116

הִדִּיחַ to thrust away (4·27·43) 623

חָקַר 15 to search [for] (1·22·27) 350

הֶחֱרִים 16 to devote to destruction (6·46·49) 355

רְחוֹב 17 broad open place, plaza (1·43) 932

כָּלִיל whole offering (2·15) 483

תֵּל mound (1·5) 1068

מְאוּמָה 18 anything (2·32) 548

חֵרֶם ban, devoted thing (3·29) 356

חָרוֹן [burning of] anger (1·41) 354

רַחֲמִים compassion (1·38) 933

רִחַם to have compassion (2·41·46) 933

Chapter 14

הִתְגֹּדֵד 1 to cut oneself (1·7·8) 151

קָרְחָה baldness, bald spot [made in mourning] (1·11) 901

סְגֻלָּה 2 property (3·8) 688

שֶׂה 4 sheep, goat (5·44) 961

כֶּשֶׂב lamb (1·13) 461

אַיָּל 5 hart, deer (4·11) 19

צְבִי gazelle (4·11) 840

</td></tr>
</table>

יַחְמוּר	roebuck (1·2) 331
אַקּוֹ	wild goat (1·1) 70
דִּישֹׁן	a clean animal, antelope|?| (1·1) 190
תְּאוֹ	antelope (1·2) 1060
זֶמֶר	an animal allowed as food, probably mountain sheep (1·1) 275
הִפְרִיס	6 to divide (4·12·14) 828
פַּרְסָה	hoof (5·21) 828
שֹׁסַע	to divide, cleave (2·5·8) 1042
שֶׁסַע	cleft (1·4) 1043
גֵּרָה	cud (4·11) 176
גֵּרָה	7 cud (4·11) 176
הִפְרִיס	to divide (4·12·14) 828
פַּרְסָה	hoof (5·21) 828
שֹׁסַע	to divide, cleave (2·5·8) 1042
אַרְנֶבֶת	hare (1·2) 58
שָׁפָן	rock badger (1·4) 1050
חֲזִיר	8 swine (1·7) 306
הִפְרִיס	to divide (4·12·14) 828
פַּרְסָה	hoof (5·21) 828
גֵּרָה	cud (4·11) 176
נְבֵלָה	corpse (4·48) 615
סְנַפִּיר	9 fin (2·5) 703
קַשְׂקֶשֶׂת	scale |of fish| (2·8) 903
סְנַפִּיר	10 fin (2·5) 703
קַשְׂקֶשֶׂת	scale |of fish| (2·8) 903
צִפּוֹר	11 bird|s| (3·40) 861
נֶשֶׁר	12 eagle (3·26) 676
פֶּרֶס	bearded vulture (1·2) 828
עָזְנִיָּה	unclean bird of prey (1·2) 740
רָאָה	13 bird of prey, perhaps kite (1·1) 178
אַיָּה	hawk, falcon, kite (1·3) 17
דַּיָּה	a bird of prey (1·1) 178
מִין	species (4·31) 568
עֹרֵב	14 raven (1·12) 788
מִין	species (4·31) 568
יַעֲנָה	15 ostrich (1·8) 419
תַּחְמָס	male ostrich (1·2) 329
שַׁחַף	sea mew, gull (1·2) 1006
נֵץ	bird of prey (1·3) 665
מִין	species (4·31) 568
כּוֹס	16 a kind of owl (1·3) 468
יַנְשׁוּף	a bird (1·3) 676
תִּנְשֶׁמֶת	unclean bird (1·2) 675
קָאָת	17 bird, usually a pelican (1·5) 866
רָחָמָה	carrion vulture (1·2) 934
שָׁלָךְ	cormorant (1·2) 1021
חֲסִידָה	18 stork (1·6) 339
אֲנָפָה	an unclean bird (1·2) 60
מִין	species (4·31) 568
דּוּכִיפַת	an unclean bird (1·2) 189
עֲטַלֵּף	bat (1·3) 742
שֶׁרֶץ	19 swarmers, swarming things (1·15) 1056
נְבֵלָה	21 corpse (4·48) 615
נָכְרִי	foreigner (5·45) 648
בִּשֵּׁל	to boil (2·20·27) 143
גְּדִי	kid (1·16) 152
חָלָב	milk (8·44) 316
עִשֵּׂר	22 to give tithe (2·5·9) 797
תְּבוּאָה	product, yield (6·43) 100
מַעֲשֵׂר	23 tithe (7·31) 798
דָּגָן	grain (7·40) 186
תִּירוֹשׁ	fresh or new wine (7·38) 440
יִצְהָר	fresh oil (6·23) 844
צוּר	25 to confine, secure (3·31·31) 848
אִוָּה	26 to desire (2·11·27) 16
שֵׁכָר	intoxicating drink, strong drink (2·23) 1016
מַעֲשֵׂר	28 tithe (7·31) 798
תְּבוּאָה	product, yield (6·43) 100
יָתוֹם	29 orphan (11·42) 450

Chapter 15

שְׁמִטָּה	1 a letting drop [of exactions], a remitting (5·5) 1030

שְׁמִטָּה	2 a letting drop [of exactions], a remitting (5·5) 1030
שמט	to let drop, fall (1·7·9) 1030
מַשֶּׁה	loan (1·1) 674`
נגשׂ	to exact (2·4·7) 620
נָכְרִי	3 foreigner (5·45) 648
נגשׂ	to exact (2·4·7) 620
הִשְׁמִיט	to cause to let drop (1·1·9) 1030
אֶפֶס	4 אֶפֶס כִּי save that, howbeit (3·43) 67
הֶעֱבִיט	6 to cause to give pledge (3·3·5) 716
עבט	to give pledge (2·2·5) 716
אמץ	7 to harden, make obstinate (3·19·41) 54
קָפַץ	to draw together, shut (1·5·7) 891
הֶעֱבִיט	8 to lend (3·3·5) 716
דַּי	sufficiency, enough for (1·12) 191
מַחְסֹר	need (1·13) 341
חָסֵר	to lack, decrease (3·20·24) 341
בְּלִיַּעַל	9 worthlesness (2·27) 116
שְׁמִטָּה	a letting drop [of exactions], a remitting (5·5) 1030
חֵטְא	sin, guilt of sin (8·33) 307
בִּגְלַל	10 on account of (3·10) 164
מִשְׁלַח	outstretching (6·7) 1020
חָפְשִׁי	12 free (3·17) 344
חָפְשִׁי	13 free (3·17) 344
רֵיקָם	in empty condition, empty (2·16) 938
הַעֲנִיק	14 to make a necklace (2·2·3) 778
גֹּרֶן	threshing floor (2·34) 175
יֶקֶב	wine vat (2·16) 248
מַרְצֵעַ	17 awl (1·2) 954
קָשָׁה	18 to be hard, severe (2·5·28) 904
חָפְשִׁי	free (3·17) 344
מִשְׁנֶה	double (2·35) 1041
שָׂכָר	hire, wages (2·29) 969
שָׂכִיר	hireling, hired laborer (2·18) 969
גָּזַז	19 to shear (1·14·15) 159

מוּם	21 defect (4·21[?]) 548
פִּסֵּחַ	lame (1·14) 820
עִוֵּר	blind (3·25) 734
צְבִי	22 gazelle (4·11) 840
אַיָּל	hart, deer (4·11) 19

Chapter 16

אָבִיב	1 month of ear forming or growing (2·8) 1
פֶּסַח	passover (4·49) 820
פֶּסַח	2 passover (4·49) 820
חָמֵץ	3 that which is leavened (1·11) 329
עֳנִי	affliction (2·36) 777
חִפָּזוֹן	hurried flight (1·3) 342
שְׂאֹר	4 leaven (1·5) 959
פֶּסַח	5 passover (4·49) 820
פֶּסַח	6 passover (4·49) 820
בשׁל	7 to boil (2·20·27) 143
עֲצֶרֶת	8 assembly (1·11) 783
שָׁבוּעַ	9 week (4·20) 988
חֶרְמֵשׁ	sickle (2·2) 357
קָמָה	standing grain (3·10) 879
שָׁבוּעַ	10 week (4·20) 988
מִסָּה	sufficiency (1·1) 588
נְדָבָה	freewill offering (4·27) 621
יָתוֹם	11 orphan (11·42) 450
סֻכָּה	13 booth (3·31) 697
גֹּרֶן	threshing floor (2·34) 175
יֶקֶב	wine vat (2·16) 428
יָתוֹם	14 orphan (11·42) 450
חגג	15 to keep a pilgrim feast (1·16·16) 290
תְּבוּאָה	product, yield (6·43) 100
שָׂמֵחַ	glad, joyful, merry (1·21) 970
זָכוּר	16 male (2·4) 271
שָׁבוּעַ	week (4·20) 988
סֻכָּה	booth (3·31) 697
רֵיקָם	empty (2·16) 938

מַתָּנָה 17 gift (1·17) 682

שֹׁטֵר 18 official, officer (7·25) 1009

הִכִּיר 19 to regard (4·37·40) 647

שֹׁחַד bribe (4·23) 1005

עִוֵּר to make blind (1·5·5) 734

סלף to pervert (1·7·7) 701

אֲשֵׁרָה 21 a sacred tree, pole symbol of Canaanite goddess (3·40) 81

מַצֵּבָה 22 pillar (3·35) 663

Chapter 17

שֶׂה 1 sheep, goat (5·44) 961

מוּם defect (4·21[?]) 548

יָרֵחַ 3 moon (2·27) 437

סקל 5 to stone (4·12·22) 509

בָּעֵר 7 to consume (12·26·28) 129

נפלא 8 to be too difficult for (2·13·24) 810

דִּין judgement (1·19) 192

הורה 10 to teach (4·45[?]·45[?]) 434

הורה 11 to teach (4·45[?]·45[?]) 434

זָדוֹן 12 proudly, pride (2·20) 267

בָּעֵר 13 to consume (12·26·28) 129

הזיד to act presumptuously (3·8·10) 267

נָכְרִי 15 foreign (5·48) 648

מִשְׁנֶה 18 copy (2·35) 1041

הֶאֱרִיךְ 20 to prolong (11·31·34) 73

Chapter 18

שֶׂה 3 sheep, goat (5·44) 961

קֵבָה stomach, belly (1·2) 867

דָּגָן 4 grain (7·40) 186

תִּירוֹשׁ fresh or new wine (7·38) 440

יִצְהָר fresh oil (6·23) 844

גֵּז shearing (1·4) 159

אַוָּה 6 desire, will (4·7) 16

מִמְכָּר 8 sale (7·10) 569

קֹסֵם 10 to practice divination (1·11·11) 890

קֶסֶם divination (1·11) 890

עוֹנֵן to practice soothsaying (2·10·11) 778

נחשׁ to practice divination (1·9·9) 638

כָּשֵׁף to practice sorcery (1·6·6) 506

חבר 11 to tie magic knots, charm (1·11·28) 287

חֶבֶר spell, company (1·7) 288

אוֹב necromancer (1·6) 15

יִדְּעֹנִי familiar spirit (1·11) 396

בִּגְלַל 12 on account of (2·9) 164

עוֹנֵן 14 to practice soothsaying (2·10·11) 778

קֹסֵם false prophet (1·9) 890

הֵזִיד 20 to act presumptuously (3·8·10) 267

אֵיכָה 21 in what manner (5·18) 32

זָדוֹן 22 proudly, pride (2·10[?]) 267

יגר to be afraid (2·5·5) 388

or

גור to dread, be afraid of (3·10·10) 158

Chapter 19

הִבְדִּיל 2 to separate, make a distinction between (6·32·42) 95

שׁלשׁ 3 to do a third time, divide into three parts (1·4·9) 1026

רָצַח to murder, slay (7·38·43) 953

רָצַח 4 to murder, slay (7·38·43) 953

בִּבְלִי without (2·5) 115

שֹׂנֵא enemy (9·41) 971

תְּמוֹל aforetime (3·23) 1069

שִׁלְשׁוֹם aforetime, previously (3·25) 1026

חטב 5 to cut or gather wood (1·2·3) 310

נדח to be impelled (4·13·43) 623

גַּרְזֶן axe (2·4) 173

נָשַׁל to drop off (4·6·7) 675

גֹּאֵל 6 kinsman (2·44[?]) 145

רָצַח to murder, slay (7·38·43) 953

חמם to be or grow warm (1·23·26) 328

הִשִּׂיג	to overtake (4·48·48) 673		זְכוּר	13 male (2·4) 271
שֹׂנֵא	enemy (9·41) 971		טַף	14 children (7·41) 381
תְּמוֹל	aforetime (3·23) 1069		בָּזַז	to plunder (3·37·40) 102
שִׁלְשׁוֹם	aforetime, previously (3·25) 1026		נְשָׁמָה	16 breathing things (1·24) 675
הִבְדִּיל	7 to separate, make a distinction between (6·32·42) 95		הֶחֱרִים	17 to devote to destruction (6·46·49) 355
הִרְחִיב	to enlarge (3·21·25) 931		צור	19 to shut in, besiege (3·31·31) 848
נָקִי	10 exempt (6·43) 667		נדח	to impell (1·1·43) 623
שֹׂנֵא	11 enemy (9·41) 971		גַּרְזֶן	axe (2·4) 173
אָרַב	to lie in wait (1·20·23) 70		מָצוּר	siege (5·25) 848
גֹּאֵל	12 kinsman (2·44[?]) 145		מַאֲכָל	20 food (2·30) 38
אֵל	these (3·10) 41		מָצוֹר	siege works (5·25) 848
חוס	13 to pity (5·24·24) 299			

Chapter 21

נָקִי	exempt (6·43) 667		עֶגְלָה	3 heifer (4·12) 722
בָּעַר	to consume (12·26·28) 129		מָשַׁךְ	to draw (1·30·36) 604
הִסִּיג	14 to displace (2·7·19) 690		עֹל	yoke (2·40) 760
גבל	to bound, border (1·3·5) 148		עֶגְלָה	4 heifer (4·12) 722
חֵטְא	15 sin, guilt of sin (8·33) 307		אֵיתָן	ever-flowing, permanent (1·14) 450
סָרָה	16 defection (2·7[?]) 694		ערף	to break the neck (2·6·6) 791
זָמַם	19 to purpose, devise (1·13 13) 273		עֶגְלָה	heifer (4·12) 722
בָּעַר	to consume (12·26·28) 129		ערף	to break the neck (2·6·6) 791
חוס	21 to pity (5·24·24) 299		נָקִי	8 exempt (6·43) 667
			בָּעַר	9 to consume (12·26·28) 129

Chapter 20

קָרֵב	3 approaching (1·11) 898		נָקִי	exempt (6·43) 667
רכך	to be timid, fearful (1·6·8) 939		שָׁבָה	10 to take captive (1·29·37) 985
חפז	to be alarmed (1·6·10) 342		שְׁבִי	captive (3·46) 985
ערץ	to tremble (4·11·14) 792		שִׁבְיָה	11 captives (2·9) 986
שֹׁטֵר	5 official, officer (7·25) 1009		יָפֶה	beautiful (1·40) 421
חנך	to dedicate (2·5·5) 335		תֹּאַר	outline, form (1·15) 1061
אָרַשׂ	7 to betroth (2·6·11) 76		חָשַׁק	to love (3·8·11) 365
שֹׁטֵר	8 official, officer (7·25) 1009		גִּלַּח	12 to shave (1·18·23) 164
יָרֵא	fearing (1·45) 431		צִפֹּרֶן	fingernail (1·2) 862
רַךְ	tender, delicate, soft (3·16) 940		שִׂמְלָה	13 wrapper, mantle (6·29) 971
נָמֵס	to melt (1·19·21) 587		שְׁבִי	captivity, captive (3·46) 985
שֹׁטֵר	9 official, officer (7·25) 1009		יֶרַח	month (2·12) 437
מַס	11 slave gangs (1·23) 586		בָּעַל	to marry (2·10·12) 127
צור	12 to shut in, besiege (3·31·31) 848		הִתְעַמֵּר	14 to deal tyrannically (2·2·2) 771

שָׂנִיא 15 hated, held in aversion (1·1) 971

בכר 16 to constitute as firstborn (1·2·4) 114

הִכִּיר 17 to acknowledge (4·37·40) 647

אוֹן manly vigour (1·10) 20

בְּכֹרָה right of first-born (1·10) 114

סרר 18 to be stubborn (2·16·16) 710

מָרָה to be rebellious (2·21·43) 598

יִסַּר to discipline (5·30·41) 415

סרר 20 to be stubborn (2·16·16) 710

מָרָה to be rebellious (2·21·43) 598

זֹלֵל squandering (1·6[?]) 272

סֹבֵא drunkard (1·3) 684

רגם 21 to kill by stoning, to stone (1·15·15) 920

בְּעֵר to consume (12·26·28) 129

חֵטְא 22 sin, guilt of sin (8·33) 307

תָּלָה 22 to execute by hanging (2·23·27) 1067

נְבֵלָה 23 corpse (4·48) 615

תָּלָה to execute by hanging (2·23·27) 1067

קְלָלָה curse (11·33) 887

Chapter 22

שֶׂה 1 sheep, goat (5·44) 961

נדח to be driven away (4·13·43) 623

הִתְעַלֵּם to hide oneself (3·6·29) 761

שִׂמְלָה 3 wrapper, mantle (6·29) 971

אֲבֵדָה a lost thing (1·4) 2

הִתְעַלֵּם to hide oneself (3·6·29) 761

הִתְעַלֵּם 4 to hide oneself (3·6·29) 761

שִׂמְלָה 5 wrapper, mantle (6·29) 971

קַן 6 nest (2·13) 890

צִפּוֹר bird|s| (3·40) 861

אֶפְרֹחַ young one (2·4) 827

בֵּיצָה egg (2·6) 101

רָבַץ to stretch oneself out, lie down (3·24·30) 918

הַאֲרִיךְ 7 to prolong (11·31·34) 73

מַעֲקֶה 8 parapet (1·1) 785

גָּג roof (1·29) 150

כִּלְאַיִם 9 two kinds (1·4) 476

תְּבוּאָה product, yield (6·43) 100

חרש 10 to plow (1·21·24) 360

שַׁעַטְנֵז 11 mixed stuff (1·2) 1043

צֶמֶר wool (1·16) 856

פֵּשֶׁת flax, linen (1·16) 833

גְּדִל 12 tassel (1·2) 153

כְּסוּת covering (1·8) 492

עֲלִילָה 14 wantonness (2·24) 760

בְּתוּלִים tokens of virginity (5·10) 144

בְּתוּלִים 15 tokens of virginity (5·10) 144

עֲלִילָה 17 wantonness (2·24) 760

בְּתוּלִים tokens of virginity (5·10) 144

שִׂמְלָה [bed]covering (6·29) 971

יִסַּר 18 to discipline (5·30·41) 415

ענש 19 to fine, punish (1·6·9) 778

בְּתוּלָה virgin (4·50) 143

בְּתוּלִים 20 tokens of virginity (5·10) 144

סקל 21 to stone (4·12·22) 709

נְבָלָה disgraceful folly (1·13) 615

בְּעֵר to consume (12·26·28) 129

בְּעוּלָה 22 married woman (1·4[?]) 127

בְּעֵר to consume (12·26·28) 129

בְּתוּלָה 23 virgin (4·50) 143

ארש to be betrothed (4·5·11) 76

סקל 24 to stone (4·12·12) 709

בְּעֵר to consume (12·26·28) 129

ארש 25 to be betrothed (4·5·11) 76

חֵטְא 26 sin, guilt of sin (8·33) 307

רָצַח to murder, slay (7·38·43) 953

ארש 27 to be betrothed (4·5·11) 76

מוֹשִׁיעַ savior (3·27) 446

בְּתוּלָה 28 virgin (4·50) 143

ארש to be betrothed (4·5·11) 76

Chapter 23

פָּצַע 2 to wound, wound by bruising (1·3·3) 822

דַּכָּא crushing (1·1) 194

שָׁפְכָה male organ (1·1) 1050

מַמְזֵר 3 bastard (1·2) 561

קִדֵּם 5 to come to meet (1·24·26) 869

שָׂכַר to live (1·17·20) 968

קְלָלָה 6 curse (11·33) 887

תָּעֵב 8 to regard as an abomination, abhor (3·14·21) 1073

קָרֶה 11 chance, accident (1·1) 899

יָתֵד 14 peg (1·24) 450

אָזֵן tools, implements (1·1) 24

חָפַר to search for (2·22·22) 343

צֵאָה filth, excrement (1·2) 844

הוֹנָה 17 oppress (1·14·18) 413

קָדֵשׁ 18 temple prostitute (2·11) 873

אֶתְנַן 19 hire of harlot (1·11) 1072

זוֹנָה harlot (1·33[?]) 275

מְחִיר hire (1·15) 564

כֶּלֶב dog (1·32) 476

הִשִּׁיךְ 20 to make one give interest (3·3·4) 675

נֶשֶׁךְ interest (3·12) 675

אֹכֶל food (3·44) 38

נֶשֶׁךְ אֹכֶל = usuary of food 38

נשׁך to give interest (1·1·4) 675

נָכְרִי 21 foreigner (5·45) 648

הִשִּׁיךְ to make one give interest (3·3·4) 675

מִשְׁלָח outstretching (6·7) 1020

נָדַר 22 to vow (5·30·30) 623

אִחַר to keep back, bring late (2·15·17) 29

חֵטְא sin, guilt of sin (8·33) 307

נָדַר 23 to vow (5·30·30) 623

חֵטְא sin, guilt of sin (8·33) 307

מוֹצָא 24 that which goes forth (2·27) 425

נָדַר to vow (5·30·30) 623

נְדָבָה voluntariness (4·27) 621

עֵנָב 25 grapes (4·19) 772

שָׂבַע appetite, fill (1·8) 959

קָמָה 26 standing grain (3·10) 879

קָטַף to pluck off (1·4·5) 882

מְלִילָה ear of wheat (1·1) 576

חֶרְמֵשׁ sickle (2·2) 357

הֵנִיף to wield (2·32·34[?]) 631

Chapter 24

בָּעַל 1 to marry (2·10·12) 127

כְּרִיתוּת divorcement (2·4) 504

כְּרִיתוּת 3 divorcement (2·4) 504

נָקִי 5 exempt (6·43) 667

חבל 6 to bind by a pledge (3·11·12) 286

רֵחַיִם [hand]mill (1·5) 932

גנב 7 to steal, take by stealth (2·30·39) 170

הִתְעַמֵּר to deal tyranically (2·2·2) 771

גַּנָּב thief (1·17) 170

בֵּעַר to consume (12·26·28) 129

צָרַעַת 8 leprosy (1·35) 863

הוֹרָה to teach (4·45[?]·45[?]) 434

הִשָּׁה 10 to lend (2·2·11[?]) 674

מְאוּמָה anything (2·32) 548

עבט to take pledge [the thing pledged] (2·2·5) 716

עֲבוֹט pledge, article pledged (4·4) 716

נשׁה 11 to lend (1·9·11[?]) 674

עֲבוֹט pledge, article pledged (4·4) 716

עֲבוֹט 12 pledge, article pledged (4·4) 716

עֲבוֹט 13 pledge, article pledged (4·4) 716

שַׂלְמָה outer garment (2·16) 971

עָשַׁק 14 to oppress, wrong (3·36·37) 798

שָׂכִיר hireling, hired laborer (2·18) 969

שָׂכָר 15 hire, wages (2·29) 969

חֵטְא guilt of sin (8·33) 307

חֵטְא 16 guilt of sin (8 · 33) 307

יָתוֹם 17 orphan (11 · 42) 450

חבל   to bind by a pledge (3 · 11 · 12) 286

קצר 19 to reap, harvest (1 · 24 · 24) 894

קָצִיר   harvest (1 · 49) 894

עֹמֶר   sheaf (1 · 8) 771

יָתוֹם   orphan (11 · 12) 450

חבט 20 to beat off (1 · 4 · 5) 286

זַיִת   olive, olive tree (5 · 38) 268

פאר   to go over the boughs, glean (1 · 1 · 1) 802

יָתוֹם   orphan (11 · 42) 450

בצר 21 to cut off |grapes| (1 · 7 · 7[?]) 130

עולל   to glean (1 · 8 · 17) 760

יָתוֹם   orphan (11 · 42) 450

Chapter 25

הצדיק   to declare righteous, justify (1 · 12 · 41) 842

הרשׁיע   to condemn as guilty (1 · 25 · 34) 957

כְּדֵי 2 according to the sufficiency, as much as it demands (1 · 5) 191

מַכָּה 3 plague (6 · 48) 642

נקְלָה   to be lightly esteemed, dishonored (1 · 5 · 6) 885

חסם 4 to muzzle (1 · 2 · 2) 340

דָּשׁ   to tread, thresh (1 · 12 · 15) 190

יָבָם 5 husband's brother (2 · 2) 386

יבם   to do the duty of a husband's brother (2 · 3 · 3) 386

נמחה 6 to be blotted out (1 · 9 · 35) 562

יְבָמָה 7 sister in law (2 · 4) 386

מֵאֵן   to refuse (1 · 45 · 45) 549

יָבָם   husband's brother (2 · 2) 386

יבם   to do the duty of a husband's brother (2 · 3 · 3) 386

בְּאֵר 8 to make plain (2 · 3) 91

יְבָמָה 9 sister-in-law (2 · 4) 386

חָלַץ   to draw, draw off (2 · 5 · 27) 322

יָרַק   to spit (1 · 2 · 2) 439

בִּפְנֵי   in the face of (5 · 17) 816

כָּכָה   thus (2 · 34) 462

חָלַץ 10 to draw, draw off (2 · 5 · 27) 322

נַעַל   sandal (3 · 22) 653

נצה 11 to struggle with each other (1 · 5 · 8) 663

מְבוּשִׁים   privates (1 · 1) 102

קצץ 12 to cut off (1 · 4 · 14) 893

חוס   to pity (5 · 24 · 24) 299

כִּיס 13 bag (1 · 5) 476

קָטָן   small, small things (2 · 47) 881

אֵיפָה 14 ephah, measure or receptacle holding an ephah (3 · 38) 35

קָטָן   small, small things (2 · 47) 881

שָׁלֵם 15 complete, full, perfect (3 · 28) 1023

אֵיפָה   ephah, measure or receptacle holding an ephah (3 · 38) 35

הֶאֱרִיךְ   to prolong (11 · 31 · 34) 73

עָוֶל 16 injustice, unrighteousness (2 · 21) 732

קרה 18 to encounter, meet (1 · 13 · 27) 899

זנב   to cut off the tail, attack the rear (1 · 2 · 2) 275

נחשל   to shatter (1 · 1 · 1) 365

עָיֵף   faint, weary (1 · 17) 746

יָגֵעַ   weary, warisome (1 · 3) 388

מחה 19 to blot out (3 · 22 · 35) 562

זֵכֶר   remembrance (2 · 23) 271

Chapter 26

טֶנֶא 2 basket (4 · 4) 380

טֶנֶא 4 basket (4 · 4) 380

מַת 5 man (6 · 21) 607

עָצוּם 5 mighty |strong| (6 · 31) 783

קָשֶׁה 6 severe (4 · 36) 904

עֳנִי 7 affliction (2 · 36) 777

לַחַץ   oppression (1 · 11) 537

118

מוֹרָא	8 awe-inspiring spectacle (4·12) 432	
מוֹפֵת	wonder (9·36) 68	
זָב	9 to flow (6·29·29) 264	
חָלָב	milk (8·44) 316	
הֶעָשִׁיר	12 to tithe (1·2·9) 797	
מַעֲשֵׂר	tithe (7·31) 798	
תְּבוּאָה	product, yield (6·43) 100	
יָתוֹם	orphan (11·42) 450	
בָּעֵר	13 to consume (12·26·28) 129	
יָתוֹם	orphan (11·42) 450	
אֹנֶה	14 mourning[?] not in BDB (1·2)	
בָּעֵר	to consume (12·26·28) 129	
הִשְׁקִיף	15 to over hang, look out and down (1·12·22) 1054	
מָעוֹן	dwelling (1·18) 732	
זָב	to flow (6·29·29) 264	
חָלָב	milk (8·44) 316	
סְגֻלָּה	18 property (3·8) 688	

Chapter 27

שִׂיד	2 to whitewash (2·2·2) 966
שִׂיד	lime, whitewash (2·4) 966
זָב	3 to flow (6·29·29) 264
חָלָב	milk (8·44) 316
שִׂיד	4 to whitewash (2·2·2) 966
שִׂיד	lime, whitewash (2·4) 966
הֵנִיף	5 to wield (2·32·34[?]) 631
שָׁלֵם	6 complete, full, perfect (3·28) 1023
בֵּאֵר	8 to make plain (2·3·3) 91
הִסְכִּית	9 to keep silence (1·1·1) 698
קְלָלָה	13 curse (11·33) 887
רָם	14 uplifted (7·31[?]) 926
פֶּסֶל	15 idol, image (5·31) 820
מַסֵּכָה	molten image (3·25) 651
חָרָשׁ	graver, artificer (1·38) 360
סֵתֶר	secrecy (4·35) 712
אָמֵן	truly (12·26) 53
הִקְלָה	16 to treat with contempt, dishonor

	(1·1·16) 885	
אָמֵן	truly (12·26) 53	
הִסִּיג	17 to displace (2·7·19) 690	
אָמֵן	truly (12·26) 53	
הִשְׁגָּה	18 to lead astray (1·4·21) 993	
עִוֵּר	blind (3·25) 734	
אָמֵן	truly (12·26) 53	
יָתוֹם	19 orphan (11·42) 450	
אָמֵן	truly (12·26) 53	
אָמֵן	20 truly (12·26) 53	
אָמֵן	21 truly (12·26) 53	
אָמֵן	22 truly (12·26) 53	
חֹתֶנֶת	23 wife's mother (1·1[?]) 368	
אָמֵן	truly (12·26) 53	
סֵתֶר	24 secrecy (4·35) 712	
אָמֵן	truly (12·26) 53	
שֹׁחַד	25 bribe (4·23) 1005	
נָקִי	exempt (6·43) 667	
אָמֵן	truly (12·26) 53	
אָמֵן	26 truly (12·26) 53	

Chapter 28

הִשִּׂיג	2 to overtake (4·48·48) 673
שֶׁגֶר	4 offspring, young [of beasts] (4·5) 993
אֶלֶף	cattle (4·8) 48
עַשְׁתָּרוֹת	ewes, young (4·4) 800
טֶנֶא	5 basket (4·4) 380
מִשְׁאֶרֶת	kneading trough (2·4) 602
נִגַּף	7 to be smitten (3·23·48) 619
אָסָם	8 storehouse (1·2) 62
מִשְׁלַח	outstretching (6·7) 1020
מָטָר	12 rain (6·37) 564
הִלְוָה	to lend (3·9·14) 531
לָוָה	to borrow (1·5·14) 531
זָנָב	13 tail, end (2·11) 275
לְמַעְלָה	upwards (1·34) 751
לְמַטָּה	downwards (1·10) 641
קְלָלָה	15 curse (11·33) 887

119

הַשִּׂיג	to overtake (4·48·48) 673	
טֶנֶא	17 basket (4·4) 380	
מִשְׁאֶרֶת	kneading trough (2·4) 602	
שֶׁגֶר	18 offspring, young [of beasts] (4·5) 993	
אֶלֶף	cattle (4·8) 48	
עַשְׁתָּרוֹת	ewes, young (4·4) 800	
מְאֵרָה	20 curse (1·5) 73	
מְהוּמָה	discomfiture (2·12) 223	
מִגְעֶרֶת	rebuke (1·1) 172	
מִשְׁלַח	outstretching (6·7) 1020	
רֹעַ	evil, badness (1·19) 947	
מַעֲלָל	practice (1·41) 760	
דֶּבֶר	21 pestilence, plague (1·46) 184	
שַׁחֶפֶת	22 consumption (1·2) 1006	
קַדַּחַת	fever (1·2) 869	
דַּלֶּקֶת	inflamation (1·1) 196	
חַרְחֻר	violent heat, fever (1·1) 359	
שִׁדָּפוֹן	smut (1·5) 995	
יֵרָקוֹן	rust (1·6) 439	
מָטָר	24 rain (6·37) 564	
אָבָק	dust (1·6) 7	
נִגָּף	25 to be smitten (3·23·48) 619	
זַעֲוָה	terror, object of trembling (1·7) 266	
נְבֵלָה	26 carcass (4·48) 615	
מַאֲכָל	food (2·30) 38	
הֶחֱרִיד	to drive in terror, rout an army (1·16·39) 353	
שְׁחִין	27 boil (2·13) 1006	
עֹפֶל	hemorrhoid (1·6) 779	
גָּרָב	itch, scab (1·3) 173	
חֶרֶס	an eruptive disease (1·1) 360	
שִׁגָּעוֹן	28 madness (1·3) 993	
עִוָּרוֹן	blindness (1·2) 734	
תִּמָּהוֹן	bewilderment (1·2) 1069	
מְשַׁשׁ	29 to grope (2·6·8[?]) 606	
צָהֳרַיִם	midday, noon (1·23) 843	
עִוֵּר	blind (3·25) 734	
אֲפֵלָה	darkness (1·10) 66	

עָשַׁק	to oppress, wrong (3·36·37) 798	
גָּזַל	to seize, tear away (2·29·30) 159	
מוֹשִׁיעַ	savior (3·27) 446	
אֵרַשׂ	30 to betroth (2·6·11) 76	
שָׁגַל	to violate, ravish (1·1·4) 993	
טָבַח	31 to slaughter (1·11·11) 370	
גָּזַל	to seize, tear away (2·29·30) 159	
מוֹשִׁיעַ	savior (3·27) 446	
אֵל	32 strength, power (1·5) 43	
יְגִיעַ	33 produce (1·16) 388	
עָשַׁק	to oppress, wrong (3·36·37) 798	
רָצַץ	to crush (1·11·19) 954	
שֻׁגַּע	34 to be maddened (1·5·7) 993	
שְׁחִין	35 boil (2·13) 1006	
בֶּרֶךְ	knee (1·25) 139	
שׁוֹק	leg (1·19) 1003	
קָדְקֹד	scalp, hairy crown (3·11) 869	
שַׁמָּה	37 appalment, horror (1·39) 1031	
מָשָׁל	byword (1·39) 605	
שְׁנִינָה	sharp [cutting] word, taunt (1·4) 1042	
נָהַג	to lead off (2·10·30) 624	
הֶחָסִיל	38 to consume (1·1·1) 340	
אַרְבֶּה	locust (1·24) 916	
אָגַר	39 to gather [food] (1·3·3) 8	
תּוֹלֵעָה	worm, grub (1·41) 1069	
זַיִת	40 olive, olive tree (5·38) 268	
סוּךְ	to annoint oneself (1·8·9) 691	
נָשַׁל	to drop off (4·6·7) 675	
שְׁבִי	41 captivity (3·46) 985	
צְלָצַל	42 whirring locust (1·2) 852	
מַטָּה	43 downwards (2·3) 641	
לוה	44 to borrow (1·5·14) 531	
הִלְוָה	to lend (3·9·14) 531	
זָנָב	tail, end (2·11) 275	
קְלָלָה	45 curse (11·33) 887	
הַשִּׂיג	to overtake (4·48·48) 673	
מוֹפֵת	46 wonder (9·36) 68	

120

טוֹב	47	goodness [of heart], joy (2·32) 375
צָמָא	48	thirst (1·17) 854
עֵירֹם		nakedness (1·10) 735
חֹסֶר		want, lack (2·3) 341
עֹל		yoke (2·40) 760
צַוָּאר		neck, back of the neck (1·41) 848
דָּאָה	49	to fly swiftly (1·4·4) 178
נֶשֶׁר		eagle (3·26) 676
עַז	50	strong, mighty, fierce (1·22) 738
דָּגָן	51	grain (7·40) 186
תִּירוֹשׁ		fresh or new wine (7·38) 440
יִצְהָר		fresh oil (6·23) 844
שֶׁגֶר		offspring, young [of beasts] (4·5) 993
אֶלֶף		cattle (4·8) 48
עַשְׁתָּרוֹת		ewes, young (4·4) 800
גָּבֹהַּ	52	high (2·41) 147
בָּצוּר		made inaccessible, fortified (4·25) 130
מָצוֹר	53	siege (5·25) 848
מָצוֹק		stress (3·6) 848
הֵצִיק		to constrain, bring into straits (3·11·11) 847
רַךְ	54	tender, delicate, soft (3·16) 940
עָנֹג		dainty (2·3) 772
חֵיק		fold of the garment at the breast (3·38) 300
מִבְּלִי	55	from want of (2·25) 115
מָצוֹר		siege (5·25) 848
מָצוֹק		stress (3·6) 848
הֵצִיק		to constrain, bring into straits (3·11·11) 847
רַךְ	56	tender, delicate, soft (3·16) 940
עָנֹג		dainty (2·3) 772
נִסָּה		to try (8·36·36) 650
הַצִּיג		to set (1·5·16) 426
הִתְעַנֵּג		to be of dainty habit (1·9·10) 772
רֹךְ		tenderness, delicacy (1·1) 940

חֵיק		fold of the garment at the breast (3·38) 300
שִׁלְיָה	57	after birth (1·1) 1017
מִבֵּין		from between (1·21) 107
חֹסֶר		want, lack (2·3) 341
סֵתֶר		secrecy (4·35) 712
מָצוֹר		siege (5·25) 848
מָצוֹק		stress (3·6) 848
הֵצִיק		to constrain, bring into straits (3·11·11) 847
נוֹרָא	58	fearful (6·44) 431
הִפְלִיא	59	to do something exceptional, wonderful (1·10·24) 810
מַכָּה		plague (6·48) 642
חֳלִי		sickness (3·24) 318
מַדְוֶה	60	sickness (2·2) 188
יגר		to be afraid (2·5·5) 388
חֳלִי	61	sickness (3·24) 318
מַכָּה		plague (6·48) 642
הֶעְלִים		to conceal, hide (1·11·29) 761
מַת	62	man (6·21) 607
כּוֹכָב		star (4·37) 456
שׂוּשׂ	63	to exult, display joy (4·26·26) 965
נסח		to be torn away (1·1·4) 650
הִרְגִּיעַ	65	to rest, repose (1·8·13) 921
מָנוֹחַ		resting place (1·7) 629
רַגָּז		quivering, quaking (1·1) 919
כִּלָּיוֹן		failing (1·2) 479
דְּאָבוֹן		faintness (1·1) 178
תלא	66	to hang (1·3·3) 1067
מִנֶּגֶד		in front (2·26) 617
פָּחַד		to be in dread (2·23·26) 808
פַּחַד	67	dread (3·49) 808
פָּחַד		to be in dread (2·23·26) 808
אֳנִיָּה	68	a ship (1·31) 58
קָנָה		owner [as purchaser] (1·7) 888
מִלְּבַד	69	besides (2·33) 94

121

Chapter 29

מַסָּה	2 trial (3·3) 650	
מוֹפֵת	wonder (9·36) 68	
בלה	4 to become old and worn out (3·11·16) 115	
שַׂלְמָה	clothes (2·16) 971	
נַעַל	sandal (3·22) 653	
שֵׁכָר	5 intoxicating drink, strong drink (2·23) 1016	
שֹׁטֵר	9 official, officer (7·25) 1009	
טַף	10 children (7·41) 381	
חֹטֵב	cutter of wood (1·6[?]) 310	
שֹׁאֵב	water drawer (1·5) 980	
אָלָה	11 oath, curse (6·36) 46	
אָלָה	13 oath, curse (6·36) 46	
פֹּה	14 here, hither (4·44) 805	
שִׁקּוּץ	16 detested thing (1·28) 1055	
גִּלּוּל	idol (1·48) 165	
שֹׁרֶשׁ	17 root (1·33) 1057	
פרה	to be fruitful, bear fruit (1·22·29) 826	
רֹאשׁ	bitter and poisonous herb (3·12) 912	
לַעֲנָה	wormwood (1·8) 542	
אָלָה	18 curse, oath (6·36) 46	
שְׁרִירוּת	stubborness (1·10) 1057	
ספה	18 to snatch away (1·8·18) 705	
רָוֶה	watered (1·3) 924	
צָמֵא	thirsty (1·9) 854	
סלח	19 to forgive (1·33·46) 699	
עָשַׁן	to smoke (1·6·6) 798	
קִנְאָה	anger (1·43) 888	
רָבַץ	to stretch oneself out, lie down (3·24·30) 918	
אָלָה	curse, oath (6·36) 46	
מָחָה	to blot out (3·22·35) 562	
הִבְדִּיל	20 to separate, make a distinction	

	between (6·32·42) 95	
אָלָה	curse, oath (6·36) 46	
נָכְרִי	21 foreigner (5·45) 648	
מַכָּה	plague (6·48) 646	
תַּחֲלֻאִים	diseases (1·5) 316	
גָּפְרִית	22 brimstone, pitch (1·7) 172	
מֶלַח	salt (2·28) 571	
שְׂרֵפָה	burning (1·13) 977	
הִצְמִיחַ	to cause to grow (1·14·33) 855	
עֵשֶׂב	herb, herbage (3·33) 793	
מַהְפֵּכָה	overthrow (1·6) 246	
כָּכָה	23 thus (2·34) 462	
חֳרִי	burning (1·6) 354	
קְלָלָה	26 curse (11·33) 887	
נָתַשׁ	27 to pull up (1·17·22) 684	
קֶצֶף	wrath (1·29) 893	

Chapter 30

קְלָלָה	1 curse (11·33) 887	
הִדִּיחַ	to thrust out (4·27·43) 623	
שְׁבוּת	3 captivity (1·26) 986	
רִחַם	to have compassion (2·41·46) 933	
נדח	4 to be thrust out (4·13·43) 623	
מול	6 to circumcise (2·12·29) 557	
אָלָה	7 curse, oath (6·36) 46	
שֹׂנֵא	enemy (9·41) 971	
שׂושׂ	9 to exult, display joy (4·26·26) 965	
נפלא	11 to be too difficult for (2·13·24) 810	
נדח	17 to be thrust aside (4·13·43) 623	
הֶאֱרִיךְ	18 to prolong (11·31·34) 73	
הֵעִיד	19 to call as witness (5·39·44) 729	
קְלָלָה	curse (11·33) 887	

Chapter 31

אמץ	6 to be strong (3·16·41) 54	
ערץ	to tremble (4·11·14) 792	
הרפה	to abandon, forsake (4·21·44) 951	
אמץ	7 to be strong (3·16·41) 54	

הרפה 8 to abandon, forsake (4·22·44) 951

שְׁמִטָּה 10 a letting drop of exactions, a remitting (5·5) 1030

סֻכָּה booth (3·31) 697

נפלא 11 to be too difficult for (2·13·24) 810

הקהיל 12 to summon as assembly (3·20·39) 874

טַף children (7·41) 381

הִתְיַצֵּב 14 to hold one's ground, take one's stand (5·48·48) 426

נֵכָר 16 that which is foreign (2·36) 648

הֵפֵר to break, frustrate (2·41·44) 830

שִׁירָה 19 song (6·13) 1010

זָב 20 to flow (6·29·29) 264

חָלָב milk (8·44) 316

דָּשֵׁן to be fat, grow fat (1·1·11) 206

נָאַץ to spurn (1·15·24) 610

הֵפֵר to break, frustrate (2·41·44) 830

שִׁירָה 21 song (6·13) 1010

יֵצֶר imagination (1·9) 428

בְּטֶרֶם before (1·39) 382

שִׁירָה 22 song (6·13) 1010

אמץ 23 to be strong (3·16·41) 54

צַד 26 side (1·31) 841

מְרִי 27 rebellion (1·22) 598

מָרָה to be rebellious (2·21·43) 598

עֹרֶף neck (4·33) 791

קָשֶׁה stiff, stubborn (4·36) 904

בְּעוֹד while, yet (1·20) 728

המרה to show rebelliousness (6·22·43) 698

הקהיל 28 to summon an assembly (3·20·39) 874

שֹׁטֵר official, officer (7·25) 1009

הֵעִיד to call as witness (5·39·44) 729

שִׁירָה 30 song (6·13) 1010

Chapter 32

הַאֲזִין 1 to give ear, hear (2·41·41[?]) 24

אֵמֶר speech, word (1·48) 56

עָרַף 2 to drip, drop (2·2·2) 791

מָטָר rain (6·37) 564

לֶקַח teaching (1·9) 544

נזל to distil (1·8·9) 633

טַל dew (3·31) 378

אִמְרָה speech, word (2·30) 57

שְׂעִירִים rain|drops| (1·1) 973

דֶּשֶׁא grass (1·14) 206

רְבִיבִים copious showers (1·6) 914

עֵשֶׂב herbage, herb (3·33) 793

יהב 3 to give, ascribe (2·31·31) 396

גֹּדֶל greatness (6·14) 152

פֹּעַל 4 deed, thing done (2·37) 821

עָוֶל injustice, unrighteousness (2·21) 732

מוּם 5 defect (4·21[?]) 541

עִקֵּשׁ twisted, perverted (1·11) 786

פְּתַלְתֹּל tortuous (1·1) 836

גמל 6 to repay (2·34·37) 168

נָבָל foolish (2·18) 614

קָנָה to get, acquire (1·5·5) 888

הִפְרִיד 8 to divide (1·7·26) 828

גְּבוּלָה border, boundary (1·10) 148

חֶבֶל 9 lot, region (4·49) 286

תֹּהוּ 10 nothingness, waste (1·20) 1062

יְלֵל howling (1·1) 410

יְשִׁימוֹן wilderness (1·13) 445

אִישׁוֹן pupil |of eye| (1·4) 36

נֶשֶׁר eagle (3·26) 676

קֵן nestlings (2·13) 890

גּוֹזָל young of a bird (1·2) 160

רחף to hover (1·3·3) 934

אֶבְרָה pinion (1·4) 7

בָּדָד 12 isolation, alone (2·11) 94

נֵכָר that which is foreign (2·36) 648

הנחה to lead, guide (1·26·40) 634

תְּנוּבָה 13 fruit, produce (1·5) 626

שָׂדַי   field, land (1 · 13) 961

הֵינִיק   to nurse, give suck (1 · 10 · 18) 413

חַלָּמִישׁ   flint (2 · 5) 321

חֶמְאָה   14 curd (1 · 10) 326

חָלָב   milk (8 · 44) 316

כַּר   he-lamb (1 · 11) 503

עַתּוּד   he-goat (1 · 29) 800

כִּלְיָה   kidney (1 · 30) 480

חִטָּה   wheat (2 · 30) 334

עֵנָב   grapes (4 · 19) 772

חֶמֶר   wine (1 · 2) 330

שׁמן   15 to grow fat (2 · 3 · 5) 1031

בעט   to kick (1 · 2 · 2) 127

עָבָה   15 to be thick, gross (of rebellion) (1 · 3 · 3) 716

כשׂה   to be sated (1 · 1 · 1) 505

נטשׁ   to abandon (1 · 33 · 40) 643

נבל   to be foolish (1 · 4 · 24[?]) 614

הִקְנִיא   16 to provoke to jealous anger (2 · 4 · 34) 888

שֵׁד   17 demon (1 · 2) 993

שׂער   to be acquainted with (1 · 1 · 1) 973

שׁיה   18 read נשׁה, to forget (1 · 1 · 1) 1009

נָאַץ   19 to spurn (1 · 8 · 24) 610

כַּעַס   vexation, anger (2 · 25) 495

תַּהְפֻּכָה   20 perversity, perverse thing (1 · 10) 246

אֵמוּן   trusting (1 · 1[?]) 53

קִנֵּא   21 to excite to jealous anger (1 · 30 · 34) 88

הִקְנִיא   to provoke to jealous anger (2 · 4 · 34) 888

נָבָל   foolish (2 · 18) 614

קדח   22 to be kindled (1 · 5 · 5) 869

יקד   to be kindled (1 · 3 · 8) 428

תַּחְתִּי   lower, lowest (1 · 19) 1066

יְבוּל   produce (2 · 13) 385

לְהַט   to set ablaze (1 · 9 · 11) 529

מוֹסָד   foundation (1 · 13) 414

הספה   23 to catch up, or perhaps read אסף, to gather (1 · 1 · 18) 705

מָזֶה   24 empty (1 · 1) 561

לחם   to eat (1 · 6 · 6) 536

רֶשֶׁף   firebolt (1 · 7) 958

קֶטֶב   destruction (1 · 4) 881

מְרִירִי   bitter (1 · 1) 601

זחל   to crawl (1 · 3 · 3[?]) 267

שׁכל   25 to make childless (1 · 18 · 24) 1013

חֶדֶר   chamber, room (1 · 34) 293

אֵימָה   terror, dread (1 · 16 · 17) 33

בָּחוּר   young man (1 · 45) 104

בְּתוּלָה   virgin (4 · 50) 143

יוֹנֵק   suckling (1 · 11) 413

שֵׂיבָה   gray hair, hoary head (1 · 20[?]) 966

הפאה   26 to cleave in pieces (1 · 1 · 1) 802

אֱנוֹשׁ   man, mankind (1 · 42) 60

זֵכֶר   remembrance (2 · 23) 271

לוּלֵי   27 if not, unless (1 · 10) 530

כַּעַס   vexation, anger (2 · 25) 495

יגר   to be afraid of (2 · 5 · 5) 388

or

גור   to be afraid of (3 · 10 · 10) 158

נכר   to misconstrue (1 · 4 · 8) 649

רָם   high, lifted, exalted (7 · 31[?]) 926

תְּבוּנָה   28 understanding (1 · 42) 108

לוּ   29 if (1 · 19) 530

חכם   to be wise (1 · 18 · 26) 314

אֵיכָה   30 in what manner (5 · 18) 32

רְבָבָה   myriad (3 · 16) 914

פָּלִיל   31 judge (1 · 3) 813

שְׁדֵמָה   32 field (1 · 6) 995

עֵנָב   grapes (4 · 19) 772

רוֹשׁ   bitter and poisonous herb (3 · 12) 912

אֶשְׁכֹּל   cluster (1 · 9) 79

מְרֹר   bitter thing, bitter herb (1 · 5) 601

תַּנִּין   33 serpent (1 · 15) 1072

ראש venom (3·12) 912

פֶּתֶן venemous serpent, perhaps the cobra (1·6) 837

אַכְזָר cruel fierce (1·4) 470

כמס 34 to store up (1·1·1) 485

חתם to seal (1·23·27) 367

נָקָם 35 vengeance (3·17) 668

שָׁלֵם recompense (1·1) 1024

מוט to slip (1·15·39) 556

אֵיד distress, calamity (1·24) 15

חָשׁ to make haste (1·15·21) 301

עָתִיד prepared (1·5) 800

דִּין 36 to judge (1·23·24) 192

אזל to be gone, used up (1·6·6) 23

אֶפֶס end, i.e., extreme limit (3·43) 67

עָצַר to restrain, refrain (2·36·46) 783

אֵי 37 where (1·39) 32

חָסָה to seek refuge (1·37·37) 340

נֶסִיךְ 38 drink offering, libation (1·6) 651

סתרה shelter (1·1) 712

מָחַץ 39 to shatter (2·14·14) 563

שנן 41 to whet, sharpen (1·7·9) 1041

בָּרָק lightning, flashing (1·20) 140

נָקָם vengeance (3·17) 668

השכיר 42 to make drunk (1·6·20) 1016

שִׁבְיָה captives (2·9) 986

פֶּרַע leader [perh.] (1·2) 828

נקם 43 to avenge (1·13·34) 667

נָקָם vengeance (3·17) 668

שִׁירָה 44 song (3·13) 1010

הֵעִיד 46 to enjoin solemnly (5·39·44) 729

רֵיק 47 empty, idle, worthless (1·14) 938

הֶאֱרִיךְ to prolong (11·31·34) 73

בְּעֶצֶם 48 selfsame, itself (1·17) 782

עַם 50 kinsman (2·34) 769

מעל 51 to act unfaithfully (1·35·35) 591

מִנֶּגֶד 52 some way off from, at a distance (2·26) 617

Chapter 33

זָרַח 2 to rise, come forth (1·18·18) 280

הוֹפִיעַ to shine forth (1·8·8) 422

אָתָה to come (2·19·21) 87

רְבָבָה myriad (3·16) 914

אשדת = אש דת , (1·1) דת law decree (1·22) 206

חבב 3 to love (1·1·1) 285

תכה to be lead[dub.?], to be assembled [dub.?] (1·1·1) 1067

דַּבְּרֶת word (1·1) 184

מוֹרָשָׁה 4 possession (1·9) 440

קְהִלָּה assembly, congregation (1·2) 875

מַת 6 man (6·21) 607

עֵזֶר help, succour (3·21) 740

תֻּמִּים 8 Thummin [dub.] (1·5) 1070

אוּר Urim (1·7) 22

חָסִיד pious, godly (1·32) 339

נִסָּה to try (8·36·36) 650

הִכִּיר 9 to acknowledge (4·37·40) 647

אִמְרָה speech, word (2·30) 57

הורה 10 to teach (4·45[?]·45[?]) 434

קְטוֹרָה smoke of sacrifice (1·1) 882

כָּלִיל whole offering (2·15) 483

פֹּעַל 11 deed, thing done (2·37) 821

מָחַץ to shatter (2·14·14) 563

קָם adversary (1·12) 878

יָדִיד 12 beloved (1·8) 391

בֶּטַח securely (3·43) 105

חפף to enclose, cover (1·1·1) 342

מֶגֶד 13 excellence (5·8) 550

טַל dew (3·31) 378

תְּהוֹם deep, sea, abys (2·36) 1062

רָבַץ to stretch oneself out, lie down (3·24·30) 918

מֶגֶד 14 excellence (5·8) 550

תְּבוּאָה	product, yield (6·43) 100
גֶּרֶשׁ	yield (1·1) 177
יֶרַח	calendar month (2·12) 437
מֶגֶד	15 excellence (5·8) 550
מֶגֶד	16 excellence (5·8) 550
סְנֶה	blackberry bush (1·6) 702
תְּבוּאָה	product, yield (6·43) 100
קָדְקֹד	scalp, hairy crown (3·11) 869
נָזִיר	one devoted (1·15) 634
הָדָר	17 splendor, majesty (1·30) 214
רְאֵם	wild ox (1·9) 910
נגח	to thrust (1·6·11) 618
אֶפֶס	end, extremity (3·43) 67
רְבָבָה	myriad (3·16) 914
שֶׁפַע	19 abundance (1·1) 1051
ינק	to suck (1·8·18) 413
שׂפן	to be hidden (1·1) 706
טָמַן	to hide (1·28·31) 380
חוֹל	sand (1·22) 297
הִרְחִיב	20 to enlarge (3·21·25) 931
לָבִיא	lioness (1·11) 522
טָרַף	to tear (1·19·24) 382
קָדְקֹד	scalp, hairy crown (3·11) 869
חֶלְקָה	21 portion of ground (1·24) 324
מְחֹקֵק	commander (1·7) 349
ספן	to cover (1·6·6) 706
אתה	to come (2·19·21) 87
גוּר	22 young, whelp (1·7) 158
אַרְיֵה	lion (1·45) 71
זנק	to leap (1·1·1) 276
שָׂבֵעַ	23 abounding (1·10) 960
דָּרוֹם	south (1·17) 204

טָבַל	24 to dip (1·15·16) 371
מִנְעָל	25 bolt (1·1) 653
דֹּבֶא	rest[?] (1·1) 179
עֵזֶר	26 help, succour (3·21) 740
גַּאֲוָה	majesty (2·19) 144
שַׁחַק	cloud (1·21) 1007
מְעֹנָה	27 refuge (1·9) 733
גרש	to drive out (1·34·48) 176
בֶּטַח	28 securely (3·43) 105
בָּדָד	isolation, alone (2·11) 94
דָּגָן	grain (7·40) 186
תִּירוֹשׁ	fresh or new wine (7·38) 440
ערף	to drip, drop (2·2·2) 791
טַל	dew (3·31) 378
אֶשֶׁר	29 happiness, blessedness (1·44) 80
עֵזֶר	help, succour (3·21) 740
גַּאֲוָה	majesty (2·19) 144
נכחש	to cringe (1·1·22) 471

Chapter 34

בִּקְעָה	3 valley, plain (3·19) 132
תָּמָר	palm tree, date palm (1·12) 1071
גַּיְא	6 valley (3·47) 161
מוּל	in front of (5·25) 557
קְבֻרָה	grave (1·14) 869
כהה	7 to grow faint (1·5·8[?]) 462
לֵחַ	freshness (1·1) 535
בְּכִי	8 weeping (1·30) 113
אֵבֶל	mourning (1·24) 5
סָמַךְ	9 to lay (1·41·48) 701
מוֹפֵת	11 wonder (9·36) 68
מוֹרָא	12 awe-inspiring spectacle (4·12) 432

JOSHUA

Chapter 1

מְשָׁרֵת 1 servant (1·20) 1058

מָבוֹא 4 entering (2·23) 99

הַתְיַצֵּב 5 to take one's stand (2·48·48) 426

הַרְפָּה to abandon, forsake (2·21·44) 951

אמץ 6 to be strong, bold (5·16·41) 54

אמץ 7 to be strong, bold (5·16·41) 54

מוּשׁ 8 to depart (1·20[?]·20) 559

הגה to meditate, muse (1·22·24) 211

אמץ 9 to be strong, bold (5·16·41) 54

ערץ to tremble (1·11·14) 792

שׁטֵר 10 official, officer (5·25) 1009

צֵידָה 11 provision (2·9) 845

בְּעוֹד within yet (1·20) 728

טַף 14 children (2·41) 381

חמשׁ ptc.: in battle array (2·4·5) 332

יְרֻשָּׁה 15 possession (3·14) 440

מרה 18 to show rebelliousness (1·22·43) 598

אמץ to be strong, bold (5·16·41) 54

Chapter 2

מְרַגֵּל 1 spy (1·10) 920

חֶרֶשׁ silently, secretly (1·1) 361

זוֹנָה harlot (4·33[?]) 275

הֵנָּה 2 hither, here (5·49) 244

חפר to search (2·22·22) 343

חפר 3 to search (2·22·22) 343

צָפַן 4 to hide (1·23·28) 860

מֵאַיִן whence? (2·48) 32

אָנָה 5 whence? whither? (2·39) 33

הִשִּׂיג to overtake (1·48·48) 673

גָּג roof (3·29) 150

טָמַן to hide (3·28·31) 380

פֶּשֶׁת flax, linen (1·16) 833

מַעְבָּרָה 7 ford (1·8) 721

טֶרֶם 8 not yet (2·16) 382

גָּג roof (3·29) 150

אֵימָה 9 terror, dread (1·17) 33

נָמוֹג to melt (2·8·17) 556

הֶחֱרִים 10 to devote to destruction (14·46·49) 335

נָמֵס 11 to melt, grow fearful (3·19·21) 587

מִמַּעַל above, on top of (1·29) 751

חֶבֶל 15 cord (5·49) 286

חַלּוֹן window (3·30) 319

פָּגַע 16 to fall upon (10·40·46) 803

נֶחְבָּא to hide oneself, be hidden (2·16·34) 285

נָקִי 17 free, exempt from obligations (3·43) 667

שְׁבוּעָה oath (3·30) 989

תִּקְוָה 18 cord (2·2) 876

חוּט cord, thread (1·7) 296

שָׁנִי scarlet (2·42) 1040

קָשַׁר to bind (2·36·44) 905

חַלּוֹן window (3·30) 319

נָקִי 19 free, exempt from obligations (3·43) 667

נָקִי 20 free, exempt from obligations (3·43) 667

שְׁבוּעָה oath (3·30) 989

קָשַׁר 21 to bind (2·36·44) 905

תִּקְוָה cord (2·2) 876

שָׁנִי scarlet (2·42) 1040

חַלּוֹן window (3·30) 319

נָמוֹג 24 to melt (2·8·17) 556

Chapter 3

טֶרֶם 1 before, before that (2·16) 382

שׁטֵר 2 official (5·25) 1009

תְּמוֹל 4 yesterday; ת׳ שִׁלְשׁוֹם = formerly (3·23) 1069

שִׁלְשׁוֹם aforetime, previously = תְּמוֹל שׁ׳

127

נִפְלָאוֹת 5 wonderful acts (1·43) 810

הֵנָּה 9 hither, here (5·49) 244

מִלְמַעְלָה 13 above (2·24) 752

נֵד heap of waters (2·6) 622

נטבל 15 to be dipped (1·1·16) 371

גְּדְיָה riverbank (2·4) 152

קָצִיר harvest (1·49) 894

צַד 16 side (3·31) 841

מֶלַח salt (5·28) 571

חָרָבָה 17 dry ground (3·8) 351

Chapter 4

מַצָּב 3 standing place (2·10) 662

מָלוֹן lodging place (2·8) 533

שְׁכֶם 5 shoulder (1·22) 1014

זִכָּרוֹן 7 memorial (1·24) 272

מָלוֹן 8 lodging place (2·8) 533

מַצָּב 9 standing place (2·10) 622

חמש 12 ptc.: in battle array (2·4·5) 332

חֲלוּץ 13 equipped one, warrior (4·17[?]) 323

נִתַּק 18 to be drawn out (2·10·27) 683

חָרָבָה dry ground (3·8) 351

תְּמוֹל yesterday; ת׳ שִׁלְשׁוֹם = formerly (3·23) 1069

שִׁלְשׁוֹם תְּמוֹל שׁ׳ = aforetime, previously (3·25) 797

גְּדְיָה riverbank (2·4) 152

יַבָּשָׁה 22 dry ground (1·14) 387

Chapter 5

נָמֵס 1 to melt, grow fearful (3·19·21) 587

צֹר 2 flint (2·6) 866

מול to circumcise (6·12·29) 557

צֹר 3 flint (2·6) 866

מול to circumcise (6·12·29) 557

עָרְלָה foreskin (1·16) 790

מול 4 to circumcise (6·12·29) 557

מול 5 to circumcise (6·12·29) 557

יִלּוֹד born (1·5) 409

זוב 6 to flow (1·29·29) 264

חָלָב milk (1·44) 316

מול 7 to circumcise (6·12·29) 557

עָרֵל uncircumcised (1·35) 790

נִמּוֹל 8 to be circumcised (1·17·29) 557

גלל 9 to roll away (2·10·17) 164

פֶּסַח 10 passover (2·48) 820

עָבוּר 11 produce, yield (2·2) 721

מָחֳרָת the morrow (2·32) 564

פֶּסַח passover (2·48) 820

קָלָה to roast, parch (1·3·4) 885

בְּעֶצֶם selfsame, itself (1·17[?]) 783

מָן 12 manna (2·14) 557

מָחֳרָת the morrow (2·32) 564

עָבוּר produce, yield (2·2) 721

תְּבוּאָה product, yield (1·43) 100

לְנֶגֶד 13 in front of, before (1·32) 617

שָׁלַף to draw out (1·24·24) 1025

נָשַׁל 15 to draw off (1·6·7) 675

נַעַל sandal (3·22) 653

Chapter 6

הַקִּיף 3 to go around (2·16·27) 668

יוֹבֵל 4 ram (5·27) 385

מָשַׁךְ 5 to draw out, give a sound (1·30·36) 604

יוֹבֵל ram (5·27) 385

הריע to shout a war cry, alarm of battle (7·40·44) 929

תְּרוּעָה alarm [of war], war cry (2·36) 929

יוֹבֵל 6 ram (5·27) 385

חֲלוּץ 7 equipped one, warrior (4·17[?]) 323

יוֹבֵל 8 ram (5·27) 385

חֲלוּץ 9 equipped one, warrior (4·17[?]) 323

הריע 10 to shout a war cry, alarm of battle (7·40·44) 929

הַקִּיף 11 to go around (2·16·17) 668

יוֹבֵל	13	ram (5·27) 385
חָלוּץ		equipped one, warrior (4·17[?]) 323
שַׁחַר	15	dawn (1·23) 1007
הֵרִיע	16	to shout a war cry, alarm of battle (7·40·44) 929
חֵרֶם	17	devoted thing (13·29) 356
זוֹנָה		harlot (4·33[?]) 275
הֶחְבִּיא		to hide (2·6·34) 285
חֵרֶם	18	devoted thing (13·29) 356
הֶחֱרִים		to devote to destruction (14·46·49) 355
עָכַר		to disturb, trouble (3·12·14) 747
הֵרִיע	20	to shout a war cry, alarm of battle (7·40·44) 929
תְּרוּעָה		alarm [of war], war cry (2·36) 929
הֶחֱרִים	21	to devote to destruction (14·46·49) 355
שֶׂה		sheep, goat (1·44) 961
רָגַל	22	to spy (5·14·16) 920
זוֹנָה		harlot (4·33[?]) 275
רָגַל	23	to spy (5·14·16) 920
זוֹנָה	25	harlot (4·33[?]) 275
הֶחְבִּיא		to hide (2·6·34) 285
רָגַל		to spy (5·14·16) 920
יָסַד	26	to found (1·10·42) 413
צָעִיר		young (1·22) 859
שֵׁמַע	27	report (2·4) 1035

Chapter 7

מָעַל	1	to act unfaithfully (4·35·35) 591
מַעַל		unfaithful act (5·29) 591
חֵרֶם		devoted thing (13·29) 356
רָגַל	2	to spy (5·14·16) 920
שֶׁבֶר	5	perh. quarry (1·45) 991
מוֹרָד		descent (2·5) 434
נָמֵס		to melt, grow fearful (3·19·21) 587
שִׂמְלָה	6	clothes (1·29) 971
אֲהָהּ	7	alas! (1·15) 13

הוֹאִיל		to show willingness (2·18·18) 383
בִּי	8	part. of entreaty: I pray, Oh (1·12) 106
עֹרֶף		back of neck (2·33) 791
חֵרֶם	11	devoted thing (13·29) 356
גנב		to take by stealth, steal (1·30·39) 170
כִּחֵשׁ		to deceive (2·19·22) 471
עֹרֶף	12	back of neck (2·33) 791
חֵרֶם		devoted thing (13·29) 356
חֵרֶם	13	devoted thing (13·29) 356
חֵרֶם	15	devoted thing (13·29) 356
נְבָלָה		disgraceful folly (1·13) 615
תּוֹדָה	19	thanksgiving, praise (1·32) 392
כִּחֵד		to hide (1·15·30) 470
אָמְנָה	20	truly, indeed (1·3) 53
אַדֶּרֶת	21	cloak (2·12) 12
מִשְׁקָל		weight (1·48) 1054
חָמַד		to desire (1·16·21) 326
טָמַן		to hide (3·28·31) 380
טָמַן	22	to hide (3·28·31) 380
אַדֶּרֶת	24	cloak (2·12) 12
עָכַר	25	to disturb, trouble (3·12·14) 747
רגם		to kill by stoning (1·15·15) 920
סקל		to stone (1·12·22) 709
גַּל	26	heap (2·20) 164
חָרוֹן		[burning of] anger (1·41) 354

Chapter 8

בָּזַז	2	to plunder (3·37·40) 102
אֹרֵב		liers in wait (6·18[?]) 70
אָרַב	4	to lie in wait (5·20·23) 70
הִתִּיק	6	to draw away (1·2·27) 683
אֹרֵב	7	place of lying in wait, ambush (6·18[?]) 70
הִצִּית	8	to kindle (2·17·27) 428
מַאֲרָב	9	ambush (1·5) 70
גַּיְא	11	valley (3·47) 161

אֹרֵב 12 liers in wait (6·18[?]) 70

עָקֵב 13 hinder part, rear (1·14) 784

אֹרֵב 14 liers in wait (6·18[?]) 70

נִתַּק 16 to be drawn out (2·10·27) 683

כִּידוֹן 18 javelin (3·9) 475

אֹרֵב 19 liers in wait (6·18[?]) 70

הִצִּית to kindle (2·17·27) 428

עָשָׁן 20 smoke (2·25) 798

הֵנָּה הנה להנה = hither and thither (5·49) 244

אֹרֵב 21 liers in wait (6·18[?]) 70

עָשָׁן smoke (2·25) 798

בִּלְתִּי 22 not, except (4·24) 116

שָׂרִיד survivor (9·28) 975

פָּלִיט fugitive, escaped one (1·19) 812

כִּידוֹן 26 javelin (3·9) 475

הַחֲרִים to devote to destruction (14·46·49) 355

בָּזַז 27 to plunder (3·37·40) 102

תֵּל 28 mound (2·5) 1068

תָּלָה 29 to execute by hanging (3·23·27) 1067

נְבֵלָה corpse (1·48) 615

גַּל heap (2·20) 164

שָׁלֵם 31 full, perfect (1·28) 1023

הֵנִיף to wield (1·32·34[?]) 631

מִשְׁנֶה 32 copy (1·35) 1041

שֹׁטֵר 33 official, officer (5·25) 1009

אֶזְרָח native (1·17) 280

מוּל in front of (5·33) 557

קְלָלָה 34 curse (1·13) 887

טַף 35 children (2·41) 381

Chapter 9

שְׁפֵלָה 1 lowland (7·20) 1050

חוֹף shore, coast (1·7) 342

מוּל in front of (5·33) 557

עָרְמָה 4 craftily (1·5) 791

הִצְעִיר perh. to form [cause to become] 851 [or alternate root הצטיד] to supply oneself with provisions (1·1·1) 845

שָׂק sack [for grain] (1·48) 974

בָּלֶה worn out (4·5) 115

נֹאד skin (2·6) 609

נַעַל 5 sandal (3·22) 653

בָּלֶה worn out (4·5) 115

טֻלָּא to be patched (1·1·1) 378

שַׂלְמָה outer garment (3·16) 971

צֵיד provision (2·5) 845

נִקֻּד crumbs (2·3) 666

אוּלַי 7 perhaps (2·45) 19

מֵאַיִן 8 whence? (2·48) 32

שֹׁמַע 9 report (2·4) 1035

צֵידָה 11 provision (2·9) 845

חָם 12 hot (1·12) 328

הִצְטַיֵּד to take as one's provisions (1·1·1) 845

נִקֻּד crumbs (2·3) 666

נֹאד 13 skin (2·6) 609

שַׂלְמָה outer garment (3·16) 971

נַעַל sandal (3·22) 653

בלה to become old and worn out (1·11·16) 115

צֵיד 14 provision (2·5) 845

נלון 18 to murmur (1·8·18) 534

קֶצֶף 20 wrath (3·29) 893

שְׁבוּעָה oath (3·30) 989

חֹטֵב 21 cutter or gatherer of firewood (3·6[?]) 310

שֹׁאֵב water drawer (3·5) 980

רִמָּה 22 to deceive (1·8·8) 941

חֹטֵב 23 cutter or gatherer of firewood (3·6[?]) 310

שֹׁאֵב water drawer (3·5) 980

חֹטֵב 27 cutter or gatherer of firewood (3·6[?]) 310

שֹׁאֵב water drawer (3·5) 980

Chapter 10

הַחֲרִים 1 to devote to destruction (14·46·49) 355

הרפה 6 to abandon (2·21·44) 951

בִּפְנֵי 8 in the face of (3·17) 816

פִּתְאֹם 9 suddenly (2·25) 837

הָמַם 10 to confuse, rout (1·13·13) 243

מַכָּה defeat (2·48) 646

מַעֲלֵה ascent (4·19) 751

מוֹרָד 11 descent (2·5) 434

בָּרָד hail (1·29) 135

מֵאֲשֶׁר from [or than] that which (1·17) 84

דמם 12 to be still, silent (2·23·30) 198

יָרֵחַ moon (2·27) 437

דמם 13 to be still, silent (2·23·30) 198

יָרֵחַ moon (2·27) 437

נקם to avenge (1·13·34) 667

אוץ to hasten (2·8·10) 21

נֶחְבָּא 16 to hide oneself, be hidden (4·16·34) 285

מְעָרָה cave (9·40) 792

נֶחְבָּא 17 to hide oneself, be hidden (4·16·34) 285

מְעָרָה cave (9·40) 792

גלל 18 to roll (2·10·17) 164

מְעָרָה cave (9·40) 792

זנב 19 to cut off or smite the tail = attack in the rear (1·2·2) 275

מַכָּה 20 slaughter (2·48) 646

שָׂרִיד survivor (9·28) 975

שׂרד to escape (1·1·1) 974

מִבְצָר fortification (3·37) 131

חָרַץ 21 to cut, sharpen, decide (1·5·10) 358

מְעָרָה 22 cave (9·40) 792

מְעָרָה 23 cave (9·40) 792

קָצִין 24 chief, commander (1·12) 892

צַוָּאר neck, back of neck (2·41) 848

אמץ 25 to be strong, bold (5·16·41) 54

כָּכָה thus (1·34) 462

תָּלָה 26 to execute by hanging (3·27) 1067

מְעָרָה 27 cave (9·40) 792

נֶחְבָּא to hide oneself, be hidden (4·16·34) 285

הַחֲרִים 28 to devote to destruction (14·46·49) 355

שָׂרִיד survivor (9·28) 975

שָׂרִיד 30 survivor (9·28) 975

בִּלְתִּי 33 not, except (4·24) 116

שָׂרִיד survivor (9·28) 975

הַחֲרִים 35 to devote to destruction (14·46·49) 355

שָׂרִיד 37 survivor (9·28) 975

הַחֲרִים to devote to destruction (14·46·49) 355

הַחֲרִים 39 to devote to destruction (14·46·49) 355

שָׂרִיד survivor (9·28) 975

שְׁפֵלָה 40 lowland (7·20) 1050

אָשֵׁד mountain slope (4·7) 78

שָׂרִיד survivor (9·28) 975

נְשָׁמָה breathing thing (3·24) 675

הַחֲרִים to devote to destruction (14·46·49) 355

Chapter 11

שְׁפֵלָה 2 lowland (7·20) 1050

נפה height (2·4) 632

חוֹל 4 sand (1·22) 297

נועד 5 to assemble by appointment (1·18·28) 416

עָקַר 6 to hamstring (2·5·7) 785

מֶרְכָּבָה chariot (2·44) 939

פִּתְאֹם 7 suddenly (2·25) 837

בִּקְעָה 8 valley, plain (3·19) 132

בִּלְתִּי not, except (4·24) 116

שָׂרִיד survivor (9·28) 975

עָקַר 9 to hamstring (2·5·7) 785

מֶרְכָּבָה chariot (2·44) 939

הַחֲרִים 11 to devote to destruction (14·46·49) 355

נְשָׁמָה breathing thing (3·24) 675

הַחֲרִים 12 to devote to destruction (14·46·49) 355

תֵּל 13 mound (2·5) 1068

זוּלָה except that (1·16) 265

בָּזַז 14 to plunder (3·37·40) 102

נְשָׁמָה breathing thing (3·24) 675

שְׁפֵלָה 16 lowland (7·20) 1050

בִּקְעָה 17 valley, plain (3·19) 132

בִּלְתִּי 19 not, except (4·24) 116

הַחֲרִים 20 to devote to destruction (14·46·49) 355

תְּחִנָּה favor (1·25) 337

הַחֲרִים 21 to devote to destruction (14·46·49) 355

מַחֲלֹקֶת 23 division (3·44) 324

שָׁקַט to be quiet, undisturbed (2·31·41) 1052

Chapter 12

מֶלַח 3 salt (5·28) 571

תֵּימָן south (3·24) 412

יְרֵשָׁה 6 possession (3·14) 440

בִּקְעָה 7 valley, plain (3·19) 132

יְרֵשָׁה possession (3·14) 440

מַחֲלֹקֶת division (3·44) 324

שְׁפֵלָה 8 lowland (7·20) 1050

אָשֵׁד mountain slope (4·7) 78

צַד 9 side (3·31) 841

נפה 23 height (2·4) 632

Chapter 13

זָקֵן 1 to be old, become old (4·25·27) 278 165

גְּלִילָה 2 circuit, boundary, territory (4·6[?]) 165

סרן 3 lord (1·21) 710

תֵּימָן 4 south (3·24) 412

מִישׁוֹר 9 plain (5·23) 449

מִישׁוֹר 16 plain (5·23) 449

מִישׁוֹר 17 plain (5·23) 449

אָשֵׁד 20 mountain slope (4·7) 78

מִישׁוֹר 21 plain (5·23) 449

נסיך prince (1·6[?]) 651

קֶסֶם 22 necromancers, diviners (1·9) 890

חַוָּה 30 tent village (1·7) 295

Chapter 14

קִנְיָן 4 acquisition (1·9) 889

אֹדוֹת 6 cause; על א = because of (2·11) 15

רגל to spy (5·14·16) 920

המסה 8 to melt (1·4·4) 587

מֵאָז 10 from that time, time past (1·18) 23

בָּצוּר 12 fortified (1·25) 130

אוּלַי perhaps (2·45) 19

שָׁקַט 15 to be quiet, undisturbed (2·31·41) 1052

Chapter 15

תֵּימָן 1 south (3·24) 412

מֶלַח 2 salt (5·28) 571

עַקְרָב 3 scorpion (1·9) 785

מַעֲלֵה ascent (4·19) 751

תּוֹצָאָה 4 extremity, outgoing (14·23) 426

קֵדֶם 5 eastward (4·26) 870

מֶלַח salt (5·28) 571

נֹכַח 7 opposite to (2·27) 647

מַעֲלֵה ascent (4·19) 751

תּוֹצָאָה extremity, outgoing (14·23) 426

גַּיְא 8 valley (3·47) 161

תָּאַר 9 to incline (5·5·8) 1061

מַעְיָן spring (2·23) 745

תָּאַר 11 to incline (5·5·8) 1061

תּוֹצָאָה extremity, outgoing (14·23) 426

יָלִיד 14 born (1·12) 409

הֵסִית 18 to instigate (1·18·18) 694

צנח to descend (1·3·3) 856

גֻּלָּה 19 basin (3·15) 165

עִלִּי upper (1·2) 751

תַּחְתִּי lower, lowest (1·19) 1066

שְׁפֵלָה 33 lowland (7·20) 1050

מֶלַח 62 salt (5·28) 571

Chapter 16

תַּחְתּוֹן 3 lower, lowest (2·13) 1066

תּוֹצָאָה extremity, outgoing (14·23) 426

פָּגַע 7 to strike, touch (10·40·46) 803

תּוֹצָאָה 8 extremity, outgoing (14·23) 426

מבדלה 9 a separate place (1·1) 95

מַס 10 slave gang(s) (2·23) 586

Chapter 17

חֶבֶל 5 measured portion, lot (5·49) 286

תּוֹצָאָה 9 extremity, outgoing (14·23) 426

פָּגַע 10 to strike, touch (10·40·46) 803

נפת 11 height (1·1) 632

הוֹאִיל 12 to determine (2·18·18) 383

מַס 13 slave gang(s) (2·23) 586

חֶבֶל 14 measured portion, lot (5·49) 286

ברא 15 to cut down, clear (2·5·5[?]) 135

אוץ to be pressed, confined, narrow (2·8·10) 21

לַאֲשֶׁר 16 to those who (2·38) 81

ברא 18 to cut down, clear (2·5·5[?]) 135

תּוֹצָאָה extremity, outgoing (14·23) 426

Chapter 18

נקהל 1 to assemble (2·19·39) 874

נכבש to be subdued (1·5·14) 461

אָנָה 3 whence? whither? (2·39) 33

התרפה to show oneself slack (1·3·44) 951

הֵנָּה 6 hither, here (5·49) 244

יָרָה to throw (1·13·25[?]) 434

פֹּה here, hither (2·44) 805

כְּהֻנָּה 7 priesthood (1·13) 464

פֹּה 8 here, hither (2·44) 805

מַחְלְקֶת 10 division (3·44) 324

תּוֹצָאָה 12 extremity, outgoing (14·23) 426

תָּאַר 14 to incline (5·5·8) 1061

תּוֹצָאָה extremity, outgoing (14·23) 426

מַעְיָן 15 spring (2·23) 745

גַּיְא 16 valley (3·47) 161

תָּאַר 17 to incline (5·5·8) 1061

נֹכַח opposite to (2·27) 647

מַעֲלֶה ascent (4·19) 751

מוּל 18 in front of (5·33) 557

תּוֹצָאָה 19 extremity, outgoing (14·23) 426

מֶלַח salt (5·28) 571

גבל 20 to bound, border (1·3·5) 148

קדם eastward (4·26) 870

גְּבוּלָה border, boundary (2·10) 148

Chapter 19

פָּגַע 11 to strike, touch (10·40·46) 803

קדם 12 eastward (4·26) 870

קדם 13 eastward (4·26) 870

תָּאַר to reach to (1·1·8) 1061

תּוֹצָאָה 14 extremity, outgoing (14·23) 426

גַּיְא valley (3·47) 161

פָּגַע 22 to strike, touch (10·40·46) 803

תּוֹצָאָה extremity, outgoing (14·23) 426

פָּגַע 26 to strike, touch (10·40·46) 803

פָּגַע 27 to strike, touch (10·40·46) 803

גַּיְא valley (3·47) 161

מִבְצָר 29 fortification (3·37) 137

תּוֹצָאָה extremity, outgoing (14·23) 426

אֵלוֹן 33 terebinth, tall tree (1·10) 18

תּוֹצָאָה extremity, outgoing (14·23) 426

פָּגַע 34 to strike, touch (10·40·46) 803

מִבְצָר 35 fortification (3·37) 131

מוּל 46 in front of (6·25) 557

גְּבוּלָה 49 border, boundary (2·10) 148

Chapter 20

מִקְלָט 2 refuge (7·20) 886

רָצַח 3 to murder, slay (8·38·43) 953

שְׁגָגָה sin of error, inadvertance (2·9) 993

מִקְלָט refuge (7·20) 886

גֹּאֵל kinsman (3·44[?]) 145

בִּבְלִי without (2·6) 115

גֹּאֵל 5 kinsman (3·44[?]) 145

רָצַח to murder, slay (8·38·43) 953

בִּבְלִי without (2·6) 115

שֹׂנֵא enemy (1·41) 971

תְּמוֹל yesterday; ת׳ שִׁלְשׁוֹם = aforetime (3·23) 1069

שִׁלְשׁוֹם 5 תְּמוֹל שׁ׳ = aforetime, previously (3·25) 1026

רָצַח 6 to murder, slay (8·38·43) 953

מִישׁוֹר 8 plain (5·23) 449

מוּעָדָה 9 cities appointed (1·1) 418

שְׁגָגָה sin of error, inadvertance (2·9) 993

גֹּאֵל kinsman (3·44[?]) 145

Chapter 21

מִקְלָט 13 refuge (7·20) 886

רָצַח to murder, slay (8·38·43) 953

מִקְלָט 21 refuge (7·20) 886

רָצַח to murder, slay (8·38·43) 953

מִקְלָט 27 refuge (7·20) 886

רָצַח to murder, slay (8·38·43) 953

מִקְלָט 32 refuge (7·20) 886

רָצַח to murder, slay (8·38·43) 953

מִקְלָט 38 refuge (7·20) 886

רָצַח to murder, slay (8·38·43) 953

בִּפְנֵי 42 in the face of (3·17) 816

Chapter 22

נכס 8 riches (1·5) 647

שַׂלְמָה clothes (3·16) 971

גְּלִילָה 10 circuit, boundary, territory (4·6) 165

מוּל 11 in front of (6·25) 557

גְּלִילָה circuit, boundary, territory (4·6) 165

נקהל 12 to assemble (2·19·39) 874

מַעַל 16 unfaithful act (5·29) 591

מָעַל to act unfaithfully (4·35·35) 591

מָרַד to rebel (5·25·25) 597

נֶגֶף 17 plague (1·7) 620

מָרַד 18 to rebel (5·25·25) 597

קָצַף to be angry (1·28·34) 893

מָרַד 19 to rebel (5·25·25) 597

מִבַּלְעֲדֵי apart from, except, without (1·12) 116

מָעַל 20 to act unfaithfully (4·35·35) 591

מַעַל unfaithful act (5·29) 591

חֵרֶם devoted thing (13·29) 356

קֶצֶף wrath (3·29) 893

גָּוַע to expire, die (1·23·23) 157

אֶלֶף 21 thousand (3·12[?]) 48

מֶרֶד 22 revolt (1·1) 597

מַעַל unfaithful act (5·29) 591

דְּאָגָה 24 anxiety, anxious care (1·6) 178

תַּבְנִית 28 construction, structure (1·20) 125

חָלִילָה 29 far be it [from] (2·21) 321

מָרַד to rebel (5·25·25) 597

מִלְּבַד besides (1·33) 94

אֶלֶף 30 thousand (3·12[?]) 48

מָעַל 31 to act unfaithfully (4·35·35) 591

מַעַל unfaithful act (5·29) 591

Chapter 23

זָקֵן 1 to be old, become old (4·25·27) 278

שֹׁטֵר 2 official, officer (5·25) 1009

זָקֵן to be old, become old (4·25·27) 278

מָבוֹא 4 entering (2·23) 99

הָדַף 5 to thrust out, drive out (1 · 11 · 11) 213

עָצוּם 9 mighty, strong (1 · 31) 783

בִּפְנֵי in the face of (3 · 17) 816

הִתְחַתֵּן 12 to form a marriage alliance with (1 · 11 · 11) 368

פַּח 13 bird trap (1 · 25) 809

מוֹקֵשׁ lure (1 · 27) 430

שֹׁטֵט scourge (1 · 1) 1002

צַד side (3 · 31) 841

צְנִין thorn, prick (1 · 2) 856

מְהֵרָה 16 haste (3 · 20) 555

Chapter 24

שֹׁטֵר 1 official, officer (5 · 25) 1009

הִתְיַצֵּב to station oneself (2 · 48 · 48) 426

נָגַף 5 to smite (1 · 24 · 48) 619

מַאֲפֵל 7 darkness (1 · 1) 66

צִרְעָה 12 hornets (1 · 3) 864

גָּרַשׁ to drive out (2 · 34 · 48) 176

יָגַע 13 to toil (1 · 20 · 26) 388

זַיִת olives, olive tree (1 · 38) 268

חָלִילָה 16 far be it [from] (2 · 21) 321

גָּרַשׁ 18 to drive out (2 · 34 · 48) 176

קַנּוֹא 19 jealous (1 · 2) 888

נֵכָר 20 foreignness (2 · 36) 648

נֵכָר 23 foreignness (2 · 36) 648

שֹׁטֵר 24 official, officer (5 · 25) 1009

אֵלָה 26 terebinth (1 · 17) 18

עֵדָה 27 testimony, witness (1 · 3) 729

אֵמֶר speech, word (1 · 48) 56

כָּחֵשׁ to deceive (2 · 19 · 22) 471

הֶאֱרִיךְ 31 to prolong (1 · 31 · 34) 73

חֶלְקָה 32 portion of ground (1 · 24) 324

קְשִׂיטָה a unit of [unknown] value, perh. weight (1 · 3) 903

JUDGES

Chapter 1

תְּחִלָּה 1 beginning; בַּתְּ' = first, at first (3·22) 321

קצץ 6 to cut, hew off (1·9·14) 893

בֹּהֶן thumb, great toe (2·2 [?]) 97

בֹּהֶן 7 thumb, great toe (2·[2[?]) 97

קצץ to be cut or hewn off (1·1·14) 893

לקט to gather (1·21·36) 544

שְׁפֵלָה 9 lowland (1·20) 1050

לְפָנִים 10 formerly (5·21) 815

לְפָנִים 11 formerly (5·21) 815

הסית 14 to incite (1·18·18) 694

צנח to descend (2·3·3) 856

יהב 15 to give (2·27·27) 396

גֻּלָּה basin (pool, well[?]) (3·15) 165

עִלִּי upper (1·2) 751

תַּחְתִּי lower (1·9) 1066

חֹתֵן 16 wife's father (5·21) 368

תָּמָר palm tree, date palm; עִיר הַתְּמָרִים = Jericho (2·12) 1071

הֶחֱרִים 17 to devote to destruction (2·46·49) 355

הֵתִיר 23 to make reconnaissance (1·3·22) 1064

לְפָנִים formerly (5·21) 815

מָבוֹא 24 entrance (2·23) 99

מָבוֹא 25 entrance (2·23) 99

הוֹאִיל 27 to resolve, be determined (4·18·18) 383

מַס 28 labor bands (4·23) 586

מַס 30 labor bands (4·23) 586

מַס 33 labor bands (4·23) 586

לָחַץ 34 to press (3·14·15) 537

הוֹאִיל 35 to resolve, persist (4·18·18) 383

מַס labor bands (4·23) 586

מַעֲלֵה 36 ascent; מ' עַקְרַבִּים = Scorpion Pass (2·19) 751

עַקְרָב scorpion (1·9) 785

Chapter 2

הֵפֵר 1 to break, violate (1·41·44) 830

נָתַץ 2 to pull down (7·31·42) 683

גרש 3 to drive out, away (5·34·48) 176

צַד side, *prob.* = snare, trap (1·1) 841

מוֹקֵשׁ lure (2·27) 430

הֶאֱרִיךְ 7 to prolong; הֶאֱרִיךְ אַחֲרֵי = survive (1·31·34) 73

שֹׁסִים 14 plunderers (2·7) 1042

שסס to plunder (1·3·5) 1042

שֹׁסִים 16 plunderers (2·7) 1042

נאקה 18 groaning (1·4) 611

לָחַץ to oppress (3·14·15) 537

דחק oppressor (1·1[?]) 191

מעלל 19 practice (1·4) 611

קָשֶׁה stiff, stubborn (2·36) 904

נִסָּה 22 to test (4·36·36) 650

Chapter 3

נִסָּה 1 to test (4·36·36) 650

לְפָנִים 2 formerly (5·21) 815

סרן 3 lord (8·21) 710

נִסָּה 4 to test (4·36·36) 650

אֲשֵׁרָה 7 Ashera; Canaanite goddess of fortune and happiness; a sacred tree or pole (5·40) 81

מוֹשִׁיעַ 9 savior (3·27) 446

עזז 10 to be strong, prevail (2·9·11) 738

שָׁקַט 11 to be quiet, undisturbed, at peace (6·31·41) 1052

תָּמָר 13 palm tree, date palm; עִיר הַתְּמָרִים = Jericho (2·12) 1071

מוֹשִׁיעַ 15 savior (3·27) 446

136

אָטֵר shut up, bound [of right hand = left handed] (2·2) 32

גֹּמֶד 16 short cubit (1·1) 167

חגר to gird on (4·44·44) 291

מַד garment (2·12) 551

יָרֵךְ thigh (4·34) 437

בָּרִיא 17 fat (1·14) 135

פְּסִיל 19 idol, image (2·23) 820

סֵתֶר secrecy (1·35) 712

הַס interj.: hush! keep silence! (1·6) 245

עֲלִיָּה 20 roof chamber (4·20) 751

מְקֵרָה coolness (2·2) 903

יָרֵךְ 21 thigh (4·34) 437

נִצָּב 22 hilt (1·1) 662

לַהַב blade (4·12) 529

שָׁלַף to draw out (10·25·25) 1025

פַּרְשְׁדֹנָה feces [dub.] (1·1) 832

מסדרון 23 porch [dub.] (1·1) 690

עֲלִיָּה roof chamber (4·20) 751

נָעַל to bar, lock (2·7[?]·8[?]) 653

עֲלִיָּה 24 roof chamber (4·20) 751

נָעַל to bar, lock (2·7[?]·8[?]) 653

הסך to cover (1·5·18[?]) 696

חֶדֶר chamber (4·34) 293

מְקֵרָה coolness (2·2) 903

חִיל 25 to be in anxious longing (1·3·5[?]) 296

עֲלִיָּה roof chamber (4·20) 751

מַפְתֵּחַ key (1·3) 836

התמהמה 26 to linger, wait (2·9·9) 554

פְּסִיל idol, image (2·23) 820

מַעְבָּרָה 28 ford (3·8) 721

שָׁמֵן 29 stout, robust (1·10) 1032

נִכְנַע 30 to be subdued (3·25·36) 488

שָׁקַט to be quiet, undisturbed, at peace (6·31·41) 1052

מלמד 31 oxgoad (1·1) 541

Chapter 4

לָחַץ 3 to oppress (3·14·15) 537

חָזְקָה strength, force, forcibly (2·6) 306

נְבִיאָה 4 prophetess (1·6) 612

תֹּמֶר 5 palm tree (1·2) 1071

מָשַׁךְ 6 to proceed, march (4·30·36) 604

מָשַׁךְ 7 to draw, lead along (4·30·36) 604

אֶפֶס 9 אֶפֶס כִּי = save that, howbeit (1·41) 67

נפרד 11 to divide, separate (1·12·26) 825

חֹתֵן wife's father (5·21) 368

אֵלוֹן terebinth, tall tree (3·10) 18

הָמַם 15 to confuse, discomfit (1·13·13) 243

מֶרְכָּבָה chariot (2·44) 939

שְׂמִיכָה 18 rug or thick coverlet [dub.] (1·1) 970

צמא 19 to be thirsty (2·10·10) 854

נֹאד skin bottle, skin (2·6) 609

חָלָב milk (2·44) 316

פֹּה 20 here (3·46) 805

יָתֵד 21 tent peg (6·24) 450

מַקֶּבֶת hammer (1·4) 666

לָאט secrecy, בַּלָּאט = secretly (1·7) 532

רַקָּה the temple of the head (3·5) 956

צנח to go down (1·3·3) 856

נִרְדָּם to be or fall fast asleep (1·7·7) 922

עִיף to be faint (1·5·5) 746

יָתֵד 22 tent peg (6·24) 450

רַקָּה the temple of the head (3·5) 956

הִכְנִיעַ 23 to subdue (1·36) 488

קָשָׁה 24 severe (2·36) 904

Chapter 5

פֶּרַע 2 leader [dub.] (2·2) 828

פרע to act as leader, lead [dub.] (1·13·16) 828

התנדב to volunteer (2·14·17) 621

הַאֲזִין 3 to listen, give ear (1·41·41) 24

רֹזְנִים rulers (1·6) 931

137

זָמַר	to make music, to sing (1·43·43) 274
צָעַד	4 to step, march (1·7·8) 857
רָעַשׁ	to quake, shake (1·21·29) 950
נָטַף	to drop (2·9·18) 642
עָב	dark cloud (1·30) 728
נָזַל	5 to shake, quake (1·3·4) 272
נְתִיבָה	6 path (1·21) 677
עֲקַלְקַל	crooked, i.e., roundabout (1·2) 785
פְּרָזוֹן	7 coll. rural population, rustics [dub.] (2·2) 826
לָחֶם	8 war [dub.] (1·1) 535
רֹמַח	spear, lance (1·15) 942
חוֹקֵק	9 commander (1·1[?]) 349
הִתְנַדֵּב	to volunteer (2·14·17) 621
אָתוֹן	10 she ass (1·35) 87
צָחֹר	tawny (1·1) 850
מַד	cloth, carpet [dub.] (2·12) 551
שִׂיחַ	to talk, sing (1·18·20) 967
חָצַץ	11 archer (1·1·3[?]) 346
מַשְׁאָב	place for drawing water [dub.] (1·1) 980
תָּנָה	to recount (2·2·2) 1072
פְּרָזוֹן	coll. rural population, rustics [dub.] (2·2) 826
שָׁבָה	12 to lead captive (1·29·37) 985
שְׁבִי	captivity, captives (1·46) 985
שָׂרִיד	13 survivor (1·28) 975
אַדִּיר	majestic one (2·27) 12
שֹׁרֶשׁ	14 root (1·33) 1057
מְחֹקֵק	commander (1·7) 349
מָשַׁךְ	to proceed, march (4·30·36) 604
פְּלַגָּה	15 division, section [of tribe] (2·3) 811
מִשְׁפְּתַיִם	16 fire places or ash heaps [dub.] (1·2) 1046
שְׁרִיקָה	hissing [whistling, piping] (1·2) 1057
עֵדֶר	flock (1·39) 727
פְּלַגָּה	division, section [of tribe] (2·3) 811

חֵקֶר	searchings, questionings (1·12) 350
אֳנִיָּה	17 ship (1·31) 58
חוֹף	shore, coast (1·7) 342
מִפְרָץ	landing place (1·1) 830
חֵרֵף	18 to reproach, despise, scorn (2·34·38) 357
בֶּצַע	19 gain made by violence (1·23) 130
כּוֹכָב	20 star (1·37) 456
מְסִלָּה	highway (5·27) 700
גָּרַף	21 to sweep away (1·1·1) 175
קְדוּמִים	dubious (1·1) 870
הָלַם	22 to hammer, strike down (2·8·8) 240
עָקֵב	heel (1·14) 784
דַּהֲרָה	rushing, dashing (2·2) 187
אַבִּיר	mighty, valiant (1·17) 7
עֶזְרָה	23 help (2·26) 740
חָלָב	25 milk (2·44) 316
סֵפֶל	bowl (2·2) 705
אַדִּיר	majestic one (2·27) 12
חֶמְאָה	curd, curdled milk (1·10) 326
יָתֵד	26 tent peg (6·24) 450
הַלְמוּת	hammer, mallet (1·1) 240
עָמֵל	laborer, workman (1·9) 766
הָלַם	to smite (2·8·8) 240
מָחַק	to utterly destroy (1·1·1) 563
מָחַץ	to smite through (1·14·14) 563
חָלַף	to pass through, i.e., pierce (1·2·2[?]) 322
רַקָּה	the temple of the head (3·5) 956
כָּרַע	27 to bow down (4·29·35) 502
בַּאֲשֶׁר	in [the place] where (3·19) 84
חַלּוֹן	28 window (1·30) 319
נִשְׁקַף	to lean over, look through (1·10·22) 1054
יִבֵּב	to cry shrilly (1·1·1) 384
אֶשְׁנָב	window lattice (1·2) 1039
אָחַר	to delay, tarry (1·15·17) 29

מֶרְכָּבָה chariot (2·44) 939

שׂרה 29 princess (1·5) 979

אֹמֶר utterance, word (1·48) 56

רַחַם 30 a woman (2·33) 933

צֶבַע dye, dyed stuff (2·2) 840

רִקְמָה variegated stuff (2·12) 955

צַוָּאר neck, back of neck (3·41) 848

אֹהֵב 31 friend, lover (1·36[?]) 12

שָׁקַט to be quiet, undisturbed, at peace (6·31·41) 1052

Chapter 6

עזז 2 to be strong, prevail (2·9·11) 738

מנהרה dubious (1·1) 626

מְעָרָה cave (1·40) 792

מְצָד mountain fastness (1·11) 844

יְבוּל 4 produce (1·13) 385

מִחְיָה sustenance (2·8) 313

שֶׂה a sheep or goat (1·44) 961

כְּדֵי 5 according to the abundance of (1·5) 191

אַרְבֶּה locust (2·24) 916

נדלל 6 to be brought low (1·8·8) 195

אדה 7 cause; על אדות = because of (1·11) 15

לחץ 9 oppressor (2·4) 537

גרש to drive out, away (5·34·48) 176

אֵלָה 11 terebinth, tall tree (2·17) 18

חבט to beat out (1·4·5) 286

חִטָּה wheat (2·30) 334

גַּת wine press (1·5) 387

בִּי 13 part. of entreaty: I pray (3·13) 106

אַיֵּה where? (2·44) 32

נִפְלָאוֹת wonderful acts (1·43) 810

נָטַשׁ to forsake (1·33·40) 643

בִּי 15 part. of entreaty: I pray (3·13) 106

בַּמָּה by what means? (8·29) 552

אֶלֶף thousand (1·12[?]) 48

דַּל weak (1·48) 195

צָעִיר little, insignificant (1·22) 859

מוּשׁ 18 to depart (1·20?·20) 559

גְּדִי 19 kid (5·16) 152

אֵיפָה ephah, a grain measure (1·38) 35

קֶמַח flour, meal (1·14) 887

סַל basket (1·15) 700

מָרָק broth (2·3) 600

פָּרוּר pot (1·3) 807

אֵלָה terebinth, tall tree (2·17) 18

הַלָּז 20 this (1·7) 229

מָרָק broth (2·3) 600

מִשְׁעֶנֶת 21 staff (1·12) 1044

אֲהָהּ 22 alas! (2·15) 13

הָרַס 25 to throw down, tear down (1·30·43) 248

אֲשֵׁרָה Ashera; Canaanite goddess of fortune; a symbol of this goddess — sacred tree or pole (5·40) 81

מָעוֹז 26 place of safety, fastness (1·36) 731

מַעֲרָכָה row (1·18) 790

אֲשֵׁרָה a sacred tree or pole (5·40) 81

נָתַץ 28 to be torn down (1·1·42) 683

אֲשֵׁרָה a sacred tree or pole (5·40) 81

נָתַץ 30 to pull down (7·31·42) 683

אֲשֵׁרָה a sacred tree or pole (5·40) 81

נָתַץ 31 to pull down (7·31·42) 683

נָתַץ 32 to pull down (7·31·42) 683

הַצִּיג 37 to set, place (3·15·16)

גִּזָּה fleece (7·7) 159

צֶמֶר wool (1·16) 856

גֹּרֶן threshing floor (1·34) 175

טַל night mist, dew (4·31) 378

חֹרֶב dryness (3·16) 351

מָחֳרָת 38 the morrow, next day; מִמָּחֳרָת = on the morrow (3·32) 564

זור to press [twist or wring] out (1·3·3) 266

גִּזָּה fleece (7·7) 159

מָצָה   to drain (1·4·7) 594

טַל   night mist, dew (4·31) 378

סֵפֶל   bowl (2·2) 705

נָסָה   39 to test (4·36·36) 650

גִּזָּה   fleece (7·7) 159

חֹרֶב   dryness (3·16) 351

טַל   night mist, dew (4·31) 378

חֹרֶב   40 dryness (3·16) 351

גִּזָּה   fleece (7·7) 159

טַל   night mist, dew (4·31) 378

Chapter 7

הִתְפָּאר   2 to glorify oneself (1·7·13) 802

יָרֵא   3 afraid (1·45) 431

חָרֵד   trembling (1·6) 353

צפר   to depart [dub.] (1·1·1) 861

צָרַף   4 to test (1·18·21) 864

לקק   5 to lap (2·5·7) 545

כֶּלֶב   dog (1·32) 476

הִצִּיג   to set, place (3·15·16) 426

כָּרַע   to bow (4·29·35) 502

בֶּרֶךְ   knee (3·25) 139

לקק   6 to lap (2·2·7) 545

כָּרַע   to bow (4·29·35) 502

בֶּרֶךְ   knee (3·25) 139

לֹקֵק   7 to lap (2·2·7) 545

צֵידָה   8 provision (2·9) 845

חֹמֶשׁ   11 in battle array (1·4·5[?]) 332

אַרְבֶּה   12 locust (2·24) 916

חוֹל   sand (1·22) 297

שֶׁעַל   which [is] upon (2·2) 979

חָלַם   13 to dream (1·26·28[?]) 321

שְׂעֹרָה   barley (1·34) 972

לְמַעְלָה   upwards (1·34) 751

בִּלְתִּי   14 except (1·24) 116

שֶׁבֶר   15 breaking [of dream], i.e,
     interpretation (1·45) 991

חָצָה   16 to divide (2·11·15) 345

כַּד   jar (4·18) 461

רֵק   empty [of vessels] (3·14) 938

לַפִּיד   torch (5·13) 542

אַשְׁמֹרֶת   19 watch [div. of time] (1·7) 1038

תִּיכוֹן   middle (1·12) 1064

נפץ   to shatter (1·5·21) 658

כַּד   jar (4·18) 461

כַּד   20 jar (4·18) 461

לַפִּיד   torch (5·13) 542

הֵרִיעַ   21 to shout a war cry, alarm of battle
     (2·40·44) 929

עֹרֵב   raven (1·12) 788

זְאֵב   25 wolf [dub.] (1·8) 255

יֶקֶב   wine press (1·16) 428

Chapter 8

חָזְקָה   1 force, strength, severe rebuke
     (2·6) 306

עֹלֵלוֹת   2 gleaning (1·6) 760

בָּצִיר   vintage (1·7) 131

רָפָה   3 to relax, abate (2·14·44) 951

עָיֵף   4 faint, weary (2·17) 746

עָיֵף   5 faint, weary (2·17) 746

דּוּשׁ   7 to tread, thresh (1·12·15) 190

קוֹץ   thornbush (2·11) 881

בַּרְקָנִים   briers (2·2) 140

נָתַץ   9 to pull down (7·31·42) 683

מִגְדָּל   tower (9·49) 153

שָׁלַף   10 to draw out (10·25·25) 1025

בֶּטַח   11 securely (2·43) 105

הֶחֱרִיד   12 to drive in terror, rout (1·16·39) 353

מַעֲלֶה   13 ascent (2·19) 751

חֵרֵף   15 to reproach, taunt (2·34·38) 357

יָעֵף   weary, faint (1·4) 419

קוֹץ   16 thornbush (2·11) 881

בַּרְקָנִים   briers (2·2) 140

מִגְדָּל   17 tower (9·49) 153

נָתַץ   to pull down (7·31·42) 683

אֵיפֹה	18 where? of what kind? (2·25) 33
תֹּאַר	outline, form (1·15) 1061
שָׁלַף	20 to draw out (10·25·25) 1025
פָּגַע	21 to fall upon (3·40·46) 803
שַׂהֲרֹן	moon, crescent (2·3) 962
צַוָּאר	neck, back of neck (3·41) 848
שְׁאֵלָה	24 request, petition (1·13) 982
נֶזֶם	earring (4·17) 633
שִׂמְלָה	25 wrapper, mantle, covering (1·29) 971
נֶזֶם	earring (4·17) 633
מִשְׁקָל	26 weight (1·48) 1054
נֶזֶם	earring (4·17) 633
שַׂהֲרֹן	moon, crescent (2·3) 962
נטיפה	pendant (1·2) 643
אַרְגָּמָן	purple cloth (1·39) 71
שֶׁעַל	which [were] on (2·2) 979
עֲנָק	neck pendant [dub.] (1·31) 848
צַוָּאר	neck, back of neck (3·41) 848
אֵפוֹד	27 ephod (6·49) 65
הַצִּיג	to set (3·15·16) 426
מוֹקֵשׁ	lure (2·27) 430
נִכְנַע	28 to be subdued (3·25·36) 488
שָׁקַט	to be quiet, undisturbed, at peace (6·31·41) 1052
יָרֵךְ	30 thigh = loins (4·34) 437
פִּילֶגֶשׁ	31 concubine (12·37) 811
שֵׂיבָה	32 old age (1·20[?]) 966

Chapter 9

שָׂכַר	4 to hire (2·17·20) 968
רֵק	empty, idle, worthless (3·14) 938
פחז	to be wanton, reckless (1·2·2) 808
נֶחְבָּא	5 to hide oneself (1·16·34) 285
אֵלוֹן	6 terebinth, tall tree (3·10) 18
מֻצָּב	set up (1·2[?]) 662
זַיִת	8 olive, olive tree (3·38) 268
זַיִת	9 olive, olive tree (3·38) 268

דֶּשֶׁן	fatness (1·15) 206
נוּעַ	to wave (3·22·38) 631
תְּאֵנָה	10 fig tree (2·39) 1061
תְּאֵנָה	11 fig tree (2·39) 1061
מתק	sweetness (1·1) 608
תְּנוּבָה	fruit, produce (1·5) 626
נוּעַ	to wave (3·22·38) 631
תִּירוֹשׁ	13 must, new wine (1·39) 440
נוּעַ	to wave (3·22·38) 631
אָטָד	14 bramble, buckthorn (3·4) 31
אָטָד	15 bramble, buckthorn (3·4) 31
חָסָה	to seek refuge (1·37·37) 340
גְּמוּל	16 dealing (1·19) 168
מִנֶּגֶד	17 in front, straight away [i.e., hazarded it] (2·26) 617
שָׂרַר	22 to rule over (1·5·7) 979
בגד	23 to act or deal treacherously, faithlessly (1·42·42) 93
ארב	25 lier in wait (1·2·23) 70
גָּזַל	to tear away, sieze; rob, plunder (2·29·30) 159
בצר	27 to cut off [grapes] (1·7·7[?]) 130
הלולים	praise, rejoicing (1·2) 239
פָּקִיד	28 commissioner, deputy (1·13) 824
תַּרְמָה	31 treacherously [dub.] (1·1) 941
צוּר	to incite [dub.] (1·5·5) 848
אָרַב	32 to lie in wait (5·20·23) 70
זָרַח	33 to rise (1·18·18) 280
פָּשַׁט	to put off [one's shelter], i.e., make a dash [from a sheltered place] (4·24·43) 833
אָרַב	34 to lie in wait (5·20·23) 70
מַאֲרָב	35 ambush (1·5) 70
טַבּוּר	37 highest part (1·2) 371
אֵלוֹן	terebinth, tall tree (3·10) 18
עוֹנֵן	to practice soothsaying (1·10·11) 778
אַיֵּה	38 where? (2·44) 32

אֵפוֹא   then (1·15) 66

גרש 41 to drive out, away (5·34·48) 176

מָחֳרָת 42 the morrow, next day; מִמָּחֳרָת = on the morrow (3·32) 564

חָצָה 43 to divide (2·11·15) 345

אָרַב   to lie in wait (5·20·23) 70

פָּשַׁט 44 to put off [one's shelter], i.e., make a ;dash [from a sheltered place] (4·24·43) 833

נָתַץ 45 to pull down (7·31·42) 683

מֶלַח   salt (1·28) 571

מִגְדָּל 46 tower (9·49) 153

צְרִיחַ   excavation, underground chamber [dub.] (3·4) 863

מִגְדָּל 47 tower (9·49) 153

קרדם 48 axe (1·5) 899

שׂוֹכה   branch, brushwood (1·1) 962

שְׁכֶם   shoulder (1·22) 1014

שׂוֹך 49 branch, brushwood (1·1) 962

צְרִיחַ   excavation, underground chamber [dub.] (3·4) 863

הִצִּית   to kindle, set on fire (1·17·27) 428

מִגְדָּל   tower (9·49) 153

מִגְדָּל 51 tower (9·49) 153

גַּג   top, roof (2·29) 150

מִגְדָּל 52 tower (9·49) 153

פֶּלַח 53 millstone (1·6) 812

הרץ   to crush (1·1·19) 954

גֻּלְגֹּלֶת   skull (1·12) 166

שָׁלַף 54 to draw out (10·25·25) 1025

דקר   to pierce (1·7·11) 201

קְלָלָה 57 curse (1·33) 887

Chapter 10

עַיִר 4 male ass (3·9) 747

חוה   tent village (1·7) 295

רעץ 8 to shatter (1·2·2) 950

רוצץ   to grievously oppress (1·1·19) 954

לָחַץ 12 to oppress (3·14·15) 537

נֵכָר 16 that which is foreign (1·36) 648

קָצַר   to be short, impatient (2·11·13) 894

Chapter 11

זוֹנָה 1 harlot (2·33) 275

גרש 2 to drive out, away (5·34·48) 176

התלקט 3 to collect themselves (1·1·36) 544

רֵק   empty, idle, worthless (3·14) 938

קָצִין 6 chief, commander (2·12) 892

גרש 7 to drive out, away (5·34·48) 176

קָצִין 11 chief, commander (2·12) 892

נָדַר 30 to vow (2·30·30) 623

מַכָּה 33 defeat (2·48) 646

נִכְנַע   to be subdued (3·25·36) 488

תֹּף 34 timbrel, tambourine (1·17) 1074

מחולה   dancing (2·8) 298

יָחִיד   only one (1·12) 402

אֲהָהּ 35 alas! (2·15) 13

הִכְרִיעַ   to cause to bow (2·6·35) 502

עָכַר   to disturb, trouble (1·12·14) 747

פצה   to open (2·15·15) 822

פצה 36 to open (2·15·15) 822

נְקָמָה   vengeance (1·27) 668

הרפה 37 to refrain; ר' מִן = to let one alone (1·21·45) 952

בְּתוּלִים   virginity, tokens of virginity (2·10) 144

רעה   companion, attendant (2·3) 946

רעה 38 companion, attendant (2·3) 946

בְּתוּלִים   virginity, tokens of virginity (2·10) 144

נָדַר 39 to vow (2·30·30) 623

תנה 40 to recount, celebrate (2·2·2) 1072

Chapter 12

מוֹשִׁיעַ 3 savior (3·27) 446

פָּלִיט 4 fugitive (2·19) 812

מַעְבָּרָה 5 ford (3·8) 721
פָּלִיט fugitive (2·19) 812
מַעְבָּרָה 6 ford (3·8) 721
עַיִר 14 male ass (3·9) 747

Chapter 13

עָקָר 2 barren (2·11) 785
הָרָה 3 to conceive, become pregnant (1·38·40) 247
עָקָר barren (2·11) 785
שֵׁכָר 4 intoxicating, strong drink (3·23) 1016
הָרָה 5 pregnant (2·16[?]) 248
מוֹרָה razor (2·3) 559
נוֹרָא 6 fearful, awful (1·44) 431
אֵי where? אי מִזֶּה = (1·39) 32
הָרָה 7 pregnant (2·16[?]) 248
שֵׁכָר intoxicating, strong drink (3·23) 1016
טָמְאָה uncleanness (2·37) 380
עתר 8 to pray, supplicate (1·5·20) 801
בִּי part. of entreaty, I pray (3·13) 106
הורה to instruct (1·45[?]·45[?]) 434
שֵׁכָר 14 intoxicating, strong drink (3·23) 1016
טָמְאָה uncleanness (2·37) 380
עָצַר 15 to restrain, detain (2·36·46) 783
גְּדִי kid (5·16) 152
עָצַר 16 to restrain, detain (2·36·46) 783
פִּלְאִי 18 wonderful, incomprehensible (1·2) 811
גְּדִי 19 kid (5·16) 152
הִפְלִיא to work wonders (1·10·21) 810
לַהַב 20 flame (4·12) 529
לוּ 23 if (2·19) 530
פעם 25 to thrust, impel (1·1·5) 821

Chapter 14

עָרֵל 3 having foreskin, i.e., uncircumcised

(2·35) 790
יָשַׁר to be pleasing (2·13·25) 448
תֹּאֲנָה 4 opportunity (1·1) 58
כְּפִיר 5 young lion (1·31) 498
אֲרִי lion (2·34) 71
שָׁאַג to roar (1·20·20) 980
שׁסע 6 to tear in two (1·3·8) 1042
גְּדִי kid (5·16) 152
מְאוּמָה anything (1·32) 548
יָשַׁר 7 to be pleasing (1·13·25) 448
מַפֶּלֶת 8 carcass (1·8) 658
אַרְיֵה lion (3·45) 71
דְּבוֹרָה bee (1·4) 185
גְּוִיָּה carcass, corpse (2·12) 156
רָדָה 9 to scrape out (2·3·3) 922
גְּוִיָּה carcass, corpse (2·12) 156
אַרְיֵה lion (3·45) 71
מִשְׁתֶּה 10 feast (3·45) 1059
בָּחוּר young man (1·45) 104
מרע 11 companion, confidential friend (4·7) 946
חוד 12 to propound a riddle (3·4·4) 295
חִידָה riddle (8·17) 295
מִשְׁתֶּה feast (3·45) 1059
סָדִין linen wrapper (2·4) 690
חליפה a change [of raiment] (3·12) 322
סָדִין 13 linen wrapper (2·4) 690
חליפה a change [of raiment] (3·12) 322
חוד to propound a riddle (3·4·4) 295
חִידָה riddle (8·17) 295
מַאֲכָל 14 food (1·30) 38
עַז formidable, fierce (2·22) 738
מָתוֹק sweet, a sweet thing (2·12) 608
חִידָה riddle (8·17) 295
פתה 15 to entice (2·17·27) 834
חִידָה riddle (8·17) 295
חִידָה 16 riddle (8·17) 295
חוד to propound a riddle (3·4·4) 285

מִשְׁתֶּה 17 feast (3·45) 1059

הֵצִיק to distress by importunity (2·11·16) 847

חִידָה riddle (8·17) 295

בְּטֶרֶם 18 before (1·39) 382

חֶרֶס sun (1·2) 357

מָתוֹק sweet (2·12) 608

עַז formidable, fierce (2·22) 738

אֲרִי lion (2·35) 71

לוּלֵא unless (1·4) 530

חרשׁ to plough (1·21·24) 360

עֶגְלָה heifer (1·12) 722

חִידָה riddle (8·17) 295

חֲלִיצָה 19 what is stripped off a person, as plunder in war (1·2) 322

חֲלִיפָה a change [of raiment] (3·12) 322

חִידָה riddle (8·17) 295

מֵרֵעַ 20 companion, confidential friend (4·7) 946

רֵעָה to be a special friend (1·1·6) 946

Chapter 15

קָצִיר 1 time of harvest (1·49) 894

חִטָּה wheat (2·30) 334

גְּדִי kid (5·16) 152

חֶדֶר room, chamber (4·34) 293

מֵרֵעַ 2 companion, confidential friend (4·7) 946

קָטָן small, younger (1·47) 881

נקה 3 to be free from guilt (1·23·37) 667

שׁוּעָל 4 fox, perh. jackal (1·7) 1043

לַפִּיד torch (5·13) 542

זָנָב tail (3·11) 275

לַפִּיד 5 torch (5·13) 542

קָמָה standing grain (2·10) 879

גָּדִישׁ heap, stack (1·4) 155

זַיִת olive, olive tree, olive yards (3·38) 268

חָתָן 6 daughter's husband (2·20) 368

מֵרֵעַ companion, confidential friend (4·7) 946

נקם 7 to avenge oneself (2·12·34) 667

שׁוֹק 8 leg (1·19) 1003

יָרֵךְ thigh (4·34) 437

מַכָּה defeat (2·48) 646

סָעִיף cleft (2·4[?]) 703

נטשׁ 9 to be spread abroad (1·6·40) 643

סָעִיף 11 cleft (2·4[?]) 703

פָּגַע 12 to fall upon (3·40·46) 803

עֲבֹת 13 cord, rope (4·24) 721

הֵרִיעַ 14 to shout a war cry, alarm of battle (2·40·44) 929

עֲבֹת cord, rope (4·24) 721

פֵּשֶׁת flax (1·16) 833

נָמֵס to melt, drop off (1·19·21) 587

אֵסוּר band, bond (1·3) 64

לְחִי 15 jawbone (5·21) 534

טָרִי fresh (1·2) 382

לְחִי 16 jawbone (5·21) 534

חֲמוֹר heap (2·3) 331

לְחִי 17 jawbone (5·21) 534

צמא 18 to be thirsty (2·10·10) 854

תְּשׁוּעָה deliverance, victory (1·34) 448

צָמָא thirst (1·17) 854

עָרֵל having foreskin, i.e., uncircumcised (2·35) 790

מַכְתֵּשׁ 19 hollow, resembling a mortar (1·2) 509

Chapter 16

זוֹנָה 1 harlot (2·33) 275

הֵנָּה 2 hither (2·49) 244

אָרַב to lie in wait (5·20·23) 70

התחרשׁ to keep quiet (1·1·44) 361, 1123

מְזוּזָה 3 gatepost (1·20) 265

בְּרִיחַ bar(s) (1·41) 138

סֶרֶן	5 lord (8·21) 710	
פָּתָה	to entice (2·17·27) 834	
בַּמֶּה	wherein? by what means? (8·29) 552	
בַּמֶּה	6 wherein? by what means? (8·29) 552	
יֶתֶר	7 cord (3·6) 452	
לַח	new (2·6) 535	
חרב	to be dry, dried up (2·2·37[?]) 351	
סֶרֶן	8 lord (8·21) 710	
יֶתֶר	cord (3·6) 452	
לַח	new (2·6) 535	
חרב	to be dry, dried up (2·2·37[?]) 351	
אֹרֵב	liers in wait (8·18[?]) 70	
חֶדֶר	room, chamber (4·34) 293	
נתק	to tear apart, snap (2·11·27) 683	
יֶתֶר	9 cord (3·6) 452	
נתק	to be torn apart, snapped (1·10·27) 683	
פָּתִיל	cord (1·11) 836	
נְעֹרֶת	tow (1·2) 654	
הריח	to smell (1·11·14) 926	
הָתֵל	10 to mock, trifle with (3·7·8) 1068	
כָּזָב	lie (2·31) 469	
בַּמֶּה	by what means? (8·29) 552	
עֲבֹת	11 rope, cord (4·24) 721	
עֲבֹת	12 rope, cord (4·24) 721	
אֹרֵב	liers in wait (8·18[?]) 70	
חֶדֶר	room, chamber (4·34) 293	
נתק	to tear apart, snap (2·11·27) 683	
חוּט	thread (1·7) 296	
הֵנָּה	13 hitherto (2·49) 244	
הָתֵל	to mock, trifle with (3·7·8) 1068	
כָּזָב	lie (2·31) 469	
בַּמֶּה	by what means? (8·29) 552	
ארג	to weave (1·3·3) 70	
מחלפה	plait (2·2) 322	
מסכת	web (2·2) 651	
יָתֵד	14 pin (stick) (6·24) 450	
יקץ	to awake (2·11·11) 429	

שֵׁנָה	sleep (2·33) 446	
אֶרֶג	loom (1·2) 71	
מסכת	web (2·2) 651	
הָתֵל	15 to mock, trifle with (3·7·8) 1069	
בַּמֶּה	wherein? (8·29) 552	
הציק	16 to bring into straits by importunity (2·11·11) 847	
אלץ	to urge (1·1·1) 49	
קָצַר	to be short, impatient (2·11·13) 894	
מוֹרָה	17 razor (2·3) 559	
גֻּלַּח	to be shaven (2·3·23) 164	
סֶרֶן	18 lord (8·21) 710	
ישׁן	19 to make to sleep (1·1·16[?]) 445	
בֶּרֶךְ	knee (3·25) 139	
גֻּלַּח	to shave off (1·18·23) 164	
מחלפה	plait (2·2) 322	
יקץ	20 to awake (2·11·11) 429	
שֵׁנָה	sleep (2·23) 446	
ננער	to shake oneself (1·3·10) 654	
נִקַּר	21 to bore out (1·3·6) 669	
טחן	to grind (1·7·7) 377	
אָסִיר	prisoner (2·17[?]) 64	
שֵׂעָר	22 hair (1·28) 972	
צָמַח	to grow abundantly (1·4·33) 855	
גֻּלַּח	to be shaven (2·3·23) 164	
סֶרֶן	23 lord (8·21) 710	
צָמַח	to grow abundantly (1·4·33) 855	
גֻּלַּח	to be shaven (2·3·23) 164	
סֶרֶן	lord (8·21) 710	
הֶחֱרִיב	24 to make desolate (1·13·37[?]) 351	
שׂחק	25 to make sport (1·16·36) 965	
אָסִיר	prisoner (2·17[?]) 64	
צחק	to make sport (1·7·13) 850	
המישׁ	26 to feel (1·3·4[?]) 559	
נִשְׁעַן	to lean (1·22·22) 1043	
סֶרֶן	27 lord (8·21) 710	
גָּג	top, roof (2·29) 150	
שָׂחַק	to sport, play (1·18·36) 965	

145

נקם 28 to avenge oneself (2·12·34) 667

נָקָם vengeance (1·17) 668

לפת 29 to grasp (1·1·3) 542

נסמך to brace oneself (1·6·48) 701

סרן 30 lord (8·21) 710

מֵאֲשֶׁר from those, than those (1·17) 84

Chapter 17

אַתְּ 2 thou [fem.] (1·7) 61

אָלָה to curse (1·3·6) 46

פֶּסֶל 3 idol (8·31) 820

מַסֵּכָה molten image (5·25) 651

צוֹרֵף 4 smelter, refiner, goldsmith (1·10) 864

פֶּסֶל idol (8·31) 820

מַסֵּכָה molten image (5·25) 651

אֵפוֹד 5 ephod (6·49) 65

תְּרָפִים idol (5·15) 1076

בַּאֲשֶׁר 8 in [the place] where (3·20) 84

מֵאַיִן 9 whence? (2·48) 32

בַּאֲשֶׁר in [the place] where (3·19) 84

עֵרֶךְ 10 order, row, a [complete] suit of clothes (1·33) 789

מִחְיָה sustenance (2·8) 313

הוֹאִיל 11 to show willingness (4·18·18) 383

Chapter 18

קָצֶה 2 end, whole (1·7) 892

רגל to go about as explorer, spy (3·14·16) 920

חקר to search through, explore (2·22·27) 350

הִכִּיר 3 to recognize (1·37·40) 647

הֲלֹם hither (2·11) 240

פֹּה here? (3·46) 805

זֶה 4 this; כָּזֹה וְכָזֶה = thus and thus (1·11) 262

שָׂכַר to hire (2·17·20) 968

נֹכַח 6 before (3·27) 647

בֶּטַח 7 securely (2·43) 105

שָׁקַט to be quiet, undisturbed, at peace and safety (6·31·41) 1052

עֶצֶר restraint [dub.] (1·1) 783

הכלים to restrain [dub.] (1·10·38) 483

הֶחֱשָׁה 9 to show inactivity (1·9·16) 364

נעצל to be sluggish (1·1·1) 782

מַחְסוֹר 10 lack (3·13) 341

חגר 11 to gird on (4·44·44) 291

רגל 14 to go about as explorer, spy (3·14·16) 920

אֵפוֹד ephod (6·49) 65

תְּרָפִים idol (5·15) 1076

פֶּסֶל idol (8·31) 820

מַסֵּכָה molten image (5·25) 651

חגר 16 to gird on (4·44·44) 291

רגל 17 to go about as an explorer, spy (3·14·16) 920

פֶּסֶל idol (8·31) 820

אֵפוֹד ephod (6·49) 65

תְּרָפִים idol (5·15) 1076

מַסֵּכָה molten image (5·25) 651

חגר to gird on (4·44·44) 291

פֶּסֶל 18 idol (8·31) 820

אֵפוֹד ephod (6·49) 65

תְּרָפִים idol (5·15) 1076

מַסֵּכָה molten image (5·25) 651

הֶחֱרִישׁ 19 to be silent (1·38·46) 361

אֵפוֹד 20 ephod (6·49) 65

תְּרָפִים idol (5·15) 1076

פֶּסֶל idol (8·31) 820

טַף 21 children (2·41) 381

כְּבוּדָּה abundance, riches (1·3[?]) 459

פָּגַע 25 to fall upon (3·40·46) 803

מַר bitter; מָרֵי נֶפֶשׁ = fierce of temper (1·37) 600

שָׁקַט 27 to be quiet, undisturbed, at peace

and safety (6·31·41) 1052

אוּלָם 29 but, but indeed (1·19) 19

פֶּסֶל 30 idol (8·31) 820

פֶּסֶל 31 idol (8·31) 820

Chapter 19

יַרְכָה 1 extreme parts (2·28) 438

פִּילֶגֶשׁ concubine (12·37) 811

פִּילֶגֶשׁ 2 concubine (12·37) 811

צֶמֶד 3 pair (2·15) 855

חֹתֵן 4 wife's father (5·21) 368

חָתָן 5 daughter's husband (2·20) 368

סָעַד to sustain (2·12·12) 703

פַּת fragment, bit, morsel (1·14) 837

הוֹאִיל 6 to show willingness, accept an invitation (4·18·18) 383

פצר 7 to urge (1·6·7) 823

חֹתֵן wife's father (5·21) 368

סָעַד to sustain (2·12·12) 703

התמהמה to tarry (2·9·9) 554

פִּילֶגֶשׁ 9 concubine (12·37) 811

חֹתֵן wife's father (5·21) 368

רָפָה to sink, decline (2·14·44) 951

ערב to become evening (1·2·3) 788

פֹּה here (3·46) 805

נֹכַח 10 in front of; עד־נ׳ = as far as in front of (3·27) 647

צֶמֶד pair (2·15) 855

חבש to bind up, equip (1·27·31) 289

פִּילֶגֶשׁ concubine (12·37) 811

נָכְרִי 12 foreigner (1·45) 648

רְחֹב 15 broad open place, plaza (3·43) 932

אֹרַח 17 journeying, wayfaring (1·4[?]) 72

רְחֹב broad open place, plaza (3·43) 932

אָנָה whither? (1·39) 33

מֵאַיִן whence? (2·48) 32

יַרְכָה 18 extreme parts (2·28) 438

תֶּבֶן 19 straw (6·17) 1061

מִסְפּוֹא fodder (1·5) 704

מַחְסוֹר lack (3·13) 341

מַחְסוֹר 20 need, thing needed (3·13) 341

רְחֹב broad open place, plaza (3·43) 932

בלל 21 to give provender (1·1·1) 117

התדפק 22 to beat violently (1·1·3) 200

נְבָלָה 23 disgraceful folly (4·13) 615

פִּילֶגֶשׁ 24 concubine (12·37) 811

נְבָלָה disgraceful folly (4·13) 615

פִּילֶגֶשׁ 25 concubine (12·37) 811

הִתְעַלֵּל to deal wantonly, abuse (1·7·17) 759

שַׁחַר dawn (1·23) 1007

פִּילֶגֶשׁ 27 concubine (12·37) 811

סַף threshold (1·25) 706

מַאֲכֶלֶת 29 knife (1·4) 38

פִּילֶגֶשׁ concubine (12·37) 811

נָתַח to cut up (2·9·9) 677

נֵתַח piece of a divided corpse (1·2) 677

עוץ 30 to counsel, plan (1·2·2) 734

Chapter 20

נקהל 1 to assemble (1·19·39) 874

פִּנָּה 2 corner (1·30) 819

רַגְלִי on foot; אִישׁ ר׳ = footmen (1·12) 920

שָׁלַף to draw out (10·25·25) 1025

אֵיכָה 3 in what manner? (1·18) 32

נרצח 4 to be murdered (1·2·43) 953

פִּילֶגֶשׁ concubine (12·37) 811

דִּמָּה 5 to think, intend (1·13·27) 197

פִּילֶגֶשׁ concubine (12·37) 811

פִּילֶגֶשׁ concubine (12·37) 811

נָתַח to cut up (2·9·9) 677

זִמָּה wickedness (1·28) 273

נְבָלָה disgraceful folly (4·13) 615

יהב 7 to give, provide (2·27·27) 396

הֲלֹם hither (2·11) 240

רְבָבָה 10 ten thousand (1·6) 914

צֵידָה provision (2·9) 845

נְבָלָה   disgraceful folly (4·13) 615

חָבֵר   11 united (1·12) 288

שָׁלַף   15 to draw out (10·25·25) 1025

בָּחוּר   chosen (3·19) 103

בָּחוּר   16 chosen (3·19) 103

אִטֵּר   shut up, bound [of right hand = left handed] (2·2) 32

קָלַע   to sling (1·2·4) 887

שַׂעֲרָה   a hair (1·3) 972

שָׁלַף   17 to draw out (10·25·25) 1025

תְּחִלָּה   18 beginning; 'בַּתְּ = first, at first (3·22) 321

שָׁלַף   25 to draw out (10·25·25) 1025

צוֹם   26 to fast (1·20·20) 847

אֹרֵב   29 liers in wait (8·18[?]) 70

הנתק   31 to be drawn away from (1·1·27) 683

מְסִלָּה   highway (5·27) 700

נָגַף   32 to be smitten (4·23·48) 619

נתק   to draw away (1·3·27) 683

מְסִלָּה   highway (5·27) 700

אֹרֵב   33 liers in wait (8·18[?]) 70

הגיח   to burst forth (1·2·5) 161, 1121

מערה   bare space (1·1[?]) 789

מִנֶּגֶד   34 in front of (2·26) 617

בָּחוּר   chosen (3·19) 103

נָגַף   35 to smite (1·24·48) 619

שָׁלַף   to draw out (10·25·25) 1025

נָגַף   36 to be smitten (4·23·48) 619

אֹרֵב   liers in wait (8·18[?]) 70

אֹרֵב   37 liers in wait (8·18[?]) 70

החיש   to act quickly (1·6·21) 301

פשט   to put off [one's shelter] i.e., make a dash [from a sheltered place] (4·24·43) 833

מָשַׁךְ   to proceed (4·30·36) 604

אֹרֵב   38 liers in wait (8·18[?]) 70

מַשְׂאֵת   uprising (2·16) 673

עָשָׁן   smoke (2·25) 798

נָגַף   39 to be smitten (4·23·48) 619

מַשְׂאֵת   40 uprising (2·16) 673

עָשָׁן   smoke (2·25) 798

כָּלִיל   whole (1·15) 483

נִבְהַל   41 to be disturbed, dismayed, terrified (1·24·39) 96

כתר   43 to surround (1·3·6) 509

מְנוּחָה   rest, quietness [dub.] (1·21) 629

נֹכַח   in front of, 'עַד־נ = as far as in front of (3·27) 647

עוֹלֵל   45 to glean (1·8·17) 760

מְסִלָּה   highway (5·27) 700

שָׁלַף   46 to draw out (10·25·25) 1025

מְתֹם   48 soundness, entire (1·4) 1071

Chapter 21

בְּכִי   2 weeping (1·30) 113

מָחֳרָת   4 the morrow, next day מִמָּחֳרָת = on the morrow (3·32) 564

שְׁבוּעָה   5 oath (1·30) 989

לַאֲשֶׁר   concerning him who (1·37) 81

נִגְדַּע   6 to be hewn off (1·17·22) 154

טַף   10 children (2·41) 381

מִשְׁכָּב   11 act of lying down (2·46) 1012

הַחֲרִים   to devote to destruction (2·46·49) 355

מִשְׁכָּב   12 act of lying down (2·46) 1012

פֶּרֶץ   15 outburst (1·18) 829

יְרֻשָּׁה   17 possession, inheritance (1·14) 440

פְּלֵיטָה   escaped remnant (1·28) 812

נמחה   to be blotted out (1·9·33) 562

מְסִלָּה   19 highway (5·27) 700

אָרַב   20 to lie in wait (5·20·23) 70

חוּל   21 to dance (1·6·9) 296

מחולה   dancing (2·8) 298

חטף   to catch, seize (1·3·3) 310

אָשֵׁם   22 to be or become guilty (1·31·33) 79

חוֹלֵל 23 to dance (1·2·9) 296

גָּזַל to tear away, rob (2·29·30) 159

Ruth appears in volume 4, correspond-
ing to its placement in the Hebrew
Old Testament.

1 SAMUEL

Chapter 1

מָנָה   4 portion (3·12) 584

מָנָה   5 portion (3·12) 584

רֶחֶם   womb (2·33) 933

צָרָה   6 vexer, rival wife (1·1) 865

כַּעַס   vexation (2·25?) 495

בַּעֲבוּר   in order to (3·45) 721

הַרְעִים   to make to fret [dub.] (1·2·2) 947

רֶחֶם   womb (2·33) 933

מִדֵּי   7 out of the abundance of, i.e., as often as (3·15) 191

מְזוּזָה   9 doorpost (1·20) 265

מַר   10 bitter; מָרַת נ׳ = the bitterly wretched (3·37) 600

נָדַר   11 to vow (1·30·30) 623

מוֹרָה   razor (1·3) 559

נוּעַ   13 to quiver (1·20·36) 631

שָׁכֹּר   drunken, drunkard (2·13) 1016

מָתַי   14 when? עַד־מָתַי = how long? (2·40) 607

הִשְׁתַּכֵּר   to make oneself drunken (1·1·20) 1016

קָשֶׁה   15 severe (3·36) 904

שֵׁכָר   intoxicating drink, strong drink (1·23) 1016

בְּלִיַּעַל   16 worthlessness, good for nothing (6·27) 116

שִׂיחַ   anxiety, trouble (1·14) 967

כַּעַס   vexation (2·25[?]) 495

הֵנָּה   hither (3·49) 244

שֵׁלָה   17 request (1·1) 982

תְּקוּפָה   20 circuit (1·4) 880

הָרָה   to conceive, become pregnant (2·38·40) 247

נגמל   22 to be weaned (1·3·37) 168

גָּמַל   23 to wean (5·34·37) 168

הֵינִיק   to nurse (1·10·18) 413

גָּמַל   24 to wean (5·34·37) 168

אֵיפָה   ephah, quantity of wheat, barley, etc. (2·38) 35

קֶמַח   flour, meal (2·14) 887

נֵבֶל   skin of wine (4·12) 614

בִּי   26 part. of entreaty: I pray (1·13) 106

שְׁאֵלָה   27 thing asked for (2·13) 982

Chapter 2

עלץ   1 to rejoice, exult (1·8·8) 763

רָחַב   to be or grow wide (1·3·25) 931

בִּלְתִּי   2 not, except (2·24) 116

גָּבֹהַּ   3 high, haughty (4·41) 147

עָתָק   forward, arrogant (1·4) 801

נתכן   to be estimated (1·10·18) 1067

עֲלִילָה   deed (1·24) 760

חת   4 shattered (1·4) 369

אזר   to gird on (1·6·16) 25

שָׂבֵעַ   5 sated (1·10) 960

נשכר   to hire oneself out (1·1·20) 968

רָעֵב   hungry (1·19) 944

עָקָר   barren (1·11) 785

אֻמְלַל   to be or grow feeble, languish (1·15·15[?]) 51

העשיר   7 to make rich (2·14·17) 799

הִשְׁפִּיל   to lay low, humiliate (1·18·29) 1050

דַּל   8 poor (1·48) 195

אַשְׁפֹּת   ash heap [dub.] refuse heap (1·7) 1046

נָדִיב   noble (1·27) 622

מצוק   support (2·2) 848

תֵּבֵל   world (1·36) 385

חָסִיד   9 pious, godly (1·32) 339

נדמם   to be made silent (1·5·30) 199

גָּבַר   to prevail (1·17·25) 149

הַרְעִים   10 to thunder (2·8·11) 947

דִּין	to execute judgment (1·23·24[?]) 192
אֶפֶס	end, extreme limit (1·27) 67
מָשִׁיחַ	anointed (13·40) 603
בְּלִיַּעַל	12 worthlessness, good for nothing (6·27) 116
בשל	13 to boil (1·20·27) 143
מַזְלֵג	three-pronged fork [dub.] (2·2) 272
כִּיּוֹר	14 pot (1·23) 468
דּוּד	pot, kettle (1·7) 188
קַלַּחַת	caldron (1·2) 886
פָּרוּר	(1·3) 807
מַזְלֵג	three-pronged fork [dub.] (2·2) 272
כָּכָה	thus (2·34) 462
צלה	15 to roast (1·3·3) 852
בְּטֶרֶם	before (2·39) 382
בשל	to be boiled (1·4·27) 143
אָוָה	16 to desire (1·11·27) 16
חָזְקָה	strength, force (1·6) 308
נָאַץ	17 to spurn (1·14·23) 610
חגר	18 to gird (5·44·44) 291
אֵפוֹד	ephod, priestly garment (9·49) 65
בַּד	white linen (2·23) 94
מְעִיל	19 robe (7·28) 591
שְׁאֵלָה	20 thing asked for (2·13) 982
הָרָה	21 to conceive, become pregnant (2·38·40) 247
זָקֵן	22 to be old, become old (6·25·27) 278
צבא	to serve (1·12·14) 838
שְׁמוּעָה	24 report (2·27) 1035
גָּדֵל	26 becoming great (1·4) 152
אֵפוֹד	28 ephod, priestly garment (9·49) 65
בעט	29 to kick at (1·2·2) 127
מָעוֹן	dwelling (2·18) 732
הבריא	to make oneself fat (1·1·1) 135
חָלִילָה	30 far be it [from] (8·21) 321
בּוֹזֶה	despiser (1·1[?]) 102
גָּדַע	31 to hew off (1·5·22) 154

צַר	32 distress [dub.] (1·29) 865
מָעוֹן	dwelling (2·18) 732
הֶאֱדִיב	33 to cause to grieve (1·1·1) 9
מַרְבִּית	increase (1·5) 916
מָשִׁיחַ	35 anointed (13·40) 603
אֲגוֹרָה	36 payment (1·1) 8
ספח	to attach to (1·1·5) 705
כְּהֻנָּה	priesthood (1·13) 464
פַּת	bit, morsel (2·4) 837

Chapter 3

יָקָר	1 rare (1·35) 429
חָזוֹן	vision (1·35) 302
נפרץ	to spread abroad (1·1·49) 829
כהה	2 dim (1·7) 462
נֵר	3 lamp (1·44) 632
טֶרֶם	not yet (3·16) 382
כבה	to be extinguished (1·14·24) 459
טֶרֶם	7 not yet (3·16) 382
התיצב	10 to station oneself (6·48·48) 426
צלל	11 to tingle (1·4·4) 852
כהה	13 to rebuke (1·3·8[?]) 462
כָּחַד	17 to hide (3·15·30) 470
כָּחַד	18 to hide (3·15·30) 470

Chapter 4

נָטַשׁ	2 to permit [dub.] (7·33·40) 643
נִגַּף	to be smitten (3·23·48) 619
מַעֲרָכָה	battle line (15·18) 790
נָגַף	3 to smite (2·24·48) 619
הריע	5 to shout (4·40·44) 929
תְּרוּעָה	shout of joy (3·36) 929
הום	to reecho (1·3·6) 223
תְּרוּעָה	6 shout of joy (3·36) 929
אוֹי	7 woe! alas! (2·22) 17
אֶתְמוֹל	yesterday; אֶ' שִׁלְשֹׁום = formerly (4·8) 1069

שְׁלְשׁוֹם	three days ago (5·25) 1026	נשׁתר	to break out (1·1·1) 979
אוֹי	8 woe! alas! (2·22) 17	עפל	hemorrhoid (5·6) 779
אַדִּיר	majestic (1·27) 12	סרן	11 lord (11·21) 710
מַכָּה	plague (7·48) 646	מְהוּמָה	confusion (3·12) 223
נָגַף	10 to be smitten (3·23·48) 619	עפל	12 hemorrhoid (5·6) 779
מַכָּה	slaughter (7·48) 646	שַׁוְעָה	cry for help (1·11) 1003
רַגְלִי	footmen, foot soldier (2·12) 920		

מַעֲרָכָה	12 battle line (15·18) 790
מַד	garment (4·12) 551

Chapter 6

חָרֵד	13 trembling (1·6) 353	קֶסֶם	2 necromancer, diviner (1·9) 890
צפה	to watch (1·9·18) 859	בַּמֶּה	wherewith? (3·29) 552
צְעָקָה	14 cry of distress (2·21) 858	רֵיקָם	3 empty (1·16) 938
מַעֲרָכָה	16 battle line (15·18) 790	אָשָׁם	trespass offering (4·46) 79
מְבַשֵּׂר	17 bearer of tidings (1·9) 142	אָשָׁם	4 trespass offering (4·46) 79
מַגֵּפָה	slaughter (2·26) 620	סרן	lord (11·21) 710
אֲחֹרַנִּית	18 backwards (1·7) 30	עפל	hemorrhoid (5·6) 779
מפרקת	neck (1·1) 830	עַכְבָּר	mouse (4·6) 747
זָקֵן	to be old, become old (6·25·27) 278	מַגֵּפָה	plague (2·26) 620
כַּלָּה	19 daughter-in-law (1·34) 483	צֶלֶם	5 image (3·17) 853
הָרָה	pregnant (1·15?) 248	עפל	hemorrhoid (5·6) 779
שְׁמוּעָה	report, news (2·27) 1035	עַכְבָּר	mouse (4·6) 747
חם	husband's father (2·4) 327	אוּלַי	perhaps (3·45) 19
כָּרַע	to bow down (1·29·34) 502	הִתְעַלֵּל	6 to deal wantonly, ruthlessly (2·7·17) 759
צִיר	pang (1·5) 852	עֲגָלָה	7 cart (7·25) 722
חם	21 husband's father (2·4) 327	פָּרָה	cow (5·26) 831
		עוּל	to give suck (2·5·5) 732
		עֹל	yoke (1·40) 760

Chapter 5

הצּיג	2 to set, place (1·15·16) 426	עֲגָלָה	8 cart (7·25) 722
מָחֳרָת	3 the morrow, next day; מִמֳּחֳרָת = on the morrow (7·32) 564	אָשָׁם	trespass offering (4·46) 79
		אַרְגַּז	box, chest (3·3) 919
מָחֳרָת	4 the morrow, next day; מִמֳּחֳרָת = on the morrow (7·32) 564	צַד	side; מִצַּד = at the side of (5·31) 841
מִפְתָּן	threshold (2·8) 837	מִקְרֶה	9 chance, accident (2·9) 894
מִפְתָּן	5 threshold (2·8) 837	פָּרָה	10 cow (5·26) 831
עפל	6 hemorrhoid (5·6) 779	עוּל	to give suck (2·5·5) 732
קשׁה	7 to be hard, severe (1·5·28) 904	כלא	to shut up (2·14·17) 476
סרן	8 lord (11·21) 710	עֲגָלָה	cart (7·25) 722
מְהוּמָה	9 confusion (3·12) 223	עֲגָלָה	11 cart (7·25) 722

אַרְגַּז	box, chest (3·3) 919
עַכְבָּר	mouse (4·6) 747
צֶלֶם	image (3·17) 853
טְחוֹר	tumor (7·8) 377
יָשַׁר	12 to go straight (3·13·25) 448
פָּרָה	cow (5·26) 831
מְסִלָּה	highway (1·27) 700
גָּעָה	to low (1·2·2) 171
סֶרֶן	lord (11·21) 710
קָצַר	13 to reap (2·24·24) 894
קָצִיר	what is harvested, crop (3·49) 894
חִטָּה	wheat (2·30) 334
עֲגָלָה	14 cart (7·25) 722
פָּרָה	cow (5·26) 831
אַרְגַּז	15 box, chest (3·3) 919
סֶרֶן	16 lord (11·21) 710
טְחוֹר	17 tumor (7·8) 377
אָשָׁם	trespass offering (4·46) 79
עַכְבָּר	18 mouse (4·6) 747
סֶרֶן	lord (11·21) 710
מִבְצָר	fortification (1·37) 131
כֹּפֶר	a village (1·1) 499
פְּרָזִי	hamlet dweller (1·3) 826
אָבֵל	meadow [dub.] (1·1) 5
הִתְאַבֵּל	19 to mourn (3·19·38) 5
מַכָּה	slaughter (7·48) 646

Chapter 7

נָנָה	2 to mourn [dub.] (1·1·1[?]) 624
נֵכָר	3 foreignness (1·36) 648
לְבַדּוֹ	alone (2·35) 94
לְבַדּוֹ	4 alone (2·35) 94
שָׁאַב	6 to draw (2·14·14) 980
צוּם	to fast (2·20·20) 847
סֶרֶן	7 lord (11·21) 710
הֶחֱרֵשׁ	8 to be deaf (2·38·46) 361
טָלֶה	9 lamb (1·3) 378
חָלָב	milk (2·44) 316

כָּלִיל	whole [offering] (1·15) 483
הִרְעִים	10 to thunder (2·8·11) 947
הָמַם	to confuse, rout (1·13·13) 243
נִגַּף	to be smitten (3·23·48) 619
הֵנָּה	12 hither (3·49) 244
נִכְנַע	13 to be subdued (1·25·36) 488
מִדֵּי	16 out of the abundance of, hence as often as; מִדֵּי שָׁנָה בְּשָׁנָה = yearly (3·15) 191
תְּשׁוּבָה	17 return (1·8) 1000

Chapter 8

זָקֵן	1 to be old, become old (6·25·27) 278
מִשְׁנֶה	2 second [in age] (4·35) 1041
בֶּצַע	3 unjust gain (1·23) 130
שֹׁחַד	bribe (1·23) 1005
זָקֵן	5 to be old, become old (6·25·27) 278
הֵעִיד	9 to affirm solemnly, warn (2·39·44) 729
מֶרְכָּבָה	11 chariot (2·44) 939
חָרַשׁ	12 to plough (1·21·24) 360
חָרִישׁ	plowing (1·3) 361
קָצַר	to reap (2·24·24) 894
קָצִיר	what is harvested, crop (3·49) 894
רקה	13 ointment maker, perfumer (1·2) 955
טבחה	female cook (1·1) 371
אֹפֶה	baker (1·12[?]) 66
זַיִת	14 olive, olive tree (1·38) 268
עשׂר	15 to take a tenth of (2·2·9) 797
סָרִיס	eunuch (1·45) 710
בָּחוּר	16 young man (2·45) 104
עשׂר	17 to take a tenth of (2·2·9) 797
מֵאָן	19 to refuse (2·45·45) 549

Chapter 9

בָּחוּר	2 young man (2·45) 104
שְׁכֶם	shoulder (3·22) 1014

גָּבֹהַּ	high, tall (4·41) 147		נָשַׁק	to kiss (2·26·32) 676
אָתוֹן	3 she ass (8·35) 87		נָגִיד	ruler (4·44) 617
אָתוֹן	5 she ass (8·35) 87		קְבוּרָה	2 grave (1·14) 869
דָּאַג	to be anxious, concerned (2·6·6) 178		אָתוֹן	she ass (8·35) 87
אוּלַי	6 perhaps (3·45) 19		נָטַשׁ	to abandon (7·33·40) 643
אָזַל	7 to be gone, used up (1·6·6) 23		דָּאַג	to be anxious, concerned (2·6·6) 178
תְּשׁוּרָה	gift [dub.] (1·1) 1003		חָלַף	3 to pass on quickly (1·14·26) 322
רֶבַע	8 fourth part (1·7) 917		הָלְאָה	beyond (4·13) 229
לְפָנִים	9 formerly (2·22) 815		אֵלוֹן	terebinth, tall tree (1·10) 18
רֹאֶה	seer (5·12) 909		גְּדִי	kid (2·16) 152
מַעֲלֶה	11 ascent (1·19) 751		נֵבֶל	skin of wine (4·12) 614
שָׁאַב	to draw (2·14·14) 980		נְצִיב	5 deputy [dub.] (3·11) 662
רֹאֶה	seer (5·12) 909		פָּגַע	to meet (4·40·46) 803
בְּטֶרֶם	13 before (2·39) 382		חֶבֶל	band, company (2·49) 286
נָגִיד	16 ruler (4·44) 617		נֵבֶל	skin of wine (4·12) 614
צְעָקָה	cry of distress (2·21) 858		תֹּף	timbrel, tambourine (2·17) 1074
עָצַר	17 to rule over (2·36·46) 783		חָלִיל	flute, pipe (1·6) 319
אֵי	18 where? אֵי־זֶה = where, then? (4·39) 32		כִּנּוֹר	lyre (3·41) 490
			הוֹחֵל	8 to wait (2·15·42) 403
רֹאֶה	seer (5·12) 909		שְׁכֶם	9 shoulder (3·22) 1014
רֹאֶה	19 seer (5·12) 909		חֶבֶל	10 band, company (2·49) 286
אָתוֹן	20 she ass (8·35) 87		אֶתְמוֹל	11 yesterday; אֵת׳ שִׁלְשׁוֹם = (from) aforetime (4·8) 1069
שִׁלְשׁוֹם	three days ago (5·25) 1026		שִׁלְשׁוֹם	three days ago (5·25) 1026
לְמִי	to whom? whose? (2·20) 566		מָשָׁל	12 proverbial saying (2·39) 605
חֶמְדָּת	desire (1·16) 326		אָן	14 where? whither? (1·45) 33
צָעִיר	21 little, insignificant (1·22) 859		אָתוֹן	she ass (8·35) 87
לִשְׁכָּה	22 room (1·47) 545		אָתוֹן	16 she ass (8·35) 87
טַבָּח	23 cook (2·32) 371		מְלוּכָה	kingship (5·24) 574
מָנָה	portion (3·12) 584		לָחַץ	18 to oppress (1·14·15) 537
טַבָּח	24 cook (2·32) 371		מוֹשִׁיעַ	19 savior (1·27) 446
שׁוֹק	[upper] leg, hind leg (1·19) 1003		הִתְיַצֵּב	to present oneself before (6·48·48) 426
גָּג	25 roof (2·29) 150		אֶלֶף	thousand (2·12[?]) 48
שַׁחַר	26 dawn (1·23) 1007		הֲלֹם	22 hither (4·12[?]) 240
גָּג	roof (2·29) 150		נֶחְבָּא	to hide oneself (2·16·34) 285
			הִתְיַצֵּב	23 to station oneself, stand (6·48·48) 426

Chapter 10

| פַּךְ | 1 flask (1·3) 810 |

154

גָּבַהּ to be tall (1·24·34) 146

שְׁכֶם shoulder (3·22) 1014

הֵרִיעַ 24 to shout in applause (4·40·44) 929

מְלוּכָה 25 kingship (5·24) 574

בְּלִיַּעַל 27 base fellow, worthlessness (6·27) 116

בָּזָה to despise (2·31·42) 102

הֶחֱרִישׁ to be silent [dub.] (2·38·46) 361

Chapter 11

נָקַר 2 to bore or pick (1·2·6) 669

הִרְפָּה 3 to refrain, let one alone (2·21·44) 951

צֶמֶד 7 a span [of oxen] (2·15) 855

נִתַּח to cut up (1·9·9) 677

פַּחַד dread (1·49) 808

תְּשׁוּעָה 9 deliverance (3·34) 448

חֹם to be or grow warm (2·23·26) 328

מָחֳרָת 11 the morrow, next day; מִמָּחֳרָת = on the morrow (7·32) 564

אַשְׁמֹרֶת watch [div. of time] (1·7) 1038

חֹם heat (1·4[?]) 328

תְּשׁוּעָה 13 victory (3·34) 448

חִדֵּשׁ 14 to renew (1·9·10) 293

מְלוּכָה kingship (5·24) 574

Chapter 12

זָקֵן 2 to be old, become old (6·25·27) 288

שִׂיב to be hoary (1·1·2) 966

נְעוּרִים youth (2·46) 655

מָשִׁיחַ 3 anointed (13·40) 603

עָשַׁק to oppress, wrong (2·36·37) 798

רָצַץ to crush, oppress (2·11·19) 954

כֹּפֶר ransom (1·13) 497

הֶעְלִים to hide (1·11·29) 761

עָשַׁק 4 to oppress, wrong (2·36·37) 798

רָצַץ to crush, oppress (2·11·19) 954

מְאוּמָה anything (9·32) 548

מָשִׁיחַ 5 anointed (13·40) 603

מְאוּמָה anything (9·32) 548

הִתְיַצֵּב 7 to take one's stand; to stand (6·48·48) 426

בֶּטַח 11 securely (1·43) 105

הִמְרָה 14 to show rebelliousness (1·22·43) 598

מָרָה 15 to be rebellious (1·21·43) 598

הִתְיַצֵּב 16 to take one's stand; to stand (6·48·48) 426

קָצִיר 17 time of harvest (3·49) 894

חִטָּה wheat (2·30) 334

מָטָר rain (2·37) 564

מָטָר 18 rain (2·37) 564

תֹּהוּ 21 [what is] empty, unreal (2·20) 1062

הוֹעִיל to profit (1·22·22) 418

נָטַשׁ 22 to abandon (7·33·40) 643

בַּעֲבוּר for the sake of (3·45) 721

הוֹאִיל to be pleased (1·18·18) 383

חָלִילָה 23 far be it [from] (8·21) 321

הוֹרָה to instruct (1·45[?]·45[?]) 434

נִסְפָּה 25 to be swept away, destroyed (3·9·18) 705

Chapter 13

נְצִיב deputy [dub.] (3·11) 662

נְצִיב deputy [dub.] (3·11) 662

נִבְאַשׁ to make oneself odious (1·3·16) 92

חוֹל 5 sand (1·22) 297

נִגַּשׂ 6 to be hard pressed (1·3·7) 620

הִתְחַבָּא to hide oneself (4·10·34) 285

מְעָרָה cave (8·40) 792

חוֹחַ briers = thickets as hiding places (1·1[?]) 296

צְרִיחַ excavation, underground chamber (1·4) 863

חָרַד 7 to go [or come] trembling (5·23·39) 353

הוֹחִל 8 to wait (2·15·42) 403

חִלָּה 12 to entreat the favor of (1·1·1) 318

155

הִתְאַפֵּק	to compel oneself (1·7·7) 67	
נִסְכַּל	13 to act foolishly (1·4·8) 698	
נָגִיד	14 ruler (4·44) 617	
מַשְׁחִית	17 destroying band (2·19) 1008	
נִשְׁקָף	18 to overhang (1·10·22) 1054	
גַּיְא	valley (3·47) 161	
חָרָשׁ	19 engraver, artificer [worker in metal] (1·38) 360	
חֲנִית	spear (20·46) 333	
לָטַשׁ	20 to sharpen (1·4·5) 538	
מַחֲרֵשָׁה	ploughshare (3·3) 361	
אֵת	ploughshare [dub.], a cutting instrument of iron (2·5) 88	
קַרְדֹּם	axe (2·5) 899	
פְּצִירָה	21 bluntness [dub.] (1·1) 823	
מַחֲרֵשָׁה	ploughshare (3·3) 361	
אֵת	ploughshare [dub.], a cutting instrument of iron (2·5) 88	
קִלְּשׁוֹן	fine point [dub.] (1·1) 887	
קַרְדֹּם	axe (2·5) 899	
דָּרְבָן	goad (1·2) 201	
חֲנִית	22 spear (20·46) 333	
מַצָּב	23 garrison (6·10) 662	
מַעְבָּר	pass (1·3) 721	

Chapter 14

מַצָּב	1 garrison (6·10) 662	
הַלָּז	this (2·7) 229	
רִמּוֹן	2 pomegranate [tree] (1·32) 941	
אֵפוֹד	3 ephod (9·49) 65	
מַעְבָּרָה	4 pass (1·8) 721	
מַצָּב	garrison (6·10) 662	
מָצוּק	5 pillar [dub.] (2·2) 848	
מוּל	in front of (3·25) 557	
מַצָּב	6 garrison (6·10) 662	
עָרֵל	uncircumcised person (4·35) 790	
אוּלַי	perhaps (3·45) 19	

מַעְצוֹר	hindrance (1·1) 784	
דָּמַם	9 to be still [motionless] (1·3·30) 198	
מַצָּב	11 garrison (6·10) 662	
חֹר	hole (1·7) 359	
הִתְחַבֵּא	to hide oneself (3·10·34) 285	
מַצֵּבָה	12 garrison (1·1) 663	
מַכָּה	14 slaughter (7·48) 646	
מַעֲנָה	field for ploughing [dub.] (1·2) 776	
צֶמֶד	a measure of land (2·15) 855	
חֲרָדָה	15 trembling, quaking (2·9) 353	
מַצָּב	garrison (6·10) 662	
מַשְׁחִית	destroying band (2·19) 1008	
חָרַד	to tremble (5·23·39) 353	
רָגַז	to quake (1·30·41) 919	
צֹפֶה	16 watchman (1·19) 859	
נָמוֹג	to melt away (1·8·17) 556	
הֲלֹם	hither (4·12[?]) 240	
מְהוּמָה	20 rout (3·12) 223	
אֶתְמוֹל	21 yesterday; אֶת׳ שִׁלְשׁוֹם = formerly (4·8) 1069	
שִׁלְשׁוֹם	three days ago (5·25) 1026	
הִתְחַבֵּא	22 to hide oneself (3·10·34) 285	
נָקַם	24 to avenge oneself (2·12·34) 667	
טָעַם	to taste (4·11·11) 380	
הֵלֶךְ	26 a going, journey = flowing or dropping of honey (1·2) 237	
הִשִּׂיג	to cause to reach; to put (4·48·48) 673	
שְׁבוּעָה	oath (1·30) 989	
טָבַל	27 to dip (1·15·16) 371	
יַעְרָה	honeycomb (1·1) 421	
עִיֵף	28 to be faint (2·5·5) 746	
עָכַר	29 to disturb, trouble (1·12·14) 747	
אוֹר	to become light, shine (2·6·43) 21	
טָעַם	to taste (4·11·11) 380	
לוּא	30 if (1·3) 530	
מַכָּה	slaughter (7·48) 646	
עִיֵף	31 to be faint (2·5·5) 746	

בגד	33 to act or deal faithlessly, deceitfully (1·46·46) 93
גלל	to roll (1·10·18) 164
שֶׂה	34 a sheep [or goat] (4·44) 961
בָּזַז	36 to plunder (1·38·42) 102
הֲלֹם	hither (4·12[?]) 240
הֲלֹם	38 hither (4·12[?]) 240
פִּנָּה	corner (1·30) 819
בַּמֶּה	wherein? (3·29) 552
יהב	41 to give (1·27·27) 396
טָעַם	43 to taste (4·11·11) 380
חָלִילָה	45 far be it [from] (8·21) 321
שַׂעֲרָה	a hair (1·7) 972
מְלוּכָה	47 sovereignty (5·24) 574
הִרְשִׁיעַ	to act wickedly (1·25·34) 957
שסה	48 plunderer (1·7) 1042
בְּכִירָה	49 first-born (1·6) 114
קָטָן	small, younger (4·47) 881

Chapter 15

הַחֲרִים	3 to devote to destruction (7·46·49) 355
חָמַל	to spare, have compassion (4·40·40) 328
עוֹלֵל	child (2·11) 760
יוֹנֵק	suckling, babe (2·11) 413
שֶׂה	a sheep [or goat] (4·44) 961
רַגְלִי	4 footmen, foot soldiers (2·12) 920
הַחֲרִים	8 to devote to destruction (7·46·49) 355
חָמַל	9 to spare, have compassion (4·40·40) 328
מֵיטַב	the best (2·6) 406
מִשְׁנֶה	second [dub.] (4·35) 1041
כַּר	he lamb (1·11) 503
הַחֲרִים	to devote to destruction (7·46·49) 355
נִבְזֶה	9 vile, worthless (1·9) 102

נָמֵס	to melt; ptc.= wasted (1·19·21) 587
חָמַל	15 to spare, have compassion (4·40·40) 328
מֵיטַב	the best (2·6) 406
הַחֲרִים	to devote to destruction (7·46·49) 355
הִרְפָּה	16 to let alone (2·21·44) 951
הַחֲרִים	18 to devote to destruction (7·46·49) 355
חטא	sinner (1·19) 308
עיט	19 to dart greedily (1·3·3[?]) 743
הַחֲרִים	to devote to destruction (7·46·49) 355
חֵרֶם	21 devoted thing (1·29) 356
חֵפֶץ	22 delight (2·39) 343
הִקְשִׁיב	to give attention (1·45·46) 904
קֶסֶם	23 divination (1·11) 890
מְרִי	rebellion (1·22) 598
תְּרָפִים	idol (3·15) 1076
הִפְצִיר	to display pushing, i.e., arrogance, presumption (1·1·7) 823
מְעִיל	27 robe (7·28) 591
מַמְלָכוּת	28 dominion (1·9) 575
נֵצַח	29 eminence (1·42) 664
שִׁקֵּר	to deal falsely (1·5·6) 1055
מַעֲדַנּוֹת	32 bonds (1·2) 772
אָכֵן	surely (1·19) 38
מַר	bitterness (3·37) 600
שִׁכֵּל	33 to make childless (1·18·24) 1013
שכל	to be bereaved (1·4·24) 1013
שִׁסֵּף	to hew in pieces (1·1·1) 1043
הִתְאַבֵּל	35 to mourn (3·19·38) 5

Chapter 16

מָתַי	1 when? עַד־מָתַי = how long? (2·42) 607
הִתְאַבֵּל	to mourn (3·19·38) 5
עֶגְלָה	2 heifer (1·12) 722

חָרַד	4	to go [or come] trembling (5·23·39) 353
מָשִׁיחַ	6	anointed (13·40) 603
גֹּבַהּ	7	loftiness (4·41) 147
קוֹמָה		height (2·45) 879
קָטָן	11	small, youngest (4·47) 881
פֹּה		hither (3·44) 806
אַדְמוֹנִי	12	red, ruddy (2·3) 10
יָפֶה		beautiful, beauty (3·40) 421
רֳאִי		appearance (1·4) 909
בעת	14	to fall upon (2·13·16) 130
בעת	15	to fall upon (2·13·16) 130
נַגֵּן	16	to play (7·14·15) 618
כִּנּוֹר		lyre (3·41) 490
נַגֵּן	17	to play (7·14·15) 618
נַגֵּן	18	to play (7·14·15) 618
נָבוֹן		[to be] discerning (1·21) 106
תֹּאַר		form (3·15) 1061
נֹאד	20	skin (1·6) 609
גְּדִי		kid (2·16) 152
כִּנּוֹר	23	lyre (3·41) 490
נַגֵּן		to play (7·14·15) 618
רָוַח		to be spacious, i.e., there was enlargement, relief (1·2·14) 926

Chapter 17

אֵלָה	2	terebinth, tall tree (3·17) 18
גַּיְא	3	valley (3·47) 161
גֹּבַהּ	4	height (1·17) 147
זֶרֶת		span (1·7) 284
כּוֹבַע	5	helmet (1·6) 464
שִׁרְיוֹן		body armor (3·8) 1056
קַשְׂקֶשֶׂת		scale [of fish] (1·8) 903
מִשְׁקָל		weight (1·48) 1054
מצחה	6	greave[s] (1·1) 595
כִּידוֹן		javelin (2·9) 475
חֲנִית	7	spear (20·46) 333
מנור		beam (1·4) 644

אֹרֵג		weaver (1·10[?]) 70
לֶהָבָה		point, head (1·19) 529
צִנָּה		large shield (2·20) 857
מַעֲרָכָה	8	ranks = army (15·18) 790
ברו		scribal error for בחרו (1·1·1) 136
חֵרֶף	10	to reproach, taunt (5·34·38) 357
מַעֲרָכָה		ranks = army (15·18) 790
זָקֵן	12	to be old, become old (6·25·27) 278
מִשְׁנֶה	13	second in age (4·35)|1041
קָטָן	14	small, youngest (4·47) 881
הֶעֱרִיב	16	to do at evening (1·1·3)|788
הִתְיַצֵּב		to take one's stand; to stand (6·48·48) 426
אֵיפָה	17	ephah (2·38) 35
קָלִי		parched grain (2·6)|885
חָרִיץ	18	thing cut; cut of milk = cheese (1·1[?]) 358
חָלָב		milk (2·44) 316
עֲרֻבָּה		token (1·2) 786
אֵלָה	19	terebinth, tall tree (3·17)|18
נָטַשׁ	20	to leave, entrust (7·33·40) 643
מַעְגָּל		entrenchment (3·3[?]) 722
מַעֲרָכָה		battle line (15·18)|790
הֵרִיעַ		to shout a war cry, alarm of battle (4·40·44) 929
מַעֲרָכָה	21	battle line (15·18) 790
נָטַשׁ	22	to leave, entrust (7·33·40) 643
מַעֲרָכָה		battle line (15·18) 790
מַעֲרָכָה	23	ranks = army (15·18) 790
חֵרֶף	25	to reproach, taunt (5·34·38) 357
הֶעֱשִׁיר		to make rich (2·14·17) 799
עֹשֶׁר		riches (1·37) 799
חָפְשִׁי		free (1·17) 344
הַלָּז	26	this (2·7) 229
עָרֵל		uncircumcised person (4·35) 790
חֵרֶף		to reproach, taunt (5·34·38) 357
מַעֲרָכָה		ranks = army (15·18) 790

נָטַשׁ	28	to leave, entrust (7·33·40) 643
זָדוֹן		insolence (1·12) 268
רֹעַ		willfulness (1·19) 947
מֵאֵצֶל	30	from beside (2·6) 69
מוּל		in front of; אֶל־מוּל = towards the front of (2·33) 557
נְעוּרִים	33	youth (2·46) 655
אֲרִי	34	lion (3·35) 71
דֹּב		bear (3·12) 179
שֶׂה		a sheep [or goat] (4·44) 961
עֵדֶר		a flock (1·39) 727
זָקָן	35	chin [lower jaw] (2·18) 278
אֲרִי	36	lion (3·35) 71
דֹּב		bear (3·12) 179
עָרֵל		uncircumcised person (4·35) 790
חֵרֵף		to reproach, taunt (5·34·38) 357
מַעֲרָכָה		ranks = army (15·18) 790
אֲרִי	37	lion (3·35) 71
דֹּב		bear (3·12) 179
מַד	38	garment (4·12) 551
קוֹבַע		helmet (1·2) 875
שִׁרְיוֹן		body armor (3·8) 1056
חָגַר	39	to gird on (5·44·44) 291
מַד		garment (4·12) 551
הוֹאִיל		to voluntarily undertake to do (1·18·18) 383
נִסָּה		to test, try (2·36·36) 650
מַקֵּל	40	staff (2·18) 596
חָלָק		smooth (1·1) 325
יַלְקוּט		wallet [dub.] (1·1) 545
קֶלַע		sling (3·6) 887
קָרֵב	41	approaching (1·11) 898
צִנָּה		large shield (2·20) 857
בָּזָה	42	to despise (3·31·42) 102
אַדְמוֹנִי		red, ruddy (2·3) 10
יָפֶה		beautiful, beauty (3·40) 421
כֶּלֶב	43	dog (2·32) 476
מַקֵּל		staff (2·18) 596

חֲנִית	45	spear (20·46) 333
כִּידוֹן		javelin (2·9) 475
מַעֲרָכָה		ranks = army (15·18) 790
חֵרֵף		to reproach, taunt (5·34·38) 357
פֶּגֶר	46	corpse (1·22) 803
חֲנִית	47	spear (20·46) 333
מַעֲרָכָה	48	battle line (15·18) 790
קָלַע	49	to sling (2·2·4) 887
מֵצַח		forehead (2·13) 594
טָבַע		to sink (1·6·10) 371
קֶלַע	50	sling (3·6) 887
שָׁלַף	51	to draw out (2·24·24) 1025
תַּעַר		sheath (1·13) 789
הֵרִיעַ	52	to shout a war cry, alarm of battle (4·40·44) 929
גַּיְא		valley (3·47) 161
דָּלַק	53	to pursue hotly (1·7·9) 196
שָׁסַס		to plunder (1·3·5) 1042
עֶלֶם	56	young man (2·2) 761

Chapter 18

נִקְשַׁר	1	to be bound up (1·2·44) 905
הִתְפַּשֵּׁט	4	to strip oneself (1·1·43) 832
מְעִיל		robe (7·28) 591
מַד		garment (4·12) 551
חֲגוֹר		belt, girdle (1·3) 292
מְחוֹלָה	6	dancing (3·8) 298
תֹּף		timbrel, tambourine (2·17) 1074
שָׁלִישׁ		a [three-stringed(?) three-barred(?) three-cornered(?)] musical instrument, perh. sistrum or triangle (1·1) 1026
עָנָה	7	to sing (3·13·16) 777
שָׂחַק		to play (1·17·36) 965
רְבָבָה		ten thousand (4·6) 914
רְבָבָה	8	ten thousand (4·6) 914
מְלוּכָה		kingship (5·24) 574
עִין	9	to eye, look at (1·1·1) 745
הָלְאָה		onward (4·13) 229

מָחֳרָת 10 the morrow, next day; מִמָּחֳרָת = on the morrow (7·32) 564

נַגֵּן to play (7·14·15) 618

חֲנִית spear (20·46) 333

הֵטִיל 11 to cast (2·9·14) 376

חֲנִית spear (20·46) 333

גוּר 15 to be afraid of (1·10·10) 158

חָתָן 18 daughter's husband (2·20) 368

יָשַׁר 20 to be pleasing (3·13·25) 448

מוֹקֵשׁ 21 lure (1·27) 430

הִתְחַתֵּן to make oneself a daughter's husband (5·11·11) 368

לָט 22 secrecy; בַּלָּט = secretly (2·7) 532

הִתְחַתֵּן to make oneself a daughter's husband (5·11·11) 368

נִקְלָה 23 to be lightly esteemed (1·5·6) 885

הִתְחַתֵּן to make oneself a daughter's husband (5·11·11) 368

רָשׁ poor man (1·21) 930

חֵפֶץ 25 delight (2·39) 343

מֹהַר purchase price (1·3) 555

עָרְלָה foreskin (2·16) 790

נקם to avenge oneself (2·12·34) 667

יָשַׁר 26 to be pleasing (3·13·25) 448

הִתְחַתֵּן to make oneself a daughter's husband (5·11·11) 368

עָרְלָה 27 foreskin (2·16) 790

הִתְחַתֵּן to make oneself a daughter's husband (5·11·11) 368

מִדֵּי 30 out of the abundance of, hence as often as (3·15) 191

יקר to be precious, esteemed (2·9·11) 429

Chapter 19

סֵתֶר 2 hiding place (2·35) 712

נֶחְבָּא to hide oneself (2·16·34) 285

תְּשׁוּעָה 5 victory (3·34) 448

נָקִי innocent (1·43) 667

חִנָּם without cause (2·32) 336

אֶתְמוֹל 7 yesterday; אֶת׳ שִׁלְשׁוֹם = formerly (4·8) 1069

שִׁלְשׁוֹם three days ago (5·25) 1026

מַכָּה 8 slaughter (7·48) 646

חֲנִית 9 spear (20·46) 333

נַגֵּן to play (7·14·15) 618

חֲנִית 10 spear (20·46) 333

פָּטַר to remove [oneself], escape (1·7·8) 809

חַלּוֹן 12 window (1·30) 319

תְּרָפִים 13 idol (3·15) 1076

מִטָּה bed (= bier) (4·29) 641

כביר perh. quilt (2·2) 460

מְרַאֲשׁוֹת bed [=bier] (4·29) 641

מִטָּה 15 head place (6·10) 912

תְּרָפִים 16 idol (3·15) 1076

מִטָּה bed [=bier] (4·29) 641

כביר perh. quilt (2·2) 460

מְרַאֲשׁוֹת head place (6·10) 912

כָּכָה 17 thus (2·34) 462

רִמָּה to deal treacherously with, betray (2·8·8) 941

להקה 20 band, company [dub.] (1·1) 530

אֵיפֹה 22 where? (1·10) 33

פָּשַׁט 24 to strip off (6·24·43) 832

עָרֹם naked (1·16) 736

Chapter 20

חָלִילָה 2 far be it [from] (8·21) 321

נֶעֱצַב 3 to be pained (2·7·15) 780

אוּלָם but, but indeed (2·19) 19

פֶּשַׂע step (1·1) 832

חָלִילָה 9 far be it [from] (8·21) 321

קָשֶׁה 10 severe (3·36) 904

חֵקֶר	12	to search [find out one's sentiments] (1·22·27) 350
מוֹשָׁב	18	seat (3·43) 444
שָׁלֹשׁ	19	to stay three days (1·4·9) 1026
אֵזֶל		read הַלָּאז = this (1·1) 23
צַד	20	side (5·31) 841
הוֹרָה		to shoot [2·11(?)·25(?)] 434
מַטָּרָה		target (1·16) 643
הֵנָּה	21	hitherwards, i.e., on this side (3·49) 244
עֶלֶם	22	young man (2·2) 761
הָלְאָה		onward (4·13) 229
מוֹשָׁב	25	seat (3·43) 444
צַד		side; מצד = at the side of (5·31) 841
מְאוּמָה	26	anything (9·32) 548
מִקְרֶה		accident, chance (2·9) 889
בִּלְתִּי		not (2·24) 116
מָחֳרָת	27	the morrow, next day; מִמָּחֳרָת = on the morrow (7·32) 564
תְּמוֹל		yesterday (4·8) 1069
נֵעֲוֵה	30	to be bent, twisted (1·4·17?) 730
מַרְדּוּת		rebelliousness (1·1) 397
בֹּשֶׁת		shame (2·30) 102
הֵטִיל	33	to cast (2·9·14) 376
חֲנִית		spear (20·46) 333
חֳרִי	34	burning (1·6) 354
נֶעֱצַב		to be pained (2·7·15) 780
הִכְלִים		to put to shame (2·10·38) 483
הוֹרָה	36	to shoot (2·11[?]·25[?]) 434
יָרָה		to shoot (2·13·25[?]) 434
יָרָה	37	to shoot (2·13·25[?]) 434
הָלְאָה		onwards (4·13) 229
חוּשׁ	38	to make haste (1·15·22) 301
לִקֵּט		to gather up (1·21·36) 544
מְאוּמָה	39	anything (9·32) 548
מֵאֵצֶל	41	from beside (2·6) 69
נָשַׁק		to kiss (2·26·32) 676

Chapter 21

חָרַד	2	to go [or come] trembling (5·23·39) 353
מְאוּמָה	3	in anything at all (9·32) 548
פְּלֹנִי		a certain one, such a one; פְּלֹנִי אַלְמֹנִי
		מלים = such and such a place (1·6) 811
אַלְמֹנִי		some one, a certain [one] (1·3) 48
חֹל	5	profaneness, commonness (2·7) 320
עָצַר	6	to keep away (2·36·46) 783
תְּמוֹל		yesterday; כְּת׳ שִׁלְשׁוֹם = as formerly (4·8) 1069
שִׁלְשׁוֹם		three days ago (5·25) 1026
חֹל		profaneness, commonness (2·7) 320
חֹם	7	heat (1·4) 328
נֶעֱצַר	8	to be under restraint or detention (1·10·46) 783
אַבִּיר		mighty (1·17) 7
פֹּה	9	here (3·44) 805
חֲנִית		spear (20·46) 333
נָחַץ		to urge [dub.] (1·1·1) 637
אֵלָה	10	terebinth, tall tree (3·17) 18
לוֹט		to wrap (1·4·5) 532
שִׂמְלָה		covering (1·29) 971
אֵפוֹד		ephod, priestly garment (9·49) 65
זוּלָה		except besides (1·16) 265
לָזֶה	12	of, about this one (2·4) 260
מְחוֹלָה		dancing (3·8) 298
עָנָה		to sing (3·13·16) 777
רְבָבָה		ten thousand (4·6) 914
שָׁנָּה	14	to change, alter (1·9·26[?]) 1039
טַעַם		judgment (2·13) 381
תָּוָה		to make a mark (1·1·2) 1063
רִיר		spittle (1·2) 938
זָקָן		chin (2·18) 287
הִשְׁתַּגֵּעַ	15	to show madness (2·2·7) 993
חָסֵר	16	in want of (1·17) 341
שָׁגַע		to be mad (1·5·7) 993
הִשְׁתַּגֵּעַ		to show madness (2·2·7) 993

161

Chapter 22

מְעָרָה 1 cave (8·40) 792

מָצוֹק 2 straits (1·6) 848

נֹשֶׁא creditor (1·4) 674

מַר bitter; מַר נֶפֶשׁ = discontented (3·37) 600

מְצוּדָה 4 fastness (5·18) 845

מְצוּדָה 5 fastness (5·18) 845

אֵשֶׁל 6 tamarisk tree (2·3) 79

רָמָה perh. high place (1·5) 928

חֲנִית spear (20·46) 333

קָשַׁר 8 to conspire (2·36·44) 905

אֹרֵב lier in wait (2·18[?]) 70

צֵידָה 10 provision (1·9) 845

קָשַׁר 13 to conspire (2·36·44) 905

אֹרֵב lier in wait (2·18[?]) 70

חָתָן 14 daughter's husband (2·20) 368

משמעת prob. body guard (1·4) 1036

חָלִילָה 15 far be it [from] (8·21) 321

פָּגַע 17 to fall upon (4·40·46) 803

פָּגַע 18 to fall upon (4·40·46) 803

אֵפוֹד ephod, priestly garment (9·49) 65

בַּד white linen (2·13) 94

עוֹלֵל 19 child (2·11) 760

יוֹנֵק suckling (2·11) 413

שֶׂה a sheep [or goat] (4·44) 961

Chapter 23

שסה 1 to plunder (1·4·5) 1042

גֹּרֶן threshing floor (1·34) 175

פֹּה 3 here (3·44) 805

מַעֲרָכָה ranks = army (15·18) 790

נָהַג 5 to drive away (1·20·30) 624

מַכָּה slaughter (7·48) 646

אֵפוֹד 6 ephod used in consulting (9·49) 65

נִכַּר 7 to alienate [dub.] (1·4·8) 649

בְּרִיחַ bar[s] (1·41) 138

צוּר 8 to besiege (1·31·31) 848

הַחֲרִישׁ 9 to fabricate mischief (1·1·9) 360

אֵפוֹד ephod used in consulting (9·49) 65

בַּעֲבוּר 10 on account of (3·45) 721

בַּאֲשֶׁר 13 in [the place] where (1·20) 84

מְצָד 14 mountain fastness (3·11) 844

מִשְׁנֶה 17 second rank (4·35) 1041

מְצָד 19 mountain fastness (3·11) 844

אות 20 desire [good pleasure] (1·7) 16

חָמַל 21 to have compassion (4·40·40) 328

ערם 22 to be crafty (1·1·5) 791

הערים to be crafty (1·4·5) 791

מחבא 23 hiding place (1·1) 285

התחבא to hide oneself (4·10·34) 285

חפש to search for (1·8·23) 344

אֶלֶף thousand (2·12[?]) 48

צַד 26 side; מִצַּד = on the side of (5·31) 841

נחפז to become hurried (1·4·10) 342

עטר to surround (1·2·7) 742

פָּשַׁט 27 to put off [one's shelter] i.e., make a dash [from a sheltered place] (6·24·43) 832

מַחְלָקוֹת 28 smoothness (1·1) 325

Chapter 24

מְצָד 1 mountain fastness (3·11) 844

בָּחוּר 3 chosen (2·19[?]) 103

יעל mountain goat (1·3) 418

גְּדֵרָה 4 wall: גדרת צאן = shepfolds (1·8) 155

מְעָרָה cave (8·40) 792

הסך to cover (1·5·18[?]) 696

ירכה recesses (1·28) 438

מְעִיל 5 robe (7·28) 591

לָט secrecy: בַּלָּט = secretly (2·7) 532

חָלִילָה 7 far be it [from] (8·21) 321

מָשִׁיחַ anointed (13·40) 603

שסע 8 to tear in two [dub.]: perh. = restrain (1·3·8) 1042

מְעָרָה cave (8·40) 792

מְעָרָה 9 cave (8·40) 792
קדד to bow down (2·15·15) 869
מְעָרָה 11 cave (8·40) 792
חום to look on with compassion (1·24·24) 299
מָשִׁיחַ anointed (13·40) 603
מְעִיל 12 robe (7·28) 591
צָדָה to lie in wait (1·2·2) 841
נקם 13 to avenge (1·13·34) 667
מָשָׁל 14 proverb (2·39) 605
קַדְמֹנִי ancients (1·10) 870
כֶּלֶב 15 dog (2·32) 476
פַּרְעֹשׁ flea (2·2) 829
דַּיָּן 16 judge (1·2) 193
גָּמַל 18 to deal out to; to do to (5·34·37)
מְצוּדָה 23 fastness (5·18) 845

Chapter 25

ספד 1 to lament (2·27·29) 704
גזז 2 to shear (4·14·15) 159
שֵׂכֶל 3 prudence, good sense (1·16) 968
יָפֶה beautiful (3·40) 421
תֹּאַר form (3·15) 1061
קָשֶׁה rough, rude (3·36) 904
מעלל practice (1·41) 760
גזז 4 to shear (4·14·15) 159
גזז 7 to shear (4·14·15) 159
הכלים to put to shame (2·10·38) 483
מְאוּמָה anything (9·32) 548
התפרץ 10 to break away (1·1·49) 829
טְבָחָה 11 slaughtered meat (1·4) 370
טבח to slaughter (1·11·11) 370
גזז to shear (4·14·15) 159
אֵי where? אֵי־מִזֶּה = whence? (3·49) 32
חגר 13 to gird on (5·44·44) 291
עיט 14 to scream (3·3·3) 743
הכלם 15 to be insulted (1·2·38) 483
מְאוּמָה anything (9·32) 548

בְּלִיַּעַל 17 base fellow, worthlessness (6·27) 116
נֵבֶל 18 skin of wine (4·12) 614
סְאָה measure of grain (1·9) 684
קָלִי parched grain (2·6) 885
צִמּוּק bunch of raisins (2·4) 856
דְּבֵלָה lump of pressed figs (2·5) 179
סָתַר 20 cover (2·35) 712
פגש to meet (1·10·14) 803
לָזֶה 21 to this one (2·4) 260
מְאוּמָה anything (9·32) 548
השתין 23 to urinate (2·6·6) 1010
בְּלִיַּעַל 25 base fellow, worthlessness (6·27) 116
נְבָלָה senselessness, inhospitable churlishness (1·13) 615
מָנַע 26 to withhold (2·25·29) 586
צְרוֹר 29 bundle (1·7) 865
קלע to sling (2·2·4) 887
קֶלַע sling (3·6) 887
נָגִיד 30 ruler (4·44) 617
פוּקָה 31 tottering, staggering (1·1) 807
מִכְשׁוֹל stumbling block (1·14) 506
חִנָּם without cause (2·32) 336
טַעַם 33 judgment (2·13) 381
כלא to restrain (2·14·17) 476
אוּלָם 34 but, but indeed (2·19) 19
מָנַע to withhold (2·25·29) 586
לוּלֵי unless (1·10) 530
השתין to urinate (2·6·6) 1010
מִשְׁתֶּה 36 feast (2·45) 1059
שִׁכֹּר drunken (2·13) 1016
נָגַף 38 to strike (3·24·48) 619
חָשַׂךְ 39 to keep [one from evil] (1·26·28) 362

Chapter 26

בָּחוּר 2 chosen (2·19[?]) 103
מרגל 4 spy (1·10) 920
מַעְגָּל 5 entrenchment (3·3[?]) 722

יָשֵׁן   7 sleeping (2·9) 445

מַעְגָּל   entrenchment (3·3[?]) 722

חֲנִית   spear (20·46) 333

מֵעַך   to press (1·2·3) 590

מְרַאֲשׁוֹת   head place (6·10) 912

חֲנִית   8 spear (20·46) 333

שָׁנָה   to do again (1·13·26[?]) 1040

מָשִׁיחַ   9 anointed (13·40) 603

נִקָּה   to be exempt from punishment (1·23·27) 667

נָגַף   10 to strike (3·24·48) 619

נִסְפָּה   to be swept away (3·9·18) 705

חָלִילָה   11 far be it [from] (8·21) 321

מָשִׁיחַ   anointed (13·40) 333

חֲנִית   spear (20·46) 333

מְרַאֲשׁוֹת   head place (6·10) 912

צַפַּחַת   jar or jug (3·7) 860

חֲנִית   12 spear (20·46) 333

צַפַּחַת   jar or jug (3·7) 860

מְרַאֲשׁוֹת   head place (6·10) 912

הֵקִיץ   to awake (1·22·23) 884

יָשֵׁן   sleeping (2·9) 445

תַּרְדֵּמָה   deep sleep (1·7) 922

מָשִׁיחַ   16 anointed (13·40) 603

אֵי   where? (4·39) 32

חֲנִית   spear (20·46) 333

צַפַּחַת   jar or jug (3·7) 860

מְרַאֲשׁוֹת   head place (6·10) 912

הִכִּיר   17 to recognize (1·37·40) 647

הֵסִית   19 to instigate (1·18·18) 694

הֵרִיחַ   to smell (1·11·14) 926

גֵּרֵשׁ   to drive out, away (1·37·48) 176

הִסְתַּפֵּחַ   to join oneself [with] (1·1·5) 705

פַּרְעֹשׁ   20 flea (2·2) 829

קֹרֵא   partridge (1·2) 896

יָקַר   21 to be precious (2·9·11) 429

הִסְכִּיל   to play the fool (1·2·8) 698

שָׁגָה   to go astray (1·17·21) 993

חֲנִית   22 spear (20·46) 333

מָשִׁיחַ   23 anointed (13·40) 603

Chapter 27

נִסְפָּה   1 to be swept away (3·9·18) 705

נוֹאַשׁ   to despair (1·5·6) 384

פָּשַׁט   8 to put off [one's shelter], i.e., make a dash [from a sheltered place] (6·24·43) 832

פָּשַׁט   10 to put off [one's shelter] i.e., make a dash [from a sheltered place] (6·24·43) 832

הִבְאִישׁ   12 to stink, become abhorred (1·7·16) 93

Chapter 28

סָפַד   3 to lament (3·27·29) 704

אוֹב   necromancer (5·16) 15

יִדְּעֹנִי   familiar spirit (2·11) 396

חָרַד   5 to be terrified (5·23·39) 353

אוּרִים   Urim (1·7) 22

בַּעֲלָה   7 mistress (2·4) 128

אוֹב   necromancy (5·16) 15

הִתְחַפֵּשׂ   8 to disguise oneself (1·8·23) 344

קָסַם   to practice divination (1·11·11) 890

אוֹב   necromancy (5·16) 15

אוֹב   9 necromancer (5·16) 15

יִדְּעֹנִי   familiar spirit (2·11) 396

הִתְנַקֵּשׁ   to strike at (1·1·5) 669

קָרָה   10 to befall (1·13·27) 899

רִמָּה   12 to deceive (2·8·8) 941

תֹּאַר   14 form (3·15) 1061

עָטָה   to wrap [oneself] with (1·11·14) 741

מְעִיל   robe (7·28) 591

קָדַד   to bow down (2·15·15) 869

הִרְגִּיז   15 to cause disquiet = disturb (1·7·41) 919

עָר 16 adversary [dub.] (1·2) 786

חָרוֹן 18 [burning of] anger (1·41) 354

קוֹמָה 20 height, length (2·45) 879

נִבְהַל 21 to be dismayed, terrified (1·24·39) 96

פַּת 22 bit, morsel (2·14) 837

מֵאֵן 23 to refuse (2·45·45) 549

פָּרַץ perh. read פצר = to urge (1·46·49) 829, 823

מִטָּה couch, bed (4·29) 641

עֵגֶל 24 calf (1·35) 722

מַרְבֵּק stall (1·4) 918

קֶמַח flour, meal (2·14) 887

לוּשׁ to knead (1·5·5) 534

אָפָה to bake (1·9·12) 66

Chapter 29

סֶרֶן 2 lord (11·21) 710

מְאוּמָה 3 anything (9·32) 548

קָצַף 4 to be angry (1·28·34) 893

שָׂטָן adversary (1·27) 966

בַּמֶּה by what means? (3·29) 552

הִתְרַצָּה to make oneself acceptable (1·1·50[?]) 953

עָנָה 5 to sing (3·13·16) 777

רְבָבָה ten thousand (4·6) 914

מָחוֹלָה dancing (3·8) 298

סֶרֶן 6 lord (11·21) 710

סֶרֶן 7 lord (11·21) 710

אוֹר 10 to become light, shine (2·6·43) 21

Chapter 30

פָּשַׁט 1 to put off [one's shelter], i.e., make a dash [from a sheltered place] (6·24·43) 832

שָׁבָה 2 to take captive (1·29·37) 985

נָהַג to drive [away, off] (4·20·30) 624

נִשְׁבָּה 3 to be taken captive (2·8·37) 985

נִשְׁבָּה 5 to be taken captive (2·8·37) 985

סָקַל 6 to stone to death (1·12·22) 709

מָרַר to be bitter (1·6·14) 600

אֵפוֹד 7 ephod used in consulting (9·49) 65

גְּדוּד 8 marauding band (4·33) 151

הִשִּׂיג to overtake (4·48·48) 673

פָּגַר 10 to be faint (2·2·2) 803

פֶּלַח 12 split, slice (1·6) 812

דְּבֵלָה lump of pressed figs (2·5) 179

צִמּוּק bunch of raisins (2·4) 856

לְמִי 13 to whom? whose? (2·20) 566

אֵי where? אֵי־מִזֶּה = whence? (4·39) 32

פָּשַׁט 14 to put off [one's shelter], i.e., make a dash [from a sheltered place] (6·24·43) 832

גְּדוּד 15 marauding band (4·33) 151

נָטַשׁ 16 to leave, let alone (7·33·40) 643

חָגַג to enjoy oneself merrily (1·6·16) 290

נֶשֶׁף 17 twilight (1·12) 676

מָחֳרָת the following day (7·32) 564

נֶעְדָּר 19 to be lacking (1·6·7) 727

נָהַג 20 to drive [away, off] (4·20·30) 624

פָּגַר 21 to be faint (2·2·2) 803

בְּלִיַּעַל 22 worthlessness, good for nothing (6·27) 116

נָהַג to drive [away, off] (4·20·30) 624

גְּדוּד 23 marauding band (4·33) 151

לַאֲשֶׁר 27 to those who (13·38) 81

לַאֲשֶׁר 28 to those who (13·38) 81

לַאֲשֶׁר 29 to those who (13·38) 81

לַאֲשֶׁר 30 to those who (13·38) 81

לַאֲשֶׁר 31 to those who (13·38) 81

Chapter 31

מוֹרֶה 3 archer (2·4[?]) 435

165

שָׁלַף 4 to draw out (2·24·24) 1025

דקר to pierce (2·7·11) 201

עָרֵל uncircumcised person (4·35) 790

הִתְעַלֵּל to deal wantonly, ruthlessly
(2·7·17) 759

מָחֳרָת 8 the morrow; ממחרת = on the morrow
(7·32) 564

פשׁט to strip the slain (1·3·43) 832

הִפְשִׁיט 9 to strip off (1·15·43) 833

בשׂר to gladden with good tidings
(1·14·15) 142

עצב idol (1·17) 781

גְּוִיָּה 10 corpse (3·12) 156

גְּוִיָּה 12 corpse (3·12) 156

אֶשֶׁל 13 tamarisk tree (2·3) 79

צום to fast (2·20·20) 847

2 SAMUEL

Chapter 1

אֵי 3 where? (3·39) 32

נִקְרָה 6 to chance to be present (1·6·27) 899

נִשְׁעָן to lean, support oneself (1·22·22) 1043

חֲנִית spear (9·46) 333

שָׁבָץ 9 cramp [dub.] (1·1) 990

נֵזֶר 10 crown (1·23) 634

אֶצְעָדָה armlet, band clasping upper arm (1·2) 858

הֵנָּה here, hither (5·49) 244

ספד 12 to lament (3·27·29) 704

צוֹם to fast (5·20·20) 847

אֵי 13 where? (3·39) 32

מִזֶּה, אֵי מִזֶּה idiom; whence? i.e., from where? [?] 262

פָּגַע 15 to fall upon (1·10·46) 803

קוֹנֵן 17 to chant (2·8·8) 884

קִינָה elegy, dirge (1·17) 884

צְבִי 19 beauty, decoration (1·18) 840

בִּשֵּׂר 20 to gladden with good tidings (4·14·15) 142

עלז to exult, triumph (1·16·16) 759

עָרֵל uncircumcised (1·35) 790

טַל 21 dew (2·31) 378

מָטָר rain (2·37) 564

נִגְעַל to be defiled (1·1·10) 171

בְּלִי not, negation (1·23) 115

נָשׁוֹג, נָסוֹג 22 to turn oneself away, turn back (1·14·25) 690

אָחוֹר backwards, back (2·41) 30

רֵיקָם in vain, without effect (1·16) 938

נְעִים 23 delightful (2·13) 653

נפרד to be divided (1·12·26) 825

נֶשֶׁר eagle (1·26) 676

אֲרִי lion (2·35) 71

גָּבַר to be strong, prevail (2·17·25) 149

שָׁנִי 24 scarlet (1·42) 1040

עֵדֶן luxuries (1·3) 726

עֲדִי ornaments (1·13) 725

לְבוּשׁ clothing (2·39) 528

נעם 26 to be pleasant (1·8·8) 653

נפלא to be extraordinary, wonderful (2·13·24) 810

Chapter 2

אָנָה 1 whence? whither? (2·37) 33

פגשׁ 13 to meet, encounter (1·14) 803

בְּרֵכָה pool, pond (4·17) 140

מִזֶּה . . . וּמִזֶּה on one side . . . on the other side, para. 6e. זֶה 262

שָׂחַק 14 to make sport (3·17·36) 965

צַד 16 side (2·31) 841

חֶלְקָה portion of ground (6·24) 324

קָשֶׁה 17 severe (2·36) 904

נִגַּף to be smitten (4·23·48) 619

קַל 18 light, swift, fleet (1·13) 886

צְבִי gazelle (1·11) 840

חֲלִיצָה 21 what is stripped off a person [as plunder] (1·2) 322

מֵאֵן 23 to refuse (2·46·46) 549

בְּאַחֲרֵי hinder part [under plural substantive definition] (1·1) 29

חֲנִית spear (9·46) 333

חֹמֶשׁ belly (4·4) 332

אֲגֻדָּה 25 band [of men] (1·4) 8

נֶצַח 26 everlastingness (1·42) 664

מַר bitter (2·37) 600

מָתַי when? (1·42) 607

לוּלֵא 27 if not, unless (1·4) 530

בִּתְרוֹן 29 cleft, ravine, could be the proper name of a territory (1·1[?]) 144

אוֹר 32 to be or become light (1·5·40) 21

167

Chapter 3

אָרֹךְ	1	long (1·3) 74
חָזֵק		firm, strong; BDB lists as verb (1·2[?]) 304
דַּל		weak, low, poor (2·48) 195
הֹלֵךְ		getting ever [weaker et al.] para.4. 232
מִשְׁנֶה	3	second (1·35) 1041
פִּלֶגֶשׁ	7	concubine (9·37) 811
כֶּלֶב	8	dog (3·32) 476
מֵרֵעַ		friend (1·7) 946
יִרְאָה	11	fear; specific entry does not occur in BDB (2·45) 432
לְמִי	12	to whom, whose (2·20) 566
אָרַשׂ	14	to betroth (1·6·11) 76
עָרְלָה		foreskin (1·16) 790
תְּמוֹל	17	yesterday; תמול שלשום means "formerly" (2·23) 1069
שִׁלְשֹׁם		three days ago (2·25) 1026
מִשְׁתֶּה	20	feast (1·45) 1059
אַוָּה	21	to desire (1·11·27) 16
גְּדוּד	22	raid, troop (3·33) 151
פִּתָּה	25	to deceive (1·17·27) 834
מוֹצָא		a going forth (1·27) 425
מוֹבָא		incoming (1·2) 100
שֶׁלִי	27	quietness (1·1) 1017
חֹמֶשׁ		belly (4·4) 332
נָקִי	28	innocent 667
חִיל	29	to whirl about (1·6·9) 296
זָב		flow (1·13[?]) 264
מְצֹרָע		leprous (1·15) 863
פֶּלֶךְ		whirl of spindle (1·10) 813
חָסֵר		needy, lacking (1·17) 341
חגר	31	to gird, gird on (5·44·44) 291
שַׂק		sackcloth (2·48) 974
ספד		to lament (3·27·29) 704
מִטָּה		bed, bier (2·29) 641
קוֹנֵן	33	to chant (2·8·8) 884

נָבָל		foolish (2·18) 614
עַוְלָה	34	injustice, unrightcousness (2·32) 732
הברה	35	to cause to eat (2·2·5) 136
בְּעוֹד		while yet, so long as (2·20) 728
טָעַם		to taste (2·11·11) 380
מְאוּמָה		anything (2·32) 548
הִכִּיר	36	to recognize (1·37·40) 647
רַךְ	39	tender, delicate, soft (1·16) 940
קָשֶׁה		severe (2·36) 904

Chapter 4

רָפָה	1	to sink, drop (1·14·44) 951
נִבְהַל		to be disturbed, dismayed, terrified (1·24·39) 96
גְּדוּד	2	marauding band, troop (3·33) 151
נָכֶה	4	stricken (2·3) 647
שְׁמוּעָה		report (2·27) 1035
אֹמֵן		foster [mother] (1·7) 52
חפז		to be in a hurry or alarm (1·6·9) 342
נפסח		to make to limp (1·1·7) 820
חמם	5	to be[come] warm (1·23·26) 328
מִשְׁכָּב		lying down (7·46) 1012
צָהֳרַיִם		midday, noon (1·23) 843
חִטָּה	6	wheat (2·30) 334
חֹמֶשׁ		belly (4·4) 332
מִטָּה	7	bed (2·29) 641
חֶדֶר		room, chamber (3·34) 293
מִשְׁכָּב		lying down (7·46) 1012
נְקָמָה	8	vengeance (2·27) 668
מְבַשֵּׂר	10	bearer of good tidings (2·9) 142
בְּשׂוֹרָה		reward for good news, good news (5·6) 142
מִשְׁכָּב	11	bed (7·46) 1012
בָּעַר		to consume, burn (1·26·28[?]) 129
קָצַץ	12	to cut, hew off (1·9·14) 893
תָּלָה		to hang up (2·23·27) 1067
בְּרֵכָה		pool, pond (4·17) 140

Chapter 5

אֶתְמוֹל שִׁלְשׁוֹם 2 yesterday, recently (1·8) 1069 three days ago; אתמול שלשום formerly, previously, hitherto (2·25) 1026

מֵבִי = מביא

נָגִיד ruler (3·44) 617

הֵנָּה 6 here, hither (5·49) 244

עִוֵּר blind (3·25) 734

פִּסֵּחַ lame (5·14) 820

מְצוּדָה 7 stronghold (5·18) 845

צִנּוֹר 8 pipe, spout, conduit [dub.] (1·2) 857

פִּסֵּחַ lame (5·14) 820

עִוֵּר blind (3·25) 734

מְצוּדָה 9 stronghold (5·18) 845

הָלוֹךְ וְגָדוֹל 10 growing greater and greater, para. 4. 232

חָרָשׁ 11 graver, artificer (2·36[?]) 360

בַּעֲבוּר 12 on account of, for the sake of (10·45) 721

פִּלֶגֶשׁ 13 concubine (9·37) 811

יִלּוֹד 14 born (2·5) 407

מְצוּדָה 17 stronghold (5·18) 845

נטשׁ 18 to be spread abroad (2·6·40) 643

פָּרַץ 20 to break out on (4·46·49) 829

פֶּרֶץ bursting forth (2·18) 829

עָצָב 21 idol (1·17) 781

נטשׁ 22 to be spread abroad (2·6·40) 643

מִמּוּל 23 from the front of (1·9) 557

בָּכָא balsam tree (2·5) 113

צְעָדָה 24 marching (1·3) 857

בָּכָא balsam tree (2·5) 113

חרץ to act with decision (1·1·1[?]) 358

Chapter 6

בָּחוּר 1 chosen (2·19[?]) 103

עֲגָלָה 3 cart (2·25) 722

נהג to drive (1·20·30) 624

שׂחק 5 to play (3·17·36) 965

בְּרוֹשׁ cypress, fir (1·20) 141

כִּנּוֹר lyre (1·41) 490

נֵבֶל harp (1·27) 614

תֹּף timbrel, tambourine (1·17) 1074

מְנַעַנְעִים a kind of rattle [dub.] (1·1) 631

צֶלְצְלִים cymbals (1·3) 852

גֹּרֶן 6 threshing floor (5·34) 175

שׁמט to let drop, let fall (1·6·8) 1030

שַׁל 7 hastiness, error, irreverence [dub.] (1·1) 1016

פָּרַץ 8 to break out on (4·46·49) 829

פֶּרֶץ bursting forth (2·18) 811

בַּעֲבוּר 12 on account of, for the sake of (10·46) 721

צעד 13 to step, march (1·7·8) 857

צַעַד step, pace (2·14) 857

מְרִיא fatling (1·8) 597

כרכר 14 to dance (2·2·2) 502

חגר to gird on (5·44·44) 291

אֵפוֹד priestly garment (1·49) 65

בַּד white linen (1·23) 94

תְּרוּעָה 15 shout or blast of war, alarm, or joy (1·36) 929

נשׁקף 16 to lean over, look down (1·10·22) 1054

חַלּוֹן window (1·30) 319

פזז to show agility, leap (1·1·2) 802

כרכר to dance (2·2·2) 502

בָּזָה to despise (3·31·42) 102

הצּיג 17 to place (1·5·16) 426

חַלָּה 19 a kind of cake (1·14) 319

אֶשְׁפָּר cake, roll [dub.] (1·2) 80

אֲשִׁישָׁה [pressed-]raisin cake (1·5) 84

רֵיק 20 empty, worthless (1·14) 938

נָגִיד 21 ruler (3·44) 617

שׂחק to play (3·17·36) 965

169

שָׁפֵל 22 humiliated (1·18) 1050

Chapter 7

מִסָּבִיב 1 from round about, from every side (1·42) 686

נָוֶה 8 abode [of sheep] (2·45) 627

נָגִיד ruler (3·44) 617

רָגַז 10 to be disquieted (3·30·41) 919

עַוְלָה injustice, unrighteousness (2·32) 732

לְמִן 11 from (2·14) 583

מֵעֶה 12 inward parts (3·31) 588

הֶעֱוָה 14 to commit iniquity (3·9·17) 731

חִזָּיוֹן 17 vision (1·9) 303

הֲלֹם 18 hither, here (1·11 [?]) 240

קָטֹן 19 to be insignificant (1·3·4) 881

לְמֵרָחוֹק from afar = long before (1·6[?]) 583 (para. 9b. of מִן)

בַּעֲבוּר 21 on account of, for the sake of (10·45) 721

גְּדוּלָה greatness (2·12) 153

זוּלָה 22 except, only, save that (1·16) 265

גְּדוּלָה 23 greatness (2·12) 153

נוֹרָא dreadful, wonderful thing (1·44) 431

הוֹאִיל 29 to be pleased (1·18·18) 383

Chapter 8

הִכְנִיעַ 1 to subdue (1·11·36) 488

מֶתֶג bridle, control (1·5) 607

אַמָּה mother city, metropolis (1·1) 52

חֶבֶל 2 measuring cord, line (5·49) 286

רַגְלִי 4 on foot (2·12) 920

עִקֵּר to hamstring (1·5·7) 785

נְצִיב 6 deputy (3·11) 662

שֶׁלֶט 7 shield [dub.] (1·7) 1020

כָּבַשׁ 11 to subdue (1·1·14) 461

גַּיְא 13 valley (1·47) 161

מֶלַח salt (1·28) 571

נְצִיב 14 deputy (3·11) 662

מַזְכִּיר 16 recorder (2·9) 271

Chapter 9

בַּעֲבוּר 1 on account of, for the sake of (10·45) 721

אֶפֶס 3 cessation of...!, a particle of negation (2·43) 67

נָכֵה stricken (2·3) 647

אֵיפֹה 4 where? (1·10) 33

בַּעֲבוּר 7 on account of, for the sake of (10·45) 721

כֶּלֶב 8 dog (3·32) 476

קָטָן 12 young (2·47) 881

מוֹשָׁב those dwelling [collective of dweller] (1·43) 444

פִּסֵּחַ 13 lame (5·14) 820

Chapter 10

בַּעֲבוּר 3 in order to (10·45) 721

חָקַר to search through, explore (1·22·27) 350

רִגֵּל to go about as a spy, explorer (2·14·16) 920

גִּלַּח 4 to shave [off] (4·18·23) 164

זָקָן beard (3·18) 278

מַדְוֶה garment (1·2) 551

שֵׁת seat of body, buttocks (1·4) 1059

נִכְלַם 5 to be humiliated (2·26·38) 483

צָמַח to grow abundantly (1·4·33) 855

זָקָן beard (3·18) 278

נִבְאַשׁ 6 to make oneself odious, become odious (2·3·16) 92

שָׂכַר to hire (1·17·20) 968

רַגְלִי on foot (2·12) 920

אָחוֹר 9 the hinder side, back part; with מִן = behind (2·41) 30

בָּחוּר chosen (2·19[?]) 103

נִגַּף 15 to be smitten (4·23·48) 619

יַחַד together, altogether (3·44) 403

נִגַּף 19 to be smitten (4·23·48) 619

Chapter 11

תְּשׁוּבָה	1 return (1·8) 1000
צוּר	to shut in, besiege (2·31·31) 848
מִשְׁכָּב	2 bed (7·46) 1012
גָּג	roof, top (4·29) 150
טֻמְאָה	4 uncleanness (1·37) 380
הָרָה	5 to conceive, become pregnant (1·38·40) 247
הָרָה	pregnant (1·15[?]) 247
מַשְׂאָה	8 portion (1·16) 673
סֻכָּה	11 booth (2·31) 697
מָחֳרָת	12 the morrow (1·32) 564
שׁכר	13 to make drunk (1·4·20) 1016
מִשְׁכָּב	bed (7·46) 1012
יהב	15 set; elsewhere: give, ascribe, come now (2·33) 396
מוּל	the forefront of (1·25) 557
הורה	20 to shoot (2·11[?]·25[?]) 434
פֶּלַח	21 millstone (1·6) 812
גָּבַר	23 to be strong, prevail (2·17·25) 149
הורה	24 to shoot (2·11[?]·25[?]) 434
מוֹרֶה	archer (1·4[?]) 435
זֹה	25 this; כָּזֹה וְכָזֶה thus and thus (1·11) 262
הָרַס	to throw down, tear down (1·30·43) 248
ספד	26 to lament (3·27·29) 704
אֵבֶל	27 mourning (3·24) 5

Chapter 12

עָשִׁיר	1 rich (3·23) 799
רָאשׁ	poor man [men] (3·21) 930
עָשִׁיר	2 rich (3·23) 799
רָשׁ	3 poor man [men] (3·21) 930
כִּבְשָׂה	ewe lamb (3·8) 461
קָטֹן	small (2·47) 881
פַּת	fragment, bit, morsel (1·14) 837
כּוֹס	cup (1·31) 468

חֵיק	bosom, fold of garment at breast (2·38) 300
הֵלֶךְ	4 traveler (1·2) 237
עָשִׁיר	rich (3·23) 799
חָמַל	to spare, have compassion on (3·40·40) 328
אֹרֵחַ	wanderer, wayfarer (1·4) 72
כִּבְשָׂה	ewe lamb (3·8) 461
רָאשׁ	poor man [men] (3·21) 930
כִּבְשָׂה	6 ewe lamb (3·8) 461
עֵקֶב	because (2·15) 784
חָמַל	to spare, have compassion on (3·40·40) 328
חֵיק	8 bosom, fold of garment at breast (2·38) 300
כָּהֵנָּה וְכָהֵנָּה	again as much, para. 8c.* 241
בָּזָה	9 to despise (3·31·42) 102
עֵקֶב	10 because (2·15) 784
בָּזָה	to despise (3·31·42) 102
רֵעֶה	11 friend (3·5) 946
סֵתֶר	12 secrecy (1·35) 712
אֶפֶס	14 save that; howbeit, but, when followed by כִּי (2·43) 67
נָאֵץ	to cause to scorn (1·15·24) 610
ילוד	born (2·5) 409
נָגַף	15 to smite (1·24·48) 619
נאשׁ	to be sick (1·1·1[?]) 60
צוֹם	16 to fast (5·20·20) 847
צוֹם	fast, fasting (1·25) 847
בָּרָה	17 to eat (3·3·5) 136
התלחשׁ	19 to whisper together (1·2·3) 538
סוּךְ	20 to anoint oneself (1[?]·1[?]·9[?]) 691
חלף	to change (1·2·26) 322
שִׂמְלָה	wrapper, mantle (1·29) 971
בַּעֲבוּר	21 for the sake of, because of (10·46) 721
צוֹם	to fast (5·20·20) 847
בְּעוֹד	22 while yet, so long as (2·20) 728

---

* based on definition given, specific entry not listed

171

צוֹם to fast (5·20·20) 847

צוֹם 23 to fast (5·20·20) 847

בַּעֲבוּר 25 on account of, in order that, for the sake of (10·46) 721

מְלוּכָה 26 kingship (2·24) 574

עֲטָרָה 30 crown (1·23) 742

מִשְׁקָל weight (3·48) 1054

יָקָר precious (1·35) 429

מְגֵרָה 31 saw (1·3) 176

חָרִיץ sharp instrument (1·2) 358

מַגְזֵרָה axe (1·1) 160

מַלְבֵּן brick mold (1·3) 527

Chapter 13

יָפֶה 1 beautiful (3·40) 421

בַּעֲבוּר 2 on account of, for the sake of, in order that (10·46) 721

בְּתוּלָה virgin (2·50) 143

נפלא to be beyond one's power (2·13·24) 810

מְאוּמָה anything (2·32) 548

כָּכָה 4 thus (2·33) 462

דַּל weak, thin, poor, low (2·48) 195

מִשְׁכָּב 5 bed (7·46) 1012

הברה to cause to eat (2·2·5) 136

בִּרְיָה food (3·3) 136

לבב 6 to make cakes (2·2·2) 525

לְבִבָה cakes (3·3) 525

בָּרָה to eat (3·3·5) 136

בִּרְיָה 7 food (3·3[?]) 136

בָּצֵק 8 dough (1·5) 130

לוּשׁ to knead (1·5·5) 534

לבב to make cakes (2·2·2) 525

בשל to cook, boil (1·20·27) 143

לְבִבָה cakes (3·3) 525

מַשְׂרֵת 9 pan [dub.] (1·1) 602

מֵאֵן to refuse (2·45·45) 549

בִּרְיָה 10 food (3·3[?]) 136

חֶדֶר room, chamber (3·34) 293

בָּרָה to eat (3·3·5) 136

לְבִבָה cakes (3·3) 525

נְבָלָה 12 disgraceful folly (1·13) 615

אָנָה 13 where? (2·37) 33

נָבָל foolish (2·18) 614

מָנַע to withhold (1·25·29) 586

שִׂנְאָה 15 hating, hatred (2·17) 971

אֹדוֹת 16 cause, because; here BDB reconstructs the text to read אֶל אָחִי כִּי 15

מְשָׁרֵת 17 servant (2·20) 1058

נָעַל to lock (2·7[?]·8[?]) 653

כְּתֹנֶת 18 tunic (3·30) 509

פַּס* flat of hand or foot (2·5) 821

בְּתוּלָה virgin (2·50) 143

מְעִיל robe (1·28) 591

מְשָׁרֵת servant (2·20) 1058

נָעַל to lock (2·7[?]·8[?]) 653

אֵפֶר 19 ashes (1·22) 68

כְּתֹנֶת tunic (3·30) 509

פַּס* flat of hand or foot (2·5) 821

הֶחֱרִישׁ 20 to be silent (2·36·44) 361

לְמִן 22 the expression ...וְעַד למן an idiomatic expression to denote comprehensively an entire class, para. 9b.(1) מִן 583

גזז 23 to shear (2·14·15) 159

גזז 24 to shear (2·14·15) 159

פָּרַץ 25 to spread [become known] (4·46·49) 829

פָּרַץ 27 to spread [become known] (4·46·49) 829

פֶּרֶד 29 mule (4·14) 825

שְׁמוּעָה 30 report (2·27) 1035

שׁוּמָה 32 not in Lis.; BDB "perhaps n.f., token of unluckiness, scowl" (0·0[?]) 965

צֹפֶה 34 watchman (6·19) 859

צַד side (2·31) 841

בְּכִי 36 weeping (1·30) 113

הִתְאַבֵּל 37 to mourn (4·19·38) 5

Chapter 14

הִתְאַבֵּל 2 to mourn (4·19·38) 5

אָבֵל mourning (3·24) 5

סוּךְ to anoint oneself (1[?]·1[?]·9[?]) 691

אֲבָל 5 verily, truly, indeed (1·11) 6

נצה 6 to struggle with each other (1·5·8) 663

כְּתֹנֶת פַּסִּים* tunic reaching to palms and soles 821

יוֹרֵשׁ 7 heir (1·5) 439

כבה to extinguish (2·10·24) 459

גַּחֶלֶת coal (3·18) 160

נָקִי 9 free from punishment (2·43) 667

גֹּאֵל 11 kinsman, redeemer (1·44[?]) 145

שַׂעֲרָה a [single] hair (1·7) 972

אָשֵׁם 13 guilty (1·3) 79

נִדָּח banished one (2·11) 623

נגר 14 to be poured (1·4·5) 620

נדח to be thrust down; this specific cntr not in BDB (1·2·2[?]) 191

נִדָּח banished one (2·11) 623

אוּלַי 15 perhaps (2·45) 19

יַחַד 16 together, altogether (3·44) 403

מְנֻחָה 17 security, assurance (1·21) 629

כָּחֵד 18 to hide (1·15·30) 470

אִשׁ 19 there is, was, will be = יֵשׁ (1·3) 441

הֵמִין to turn to the right (1·5) 412

הִשְׂמִיל to turn to the left (1·5·5) 970

לְבַעֲבוּר 20 in order to (2·3) 721

יָפֶה 25 fair (3·40) 421

קָדְקֹד head, crown of head (1·11) 869

מוּם blemish (1·21[?]) 548

גָּלַח 26 to shave [off] (4·18·23) 164

שָׁקַל to weigh out (2·19·22) 1053

שֵׂעָר hair (1·28) 972

יָפֶה 27 beautiful (3·40) 421

חֶלְקָה 30 portion of ground (6·24) 324

שְׂעֹרָה barley (3·34) 972

הִצִּית to kindle, set on fire (3·17·27) 428

הִצִּית 31 to kindle, set on fire (3·17·27) 428

חֶלְקָה portion of ground (6·24) 324

הֵנָּה 32 here, hither (5·49) 244

נָשַׁק 33 to kiss (4·26·32) 676

Chapter 15

מֶרְכָּבָה 1 chariot (1·44) 939

אֵי 2 where? (3·39) 32

נָכֹחַ 3 right (1·8) 647

הִצְדִּיק 4 to do justice (1·12·41) 842

נָשַׁק 5 to kiss (4·26·32) 676

גנב 6 to steal away (1·2·39) 170

נָדַר 7 to vow (2·31·31) 623

נָדַר 8 to vow (2·31·31) 623

מְרַגֵּל 10 spy (1·10) 920

תֹּם 11 innocence, simplicity (1·23) 1070

יוֹעֵץ 12 counselor (1·22) 419

קֶשֶׁר conspiracy (1·14) 905

אַמִּיץ mighty (1·6) 55

פְּלֵיטָה 14 escaped remnant (1·28) 812

הִשִּׂיג to overtake (1·48·48) 673

הִדִּיחַ to thrust (1·27·43) 623

פִּלֶגֶשׁ 16 concubine (9·37) 811

מֶרְחָק 17 distance (1·18) 935

נָכְרִי 19 foreigner (1·45) 648

תְּמוֹל 20 yesterday (2·23) 1069

הֵנִיע to cause to wander (2·14·38) 631

טַף 22 children (1·41) 381

נָוֶה 25 habitation (2·45) 627

הִתְמַהְמַהּ 28 to tarry (1·9) 554

עֲבָרָה ford (2·2) 720

מַעֲלָה 30 ascent (1·19) 751

זַיִת olive tree (1·38) 268

חפה to cover (2·6·12) 341

יָחֵף barefoot (1·5) 405

חפה to cover (2·6·12) 341

קָשַׁר 31 to league together, conspire (1·36·44) 905

סִכֵּל to turn into foolishness (1·2·8) 698

כְּתֹנֶת 32 tunic (3·30) 509

מַשָּׂא 33 burden (2·43) 672

מֵאָז 34 idiom: from that time = time past [old] (1·17) 23

הֵפֵר to break, frustrate (2·41·44) 830

רֵעֶה 37 friend (3·5) 946

Chapter 16

צֶמֶד 1 couple, pair (1·15) 855

חבשׁ to bind, bind on, bind up (3·27·31) 289

צִמּוּקָה bunch of raisins (1·4) 856

קַיִץ summer fruit (2·20) 884

נֶבֶל skin (1·11) 614

קַיִץ 2 summer fruit (2·20) 884

יָעֵף weary (1·4) 419

אַיֵּה 3 where? (2·44) 32

מַמְלְכוּת dominion (1·9) 575

סִקֵל 6 to stone (2·4·22) 709

בְּלִיַּעַל 7 worthless, good-for-nothing, base fellow (4·27) 116

מְלוּכָה 8 kingship (2·24) 574

כֶּלֶב 9 dog (3·32) 476

מַה לִּי וְלָכֶם 10 idiomatic formula of repudiation, or emphatic denial: what is there (common) to me and to you? what have I to do with you? para. 1d. (c). BDB (1·6) 553

מֵעֶה 11 inward parts (3·31) 588

אוּלַי 12 perhaps (2·45) 19

קְלָלָה curse (1·33) 887

צֵלָע 13 rib [ridge] of hill (1·39) 854

לְעֻמָּה close by, side by side, with (2·32) 769

סִקֵל to stone (2·4·22) 709

עִפֵּר to keep dusting (1·1·1) 780

עָיֵף 14 faint, weary (2·17) 746

נפשׁ to refresh oneself (1·3·3) 661

רֵעֶה 16 friend (3·5) 946

לְמִי 19 to whom, whose (2·20) 566

יהב 20 with reflex ל = provide; give (2·33·33) 396

פִּלֶגֶשׁ 21 concubine (9·37) 811

נִבְאַשׁ to make oneself odious, become odious (2·3·16) 92

גָּג 22 roof, top (4·29) 150

פִּלֶגֶשׁ concubine (9·37) 811

Chapter 17

יָגֵעַ 2 weary (1·3) 388

רָפֶה slack (1·4) 952

הֶחֱרִיד to drive in terror, rout (1·16·39) 353

ישׁר 4 to be pleasing, agreeable, right (1·13·25) 448

מַר 8 bitter (2·37) 600

דֹּב bear (1·12) 179

שַׁכּוּל bereaved, robbed of offspring (1·6) 1014

נֶחְבָּא 9 to hide oneself, be hidden (1·16·34) 285

פַּחַת pit (2·10) 809

תְּחִלָּה beginning (3·22) 321

מַגֵּפָה slaughter (4·26) 620

אַרְיֵה 10 lion (1·45) 71

נָמֵס to melt (2·19·21) 587

חוֹל 11 sand (1·22) 297

קְרָב battle, war (1·8) 898

טַל 12 dew (2·31) 378

חֶבֶל 13 cord, rope (5·49) 286

סחב to drag (1·5·5) 694

צְרוֹר pebble (1·2) 866

הֵפֵר 14 to break, frustrate (2·41·44) 830

לְבַעֲבוּר in order to [+infin.] (2·3) 721

כָּזֹאת וְכָזֹאת 15 thus and thus (2·5) para. 6d. זֶה 262

בָּלַע 16 to be swallowed up, destroyed (1·2·2) 118

בְּאֵר 18 well (3·36) 91

מָסָךְ 19 covering (1·25) 697

בְּאֵר well (3·36) 91

שטח to spread, spread abroad (1·4·5) 1008

רִאפוֹת some grain or fruit (1·2) 937

אַיֵּה 20 where? (2·44) 32

מִיכָל stream (1·1) 568

בְּאֵר 21 well (3·36) 91

כָּכָה thus (2·33) 462

נֶעְדָּר 22 to be lacking (1·6·7) 727

חבש 23 to equip [a beast] for riding, to bind on (3·27·31) 289

נחנק to strangle oneself (1·1·2) 338

מִשְׁכָּב 28 bed, lying down [?] (7·46) 1012

סַף basin (1·6) 706

יוֹצֵר potter (1·17) 427

חִטָּה wheat (2·30) 334

שְׂעֹרָה barley (3·34) 972

קֶמַח flow, meal (1·14) 887

קָלִי parched grain (2·6) 885

פּוֹל beans [collective] (1·2) 806

עֲדָשָׁה lentil (2·4) 727

חֶמְאָה 29 curd, curdled milk (1·10) 326

שְׁפוֹת cream [dub.] (1·1) 1045

רָעֵב hungry (1·19) 944

עָיֵף faint, weary (2·17) 746

צָמֵא thirsty (1·9) 854

Chapter 18

אַט 5 gentleness, with לְ = gently (1·5) 31

נָגַף 7 to be smitten (4·23·48) 619

מַגֵּפָה slaughter (4·26) 620

מֵאֲשֶׁר 8 than those (1·17) 84

פֶּרֶד 9 mule (4·14) 825

שׂוֹבֶךְ network of boughs (1·1) 959

אֵלָה terebinth [tree] (4·17) 18

תָּלָה 10 to hang up, hang (2·23·27) 1067

אֵלָה terebinth [tree] (4·17) 18

חֲגֹרָה 11 girdle, loin covering, belt (1·5) 292

לֻא 12 though, if (2·17) 530

שָׁקַל to weigh out (2·19·22) 1053

נִכְחַד 13 to be hidden (1·9·30) 470

הִתְיַצֵּב to take one's stand (4·48·48) 426

מִנֶּגֶד aloof (1·26) 617

הוֹחִיל 14 to wait, tarry (1·15·42) 403

אֵלָה terebinth [tree] (4·17) 18

חָשַׂךְ 16 to withhold, refrain (1·26·28) 362

פַּחַת 17 pit (2·10) 809

גַּל heap [of stones] (1·20) 164

מַצֶּבֶת 18 pillar (2·35) 663

בַּעֲבוּר in order to [+ infin.] (10·45) 721

בִּשֵּׂר 19 to bear tidings (4·14·15) 142

בְּשׂוֹרָה 20 news, tidings (5·6) 142

בִּשֵּׂר to bear tidings (4·14·15) 142

בְּשׂוֹרָה 22 reward for good news, good news (5·6) 142

צֹפֶה 24 watchman (6·19) 859

גַּג roof, top (4·29) 150

צֹפֶה 25 watchman (6·19) 859

בְּשׂוֹרָה news, tidings (5·6) 142

קָרֵב approaching (1·11) 898

הָלוֹךְ וְקָרֵב nearer and nearer, para. 4c. (3) 233

צֹפֶה 26 watchman (6·19) 859

שֹׁעֵר porter (1·37) 1045

מְבַשֵּׂר one bearing tidings (2·9[?]) 142

צֹפֶה 27 watchman (6·19) 859

מְרוּצָה running (2·4) 930

בְּשׂוֹרָה news, tidings (5·6) 142

הִתְיַצֵּב 30 to take one's stand (4·48·48) 426

הִתְבַּשֵּׂר 31 to receive good tidings (1·1·15) 142

Chapter 19

רָגַז 1 to be excited, perturbed (3·30·41) 919

עֲלִיָּה roof chamber (1·20) 751

הִתְאַבֵּל 2 to mourn (4·19·38) 5

תְּשׁוּעָה 3 deliverance (3·34) 448

אָבֵל mourning (3·24) 5

נֶעֱצַב to be pained [for] (1·7·15) 780

הִתְגַּנֵּב 4 to go by stealth, steal away (2·2·39) 170

נִכְלָם to be put to shame (2·26·28) 483

לוֹט 5 to wrap tightly (1·4·5) 532

פִּלֶגֶשׁ 6 concubine (9·37) 811

שֹׂנֵא 7 enemy (2·41) 971

אֹהֵב friend (1·36[?]) 12

לוֹ, לָא if (2·17) 530

נְעוּרִים 8 youth (1·46) 655

נָדוֹן 10 to be at strife (1·1·23) 192

הֶחֱרִישׁ 11 to be silent (2·36·44) 361

עֲבָרָה 19 ford (2·2) 720

הֶעֱוָה 20 to commit iniquity (3·9·17) 731

שָׂטָן 23 adversary (1·27) 966

שָׂפָם 25 moustache (1·5) 974

לְמָן 26 from (2·14) 583

רִמָּה 27 to deceive, mislead (1·8·8) 941

חבשׁ to equip [a beast] for riding, bind up (3·27·31) 289

פִּסֵּחַ lame (5·14) 820

רִגֵּל 28 to slander (2·14·16) 920

זָקֵן 33 to be old, become old (1·25·27) 278

כִּלְכֵּל to sustain (3·23·36) 465

שִׂיבָה sojourn (1·1) 444

כִּלְכֵּל 34 to sustain (3·23·36) 465

כַּמָּה 35 how much? how many? (1·13) 552

טָעַם 36 to taste (2·11·11) 380

שָׁר singer (2·9) 1010

מַשָּׂא burden (2·43) 672

גָּמַל 37 to recompense, repay, deal fully with (2·34·37) 169

גְּמוּלָה dealing, recompense (1·3) 168

נָשַׁק 40 to kiss (4·26·32) 676

גָּנַב 42 to steal, take by stealth (2·30·39) 170

קָשָׁה 44 to be hard, severe (1·5·28) 904

Chapter 20

בְּלִיַּעַל 1 worthless, good-for-nothing, base fellow (4·27) 116

פִּלֶגֶשׁ 3 concubine (9·37) 811

כִּלְכֵּל to sustain (3·23·36) 465

אַלְמָנוּת widowhood (1·4) 48

חַיּוּת life, lifetime (1·1) 313

פֹּה 4 here, hither (1·44) 805

הֶאֱחִיר 5 to show delay, delay (1·1·17) 29

יָעַד to appoint (1·5·28) 416

בָּצוּר 6 fortified (1·25[?]) 130

חָגַר 8 to gird (5·44·44) 291

חֲגוֹר belt, girdle (1·3) 292

מַד garment (1·12) 551

לְבוּשׁ garment (2·31) 528

צֶמֶד to be bound (1·1·5) 855

מָתְנַיִם loins (1·50) 608

תַּעַר sheath (1·13) 789

זָקָן 9 beard (3·18) 278

נָשַׁק to kiss (4·26·32) 676

חֹמֶשׁ 10 belly (4·4) 332

מֵעָה inward parts, internal organs (3·32) 588

שָׁנָה to repeat (1·13·25) 1040

הִתְגַּלְגַּל 12 to roll oneself (1·2·17) 164

מְסִלָּה highway (3·27) 700

הָגָה 13 to thrust away (1·1·1) 387

מְסִלָּה highway (3·27) 700

נִקְהַל 14 to assemble (1·19·39) 874

צוּר 15 to shut in, besiege (2·31·31) 848

סֹלְלָה	mound (1·11) 700	
חֵל	rampart, fortress [i.e., a little wall] (1·9) 298	
הֵנָּה	16 here, hither (5·49) 244	
שָׁלֵם	19 peaceable psv. ptc. (1·1[?]) 1023	
אָמוּן	faithful one (1·3[?]) 52	
בִּלַּע	to swallow up, destroy (2·20·41) 118	
חָלִיל	20 far be it [from me, you, etc.] (2·20[?]) 321	
בִּלַּע	to swallow up, destroy (2·20·41) 118	
מַס	24 labor band (1·23) 586	
מַזְכִּיר	recorder (2·9) 271	

Chapter 21

שִׁירָה	1 song (1·13) 1010	
קִנֵּא	2 to be zealous [for] (1·28·32) 888	
בַּמֶּה	3 wherewith? (1·29) 552	
דִּמָּה	5 to imagine, devise (1·13·27) 197	
הִתְיַצֵּב	to take one's stand (4·48·48) 426	
הוֹקִיעַ	6 of some solemn form of execution; meaning uncertain (2·3·8) 429	
בָּחִיר	chosen (1·13) 104	
חָמַל	7 to spare, have compassion on (3·40·40) 328	
שְׁבוּעָה	oath (1·30) 989	
הוֹקִיעַ	9 of some solemn form of execution; meaning uncertain (2·3·8) 429	
יַחַד	together, altogether (3·44) 403	
קָצִיר	harvest (4·49) 894	
תְּחִלָּה	beginning (3·22) 321	
שְׂעֹרָה	barley (3·34) 972	
שַׂק	10 sackcloth (2·48) 974	
תְּחִלָּה	beginning (3·22) 321	
נִתַּךְ	to be poured out (1·8·21) 677	
קָצִיר	harvest (4·49) 894	
פִּלֶגֶשׁ	11 concubine (9·37) 811	
גָּנַב	12 to steal, take by stealth (2·30·39) 39	
רְחֹב	broad open place, plaza (1·43) 932	

תָּלָה	to hang (1·3·3) 1067	
הוּקַע	13 passive of Hiph. form, of some solemn form of execution; meaning uncertain (1·1·8) Qal. form means "dislocated, alienated" 429	
נֶעְתַּר	14 to be entreated (2·8·20) 801	
עָיֵף	15 to be faint, weary (1·5·5) 746	
יָלִיד	16 children, sons (2·13) 409	
מִשְׁקָל	weight (3·48) 1054	
קַיִן	spear (1·1) 883	
חָגַר	to gird on (5·44·44) 291	
כָּבָה	17 to extinguish (2·10·24) 459	
נֵר	lamp (2·44) 632	
יָלִיד	18 children, sons (2·13) 409	
חֲנִית	19 spear (9·46) 333	
מָנוֹר	beam (1·4) 644	
אֹרֵג	weaver (1·10[?]) 70	
מָדוֹן	20 stature (1·1) 551	
אֶצְבַּע	finger, toe (2·31) 840	
חֵרֵף	21 to reproach, say sharp things against (2·34·38) 357	

Chapter 22

שִׁירָה	1 song (1·13) 1010	
מְצוּדָה	2 stronghold (5·18) 845	
פִּלֵּט	to bring into security (2·24·27) 812	
חָסָה	3 to seek refuge (2·37·37) 340	
יֵשַׁע	salvation (4·36) 447	
מִשְׂגָּב	secure height (1·17) 960	
מָנוֹס	place of refuge (1·8) 631	
מוֹשִׁיעַ	savior (2·27) 446	
אפף	5 to surround, encompass (1·5·5) 67	
מִשְׁבָּר	breaker (1·5) 991	
בְּלִיַּעַל	ruin, destruction, worthlessness (4·27) 116	
בִּעֵת	to assail, fall upon (1·13·16) 129	
חֶבֶל	6 cord (5·49) 286	
קִדֵּם	to meet, confront (2·24·26) 869	

177

מוֹקֵשׁ lure (1·27) 430

שִׁוְעָה 7 cry for help (1·11) 1003

גָּעַשׁ 8 to quake (1·2·10) 172

רָעַשׁ to quake, shake (1·21·29) 950

מוֹסָד foundation (2·13) 414

רָגַז to quake (3·30·41) 919

הִתְגָּעַשׁ to shake back and forth, toss or reel to and fro, (2·5·10) 172

עָשָׁן 9 smoke (1·25) 798

גֶּחֶלֶת coal (3·18) 160

עֲרָפֶל 10 cloud, heavy cloud (1·15) 791

עוּף 11 to fly, fly away (1·18·25) 733

סֻכָּה 12 booth (2·31) 697

חַשְׁרָה collection, mass (1·1) 366

עָב cloud mass (2·30) 728

שַׁחַק cloud (1·21) 1007

נֹגַהּ 13 brightness (2·19) 618

גֶּחֶלֶת coal (3·18) 160

הִרְעִים 14 to cause to thunder (1·11·11) 947

בָּרָק 15 lightning (1·20) 140

הָמַם to confuse, rout (1·13·13) 243

אָפִיק 16 channel, stream bed, ravine (1·18) 67

מוֹסָד foundation (2·13) 414

תֵּבֵל world (1·36) 385

גְּעָרָה rebuke (1·15) 172

נְשָׁמָה breath (1·24) 675

הַמְשֵׁה 17 to draw out (1·2·3) 602

עַז 18 strong, mighty (1·22) 738

שֹׂנֵא enemy (2·41) 971

אָמֵץ to be strong, stout (1·16·41) 54

קִדֵּם 19 to meet, confront (2·24·26) 869

אֵיד distress, calamity (1·24) 15

מִשְׁעָן support (1·3) 1044

מֶרְחָב 20 broad place (1·6) 932

חָלַץ to rescue, deliver, pull out (1·14·27) 322

גָּמַל 21 to deal fully with, repay (2·34·37) 168

בֹּר cleanness, pureness (2·7[?]) 141

רָשַׁע 22 to be wicked, act wickedly (1·9·34) 957

לְנֶגֶד 23 in front of, before (2·32) 617

בֹּר 25 cleanness, pureness (2·7[?]) 141

לְנֶגֶד in the sight of, before (2·32) 617

חָסִיד 26 kind, pious (1·32) 339

הִתְחַסֵּד to be kind, good (1·2·2) 338

נָבַרר 27 to purify oneself (1·3·15) 140

הִתְבָּרַר to show oneself pure, just, kind; to purify oneself (1·3·15) 140

עִקֵּשׁ twisted, perverted (1·11) 786

הִתְפַּתָּל to deal tortuously (1·2·5[?]) 836 [BDB's suggested correction]

רָם 28 high (1·31[?]) 926

הִשְׁפִּיל to lay low, humiliate (1·18·29) 1050

נִיר 29 lamp (2·44) 632

הִגִּיהַּ to enlighten (1·3·6) 618

גְּדוּד 30 marauding band, troop (3·33) 151

דָּגַל to carry up, set up (1·4·5) 186

שׁוּר wall (1·3) 1004

אִמְרָה 31 utterance, speech, word (1·30) 57

צָרַף to smelt, refine (1·18·21) 864

חָסָה to seek refuge (2·37·37) 340

מִבַּלְעֲדֵי 32 apart from, without (2·12) 116

מָעוֹז 33 refuge (1·36) 731

הִתִּיר to set free, unbind (1·3·22[?]) BDB amends to יֹתֵן from נָתַן, "to set" 684

שִׁוָּה 34 to please, set (1·5·16) 1001

אַיָּלָה hind, doe (1·11) 19

נִחַת 35 to press down (1·3·8) 639

יֶשַׁע 36 salvation (4·36) 447

הִרְחִיב 37 to enlarge (1·21·25) 931

צַעַד step, pace (2·14) 857

מָעַד to slip (1·5·7) 588

קַרְסֹל ankle (1·2) 902

מָחַץ 39 to shatter (1·14·14) 563

אָזַר 40 to gird [on] (1·6·16) 25

הִכְרִיעַ to cause to bow down (1·6·35) 502

קָם adversary (2·12) 878

תַּתָּה 41 = נָתַתָּה 678; G.K. para. 19. i.

עֹרֶף back of neck (1·33) 791

הצמית to exterminate, annihilate (1·10·15) 856

שָׁעָה 42 to gaze [at], regard (1·12·15) 1043

מוֹשִׁיעַ savior (2·27) 446

שחק 43 to rub away, beat fine, pulverize (1·4·4) 1007

טִיט mire (1·13) 376

הֵדַק to make dust of, pulverize (1·8·13) 200

רקע to stamp down (1·6·11) 955

פלט 44 to bring into security (2·24·27) 812

נֵכָר 45 that which is foreign (2·36) 648

התכחש to come cringing (1·1·22) 471

נֵכָר 46 that which is foreign (2·36) 648

נבל to sink down (1·20·25[?]) 615

חגר to gird on (5·44·44) 291

מִסְגֶּרֶת fastness (1·17) 689

יֵשַׁע 47 salvation (4·36) 447

נְקָמָה 48 vengeance (2·27) 668

קָם 49 adversary (2·12) 878

זמר 50 to sing [in praise of] (1·43·43) 274

מִגְדּוֹל 51 tower (1·1) 154

Chapter 23

עַל 1 on high (1·7) 752

נָעִים lovely (2·13) 653

זָמִיר song (1·6) 274

מִלָּה 2 word (1·38) 576

יִרְאָה 3 fear, reverence (2·45) 432

זָרַח 4 to rise (1·18·18) 280

עָב dark cloud (2·30) 728

נֹגַהּ brightness (2·19) 618

מָטָר rain (2·37) 564

דֶּשֶׁא grass (1·14) 206

יֵשַׁע 5 welfare, prosperity, salvation (4·36) 447

חֵפֶץ desire, longing, delight (1·39) 343

הצמיח to cause to sprout, grow (1·14·33) 855

בְּלִיַּעַל 6 worthlessness (4·27) 116

קוֹץ thorn (1·1) 881

הֻדַּד to be thrust away, chased away (1·2·24) 622

חֲנִית 7 spear (9·46) 333

שֶׁבֶת place (1·7) 443

שָׁלִישׁ 8 adjutant, officer (1·16) 1026

עָדִין voluptuous (1·2) 726

עֶצֶן listed in BDB under עָדִין only, but not explained (1·1) 726

חֵרֵף 9 to reproach, say sharp things against (2·34·38) 357

יָגַע to grow weary (1·20·26) 388

תְּשׁוּעָה 10 deliverance (3·34) 448

פשט to strip (1·3·43) 833

חַיָּה 11 troop [dub.] (2·3) 312

חֶלְקָה portion of ground (6·24) 324

עֲדָשָׁה lentile (2·4) 727

התיצב 12 to station oneself (4·48·48) 426

חֶלְקָה portion of ground (6·24) 324

תְּשׁוּעָה deliverance (3·34) 448

קָצִיר 13 harvest (4·49) 894

מְעָרָה cave (1·40) 792

חַיָּה troop, community (2·3) 312

מְצוּדָה 14 stronghold (5·18) 845

מַצָּב garrison (1·10) 662

הִתְאַוָּה 15 to desire, long for, lust after (1·16·27) 16

שאב 16 to draw [water] (1·14·14) 980

הִסִּיךְ to pour out (1·13·24[?]) 650

חָלִילָה 17 far be it [from me, you, etc.] (2·20[?]) 321

179

חֲנִית	18	spear (9·46) 333
פֹּעַל	20	deed, thing done (1·37) 821
אֲרִי		lion (2·35) 71
שֶׁלֶג		snow (1·20) 1017
חֲנִית	21	spear (9·46) 333
גָּזַל		to tear away, seize, rob (1·29·30) 159
מִשְׁמַעַת	23	bodyguard (1·4) 1036

Chapter 24

הֵסִית	1	to instigate (1·18·18) 694
מָנָה		to number (1·12·28) 584
שׁוּט	2	to go, rove about (2·7·13) 1001
מִבְצָר	7	fortification (1·37) 131
שׁוּט	8	to go, rove about (2·7·13) 1001
מִפְקָד	9	muster, appointed place (1·5) 824
שָׁלַף		to draw out (1·24·24) 1025
נסכל	10	to act foolishly (1·4·8) 698
חֹזֶה	11	seer (1·17) 302
נָטַל	12	to lift (1·3·4) 642

דֶּבֶר	13	plague, pestilence (2·46) 184
רַחֲמִים	14	compassion (1·38) 933
דֶּבֶר	15	plague, pestilence (2·46) 184
הרפה	16	to let drop (1·21·44) 951
גֹּרֶן		threshing floor (5·34) 175
הֶעֱוָה	17	to commit iniquity (3·9·17) 731
גֹּרֶן	18	threshing floor (5·34) 175
הִשְׁקִיף	20	to look down (1·12·12) 1054
גֹּרֶן	21	threshing floor (5·34) 175
נעצר		to be restrained (2·10·46) 783
מַגֵּפָה		plague (4·26) 620
מוֹרַג	22	threshing sledge (1·3) 558
רצה	23	to accept, be pleased with (1·42·50) 958
מְחִיר	24	price (1·15) 564
חִנָּם		without cost, out of favor, gratis (1·32) 336
גֹּרֶן		threshing floor (5·34) 175
נֶעְתַּר	25	to be entreated (2·8·20) 801
נעצר		to be restrained (2·10·46) 783
מַגֵּפָה		plague (4·26) 620

1 KINGS

Chapter 1

זָקֵן	1	to be old, become old (2·25·27) 278
חמם		to be warm, grow warm (2·23·26) 328
בְּתוּלָה	2	virgin (1·50) 143
סֹכֶנֶת		servant [female] (2·3) 698
חֵיק		bosom (5·38) 300
חמם		to be warm, grow warm (2·23·26) 328
יָפֶה	3	beautiful (2·40) 421
יָפֶה	4	beautiful (2·40) 421
סֹכֶנֶת		servant [female] (2·3) 698
עצב	6	to pain (1·3·15) 780
כָּכָה		thus (3·33) 462
תֹּאַר		outline, form (1·15) 1061
מְרִיא	9	fatlings (3·8) 597
זֹחֶלֶת		crawling thing, serpent [meaning dub.] (1·1) 267
חֶדֶר	15	chamber, room (3·37) 293
זָקֵן		to be old, become old (2·25·27) 278
קדד	16	to bow down (2·15·15) 869
מְרִיא	19	fatlings (3·8) 597
חַטָּא	21	sinner (1·19) 308
מְרִיא	25	fatlings (3·8) 597
קדד	31	to bow down (2·15·15) 869
פִּרְדָּה	33	she-mule (3·3) 825
נָגִיד	35	ruler (3·44) 617
אָמֵן	36	verily, truly (1·26) 53
פִּרְדָּה	38	she-mule (3·3) 825
חלל	40	to play the pipe (1·1·1) 320
חָלִיל		flute, pipe (1·6) 319
שָׂמֵחַ		glad, joyful, merry (4·21) 970
קִרְיָה	41	town, city (2·30) 900
חמה		to be in a commotion, stir, (1·33·33) 242

בָּשַׂר	42	to bear tidings, bear glad tidings (1·14·15) 142
אֲבָל	43	verily, truly, indeed (1·11) 6
פִּרְדָּה	44	she-mule (3·3) 825
שָׂמֵחַ	45	glad, joyful, merry (4·21) 970
הום		to be in a stir (1·3·6) 223
קִרְיָה		town, city (2·30) 900
מְלוּכָה	46	kingship (7·24) 574
מִשְׁכָּב	47	bed (1·46) 1012
כָּכָה	48	thus (3·33) 462
חָרַד	49	to tremble (1·23·39) 353
שַׂעֲרָה	52	a hair (1·7) 972

Chapter 2

עֵדָה	3	testimony (1·32) 730
חֲגוֹרָה	5	girdle, loin covering, belt (1·5) 292
מָתְנַיִם		loins (5·50) 608
נַעַל		sandal (1·22) 653
שֵׂיבָה	6	grey hair, hoary head (3·20[?]) 966
קְלָלָה	8	curse (1·33) 887
נמרץ		to be grievous (1·3·4) 599
נקה	9	to leave unpunished (1·13·37) 667
שֵׂיבָה		grey hair, hoary head (3·20[?]) 966
מְלוּכָה	15	kingship (7·24) 574
שְׁאֵלָה	16	request, petition (2·13) 982
שְׁאֵלָה	20	request, petition (2·13) 982
קָטָן		small (4·47) 881
מְלוּכָה	22	kingship (7·24) 574
פָּגַע	25	to fall upon (6·40·46) 803
גרש	27	to drive out, away (1·34·48) 176
שְׁמוּעָה	28	report (2·27) 1035
פָּגַע	29	to fall upon (6·40·46) 803
פֹּה	30	here, hither (4·44) 805
פָּגַע	31	to fall upon (6·40·46) 803
חִנָּם		without cause (1·32) 336
פָּגַע	32	to fall upon (6·40·46) 803
פָּגַע	34	to fall upon (6·40·46) 803
אָנֶה וָאָנָה	36	where, anywhere (4·37) 33

חָבַשׁ 40 to bind up, equip [a beast] for riding (6·28·32) 289

הֵעִיד 42 to testify (3·39·44) 729

אָנֶה וָאָנָה where, anywhere (4·37) 33

שְׁבוּעָה 43 oath (1·30) 989

פָּגַע 46 to fall upon (6·40·46) 803

Chapter 3

הִתְחַתֵּן 1 to make oneself a daughter's husband, form a marriage alliance with (1·11·11) 368

יְשָׁרָה 6 uprightness (1·1) 449

נִמְנָה 8 to be able to be numbered (2·6·28) 584

כָּבֵד 9 massive, abundant (4·39) 458

עֹשֶׁר 11 riches (3·37) 799

נָבוֹן 12 Niph. ptc.: intelligent, discreet; discerning (1·21[?]) 106

עֹשֶׁר 13 riches (3·37) 799

הַאֲרִיךְ 14 to prolong (2·31·34) 73

יָקַץ 15 to awake (2·11·11) 429

מִשְׁתֶּה feast (1·45) 1059

זוֹנָה 16 ptc.: harlot (2·33[?]) 275

בִּי 17 particle of entreaty craving permission to address a superior, "excuse me" (2·12) 106

זוּלָה 18 except only, save that (2·16) 265

מֵאֵצֶל 19 from beside (2·6) 69

יָשֵׁן 20 to sleep (1·15·16[?]) 445

חֵיק bosom (5·38) 300

הֵינִיק 21 to give suck to (1·10·18) 413

גָּזַר 25 to divide, cut in two (2·6·12) 160

נִכְמַר 26 to grow warm and tender (1·4·4) 485

רֶחֶם womb (1·33) 933

בִּי craving permission to address a superior (2·12) 106

גַּם … גַּם idiom; with a negative = neither…nor, גַּם, para. 1. 169

גָּזַר to divide, cut in two (2·6·12) 160

Chapter 4

מַזְכִּיר 3 recorder (1·9) 271

נִצָּב 5 deputy (6·7) 662

רֵעֶה friend (1·5) 946

מַס 6 labor band (7·23) 586

נִצָּב 7 deputy (6·7) 662

כִּלְכֵּל to sustain (8·24·38) 465

נָפָה 11 height (1·4) 632

חַוָּה 13 tent village (1·7) 295

חֶבֶל region, measured portion (3·49) 286

בְּרִיחַ bar (1·41) 138

נָצִיב 19 prefect (1·11) 662

חוֹל 20 sand (2·22) 297

שָׂמֵחַ glad, joyful, merry (4·21) 970

Chapter 5

כֹּר* 2 a measure (4·8) 499

קֶמַח flour, meal (4·14) 887

בָּרִיא 3 fat (1·14) 135

רְעִי pasture (1·1) 945

אַיָּל hart, stag, deer (1·11) 19

צְבִי gazelle (1·11) 840

יַחְמוּר roebuck (1·2) 331

בַּרְבֻּר bird, fowl (1·1) 141

אבס to feed, fatten (1·2·2) 7

רדה 4 to have dominion, to rule (3·22·23) 921

בֶּטַח 5 securely, security (1·43) 105

תְּאֵנָה fig tree, fig (1·39) 1061

אֻרְוָה 6 manger, crib (1·3) 71

כֹּר חֹמֶר* [dry measure] = approx. 394 liters. 331

מֶרְכָּב chariot (1·3) 939

כִּלְכֵּל 7 to sustain (8·24·38) 465

נְצָב   deputy (6·7) 662

קָרֵב   approaching (1·11) 898

עדר   to leave lacking (1·1·7) 727

שְׂעֹר   8 barley (1·34) 972

תֶּבֶן   straw (1·17) 1061

רֶכֶשׁ   (coll.) steeds (1·3) 940

תְּבוּנָה   9 the object of knowledge, understanding (2·42) 108

חוֹל   sand (2·22) 297

חכם   11 to be wise, become wise (1·18·26) 314

מָשָׁל   12 poem (2·39) 605

אֵזוֹב   13 hyssop (1·10) 23

רֶמֶשׂ   creeping things (1·16) 943

דָּג   fish (1·19) 185

אֹהֵב   15 friend, lover (1·36[?]) 12

שָׂטָן   18 adversary (4·27) 966

פֶּגַע   occurrence, chance (1·2) 803

שָׂכָר   20 wages (1·29) 969

חֵפֶץ   22 desire, longing (5·39) 343

בְּרוֹשׁ   cypress of fir tree (5·20) 141

דֹּבְרוֹת   23 floats, rafts (1·1) 184

נָפַץ   to dash to pieces, to break up (1·15·21[?]) 1125

חֵפֶץ   desire, longing (5·39) 343

בְּרוֹשׁ   24 cypress, fir (5·20) 141

חֵפֶץ   desire, longing (5·39) 343

כֹּר•   25 a measure (4·8) 499

חִטָּה   wheat (1·30) 334

מַכֹּלֶת   foodstuff (1·1) 38

כָּתִית   beaten (1·5) 510

מַס   27 labor band (7·23) 586

חֲלִיפָה   28 relay, change (1·12) 322

מַס   labor band (7·23) 586

סַבָּל   29 burden-bearer (1·5) 688

חֹצֵב   ptc.: hewer of stone (1·8[?]) 345

רדה   to have dominion, to rule (3·22·23) 921

יָקָר   31 precious, costly (7·35) 429

יָסַד   to establish (2·10·42) 413

גָּזִית   a cutting, hewing (5·11) 159

פסל   32 to hew out (1·6·6) 820

Chapter 6

קוֹמָה   2 height (13·45) 879

אוּלָם   3 porch (10·49) 17

חַלּוֹן   4 window (1·30) 319

שְׁקוּף   frame, window casing (2·2) 1054

אטם   to shut, stop [up], (1·8·8[?]) 31

יָצִיעַ   5 flat surface (3·3) 427

דְּבִיר   innermost room (11·16) 184

צֵלָע   side chamber, cells (7·39) 854

יָצִיעַ   6 flat surface (3·3) 427

תַּחְתּוֹן   lower, lowest (2·13) 1066

תִּיכוֹן   middle (4·12) 1064

מִגְרָעָה   recess, ledge (1·1) 175

שָׁלֵם   7 finished (5·28) 1023

מַסָּע   quarry (1·1) 652

מַקֶּבֶת   hammer (1·4) 666

גַּרְזֶן   axe (1·4) 173

צֵלָע   8 side chamber, cell (7·39) 854

תִּיכוֹן   middle (4·12) 1064

יְמָנִי   right hand, right (3·33) 412

לוּל   shaft or enclosed space with steps or ladder (1·1) 533

ספן   9 to cover (3·6·6) 706

גֵּב   beam? rafter? (1·3[?]) 155

שְׂדֵרָה   technical terminology of architecture, meaning unknown (1·4) 690

יָצִיעַ   10 flat surface (3·3) 427

קוֹמָה   height (13·45) 879

מִבַּיִת   15 on the inside of (3·9) בֵּית, para. 8a. 110

צֵלָע   planks, boards (7·39) 854

קַרְקַע   floor (6·8) 903

סִפֻּן   ceiling (1·1) 706

צָפָה to overlay, plate (13·44·46) 860
בְּרוֹשׁ cypress, fir (5·20) 141
יַרְכָה 16 extreme parts (1·28) 438
צֶלָע planks, boards (7·39) 854
קַרְקַע floor (6·8) 903
מִבַּיִת on the inside of (3·9) בֵּית para. 8a. 110
דְּבִיר innermost room (11·16) 184
לִפְנֵי 17 anterior (1·1) 819
פְּנִימָה 18 within (1·5) 819
מִקְלַעַת carving (4·4) 887
פְּקָעִים ball or knob-shaped wood or metal ornaments (3·3) 825
פֶּטֶר to set free (4·8·9) 809
צִיץ blossom, flower (4·15) 847
דְּבִיר 19 innermost room (11·16) 184
מִפְּנִימָה within (2·3) 819
דְּבִיר 20 innermost room (11·16) 184
קוֹמָה height (13·45) 879
צָפָה to overlay, plate (13·44·46) 860
סָגוּר closed up, closely joined (5·8) 688
צָפָה 21 to overlay, plate (13·44·46) 860
מִפְּנִימָה within (2·3) 819
סָגוּר closed up, closely joined (5·8) 688
רַתּוֹק chain (1·2) 958
דְּבִיר innermost room (11·16) 184
צָפָה 22 to overlay, plate (13·44·46) 860
דְּבִיר innermost room (11·16) 184
דְּבִיר 23 innermost room (11·16) 184
קוֹמָה height (13·45) 879
קְצוֹת 24 tips (4·7) 892
קֶצֶב 25 shape (2·3) 891
קוֹמָה 26 height (13·45) 879
פְּנִימִי 27 inner (4·33) 819
צָפָה 28 to overlay, plate (13·44·46) 860
מֵסַב 29 round about (1·5) 687
קָלַע to carve (3·3·3) 887
פִּתּוּחַ engraving (1·11) 836

מִקְלַעַת carving (4·4) 887
תִּמֹּרָה palm [tree] figure (5·19) 1071
פֶּטֶר to set free (4·8·9) 809
צִצִּים blossom, flower (4·15) 847
מִלִּפְנִים within (1·1) 819
חִיצוֹן outer, external (2·25) 300
קַרְקַע 30 floor (6·8) 903
צָפָה to overlay, plate (13·44·46) 860
לִפְנִימָה within (1·5) 819
חִיצוֹן outer, external (2·25) 300
דְּבִיר 31 innermost room (11·16) 184
אַיִל projecting pillar or pilaster (1·22) 18
מְזוּזָה doorpost (3·20) 265
חֲמִשִׁית fifth part; [Lis. p. 508 "five-cornered"] (1·1[?]) 332
קָלַע 32 to carve (3·3·3) 887
מִקְלַעַת carving (4·4) 887
תִּמֹּרָה palm [tree] figure (5·19) 1071
פֶּטֶר to set free (4·8·9) 809
צִיץ blossom, flower (4·15) 847
צָפָה to overlay, plate (13·44·46) 860
הרד to beat out (1·1·3) 921
מְזוּזָה 33 doorpost (3·20) 265
בְּרוֹשׁ 34 cypress, fir (5·20) 141
צֶלָע leaves of door (7·39) 854
גָּלִיל turning, folding = revolving (2·4[?]) 165
קֶלַע curtain, hanging (1·16) 887
קָלַע 35 to carve (3·3·3) 887
תִּמֹּרָה palm [tree] figure (5·19) 1071
פֶּטֶר to set free (4·8·9) 809
צִיץ blossom, floor (4·15) 847
צָפָה to overlay, plate (13·44·46) 860
ישר to be made level (1·1·25) 448
חקה to cut in, carve; ptc. = carved work (1·3·4) 348
פְּנִימִי 36 inner (4·33) 819
טוּר row (11·26) 377

גָּזִית	a cutting, hewing (5·11) 159	
כְּרֻתֹת	hewn beams (3·3) 503	
יָסַד	37 to be founded (2·7·42) 413	
יֶרַח	calendar month (3·12) 437	
יֶרַח	38 calendar month (3·12) 437	

Chapter 7

קוֹמָה	2 height (13·45) 879
טוּר	row (11·26) 377
כְּרֻתוֹת	hewn beams (3·3) 503
ספן	3 to cover (3·6·6) 706
מִמַּעַל	above, on top of (4·29) 751
צֵלָע	side chambers, cells (7·39) 854
טוּר	row (11·26) 377
שְׁקוּף	4 frame, window casing (2·2) 1054
טוּר	row (11·26) 377
מֶחֱזָה	light (4·4) 303
מְזוּזָה	5 doorpost (3·20) 265
רבע	Qal. psv. ptc. = square, squared (1·9·12) 917
שָׁקֻף	framework, door casing (1·1) 1054
מוּל	front (1·25) 557
מֶחֱזָה	light (4·4) 303
אוּלָם	6 porch (10·49) 17
עָב	a structure of wood, perhaps projecting roof, beam (1·3) 712
אוּלָם	7 porch (10·49) 17
ספן	to cover (3·6·6) 706
קַרְקַע	floor (6·8) 903
מִבֵּית לְ	8 within (2·9) בית, para. 8b. 110
אוּלָם	porch (10·49) 17
יָקָר	9 precious, costly (7·35) 429
גָּזִית	a cutting, hewing (5·11) 159
גרר	ptc. = sawn; to drag, chew (1·1·4) 176
מְגֵרָה	saw (1·3) 176
מִבַּיִת	on the inside; see בית, para. 8a. 110
מַסָּד	foundation (1·1) 414

טֶפַח	coping [architectural term] (2·9) 381
יָסַד	10 to be founded (2·7·42) 413
יָקָר	precious, costly (7·35) 429
מִלְמַעְלָה	11 above (3·24) 751
יָקָר	costly, precious (7·35) 429
גָּזִית	a cutting, hewing (5·11) 159
טוּר	12 row (11·26) 377
גָּזִית	a cutting, hewing (5·11) 159
כְּרֻתֹת	hewn beams (3·3) 503
פְּנִימִי	inner (4·33) 819
אוּלָם	porch (10·49) 17
חרש	14 to cut in, engrave (2·23·26) 360
תְּבוּנָה	the object of knowledge (2·42) 108
צור	15 to fashion (1·2·2) 849
קוֹמָה	height (13·45) 879
חוּט	line [as a measure of length] (1·7) 296
כֹּתֶרֶת	16 capital of pillar (14·23) 509
מוּצָק	a casting (1·2) 427
קוֹמָה	height (13·45) 879
שְׂבָכָה	17 latticework, network (7·16) 959
גָּדִל	festoons on capitals of columns (1·2) 153
שַׁרְשְׁרָה	chain (1·8) 1057
כֹּתֶרֶת	capital of pillar (14·23) 509
טוּר	18 row (11·26) 377
שְׂבָכָה	latticework, network (7·16) 959
כֹּתֶרֶת	capital of pillar (14·23) 509
רִמּוֹן	pomegranate (4·32) 941
כֹּתֶרֶת	19 capital of pillar (14·23) 509
שׁוּשַׁן	lily (3·17) 1004
אוּלָם	porch (10·49) 17
כֹּתֶרֶת	20 capital of pillar (14·23) 509
מִמַּעַל	above, on top of (4·29) 751
מִלְעֻמַּת	close beside (1·1) 769
בֶּטֶן	architectural word = rounded projection, bell, cushion (1·1) para. 4. 106

שְׂבָכָה latticework, network (7·16) 959

רִמּוֹן pomegranate (4·32) 941

טוּר row (11·26) 377

אוּלָם 21 porch (10·49) 17

יְמָנִי right hand, right (3·33) 412

שְׂמָאלִי left, on the left (1·9) 970

שׁוֹשַׁן 22 lily (3·17) 1004

עָגֹל 23 round (5·6) 722

קוֹמָה height (13·45) 879

קַו line (1·17) 876

פְּקָעִים 24 ball or knob-shaped ornaments of carved wood or metal (3·3) 825

הִקִּיף to encompass (1·16·17) 668

קוֹף ape (1·2) 880

טוּר row (11·26) 377

יְצָקָה casting (2·2) 427

מִלְמַעְלָה 25 above (3·24) 751

אָחוֹר hinder part, back part (1·41) 30

בַּיְתָה inwards (1·6) בית para. 7. 110

עֲבִי 26 thickness (1·5) 716

טֶפַח span, handbreadth (2·9) 381

כּוֹס cup (1·31) 468

פֶּרַח bud, sprout (2·17) 827

שׁוּשָׁן lily (3·17) 1004

בַּת measure = 40 litres (2·13) 144

הֵכִיל to contain (3·12·38) 465

מְכוֹנָה 27 base (15·25) 467

קוֹמה height (13·45) 879

מְכוֹנָה 28 base (15·25) 467

מִסְגֶּרֶת border (7·17) 689

שְׁלַבִּים joining [of bases] (3·3) 1016

מִסְגֶּרֶת 29 border (7·17) 689

שְׁלַבִּים joining [of bases] (3·3) 1016

אֲרִי lion (5·36) 71

כֵּן pedestal (2·17) 487

מִמַּעַל above, on top of (4·29) 751

לִיָה wreath [dub.] (3·3) 531

מוֹרָד descent (1·5) 434

אוֹפַן 30 wheel (5·34) 66

מְכוֹנָה base (15·25) 467

סֶרֶן axle (1·1) 710

כִּיּוֹר basin (7·23) 468

לִיָה wreath [dub.] (3·3) 531

מִבֵּית לְ 31 inside, para. 8b. בית 110

כֹּתֶרֶת capital of pillar (14·23) 509

עָגֹל round (5·6) 722

כֵּן pedestal (2·17) 487

מִקְלַעַת carving (4·4) 887

מִסְגֶּרֶת border (7·17) 689

רבע pual ptc. = square (1·3·12) 917

אוֹפַן 32 wheel (5·34) 66

לְמִתַּחַת under, beneath (1·1) 1066

מִסְגֶּרֶת border (7·17) 689

יָד axletree, idiom inder יַד, para. 4 d. (2·2) 390

מְכוֹנָה base (15·25) 467

קוֹמָה height (13·45) 879

אוֹפַן 33 wheel (5·34) 66

מֶרְכָּבָה chariot (5·44) 939

יָד axletree, idiom inder יַד, para. 4d. (2·2) 390

גַּב rim of wheel, anything convex (1·13) 146

חִשֻּׁקִים spokes of a wheel (1·1) 366

חִשֻּׁרִים hubs of wheels (1·1) 366

פִּנָּה 34 corner (1·30) 819

מְכוֹנָה base (15·25) 467

מְכוֹנָה 35 base (15·25) 467

קוֹמָה height (13·45) 879

עָגֹל round (5·6) 722

יָד stays, idiom under יַד, para. 4e. "hand" (4·6) 390

מִסְגֶּרֶת border (7·17) 689

פתח 36 to engrave (1·8·9) 836

לוּחַ plate (2·40) 531

יָד	stays, idiom under יָד, para. 4e. "hand" (4·6) 390		מרט	to be polished (1·5·14) 598

יָד — stays, idiom under יָד, para. 4e. "hand" (4·6) 390
מִסְגֶּרֶת — border (7·17) 689
אֲרִי — lion (5·35) 71
תִּמֹרָה — palm [tree] figure (5·19) 1071
מַעַר — bare place (1·2[?]) 789
לֹיָה — wreath [dub.] (3·3) 531
מְכוֹנָה — 37 base (15·25) 467
מוּצָק — a casting (1·2) 427
קֶצֶב — shape (2·3) 891
כִּיּוֹר — 38 basin (7·23) 468
בַּת — measure = 40 litres (2·13) 144
הֵכִיל — to contain (3·12·38) 465
מְכוֹנָה — base (15·25) 467
מְכוֹנָה — 39 base (15·25) 467
יְמָנִי — right hand, right (3·33) 412
קֶדֶם — eastward (2·26) 870
מִמּוּל — from the front of (1·9) 557
כִּיּוֹר — 40 basin (7·23) 468
יָע — shovel (2·9) 418
מִזְרָק — basin (3·32) 284
גֻּלָּה — 41 bowl or globe shape, bowl, basin (3·15) 165
כֹּתֶרֶת — capital of pillar (14·23) 509
שְׂבָכָה — latticework, network (7·16) 959
גֻּלָּה — bowl or globe shape, bowl, basin (3·15) 165
רִמּוֹן — 42 pomegranate (4·32) 941
שְׂבָכָה — latticework, network (7·16) 959
טוּר — row (11·26) 377
גֻּלָּה — bowl or globe shape, bowl, basin (3·15) 165
כֹּתֶרֶת — capital of pillar (14·23) 509
מְכוֹנָה — 43 base (15·25) 467
כִּיּוֹר — basin (7·23) 468
סִיר — 45 pot (1·29) 696
יָע — shovel (2·9) 418
מִזְרָק — basin (3·32) 284

מרט — to be polished (1·5·14) 598
מַעֲבֶה — 46 compactness (1·1[?]) 716
נֶחְקַר — 47 to be searched out, found out (1·4·27) 350
מִשְׁקָל — wieght (2·48) 1054
מְנוֹרָה — 49 lampstand (1·39) 633
דְּבִיר — innermost room (11·16) 184
סָגוּר — closely joined (5·8) 688
פֶּרַח — bud, sprout (2·17) 827
נֵר — lamp (1·44) 632
מֶלְקָחַיִם — snuffers (1·6) 544
סַף — 50 basin (1·6) 706
מְזַמֶּרֶת — snuffers (1·5) 275
מִזְרָק — basin (3·32) 284
כַּף — pan, vessel [hollow] para. 4b. 497
מַחְתָּה — firepan (1·21) 367
סָגוּר — closely joined (5·8) 688
פֹּת — sockets [for door pivots, (dub.)] (1·2) 834
פְּנִימִי — inner (4·33) 819

Chapter 8

הִקְהִיל — 1 to summon an assembly (2·20·39) 874
נִקְהַל — 2 to assemble (1·19·39) 874
יֶרַח — month (3·12) 437
אֵיתָן — 4 steady flowing, month of steady flowing = 7th month [Oct–Nov] (1·14) 450
נוֹעַד — 5 to assemble by appointment (1·18·28) 416
נִמְנָה — to be numbered (2·6·28) 584
דְּבִיר — 6 innermost room (11·16) 184
סָכַךְ — 7 to cover (1·12·18[?]) 696
בַּד — pole, stave (3·41) 94
מִלְמַעְלָה — above (3·24) 751
הֶאֱרִיךְ — 8 to be long (2·31·34) 73
בַּד — pole, stave (3·41) 94

דְּבִיר		innermost room (11·16) 184
לוּחַ	9	tablet (2·40) 531
עֲרָפֶל	12	cloud, heavy cloud (1·15) 791
זְבֻל	13	elevation, height, lofty abode (1·5) 259
מָכוֹן		fixed or established place (4·17) 467
הטיב		to do well (1·3·20) 373
חֶלֶץ	19	only in dual form = loins (1·10) 323
מִמַּעַל	23	above, on top of (4·29) 751
אָמְנָם	27	verily, truly, indeed (1·5) 53
כִּלְכֵּל		to contain (8·24·38) 465
תְּחִנָּה	28	supplication for favor (9·25) 337
רִנָּה		ringing cry (2·33) 943
תְּחִנָּה	30	supplication for favor (9·25) 337
סלח		to forgive (5·33·46) 699
אָלָה	31	oath (2·36) 46
האלה		to put under oath (1·3·6) 46
הִרְשִׁיעַ	32	to condemn as guilty (1·25·34) 957
הַצְדִּיק		to declare righteous, justify (1·12·41) 842
נִגַּף	33	to be smitten (1·23·48) 619
סלח	34	to forgive (5·33·46) 699
נעצר	35	to be shut up, restrained (1·10·46) 783
מָטָר		rain (4·37) 564
סלח	36	to forgive (5·33·46) 699
הורה		to teach (1·45·45) 434
מָטָר		rain (4·37) 564
דֶּבֶר	37	plague, pestilence (1·46) 184
שִׁדָּפוֹן		smut (1·5) 995
יֵרָקוֹן		rust (1·6) 439
אַרְבֶּה		a kind of locust (1·24) 916
חָסִיל		a kind of locust (1·6) 340
מַחֲלָה		sickness, disease (1·4) 318
תְּחִנָּה	38	supplication for favor (9·25) 337
מָכוֹן	39	fixed or established place (4·17) 467
סלח		to forgive (5·33·46) 699
נָכְרִי	41	foreigner (4·45) 648

מָכוֹן	43	fixed or established place (4·17) 467
נָכְרִי		foreigner (4·45) 648
תְּחִנָּה	45	supplication for favor (9·25) 337
אנף	46	to be angry (1·8·14) 60
שָׁבָה		to take captive (2·29·37) 985
שֹׁבֶה		captives (3·9) 985
נִשְׁבָּה	47	to be taken captive (1·8·37) 985
שֹׁבֶה		captives (3·9) 985
הֶעֱוָה		to commit iniquity (1·9·17[?]) 731
רשע		to be wicked, act wickedly (1·9·34) 957
שָׁבָה	48	to take captive (2·29·37) 985
מָכוֹן	49	fixed or established placed (4·17) 467
תְּחִנָּה		supplication for favor (9·25) 337
סלח	50	to forgive (5·33·46) 699
פָּשַׁע		to transgress (2·40·41) 833
רַחֲמִים		compassion (1·38) 933
שֹׁבֶה		captives (3·9) 985
רָחַם		to have compassion (1·41·46) 933
כּוּר	51	furnace (1·8) 468
תְּחִנָּה	52	supplication for favor (9·25) 337
הִבְדִּיל	53	to separate (1·32·42) 95
תְּחִנָּה	54	supplication for favor (9·25) 337
כָּרַע		to bow (2·29·35) 502
בֶּרֶךְ		knee (3·25) 139
מְנוּחָה	56	rest (1·21) 629
נָטַשׁ	57	to forsake (1·33·40) 643
שָׁלֵם	61	complete, perfect (5·28) 1023
חָנַךְ	63	to dedicate (1·5·5) 335
הכיל		to contain (3·12·38) 465
שָׂמֵחַ	66	glad, rejoicing, merry (4·21) 970

Chapter 9

חֵשֶׁק	1	desire = thing desired (2·4) 366
תְּחִנָּה	3	supplication for favor (9·25) 337
תָּם	4	integrity (2·23) 1070
יֹשֶׁר		uprightness (1·14) 449
מָשָׁל	7	byword (2·39) 605

שְׁנִינָה	sharp word, taunt (1·4) 1042
שָׁרַק	to hiss (1·12·12) 1056
כָּכָה	thus (3·33) 462
בְּרוֹשׁ	11 cypress, fir (5·20) 141
חֵפֶץ	desire, longing (5·39) 343
יָשַׁר	12 to be pleasing (1·13·25) 448
מַס	15 labor band (7·23) 586
שִׁלּוּחִים	16 parting gift (1·3) 1019
תַּחְתּוֹן	17 lower, lowest (2·13) 1066
מִסְכְּנוֹת	19 storage (1·7) 698
חֵשֶׁק	desire = thing desired (2·4) 366
חָשַׁק	to love (1·8·11) 365
מֶמְשָׁלָה	dominion (1·17) 606
הֶחֱרִים	21 to ban, devote to destruction (1·46·49) 355
מַס	labor band (7·23) 586
שָׁלִישׁ	22 adjutant, officer (1·16) 1026
נִצָּב	23 deputy (6·7) 662
רדה	to have dominion, to rule (3·22·23) 921
אֳנִי	26 ships, fleet (6·7) 58
אֳנִי	27 ships, fleet (6·7) 58
אֳנִיָּה	ship (4·31) 58

Chapter 10

מַלְכָּה	1 queen (4·35) 573
שֵׁמַע	hearing, report (1·17) 1034
נִסָּה	to test (1·36·36) 650
חִידָה	perplexing question, riddle (1·17) 295
כָּבֵד	2 numerous (4·39) 458
בֹּשֶׂם	spice, balsam (4·30) 141
יָקָר	precious (7·35) 429
נעלם	3 to be concealed (1·11·29) 761
מַלְכָּה	4 queen (4·35) 573
מַאֲכָל	5 food (1·30) 38
מוֹשַׁב	sitting company, assembly (1·43) 444
מַעֲמָד	service (1·5) 765

מְשָׁרֵת	servant (1·20) 1058
מַלְבּוּשׁ	raiment (1·8) 528
מַשְׁקֶה	cupbearer (2[?]·19[?]) 1052
שְׁמוּעָה	7 report (2·27) 1035
אֶשֶׁר	8 happiness, blessedness (2·44) 80–81
בֹּשֶׂם	10 spice, balsam (4·30) 141
יָקָר	precious (7·35) 429
מַלְכָּה	queen (1·35) 573
אֳנִי	11 ships, fleet (6·7) 58
אַלְמֻגִּים	trees; Lis. sandalwood (3·6) 38
יָקָר	precious (7·35) 429
אַלְמֻגִּים	12 trees (3·6) 38
מִסְעָד	support (1·1) 703
כִּנּוֹר	lyre (1·41) 490
נֵבֶל	harp (1·27) 614
שָׁר	singer (1·9) 1010
מַלְכָּה	13 queen (4·35) 573
חֵפֶץ	desire, longing (5·39) 343
מִלְּבַד	besides (1·33) 94
מִשְׁקָל	14 weight (2·48) 1054
תָּר	15 merchants (1·2) 1064
מִסְחָר	merchandise [dub.] (1·1) 695
רֹכֵל	trader (1·17) 940
עֶרֶב	mixed company, i.e., foreigners (1·2) 786
פֶּחָה	governor (2·28) 808
צִנָּה	16 large shield [covering whole body] (2·20) 857
שחט	Qal. pass. ptc. = beaten, hammered (2·6·6) 1006
שחט	17 Qal pass. ptc. = beaten, hammered (2·6·6) 1006
מָנֶה	mina (1·5) 584
צִפָּה	18 to overlay, plate (13·44·46) 860
הפז	to be refined [dub.] (1·1) 808
מַעֲלָה	19 stair (2·47) 752
עָגֹל	round (5·6) 722

יָד	stays, idiom under "hand," para. 4e. יָד (4·6) 390		שָׁלֵם	complete, perfect (5·28) 1023
מִזֶּה וּמִזֶּה	on the one side ... on the other, para. 6e. זֶה 262		שִׁקֵּץ	5 detested thing (3·28) 1055
אֲרִי	lion (5·36) 71		שִׁקֵּץ	7 detested thing (3·28) 1055
אֲרִי	20 lion (5·36) 71		נָכְרִי	8 foreign (4·45) 648
מַעֲלָה	stair (2·47[?]) 752		הִתְאַנַּף	9 to be angry (1·6·14) 60
מִזֶּה וּמִזֶּה	on the one side ... on the other, para. 6e. זֶה 262		שָׂטָן	14 adversary (4·27) 966
מַשְׁקֶה	21 drink (2·19[?]) 1052		קָטֹן	17 young (4·47) 881
סָגוּר	closely joined (5·8) 688		גְּבִירָה	19 queen (2·15) 150
לִמְאוּמָה	anything (1·2) 548		גָּמַל	20 to wean (1·34·37) 168
אֳנִי	22 ships, fleet (6·7) 58		חָסֵר	22 lacking (1·17) 341
שֶׁנְהַבִּים	ivory (1·2) 1042		שָׂטָן	23 adversary (4·27) 966
קוֹף	ape (1·2) 880		גְּדוּד	24 band, troop (1·33) 151
תֻּכִּיִּים	peacocks (1·2) 1067		שָׂטָן	25 adversary (4·27) 966
עֹשֶׁר	23 riches (3·37) 799		קוּץ	to feel a loathing, to abhor (1·8·8) 880
שַׂלְמָה	25 clothes (3·16) 971		פֶּרֶץ	27 breach (1·18) 829
נֶשֶׁק	equipment, weapons (1·10) 676		סֵבֶל	28 burden, burdensome labor (1·3) 687
בֹּשֶׂם	spice, balsam (4·30) 141		שַׂלְמָה	29 outer garment (3·16) 971
פֶּרֶד	mule (2·14) 825		שַׂלְמָה	30 outer garment (3·16) 971
הנחה	26 to lead (1·26·40) 634		קְרָעִים	torn piece [of garment], rag (2·4) 902
נתן כְּ...	27 to make [to be] like, para. 3c. נתן 681		קְרָעִים	31 torn piece [of garment], rag (2·4) 902
שִׁקְמָה	sycamore tree (1·7) 1054		מְלוּכָה	35 kingship (7·27) 574
שְׁפֵלָה	lowland (1·20) 1050		נִיר	36 lamp (2·5) 633
מוֹצָא	28 that which goes forth, export (1·27) 425		אָוָה	37 to desire (1·16·27) 16
מִקְוֵה	collection, company (2·7) 876			
סֹחֵר	trader (1·16) 695			
מְחִיר	price (2·15) 564			
מֶרְכָּבָה	29 chariot (5·44) 939			

Chapter 12

הִקְשָׁה	4 to make severe (1·21·28) 904
עֹל	yoke (8·40) 760
כָּבֵד	heavy (4·39) 458
קָשָׁה	severe (3·36) 904
עֹל	9 yoke (8·40) 760
עֹל	10 yoke (8·40) 760
קֹטֶן	little [finger] (1·2) 882
עבה	to be thick (1·3·3) 716
מָתְנַיִם	loins (5·50) 608
הֶעְמִיס	11 to load (1·2·9) 1126/770
עֹל	yoke (8·40) 760
כָּבֵד	heavy (4·39) 458

Chapter 11

נָכְרִי	1 foreign (4·45) 648
אָכֵן	2 surely, truly (1·19) 38
שָׂרָה	3 princess, noble lady (1·5) 979
פִּלֶגֶשׁ	concubine (1·37) 811
זִקְנָה	4 old age (2·6) 279

יִסֵּר to chasten (4·30·41) 415

שׁוֹט whip, scourge (2·8) 1002

עַקְרָב scorpion (2·9) 785

קָשֶׁה 13 severe (3·36) 904

עֹל 14 yoke (8·40) 760

יִסֵּר to chasten (4·30·41) 415

שׁוֹט whip, scourge (2·8) 1002

עַקְרָב scorpion (2·9) 785

סִבָּה 15 turn [of affairs] (1·1) 686

מַס 18 labor band (7·23) 586

רגם to kill by stoning, to stone (1·15·15) 920

הִתְאַמֵּץ to make oneself alert, make haste (1·4·41) 54

מֶרְכָּבָה chariot (5·44) 939

פָּשַׁע 19 to rebel, revolt (2·41) 833

זוּלָה 20 except, besides (2·16) 265

הַקְהִיל 21 to summon an assembly (2·20·39) 874

בָּחוּר chosen (1·19[?]) 103

מְלוּכָה kingship (7·24) 574

עֵגֶל 28 calf (2·35) 722

קְצוֹת 31 whole (4·7) 892

עֵגֶל 32 calf (2·35) 722

בָּרָא 33 to devise (1·2·2) 94

Chapter 13

מוֹפֵת 3 sign (3·36) 68

דֶּשֶׁן fat ashes (2·15) 206

דֶּשֶׁן 5 fat ashes (2·15) 206

מוֹפֵת sign (3·36) 68

סָעַד 7 to sustain (1·12·12) 703

מַתָּת gift (1·6) 682

אֵי 12 where? (2·39) 32

חבש 13 to bind up, equip [a beast] for riding (6·28·32) 289

אֵלָה 14 terebinth, a deciduous tree with pinnate leaves and red berries; grows

to great age (1·17) 18

כָּחַשׁ 18 to deceive (1·19·22) 471

מָרָה 21 to be rebellious (2·21·43) 598

נְבֵלָה 22 corpse (10·48) 615

חבש 23 to bind up, equip [a beast] for riding (6·28·32) 289

אַרְיֵה 24 lion (8·45) 71

נְבֵלָה corpse (10·48) 615

נְבֵלָה 25 corpse (10·48) 615

אַרְיֵה lion (8·45) 71

מָרָה 26 to be rebellious (2·21·43) 598

אַרְיֵה lion (8·45) 71

חבש 27 to bind up, equip [a beast] for riding (6·28·32) 289

נְבֵלָה 28 corpse (10·48) 615

אַרְיֵה lion (8·45) 71

נְבֵלָה 29 corpse (10·48) 615

ספד to lament (4·27·29) 704

נְבֵלָה 30 corpse (10·48) 615

ספד to lament (4·27·29) 704

קָצוֹת 33 whole (4·7) 892

חָפֵץ delight in, have pleasure in (2·12) 343

הִכְחִיד 34 to annihilate (1·6·30) 470

Chapter 14

הִשְׁתַּנָּה 2 to disguise oneself (1·1·26[?]) 1039

אַתְּ you [fem.; old form] (1·7) 61

נָקֻד 3 a kind of [hard] biscuit or cake [?] (1·3) 666

בַּקְבֻּק flask (1·3) 132

קוּם 4 idiomatic use of קוּם here meaning to be set, fixed, without vision. Qal. para. 7j. 878

שִׂיב old [hoary] age (3·20[?]) 966

זֹה 5 this; this and thus כָּזֹה כָזֶה (1·11) 272

הִתְנַכֵּר to feign to be a stranger (2·3·8) 649

הִתְנַכֵּר 6 to feign to be a stranger (2·3·8) 649

קָשֶׁה   severe, with a severe message (3·36) 904

נָגִיד   7 ruler (3·44) 617

מַסֵּכָה   9 molten image (1·25) 651

גַּו   back (1·3); הִשְׁלִיךְ אַחֲרֵי גַו = to put out of mind, ignore, reject 156

הִשְׁתִּין   10 to urinate, מַשְׁתִּין בְּקִיר = a male person (3·6·6) 1010

עָצַר   to restrain, retain (3·36·46) 783

בָּעַר   to burn, consume (4·26·28) 129

גָּלָל   dung (1·2) 165

כֶּלֶב   11 dog (7·32) 476

ספד   13 to lament (4·27·29) 704

נוד   15 to waver (1·19·26) 626

נָתַשׁ   to pull up (1·17·22) 684

זרה   to scatter, disperse (1·25·38) 279

אֲשֵׁרָה   Canaanite goddess of fortune and happiness; sacred pole representing her (5·40) 81

בִּגְלַל   16 on account of (1·10) 164

סַף   17 threshold (1·25) 706

ספד   18 to lament (4·27·29) 704

קָנָא   22 to excite to jealous anger (5·30·34) 888

מַצֵּבָה   23 stump (1·35) 663

אֲשֵׁרָה   Canaanite goddess of fortune and happiness (5·40) 81

גָּבֹהַּ   high, exalted (1·41) 147

רַעֲנָן   luxuriant, fresh (1·19) 947

קָדֵשׁ   24 temple prostitute [male] (3·11) 873

רָץ   27 runner (3·25) 930

מִדֵּי   28 out of the abundance of, i.e., as often as (1·15) 191

רָץ   runner (3·25) 930

תָּא   chamber (1·13) 1060

Chapter 15

שָׁלֵם   3 complete, perfect (5·28) 1023

נִיר   4 lamp (2·5) 633

קָדֵשׁ   12 temple prostitute [male] (3·11) 873

גִּלּוּל   idol (2·48) 165

גְּבִרָה   13 queen mother (2·15) 150

מִפְלֶצֶת   horrid thing (2·4) 814

אֲשֵׁרָה   Canaanite goddess of fortune and happiness (5·40) 81

שָׁלֵם   14 complete, perfect (5·28) 1023

שֹׁחַד   19 present, bribe (1·23) 1005

הֵפֵר   to break, frustrate (1·41·43) 830

נָקִי   22 exempt from obligations (1·43) 667

זִקְנָה   23 old age (2·6) 279

קָשַׁר   27 to conspire (4·36·44) 905

צוּר   to shut in, besiege (3·31·31) 848

נְשָׁמָה   29 every breathing thing (2·24) 675

כַּעַס   30 vexation, anger (2·25[?]) 495

Chapter 16

נָגִיד   2 ruler (3·44) 617

הבעיר   3 to consume, destroy (1·2·28) 129

כֶּלֶב   4 dog (7·32) 476

קָשַׁר   9 to conspire (4·36·44) 905

מַחֲצִית   half (1·16) 345

שִׁכּוֹר   drunken (2·13) 1016

הִשְׁתִּין   11 to urinate, מַשְׁתִּין בְּקִיר = a male person (3·6·6) 1010

גָּאַל   [redeemer-] kinsman (1·44[?]) 145

קָשַׁר   16 to conspire (4·36·44) 905

צוּר   17 to shut in, beseige (3·31·31) 848

אַרְמוֹן   18 citadel, stronghold, palace (1·33) 74

קֶשֶׁר   20 conspiracy (1·14) 905

קָשַׁר   to conspire (4·36·44) 905

אֲשֵׁרָה   33 sacred tree or pole representing Canaanite goddess of fortune and happiness (5·40) 81

יִסַּד   34 to found (2·10·42) 413

צָעִיר   little, young (1·22) 859

Chapter 17

תּוֹשָׁב	1 sojourner (1·14) 444
טַל	dew (1·31) 378
מָטָר	rain (4·37) 564
קֶדֶם	3 eastward (2·26) 870
עֹרֵב	4 raven (2·12) 788
כִּלְכֵּל	to sustain (8·24·38) 465
עֹרֵב	6 raven (2·12) 788
גֶּשֶׁם	7 rain, shower (5·35) 177
כִּלְכֵּל	9 to sustain (8·24·38) 465
קוֹשֵׁשׁ	10 to gather stubble (2·6·8) 905
פַּת	11 fragment, bit, morsel (1·14) 837
מָעוֹג	12 cake (1·2) 728
מְלֹא	fullness (1·38) 571
קֶמַח	flour, meal (4·14) 887
כַּד	jar (4·18) 461
צַפַּחַת	jar, jug (4·7) 860
קוֹשֵׁשׁ	to gather stubble (2·6·8) 905
עֻגָה	13 cake of bread (2·7) 728
קָטֹן	small (4·47) 881
כַּד	14 jar (4·18) 461
קֶמַח	flour, meal (4·14) 887
צַפַּחַת	jar, jug (4·7) 860
חָסֵר	to be lacking, to need (2·20·24) 341
גֶּשֶׁם	rain (5·35) 177
כַּד	16 jar (4·18) 461
קֶמַח	flour, meal (4·14) 887
צַפַּחַת	jar, jug (4·7) 860
חָסֵר	to be lacking, to need (2·20·24) 341
בַּעֲלָה	17 mistress (1·4) 128
חֳלִי	sickness (1·24) 318
נְשָׁמָה	breath (2·24) 675
מַה לִּי וָלָךְ	18 what have I to do with you? מַה, para. 1d. 553
חֵיק	bosom (5·38) 300
עֲלִיָּה	roof chamber (2·20) 751
מִטָּה	bed (2·29) 641
עֲלִיָּה	23 roof chamber (2·20) 751

Chapter 18

מָטָר	1 rain (4·37) 564
הֶחְבִּיא	4 to hide (2·6·34) 285
מְעָרָה	cave (4·40) 792
כִּלְכֵּל	to sustain (8·24·38) 465
מַעְיָן	5 spring (1·23) 745
אוּלַי	perhaps (3·45) 19
חָצִיר	green grass, herbage (1·18[?]) 348
פֶּרֶד	mule (2·14) 825
הִכִּיר	7 to recognize (2·37·40) 647
נְעוּרִים	12 youth (1·46) 655
הֶחְבִּיא	13 to hide (2·6·34) 285
מְעָרָה	cave (4·40) 792
כִּלְכֵּל	to sustain (8·24·38) 465
עָכַר	17 to disturb, trouble (2·12·14) 747
עָכַר	18 to disturb, trouble (2·12·14) 747
אֲשֵׁרָה	19 Canaanite goddess of fortune and happiness (5·40) 81
מָתַי	21 when? with עד before = until when? how long? (1·42) 607
פסח	to limp (1·5·7) 820
סְעִיפָה	division, divided opinion (1·1) 704
נִתַּח	23 to cut up into pieces (2·9·9) 677
צָהֳרַיִם	26 midday, noon (4·23) 843
פסח	to go limping (1·1·7) 820
צָהֳרַיִם	27 midday, noon (4·23) 843
הִתֵּל	to deceive, mock (1·1·1) 251
שִׂיחַ	musing (1·14) 967
שִׂיג	a moving back, away (1·1) 691
אוּלַי	perhaps (3·45) 19
יָשֵׁן	sleeping (2·9) 445
יקץ	to awake (2·11·11) 429
הִתְגֹּדֵד	28 to cut oneself (1·7·8) 151
רֹמַח	spear, lance (1·15) 942
צָהֳרַיִם	29 midday, noon (4·23) 843
קֶשֶׁב	attention, one who pays attention, attentiveness (1·4) 904
הָרַס	30 to throw down (3·30·43) 248

193

תְּעָלָה	32 trench (3·9) 752
סְאָה	a measure of grain (1·9)
כְּבֵית סָאתַיִם	like a receptacle holding 2 seahs. בַּיִת, para. 3. 109
נָתַח	33 to cut up into pieces (2·9·9) 677
כַּד	34 jar (4·18) 461
שָׁנָה	to repeat (2·13·26[?]) 1040
שִׁלֵּשׁ	to do a third time (2·4·9) 1026
תְּעָלָה	35 trench (3·9) 752
אֲחֹרַנִּית	37 backwards (1·7) 30
תְּעָלָה	38 trench (3·9) 752
לָחַךְ	to lick up (1·5·6) 535
גֶּשֶׁם	41 rain, shower (5·35) 177
גָּהַר	42 to bend, crouch (1·3·3) 155
בֶּרֶךְ	knee (3·25) 139
מְאוּמָה	43 anything (2·32) 548
עָב	44 dark cloud (2·30) 728
קָטֹן	small (4·47) 881
עָצַר	to restrain, retain (3·36·46) 783
גֶּשֶׁם	rain, shower (5·35) 177
עַד כֹּה וְעַד כֹּה	45 till now and till then, i.e., meanwhile (1·1) כֹּה, para. 3. 462
הִתְקַדֵּר	to grow dark (1·1·17) 871
עָב	dark cloud (2·30) 728
גֶּשֶׁם	rain, shower (5·35) 177
שִׁנֵּס	46 to gird up (1·1·1) 1042
מָתְנַיִם	loins (5·50) 608

Chapter 19

רֹתֶם	4 broom plant, retem (2·4) 958
יָשֵׁן	5 to sleep (1·15·16[?]) 445
רֹתֶם	broom plant, retem (2·4) 958
מְרַאֲשׁוֹת	6 place at the head (1·10) 912
עֻגָה	cake of bread (2·7) 728
רֶצֶף	glowing stone, coal (1·2) 954
צַפַּחַת	jar, jug (4·7) 860
אֲכִילָה	8 a meal (1·1) 38
מְעָרָה	9 cave (4·40) 792

פֹּה	here, hither (4·44) 805
קִנֵּא	10 to be zealous (5·30·34) 888
הָרַס	to tear down, throw down (3·30·43) 248
פָּרַק	11 to tear off (1·3·10) 830
רַעַשׁ	earthquake (3·17) 950
רַעַשׁ	12 earthquake (3·17) 950
דְּמָמָה	whisper, silence (1·3) 199
דַּק	small, thin (1·14) 201
הֵלִיט	13 to wrap (1·1·5) 532
אַדֶּרֶת	cloak, mantle (2·12) 12
מְעָרָה	cave (4·40) 792
פֹּה	here, hither (4·44) 805
קִנֵּא	14 to be zealous, to tear down (5·30·43) 888
הָרַס	to tear down, throw down (3·30·43) 248
בֶּרֶךְ	18 knee (3·25) 139
כָּרַע	to bow (2·29·35) 502
נָשַׁק	to kiss (2·26·32) 676
חָרַשׁ	19 to plough (2·23·26) 360
צֶמֶד	couple, pair; span [of oxen] (2·15) 855
אַדֶּרֶת	cloak, mantle (2·12) 12
נָשַׁק	20 to kiss (2·26·32) 676
צֶמֶד	21 couple, pair, span [of oxen] (2·15) 855
בִּשֵּׁל	to cook (1·20·27) 143

Chapter 20

צוּר	1 to shut in, besiege (3·31·31) 848
חִפֵּשׂ	6 to search through, search (1·8·23) 344
מַחְמָד	desire (1·13) 326
מָנַע	7 to withhold (1·25·29) 586
שָׂפַק	10 to suffice (1·1·1[?]) 974
שֹׁעַל	handful (1·3) 1043
חָגַר	11 to gird on (2·44·44) 291

סֻכָּה	12 booth (2·31) 697
בְּמִי	14 by whom? (1·1) 566
אֱסֹר הַמִּלְחָמָה	to begin the battle [?·?] 536
צָהֳרַיִם	16 midday, noon (4·23) 843
שִׁכּוֹר	drunken (2·13) 1016
סֻכָּה	booth (2·31) 697
מַכָּה	21 slaughter (2·48) 646
תְּשׁוּבָה	22 return (2·8) 1000
אוּלָם	23 but, but indeed (1·19) 19
מִישׁוֹר	plain (2·23) 449
פֶּחָה	24 governor (2·28) 808
מָנָה	25 to number (1·12·28) 584
מִישׁוֹר	plain (2·23) 449
תְּשׁוּבָה	26 return (2·8) 1000
כַּלְכֵּל	27 to be supplied (1·1·36) 465
חֲשִׂיף	little flock [dub.] (1·1) [based on versions] 362
נֹכַח	29 opposite to, in front of (2·22) 647
רַגְלִי	on foot; as substantive = foot soldiery, infantry (1·12) 920
חֶדֶר	30 room, chamber (3·37) 293
שַׂק	31 sack cloth (4·48) 974
מָתְנַיִם	loins (5·50) 608
חֶבֶל	cord (3·49) 286
אוּלַי	perhaps (3·45) 19
חָגַר	32 to gird on (2·44·44) 291
שַׂק	sack cloth (4·48) 974
מָתְנַיִם	loins (5·50) 608
חֶבֶל	cord (3·49) 286
נָחֵשׁ	33 to observe signs (1·9·9) 638
חלט	to snatch, catch (1·1·1) 319
מֶרְכָּבָה	chariot (5·44) 939
מֵאֵן	35 to refuse (2·45·45) 549
אַרְיֵה	36 lion (8·45) 71
מֵאֵצֶל	from beside (2·6) 69
פצע	37 to wound [by bruising] (1·3·3) 822
הִתְחַפֵּשׂ	38 to disguise oneself [let one be searched for] (3·8·23) 344

אֲפֵר	covering, bandage (2·2) 68
שָׁקַל	39 to weigh out (1·19·22) 1053
הֵנָּה וָהֵנָּה	40 hitherwards and thitherwards = in different directions (2·49) 244
חָרַץ	to decide, cut, sharpen (1·5·10) 358
אֲפֵר	41 covering, bandage (2·2) 68
הִכִּיר	to recognize (2·37·40) 647
חֵרֶם	42 devotion, ban involving destruction (1·29) 356
סַר	43 sullen, stubborn, resentful (3·3) 711
זָעֵף	out of humor, vexed (2·2) 277

Chapter 21

גַּן	2 garden (1·41) 171
יָרָק	herbs (1·3) 438
מְחִיר	price (2·15) 564
חָלִילָה	3 far be it [from me, you etc.] (1·21) 321
סַר	4 sullen, stubborn, resentful (3·3) 711
זָעֵף	out of humor, vexed (2·2) 277
מִטָּה	bed (2·29) 641
סַר	5 sullen, stubborn, resentful (3·3) 711
חָפֵץ	6 delighting in, having pleasure in (2·12) 343
מְלוּכָה	7 kingship (7·24) 574
חתם	8 to seal, affix one's seal (1·23·27) 367
חֹתָם	seal, signet ring (1·13) 368
חֹר	noble (2·13) 359
צוֹם	9 fast, fasting (2·25) 847
בְּלִיַּעַל	10 good for nothing, worthless (3·27) 116
הֵעִיד	to testify (3·39·44) 729
סקל	to stone (2·12·22) 709
ברך*	see note on p. 70
חֹר	11 noble (2·13) 359
צוֹם	12 fast, fasting (2·25) 847
בְּלִיַּעַל	13 good for nothing, worthless (3·27) 116
הֵעִיד	to testify (3·39·44) 729

סקל		to stone (2·12·22) 709	פתה	20 to deceive (3·17·27) 834
בּרךּ*		see note below	בְּ כֹה . . . בְּ כֹה	in this way . . . in that way (2·2) 462
סָקַל	14	to be stoned (2·2·22) 709	פתה	21 to deceive (3·17·27) 834
סָקַל	15	to be stoned (2·2·22) 709	בַּמָּה	by what means? (1·29) 552
מֵאֵן		to refuse (2·45·45) 549	פתה	22 to deceive (3·17·27) 834
רָצַח	19	to murder, slay (1·38·43) 953	לְחִי	24 cheek (1·21) 534
לקק		to lick (3·5·7) 545	אֵי	where? (2·39) 32
כֶּלֶב		dog (7·32) 476	חֶדֶר	25 chamber, room (5·37) 293
בָּעַר	21	to burn, consume (4·26·28) 129	נֶחְבָּה	to withdraw, hide oneself (1·3·4) 285
הַשְׁתִּין		to urinate, מַשְׁתִּין בְּקִיר = a male person (3·6·6) 1010	כֶּלֶא	27 imprisonment (1·10) 476
עָצַר		to restrain, retain (3·36·46) 783	לַחַץ	oppression (2·11) 537
כַּעַס	22	vexation, anger (2·25[?]) 495	הִתְחַפֵּשׂ	30 to disguise oneself [let one be searched for] (3·8·23) 344
כֶּלֶב	23	dog (7·32) 476	מָשַׁךְ	34 to draw (1·30·36) 604
חֵיל		rampart [dub.] (1·9) 298	תֹּם	innocence, simplicity (2·23) 1070
כֶּלֶב	24	dog (7·32) 476	דֶּבֶק	appendage, joining, soldering (1·3) 180
הִסִּית	25	to instigate (1·18·18) 694	שִׁרְיוֹן	body armor (1·8) 1056
הִתְעִיב	26	to do abominably (1·4·21) 1073	רַכָּב	charioteer (1·3) 939
גִּלּוּל		idol (2·48) 165	מֶרְכָּבָה	35 chariot (5·44) 939
שַׂק	27	sackcloth (4·48) 974	נֹכַח	opposite to, in front of (2·22) 647
צוֹם		to abstain from food, fast (1·1·20) 847	מַכָּה	wound (2·48) 646
אַט		softly, gentleness (1·5) 31	חֵיק	bosom = interior (5·38) 300
נִכְנַע	28	to humble oneself (2·25·36) 488	רִנָּה	36 ringing cry (2·33) 943
			שָׁטַף	38 to rinse, wash off (1·28·31) 1009
		Chapter 22	בְּרֵכָה	pool, pond (1·17) 140
הֶחֱשָׁה	3	to show inactivity (1·9·16) 364	לקק	to lick (3·5·7) 545
פֹּה	7	here, hither (4·44) 805	כֶּלֶב	dog (7·32) 476
סָרִיס	9	eunuch (1·45) 710	זוֹנָה	harlot (2·33[?]) 275
גֹּרֶן	10	threshing floor (1·34) 175	קָדֵשׁ	47 temple prostitute [male] (3·11) 873
נגח	11	to push (1·6·11) 618	בָּעֵר	to consume, burn (4·26·28) 129
(עַד) כַּמֶּה	16	how many? (1·13) 552	נִצָּב	48 deputy (6·7) 662
נפץ	17	BDB lists under פוּץ niphal — "to be scattered" (1·15·21) 806	אֳנִיָּה	ship (4·31) 58
			אֳנִיָּה	50 ship (4·31) 58

בֵּרֵךְ*	to bless; used here in the vulgar sense, it actually means "to curse," Piel (2·2), para. 5. 189

2 KINGS

Chapter 1

פָּשַׁע	1 to rebel, revolt (6·40·41) 833
שְׂבָכָה	2 [window] lattice (3·16) 959
עֲלִיָּה	roof chamber (4·20) 751
זְבוּב	flies; בעל ז׳ = lord of the flies (4·6) 256 and 127
חֲלִי	sickness (4·24) 318
מִבְּלִי	3 on account of (3·25) 115
זְבוּב	flies; see vs. 2 (4·6) 256 and 127
מִטָּה	4 bed (7·29) 641
מִבְּלִי	6 on account of (3·25) 115
זְבוּב	flies; see vs. 2 (4·6) 256 and 127
מִטָּה	bed (7·29) 641
שֵׂעָר	8 hair (1·28) 972
אֵזוֹר	waist cloth (1·14) 25
אזר	to gird on (1·6·16) 25
מָתְנַיִם	loins (3·50) 608
כָּרַע	13 to bow (2·29·35) 502
בֶּרֶךְ	knee (2·25) 139
לְנֶגֶד	in front of, before (1·32) 617
יקר	to be precious (2·9·11) 429
יקר	14 to be precious (2·9·11) 429
זְבוּב	16 flies; see vs. 2 (4·6) 256 and 127
מִבְּלִי	on account of (3·25) 115
מִטָּה	bed (2·29) 641

Chapter 2

סְעָרָה	1 tempest, storm-wind (2·15) 704
פֹּה	2 here, hither (8·44) 805
החשה	3 to be silent (3·9·16) 364
פֹּה	4 here, hither (8·44) 805
החשה	5 to be silent (3·9·16) 364
פֹּה	6 here, hither (8·44) 805
מִנֶּגֶד	7 opposite (4·26) 617
אַדֶּרֶת	8 cloak, mantle (3·12) 12

גלם	to wrap up, fold, fold together (1·1·1) 166
נחצה	to be divided (2·4·15) 345
הֵנָּה	hither; ה׳ וה׳ = hither and thither (7·49) 244
חָרָבָה	dry ground (1·8) 351
בְּטֶרֶם	9 before (2·39) 382
הִקְשָׁה	10 to make difficult (2·21·28) 904
הִפְרִיד	11 to make a division, separation (1·7·26) 825
סְעָרָה	tempest, storm-wind (2·15) 704
קְרָעִים	12 torn piece, rag (1·4) 902
אַדֶּרֶת	13 cloak, mantle (3·12) 12
אַדֶּרֶת	14 cloak, mantle (3·12) 12
אַיֵּה	where? (3·44) 32
נחצה	to be divided (2·4·15) 345
הֵנָּה	hither; ה׳ וה׳ = hither and thither (7·49) 244
מִנֶּגֶד	15 some way off from, at a distance (4·26) 617
גַּיְא	16 valley (3·48) 161
פצר	17 to urge (2·6·7) 823
מוֹשָׁב	19 situation (1·43) 444
שכל	to make childless (2·18·24) 1013
צְלֹחִית	20 jar (1·1) 852
מֶלַח	salt (3·28) 571
מוֹצָא	21 place of going forth (1·27) 425
מֶלַח	salt (3·28) 571
שכל	to make childless (2·18·24) 1013
קָטָן	23 small, young (4·47) 881
התקלס	to scoff, mock, deride (1·3·4) 887
קֵרֵחַ	bald (2·3) 901
דֹּב	24 bear (1·12) 179

Chapter 3

מַצֵּבָה	2 pillar (6·35) 663
נֹקֵד	4 sheep raiser (1·2) 667
כַּר	he-lamb (1·11) 503

צֶמֶר — wool (1·16) 856

פָּשַׁע — 5 to rebel, revolt (6·40·41) 833

פָּשַׁע — 7 to rebel, revolt (6·40·41) 833

אֵי — 8 where? אֵי־זֶה = which? (2·39) 32

אֲהָהּ — 10 alas! (3·15) 13

פֹּה — 11 here, hither (8·44) 805

לוּלֵי — 14 if not, unless (1·10) 530

נָגַן — 15 to play [a stringed instrument] (3·14·15) 618

גֵּב — 16 pit, ditch, trench (1·3[?]) 155

גֶּשֶׁם — 17 rain, shower (1·35) 177

מִבְצָר — 19 fortification (5·37) 131

מִבְחוֹר — choice (2·2) 104

מַעְיָן — spring (2·23) 745

סָתַם — to stop up (2·10·13) 711

חֶלְקָה — portion of ground (6·24) 324

הֵכְאִיב — to mar (1·4·8) 456

חָגַר — 21 to gird on (3·44·44) 291

חֲגֹרָה — girdle, loin covering, belt (1·5) 292

זָרַח — 22 to rise (1·18·18) 280

מִנֶּגֶד — some way off from, at a distance (4·26) 617

אָדֹם — red (1·9) 10

הֶחֱרַב — 23 to attack one another (1·3·37[?]) 352

נֶחְרַב — to fight together (1·1·3[?]) 352

הָרַס — 25 to throw down, tear down (1·30·33) 248

חֶלְקָה — portion of ground (6·24) 324

מַעְיָן — spring (2·23) 745

סָתַם — to stop up (2·10·13) 711

קַלָּע — slinger (1·1) 887

שָׁלַף — 26 to draw out (1·24·24) 1025

קֶצֶף — 27 wrath (1·29) 893

Chapter 4

נֹשֶׁה — 1 creditor (1·4) 674

אָסוּךְ — 2 flask (1·1) 692

שְׁכֵנֵךְ — 3 K, שְׁכֵן Q, neighbor (1·20) 1015

רֵיק — empty (1·14) 938

הַמְעִיט — to make few (1·13·22) 589

נְשִׁי — 7 debt (1·1) 674

מִדֵּי — 8 out of the abundance of, i.e., as often as (1·15) 191

עֲלִיָּה — 10 roof chamber (4·20) 751

קָטָן — small (4·47) 881

מִטָּה — bed (7·29) 641

מְנוֹרָה — lampstand (1·39) 633

עֲלִיָּה — 11 roof chamber (4·20) 751

חָרַד — 13 to be anxiously careful (1·23·39) 353

חֲרָדָה — anxious care (1·9) 353

עַם — kinsman (1·34) 769

אֲבָל — 14 verily, of a truth (1·11) 6

זָקֵן — to be old, become old (1·25·27) 278

אַתְּי — 16 you [2nd, fem.] (3·7) 61

חבק — to embrace (1·3·13) 287

כָּזַב — to tell a lie (1·12·16) 469

קֹצֵר — 18 reaper (1·10[?]) 894

בֶּרֶךְ — 20 knee (2·25) 139

צָהֳרַיִם — midday, noon (1·23) 843

מִטָּה — 21 bed (7·29) 641

אָתוֹן — 22 she-ass (2·35) 87

אַתְּי — 23 you [2nd, fem.] (3·7) 61

חרש — 24 to bind on, i.e., to saddle (1·27·31) 289

אָתוֹן — she-ass (2·35) 87

נָהַג — to drive (2·20·30) 624

עָצַר — to restrain, retain (4·36·46) 783

מִנֶּגֶד — 25 some way off from, at a distance (4·26) 617

הַלָּז — this (2·7) 229

הרף — 27 to push away, thrust (1·11·11) 213

הרפה — to refrain, let alone (1·21·44) 951

מָרַר — to be bitter (1·6·14) 600

הֶעְלִים — to conceal, hide (1·11·29) 761

הַשְׁלָה 28 to mislead [one] (1·1·7) 1017

חֲגֹר 29 to gird up (3·44·44) 291

מָתְנַיִם loins (3·50) 608

מִשְׁעֶנֶת staff (4·12) 1044

מִשְׁעֶנֶת 31 staff (4·12) 1044

קֶשֶׁב attentiveness (1·3) 904

הָקִיץ to awake (1·22·23) 884

מִטָּה 32 bed (7·29) 641

גָּהַר 34 to bend, crouch (2·3·3) 155

חָמַם to grow warm (1·23·26) 328

הֵנָּה 35 hither; וה' ה' hither and thither (7·49) 244

גָּהַר to bend, crouch (2·3·3) 155

זָרַר to sneeze (1·1·1) 284

פָּקַח to open (6·17·20) 824

שָׁפַת 38 to set [on the fire] (1·4·4) 1046

סִיר pot (6·29) 696

בִּשֵּׁל to boil (2·20·27) 143

נָזִיד pottage (3·6) 268

לָקַט 39 to gather (2·21·36) 544

אֹרָה herb (1·2) 21

פַּקֻּעֹת gourds (1·1) 825

מְלֹא fullness (1·38) 571

פִּלַּח to cleave open, cleave through (1·4·5) 812

סִיר pot (6·29) 696

נָזִיד pottage (3·6) 268

נָזִיד 40 pottage (3·6) 268

סִיר pot (6·29) 696

קֶמַח 41 flour, meal (1·14) 887

סִיר pot (6·29) 696

בִּכּוּרִים 42 first fruits (1·17) 114

שְׂעֹרָה barley (4·34) 972

כַּרְמֶל fruit, garden growth (1·3[?]) 502

צִקָּלֹן garment, wallet [dub.] (1·1) 862

מְשָׁרֵת 43 servant (2·20) 1058

Chapter 5

תְּשׁוּעָה 1 deliverance (3·34) 448

מְצֹרָע leprous (6·15) 863

גְּדוּד 2 band, troop (8·33) 151

שָׁבָה to take captive (2·29·37) 985

קָטֹן small, young (4·47) 881

גְּבֶרֶת 3 mistress over servants (2·15[?]) 150

אַחֲלֵי oh that! (1·2) 25

צָרַעַת leprosy (4·35) 863

חֲלִיפָה 5 change [of raiment] (3·12) 322

צָרַעַת 6 leprosy (4·35) 863

צָרַעַת 7 leprosy (4·35) 863

הִתְאַנָּה to seek an occasion (1·1·4) 58

קָצַף 11 to be angry (2·28·34) 893

הֵנִיף to wave (1·32·34[?]) 631

מְצֹרָע leprous (6·15) 863

טָבַל 14 to dip (2·15·16) 371

פָּצַר 16 to urge (2·6·7) 823

מֵאֵן to refuse (1·45·45) 549

מַשָּׂא 17 load (2·43) 672

צֶמֶד couple, pair (2·15) 855

פֶּרֶד mule (1·14) 825

סָלַח 18 to forgive (3·33·46) 699

נִשְׁעַן to lean, support oneself (3·22·22) 1043

כִּבְרָה 19 a distance (1·3) 460

חָשַׂךְ 20 to spare (1·26·28) 362

מְאוּמָה anything (1·32) 548

מֶרְכָּבָה 21 chariot (5·44) 939

חֲלִיפָה 22 change [of raiment] (3·12) 322

הוֹאִיל 23 to show willingness (2·18·18) 383

פָּרַץ to urge (2·46·49) 823

צוּר to confine, secure (8·31·31) 848

חָרִיט bag, purse (1·2) 355

חֲלִיפָה change [of raiment] (3·12) 322

עֹפֶל 24 mound, hill (1·8) 779

מֵאַן 25 whence? from where? (3·48[?]) 33

אָנֶה where? — אָנֶה וְאָנָה — anywhere (3·39) 33

מֶרְכָּבָה 26 chariot (5·44) 939

זַיִת olive tree, olive (2·38) 268

צָרַעַת 27 leprosy (4·35) 863

מְצֹרָע leprous (6·15) 863

שֶׁלֶג snow (1·20) 1017

Chapter 6

צַר 1 narrow, tight (1·20) 865

קוֹרָה 2 beam (2·5) 900

הוֹאִיל 3 to show willingness (2·18·18) 383

גָּזַר 4 to cut down, cut, divide (1·6·12) 160

קוֹרָה 5 beam (2·5) 900

אֲהָהּ alas! (3·15) 13

אָנֶה 6 whence? whither? (3·39) 33

קצב to cut off, shear (1·2) 891

הֵצִיף to cause to float (1·2·3) 847

פְּלֹנִי 8 a certain one; פ' = אַלְמֹנִי = such a one (1·6) 811

אַלְמֹנִי someone, a certain one (1·3) 48

תַּחֲנוֹת encampment (1·1) 334

נָחֵת 9 descending (1·1) 639

הִזְהִיר 10 to warn (1·13·21) 264

נסער 11 to be enraged (1·1·7) 704

מִשֶּׁלָּנוּ = מִן + שֶׁ + לְ + נוּ = of those that are ours 979 (שֶׁ, 4c)

חֶדֶר 12 chamber, room (3·37) 293

מִשְׁכָּב lying down (1·46) 1012

אֵיכָה 13 where? (2·18) 32

כָּבֵד 14 numerous (2·39) 458

הִקִּיף to surround (2·16·17) 668

מְשָׁרֵת 15 servant (2·20) 1058

אֲהָהּ alas! (3·15) 13

אֵיכָה what? in what manner? (2·18) 32

מֵאֲשֶׁר 16 than those who (1·17) 84

פָּקַח 17 to open (6·17·20) 824

סַנְוֵרִים 18 sudden blindness (2·3) 703

זֹה 19 this (1·11) 262

פָּקַח 20 to open (6·17·20) 824

שָׁבָה 22 to take captive (2·29·37) 985

כרה 23 to give a feast (1·1·1) 500

כֵּרָה feast (1·1) 500

גְּדוּד band, troop (8·33) 151

צוּר 24 to shut in, besiege (8·31·31) 848

צוּר 25 to shut in, besiege (8·31·31) 848

רֹבַע fourth part (1·1) 917

קַב kab [unit of dry measure] (1·1) 866

חֲרִי dung (2·3) 351

יוֹנָה dove (1·33) 401 [דִּבְיוֹנִים Q dove's dung (1·1) 179]

מֵאַיִן 27 whence? from where? (3·48[?]) 32

גֹּרֶן threshing floor (1·34) 175

יֶקֶב wine vat (1·16) 428

בִּשֵּׁל 29 to cook, boil (2·20·27) 143

הֶחְבִּיא to hide (1·6·34) 285

שַׂק 30 sackcloth (3·48) 974

בְּטֶרֶם 32 before (2·39) 382

מְרַצֵּחַ murderer (1·2) 954

לחץ to squeeze, press (3·14·15) 537

הוֹחִיל 33 to wait (1·15·42) 403

Chapter 7

סְאָה 1 a measure of grain (6·9) 684

שְׂעֹרָה barley (4·34) 972

שָׁלִישׁ 2 adjutant, officer (7·16) 1026

נִשְׁעָן to lean, support oneself (3·22·22) 1043

אֲרֻבָּה lattice, window (1·8) 70

הִנְּכָה = הֵן + ךָ = הִנְּךָ = behold you!

מְצֹרָע 3 leprous (6·15) 865

פֹּה here, hither (8·44) 805

פֹּה 4 here, hither (8·44) 805

נֶשֶׁף 5 twilight (2·12) 676

שָׂכַר 6 to hire (1·17·20) 968

נֶשֶׁף 7 twilight (2·12) 676

מְצֹרָע 8 leprous (6·15) 865

הטמין to hide something (2·2·31) 380

בְּשֹׂרָה 9 good tidings (1·6) 142

החשה to be silent (3·9·16) 364

חכּה to wait, tarry (2·13·14) 314

שֹׁעֵר 10 porter (2·37) 1045

שֹׁעֵר 11 porter (2·37) 1045

פְּנִימָה within (1·5) 819

רָעֵב 12 hungry (1·19) 944

נֶחְבָּה to withdraw, hide oneself (1·3·4) 285

בְּהִחָפְזָם 15 K, בְּחָפְזָם, Q, חפז to hurry away (1·6·9) 342

בָּזַז 16 to spoil, plunder (1·37·40) 102

סְאָה a measure of grain (6·9) 684

שְׂעֹרָה barley (4·34) 972

שָׁלִישׁ 17 adjutant, officer (7·16) 1026

נִשְׁעָן to lean, support oneself (3·22·22) 1043

רָמַס to trample (4·17·18) 942

סְאָה 18 a measure of grain (6·9) 684

שְׂעֹרָה barley (4·34) 972

שָׁלִישׁ 19 adjutant, officer (7·16) 1026

אֲרֻבָּה lattice, window (1·8) 70

רָמַס 20 to trample (4·17·18) 942

Chapter 8

אַתְּ 1 you [2nd, fem.] (3·7) 61

בַּאֲשֶׁר in where (1·19) 84

סָרִיס 6 eunuch (8·45) 710

תְּבוּאָה product, yield (1·43) 100

הֵנָּה 7 hither (7·49) 244

חֳלִי 8 sickness (4·24) 318

טוּב 9 goods (1·32) 375

מַשָּׂא load (2·43) 672

חֳלִי sickness (4·24) 318

מִבְצָר 12 fortifications (5·37) 131

בָּחוּר young man (1·45) 104

עוֹלֵל child (1·11) 760

רטש to dash in pieces (1·2·4) 936

הָרָה pregnant (2·15[?]) 247

כֶּלֶב 13 dog (3·32) 476

מָחֳרָת 15 the morrow (1·32) 564

מַכְבֵּר a netted cloth or coverlet (1·1) 460

טָבַל to dip (2·15·16) 371

נִיר 19 lamp (2·5) 633

פָּשַׁע 20 to transgress (6·40·41) 833

פָּשַׁע 22 to transgress (6·40·41) 833

חָתָן 27 son-in-law, bridegroom (1·20) 368

מַכָּה 29 wound (2·48) 646

Chapter 9

חגר 1 to gird up (3·44·44) 291

מָתְנַיִם loins (3·50) 608

פַּךְ phial, flask (1·3) 810

חֶדֶר 2 chamber, room (3·37) 293

פַּךְ 3 phial, flask (1·3) 810

חכּה to wait, tarry (2·13·14) 314

נקם 7 to avenge (1·2·34) 667

השתין 8 to urinate (1·6·6) 1010

עָצַר to restrain, retain (4·36·46) 783

כֶּלֶב 10 dog (3·32) 476

שׁגע 11 to be maddened (1·5·7) 993

שִׂיחַ the way in which he talks (1·14) 967

גֶּרֶם 13 self [dub.] ג' המעלות idiom for "the steps themselves" (1·5) 175

מַעֲלָה step (8·47[?]) 752

התקשׁר 14 to conspire (1·3·44) 905

מַכָּה 15 wound (2·48) 646

פָּלִיט fugitive (1·19) 812

צֹפֶה 17 watchman (3·19) 859

מִגְדָּל tower (3·49) 154

שִׁפְעָה multitude (2·6) 1051

רַכָּב horseman (1·3) 939

צֹפֶה 18 watchman (3·19) 859

צֹפֶה 20 watchman (3·19) 859

מִנְהַג driving (2·2) 624

שִׁגָּעוֹן madness (1·3) 993

נָהַג to drive (2·20·30) 624

חֶלְקָה 21 portion of ground (6·24) 324

זְנוּנִים 22 fornication [religious] (1·11) 276

כֶּשֶׁף sorcery (1·6) 506

מִרְמָה 23 treachery (1·39) 941

חֵצִי 24 arrow (1·4) 345

כָּרַע to bow down (2·29·35) 502

שָׁלִישׁ 25 adjutant, officer (7·16) 1026

חֶלְקָה portion of ground (6·24) 324

צֶמֶד couple, pair (2·15) 855

מַשָּׂא burden (2·43) 672

אֶמֶשׁ 26 yesterday (1·5) 57

חֶלְקָה portion of ground (6·24) 324

גַּן 27 garden (4·41) 171

מֶרְכָּבָה chariot (5·44) 939

מַעֲלֵה ascent (1·19) 751

קְבֻרָה 28 grave (3·14) 869

פּוּךְ 30 antimony, stibium (1·4) 806

הִשְׁקִיף to look down (2·12·22) 1054

חַלּוֹן window (3·30) 313

חַלּוֹן 32 window (3·30) 313

הִשְׁקִיף to look down (2·12·22) 1054

סָרִיס eunuch (8·45) 710

שמט 33 to let drop, let fall (2·7·9) 1030

נזה to spatter (1·4·24) 633

רָמַס to trample (4·17·18) 942

גֻּלְגֹּלֶת 35 skull, head (1·12) 166

כֶּלֶב 36 dog (3·32) 476

נְבֵלָה 37 corpse (1·48) 615

דֹּמֶן dung (1·6) 199

Chapter 10

אֹמֵן 1 nourisher, supporter (2·7[?]) 52

מִבְצָר 2 fortifications (5·37) 131

נֶשֶׁק weapons (1·10) 676

אֹמֵן 5 nourisher, supporter (2·7[?]) 52

דּוּד 7 basket, pot (1·7) 188

צִבּוּר 8 heap (1·1) 840

קָשַׁר 9 to conspire (9·36·44) 905

אֵפוֹא 10 then (1·15) 66

בִּלְתִּי 11 not, without (1·24) 116

שָׂרִיד survivor (1·28) 975

גְּבִירָה 13 queen mother, queen (2·15) 150

מֶרְכָּבָה 15 chariot (5·44) 939

קִנְאָה 16 zeal (2·43) 888

עָקְבָה 19 insidiousness (1·1) 784

עֲצָרָה 20 assembly (1·11) 783

לָאֶשֶׁר 22 to the one (1·38) 81

מֶלְתָּחָה wardrobe (1·1) 547

לְבוּשׁ raiment (1·31) 528

מַלְבּוּשׁ attire (1·8) 528

חפשׂ 23 to search through, search (1·8·23) 344

פֹּה here, hither (8·44) 805

רָץ 25 runner (8·25) 930

שָׁלִישׁ adjutant, officer (7·16) 1026

מַצֵּבָה 26 pillar (6·35) 663

נָתַץ 27 to pull down (8·31·42) 683

מַצֵּבָה pillar (6·35) 663

מַחֲרָאָה cesspool (1·1) 1123 n. 351a

חֵטְא 29 sin (2·33) 307

עֵגֶל calf (2·35) 722

הֵטִיב 30 to do well (1·3·20) 373

קָצָה 32 to cut off (1·2·5) 891

Chapter 11

גנב 2 to steal (1·30·39) 170

מֵינֶקֶת nurse (1·5) 413

חֶדֶר room, chamber (3·37) 293

מִטָּה bed (7·29) 641

התחבא 3 to hide oneself, draw back (1·10·34) 285

רָץ 4 runner (8·25) 930

רָץ 6 runner (8·25) 930

מַסָּח	defense [dub.] (1·1) 587		בֹּנֶה	builder (2·9[?]) 124
הִקִּיף	8 to surround (2·16·17) 668		גֹּדֵר	13 masons, wall builders (2·3[?]) 154
שְׂדֵרָה	rows, ranks (2·4) 690		חֹצֵב	hewer (1·8[?]) 345
חֲנִית	10 spear (1·46) 333		מַחְצֵב	hewing (2·3) 345
שֶׁלֶט	perh. shield (1·7) 1020		בֶּדֶק	fissure, rent, breach (8·10) 96
רָץ	11 runner (8·25) 930		חָזְקָה	perh. repairing (1·6[?]) 306
שְׂמֹאלִי	left, on the left (1·9) 970		סַף	14 bowl (1·6) 706
נֵזֶר	12 crown (1·24) 634		מְזַמֶּרֶת	snuffers (1·5) 275
רָץ	13 runner (8·25) 930		מִזְרָק	basin (3·32) 284
חֲצֹצְרָה	14 clarion trumpet (3·29) 348		חֲצֹצְרָה	clarion trumpet (3·29) 348
שָׂמֵחַ	glad, joyful, merry (1·21) 970		אָשָׁם	17 guilt offering (1·46) 79
קֶשֶׁר	conspiracy (6·14) 905		קָשַׁר	21 to conspire (9·36·44) 905
שְׂדֵרָה	15 rows, ranks (2·4) 690		קֶשֶׁר	conspiracy (6·14) 905
מָבוֹא	16 entrance (2·23) 99			
נָתַץ	18 to pull down (8·31·42) 683			
צֶלֶם	image (1·17) 853			

Chapter 13

פְּקֻדָּה	overseer (1·32) 824
רָץ	19 runner (8·25) 930
שָׁקַט	20 to be quiet, undisturbed (1·31·41) 1052

Chapter 12

הורה	3 to instruct (3·45·45[?]) 434		לַחַץ	4 oppression (1·11) 537
עֵרֶךְ	estimate, valuation (2·33) 789		לָחַץ	to oppress (3·14·15) 537
מַכָּר	6 acquaintance (2·2) 648		מוֹשִׁיעַ	5 savior (1·27) 446
בֶּדֶק	fissure, rent, breach (8·10) 96		תְּמוֹל	yesterday; כת׳ שלשום = as formerly (1·23) 1069
בֶּדֶק	7 fissure, rent, breach (8·10) 96		שִׁלְשׁוֹם	three days ago (1·25) 1026
בֶּדֶק	8 fissure, rent, breach (8·10) 96		אֲשֵׁרָה	6 sacred tree or pole representing Canaanite goddess of fortune and happiness (11·40) 81
מַכָּר	acquaintance (2·2) 648		רַגְלִי	7 on foot (1·12) 920
אות	9 to consent, agree (1·4·4) 22		דוש	to tread, thresh (1·12·15) 190
בֶּדֶק	fissure, rent, breach (8·10) 96		חֳלִי	14 sickness (4·24) 318
נקב	10 to pierce (2·13·19) 666		חַלּוֹן	17 window (3·30) 319
חֹר	hole (1·7) 359		קֶדֶם	eastward (1·26) 870
סַף	threshold (4·25) 706		יָרָה	to shoot (1·13·25[?]) 434
צוּר	11 to confine, secure (8·31·31) 848		הורה	to shoot (2·11·25[?]) 434
מָנָה	to count (1·12·28) 584		תְּשׁוּעָה	deliverance (3·34) 448
תכן	12 to be measured out (1·1·18) 1067		קָצַף	19 to be angry (2·28·34) 893
חָרָשׁ	artificer, engraver (4·38) 360		גְּדוּד	20 band, troop (8·33) 151
			גְּדוּד	21 band, troop (8·33) 151
			לָחַץ	22 to oppress (3·14·15) 537
			רִחַם	23 to have compassion (1·41·46) 933

Chapter 14

חָטָא   6 sin (2·33) 307

גַּיְא   7 valley (3·48) 161

מֶלַח   salt (3·28) 571

חוֹחַ   9 brier, bramble (2·11[?]) 296

רָמַס   to trample (4·17·18) 942

התגרה   10 to engage in strife (1·11·14) 173

נָגַף   12 to be smitten (1·23·48) 619

פָּרַץ   13 to make a breach (2·46·49) 829

פִּנָּה   corner (1·30) 819

תַּעֲרוּבָה   14 pledge; בני הת׳ = hostage (1·2) 787

קָשַׁר   19 to conspire (9·36·44) 905

קֶשֶׁר   conspiracy (6·14) 905

עֳנִי   26 affliction (1·36) 777

מָרָה   to be rebellious (1·21·43) 598

אֶפֶס   [there is] no, i.e., an end of (2·43) 67

עָצַר   to restrain, retain (4·36·46) 783

עֹזֵר   help (1·19[?]) 740

מָחָה   27 to blot out (4·21·33) 562

Chapter 15

מְצֹרָע   5 leprous (6·15) 863

חָפְשִׁית   freedom, separateness (1·2) 345

קָשַׁר   10 to conspire (9·36·44) 905

קָבָל   [cs. קְבָל] before [dub.] (1·2[?]) 867

יֶרַח   13 month (1·12) 437

קֶשֶׁר   15 conspiracy (6·14) 905

קָשַׁר   to conspire (9·36·44) 905

הָרָה   16 pregnant (2·15[?]) 247

קָשַׁר   25 to conspire (9·36·44) 905

שָׁלִישׁ   adjutant, officer (7·16) 1026

אַרְמוֹן   citadel, stronghold (1·33) 74

קָשַׁר   30 to conspire (9·36·44) 905

קֶשֶׁר   conspiracy (6·14) 905

Chapter 16

רַעֲנָן   4 luxuriant, fresh (2·19) 947

צוּר   5 to shut in, besiege (8·31·31) 848

נָשַׁל   6 to clear out entirely (1·1·7) 675

שֹׁחַד   8 bribe (1·23) 1005

דְּמוּת   10 likeness (1·25) 198

תַּבְנִית   pattern (1·20) 125

הִסִּיךְ   13 to pour out (1·13·24[?]) 650

זָרַק   to throw, scatter abundantly (2·32·34) 284

מִבֵּין   14 from between (2·21) 107

יָרֵךְ   side (1·34) 437

זָרַק   15 to throw, scatter abundantly (2·32·34) 284

בִּקֵּר   to consider, seek, inquire (1·7·7) 133

קָצַץ   17 to cut in pieces (3·9·14) 893

מִסְגֶּרֶת   border (1·17) 689

מְכוֹנָה   base (3·25) 467

כִּיּוֹר   basin (1·23) 468

מַרְצֶפֶת   pavement (1·1) 954

מוּסָךְ   18 architectural term of some covered structure (1·1) 697

מָבוֹא   entrance (2·23) 99

חִיצוֹן   outer, external (1·25) 300

Chapter 17

קֶשֶׁר   4 conspiracy (6·14) 905

עָצַר   to shut up (4·36·46) 783

כֶּלֶא   confinement (3·10) 476

צוּר   5 to shut in, besiege (8·31·31) 848

חָפָא   9 to do secretly (1·1·1) 341

מִגְדָּל   tower (3·49) 159

מִבְצָר   fortification (5·37) 131

מַצֵּבָה   10 pillar (6·35) 663

אֲשֵׁרָה   sacred tree or pole representing Canaanite goddess of fortune and happiness (11·40) 81

גָּבֹהַּ   high, exalted (1·41) 147

רַעֲנָן   luxuriant, fresh (2·19) 947

גִּלּוּל   12 idol (4·48) 165

204

הֵעִיד 13 to exhort solemnly, admonish (2·39·44) 729

חֹזֶה seer (1·17) 302

הִקְשָׁה 14 to make stiff, stubborn (2·21·28) 904

עֹרֶף neck (2·33) 791

הֵעִיד 15 to enjoin solemnly (2·39·44) 729

הבל to become vain (1·4·5) 211

מַסֵּכָה 16 molten image (1·25) 651

עֵגֶל calf (2·35) 722

אֲשֵׁרָה sacred tree or pole representing Canaanite goddess of fortune and happiness (11·40) 81

קסם 17 to practice divination (1·11·11) 890

קֶסֶם divination (1·11) 890

נחֵשׁ to practice divination, observe signs (2·9·9) 638

הִתְאַנַּף 18 to be angry (1·6·14) 60

שֹׁסֶה 20 plunderers, spoilers (1·7) 1042

יַדָּא 21 K, יַדַּח Q, הִדִּיחַ to thrust away (1·27·43) 623

חֲטָאָה sin (1·8) 308

תְּחִלָּה 25 beginning (1·22) 321

אֲרִי lion (2·36) 71

אֲרִי 26 lion (2·36) 71

הורה 27 to teach (3·45·45[?]) 434

הורה 28 to teach (3·45·45[?]) 434

קָצֶה 32 whole, מקצותם = from the whole of them, i.e., from among them (1·7) 892

פָּסִיל 41 idol, image (1·23) 820

Chapter 18

מַצֵּבָה 4 pillar (6·35) 663

אֲשֵׁרָה sacred tree or pole representing Canaanite goddess of fortune and happiness (11·40) 81

כִּתַּת to crush (1·5·17) 510

נָחָשׁ serpent (1·31) 638

מָרַד 7 to rebel (4·25·25) 597

מִגְדָּל 8 tower (3·49) 154

מִבְצָר fortification (5·37) 131

צוּר 9 to shut in, besiege (8·31·31) 848

הנחה 11 to lead, guide (1·26·40) 634

בָּצוּר 13 fortified, made inaccessible (2·25[?]) 130

קִצֵּץ 16 to cut in pieces (3·9·14) 893

אֹמְנָה pillars, supporters of the door (1·1[?]) 52

צִפָּה to overlay, plate (1·44·46) 860

תַּרְתָּן 17 field marshal [title of Assyrian general] (1·2) 1077

כָּבֵד numerous (2·39) 458

תְּעָלָה conduit (2·9) 752

בְּרֵכָה pool, pond (2·17) 140

מְסִלָּה highway (1·27) 700

מַזְכִּיר 18 recorder (2·9) 271

בִּטָּחוֹן 19 trust (1·3) 105

מָרַד 20 to rebel (4·25·25) 597

מִשְׁעֶנֶת 21 staff (4·12) 1044

רצץ to crush (1·11·19) 954

נסמך to support oneself (1·6·48) 701

נקב to pierce (2·13·19) 666

התערב 23 to exchange pledges (1·2·17) 786

פֶּחָה 24 governor (1·28) 808

קָטָן small (4·47) 881

מִבַּלְעֲדֵי 25 apart from, without (1·12) 116

אֲרָמִית 26 in Aramaic (1·5) 74

יְהוּדִית in Jewish (2·6) 397

חֲרֵא 27 K, dung (2·3) 351 [צֹאָה Q, filth (1·5) 844]

שַׁיִן urine (1·2) 1010

יְהוּדִית 28 in Jewish (2·6) 397

הִשִּׁיא 29 to deceive (2·14·15) 674

תְּאֵנָה 31 fig, fig tree (2·39) 1061

דָּגָן 32 corn, grain (1·40) 186

תִּירוֹשׁ must, fresh or new wine (1·38) 440

זַיִת		olive tree, olive (2·38) 268
יִצְהָר		fresh oil, oil (1·23) 844
הֵסִית		to instigate (1·18·18) 694
אַיֵּה	34	where? (3·44) 32
הֶחֱרִישׁ	36	to be silent (1·38·46) 361
מַזְכִּיר	37	recorder (2·9) 271

Chapter 19

שַׂק	1	sackcloth (3·48) 974
שַׂק	2	sackcloth (3·48) 974
תּוֹכֵחָה	3	rebuke, correction (1·4) 407
נְאָצָה		contempt (1·2) 611
מַשְׁבֵּר		breach (1·3) 991
אוּלַי	4	perhaps (1·45) 19
חֵרֵף		to reproach (4·34·38) 357
גִּדֵּף	6	to revile, blaspheme (2·7·7) 154
שְׁמוּעָה	7	report (1·27) 1035
הִשִּׁיא	10	to deceive (2·14·15) 674
הֶחֱרִים	11	to destroy, devote to destruction (1·46·49) 355
אֵי	13	where? (2·39) 32
פָּקַח	16	to open (6·17·20) 824
חֵרֵף		to reproach (4·34·38) 357
אָמְנָם	17	verily, truly (1·9) 53
הֶחֱרִיב		to lay waste, make desolate (2·13·37[?]) 351
בּוּז	21	to despise (1·13·13) 100
לָעַג		to mock, deride (1·12·18) 541
בְּתוּלָה		virgin (1·50) 143
הֵנִיעַ		to shake (2·14·38) 631
חֵרֵף	22	to reproach (4·34·38) 357
גִּדֵּף		to blaspheme (2·7·7) 154
חֵרֵף	23	to reproach (4·34·38) 357
יַרְכָה		extreme parts (1·28) 438
קוֹמָה		height (3·45) 879
מִבְחוֹר		choice (2·2) 104
בְּרוֹשׁ		cypress, fir (1·20) 141
מָלוֹן		lodging place (1·8) 533

כַּרְמֶל		garden land; כ׳ יער = gardenlike forest (1·14[?]) 502
קוּר	24	to bore, dig (1·2·2) 881
הֶחֱרִיב		to dry up (2·13·37[?]) 351
יָצַר	25	to preordain, plan (1·41·44) 427
הִשָּׁאָה		[Inf. cs. = לַהְשׁוֹת] to cause to crash (1·2·6) 980
גַּל		heap, wave, billow (1·20) 164
נָצָה		to be fallen in ruins (1·4·5) 663
בָּצוּר		fortified, made inaccessible (2·25[?]) 131
קָצֵר	26	short (1·5) 894
עֵשֶׂב		herb (1·33) 793
יָרָק		green (1·8) 438
דֶּשֶׁא		grass (1·14) 206
חָצִיר		green grass, herbage (1·18[?]) 348
גָּג		roof (2·29) 150
שְׁדֵפָה		blighted or blasted thing (1·1) 995
קָמָה		standing grain, i.e., maturity (1·10) 879
הִתְרַגֵּז	27	to excite oneself [to rage] (2·4·41) 919
הִתְרַגֵּז	28	to excite oneself [to rage] (2·4·41) 919
שַׁאֲנָן		arrogance (1·11) 983
חָח		hook, ring (1·7) 296
מֶתֶג		bridle (1·5) 607
סָפִיחַ	29	growth from spilled kernels (1·4) 705
סָחִישׁ		grain that shoots up of itself in the second year (1·2) 695
קָצַר		to reap, harvest (1·24·24) 894
פְּלֵיטָה	30	escaped remnant (2·28) 812
שֹׁרֶשׁ		root (1·33) 1057
לְמַטָּה		downward (1·10) 641
לְמַעְלָה		upward (1·34) 751
פְּלֵיטָה	31	escaped remnant (2·28) 812
קִנְאָה		zeal (2·43) 888
הוֹרָה	32	to shoot (2·11·25[?]) 434

קִדֵּם   to meet, confront (1·24·26) 869

סֹלְלָה   a mound (1·11) 700

גָּנַן   34 to defend, surround (2·8·8) 170

פֶּגֶר   35 corpse, carcass (1·22) 803

Chapter 20

אָנָּה   3 ah, now! I [or we] beseech thee! (1·6) 58 (אָנָּא)

שָׁלֵם   complete, perfect (1·28) 1023

בְּכִי   weeping (1·30) 113

עִיר   4 K, חָצֵר Q, court 347

תִּיכוֹן   middle (1·12) 1064

נָגִיד   5 ruler (1·44) 617

דִּמְעָה   coll. tears [from eyes] (1·23) 199

גָּנַן   6 to defend (2·8·8) 170

דְּבֵלָה   7 pressed fig cake (1·5) 179

תְּאֵנָה   fig, fig tree (2·39) 1061

שְׁחִין   boil (1·13) 1006

מַעֲלָה   9 step (8·47[?]) 752

מַעֲלָה   10 step (8·47[?]) 752

אֲחֹרַנִּית   backwards (2·7) 30

מַעֲלָה   11 step (8·47[?]) 752

אֲחֹרַנִּית   backwards (2·7) 30

נְכֹת   13 treasure (1·2) 649

בֹּשֶׂם   spice, balsalm (1·30) 141

מֶמְשָׁלָה   realm (1·17) 606

מֵאַיִן   14 whence? from where? (3·48[?]) 32

אָצַר   17 to store up, treasure (1·3·5) 69

סָרִיס   18 eunuch (8·45) 710

בְּרֵכָה   20 pool, pond (2·17) 140

תְּעָלָה   conduit (2·9) 752

Chapter 21

אֲשֵׁרָה   3 sacred tree or pole representing Canaanite goddess of fortune and happiness (11·40) 81

עוֹנֵן   6 to practice soothsaying (1·10·11) 778

נָחֵשׁ   to practice divination (2·9·9) 638

אוֹב   necromancer (2·16) 15

יִדְּעֹנִי   familiar spirit (2·11) 396

פֶּסֶל   7 idol, image (1·31) 820

אֲשֵׁרָה   sacred tree or pole representing Canaanite goddess of fortune and happiness (11·40) 81

הֵנִיד   8 to cause to wander (1·3·26) 626

הִתְעָה   9 to cause to err, to mislead (1·21·49) 1073

גִּלּוּל   11 idol (4·48) 165

צָלַל   12 to tingle (1·4·4) 852

קַו   13 line (1·17) 876

מִשְׁקֹלֶת   leveling instrument (1·2) 1054

מָחָה   to wipe (4·21·33) 562

צַלַּחַת   dish (1·4) 852

נָטַשׁ   14 to abandon (1·33·40) 643

בַּז   spoil, plunder (1·27) 103

מְשִׁסָּה   plunder (1·6) 1042

נָקִי   16 innocent (3·43) 667

גַּן   18 garden (4·41) 171

גִּלּוּל   21 idol (4·48) 165

קָשַׁר   23 to conspire (9·36·44) 905

קָשַׁר   24 to conspire (9·36·44) 905

קְבֻרָה   26 grave (3·14) 869

גַּן   garden (4·41) 171

Chapter 22

סַף   4 threshold (4·25) 706

בֶּדֶק   5 fissure, rent, breach (8·10) 96

חָרָשׁ   6 engraver, artificer (4·38) 360

גֹּדֵר   masons, wall builders (2·3[?]) 154

מַחְצֵב   hewing (2·3) 345

הִתִּיךְ   9 to pour out (1·5·21) 677

נוּצַת   13 to be kindled (2·6·27) 428

נְבִיאָה   14 prophetess (1·6) 612

מִשְׁנֶה   second quarter, district (3·35) 1041

נוּצַת   17 to be kindled (2·6·27) 428

כבה to be quenched (1·14·24) 459

רכך 19 to be softened, penitent (1·6·8) 939

נִכְנַע to humble oneself (1·25·36) 488

שַׁמָּה horror, dismay (1·39) 1031

קְלָלָה curse (1·33) 887

Chapter 23

עֵדָה 3 testimony (1·32) 730

מִשְׁנֶה 4 second (3·35) 1041

סַף threshold (4·25) 706

אֲשֵׁרָה sacred tree or pole representing Canaanite goddess of fortune and happiness (11·40) 81

שְׁדֵמָה field (1·6) 995

כמר 5 priest (1·3) 485

מֵסַב that which surrounds (1·5) 687

יָרֵחַ moon (1·27) 437

מַזָּלוֹת constellations (1·1) 561

אֲשֵׁרָה 6 sacred tree or pole representing Canaanite goddess of fortune and happiness (11·40) 81

הדקיק to pulverize (2·8·13) 200

נָתַץ 7 to pull down (8·31·42) 683

קָדֵשׁ temple prostitute [male] (1·11) 873

ארג to weave (1·3·3) 70

אֲשֵׁרָה sacred tree or pole representing Canaanite goddess of fortune and happiness (11·40) 81

נָתַץ 8 to pull down (8·31·42) 683

גַּיְא 10 valley (3·48) 161

לִשְׁכָּה 11 room, chamber (1·47) 545

סָרִיס eunuch (8·45) 710

פַּרְוָרִים structure (colonnade[?]) attached to west side of Solomon's temple (1·3) 826

מֶרְכָּבָה chariot (5·44) 939

גָּג 12 roof (2·29) 150

עֲלִיָּה roof chamber (4·20) 751

נָתַץ to pull down (8·31·42) 683

מַשְׁחִית 13 corruption (1·19) 1008

שִׁקֻץ detested thing (3·28) 1055

מַצֵּבָה 14 pillar (6·35) 663

אֲשֵׁרָה sacred tree or pole representing Canaanite goddess of fortune and happiness (11·40) 81

נָתַץ 15 to pull down (8·31·42) 683

הֵדַק to pulverize (2·8·13) 200

אֲשֵׁרָה sacred tree or pole representing Canaanite goddess of fortune and happiness (11·40) 81

צִיּוּן 17 signpost, monument (1·3) 846

הַלָּז this (2·7) 229

הֵנִיעַ 18 to shake (2·14·38) 631

פֶּסַח 21 passover (3·49) 820

פֶּסַח 22 passover (3·49) 820

פֶּסַח 23 passover (3·49) 820

אוֹב 24 necromancer (2·16) 15

יִדְּעֹנִי familiar spirit (2·11) 396

תְּרָפִים idol (1·15) 1076

גִּלּוּל idol (4·48) 165

שִׁקֻץ detested thing (3·28) 1055

חָרוֹן 26 [burning of] anger (1·41) 354

כַּעַס vexation, anger (1·25[?]) 495

קְבֻרָה 30 grave (3·14) 869

עֹנֶשׁ 33 indemnity, fine (1·2) 778

עֵרֶךְ 35 estimate, valuation (2·33) 789

נגשׂ to exact (1·4·7) 620

Chapter 24

מָרַד 1 to rebel (4·25·25) 597

גְּדוּד 2 band, troop (8·33) 151

נָקִי 4 innocent (3·43) 667

סלח to forgive (3·33·46) 699

מָצוֹר 10 siege (2·25) 848

צור 11 to shut in, besiege (8·31·31) 848

סָרִיס 12 eunuch (8·45) 710

208

קָצַץ 13 to cut in pieces (3·9·14) 893

חָרָשׁ 14 engraver, artificer (4·38) 360

מַסְגֵּר smiths (2·7) 689

זוּלָה except, besides (1·16) 265

דַּלָּה poor, weak, helpless one (2·5) 195

סָרִיס 15 eunuch (8·45) 710

אוּלַי K, אילי Q, leading man (1·1) 17

גּוֹלָה exiles, exile (2·42) 163

חָרָשׁ 16 engraver, artificer (4·38) 360

מַסְגֵּר smiths (2·7) 689

גּוֹלָה exiles, exile (2·42) 163

מָרַד 20 to rebel (4·25·25) 597

Chapter 25

עָשׂוֹר 1 tenth day [of month] (1·15) 797

דָּיֵק bulwark, siege wall (1·6) 189

מָצוֹר 2 siege (2·25) 848

גַּן 4 garden (4·41) 171

הִשִּׂיג 5 to overtake (1·49·49) 673

עִוֵּר 7 to blind (1·5·5) 734

טַבָּח 8 guardsman (7·32) 371

נָתַץ 10 to pull down (8·31·42) 683

טַבָּח guardsman (7·32) 371

טַבָּח 11 guardsman (7·32) 371

דַּלָּה 12 poor, weak, helpless one (2·5) 195

טַבָּח guardsman (7·32) 371

כרם vinedresser (1·5) 501

יגב to be a husbandman (1·2·2) 387

מְכוֹנָה 13 base stand (3·25) 467

סִיר 14 pot (6·29) 696

יָע shovel (1·9) 418

מְזַמֶּרֶת snuffers (2·5) 275

מַחְתָּה 15 fire pan (1·21) 367

מִזְרָק basin (2·32) 284

טַבָּח guardsman (7·32) 371

מְכוֹנָה 16 base, stand (3·25) 467

מִשְׁקָל weight (1·48) 1054

קוֹמָה 17 height (3·45) 879

כֹּתֶרֶת capital of pillar (3·23) 509

שְׂבָכָה lattice work, network (3·16) 959

רִמּוֹן pomegranate (1·32) 941

טַבָּח 18 guardsman (7·32) 371

מִשְׁנֶה second (3·35) 1041

סַף threshold (4·25) 706

סָרִיס 19 eunuch (8·45) 710

פָּקִיד commissioner, deputy, overseer (1·13) 824

הצבא to muster [dub.] (1·2·14) 838

טַבָּח 20 guardsman (7·32) 371

מְלוּכָה 25 royalty (1·24) 574

גָּלוּת 27 exile, exiles (1·15) 163

כֶּלֶא imprisonment (3·10) 476

שָׁנָה 29 to change, alter (1·9·26) 1039

כֶּלֶא imprisonment (3·10) 476

אֲרֻחָה 30 meal, allowance (2·6) 73

ISAIAH

Chapter 1

חָזוֹן	1 vision (2 · 35) 302
הַאֲזִין	2 to give ear, listen (8 · 41 · 41) 24
פָּשַׁע	to rebel (9 · 40 · 41) 833
קֹנֶה	3 owner (2 · 7) 888 קנה
אֵבוּס	crib (1 · 3) 7
כָּבֵד	4 heavy (3 · 40) 458
מֵרַע	evildoer (4 · 18) 949
נָאֵץ	to spurn (3 · 15 · 24) 610
נָזוֹר	to be estranged (1 · 2 · 6[?]) 266
אָחוֹר	backwards (9 · 41) 30
סָרָה	5 apostasy (3 · 7[?]) 694
חֳלִי	sickness (4 · 24) 318
דַּוָּי	faint (1 · 3) 188
מְתֹם	6 soundness (1 · 4) 1071
פֶּצַע	bruise, wound (1 · 8) 822
חַבּוּרָה	stripe, blow (2 · 7) 289
מַכָּה	wound (5 · 48) 646
טָרִי	fresh (1 · 2) 382
זוּר	to press out (1 · 1 · 1[?]) 266 III. זור
חֻבַּשׁ	to be bound up (1 · 2 · 32) 289
רֻכְּךְ	to be softened (1 · 1 · 8) 939
לְנֶגֶד	7 in front of, before (1 · 32) 617
מַהְפֵּכָה	overthrow (2 · 6) 246
סֻכָּה	8 booth (2 · 31) 697
מְלוּנָה	hut (2 · 2) 534
מִקְשָׁה	field of cucumbers (1 · 2) 903
לוּלֵי	9 unless (1 · 10) 530
שָׂרִיד	survivor (1 · 28) 975
דָּמָה	to be like (2 · 13 · 27) 197
קָצִין	10 ruler (4 · 12) 892
הַאֲזִין	to give ear, listen (8 · 41 · 41) 24
מְרִיא	11 fatling (2 · 8) 597
עַתּוּד	he-goat (3 · 29) 800
רָמַס	12 to trample (4 · 17 · 18) 942
מִקְרָא	13 convocation (2 · 22) 896
עֲצָרָה	assembly (1 · 11) 783

טֹרַח	14 burden (1 · 2) 382
נִלְאָה	to be weary (3 · 10 · 19) 521
הֶעְלִים	15 to hide, conceal (1 · 11 · 29) 761
הִתְזַכָּה	16 to make oneself clean (1 · 1 · 8) 269
רֹעַ	evil, badness (1 · 19) 947
מַעֲלָל	practice (3 · 41) 760
מִנֶּגֶד	from, from before (1 · 26) 617
אִשֵּׁר	17 to set right (3 · 5 · 7) 80
חָמוֹץ	the ruthless [coll.] (1 · 1) 330
יָתוֹם	orphan (4 · 42) 450
חֵטְא	18 sin, guilt of sin (4 · 33) 307
שָׁנִי	scarlet (1 · 42) 1040
שֶׁלֶג	snow (2 · 20) 1017
הִלְבִּין	to grow white (1 · 4 · 5) 526
הֶאְדִּים	to emit [show] redness (1 · 1 · 10) 10
תּוֹלָע	scarlet stuff (1 · 2) 1068
צֶמֶר	wool (2 · 16) 856
טוּב	19 good things, produce; goods (3 · 32) 375
מֵאֵן	20 to refuse (2 · 45 · 45) 549
מָרָה	to be stubborn (3 · 21 · 43) 598
אֵיכָה	21 how! (1 · 18) 32
זוֹנָה	harlot (3 · 33[?]) 275
קִרְיָה	town, city (10 · 30) 900
מְרַצֵּחַ	assassin (1 · 2) 954
סִיג	22 dross (2 · 8) 691
סֹבֶא	liquor (1 · 3) 685
מָהַל	to weaken (1 · 1 · 1) 554
סָרַר	23 to be stubborn (3 · 17 · 17) 710
חָבֵר	associate, companion (2 · 12) 288
גַּנָּב	thief (1 · 17) 170
שֹׁחַד	bribe (4 · 23) 1005
שַׁלְמֹן	reward, bribe (1 · 1) 1024
יָתוֹם	orphan (4 · 42) 450
אָבִיר	24 strong [one] (3 · 6) 7
נִקַּם	to avenge oneself (1 · 12 · 34) 667
צָרַף	25 to smelt away (3 · 19 · 22) 864
בֹּר	lye (1 · 7) 141
סִיג	dross (2 · 8) 691
בְּדִיל	alloy, tin, dross (1 · 1[?]) 95

יוֹעֵץ 26 counselor (5 · 22) 419

תְּחִלָּה beginning (1 · 22) 321

קִרְיָה town, city (10 · 30) 900

שֶׁבֶר 28 breaking (9 · 45) 991

פֶּשַׁע to transgress, rebel (9 · 40 · 41) 833

חַטָּא sinners (3 · 19) 308

אַיִל 29 terebinth [a deciduous tree] (3 · 4) 18

חָמַד to desire, take pleasure in (3 · 16 · 21) 326

חפר to be ashamed (2 · 13 · 17) 344

גַּנָּה garden (5 · 16) 171

אֵלָה 30 terebinth [a deciduous tree] (2 · 17) 18

נָבֵל to wither, fall (11 · 21 · 25) 615

עָלֶה leaf, leafage (3 · 18) 750

גַּנָּה garden (5 · 16) 171

חָסֹן 31 strong (1 · 2) 340

נִיצוֹץ spark (1 · 1) 665

נְעֹרֶת tow [fiber of flax, hemp, or jute] (1 · 2) 654

פֹּעַל work, thing made (6 · 37) 821

כבה to extinguish (2 · 10 · 24) 459

Chapter 2

נהר 2 to stream (1 · 3[?] · 3[?]) 625

הורה 3 to teach (4 · 45[?] · 45[?]) 434

כָּתַּת 4 to hammer (1 · 5 · 17) 510

אֵת cutting instrument of iron, usu. plowshare (1 · 5) 88

חֲנִית spear (1 · 46) 333

מַזְמֵרָה pruning knife (2 · 4) 275

נָטַשׁ 6 to abandon (2 · 33 · 40) 643

עוֹנֵן to practice soothsaying (2 · 10 · 11) 778

נָכְרִי foreigner (2 · 45) 648

הִשְׂפִּיק to cause to clap (1 · 1 · 2[?]) 706 ספק

קָצֶה 7 end (2 · 5) 892

מֶרְכָּבָה chariot (3 · 44) 939

אֱלִיל 8 worthlessness, worthless gods, idols (10 · 20) 47

לַאֲשֶׁר that which (4 · 38) 81 אֲשֶׁר 4.c.

אֶצְבַּע finger (4 · 31) 840

נשחח 9 to be humbled (3 · 4 · 18[?]) 1005

שָׁפֵל to become low, be humiliated (10 · 11 · 30) 1050

נטמן 10 to hide oneself (1 · 1 · 31) 380

פַּחַד dread (5 · 49) 808

הָדָר splendor, majesty (7 · 30) 214

גָּאוֹן exaltation, majesty (12 · 49) 144

גַּבְהוּת 11 haughtiness (2 · 2) 147

שָׁפֵל to become low, be humiliated (10 · 11 · 30) 1050

שַׁח to be humbled (3 · 12 · 18[?]) 1005

רוּם haughtiness, height (3 · 6) 927

נִשְׂגָּב to be exalted (6 · 10 · 20) 960

לְבַדּוֹ alone (2 · 36) 94

גֵּאֶה 12 proud (1 · 8) 144

רָם high, exalted (7 · 31[?]) 926 רום

שָׁפֵל to become low, be humiliated (10 · 11 · 30) 1050

רָם 13 high, exalted (7 · 31[?]) 926 רום

אַלּוֹן oak (3 · 9) 47

רָם 14 high, exalted (7 · 31[?]) 926 רום

מִגְדָּל 15 tower (4 · 49) 154

גָּבֹהַּ tall, high, lofty (6 · 41) 147

בָּצוּר cut off, made inaccessible; i.e., fortified (5 · 25[?]) 130 בצר

אֳנִיָּה 16 ship (5 · 31) 58

שְׂכִיָּה standard, ship, watchtower [very dub.] (1 · 1) 967

חֶמְדָּה desire, delight (1 · 16) 326

שַׁח 17 to be humbled (3 · 12 · 18[?]) 1005 שחח

גַּבְהוּת haughtiness (2 · 2) 147

שָׁפֵל to become low, be humiliated (10 · 11 · 30) 1050

רוּם haughtiness, height (3 · 6) 927

211

נִשְׂגַּב		to be exalted (6 · 10 · 20) 960
לְבַדּוֹ		alone (2 · 36) 94
אֱלִיל	18	worthlessness, worthless idols (10 · 20) 47
כָּלִיל		entirety (1 · 15) 483
חָלַף		to vanish, pass away (4 · 14 · 26) 322
מְעָרָה	19	cave (1 · 40) 792
מְחִלָּה		hole (1 · 1) 320
פַּחַד		dread (5 · 49) 808
הָדָר		splendor, majesty (7 · 30) 214
גָּאוֹן		exaltation, majesty (12 · 49) 144
ערץ		to cause to tremble (3 · 11 · 14) 791
אֱלִיל	20	worthlessness, idols (10 · 20) 47
חָפַר		to dig, search for (1 · 23 · 23) 343
חֲפֹר פֵּרוֹת → חֲפַרְפָּרוֹת		mole (1 · 1) 344
עֲטַלֵּף		bat (1 · 3) 742
נְקָרָה	21	hole, crevice (1 · 2) 669
סָעִיף		cleft (2[?] · 4[?]) 703
פַּחַד		dread (5 · 49) 808
הָדָר		splendor, majesty (7 · 30) 214
גָּאוֹן		exaltation, majesty (12 · 49) 144
ערץ		to cause to tremble (3 · 11 · 14) 791
נְשָׁמָה	22	breath (4 · 24) 675
בַּמֶּה		in what (1 · 29) 552

Chapter 3

מַשְׁעֵן	1	support (1 · 1) 1044
מִשְׁעֵנָה		staff (2 · 12) 1044
מַשְׁעָן		support, staff (2 · 4) 1044
קֹסֵם	2	diviner (1 · 9[?]) 890 קסם
יוֹעֵץ	3	counselor (5 · 22) 419
חָרָשׁ		magic art, or perh. magic drug (1 · 1) 361
נָבוֹן		intelligent, discerning (3 · 21) 106
לַחַשׁ		serpent charming (3 · 5) 538
תַּעֲלוּלִים	4	caprice (2 · 2) 760
נָגַשׂ	5	to tyrannize over each other (2 · 3 · 7) 620

רהב		to storm against (1 · 2 · 4) 923
נְקָלָה		to be lightly esteemed (2 · 5 · 6) 885
שִׂמְלָה	6	wrapper, mantle (4 · 29) 971
קָצִין		dictator (4 · 12) 892
מַכְשֵׁלָה		overthrown mass (1 · 2) 506
חֹבֵשׁ	7	one who binds (1 · 1[?]) 289
שִׂמְלָה		wrapper, mantle (4 · 29) 971
קָצִין		dictator (4 · 12) 892
מַעֲלָל	8	practice (3 · 41) 760
המרה		to show disobedience, rebelliousness (1 · 22 · 43) 598
הַכָּרָה	9	a look, expression (1 · 1) 648
כָּחֵד		to hide (1 · 15 · 30) 470
אוֹי		Woe! Alas! (4 · 25) 17
גָּמַל		to deal out to, to do (6 · 34 · 37) 168
מַעֲלָל	10	practice (3 · 41) 760
אוֹי	11	Woe! Alas! (4 · 25) 17
גְּמוּל		dealing, recompense, benefit (5 · 19) 168
נֹגֵשׂ	12	ruler (5 · 15) 620
עוֹלֵל		to play the child (1 · 1 · 1) 760
אשׁר		to lead on (3 · 5 · 7) 80
התעה		to mislead (6 · 21 · 50) 1073
בלע		to swallow up, engulf (2 · 3 · 6[?]) 118
דִּין	13	to minister judgment (1 · 23 · 24) 192
בֵּעֵר	14	to consume, devour (4 · 26 · 28[?]) 129
גְּזֵלָה		plunder, spoil (1 · 6) 160
דָּכָא	15	to crush (2 · 11 · 18) 194
טחן		to grind (2 · 7 · 7) 377
גָּבַהּ	16	to be haughty, be high (5 · 24 · 34) 146
גָּרוֹן		neck, throat (2 · 8) 173
שָׁקַר		to ogle, to eye (1 · 1 · 1) 974
טפף		to take quick little steps (1 · 1 · 1) 381
עכס		to shake bangles (1 · 1 · 1) 747
שִׂפַּח	17	to smite with a scab (1 · 1 · 1) 705
קָדְקֹד		crown of head, scalp (1 · 11) 869

פֹּת		secret parts [dub.] (1 · 1) 834
עֶרְוָה		to lay bare (2 · 9 · 15) 788
תִּפְאֶרֶת	18	beauty, finery (18 · 50) 802
עֶכֶס		anklet, bangle (1 · 2) 747
שָׁבִיס		front band (1 · 1) 987
שַׂהֲרֹן		crescent, moon [ornaments] (1 · 3) 962
נְטִיפָה	19	drop, pendant (1 · 2) 643
שֵׁרָה		bracelet (1 · 1) 1057
רְעָלָה		veil (1 · 1) 947
פְּאֵר	20	turban (3 · 7) 802
צְעָדָה		armlet (1 · 3) 857
קִשֻּׁרִים		bands, sashes (1 · 2) 905
לַחַשׁ		charms, amulets (3 · 5) 538
טַבַּעַת	21	signet ring (1 · 49) 371
נֶזֶם		ring, nose ring (1 · 17) 633
מַחֲלָצָה	22	robe of state (1 · 2) 323
מַעֲטָפָה		overtunic (1 · 1) 742
מִטְפַּחַת		cloak (1 · 2) 381
חָרִיט		bag, purse (1 · 2) 355
גִּלָּיוֹן	23	tablet, tablets of polished metal, mirrors [dub.] (2 · 2) 163
סָדִין		linen wrapper (1 · 4) 690
צָנִיף		turban (2 · 5) 857
רְדִיד		wide wrapper, large veil (1 · 2) 921
בֹּשֶׂם	24	perfume (2 · 30) 141
מַק		rottenness (2 · 2) 597
חֲגוֹרָה		loin covering, girdle, belt (1 · 5) 292
נִקְפָּה		encircling rope (1 · 1) 669
מִקְשֶׁה		artistic hair arrangement (1 · 1) 904
קָרְחָה		bald spot (3 · 11) 901
פְּתִיגִיל		rich robe [dub.] (1 · 1) 836
מַחֲגֹרֶת		a girdling (1 · 1) 292
שַׂק		sackcloth (8 · 48) 974
כִּי		burning, branding (1 · 1) 465
יֳפִי		beauty (2 · 19) 421
מַת	25	man, male (3 · 21) 607
אנה	26	to mourn (2 · 2 · 2) 58
אָבַל		to mourn (5 · 18 · 38) 5
נקה		to be cleaned out (1 · 23 · 37) 667

Chapter 4

שִׂמְלָה	1	clothes (4 · 29) 971
צֶמַח	2	sprouting, growth (2 · 12) 855
צְבִי		beauty (7 · 18) 840
גָּאוֹן		majesty, exaltation (12 · 49) 144
תִּפְאֶרֶת		glory (18 · 50) 802
פְּלֵיטָה		escaped remnant (5 · 28) 812
צֹאָה	4	filth (3 · 5) 844
הֵדִיחַ		to cleanse by washing (1 · 4 · 4) 188
בָּעֵר		to consume, devour (4 · 26 · 28[?]) 129
בָּרָא	5	to create, shape (20 · 38 · 48) 135
מָכוֹן		established place (2 · 17) 467
מִקְרָא		convocation (2 · 22) 896
עָשָׁן		smoke (7 · 25) 798
נֹגַהּ		brightness (5 · 19) 618
לֶהָבָה		flame (5 · 19) 529
חֻפָּה		canopy, chamber (1 · 3) 342
סֻכָּה	6	booth (2 · 31) 697
חֹרֶב		parching heat (5 · 16) 351
מַחְסֶה		shelter (4 · 20) 340
מִסְתּוֹר		hiding place (1 · 1) 712
זֶרֶם		rain storm, flood of rain, downpour (7 · 9) 281
מָטָר		rain (3 · 38) 564

Chapter 5

יָדִיד	1	beloved (2 · 8) 391
שִׁירָה		song (2 · 13) 1010
עזק	2	to dig about (1 · 1 · 1) 740
סִקֵּל		to free from stones (2 · 4 · 22) 709
שֹׂרֵק		choice species of vine (1 · 2) 977
מִגְדָּל		tower (4 · 49) 154
יֶקֶב		wine vat (2 · 16) 428
חָצֵב		to hew out (4 · 14 · 17) 345
קוה		to wait (13 · 39 · 45) 875
עֵנָב		grape (2 · 19) 772
בְּאֻשִׁים		stinking or worthless things, wild grapes (2 · 2) 93

213

קַוֵּה 4 to wait (13 · 39 · 45) 875

עֵנָב grape (2 · 19) 772

בְּאֻשִׁים stinking or worthless things, wild grapes (2 · 2) 93

מְשׂוּכָה 5 hedge (1 · 1) 968

בָּעֵר to consume, devour, burn (4 · 26 · 28) 129

פָּרַץ to break down (2 · 46 · 49) 829

גָּדֵר wall, fence (1 · 13) 154

מִרְמָס trampling (4 · 7) 942

בָּתָה 6 end, destruction (1 · 1) 144

נִזְמַר to be pruned (1 · 1 · 3) 274

נֶגְדַּר to be hoed (2 · 2 · 2) 727

שָׁמִיר thorns (8 · 11) 1038

שַׁיִת thorn bushes (7 · 7) 1011

עָב dark cloud (7 · 30) 728

הִמְטִיר to send rain (1 · 16 · 17) 565

מָטָר rain (3 · 38) 564

נֶטַע 7 plantation (3 · 4) 642

שַׁעֲשׁוּעִים delight (1 · 9) 1044

קַוֵּה to wait (13 · 39 · 45) 875

מִשְׂפָּח bloodshed (1 · 1) 705

צְעָקָה cry of distress (1 · 21) 858

אֶפֶס 8 an end of (14 · 43) 67

שְׁמָּה 9 a waste (3 · 39) 1031

מֵאֵין without (6 · 48[?]) 34 אין 6.d.

צֶמֶד 10 square measure of land (3 · 15) 855

בַּת bath [liquid measure] = 40 liters (1 · 13) 144

חֹמֶר homer [dry measure] = 10 ephahs = 393.9 liters (1 · 13[?]) 330

אֵיפָה ephah [grain measure] (1 · 38) 35

שֵׁכָר 11 strong drink (8 · 23) 1016

אָחַר to tarry (2 · 15 · 17) 29

נֶשֶׁף twilight (3 · 12) 676

הִדְלִיק to inflame (1 · 2 · 9) 196

כִּנּוֹר 12 lyre (5 · 41) 490

נֶבֶל harp (2 · 27) 614

תֹּף timbrel (3 · 17) 1074

חָלִיל flute, pipe (2 · 6) 319

מִשְׁתֶּה feast (3 · 45) 1059

פֹּעַל deed (6 · 37) 821

מִבְּלִי 13 from want of; here = unawares, suddenly (1 · 25) 115

מַת man, male (3 · 21) 607

צִחֵה parched (1 · 1) 850

צָמָא thirst (3 · 17) 854

הִרְחִיב 14 to enlarge (5 · 21 · 25) 931

פָּעַר to open wide (1 · 4 · 4) 822

לִבְלִי without (1 · 3) 115

הָדָר splendor (7 · 30) 214

שָׁאוֹן uproar (8 · 18) 981

עָלֵז jubilant (1 · 1) 759

נִשְׁחַח 15 to be humbled (3 · 4 · 18[?]) 1005

שָׁפֵל to be humiliated (10 · 11 · 15) 1050

גָּבֹהַּ haughty (6 · 41) 147

גָּבַהּ 16 to be exalted, be high (5 · 24 · 34) 146

דֹּבֶר 17 pasture (1 · 2) 184

חָרְבָּה waste, waste place amid ruins (9 · 42) 352

מֵחַ fatling (1 · 2) 562

מָשַׁךְ 18 to draw (2 · 30 · 36) 604

חֶבֶל cord (3 · 49) 286

עֲבֹת rope (1 · 24) 721

עֲגָלָה cart rope (3 · 25) 722

חַטָּאָה sin, sinful thing (1 · 2) 308

הֵחִישׁ 19 to hasten (3 · 6 · 21) 301

מַר 20 bitter, injurious, hurtful (6 · 38) 600

מָתוֹק sweet (2 · 12) 608

נָבוֹן 21 intelligent, discerning (3 · 21) 106 בין niph.

מָסַךְ 22 to mix (2 · 5 · 5) 587

שֵׁכָר strong drink (8 · 23) 1016

הַצְדִּיק 23 to declare righteous (3 · 12 · 41) 842

עֵקֶב because of (1 · 15) 784

שֹׁחַד bribe (4 · 23) 1005

קַשׁ 24 stubble, chaff (5 · 16) 905

חֲשַׁשׁ chaff (2 · 2) 366

לֶהָבָה flame (5 · 19) 529

רָפָה   to sink down (2 · 14 · 45) 951

שֹׁרֶשׁ   root (7 · 33) 1057

מַק   rottenness (2 · 2) 597

פֶּרַח   bud (2 · 17) 827

אָבָק   dust (2 · 6) 7

אִמְרָה   word[s] (5 · 30) 57

נָאֵץ   spurn (3 · 15 · 24) 610

רָגַז   25 to quake (6 · 30 · 41) 919

נְבֵלָה   corpse (2 · 48) 615

סוּחָה   offal (1 · 1) 691

מֶרְחֹק   26 at a distance (12 · 34) 935

נֵס   standard (10 · 21) 651

שָׁרַק   to hiss (2 · 12 · 12) 1056

מְהֵרָה   hastily, quickly; haste (2 · 20) 555

קַל   swift, swiftly (4 · 13) 886

עָיֵף   27 faint, weary (5 · 17) 746

נוּם   to be drowsy, to slumber (2 · 6 · 6) 630

יָשֵׁן   to sleep (1 · 15 · 16[?]) 445

אֵזוֹר   waistcloth, girdle (3 · 14) 25

חָלָץ   loins (3 · 10) 323

נִתַּק   to be torn apart (2 · 10 · 27) 683

שְׂרוֹךְ   [sandal] thong (1 · 2) 976

נַעַל   sandal (3 · 22) 653

שָׁנַן   28 to sharpen (1 · 7 · 9) 1041

פַּרְסָה   hoof (1 · 21) 828

צַר   flint (1 · 1) 866

גַּלְגַּל   wheel (2 · 11) 165

סוּפָה   storm wind (5 · 15) 693

שְׁאָגָה   29 roaring (1 · 7) 980

שָׁאַג   to roar (1 · 20 · 20) 980

לָבִיא   lioness (2 · 11) 522

כְּפִיר   young lion (3 · 31) 498

נהם   to growl (2 · 5 · 5) 625

טֶרֶף   prey (2 · 17) 383

הפליט   to bring into security (1 · 2 · 27) 812

נהם   30 to growl (2 · 5 · 5) 625

נְהָמָה   growling (1 · 2) 625

צַר   straits, distress (5[?] · 20[?]) 865

חָשַׁךְ   to be or grow dark (2 · 11 · 17) 364

עָרִיף   cloud (1 · 1) 791

Chapter 6

רָם   1 high, exalted (7 · 31[?]) 926   רום

שׁוּל   skirt [of robe] (1 · 11) 1002

שְׂרָפִים   2 seraphim (4[?] · 7[?]) 977

מִמַּעַל   with לְ = on the top of, above (2 · 29) 751   II מַעַל 1.b.

עוֹפֵף   to fly about (3 · 5 · 25) 733

מְלֹא   3 fullness, entire contents (5 · 38) 571

נוּעַ   4 to tremble (6 · 22 · 38) 631

אַמָּה   support, foundation [dub.] (1 · 1) 52

סַף   threshold (1 · 25) 706

עָשָׁן   smoke (7 · 25) 798

אוֹי   5 Alas! Woe! (4 · 25) 17

נִדְמָה   to be ruined, cut off, undone (3 · 12 · 16) 198

עוּף   6 to fly (4 · 18 · 25) 733

שְׂרָפִים   seraphim (4[?] · 7[?]) 977

רִצְפָּה   glowing stone (1 · 2) 954

מֶלְקָחַיִם   tongs (1 · 6) 544

הַשְׁמִין   10 to make fat (1 · 2 · 5) 1031

השע   to besmear (1 · 1 · 3) 1044

מָתַי   when? (1 · 42) 607

שָׁאָה   11 to crash into ruin (1 · 1 · 6) 980

מֵאֵין   without (6 · 48[?]) 34   אִין 6.d.

נִשְׁאָה   to be ruined (3 · 3 · 6) 980

רבב   12 to become great (4 · 23 · 24) 912

בָּעֵר   13 to consume, devour, burn (4 · 26 · 28[?]) 129

אֵלָה   terebinth [deciduous tree] (2 · 17) 18

אַלּוֹן   oak (3 · 9) 47

שַׁלֶּכֶת   felling [of tree] (1 · 1) 1021

מַצֶּבֶת   stump (2 · 2) 663

215

Chapter 7

נוּעַ	2 to tremble (6 · 22 · 38) 631
תְּעָלָה	3 conduit, trench (2 · 9) 752
בְּרֵכָה	pool (4 · 17) 140
מְסִלָּה	highway (9 · 27) 700
הִשָּׁקֵט	4 to show quietness (4 · 10 · 41) 1052
רכך	to be fearful (1 · 6 · 8) 939
זָנָב	end, stump (4 · 11) 275
אוּד	firebrand (1 · 3) 15
חֳרִי	burning (1 · 6) 354
עָשֵׁן	smoking (1 · 2) 798
הָקִיץ	6 to cause sickening dread (1[?]-1[?]-1[?]) 880
בְּעוֹד	8 within yet (3 · 20) 728 עוֹד 2.a.
הֶעְמִיק	11 to make deep (4 · 8 · 9) 770
שְׁאֹלָה	underworld (1 · 1) 982
הַגְבֵּהַּ	to make high, exalt (1 · 10 · 34) 146
לְמַעְלָה	upward (3 · 34) 751 מַעַל 2.c.
נִסָּה	12 to test (1 · 36 · 36) 650
הִלְאָה	13 to exhaust (2 · 6 · 19) 521
עַלְמָה	14 young woman (1 · 9) 761
הָרָה	pregnant (2 · 15) 248
חֶמְאָה	15 curd (3 · 10) 326
בְּטֶרֶם	16 before (7 · 39) 382
קוּץ	to feel a sickening dread (1 · 8 · 8 [?]) 880
שָׁרַק	18 to hiss (2 · 12 · 12) 1056
זְבוּב	fly (1 · 6) 256
דְּבוֹרָה	bee (1 · 4) 184
בַּתָּה	19 precipice, steep (1 · 1) 144
נָקִיק	cleft of rock (1 · 3) 669
נַעֲצוּץ	thorn bush (2 · 2) 654
נַהֲלֹל	pasture (1 · 1) 625
גִּלַּח	20 to shave off (1 · 18 · 23) 164
תַּעַר	razor (1 · 13) 789
שָׂכִיר	hired (3 · 18) 969
שֵׂעָר	hair (1 · 28) 972
זָקָן	beard (2 · 18) 278
ספה	to sweep away (2 · 8 · 18) 705

עֶגְלָה	21 heifer (1 · 12) 722
חָלָב	22 milk (4 · 44) 316
חֶמְאָה	curd (3 · 10) 326
שָׁמִיר	23 thorns (8 · 11) 1038
שַׁיִת	thorn bushes (7 · 7) 1011
שָׁמִיר	24 thorns (8 · 11) 1038
שַׁיִת	thorn bushes (7 · 7) 1011
מַעְדֵּר	25 hoe (1 · 1) 727
נעדר	to be hoed (2 · 2 · 2) 727
יִרְאָה	fear, terror (5 · 45) 432
שָׁמִיר	thorns (8 · 11) 1038
שַׁיִת	thorn bushes (7 · 7) 1011
מִשְׁלַח	place of letting loose (1 · 7) 1020
מִרְמָס	trampling place (4 · 7) 942
שֶׂה	a sheep [or goat] (4 · 45) 961

Chapter 8

גִּלָּיוֹן	1 tablet [for writing] (2 · 2) 163
חֶרֶט	stylus, graving tool (1 · 2) 354
אֱנוֹשׁ	men, man, mankind (8 · 42) 60
חָשׁ	to make haste (2 · 15 · 21) 301 חוש
בַּז	plunder, spoil (5 · 27) 103
הֵעִיד	2 to take as witness (1 · 39 · 44) 729
נְבִיאָה	3 prophetess (1 · 6) 612
הָרָה	to conceive, become pregnant (4 · 38 · 40) 247
חָשׁ	to make haste (2 · 15 · 21) 301 חוש
בַּז	plunder, spoil (5 · 27) 103
בְּטֶרֶם	4 before (7 · 38) 382
אַט	6 gentleness; with ל = gently (1 · 5) 31
מָשׂוֹשׂ	exultation (10 · 17) 965
עָצוּם	7 mighty (3 · 31) 783
אָפִיק	channel, stream bed (1 · 18) 67
גָּדָה	bank of river (1 · 4) 152
חָלַף	8 to move or sweep on, pass on quickly (4 · 14 · 26) 322
שָׁטַף	to overflow (9 · 28 · 31) 1009
צַוָּאר	neck (4 · 41) 848

216

מֵטָה outspreading (1 · 1) 642

מְלֹא fullness, entire contents (5 · 38) 571

הַאֲזִין 9 to give ear, hear, listen (8 · 41 · 41) 24

מֶרְחָק distant place (7 · 18) 935

הִתְאַזַּר to gird oneself (2 · 3 · 16) 25

עוּץ 10 to plan (1 · 2 · 2) 734

הוּפַר to be frustrated (1 · 3 · 45) 830

חֶזְקָה 11 strength, force (1 · 4) 305

יַסֵּר to discipline (1 · 30 · 41) 415

קֶשֶׁר 12 conspiracy (2 · 16) 905

מוֹרָא object of reverence (2 · 12) 432

הֶעֱרִיץ to treat with awe (2 · 2 · 14) 791

מוֹרָא 13 object of reverence (2 · 12) 432

מַעֲרִיץ awe inspirer (1 · 1) 793 עָרַץ

נֶגֶף 14 striking (1 · 7) 620

מִכְשׁוֹל stumbling (2 · 14) 506

פַּח bird trap (3 · 25) 809

מוֹקֵשׁ lure (1 · 27) 430

נוֹקַשׁ 15 to be ensnared (2 · 4 · 8) 430

תְּעוּדָה 16 testimony (2 · 3) 730

חָתַם to seal up (3 · 23 · 27) 367

לִמֵּד taught (4 · 6) 541

חִכָּה 17 to await, wait for (3 · 13 · 14) 314

קִוָּה to wait for (13 · 39 · 45) 875

מוֹפֵת 18 sign [of future event] (2 · 36) 68

אוֹב 19 necromancer; i.e., medium (3 · 16) 15

יִדְּעֹנִי familiar spirit (2 · 11) 396

צִפְצֵף to chirp, peep (4 · 4 · 4) 861

הֶהְגָּה to mutter; ptc. = one who makes mutterings (1 · 1 · 25) 211

תְּעוּדָה 20 testimony (2 · 3) 730

שַׁחַר dawn (3 · 23) 1007

נִקְשָׁה 21 to be hard pressed (1 · 1 · 28) 904

רָעֵב hungry (5 · 19) 944

רָעֵב to be hungry (5 · 12 · 14) 944

הִתְקַצַּף to put oneself in a rage (1 · 1 · 34) 893

לְמַעְלָה upward (3 · 34) 751 מַעַל 2.c.

חֲשֵׁכָה 22 darkness, distress (2 · 6) 365

מָעוּף gloom (1 · 1) 734

צוּקָה distress (2 · 3) 848

אֲפֵלָה darkness; fig. of calamity (3 · 10) 66

נִדָּח to be thrust (1 · 1 · 43) 623

מוּעָף 23 gloom (1 · 1) 734

לַאֲשֶׁר to whom (4 · 38) 81 אֲשֶׁר 4.c.

מוּצָק distress (1 · 3) 848

Chapter 9

צַלְמָוֶת 1 deep shadow, darkness (1 · 18) 853

נָגַהּ to shine (1 · 3 · 6) 618

קָצִיר 2 harvest, time of harvest (7 · 49) 894

גִּיל to rejoice (11 · 45 · 45) 162

עֹל 3 yoke (5 · 40) 760

סֵבֶל burden (3 · 3) 687

שְׁכֶם shoulder (5 · 22) 1014

נֹגֵשׂ oppressor (5 · 15) 620

סְאוֹן 4 sandal, boot of soldier (1 · 1) 684

סָאַן to tread, tramp (1 · 1 · 1) 684

רַעַשׁ shaking (2 · 17) 950

שִׂמְלָה wrapper, mantle (4 · 29) 971

גָּלַל to be rolled (1 · 1 · 17) 164

שְׂרֵפָה burning (2 · 13) 977

מַאֲכֹלֶת fuel (2 · 2) 38

מִשְׂרָה 5 rule, dominion (2 · 2) 976

שְׁכֶם shoulder (5 · 22) 1014

פֶּלֶא wonder (3 · 13) 810

יוֹעֵץ counselor (5 · 22) 419

עַד eternal, everlasting (8 · 48) 723 I & II עַד

מַרְבֶּה 6 increase (1 · 2) 916

מִשְׂרָה rule, dominion (2 · 2) 976

סָעַד to support (1 · 12 · 12) 703

קִנְאָה zeal (7 · 43) 888

גַּאֲוָה 8 pride, haughtiness (5 · 19) 144

גֹּדֶל greatness, pride, insolence [of heart] (2 · 14) 152

לְבֵנָה 9 brick (2 · 12) 527

גָּזִית hewing, hewn stones (1 · 11) 159

שִׁקְמָה ·sycamore tree (1 · 7) 1054

גָּדַע to be hewn down (1 · 1 · 22) 154

הֶחֱלִיף to substitute, cause to succeed (3 · 10 · 26) 322

שָׂגַב 10 to exalt (1 · 6 · 20) 960

סִכְסֵךְ to prick or spur on (2 · 2 · 4[?]) 968, 1127

מֵאָחוֹר 11 behind [= on the west] (1 · 2[?]) 30

זָנָב 13 tail (4 · 11) 275

כִּפָּה branch, frond (2 · 4[?]) 497

אַגְמוֹן rush, bulrush [used as metaph. of the lowly] (3 · 5) 8

הוֹרָה 14 to teach (4 · 45[?] · 45[?]) 434

זָנָב tail, end, stump (4 · 11) 275

אִשֵּׁר 15 to lead on (3 · 5 · 7) 80

הִתְעָה to mislead (6 · 21 · 50) 1073

אֻשַּׁר to be led on (1 · 1 · 7) 80

בֻּלַּע to be swallowed up (1 · 1 · 6) 118

בָּחוּר 16 young man (6 · 45) 104

יָתוֹם orphan (4 · 42) 450

רִחַם to have compassion (12 · 42 · 47) 933

חָנֵף profane, godless man (3 · 13) 338

מֵרַע evildoer (4 · 18) 949

נְבָלָה disgraceful folly (2 · 13) 615

רִשְׁעָה 17 wickedness (1 · 15) 958

שָׁמִיר thorns (8 · 11) 1038

שַׁיִת thorn bushes (7 · 7) 1011

יָצַת to kindle (2 · 4 · 27) 428

סְבַךְ thicket (2 · 3) 687

הִתְאַבֵּךְ to roll, roll up (1 · 1 · 1) 5

גֵּאוּת column, lifting up (5 · 8) 145

עָשָׁן smoke (7 · 25) 798

עֶבְרָה 18 fury (6 · 34) 720

נֶעְתַּם to be scorched, burned up [dub.] (1 · 1 · 1) 801

מַאֲכֹלֶת fuel (2 · 2) 38

חָמַל to spare, have compassion (22 · 40 · 40) 328

גָּזַר 19 to cut off (1 · 1 · 1[?]) 160

רָעֵב to be hungry (5 · 12 · 14) 944

Chapter 10

חָקַק 1 to engrave, enact, decree (4 · 8 · 11) 349

דִּין 2 cause, plea, judgment (1 · 19) 192

דַּל helpless, poor (5 · 48) 195

גָּזַל to seize, rob, tear away (1 · 29 · 30) 159

יָתוֹם orphan (4 · 42) 450

בָּזַז to spoil, plunder (7 · 37 · 41) 102

פְּקֻדָּה 3 visitation (3 · 32) 824

שׁוֹאָה devastation (2 · 12) 996

מֶרְחָק distance ממרחק = from afar (7 · 18) 935

עֶזְרָה help (4 · 26) 740

אָנָה whither? (1 · 39) 33 אָן

בִּלְתִּי 4 except (2 · 24) 116

כָּרַע to bow down (5 · 30 · 36) 502

אַסִּיר [coll.] prisoners (4 · 17[?]) 64

זַעַם 5 indignation (5 · 22) 276

חָנֵף 6 profane, godless (3 · 13) 338

עֶבְרָה fury (6 · 34) 720

שָׁלָל to plunder (1 · 13 · 15) 1021

בָּזַז to spoil, plunder (7 · 37 · 41) 102

בַּז booty, spoil (5 · 27) 103

מִרְמָס trampling (4 · 7) 942

חֹמֶר clay, mire (5 · 17) 330

דָּמָה 7 to think, intend (5 · 13 · 27) 197

אֱלִיל 10 idolatrous, worthlessness (10 · 20) 47

פָּסִיל idol (4 · 23) 820

אֱלִיל 11 pl. = worthless gods (10 · 20) 47

עָצָב idol (2 · 17) 781

בָּצַע 12 to finish, complete, cut off (2 · 6 · 16) 130

גֹּדֶל greatness, pride, insolence of heart (2 · 14) 152

תִּפְאֶרֶת glorying, boasting (18 · 50) 802

רוּם	loftiness, height; fig. of haughtiness (3 · 6) 927		שָׁטַף	to overflow (9 · 28 · 31) 1009
גְּבוּלָה	13 border, boundary (2 · 10) 148		כָּלָה	23 complete destruction (2 · 22) 428
עָתִיד	Q עָתוּד prepared; i.e., stores (1 · 1) 800		נֶחֱרָץ	ptc. = decisive (2 · 5 · 10) 358
שׁוֹשֵׁתִי	"I plundered"; שסה to plunder (1 · 1 · 5) 1042		מִזְעָר	25 a little (4 · 4) 277
			זַעַם	indignation (5 · 22) 276
אַבִּיר	mighty (3 · 17) 7		תַּבְלִית	destruction (1 · 1) 115
קֵן	14 nest (2 · 13) 890		שׁוֹט	26 scourge (1[?] · 8[?]) 1002
בֵּיצָה	egg (3 · 6) 101		מַכָּה	beating, scourging (5 · 48) 646
נדד	to flutter, elsewhere = to flee, retreat (8 · 20 · 24) 622		עֹרֵב	raven (2 · 12) 788, 1126
פצה	to open, part (1 · 15 · 15) 822		סֹבֶל	27 burden (3 · 3) 687
צפצף	to chirp, peep (4 · 4 · 4) 861		שְׁכֶם	shoulder (5 · 22) 1014
הִתְפָּאֵר	15 to glorify oneself (5 · 7 · 13) 802		עֹל	yoke (5 · 40) 760
גַּרְזֶן	axe (1 · 4) 173		צַוָּאר	neck (4 · 41) 848
חָצַב	to hew wood (4 · 14 · 17) 345		חֻבַּל	to be ruined, broken (1 · 2 · 10) 287
מַשּׂוֹר	saw (1 · 1) 673		מַעְבָּרָה	29 pass (2 · 8) 721
הֵנִיף	to wield (5 · 32 · 34[?]) 631		מָלוֹן	lodging place (1 · 8) 533
מִשְׁמָן	16 fatness; stout, vigorous ones (2 · 4) 1032		חָרַד	to be terrified (4 · 23 · 39) 353
רָזוֹן	leanness (1 · 3) 931		צהל	30 to cry shrilly (1 · 1 · 8) 843
יקד	to be kindled (2 · 3 · 8) 428		הִקְשִׁיב	to give attention (8 · 45 · 46) 904
יְקוֹד	a burning (2 · 2) 423		נדד	31 to retreat, flee (8 · 20 · 24) 622
לֶהָבָה	17 flame (5 · 19) 529		הֵעִיז	to bring into safety (1 · 4 · 5) 731
שַׁיִת	thorn bushes (7 · 7) 1011		נוֹפֵף	32 to brandish (1 · 1 · 34[?]) 631
שָׁמִיר	thorns (8 · 11) 1038		סָעֵף	33 to lop off (1 · 1 · 1) 703
כַּרְמֶל	18 plantation, garden land (8 · 14[?]) 502		פֻּארָה	[coll.] boughs (1 · 1) 802
מסס	to melt (1 · 1 · 21) 587		מַעֲרָצָה	awful shock, crash (1 · 1) 792
נסס	to be sick (1 · 1 · 3[?]) 651		רָם	high, exalted (7 · 31[?]) 926 רום
שְׁאָר	19 remainder (12 · 26) 984		קוֹמָה	height (2 · 45) 879
שְׁאָר	20 remnant (12 · 26) 984		גָּדַע	to hew, cut in two (1 · 5 · 22) 154
פְּלֵיטָה	escaped remnant (5 · 28) 812		גָּבֹהַּ	high, haughty (6 · 41) 147
נִשְׁעָן	to lean (5 · 22 · 22) 1043		שָׁפֵל	to become low (10 · 11 · 30) 1050
שְׁאָר	21 remnant (12 · 26) 984		נִקַּף	34 to be struck away (1 · 2[?] · 2) 668
חוֹל	22 sand (2 · 22) 297		סְבַךְ	thicket (2 · 3) 687
שְׁאָר	remnant (12 · 26) 984		אַדִּיר	majestic one (3 · 27) 12
כִּלָּיוֹן	annihilation (1 · 2) 479			
חָרַץ	to decide (1 · 5 · 10) 358			

Chapter 11

חֹטֶר	1 branch, twig (1 · 2) 310
גֶּזַע	stem, stock (2 · 3) 160
נֵצֶר	sprout, shoot (3 · 4) 666
שֹׁרֶשׁ	root (7 · 33) 1057

פרה to bear fruit (4 · 22 · 29) 826

בִּינָה 2 understanding, object of knowledge (5 · 37) 108

יִרְאָה fear of God, reverence, piety (5 · 45) 432

הריח 3 to smell; metaph. = delight in [cf. Am 5:21] (1 · 11 · 14) 926

יִרְאָה fear, reverence, piety (5 · 45) 432

מִשְׁמָע thing heard (1 · 1) 1036

דַּל 4 reduced, weak, helpless (5 · 48) 195

מִישׁוֹר uprightness, level place (3 · 23) 449

עָנָו poor and weak (3[?] · 21[?]) 776

אֵזוֹר 5 waistcloth (3 · 14) 25

מָתְנַיִם loins (4 · 47) 608

חָלָץ dual = loins (3 · 10) 323

זְאֵב 6 wolf (2 · 8) 255

נָמֵר leopard (1 · 6) 649

גְּדִי kid (1 · 16) 152

רָבַץ to lie down, stretch out (6 · 24 · 30) 918

עֵגֶל calf (2 · 35) 722

כְּפִיר young lion [old enough to hunt] (3 · 31) 498

מְרִיא fatling (2 · 8) 597

נָהַג to drive, conduct (3 · 20 · 30) 624

פָּרָה 7 heifer, cow (1 · 26) 831

דֹּב bear (2 · 12) 179

רָבַץ to lie down, stretch out (6 · 24 · 30) 918

אַרְיֵה lion (6 · 45) 71

תֶּבֶן straw, food for livestock (2 · 17) 1061

שֵׁעֲשַׁע 8 to sport, take delight (1 · 3 · 6) 1044

יוֹנֵק suckling, babe (2[?] · 11[?]) 413 ינק

חֻר hole (2 · 2[?]) 359

פֶּתֶן venomous serpent, perh. cobra (1 · 6) 837

מְאוּרָה light-hole = den of great viper (1 · 1) 22

צִפְעוֹנִי a poisonous serpent (3 · 5) 861

גָּמַל to wean; ptc. pass. = weaned child (6 · 34 · 37) 168

הָדָה to stretch out (1 · 1 · 1) 213

דֵּעָה 9 knowledge (2 · 6) 395

שֹׁרֶשׁ 10 root (7 · 33) 1057

נֵס standard, ensign (10 · 21) 651

מְנוּחָה resting place (4 · 21) 629

שְׁאָר 11 remnant, remainder (12 · 26) 984

אִי coastlands [and islands] (17 · 36) 15

נֵס 12 standard, ensign (10 · 21) 651

נָדַח to be thrust out, banished; ptc. = banished one, outcast (5 · 11) 623

נָפַץ to disperse, be scattered (1 · 5 · 21 [?]) 659

קִנְאָה jealousy, rivalry (7 · 43) 888

צֹרֵר vexer, harasser (1 · 17) 865 III צור

קָנָא to be jealous of (1 · 30 · 34) 888

צרר to show hostility toward, treat with enmity (1 · 10 · 10) 865

עוּף 14 to fly (4 · 18 · 25) 733

בָּזַז to plunder, despoil (7 · 37 · 41) 102

מִשְׁלוֹחַ outstretching, sending (1 · 3) 1020

מִשְׁמַעַת subjects, obedient band (1 · 4) 1036

הֶחֱרִים 15 to devote to destruction, destroy (3 · 46 · 49) 355

הֵנִיף to shake, wave, brandish against (5 · 32 · 34) 631

עָיָם [dub.] glow (1 · 1) 744

נַעַל sandal, shoe (3 · 22) 653

מְסִלָּה 16 highway, public road (9 · 27) 700

שְׁאָר remnant, residue, remainder (12 · 26) 984

Chapter 12

אָנַף 1 to be angry (1 · 8 · 14) 60

פָּחַד 2 to be in dread (7 · 23 · 26) 808

זִמְרָה melody, song (1[?] · 4[?]) 274

שׁאב 3 to draw [water] (1 · 14 · 14) 980

שָׂשׂוֹן exultation, rejoicing, joy (6 · 22) 965

מַעְיָן spring (2 · 23) 745

עֲלִילָה 4 deed (1 · 24) 760

נִשְׂגָּב to be exalted, high (6 · 10 · 20) 960

זִמֵּר 5 to praise in song (1 · 43 · 43) 274

גֵּאוּת majesty; here as adv. = majestical-
ly (5 · 8) 145

צָהַל 6 to cry shrilly (3 · 7 · 8) 843

Chapter 13

מַשָּׂא 1 utterance, oracle (11 · 21) 672

נִשְׁפָּה 2 to be windswept, bare (1 · 1 · 2) 1045

נֵס standard, ensign (10 · 21) 651

הֵנִיף to wave [as a signal] (5 · 32 · 34) 631

נָדִיב noble, princely, generous (3 · 27)
622

עַלִּיז 3 exultant, jubilant (5 · 7) 759

גַּאֲוָה proud one, pride, haughtiness
(5 · 19) 144

דְּמוּת 4 likeness, similitude; here adverbial-
ly = in likeness of, like (2 · 25) 198

שָׁאוֹן roar, uproar, din (8 · 18) 981

מֶרְחָק 5 distant place, distance (7 · 18) 935

זַעַם indignation (5 · 22) 276

חִבֵּל to ruin, destroy (3 · 6 · 10) 287

הֵילִל 6 to utter or make a howling, give a
howl (11 · 30 · 30) 410

שֹׁד devastation, ruin (6 · 25) 994

שַׁדַּי name of God = (1) self-sufficient,
(2) almighty, or (3) my sovereign
(1 · 48) 994 · 995

רָפָה 7 to sink, drop; of hands = to lose
heart, energy (2 · 14 · 45) 951

אֱנוֹשׁ man, mankind (8 · 42) 60

נָמֵס to melt, dissolve; of heart = faint,
grow fearful (3 · 19 · 21) 587

נִבְהַל 8 to be disturbed, dismayed, terrified
(2 · 24 · 39) 96

צִיר pang [writhing] (3 · 5) 852

חֵבֶל pains of travail, anguish (3 · 7) 286

חִיל to twist, writhe; fig. = be in
severe pain, anguish (9 · 30 · 47) 296

תָּמַהּ to be astounded (2 · 8 · 9) 1069

לַהַב flame; w. פֶּה = hot with excitement (4 · 12) 529

אַכְזָרִי 9 cruel, cruelty (1 · 8) 470

עֶבְרָה overflowing rage, fury (6 · 34) 720

חָרוֹן [burning of] anger (2 · 41) 354

שַׁמָּה waste [of land] (3 · 39) 1031

חַטָּא sinner[s], sinful (3 · 19) 308

כּוֹכָב 10 star (3 · 37) 456

כְּסִיל Orion, or constellations of same
brilliancy (1 · 4) 493

הֵהֵלִיל to flash forth light, shine (1 · 4 · 4)
237

חָשַׁךְ to be dark, grow dark (2 · 11 · 17)
364

יָרֵחַ moon (3 · 27) 437

הִגִּיהַ to cause to shine (1 · 3 · 6) 618

תֵּבֵל 11 world (9 · 36) 385

גָּאוֹן exaltation, majesty, excellence
(12 · 49) 144

זֵד insolent one, insolent, presumptuous (1 · 13) 267

גַּאֲוָה pride, haughtiness (5 · 19) 144

עָרִיץ ruthless, terror-striking (7 · 20[?])
792

הִשְׁפִּיל to lay low, humiliate (6 · 19 · 30)
1050

הֹקִיר 12 to make rare, precious (1 · 2 · 11)
429

אֱנוֹשׁ man (8 · 42) 60

פַּז refined, pure gold (1 · 9) 808

כֶּתֶם gold (1 · 9) 508

הִרְגִּיז 13 to cause to quake (3 · 7 · 41) 919

רָעַשׁ to quake, shake (2 · 21 · 29) 950

עֶבְרָה overflowing rage, fury (6 · 34) 720

חָרוֹן [burning of] anger (2 · 41) 354

צְבִי 14 gazelle (1 · 11) 840

הֻדָּח ptc. = chased, hunted (1 · 1 · 43) 623

221

נדקר 15 to be pierced through, slain
(1 · 1 · 11) 201

נִסְפָּה to be caught up, captured; to be
swept away (1 · 9 · 18) 705

עוֹלֵל 16 child (1 · 11) 760

רטש to be dashed in pieces (1 · 4 · 6) 936

נשסס to be plundered, rifled (1 · 2 · 5)
1042

נשגל to violate, ravish [Mass. regarded
verb obscene and subst. שכב]
(1 · 2 · 4) 993

רטש 18 to dash in pieces (1 · 2 · 6) 936

רחם to have compassion, be compassionate (12 · 42 · 47) 933

חוּס to look with compassion or pity on
(1 · 24 · 24) 299

צְבִי 19 beauty, honor (7 · 18) 840

תִּפְאָרָה glorying, boasting, beauty, glory
(18 · 50) 802

גָּאוֹן exaltation, majesty, excellence
(12 · 49) 144

מַהְפֵּכָה overthrow (2 · 6) 246

נֶצַח 20 everlastingness; w. ל = forever
(7 · 43) 664

אהל to pitch one's tent (1 · 1 · 3) 14

הרביץ to cause to lie down (2 · 6 · 30)
918

רָבַץ 21 to lie down = make lair, abode
(6 · 24 · 30) 918

צִי a wild beast, desert-dweller, yelper
(3 · 6) 850

אֹחַ jackal (1 · 1) 28

יַעֲנָה ostrich (3 · 8) 419

שָׂעִיר satyr, demon [with he-goat form]
(2 · 4) 972 Note: שָׂעִיר is often used
as merely a he-goat 972 II

רקד to dance, leap (1 · 5 · 9) 955

ענה 22 to sing (1 · 13 · 16) 777 IV; but
perh. to dwell 732 עון

אִי jackal (2 · 3) 17

אלמון → אַרְמוֹן castle, palace, citadel (5 · 33)
74

תַּן jackal (4 · 14) 1072

עֹנֶג daintiness, exquisite delight (2 · 2)
772

נמשך to be prolonged, postponed, drawn
out (1 · 3 · 36) 604

Chapter 14

רָחַם 1 to have compassion, be compassionate (12 · 42 · 47) 933

נִלְוָה to join oneself or be joined [to]
(3 · 11 · 12) 530

נספח to attach oneself to (1 · 1 · 5) 705

שָׁבָה 2 to take captive; ptc. = captive,
captor (1 · 30 · 38) 985

שֹׁבֶה captive, captor (2 · 9) 985

רדה to have dominion, rule (2 · 22 · 23)
921

נֹגֵשׂ oppressor, tyrant (5 · 15) 620 נגש

עֹצֶר 3 pain (1 · 3) 780

רֹגֶז disquiet, turmoil (1 · 7) 919

קָשֶׁה severe, hard (6 · 36) 904

מָשָׁל 4 parable, proverb (1 · 39) 605

נֹגֵשׂ oppressor, tyrant (5 · 15) 620 נגש

מַדְהֵבָה → מרהבה boisterous, raging behavior
(1 · 1) 923

מֹשֵׁל 5 ruler (4 · 24) 605 III (משל)

עֶבְרָה 6 overflowing rage, fury (6 · 34) 720

מַכָּה conquest, defeat [of enemy],
slaughter (5 · 48) 646

בִּלְתִּי not; here w. סרה = never-ceasing
(2 · 24) 116

סָרָה withdrawal, turning aside (1[?] · 1
[?]) 694

רדה to have dominion, rule (2 · 22 · 23)
921

מֻרְדָּף persecution (1 · 1) 923

בְּלִי adv. of negation, not (3 · 23) 115

222

חָשַׂךְ	to hinder, withhold, refrain (3 · 26 · 28) 362		הִרְגִּיז	to cause to quake (3 · 7 · 41) 919
			הִרְעִישׁ	to cause to quake (1 · 7 · 29) 950
שָׁקַט	7 to be at peace, quiet (3 · 31 · 41) 1052		תֵּבֵל	17 world (9 · 36) 385
פָּצַח	to break forth with (6 · 7 · 7[?]) 822		הָרַס	to throw down, tear down (2 · 30 · 43) 248
רִנָּה	ringing cry (9 · 33) 943		אָסִיר	prisoner (4 · 17[?]) 64
בְּרוֹשׁ	8 cypress, fir (5 · 20) 141		נֵצֶר	19 sprout, shoot (3 · 4) 666
מֵאָז	since, from that time (8 · 18) 23		נִתְעָב	to be abhorred, rejected (1 · 3 · 22) 1073
רָגַז	9 to be excited, perturbed, agitated (6 · 30 · 41) 919		לְבוּשׁ	garment, clothing (3 · 47) 528
רְפָאִים	shades, ghosts; name of dead in She ól (3 · 8) 952		טען	to be pierced; ptc. = pierced (1 · 1 · 1) 381
עַתּוּד	he-goat; here fig. of chiefs or princes (3 · 29) 800		פֶּגֶר	corpse, carcass (4 · 22) 803
נִמְשַׁל	10 to be like, similar (1 · 5 · 15) 605		הבוס	to be trodden down; ptc. = trodden down (1 · 1 · 12) 101
גָּאוֹן	11 exaltation, majesty, excellence (12 · 49) 144		יחד	20 to be united (1 · 2 · 3) 402
הֶמְיָה	sound, music (1 · 1) 242		קְבוּרָה	burial, grave (1 · 14) 869
נֵבֶל	portable harp, lute (2 · 27) 614		מֵרַע	evildoer (4 · 18) 949 רעע vb. denom.
הוּצַע	to be laid, spread (1 · 2 · 4) 426			
רִמָּה	worm [that feeds on the dead] (1 · 7) 942		מַטְבֵּחַ	21 place of slaughter (1 · 1) 371
מְכַסֶּה	covering (2 · 4) 492		תֵּבֵל	world (9 · 36) 385
תּוֹלֵעָה	worm, grub (3 · 41) 1069		שְׁאָר	22 rest, residue, remainder (12 · 26) 984
הֵילֵל	12 shining one; i.e., star of the morning (1 · 1) 237		נִין	offspring, posterity (1 · 3) 630
שַׁחַר	dawn (3 · 23) 1007		נֶכֶד	progeny, posterity (1 · 3) 645
נִגְדַּע	to be hewn off, severed (2 · 7 · 22) 154		מוֹרָשׁ	23 possession (1 · 3) 440
חלשׁ	to disable, prostrate (1 · 3 · 3) 325		קִפֹּד	porcupine (2-3) 891
מִמַּעַל	13 with ל = on the top of, above (3 · 29) 751		אֲגַם	troubled or muddy pool, marsh (4 · 8) 8
כּוֹכָב	star (3 · 37) 456		טאטא	to sweep (1 · 1 · 1) 370
יַרְכָה	remote part, extreme part, recesses (3 · 28) 438		מַטְאֲטֵא	broom (1 · 1) 370
עָב	14 dark cloud (7 · 30) 728		דִּמָּה	24 to imagine, think, intend (5 · 13 · 27) 197
הִדַּמָּה	to make oneself like, become like (1 · 1 · 27) 198		בוס	25 to tread down, trample (2 · 7 · 12) 100
יַרְכָה	15 remote part, recesses or innermost part (3 · 28) 438		עֹל	yoke (5 · 40) 760
			סֵבֶל	burden [always fig. of tyranny] (3 · 3) 687
הִשְׁגִּיחַ	16 to gaze (1 · 3 · 3) 993		שְׁכֶם	shoulder (5 · 22) 1014
			הֵפֵר	27 to frustrate, make ineffectual (4 · 42 · 45) 830

223

מַשָּׂא 28 utterance, oracle (11 · 21) 672 III
שֹׁרֶשׁ 29 root (7 · 33) 1057
נָחָשׁ serpent (4 · 31) 638
צֶפַע poisonous serpent (3 · 5) 861
שָׂרָף fiery serpent (4 · 7[?]) 977
עוֹפֵף to fly about, to and fro (3 · 5 · 25) 733
דַּל 30 reduced, poor; בכורי ד' = poor (5 · 48) 195
בֶּטַח security; with ל = securely (4 · 43) 105
רָבַץ to lie down, repose (6 · 24 · 30) 918
שֹׁרֶשׁ root (7 · 33) 1057
הֵילִיל 31 to make a howling, give a howl (11 · 30 · 30) 410
נָמוֹג to melt away, be helpless (1 · 8 · 17) 556
עָשָׁן smoke (7 · 25) 798
בֹּדֵד to be separate, isolated; ptc. = straggler (1 · 3 · 3) 94
מוֹעֵד appointed place (1 · 1) 418
יִסַּד 32 to found (2 · 10 · 41) 414
חָסָה to seek refuge (3 · 37 · 37) 340

Chapter 15

מַשָּׂא 1 utterance, oracle (11 · 21) 672 III
נִדְמָה to be cut off, destroyed, ruined (3 · 12 · 16) 198
בְּכִי 2 weeping (8 · 32) 113
הֵילִיל to make a howling, to give a howl (11 · 30 · 30) 410
קָרְחָה baldness, bald spot [made in mourning] (3 · 11) 901
זָקָן beard (2 · 18) 278
גָּרַע to diminish; ptc. pass. = diminished, clipped (1 · 14 · 22) 175
חָגַר 3 to gird on, bind on (3 · 44 · 44) 291
שַׂק sackcloth (8 · 48) 974
גָּג roof (3 · 29) 150

רְחֹב broad open place, plaza (2 · 43) 932
הֵילִיל to make a howling, give a howl (11 · 30 · 30) 410
בְּכִי weeping (8 · 32) 113
חלץ 4 to equip for war; ptc. pass. = equipped one, warrior (1 · 17[?]) 323
הֵרִיע to cry out in distress (3 · 40 · 44) 929
יָרַע to quiver (1 · 1 · 1) 438
בָּרִיחַ 5 fugitive, fleeing (3 · 4[?]) 138
בָּרִיחַ bar [of city gates] (2 · 41) 138; but perh. בריח = fleeing, fugitive 138 I
מַעֲלֶה ascent (1 · 19) 751
בְּכִי weeping (8 · 32) 113
זְעָקָה cry, cry of distress (3 · 18) 227
שֶׁבֶר shattering, crushing, breaking (9 · 45) 991
עער = Pilp. form of עוּר, to rouse 735
מְשַׁמָּה 6 devastation, waste (1 · 8) 1031
חָצִיר grass (8 · 18) 348
דֶּשֶׁא grass (3 · 14) 206
יָרָק green thing, grass (2 · 8) 438
יִתְרָה 7 abundance, riches (1 · 2) 452
פְּקֻדָּה store, things laid up (3 · 32) 824
עֲרָבָה poplar, Euphrates poplar (2 · 5) 788
הִקִּיף 8 to go about, go around (1 · 16 · 17) 669
זְעָקָה cry of distress, outcry (3 · 18) 277
יְלָלָה howling (2 · 5) 410
פְּלֵיטָה 9 escaped remnant (5 · 28) 812
אַרְיֵה lion (6 · 45) 71

Chapter 16

כַּר 1 he-lamb; here lamb of ruler = tribute lamb (2 · 11) 503
מֹשֵׁל ruler (4 · 24) 605 III משל
נדד 2 to wander, stray (8 · 20 · 24) 622
קֵן nestling, nest (2 · 13) 890
מַעְבָּרָה ford, pass, passage (2 · 8) 721

פְּלִילָה 3 office of judge or umpire (1 · 1) 813

צָהֳרַיִם noon, midday (3 · 23) 843

נדח banished one, outcast (5 · 11) 623
נדח

נדד to retreat, flee, stray; ptc. = fugitive (8 · 20 · 24) 622

נִדָּח 4 banished one, outcast (5 · 11) 623
נדח

הוה to become (1 · 5 · 5) 217

סֵתֶר hiding place (5 · 35) 712

אָפֵס to cease, fail, come to an end (2 · 5 · 5) 67

מֵץ squeezer, extortioner, oppressor (1 · 1) 568

שֹׁד devastation, ruin (6 · 25) 994

רֹמֵס trampler (1 · 1) 942 רָמַס

מָהִיר 5 prompt, quick, ready (1 · 4) 555

גָּאוֹן 6 pride [in bad sense] (12 · 49) 145

גֵּא proud, = גאה (1 · 1[?]) 144

גַּאֲוָה majesty, pride (5 · 19) 144

עֶבְרָה arrogance, fury (6 · 34) 720

כֵּן veritable, true (1 · 24) 467

בַּד empty, idle talk (2 · 6) 95

הֵילִל 7 to make a howling, give a howl (11 · 30 · 30) 410

אֲשִׁישָׁה raisin cake (1 · 5) 84

הָגָה to moan for, sigh (7 · 23 · 25) 211

נָכָא stricken (1 · 1) 644

שְׁדֵמָה 8 field (2 · 6) 995

אָמְלַל to be or grow feeble, languish (6 · 15[?] · 15[?]) 51

הלם to smite, strike down, hammer (3 · 8 · 8) 240

שָׂרֵק vine tendrils [or clusters] (1 · 2) 977

תָּעָה to wander about, err (8 · 27 · 50) 1073

שְׁלֻחָה shoot, branch (1 · 1) 1020

נטש to be spread abroad, let go (2 · 6 · 40) 644

בְּכִי 9 weeping (8 · 32) 113

רוה to drench, water abundantly (3 · 6 · 14) 924

דִּמְעָה tears (3 · 23) 199

קַיִץ summer fruit, summer (2 · 20) 884

קָצִיר harvested crop, harvest (7 · 49) 894

הֵידָד shouting, shout (2 · 7) 212

גִּיל 10 rejoicing (1 · 8) 162

כַּרְמֶל garden land (8 · 14) 502

רעע to utter a shout (1 · 1 · 44) 929

יֶקֶב wine press, wine vat (2 · 16) 428

הֵידָד shout, shouting (2 · 6) 212

מֵעֶה 11 internal organs, inward parts (4 · 32) 588

כִּנּוֹר lyre, stringed instrument (5 · 41) 490

המה to murmur, growl, roar (5 · 33 · 33) 242

נִלְאָה 12 to weary oneself (3 · 10 · 19) 521

מֵאָז 13 in time past = of old (8 · 18) 23

שָׂכִיר 14 hireling, hired laborer (3 · 18) 969

נִקְלָה to be lightly esteemed (2 · 5 · 6) 885

שְׁאָר rest, residue, remainder, remnant (12 · 26) 984

מִזְעָר a remnant, very few, a little (4 · 4) 277

כַּבִּיר much, great, mighty (3[?] · 10[?]) 460

Chapter 17

מַשָּׂא 1 utterance, oracle (11 · 21) 672 III

מְעִי = עִי ruin heap (1 · 1) 590

מַפָּלָה ruin (3 · 3) 658

עֵדֶר 2 flock (3 · 39) 727

רָבַץ to lie down, lie (6 · 24 · 30) 918

הֶחֱרִיד to terrify (1 · 16 · 39) 353

מִבְצָר 3 fortress, stronghold (3 · 37) 131

שְׁאָר rest, remainder, residue (12 · 26) 984

נדל 4 to be brought low (1 · 8 · 8[?]) 195
דלל

מִשְׁמָן fatness (2 · 4) 1032

נרזה to be made lean (1 · 1 · 2) 931

קָצִיר 5 what is harvested, crop (7 · 49) 894

קָמָה standing grain (2 · 10) 879

שִׁבֹּלֶת ear of grain (3[?] · 20[?]) 987 II

קָצַר to reap (2 · 24 · 24) 894 II

לקט to glean, gather up, pick up (1 · 21 · 37) 544

רְפָאִים shades, ghosts (3 · 8) 952 I

עוֹלֵלוֹת 6 gleaning [fig. of remnant] (2 · 6) 760

נֹקֶף striking off (2 · 2) 668

זַיִת olive tree, olive (2 · 38) 268

גַּרְגַּר berry (1 · 1) 176

אָמִיר top, summit (2 · 2[?]) 57

סָעִיף branch (2 · 2) 703

פרה to bear fruit; ptc. = fruit bearer (4 · 22 · 29) 826

שָׁעָה 7 to regard [w. trust], gaze [at] (5 · 12 · 15) 1043

שָׁעָה 8 to regard, gaze [at] (5 · 12 · 15) 1043

אֶצְבַּע finger (4 · 31) 840

אֲשֵׁרָה sacred tree or pole (2 · 40) 81

חַמָּן sun pillar [used in idolatrous worship] (2 · 8) 329

מָעוֹז 9 refuge, place of safety (10 · 36) 731

עֲזוּבָה ptc. as subst. = deserted region (>50) 737; 736 I עזר, Qal. 2.a.

חֹרֶשׁ wooded height (1 · 3) 361

אָמִיר top, summit (2 · 2)[?]) 57

יֵשַׁע 10 salvation, deliverance (5 · 36) 447

מָעוֹז place of safety (10 · 36) 731

נֶטַע plantation (3 · 4) 642

נַעֲמָן pleasantness; but perh. epithet of Adonis (1 · 1) 654

זְמוֹרָה twig, branch, shoot; זור = twigs of a strange one; i.e., of strange god (1 · 5) 274

נֶטַע 11 act of planting (3 · 4) 642

שגשג to fence carefully about (1 · 1 · 1[?]) 691 סוג

הפריח to cause to bud or sprout (1 · 5 · 34) 827

נֵד heap (1 · 6) 622

קָצִיר what is reaped, harvested; crop (7 · 49) 894 I

נַחֲלָה severe, sore (1 · 5[5]) 317 I

כְּאֵב pain (2 · 6) 456

אנש to be weak, sick; ptc. pass. = incurable (1 · 8 · 8[?]) 60

הָמָה 12 to roar, murmur, growl (5 · 33 · 33) 242

שָׁאוֹן roar, din (8 · 18) 981

לְאֹם people (11 · 35) 522

כַּבִּיר great, mighty, much (3[?] · 10[?]) 460

נשאה to be in uproar (3 · 3 · 6) 980

לְאֹם 13 people (11 · 35) 522

שָׁאוֹן roar, din (8 · 18) 981

נשאה to be in uproar (3 · 3 · 6) 980

גָּעַר to rebuke (2 · 14 · 14) 172

מֶרְחָק distance, distant place; to a distance (7 · 18) 935

מֹץ chaff (3 · 8) 558

גַּלְגַּל whirl [of dust or chaff], whirlwind; dust (2 · 11) 165

סוּפָה storm wind (5 · 15) 693

בַּלָּהָה 14 calamity, destruction, terror (1 · 10) 117

בְּטֶרֶם before (7 · 39) 382

שֹׁסֶה plunderer, spoiler (1 · 7) 1042 שסה

בָּזַז to plunder, despoil (7 · 37 · 41) 102

Chapter 18

צְלָצַל 1 whirring, buzzing (1 · 1) 852

צִיר 2 envoy, messenger (2 · 6) 851

גֹּמֶא papyrus, paper reed (2 · 4) 167

קַל swift, fleet (4 · 13) 886

מָשַׁךְ to be long, drawn out; of persons = tall (2 · 3 · 36) 604

מרט ptc. = polished, smooth pual ptc. [G.K. 52S] (2 · 5 · 14) 599

נוֹרָא fearful, wonderful (4 · 44) 431 ירא

הָלְאָה onwards, further (2 · 13) 229

קו might [dub.] (16 · 25[?]) 876 קוקו

מְבוּסָה downtreading, subjugation (3 · 3) 101

בְזָא to divide, cut through (2 · 2 · 2) 102

תֵּבֵל 3 world (9 · 36) 385

נֵס standard, ensign (10 · 21) 651

שָׁקַט 4 to be quiet, inactive (3 · 31 · 41) 1052

מָכוֹן fixed place, established place (2 · 17) 467

חמם חֹם = heat; to be or grow warm (5 · 23 · 26[?]) 328 חֹם

צַח glowing, dazzling (2 · 4) 850

עָב dark cloud (7 · 30) 728

טַל mist, dew (3 · 31) 378

קָצִיר harvest, time of harvest (7 · 49) 894

קָצִיר 5 time of harvest, harvest (7 · 49) 894

פֶּרַח bud, sprout (2 · 17) 827

בֹּסֶר unripe grapes (1 · 5) 126

גָּמַל to become ripe (6 · 34 · 37) 168

נִצָּה blossom (1 · 4) 665

זַלְזַל tendrils (1 · 1) 272

מַזְמֵרָה pruning knife (2 · 4) 275

נְטִישָׁה twig, tendril (1 · 3) 644

הֵתַז to strike away (1 · 1 · 1) 1064 תזז

עַיִט 6 bird[s] of prey (3 · 8) 743

קָץ to spend the summer (1 · 1 · 23[?]) 884 II קיץ

חֹרֶף to remain in harvest time (1 · 1 · 2 [?]) 358

הוּבִיל 7 to be borne [carried] along (3 · 11 · 18) 384 יבל

שַׁי gift [offered as homage] (1 · 3) 1009

מְשֻׁךְ to be long, drawn out; of persons = tall (2 · 3 · 36) 604

מרט polished, smooth; pual ptc. [G.K 52S] (2 · 5 · 14) 598

נוֹרָא fearful, dreadful, wonderful (4 · 44) 431 ירא

הָלְאָה onwards, further (2 · 13) 229

קו might [dub.] (16 · 25[?]) 876 קוקו

מְבוּסָה downtreading, subjugation (3 · 3) 101

בְזָא to divide, cut through (2 · 2 · 2) 102

Chapter 19

מַשָּׂא 1 utterance, oracle (11 · 21) 672 III

עָב dark cloud (7 · 30) 728

קַל swift, fleet (4 · 13) 886

נוע to tremble (6 · 22 · 38) 631

אֱלִיל idolatrous worthlessness, worthless gods, idols (10 · 20) 47

נָמֵס to melt, dissolve; of heart = to be faint, grow fearful (3 · 19 · 21) 587 מסס

סִכְסֵךְ 2 to prick or spur on [pilpel שׂכך] (2 · 2 · 4[?]) 1127

נבק 3 to be emptied [laid waste] (2 · 2 · 7) 132 בקק

בִּלַּע to swallow up, engulf; i.e., confuse, confound (2 · 3 · 6[?]) 118

אֱלִיל idolatrous worthlessness, worthless gods, idols (10 · 20) 47

אִטִּי mutterer, whisperer of charms (1 · 1) 31

אוֹב necromancer, one who seeks the dead for instruction (3 · 16) 15

יִדְּעֹנִי familiar spirit (2 · 11) 396

סִכַּר 4 to shut up, deliver (1 · 1 · 3) 698

קָשֶׁה severe, rough, hard (6 · 36) 904

עַז formidable, fierce, mighty (4 · 22) 738

נִשַּׁת 5 to be dried up (1[?] · 1[?] · 3[?]) 677

חרב to be dried up (6 · 17 · 37[?]) 351

הֶזְנִיחַ 6 to stink, emit stench (1 · 1 · 1) 276

דָּלַל to be low (2 · 8 · 8[?]) 195

חרב to be dried up (6 · 17 · 37[?]) 351

סוּף rushes, reeds (1 · 4) 693

קָמַל — to be decayed (2 · 2 · 2) 888

עָרָה — 7 bare place [dub., LXX, reeds] (1 · 1) 788

מִזְרָע — place of sowing, seedland (1 · 1) 283

נִדַּף — to be driven, driven about (2 · 6 · 9) 623

אָנָה — 8 to mourn (2 · 2 · 2) 58

דַּיָּג — fisherman (1 · 2[?]) 186

אָבַל — to mourn, lament (5 · 18 · 38) 5

חַכָּה — hook, fishhook (1 · 3) 335

מִכְמֹרֶת — net, fishing net (1 · 3) 485

אֻמְלַל — to languish, grow feeble (6 · 15 [?] · 15[?]) 51

פֵּשֶׁת — 9 flax, linen (1 · 16) 833

שָׂרִיק — carded, combed (1 · 1) 977

אֹרֵג — to weave; ptc. = weaver (2 · 10[?]) 70

חוֹרָי — white stuff (1 · 1) 301

שָׁת — foundation, stay [of society] (2 [?] · 4[?]) 1011

דכא — to be crushed; ptc. = crushed, broken (2 · 4 · 18) 194

שֶׂכֶר — hire, wages (1 · 2) 969

אָגֵם — sad (1 · 1) 8

אֱוִיל — 11 fool, foolish (2 · 26) 17

יוֹעֵץ — counselor (5 · 22) 419

נִבְעַר — to be brutish, stupid; ptc. = stupid, brutish (1 · 4 · 7) 129

אֵי — 12 where? אַיָּם = where are they? (4 · 39) 32 אי

אֵפוֹא — pray (2 · 15) 66

נואל — 13 to become fools (1 · 4 · 4) 383 I יאל

נשׁא — to be beguiled (1 · 1 · 16) 674 II

הִתְעָה — to cause to wander about (6 · 21 · 50) 1073

פִּנָּה — corner [fig. for support, defense] (2 · 30) 819

מָסַךְ — 14 pour, mix (2 · 5 · 5) 587

עִוְעִים — distorting, רוּחַ ע׳ = warped judgment (1 · 1) 730

הִתְעָה — to cause to wander about (6 · 21 · 50) 1073

נִתְעָה — to be made to wander about (1 · 2 · 50) 1073

שִׁכּוֹר — drunken one, drunkard (4 · 13) 1016

קִיא — vomit (2 · 3) 883

זָנָב — 15 tail, end (4[?] · 11[?]) 275

כִּפָּה — branch, frond [prob. of palm tree] (2 · 3) 497

אַגְמוֹן — rush, bulrush [fig. = lowly persons] (3 · 5) 8

הָרַד — 16 to be terrified, tremble (4 · 23 · 39) 353

פָּחַד — to be in dread, to dread (7 · 23 · 26) 808

תְּנוּפָה — a brandishing, swinging (2 · 30) 632

הֵנִיף — to shake, wave, brandish against (5 · 32 · 34) 631 נוף

חָגָּא — 17 reeling (1 · 1) 291

פָּחַד — to be in dread, to dread (7 · 23 · 26) 808

הֶרֶס — 18 overthrow, destruction; [word-play allusion to On–Heliopolis] (1 · 1) 249

מַצֵּבָה — 19 pillar, sacred stone (1[?] · 36[?]) 663

לֹחֵץ — 20 oppressor (1 · 4[?]) 537 לחץ

מוֹשִׁיעַ — savior (9 · 27[?]) 446 ישׁב

נָדַר — 21 to vow (1 · 31 · 31) 623

נָגַף — 22 to strike, smite (2 · 25 · 48) 619

נֶעְתַּר — to be supplicated, entreated (1 · 8 · 20) 801

מְסִלָּה — 23 highway (9 · 27) 700

Chapter 20

תַּרְתָּן — 1 field marshal, title of Assyrian general (1 · 2[?]) 1077

שַׂק — 2 sackcloth (8 · 48) 974

מָתְנַיִם — loins (4 · 47) 608

נַעַל — sandal, shoe (3 · 22) 653

חָלַץ — to draw, draw off (1 · 5 · 27) 322

עָרוֹם — naked (4 · 16) 736

יָחֵף — barefoot (3 · 5) 405

228

עָרוֹם 3 naked (4 · 16) 736

יָחֵף barefoot (3 · 5) 405

מוֹפֵת sign, token of future event, symbolic act (2 · 36) 68

נָהַג 4 to drive away, off; to conduct (3 · 20 · 30) 624

שְׁבִי captives [coll.] (4 · 49) 985

גָּלוּת exiles [coll.] (2 · 15) 163

עָרוֹם naked (4 · 16) 736

יָחֵף barefoot (3 · 5) 405

חֲשׂוּפַי stripped, bared (1 · 1[?]) 362 חשׂף

שֵׁת seat, buttocks (2[?] · 4[?]) 1059

מַבָּט 5 expectation, thing looked to for hope (2 · 3) 613

תִּפְאָרָה glorying, boasting; beauty, glory (18 · 50) 802

אִי 6 coast, border, region (17 · 36) 15

מַבָּט expectation, thing looked to for hope (2 · 3) 613

עֶזְרָה help, succor (4 · 26) 740

Chapter 21

מַשָּׂא 1 utterance, oracle (11 · 21) 672

סוּפָה storm wind (5 · 15) 693

חָלַף to move on, sweep on (4 · 14 · 26) 322

נוֹרָא fearful, dreadful; wonderful (4 · 44) 431

חָזוּת 2 vision (3 · 5) 303

קָשֶׁה severe, hard (6 · 36) 904

בָּגַד to act treacherously (12 · 49 · 49) 93

צוּר to shut in, besiege (3 · 31 · 31) 848

אֲנָחָה sighing, groaning (3 · 11) 58

מָתְנַיִם 3 loins [seat of keenest pain] (4 · 47) 608

חַלְחָלָה anguish (1 · 4) 298

צִיר pang, writhing (3 · 5) 852

נעוה to be bent, bowed down (1 · 4 · 17) 730

נִבְהַל to be disturbed, dismayed, terrified (2 · 24 · 39) 96

תָּעָה 4 to wander about (8 · 27 · 50) 1073

פַּלָּצוּת shuddering (1 · 4) 814

בעת to overwhelm (1 · 13 · 16) 130

נֶשֶׁף twilight (3 · 12) 676

חֵשֶׁק desire (1 · 4) 366

חֲרָדָה trembling, fear, anxiety (1 · 9) 353

צפה 5 to lay out (1 · 9 · 18) 860

צָפִית rug, carpet (1 · 1) 860

צפה 6 to keep watch; ptc. = watchman (1 · 9 · 18) 859

צֶמֶד 7 pair, couple (3 · 15) 855

הִקְשִׁיב to give attention [or cause to give attention] (8 · 45 · 46) 904

קֶשֶׁב attentiveness (2 · 4) 904

אַרְיֵה 8 lion (6 · 45) 71

מִצְפֶּה watchtower (1 · 2) 859

צֶמֶד 9 pair, couple (3 · 15) 855

פָּסִיל idol, image (4 · 23) 820

מְדֻשָׁה 10 that which is threshed (1 · 1) 190

גֹּרֶן threshing floor (1 · 34) 175

מַשָּׂא 11 utterance, oracle (11 · 21) 672

דּוּמָה = Edom [name of Edom with a mystic ring; e.g., silence of death, desolation] 189

מַה מִלַּיְלָה [idiom] how much of the night is past? 552 מָה 1.a.

אָתָה 12 to come (9 · 19 · 21) 87

בעה to seek, inquire (2 · 2 · 4) 126

מַשָּׂא 13 utterance, oracle (11 · 21) 672

אֹרְחָה traveling company, caravan (1 · 3) 73

צָמֵא 14 thirsty one, thirsty (5 · 9) 854

האתה to bring (1 · 2 · 21) 87

קדם to come to meet (2 · 24 · 26) 869

נדד to retreat, flee; ptc. = fugitive (8 · 20 · 24) 622

נדד 15 to retreat, flee (8 · 20 · 24) 622

נָטַשׁ to leave, forsake, permit (2 · 33 · 40) 643

כֹּבֶד		vehemence, heaviness (2 · 4) 458
בְּעוֹד	16	within yet (3 · 20) 728 עוֹד, 2.a.
שָׂכִיר		hireling, hired laborer (3 · 18) 969
שְׁאָר	17	rest, residue, last remnant (12 · 26) 984
מעט		to become few, small (1 · 8 · 22) 589

Chapter 22

מַשָּׂא	1	utterance, oracle (11 · 21) 672
גַּיְא		valley (5 · 47) 161
חִזָּיוֹן		vision (2 · 9) 303
אֵפוֹא		pray [enclitic part.] (2 · 15) 66
גָּג		roof (3 · 29) 150
תְּשֻׁאוֹת	2	noise (1 · 4) 996 תְּשֻׁאָה
המה		to be in commotion, stir [roar, murmur] (5 · 33 · 33) 242
קִרְיָה		town, city (10 · 30) 900
עַלִּיז		jubilant, exultant (5 · 7) 759
קָצִין	3	ruler, chief (4 · 12) 892
נדד		to retreat, flee (8 · 20 · 24) 622
יַחַד		all together (7 · 44) 403
מֵרָחֹק		to a distance, at a distance (12 · 34) 935 רָחַק 2.a.(3).
שָׁעָה	4	to gaze; w. מִן = to turn gaze away (5 · 12 · 15) 1043
מרר		to show bitterness (1 · 3 · 16) 600
בְּכִי		weeping (8 · 32) 113
האיץ		to hasten (1 · 2 · 10) 21
שֹׁד		devastation, ruin (6 · 25) 994
מְהוּמָה	5	discomfiture, disquietude (1 · 12) 223
מְבוּסָה		downtreading, subjugation (3 · 3) 101
מְבוּכָה		confusion (1 · 2) 100
גַּיְא		valley (5 · 47) 161
חִזָּיוֹן		vision (2 · 9) 303
קרקר		to tear down (1 · 1 · 3) 903 II קרר
שׁוֹעַ		cry; perh. war cry, cry for help (1 · 1) 1003

אַשְׁפָּה	6	quiver for arrows (2 · 6) 80
עָרָה		to lay bare (2 · 9 · 15) 788
מִבְחָר	7	choicest, best (2 · 12) 104
מָסָךְ	8	covering, fig. for protection; eye-screen (1 · 25) 697
נֶשֶׁק		equipment, weapons (1 · 10) 676
בְּקִיעַ	9	fissure, breach (1 · 2) 132
רב		to be [become] many (4 · 23 · 24) 912 רבב I
בְּרֵכָה		pool, pond (4 · 17) 140
תַּחְתּוֹן		lower (1 · 13) 1066
נָתַץ	10	to pull down (1 · 31 · 42) 683
נִבְצַר		to fortify (1 · 2 · 4[?]) 130
מִקְוָה	11	reservoir (1 · 1) 876
בְּרֵכָה		pool, pond (4 · 17) 140
יָשָׁן		old (1 · 8) 445
עֹשֶׂה		maker, creator (6 · 24[?]) 793 עשה I
יָצַר		to form, fashion; fig. for frame, preordain, plan (22 · 41 · 44) 427
מֵרָחֹק		long ago, at a distance (12 · 34) 935
בְּכִי	12	weeping (8 · 32) 113
מִסְפֵּד		wailing (1 · 16) 704
קָרְחָה		baldness (3 · 11) 901
חגר		to gird on, bind on (3 · 44 · 44) 291
שָׂק		sackcloth (8 · 48) 974
שָׂשׂוֹן	13	exultation, joy (6 · 22) 965
סֹכֵן	15	servitor, steward (1 · 3[?]) 698 סכן
פֹּה	16	here (2 · 44) 805
מַה לְּךָ פֹה		[idiom] what have you here? 552 מה, 1.a.(d).
מִי לְךָ פֹה		[idiom] who do you have here? 552
חָצֵב		to hew out (4 · 14 · 17) 345
חקק		to cut in, inscribe (4 · 8 · 11) 349
טַלְטֵל	17	to hurl, cast (1 · 1 · 14) 376, טול
טַלְטֵלָה		a hurling (1 · 1) 376
עטה		to grasp; inf. abs. + ptc. = grasp forcibly (2 · 4 · 4) 742
צָנַף	18	to wind up, wrap (2 · 3 · 3) 857
צְנֵפָה		winding (1 · 1) 857
דּוּר		ball, circle (2 · 2) 189

רָחָב wide, broad (2 · 21) 932

רַחֲבָה יָדַיִם [idiom] = wide on both hands = wide in both directions 388 יָד 3.d.

מֶרְכָּבָה chariot (3 · 44) 939

קָלוֹן dishonor, disgrace (1 · 17) 885

הָדַף 19 to depose, thrust out (1 · 11 · 11) 213

מַצָּב station, office (1 · 10) 662

מַעֲמָד station, office, post (1 · 5) 765

הָרַס to cast down, throw down (2 · 30 · 43) 248

כֻּתֹּנֶת 21 tunic (1 · 29) 509

אַבְנֵט girdle (1 · 9) 126

מֶמְשָׁלָה rule, dominion (2 · 17) 606

מַפְתֵּחַ 22 key (1 · 3) 836

שְׁכֶם shoulder (5 · 22) 1014

יָתֵד 23 peg (4 · 23) 450

תָּלָה 24 to hang, hang up (1 · 23 · 27) 1067

צֶאֱצָא offspring (7 · 11) 425

צְפִיעָה offshoot [dub.] (1 · 1) 861

קָטָן small size, small (2 · 47) 881

אַגָּן bowl (1 · 3) 8

נֵבֶל [earthen] jar, pitcher (2 · 11) 614

מוּשׁ 25 to depart, remove (5 · 20[?] · 20[?]) 559

יָתֵד peg (4 · 23) 450

נִגְדַּע to be hewn off (2 · 7 · 22) 154

מַשָּׂא load, burden (3 · 42) 672

Chapter 23

מַשָּׂא 1 utterance, oracle (11 · 21) 672

הֵילִל to howl (11 · 30 · 30) 410

אֳנִיָּה ship (5 · 31) 58

דָּמַם 2 to be struck dumb, be astounded, be silent (1 · 23 · 30) 198   I דמם

אִי coast, region (17 · 36) 15

סֹחֵר trafficker, trader (3 · 16) 695   סחר

שִׁיחוֹר 3 Nile (1 · 4) 1009

קָצִיר harvested crop, harvest (7 · 49) 894

תְּבוּאָה income, revenue (2 · 43) 100

סַחַר traffic, gain from traffic (4 · 8) 695

מָעוֹז 4 place of safety, harbor (10 · 36) 731

חוּל to twist, writhe (9 · 30 · 47) 297

בָּחוּר young man (6 · 45) 104

בְּתוּלָה virgin (5 · 50) 143

שֵׁמַע 5 report, tidings (3 · 17) 1034

חוּל to be in severe pain, anguish (9 · 30 · 47) 297

הֵילִל 6 to howl (11 · 30 · 30) 410

אִי coast, region (17 · 36) 15

עַלִּיז 7 exultant, jubilant (5 · 7) 759

קַדְמָה antiquity, beginning (1 · 6) 870

הֵיבִל to carry away (1 · 7 · 18) 384

מֵרָחוֹק to a distance, at a distance (12 · 34) 935

הַעֲטִיר 8 to bestow a crown (1 · 1 · 7) 742

סֹחֵר trafficker, trader (3 · 16) 695   סחר

כְּנַעֲנִי trader, merchant (1 · 4) 489, 1124

גָּאוֹן 9 exaltation, majesty, excellence; pride (12 · 49) 144

צְבִי beauty, decoration (7 · 18) 840

מֵזַח 10 girdle [dub.]; fig. for restraint (1 · 1) 561

הִרְגִּיז 11 to shake, cause to quake (3 · 7 · 41) 919

מָעוֹז place of safety, fastness (10 · 36) 731

עָלַז 12 to exult, triumph (1 · 16 · 16) 759

עֻשַּׁק to be crushed (1 · 1 · 37) 798

בְּתוּלָה virgin (5 · 50) 143

יָסַד 13 to appoint, establish (5 · 20 · 41) 413

צִי wild beast, desert dweller (3 · 6) 850

בַּחוּן siege tower (1 · 1) 103

עוֹרֵר to lay bare (1 · 1 · 4) 792   II

אַרְמוֹן palace, castle, citadel (5 · 33) 74

מַפֵּלָה ruin (3 · 3) 658

הֵילִל 14 to howl (11 · 30 · 30) 410

אֳנִיָּה ship (5 · 31) 58

מָעוֹז place of safety, fastness (10 · 36) 731

שִׁירָה 15 song, ode (2 · 13) 1010
זוֹנָה harlot (3 · 33[?]) 275 זנה
כִּנּוֹר 16 lyre (5 · 41) 490
זוֹנָה harlot (3 · 33[?]) 275 זנה
נָגַן to play a stringed instrument (2 · 13 · 14) 618
אֶתְנַן 17 hire of harlot (2 · 11) 1072
סַחַר 18 traffic, gain (4 · 18) 695
אֶתְנַן hire of harlot (2 · 11) 1072
נֶאֱצַר to be stored up (1 · 1 · 5) 69
נחסן to be treasured up, hoarded (1 · 1 · 1) 1123 (340 b)
שָׂבְעָה satiety, one's fill (3 · 7[?]) 960
מְכַסֶּה covering (2 · 4) 492
עָתִיק eminent, surpassing (1 · 1) 801

Chapter 24

בקק 1 to empty, lay waste (1 · 4 · 7) 132
בלק to lay waste [Pual ptc.] (1 · 1 · 2) 118
עָוָה to distort, twist (1 · 2 · 17) 730
גְּבֶרֶת 2 mistress (3 · 15) 150
קוֹנֶה buyer (2 · 7) 888 קנה
הלוה to cause to borrow, lend (1 · 9 · 14) 530 II לוה
לוה to borrow (1 · 5 · 14) 530 II
נשה to lend; ptc. = creditor (1 · 10 · 12) 674 I
נשא creditor (1 · 5) 673 נשא
נבק 3 to be emptied (2 · 2 · 7) 132 בקק II
תִּבּוֹז to be spoiled, plundered; here = Niph. impf. 2 ms. (2 · 3 · 41) 102 בזז
אָבַל 4 to mourn (5 · 18 · 38) 5
נָבֵל to droop, wither and fall, fade (11 · 21 · 25) 615
אֻמְלַל to be or grow feeble, languish (6 · 15[?] · 15[?]) 51
תֵּבֵל world (9 · 36) 385
חנף 5 to be polluted (1 · 6 · 10) 337

חָלַף to overstep, transgress, pass on (4 · 14 · 26) 322
הֵפֵר to break, violate (4 · 42 · 45) 830 I פור
אָלָה 6 curse (1 · 36) 46
אָשֵׁם to be held guilty, be guilty (1 · 31 · 33) 79
חר to burn, be burned (1 · 3 · 9) 359 I חרר
אֱנוֹשׁ men (8 · 42) 60
מִזְעָר a little; מְעַט מִזְעָר = a very little while (4 · 4) 277
אָבַל 7 to mourn (5 · 18 · 38) 5
תִּירוֹשׁ fresh or new wine (4 · 38) 440
אֻמְלַל to be or grow feeble, languish (6 · 15[?] · 15[?]) 51
נֶאֱנַח to sigh (1 · 12 · 12) 58
שָׂמֵחַ glad, joyful, merry (1 · 21) 970
מָשׂוֹשׂ 8 exultation (10 · 17) 965
תֹּף timbrel, tambourine (3 · 17) 1074
שָׁאוֹן uproar (8 · 18) 981
עַלִּיז exultant, jubilant (5 · 7) 759
כִּנּוֹר lyre (5 · 41) 490
מַר 9 to be bitter (1 · 6 · 16) 600 מרר
שֵׁכָר intoxicating drink, strong drink (8 · 23) 1016
קִרְיָה 10 town, city (10 · 30) 900
תֹּהוּ formlessness, primeval chaos (11 · 20) 1062
צְוָחָה 11 outcry (1 · 4) 846
ערב to grow dark, become evening (1 · 2 · 3) 788
מָשׂוֹשׂ exultation (10 · 17) 965
שַׁמָּה 12 a waste (3 · 39) 1031
שְׁאִיָּה ruin (1 · 1) 981
הכת to be crushed (1 · 4 · 17) 510 כתת
נֹקֶף 13 striking off (2 · 2) 668
זַיִת olive tree (2 · 38) 268
עוֹלֵלוֹת gleaning (2 · 6) 760
בָּצִיר vintage (2 · 7) 131

גָּאוֹן 14 exaltation, majesty (12 · 49) 144

צהל to cry shrilly (3 · 7 · 8) 843

אֻרִים 15 region of light, East (5 · 6[?]) 22

אִי coastland, island (17 · 36) 15

זָמִיר 16 song (2 · 6) 274

צְבִי honor (7 · 18) 840

רָזִי leanness, wasting (2 · 2) 931

אוֹי Woe! Alas! (4 · 25) 17

בָּגַד to act treacherously; ptc. = treacherous one (12 · 49 · 49) 93

בֶּגֶד treachery (1 · 2) 93

פַּחַד 17 dread (5 · 49) 808

פַּחַת pit (3 · 10) 809

פַּח bird trap (3 · 25) 809

פַּחַד 18 dread (5 · 49) 808

פַּחַת pit (3 · 10) 809

פַּח bird trap (3 · 25) 809

אֲרֻבָּה lattice, window (2 · 9) 70

רעש to quake, shake (2 · 21 · 29) 950

מוֹסָד foundation (3 · 13) 414

רֹעָה 19 breaking (1 · 1) 949 II רעע

התרעע to be broken in pieces (1 · 2 · 5[?]) 949 II רעע

פרר to split, divide (1 · 1 · 4) 830

התפוֹרר to be cracked through (1 · 1 · 4) 830 II פרר

מוֹט to totter, shake (3 · 15 · 39) 556

התמוֹטט to be shaken (1 · 1 · 39) 556 מוט

נוּעַ 20 to tremble (6 · 22 · 38) 631

שִׁכּוֹר drunken one, drunken (4 · 13) 1016

התנוֹדד to sway, totter (1 · 4 · 27) 626 נוד

מְלוּנָה hut; frail, insecure structure (2 · 2) 534

אֲסֵפָה 22 gathering (1 · 1) 63

אַסִּיר prisoners (4 · 17[?]) 64

מַסְגֵּר dungeon (2 · 7) 689

חפר 23 to be abashed, ashamed (2 · 13 · 17) 344

לְבָנָה moon [poet.] (2 · 3) 526

חַמָּה sun, heat (3 · 6) 328

Chapter 25

פֶּלֶא 1 wonder (3 · 13) 810

מֵרָחֹק long ago, of long standing (12 · 34) 935

אֹמֶן faithfulness; אֱמוּנָה אֹמֶן = perfect faithfulness (1 · 1) 53

גַּל 2 heap (2 · 20) 164

קִרְיָה town, city (10 · 30) 900

בָּצוּר cut off, made inaccessible (5 · 25) 130 בצר

מַפֵּלָה ruin (3 · 3) 658

אַרְמוֹן palace, castle, citadel (5 · 33) 74

עַז 3 fierce, formidable, strong (4 · 22) 738

קִרְיָה town, city (10 · 30) 900

עָרִיץ awe inspiring; terror striking (7 · 20) 792

מָעוֹז 4 refuge (10 · 36) 731

דַּל poor (5 · 48) 195

צַר distress, straits (6 · 21[?]) 865 II צר

מַחְסֶה shelter, refuge (4 · 20) 340

זֶרֶם rain storm (7 · 9) 281

חֹרֶב parching heat (5 · 16) 351

עָרִיץ awe inspiring; terror striking (7 · 20) 792

חֹרֶב 5 parching heat (5 · 16) 351

צָיוֹן dryness, parched ground (2 · 2) 851

שָׁאוֹן roar, din (8 · 18) 981

הִכְנִיעַ to humble (1 · 11 · 35) 488

עָב dark cloud (7 · 30) 728

זָמִיר song (2 · 6) 274

עָרִיץ awe inspiring; terror striking (7 · 20) 792

מִשְׁתֶּה 6 feast (3 · 45) 1059

שֶׁמֶר dregs (2 · 5) 1038

מחה ptc. only = full of marrow (1 · 1 · 1) 526 IV מחה

זקק to be refined; here = Pual. ptc. = refined (1 · 4 · 7) 279

בָּלַע 7 to swallow up, engulf (3 · 20 · 41) 118

לוֹט envelope, covering (1 · 1) 532

לוֹט to cover, enwrap, envelop (1 · 3 · 4) 532

מַסֵּכָה woven stuff, web (2[?] · 2[?]) 651

נסךְ to weave (1 · 1 · 1) 651

בָּלַע 8 to swallow up, engulf (3 · 20 · 41) 118

נֶצַח everlastingness; w. לְ = forever (7 · 43) 664

מָחָה to wipe, wipe out (3 · 22 · 34) 562 I

דִּמְעָה tears (3 · 23) 199

קָוָה 9 to wait or look eagerly for (13 · 39 · 45) 875

גִּיל to rejoice (11 · 45 · 45) 162

נָדוֹשׁ 10 to be trampled down (2 · 2 · 16) 190

מַתְבֵּן straw heap (1 · 1) 1062

בְּמִי = בְּמוֹ poetic for בְּ (4 · 10) 91

מַדְמֵנָה dung place, dung pit (1 · 1) 198

שׂחה 11 to swim (2 · 2 · 3) 965

הִשְׁפִּיל to lay low (6 · 19 · 30) 1050

גַּאֲוָה pride, haughtiness (5 · 19) 144

אָרְבָּה tricks, artifice (1 · 1) 70

מִבְצָר 12 fortress, stronghold (3 · 37) 131

מִשְׂגָּב stronghold, secure height, retreat (2 · 17) 960

הֵשַׁח to prostrate, lay low (2 · 2 · 18[?]) 1005 שׁחח

הִשְׁפִּיל to lay low, humiliate (6 · 19 · 30) 1050

Chapter 26

חֵל 1 rampart, little wall, fortress (1 · 9) 298

יֵצֶר 3 purpose, device, imagination (2 · 9) 428

סָמַךְ to sustain, uphold (4 · 41 · 48) 701

בָּטוּחַ trusted, trusts (1 · 2[?]) 105 I בטח

עֲדֵי 4 as far as, until (poetic for עַד) (1 · 12) 723 III עד

עַד forever, eternity (8 · 48) 723 I עד

עֲדֵי־עַד continuous existence, forever 723 [see above]

הֵשַׁח 5 to prostrate, lay low (2 · 2 · 18[?]) 1005

קִרְיָה town, city (10 · 30) 900

נִשְׂגָּב to be high (6 · 10 · 20) 960

הִשְׁפִּיל to lay low (6 · 19 · 30) 1050

רָמַס 6 to trample down (4 · 17 · 18) 942

דַּל reduced, weak, helpless (5 · 48) 195

מֵישָׁר 7 evenness, level (3 · 19) 449

מַעְגָּל track, course of action or life (2 · 13) 722

פִּלֵּס to make level, smooth (1 · 6 · 6) 814

קָוָה 8 to wait or look eagerly for (13 · 39 · 45) 875

זֵכֶר memorial, memory (2 · 23) 271

תַּאֲוָה desire, wish (1 · 21) 16

אָוָה 9 to desire (1 · 11 · 27) 16

שׁחר to seek (2 · 12 · 13) 1007

תֵּבֵל world (9 · 36) 385

נָכֹחַ 10 true, honest, straight (4 · 8) 647

עוּל to act wrongfully (1 · 2 · 2) 732

גֵּאוּת majesty (5 · 8) 145

רָם 11 high, exalted (7 · 31[?]) 926 רום

קִנְאָה [ardor of] anger (7 · 43) 888

שׁפת 12 to ordain, establish (1 · 5 · 5) 1046

בָּעַל 13 to rule over; to marry (4 · 10 · 12) 127

זוּלָה other than (4 · 16) 265

רְפָאִים 14 shades, ghosts (3 · 8) 952

זֵכֶר remembrance, memory (2 · 23) 271

קָצוּ 15 end, boundary (1 · 3) 892

צַר 16 straits, distress (5[?] · 20[?]) 865

צוּק to pour out (1 · 3 · 3) 848

לַחַשׁ whisper of prayer, whisper, charm (3 · 5) 538

מוּסָר chastening, chastisement (2 · 50) 416

הָרָה 17 pregnant (2 · 15) 247
חוּל to twist, writhe (9 · 30 · 47) 296
חֵבֶל pain, pang (3 · 7) 286
הָרָה 18 to conceive, become pregnant (4 · 38 · 40) 247
חוּל to twist, writhe (9 · 30 · 47) 296
תֵּבֵל world (9 · 36) 385
נְבֵלָה 19 corpse, carcass (2 · 48) 615
הֵקִיץ to awake (3 · 22 · 23) 884 I קיץ
טַל dew, night mist (3 · 31) 378
אוֹרָה herb (1 · 2) 21
רְפָאִים shades, ghosts; here of righteous (3 · 8) 952
הִפִּיל [idiom] bring to life [drop one's young] (>50) 658 נפל 6.
חֶדֶר 20 chamber, room (1 · 37) 293
חבה to withdraw, hide (1 · 1 · 4) 285
רֶגַע moment (5 · 22) 921
זַעַם indignation (5 · 22) 276

Chapter 27

קָשֶׁה 1 fierce, relentless, severe (6 · 36) 904
לִוְיָתָן serpent, dragon, leviathon (2 · 6) 531
נָחָשׁ serpent (4 · 31) 638
בָּרִחַ fleeing (2 · 3) 138
עֲקַלָּתוֹן crooked (1 · 1) 785
תַּנִּין sea monster, serpent, dragon (2 · 15) 1072
חֶמֶר 2 wine (1 · 2) 330
ענה to sing sweetly (1 · 3 · 16) 777
רֶגַע 3 moment; ל + pl. = every moment (5 · 22) 921
שָׁמִיר 4 thorns, thorn bushes (8 · 11) 1038
שַׁיִת thorn bushes (7 · 7) 1011
פָּשַׂע to step, march (1 · 1 · 1) 832
הִצִּית to kindle, set on fire (1 · 1 · 1[?]) 428 יצת
יַחַד altogether (7 · 44) 403

מָעוֹז 5 refuge (10 · 36) 731
הִשְׁרִישׁ 6 to take root (1 · 3 · 8)a 1057
צִיץ to blossom (1 · 7 · 8) 847
פָּרַח to bud, sprout (5 · 28 · 34) 827
תֵּבֵל world (9 · 36) 385
תְּנוּבָה fruit, produce (1 · 5) 626
מַכָּה blow, wound, slaughter (5 · 48) 646
הֶרֶג slaughter (2 · 5) 247
סָאסָא 8 to drive away (1 · 1 · 1) 684
הָגָה to remove (1 · 3 · 3) 212
קָשֶׁה severe, hard (6 · 36) 904
גִּר 9 chalk, lime (1 · 1) 162
נפץ to be pulverized (1 · 1 · 21) 658
אֲשֵׁרָה sacred trees or poles; symbol of Canaanitish goddess of fortune (2 · 40) 81
חַמָּן sun pillar, used in idolatrous worship (2 · 8) 329
בצר 10 to cut off, make inaccessible; ptc. = cut off, made inaccessible; fortified (5 · 25 · 25) 130
בָּדָד isolation, separation (1 · 11) 94
נָוֶה habitation (6 · 45) 627
עֵגֶל calf (2 · 35) 722
רָבַץ to lie down (6 · 24 · 30) 918
סָעִיף branches, boughs (2 · 2) 703
קָצִיר 11 boughs, branches (1 · 5) 894 II
הֵאִיר to light [ignite] (2 · 24 · 40) 21 אור
בִּינָה understanding (5 · 37) 108
רְחַם to have compassion, be compassionate (12 · 42 · 47) 933
עֹשֶׂה maker, creator (6 · 24) 793 I עשה
יָצַר to form, fashion (22 · 41 · 44) 427
חבט 12 to beat out (1 · 4 · 5) 286
שִׁבֹּלֶת flowing stream (3[?] · 20[?]) 987 I
לקט to be picked up (1 · 1 · 37) 544
נִדָּח 13 banished one, outcast (5 · 11) 623 נדח

235

Chapter 28

עֲטָרָה 1 crown (4 · 23) 742

גֵּאוּת majesty (5 · 8) 145

שָׁכוּר drunken one, drunken (4 · 13) 1016

צִיץ blossom, flower (4 · 15) 847

נָבֵל to wither and fall, fade (11 · 21 · 25) 615

צְבִי beauty, decoration (7 · 18) 840

תִּפְאָרָה beauty, finery, glory (18 · 50) 802

גַּיְא valley (5 · 47) 161

הָלַם to smite down, strike down, hammer (3 · 8 · 8) 240

אַמִּיץ 2 mighty (2 · 6) 55

זֶרֶם rain storm (7 · 9) 281

בָּרָד hail (3 · 29) 135

שַׂעַר storm (1 · 1) 973

קֶטֶב destruction (1 · 4) 881

כַּבִּיר great, mighty, much (3 · 10) 460

שָׁטַף to overflow (9 · 28 · 31) 1009

נרמס 3 to be trampled (1 · 1 · 18) 942

עֲטָרָה crown (4 · 23) 742

גֵּאוּת majesty (5 · 8) 145

שָׁכוּר drunken one, drunken (4 · 13) 1016

צִיצָה 4 blossom, flower (1 · 1[?]) 847

נָבֵל to wither and fall, fade (11 · 21 · 25) 615

צְבִי beauty, decoration (7 · 18) 840

תִּפְאָרָה beauty, finery, glory (18 · 50) 802

גַּיְא valley (5 · 47) 161

בִּכּוּרָה first ripe fig, early fig (1 · 4) 114

בְּטֶרֶם before (8 · 39) 382

קַיִץ summer, summer fruit (2 · 20) 884

בְּעוֹד while yet (3 · 20) 728 עוד 2.a.

בָּלַע to swallow down (1 · 20 · 41) 118

עֲטָרָה 5 crown (4 · 23) 742

צְבִי beauty, decoration (7 · 18) 840

צְפִירָה diadem, coronet (1 · 3) 862

תִּפְאָרָה beauty, finery, glory (18 · 50) 802

שְׁאָר remnant (12 · 26) 984

שׁגה 7 to reel, roll [in drunkenness] (3 · 17 · 21) 993

שֵׁכָר intoxicating drink, strong drink (8 · 23) 1016

תָּעָה to wander about (8 · 27 · 50) 1073

נִבְלַע to be swallowed up (1 · 1 · 6[?]) 118

רֹאֶה seer (2 · 12) 909

פּוּק to reel, totter (1 · 1 · 9) 807

פְּלִילִיָּה the giving of a decision (1 · 1) 813

קִיא 8 vomit (2 · 3) 883

צֹאָה filth (3 · 5) 844

בְּלִי without (3 · 23) 115

הוֹרָה 9 to direct, teach (4[?] · 45[?] · 45[?]) 434 ירה

דֵּעָה knowledge (2 · 6) 395

שְׁמוּעָה report (4 · 27) 1035

גָּמַל to wean (6 · 34 · 37) 168

חָלָב milk (4 · 44) 316

עַתִּיק removed (1 · 2) 801

שָׁד breast (2 · 21) 994

צַו 10 command [dub.] (8 · 9) 846

קַו mimicry of Isaiah's words (875), or line, measuring line (16 · [?] · 25[?]) 876

זְעֵיר a little (4 · 5) 277

לַעַג 11 mocking or לעג stammerings (1 [?] · 2[?]) 541

מְנוּחָה 12 rest, quietness (4 · 21) 629

עָיֵף faint, weary (5 · 17) 746

מַרְגֵּעָה rest, repose (1 · 1) 921

צַו 13 command [dub.] (8 · 9) 846

קַו mimicry of Isaiah's words (875), or line, measuring line (16[?] · 25[?]) 876

זְעֵיר a little (4 · 5) 277

אָחוֹר backwards (9 · 41) 30

נוקש to be caught by a bait, ensnared (2 · 4 · 8) 430 יקש

לָצוֹן 14 scorner, scorning (1 · 3) 539

משׁל ruler (1 · 2) 605 משׁל

236

חֹזֶה 15 vision (3 · 17) 304

שִׁיט scourge, whip (2 · 3[?]) 1002 שׁוט

שָׁטַף to overflow (9 · 28 · 31) 1009

כָּזָב lie, falsehood (2 · 31) 469

מַחְסֶה refuge (4 · 20) 340

יִסַּד 16 to found, establish (2 · 10 · 41) 413

בֹּחַן tested, tried (1 · 1) 103

פִּנָּה corner, cornerstone (2 · 30) 819

מוּסָד foundation (1 · 2) 414

הוּסָד hoph. ptc. = founded (1 · 3 · 41) 413 יסד

הֵחִישׁ to hasten, come quickly (3 · 6 · 21) 301 חושׁ

קָו 17 line, measuring line (16[?] · 25[?]) 876

מִשְׁקֶלֶת leveling instrument, level (1 · 2) 1054

יָעָה to sweep together (1 · 1 · 1) 418

בָּרָד hail (3 · 29) 135

מַחְסֶה refuge (4 · 20) 340

כָּזָב lie, falsehood (2 · 31) 469

סֵתֶר hiding place (5 · 35) 712

שָׁטַף to overflow (9 · 28 · 31) 1009

חָזוּת 18 vision; perh. here = agreement (3 · 5) 303

שׁוֹט scourge, whip (2 · 3[?]) 1002

שָׁטַף to overflow (9 · 28 · 31) 1009

מִרְמָס trampling (4 · 7) 942

מִדֵּי 19 out of the abundance of, as often as (3 · 15) 191 דַּי 2.c

בַּבֹּ קֶר בַּבֹּקֶר [idiom] morning by morning 133 בֹּקֶר 1.f.

זְוָעָה object of trembling, terror (1 · 1) 266

שְׁמוּעָה report (4 · 27) 1035

קָצַר 20 to be short (4 · 12 · 14) 894

מַצָּע couch, bed (1 · 1) 427

הִשְׂתָּרֵעַ to stretch oneself (1 · 1 · 3) 976

מַסֵּכָה covering, woven stuff (2[?] · 2[?]) 651

הִתְכַּנֵּס to gather oneself together (1 · 1 · 11) 488

רָגַז 21 to be excited, perturbed (6 · 30 · 41) 919

נָכְרִי strange; foreign, alien (2 · 45) 648

הִתְלוֹצֵץ 22 to act as a scorner, show oneself a mocker (1 · 1 · 12) 539 ליץ

מוֹסֵר bond, band (2 · 12) 64

כָּלָה complete destruction; completion (2 · 22) 478

נֶחֱרָץ Niph. ptc. = decisive (2 · 5 · 10) 358

הַאֲזִין 23 to give ear, hear (8 · 41 · 41) 24

הִקְשִׁיב to give attention (8 · 45 · 46) 904

אִמְרָה word, speech, utterance (5 · 30) 57

חָרַשׁ 24 to plough (2 · 23 · 26) 360

שִׂדֵּד to harrow (1 · 3 · 3) 961

שִׁוָּה 25 to level (2 · 5 · 16) 1000

קֶצַח black cumin, condiment (3 · 3) 892

כַּמֹּן cumin, condiment (3 · 3) 485

זָרַק to scatter, throw (1 · 32 · 34) 284

חִטָּה wheat (1 · 30) 334

שׂוֹרָה in rows [dub.] (1 · 1) 965

שְׂעֹרָה barley (1 · 34) 972

נִסְמָן ptc. = an appointed place, or determined portion (1 · 1 · 1) 702

כֻּסֶּמֶת spelt (1 · 3) 493

גְּבוּלָה border, boundary (2 · 10) 148

יִסַּר 26 to discipline, correct (1 · 27 · 38) 415

הוֹרָה to teach, direct (4[?] · 45[?] · 45[?]) 435 ירה

חָרוּץ 27 sharp (2 · 4) 358

הוּדַשׁ to be threshed (1 · 1 · 15) 190 דושׁ

קֶצַח black cumin, condiment (3 · 3) 892

אוֹפָן wheel (1 · 34) 66

עֲגָלָה cart, wagon (3 · 25) 722

כַּמֹּן cumin, condiment (3 · 3) 485

נֶחְבַּט to be beat out (1 · 1 · 5) 286

הוּדַק 28 to be crushed (1 · 1 · 13) 200 דקק

נֶצַח everlastingness; with ל = forever (7 · 43) 664

אדש	inf. only = to thresh (1·1·1) 12
הָמַם	to move noisily, make a noise (1·13·13) 243
גּלְגּל	wheel (1·1) 166
עֲגָלָה	cart, wagon (3·25) 722
דקק	to crush, pulverize (2·4·13) 200
הדק	to be crushed (1·1·13) 200
הִפְלִיא	29 to make wonderful, do wondrously (2·10·24) 810
תּוּשִׁיָּה	sound wisdom, abiding success (1·12) 444

Chapter 29

קִרְיָה	1 town, city (10·30) 900
נקף	to go around, to run the round of the year (1·1·17) 668
הֵצִיק	2 to bring into straits, press upon (2·11·11) 847
תַּאֲנִיָּה	mourning (1·2) 58
אֲנִיָּה	mourning (1·2) 58
דּוּר	3 circle (2·2) 189
צוּר	to shut in, besiege (3·31·31) 848
מַצָּב	palisade, intrenchment (1·2[?]) 663
מְצוּרָה	siege works, rampart (1·8) 849
שָׁפֵל	4 to become low, be humiliated (10·11·30) 1050
נשׁחח	to proceed humbly; be humbled, reduced (3·34·18[?]) 1005
אִמְרָה	word, speech, utterance (5·30) 57
אוֹב	ghost [here only] (3·16) 15
צפצף	to chirp, peep (4·4·4) 861 צפף
אָבָק	5 dust (2·6) 7
דַּק	small, fine [dust] (2·14) 201
מֹץ	chaff (3·8) 558
עָרִיץ	awe inspiring; terror striking (7·20) 792
פֶּתַע	suddenness; w. פתאם = at an instant (2·7) 837
פִּתְאֹם	suddenly (4·25) 837

רַעַם	6 thunder (1·6) 947
רַעַשׁ	earthquake (2·17) 950
סוּפָה	storm wind (5·15) 693
סְעָרָה	tempest, storm wind (3·16) 704
לַהַב	flame (4·12) 529
חָזוֹן	7 vision (2·35) 302
צבא	to wage war (4·12·14) 838
מְצוֹדָה	fastness, stronghold (1·3) 845
הֵצִיק	to bring into straits, press upon (4·11·11) 847 צוק I
חָלַם	8 to dream (2·26·28) 321
רָעֵב	hungry, hungry one (5·19) 944
הֵקִיץ	to awake (3·22·23) 884 קיץ
רֵיק	empty, vain (1·14) 938
צָמֵא	thirsty one, thirsty (5·9) 854
עָיֵף	faint, weary (5·17) 746
שׁקק	to run, run about, rush (2·5·6) 1055
צבא	to wage war (4·12·14) 838
הִתְמַהְמַהּ	9 to linger, tarry, wait (1·9·9) 554 מהה
תָּמַהּ	to be astounded (2·8·9) 1069
הִשְׁתַּעְשֵׁע	to blind yourselves (1·1·3) 1044 I שׁעע
שׁעע	to be blind (1·1·3) 1044 I
שׁכר	to become drunken (2·9·18) 1016
נוע	to stagger (6·22·38) 631
שֵׁכָר	intoxicating drink, strong drink (8·23) 1016
נָסַךְ	10 to pour out (4·7·25) 650
תַּרְדֵּמָה	deep sleep (1·7) 922
עצם	to shut tightly (1·1·2) 783
חֹזֶה	seer (3·17) 302
חָזוּת	11 vision (3·5) 303
חתם	to seal up (3·23·27) 367
הִפְלִיא	14 to make wonderful, do wondrously (2·10·24) 810
פֶּלֶא	wonder (3·13) 810
בִּינָה	understanding (5·37) 108
נָבוֹן	intelligent, discerning (3·21) 106 בין

הַעְמִיק 15 to make deep (4 · 8 · 9) 770

מַחְשָׁךְ dark place (2 · 7) 365

הֶפֶךְ 16 perversity, contrariness; w. suffix = Oh, your perversity! (1 · 3) 246

חֹמֶר clay, mortar (5 · 17) 330

יוֹצֵר potter (3 · 17[?]) 427 יצר

עֹשֶׂה maker, creator (6 · 24[?]) 793 I עשׂה

יֵצֶר pottery (2 · 9) 428

יָצַר to form (22 · 41 · 44) 427

מִזְעָר 17 a little; מעט מזער = a very little while (4 · 4) 277

כַּרְמֶל garden land (8 · 14) 502

חֵרֵשׁ 18 deaf (5 · 9) 361

אֹפֶל darkness, gloom (1 · 9) 66

עִוֵּר blind (11 · 26) 734

עָנָו 19 poor and weak (3[?] · 21[?]) 776

גִּיל to rejoice (11 · 45 · 45) 162

אָפֵס 20 to cease, fail, come to an end (2 · 5 · 5) 67

עָרִיץ ruthless, terror-striking (7 · 20) 792

לֵץ scorner (1 · 16) 539 ליץ

שָׁקַד to keep watch, be wakeful over (1 · 11 · 17) 1052

קוֹשׁ 21 to lay bait or lure (1 · 1 · 1) 881

תֹּהוּ unreality, emptiness (11 · 20) 1062

חוּר 22 to be or grow white, pale (1 · 1 · 1) 301

הֶעֱרִיץ 23 to regard or treat with awe (2 · 2 · 14) 791

תָּעָה 24 to wander about (8 · 27 · 50) 1073

בִּינָה understanding (5 · 37) 108

רָגַן to murmur (1 · 1 · 3) 920

לֶקַח instruction, learning, teaching (1 · 9) 544

Chapter 30

סָרַר 1 to be stubborn, rebellious (3 · 17 · 17) 710

נָסַךְ to pour out (4 · 7 · 25) 650

מַסֵּכָה libation (in a covenant formation) (1[?] · 1[?]) 651

ספה to snatch away; sweep away (2 · 8 · 18) 705

עוֹז 2 to take or seek refuge (1 · 1 · 5) 781

מָעוֹז protection (10 · 36) 731

חָסָה to seek refuge (3 · 37 · 37) 340

מָעוֹז 3 protection (10 · 36) 731

בֹּשֶׁת shame (5 · 30) 102

חָסוּת refuge (1 · 1) 340

כְּלִמָּה ignominy, reproach (4 · 30) 484

הוֹעִיל 5 to profit, avail, benefit (8 · 23 · 23) 418

עֵזֶר help, succour (1 · 21) 740

בֹּשֶׁת shame (5 · 30) 102

מַשָּׂא 6 utterance, oracle (11 · 21) 672

צוּקָה pressure, distress (2 · 3) 848

לָבִיא lion, lioness (2 · 11) 522

לַיִשׁ lion (1 · 3) 539

אֶפְעֶה a kind of viper (2 · 3) 821

שָׂרָף fiery serpent (4 · 7[?]) 977

עוֹפֵף to fly about, to and fro (3 · 5 · 25) 733

עַיִר male ass (2 · 9) 747

דַּבֶּשֶׁת hump [of camel] (1 · 1) 185

הוֹעִיל to profit, avail, benefit (8 · 23 · 23) 418 יעל

רִיק 7 emptiness, vanity (3 · 12) 938

רַהַב storm, arrogance (2 · 7) 923

שֶׁבֶת cessation [dub.] (1 · 7[?]) 992

לוּחַ 8 tablet, plate (1 · 43) 531

הקק to cut in or on, inscribe (4 · 8 · 11) 349

עַד forever (8 · 48) 723 I עד

מְרִי 9 rebellion (1 · 22) 598

כֶּחָשׁ deceptive, false (1 · 1) 471

רֹאֶה seer (2 · 12) 909

נָכֹחַ true, honest (4 · 8) 647

חֹזֶה seer (3 · 17) 302

חָלָק smoothness = flattery (2[?] · 12[?]) 325

239

מַהֲתַלּוֹת 10 deceptions (1 · 1) 251, 1122

עֹשֶׁק 12 extortion, oppression (3 · 15) 799

נָלוֹז ptc. = devious, crooked (1 · 4 · 6) 531

נִשְׁעָן to lean, support oneself (5 · 22 · 22) 1043

פֶּרֶץ 13 broken wall, breach (2 · 19) 829

נִבְעֶה ptc. = swelling (1 · 2 · 4) 126

נִשְׂגָּב to be high (6 · 10 · 20) 960

פִּתְאֹם suddenly (4 · 25) 837

פֶּתַע suddenness; w. פתאם = at an instant, suddenly (2 · 7) 837

שֶׁבֶר shattering, breaking (9 · 45) 991

שֶׁבֶר 14 breaking (9 · 45) 991

נֵבֶל [earthen] jar, pitcher (2 · 11) 614

יוֹצֵר potter, activity of potter (3 · 17) 427 יצר

כָּתַת to beat or crush fine (1 · 5 · 17) 510

חָמַל to spare, have compassion (2 · 40 · 40) 328

מְכִתָּה crushed fragments (1 · 1) 510

חֶרֶשׂ a fragment of earthenware, sherd (3 · 17) 360

חָתָה to snatch up (1 · 3 · 3) 367

יָקוּד kindled, as subst. = what is kindled (1[?] · 1[?]) 428 יקד

חָשַׂף to draw, skim, take from the surface (3 · 10 · 10) 362

גֶּבֶא cistern, pool (1 · 2) 146

שׁוּבָה 15 retirement, withdrawal (1 · 1) 1000

נַחַת quietness, quiet attitude (1 · 7) 629

הַשְׁקֵט to show quietness, display quietness; inf. abs. = subst., quietness (4 · 10 · 41) 1052

בִּטְחָה trusting (1 · 1) 105

קַל 16 swift, light (4 · 13) 886

אֶלֶף 17 [pl. only] cattle (1 · 8) 48

גַּעֲרָה rebuke (6 · 15) 172

תֹּרֶן mast, flagstaff (2 · 3) 1076

נֵס standard, signal (10 · 21) 651

חִכָּה 18 to wait (3 · 13 · 14) 314

רָחַם to have compassion, be compassionate (12 · 42 · 47) 933

אֶשֶׁר blessedness, happiness (3 · 45[?]) 80

חכה to wait for (1 · 1 · 14) 314

צַר 20 distress, straits (5[?] · 20[?]) 865

לַחַץ oppression, distress (1 · 12) 537

נִכְנָף to be thrust into a corner, cornered (1 · 1 · 1) 489

מוֹרֶה teacher (2 · 9) 435

תַּאֲמִינוּ 21 you go to the right (1 · 5 · 5) 412 ימן

הִשְׂמְאִיל to turn [aside] to the left [fr. true way] (1 · 5 · 5) 970 שמאל

צִפּוּי 22 plating (1 · 5) 860

פָּסִיל idol, image (4 · 23) 820

אֲפֻדָּה ephod [of sheathing of idol images] (1 · 3) 65

מַסֵּכָה molten metal, or image (2 · 25) 651

זרה to scatter (3 · 9 · 38) 279

דָּוֶה unwell, menstruous (1 · 5) 188

מָטָר 23 rain (3 · 38) 564

תְּבוּאָה product, yield (2 · 43) 100

דָּשֵׁן fat (1 · 3) 206

שָׁמֵן fat, rich (1 · 10) 1032

כַּר pasture (1 · 3) 499

נרחב to be broad, roomy (1 · 1 · 25) 931

אֶלֶף 24 pl. only = cattle (1 · 8) 48

עַיִר male ass (2 · 9) 747

בְּלִיל fodder (1 · 3) 117

חָמִיץ seasoned; of provender for cattle (1 · 1) 330

זרה to scatter, winnow (3 · 9 · 38) 279

רַחַת winnowing shovel (1 · 1) 935

מִזְרֶה pitch fork (1 · 2) 280

גָּבֹהַּ 25 high (6 · 41) 147

פֶּלֶג channel, canal (2 · 10) 811

יָבָל watercourse, stream (2 · 2) 385

הֶרֶג slaughter (2 · 5) 247

מִגְדָּל tower (4 · 49) 153

לְבָנָה	26	moon [poet.] (2 · 3) 526
חַמָּה		sun; heat [poet.] (3 · 6) 328
חבש		to bind up (2 · 28 · 32) 289
שֶׁבֶר		fracture, breaking (9 · 45) 991
מַחַץ		severe wound (1 · 1) 563
מַכָּה		beating, scourging, wound (5 · 48) 646
מֶרְחָק	27	distant place, far country (7 · 18) 935
כֹּבֶד		vehemence, heaviness (2 · 4) 458
מַשָּׂאָה		the uplifted [cloud] (1[?] · 16[?]) 673
זַעַם		indignation (5 · 22) 276
שָׁטַף	28	to overflow (9 · 28 · 31) 1009
צַוָּאר		neck, back of neck (4 · 41) 848
חָצָה		to halve (1 · 11 · 15) 345
נָפָה		sieve, or other winnowing implement (1 · 1) 632
רֶסֶן		halter (1 · 4) 943
הִתְעָה		to cause to wander about (6 · 21 · 50) 1073
לְחִי		jaw, cheek (2 · 21) 534
חָלִיל	29	flute, pipe (2 · 6) 319
הוֹד	30	splendor, majesty (1 · 24) 217
נַחַת		descent (1 · 1) 639
זַעַף		rage (1 · 7) 277
לַהַב		flame (4 · 12) 529
נֶפֶץ		driving storm, bursting of clouds (1 · 1) 658
זֶרֶם		rain storm (7 · 9) 281
בָּרָד		hail (3 · 29) 135
מַעֲבָר	32	passing, sweep (1 · 3) 721
מוּסָדָה		appointment, foundation (1 · 2) 414
תֹּף		timbrel, tambourine (3 · 17) 1074
כִּנּוֹר		lyre (5 · 41) 490
תְּנוּפָה		a brandishing, waving (2 · 30) 632
אֶתְמוֹל	33	yesterday; w. מִן from yesterday = already (1 · 8) 1069
הֶעֱמִיק		to make deep (4 · 8 · 9) 770
הִרְחִיב		to make large (5 · 21 · 25) 931
מְדוּרָה		pile, pyre (1 · 2) 190
נִשְׁמָה		breath; spirit (4 · 24) 675

גָּפְרִית		brimstone (2 · 7) 172

Chapter 31

עֶזְרָה	1	help, succour, assistance (4 · 26) 740
נִשְׁעַן		to lean, support oneself (5 · 22 · 22) 1043
עָצַם		to be numerous (1 · 16 · 18) 782
שָׁעָה		to regard, gaze at (5 · 12 · 15) 1043
מֵרַע	2	evildoer (4 · 18) 949 רעע vb. denom.
עֶזְרָה		help, succour, assistance (4 · 26) 740
הָגָה	4	to growl, moan (7 · 23 · 25) 211
אַרְיֵה		lion (6 · 45) 71
כְּפִיר		young lion (3 · 31) 498
טֶרֶף		prey, food (2 · 17) 383
מְלֹא		mass, fullness (5 · 38) 571
צבא		to wage war (4 · 12 · 14) 838
צִפּוֹר	5	[coll.] bird[s] (1 · 40) 861
עוּף		to hover, fly (4 · 18 · 25) 733
גנן		to defend (4 · 8[?] · 8[?]) 170
פָּסַח		to pass or spring over (1 · 5 · 7[?]) 820
לַאֲשֶׁר	6	to whom (4 · 38) 82 אשר 4.c.
הֶעֱמִיק		to make deep (4 · 8 · 9) 770
סָרָה		apostasy, withdrawal, defection (3 · 7) 694
אֱלִיל	7	worthless idols (10 · 20) 47
חֵטְא		sin (4 · 33) 307
בָּחוּר	8	young man (6 · 45) 104
מַס		labor bands, slave gangs (1 · 23) 587
מָגוֹר	9	fear, terror (1-8) 159
נֵס		standard, signal (10 · 21) 651
אוּר		fire (5 · 6) 22
תַּנּוּר		fire pot, portable stove (1 · 15) 1072

Chapter 32

שׂרר	1	to govern, rule, act as prince (1 · 5 · 8) 979
מַחֲבֵא	2	hiding place (1 · 1) 285

241

סֵתֶר	hiding place (5 · 35) 712
זֶרֶם	rain storm (7 · 9) 281
פֶּלֶג	channel, canal (2 · 10) 811
צָיוֹן	dryness, parched ground (2 · 2) 851
כָּבֵד	heavy (3 · 40) 458
עָיֵף	faint, weary (5 · 17) 746
שָׁעָה	3 to be blinded (5 · 12 · 15) 1043 (1044 שעע)
קָשַׁב	to incline, attend (1 · 1 · 46) 904
עָלֵג	4 speaking inarticulately (1 · 1) 748
צַח	clear, glowing (2 · 4) 850
נָבָל	5 fool, impious or presumptuous person (2 · 18) 614
נָדִיב	noble in mind, generous (3 · 27) 622
כִּילַי	knave (2 · 2) 647
שׁוֹעַ	noble (1 · 2) 447
נָבָל	6 fool, impious or presumptuous person (2 · 18) 614
נְבָלָה	disgraceful folly, senselessness (2 · 13) 615
חֹנֶף	profaneness (1 · 1) 338
תּוֹעָה	error, wandering (1 · 2) 1073
הֵרִיק	to empty, keep empty (1 · 17 · 19) 937
רָעֵב	hungry, hungry one (5 · 19) 944
מַשְׁקֶה	drink (1 · 19[?]) 1052
צָמֵא	thirsty one, thirsty (5 · 9) 854
הֶחְסִיר	to cause to be lacking, fail (1 · 2 · 23[?]) 341
כִּילַי	7 knave (2 · 2) 647
זִמָּה	evil device, plan (1 · 28[?]) 273
חִבֵּל	to ruin, destroy (3 · 6 · 10) 287
עָנָו	poor, weak (3 · 12) 776
אֹמֶר	speech, word (2 · 48[?]) 56
נָדִיב	8 noble in mind, generous (3 · 27) 622
נְדִיבָה	nobility, nobleness (2 · 3) 622
שַׁאֲנָן	9 at ease, carelessly at ease (5 · 11) 983
הַאֲזִין	to give ear, hear, listen (8 · 41 · 41) 24
אִמְרָה	word, speech, utterance (5 · 30) 57
רָגַז	10 to come quivering, quake (6 · 30 · 41) 919
בָּצִיר	vintage (2 · 7) 131
אֹסֶף	gathering (2 · 3) 63
בְּלִי	not; particle of negation (3 · 23) 115
חָרַד	11 to tremble, be terrified (4 · 23 · 39) 353
שַׁאֲנָן	at ease, carelessly at ease (5 · 11) 983
רָגַז	to come quivering, quake (6 · 30 · 41) 919
פָּשַׁט	to strip off, put off (1 · 24 · 43) 832
ערר	to strip oneself (1 · 1 · 4) 792
חגר	to gird on (3 · 44 · 44) 291
חָלָץ	[dual] = loins (3 · 10) 323
שַׁד	12 breast (2 · 21) 994
ספד	to wail, lament (1 · 28 · 30) 704
חֶמֶד	desire, delight (1 · 5) 326
פרה	to bear fruit, be fruitful (4 · 22 · 29) 826
קוֹץ	13 thornbush (2 · 11) 881
שָׁמִיר	thorns, thornbushes (8 · 11) 1038
מָשׂוֹשׂ	exultation (10 · 17) 965
קִרְיָה	town, city (10 · 30) 900
עַלִּיז	exultant, jubilant (5 · 7) 759
אַרְמוֹן	14 palace, castle, citadel (5 · 33) 74
נֻטַּשׁ	to be abandoned, deserted (1 · 1 · 40) 643
עֹפֶל	mound, hill (1 · 8) 779
בַּחַן	watchtower (1 · 1) 103
בְּעַד	on behalf of = take the place of, serve as (>50) 126
מְעָרָה	den, cave (1[?] · 1[?]) 792
מָשׂוֹשׂ	exultation (10 · 17) 965
פֶּרֶא	wild ass (1 · 10) 825
מִרְעֶה	pasture (1 · 13) 945
עֵדֶר	flock, herd (3 · 39) 727
נערה	15 to be poured out (1 · 1 · 15) 788
כַּרְמֶל	garden land (8 · 14) 502

242

כַּרְמֶל 16 garden land (8 · 14) 502

הַשְׁקֵט 17 to show quietness; inf. abs. =
subst. = quietness (4 · 10 · 41) 105

בֶּטַח security (3 · 43) 105

נָוֶה 18 habitation (6 · 45) 627

מִבְטָח confidence (1 · 15) 105

מְנוּחָה resting place, rest (4 · 21) 629

שַׁאֲנָן secure; at ease (5 · 11) 983

בָּרַד 19 to hail (1 · 1 · 1) 136

שִׁפְלָה humiliation (1 · 1) 1050

שָׁפֵל to be humiliated, brought low
(10 · 11 · 30) 1050

אֶשֶׁר 20 happiness, blessedness (3 · 45[?]) 80

Chapter 33

בָּגַד 1 to act treacherously (12 · 49 · 49) 93

כַּנְלֹתְךָ [dub.] when you cease, finish
(1 · 1) 649 נלה

קִוָּה 2 to wait or look eagerly for
(13 · 39 · 45) 875

נָדַד 3 to retreat, flee (8 · 20 · 24) 622

רוֹמְמוּת uplifting, arising (1 · 1) 928

נָפַץ to be scattered (1 · 5 · 21) 659 II

אֹסֶף 4 gathering (2 · 3) 63

חָסִיל [a kind of] locust (1 · 6) 340

מַשָּׁק running, rushing (1 · 1) 1055

גֵּב locust (1 · 1) 146

שָׁקַק to run, run about, rush (2 · 5 · 6) 1055

נִשְׂגָּב 5 to be exalted, high (6 · 10 · 20) 960

חֹסֶן 6 wealth, treasure (1 · 5) 340

יִרְאָה fear, reverence; terror (5 · 45) 432

אֶרְאֶלָּם 7 heroes [dub.] (1 · 1 · 1) 72 אראל

מַר bitter, bitterness; bitterly (6 · 38) 600

מְסִלָּה 8 highway, public road (9 · 27) 700

הֵפֵר to break, violate (4 · 42 · 45) 830 פרר

אֱנוֹשׁ men (8 · 42) 60

אָבַל 9 to mourn (5 · 18 · 38) 5

אֻמְלַל to be or grow feeble, languish
(6 · 15[?] · 15[?]) 51

הֶחְפִּיר to display shame (2 · 4 · 17) 344

קָמַל to be decayed (2 · 2 · 2) 888

נָעַר to shake, shake out, shake off
(2 · 4 · 11) 654

הָרָה 11 to conceive, become pregnant
(4 · 38 · 40) 247

חֲשַׁשׁ chaff (2 · 2) 366

קַשׁ stubble, chaff (5 · 16) 905

מִשְׂרְפוֹת 12 burning (1 · 2) 977

שִׂיד lime (1 · 4) 966

קוֹץ thornbush (2 · 11) 881

כָּסַח to cut off or away (1 · 2 · 2) 492

יָצַת to kindle, be kindled (2 · 4 · 27) 428

מֵרָחֹק 13 distant, at a distance (12 · 34) 935

פָּחַד 14 to be in dread (7 · 23 · 26) 808

חַטָּא sinners (3 · 19) 308

רְעָדָה trembling (1 · 4) 944

חָנֵף profane, godless (3 · 13) 338

מוֹקֵד a burning mass (1 · 3) 428

מֵישָׁר 15 uprightness, equity (3 · 19) 449

בֶּצַע unjust gain, gain made by violence
(3 · 23) 130

מַעֲשַׁקּוֹת extortionate act[s] (1 · 2) 799

נָעַר to shake off, shake (2 · 4 · 11) 654

תָּמַךְ to lay hold of, grasp (3 · 20 · 21) 1069

שֹׁחַד bribe, present (4 · 23) 1005

אָטַם to shut (1 · 8 · 8) 31

עָצַם to shut (1 · 1 · 2) 783 III

מְצָד 16 mountain fastness, stronghold
(1 · 11) 844

מִשְׂגָּב secure height, retreat (2 · 17) 960

יָפִי 17 beauty (2 · 19) 421

מֶרְחָק distant place, distance (7 · 18) 935

הָגָה 18 to meditate, muse, moan
(7 · 23 · 25) 211

אֵימָה terror, dread (1 · 16 · 17) 33

אַיֵּה where? (9 · 44) 32

שָׁקַל to weigh (4 · 19 · 22) 1053

מִגְדָּל tower (4 · 49) 153

נוֹעֵז 19 ptc. = barbarous [dub.] (1 · 1 · 1) יעז 418

עָמֵק deep, unfathomable; עִמְקֵי שָׂפָה unintelligible of speech (1 · 3) 771

נִלְעַג to stammer, ptc. = stammering (1 · 1 · 18) 541

בִּינָה understanding (5 · 37) 108

קִרְיָה 20 town, city (10 · 30) 900

נָוֶה habitation (6 · 45) 627

שַׁאֲנָן secure, at ease (5 · 11) 983

צָעַן to travel, wander (1 · 1 · 1) 858

יָתֵד tent pin, peg (4 · 23) 450

נֶצַח everlastingness; with ל = forever (7 · 43) 664

חֶבֶל cord, rope (3 · 49) 286

נִתַּק to be torn apart, torn in two (2 · 10 · 27) 683

אַדִּיר 21 majestic (3 · 27) 12

רָחָב wide, broad (2 · 21) 932

רְחַב־יָדַיִם [idiom] wide in both directions 390 יָד 3.d.

אֳנִי ships, fleet (1 · 7) 58

שַׁיִט rowing (1[?] · 1[?]) 1002

צִי ship (1 · 4) 850

מְחֹקֵק 22 prescriber [of laws], commander (1 · 7) 349 חקק

נֻטַּשׁ 23 to be loosened, loose; let alone (2 · 6 · 40) 643

חֶבֶל cord, rope (3 · 49) 286

כֵּן base, pedestal (1 · 17) 487

תֹּרֶן mast, flagstaff (2 · 3) 1076

נֵס sail, ensign, standard (10 · 21) 651

עַד booty, prey (1 · 3) 723

מַרְבֶּה abundance, increase (2 · 2) 916

פִּסֵּחַ lame (2 · 14) 820

בָּזַז to plunder, dispoil (7 · 37 · 41) 102

בַּז spoil, booty, plunder (5 · 27) 103

שָׁכֵן 24 inhabitant (1 · 20) 1015

Chapter 34

לְאֹם 1 people (11 · 35) 522

הִקְשִׁיב to give attention (8 · 45 · 46) 904

מְלֹא fullness, entire contents (5 · 38) 571

תֵּבֵל world (9 · 36) 385

צֶאֱצָא produce, offspring (7 · 11) 425

קֶצֶף 2 wrath (3 · 28) 893

הֶחֱרִים to destroy, exterminate; to be devoted (3 · 46 · 49) 355

טֶבַח slaughter (4 · 12) 370

פֶּגֶר 3 corpse, carcass (4 · 22) 803

בְּאֹשׁ stench (1 · 3) 93

נָמֵס to melt, dissolve (3 · 19 · 21) 587 מסס

נָמֵק 4 to molder away, rot away (1 · 9 · 10) 596

נָגֹלל to roll (1 · 2 · 17) 164

נָבֵל to wither and fall, fade (11 · 21 · 25) 615

עָלֶה leaf, leafage (3 · 18) 750

תְּאֵנָה fig tree (3 · 39) 1061

רִוָּה 5 to be intoxicated, drunk, saturated (3 · 6 · 14) 924

חֵרֶם devotion, ban involving destruction (2 · 29) 356

הֻדַּשַׁן 6 hothp., to make oneself fat (1 · 1 · 11) 206

כַּר male lamb (2 · 11) 503

עַתּוּד male goat (3 · 29) 800

כִּלְיָה kidney (1 · 31) 480

טֶבַח slaughter (4 · 12) 370

רְאֵם 7 wild ox (1 · 9) 910

אַבִּיר mighty (3 · 17) 7

רִוָּה to be intoxicated, drunk, saturated (3 · 6 · 14) 924

דִּשֵּׁן to be made fat (1 · 4 · 11) 206

נָקָם 8 vengeance (6 · 17) 668

שִׁלּוּם requital, retribution, reward (1 · 3) 1024

זֶפֶת 9 pitch (2 · 3) 278

244

גׇּפְרִית	brimstone, pitch, sulphur (2 · 7) 172	דַּיָּה	bird of prey, possibly a kite (1 · 2) 178
כבה	10 to be quenched, extinguished (3 · 14 · 24) 459	רְעוּת	fellow [woman] (2 · 6) 946
עָשָׁן	smoke (7 · 25) 798	נֶעְדַּר	16 to be lacking (3 · 6 · 7) 727
חׇרֵב	to be waste, desolate (6 · 17 · 37[?]) 351	רְעוּת	fellow [woman] (2 · 6) 946
נֶצַח	everlastingness (7 · 43) 664	קַו	17 line, measuring line (16[?] · 25[?]) 876
קָאַת	11 bird, usually a pelican (1 · 5) 886		
קִפֹּד	porcupine (2 · 3) 891		
יַנְשׁוֹף	bird, prob. a kind of owl (1 · 3) 676	**Chapter 35**	
עֹרֵב	raven (2 · 12) 788	שׂוֹשׂ	1 to exult, display joy (9 · 27 · 27) 965
קַו	line, measuring line (16[?] · 25[?]) 876	שׂוּשׂ	
תֹהוּ	formlessness, primeval chaos (11 · 20) 1062	צִיָּה	desert, dryness (3 · 16) 851
בֹּהוּ	emptiness, wasteness (1 · 3) 96	גִּיל	to rejoice (11 · 45 · 45) 162
חֹר	12 noble (1 · 13) 359	פָּרַח	to bud, sprout (5 · 28 · 34) 827
מְלוּכָה	kingship, kingly office, royalty (2 · 24) 574	חֲבַצֶּלֶה	meadow saffron, or crocus (1 · 2) 287
אֶפֶס	nought; i.e., nothing (14 · 43) 67	פָּרַח	2 to bud, sprout (5 · 28 · 34) 827
אַרְמוֹן	13 palace, citadel, castle (5 · 33) 74	גִּיל	to rejoice (11 · 45 · 45) 162
סִיר	thorn, hook (1 · 5) 696	גִּילָה	rejoicing (2 · 2) 162
קִמּוֹשׂ	thistles, nettles [coll.] (1 · 3) 888	הָדָר	splendor, majesty (7 · 30) 214
חוֹחַ	brier, bramble (1 · 11) 296	רָפֶה	3 slack (1 · 4) 952
מִבְצָר	fortress, stronghold (3 · 37) 131	בֶּרֶךְ	knee (3 · 25) 139
נָוֶה	habitation (6 · 45) 627	אמץ	to make firm, strengthen (3 · 19 · 41)
תַּן	jackal (4 · 14) 1072	נָקָם	4 vengeance (6 · 17) 668
חָצִיר	green grass (8 · 18[?]) 348	גְּמוּל	dealing, recompense, benefit (5 · 19) 168
יַעֲנָה	ostrich (3 · 8) 418	נפקח	5 to be opened (1 · 3 · 20) 824
פגשׁ	14 to meet, encounter (1 · 10 · 14) 803	עִוֵּר	blind (11 · 26) 734
צִי	wild beast, desert dweller (3 · 6) 850	חֵרֵשׁ	deaf (5 · 9) 361
אִי	jackal (2 · 3) 17	דלג	6 to leap, leap over (1 · 4 · 5) 194
שָׂעִיר	satyr [demon w. goat form] (2 · 4) 972	אַיָּל	hart, stag, deer (1 · 11) 19
הרגיע	to rest, repose (2 · 8 · 13) 921 II	פִּסֵּחַ	lame (2 · 14) 820
לִילִית	Lilith [female night demon] (1 · 1) 539	אִלֵּם	dumb, unable to speak (2 · 6) 48
מָנוֹחַ	resting place (1 · 7) 629	שָׁרָב	7 parched ground, burning heat (2 · 2) 1055
קנן	15 to make a nest (1 · 4 · 5) 890	אֲגַם	troubled pool (4 · 8) 8
קִפּוֹז	arrow snake (1 · 1) 891	צִמָּאוֹן	thirsty ground (1 · 3) 855
דגר	to gather together as a brood (1 · 2 · 2) 186	מַבּוּעַ	spring of water (2 · 3) 616

נָוֶה   habitation (6 · 45) 627

תַּן   jackal (4 · 14) 1072

רֵבֶץ   resting place, place of lying down (2 · 4) 918

חָצִיר   an abode, home (2 · 3[?]) 347

גֹּמֶא   rush, paper reeds (2 · 4) 167

מַסְלוּל   8 highway (1 · 1) 700

אֱוִיל   foolish (2 · 26) 17

תָּעָה   to wander about (8 · 27 · 50) 1073

אַרְיֵה   9 lion (6 · 45) 71

פָּרִיץ   violent one (1 · 6) 829

רִנָּה   10 ringing cry [in joy] (9 · 33) 943

שָׂשׂוֹן   exultation, joy (6 · 22) 965

הִשִּׂיג   to reach, attain; to overtake (3 · 49 · 49) 673

יָגוֹן   grief, sorrow (2 · 14) 387

אֲנָחָה   sighing, groaning (3 · 11) 58

Chapter 36

בָּצוּר   1 cut off, made inaccessible (5 · 25) בצר 130

כָּבֵד   2 massive, abundant, numerous; heavy (3 · 40) 458

תְּעָלָה   conduit, watercourse, trench (2 · 9) 752

בְּרֵכָה   pool, pond (4 · 17) 140

מְסִלָּה   highway, public road (9 · 27) 700

מַזְכִּיר   3 recorder, title of public officer (2 · 9) 271 זכר

בִּטָּחוֹן   4 trust (1 · 3) 105

מָרַד   5 to rebel, revolt (1 · 25 · 25) 597

מִשְׁעֶנֶת   6 staff (2 · 12) 1044

רצץ   to crush, ptc. pass. = crushed (4 · 11 · 19) 954

נסמך   to support oneself, brace oneself (2 · 6 · 48) 702

נקב   to pierce, bore (2 · 13 · 19) 666

התערב   8 to exchange pledges; hence = make a bargain (1 · 2 · 17) 786

פֶּחָה   9 governor (1 · 28) 808

קָטֹן   small [with added idea of weakness] (2 · 47) 881

מִבַּלְעֲדִי   10 apart from, without (5 · 12) 116 בלעדי b.

אֲרָמִית   11 Aramaic (1 · 4) 74

יְהוּדִית   Jewish (2 · 6) 397

חֲרָאִים   12 dung (1 · 3) 351 חֲרֵא

[Q צֹאָה   excrement, filth (3 · 5) 844]

שַׁיִן   urine (1 · 2) 1010

יְהוּדִית   13 Jewish (2 · 6) 397

הִשִּׁיא   14 to beguile (2 · 15 · 16) 674 נשא

בְּרֵכָה   16 pond, pool (4 · 17) 140

תְּאֵנָה   fig tree (3 · 39) 1061

דָּגָן   17 corn, grain (2 · 40) 186

תִּירוֹשׁ   fresh or new wine (4 · 38) 440

הֵסִית   18 to instigate, allure, incite (1 · 18 · 18) 694

אַיֵּה   19 where? (9 · 44) 32

הֶחֱרִישׁ   21 to be silent (3 · 38 · 46) 361

מַזְכִּיר   22 recorder, title for public officer (2 · 9) 271 זכר

Chapter 37

שַׂק   1 sackcloth (8 · 48) 974

שַׂק   2 sackcloth (8 · 48) 974

תּוֹכֵחָה   3 rebuke, correction (1 · 4) 407

נְאָצָה   contempt (1 · 2) 611

מַשְׁבֵּר   breach, mouth of womb (1 · 3) 991

לֵדָה   give birth (inf. cs.) (1 · 4[?]) 408 ילד

אוּלַי   4 perhaps (3 · 45) 19

חֵרֵף   to reproach, say sharp things against, taunt (5 · 34 · 38) 357

גִּדֵּף   6 to blaspheme (2 · 7 · 7) 154

שְׁמוּעָה   7 report (4 · 27) 1035

הִשִּׂיא   10 to beguile (2 · 15 · 16) 674

הֶחֱרִים   11 to destroy, exterminate, be devoted (3 · 46 · 49) 355

אַיֵּה   13 where? (9 · 44) 32

פָּקַח 17 to open (3 · 17 · 20) 824

חָרַף to reproach, say sharp things against, taunt (5 · 34 · 38) 357

אָמְנָם 18 verily, truly (1 · 9) 53

הֶחֱרִיב to lay waste, make desolate (6 · 13 · 37[?]) 351

בָּז 22 to despise (1 · 13 · 13[?]) 100

לָעַג to mock or deride (1 · 12 · 18) 541

בְּתוּלָה virgin (5 · 50) 143

הֵנִיעַ to shake, wag (1 · 14 · 38) 631

חָרַף 23 to reproach, say sharp things against, taunt (5 · 34 · 38) 357

גִּדֵּף to blaspheme (2 · 7 · 7) 154

חָרַף 24 to reproach, say sharp things against, taunt (5 · 34 · 38) 357

יַרְכָּה angle, recess, extreme part (3 · 28) 438

קוֹמָה height (2 · 45) 879

מִבְחָר choicest, best (2 · 12) 104

בְּרוֹשׁ cypress or fir (5 · 20) 141

כַּרְמֶל gardenlike; garden land; w. יַעַר = fertile forest (8 · 14) 502

קוּר 25 to bore, dig (1 · 2 · 2) 881

הֶחֱרִיב to dry up (6 · 13 · 37[?]) 351

לְמֵרָחוֹק 26 long ago; from afar (1 · 8) 935 רָחֹק 2.b.

יָצַר to form, fashion; fig. for to frame, preordain, plan (22 · 41 · 44) 427

הִשְׁאָה to cause to crash (1 · 2 · 6) 980

גַּל heap (2 · 20) 164

נָצָה to be ruined; ptc. = ruined (1 · 4 · 5) 663

בָּצוּר made inaccessible, cut off, fortified (5 · 25) 130 בצר

קָצֵר 27 short (1 · 5) 894

עֵשֶׂב herb, herbage (2 · 33) 793

יָרָק herbs [coll.], herbage (2 · 8[?]) 438

דֶּשֶׁא grass (3 · 14) 206

חָצִיר green grass (8 · 18[?]) 348

גָּג roof (3 · 29) 150

שְׁדֵמָה field (2 · 6) 995

קָמָה standing grain (2 · 10) 879

הִתְרַגֵּז 28 to excite oneself (2 · 4 · 41) 919

הִתְרַגֵּז 29 to excite oneself (2 · 4 · 41) 919

שַׁאֲנָן as subst. = arrogance; at ease, carelessly at ease (5 · 11) 983

חָח hook, ring (1 · 7) 296

מֶתֶג bridle (1 · 5) 607

סָפִיחַ 30 growth from spilled kernels (1 · 4) 705

שָׁחִים grain that shoots up of itself in second year (1 · 2) 695 סחיש

קָצַר to reap (2 · 24 · 24) 984

פְּלֵיטָה 31 escaped remnant (5 · 28) 812

שֹׁרֶשׁ root (7 · 33) 1057

לְמַטָּה downward (1 · 10) 641 מטה 2.a.

לְמָעְלָה upward (3 · 34) 751 מעל 2.c.

פְּלֵיטָה 32 escaped remnant (5 · 28) 812

קִנְאָה zeal (7 · 43) 888

הוֹרָה 33 to shoot (1 · 11 · 25) 435

קִדֵּם to meet, confront (with hostility) (2 · 24 · 26) 869

סֹלְלָה mound (1 · 11) 700

גָּנַן 35 to defend (4 · 8[?] · 8[?]) 170

פֶּגֶר 36 corpse, carcass (4 · 22) 803

Chapter 38

אָנָּה 3 Ah, now!; I beseech thee! (1 · 6) 58 אנא

שָׁלֵם at peace, complete, perfect (1 · 28) 1023

בְּכִי weeping (8 · 32) 113

דִּמְעָה 5 tears (3 · 23) 199

גָּנַן 6 to defend (4 · 8[?] · 8[?]) 170

מַעֲלָה 8 step, stair, ascent (5 · 47) 752

אֲחֹרַנִּית backwards (1 · 7) 30

מִכְתָּב 9 writing, thing written (1 · 9) 508

חֳלִי sickness, disease (4 · 24) 318

דֳּמִי 10 quiet, peacefulness (1 · 1[?]) 198

247

חָדֵל 11 cessation, land of cessation = Sheol (1 · 1) 293

דּוֹר 12 dwelling place, habitation (1 · 1[?]) 189

רֵעִי m. pl. cs. of רעה (>50)

קפד to gather together, roll up (1 · 1 · 1) 891

אֹרֵג weaver (2 · 10[?]) 70 ארג

דַּלָּה hair, thrum; threads of warp hanging in loom (1 · 2) 195

בָּצַע to cut off (2 · 6 · 16) 130

שִׁוָּה 13 to make smooth, gain composure (2 · 5 · 16) 1000

אֲרִי lion (1 · 36) 71

סוּס 14 swallow, swift (a bird) (1 · 1) 692

עָגוּר a name of a bird, crane [dub.] (1 · 2) 723

צפצף to chirp, peep (4 · 4 · 4) 861

הָגָה to groan, moan (7 · 23 · 25) 211

יוֹנָה dove (3 · 33) 401

דלל to languish, be low; of eyes = look languishingly (3 · 8 · 8[?]) 195

עָשְׁקָה oppression, distress (1 · 1) 799

עָרַב to take on pledge; be surety for (1 · 15 · 17) 786

הִתְדַּדָּה 15 to walk deliberately (1 · 2[?] · 2[?]) 186

מַר bitterness (6 · 38) 600

הַחֲלִים 16 to restore to health (1 · 2 · 28) 321

מַר 17 bitter (6[?] · 38[?]) 600 מרר

חָשַׁק to be attached to, love (1 · 8 · 11) 365

שַׁחַת pit (2 · 23) 1001

בְּלִי destruction (1 · 1) 115

גֵּו back (3 · 6) 156

חֵטְא sin (4 · 33) 307

שָׂבַר 18 to hope, wait (1 · 6 · 8) 960

נְגִינָה 20 music (1 · 14) 618

נִגֵּן to play a stringed instrument (2 · 13 · 14) 618

דְּבֵלָה 21 pressed fig cake (1 · 5) 179

תְּאֵנָה fig (3 · 39) 1061

מרח to rub (1 · 1 · 1) 598

שְׁחִין boil, eruption (1 · 13) 1006

Chapter 39

נְכֹת 2 treasure (1 · 2) 649

בֹּשֶׂם spice[s] (2 · 30) 141

טוֹב precious (1 · 3[?]) 373 II טוב 3.c.

מֶמְשָׁלָה realm, domain (2 · 17) 606

מֵאַיִן 3 whence? from where? (6 · 48[?]) 32 אין

אצר 6 to store up, treasure (1 · 3 · 5) 69

סָרִיס 7 eunuch, military official (3 · 45) 710

Chapter 40

נִרְצָה 2 to be accepted [as satisfactory] (1 · 1 · 7) 953

כֶּפֶל double, the double (1 · 3) 495

פַּנָּה דֶרֶךְ 3 [idiom] to make clear, free from obstacles 815 פנה, pi.

ישׁר to make smooth, straight (3 · 9 · 25) 448

מְסִלָּה highway, public road (9 · 27) 700

גִּיא 4 valley (5 · 47) 161

שָׁפֵל to become low, be brought low (10 · 11 · 30) 1050

עָקֹב steep, hilly (1 · 3[?]) 784

מִישׁוֹר level country, plain (3 · 23) 449

רֶכֶס roughness; i.e., the impassable [dub.] (1 · 1) 940

בִּקְעָה valley (3 · 19) 132

חָצִיר 6 green grass [fig. for quickly perishing] (8 · 18[?]) 348

חֶסֶד only here = loveliness, lovely appearance (>50) 338

צִיץ blossom, flower (4 · 15) 847

חָצִיר 7 green grass [fig. for quickly perishing] (8 · 18[?]) 348

נָבֵל	to wither and fall, fade (11 · 21 · 25) 615		אִי	coastlands, islands, coast (17 · 36) 15
צִיץ	blossom, flower (4 · 15) 847		דַּק	small, fine [dust] (2 · 14) 201
נשׁב	to blow (1 · 1 · 3) 674		נָטַל	to life, bear (1 · 3 · 4) 642
אָכֵן	surely, truly (4 · 18) 38		דַּי 16	enough, sufficiency (2 · 12) 191
חָצִיר 8	green grass [fig. for quickly perishing] (8 · 18[?]) 348		כְּאַיִן 17	as nothing (4 · 7) 34 אין, 1.
נָבֵל	to wither and fall, fade (11 · 21 · 25) 615		אֶפֶס	nought; מאפס ותהו = as made of nought and worthlessness (14 · 43) 67
צִיץ	blossom, flower (4 · 15) 847		תֹּהוּ	unreality, thing of nought (11 · 20) 1062
גָּבֹהַּ 9	high, lofty, tall (6 · 41) 147		דָּמָה 18	to liken, compare (5 · 13 · 27) 197
מְבַשֵּׂר	preach, herald as glad tidings (4 · 9) 142 בשר Piel. 3.		דְּמוּת	likeness, similitude (2 · 25) 198
שָׂכָר 10	reward, hire, wages (2 · 29) 969		פֶּסֶל 19	idol, image (9 · 31) 820
פְּעֻלָּה	reward, wages, recompense; work (5 · 14) 821		נָסַךְ	to cast, pour out; w. פסל = to cast metal images (4 · 7 · 25) 650
עֵדֶר 11	flock, herd (3 · 39) 727		חָרָשׁ	graver, artificer [here in metal] (8 · 38) 360
טָלָא	lamb (2 · 3) 378 טלה		צֹרֵף	smelter, refiner (3 · 10[?]) 864 צרף
חֵיק	bosom (3 · 38) 300		צָרַף	to smelt, refine, test (3 · 19 · 22) 864
עוּל	to give suck (1 · 5 · 5) 732		רקע	to beat out; i.e., to overlay (1 · 3 · 11) 955
נהל	to lead or guide to a watering place and cause to rest there (3 · 9 · 10) 625		רְתֻקָה	chain [dub.] (1 · 1) 958
שֹׁעַל 12	hollow hand, handful (1 · 3) 1043		סכן 20	ptc. pass. = poor, impoverished [dub.] (1 · 1 · 1) 698
זֶרֶת	span (1 · 7) 284		רקב	to rot (1 · 2 · 2) 955
תִּכֵּן	to mete out, regulate (2 · 4 · 18) 1067		חָרָשׁ	graver, artificer (here, in wood) (8 · 38) 360
כּוּל	to comprehend, contain (1 · 1 · 38) 465		פֶּסֶל	idol, image (9 · 31) 820
שָׁלִשׁ	third [part, = 13 ephah—dub.] (1 · 2) 1026		נמוט	to be shaken, moved (2 · 22 · 39) 556
שָׁקַל	to weigh (4 · 19 · 22) 1053		מוֹסָד 21	foundation (3 · 13) 414
פֶּלֶס	balance, scale (1 · 2) 813		חוּג 22	vault, horizon (1 · 3) 295
מֹאזְנַיִם	balances, scales (2 · 15) 24		חָגָב	locust, grasshopper (1 · 5) 290
תִּכֵּן 13	to mete out, regulate (2 · 4 · 18) 1067		דֹּק	veil, curtain (1 · 1) 201
תְּבוּנָה 14	the faculty of understanding, understanding (3 · 42) 108		מתח	to spread out (1 · 1 · 1) 607
מַר 15	drop (1 · 1) 601		רֹזֵן 23	ruler, potentate (1 · 6) 931 רזן
דְּלִי	bucket (1 · 2) 194		תֹּהוּ	unreality, thing of nought (11 · 20) 1062
שַׁחַק	fine dust, cloud (2 · 21) 1007		שֹׁרֵשׁ 24	to take root (1 · 1 · 8) 1057
מֹאזְנַיִם	balances, scales (2-15) 24		גֶּזַע	stock, stem (2 · 3) 160

נָשַׁף	to blow (1 · 2 · 2) 676
סְעָרָה	tempest, storm wind (3 · 16) 704
קַשׁ	stubble, chaff (5 · 16) 905
דָּמָה	25 to liken, compare (5 · 13 · 27) 197
שָׁוָה	to be like (1 · 8 · 16) 1000
בָּרָא	26 to shape, fashion, create (20 · 38 · 48) 135
אוֹן	strength (2 · 10) 20
אַמִּיץ	mighty (2 · 6) 55
נֶעְדָּר	to be lacking (3 · 6 · 7) 727
בָּרָא	28 to shape, fashion, create (20 · 38 · 48) 135
קָצֶה	end (3 · 28) 892
יָעֵף	to be weary, faint (4 · 8 · 9) 419
יגע	to grow or be weary (10 · 20 · 26) 388
חֵקֶר	thing [to be] searched out; אֵין ח׳ = it is unsearchable (1 · 12) 350
תְּבוּנָה	the object of knowledge; understanding, faculty of understanding (3 · 42) 108
יָעֵף	29 weary, faint (2 · 4) 419
לְאֵין	without (1 · 9) 34 אין, 6.c.
אוֹן	strength (2 · 10) 20
עָצְמָה	might (2 · 2[?]) 782
יָעֵף	30 to be weary, faint (4 · 8 · 9) 419
יגע	to grow or be weary (10 · 20 · 26) 388
בָּחוּר	young man (6 · 45) 104
קוה	31 to wait, look eagerly for (2 · 6 · 45) 875
הֶחֱלִף	to renew, change for the better (3 · 10 · 26) 322
אֵבֶר	pinions (1 · 3) 7
נֶשֶׁר	griffin vulture, eagle (1 · 26) 676
יגע	to grow or be weary (10 · 20 · 26) 388
יעף	to be weary, faint (4 · 8 · 9) 419

Chapter 41

הֶחֱרִישׁ	1 to keep silence, come silently (3 · 38 · 46) 361
אִי	coast (17 · 36) 15
לְאֹם	people (11 · 35) 522
הֶחֱלִף	to change, renew (3 · 10 · 26) 322
יַרְדְּ	2 read: יָרֹד subdues (1 · 1 · 23[?]) 921 רדד
קַשׁ	stubble, chaff (5 · 16) 905
נִדָּף	to be driven (2 · 6 · 9) 623
אִי	5 coast (17 · 36) 15
קָצֶה	end (3 · 28) 892
חָרַד	to tremble, quake (4 · 23 · 39) 353
אָתָה	to come (9 · 19 · 21) 87
חָרָשׁ	7 graver, artificer (8 · 38) 360
צֹרֵף	smelter, refiner (3 · 10[?]) 864 צרף
הֶחֱלִיק	to make smooth (1 · 7 · 9) 325
פַּטִּישׁ	forge hammer (1 · 3) 809
הלם	to strike (3 · 8 · 8) 240
פַּעַם	anvil (>50) 821 פעם 2.
דֶּבֶק	joining, soldering (1 · 3) 180
מַסְמֵר	nail (1 · 5) 702
נמוט	to be shaken, moved (2 · 22 · 39) 556
אֹהֵב	8 friend (2 · 36) 12 אָהֵב Qal 4.(b)
קָצֶה	9 end (3 · 28) 892
אָצִיל	sides [borders] (1 · 1) 69
הִשְׁתָּעָה	10 to gaze about [in anxiety] (2 · 2 · 15) 1043 שעה
אִמֵּץ	to make firm, strengthen (3 · 19 · 41) 54
תמך	to hold up, support (3 · 20 · 21) 1069
נכלם	11 to be put to shame (5 · 26 · 38) 483
כְּאַיִן	as nothing (4 · 7) 34 אַיִן 1.
מַצּוּת	12 strife, contention (1 · 1) 663
כְּאַיִן	as nothing (4 · 7) 34 אַיִן 1.
אֶפֶס	nought (13 · 27) 67
תּוֹלַעַת	14 worm, grub (3 · 41) 1069 תּוֹלֵעָה
מַת	man, male (3 · 21) 607
גֹּאֵל	redeemer (13 · 44[?]) 145 גָּאַל

250

מוֹרַג 15 threshing sledge (1 · 3[?]) 558

חָרוּץ sharp (2 · 4) 358

פִּיפִיּוֹת־ בַּעַל [idiom] = double edged 127 I בַּעַל 5.a.

פִּיפִיּוֹת edges [pl. form of פֶּה] (1 · 2) 804 פֶּה

דָּשׁ to thresh, tread (4 · 13 · 16) 190 דושׁ

דָּק to crush (2 · 4 · 13) 200 דקק

מֹץ chaff (3 · 8) 558

זרה 16 to fan, winnow (3 · 9 · 38) 279

סְעָרָה tempest, storm wind (3 · 16) 704

גִּיל to rejoice (11 · 45 · 45) 162

צָמֵא 17 thirst (3 · 17) 854

נשׁת to be dry, parched (1 · 2 · 3) 677

שְׁפִי 18 bare place, height (2 · 10) 1046

בִּקְעָת valley (3 · 19) 132

מַעְיָן spring (2 · 23) 745

אֲגַם pool, pond; troubled pond (4 · 8) 8

צִיָּה land of drought, desert (3 · 16) 851

מוֹצָא spring, source, going forth (2 · 27) 425

שִׁטָּה 19 acacia tree (1 · 28) 1008

הֲדַס myrtle tree (2 · 6) 213

בְּרוֹשׁ cypress or fir (5 · 20) 141

תִּדְהָר name of tree, prob. elm or pine (2 · 2) 187.

תְּאַשּׁוּר box tree, small evergreen tree (2 · 3) 81

שִׂים (לֵב) 20 [idiom] "to pay attention to" 962 שׂום Qal 2.b.

בָּרָא to transform, create (20 · 38 · 48) 135

עָצְמָה 21 defense, defensive argument (1 · 1) 783

קרה 22 to befall (1 · 13 · 28) 899

שִׂים (לֵב) [idiom] "to pay attention to" 962 שׂום Qal 2.b.

אָתָה 23 to come; here, ptc. pl. fem. as subst. = things to come (9 · 19 · 21) 87

אָחוֹר with לְ = hereafter (9 · 41) 30

הִשְׁתָּעָה to gaze at one another [in rivalry] (2 · 2 · 15) 1043 שׁעה

מֵאַיִן 24 whence? from where? (6 · 48[?]) 32 אין

פַּעַל deed, thing done (6 · 37) 821

מֵאָפַע nought; nonexistence (1 · 1) 67 אֶפֶס 2.a.

אָתָה 25 to come (9 · 19 · 21) 87

סָגָן prefect, ruler (1 · 17) 688

חֹמֶר mire, clay, mortar (5 · 17) 330

יוֹצֵר potter (3 · 17) 427 יצר

רָמַס to trample (4 · 17 · 18) 942

טִיט clay, mud (2 · 13) 376

אֹמֶר 26 utterance, word (2 · 48) 56

מְבַשֵּׂר 27 one bringing glad tidings (4 · 9) 142 בשׂר

יוֹעֵץ 28 counselor (5 · 22) 419

אֶפֶס 29 nought, nothing (13 · 27) 67

תֹּהוּ that which is empty, unreal; confusion, formlessness (11 · 20) 1062

נֶסֶךְ here = molten image (>50) 651

Chapter 42

תמך 1 to hold up, support (3 · 20 · 21) 1069

בָּחִיר chosen, elect (6 · 13) 104

רָצָה to be pleased with, favorable to (1 · 42 · 50) 953

רצץ 3 to crush, ptc. pass. = crushed (4 · 11 · 19) 954

פִּשְׁתָּה flax; i.e., wick (2 · 4) 834

כֵּהֶה dim, faint (2 · 7) 462

כבה to quench, extinguish (2 · 10 · 24) 459

כהה 4 to grow dim, faint (1 · 5 · 9) 462

רצץ to get crushed out (4 · 11 · 19) 954

אִי pl. = coastlands and islands (17 · 36) 15

יחל to wait for = hope for (2 · 25 · 42) 404

בָּרָא 5 to shape, fashion, create
(20 · 38 · 48) 135

רקע to spread out (2 · 6 · 11) 955

צֶאֱצָא produce, offspring (7 · 11) 425

נְשָׁמָה breath, spirit (4 · 24) 675

פָּקַח 7 to open (3 · 17 · 20) 824

עִוֵּר blind (11 · 26) 734

מַסְגֵּר dungeon (2 · 7) 689

אַסִּיר [coll.] prisoner (4 · 17) 64

כֶּלֶא confinement, imprisonment (2 · 10)
476

פָּסִיל 8 idol, image (4 · 23) 820

בְּטֶרֶם 9 before (8 · 39) 382

צָמַח to sprout, spring up (4 · 15 · 33)
855

מְלֹא 10 fullness, entire contents (5 · 38) 571

אִי pl. = coastlands and islands
(17 · 36) 15

צוח 11 to cry aloud (1 · 1 · 1) 846

אִי 12 pl. = coastlands and islands
(17 · 36) 15

קִנְאָה 13 zeal (7 · 43) 888

הֵרִיעַ to shout a war cry, alarm of battle
(3 · 40 · 44) 929 רוע

הִצְרִיחַ to utter a roar (1 · 1 · 2) 863

הִתְגַּבֵּר to show oneself mighty (1 · 3 · 25)
149

הֶחֱשָׁה 14 to be silent (2 · 9 · 16) 364

הֶחֱרִישׁ to be silent (3 · 38 · 46) 361

הִתְאַפֵּק to restrain oneself, refrain (3 · 7 · 7)
67

פעה to groan (1 · 1 · 1) 821

נשם to pant (1 · 1 · 1) 675

שָׁאַף to gasp (1 · 14 · 14) 983

יַחַד together (7 · 44) 403

הֶחֱרִיב 15 to lay waste, make desolate
(6 · 13 · 37[?]) 351

עֵשֶׂב herb, herbage (2 · 33) 793

אִי coasts, banks (17 · 36) 15

אֲגַם pool, pond (4 · 8) 8

עִוֵּר 16 blind (11 · 26) 734

נְתִיבָה path, course of life (4 · 21) 677

מַחְשָׁךְ dark region, dark place (2 · 7) 365

מַעֲקָשׁ twisted, crooked place (1 · 1) 786

מִישׁוֹר level country, plain (3 · 23) 449

נָסוֹג 17 to be turned, driven back
(3 · 14 · 25) 690 סוג

אָחוֹר with ל = hereafter (9 · 41) 30

בֹּשֶׁת shame (5 · 30) 102

פֶּסֶל idol, image (9 · 31) 820

מַסֵּכָה molten metal, image (2 · 25) 651

חֵרֵשׁ 18 deaf (5 · 9) 361

עִוֵּר blind (11 · 26) 734

עִוֵּר 19 blind (11 · 26) 734

חֵרֵשׁ deaf (5 · 9) 361

מְשֻׁלָּם ptc. = one in covenant of peace
1023 שלם

פָּקַח 20 to open (3 · 17 · 20) 824

הַאְדִּיר 21 to make glorious (1 · 1 · 3) 12

בָּזַז 22 to plunder, despoil (7 · 37 · 41)
102

שָׁסָה to spoil, plunder (1 · 4 · 5) 1042

הִפַח to ensnare (1 · 1 · 1) 809 פחח

חוּר hole (2 · 2) 359

כֶּלֶא confinement, imprisonment (2 · 10)
476

הָחְבָּא to be hidden (1 · 1 · 34) 285

בַּז spoil, booty, plunder (5 · 27) 103

מְשִׁסָּה plunder, spoil, prey (2 · 6) 1042

הַאֲזִין 23 to give ear, listen (8 · 41 · 41) 24

הִקְשִׁיב to give attention (8 · 45 · 46) 904

אָחוֹר with ל = hereafter (9 · 41) 30

מְשִׁסָּה 24 K משוסה booty, plunder (2 · 6) 1042

בָּזַז to plunder (7 · 37 · 41) 102

זוּ which, who (2 · 14) 262

עֱזוּז 25 fierceness, might (1 · 3) 739

להט to set ablaze (1 · 9 · 11) 529

מִסָּבִיב on every side (1 · 42) 687

252

Chapter 43

בָּרָא 1 to shape, fashion, create (20 · 38 · 48) 135

יָצַר to form, fashion (22 · 41 · 44) 427

שָׁטַף 2 to overflow (9 · 28 · 31) 1009

בְּמוֹ poet. for בְּ (4 · 10) 91

נכוה to be scorched (1 · 2 · 2) 464

לֶהָבָה flame (5 · 19) 529

מוֹשִׁיעַ 3 savior, deliverer (9 · 27) 446 ישע

כֹּפֶר ransom, the price of a life (1 · 13) 497

מֵאֲשֶׁר 4 from that, since (2 · 17) 84

יקר to be highly valued, esteemed, precious (1 · 9 · 11) 429

לְאֹם people (11 · 35) 522

מַעֲרָב 5 west, place of sunset (3 · 14) 788

תֵּימָן 6 south, southern quarter (1 · 24) 412

כלא to withhold (1 · 14 · 17) 476

מֵרָחוֹק from a distance (12 · 34) 935

בָּרָא 7 to shape, fashion, create (20 · 38 · 48) 135

יָצַר to form, fashion (22 · 41 · 44) 427

עִוֵּר 8 blind (11 · 26) 734

חֵרֵשׁ deaf (5 · 9) 361

לְאֹם 9 people (11 · 35) 522

צדק to be justified (3 · 22 · 41) 842

נוֹצַר 10 to be formed (1 · 1 · 44) 428

מִבַּלְעָדַי 11 apart from, without (5 · 12) 116 בלעדי b.

מוֹשִׁיעַ savior, deliverer (9 · 27) 446 ישע

גֹּאֵל 14 redeemer (13 · 44) 145 גאל

בָּרִיחַ fugitive, fleeing one (2 · 3) 138

אֳנִיָּה ship (5 · 31) 58

רִנָּה ringing cry, exultation (9 · 33) 943

בָּרָא 15 to shape, fashion, create (20 · 38 · 48) 135

עַז 16 strong, mighty, fierce (4 · 22) 738

נְתִיבָה path (4 · 21) 677

עִזּוּז 17 mighty, powerful (1 · 2) 739

דָּעַךְ to go out, be extinguished (1 · 7 · 9) 200

פִּשְׁתָּה flax; i.e., wick (2 · 4) 834

כבה to be quenched, extinguished (3 · 14 · 24) 459

קַדְמֹנִי 18 former things, former (1 · 10) 870

צָמַח 19 to sprout, spring up (4 · 15 · 33) 855

יְשִׁימֹן waste, wilderness (2 · 13) 445

תַּן 20 jackal (4 · 14) 1072

יַעֲנָה ostrich (3 · 8) 419

יְשִׁימֹן waste, wilderness (2 · 13) 445

בָּחִיר chosen, elect (6 · 13) 104

זוּ 21 who, which (2 · 14) 262

יָצַר to form, fashion (22 · 41 · 44) 427

יגע 22 to grow or be weary (10 · 20 · 26) 388

שֶׂה 23 a sheep, goat (4 · 45) 961

הוֹגִיעַ to make to toil, to weary (2 · 4 · 26) 388

לְבוֹנָה frankincense (3 · 21) 526

הִרְוָה 24 to cause to drink (2 · 5 · 14) 924

הוֹגִיעַ to make to toil, to weary (2 · 4 · 26) 388

מָחָה 25 to blot out, obliterate (3 · 22 · 34) 562

יַחַד 26 together (7 · 44) 403

צדק to be justified (3 · 22 · 41) 842

הֵלִיץ 27 *Hiph.* ptc. = interpreter, intermediary; vb. = to deride (1 · 9 · 12) 539

פָּשַׁע to transgress, rebel (9 · 40 · 41) 833

חֵרֶם 28 devotion, ban involving destruction (2 · 29) 356

גִּדּוּפִים revilings, reviling words (2 · 2) 154

Chapter 44

עֹשֶׂה 2 maker, creator (6 · 24[?]) 793 I. עשה

יָצַר to form, fashion (22 · 41 · 44) 427

צָמֵא 3 thirsty place, thirsty (5 · 9) 854

נֹזֵל streams, flows (1 · 6) 633 נזל

יַבָּשָׁה dry land, dry ground (1 · 14) 387

צֶאֱצָא offspring (7 · 11) 425

צָמַח 4 to sprout, spring up (4 · 15 · 33) 855

בְּבֵין in the midst of, among (1 · 1) 107

חָצִיר green grass (2[?] · 3[?]) 348

עֲרָבָה poplar, Euphrates poplar (2 · 5) 788

יָבָל watercourse, stream (2 · 2) 385

כנה 5 to title, give an epithet (2 · 4 · 4) 487

גֹּאֵל 6 redeemer, kinsman (13 · 44) 145 גאל

מִבַּלְעֲדֵי apart from, without (5 · 12) 116 בלעדי b.

אתה 7 to come; ptc. pl. = things to come (9 · 19 · 21) 87

פָּחַד 8 to be in dread (7 · 23 · 26) 808

רהה to fear [dub.] (1 · 1 · 1) 923

מֵאָז in time past = of old (8 · 18) 23

מִבַּלְעֲדֵי apart from, without (5 · 12) 116 בלעדי b.

יָצַר 9 to form; ptc. = carver, graver (22 · 41 · 44) 427

פֶּסֶל idol, image (9 · 31) 820

תֹּהוּ what is empty, unreal (11 · 20) 1062

חָמַד to take pleasure in, desire (3 · 16 · 21) 326

הוֹעִיל to profit, avail, benefit (8 · 23 · 23) 418

יָצַר 10 to form, fashion (22 · 41 · 44) 427

פֶּסֶל idol, image (9 · 31) 820

נָסַךְ to cast, pour out; with פסל, to cast metal images (4 · 7 · 25) 650

הוֹעִיל to profit, avail, benefit (8 · 23 · 23) 418

חָבֵר 11 worshiping associate, worshiping companion (2 · 12) 288

חָרָשׁ graver, artificer, idol maker (8 · 38) 360

פָּחַד to be in dread (7 · 23 · 26) 808

יַחַד together, altogether (7 · 44) 403

חָרָשׁ 12 graver, artificer (8 · 38) 360

מַעֲצָד axe (1 · 2) 781

פֶּחָם coal (2 · 3) 809

מַקָּבֶת hammer (1 · 4) 666

יָצַר to form, fashion (22 · 41 · 44) 427

רָעֵב to be hungry (5 · 12 · 14) 944

יָעֵף to be weary, faint (4 · 8 · 9) 419

חָרָשׁ 13 graver, artificer (8 · 38) 360

קַו measuring line, line (16[?] · 25[?]) 876

תאר to draw in outline, trace out (2 · 2 · 8[?]) 1061

שֶׂרֶד marking tool for wood, stylus (1 · 1) 975

מַקְצוּעָה scraping tool (1 · 1) 893

מְחוּגָה compass (1 · 1) 295

תַּבְנִית figure, image, pattern (1 · 20) 125

תִּפְאֶרֶת beauty, finery, glory (18 · 50) 802

תִּרְזָה 14 tree, cypress [dub.] (1 · 1) 1076

אַלּוֹן oak (3 · 9) 47

אמץ to assure or secure for oneself; to make firm (3 · 19 · 41) 54

אֹרֶן fir or cedar (1 · 1) 75

גֶּשֶׁם rain, shower (2 · 35) 177

חָם 15 to be or grow warm (5 · 23 · 26) 328 חמם

הִשִּׂיק to make a fire burn (1 · 2 · 3[?]) 969 שלק

אָפָה to bake (2 · 10 · 13) 66

פֶּסֶל idol, image (9 · 31) 820

סגד to prostrate oneself in worship (4 · 4 · 4) 688

בְּמוֹ 16 poetic for ב (4 · 10) 91

צלה to roast (2 · 3 · 3) 852

צָלִי roast, roasted (1 · 3) 852

חָם	to be or grow warm (5 · 23 · 26) 328 חמם	שָׂכַל	to turn into foolishness (1 · 2 · 8) 698 סכל
הָאָח	Aha! interjection expressing joy (1 · 9) 210	חָרְבָּה	26 waste, ruin (9 · 42) 352
פֶּסֶל	17 idol, image (9 · 31) 820	צוּלָה	27 ocean deep (1 · 1) 846
סגד	to prostrate oneself in worship (4 · 4 · 4) 688	חרב	to be waste, desolate (6 · 17 · 37[?]) 351
טָח	18 to be smeared (1 · 1 · 1) 377 טחח	חֵפֶץ	28 good pleasure, delight (9 · 39) 343
תְּבוּנָה	19 the faculty of understanding, understanding (3 · 42) 108	נוֹסַד	to be founded (1 · 2 · 41) 413 יסד

בְּמוֹ	poetic for ב (4 · 10) 91
אָפָה	to bake (2 · 10 · 13) 66
גַּחֶלֶת	coal (2 · 18) 160
צלה	to roast (2 · 3 · 3) 852
בּוּל	produce, outgrowth (1 · 2) 385
סגד	to prostrate oneself in worship (4 · 4 · 4) 688
אֵפֶר	20 ashes (3 · 22) 68
הוּתַל	to be deceived (1 · 1 · 9) 1068
יָצַר	21 to form, fashion (22 · 41 · 44) 427
נשׁה	to be forgotten (1 · 1 · 5) 674
מָחָה	22 to blot out (3 · 22 · 34) 562
עָב	dark cloud (7 · 30) 728
הֵרִיעַ	23 to shout, cry out (3 · 40 · 44) 929
תַּחְתִּי	lowest [place] (1 · 19) 1066
פצח	to break forth with (6 · 7 · 7) 822
רִנָּה	ringing cry [in joy] (9 · 33) 943
התפאר	to get glory to oneself, be glorified by means of [ב] (5 · 7 · 13) 802
גֹּאֵל	24 redeemer, kinsman (13 · 44) 145
יָצַר	to form, fashion (22 · 41 · 44) 427
רקע	to spread out, beat out (2 · 6 · 11) 955
הֵפֵר	25 to frustrate, make ineffectual (4 · 42 · 45) 830 פרר
בַּד	empty talker, prater (2 · 6) 95
קֹסֵם	diviner (1 · 9[?]) 890 קסם
הוֹלֵל	to make into a fool (1 · 4 · 14[?]) 239 הלל
אָחוֹר	backwards; back part (9 · 41) 30

Chapter 45

מָשִׁיחַ	1 anointed, commissioned one (1 · 39) 603
רדד	to beat down (1 · 2 · 3) 921
מָתְנַיִם	loins, place where sword (et al.) is attached (4 · 47) 608
הדר	2 to swell, honor; ptc. (1 · 1) = swells of land (1 · 4 · 6) 213
ישׁר	to make smooth, strait (3 · 9 · 25) 448
נְחוּשָׁה	copper, bronze (2 · 10) 639
בְּרִיחַ	bar (2 · 41) 138
גָּדַע	to hew off, [cut] down, [cut] in two (1 · 9 · 22) 154
מַטְמוֹן	3 hidden treasure, treasure (1 · 5) 380
מִסְתָּר	secret place, hiding place (1 · 10) 712
בָּחִיר	4 chosen, elect (6 · 13) 104
כנה	to title, give an epithet (2 · 4 · 4) 487
זוּלָה	5 except, besides (4 · 16) 265
אזר	to gird (2 · 6 · 16) 25
מַעֲרָב	6 west, place of sunset (3 · 14) 788
אֶפֶס	nonexistence; cessation of (13 · 27) 67
בִּלְעֲדֵי	except, besides, apart from (1 · 4) 116
יָצַר	7 to form, fashion (22 · 41 · 44) 427
בָּרָא	to create, shape, fashion (20 · 38 · 48) 135
הִרְעִיף	8 to trickle (1 · 1 · 5) 950
מִמַּעַל	above (3 · 29) 751 מעל 1.

שַׁחַק	cloud, fine dust (2 · 21) 1007	כְּלִימָה	reproach, ignominy (4 · 30) 484
נזל	to flow, stream (1 · 8 · 9) 633	חָרָשׁ	idol maker, graver, artificer (8 · 38) 360
פרה	to be fruitful, bear fruit (4 · 22 · 29) 826	צִיר	image (1 · 1) 849
יֶשַׁע	salvation, deliverance, rescue (5 · 36) 447	תְּשׁוּעָה	17 deliverance, salvation (3 · 34) 448
הצמיח	to cause to sprout, grow (4 · 14 · 33) 855	נכלם	to be humiliated, ashamed (5 · 26 · 38) 483
יַחַד	together (7 · 44) 403	עַד	forever (8 · 48) 723 I. עד
בָּרָא	to create, shape, fashion (20 · 38 · 48) 135	בָּרָא	18 to shape, fashion, create (20 · 38 · 48) 135
יָצַר	9 to form, fashion; oft. ptc. = potter (22 · 41 · 44) 427	יָצַר	to form, fashion (22 · 41 · 44) 427
חֶרֶשׂ	earthen vessels (3 · 17) 360	תֹּהוּ	formlessness, primeval chaos (11 · 20) 1062
חֹמֶר	clay, mortar, cement (5 · 17) 330	סֵתֶר	19 secrecy; with ב = secretly (5 · 35) 712
פֹּעַל	work, thing made (6 · 37) 821		
חִיל	10 to twist, writhe [in childbirth] (9 · 30 · 47) 296 חול	תֹּהוּ	worthlessness, what is unreal (11 · 20) 1062
יָצַר	11 to form, fashion; oft. ptc. = potter (22 · 41 · 44) 427	מֵישָׁר	uprightness, equity (3 · 19) 449
		פָּלִיט	20 escaped one, fugitive (1 · 19) 812
אתה	to come; ptc. pl. = things to come (9 · 19 · 21) 87	פֶּסֶל	idol, image (9 · 31) 820
פֹּעַל	work, thing made (6 · 37) 821	מֵאָז	21 in time past = of old (8 · 18) 23
בָּרָא	12 to shape, fashion, create (20 · 38 · 48) 135	מִבַּלְעֲדֵי	apart from, without (5 · 12) 116 בלעדי b.
יֹשֶׁר	13 to make smooth, strait (3 · 9 · 25) 448	מוֹשִׁיעַ	savior, deliverer (9 · 27) 446 ישׁע
גָּלוּת	[coll.] exiles (2 · 15) 163	זוּלָה	except, besides (4 · 16) 265
מְחִיר	reward, gain, hire, price (2 · 15) 564	אֶפֶס	22 end, extremity (13 · 27) 67
שֹׁחַד	bribe, present (4 · 23) 1005	כָּרַע	23 to bow, bow down (5 · 30 · 36) 502
יְגִיעַ	14 product, produce, acquired property (2 · 16) 388	בֶּרֶךְ	knee (3 · 25) 139
סַחַר	traffic, gain (4 · 8) 695	צדק	25 to be justified, be just (3 · 22 · 41) 842
זֵק	fetter; only זקים (1 · 4) 279		
אֶפֶס	nonexistence, cessation of (13 · 27) 67		Chapter 46
אָכֵן	15 surely, truly (4 · 18) 38	כָּרַע	1 to bow down, bow (5 · 30 · 36) 502
מוֹשִׁיעַ	savior, deliverer (9 · 27) 446 ישׁע	קרס	to bend down, stoop, crouch (2 · 2 · 2) 902
נכלם	16 to be put to shame, dishonored (5 · 26 · 38) 483	עָצָב	idol (2 · 17) 781
		נְשׂוּאָה	things borne about (1 · 1[?]) 672
		עמס	Qal pass. ptc. = being a load; i.e., burdensome (2 · 7 · 9) 770

מַשָּׂא   load, burden (3 · 42) 672

עָיֵף   faint, weary (5 · 17) 746

קָרַס   2 to bend down, stoop, crouch (2 · 2 · 2) 902

כָּרַע   to bow down, bow (5 · 30 · 36) 502

מַשָּׂא   load, burden (3 · 42) 672

שְׁבִי   captivity, captives (4 · 49) 985

עמס   3 *Qal* pass. ptc. = to be carried as a load (2 · 7 · 9) 770

רֶחֶם   womb (1 · 33) 933

זִקְנָה   4 old age (1 · 6) 279

שֵׂיבָה   gray hair, hoary head, old age (1 · 20[?]) 966

סבל   to bear a load, carry (5 · 7 · 9) 687

לְמִי   5 to whom (1 · 20) 566

דָּמָה   to liken to, consider to be like (5 · 13 · 26) 197

הִשְׁוָה   to make like (1 · 2 · 16) 1000

הַמְשִׁיל   to compare (1 · 1 · 15) 605

דָּמָה   to be like, resemble (2 · 13 · 27) 197

זול   6 to lavish (1 · 1 · 1) 266

כִּיס   bag, purse (1 · 5) 476

קָנֶה   beam [of scales]; here used idiomatically of scales (>50) 889 קנה 4.c.

שָׁקַל   to weigh (4 · 19 · 22) 1053

שָׂכַר   to hire (1 · 17 · 20) 968

צָרַף   smelter, refiner (3 · 10) 864 צרף

סגד   to prostrate oneself in worship (4 · 4 · 4) 688

סבל   7 to carry, bear (5 · 7 · 9) 687

הֵמִישׁ   to leave its place, depart (5 · 20 [?] · 20[?]) 559 מוש

הִתְאֹשֵׁשׁ   8 to show oneself firm (1 · 1 · 1) 84

פָּשַׁע   to transgress, rebel (9 · 40 · 41) 833

אֶפֶס   9 end of, nonexistence of, cessation of (13 · 27) 67

חֵפֶץ   10 will, purpose, good pleasure, delight (9 · 39) 343

עַיִט   11 bird[s] of prey (3 · 8) 743

מֶרְחָק   distant place, far country (7 · 18) 935

יָצַר   to form, fashion; fig. for preordain, plan (22 · 41 · 44) 427

אַבִּיר   12 strong, the strong one (3 · 17) 7

תְּשׁוּעָה   13 deliverance, salvation (3 · 34) 448

אִחַר   to delay, tarry (2 · 15 · 17) 29

תִּפְאֶרֶת   glory, beauty (18 · 50) 802

Chapter 47

בְּתוּלָה   1 virgin (5 · 50) 143

רַךְ   tender, delicate, soft (1 · 16) 940

עָנֹג   dainty (1 · 3) 772

רֵחַיִם   2 [hand] mill (1 · 5) 932 רחה

טחן   to grind (2 · 7 · 7) 377

קֶמַח   flour, meal (1 · 14) 887

צַמָּה   woman's veil (1 · 4) 855

חָשַׂף   to strip off, make bare (3 · 10 · 10) 362

שֹׁבֶל   flowing skirt, train (1 · 1) 987

שׁוֹק   leg, lower leg, calf (1 · 19) 1003

נָקָם   3 vengeance (6 · 17) 668

פָּגַע   to meet (2 · 40 · 46) 803

גָּאַל   4 redeemer, kinsman (13 · 44) 145 גאל

דּוּמָם   5 in silence, silent; silence (1 · 3) 189

גְּבֶרֶת   lady, queen; mistress (3 · 15[?]) 150

קָצַף   6 to be angry (7 · 28 · 34) 893

רַחֲמִים   compassion (4 · 38) 933

עֹל   yoke (5 · 40) 760

גְּבֶרֶת   7 lady, queen; mistress (3 · 15[?]) 150

עַד   forever (8 · 48) 723 I. עד

עֲדִין   8 voluptuous (1 · 2) 726

בֶּטַח   security; w. ל = securely (3 · 43) 105

אֶפֶס   nonexistence; w. עוד = none besides (13 · 27[?]) 67

שְׁכוֹל   bereavement, loss of children (2 · 3) 1013

רֶגַע   9 in a moment, suddenly (5 · 22) 921

שָׁכוֹל	bereavement, loss of children (2 · 3) 1013
אַלְמֹן	widowhood (1 · 1) 48
תֹּם	completeness, fullness, integrity (1-23) 1070
כֶּשֶׁף	sorcery (2 · 6) 506
עָצְמָה	might (2 · 2[?]) 782
חֶבֶר	spell; association, company (2 · 7) 288
אֶפֶס	10 nonexistence; w. עוֹד = none besides (13 · 27[?]) 67
שַׁחַר	11 perh. dawn; i.e., origin (2 · 12 · 13 [?]) 1007 שׁחר
הֹוָה	ruin, disaster (1 · 3) 217
פִּתְאֹם	suddenly (4 · 25) 837
שׁוֹאָה	devastation, ruin (2 · 13) 996
חֶבֶר	12 spell; association, company (2 · 7) 288
כֶּשֶׁף	sorcery (2 · 6) 506
בַּאֲשֶׁר	in [that] which (4 · 19) 84
יגע	to toil, labor (10 · 20 · 26) 388
נְעוּרִים	youth, early life (3 · 46) 655
אוּלַי	perhaps (3 · 45) 19
הוֹעִיל	to gain profit (8 · 23 · 23) 418
ערץ	to cause to tremble = to inspire awe (3 · 11 · 14) 791
נִלְאָה	13 to be weary, weary oneself (3 · 10 · 19) 521
הבר	to divide [dub.] (1 · 1 · 1) 211
כּוֹכָב	star (3 · 37) 456
מֵאֲשֶׁר	from [that] which (2 · 17) 84
קַשׁ	14 stubble, chaff (5 · 16) 905
לֶהָבָה	flame [error in B.H.³ reads להבד] (5 · 19) 529
גַּחֶלֶת	coal (2 · 18) 160
יגע	15 to toil, labor (10 · 20 · 26) 388
סֹחֵר	trafficker, trader (3 · 16) 695 סחר
נְעוּרִים	youth, early life (3 · 46) 655
תָּעָה	to wander about, err (8 · 27 · 50) 1073
מוֹשִׁיעַ	savior, deliverer (9 · 27[?]) 446 ישע

Chapter 48

נסמך	2 to support oneself (2 · 6 · 48) 701
מֵאָז	3 in time past = of old (8 · 18) 23
פִּתְאֹם	suddenly (4 · 25) 837
קָשֶׁה	4 stubborn, hard (6 · 36) 904
גִּיד	sinew (1 · 7) 161
עֹרֶף	neck (1 · 33) 791
מֵצַח	brow, forehead (1 · 13) 594
נְחוּשָׁה	bronze (2 · 10) 639
מֵאָז	5 in time past = of old (8 · 18) 23
בְּטֶרֶם	before (8 · 39) 382
עָצָב	idol (1 · 1) 781
פֶּסֶל	idol, image (9 · 31) 820
נברא	7 to be created (1 · 10 · 48) 135
מֵאָז	in time past = of old (8 · 18) 23
מֵאָז	8 in time past = of old (8 · 18) 23
בגד	to deal treacherously (12 · 49 · 49) 93
פָּשַׁע	to transgress, rebel (9 · 40 · 41) 833
הֶאֱרִיךְ	9 to postpone, prolong (4 · 31 · 34) 73
חטם	to restrain, hold in (1 · 1 · 1) 310
צָרַף	10 to test, refine, smelt (3 · 19 · 22) 864
בחר	to test, try (>50) 103 בחר Qal 8.
כּוּר	smelting pot, furnace (1 · 9) 468
עֹנִי	affliction (1 · 36) 777
יָסַד	13 to found, establish (5 · 20 · 41) 413
טפח	to spread out (1 · 1 · 1[?]) 381
חֵפֶץ	14 will, purpose; good pleasure, delight (9 · 39) 343
סֵתֶר	16 secrecy, with בְּ = secretly (5 · 35) 712
גֹּאֵל	17 redeemer, kinsman (13 · 44) 145 גאל
הוֹעִיל	to gain profit (8 · 23 · 23) 418
לוּא	18 if only! (2 · 3) 530
הִקְשִׁיב	to give attention (8 · 45 · 46) 904
גַּל	heap; pl., waves (2[?] · 16[?]) 164
חוֹל	sand (2 · 22) 297
צֶאֱצָא	19 offspring, produce (7 · 11) 425
מֵעֶה	inward parts (4 · 32) 588

מֵעָה grain [of sand] (1 · 1) 589

רִנָּה 20 ringing cry [in joy] (9 · 33) 943

צמא 21 to be thirsty (3 · 10 · 10) 854

חָרְבָּה desert, waste place, desolation (9 · 42) 352

הִזִּיל to cause to flow (1 · 1 · 9) 633

זוב to flow, gush (1 · 29 · 29) 264

Chapter 49

אִי 1 coast; אִיֵּי הַיָּם = coastlands and islands (17 · 36) 15

הִקְשִׁיב to give attention (8 · 45 · 46) 904

לְאֹם people (11 · 35) 522

מֵרָחוֹק from a distance (12 · 134) 935

מֵעֶה womb, internal organs (4 · 32) 588

חַד 2 sharp (1 · 4) 292

הֶחְבִּיא to hide (1 · 6 · 34) 285

ברר to cleanse, polish (1 · 1 · 2) 140

אַשְׁפָּה quiver (2 · 6) 80

הִתְפָּאֵר 3 to be glorified by means of [בְּ] (5 · 7 · 13) 802

רִיק 4 emptiness, vanity; w. לְ = in vain (3 · 12) 938

יגע to toil, labor (10 · 20 · 26) 388

תֹּהוּ worthlessness (11 · 20) 1062

אָכֵן but indeed, but in fact (4 · 18) 38

פְּעֻלָּה reward, wages (5 · 14) 821

יָצַר 5 to form, fashion (22 · 41 · 44) 427

גֹּאֵל 7 redeemer, kinsman (13 · 44) 145 גאל

בָּזָה to despise (1 · 31 · 42) 102

תעב to cause to be an abomination (1 · 15 · 22) 1073

מֹשֵׁל ruler (4 · 24) 605 מָשַׁל

לַאֲשֶׁר 9 to him who, those who (4 · 38) 81 אשר 4.c.

שְׁפִי bare place, height (2 · 10) 1046

מַרְעִית pasturage (1 · 10) 945

רָעֵב 10 to be hungry (5 · 12 · 14) 944

צמא to be thirsty (3 · 10 · 10) 854

שָׁרָב burning heat (2 · 2) 1055

רחם to have compassion (12 · 42 · 47) 933

נהג to lead on, guide (2 · 10 · 30) 624

מַבּוּעַ spring of water (2 · 3) 616

נהל to lead to a watering place and cause to rest there (3 · 9 · 10) 624

מְסִלָּה 11 raised way, highway (9 · 27) 700

מֵרָחוֹק 12 from a distance (12 · 34) 935

גִיל 13 to rejoice (11 · 45 · 45) 162

פצח to break forth with (6 · 7 · 7) 822

רִנָּה ringing cry (9 · 33) 943

רחם to have compassion (12 · 42 · 47) 933

עוּל 15 suckling child (2 · 2) 732

רחם to have compassion (12 · 42 · 47) 933

חקק 16 to engrave, inscribe (4 · 8 · 11) 349

הרס 17 to destroy, tear down (1 · 3 · 43) 248

הֶחֱרִיב to lay waste, make desolate (6 · 13 · 37[?]) 351

מִמֵּךְ redupl. of מִן w. suffix 577

עֲדִי 18 ornaments (1 · 14) 725

קשר to bind on (1 · 2 · 44) 905

כַּלָּה bride, daughter-in-law (3 · 34) 483

חָרְבָּה 19 waste, ruin (9 · 42) 352

הֲרִסוּת overthrow, destruction, ruin (1 · 1) 249

בְּלַע to swallow up, engulf (3 · 10 · 41) 118

שִׁכֻּלִים 20 bereavement, childlessness (1 · 1) 1014

צַר narrow, tight (5[?] · 20[?]) 865

שָׁכוּל 21 childless (1 · 1) 1014

גַּלְמוּד barren (1 · 4) 166

גּוֹלָה exile, exiles (1 · 43) 163

סוּרָה one made to depart, thrust away (1 · 3) 693 סור Qal 2.

אֵיפֹה where? (1 · 10) 33

נֵס 22 standard (10 · 21) 651

חֹצֶן bosom (1 · 3) 346

אֹמֵן 23 foster father (1 · 7) 52 אמן Qal 2.

שָׂרָה princess, noble lady (1 · 5) 979

מֵינֶקֶת nursing; אשה מ = a nursing woman, a nurse (1 · 5) 413 ינק

לחך to lick (1 · 5 · 6) 535

קוה to wait for; ptc. pl. = those waiting for (2 · 6 · 45) 875

מַלְקוֹחַ 24 booty, prey (2 · 6) 544

שְׁבִי [coll.] captives, captivity (4 · 49) 985

שְׁבִי 25 [coll.] captives, captivity (4 · 49) 985

מַלְקוֹחַ booty, prey (2 · 6) 544

עָרִיץ awe inspiring, terror striking (7 · 20) 792

יָרִיב opponent, adversary (1 · 3) 937

הוֹנָה 26 to oppress, maltreat (1 · 14 · 18) 413

עָסִיס sweet wine (1 · 5) 779

שָׁכַר to become drunken (2 · 9 · 18) 1016

מוֹשִׁיעַ savior, deliverer (9 · 27) 446 ישע Hiph. 1.b.

גָּאַל kinsman, redeemer (13 · 44) 145 גאל

אָבִיר strong, the Strong One (3 · 17) 7

Chapter 50

אֵי 1 where? (4 · 39) 32 אי

אֵי זֶה idiom = where, then? 261 זֶה 4.a.

כְּרִיתוּת divorcement (1 · 4) 504

נֹשֶׁא creditor (1 · 5) 674 נשה

קָצַר 2 to be short; short of hand = powerless (4 · 12 · 14) 894

פְּדוּת ransom (1 · 4) 804

גְּעָרָה rebuke (6 · 15) 172

הֶחֱרִיב to dry up (6 · 13 · 37[?]) 351

בָּאַשׁ to have a bad smell, stink (1 · 5 · 16) 92

דָּגָה fish [coll.] (1 · 15) 185

מֵאֵין from lack of (6 · 48[?]) 34 אין 6.d.

צָמָא thirst (3 · 17) 854

קַדְרוּת 3 darkness, gloom (1 · 1) 871

שָׂק sackcloth (8 · 48) 974

כְּסוּת clothing, covering (1 · 8) 492

לִמֻּד 4 taught [one]; i.e., a disciple (4 · 6) 541

עוּת to help [dub.] (1 · 1 · 1) 736

יָעֵף weary, faint (2 · 4) 419

בַּבֹּקֶר בַּבֹּקֶר idiom = morning by morning, every morning 134 בקר 1.f.

מָרָה 5 to be disobedient, rebellious (3 · 21 · 43) 598

אָחוֹר backwards; back part (9 · 41) 30

נָסוֹג to turn oneself away, turn back, prove faithless (3 · 14 · 25) 690

גַּו 6 back (3 · 6) 156

לְחִי cheek, jaw (2 · 21) 534

מרט to make bare, bald, smooth (1 · 7 · 14) 598

כְּלִמָּה reproach, ignominy (4 · 30) 484

רֹק spittle (1 · 3) 956

נכלם 7 to be humiliated, ashamed (5 · 26 · 38) 483

חַלָּמִישׁ flint (1 · 5) 321

הַצְדִּיק 8 to justify, vindicate (3 · 12 · 41) 842

יַחַד together (7 · 44) 403

הִרְשִׁיעַ 9 to condemn as guilty (2 · 25 · 34) 957

בלה to wear out (2 · 11 · 16) 115

עָשׁ moth (2 · 7) 799

יָרֵא 10 fear, reverence, honor (1[?] · 45) 431 ירא

חֲשֵׁכָה darkness (2 · 6) 365

נֹגַהּ brightness (5 · 19) 618

נִשְׁעַן to lean, support oneself (5 · 22 · 22) 1043

קדח 11 to kindle (2 · 5 · 5) 869

אזר to gird (2 · 6 · 16) 25

זִיקוֹת sparks, brands (2 · 2) 278 זק

מַעֲצֵבָה place of pain (1 · 1) 781

Chapter 51

חָצַב 1 to be hewn (1 · 1 · 17) 345

מַקֶּבֶת hole, excavation (1 · 1) 666

נָקַר to be dug (1 · 1 · 6) 669

חוֹלֵל 2 to writhe in travail with, bear, bring forth (1 · 7 · 47) 296

חָרְבָּה 3 waste place, ruin (9 · 42) 352

גַּן garden (2 · 42) 171

שָׂשׂוֹן exultation, joy (6 · 22) 965

תּוֹדָה thanksgiving in songs of liturgical worship, thanksgiving (1 · 32) 392

הַקְשִׁיב 4 to give attention (8 · 45 · 46) 904

לְאֹם people (11 · 35) 522

הַאֲזִין to hear, give ear (8 · 41 · 41) 24

הִרְגִּיעַ to give rest to [but use here idiomatic and uncertain] (2 · 8 · 13[?]) 921 II

יֶשַׁע 5 salvation, deliverance, rescue (5 · 36) 447

אִי coastlands, islands (17 · 36) 15

קִוָּה to wait, look eagerly for (13 · 39 · 45) 875

יִחֵל to wait for, hope for (2 · 25 · 42) 404

עָשָׁן 6 smoke (7 · 25) 798

נִמְלַח to be dispersed in fragments, dissipated (1 · 1 · 1) 571

בָּלָה to wear out (2 · 11 · 16) 115

כֵּן gnat, gnats, gnat swarm [dub.] (1 · 5) 48

אֱנוֹשׁ 7 men; man, mankind (8 · 42) 60

גִּדּוּפִים revilings, reviling words (2 · 3) 154

עָשׁ 8 moth (2 · 7) 799

צֶמֶר wool (2 · 16) 856

סָס moth (1 · 1) 703

הַחֲצִיב 9 to hew in pieces (1 · 1 · 17) 345

רַהַב storm, arrogance [here used for mythical sea monster] (2 · 7) 923

חוֹלֵל to pierce (2 · 3 · 7) 319

תַּנִּין sea monster, serpent, dragon (2 · 15) 1072

הֶחֱרִיב 10 to dry up (6 · 13 · 37[?]) 351

תְּהוֹם deep, sea, abyss (2 · 36) 1062

מַעֲמַקִּים depths (1 · 5) 771

רִנָּה 11 ringing cry [in joy] (9 · 33) 943

שָׂשׂוֹן exultation, joy (6 · 22) 965

הִשִּׂיג to reach, attain, overtake (3 · 49 · 49) 673

יָגוֹן grief, sorrow (2 · 14) 387

אֲנָחָה sighing, groaning (3 · 11) 58

אֱנוֹשׁ 12 man, mankind (8 · 42) 60

חָצִיר green grass, herbage (8 · 18[?]) 348

עֹשֶׂה 13 maker, creator (6 · 24) 793 I. עשה

יָסַד to found, establish (5 · 20 · 41) 413

פָּחַד to be in great dread (1 · 2 · 26) 808

הֵצִיק to bring into straits; ptc. = oppressor (4 · 11 · 11) 847

אַיֵּה where? (9 · 44) 32

צָעָה 14 to stoop, bend, incline (2 · 4 · 5) 858

שַׁחַת pit (2 · 23) 1001

חָסֵר to be lacking (1 · 19 · 23) 341

רָגַע 15 to disturb (1 · 4 · 13) 920 I.

הָמָה to roar, be boisterous, growl, murmur (5 · 33 · 33) 242

גַּל wave, billow, heap (2 · 16) 164

יָסַד 16 to found, establish (5 · 20 · 41) 413

כּוֹס 17 cup (4 · 31) 468

קֻבַּעַת cup (2 · 2) 867

תַּרְעֵלָה reeling (2 · 3) 947

מָצָה to drain, drain out (1 · 4 · 7) 594

נָהַל 18 to lead or guide (3 · 9 · 10) 624

נוּד 19 to show grief; i.e., by shaking or nodding head (1 · 20 · 27) 626

שֹׁד devastation, ruin (6 · 25) 994

שֶׁבֶר shattering, crushing, breach (9 · 45) 991

עֻלַּף 20 to be covered [i.e., to have senses obscured]; to have fainted (1 · 2 · 5 [?]) 763

תּוֹא antelope (1 · 2) 1060

מִכְמָר net, snare (1 · 2) 485

גְּעָרָה rebuke (6 · 15) 172

שָׁכוּר 21 ptc. pass. = drunk (1 · 1) 1016 שכר

כּוֹס 22 cup (4 · 31) 468

תַּרְעֵלָה reeling (2 · 3) 947

קֻבַּעַת cup (2 · 2) 867

הוֹגָה 23 to cause grief or sorrow (1 · 5 · 8) 387

שְׁחִי only *Qal* form of השתחוה; here = bow down! 1005

גֵּו back (3 · 6) 156

Chapter 52

תִּפְאֶרֶת 1 beauty, finery, glory (18 · 50) 802

עָרֵל uncircumcised (1 · 35) 790

התנער 2 to shake oneself [free] (1 · 1 · 11) 654

מוֹסֵר bond [of captivity] (2 · 12) 64

צַוָּאר neck, back of neck (4 · 41) 848

שְׁבִי captive (1 · 1) 985

חִנָּם 3 for nothing, gratis; without cause (2 · 32) 336

אֶפֶס 4 nought, nonexistence (13 · 27) 67

עָשַׁק to oppress (1 · 36 · 37) 798

פֹּה 5 here (2 · 44) 805

מַה־לִּי־פֹה idiom = What have I here? 552 מָה 1.a. (d.)

חִנָּם for nothing, gratis; without cause (2 · 32) 336

מֹשֵׁל ruler (4 · 24) 605 III מָשַׁל

הֵילִיל to howl (11 · 30 · 30) 410

מְנֹאָץ = Hith. ptc. = contemned; to be contemned, spurned (1 · 1 · 24) 610 נאץ

נָאוָה 7 to be comely, fitting; *Pilel* form (1 · 3 · 3[?]) 610

מְבַשֵּׂר one bringing glad tidings (4 · 9) 142 בשׂר

בִּשֵּׂר to herald as glad tidings (3 · 14 · 15) 142

צֹפֶה 8 watchman (2 · 19)[?]) 859

עַיִן בְּעַיִן idiom = eye to eye; eye for an eye 745 עין 5.

פָּצַח 9 to break forth with, burst forth (6 · 7 · 7) 822

חָרְבָּה waste, ruin (9 · 42) 352

חָשַׂף 10 to strip, lay bare (3 · 10 · 10) 362

אֶפֶס end, extreme limits, non-existence (13 · 27) 67

נברר 11 to purify oneself (1 · 3 · 15[?]) 140

חִפָּזוֹן 12 trepidation, hurried flight (1 · 3) 342

מְנוּסָה flight; i.e., escape (1 · 2) 631

גָּבַהּ 13 to be exalted, high (5 · 24 · 34) 146

מִשְׁחַת 14 disfigurement (1 · 1) 1008

תֹּאַר form, outline (2 · 15) 1061

הִזָּה 15 to cause to leap; i.e., startle; or to sprinkle (1 · 20 · 24[?]) 633 I & II נזה

קָפַץ to shut, draw together (1 · 5 · 7) 891

Chapter 53

שְׁמוּעָה 1 report (4 · 27) 1035

יוֹנֵק 2 young plant, sapling (2[?] · 11[?]) 413

שֹׁרֶשׁ root (7 · 33) 1057

צִיָּה land of drought, desert (3 · 16) 851

תֹּאַר form, outline (2 · 15) 1061

הָדָר splendor, majesty (7 · 30) 214

חָמַד to desire, take pleasure in (3 · 16 · 21) 326

נבזה 3 to be despised; ptc. = despised, vile, worthless (2 · 10 · 42) 102

חָדֵל lacking; here w. "men" = forsaken (1 · 3) 293

מַכְאוֹב pain, mental pain (2 · 16) 456

חֳלִי sickness, disease (4 · 24) 318

מַסְתֵּר hiding, act of hiding (1 · 1) 712

אָכֵן 4 surely, truly, but indeed (4 · 18) 38

חֳלִי sickness, disease (4 · 24) 318

262

מַכְאוֹב pain, mental pain (2 · 16) 456

סֵבֶל to carry, bear (5 · 7 · 9) 687

חוֹלֵל 5 to be pierced, wounded (2 · 3 · 7) 319 I.

דֻּכָּא to be crushed; ptc. crushed (2 · 4 · 18) 193

מוּסָר chastisement (2 · 50) 416

חַבּוּרָה stripe, blow, stroke (2 · 7) 289

תָּעָה 6 to wander about, err (8 · 27 · 50) 1073

הִפְגִּיעַ to cause to light upon, cause one to entreat, interpose (3 · 6 · 46) 803

נִגַּשׂ 7 to be treated harshly (2 · 3 · 7) 620

שֶׂה a sheep, goat (4 · 45) 961

טֶבַח slaughtering, slaughter (4 · 12) 370

הוּבַל to be led, conducted (3 · 11 · 18) 384

רָחֵל ewe (1 · 4) 932

גָּזַז to shear; ptc. = sheep-shearer (1 · 14 · 15) 159

נֶאֱלַם to be dumb, unable to speak, bound (1 · 8 · 9) 47

עֹצֶר 8 coercion, restraint (1 · 3) 783

שׂוֹחֵחַ to meditate, consider (1 · 2 · 20) 967

נִגְזַר to be cut off, separated, excluded (1 · 6 · 12) 160

עָשִׁיר 9 rich (1 · 23) 799

מִרְמָה deceit, treachery (1 · 39) 941

דִּכָּא 10 to crush (2 · 11 · 18) 193

אָשָׁם trespass offering, substitute (1 · 46) 79

הֶאֱרִיךְ to prolong (4 · 31 · 34) 73

חֵפֶץ cause, purpose, good pleasure, delight (9 · 39) 343

הִצְדִּיק 11 to justify, vindicate the cause of, save (3 · 12 · 41) 842

סֵבֶל to carry, bear (5 · 7 · 9) 687

עָצוּם 12 numerous, countless, many (3 · 31) 783

תַּחַת אֲשֶׁר idiom = because that, instead of that 1066 תַּחַת II. 3.a.

הֶעֱרָה to pour out; elsewhere = make naked (1 · 3 · 15) 788

פָּשַׁע to transgress, rebel (9 · 40 · 41) 833

נִמְנָה to be reckoned, assigned (1 · 6 · 28) 584

חֵטְא punishment for sin, sin (4 · 33) 307

הִפְגִּיעַ to interpose, make entreaty (3 · 6 · 46) 803

Chapter 54

עָקָר 1 barren (1 · 11) 785

פָּצַח to break forth with, burst forth (6 · 7 · 7) 822

רִנָּה ringing cry [in joy] (9 · 33) 943

צָהַל to cry shrilly (3 · 7 · 8) 843

חוּל to twist, writhe [in childbirth] (9 · 30 · 47) 296

בְּעוּלָה married (2 · 4) 127 בעל

הִרְחִיב 2 to enlarge (5 · 21 · 25) 931

חָשַׂךְ to refrain, keep back (3 · 26 · 28) 362

הַאֲרִיךְ to make long (4 · 31 · 34) 73

מֵיתָר cord, string (1 · 9) 452

יָתֵד tent pin, peg (4 · 23) 450

פָּרַץ 3 to break over, increase (2 · 46 · 49) 829

נִכְלַם 4 to be humiliated, ashamed (5 · 26 · 38) 483

הֶחְפִּיר to display shame (2 · 4 · 17) 344

בֹּשֶׁת shame (5 · 30) 102

עֲלוּמִים youth, youthful vigor (1 · 4) 761

אַלְמָנוּת widowhood (1 · 4) 48

בָּעַל 5 to marry (4 · 10 · 12) 127

עֹשֶׂה maker, creator (6 · 24) 793 I. עשה

גֹּאֵל redeemer, kinsman (13 · 44) 145 גאל

עָצֵב 6 to hurt, grieve; here ptc. pass. (1 · 3 · 15) 780

נְעוּרִים youth, early life (3 · 46) 655

רֶגַע 7 a moment (5 · 22) 921

רַחֲמִים compassion (4 · 38) 933

263

שֶׁצֶף 8 flood (1 · 1[?]) 1009 שטף

קֶצֶף wrath (3 · 28) 893

רֶגַע moment, one moment (5 · 22) 921

רָחַם to have compassion, be compassionate (12 · 42 · 47) 933

גֹּאֵל redeemer, kinsman (13 · 44) 145 גאל

קָצַף 9 to be angry (7 · 28 · 34) 893

גָּעַר to rebuke (2 · 14 · 14) 172

מוּשׁ 10 to depart, be removed (5 · 20[?] · 20 [?]) 559

מוֹט to totter, shake (3 · 15 · 39) 556

רָחַם to have compassion, be compassionate (12 · 42 · 47) 933

סֹעַר 11 to storm, rage (1[?] · 1[?] · 7[?]) 704

הרביץ to lay, to cause to lie down (2 · 6 · 30) 918

פּוּךְ antimony, stibium (1 · 4) 806

יָסַד to found, establish (5 · 20 · 41) 413

סַפִּיר sapphire, lapis lazuli (1 · 11) 705

כַּדְכֹד 12 a precious stone; perh. ruby (1 · 2) 461

אֶקְדָּח fiery glow, sparkle (1 · 1) 869

חֵפֶץ delight, good pleasure (9 · 39) 343

לִמֻּד 13 taught one; i.e., a disciple (4 · 6) 541

עֹשֶׁק 14 oppression (3 · 15) 799

מְחִתָּה terror, destruction, ruin (1 · 11) 369

אֶפֶס 15 cessation of, nonexistence of, end of (13 · 27) 67

בָּרָא 16 to shape, fashion, create (20 · 38 · 48) 135

חָרָשׁ graver, artificer (8 · 38) 360

נפח to breathe, blow (1 · 9 · 12) 655

פֶּחָם coal (2 · 3) 809

מַשְׁחִית destroyer (1 · 19) 1007 שחת

חבל to ruin, destroy (3 · 6 · 11) 287 II.

הוּצַר 17 to be formed (1 · 1 · 44) 427

הִרְשִׁיעַ to condemn as guilty (2 · 25 · 34) 957

Chapter 55

צָמֵא 1 thirsty, thirsty one (5 · 9) 854

שבר to buy grain (2 · 16 · 21) 991

בְּלוֹא without (4 · 30) 518 לא 4.a.

מְחִיר price (2 · 15) 564

חָלָב milk (4 · 44) 316

שָׁקַל 2 to weigh out [a price] (4 · 19 · 22) 1053

בְּלוֹא for what is not, for what does not (4 · 30) 518 לא 4.a.

יְגִיעַ toil, produce, acquired property (2 · 16) 388

שָׂבְעָה satiety (3 · 7[?]) 960

התענג to take exquisite delight (4 · 9 · 10) 772

דֶּשֶׁן fatness (1 · 15) 206

לְאֹם 4 people (11 · 35) 522

נָגִיד ruler, prince (1 · 44) 617

פָּאַר 5 to beautify, glorify (4 · 6 · 13) 802

רָחַם 7 to have compassion (12 · 42 · 47) 933

סלח to forgive, pardon (1 · 33 · 46) 699

גָּבַהּ 9 to be high (5 · 24 · 34) 146

גֶּשֶׁם 10 rain (2 · 35) 177

שֶׁלֶג snow (2 · 20) 1017

הִרְוָה to saturate, water (2 · 5 · 14) 924

הצמיח to cause to sprout, grow (4 · 14 · 33) 855

רֵיקָם 11 in vain (1 · 16) 938

הובל 12 to be led, conducted (3 · 11 · 18) 384

פצח to break forth (6 · 7 · 7) 822

רִנָּה ringing cry [in joy] (9 · 33) 943

מחא to clap (1 · 2 · 3) 561

נַעֲצוּץ 13 thornbush (2 · 2) 654

בְּרוֹשׁ cypress or fir (5 · 20) 141

סִרְפַּד a desert plant (1 · 1) 710

הֲדַס myrtle (2 · 6) 213

Chapter 56

אָשֶׁר 2 happiness; אַשְׁרֵי = 0 the happiness of (3·45)80

אֱנוֹשׁ man (8·42)60

נֵכָר 3 foreignness, foreigner (5·36)648

נִלְוָה to join oneself to, be joined (3·11·12)530

הִבְדִּיל to separate (2·32·42)95

סָרִיס eunuch (3·45)710

יָבֵשׁ dry (1·9)386

סָרִיס 4 eunuch (3·45)710

בַּאֲשֶׁר in [that] which (4·19)84

נֵכָר 6 foreignness, foreigner (5·36)648

נִלְוָה to join oneself or be joined (3·11·12)530

נִדָּח 8 banished ones[s], outcast[s] (5·11) נדח 623

שָׂדַי 9 field (1·13)961

אָתָה to come (9·19·21)87

צֹפֶה 10 watchman (2·19[?])859 I. צפה

עִוֵּר blind (11·26)734

כֶּלֶב dog (3·32)476

אִלֵּם dumb (2·6)48

נבח to bark (1·1·1)613

הזה to dream, rave (1·1·1)223

נום to be drowsy, slumber (2·6·6)630

כֶּלֶב 11 dog (3·32)476

עַז fierce, strong (4·22)738

שָׂבְעָה satiety (3·7[?])960

בֶּצַע unjust gain (3·23)130

אָתָה 12 to come (9·19·21)87

סבא to imbibe (1·2·2)684

שֵׁכָר strong drink (8-23)1016

Chapter 57

בְּאֵין 1 in defect of, for want of, without (1·10)35 II אין 6.a.

מִשְׁכָּב 2 couch, bed (4·46)1012

נָכֹחַ straightness, straight, right (4·8) 647

הֵנָּה 3 hither (1·49)244

עוֹנֵן to practice soothsaying; fem. ptc. = soothsaying woman (2·10·11) 778

נאף to commit adultery (1·14·31)610

התענג 4 to make merry over, make sport of, take exquisite delight in (4·9·10) 772

הִרְחִיב to enlarge, open wide (5·21·25) 931

הֶאֱרִיךְ to make long, stretch out (4·31·34)73

אַיִל 5 terebinth [deciduous tree] (3·4)18

רַעֲנָן luxuriant (1·19)947

סָעִיף cleft (2[?]·4[?])703

חָלָק 6 smooth (2[?]·12[?])325

גָּבֹהַּ 7 high, lofty, tall (6·41)147

מִשְׁכָּב couch, bed (4·46)1012

מְזוּזָה 8 doorpost, gatepost (1·20)265

זִכָּרוֹן memorial, reminder (1·24)272

הִרְחִיב to make wide, make large (5·21·25)931

מִשְׁכָּב couch, bed (4·46)1012

יָד idiomatic [dub.] phallus 388 יָד 4.g.

שׁוּר 9 perh. to travel, journey (1·1·1[?]) 1003 I.

רִקּוּחַ perfumery, ointment (1·1)955

צִיר envoy, messenger (2·6)851

מֵרָחֹק to a distance, at a distance (12·34) 935

הִשְׁפִּיל to set in a lower place, to show abasement (6·19·30)1050

יגע 10 to grow or be weary, toil (10·20·26)388

נוֹאָשׁ to despair, be desperate, have no hope (1·5·6)384

הִיָּה revival, renewal; w. יד = renewal of strength (1·12)312

דָּאַג 11 to fear, dread, be anxious, concerned (1 · 7 · 7) 178

כָּזַב to lie (2 · 12 · 16) 469

הֶחֱשָׁה to be silent (2 · 9 · 16) 364

הוֹעִיל 12 to profit, avail, benefit (8 · 23 · 23)
418

קִבּוּץ 13 assemblage, masses (1 · 1) 868

חָסָה to seek refuge (3 · 37 · 37) 340

סָלַל 14 to cast up, lift up (4 · 10 · 12) 699

פַּנָּה דָרֶךְ [idiom] to make clear, free from
obstacles 815

מִכְשׁוֹל means or occasion of stumbling,
stumbling block (2 · 14) 506

רָם 15 high, exalted (7 · 31[?]) 926 רום

עַד forever (8 · 48) 723 עד I.

דַּכָּא contrite, crushed (1 · 1) 194

שָׁפָל lowly (2 · 18) 1050

נדכא ptc. = crushed (1 · 1 · 18) 193 דכא

נֶצַח 16 everlastingness; with לְ = forever
(7 · 43) 664

קָצַף to be angry (7 · 28 · 34) 893

עטף to be feeble, faint (1 · 3 · 11) 742

נְשָׁמָה breathing thing, breath, spirit
(4 · 24) 675

בֶּצַע 17 unjust gain; gain made by violence
(3 · 23) 130

קָצַף to be angry (7 · 28 · 34) 893

שׁוֹבָב back turning, apostate (1 · 3) 1000

הנחה 18 to guide, lead (1 · 26 · 40) 634

נֶחֻמִים comfort (1 · 3) 637 נחם

אָבֵל mourner, mourning (3 · 8) 5

בָּרָא 19 to shape, fashion, create
(20 · 38 · 48) 135

נִיב fruit (1 · 2) 626

לָרָחוֹק distant (1 · 1) 935

לָקָרוֹב near 898 קרב 2.b.

נגרש 20 to be driven, tossed (1 · 3 · 48) 176

השקיט to show quietness (4 · 10 · 41) 1052

גרש to cast out, thrust out (1 · 8 · 48)
176

רֶפֶשׁ mire (1 · 1) 952

טִיט mire, mud, clay (2 · 13) 376

Chapter 58

גָּרוֹן 1 throat (2 · 8) 173

חָשַׂךְ to refrain, keep back (3 · 26 · 28) 362

קִרְבָה 2 approach (1 · 2) 898

צוֹם 3 to abstain from food, fast
(3 · 20 · 20) 847

צוֹם fasting, fast (4 · 26) 847

חֵפֶץ business, cause, good pleasure, delight (9 · 39) 343

עָצֵב toiler (1 · 1) 780

נָגַשׂ to press, drive (1 · 4 · 7) 620

מַצָּה 4 strife, contention (1 · 3) 663

צוֹם to abstain from food, fast
(3 · 20 · 20) 847

אֶגְרֹף fist (1 · 2) 175

רֶשַׁע wickedness (2 · 30) 957

צוֹם 5 fast, fasting (4 · 26) 847

כָּפַף to bend, bend down (1 · 4 · 5) 496

אַגְמֹן rush, bulrush (3 · 5) 8

שַׂק sackcloth (8 · 48) 974

אֵפֶר ashes (3 · 22) 68

הִצִּיעַ to lay out, spread out (1 · 2 · 4) 426
יצע

צוֹם 6 fast, fasting (4 · 26) 847

חַרְצֻבּוֹת bond, fetter, pang (1 · 2) 359

רֶשַׁע wickedness (2 · 30) 957

הִתִּיר to unfasten, loosen (1 · 5 · 7) 684

אֲגֻדָּה band (1 · 4) 8

מוֹטָה bar of yoke (3 · 11) 557

רצץ crush; ptc. pass. = oppressed
(4 · 11 · 19) 954

חָפְשִׁי free (1 · 17) 344

נתק to tear apart, snap (1 · 11 · 27) 683

פָּרַס 7 to divide, break in two (1 · 2 · 14)
828

רָעֵב hungry, hungry one (5 · 19) 944

מָרוּד   restlessness, straying, wandering poor (1 · 3) 924

עָרֹם   naked (4 · 16) 736 עֵרֹם

הִתְעַלֵּם   to hide oneself (1 · 6 · 29) 761

שַׁחַר   8 dawn (3 · 23) 1007

אֲרֻכָה   healing, restoration (1 · 6) 74 אֲרוכה

מְהֵרָה   hastily, quickly; haste (2 · 20) 555

צָמַח   to sprout, spring up (4 · 15 · 33) 855

אָסַף   [idiom] bring up the rear of, be rear guard for 62 אסף Qal 3.

שׁוּעַ   9 to cry for help (1 · 21 · 21[?]) 1002

מוֹטָה   bar of yoke (3 · 11) 557

אֶצְבַּע   finger, forefinger (4 · 31) 840

הָפִיק   10 ותפק to produce, furnish (1[?] · 8 [?] · 9[?]) 807 II. פוק

רָעֵב   hungry, hungry one (5 · 19) 944

זָרַח   to rise, come forth (3 · 18 · 18) 280

אֲפֵלָה   calamity, darkness, gloom (3 · 10) 66

צָהֳרַיִם   noon, midday (3 · 23) 843

נָחָה   11 to lead, guide (2[?] · 14[?] · 40[?]) 634

צַחְצָחָה   scorched region (1 · 1) 850

הֶחֱלִיץ   to brace up, invigorate (1 · 1 · 27) 323

גַּן   garden (2 · 42) 171

רָוֶה   watered (1 · 3) 924

מוֹצָא   source, spring, going forth (2 · 27) 425

כָּזַב   to disappoint, fail (2 · 12 · 16) 469

חָרְבָּה   12 waste, ruin (9 · 42) 352

מוֹסָד   foundation (3 · 13) 414

גָּדֵר   mason [wall builder] (1 · 3) 154 גדר

פֶּרֶץ   breach, bursting forth (2 · 19) 829

נְתִיבָה   path (4 · 21) 677

חֵפֶץ   13 affairs, good pleasure, delight (9 · 39) 343

עֹנֶג   daintiness, exquisite delight (2 · 2) 772

הִתְעַנֵּג   14 to take exquisite delight in (4 · 9 · 10) 772

Chapter 59

קָצַר   1 to be short (4 · 12 · 14) 894

הִבְדִּיל   2 to separate (3 · 32 · 42) 95

לְבֵין   and between (1 · 1) 107 בֵּין 1.d.

נְגֹאַל   3 to be defiled (1 · 3 · 11) 146

אֶצְבַּע   finger, forefinger (4 · 31) 840

עַוְלָה   injustice, wrong (1[?] · 32[?]) 732

הָגָה   to utter, groan, moan, growl (7 · 23 · 25) 211

תֹּהוּ   4 [moral] unreality or falsehood (11 · 20) 1062

הָרָה   to conceive, become pregnant (4 · 38 · 40) 247

בֵּיצָה   5 egg (3 · 6) 101

צִפְעוֹנִי   a poisonous serpent (3 · 5) 861

קוּר   thread (2 · 2) 881

עַכָּבִישׁ   spider (1 · 2) 747

אָרַג   to weave; [metaph.] weave a spider's web = intrigue (1 · 3 · 3) 70

זוּר   to press down (1 · 3 · 3) 266

אֶפְעֶה   a kind of viper (2 · 3) 821

קוּר   6 thread (2 · 2) 881

פֹּעַל   dead, thing done (6 · 37) 821

נָקִי   7 free from guilt, clean, innocent (1 · 43) 667

שֹׁד   violence, havoc, devastation (6 · 25) 994

שֶׁבֶר   shattering, crushing, breach (9 · 45) 991

מְסִלָּה   highway, public road (9 · 27) 700

מַעְגָּל   8 track, course of action or life (2 · 13) 722

נְתִיבָה   path (4 · 21) 677

עִקֵּשׁ   to twist, make crooked (1 · 3 · 5) 786

הִשִּׂיג   9 to overtake, reach, attain (3 · 49 · 49) 673

קָוָה   to wait or look eagerly for (13 · 39 · 45) 875

נְגֹהָה   brightness (1 · 1) 618

267

אֲפֵלָה calamity, darkness, gloom (3 · 10) 66

גָּשַׁשׁ 10 to grope, grope for, feel with the hand (2 · 2 · 2) 178

עִוֵּר blind (11 · 26) 734

כְּאֵין as no ... (4 · 7) 34 אַיִן 6.b.

צָהֳרַיִם noon, midday (3 · 23) 843

נֶשֶׁף evening twilight, morning twilight (3 · 12) 676

אַשְׁמַנִּים stout, lusty [dub.] (1 · 1) 1032

הָמָה 11 to growl, groan, roar (5 · 33 · 33) 242

דֹּב bear (2 · 12) 179

יוֹנָה dove (3 · 33) 401

הָגָה to groan, moan, utter, growl (7 · 23 · 25) 211

קָוָה to wait or look eagerly for (13 · 39 · 45) 875

רָבַב 12 to be [become] many (4 · 23 · 24) 912

פָּשַׁע 13 to transgress, rebel (9 · 40 · 41) 833

כָּחֵשׁ • to act deceptively against, deceive (1 · 19 · 22) 471

נָסוֹג to turn oneself away, turn back, prove faithless (3 · 14 · 25) 690

עֹשֶׁק extortion, oppression (3 · 15) 799

סָרָה defection, apostasy, withdrawal (3 · 7) 694

הָרֹה to conceive, contrive, devise (1 · 1 · 40) 247

הוֹגֶה to moan, utter; here inf. abs. = uttering (1 · 1 · 25) 211 הגה

הֻסַּג 14 to be driven back (1 · 1 · 25) 690

אָחוֹר backwards; back part (9 · 41) 30

רָחוֹק distance; distant; מר׳ = at a distance (12 · 34) 935 2.a. (2)

רְחוֹב broad open place, plaza (2 · 43) 932

נְכֹחַ straightforwardness, honesty (4 · 8) 647

נֶעְדָּר 15 to be lacking (3 · 6 · 7) 727

הִשְׁתּׂלֵל to be despoiled (1 · 2 · 15) 1021 II. שׁלל

הִפְגִּיעַ 16 to interpose, to make entreaty; ptc. = one interposing (3 · 6 · 46) 803

סָמַךְ to uphold, sustain (4 · 41 · 48) 701

שִׁרְיָן 17 body armor (1 · 8) 1056

כּוֹבַע helmet (1 · 6) 464

נָקָם vengeance (6 · 17) 668

תִּלְבֹּשֶׁת raiment, clothing (1 · 1) 528

עָטָה to wrap oneself, envelop oneself (1 · 11 · 14) 741

מְעִיל robe (2 · 28) 839

קִנְאָה zeal (7 · 43) 888

כְּעַל 18 according to, like (3 · 5) 758 עַל IV. 1.

גְּמוּלָה dealing, recompense (1 · 3) 168

גְּמוּל dealing, recompense (5 · 19) 168

אִי coastland, island (17 · 36) 15

מַעֲרָב 19 west, place of sunset (3 · 14) 788

צוּר to besiege, bind (3 · 31 · 31) 848; but perh. contracted; hence, swift [river] 865 I. צר

גָּאַל 20 redeemer, kinsman (13 · 44) 145 גאל

מוּשׁ 21 to depart, be removed (5 · 20[?] · 20 [?]) 559

Chapter 60

אוֹר 1 to shine (1 · 5 · 40) 21

זָרַח to rise, come forth (3 · 18 · 18) 280

עֲרָפֶל 2 cloud, heavy cloud (1 · 15) 791

לְאֹם people (11 · 35) 522

זָרַח to rise, come forth (3 · 18 · 18) 280

נֹגַהּ 3 brightness (5 · 19) 618

זֶרַח dawning, shining (1 · 1) 280

מֵרָחֹק 4 from a distance, at a distance (12 · 34) 935

צַד side, possibly hip (2 · 32) 841

נֶאֱמַן [idiom] to be carried 52

נָהַר 5 to shine, beam (1[?] · 3[?] · 3[?]) 626

פָּחַד to be in awe, dread (7 · 23 · 26) 808

רָחַב to be widened, expanded [with joy] (1 · 3 · 25) 931

שִׁפְעָה 6 multitude, abundance, quantity (1 · 6) 1051

בִּכְרָה young camel, dromedary (1 · 1) 114

לְבוֹנָה frankincense (3 · 21) 526

בִּשֵּׂר to herald as good news (3 · 14 · 15) 142

תִּפְאֶרֶת 7 glory (18 · 50) 802

פָּאַר to beautify, glorify (4 · 6 · 13) 802

עָב 8 dark cloud (7 · 30) 728

עוּף to fly (4 · 18 · 25) 733

יוֹנָה dove (3 · 33) 401

אֲרֻבָּה opening, lattice, window (2 · 9) 70

אִי 9 coastland, island (17 · 36) 15

קָוָה to wait or look eagerly for (13 · 39 · 45) 875

אֳנִיָּה ship (5 · 31) 58

מֵרָחוֹק from a distance, at a distance (12 · 34) 935

פָּאַר to beautify, glorify (4 · 6 · 13) 802

קֶצֶף 10 wrath (3 · 28) 893

רָחַם to have compassion, be compassionate (12 · 42 · 47) 933

נָהַג 11 to drive, conduct; ptc. pass. led (3 · 20 · 30) 624

חרב 12 to be waste, desolate (6 · 17 · 37) 351

בְּרוֹשׁ 13 cypress, fir (5 · 20) 141

תִּדְהָר tree, prob. elm or pine (2 · 2) 187

תְּאַשּׁוּר box tree; a small evergreen (2 · 3) 81

פָּאַר to beautify, glorify (4 · 6 · 13) 802

שָׁחַ 14 to bow [in homage] (3 · 12 · 18) 1005
שחח

נָאַץ to cause to spurn, blaspheme (3 · 15 · 24) 610

גָּאוֹן 15 excellency, majesty, pride (12 · 49) 144

מָשׂוֹשׂ exultation (10 · 17) 965

יָנַק 16 to suck (4 · 8 · 18) 413

חָלָב milk (4 · 44) 316

שֹׁד female breast (2 · 3) 994

מוֹשִׁיעַ savior, deliverer (9 · 27) 446 ישע

גָּאַל redeemer, kinsman (13 · 44) 145 גאל

אָבִיר strong, the Strong One, old name for God (3 · 6) 7

פְּקֻדָּה 17 overseer, oversight, visitation (3 · 32) 824

נֹגֵשׂ lord, ruler (5 · 15) 620 נגש

שֹׁד 18 violence, havoc, devastation (6 · 25) 994

שֶׁבֶר shattering, crushing, breach (9 · 45) 991

נֹגַהּ 19 brightness (5 · 19) 618

יָרֵחַ moon (3 · 27) 437

הֵאִיר to give light (2 · 34 · 40) 21

תִּפְאֶרֶת glory, beauty (18 · 50) 802

יָרֵחַ 20 moon (3 · 27) 437

נֶאֱסַף [idiom] of moon = to withdraw itself (>50) 62

אֵבֶל mourning (2 · 24) 5

נֵצֶר 21 sprout, shoot (3 · 4) 666

מַטָּע act of planting, place of planting (2 · 6) 642

הִתְפָּאֵר to be glorified (5 · 17 · 13) 802

אֶלֶף 22 thousand (1 · 12) 48

צָעִיר little, insignificant, young (1 · 22) 859

עָצוּם mighty, numerous (3 · 31) 783

הֵחִישׁ to hasten, act quickly (3 · 6 · 21) 301

Chapter 61

בִּשֵּׂר 1 to herald as glad tidings (3 · 14 · 15) 142

עָנָו poor, weak, afflicted (3[?] · 21[?]) 776

חבש to bind up, bind on (2 · 28 · 32) 289

269

שָׁבָה to take captive; ptc. = captive (1 · 30 · 38) 985

דְּרוֹר liberty, free run (1 · 7) 204

פְּקַח־קוֹחַ opening; fig. of freeing (1 · 1) 824

נָקָם 2 vengeance (6 · 17) 668

אָבֵל mourner, mourning (3 · 8) 5

אָבֵל 3 mourner, mourning (3 · 8) 5

אֵבֶל mourning (2 · 24) 5

פְּאֵר headdress, turban (3 · 7) 802

אֵפֶר ashes (3 · 22) 68

שָׂשׂוֹן exultation, joy (6 · 22) 965

מַעֲטֶה wrap, mantle (1 · 1) 742

כֵּהֶה faint, dim, dull (2 · 7) 462

אַיִל terebinth, a deciduous tree (3 · 4) 18

מַטָּע plantation, place of planting, act of planting (2 · 6) 642

הִתְפָּאֵר to be glorified (5 · 7 · 13) 802

חָרְבָּה 4 waste place, ruin (9 · 42) 352

חִדֵּשׁ to repair, renew (1 · 9 · 10) 293

חֹרֶב desolation (5 · 16) 351

נֵכָר 5 foreigner (5 · 36) 648

אִכָּר plowman, husband (1 · 7) 38

כֹּרֵם vinedressers (1 · 5) 501 כרם

מְשָׁרֵת 6 minister (1 · 20) 1058 שרת

תִּתְיַמָּרוּ to boast (1 · 1 · 1[?]) 55 אמר Hithp.

בֹּשֶׁת 7 shame (5 · 30) 102

מִשְׁנֶה double portion, double, copy, second (2 · 36) 1041

כְּלִמָּה reproach, ignominy (4 · 30) 484

גָּזֵל 8 robbery, thing plundered (1 · 4) 160

עַוְלָה violent deeds of injustice (1[?] · 32 [?]) 732

פְּעֻלָּה reward, wages; work (5 · 14) 821

צֶאֱצָא 9 offspring (7 · 11) 425

הִכִּיר to be willing to recognize, acknowledge; to regard, observe (2 · 38 · 40) 647

שׂוֹשׂ 10 to exult, display joy (9 · 27 · 27) 965 שׂושׂ

גִּיל to rejoice (11 · 45 · 45) 162

יֵשַׁע salvation, deliverance, rescue (5 · 36) 447

מְעִיל robe (2 · 28) 591

הֶעְטָה to wrap, envelop (1 · 3 · 14) 742

חָתָן bridegroom; daughter's husband (2 · 20) 368

כִּהֵן to play the priest, to deck oneself out like a priest (1 · 23 · 23) 464

פְּאֵר headdress, turban (3 · 7) 802

כַּלָּה bride; daughter-in-law (3 · 34) 483

עדה to deck oneself with ornaments (1 · 8 · 8) 725

צֶמַח 11 sprout, growth (2 · 11) 855

גַּנָּה garden (5 · 16) 171

זֵרוּעַ sowing, thing sown (1 · 2) 283

הִצְמִיחַ to cause to sprout, grow (4 · 14 · 33) 855

Chapter 62

חָשָׁה 1 to be silent, still (4 · 7 · 16) 364

שָׁקַט to be quiet (3 · 31 · 41) 1052

נֹגַהּ brightness (5 · 19) 618

לַפִּיד torch (1 · 13) 542

נקב 2 to prick off, designate, to pierce (2 · 13 · 19) 666

עֲטָרָה 3 crown (4 · 23) 742

תִּפְאֶרֶת glory, beauty (18 · 50) 802

צָנוּף turban (2 · 5) 857 צניף

מְלוּכָה kingship, kingly office, royalty (2 · 24) 574

חֵפֶץ 4 delight, pleasure, good cause (9 · 39) 343

בְּעוּלָה married (2 · 4) 127 בעל

נִבְעַל to be married (1 · 2 · 12) 127

בָּעַל 5 to marry (4 · 10 · 12) 127

בָּחוּר young man (6 · 45) 104

בְּתוּלָה virgin (5 · 50) 143

מָשׂוֹשׂ exultation (10 · 17) 965

חָתָן bridegroom; daughter's husband (2 · 20) 368

כַּלָּה	bride; daughter-in-law (3 · 34) 483	גְּאוּלִים	redemption (1 · 1) 145
שׂוֹשׂ	to exult, display joy (9 · 27 · 27) שׂוּשׂ 965	עֹזֵר	5 helper (1 · 19) 740 I. עזר
חשׁה	6 to be silent, still (4 · 7 · 16) 364	סָמַךְ	to uphold, support, sustain (4 · 41 · 48) 701
דֳמִי	quiet, rest, pause (2 · 3) 198	בוס	6 to tread down, trample (2 · 7 · 12) 100
דֳמִי	7 rest, quiet, pause (2 · 3) 198	שׁכר	to make drunk (1 · 4 · 18) 1016
דָּגָן	8 corn, grain (2 · 40) 186	נֵצַח	juice of grapes; fig. of blood, gore (2 · 2) 664
מַאֲכָל	food (1 · 30) 38		
נֵכָר	foreigner (5 · 36) 645	כְּעַל	7 according to (3 · 5) 758 עַל IV. 1.
תִּירוֹשׁ	fresh or new wine (4 · 38) 440	גמל	to deal out to, deal fully with (6 · 34 · 37) 168
יגע	to toil, labor (10 · 20 · 26) 388		
פַּנָּה דֶרֶךְ	10 [idiom] to make clear, clear from obstacles 815 פנה Pi.	טוב	goodness, goods, good things (3 · 32) 375
סלל	to cast up, lift up (4 · 10 · 12) 699	רַחֲמִים	compassion (4 · 38) 933
מְסִלָּה	highway, public road (9 · 27) 700	שׁקר	8 to deal falsely (1 · 5 · 6) 1055
סקל	to free from stones; to pelt w. stones (2 · 4 · 22) 709	מוֹשִׁיעַ	savior, deliverer (9 · 27) 446 ישׁע
נֵס	standard, ensign, signal (10 · 21) 651	צַר	9 distress (5[?] · 20[?]) 865
יֵשַׁע	11 salvation, deliverance, rescue (5 · 36) 447	חֶמְלָה	compassion, mercy (1 · 2) 328
		נטל	to bear, lift up (1 · 1 · 4) 642
שָׂכָר	reward, hire, wages (2 · 29) 969	מָרָה	10 to be disobedient, rebellious (3 · 21 · 43) 598
פְּעֻלָּה	reward, wages; work (5 · 14) 821	עצב	to vex (1 · 2 · 15) 780
		אַיֵּה	11 where? (9 · 44) 32
Chapter 63		תִּפְאֶרֶת	12 glory, beauty (18 · 50) 802
		תְּהוֹם	13 abyss of sea, deep, sea (2 · 36) 1062
חָמוּץ	1 ptc. pass. = red (1 · 1) 330 II. חמץ	בִּקְעָה	14 valley (3 · 19) 132
הדר	to adorn, honor, swell (1 · 4 · 6) 213	נהג	to lead on, guide (2 · 10 · 30) 624
לְבוּשׁ	garment, clothing (3 · 47) 528	תִּפְאֶרֶת	glory, beauty (18 · 50) 802
צעה	to bend, stoop, incline (2 · 4 · 5) 858	זְבֻל	15 dwelling, lofty abode; elevation, height (1 · 5) 259
אָדֹם	2 red (1 · 9) 10		
לְבוּשׁ	garment, clothing (3 · 47) 528	תִּפְאֶרֶת	glory, beauty (18 · 50) 802
גַּת	wine press (1 · 5) 387	אַיֵּה	where? (9 · 44) 32
פּוּרָה	3 wine press (1 · 2) 807	קִנְאָה	zeal (7 · 43) 888
רָמַס	to trample down (4 · 17 · 18) 942	מֵעֶה	seat of emotions, inward parts, internal organs (4 · 32) 588
נזה	to spurt, spatter (1 · 4 · 24[?]) 633		
נֵצַח	juice of grapes; fig. of blood, gore (2 · 2) 664	רַחֲמִים	compassion (4 · 38) 933
מַלְבּוּשׁ	raiment, attire (1 · 8) 528	התאפק	to restrain oneself (3 · 7 · 7) 67
גאל	to pollute, stain (1 · 1 · 11) 146	הִכִּיר	16 to be willing to recognize, acknowledge; to regard, observe (2 · 38 · 40) 647
נָקָם	4 vengeance (6 · 17) 668		

271

גָּאַל redeemer, kinsman (13 · 44) 145 גאל

הִתְעָה 17 to cause to err, mislead (6 · 21 · 50) 1073

הִקְשִׁיחַ to make hard, stubborn (1 · 2 · 2) 905

יִרְאָה fear, reverence, piety (5 · 45) 432

מִצְעָר 18 little while; small thing (1 · 6) 859

בּוּס to tread down (1 · 2 · 12) 100

לוּא 19 O that!, if only . . . ! (2 · 3) 530

נָזַל to shake, quake (2 · 3 · 4) 272

Chapter 64

קָדַח 1 to kindle (2 · 5 · 5) 869

הֲמָסִים brushwood (1 · 1) 243

בָּעָה to cause to boil up; to inquire (2 · 2 · 4) 126

רָגַז to quake (6 · 30 · 41) 919

נוֹרָא 2 wonderful thing; fearful, dreadful (4 · 44) 431

קִוָּה to wait or look eagerly for (13 · 39 · 45) 875

נָזַל shake, quake (2 · 3 · 4) 272

הֶאֱזִין 3 to hear, give ear (8 · 41 · 41) 24

זוּלָה except, besides (4 · 16) 265

חִכָּה to wait for, await (3 · 13 · 14) 314

פָּגַע 4 to meet (2 · 40 · 46) 803

שָׂשׂ to exult, display joy (9 · 27 · 27) 965 שוש

קָצַף to be angry (7 · 28 · 34) 893

עִדָּה 5 menstruation (1 · 1) 723

נָבֵל to wither and fall, fade (11 · 21 · 25) 615

עָלֶה leaf, leafage (3 · 18) 750

מוּג 6 to cause to melt (1 · 4 · 17) 556

חֹמֶר 7 clay, mortar, cement (5 · 7) 330

יָצַר to form; ptc. = potter (22 · 41 · 44) 427

קָצַף 8 to be angry (7 · 28 · 34) 893

עַד־מְאֹד to a great degree, exceedingly (2 · 16) 547 מאד 2.b.

עַד forever (8 · 48) 723 עד I.

תִּפְאָרֶת 10 glory, beauty (18 · 50) 802

שְׂרֵפָה burning (2 · 13) 977

מַחְמַד desirable thing, precious thing (1 · 13) 326

חָרְבָּה waste place, ruin (9 · 42) 352

הִתְאַפַּק 11 to restrain oneself, refrain (3 · 7 · 7) 67

חָשָׁה to be silent, inactive (4 · 7 · 16) 364

עַד־מְאֹד to a great degree, exceedingly (2 · 16) 547 מאד 2.b.

Chapter 65

לְלוֹא 1 without (2 · 11) 518 לא 4.e.

סָרַר 2 to be stubborn, rebellious (3 · 17 · 17) 710

גַּנָּה 3 garden (5 · 16) 171

לְבֵנָה brick, tile (2 · 12) 527

נְצוּרִים 4 secret places (1 · 1) 665 נצר I. 4.

חֲזִיר swine, boar (3 · 7) 306

פָּרָק fragment (1 · 1) 830; Q מרק broth (1 · 3) 600

פִּגֻּל foul thing, refuse (1 · 4) 803

קָרַב אֵלֶיךָ 5 [idiom] to keep to yourself 897

עָשָׁן smoke (7 · 25) 798

יָקַד to be kindled, burned (2 · 3 · 8) 428

חָשָׁה 6 to be silent, inactive, still (4 · 7 · 16) 364

חֵיק bosom (3 · 38) 300

חֵרֵף 7 to reproach, say sharp things against, taunt (5 · 34 · 38) 357

פְּעֻלָּה work; recompense (5 · 14) 821

חֵיק bosom (3 · 38) 300

תִּירוֹשׁ 8 fresh or new wine (4 · 38) 440

אֶשְׁכּוֹל cluster (1 · 9) 79

בָּחִיר 9 chosen, elect (6 · 13) 104

נָוֶה 10 abode of sheep, habitation (6 : 45) 627

רִבֵץ	resting place, place of lying down (2 · 4) 918		child, suckling a few days old (2 · 2) 732
שָׁכֵחַ 11	forgetting, forgetful (1 · 2) 1013	בלה 22	to wear out by use, use to the full (1 · 5 · 16) 115
גַּד	fortune, god of fortune (1 · 2) 151		
מְנִי	god of fate (1 · 1) 584	בָּחִיר	chosen, elect (6 · 13) 104
מִמְסָךְ	mixed drink, mixed wine (1 · 2) 587	יגע 23	to toil, labor (10 · 20 · 26) 388
מָנָה 12	to reckon, assign, appoint (1 · 12 · 28) 584	רִיק	emptiness, vanity; w. ל = in vain (3 · 12) 938
טֶבַח	slaughtering, slaughter (4 · 12) 370	בֶּהָלָה	sudden terror, ruin, dismay (1 · 4) 96
כָּרַע	to bow down, bow (5 · 30 · 36) 502		
בַּאֲשֶׁר	in [that] which (4 · 19) 84	צֶאֱצָא	offspring (7 · 11) 425
רָעֵב 13	to be hungry (5 · 12 · 14) 944	טֶרֶם 24	before (1 · 16) 382
צמא	to be thirsty (3 · 10 · 10) 854	זְאֵב 25	wolf (2 · 8) 255
טוּב 14	joy, fairness, beauty, good things (3 · 32) 375	טָלֶה	lamb (2 · 3) 378
		אַרְיֵה	lion (6 · 45) 71
כְּאֵב	pain (2 · 6) 456	תֶּבֶן	straw (2 · 17) 1061
שֶׁבֶר	breaking, crushing (9 · 45) 991	נָחָשׁ	serpent (4 · 31) 638
הֵילִיל	to howl (11 · 30 · 30) 410		
שְׁבוּעָה 15	curse, oath (1 · 30) 989		
בָּחִיר	chosen, elect (6 · 13) 104		**Chapter 66**
אָמֵן 16	verily, truly; amen (2 · 30) 53	הֲדֹם 1	footstool (1 · 6) 213
בָּרָא 17	to shape, fashion, create (20 · 38 · 48) 135	אֵי	where? (4 · 39) 32 אי
		מְנוּחָה	resting place, rest (4 · 21) 629
שָׂשׂ 18	to exult, rejoice, display joy (9 · 27 · 27) 965 שוש	נָכֵה 2	contrite, smitten, stricken (1 · 3) 646
		חָרֵד	trembling (2 · 6) 353
גִּיל	to rejoice (11 · 45 · 45) 162	שֶׂה 3	a sheep, goat (4 · 45) 961
גִּילָה	rejoicing (2 · 2) 162	ערף	to break the neck (1 · 6 · 6) 791
עֲדִי	as far as, until [poetic for עַד] (1 · 12) 723 III. עד	כֶּלֶב	dog (3 · 32) 476
		חֲזִיר	swine, boar (3 · 7) 306
עַד	forever, eternity (8 · 48) 723 I. עד	לְבֹנָה	frankincense, incense (3 · 21) 526
עֲדֵי־עַד	continuous existence, forever	שִׁקּוּץ	detested thing (1 · 28) 1055
בָּרָא	to shape, fashion, create (20 · 38 · 48) 135	תַּעֲלוּלִים 4	wantonness, wanton dealing, caprice (2 · 2) 760
מָשׂוֹשׂ	exultation (10 · 17) 965	מְגוֹרָה	fear, terror (1 · 3) 159
גִּיל 19	to rejoice (11 · 45 · 45) 162	בַּאֲשֶׁר	in [that] which (4 · 19) 84
שָׂשׂ	to exult, rejoice, display joy (9 · 27 · 27) 965 שוש	חָרֵד 5	trembling (2 · 6) 353
בְּכִי	weeping (8 · 32) 113	שֹׂנֵא	hating; enemy (1 · 41[?]) 971 שנא
זְעָקָה	cry of distress (3 · 19) 277	נדה	to thrust away, exclude (1 · 2 · 2) 622
עוּל 20	suckling child; עוּל־יָמִים a short-lived	שָׁאוֹן 6	roar, din (8 · 18) 981

273

גְּמוּל	recompense, dealing (5 · 19) 168
בְּטֶרֶם	7 before (8 · 39) 382
חוּל	to twist, writhe [in labor] (9 · 30 · 47) 296
חֵבֶל	pains of travail, pain (3 · 7) 286
הִמְלִיט	[idiom] to give birth 572 מלט
הוּחַל	8 to be born (1 · 1 · 47) 296
חוּל	to twist, writhe [in labor] (9 · 30 · 47) 296
עָצַר	9 to restrain (1 · 36 · 46) 783
גִּיל	10 to rejoice (11 · 45 · 45) 162
אֹהֵב	one who loves; friend (2 · 36) 12
שׂוּשׂ	to exult, rejoice, display joy (9 · 27 · 27) 965 שׂושׂ
מָשׂושׂ	exultation (10 · 17) 965
הִתְאַבֵּל	to mourn (1 · 19 · 38) 5
יָנַק	11 to suck (4 · 8 · 18) 413
שַׁד	female breast (2 · 3) 994
תַּנְחוּם	consolation (1 · 5) 637
מָצַץ	to drain out (1 · 1 · 1) 595
הִתְעַנֵּג	to take exquisite delight in (4 · 9 · 10) 772
זִיז	abundance, fullness; if cogn. to Ar. = breast, teat (1 · 1) 265 II.
שָׁטַף	12 to overflow (9 · 28 · 31) 1009
יָנַק	to suck (4 · 8 · 18) 413
צַד	side, possibly hip (2 · 32) 841
בֶּרֶךְ	knee (3 · 25) 139
שִׁעֲשַׁע	to be fondled (1 · 1 · 6) 1044 II. שעע
שָׂשׂ	13 to exult, rejoice, display joy (9 · 27 · 27) 965 שׂושׂ

דֶּשֶׁא	grass (3 · 14) 206
פָּרַח	to bud, sprout (5 · 28 · 34) 827
זָעַם	to be indignant (1 · 11 · 12) 276
סוּפָה	15 storm wind (5 · 15) 693
מֶרְכָּבָה	chariot (3 · 44) 939
גְּעָרָה	rebuke (6 · 15) 172
לַהַב	flame (4 · 12) 529
רבב	16 to be [become] many (4 · 23 · 24) 912
גַּנָּה	17 garden (5 · 16) 171
חֲזִיר	swine, boar (3 · 7) 306
שֶׁקֶץ	detestible thing (1 · 11) 1054
עַכְבָּר	mouse (1 · 6) 747
סוּף	to come to an end (1 · 4 · 8) 692
פָּלִיט	19 escaped one, fugitive (1 · 5) 812
מָשַׁךְ	to draw, draw out, draw off (2 · 30 · 36) 604
אִי	coastland, island (17 · 36) 15
שֵׁמַע	report (3 · 17) 1034
צָב	20 pl. = litters (1 · 2) 839
פֶּרֶד	mule (1 · 14) 825
כִּרְכָּרָה	dromedary, camel (1 · 1) 503
מִדֵּי	23 as often as (3 · 15) 191 דִּי 2.c.
פֶּגֶר	24 corpse, carcass (4 · 22) 803
פָּשַׁע	to transgress, rebel (9 · 40 · 41) 833
תּוֹלֵעָה	worm, grub (3 · 41) 1069
כבה	to be quenched, extinguished (3 · 14 · 24) 459
דֵּרָאוֹן	aversion, abhorrence, object of abhorrence (1 · 2) 201

JEREMIAH

Chapter 1

בְּטֶרֶם 5 before (6 · 39) 382

יָצַר to form, fashion (4 · 41 · 44[?]) 427

רֶחֶם womb (4 · 33) 933

אֲהָהּ 6 Alas! (4 · 15) 13

נָתַשׁ 10 to pull up, pluck up (11 · 16 · 21) 684

נָתַץ to pull down, break down (6 · 31 · 42) 683

הָרַס to tear down, throw down (5 · 30 · 43) 248

מַקֵּל 11 rod, stick, staff (2 · 18) 596

שָׁקֵד almond tree (1 · 4) 1052

שָׁקַד 12 to keep watch (5 · 11 · 17) 1052

סִיר 13 pot (3 · 29) 696 I

נפח to blow; ptc. = blown (i.e., well heated, boiling) (2 · 9 · 12) 655

אזר 17 to gird, gird on (1 · 6 · 16) 25

מָתְנַיִם loins (6 · 47) 608

מִבְצָר 18 fortification (7 · 37) 131

Chapter 2

נְעוּרִים 2 youth (7 · 46) 655

כְּלוּלָה betrothal, betrothal time (1 · 1) 483

תְּבוּאָה 3 product, yield (2 · 43) 100

אָשׁם to be held guilty, be guilty (2 · 33 · 35) 79

עָוֶל 5 injustice, unrighteousness (1 · 21) 732

הבל to become vain, act emptily (1 · 4 · 5) 211

אַיֵּה 6 where? (6 · 44) 32

שׁוּחָה pit (3 · 5) 1001

צִיָּה drought (3 · 16) 851

צַלְמָוֶת deep shadow, darkness (2 · 18) 853

כַּרְמֶל 7 garden land (3 · 14) 502 I

טוּב good things (3 · 32) 375

אַיֵּה 8 where? (6 · 44) 32

פָּשַׁע to transgress (4 · 40 · 41) 833

הוֹעִיל to profit, avail, benefit (7 · 23 · 23) 418

אִי 10 coast, border, region (4 · 36) 15

הֵמִיר 11 to exchange, change (2 · 13 · 14) 558

בְּלוֹא for not (4 · 30) 518 לֹא 4. a.(c)

הוֹעִיל to profit, avail, benefit (7 · 23 · 23) 418

שׂער 12 to bristle [with horror] (1 · 3 · 3) 972

חרב to be waste, desolate (2 · 17 · 37) 351

מָקוֹר 13 spring, fountain, source (4 · 18) 881

חָצֵב to hew out, dig (1 · 14 · 17) 345

בֹּאר cistern, pit, well (2 · 5) 92

הכיל to contain, hold in (3 · 12 · 38) 465

יָלִיד 14 born; יליד בית = born in [one's] house (1 · 13) 409

בַּז spoil, booty, plunder (5 · 27) 103

שָׁאַג 15 to roar (5 · 20 · 20) 980

כְּפִיר young lion (3 · 31) 498

נָתַן [idiom] with קול = to lift up the voice 678 Qal 1.x.

שַׁמָּה waste (24 · 39) 1031

נצת to be kindled, burned (2 · 6 · 27) 428

מִבְּלִי so that there is no (4 · 25) 115 בְּלִי

יִרְעוּךְ 16 from רעה, to graze 944

קָדְקֹד hairy crown, scalp (2 · 11) 869

שִׁיחוֹן 18 Nile (1 · 4) 1009

יסר 19 to chastise, chasten, correct (5 · 27 · 38) 415

מְשֻׁבָה turning back, apostacy (9 · 12) 1000 משובה

מַר bitter (2 · 39) 600

פַּחְדָּה awe, dread (1 · 1) 808

עֹל 20 yoke (10 · 40) 760

נתק to tear apart, snap (3 · 11 · 27) 683

מוֹסֵר band or bond of restraint (4 · 12) 64

גָּבֹהַּ high, lofty, tall (4 · 41) 147

275

רַעֲנָן luxuriant, fresh (6 · 19) 947

צעה to stoop, bend (2 · 4 · 5) 858

שׂרֵק 21 vine [choice species] (1 · 2) 977

סוּר degenerate (2 · 3) 693 סוּר *Qal* 1.

נָכְרִי foreign, alien (1 · 45) 648

נֶתֶר 22 natron [carbonate of soda] (1 · 2) 684

בֹּרִית lye, alkali, soap (1 · 2) 141

נִכְתָּם to be stained; ptc. = stained
(1 · 1 · 1) 508 I. כתם

גַּיְא 23 valley (4 · 48) 161

בִּכְרָה young camel, dromedary (1 · 1) 114

קַל swift, fleet (2 · 13) 886

שׂרֵךְ to twist, ptc. = entangling
(1 · 1 · 1) 976

פֶּרֶא 24 wild ass (2 · 10) 825

לֻמָּד taught, accustomed (2 · 6) 541

אַוָּה desire (1 · 7) 16

שָׁאַף to pant after (2 · 14 · 14) 983

תַּאֲנָה occasion or time of copulation
(1 · 1) 58

יעף to be weary, faint (3 · 8 · 9) 419

מָנַע 25 to withhold, hold back (5 · 25 · 29)
586

יָחֵף barefoot (1 · 5) 405

גָּרוֹן throat, neck (1 · 8) 173

צִמְאָה parched condition (1 · 1) 854

נוֹאָשׁ to despair (2 · 5 · 6) 384

בֹּשֶׁת 26 shame (6 · 30) 102

גַּנָּב thief (3 · 17) 170

עֹרֶף 27 back of neck (7 · 33) 791

אַיֵּה 28 where? (6 · 44) 32

פָּשַׁע 29 to transgress (4 · 40 · 41) 833

מוּסָר 30 chastisement, discipline (8 · 50) 416

אַרְיֵה lion (6 · 45) 71

מַאְפֵּלְיָה 31 deep darkness (1 · 1) 66

רוד to wander restlessly, roam (1 · 2 · 4)
923

בְּתוּלָה 32 virgin (8 · 50) 143

עֲדִי ornaments (2 · 13) 725

כַּלָּה bride; daughter-in-law (5 · 34) 483

קִשֻּׁרִים bands, sashes (1 · 2) 905

נָקִי 34 innocent, free from guilt (6 · 43) 667

מַחְתֶּרֶת burglary, a breaking in (1 · 2) 369

נָקָה 35 to be clean, free from guilt, innocent (6 · 24 · 43) 667

אָזַל 36 to go about, go (1 · 5 · 5) 23

שָׁנָה to change, alter (2 · 9 · 26) 1040

מִבְטָח 37 object of confidence, confidence
(3 · 15) 105

Chapter 3

חנף 1 to be polluted (4 · 7 · 11) 337

שְׁפִי 2 bare place, height (6 · 10) 1046

אֵיפֹה where? (2 · 10) 33

שׁגל to be ravished (1 · 1 · 4) 993

החניף to pollute (1 · 4 · 11) 337

זְנוּת fornication (3 · 9) 276

נִמְנַע 3 to be withheld (1 · 4 · 29) 586

רְבִיבִים copious showers; i.e., plentiful
showers (2 · 6) 914

מַלְקוֹשׁ spring rain, latter rain (2 · 8) 545

מֵצַח brow, forehead (1 · 13) 594

זוֹנָה harlot (2 · 33[?]) 275 זָנָה

מֵאֵן to refuse (12 · 46) 549

נכלם to be humiliated, ashamed
(4 · 26 · 38) 483

מֵעַתָּה 4 from now, henceforth (1 · 14) 773
עַתָּה 2.e.

אַלּוּף friend, intimate; tame (3 · 9) 48

נְעוּרִים youth (7 · 46) 655

נטר 5 to keep, maintain; i.e., keep anger
(2 · 5 · 5) 643

נֶצַח everlastingness, ever; לָנֶצַח = forever (3 · 42) 664

יָכֹל to prevail, have one's way (>50)
407 2.a.

מְשֻׁבָה 6 turning back, apostasy (9 · 12) 1000
מְשׁוּבָה

גָּבֹהַּ high, lofty, tall (4 · 41) 147

276

רַעֲנָן	luxuriant, fresh (6 · 19) 947	שְׁרִירוּת	stubbornness (8 · 10) 1057
בָּגוֹדָה	7 treacherous (2 · 2) 93 בָּגוֹד	חֶמְדָּה	19 desire (3 · 16) 326
אוֹדֹת	8 cause; עַל־כָּל־אֹ׳ = because of all (1 · 11) 15	צְבִי	decoration, beauty (pl. cstr. = צְבָאוֹת) (1 · 18) 840
נאף	to commit adultery (5 · 17 · 31) 610	אָכֵן	20 surely, truly (5 · 18) 38
מְשֻׁבָה	turning back, apostacy (9 · 12) 1000 מְשׁוּבָה	בגד	to act or deal treacherously (8 · 49 · 49) 93
כְּרִיתוּת	divorcement (1 · 4) 504	שְׁפִי	21 bare place, height (6 · 10) 1046
בתד	to act or deal treacherously (8 · 49 · 49) 93	בְּכִי	weeping (8 · 30) 113
קל	9 lightness, frivolity (1 · 1) 887	תַּחֲנוּן	supplication for favor (2 · 18) 337
זְנוּת	fornication (3 · 9) 276	הֶעֱוָה	to pervert (2 · 9 · 17[?]) 730
חנף	to be profane, godless; to be polluted (4 · 7 · 11) 337	שׁוֹבָב	22 recusant, apostate (2 · 3) 1000
		מְשׁוּבָה	turning back, apostacy (9 · 12) 1000
נאף	to commit adultery (5 · 17 · 31) 610	אָתָה	to come (1 · 19 · 21) 87
בָּגוֹד	10 treacherous (2 · 2) 93	אָכֵן	23 surely, truly (5 · 18) 38
צדק	11 to make to appear righteous (1 · 5 · 41) 842	תְּשׁוּעָה	deliverance (1 · 34) 448
מְשֻׁבָה	turning back, apostacy (9 · 12) 1000 מְשׁוּבָה	בֹּשֶׁת	24 shameful thing, shame (6 · 30) 102
		יְגִיעַ	product, toil (2 · 16) 388
בגד	to act or deal treacherously (8 · 49 · 49) 93	נְעוּרִים	youth (7 · 46) 655
מְשֻׁבָה	12 turning back, apostacy (9 · 12) 1000 מְשׁוּבָה	בֹּשֶׁת	25 shame (6 · 30) 102
אַפִּיל פָּנַי	[idiom] to look displeased נָפַל 656 Hiph. 5	כְּלִמָּה	reproach, ignominy, insult (3 · 30) 484
		נְעוּרִים	youth (7 · 46) 655
חָסִיד	kind, pious (1 · 32) 339		
נטר	to keep, maintain; i.e., keep anger (2 · 5 · 5) 643		Chapter 4
פָּשַׁע	13 to transgress (4 · 40 · 41) 833	שִׁקּוּץ	1 detested thing (5 · 28) 1055
פּוּר	to scatter (1 · 7 · 10) 808	נָד	to move to and fro, wander (8 · 19 · 26) 626 נוד
רַעֲנָן	luxuriant, fresh (6 · 19) 947		
שׁוֹבָב	14 recusant, apostate (2 · 3) 1000	ניר	3 to break up, freshly till (1 · 1 · 2) 644 I.
בָּעַל	to be lord [over], husband [of] (2 · 10 · 12[?]) 127	ניר	untilled, tillable (1 · 3) 644
		קוֹץ	thornbush (2 · 11) 881
דֵּעָה	15 knowledge (1 · 6) 395	נִמֹּל	4 to circumcise yourself (1 · 17 · 29) 557
פרה	16 to be fruitful (2 · 22 · 29) 826	עָרְלָה	foreskin (2 · 16) 790
פקד	to seek in vain, miss (>50) 823 Qal A.1.d.	כבה	to quench, extinguish (2 · 10 · 24) 459
		רַע	evil, badness (11 · 19) 947
נקוה	17 to be collected (1 · 2 · 2) 876	מַעֲלָל	practice, deed (17 · 41) 760

277

מִבְצָר 5 fortification (7 · 37) 131

נֵס 6 standard, signal (5 · 21) 651

הֵעִיז to bring into safety (2 · 4 · 5) 731

שֶׁבֶר shattering (15 · 45) 991

אַרְיֵה 7 lion (6 · 45) 71

סְבָךְ thicket (1 · 2) 687

שַׁמָּה waste (24 · 39) 1031

נצה to fall in ruins (1 · 1 · 5) 663 III.

מֵאֵין without (2 · 48[?]) 34 אֵין 6.d.

חגר 8 to gird on, bind on (3 · 44 · 44) 291

שַׂק sackcloth (4 · 48) 974

ספד to wail, lament (7 · 28 · 30) 704

הֵילִל to give a howl (8 · 30 · 30) 410

חָרוֹן [burning of] anger; ח׳ אף = burning anger (9 · 41) 354

תמה 9 to be astounded (1 · 8 · 9) 1069

אֲהָהּ 10 Alas! (4 · 15) 13

אָכֵן surely, truly (5 · 18) 38

הִשִּׁיא to beguile (5 · 15 · 16) 674

צַח 11 glowing, clear (1 · 4) 850

שְׁפִי bare place, height (6 · 10) 1046

זרה to fan, winnow (2 · 9 · 38) 279

הבריר to purify, cleanse (1 · 1 · 15) 140

סוּפָה 13 storm wind (1 · 15) 693

מֶרְכָּבָה war chariot, chariot (1 · 44) 939

נֶשֶׁר vulture, eagle (4 · 26) 676

אוֹי Woe! Alas! (8 · 25) 17

מָתַי 14 when? עד-מ׳ = how long? (7 · 42) 607

נצר to keep closed, blockade (>50) 665 Qal 5.

מֶרְחָק 16 distant place, far country (5 · 18) 935

שָׂדַי 17 land, field (2 · 13) 961

מָרָה to be disobedient, rebellious (2 · 21 · 43) 598

מַעֲלָל 18 practice, deed (17 · 41) 760

מַר bitter (2 · 39) 600

מֵעָה 19 seat of emotions, internal organs (3 · 32) 589

הוֹחִיל] Q to wait, tarry (1 · 15 · 42) 403 יחל Hiph.]

חול to be in anguish, twist, writhe (5 · 30 · 47) 296

הָמָה to murmur, growl (9 · 33 · 33) 242

הֶחֱרִישׁ to be silent (2 · 38 · 46) 361

תְּרוּעָה alarm, war cry (3 · 36) 929

שֶׁבֶר 20 shattering (15 · 45) 991

פִּתְאוֹם suddenly (5 · 25) 837

רֶגַע moment (3 · 22) 921

מָתַי 21 when? עד-מ׳ = how long? (7 · 42) 607

נֵס standard, signal (5 · 21) 651

אֱוִיל 22 fool [always morally bad] (1 · 26) 17

סָכָל fool (2 · 7) 698

נָבוֹן discreet, discerning, intelligent (1 · 21) 106 בִּין Niph. ptc.

תֹהוּ 23 formlessness, waste (1 · 20) 1062

בֹּהוּ emptiness (1 · 3) 96

רעש 24 to quake, shake (5 · 21 · 29) 950

נדד 25 to retreat, flee (3 · 21 · 24) 622

כַּרְמֶל 26 garden land (3 · 14) 502

נתץ to be pulled down, broken down (1 · 3 · 42) 683

חָיוֹן [burning of] anger; ח׳אף burning anger (9 · 41) 354

כָּלָה 27 complete destruction (7 · 22) 478

אָבַל 28 to mourn (5 · 18 · 38) 5

קָדַר to be dark (3 · 13 · 17) 871

מִמַּעַל above, on the top of (4 · 29) 751

זָמַם to purpose, devise (2 · 13 · 13) 273

רָמָה 29 to shoot (1 · 4 · 4) 941

עָב thicket (1 · 1[?]) 728

כֵּף rock (1 · 2) 495

אַתְּי 30 you [fem.] (1 · 7) 61

שָׁנִי scarlet (1 · 42) 1040

עָדָה to deck oneself, ornament (2 · 8 · 8) 725

עֲדִי ornaments (2 · 13) 725

קָרַע to make wide, large (>50) 902 Qal 3.b.

פּוּךְ	antimony, stibium [a black mineral powder] (1 · 4) 806
הִתְיַפָּה	to beautify oneself (1 · 1 · 8) 421
עגב	to lust; ptc. = ''paramour'' (1 · 7 · 7) 721
חול 31	to twist, writhe [in child birth] (5 · 30 · 47) 296
הַבְּכִיר	ptc. = one bearing her first child (1 · 1 · 4) 114
הִתְיַפַּח	to gasp for breath (1 · 1 · 1) 422
אוֹי	Woe! Alas! (8 · 25) 17
עָיֵף	to be faint (1 · 5 · 5) 746

Chapter 5

שׁוֹטֵט 1	to go eagerly and quickly to and fro (1 · 5 · 13) 1001
רְחוֹב	broad open place (5 · 43) 932
סלח	to forgive, pardon (1 · 6 · 46) 699
הל 3	to be in severe pain, anguish; to twist, writhe (5 · 30 · 47) 296 חול
מֵאֵן	to refuse (12 · 46) 549
מוּסָר	chastisement, discipline (8 · 50) 416
דַּל 4	reduced, poor, low (2 · 48) 195
נואל	to show wicked folly, act foolishly (2 · 4 · 4) 383
עֹל 5	yoke (10 · 40) 760
נתק	to tear apart, snap (3 · 11 · 27) 683
מוֹסֵר	band or bond of restraint (4 · 12) 64
אַרְיֵה 6	lion (6 · 45) 71
זְאֵב	wolf (1 · 8) 255
נָמֵר	leopard (2 · 6) 649
שָׁקַד	to keep watch, to be wakeful (5 · 11 · 17) 1052
נטרף	to be torn (1 · 2 · 24) 382
רבב	to be, become, many (3 · 23 · 24) 912
עָצַם	to be numerous (4 · 16 · 18) 782
מְשֻׁבָה	turning back, apostasy (9 · 12) 1000 מְשׁוּבָה

אֵי 7	where?; אֵי־לָזֹאת = on what ground? how? (3 · 39) 32 אֵי 2.c.
סלח	to forgive, pardon (6 · 33 · 46) 699
בְּלוֹא	by no, by not (4 · 30) 518
נאף	to commit adultery (5 · 17 · 31) 610
זוֹנָה	ptc. = harlot; vb. to commit fornication (2 · 33) 275
הִתְגֹּדֵד	to gather in troops or bands, to go in troops or throngs (4 · 7 · 8) 151
מְיֻזָּנִים 8	[dub.] ruttish (1 · 1) 402
הִשְׁכָּה	ptc. = lustful (1 · 1 · 1) 1013
צהל	to neigh (3 · 7 · 8) 843
הִתְנַקֵּם 9	to avenge oneself (3 · 5 · 35) 667
שׁוּרָה 10	row [of vines] (1 · 2) 1004
כָּלָה	complete destruction, annihilation (7 · 22) 478
נְטִישָׁה	twig, tendril (2 · 3) 644
בגד 11	to act or deal treacherously (8 · 49 · 49) 93
כָּחֵשׁ 12	to act deceptively against, deceive (1 · 19 · 22) 471
דִּבֶּר 13	speaking (2 · 2) 184
מֶרְחָק 15	distant place, distance (5 · 18) 935
אֵיתָן	permanent, enduring, everflowing (3 · 14) 450
אַשְׁפָּה 16	quiver for arrows (1 · 6) 80
קָצִיר 17	harvest (5 · 49) 894
תְּאֵנָה	fig, fig tree (12 · 39) 1061
רשׁשׁ	to beat down, shatter (1 · 1 · 2) 958
מִבְצָר	fortification (7 · 37) 131
כָּלָה 18	complete destruction, annihilation (7 · 22) 478
נֵכָר 19	foreign (2 · 36) 648
סָכָל 21	fool (2 · 7) 698
חיל 22	to be in severe pain or anguish; to twist, writhe (5 · 30 · 47) 296 חול
חוֹל	sand (3 · 22) 297
הִתְגָּעֵשׁ	to shake back and forth, reel to and fro (2 · 5 · 10) 172

הָמָה to roar, murmur, growl (9 · 33 · 33) 242

גַּל wave of water, roller, heap (4 · 16) 164

סָרַר 23 to be stubborn, rebellious (3 · 18 · 18) 710

מָרָה to be disobedient, rebellious (2 · 21 · 43) 598

גֶּשֶׁם 24 shower, rain (2 · 35) 177

יוֹרֶה early rain (1 · 2) 435

מַלְקוֹשׁ latter rain, spring rain (2 · 8) 545

שָׁבוּעַ week (1 · 20) 988

קָצִיר harvest (5 · 49) 894

הִטּוּ *Hiph.* perf. נטה; here = to turn (>50) 639 *Hiph.* 3.h.

מָנַע 25 to withhold, hold back (5 · 25 · 29) 586

שׁוּר 26 to lie in wait, watch (1 · 16 · 16) 1003

שָׁכַךְ to bend, crouch (1 · 4 · 5) 1013

יָקוּשׁ fowler, bait layer (1 · 4) 430

מַשְׁחִית destroyer, ravager; fig. for snare, trap (4 · 19) 1008

כְּלוּב 27 basket, cage (1 · 3) 477

מִרְמָה deceit, treachery (4 · 39) 941

הֶעָשִׁיר to cause to be [become] rich (1 · 14 · 17) 799

שָׁמֵן 28 to grow fat (1 · 3 · 5) 1031

עָשְׁתוּ [dub.] to be smooth, shiny (1 · 1 · 1) 799

דִּין cause, plea, judgment (4 · 19) 192

דָּן to plead the cause, administer judgment (4 · 23 · 24) 192 דין

יָתוֹם orphan (4 · 42) 450

הִתְנַקֵּם 29 to avenge oneself (3 · 5 · 35) 667

שַׁמָּה 30 horror, an appalling thing (24 · 39) 1031

שַׁעֲרוּר horrible thing (2 · 2) 1045

רָדָה 31 to rule, have dominion (1 · 3 · 3[?]) 921

Chapter 6

הָעִיז 1 to bring into safety (2 · 4 · 5) 731

מַשְׂאֵת signal (2 · 16) 673 1.b.

נִשְׁקַף to lean over, look down (1 · 10 · 22) 1054

שֶׁבֶר shattering (15 · 45) 991

נָוֶה 2 comely, beautiful (1 · 2[?]) 610 נָאוֶה

עֻנַּג to be daintily bred (1 · 1 · 10) 772

דָּמָה to cause to cease, cut off; cease (2 · 4 · 16) 198

עֵדֶר 3 flock (6 · 39) 727

תָּקַע to pitch (>50) 1075 *Qal* 1.

צָהֳרַיִם 4 midday, noon (3 · 23) 843

אוֹי Woe! Alas! (8 · 25) 17

אַרְמוֹן 5 citadel, castle (5 · 33) 74

עֵצָה 6 [coll.] trees (1 · 1) 782

סֹלְלָה mound (3 · 11) 700

עֹשֶׁק oppression, extortion (2 · 15) 799

הָקַר 7 to make or keep cool (2 · 2 · 3) 903

בַּיִר בּוֹר well (>50) 92

שֹׁד violence, havoc (3 · 25) 994

חֳלִי wound, sickness, disease (2 · 24) 318

מַכָּה wound, blow (10 · 48) 646

נוֹסַר 8 to let oneself be corrected, chastened (2 · 5 · 38) 415

יָקַע to be torn away, alienated (1 · 4 · 8) 429

עוֹלֵל 9 to glean (1 · 8 · 17) 760

בֹּצֵר ptc. = grape-gatherer (2 · 7 · 7) 130

סַלְסִלָּה shoot, branch (1 · 1) 700

הֵעִיד 10 to protest, warn (8 · 39 · 44) 729

עָרֵל uncircumcised (3 · 35) 790

הִקְשִׁיב to give attention (8 · 45 · 46) 904

נִלְאָה 11 to be weary, make oneself weary (4 · 10 · 19) 521

הָכִיל to contain, hold in (3 · 12 · 38) 465

עוֹלָל child (2 · 9) 760

סוֹד circle, council (4 · 21) 691

בָּחוּר young man (11 · 45) 104

קָטָן 13 insignificant (3 · 47) 881

בָּצַע to cut off, gain by violence; ptc. = robber (2 · 10 · 16) 130

בֶּצַע unjust gain, gain made by violence (4 · 23) 130

שֶׁבֶר 14 fracture, breaking (15 · 45) 991

נְקַלָּה *Niph.* קלל to be trifling (>50) 886

הכלים 15 to exhibit shame, put to shame (1 · 10 · 38) 483

נְתִיבָה 16 path (2 · 21) 677

אֵי where?; אי זה = where, then? (3 · 39) 32 אי 1.b.

מַרְגּוֹעַ rest (1 · 1) 921

צֹפֶה 17 watchman (1 · 19[?]) 859

הִקְשִׁיב to give attention (8 · 45 · 46) 904

הִקְשִׁיב 19 to give attention (8 · 45 · 46) 904

לְבוֹנָה 20 frankincense (3 · 21) 526

טוב sweet-scented, fragrant (>50) 373 II. טוב 1.c.

מֶרְחָק distance, distant place (5 · 18) 935

ערב to be pleasing, sweet (2 · 8 · 8) 787

מִכְשׁוֹל 21 stumbling block, means or occasion of stumbling (1 · 14) 506

שָׁכֵן neighbor (5 · 20) 1015

יַרְכָה 22 remote part, side (4 · 28) 438

כִּידוֹן 23 dart, javelin (2 · 9) 475

אַכְזָרִי cruel (3 · 8) 470

רחם to have compassion (9 · 41 · 46) 933

המה to roar, growl, murmur (9 · 33 · 33) 242

שֵׁמַע 24 report (1 · 4) 1035

רָפָה to sink, drop (3 · 14 · 45) 951

חִיל anguish, writhing (3 · 6) 297

מָגוֹר 25 terror, fear (6 · 8) 159

חגר 26 to gird on, bind on (3 · 44 · 44) 291

שַׂק sackcloth (4 · 48) 974

התפלש to roll in (2 · 4 · 4) 814

אֵפֶר ashes (1 · 22) 68

אֵבֶל mourning (3 · 24) 5

יָחִיד only one (e.g., only son) (1 · 12) 402

מִסְפֵּד wailing (2 · 16) 704

תַּמְרוּרִים bitterness (2 · 3) 601

פִּתְאוֹם suddenly (5 · 25) 837

בָּחוֹן 27 assayer, one who tries metals (1 · 1) 103

מִבְצָר fortification [fortified city] (7 · 37) 131

בחן to prove, test, try (6 · 24 · 28) 103

סָרַר 28 to be stubborn, rebellious (2 · 18 · 18) 710

רָכִיל slander; talebearer, informer (2 · 6) 940

נָחַר 29 to be scorched (1 · 5 · 9) 359 חרר

מַפֻּחַ bellows (1 · 1) 656

אֵשָׁה fire (1 · 1) 77

עֹפֶרֶת lead (1 · 9) 780

צָרַף to smelt, refine (2 · 18 · 26[?]) 864

נִתַּק to be separated (2 · 10 · 27) 683

Chapter 7

מַעֲלָל 3 practice, deed (17 · 41) 760

מַעֲלָל 5 practice, deed (17 · 41) 760

יָתוֹם 6 orphan (4 · 42) 450

עָשַׁק to oppress, wrong (3 · 36 · 37) 798

נָקִי innocent, free from guilt (6 · 43) 667

לְמַן 7 from (4 · 14) 577 מן 9.b.(2)

הוֹעִיל 8 to profit, benefit (7 · 23 · 23) 418

גנב 9 to take by stealth, steal (1 · 30 · 39) 170

רָצַח to murder, slay (1 · 38 · 43) 953

נאף to commit adultery (5 · 17 · 31) 610

מְעָרָה 11 cave (1 · 40) 792

פָּרִיץ violent one (1 · 6) 829

רִנָּה 16 ringing cry (3 · 33) 943

פָּגַע to entreat (2 · 40 · 46) 803

לקט 18 to gather, gather up (1 · 21 · 37) 544

לוש to knead (1 · 5 · 5) 534

בָּצֵק dough (1 · 5) 130

כַּוָּן cake, sacrificial cake (2 · 2) 467

מְלֶכֶת queen (5 · 5) 573

הַסִּיךְ to pour out libations (8 · 14 · 25) 650 נסך

בֹּשֶׁת 19 shame (6 · 30) 102

נִתַּךְ 20 to be poured out (2 · 8 · 21) 677

כבה to be quenched, extinguished (2 · 14 · 24) 459

הַטּוּ *Hiph.* נטה (>50) 639

מוֹעֵצָה 24 counsel, plan, principle (1 · 7) 420

שְׁרִירוּת stubbornness (8 · 10) 1057

אָחוֹר with לְ = backwards (4 · 41) 30

לְמִן 25 from (4 · 14) 577 מִן 9.b.

הַקְשָׁה 26 to make stiff, stubborn (3 · 21 · 28) 904

עֹרֶף back of neck (7 · 33) 791

מוּסָר 28 chastisement, discipline (8 · 50) 416

גזז 29 to shear (1 · 14 · 15) 159

גֵּזֶר hair; consecration (1 · 25) 634

שְׁפִי bare place, height (6 · 10) 1046

קִינָה ·elegy, dirge (3 · 17) 884

נָטַשׁ to abandon, forsake (5 · 33 · 40) 643

עֶבְרָה overflowing rage, fury (2 · 34) 720

שִׁקּוּץ 30 detested thing (5 · 28) 1055

גַּיְא 32 valley (4 · 48) 161

הֲרֵגָה slaughter (3 · 5) 247

מֵאֵין from lack of (20 · 48[?]) 34 אִין 6.d.

נְבֵלָה carcass, corpse (8 · 48) 615

מַאֲכָל food (4 · 30) 38

הֶחֱרִיד to terrify, drive in terror (3 · 16 · 39) 353

שָׂשׂוֹן 34 joy, exultation (7 · 22) 965

חָתָן bridegroom (4 · 20) 368

כַּלָּה bride; daughter-in-law (5 · 34) 483

חָרְבָּה waste, desolation (10 · 42) 352

Chapter 8

שטח 2 to spread abroad (1 · 4 · 5) 1008

יָרֵחַ moon (2 · 27) 437

דֹּמֶן dung (4 · 6) 199

הַדִּיחַ 3 to thrust out, banish (13 · 27 · 43) 623

מְשֻׁבָה 5 turning back, apostacy (9 · 12) 1000 מְשׁוּבָה

נצח ptc. = enduring (1 · 1 · 8) 663

תַּרְמִית deceitfulness (3 · 5) 941

מֵאֵן to refuse (12 · 46) 549

הִקְשִׁיב 6 to give attention (8 · 45 · 46) 904

כֵּן right, honest, true (4 · 24) 467

מְרוּצָה course, running (2 · 4) 930

שָׁטַף to overflow [fig. of dashing, rushing] (3 · 28 · 31) 1009

חֲסִידָה 7 stork (1 · 6) 339

תּוֹר turtle dove (1 · 14) 1076

סוּס swallow or swift (1 · 1) 692 סִיס

עָגוּר [dub.] crane (1 · 2) 723

אֵיכָה 8 in what manner? (2 · 18) 32

אָכֵן surely, truly (5 · 18) 38

עֵט stylus (2 · 4) 741

יוֹרֵשׁ 10 heir, inheritor (3 · 5) 439

בָּצַע to gain by violence, ptc. = robber (2 · 10 · 16) 130

בֶּצַע gain made by violence, unjust gain (4 · 23) 130

שֶׁבֶר 11 breaking (15 · 45) 991

נכלם 12 to be put to shame, dishonored, humiliated (4 · 26 · 38) 483

פְּקֻדָּה visitation (9 · 32) 824

הֵסִיף 13 to make an end of (2 · 6 · 10) 692

עֵנָב grape[s] (1 · 19) 772

תְּאֵנָה fig, fig tree (12 · 39) 1061

עלה leaf, leafage (2 · 17) 750

נָבֵל to droop, wither and fall, fade (1 · 19 · 23) 615

מִבְצָר 14 fortification (7 · 37) 131

דמם to perish; to be still, silent (3 · 23 · 30) 198

הדמים	to silence = cause to perish (1 · 1 · 30) 198
רֹאשׁ	bitter, poisonous herb (3 · 12) 912
קוה	15 to wait, look eagerly for (5 · 39 · 45) 875
מַרְפֵּה	healing, cure (4 · 13) 951 מַרְפֵּא
בְּעָתָה	terror, dismay (2 · 2) 130
נַחְרָה	16 snorting (1 · 1) 637
מִצְהָלָה	neighing (2 · 2) 843
אַבִּיר	mighty, valiant (4 · 17) 7
רעשׁ	to quake, shake (5 · 21 · 29) 950
מְלוֹא	fullness, entire contents (2 · 38) 571
נָחָשׁ	17 serpent (2 · 31) 638 I.
צֶפַע	[dub.] venomous viper (1 · 5[?]) 861
לַחַשׁ	serpent-charming, whispering (1 · 5) 538
נשׁך	to bite fatally (1 · 2 · 12) 675
מַבְלִיגִית	18 smiling, cheerfulness, source of brightening (1 · 1) 114
יָגוֹן	grief, sorrow (4 · 14) 387
דַּוָּי	faint [adj.] (1 · 3) 188
שַׁוְעָה	19 cry for help (1 · 11) 1003
מֶרְחָק	distance, distant place (5 · 18) 935
פָּסִיל	idol, image (4 · 23) 820
נֵכָר	foreign (2 · 36) 648
קָצִיר	20 harvest (5 · 49) 894
קַיִץ	summer (4 · 20) 884
שֶׁבֶר	21 breaking (15 · 45) 991
קָדַר	to be dark; fig. of mourning (3 · 13 · 17) 871
שַׁמָּה	horror, an appalling thing (24 · 39) 1031
צֱרִי	22 a kind of balsam [for medication] (3 · 6) 863
רֹפֵא	physician (1 · 5[?]) 950
אֲרוּכָה	healing, restoration (3 · 6) 74
מִי יִתֵּן	23 here rhetorical = O that I had (>50) 678 נתן Qal 1.e.
מָקוֹר	spring, fountain, source (4 · 18) 881
דִּמְעָה	tears (5 · 23) 199

Chapter 9

מָלוֹן	1 lodging place, inn (1 · 8) 533
אֹרֵחַ	wayfarer, wanderer (2 · 4[?]) 72 אָרַה
נאף	to commit adultery (3 · 14 · 31) 610
עֲצֶרֶת	company, assemblage (1 · 11) 783
בגד	to act or deal treacherously (8 · 49 · 49) 93
הדריך	2 here = bending [the bow] (>50) 201 Hiph. 2.
גָּבַר	to prevail, be strong (1 · 17 · 25) 149
עָקַב	3 to overreach (1 · 3 · 3[?]) 784
רָכִיל	slander; tale bearer, informer (2 · 6) 940
חָתַל	to mock, trifle with (1 · 7 · 8) 1068
הֶעֱוָה	to commit iniquity (2 · 9 · 17[?]) 731
נִלְאָה	to be weary, make oneself weary (4 · 10 · 19) 521
שֶׁבֶת	5 dwelling (1 · 7[?]) 442 ישׁב
מִרְמָה	deceit, treachery (4 · 39) 941
מֵאֵן	to refuse (12 · 46) 549
צָרַף	6 to test (2 · 18 · 21) 864
בחן	to prove, test, try (6 · 24 · 28) 103
שׁחט	7 Qal pass. ptc. = hammered; i.e., sharpened (1 · 6 · 6[?]) 1006
מִרְמָה	deceit, treachery (4 · 39) 941
דִּבֵּר	speaking (2 · 2) 184
אֹרֶב	ambuscade, treachery (1 · 2) 70
התנקם	8 to avenge oneself (3 · 5 · 35) 667
בְּכִי	9 weeping (8 · 30) 113
נְהִי	wailing, lamentation (4 · 7) 624
נְאוֹת	pasture, meadow (14 · 45[?]) 627 בְּרָה
קִינָה	elegy, dirge (3 · 17) 884
נצת	to be kindled, burned (2 · 6 · 27) 428
מִבְּלִי	so that there is no (4 · 25) 115 בְּלִי
נדד	to retreat, flee (3 · 21 · 24) 622
גַּל	heap, pile (2 · 20) 164
מָעוֹן	lair, refuge, habitation (5 · 18) 732
תַּן	jackal (5 · 14) 1072

283

מִבְּלִי   so that there is no (4 · 25) 115   בְּלִי

נִצָּה 11 to be desolated (2 · 4 · 5[?]) 428   יצת
Niph.

מִבְּלִי   so that there is no (4 · 25) 115   בְּלִי

שְׁרִירוּת 13 stubbornness (8 · 10) 1057

לַעֲנָה 14 wormwood (2 · 8) 542

רֹאשׁ   bitter, poisonous herb (3 · 12) 912

קוֹנֵן 16 to chant (1 · 8 · 8) 884

חכם   skillful [here as mourners] (>50) 314

נֶהִי 17 wailing, lamentation (4 · 7) 624

דִּמְעָה   tears (5 · 23) 199

עַפְעַף   eyelid (1 · 10) 733

נזל   to flow, trickle, drop (2 · 8 · 9) 633

נֶהִי 18 wailing, lamentation (4 · 7) 624

נֶהִי 19 mourning song, lamentation (4 · 7) 624

רְעוּת   fellow [woman] (1 · 6) 946

קִינָה   elegy, dirge (3 · 17) 884

חַלּוֹן 20 window (1 · 30) 319

אַרְמוֹן   castle, palace (5 · 33) 74

עוֹלָל   child (2 · 9) 760

בָּחוּר   young man (11 · 45) 104

רְחוֹב   broad open place (5 · 43) 932

נְבֵלָה 21 carcass, corpse (8 · 48) 615

דֹּמֶן   dung (4 · 6) 199

עָמִיר   swath, row of fallen grain (1 · 4) 771

קֹצֵר   reaper (1 · 10[?]) 894

עָשִׁיר 22 rich (1 · 23) 799

עֹשֶׁר   riches (2 · 37) 799

מוּל 24 to circumcise (1 · 12 · 29) 557

עָרְלָה   foreskin (2 · 16) 790

קָצַץ 25 to cut off (3 · 4 · 14) 893

עָרֵל   uncircumcised (3 · 35) 790

Chapter 10

חָרָשׁ 3 artificer, graver (4 · 38) 360

מַעֲצָד   axe (1 · 2) 781

יפה 4 to beautify (1 · 1 · 8) 421

מַסְמֵר   nail (1 · 5) 702

מַקֶּבֶת   hammer (1 · 4) 666

הפיק   to totter (1 · 8 · 9) 807

תֹּמֶר 5 palm tree, post (1 · 2) 1071

מִקְשָׁה   place or field of cucumbers (1 · 2) 903

צעד   to step, march (1 · 7 · 8) 857

מֵאַיִן 6 none at all or whence [is any] (28 · 48[?]) 34   אַיִן 6.d.

יאה 7 to be befitting (1 · 1 · 1) 383

מֵאַיִן   none at all or whence [is any] (20 · 48[?]) 34   אַיִן 6.d.

בער 8 to be stupid, dullhearted, unreceptive (1 · 3 · 7) 129

כסל   to be, become stupid (1 · 1 · 1) 492

מוּסָר   discipline, chastisement (8 · 50) 416

רקע 9 to be beaten (1 · 1 · 11) 955

חָרָשׁ   artificer, graver (4 · 38) 360

צֹרֵף   smelter; i.e., goldsmith (3 · 10[?]) 864

תְּכֵלֶה   violet stuff, fabric (1 · 49) 1067

אַרְגָּמָן   wool dyed with red purple, purple (1 · 39) 71

לְבוּשׁ   garment, clothing, raiment (1 · 31) 528

קֶצֶף 10 wrath (4 · 29) 893

רעשׁ   to quake, shake (5 · 21 · 29) 950

הכיל   to sustain, endure, contain, hold in (2 · 12 · 38) 465

זעם   indignation (3 · 22) 276

דְּנָה 11 [Aram.] this; כִּדְנָה = thus (1 · 43) 1088

אֲמַר   [Aram.] to say (1 · 1 · 72) 1081

לְהוֹם   [Aram.] to them, לְ + 3 mp. suffix

אֱלָה   [Aram.] god (1 · 92) 1080

דִּי   [Aram.] who, that (1 · 310) 1087

שְׁמַיָּא   [Aram.] heavens (2 · 38) 1116

אֲרַק   [Aram.] earth (1 · 21) 1083

לָא   [Aram.] not (1 · 80) 1098

עֲבַד   [Aram.] to make (1 · 19 · 28) 1104

אֲבַד [Aram.] to perish (1 · 1 · 7) 1078

אֲרַע [Aram.] earth (1 · 21) 1083

מִן [Aram.] from (1 · 101) 1100

תְּחוֹת [Aram.] under (1 · 5) 1117

אֵלֶּה [Aram.] these (1 · 2) 1080

תֵּבֵל 12 world (2 · 36) 385

תְּבוּנָה understanding (2 · 42) 108

נָשִׂיא 13 vapor (2 · 4) 672 II.

בָּרָק lightning (2 · 21) 140

מָטָר rain (2 · 38) 564

נִבְעַר 14 to be brutish, stupid (3 · 4 · 7) 129

צֹרֵף smelter; i.e., goldsmith (3 · 10[?]) 864

תַּעְתֻּעִים 15 mockery (2 · 2) 1074

פְּקֻדָּה visitation (9 · 32) 824

יָצַר 16 to form, fashion (4 · 41 · 44) 427

כְּנֻעָה 17 bundle, pack (1 · 1) 488

מָצוֹר siege; siegeworks (3 · 25) 848

קֶלַע 18 to sling (1 · 2 · 4) 887

אוֹי 19 Woe! Alas! (8 · 25) 17

שֶׁבֶר breaking (15 · 45) 991

נַחְלָה serious, sore; diseased (3 · 5[?]) 317
חלה Niph.

מַכָּה wound, blow (10 · 48) 646

חֳלִי sickness, disease (2 · 24) 318

מֵיתָר 20 cord, string (1 · 9) 452

נִתַּק to be torn apart or in two (2 · 10 · 27) 683

נִבְעַר 21 to be brutish, stupid, dull-hearted (3 · 4 · 7) 129

מַרְעִית pasturage, pasturing; here = flock (3 · 10) 945

שְׁמוּעָה 22 report (6 · 27) 808

רַעַשׁ quaking, shaking (2 · 17) 950

מָעוֹן lair, refuge, habitation (5 · 18) 732

תַּן jackal (5 · 14) 1072

צַעַד 23 step, steps (1 · 14) 857

יָסַר 24 to chasten, chastise (5 · 27 · 38) 415

הַמְעִיט to make small or few, diminish (1 · 13 · 22) 589

נָוֶה 25 habitation (14 · 45[?]) 627

Chapter 11

כּוּר 4 furnace [for smelting metals] (1 · 9) 468

שְׁבוּעָה 5 oath (1 · 30) 989

זוּב to flow (3 · 29 · 29) 264

חָלָב milk (2 · 44) 316

אָמֵן verily, truly (2 · 30) 53

הֵעִיד 7 to admonish (8 · 39 · 44) 729

שְׁרִירוּת 8 stubbornness (8 · 10) 1057

קֶשֶׁר 9 conspiracy (1 · 14) 905

מֵאֵן 10 to refuse (12 · 46) 549

הֵפֵר to break, frustrate (4 · 41 · 44[?]) 380

בֹּשֶׁת 13 shameful things, shame (6 · 30) 102

רִנָּה 14 ringing cry (3 · 33) 943

יָדִיד 15 beloved, lovely (1 · 8) 391

מְזִמָּה wickedness; purpose, discretion (4 · 19) 273

עָלַז to exult, triumph (4 · 16 · 16) 759

זַיִת 16 olive tree (1 · 38) 268

רַעֲנָן luxuriant, fresh (6 · 19) 947

יָפֶה fair, beautiful (1 · 41) 421

תֹּאַר form, outline (1 · 15) 1061

הֲמוּלָה rainstorm, rushing or roaring sound (1 · 2) 242

הִצִּית to kindle, set on fire (8 · 17 · 27) 428

דָּלִית branch, bough (1 · 8) 194

בִּגְלַל 17 on account of (2 · 10) 164 I. גָּלַל

מַעֲלָל 18 practice, deed (17 · 41) 760

אַלּוּף 19 docile, tame; friend (3 · 9) 48

הוּבַל to be led, conducted, borne (1 · 11 · 18) 384

טֶבַח to slaughter, butcher (3 · 11 · 11) 370

בֹּהַן 20 to prove, test, try (6 · 24 · 28) 103

כִּלְיָה (pl. only) kidneys, affections (4 · 31) 480

נְקָמָה vengeance (11 · 27) 668

בָּחוּר 22 young man (11 · 45) 104

285

פְּקֻדָּה 23 visitation (9 · 32) 824

Chapter 12

שָׁלָה 1 to be at ease, prosper (1 · 5 · 7) 1017

בגד to act or deal treacherously (8 · 49 · 49) 93

בֶּגֶד treachery (1 · 2) 93

שָׁרַשׁ 2 to take root (1 · 1 · 8) 1057

הָלַךְ to grow (>50) 229 *Qal* I.3.

כִּלְיָה (pl. only) kidneys, affections (4 · 31) 480

בָּחַן 3 to prove, test, try (6 · 24 · 28) 103

הִתִּיק to drag away (1 · 2 · 27) 683

טִבְחָה slaughter (1 · 4) 370

הֲרֵגָה slaughter (3 · 5) 247

מָתַי 4 when? (7 · 42) 607

אבל to mourn, lament (5 · 18 · 38) 5

עֵשֶׂב herb, herbage (2 · 33) 793

ספה to be snatched away (1 · 8 · 18) 705

רַגְלִי 5 on foot; as subst. = foot soldiery, infantry (1 · 12) 920

הִלְאָה to weary, make weary, exhaust (1 · 6 · 19) 521

הִתְחָרָה to contend hotly (>50) 354

גָּאוֹן majesty, exaltation, pride (7 · 49) 144

בגד 6 to act or deal treacherously (8 · 49 · 49) 93

נָטַשׁ 7 to abandon, forsake (5 · 33 · 40) 643

יְדִדוּת love, beloved one (1 · 1) 392

אַרְיֵה 8 lion (6 · 45) 71

עַיִט 9 bird[s] of prey (1 · 8) 743

צָבוּעַ colored, variegated (1 · 1) 840

הֵתָיוּ Bring! [impv.] (1 · 2 · 21) 87 אתה

אכלה food (1 · 18) 38; or to eat (>50) 37

בּוּסס 10 to tread down (1 · 2 · 12) 100

חֶלְקָה portion of ground (2 · 24) 324

חֶמְדָּה desire, desirable thing (3 · 16) 326

אָבֵל 11 to mourn, lament (5 · 8 · 38) 5

שָׁמֵם devastated (1 · 3) 1031

שְׁפִי 12 bare place, height (6 · 10) 1046

חִטָּה 13 wheat (2 · 30) 334

קוֹץ thorn bush (2 · 11) 881

קצר to reap, harvest (1 · 24 · 24) 894

הוֹעִיל to gain profit, benefit (7 · 23 · 23) 418

תְּבוּאָה product (2 · 43) 100

חָרוֹן [burning of] anger; ח' אַף = burning anger (9 · 41) 354

שָׁכֵן 14 neighbor (5 · 20) 1015

נָתַשׁ to pull up, pluck up (11 · 16 · 21) 684

נָתַשׁ 15 to pull up, pluck up (11 · 16 · 21) 684

רחם to have compassion (9 · 41 · 46) 933

נָתַשׁ 17 to pull up, pluck up (11 · 16 · 21) 684

Chapter 13

אֵזוֹר 1 waistcloth (8 · 14) 25

פֵּשֶׁת flax, linen (1 · 16) 833

מָתְנַיִם loins (6 · 47) 608

אֵזוֹר 2 waistcloth (8 · 14) 25

מָתְנַיִם loins (6 · 47) 608

אֵזוֹר 4 waistcloth (8 · 14) 25

מָתְנַיִם loins (6 · 47) 608

טָמַן to hide (7 · 28 · 31) 380

נָקִיק cleft (2 · 3) 669

טָמַן 5 to hide (7 · 28 · 31) 380

אֵזוֹר 6 waistcloth (8 · 14) 25

טָמַן to hide (7 · 28 · 31) 380

חָפַר 7 to dig, search for (1 · 23 · 23) 343

אֵזוֹר waistcloth (8 · 14) 25

טָמַן to hide (7 · 28 · 31) 380

צלח w. לְ = to be good for (>50) 852 II.

כָּכָה 9 thus (5 · 34) 462

286

גָּאוֹן   majesty, excellence, pride (7 · 49) 144

מָאֵן   10   to refuse (12 · 46) 549

שְׁרִירוּת   stubbornness (8 · 10) 1057

אֵזוֹר   waistcloth (8 · 14) 25

אֵזוֹר   11   waistcloth (8 · 14) 25

מָתְנַיִם   loins (6 · 47) 608

נֵבֶל   12   skin bottle, skin (3 · 11) 614

שִׁכָּרוֹן   13   drunkenness (1 · 3) 1016

נָפַץ   14   to dash to pieces (11 · 15 · 21) 658

חָמַל   to spare, have compassion on (5 · 40 · 40) 328

חוּס   to pity, look with compassion (2 · 24 · 24) 299

רָחַם   to have compassion (9 · 41 · 46) 933

הַאֲזִין   15   to give ear, hearken to = be obedient to (1 · 41 · 41) 24

גָּבַהּ   to be haughty, exalted, high (1 · 24 · 34) 146

בְּטֶרֶם   16   before (6 · 39) 382   טֶרֶם 2.

הֶחְשִׁיךְ   to cause darkness, make dark (1 · 6 · 17) 364

הִתְנַגֵּף   to stumble (1 · 1 · 48) 619

נֶשֶׁף   evening twilight (1 · 12) 676

קרה   to wait, look eagerly for (5 · 39 · 45) 875

צַלְמָוֶת   deep shadow, darkness (2 · 18) 853

עֲרָפֶל   cloud, heavy cloud (1 · 15) 791

מִסְתָּר   17   secret place, hiding place (3 · 10) 712

גֵּוָה   pride, lifting up (1 · 3) 145

דמע   to weep (2 · 2 · 2) 199

דִּמְעָה   tears (5 · 23) 199

נִשְׁבָּה   to be taken captive (1 · 8 · 37) 985

עֵדֶר   flock (6 · 39) 727

גְּבִירָה   18   queen mother, queen, lady (2 · 15) 150

הִשְׁפִּיל   to make low, sit down (1 · 18 · 29) 1050

מַרְאֲשׁוֹת   place at the head, head place (1 · 10) 912

עֲטָרָה   crown, [wreath] (1 · 23) 742

אַיֵּה   20   where? (6 · 44) 32

עֵדֶר   flock (6 · 39) 727

אַלּוּף   21   friend, intimate (3 · 9) 48

חֵבֶל   pains of travail (3 · 7) 286

לֵדָה   bringing forth (1 · 4) 408   יָלַד

שׁוּל   22   skirt (2 · 11) 1002

נחמס   to suffer violence (1 · 1 · 8) 329

עָקֵב   heel, foot print (1 · 14) 784

נָמֵר   23   leopard (2 · 6) 649

חֲבַרְבֻּרָה   (pl.) stripes, marks (1 · 1) 289

לֻמַּד   accustomed, taught (2 · 6) 541

קַשׁ   24   stubble, chaff (1 · 16) 905

מָנָת   25   portion (1 · 9) 584

מַד   measure (1 · 12) 551

חָשַׂף   26   to strip off, make bare (2 · 10 · 10) 362

שׁוּל   skirt (2 · 11) 1002

קָלוֹן   ignominy, dishonor (2 · 17) 885

נָאַף   27   adultery (1 · 2) 610

מִצְהָלָה   neighing (2 · 2) 843

זִמָּה   wickedness, evil device (1 · 28) 273

זְנוּת   fornication (3 · 9) 276

שִׁקּוּץ   detested thing (5 · 28) 1055

אוֹי   Woe! Alas! (8 · 25) 17

מָתַי   when? אַחֲרֵי מ׳ עֹד = after how long yet? when? (7 · 42) 607   d.

Chapter 14

בַּצָּרָה   1   dearth, destitution (1 · 2) 131

אָבַל   2   to mourn, lament (5 · 18 · 38) 5

אֻמְלַל   to be or grow feeble, languish (2 · 15 · 15) 51

קָדַר   to be dark; fig. of mourning (3 · 13 · 17) 871

צְוָחָה   outcry (2 · 4) 846

אַדִּיר   3   subst. = majestic one [used of nobles, chieftains, etc.] (5 · 27) 12

צָעִיר insignificant, mean [as subst. here] (4 · 22) 859

גֵּב pit, ditch, cistern (1 · 3) 155

רֵיקָם in vain, without effect (2 · 16) 938

הכלם to be put to shame, dishonored; be humiliated (1 · 2 · 38) 484

חפה to cover (2 · 6 · 12) 341

בַּעֲבוּר 4 because of (1 · 45) 721 II. עֲבוּר

גֶּשֶׁם shower, rain (2 · 35) 177

אִכָּר plowman, husbandman (3 · 7) 38

חפה to cover (2 · 6 · 12) 341

אַיָּלָה 5 hind, doe (1 · 11) 19

דֶּשֶׁא grass (1 · 14) 206

פֶּרֶא 6 wild ass (2 · 10) 825

שְׁפִי bare place, height (6 · 10) 1046

שָׁאַף to pant after (2 · 14 · 14) 983

תַּן jackal (5 · 14) 1072

עֵשֶׂב herb, herbage (2 · 33) 793

רבב 7 to be, become many (3 · 23 · 24) 912

מְשׁוּבָה turning back, apostasy (9 · 12) 1000

מִקְוֵה 8 hope (3 · 5) 876

מוֹשִׁיעַ savior (1 · 27) 446 ישע *Hiph.* ptc.

אֹרֵחַ wanderer, traveler (2 · 4) 72

נדהם 9 to be astounded (1 · 1 · 1) 187

תַּנַּחֵנוּ fr. נוח to abandon (>50) 628 *Hiph.* B.4.

נוע 10 to err, sin (1 · 22 · 38) 631

חָשַׂךְ to hold in check, withhold (1 · 26 · 28) 362

צום 12 to fast (1 · 20 · 20) 847

רִנָּה ringing cry (3 · 33) 943

דֶּבֶר plague (17 · 46) 184

אֲהָהּ 13 Alas! (4 · 15) 13

חָזוֹן 14 vision (2 · 35) 302

קֶסֶם divination (1 · 11) 890

אֱלִיל worthlessness (1 · 20) 47

תַּרְמִית deceitfulness (3 · 5) 941

דִּמְעָה 17 tears (5 · 23) 199

דמה to cease, cause to cease (2 · 4 · 16) 198

שֶׁבֶר breaking (15 · 45) 991

בְּתוּלָה virgin (8 · 50) 143

מַכָּה wound, blow (10 · 48) 646

נַחְלָה serious, sore; diseased (3 · 5[?]) חלה *Niph.*

תַּחֲלֻאִים 18 diseases (2 · 5) 316

סחר to go about; i.e., go about one's affairs (1 · 4 · 5[?]) 695

געל 19 to abhor, loathe (1 · 8 · 10) 171

מַרְפֵּא healing, cure (4 · 13) 951

קרה to wait, look eagerly for (5 · 39 · 45) 875

בְּעָתָה terror, dismay (2 · 2) 130

רֶשַׁע 20 wickedness (1 · 30) 957

נָאַץ 21 to contemn [treat with contempt] (2 · 8 · 24) 610

נבל to regard or treat as a foolish one (1 · 4 · 23[?]) 614 II. [נָבֵל] [נָבַל]

חפר to break, frustrate (4 · 41 · 44[?]) 830

הגשים 22 to cause or send rain (1 · 1 · 1) 177

הֶבֶל here pl. = false gods (>50) 210

רְבִיבִים copious showers (2 · 6) 914

קוה to wait, look eagerly for (4 · 39 · 45) 875

Chapter 15

אנה 2 whither? where? (2 · 39) 33

שְׁבִי captivity (8 · 46) 985

מִשְׁפָּחָה 3 kind, species (>50) 1046 3.

כֶּלֶב dog (1 · 32) 476

סחב to drag (4 · 5 · 5) 694

זְוָעָה 4 object of trembling, terror (4 · 7) 266

בִּגְלַל on account of (2 · 10) 164 I. גלל

חָמַל 5 to spare, have compassion (5 · 40 · 40) 328

נָד to lament, show grief (8 · 19 · 26) 626

נָטַשׁ 6 to forsake, abandon (5 · 33 · 40) 643

אָחוֹר backwards (4 · 41) 30

אָט	*Hiph.* of נטה, to stretch out (>50) 639
נִלְאָה	to be weary, make oneself weary (4 · 10 · 19) 521
זרה	7 to fan, winnow (2 · 9 · 38) 279
מִזְרֶה	pitchfork (1 · 2) 280
שִׁכֵּל	to make childless (1 · 18 · 24) 1013
עָצַם	8 to be numerous (4 · 16 · 18) 782
חוֹל	sand (3 · 22) 297
בָּחוּר	[coll.] young men; young man (11 · 45) 104
צָהֳרַיִם	midday, noon (3 · 23) 843
פִּתְאֹם	suddenly (5 · 25) 837
עִיר	agitation [of terror] (1 · 2) 735
בֶּהָלָה	sudden terror, dismay (1 · 4) 96
אֻמְלַל	9 to be or grow feeble, languish (2 · 15 · 15) 51
נפח	to breathe; here = breathe out (2 · 9 · 12) 655
בְּעֹד	while, so long as (3 · 20) 728 2.a.
חפר	to be abashed, ashamed (2 · 17 · 17) 344
אוֹי	10 Woe! Alas! (8 · 25) 17
מָדוֹן	contention, strife (1 · 12) 193
נשה	to lend (4 · 12 · 14[?]) 674 I. נשה
שרה	11 [dub.] to set free (1 · 1 · 2) 1056
הִפְגִּיעַ	to cause one to entreat (2 · 6 · 46) 803
רעע	12 to break (1 · 3 · 5[?]) 949
בַּז	13 spoil, booty, plunder (5 · 27) 103
מְחִיר	price, hire (1 · 15) 564
קדח	14 to be kindled (2 · 5 · 5) 869
הוּקַד	to be burning, burn (2 · 5 · 8) 428 יקד
נקם	15 to avenge oneself (3 · 12 · 35) 667
אָרֵךְ	long; w. אף = slow to anger (1 · 15) 74
שָׂשׂוֹן	16 joy, exultation (7 · 22) 965
סוֹד	17 intimate circle, council (4 · 21) 691
שׂחק	to play (3 · 17 · 36) 965

עלז	to exult, triumph (4 · 16 · 16) 759
בָּדָד	isolation, separation (2 · 11) 94
זַעַם	indignation (3 · 22) 276
כְּאֵב	18 pain (1 · 6) 456
נֶצַח	everlastingness, ever (3 · 42) 664
מַכָּה	wound, blow (10 · 48) 646
אָנוּשׁ	incurable (5 · 8) 60 אנש
מֵאֵן	to refuse (12 · 46) 549
אַכְזָב	deceptive, disappointing (1 · 2) 469
יָקָר	19 precious, highly valued (1 · 35) 429
זוֹלֵל	worthless, insignificant (1 · 6) 272 זלל
כְּפִי	according to my mouth, as my mouth (1 · 16) 804 פֶּה 6.b.
בָּצוּר	20 made inaccessible, fortified (2 · 25) 130 בצר
עָרִיץ	21 awe inspiring, terror striking (2 · 20) 792

Chapter 16

יִלּוֹד	3 born (1 · 5) 409
מָמוֹת	4 death [of painful death] (1 · 2) 560
תַּחֲלֻאִים	diseases (2 · 5) 316
נספד	to be bewailed (2 · 2 · 30) 704
דֹּמֶן	dung (4 · 6) 199
נְבֵלָה	carcass, corpse (8 · 48) 615
מַאֲכָל	food (4 · 30) 38
מַרְזֵחַ	5 mourning cry (1 · 2) 931
ספד	to wail, lament (7 · 28 · 30) 704
נָד	to lament, show grief (8 · 19 · 26) 626
רַחֲמִים	compassion (2 · 38) 933
קָטָן	6 young (3 · 47) 881
ספד	to wail, lament (7 · 28 · 30) 704
הִתְגֹּדֵד	to cut oneself [as relig. practice]; to gather in troops or bands (4 · 7 · 8) 151
נקרח	to make themselves bald (1 · 1 · 5) 901

289

פָּרַס 7 to break (1 · 2 · 14) 828

אֵבֶל mourning (3 · 24) 5

כּוֹס cup (7 · 31) 468

תַּנְחוּם consolation (1 · 5) 637

מִשְׁתֶּה 8 feast, banquet, drink (2 · 46) 1059

שָׂשׂוֹן 9 joy, exultation (7 · 22) 965

חָתָן bridegroom (4 · 20) 368

כַּלָּה bride; daughter-in-law (5 · 34) 483

שְׁרִירוּת 12 stubbornness (8 · 10) 1057

הֵטִיל 13 to hurl, cast, cast out (2 · 9 · 14) 376

חֲנִינָה favor (1 · 1) 337

הֵדִיחַ 15 to thrust out, banish (13 · 27 · 43) 623

דַּיָּג 16 fisherman (1 · 2) 186

דִּיג to fish for, catch (1 · 1 · 1) 185

צַיָּד hunter (1 · 1) 844

צוּד to hunt (1 · 12 · 16) 844

נָקִיק cleft (2 · 3) 669

נִצְפַּן 17 to be hidden (1 · 3 · 28) 860

מִגֶּגֶד from before (1 · 26) 617 גֶּגֶד 2.c.

מִשְׁנֶה 18 double, copy (3 · 36) 1041

נְבֵלָה carcass, corpse (8 · 48) 615

שִׁקּוּץ detested thing (5 · 28) 1055

מָעוֹז 19 refuge, place of safety (1 · 36) 731

מָנוֹס place of escape, refuge; flight (3 · 8) 631

אֶפֶס end, extremity (1 · 27) 67

הוֹעִיל to profit, benefit (7 · 23 · 23) 418

Chapter 17

עֵט 1 stylus (2 · 4) 741

צִפֹּרֶן point (1 · 2) 862

שָׁמִיר adamant, flint (1 · 11) 1038

חָרַשׁ to cut in, engrave (1 · 23 · 26) 360

לוּחַ tablet, board, plank (1 · 43) 531

אֲשֵׁרָה 2 sacred tree or pole as symbol of Canaanitish goddess (1 · 40) 81

רַעֲנָן luxuriant, fresh (6 · 19) 947

גָּבֹהַּ high, lofty, tall (4 · 41) 147

בַּז 3 spoil, booty, plunder (5 · 27) 103

שָׁמַט 4 to let fall, drop (1 · 7 · 9) 1030

קָדָה to be kindled (2 · 5 · 5) 869

הוּקַד to be burning, burn (2 · 5 · 8) 428 יקד

עַרְעָר 6 tree or bush (1 · 2) 792 עֲרוֹעֵר

חֲרֵרִים parched places (1 · 1) 359

מְלֵחָה saltiness, barrenness (1 · 2) 572

מִבְטָח 7 object of confidence, confidence (3 · 15) 105

שָׁתַל 8 to transplant (1 · 10 · 10) 1060

יוּבַל stream (1 · 1) 385

שֹׁרֶשׁ root (1 · 33) 1057

חֹם heat (1 · 4) 328

עָלֶה leaf, leafage (2 · 17) 750

רַעֲנָן luxuriant, fresh (6 · 19) 947

בַּצֹּרֶת dearth (2 · 2) 131

דָּאַג to be anxious, concerned (3 · 7 · 7) 178

הֵמִישׁ to cease from, depart (2 · 20 · 20) 559 מוּשׁ I.

עָקֹב 9 deceitful, insidious (1 · 3[?]) 784

אָנוּשׁ incurable, sick (5 · 8) 60

חָקַר 10 to search (1 · 22 · 27) 350

בָּחַן to prove, test, try (6 · 24 · 28) 103

כִּלְיָה pl. only, kidneys, affections (4 · 31) 480

מַעֲלָל practice, deed (17 · 41) 760

קֹרֵא 11 partridge (1 · 2) 896

דָּגַר to gather together as a brood (1 · 22) 186

עֹשֶׁר riches (2 · 37) 799

נָבָל foolish, senseless (1 · 18) 614

מִקְוֶה 13 hope (3 · 5) 876

יְסוּרַי read: those revolting from Me [with Q] (2 · 3) 693 סוּר Qal 1.

מָקוֹר spring, fountain, source (4 · 18) 881

אַיֵּה 15 where[?] (6 · 44) 32

אָץ 16 to hasten, make haste (1 · 8 · 10) 21 אוּץ

אָנוּשׁ incurable (5 · 8) 60 אנשׁ

הִתְאַוָּה   to desire, long for, lust after (1 · 16 · 27) 16

מוֹצָא   utterance, that which goes forth (1 · 27) 425

נֹכַח   before (1 · 22) 647

17 מְחִתָּה   terror, destruction, ruin (2 · 11) 369

מַחְסֶה   refuge, shelter (1 · 20) 340

18 מִשְׁנֶה   double, copy, second (3 · 36) 1041

שִׁבָּרוֹן   breaking, crushing (1 · 2) 991

21 מַשָּׂא   load, burden (12 · 45) 672 III.

22 מַשָּׂא   load, burden (12 · 45) 672 III.

23 הִקְשָׁה   to make stiff, stubborn (3 · 21 · 28) 904

עֹרֶף   back of neck (7 · 33) 791

מוּסָר   discipline, correction; chastisement (8 · 50) 416

24 מַשָּׂא   load, burden (12 · 45) 672 III.

26 שְׁפֵלָה   lowland (3 · 20) 1050

לְבוֹנָה   frankincense (3 · 21) 526

תּוֹדָה   sacrifice of thanksgiving (3 · 32) 392

27 מַשָּׂא   load, burden (12 · 45) 672 III.

הִצִּית   to kindle, set on fire (8 · 17 · 27) 428

אַרְמוֹן   palace, citadel (5 · 33) 74

כבה   to be quenched, extinguished (2 · 14 · 24) 459

Chapter 18

2 יוֹצֵר   ptc. = potter, former (8 · 17) 427 יצר

3 יוֹצֵר   ptc. = potter, former (8 · 17) 427 יצר

אֹבֶן   potter's wheel, disc (1 · 2) 7

4 חֹמֶר   clay (2 · 17) 330

יוֹצֵר   ptc. = potter, former (8 · 17) 427 יצר

יָשַׁר   to be pleasing, right, straight (2 · 13 · 25) 448

6 יוֹצֵר   ptc. = potter, former (8 · 17) 427 יצר

חֹמֶר   clay (2 · 17) 330

7 רֶגַע   moment (3 · 22) 921

נָתַשׁ   to pull up, pluck up (11 · 16 · 21) 684

נָתַץ   to pull down, break down (6 · 31 · 42) 683

9 רֶגַע   moment (3 · 22) 921

11 יָצַר   to form, fashion (4 · 41 · 44) 427

מַעֲלָל   practice, deed (17 · 41) 760

12 נוֹאָשׁ   to despair (2 · 5 · 6) 384

שְׁרִירוּת   stubbornness (8 · 10) 1057

13 שַׁעֲרוּרִי   horrible thing (1 · 2) 1045

בְּתוּלָה   virgin (8 · 50) 143

14 שָׂדַי   land, field (2 · 13) 961

שֶׁלֶג   snow (1 · 20) 1017

נתש   to be rooted up (2 · 4 · 21) 684; to be dried up 677 נשׁת

קַר   cool (1 · 3) 903

נזל   to flow (2 · 8 · 9) 633

15 שְׁבִיל   way, path (1 · 2) 987

נְתִיבָה   path, bypath (2 · 21) 677

סלל   to cast up (2 · 10 · 12) 699

16 שַׁמָּה   waste (24 · 39) 1031

שְׁרִיקֹת   hissing (1 · 2) 1057 שְׁרִיקָה

הנוד   to wag (1 · 3 · 26) 626

17 עֹרֶף   neck (7 · 33) 791

אֵיד   distress, calamity (5 · 24) 15

18 הִקְשִׁיב   to give attention (8 · 45 · 46) 904

19 הִקְשִׁיב   to give attention (8 · 45 · 46) 904

יָרִיב   opponent, adversary (1 · 3) 937

20 כָּרָה   to dig (2 · 13 · 14) 500

שׁוּחָה   pit (3 · 5) 1001

21 הִגִּיר   to deliver over to (1 · 5 · 10) 620

שַׁכּוּל   bereaved, robbed of offspring (1 · 6) 1014

בָּחוּר   young man (11 · 45) 104

22 זְעָקָה   cry of distress (6 · 18) 277

גְּדוּד   marauding band, troop (1 · 33) 151

פִּתְאֹם   suddenly (5 · 25) 837

כָּרָה   to dig (2 · 13 · 14) 500

שִׁיחָה   pit (3 · 5) 1001   שׁוּחָה

פַּח   bird trap (3 · 25) 809

טָמַן   to hide, conceal (7 · 28 · 31) 380

הִמְחָה 23 to blot out (1 · 3 · 34) 562

Chapter 19

בַּקְבֻּק 1 flask (2 · 3) 132

יוֹצֵר   potter, former (8 · 17) 427   יצר

חֶרֶשׂ   earthenware, earthen vessel (2 · 17) 360

גַּיְא 2 valley (4 · 48) 161

חַרְסוּת   potsherd (1 · 1) 360

צָלַל 3 to tingle (1 · 4 · 4) 852

נכר 4 to treat as foreign (1 · 4 · 8) 649

נָקִי   innocent, free from guilt, clean (6 · 43) 667

גַּיְא 6 valley (4 · 48) 161

הֲרֵגָה   slaughter (3 · 5) 247

בקק 7 to make void, lay waste (1 · 4 · 7) 132

נְבֵלָה   carcass, corpse (8 · 48) 615

מַאֲכָל   food (4 · 30) 38

שַׁמָּה 8 waste (24 · 39) 1031

שְׁרֵקָה   hissing (5 · 7) 1056

שָׁרַק   to hiss (3 · 12 · 12) 1056

מַכָּה   wound, blow (10 · 48) 646

מָצוֹר 9 siege, siege works (3 · 25) 848

מָצוֹק   stress, straits (1 · 6) 848

הֵצִיק   to bring into straits, constrain, press upon (1 · 11 · 11) 847

בַּקְבֻּק 10 flask (2 · 3) 132

כָּכָה 11 thus (5 · 34) 462

יוֹצֵר   potter, former (8 · 17) 427   יצר

מֵאֵין   without (20 · 48[?]) 34   אֵין 6.d.

גַּג 13 roof, top (3 · 29) 150

הִסִּיךְ   to pour out libations (8 · 14 · 25) 650

מֵבִי   K, מֵבִיא Q Hiph. ptc. (>50) 97

עֹרֶף 15 to make stiff, stubborn (3 · 21 · 28) 904

עֹרֶף   neck, back of neck (7 · 33) 791

Chapter 20

פָּקִיד 1 commissioner, deputy, overseer (3 · 13) 824

נָגִיד   prince, leader (1 · 44) 617

מַהְפֶּכֶת 2 stocks [or similar instrument of punishment] (3 · 4) 246

מָחֳרָת 3 with מִן = on the morrow (1 · 32) 564

מַהְפֶּכֶת   stocks; cf. vs. 2. (3 · 4) 246

מָגוֹר   terror, fear (6 · 8) 159

מָגוֹר 4 terror, fear (6 · 8) 159

אֹהֵב   friend, lover (2 · 36) 12   אָהֵב

חֹסֶן 5 wealth, treasure (1 · 5) 340

יְגִיעַ   product, toil (2 · 16) 388

יְקָר   precious things; preciousness, price, honor (1 · 17) 430

בָּזַז   to spoil, plunder (2 · 37 · 41) 102

שְׁבִי 6 captivity (8 · 46) 985

אֹהֵב   friend, lover (2 · 36) 12   אָהֵב

פתה 7 to deceive (1 · 17 · 27) 834

נִפְתָּה   to be deceived (1 · 2 · 27) 834

שְׂחוֹק   derision (4 · 15) 966

לעג   to mock, have in derision (1 · 12 · 18) 541

מִדֵּי 8 as often as (3 · 15) 191   דַּי 2.c.

שֹׁד   violence, havoc (3 · 25) 994

קֶלֶס   derision (1 · 3) 887

עָצַר 9 to shut up (4 · 36 · 46) 783

נִלְאָה   to be weary, make oneself weary (4 · 10 · 19) 521

כִּלְכֵּל   to contain, hold in, restrain; sustain (1 · 24 · 38) 465

דִּבָּה   whispering, evil report (1 · 9) 179

מָגוֹר   terror, fear (6 · 8) 159

הִגִּיד   to inform of (>50) 616   נגד Hiph. 3.

אֱנוֹשׁ   man, mankind (1 · 42) 60

צֶלַע	limping, stumbling (1 · 4) 854
אוּלַי	perhaps (6 · 45) 19
פתה	to be deceived (1 · 3 · 27) 834
נְקָמָה	vengeance (11 · 27) 668
עָרִיץ	11 awe inspiring, terror striking (2 · 20) 792
כְּלִמָּה	ignominy, reproach, insult (3 · 30) 484
בחן	12 to prove, test, try (6 · 24 · 28) 103
כִּלְיָה	pl. only = kidneys, affection (4 · 31) 480
נְקָמָה	vengeance (11 · 27) 668
מֵרַע	13 evildoer (2 · 18) 949 מרע Hiph.
בִּשֵּׂר	15 to gladden with good tidings (1 · 14 · 15) 142
זְעָקָה	16 cry of distress (6 · 18) 277
תְּרוּעָה	alarm, war cry (3 · 36) 929
צָהֳרַים	midday, noon (3 · 23) 843
רֶחֶם	17 womb (4 · 33) 933
הָרָה	pregnant, woman with child (2 · 15) 248
רֶחֶם	18 womb (4 · 33) 933
יָגוֹן	grief, sorrow (4 · 14) 387
בּשֶׁת	shame (6 · 30) 102

Chapter 21

אוּלַי	2 perhaps (6 · 45) 19
נִפְלָאוֹת	wonderful acts (1 · 44[?]) 810 פלא Niph. 4.
צוּר	4 to besiege, shut in (5 · 31 · 31) 848
קֶצֶף	5 wrath (4 · 29) 893
דֶּבֶר	6 plague, pestilence (17 · 46) 184
דֶּבֶר	7 plague, pestilence (17 · 46) 184
חוס	to pity, look upon with compassion (2 · 24 · 24) 299
חמל	to spare, have compassion (5 · 40 · 40) 328
רחם	to have compassion (9 · 41 · 46) 933
דֶּבֶר	9 plague, pestilence (17 · 46) 184

צוּר	to shut in, besiege (5 · 31 · 31) 848
דִּין	12 to execute judgment, plead the cause, judge (4 · 23 · 24) 192
גָּזַל	to tear away, seize, plunder (2 · 29 · 30) 159
עָשַׁק	to oppress (3 · 36 · 37) 798
כבה	to quench, extinguish (2 · 10 · 24) 459
רֹעַ	evil, badness (11 · 19) 947
מַעֲלָל	practice, deed (17 · 41) 760
מִישׁוֹר	13 tableland, level country (3 · 23) 449
נחת	to go down, descend (1 · 3 · 8) 639
מְעֹנָה	den, lair, habitation (1 · 9) 733
מַעֲלָל	14 practice, deed (17 · 41) 760
הִצִּית	to kindle, set on fire (8 · 17 · 27) 428

Chapter 22

גָּזַל	3 to tear away, seize, plunder (2 · 29 · 30) 159
עָשׁוֹק	oppressor, extortioner (1 · 1) 799
יָתוֹם	orphan (4 · 42) 450
הוֹנָה	to oppress, maltreat (1 · 14 · 18) 413
חמס	to treat violently, wrong (2 · 8 · 8) 329
נָקִי	innocent, free from guilt, clean (6 · 43) 667
הָרְבָּה	5 waste, ruin (10 · 42) 352
מַשְׁחִית	7 destroyer (4 · 19) 1008
מִבְחָר	choicest, best (2 · 12) 104
כָּכָה	8 thus (5 · 34) 462
נוד	10 to lament, show grief (8 · 19 · 26) 626
מוֹלֶדֶת	kindred, birth, offspring (2 · 22) 409
בְּלֹא	13 without (4 · 30) 518
עֲלִיָּה	roof chamber (2 · 20) 751
חִנָּם	for naught (1 · 32) 336
פֹּעַל	wages (3 · 37) 821
מִדָּה	size (>50) 551
עֲלִיָּה	14 roof chamber (2 · 20) 751

293

רָוַח	*Pual* ptc. = spacious (1 · 1 · 14[?]) 926
חַלּוֹן	window (1 · 1[?]) 319
סָפַן	to cover in, panel (1 · 6 · 6) 706
שָׁשַׁר	red color, vermilion (1 · 2) 1059
הִתְחָרָה	15 to strive eagerly [dub.] (>50) 354
דָּן	16 to plead the cause, minister judgment, judge (4 · 23 · 24) 192 דין
דִּין	cause, plea; judgment (4 · 19) 192
בֶּצַע	17 unjust gain, gain made by violence (4 · 23) 130
נָקִי	innocent, free from guilt, clean (6 · 43) 667
עֹשֶׁק	oppression, extortion (2 · 15) 799
מְרוּצָה	crushing, oppression (1 · 1) 954
סָפַד	18 to wail, lament (7 · 28 · 30) 704
הוֹד	splendor, majesty (1 · 24) 217
קְבוּרָה	19 burial (1 · 14) 869
סָחַב	to drag (4 · 5 · 5) 694
מֵהָלְאָה	beyond (1 · 3) 229 הָלְאָה
תְּנִי	20 lift up! (>50) 678 נתן *Qal* 1. x.
מְאַהֵב	lover, friend (3 · 16) 12
שַׁלְוָה	21 prosperity (1 · 8) 1017
נְעוּרִים	youth (7 · 46) 655
מְאַהֵב	22 lover, friend (3 · 16) 12
שְׁבִי	captivity (8 · 46) 985
נכלם	to be put to shame, dishonored, humiliated (4 · 26 · 38) 483
קָנַן	23 to be nested (1 · 4 · 5) 890
נֵחַנְתְּ	to be pitied (>50) 335 חנן *Niph.*
חֵבֶל	pains of travail (3 · 7) 286
חִיל	anguish, writhing (3 · 6) 297
חוֹתָם	24 seal, signet ring (1 · 14) 368
נתק	to draw off, pull off (1 · 3 · 27) 683
יָגוֹר	25 fearing (2 · 2) 388
הֵטִיל	26 to hurl, cast out (2 · 9 · 14) 376
עֶצֶב	28 vessel (1 · 1) 781
נבזה	ptc. = despised (1 · 10 · 42) 102
נפץ	to shatter (1 · 5 · 21) 658
חֵפֶץ	pleasure, delight (2 · 39) 343

הוטל	to be hurled, hurled down (1 · 4 · 14) 376
עֲרִירִי	30 childless (1 · 4) 792

Chapter 23

מַרְעִית	1 pasturing, pasturage (3 · 10) 945
הִדִּיחַ	2 to thrust out, banish (13 · 27 · 43) 623
רֹעַ	evil, badness (11 · 19) 947
מַעֲלָל	practice, deed (17 · 41) 760
הִדִּיחַ	3 to thrust out, banish (13 · 27 · 43) 623
נָוֶה	abode, habitation (14 · 45[?]) 627
פרה	to be fruitful (2 · 22 · 29) 826
צֶמַח	5 growth, sprout (2 · 12) 855
בֶּטַח	6 security, as adv. = securely (5 · 43) 105
הִדִּיחַ	8 to thrust out, banish (13 · 27 · 43) 623
רחף	9 to grow soft, relax (1 · 1 · 3[?]) 934
שִׁכּוֹר	drunken (1 · 13) 1016
נאף	10 to commit adultery (3 · 14 · 31) 610
אלה	curse, oath (4 · 36) 46
אבל	to mourn, lament (5 · 18 · 38) 5
נוה	cs. נְאוֹת, pasture, meadow (14 · 45[?]) 627
מְרוּצָה	course, running (2 · 4) 930
כֵּן	right, honest, true (4 · 24) 467
חנף	11 to be profane, godless (4 · 7 · 11) 337
חֲלַקְלַקּוֹת	12 slipperiness (1 · 4) 325
אֲפֵלָה	darkness, gloominess (2 · 12) 66
נדחח	to push, push violently (1 · 2 · 2) 190 דחח
פְּקֻדָּה	visitation (9 · 32) 824
תִּפְלָה	13 unseemliness (1 · 3) 1074
הִתְעָה	to cause to err, mislead (4 · 21 · 50) 1073
שַׁעֲרוּר	14 horrible thing (2 · 2) 1045

נָאַף	to commit adultery (5 · 17 · 31) 610	
מֵרַע	evildoer (2 · 18) 949 רעע *Hiph.* 2.	
לַעֲנָה	15 wormwood (2 · 8) 542	
רֹאשׁ	bitter, poisonous herb (3 · 12) 912	
חֲנֻפָּה	profaneness, pollution (1 · 1) 338	
הֶהְבִּיל	16 to cause to become vain (1 · 1 · 5) 211	
חָזוֹן	vision (2 · 35) 302	
נָאַץ	17 to contemn, spurn (1 · 15 · 24) 610	
שְׁרִירוּת	stubbornness (8 · 10) 1057	
סוֹ	18 intimate circle, council (4 · 21) 691	
הִקְשִׁית	to give attention (8 · 45 · 46) 904	
סְעָרָה	19 tempest, storm wind (2 · 16) 704	
סַעַר	tempest (3 · 8) 704	
הִתְחוֹלֵל	ptc. = whirling (1 · 1 · 9) 296 I. חול	
חוּל	to whirl (2 · 6 · 9) 296 I.	
מְזִמָּה	20 purpose, device (4 · 19) 273	
בִּינָה	the act of understanding; understanding (1 · 37) 108	
סוֹד	22 intimate circle, council (4 · 21) 691	
רֹעַ	evil, badness (11 · 19) 947	
מַעֲלָל	practice, deed (17 · 41) 760	
מִסְתָּר	24 hiding place, secret place (3 · 10) 712	
חָלַם	25 to dream (2 · 27 · 29) 321	
מָתַי	26 when? (2 · 42) 607	
תַּרְמִית	deceitfulness (3 · 5) 941	
תֶּבֶן	28 straw (1 · 17) 1061	
בַּר	grain, corn (1 · 14) 141	
פַּטִּישׁ	29 forge hammer (2 · 3) 809	
פָּצַץ	to shatter (1 · 1 · 3) 823	
גָּנַב	30 to steal away [transitive] (1 · 2 · 40) 170	
נָאַם	31 utter a prophecy, speak as a prophet (1 · 1) 610	
הִתְעָה	32 to cause to err, mislead (4 · 21 · 50) 1073	
פַּחֲזוּת	recklessness, extravagance (1 · 1) 808	
הוֹעִיל	to profit, benefit (7 · 23 · 23) 418	

מַשָּׂא	33 utterance, oracle (12 · 45) 672 III.	
נָטַשׁ	to abandon, forsake (5 · 33 · 40) 643	
מַשָּׂא	34 utterance, oracle (12 · 45) 672 III.	
מַשָּׂא	36 utterance, oracle (12 · 45) 672 III.	
מַשָּׂא	38 utterance, oracle (12 · 45) 672 III.	
נָשָׁה	39 to forget (4 · 12 · 14[?]) 674 II. נשה	
נָטַשׁ	to abandon, forsake (5 · 33 · 40) 643	
כְּלִמּוּת	40 ignominy (1 · 1) 484	

Chapter 24

דּוּד	1 basket, pot, jar (1 · 1) 188	
תְּאֵנָה	fig, fig tree (12 · 39) 1061	
הוּעַד	ptc. = set, placed (1 · 2 · 28) 416 יעד	
חָרָשׁ	artificer, graver (4 · 38) 360	
מַסְגֵּר	[coll.] smiths, locksmiths (2 · 7) 689	
דּוּד	2 basket, pot, jar (2 · 7) 188	
תְּאֵנָה	fig, fig tree (12 · 39) 1061	
בְּכּוּרָה	first ripe fig (1 · 4) 114	
רֹעַ	badness, bad quality (11 · 19) 947	
תְּאֵנָה	3 fig, fig tree (12 · 39) 1061	
רֹעַ	badness, bad quality (11 · 19) 947	
תְּאֵנָה	5 fig, fig tree (12 · 39) 1061	
הִכִּיר	to regard (1 · 37 · 40) 647	
גָּלוּת	exile; [coll.] exiles (5 · 15) 163	
הָרַס	6 to tear, throw down (5 · 30 · 43) 248	
נָתַשׁ	to pull up, pluck up (11 · 16 · 21) 684	
תְּאֵנָה	8 fig, fig tree (12 · 39) 1061	
רֹעַ	badness, bad quality (11 · 19) 947	
זְוָעָה	9 object of trembling, terror (K 4 · 4) (Q 4 · 7) 266	
מָשָׁל	byword, proverb, parable (1 · 39) 605	
שְׁנִינָה	sharp word, taunt (1 · 4) 1042	
קְלָלָה	curse (9 · 33) 887	
הִדִּיחַ	to thrust out, banish (13 · 27 · 43) 623	
דֶּבֶר	10 plague, pestilence (17 · 46) 184	

Chapter 25

רֵאשִׁנִי 1 first (1 · 1) 912

רֹעַ 5 evil, badness (11 · 19) 947

מַעֲלָל practice, deed (17 · 41) 760

לְמֶן from (4 · 14) 577 מִן 9.b.

הַחֲרִים 9 to destroy, devote to destruction (5 · 46 · 49) 355

שַׁמָּה horror, an appalling thing (24 · 39) 1031

שְׁרֵקָה hissing (5 · 7) 1056

חָרְבָּה waste, ruin (10 · 42) 352

שָׂשׂוֹן 10 joy, exultation (7 · 22) 965

חָתָן bridegroom (4 · 20) 368

כַּלָּה bride; daughter-in-law (5 · 34) 483

רֵחַיִם hand mill (1 · 5) 932

נֵר lamp (1 · 44) 632

חָרְבָּה 11 waste, ruin (10 · 42) 352

שַׁמָּה horror, an appalling thing (24 · 39) 1031

פֹּעַל 14 deed, thing done (3 · 37) 821

כּוֹס 15 cup (7 · 31) 468

הִתְגֹּעֲשׁ 16 to reel to and fro (2 · 2 · 10) 172

הִתְהֹלֵל to act like a madman (4 · 6 · 14) 237 II. הלל *Hithpo.*

כּוֹס 17 cup (7 · 31) 468

חָרְבָּה 18 waste, ruin (10 · 42) 352

שַׁמָּה horror, an appalling thing (24 · 39) 1031

שְׁרֵקָה hissing (5 · 7) 1056

קְלָלָה curse (9 · 33) 887

עֶרֶב 20 mixture, mixed company (2 · 5) 786

אִי 22 coast, border, region (4 · 36) 15

קָצַץ 23 to cut off (3 · 4 · 14) 893

עֶרֶב 24 mixture, mixed company (2 · 5) 786

שָׁכַר 27 to be, become drunk (1 · 9 · 20) 1016

קיה to vomit (1 · 1 · 1) 883

מֵאֵן 28 to refuse (12 · 46) 549

כּוֹס cup (7 · 31) 468

נָקָה 29 to be free, exempt from punish-

ment (6 · 24 · 43) 667

שָׁאַג 30 to roar (5 · 20 · 20) 980

מָעוֹן dwelling, refuge, lair (5 · 18) 732

נָוֶה habitation (14 · 45[?]) 627

הֵידָד shout, shouting, cheer (5 · 7) 212

ענה to sing (2 · 13 · 16) 777

שָׁאוֹן 31 roar, din (4 · 17) 981

סַעַר 32 tempest (3 · 8) 704

יַרְכָה remote part, side (4 · 28) 438

נספד 33 to be bewailed (2 · 2 · 30) 704

דֹּמֶן dung (4 · 6) 199

הֵילִיל 34 to give a howl (8 · 30 · 30) 410

הִתְפַּלֵּשׁ to roll in (2 · 4 · 4) 814

אַדִּיר [subst.] majestic one [used of nobles, chieftains, etc.] (5 · 27) 12

טבח to slaughter, butcher (3 · 11 · 11) 370

תְּפוֹצָה dispersion (1 · 1) 807

חֶמְדָּה desire (3 · 16) 326

מָנוֹס 35 place of escape, refuge; flight (3 · 8) 631

פְּלֵיטָה escape, deliverance (2 · 28) 812

אַדִּיר [subst.] majestic one [used of nobles, chieftains, etc.] (5 · 27) 12

צְעָקָה 36 cry of distress (4 · 21) 858

יְלָלָה howling (1 · 5) 410

אַדִּיר [subst.] majestic one [used of nobles, chieftains, etc.] (5 · 27) 12

מַרְעִית pasturage, pasturing (3 · 10) 945

נדמם 37 to be made silent (4 · 5 · 30) 198

נָוֶה cstr. נְאוֹת, meadow, pasture (14 · 45 [?]) 627 II.

חָרוֹן [burning of] anger; ח׳ אף = burning anger (9 · 41) 354

כְּפִיר 38 young lion (3 · 31) 498

סֹךְ lair (1 · 4) 697

שַׁמָּה horror, an appalling thing (24 · 39) 1031

חָרוֹן [burning of] anger (9 · 41) 354

ינה ptc. = oppressor (3 · 4 · 18) 413

Chapter 26

מַמְלָכוּת 1 dominion, kingdom (1 · 9) 575
גָּרַע 2 to diminish (2 · 14 · 22) 175
אוּלַי 3 perhaps (6 · 45) 19
רֹעַ evil, badness (11 · 19) 947
מַעֲלָל practice, deed (17 · 41) 760
קְלָלָה 6 curse (9 · 33) 887
חָרֵב 9 to be waste, desolate (2 · 17 · 37) 351
מֵאֵין without (20 · 48[?]) 34   אַיִן 6.d.
נִקְהַל to assemble (1 · 19 · 39)
מַעֲלָל 13 practice, deed (17 · 41) 760
נָקִי 15 free from guilt, clean, innocent (6 · 43) 667
נֶחֱרַשׁ 18 to be plowed (1 · 2 · 26) 360
עִי ruin, heap of ruins (1 · 5) 730
נְבֵלָה 23 carcass, corpse (8 · 48) 615

Chapter 27

מוֹסֵר 2 band or bond of restraint (4 · 12) 64
מוֹטָה bar of yoke (5 · 11) 557
צַוָּאר neck, back of neck (9 · 41) 848
לַאֲשֶׁר 5 to him who (3 · 38) 81   עָשָׂה
יָשַׁר to be pleasing, agreeable, right (2 · 13 · 25) 448
צַוָּאר 8 neck (9 · 41) 848
עֹל yoke (10 · 40) 760
דֶּבֶר plague, pestilence (17 · 46) 184
קֹסֵם 9 false prophet, diviners (2 · 9[?]) 890
עֹנֵן to practice soothsaying (1 · 10 · 11) 778
כַּשָּׁף sorcerer (1 · 1) 506
הִדִּיחַ 10 to thrust out, banish (13 · 27 · 43) 623
צַוָּאר 11 neck, back of neck (9 · 41) 848
עֹל yoke (10 · 40) 760
צַוָּאר 12 neck, back of neck (9 · 41) 848
עֹל yoke (10 · 40) 760

דֶּבֶר 13 plague, pestilence (17 · 46) 184
הִדִּיחַ 15 to thrust out, banish (13 · 27 · 43) 623
מְהֵרָה 16 hastily, quickly (1 · 20) 555
חָרְבָּה 17 waste, ruin (10 · 42) 352
פָּגַע 18 to entreat (2 · 40 · 46) 803
מְכוֹנָה 19 base, stand (3 · 25) 467
חֹר 20 noble (2 · 13) 359

Chapter 28

עֹל 2 yoke (10 · 40) 760
בְּעוֹד 3 within yet (3 · 20) 728   עוֹד 2.a.
יָמִים time; שְׁנָתַיִם יָמִ׳ = two years' time (>50) 398   יוֹם 6.b.
גָּלוּת 4 exile; [coll.] exiles (5 · 15) 163
עֹל yoke (10 · 40) 760
אָמֵן 6 verily, truly (2 · 30) 53
גּוֹלָה exile; [coll.] exiles (10 · 42) 163
דֶּבֶר 8 plague, pestilence (17 · 46) 184
מוֹטָה 10 bar of yoke (5 · 11) 557
צַוָּאר neck, back of neck (9 · 41) 848
כָּכָה 11 thus (5 · 34) 462
עֹל yoke (10 · 40) 760
בְּעוֹד within yet (3 · 20) 728   עוֹד 2.a.
יָמִים time; שְׁנָתַיִם יָמִ׳ = two years' time (>50) 398   יוֹם 6.b.
צַוָּאר neck, back of neck (9 · 41) 848
מוֹטָה 12 bar of yoke (5 · 11) 557
צַוָּאר neck, back of neck (9 · 41) 848
מוֹטָה 13 bar of yoke (5 · 11) 557
עֹל 14 yoke (10 · 40) 760
צַוָּאר neck, back of neck (9 · 41) 848
סָרָה 16 apostasy (2 · 7) 694

Chapter 29

גּוֹלָה 1 exile; [coll.] exiles (10 · 42) 163
צֵאת 2 *Qal* inf. cstr. of יצא (>50) 422
גְּבִירָה queen mother; queen, lady (2 · 15) 150

297

סָרִיס	eunuch (7 · 45) 710	
חָרָשׁ	artificer, graver (4 · 38) 360	
מַסְגֵּר	[coll.] smiths, locksmith; dungeon (2 · 7) 689	
גּוֹלָה	4 exile; [coll.] exiles (10 · 42) 163	
גַּנָּה	5 garden, orchard (2 · 16) 171	
מעט	6 to be, become small, few (2 · 8 · 22) 589	
הִשִּׁיא	8 to beguile (5 · 15 · 16) 674	
קֹסֵם	false prophet, diviner (2 · 9) 890	
הַחֲלִים	to dream (1 · 2 · 29) 321	
תִּקְוָה	11 hope (2 · 32) 876	
שְׁבִית	14 captivity (12 · 26) 986	
הִדִּיחַ	to thrust out, banish (13 · 27 · 43) 623	
גּוֹלָה	16 exile; [coll.] exiles (10 · 42) 163	
דֶּבֶר	17 plague, pestilence (17 · 46) 184	
תְּאֵנָה	fig, fig tree (12 · 39) 1061	
שֹׁעָר	horrid, disgusting (1 · 1) 1045	
רֹעַ	badness, bad quality (11 · 19) 947	
דֶּבֶר	18 plague, pestilence (17 · 46) 184	
זְוָעָה	object of trembling, terror (K. 4 · 4) (Q. 4 · 7) 266	
אלה	execration, curse, oath (4 · 36) 46	
שַׁמָּה	horror, an appalling thing (24 · 39) 1031	
שְׁרֵקָה	hissing (5 · 7) 1056	
הִדִּיחַ	to thrust out, banish (13 · 27 · 43) 623	
גּוֹלָה	20 exile; [coll.] exiles (10 · 42) 163	
קְלָלָה	22 curse (9 · 33) 887	
גָּלוּת	exile; [coll.] exiles (5 · 15) 163	
קלה	to roast, parch (1 · 3 · 4) 885	
נְבָלָה	23 disgraceful folly, senselessness (1 · 13) 615	
נאף	to commit adultery (3 · 14 · 31) 610	
פָּקִיד	26 commissioner, deputy, overseer (3 · 13) 824	
שׁגע	to be maddened (1 · 5 · 7) 993	

מַהְפֶּכֶת	stocks [or similar instrument of punishment] (3 · 4) 246	
צִינֹק	pillory (1 · 1) 857	
גָּעַר	27 to rebuke (1 · 14 · 14) 172	
אָרֵךְ	28 long (1 · 3) 74	
גַּנָּה	garden, orchard (2 · 16) 170	
גּוֹלָה	31 exile; [coll.] exiles (10 · 42) 163	
סָרָה	32 apostasy (2 · 7) 694	

Chapter 30

שְׁבוּת	3 captivity (12 · 26) 986	
חֲרָדָה	5 trembling, fear (1 · 9) 353	
פַּחַד	dread (4 · 49) 808	
חָלָץ	6 [dual only] loins (1 · 10) 323	
יֵרָקוֹן	paleness, mildew, lividness (1 · 6) 439	
עֹל	8 yoke (10 · 40) 760	
צַוָּאר	neck, back of neck (9 · 41) 848	
מוֹסֵר	band or bond of restraint (4 · 12) 64	
נתק	to tear apart, snap (3 · 11 · 27) 683	
שְׁבִי	10 captivity (8 · 46) 985	
שָׁקַט	to be undisturbed, quiet (5 · 31 · 41) 1052	
שַׁאֲנַן	to be at ease, secure (3 · 5 · 5) 983	
הֶחֱרִיד	to terrify, drive in terror (3 · 16 · 39) 353	
כָּלָה	11 complete destruction, annihilation (7 · 27) 478	
יִסַּר	to chasten, chastise (5 · 27 · 38) 415	
נקה	to leave unpunished (4 · 18 · 43) 667	
אָנוּשׁ	12 incurable, sick (5 · 8) 60 I. אנשׁ	
שֶׁבֶר	breaking (15 · 45) 991	
נַחְלָה	serious, sore, diseased (3 · 5[?]) 317 חלה Niph.	
מַכָּה	wound, blow (10 · 48) 646	
דָּן	13 to plead the cause, minister judgment, judge (4 · 23 · 24) 192 דין	
דִּין	plea, cause; judgment (4 · 19) 192	
מָזוֹר	wound (1 · 3) 267	
רְפֻאָה	remedy, medicine (2 · 3) 951	

תְּעָלָה   healing (2 · 2) 752

מְאַהֵב   14 lover, friend (3 · 16) 12   אהב

מַכָּה   wound, blow (10 · 48) 646

מוּסָר   chastisement, discipline, correction (8 · 50) 416

אַכְזָרִי   cruel (3 · 8) 470

עצם   to be numerous (4 · 16 · 18) 782

שֶׁבֶר   15 breaking (15 · 45) 991

אָנוּשׁ   incurable, sick (5 · 8) 60

מַכְאוֹב   pain (3 · 16) 456

עָצַם   to be numerous (4 · 16 · 18) 782

שְׁבִי   16 captivity (8 · 46) 985

שֹׁאסַיִךְ   ptc. = those who plunder you (2 · 7[?]) 1042   שׁסס

מְשִׁסָּה   plunder, spoil, prey (1 · 6) 1042

בָּזַז   to spoil, plunder (2 · 37 · 41) 102

בַּז   spoil, booty, plunder (5 · 27) 103

אֲרוּכָה   17 healing, restoration (3 · 6) 74

מַכָּה   wound, blow (10 · 48) 646

נדח   to be banished, thrust out; here ptc. = outcast (4 · 13 · 43) 623

רְחַם   18 to have compassion (9 · 41 · 46) 933

תֵּל   mound (2 · 5) 1068

אַרְמוֹן   citadel, palace (5 · 33) 74

תּוֹדָה   19 thanksgiving, praise (3 · 32) 392

שׂחק   to play (17 · 36) 965

מעט   to be, become small, few (2 · 8 · 22) 589

צער   to be or grow insignificant (1 · 3 · 3) 858

לֹחֵץ   20 oppressing, oppressor (1 · 4) 537   לחץ

אַדִּיר   21 [subst.] majestic one [used of nobles, chieftains, etc.] (5 · 27) 12

מֹשֵׁל   ruling, ruler (4 · 24) 605   III. מָשַׁל

עָרַב   to give in pledge (1 · 15 · 17) 786

סְעָרָה   23 tempest, storm wind (2 · 16) 704

סַעַר   tempest (3 · 8) 704

הִתְגּוֹרֵר   sweeping, roaring (1 · 1 · 5) 176   גרר

חוּל   to whirl, whirl about (2 · 6 · 9) 297

חָרוֹן   24 [burning of] anger; ח׳ אף = burning anger (9 · 41) 354

מְזִמָּה   purpose, devise (4 · 19) 273

Chapter 31

שָׂרִיד   2 survivor (4 · 28) 975

הרגיע   to give rest (4 · 8 · 13[?]) 921   II.

מָשַׁךְ   3 to draw out, prolong; draw (2 · 30 · 36) 604

בְּתוּלָה   4 virgin (8 · 50) 143

עָדָה   to deck oneself, ornament (2 · 8 · 8) 725

תֹּף   timbrel, tambourine (1 · 17) 1074

מָחוֹל   dance (2 · 6) 298

שׂחק   to play (3 · 17 · 36) 965

חלל   5 i.e., to begin to use the fruit (>50) 320 Piel 4.

צהל   7 to cry shrilly (3 · 7 · 8) 843

יַרְכָה   8 remote part, side (4 · 28) 438

עִוֵּר   blind (1 · 25) 734

פִּסֵּחַ   lame (1 · 14) 820

הָרָה   pregnant, woman with child (2 · 15) 248 II.

הֵנָּה   hither (4 · 49) 244

בְּכִי   weeping (8 · 30) 113

תַּחֲנוּן   supplication (2 · 18) 337

הוֹבִיל   to lead, conduct; bear along (1 · 7 · 18) 384

אִי   10 coast, border, region, island (4 · 36) 15

מֶרְחָק   distance, distant place (5 · 18) 935

זרה   to scatter, disperse (4 · 25 · 38) 279

עֵדֶר   flock (6 · 39) 727

נהר   12 to flow, stream (1 · 3 · 3[?]) 625

טוּב   good things (3 · 32) 375

דָּגָן   corn, grain (1 · 40) 186

תִּירוֹשׁ   fresh or new wine (1 · 38) 440

יִצְהָר   fresh oil (1 · 23) 844

גַּן   garden (3 · 42) 171

רָוֶה   watered (1 · 3) 924

דָּאַב	to become faint, languish (2 · 3 · 3) 178
בְּתוּלָה 13	virgin (8 · 50) 143
מָחוֹל	dance (2 · 6) 298
בָּחוּר	young man (11 · 45) 104
אֵבֶל	mourning (3 · 24) 5
שָׂשׂוֹן	joy, exultation (7 · 22) 965
יָגוֹן	grief, sorrow (4 · 14) 387
רָוָה 14	to water abundantly, drench (1 · 6 · 14) 924
דֶּשֶׁן	fatness, abundance; ashes mixed w. fat (2 · 15) 206
טוּב	good things (3 · 32) 375
נְהִי 15	lamentation, wailing (5 · 8) 624
בְּכִי	weeping (8 · 30) 113
תַּמְרוּרִים	bitterness (2 · 3) 601
מֵאֵן	to refuse (12 · 46) 549
מָנַע 16	to withhold, hold back (5 · 25 · 29) 586
בְּכִי	weeping (8 · 30) 113
דִּמְעָה	tears (5 · 23) 199
שָׂכָר	hire, wages (1 · 29) 969
פְּעֻלָּה	work (1 · 14) 821
תִּקְוָה 17	hope (2 · 32) 876
הִתְנוֹדֵד 18	to bemoan oneself (2 · 4 · 26) 626
יָסַר	to chasten, chastise (5 · 27 · 38) 415
נוֹסַר	to let oneself be chastened, admonished (2 · 5 · 38) 415
עֵגֶל	calf (4 · 35) 722
סָפַק 19	to slap (1 · 6 · 6) 706
יָרֵךְ	thigh, loin, side (1 · 34) 437
נכלם	to be put to shame, dishonored, humiliated (4 · 26 · 38) 483
נְעוּרִים	youth (7 · 46) 655
יַקִּיר 20	very precious, dear (1 · 1) 430
שַׁעֲשׁוּעִים	delight (1 · 9) 1044
מִדֵּי	as often as (3 · 15) 191 דַּי 2.c.
המה	to murmur, growl, roar (9 · 33 · 33) 242
מעה	inward parts; i.e., compassion; in-

	ternal organs (3 · 32) 589
רָחַם	to have compassion (9 · 41 · 46) 933
צִיּוּן 21	signpost, monument (1 · 3) 846
תַּמְרוּרִים	signposts (1 · 1) 1071
מְסִלָּה	highway (1 · 27) 700
בְּתוּלָה	virgin (8 · 50) 143
מָתַי 22	when? (7 · 42) 607
הִתְחַמֵּק	to turn here and there (1 · 1 · 2) 330
שׁוֹבֵב	backturning, apostate (2 · 3) 1000
בָּרָא	to shape, fashion, create (1 · 38 · 48) 135
נְקֵבָה	woman (1 · 22) 666
שְׁבוּת 23	captivity (12 · 26) 986
נָוֶה	habitation (14 · 45[?]) 627
אִכָּר 24	plowman, husbandman (3 · 7) 38
עֵדֶר	flock (6 · 39) 727
הִרְוָה 25	to cause to drink (1 · 5 · 14) 924
עָיֵף	weary, faint (1 · 17) 746
דָּאַב	to become faint, languish (2 · 3 · 3) 178
הֵקִיץ 26	to awake (3 · 22 · 23) 884
שֵׁנָה	sleep (3 · 23) 446
ערב	to be pleasing, sweet (2 · 8 · 8) 787
שָׁקַד 28	to keep watch, to be wakeful (5 · 11 · 17) 1052
נָתַשׁ	to pull up, pluck up (11 · 16 · 21) 684
נָתַץ	to pull down, break down (6 · 31 · 42) 683
הָרַס	to tear down, throw down (5 · 30 · 43) 248
בֹּסֶר 29	unripe or sour grapes (2 · 5) 126
קהה	to be blunt, dull (2 · 3 · 4) 874
בֹּסֶר 30	unripe or sour grapes (2 · 5) 126
קהה	to be blunt, dull (2 · 3 · 4) 874
הֵפֵר 32	to break, frustrate (4 · 41 · 44[?]) bd 830
בָּעַל	to be lord [over], husband [of] (2 · 10 · 12) 127
קָטָן 34	insignificant (3 · 47) 881

סלח   to forgive, pardon (6 · 33 · 46) 699

יָרֵחַ 35   moon (2 · 27) 437

כּוֹכָב   star (1 · 37) 456

רָגַע   to disturb (1 · 4 · 13[?]) 920

המה   to roar, murmur, growl (9 · 33 · 33) 242

גַּל   wave [of water], billow; heap (4 · 16) 164

מוֹשׁ 36   to depart, be removed (2 · 20 · 20) 559

מִלְמַעְלָה 37   above (1 · 24) 751   מַעַל 2.d.

נֶחְקַר   to be searched out, found (2 · 4 · 27) 350

מוֹסָד   foundation (2 · 13) 414

לְמַטָּה   downward (1 · 10) 641   מִמַּה 2.

מִגְדָּל 38   tower (1 · 49) 153

פִּנָּה   corner (3 · 30) 819

קוה 39   line (1 · 17) 876   קַו

פֶּגֶד 40   corpse, carcass (3 · 22) 803

דֶּשֶׁן   ashes mixed with fat; fatness, abundance (2 · 15) 206

שְׁרֵמָה   field (1 · 6) 995   שְׁדֵמָה

פִּנָּה   corner (3 · 30) 819

נתש   to be rooted up (2 · 4 · 21) 684

נהרס   to be thrown or torn down (2 · 10 · 43) 248

Chapter 32

צור 2   to shut in, besiege (5 · 31 · 31) 848

כלא   to shut up, restrain (2 · 14 · 17) 476

מַטָּרָה   guard, ward, prison (11 · 16) 643

כלא 3   to shut up, restrain (2 · 14 · 17) 476

גְּאֻלָּה 7   right of redemption, redemption (2 · 14) 145

מַטָּרָה 8   guard, ward, prison (11 · 16) 643

יְרֻשָּׁה   possession, inheritance (1 · 14) 440

גְּאֻלָּה   right of redemption, redemption (2 · 14) 145

שָׁקַל 9   to weigh out (2 · 19 · 22) 1053

חתם 10   to seal up, fasten up by sealing (4 · 23 · 27) 367

הֵעִיד   to cause to testify (8 · 39 · 44) 729

שָׁקַל   to weigh out (2 · 19 · 22) 1053

מֹאזְנַיִם   balances, scales (1 · 15) 24

מִקְנָה 11   purchase; w. ספר = document of purchase (5 · 15) 889

חתם   to seal up, fasten up by sealing (4 · 23 · 27) 367

מקנה 12   purchase; cf. vs. 11 (5 · 15) 889

מַטָּרָה   guard, ward, prison (11 · 16) 643

מִקְנָה 14   purchase; cf. vs. 11 (5 · 15) 889

חתם   to seal up, fasten up by sealing (4 · 23 · 27) 367

חֶרֶשׂ   earthenware, earthen vessel (2 · 17) 360

מִקְנָה 16   purchase; cf. vs. 11 (5 · 15) 889

אֲהָהּ 17   Alas! (4 · 15) 13

נפלא   to be too difficult for (2 · 13 · 24) 810

חֵיק 18   bosom, fold of garment at breast (1 · 38) 300

עֲלִילִיָּה 19   deed (1 · 1) 760

פָּקַח   to open (1 · 17 · 20) 824

מַעֲלָל   practice, deed (17 · 41) 760

מוֹפֵת 20   wonder, sign, token (2 · 36) 68

מוֹפֵת 21   wonder, sign, token (2 · 36) 68

אֶזְרוֹעַ   arm (1 · 2) 284

מוֹרָא   awe-inspiring spectacle or deed (1 · 12) 432

זוּב 22   to flow (3 · 29 · 29) 264

חלב   milk (2 · 44) 316

סֹלְלָה 24   mound (3 · 11) 700

דֶּבֶר   plague, pestilence (17 · 46) 184

הֵעִיר 25   to cause to testify (8 · 39 · 44) 729

נפלא 27   to be too difficult for (2 · 13 · 24) 810

הִצִּית 29   to kindle, set on fire (8 · 17 · 27) 428

גָּג   roof, top (3 · 29) 150

הִסִּיךְ   to pour out libations (8 · 14 · 25) 650   נסך

נְעוּרִים 30 youth (8 · 46) 655

לְמִן 31 from (4 · 14) 577 מִן 9.b.

עֹרֶף 33 neck (7 · 33) 791

מוּסָר discipline, correction, chastisement
(8 · 50) 416

שִׁקּוּץ 34 detested thing (5 · 28) 1055

דֶּבֶר 36 plague, pestilence (17 · 46) 184

הִדִּיחַ 37 to thrust out, banish (13 · 27 · 43)
623

קֶצֶף wrath (4 · 29) 893

בֶּטַח security, as adv. = securely
(5 · 43) 105

יִרְאָה 40 reverence, fear (1 · 45) 432

שׂוּשׂ 41 to exult, rejoice (1 · 26 · 26) 965

מֵאֵין 43 without (20 · 48[?]) 34 אַיִן 6.d.

חתם 44 to seal up, fasten up by sealing
(4 · 23 · 27) 367

הֵעִיד to cause to testify (8 · 39 · 44)
729

שְׁפֵלָה lowland (3 · 20) 1050

שְׁבוּת captivity (12 · 26) 986

Chapter 33

עָצַר 1 to shut up (4 · 36 · 46) 783

מַטָּרָה guard, prison, ward (11 · 16) 643

יָצַר 2 to devise, plan; to form (4 · 41 · 44)
427

בָּצוּר 3 secret things; elsewhere = cut off,
made inaccessible (2 · 25) 130 בצר

נתץ 4 to pull down, break down
(6 · 31 · 42) 683

סֹלְלָה mound (3 · 11) 700

פֶּגֶר 5 corpse, carcass (3 · 22) 803

מַרְפֵּא 6 healing, cure (4 · 13) 951

אֲרוּכָה healing, restoration (3 · 6) 74

עֲתֶרֶת abundance (1 · 1) 801

שְׁבוּת 7 captivity (12 · 26) 986

סלח 8 to forgive, pardon (6 · 33 · 46) 699

פָּשַׁע to transgress (4 · 40 · 41) 833

שָׂשׂוֹן 9 joy, exultation (7 · 22) 965

פָּחַד to be in dread (3 · 23 · 26) 808

רגז to quake (1 · 30 · 41) 919

חָרֵב 10 waste, desolate (2 · 10) 351

מֵאֵין without (20 · 48[?]) 34 אַיִן 6.d.

שָׂשׂוֹן 11 joy, exultation (7 · 22) 965

חָתָן bridegroom (4 · 20) 368

כַּלָּה bride; daughter-in-law (5 · 34) 483

תּוֹדָה sacrifice of thanksgiving (3 · 32) 392

שְׁבוּת captivity (12 · 26) 986

חָרֵב 12 waste, desolate (2 · 10) 351

מֵאֵין without (20 · 48[?]) 34 אַיִן 6.d.

נָוֶה abode of shepherds (14 · 45[?]) 627

הִרְבִּיץ to cause to lie down (1 · 6 · 30) 918

שְׁפֵלָה 13 lowland (3 · 20) 1050

מָנָה to count, number (1 · 12 · 28) 584

הִצְמִיחַ 15 to cause to grow (1 · 14 · 33) 855

צֶמַח growth, sprout (2 · 12) 855

בֶּטַח 16 security; as adv. = securely
(5 · 43) 105

הֵפֵר 20 to break, frustrate (4 · 41 · 44[?]) 830

הֻפַר 21 to be broken (1 · 3 · 44[?]) 830

מְשָׁרֵת minister, ministering (1 · 20) 1058
שׁרת

חוֹל 22 sand (3 · 22) 297

נאץ 24 to contemn, spurn (2 · 8 · 24) 610

מֹשֵׁל 26 ruling, ruler (4 · 24) 605 III. מָשַׁל

שְׁבוּת captivity (12 · 26) 986

רִחַם to have compassion (9 · 41 · 46) 933

Chapter 34

מֶמְשָׁלָה 1 dominion, rule (2 · 17) 606

מַשְׂרֵפָה 5 burning (1 · 2) 977

ספד to wail, lament (7 · 28 · 30) 704

מבצר 7 fortification (7 · 37) 131

דְּרוֹר 8 liberty; w. קרא, to proclaim liberty
(4 · 7) 204

חָפְשִׁי 9 free [from slavery] (5 · 17) 344

חָפְשִׁי 10 free [from slavery] (5 · 17) 344

302

חָפְשִׁי 11 free [from slavery] (5 · 17) 344

כבש to bring into bondage (2 · 8 · 14) 461

חָפְשִׁי 14 free [from slavery] (5 · 17) 344

דְּרוֹר 15 liberty; w. קרא, to proclaim liberty (4 · 7) 204

חָפְשִׁי 16 free [from slavery] (5 · 17) 344

כבש to bring into bondage (2 · 8 · 14) 461

דְּרוֹר 17 liberty; w. קרא, = to proclaim liberty (4 · 7) 204

דֶּבֶר plague, pestilence (17 · 46) 184

זְוָעָה object of trembling, terror (K 4 · 4) (Q 4 · 7) 266

עֵגֶל 18 calf (4 · 35) 722

בֶּתֶר part, piece (2 · 3) 144

סָרִיס 19 eunuch (7 · 45) 710

בֶּתֶר part, piece (2 · 3) 144

עֵגֶל calf (4 · 35) 722

נְבֵלָה 20 carcass, corpse (8 · 48) 615

מַאֲכָל food (4 · 30) 38

מֵאֵין 22 without (20 · 48[?]) 34 אֵין 6.d.

Chapter 35

לִשְׁכָּה 2 chamber, room (8 · 47) 545

לִשְׁכָּה 4 chamber, room (8 · 47) 545

מִמַּעַל above, on the top of (4 · 29) 751 II. מַעַל

סַף threshold; שֹׁמֵר הַסַּף = doorkeeper (2 · 25) 706 II.

גָּבִיעַ 5 bowl, cup (1 · 14) 149

כּוֹס cup (7 · 31) 468

מוּסָר 13 discipline, correction, chastisement (8 · 50) 416

מַעֲלָל 15 practice, deed (17 · 41) 760

Chapter 36

מְגִלָּה 2 roll (14 · 21) 166

אוּלַי 3 perhaps (6 · 45) 19

סלח to forgive, pardon (6 · 33 · 46) 699

מְגִלָּה 4 roll (14 · 21) 166

עָצַר 5 to shut up (4 · 36 · 46) 783

מְגִלָּה 6 roll (14 · 21) 166

צוֹם fast, fasting (2 · 25) 847

אוּלַי 7 perhaps (6 · 45) 19

תְּחִנָּה supplication for favor (5 · 25) 337

צוֹם 9 fast, fasting (2 · 25) 847

לִשְׁכָּה 10 chamber, room (8 · 47) 545

לִשְׁכָּה 12 chamber, room (8 · 47) 545

מְגִלָּה 14 roll (14 · 21) 166

פָּחַד 16 to be in dread (3 · 23 · 26) 808

דְּיוֹ 18 ink (1 · 1) 188

אֵיפֹה 19 where? (2 · 10) 33

מְגִלָּה 20 roll (14 · 21) 166

לִשְׁכָּה chamber, room (8 · 47) 545

מְגִלָּה 21 roll (14 · 21) 166

לִשְׁכָּה chamber, room (8 · 47) 545

חֹרֶף 22 autumn; w. בית = autumn house, palace (1 · 7) 358

אָח brazier, firepot (3 · 3) 28

דֶּלֶת fig. for column of MS (>50) 195 4.

תַּעַר 23 razor (2 · 13) 789

אָח brazier, firepot (3 · 3) 28

מְגִלָּה roll (14 · 21) 166

פָּחַד 24 to be in dread; w. אל = to turn in dread (3 · 23 · 26) 808

הִפְגִּיעַ 25 to make entreaty (2 · 6 · 46)

מְגִלָּה roll (14 · 21) 166

מְגִלָּה 27 roll (14 · 21) 166

מְגִלָּה 28 roll (14 · 21) 166

מְגִלָּה 29 roll (14 · 21) 166

נְבֵלָה 30 carcass, corpse (8 · 48) 615

חֹרֶב parching heat (3 · 16) 351

קֶרַח frost (1 · 7) 901

מְגִלָּה 32 roll (14 · 21) 166

Chapter 37

כְּלִיא 4 confinement, imprisonment (2 · 2)
כלוא 476

צוּר 5 to shut in, besiege (5 · 31 · 31) 848

שֶׁמַע report, hearing (2 · 17) 1034

עֶזְרָה 7 help (1 · 26) 740

הִשִּׁיא 9 to beguile (5 · 15 · 16) 674

דִּקֻר 10 ptc. = pierced, riddled (2 · 3 · 11) 201

עַם 12 kinsman (1 · 34) 769

פְּקֻדַת 13 sentinel, oversight (1 · 1) 824

קָצַף 15 to be wroth (1 · 28 · 34) 893

אֵסוּר band, bond; w. בֵּית = prison (1 · 3) 64

כֶּלֶא confinement, restraint, imprisonment (3 · 10) 476

חָנוּת 16 cell (1 · 1) 333

סֵתֶר 17 secretly; 'בַּס = in secrecy (3 · 35) 712

כֶּלֶא 18 confinement, restraint, imprisonment (3 · 10) 476

אַיֵּו 19 where? (6 · 44) 32 אַיֵּה

תְּחִנָּה 20 supplication for favor (5 · 23) 337

מַטָּרָה 21 guard, ward, prison (11 · 16) 643

אֹפֶה baker (1 · 12) 66 אָפָה

Chapter 38

דֶּבֶר 2 plague, pestilence (17 · 46) 184

רָפָה 4 to enfeeble, dishearten (1 · 5 · 45) 951

מַטָּרָה 6 guard, ward, prison (11 · 16) 643

חֶבֶל cord, rope (4 · 49) 286

טִיט mud, mire (2 · 13) 376

טָבַע to sink down (1 · 6 · 10) 371

סָרִיס 7 eunuch (7 · 45) 710

בְּטֶרֶם 10 before (6 · 39) 382 טֶרֶם

בְּלוֹא 11 worn out thing, rag; pl. cs. בְּלוֹי (3 · 3) 115

סְחָבָה rag, clout (2 · 2) 695

מֶלַח rag (2 · 2) 571

חֶבֶל cord, rope (4 · 49) 286

בְּלוֹא 12 worn out thing, rag (3 · 3) 115

סְחָבָה rag, clout (2 · 2) 695

מֶלַח rag (2 · 2) 571

אַצִּיל joint, joining (1 · 3) 69

חֶבֶל cord, rope (4 · 49) 286

מָשַׁד 13 to draw, drag (2 · 30 · 36) 604

חֶבֶל cord, rope (4 · 49) 286

מַטָּרָה guard, ward, prison (11 · 16) 643

מָבוֹא 14 entrance, a coming in (1 · 23) 99

כָּחַד to hide, conceal (3 · 15 · 32) 470

סֵתֶר 16 secretly; 'בַּס = in secrecy (3 · 35) 712

דָּאַג 19 to fear, dread, be anxious (3 · 7 · 7) 178

הִתְעַלֵּל to deal wantonly, ruthlessly (1 · 7 · 17) 759

לַאֲשֶׁר 20 in what (3 · 38) 81 אֲשֶׁר

מֵאֵן 21 to refuse (12 · 46) 549

הֵסִית 22 to instigate, incite, allure (2 · 18 · 18) 694 סות

הָטְבַּע to be sunk (1 · 3 · 10) 371

בֹּץ mire (1 · 1) 130

נָסוֹג to turn oneself away, turn back; fig. = prove faithless (2 · 14 · 25) 690

אָחוֹר backwards (4 · 41) 30

כָּחַד 25 to hide, conceal (3 · 15 · 32) 470

תְּחִנָּה 26 supplication for favor (5 · 25) 337

הֶחֱרִישׁ 27 to cease to speak (2 · 38 · 46) 361

מַטָּרָה 28 guard, ward, prison (11 · 16) 643

Chapter 39

צוּר 1 to shut in, besiege (5 · 31 · 31) 848

סָרִיס 3 eunuch (7 · 45) 710

רַב־מָג chief soothsayer (2 · 2) 913 II. רַב

גַּן 4 garden (3 · 42) 171

304

הִשִּׂיג 5 to overtake (3 · 49 · 49) 673

חֹר 6 noble (2 · 13) 359

עִוֵּר 7 to blind (2 · 5 · 5) 734

נָתַץ 8 to pull down, break down (6 · 31 · 42) 683

טַבָּח 9 bodyguard (17 · 32) 371

דַּל 10 reduced, poor, low (2 · 48) 195

מְאוּמָה anything (2 · 32) 548

טַבָּח bodyguard (17 · 32) 371

יָגֵב field (1 · 1) 387

טַבָּח 11 bodyguard (10 · 32) 371

מְאוּמָה 12 anything (2 · 32) 548

טַבָּח 13 bodyguard (17 · 32) 371

סָרִיס eunuch (7 · 45) 710

רַב־מָג chief soothsayer (2 · 2) 913 II. רב

מַטָּרָה 14 guard, ward, prison (11 · 16) 643

עָצַר 15 to shut up (4 · 36 · 46) 783

מַטָּרָה guard, ward, prison (11 · 16) 643

מֵבִי 16 K. for מֵבִיא 97 בוא Hiph.

יָגוֹר 17 fearing (2 · 2) 388

Chapter 40

טַבָּח 1 bodyguard (17 · 32) 371

אֵזֶק manacle [fetter] (2 · 2) 279

גָּלוּת exile; [coll.] exiles (5 · 15) 163

טַבָּח 2 bodyguard (17 · 32) 371

אֵזֶק 4 manacle [fetter] (2 · 2) 279

טַבָּח 5 bodyguard (17 · 32) 371

אֲרֻחָה meal, allowance [of food] (3 · 7) 73

מַשְׂאֵת present, portion, uplifting (2 · 16) 673

טַף 7 children, little ones (3 · 42) 381

דַּלָּה the poor (3 · 5) 195

מֵאֲשֶׁר who (1 · 17) 84

קַיִץ 10 summer fruit (4 · 20) 884

נדח 12 to be thrust out, banished (4 · 13 · 43) 623

קַיִץ summer fruit (4 · 20) 884

סֵתֶר 15 secretly; בַּסֵּ׳ = in secrecy (3 · 35) 712

Chapter 41

מְלוּכָה 1 kingship, royalty (1 · 24) 574

גֻּלַּח 5 to be shaven (1 · 3 · 23) 164

זָקָן beard (2 · 19) 278

התגדד to cut oneself [in relig. practice]; to gather in troops or bands (4 · 7 · 8) 151

לְבוֹנָה frankincense (3 · 21) 526

פגש 6 to meet, encounter (1 · 10 · 14) 803

מַטְמוֹן 8 hidden treasure, treasure (1 · 5) 380

חִטָּה wheat (2 · 30) 334

שְׂעֹרָה barley (1 · 34) 972

פֶּגֶר 9 corpse, carcass (3 · 22) 803

שָׁבָה 10 to take captive (4 · 29 · 37) 985

טַבָּח bodyguard (17 · 32) 371

שָׁבָה to take captive (4 · 29 · 37) 985

שָׁבָה 14 to take captive (4 · 29 · 37) 985

טַף 16 children, little ones (3 · 42) 381

סָרִיס eunuch (7 · 45) 710

גֵּרוּת 17 lodging place, inn (1 · 1) 158

Chapter 42

תְּחִנָּה 2 supplication for favor (5 · 25) 337

מָנַע 4 to withhold, hold back (5 · 25 · 29) 586

תְּחִנָּה 9 supplication for favor (5 · 25) 337

הָרַס 10 to tear, throw down (5 · 30 · 43) 248

נָתַשׁ to pull up, pluck up (11 · 16 · 21) 684

רַחֲמִים 12 compassion (2 · 38) 933

רחם to have compassion (9 · 41 · 46) 933

רָעֵב 14 to be hungry (1 · 12 · 14) 944

הִשִּׂיג 16 to overtake (3 · 49 · 49) 673

דאג to be anxious, concerned (3 · 7 · 7) 178

דֶּבֶר 17 plague, pestilence (17 · 46) 184

שָׂרִיד		survivor (4 · 28) 975
פָּלִיט		fugitive (3 · 19) 812
נִתַּךְ	18	to be poured out (2 · 8 · 21) 677
נתך		to pour forth (2 · 7 · 21) 677
אָלָה		execration, curse, oath (4 · 36) 46
שַׁמָּה		horror, an appalling thing (24 · 39) 1031
קְלָלָה		curse (9 · 33) 887
הֵעִיד	19	to protest, warn (8 · 39 · 44) 729 עוד
הִתְעָה	20	w. בְּ = to err at cost of (4 · 21 · 50) 1073
דֶּבֶר	22	plague, pestilence (17 · 46) 184

Chapter 43

זֵד	2	insolent, presumptuous (1 · 13) 267
הֵסִית	3	to instigate (2 · 18 · 18) 694
נדח	5	to be thrust out, banished (4 · 13 · 43) 623
טַף	6	children, little ones (3 · 42) 381
טַבָּח		bodyguard (17 · 32) 371
טָמַן	9	to hide, conceal (7 · 28 · 31) 380
מֶלֶט		mortar, cement (1 · 1) 572
מַלְבֵּן		quadrangle; brick mold (1 · 3) 527
מִמַּעַל	10	above, on the top of (4 · 29) 751 II. מַעַל
טָמַן		to hide, conceal (7 · 28 · 31) 380
שַׁפְרִיר		[dub.] carpet, splendor; pavilion, canopy (1 · 1) 1051
שְׁבִי	11	captivity (8 · 46) 985
הִצִּית	12	to kindle, set on fire (8 · 17 · 27) 428
שָׁבָה		to take captive (4 · 29 · 37) 985
עטה		to grasp (2 · 44) 742
מַצֵּבָה	13	pillar, sacred pillar, stump (1 · 36) 663

Chapter 44

חָרְבָּה	2	waste, ruin (10 · 42) 352
נתך	6	to pour forth (2 · 7 · 21) 677

חָרְבָּה		waste, ruin (10 · 42) 352
עוֹלֵל	7	child (1 · 11) 760
יוֹנֵק		suckling, babe (1 · 11) 413 ינק
קְלָלָה	8	curse (9 · 33) 887
דכא	10	to be crushed; to be made humble, contrite (1 · 4 · 18) 193
אָלָה	12	execration, curse, oath (4 · 36) 46
שַׁמָּה		horror, an appalling thing (24 · 39) 1031
קְלָלָה		curse (9 · 33) 887
דֶּבֶר	13	plague, pestilence (17 · 46) 184
פָּלִיט	14	fugitive (3 · 19) 812
שָׂרִיד		survivor (4 · 28) 975
פָּלִיט		escaped one, fugitive (3 · 5) 812
מְלֶכֶת	17	queen (5 · 5) 573
הִסִּיךְ		to pour out (8 · 14 · 25) 650 I. נסך
מְלֶכֶת	18	queen (5 · 5) 573
הִסִּיךְ		to pour out (8 · 14 · 25) 650 I. נסך
חָסֵר		to lack, need (1 · 19 · 23) 341
מְלֶכֶת	19	queen (5 · 5) 573
הִסִּיךְ		to pour out (8 · 14 · 25) 650 I. נסך
מִבַּלְעֲדֵי		without, apart from (1 · 12) 116 בִּלְעֲדֵי
כַּוָּן		cake, sacrificial cake (2 · 2) 467
הֶעֱצִיב		to shape, fashion (1 · 1 · 2) 781
קְטֹר	21	incense (1 · 1) 883
רֹעַ	22	evil, badness (11 · 19) 947
מַעֲלָל		practice, deed (17 · 41) 760
חָרְבָּה		waste, desolation (10 · 42) 352
שַׁמָּה		appalling waste (24 · 39) 1031
קְלָלָה		curse (9 · 33) 887
מֵאֵין		without (20 · 48[?]) 34 אַיִן 6.d.
נָדַר	25	to vow (1 · 30) 623
מְלֶכֶת		queen (5 · 5) 573
הִסִּיךְ		to pour out (8 · 14 · 25) 650 I. נסך
שָׁקַד	27	to keep watch, be wakeful (5 · 11 · 16) 1052
פָּלִיט	28	fugitive (3 · 19) 812
מַת		male, man (1 · 22) 607

306

Chapter 45

אוֹי 3 Woe! Alas! (8 · 25) 17

יָגוֹן grief, sorrow (4 · 14) 387

מַכְאוֹב pain (3 · 16) 456

יגע to grow or be weary (2 · 20 · 26) 388

אנחה sighing, groaning (1 · 11) 58

מְנוּחָה rest, resting-place (2 · 21) 629

הָרַס 4 to tear down, throw down (5 · 30 · 43) 248

נָתַשׁ to pull up, pluck up (11 · 16 · 21) 684

Chapter 46

צִנָּה 3 large shield (1 · 20) 857

הִתְיַצֵּב 4 to station oneself, take one's stand (2 · 48 · 48) 426

כּוֹבַע helmet (1 · 6) 464

מרק to polish, scour (1 · 2 · 4) 599

רֹמַח spear, lance (1 · 15) 942

סִרְיֹן armor (2 · 2) 710

חַת 5 dismayed (1 · 4) 369

נָסוֹג to be turned or driven back, be repulsed (2 · 14 · 25) 690

אָחוֹר backwards (4 · 41) 30

הֻכַּתת Hoph. to be crushed (1 · 4 · 17) 510

מָנוֹס flight; refuge, place of escape (3 · 8) 631

מָגוֹר fear, terror (6 · 8) 159

קַל 6 swift, fleet (2 · 13) 886

הִתְגַּעֵשׁ 7 to shake back and forth, toss or reel to and fro (2 · 5 · 10) 172

הִתְגַּעֵשׁ 8 to shake back and forth, toss or reel to and fro (2 · 2 · 10) 172

הִתְהֹלֵל 9 to act like a madman (4 · 6 · 14) 237 II.

נְקָמָה 10 vengeance (11 · 27) 668

נקם to avenge oneself (3 · 12 · 35) 667

רוח to be saturated, take one's fill (1 · 3 · 14) 924

צֳרִי 11 a kind of balsam [used as medicine] (3 · 6) 863

בְּתוּלָה virgin (8 · 50) 143

רְפֻאָה remedy, medicine (2 · 3) 951

תְּעָלָה healing (2 · 2) 752

קָלוֹן 12 ignominy, dishonor (2 · 17) 885

צְוָחָה outcry (2 · 4) 846

הִתְיַצֵּב 14 to station oneself, take one's stand (2 · 48 · 48) 426

נִסְחַף 15 to be prostrate, (1 · 1 · 2) 695

אַבִּיר mighty, valiant (4 · 17) 7

הדף to thrust out, drive out, push (1 · 11 · 11) 213

מוֹלֶדֶת 16 kindred, birth, offspring (2 · 22) 409

ינה ptc. = oppressor (3 · 4 · 18) 413

שָׁאוֹן 17 roar, din (4 · 17) 981

גּוֹלָה 19 exile; [coll.] exiles (10 · 42) 163

שַׁמָּה waste (24 · 39) 1031

נצת to be desolated, burned (2 · 4 · 5[?]) 428 יצת Niph.

מֵאֵין without (20 · 48[?]) 34 אֵין 6.d.

עֶגְלָה 20 heifer (2 · 12) 722

יְפֵה־פִיָּה pretty (1 · 1) 421

קֶרֶץ [dub.] gadfly (1 · 1) 903

שָׂכִיר 21 hireling, hired laborer (1 · 18) 969

עֵגֶל calf (4 · 35) 722

מַרְבֵּק stall; w. עגל = fatted [stall-fed] calf (1 · 4) 918

אֵיד distress, calamity (5 · 24) 15

פְּקֻדָּה visitation (9 · 32) 824

נָחָשׁ 22 serpent (2 · 31) 638 I.

קַרְדֹּם axe (1 · 5) 899

חֹטֵב cutter; ח׳ עֵץ = wood cutter (1 · 6) 310 I. חטב

נֶחְקַר 23 to be searched out, found out, ascertained (2 · 4 · 27) 350

רבב to be, become many (3 · 23 · 24) 912

אַרְבֶּה   locust (1 · 24) 916

שְׁבִי   27 captivity (8 · 46) 985

שָׁקַט   to be undisturbed, quiet (5 · 31 · 41) 1052

שַׁאֲנַן   to be at ease, secure (3 · 5) 983

הֶחֱרִיד   to terrify, drive in terror (3 · 16 · 39) 353

כָּלָה   28 complete destruction, annihilation (7 · 22) 478

הִדִּיחַ   to thrust out, banish (13 · 27 · 43) 623

יִסַּר   to chasten, chastise (5 · 27 · 38) 415

נקה   to leave unpunished (4 · 18 · 43) 667

אָנָה   6 where? עַד אָנָ׳ = how long? (2 · 39)

אָן   33

שָׁקַט   to be quiet, inactive (5 · 31 · 41) 1052

תַּעַר   sheath (2 · 13) 789

נרגע   to repose, be at rest (1 · 1 · 13[?]) 921

דמם   to be still, motionless, stand still (3 · 23 · 30) 198

שָׁקַט   7 to be quiet, inactive (5 · 31 · 41) 1052

חוֹף   shore, coast (1 · 7) 342

יָעַד   to appoint (1 · 5 · 28) 416

Chapter 47

בְּטֶרֶם   1 before (6 · 39) 382   טֶרֶם

שָׁטַף   2 to overflow, rinse or wash off (3 · 28 · 31) 1009

מְלוֹא   that which fills, entire contents (2 · 38) 571

הֵילִל   to give a howl (8 · 30 · 30) 410

שַׁעֲטָה   3 stamping (1 · 1) 1043

פַּרְסָה   hoof (1 · 21) 828

אַבִּיר   mighty, valiant [here of horses] (4 · 17) 7

רַעַשׁ   earthquake (2 · 17) 950

גִּלְגַּל   wheel (1 · 11) 165

רִפָּיוֹן   sinking (1 · 1) 952

שָׂרִיד   4 survivor (4 · 28) 975

עֹזֵר   helper (1 · 19[?]) 740   I. עזר

אִי   coast, border, region (4 · 36) 15

קָרְחָה   5 baldness (2 · 11) 901

נִדְמָה   to be cut off, destroyed, ruined (1 · 12 · 16) 198

מָתַי   when[?] עַד מָ׳ = how long[?] (7 · 42) 607

הִתְגֹּדֵד   to cut oneself [as relig. practice]; to gather in troops or bands (4 · 7 · 8) 151

Chapter 48

מִשְׂגָּב   1 stronghold, refuge (1 · 17) 960 I. & II.

דמם   2 to be still, silent (3 · 23 · 30) 198

צְעָקָה   3 cry of distress (4 · 21) 858

שֹׁד   devastation, ruin (3 · 25) 994

שֶׁבֶר   shattering (15 · 45) 991

זְעָקָה   4 cry of distress (6 · 18) 277

צָעִיר   young (4 · 22) 859

מַעֲלֶה   5 ascent, stairs (1 · 19) 751

בְּכִי   weeping (8 · 30) 113

מוֹרָד   descent, slope (1 · 5) 434

צְעָקָה   cry of distress (4 · 21) 858

שֶׁבֶר   shattering (15 · 45) 991

עֲרוֹעֵר   6 tree, bush; perh. juniper (1 · 1) 792

בֶּטַח   7 security (5 · 43) 105

גּוֹלָה   exile; [coll.] exiles (10 · 42) 163

יַחַד   together, altogether (1 · 44) 403   יַחְדָּו

מִישׁוֹר   8 tableland, level country (3 · 23) 449

צִיץ   9 [dub.] [coll.] wings (1 · 15) 851 II.

נצא   to fly (1 · 1 · 1) 661

שַׁמָּה   waste (24 · 39) 1031

מֵאֵין   without (20 · 48[?]) 34   אַיִן 6.d.

רְמִיָּה   10 deceit, treachery (1 · 15) 941

מָנַע   to withhold, hold back (5 · 25 · 29) 586

שַׁאֲנָן	11	at ease, secure (3 · 5) 983
נְעוּרִים		youth (7 · 46) 655
שָׁקַט		to be undisturbed, quiet (5 · 31 · 41) 1052
שֶׁמֶר		lees, dregs (1 · 5) 1038
הוּרַק		to be emptied out (1 · 2 · 19) 937
גּוֹלָה		exile; [coll.] exiles (10 · 42) 163
טַעַם		taste, discernment (1 · 13) 381
נָמַר		to be changed (1 · 1 · 14) 558 מור
צֹעֶה	12	ptc. pl. = tippers (2 · 4 · 5) 858
צעה		to tip over (1 · 1 · 5) 858
הֵרִיק		to empty (1 · 17 · 19) 937
נֵבֶל		jar, pitcher (3 · 11) 614
נֶפֶץ		to dash to pieces (11 · 15 · 21) 658
מִבְטָח	13	confidence, object of confidence (3 · 15) 105
מִבְחָר	15	choicest, best (2 · 12) 104
בָּחוּר		young man (11 · 45) 104
טֶבַח		a slaughter, slaughtering (2 · 12) 370
אֵיד	16	distress, calamity (5 · 24) 15
נָד	17	to lament, show grief (8 · 19 · 26) 626 נוד
אֵיכָה		how! (2 · 18) 32
מַקֵּל		rod, stick, staff (2 · 18) 596
צָמָא	18	thirst (1 · 17) 854
מִבְצָר		fortress, stronghold (7 · 37) 131
צִפָּה	19	to watch, look (1 · 9 · 18) 859
הֵילִיל	20	to give a howl (8 · 30 · 30) 410
מִישׁוֹר	21	tableland, level country (3 · 23) 449
נִגְדַּע	25	to be hewn off (2 · 7 · 22) 154
הִשְׁכִּיר	26	to make drunken (5 · 6 · 20) 1016
סָפַק		to splash; i.e., to fall with a splash (1 · 1 · 1[?]) 706
קִיא		vomit (1 · 3) 883
שְׂחֹק		derision (4 · 15) 966
שְׂחֹק	27	derision (4 · 15) 966
גַּנָּב		thief (3 · 17) 170
מִדֵּי		as often as (3 · 15) 191 דֵּי 2.c.
הִתְנוֹדֵד		to shake oneself (2 · 4 · 26) 626

יוֹנָה	28	dove (1 · 33) 401
קִנֵּן		to make a nest (1 · 4 · 5) 890
פַּחַת		pit (4 · 10) 809
גָּאוֹן	29	pride, majesty, excellence (7 · 49) 144
גֵּאֶה		proud (1 · 8) 144
גֹּבַהּ		haughtiness, height (1 · 17) 147
גַּאֲוָה		majesty, pride (1 · 19) 144
רֻם		height, loftiness (1 · 6) 927
עֶבְרָה	30	arrogance (2 · 34) 720
בַּד		empty talker, prater; empty talk (2 · 6) 95
כֵּן		veritable, true, honest, right (4 · 24) 467
הֵילִיל	31	to give a howl (8 · 30 · 30) 410
הָגָה		to groan, moan (1 · 23 · 25) 211
בְּכִי	32	weeping (8 · 30) 113
נְטִישָׁה		twig, tendril (2 · 3) 644
קַיִץ		summer fruit (4 · 20) 884
בָּצִיר		vintage (1 · 7) 131
גִּיל	33	rejoicing (1 · 8) 162
כַּרְמֶל		garden land (3 · 14) 502
יֶקֶב		winepress, wine vat (1 · 16) 428
הֵידָד		shout, shouting, cheer (5 · 7) 212
זְעָקָה	34	cry of distress (6 · 18) 277
מְשַׁמָּה		devastation, waste (1 · 7) 1031
חָלִיל	36	flute, pipe (2 · 6) 319
הָמָה		to murmur, roar, growl (9 · 33 · 33) 242
יִתְרָה		abundance, riches (1 · 2) 452
קָרְחָה	37	baldness, bald spot (2 · 11) 901
זָקָן		beard (2 · 19) 278
גָּרַע		to diminish, clip (2 · 14 · 22) 175
גְּדֻדָה		cutting; furrow (1[?] · 1[?]) 151
מָתְנַיִם		loins (6 · 47) 608
שַׂק		sackcloth (4 · 48) 974
גָּג	38	roof, top (3 · 29) 150
רְחוֹב		broad open place (5 · 43) 932
מִסְפֵּד		wailing (2 · 16) 704
חֵפֶץ		pleasure, delight (2 · 39) 343

הֵילִל 39 to give a howl (8 · 30 · 30) 410

עֹרֶף neck (7 · 33) 791

שְׂחֹק derision (4 · 15) 966

מְחִתָּה terror, object of terror; ruin (2 · 11) 369

נֶשֶׁר 40 eagle, vulture (4 · 26) 676

דאה to fly swiftly, dart (2 · 4 · 4) 178

קִרְיָה 41 town, city (2 · 30) 900

מְצָד stronghold, mountain fastness (2 · 11) 844

מְצָרָה *Hiph.* ptc. of צרר (>50) 864

פַּחַד 43 dread (4 · 49) 808

פַּחַת pit (4 · 10) 809

פַּח bird trap (3 · 25) 809

הַנִּיס 44 Q הֵנַס (>50) 630 נוס

פַּחַד dread (4 · 49) 808

פַּחַת pit (4 · 10) 809

פַּח bird trap (3 · 25) 809

פְּקֻדָּה visitation (9 · 32) 824

לֶחָבָה 45 flame (1 · 19) 529

מִבֵּין from the midst (1 · 21) 107 בֵּין 2.d.

פֵּאָה temples [of lead] (>50) 802

קָדְקֹד hairy crown, scalp (2 · 11) 869

שָׁאוֹן roar, din (4 · 17) 981

אוֹי 46 Woe! Alas! (8 · 25) 17

שְׁבִי captivity (8 · 46) 985

שִׁבְיָה captivity (1 · 9) 986

שְׁבוּת 47 captivity (12 · 26) 986

הֵנָּה hither; 'עַד ה = to this point (4 · 49) 244

Chapter 49

יוֹרֵשׁ 1 heir, inheritor (3 · 5) 439 יָרַשׁ

תְּרוּעָה 2 alarm, war cry (3 · 36) 929

תֵּל mound (2 · 5) 1068

בָּנוֹת villages (>50) 123 I. בַּת

יצת to be kindled (2 · 4 · 27) 428

יוֹרֵשׁ heir, inheritor, possessor (3 · 5) 439 יָרַשׁ

הֵילִל 3 to give a howl (8 · 30 · 30) 410

חגר to gird on, bind on (3 · 44 · 44) 291

שַׂק sackcloth (4 · 48) 974

ספד to wail, lament (7 · 28 · 30) 704

התשוטט to run to and fro (1 · 5 · 13) 1001

גְּדֵרָה wall, hedge (1 · 8) 155

גּוֹלָה exile; [coll.] exiles (10 · 42) 163

זוב 4 to flow (3 · 29 · 29) 264

שׁוֹבֵב backturning; apostate (2 · 3) 1000

פַּחַד 5 dread (4 · 49) 808

נדח to be thrust out, banished (4 · 13 · 43) 623

נדד to retreat, flee (3 · 21 · 24) 622

שְׁבוּת 6 captivity (12 · 26) 986

נסרח 7 to be let loose (1 · 1 · 4) 710

הֶעְמִיק 8 to make deep (2 · 8 · 9) 770

אֵיד distress, calamity (5 · 24) 15

בצר 9 to cut off, gather grapes (2 · 7 · 7) 130

עֹלֵלוֹת gleaning (1 · 6) 760

גַּנָּב thief (3 · 17) 170

דַּי sufficiency, enough (1 · 12) 191

חָשַׂף 10 to strip off, make bare (2 · 10 · 10) 362

מִסְתָּר hiding place, secret place (3 · 10) 712

נֶחְבָּה to withdraw, hide oneself (1 · 3 · 4) 285

שָׁכֵן neighbor (5 · 20) 1015

יָתוֹם 11 orphan (4 · 42) 450

כּוֹס 12 cup (7 · 31) 468

נקה to be empty, clean (1 · 1 · 43) 667

נקה to be free, exempt from punishment (6 · 24 · 43) 667

שַׁמָּה 13 horror, an appalling thing (24 · 39) 1031

חֹרֶב desolation (3 · 16) 351

קְלָלָה curse (9 · 33) 887

חָרְבָּה ruin, desolation (10 · 42) 352

שְׁמוּעָה 14 report (6 · 27) 1035

310

צִיר	envoy (1 · 6) 851
בָּזָה	15 to despise, regard with contempt (1 · 31 · 42) 102
תִּפְלֶצֶת	16 shuddering, horror (1 · 1) 814
הִשִּׁיא	to beguile (5 · 15 · 16) 674
זָדוֹן	insolence, presumptuousness (3 · 10) 268
חֲגוּ	retreat, place of concealment (1 · 3) 291
הגבה	to make high, exalt (1 · 10 · 34) 146
נֶשֶׁר	vulture, eagle (4 · 26) 676
קֵן	nest (1 · 13) 890
שַׁמָּה	17 horror, an appalling thing (24 · 39) 1031
שָׁרַק	to hiss (3 · 12 · 12) 1056
מַכָּה	wound, blow (10 · 48) 646
מַהְפֵּכָה	18 overthrow (2 · 6) 246
שָׁכֵן	neighbor (5 · 20) 1015
אַרְיֵה	19 lion (6 · 45) 71
גָּאוֹן	majesty, excellence, pride (7 · 49) 144
נָוֶה	habitation (14 · 45[?]) 627
אֵיתָן	permanent, enduring, everflowing (3 · 14) 450
הרגיע	to make a twinkling, to twinkle (4 · 8 · 13) 920
בָּחוּר	chosen (2 · 19) 103 בָּחַר
הוֹעִיד	to summon, arraign (2 · 3 · 28) 416
סחב	20 to drag (4 · 5 · 5) 694
צָעִיר	young (4 · 22) 859
נָוֶה	abode (14 · 45[?]) 627
רעש	21 to quake, shake (5 · 21 · 29) 950
צְעָקָה	cry of distress (4 · 21) 858
נֶשֶׁר	22 vulture, eagle (4 · 26) 676
דאה	to fly swiftly, dart (2 · 4 · 4) 178
מְצֵרָה	Hiph. ptc. of צרר (>50) 864
שְׁמוּעָה	23 report (6 · 27) 1035
נָמוֹג	to melt away (1 · 8 · 17) 556
דְּאָגָה	anxious care (1 · 6) 178
השקיט	to show quietness (1 · 10 · 41) 1052

רָפָה	24 to sink, drop (3 · 14 · 45) 951
רֶטֶט	trembling panic (1 · 1) 936
חֵבֶל	pains of travail (3 · 7) 286
קִרְיָה	25 city, town (2 · 30) 900
מָשׂוֹשׂ	exultation, joy (1 · 17) 965
בָּחוּר	26 young man (11 · 45) 104
רְחוֹב	broad open place (5 · 43) 932
נדמם	to be made silent, quiet (4 · 5 · 30) 198
הִצִּית	27 to kindle, set on fire (8 · 17 · 27) 428
אַרְמוֹן	palace, citadel (5 · 33) 74
מָגוֹר	29 fear, terror (6 · 8) 159
נָד	30 to take flight (8 · 19 · 26) 626 נוד
הֶעְמִיק	to make deep (2 · 8 · 9) 770
שְׁלֵי	31 at ease (1 · 8) 1017
בֶּטַח	security; as adv. = securely (5 · 43) 105
בְּרִיחַ	bar (2 · 41) 138
בָּדָד	alone; isolation, separation (2 · 11) 94
בַּז	32 spoil, booty, plunder (5 · 27) 103
זרה	to scatter, disperse (4 · 25 · 38) 279
קצץ	to cut off (3 · 4 · 14) 893
אֵיד	distress, calamity (5 · 24) 15
מָעוֹן	33 lair, refuge, habitation (5 · 18) 732
תַּן	jackal (5 · 14) 1072
קָצֶה	36 end (1 · 28[?]) 892
זרה	to scatter, disperse (4 · 25 · 38) 279
נִדָּח	banished one, outcast (1 · 11[?]) 623 נדח
חָרוֹן	37 [burning of] anger; ח׳ אף = fierce anger (9 · 41) 354, 60 I. אף 3.
שְׁבִית	39 captivity (12 · 26) 986 שבות

Chapter 50

נֵס	2 standard, signal (5 · 21) 651
כָּחַד	to hide, conceal from (3 · 15 · 32) 470
עָצָב	idol (1 · 17) 781

גִּלּוּל idol (1 · 48) 165

שַׁמָּה 3 waste (24 · 39) 1031

נָד to wander, take flight (8 · 19 · 26) נוד 626

הֵנָּה 5 hither (4 · 49) 244

נִלְוָה to join oneself, be joined to (1 · 11 · 12) 530

אָבַד to be lost (>50) 1

הִתְעָה 6 to cause to wander about (4 · 21 · 50) 1073

רֵבֶץ resting place, dwelling place (1 · 4) 918

אָשֵׁם 7 to be or become guilty (2 · 33 · 35) 79

נָוֶה habitation (14 · 45[?]) 627

מִקְוֶה hope (3 · 5) 876

נָד 8 to wander, take flight (8 · 19 · 26) נוד 626

עַתּוּד he-goat (2 · 29) 800

הִשְׂכִּיל 9 to make childless (1 · 2 · 24) 1013

רֵיקָם in vain, without effect (2 · 16) 938

שָׁלַל 10 to spoil, plunder (1 · 12 · 14) 1021

עָלַז 11 to exalt, triumph (4 · 16 · 16) 759

שֹׁסֶה spoiler, plunderer (2 · 7[?]) 1042 שסה

פּוּשׁ to spring about (1 · 3 · 3) 807

עֶגְלָה heifer (2 · 12) 722

דּוּשׁ to tread on, trample on (1 · 13 · 16) 190

צָהַל to neigh (3 · 7 · 8) 843

אַבִּיר mighty, valiant [of horses] (4 · 17) 7

חָפֵר 12 to be abashed, ashamed (2 · 17 · 17) 344

צִיָּה drought (3 · 16) 851

קֶצֶף 13 wrath (4 · 29) 893

שָׁרַק to hiss (3 · 12 · 12) 1056

מַכָּה wound, blow (10 · 48) 646

ידה 14 to shoot (1 · 1 · 3) 392

חָמַל to spare, have compassion (5 · 40 · 40) 328

הָרִיעַ 15 to shout in triumph (1 · 40 · 44) 929

אָשְׁיָה buttress, support (1 · 1) 78

נֶהֱרַס to be thrown down, torn down (2 · 10 · 43) 248

נְקָמָה vengeance (11 · 27) 668

נָקַם to avenge oneself (3 · 12 · 35) 667

מַגָּל 16 sickle (1 · 2) 618

קָצִיר harvest (5 · 49) 894

יוֹנָה oppressor (3 · 4 · 18) 413 ינה

שֶׂה 17 flock (1 · 45) 961

פָּזַר Qal. ptc. pass. = scattered (1 · 1 · 10) 808

אֲרִי lion (2 · 35) 71

חִדִּיחַ to thrust out, banish (13 · 27 · 43) 623

עִצֵּם to break the bones (1 · 1 · 1) 782

נָוֶה 19 abode, habitation (14 · 45[?]) 627

סָלַח 20 to forgive, pardon (6 · 33 · 46) 699

לַאֲשֶׁר those whom (3 · 38) 81 אֲשֶׁר

חָרַב 21 to attack, smite down (2 · 2 · 3) 352

הֶחֱרִים to destroy, exterminate, ban (5 · 46 · 49) 355

שֶׁבֶר 22 crashing, breaking (15 · 45) 991 I.

נִגְדַּע 23 to be hewn off (2 · 7 · 22) 154

פַּטִּישׁ forge hammer (2 · 3) 809

שַׁמָּה horror, an appalling thing (24 · 39) 1031

יָקשׁ 24 to lay snares, bait (1 · 3 · 8) 430

הִתְגָּרָה to excite oneself, engage in strife (1 · 11 · 14) 173

זַעַם 25 indignation (3 · 22) 276

מַאֲבוּס 26 granary (1 · 1) 7

סָלַל to cast up (2 · 10 · 12) 699

עֲרֵמָה heap (1 · 10) 790

הֶחֱרִים to destroy, exterminate, ban (5 · 46 · 49) 355

חָרַב 27 to attack, smite down (2 · 2 · 3) 352

טֶבַח a slaughtering, slaughter (2 · 12) 370

פְּקֻדָּה visitation (9 · 32) 824

פָּלִיט 28 escaped one, fugitive (3 · 5) 812

נְקָמָה	vengeance (11 · 27) 668
רַב 29	archer (1 · 2) 914 III.
פְּלֵיטָה	escaped remnant (2 · 28) 812
פֹּעַל	deed, thing done (3 · 37) 821
זִיד	to act presumptuously, rebelliously (1 · 2 · 10) 267
בָּחוּר 30	young man (11 · 45) 104
רְחוֹב	broad open place (5 · 43) 932
נדמם	to be made silent, quiet (4 · 5 · 30) 198
זָדוֹן 31	presumption, insolence (3 · 10) 268
זָדוֹן 32	presumption, insolence (3 · 10) 268
הִצִּית	to kindle, set on fire (8 · 17 · 27) 428
עָשַׁק 33	to oppress; ptc. pass. = oppressed one (3 · 35 · 37) 798
שֹׁבֶה	captives (1 · 9) 985
מֵאֵן	to refuse (12 · 46) 549
גֹּאֵל 34	redeemer, kinsman (1 · 44) 145 גָּאַל
הרגיע	to give rest to (4 · 8 · 13[?]) 921
הרגיז	to cause disquiet (1 · 7 · 41) 919
בַּד 36	empty, idle talk, imaginary claim (2 · 6) 95
נואל	to become fools, show wicked folly (2 · 4 · 4) 383
עֶרֶב 37	mixture, mixed company (2 · 5) 786
בזז	to be taken as spoil (1 · 1 · 41) 102
חֹרֶב 38	dryness, drought, heat (3 · 16) 351
פָּסִיל	idol, image (4 · 23) 820
אֵימָה	terror, dread (1 · 17) 33
התהלל	to act like a madman (4 · 6 · 14) 237
צִי 39	wild beast (1 · 6) 850
אִי	jackal (1 · 3) 17
יַעֲנָה	ostrich (1 · 8) 419
נֵצַח	evelastingness, ever; לָנֶצַח = for-ever (3 · 42) 664
מַהְפֵּכָה 40	overthrow (2 · 6) 246
שָׁכֵן	neighbor (5 · 20) 1015
יַרְכָה 41	remote part, side (4 · 28) 438
כִּידוֹן 42	dart, javelin (2 · 9) 475
אַכְזָרִי	cruel (3 · 8) 470

רָחַם	to have compassion (9 · 41 · 46) 933
הָמָה	to roar, murmur, growl (9 · 33 · 33) 242
שֵׁמַע 43	hearing report (2 · 17) 1034
רָפָה	to sink, drop (3 · 14 · 45) 951
חִיל	anguish, writhing (3 · 6) 297
אַרְיֵה 44	lion (6 · 45) 71
גָּאוֹן	majesty, excellence, pride (7 · 49) 144
נָוֶד	habitation (14 · 45[?]) 627
אֵיתָן	permanent, enduring, ever-flowing (3 · 14) 450
הרגיע	to make a twinkling, to twinkle (4 · 8 · 13[?]) 920
בָּחוּר	chosen (2 · 19) 103 בָּחַר
הוֹעִיד	to summon, arraign (2 · 3 · 28) 416
סחב 45	to drag (4 · 5 · 5) 694
צָעִיר	young (4 · 22) 859
נָוֶה	abode (14 · 45[?]) 627
נרעש 46	to be made to quake (1 · 1 · 29) 950
זְעָקָה	cry of distress (6 · 18) 277

Chapter 51

קָם 1	adversary (1 · 12) 878 קום
מַשְׁחִית	destroyer (4 · 19) 1007 שחת Hiph. ptc.
זרה 2	to scatter, disperse (4 · 25 · 38) 279
בקק	to empty out, devastate (1 · 1 · 7) 132
סִרְיוֹ 3	armor (2 · 2) 710
חָמַל	to spare, have compassion (5 · 40 · 40) 328
בָּחוּר	young man (11 · 45) 104
הֶחֱרִים	to destroy, exterminate; ban (5 · 46 · 49) 355
דִּקָּר 4	ptc. = pierced, riddled (2 · 3 · 11) 201
אַלְמָן 5	widowed (1 · 1) 48
אָשָׁם	guilt, guilt offering (1 · 47) 79

נדמם 6 to be made silent, quiet (4 · 5 · 30) 198

נִקְמָם vengeance (11 · 27) 668

גְמוּל recompense, what is gained from dealing; dealing (1 · 19) 168

כּוֹס 7 cup (7 · 31) 468

שׁכר to make drunken (1 · 4 · 20) 1016

התהלל to act like a madman (4 · 6 · 14[?]) 237 *Hithpo.*

פִּתְאֹם 8 suddenly (5 · 25) 837

הֵילֵל to give a howl (8 · 30 · 30) 410

צֳרִי a kind of balsam (3 · 6) 863

מַכְאוֹב pain (3 · 16) 456

אוּלַי perhaps (6 · 45) 19

שַׁחַק 9 cloud (1 · 21) 1007

הברּיר 11 to polish (1 · 1 · 2) 140

שֶׁלֶט perh. shield; quiver, equipment (1 · 7) 1020

מְזִמָּה purpose, device (4 · 19) 273

נְקִמָה vengeance (11 · 27) 668

נֵס 12 standard, signal (5 · 21) 651

מִשְׁמָר guard, prison (1 · 22) 1038

אֹרֵב lier-in-wait = ambusher (1 · 18) 70 אָרב

זָמַם to purpose, devise (2 · 13 · 13) 273

בֶּצַע 13 unjust gain, gain made by violence (4 · 23) 130

יֶלֶק 14 [a kind of] locust (2 · 9) 410

ענה to sing (2 · 13 · 16) 777

הֵידָד shout, shouting, cheer (5 · 7) 212

תֵּבֵל 15 world (2 · 36) 385

תְּבוּנָה understanding (2 · 42) 108

נָשִׂיא 16 vapor (2 · 4) 672 II.

בָּרָק lightning (2 · 21) 140

מָטָר rain (2 · 38) 564

נבְעַר 17 to be dull hearted, brutish, stupid (3 · 4 · 7) 129

צֹרֵף smelter; i.e., goldsmith (3 · 10[?]) 864

פֶּסֶל idol, image (2 · 31) 820

תַּעְתֻּעִים 18 mockery (2 · 2) 1074

פְּקֻדָּה visitation (9 · 32) 824

יָצַר 19 to form, fashion (4 · 41 · 44) 427

מַפֵּץ 20 war club (1 · 1) 659

נפֵּץ to dash to pieces (11 · 15 · 21) 658

נפֵּץ 21 to dash to pieces (11 · 15 · 21) 658

נפֵּץ 22 to dash to pieces (11 · 15 · 21) 658

בָּחוּר [coll.] young men, young man (11 · 45) 104

בְּתוּלָה virgin (8 · 50) 143

נפֵּץ 23 to dash to pieces (11 · 15 · 21) 658

עֵדֶר flock (6 · 39) 727

אִכָּר plowman, husbandman (3 · 7) 38

צֶמֶד span; couple, pair (1 · 15) 855

פֶּחָה governor (3 · 28) 802

סָגָן perfect, ruler (3 · 17) 688

מַשְׁחִית 25 destroyer, destruction (4 · 19) 1008

גלגל to roll down (1 · 1 · 17) 164

שְׂרֵפָה burning (1 · 13) 977

פִּנָּה 26 corner (3 · 30) 819

מוֹסָד foundation (2 · 13) 414

נֵס 27 standard, signal (5 · 21) 651

טִפְסָר marshal, scribe (1 · 2) 381

יֶלֶק [a kind of] locust (2 · 9) 410

סָמָר bristling, rough (1 · 1) 702

פֶּחָה 28 governor (3 · 28) 808

סָגָן perfect, ruler (3 · 17) 688

מֶמְשָׁלָה dominion, rule (2 · 17) 606

רעשׁ 29 to quake, shake (5 · 21 · 29) 950

חול to be in severe pain, or anguish, twist, writhe (5 · 30 · 47) 296

שַׁמָּה waste (24 · 39) 1031

מֵאֵין without (20 · 48[?]) 34 אֵין 6.d.

מְצָד 30 stronghold, mountain fastness (2 · 11) 844

נשׁת to be dry (1 · 2 · 3) 677

הִצִּית to kindle, set on fire (8 · 17 · 27) 428

בָּרִיחַ bar (2 · 41) 138

נָץ 31 runner (2 · 25) 930

מַעְבָּרָה 32 passage, ford, pass (1 · 8) 721

אֲגַם   swamp reed, rush; troubled pool (1 [?] · 1[?]) 8

נִבְהַל   to be disturbed, dismayed, terrified (1 · 24 · 39) 96

גֹּרֶן 33   threshing floor (1 · 34) 175

קָצִיר   harvest (5 · 49) 894

הָמַם 34   to confuse, discomfit; to make a noise (1 · 13 · 13) 243

הִצִּיג   to set, place (1 · 16 · 16) 426 יצג

רִיק   vanity, emptiness (2 · 12) 938

בָּלַע   to swallow up, engulf (1 · 20 · 41) 118

תַּנִּין   dragon (1 · 15) 1072

כָּרֵשׂ   belly (1 · 1) 503

עֵדֶן   dainties (1 · 3) 726

הֵדִיחַ   to rinse, cleanse (1 · 4 · 4) 188

שְׁאָר 35   flesh (1 · 16) 984

נקם 36   to take vengeance (1 · 2 · 35) 667

נְקָמָה   vengeance (11 · 27) 668

הֶחֱרִיב   to dry up (1 · 13 · 37) 351

מָקוֹר   spring, fountain (4 · 18) 881

גַּל 37   heap, pile (2 · 20) 164

מָעוֹן   lair, refuge, habitation (5 · 18) 732

תַּן   jackal (5 · 14) 1072

שַׁמָּה   horror, an appalling thing (24 · 39) 1031

שְׁרֵקָה   hissing (5 · 7) 1056

מֵאֵין   without (20 · 48[?]) 34 אַיִן 6.d.

כְּפִיר 38   young lion (3 · 31) 498

שָׁאַג   to roar (5 · 20 · 20) 980

נער   to growl (1 · 1 · 1) 654

גּוּר   whelp, young of an animal (1 · 2) 158

אֲרִי   lion (2 · 35) 71

חמם 39   to be or grow warm (1 · 23 · 26) 328

מִשְׁתֶּה   feast, banquet, drink (2 · 46) 1059

הִשְׁכִּיר   to make drunken (5 · 6 · 20) 1016

עלז   to exult, triumph (4 · 16 · 16) 759

ישׁן   to sleep, go to sleep (2 · 15 · 16) 445

שֵׁנָה   sleep (3 · 23) 446

הֵקִיץ   to awake (3 · 22 · 23) 884

כַּר 40   he-lamb; battering ram (1 · 12) 503

טבח   to slaughter (3 · 11 · 11) 370

עַתּוּד   he-goat (2 · 29) 800

שַׁמָּה 41   horror, an appalling thing (24 · 39) 1031

גַּל 42   wave [of water], roller; heap (4 · 16) 164

שַׁמָּה 43   waste (24 · 39) 1031

צִיָּה   draught (3 · 16) 851

בֶּלַע 44   thing swallowed (1 · 1) 118

נהר   to flow, stream (1 · 3 · 3[?]) 625

חָרוֹן 45   [burning of] anger; אף ח׳ = fierce anger (9 · 41) 354, 60 אַף 3.

רכך 46   to be timid, fearful (1 · 6 · 8) 939

שְׁמוּעָה   report (6 · 27) 1035

מֹשֵׁל   ruler (4 · 24) 605 III. מָשַׁל

פָּסִיל 47   idol, image (4 · 23) 820

פָּלִיט 50   escaped one, fugitive (6 · 24) 812

כְּלִמָּה 51   ignominy, reproach, insult (3 · 30) 484

פָּסִיל 52   idol, image (4 · 23) 820

אנק   to cry, groan (1 · 2 · 4) 60

בצר 53   to fortify (1 · 2 · 4) 130

זְעָקָה 54   cry of distress (6 · 18) 277

שֶׁבֶר   crashing (15 · 45) 991

המה 55   to roar, murmur, growl (9 · 33 · 33) 242

גַּל   wave [of water], roller; (4 · 16) 164

שָׁאוֹן   roar, din (4 · 17) 981

גְּמוּלָה 56   recompense, dealing (1 · 3) 168

הִשְׁכִּיר 57   to make drunken (5 · 6 · 20) 1016

פֶּחָה   governor (3 · 28) 808

סָגָן   prefect, ruler (3 · 17) 688

ישׁן   to sleep, go to sleep (2 · 15 · 16) 445

שֵׁנָה   sleep (3 · 23) 446

הֵקִיץ   to awake (3 · 22 · 23) 884

רָחָב 58   thick (1 · 21) 932

ערער   to lay bare (1 · 1 · 4) 792

הִתְעַרְעַר   to be laid bare (1 · 1 · 4) 792

גָּבֹהַּ   high, lofty, tall (4 · 41) 147

יצח   to be burned, to kindle (2 · 4 · 27) 428

315

יָגַע to toil, labor, be or grow weary (2 · 20 · 26) 388

בְּדֵי for what suffices for, for (2 · 6) 191 דַּי 2.a.

רִיק vanity, emptiness (2 · 12) 938

לְאוֹם people (1 · 35) 522

יָעֵף to be weary, faint (3 · 8 · 9) 419

מְנוּחָה 59 resting place, rest (2 · 21) 629

קָשַׁר 63 to bind (1 · 36 · 44) 905

כָּכָה 64 thus (5 · 34) 462

שָׁקַע to sink down (1 · 3 · 6) 1054

יָעֵף to be weary, faint (3 · 8 · 9) 419

הֵנָּה hither (4 · 49) 244

Chapter 52

מָרַד 3 to rebel, revolt (1 · 25 · 25) 597

עָשׂוֹר 4 tenth day (1 · 15) 797

דָּיֵק bulwark, siege wall (1 · 6) 189

מָצוֹר 5 siege, siege works (3 · 25) 848

גַּן 7 garden (3 · 42) 171

הִשִּׂיג 8 to overtake (3 · 49 · 49) 673

עִוֵּר 11 to blind (2 · 5 · 5) 734

פְּקֻדָּה visitation (9 · 32) 824

עָשׂוֹר 12 tenth day (1 · 15) 797

טַבָּח bodyguard (17 · 32) 371

נָתַץ 14 to pull down, break down (6 · 31 · 42) 683

טַבָּח bodyguard (17 · 32) 371

דַּלָּה 15 the poor (3 · 5) 195

אָמוֹן master workman, architect (1 · 2) 54 II.

טַבָּח bodyguard (17 · 32) 371

דַּלָּה 16 the poor (3 · 5) 195

טַבָּח bodyguard (17 · 32) 371

כֹּרֶם vine dresser (1 · 5) 501 כרם

יָגַב to till, be husbandman (1 · 2 · 2) 387

מְכוֹנָה 17 base, stand (3 · 25) 467

סִיר 18 pot (3 · 29) 696 I.

יָע shovels (1 · 9) 418

מְזַמֶּרֶת snuffers (1 · 5) 275

מִזְרָק bowl, basin (2 · 32) 284

סַף 19 basin, goblet (1 · 6) 706 I.

מַחְתָּה fire pan, censer (1 · 22) 367

מִזְרָק bowl, basin (2 · 32) 284

סִיר pot (3 · 29) 696 I.

מְנוֹרָה lampstand (1 · 40) 633

מְנַקִּית sacrificial bowl (1 · 4) 667

טַבָּח bodyguard (17 · 32) 371

מְכוֹנָה 20 base, stand (3 · 25) 467

מִשְׁקָל weight (1 · 49) 1054

קוֹמָה 21 height (2 · 45) 879

חוּט measuring line, cord (1 · 7) 296

עֳבִי thickness (1 · 5) 716

אֶצְבַּע finger (1 · 31) 840

נבב to hollow out (1 · 4 · 4) 612

כֹּתֶרֶת 22 capital [of pillar] (3 · 24) 509

קוֹמָה height (2 · 45) 879

שְׂבָכָה lattice work, network (2 · 16) 959

רִמּוֹן pomegranate (4 · 32) 941

רִמּוֹן 23 pomegranate (4 · 32) 941

שְׂבָכָה lattice work, network (2 · 16) 959

טַבָּח 24 bodyguard (17 · 32) 371

מִשְׁנֶה second in rank; double, copy (3 · 36) 1041

סַף threshold; שֹׁמֵר הַסַּף = doorkeeper (2 · 25) 706 II.

סָרִיס 25 eunuch (7 · 45) 710

פָּקִיד commissioner, deputy, overseer (3 · 13) 824

הַצֹּבִא to muster (1 · 2 · 14) 838

טַבָּח 26 bodyguard (17 · 32) 371

טַבָּח 30 bodyguard (17 · 32) 371

גָּלוּת 31 exile; [coll.] exiles (5 · 15) 163

כְּלִיא confinement, imprisonment (2 · 2) כלוא 476

מִמַּעַל 32 above, on the top of (4 · 29) 751 מַעַל

שִׁנָּה 33 to change, alter (2 · 9 · 26) 1040

כֶּלֶא imprisonment, confinement (3 · 10) 476

אֲרֻחָה 34 meal, allowance [of food] (3 · 7) 73

316

EZEKIEL

Chapter 1

גּוֹלָה	1	[coll.] exiles (11 · 42) 163
מַרְאָה		vision (4 · 12) 909 I.
גָּלוּת	2	exile (3 · 15) 163
סְעָרָה	4	tempest, storm (3 · 16) 704
נֹגַהּ		brightness (5 · 19) 618
עַיִן		gleam, sparkle (so in ch. 1.) (>50) 744 עַיִן 4.c.
חַשְׁמַל		[dub.] amber (3 · 3) 365
דְּמוּת	5	likeness, similitude (16 · 25) 198
עֵגֶל	7	calf (1 · 35) 722
נצץ		to shine, sparkle (1 · 1 · 4) 665 I.
קָלָל		burnished (1 · 2) 887
רֶבַע	8	pl. = four sides (5 · 7) 917
חבר	9	to unite, be joined (2 · 11) 287
דְּמוּת	10	likeness, similitude (16 · 25) 198
אַרְיֵה		lion (2 · 45) 71
נֶשֶׁר		vulture, eagle (4 · 26) 676
פרד	11	ptc. pass. = divided; i.e., spread (1 · 1 · 26) 825
מִלְמָעְלָה		above (6 · 24) 751 II. מַעַל 2.d.
חבר		to unite, be joined (2 · 11 · 28) 287
גְּוִיָּה		body (2 · 13) 156
דְּמוּת	13	likeness, similitude (16 · 25) 198
גַּחֶלֶת		cool (3 · 18) 160
לַפִּיד		torch (1 · 13) 542
נֹגַהּ		brightness (5 · 19) 618
בָּרָק		lightning (4 · 21) 140
רצא	14	to run (1 · 1 · 1) 952
בָּזָק		lightning flash [dub.] (1 · 1) 103
אוֹפַן	15	wheel (25 · 35) 66
אוֹפַן	16	wheel (25 · 35) 66
תַּרְשִׁישׁ		[perh.] yellow jasper (3 · 7) 1076
דְּמוּת		likeness, similitude (16 · 25) 198
רֶבַע	17	pl. = four sides (5 · 7) 917
גַּב	18	rim (7 · 13) 146
גֹּבַהּ		height (6 · 17) 147
יִרְאָה		a terror = obj. of terror (2 · 45) 432
אוֹפַן	19	wheel (25 · 35) 66
אוֹפַן	20	wheel (25 · 35) 66
לְעֻמָּה		side by side with (15 · 31) 769 I. עֻמָּה
אוֹפַן	21	wheel (25 · 35) 66
לְעֻמָּה		side by side with (15 · 31) 769 I. עֻמָּה
דְּמוּת	22	likeness, similitude (16 · 25) 198
רָקִיעַ		expanse (5 · 17) 956
קֶרַח		ice (1 · 7) 901
נוֹרָא		awe inspiring, awful (1 · 44) 431 יָרֵא Niph.
מִלְמָעְלָה		above (6 · 24) 751 II. מַעַל 2.d.
רָקִיעַ	23	expanse (5 · 17) 956
גְּוִיָּה		body (2 · 13) 156
שַׁדַּי	24	name of God (2 · 48) 994
הֲמֻלָּה		rushing or roaring sound [dub.] (1 · 2) 242
רָפָה		to let drop (2 · 5 · 45) 951
רָקִיעַ	25	expanse (5 · 17) 956
רָפָה		to let drop (2 · 5 · 45) 951
מִמַּעַל	26	above, on the top (1 · 29) 751 II. מַעַל 1.
רָקִיעַ		expanse (5 · 17) 956
סַפִּיר		sapphire (3 · 11) 705
דְּמוּת		likeness, similitude (16 · 25) 198
מִלְמָעְלָה		above (6 · 24) 751 II מַעַל 2.d.
חַשְׁמַל	27	[dub.] amber (3 · 3) 365
מָתְנַיִם		loins (12 · 47) 608
לְמַעְלָה		upward (8 · 34) 751 מַעַל 2.c.
לְמַטָּה		downward (2 · 10) 641 מַטָּה 2.
נֹגַהּ		brightness (5 · 19) 618
גֶּשֶׁם	28	rain, shower (6 · 35) 177
נֹגַהּ		brightness (5 · 19) 618
דְּמוּת		likeness, similitude (16 · 25) 198

Chapter 2

מָרַד	3	to rebel, revolt (4 · 25 · 25) 597
פָּשַׁע		to transgress (3 · 40 · 41) 833
קְשִׁי	4	stiff, stubborn (2 · 36) 904 קָשֶׁה

מְרִי	5	rebellion (15 · 22) 598
סָרָב	6	rebel; resistance; briers (1 · 1) 709
סַלּוֹן		brier (2 · 2) 699
עַקְרָב		scorpion (1 · 9) 785
מְרִי		rebellion (15 · 22) 598
מְרִי	7	rebellion (15 · 22) 598
מְרִי	8	rebellion (15 · 22) 598
פצה		to part, open (1 · 15 · 15) 822
מְגִלָּה	9	roll [writing, book] (4 · 21) 166
אָחוֹר	10	behind (2 · 41) 30
קִינָה		elegy, dirge (9 · 17) 884
הֶגֶה		a moaning (1 · 3) 211
הִי		lamentation, wailing (1 · 1) 223

Chapter 3

מְגִלָּה	1	roll [writing, book] (4 · 21) 166
מְגִלָּה	2	roll [writing, book] (4 · 21) 166
מֵעֶה	3	stomach, belly (2 · 32) 588
מְגִלָּה		roll [writing, book] (4 · 21) 166
מָתוֹק		sweetness (1 · 12) 608
עָמֵק	5	deep, unfathomable (2 · 3) 771
כָּבֵד		burdensome, heavy (2 · 39) 458
עָמֵק	6	deep, unfathomable (2 · 3) 771
כָּבֵד		burdensome, heavy (2 · 39) 458
מֵצָה	7	forehead (5 · 13) 594
קָשֵׁי		stiff, stubborn (2 · 36) 904
לְעֻמָּה	8	side by side with (15 · 31) 769 I. עמה
מֵצַח		forehead (5 · 13) 594
שָׁמִיר	9	adamant, thorns (1 · 11) 1038
צֹר		flint (1 · 6) 866
מֵצַח		forehead (5 · 13) 594
מְרִי		rebellion (15 · 22) 598
גּוֹלָה	11	[coll.] exiles (11 · 42) 163
רַעַשׁ	12	earthquake (5 · 17) 950
מַשִּׁיקוֹת	13	ptc. = gently touching (1 · 1 · 32) 676 I. שׁק וְ Hiph.
אוֹפַן		wheel (25 · 35) 66
לְעֻמָּה		side by side with (15 · 31) 769 I. עמה
רַעַשׁ		earthquake (5 · 17) 950

מַר	14	bitterly; bitter (3 · 38) 600 I.
גּוֹלָה	15	[coll.] exiles (11 · 42) 163
צֹפֶה	17	watchman (5 · 19[?]) 859 I. צפה
הִזְהִיר		to warn, give a warning (10 · 13 · 21) 264 II.
הִזְהִיר	18	to warn, give a warning (10 · 13 · 21) 264 II.
הִזְהִיר	19	to warn, give a warning (10 · 13 · 21) 264 II.
רֶשַׁע		wickedness (4 · 30) 957
עָוֶל	20	injustice, unrighteousness (10 · 21) 732
מִכְשׁוֹל		stumbling block, means or occasion of stumbling (8 · 14) 506
הִזְהִיר		to warn, give a warning (10 · 13 · 21) 264 II.
הִזְהִיר	21	to warn, give a warning (10 · 13 · 21) 264 II.
נִזְהַר		to take warning (5 · 8 · 21) 264 II.
בִּקְעָה	22	plain (5 · 19) 132
בִּקְעָה	23	plain (5 · 19) 132
עֲבֹת	25	cord, rope (6 · 24) 721
חֵךְ	26	palate, roof of mouth (1 · 18) 335
נאלם		to be dumb (3 · 8 · 9) 47
מְרִי		rebellion (15 · 25) 598
מְרִי	27	rebellion (15 · 25) 598
חָדֵל		forbearing, lacking (1 · 3) 293

Chapter 4

לְבֵנָה	1	tile, brick (1 · 12) 527
חקק		to engrave, inscribe (2 · 8 · 11) 349
מָצוֹר	2	siege, entrenchment (5 · 25) 848 I.
דָּיֵק		bulwark, siege wall (4 · 6) 189
סֹלְלָה		mound (4 · 11) 700
כַּר		battering ram (5 · 12) 305 III.
מַחֲבַת	3	plate (1 · 5) 290
מָצוֹר		siege (5 · 25) 848 I.
צוּר		to besiege (2 · 31 · 31) 848
צַד	4	side (6 · 32) 841

שְׂמָאלִי		left, on the left (1 · 9) 970
צַד	6	side (6 · 32) 841
יְמָנִי		right, right hand (3 · 33) 412
מָצוֹר	7	siege (5 · 25) 848 I.
חָשַׂף		to strip, lay bare (1 · 10 · 10) 362
עֲבֹת	8	cord, rope (6 · 24) 721
צַד		side (6 · 32) 841
מָצוֹר		siege (5 · 25) 848 I.
חִטִּין	9	wheat (3 · 30) 334 חטה
שְׂעֹרָה		barley (4 · 34) 972
פוֹל		bean[s] (1 · 2) 806
עֲדָשָׁה		lentil (1 · 4) 727
דֹּחַן		millet (1 · 1) 191
כֻּסֶּמֶת		spelt (1 · 3) 493
צַד		side (6 · 32) 841
מַאֲכָל	10	food (3 · 30) 38
מִשְׁקוֹל		weight, heaviness (1 · 1) 1054
מְשׂוּרָה	11	measure [of liquids] (2 · 4) 601
הִין		hin [liquid measure] (6 · 22) 228
עֻגָה	12	cake of bread (1 · 7) 728
שְׂעֹרָה		barley (4 · 34) 972
גֵּל		dung; pl. cstr. גֶּלְלֵי (2 · 3) 165
צֵאָה		filth, human excrement (1 · 2) 844
עוּג		to bake (1 · 1 · 1) 728
כָּכָה	13	thus (2 · 34) 462
אדיח		to thrust out, banish (1 · 27 · 43) 623 הדּיח
אֲהָהּ	14	Alas! (4 · 15) 13
נְבֵלָה		carcass, corpse (2 · 48) 615
טְרֵפָה		animal torn [by wild beasts] (2 · 9) 383
נְעוּרִים		youth (9 · 46) 655
פִּגּוּל		foul thing, refuse (1 · 4) 803
צָפוּעַ	15	Q., dung (1 · 1) 861 צְפִיעַ
גֵּל		dung; pl. cstr. גֶּלְלֵי (2 · 3) 165
מִשְׁקָל	16	weight (2 · 49) 1054
דְּאָגָה		anxiety, anxious care (3 · 6) 178
מְשׂוּרָה		measure [of liquids] (2 · 4) 601
שִׁמָּמוֹן		horror, an appalling thing (2 · 2) 1031

חָסֵר	17	to lack, need, be lacking (1 · 19 · 23) 341
נמוק		to pine away (3 · 9 · 10) 596 מקק

Chapter 5

חַד	1	sharp (1 · 4) 292
תַּעַר		razor (5 · 13) 789
גַּלָּב		barber (1 · 1) 162
זָקָן		chin; beard (1 · 19) 278
מֹאזְנַיִם		balances, scales (2 · 15) 24 מאזן
מִשְׁקָל		weight (2 · 49) 1054
אוּר	2	flame (1 · 6) 22
מָצוֹר		siege (5 · 25) 848 I.
זרה		to scatter (1 · 9 · 38) 279
הריק		to empty out (5 · 17 · 19) 937
צור	3	to secure (2 · 31 · 31) 848
תֶּמֶר	6	*Hiph.* impf. 2fs, to show disobedience, rebelliousness (4 · 22 · 43) 598 מרה
רִשְׁעָה		wickedness (5 · 15) 958
הָמָנְכֶם	7	inf. of המן to rage, be turbulent (1 · 1) 243
שֶׁפֶט	10	judgment (10 · 16) 1048
זרה		to scatter, disperse (10 · 25 · 38) 279
שִׁקּוּץ	11	detested thing (8 · 28) 1055
גרע		to withdraw (2 · 14 · 22) 175
חוס		to pity, look upon with compassion (9 · 24 · 24) 299
חָמַל		to spare, have compassion (7 · 40 · 40) 328
דֶּבֶר	12	plague, pestilence (12 · 46) 184
זרה		to scatter, disperse (10 · 25 · 38) 279
הריק		to empty out (5 · 17 · 19) 937
קִנְאָה	13	anger (10 · 43) 888
חָרְבָּה	14	waste, ruin (14 · 42) 352
גְּדוּפָה	15	taunt (1 · 1) 154
מוּסָר		discipline; i.e., warning (1 · 50) 416
מְשַׁמָּה		horror (5 · 7) 1031
שֶׁפֶט		judgment (10 · 16) 1048

תּוֹכַחַת	correction, rebuke (2 · 24) 407
מַשְׁחִית	16 ruin, destruction (4 · 19) 1008
שָׁכֹל	17 to make childless (5 · 18 · 24) 1013
דֶּבֶר	plague, pestilence (12 · 46) 184

Chapter 6

אָפִיק	3 channel (7 · 18) 67
גַּיְא	valley (10 · 47) 161
חַמָּן	4 sun pillar [for idolatrous worship] (2 · 8) 329
גִּלּוּל	idol (39 · 48) 165
פֶּגֶר	5 a corpse, carcass (3 · 22) 803
גִּלּוּל	idol (39 · 48) 165
זרה	to scatter, disperse (10 · 25 · 38) 279
מוֹשָׁב	6 dwelling, habitable place (7 · 44) 444
חרב	to waste, desolate (3 · 17 · 37) 351 II.
אשם	to be held guilty, bear punishment (4 · 33 · 35) 79
גִּלּוּל	idol (39 · 48) 165
נִגְדַּע	to be hewn off (1 · 5 · 22) 154
חַמָּן	sun pillar [for idolatrous worship] (2 · 8) 329
נמחה	to be exterminated (1 · 9 · 34) 562 I.
פָּלִיט	8 fugitive (7 · 19) 812
נזרה	to be scattered, dispersed (2 · 2 · 38) 279
פָּלִיט	9 fugitive (7 · 19) 812
נשבה	to be taken captive (1 · 8 · 37) 985
גִּלּוּל	idol (39 · 48) 165
נקוט	to feel loathing (3 · 4 · 7) 876
בִּפְנֵי	against (4 · 17) 816 פָּנֶה II.3.
חִנָּם	10 for no purpose, in vain (2 · 32) 336
רקע	11 to stomp down (2 · 6 · 11) 955
אָח	Ah! Alas! (2 · 2) 25 III.
דֶּבֶר	plague, pestilence (12 · 46) 184
דֶּבֶר	12 plague, pestilence (12 · 46) 184
גִּלּוּל	13 idol (39 · 48) 165
רָם	high (5 · 31[?]) 926 רום

רַעֲנָן	luxuriant, fresh (1 · 19) 947
אֵלָה	terebinth [a deciduous tree] (1 · 17) 18 I.
עָבוֹת	leafy (2 · 4) 721
נִיחֹחַ	a soothing, tranquilizing (4 · 43) 629
מְשַׁמָּה	14 devastation, waste (5 · 7) 1031
מוֹשָׁב	dwelling place (7 · 44) 44

Chapter 7

חוס	4 to pity, look upon with compassion (9 · 24 · 24) 299
חָמַל	to spare, have compassion (7 · 40 · 40) 328
הֵקִיץ	6 to awake (1 · 22 · 23) 884
צְפִירָה	7 [dub.] plait, chaplet (2 · 3) 862
מְהוּמָה	tumult, confusion, panic (2 · 12) 223
הֵד	shout, shouting, cheer (1 · 1) 212
חוס	9 to pity, look upon with compassion (9 · 24 · 24) 299
חָמַל	to spare, have compassion (7 · 40 · 40) 328
צְפִירָה	10 [dub.] plait, chaplet (2 · 3) 862
צָץ	to blossom (1 · 7 · 8) 847 I. צוץ
פָּרַח	to bud, sprout (1 · 29 · 34) 827
זָדוֹן	insolence (1 · 10) 268
רֶשַׁע	11 wickedness (4 · 30) 957
מֵהֲמֵהֶם	[dub.] wealth (1 · 1) 241 הָם[?]
נֹהַּ	eminency, distinction (1 · 1) 627
קֹנֶה	12 owner (1 · 7[?]) 888 קָנָה
הִתְאַבֵּל	to mourn (2 · 19 · 38) 5 I.
חָרוֹן	[burning of] anger (2 · 41) 354
מִמְכָּר	13 ware, thing sold, merchandise (1 · 10) 569
חַיָּה	life (2 · 12) 312 I. חַיָּה 2.
חָזוֹן	vision (7 · 35) 302
תָּקוֹעַ	14 blast instrument (1 · 1) 1075
חָרוֹן	[burning of] anger (2 · 41) 354
דֶּבֶר	15 plague, pestilence (12 · 46) 184
פלט	16 to escape (1 · 1 · 27) 812

פָּלִיט	fugitive (7 · 19) 812	לְמַטָּה	downward (2 · 10) 641 מַטֶּה
יוֹנָה	dove (1 · 33) 401	לְמַעְלָה	upward (8 · 34) 751 מַעַל 2.c.
גַּיְא	valley (10 · 47) 161	זֹהַר	shining, brightness (1 · 2) 264
הָמָה	to groan, murmur (1 · 33 · 33) 242	חַשְׁמַל	[dub.] amber (3 · 3) 365
רָפָה	17 to lose heart (2 · 14 · 45) 951	תַּבְנִית	3 figure, image (3 · 20) 125
בֶּרֶךְ	knee (3 · 25) 139	צִיצַת	lock (1 · 4) 851
חָגַר	18 to gird on, bind on (3 · 44 · 44) 291	מַרְאָה	vision (4 · 12) 909 I.
שַׂק	sackcloth (2 · 48) 974	פְּנִימִי	inner (24 · 33) 819
פַּלָּצוּת	shuddering (1 · 4) 814	מוֹשָׁב	location, dwelling (7 · 44) 444
בּוּשָׁה	shame (1 · 4) 102	סֵמֶל	statue (2 · 5) 702
קָרְחָה	baldness, bald spot (2 · 11) 901	קִנְאָה	anger (10 · 43) 888
נִדָּה	19 impure thing (5 · 30) 622	הִקְנָא	to provoke to jealous anger (1 · 4 · 34) 888
עֶבְרָה	rage, fury (5 · 34) 720	בִּקְעָה	4 plain (5 · 19) 132
מֵעֶה	stomach, belly (2 · 32) 588	סֵמֶל	5 image, figure (2 · 5) 702
מִכְשׁוֹל	stumbling block (8 · 14) 506	קִנְאָה	anger (10 · 43) 888
צְבִי	20 beauty, decoration (5 · 18) 840	בָּאָה	entrance, entry (1 · 1) 99
עֶדִי	[coll.] ornaments (5 · 14) 725	פֹּה	6 here, hither (3 · 44) 805
גָּאוֹן	pride (9 · 49) 144	חֹר	7 hole (1 · 7) 359 III.
צֶלֶם	image (3 · 17) 853	חָתַר	8 to dig (5 · 8 · 8) 369
שִׁקּוּץ	detested thing (8 · 28) 1055	פֹּה	9 here, hither (3 · 44) 805
נִדָּה	impure thing (5 · 30) 622	תַּבְנִית	10 figure, image (3 · 20) 125
בַּז	21 spoiling, robbery (12 · 27) 103	רֶמֶשׂ	creeping things (2 · 16) 943
צָפוּן	22 treasured, cherished place (1 · 3[?]) 860 צָפַן	שֶׁקֶץ	detestable (1 · 11) 1054
פָּרִיץ	violent one (2 · 6) 829	גִּלּוּל	idol (39 · 48) 165
רַתּוֹק	23 chain (1 · 2) 958	מְחֻקֶּה	*Pual* ptc. = carved (2 · 3 · 4) 348
גָּאוֹן	24 pride, exaltation (9 · 49) 144	מְקַטֶּרֶת	11 censer (1 · 2) 883
עַז	strong, mighty, fierce (1 · 22) 738	עָתָר	odor (1 · 1) 801
קְפָדָה	25 shuddering (1 · 1) 891	חֶדֶר	12 chamber, room (1 · 37) 293
הֹוָה	26 ruin, disaster (2 · 3) 217	מַשְׂכִּית	showpiece, figure (1 · 6) 967
שְׁמוּעָה	report (4 · 27) 1035	פְּנִימִי	16 inner (24 · 33) 819
חָזוֹן	vision (7 · 35) 302	אוּלָם	porch (32 · 49) 17 I.
הִתְאַבֵּל	27 to mourn (2 · 19 · 38) 5 I.	אָחוֹר	pl. cs. אַחֲרֵי = hinder part (2 · 41) 30
נִבְהַל	to be disturbed, dismayed, terrified (2 · 24 · 39) 96	קֶדֶם	קֵדְמָה = eastward (3 · 26) 870
		פֹּה	17 here, hither (3 · 44) 805

Chapter 8

דְּמוּת	2 likeness, similitude (16 · 25) 198	זְמוֹרָה	branch, twig (2 · 5) 274
מָתְנַיִם	loins (12 · 47) 608	חוּס	18 to pity, look upon with compassion (9 · 24 · 24) 299

חָמַל to spare, have compassion (7 · 40 · 40) 328	קֶסֶת pot, ink horn (3 · 3) 903
	מָתְנַיִם loins (12 · 47) 608

Chapter 9

פְּקֻדָּה 1 visitation (2 · 32) 824

מַשְׁחֵת destruction, ruin (1 · 1) 1008

מַפָּץ 2 shattering (1 · 1) 658

לָבוּשׁ clothed with (9 · 16[?]) 527 לבש

בַּד white linen (6 · 23) 94 I.

קֶסֶת pot, ink horn (3 · 3) 903

מָתְנַיִם loins (12 · 47) 608

מִפְתָּן 3 threshold (5 · 8) 837

לָבוּשׁ clothed with (9 · 16[?]) 527 לבש

בַּד white linen (6 · 23) 94 I.

קֶסֶת pot, ink horn (3 · 3) 903

מָתְנַיִם loins (12 · 47) 608

הִתְוָיה 4 to make a mark (1 · 1 · 2) 1063

תָּו mark (2 · 3) 1063

מֵצַח forehead (5 · 13) 594

נֶאֱנַח to sigh (4 · 12 · 12) 58

נֶאֱנַק to cry, groan (2 · 4 · 4) 60

חוּס 5 to pity, look upon with compassion (9 · 24 · 24) 299

חָמַל to spare, have compassion (7 · 40 · 40) 328

בָּחוּר 6 young man (5 · 45) 104

בְּתוּלָה virgin (1 · 50) 143

טַף [coll.] children (1 · 42) 381

מַשְׁחִית destruction, ruin (4 · 19) 1008

תָּו mark (2 · 3) 1063

אֲהָהּ 8 Alas! (4 · 15) 13

מַטֶּה 9 perverseness, perversion (1 · 1) 642

חוּס 10 to pity, look upon with compassion (9 · 24 · 24) 299

חָמַל to spare, have compassion (7 · 40 · 40) 328

לָבוּשׁ 11 clothed with (9 · 16) 527 לבש

בַּד white linen (6 · 23) 94 I.

Chapter 10

רָקִיעַ 1 expanse (5 · 17) 956

סַפִּיר sapphire (3 · 11) 705

דְּמוּת likeness, similitude (16 · 25) 198

לָבוּשׁ 2 clothed with (9 · 16) 527 לבש

בַּד white linen (6 · 23) 94 I.

גַּלְגַּל wheel, whirling (5 · 11) 165

חֹפֶן hollow of hand (2 · 6) 342

גַּחֶלֶת coal (3 · 18) 160

מִבֵּין from between (9 · 21) 107 בַּיִן 2.a.

זָרַק to toss, throw (3 · 32 · 34) 284

פְּנִימִי 3 inner (24 · 33) 819

מִפְתָּן 4 threshold (5 · 8) 837

נֹגַהּ brightness (5 · 19) 618

חִיצוֹן 5 outer (18 · 25) 300

שַׁדַּי name of God (2 · 48) 994

לָבוּשׁ 6 clothed with (9 · 16) 527 לבש

בַּד white linen (6 · 23) 94 I.

מִבֵּין from between (9 · 21) 107 בַּיִן 2.a.

גַּלְגַּל wheel, whirling (5 · 11) 165

אוֹפַן wheel (25 · 35) 66

מִבֵּין 7 from between (9 · 21) 107 בַּיִן 2.a.

חֹפֶן hollow of hand (2 · 6) 342

לָבוּשׁ clothed with (9 · 16) 527 לבש

בַּד white linen (6 · 23) 94 I.

תַּבְנִית 8 figure, image (3 · 20) 125

אוֹפַן 9 wheel (25 · 35) 66

תַּרְשִׁישׁ [perh.] yellow jasper (3 · 7) 1076

דְּמוּת 10 likeness, similitude (16 · 25) 198

אוֹפַן wheel (25 · 35) 66

רֶבַע 11 pl. = four sides (5 · 7) 917 I.

גַּב 12 back (7 · 13) 146

אוֹפַן wheel (25 · 35) 66

אוֹפַן 13 wheel (25 · 35) 66

גַּלְגַּל wheel, whirling (5 · 11) 165

אַרְיֵה 14 lion (2 · 45) 71

נֶשֶׁר		vulture, eagle (4 · 26) 676
נרמם	15	to rise up (3 · 4 · 5) 942
אוֹפָן	16	wheel (25 · 35) 66
מֵאֵצֶל		beside (2 · 6) 69 I. אֵצֶל
נרמם	17	to rise up (3 · 4 · 5) 942
מִפְתָּן	18	threshold (5 · 8) 837
נרמם	19	to rise up (3 · 4 · 5) 942
אוֹפָן		wheel (25 · 35) 66
לְעֻמָּה		side by side with (15 · 31) 769 עֻמָּה
קַדְמֹנִי		eastern (4 · 10) 870
מִלְמָעְלָה		above (6 · 24) 751 II. מַעַל 2.d.
דְּמוּת	21	likeness, similitude (16 · 25) 198
דְּמוּת	22	likeness, similitude (16 · 25) 198

Chapter 11

קַדְמֹנִי	1	eastern (4 · 10) 870
סִיר	3	pot (5 · 29) 696
מַעֲלָה	5	ascent, step, stair (9 · 47) 752
סִיר	7	pot (5 · 29) 696
שֶׁפֶט	9	judgment (10 · 16) 1048
סִיר	11	pot (5 · 29) 696
אֲהָהּ	13	Alas! (4 · 15) 13
כָּלָה		complete destruction, annihilation (3 · 22) 478
גְּאֻלָּה	15	kin, kindred (1 · 14) 145
מוֹרָשָׁה		a possession (7 · 9) 440
שִׁקּוּץ	18	detested thing (8 · 28) 1055
שִׁקּוּץ	21	detested thing (8 · 28) 1055
אוֹפָן	22	wheel (25 · 35) 66
לְעֻמָּה		side by side with (15 · 31) 769 עֻמָּה
מִלְמָעְלָה		above (6 · 24) 751 מַעַל 2.d.
גּוֹלָה	24	[coll.] exiles (11 · 42) 163
גּוֹלָה	25	[coll.] exiles (11 · 42) 163

Chapter 12

מְרִי	2	rebellion (15 · 22) 598
גּוֹלָה	3	exile (11 · 42) 163
אוּלַי		perhaps (1 · 45) 19

מְרִי		rebellion (15 · 22) 598
גּוֹלָה	4	exile (11 · 42) 163
מוֹצָא		a going forth (4 · 27) 425 I.
חָתַר	5	to dig (5 · 8 · 8) 369
עֲלָטָה	6	thick darkness (3 · 4) 759
מוֹפֵת		sign, wonder (4 · 36) 68
גּוֹלָה	7	exile (11 · 42) 163
חָתַר		to dig (5 · 8 · 8) 369
עֲלָטָה		thick darkness (3 · 4) 759
מְרִי	9	rebellion (15 · 22) 598
מַשָּׂא	10	utterance (2 · 45) 672 III.
מוֹפֵת	11	sign, wonder (4 · 36) 68
גּוֹלָה		exile (11 · 42) 163
שְׁבִי		captivity (3 · 46) 985
עֲלָטָה	12	thick darkness (3 · 4) 759
חָתַר		to dig (5 · 8 · 8) 369
רֶשֶׁת	13	net (4 · 22) 440
מְצוּדָה		net (3 · 3) 845
עֵזֶר	14	help (1 · 21) 740
אֲגַף		bands, armies (7 · 7) 8
זרה		to scatter, disperse (10 · 25 · 38) 279
הריק		to empty out; i.e., draw (5 · 17 · 19) 937
זרה	15	to scatter, disperse (10 · 25 · 38) 279
דֶּבֶר	16	plague, pestilence (12 · 46) 184
רַעַשׁ	18	quaking, trembling (5 · 17) 950
רָגְזָה		quivering, shaking (1 · 1) 919
דְּאָגָה		anxiety, anxious care (3 · 6) 178
דְּאָגָה	19	anxiety, anxious care (3 · 6) 178
שִׁמָּמוֹן		horror, an appalling thing (2 · 2) 1031
מְלֹא		fullness (5 · 38) 571
חרב	20	to be waste, desolate (3 · 17 · 37) 351 II.
מָשָׁל	22	proverbial saying (8 · 39) 605 III.
ארך		to be long (2 · 3 · 34) 73
חָזוֹן		vision (7 · 35) 302
מָשָׁל	23	proverbial saying (8 · 39) 605 II.
משׁל		to use a proverb (6 · 7 · 15) 605 II.
חָזוֹן		vision (7 · 35) 302

323

חָזוֹן 24 vision (7 · 35) 302

מִקְסָם divination (2 · 2) 890

חֵלֶק flattery (1 · 12) 325

נמשׁךְ 25 to be postponed (2 · 3 · 36) 604

מְרִי rebellion (15 · 22) 598

חָזוֹן 27 vision (7 · 35) 302

נמשׁךְ 28 to be postponed (2 · 3 · 36) 604

Chapter 13

נָבָל 3 senseless (1 · 18) 614 I.

שׁוּעָל 4 fox (1 · 7) 1043

חָרְבָּה waste, ruin (14 · 42) 352

פֶּרֶץ 5 breach (2 · 18) 829

גָּדַר to wall up, shut off (2 · 7 · 7) 154

גָּדֵר wall, fence (4 · 14) 154

קֶסֶם 6 divination (4 · 11) 890

כָּזָב lie, falsehood (7 · 31) 469

יחל to wait for = hope for (1 · 25 · 42) 403

מַחֲזֶה 7 vision (1 · 4) 303

מִקְסָם divination (2 · 2) 890

כָּזָב lie, falsehood (7 · 31) 469

כָּזָב 8 lie, falsehood (7 · 31) 469

קסם 9 to practice divination (6 · 11 · 11) 890

כָּזָב lie, falsehood (7 · 31) 469

סוֹד assembly, company (1 · 21) 691

כְּתָב register, enrollment (1 · 17) 508

בְּיַעַן 10 by the cause (2 · 3) 774

הטעה to lead astray (1 · 1 · 1) 380

חַיִץ thin or party wall (1 · 1) 300

טוח to coat, overlay (7 · 9 · 11) 376

תָּפֵל whitewash (5 · 6[?]) 1074

טוח 11 to coat, overlay (7 · 9 · 11) 376

תָּפֵל whitewash (5 · 6[?]) 1074

גֶּשֶׁם rain, shower (6 · 35) 177

שָׁטַף to overflow, rinse or wash off (4 · 28 · 31) 1009

אֶלְגָּבִישׁ hail (3 · 3) 38

סְעָרָה tempest, storm wind (3 · 16) 704

אַיֵּה 12 where? (1 · 44) 32

טִיחַ a coating (1 · 1) 376

טוח to coat, overlay (7 · 9 · 11) 376

סְעָרָה 13 tempest, storm wind (3 · 16) 704

גֶּשֶׁם rain, shower (6 · 35) 177

שָׁטַף to overflow, rinse or wash off (4 · 28 · 31) 1009

אֶלְגָּבִישׁ hail (3 · 3) 38

כָּלָה complete destruction, annihilation (3 · 22) 478

הָרַס 14 to throw down, tear down (4 · 30 · 33) 248

טוח to coat, overlay (7 · 9 · 11) 376

תָּפֵל whitewash (5 · 6[?]) 1074

יְסוֹד foundation, base (2 · 19) 414

טוח 15 to coat, overlay (7 · 9 · 11) 376

תָּפֵל whitewash (5 · 6[?]) 1074

חָזוֹן 16 vision (7 · 35) 302

תפר 18 to keep sewing (1 · 1 · 4) 1074

כֶּסֶת band, fillets (2 · 2) 492

אַצִּיל joint; i.e., elbow (2 · 3) 69

מִסְפָּחָה long veil (2 · 2) 705

קוֹמָה height (8 · 45) 879

צוֹדֵד to hunt (4 · 4 · 16) 844

שֹׁעַל 19 handful (1 · 3) 1043

שְׂעֹרָה barley (4 · 34) 972

פְּתוֹת fragment, bit, morsel (1 · 1) 837

כּזֵּב to lie (1 · 12 · 16) 469

כָּזָב lie, falsehood (7 · 31) 469

כֶּסֶת 20 band, fillet (2 · 2) 492

צוֹתֵת to hunt (4 · 4 · 16) 844

פרח to fly (2 · 2 · 2) 827

מִסְפָּחָה 21 long veil (2 · 2) 705

מְצוּדָה prey, net (3 · 3) 845

הכאה 22 to cause to be disheartened (1 · 1 · 3) 456

הכאיב to pain, mar (2 · 4 · 8) 456

קֶסֶם 23 divination (4 · 11) 890

קסם to practice divination (6 · 11 · 11) 890

Chapter 14		Chapter 15	
גִּלּוּג	3 idol (39 · 48) 165	זְמוֹרָה	2 branch, twig (2 · 5) 274
מִכְשׁוֹל	stumbling block (8 · 14) 506	יָתֵד	3 peg, pin (1 · 24) 450
נֹכַח	before (5 · 22) 647	תָּלָה	to hang up (1 · 23 · 27) 1067
גִּלּוּג	4 idol (39 · 48) 165	אָכְלָה	4 consuming, eating (10 · 18) 38
מִכְשׁוֹל	stumbling block (8 · 14) 506	נחר	to be scorched, charred (3 · 5 · 9) 359 I. חרר
נֹכַח	before (5 · 22) 647		
נזור	5 to be estranged (1 · 2 · 6) 266 I. זור	נחר	5 to be scorched, charred (3 · 5 · 9) 359 I. חרר
גִּלּוּל	idol (39 · 48) 165	אָכְלָה	6 consuming, eating (10 · 18) 38
גִּלּוּל	6 idol (39 · 48) 165	מָעַל	8 to act unfaithfully, treacherously (7 · 35 · 35) 591
נזר	7 to devote oneself, dedicate oneself (1 · 4 · 10) 634	מַעַל	unfaithful, treacherous act (6 · 29) 591
גִּלּוּל	idol (39 · 48) 165		
מִכְשׁוֹל	stumbling block (8 · 14) 506		
נֹכַח	before (5 · 22) 647		
מָשָׁל	8 byword (8 · 39) 605 II.		**Chapter 16**
פתה	9 to be deceived (1 · 3 · 27) 834	מְכֹרָה	3 origin (3 · 3) 468
פתה	to deceive (1 · 17 · 27) 834	מוֹלֶדֶת	circumstances of birth, birth (3 · 22) 409
תָּעָה	11 to err (7 · 27 · 50) 1073		
מָעַל	13 to act unfaithfully, treacherously (7 · 35 · 35) 591	מוֹלֶדֶת	4 circumstances of birth, birth (3 · 22) 409
מַעַל	unfaithful, treacherous act (6 · 29) 591	שֹׁר	navel cord (1 · 3) 1057
לוּ	15 if (1 · 19) 530	מִשְׁעִי	cleansing (1 · 1) 606
שׁכּל	to make childless (5 · 18 · 24) 1013	המלח	המלח לא המלחת = not at all were you rubbed, washed, with salt (2 · 2 · 4) 572 III.
מִבְּלִי	so that there is no (2 · 25) 115		
דֶּבֶר	19 plague, pestilence (12 · 46) 184	החתיל	החתל לא חתלת = not at all were you swaddled (1 · 1 · 2) 367
שֶׁפֶט	21 judgment (10 · 16) 1048		
דֶּבֶר	plague, pestilence (12 · 46) 184	חוס	5 to pity, look upon with compassion (9 · 24 · 24) 299
פְּלֵיטָה	22 escaped remnant (1 · 28) 812	חֶמְלָה	compassion (1 · 1) 328 חמל
עֲלִילָה	deed (8 · 24) 760	גֹּעַל	loathing (1 · 1) 172
עֲלִילָה	23 deed (8 · 24) 760	מִתְבּוֹסֶסֶת	6 ptc. = kick out (2 · 2 · 12) 100
חִנָּם	without cause, undeservedly (2 · 32) 336	רְבָבָה	7 myriad (1 · 16) 914
		צֶמַח	growth, sprout (3 · 12) 855
		עֲדִי	ornament (5 · 14) 725
		שַׁד	breast (4 · 21) 994
		שֵׂעָר	hair (1 · 28) 972

צָמַח	to grow abundantly (1 · 4 · 33) 855	
עֵירֹם	nakedness (6 · 10) 735	
עֶרְיָה	nakedness (4 · 6) 789	
שָׁטַף	9 to overflow, rinse or wash off (4 · 28 · 31) 1009	
סוּךְ	to anoint (1 · 7 · 9) 691 I.	
רִקְמָה	10 variegated stuff (8 · 12) 955	
נָעַל	to shoe (1 · 7 · 8) 653	
תַּחַשׁ	a kind of leather or skin (1 · 14) 1065	
חבשׁ	to bind, bind on (6 · 28 · 32) 289	
שֵׁשׁ	linen (3 · 38) 1058	
מֶשִׁי	[dub.] silk (2 · 2) 603	
עָדָה	11 to ornament, deck (3 · 8 · 8) 725	
עֲדִי	ornament (5 · 14) 725	
צָמִיד	bracelet (2 · 6) 855	
רָבִיד	chain (1 · 2) 914	
גָּרוֹן	neck, throat (1 · 8) 173	
נֶזֶם	12 ring (1 · 17) 633	
עָגִיל	hoop, ring (1 · 2) 722	
עֲטָרָה	crown (3 · 23) 742	
עָדָה	13 to ornament, deck oneself (3 · 8 · 8) 725	
מַלְבּוּשׁ	raiment, attire (1 · 8) 528	
שֵׁשׁ	linen (3 · 38) 1058	
מֶשִׁי	[dub.] silk (2 · 2) 603	
רִקְמָה	variegated stuff (8 · 12) 955	
יפה	to be beautiful (2 · 6 · 8) 421	
מְלוּכָה	kingship, royalty (2 · 24) 574	
יְפִי	14 beauty (10 · 19) 421	
כָּלִיל	entire, whole (3 · 15) 483	
הָדָר	ornament, honor (2 · 30) 214	
יְפִי	15 beauty (10 · 19) 421	
תַּזְנוּת	fornication (20 · 20) 276	
טָלוּא	16 variegated (1 · 7[?]) 378 טלא	
צֶלֶם	17 image (3 · 17) 853	
רִקְמָה	18 variegated stuff (8 · 12) 955	
נִיחֹחַ	19 a soothing, tranquilizing (4 · 43) 629	
תַּזְנוּת	20 fornication (20 · 20) 276	
תַּזְנוּת	22 fornication (20 · 20) 276	

נְעוּרִים	youth (9 · 46) 655	
עֵירֹם	nakedness (6 · 10) 735	
עֶרְיָה	nakedness (4 · 6) 789	
מִתְבּוֹסֶסֶת	ptc. = kick out (2 · 2 · 12) 100	
אוֹי	23 Woe! Alas! (4 · 25) 17	
גַּב	24 mound (7 · 13) 146	
רָמָה	high place (4 · 5) 928	
רְחוֹב	broad open place, plaza (2 · 43) 93	
רָמָה	25 high place (4 · 5) 928	
תעב	to cause to be an abomination (1 · 14 · 21) 107	
יֳפִי	beauty (10 · 19) 421	
פשׂק	to part, open wide (1 · 1 · 2) 832	
תַּזְנוּת	fornication (20 · 20) 276	
שָׁכֵן	26 neighbor (1 · 20) 1015	
גָּדֵל	great (1 · 4) 152	
תַּזְנוּת	fornication (20 · 20) 276	
גרע	27 to diminish (2 · 14 · 22) 175	
שֹׂנֵא	enemy (1 · 41[?]) 971	
נכלם	to be humiliated, ashamed (6 · 26 · 38) 483	
זִמָּה	wickedness (14 · 28) 273 I.	
מִבִּלְתִּי	28 on account of, not (1 · 2) 116 בֶּלֶת 4.b.	
שָׂבְעָה	satiety (3 · 7[?]) 960	
תַּזְנוּת	29 fornication (20 · 20) 276	
כְּנַעַן	merchant[s] (2 · 4) 488	
אֲמֻלָה	30 weak (1 · 1[?]) 51 עמל Qal.	
לִבָּה	anger (1 · 1) 525	
זוֹנָה	harlot (6 · 33) 275 זנה Qal. 1.	
שַׁלֶּטֶת	domineering, imperious (1 · 1[?]) 1020	
גַּב	31 mound (7 · 13) 146	
רָמָה	high place (4 · 5) 928	
רְחוֹב	broad open place, plaza (2 · 43) 932	
זוֹנָה	harlot (6 · 33) 275 זנה Qal. 1.	
קלס	to scoff, mock (1 · 1 · 4) 887	
אֶתְנַן	hire [a harlot's earnings] (4 · 11) 1072	
נאף	32 to commit adultery (3 · 14 · 31) 610	

זוֹנָה	33	harlot (6 · 33) 275 זנה *Qal*. 1.
נֶדֶה		gift (1 · 1) 622
נָדָן		gift (1 · 1) 623 I.
מְאַהֵב		lover (6 · 16) 12 אהב *Piel*
שֹׁחַד		to bribe (1 · 2) 1005
תַּזְנוּת		fornication (20 · 20) 276
הֵפֶךְ	34	the contrary, opposite thing (2 · 3) 246
תַּזְנוּת		fornication (20 · 20) 276
זוּנָּה		לֹא זֹ fornication was not done (>50) 275 *Pual*
אֶתְנַן		hire [a harlot's earnings] (4 · 11) 1072
זוֹנָה	35	harlot (6 · 33) 275 זנה *Qal*. 3.
נְחֹשֶׁת	36	lust, harlotry (1 · 1) 639
תַּזְנוּת		fornication (20 · 20) 276
מְאַהֵב		lover (6 · 16) 12 אהב *Piel*
גִּלּוּל		idol (39 · 48) 165
מְאַהֵב	37	lover (6 · 16) 12 אהב *Piel*
עָרֵב		to be sweet, pleasing (1 · 8 · 8) 787
נָאַף	38	to commit adultery (3 · 17 · 31) 610
קִנְאָה		anger (10 · 43) 888
הָרַס	39	to throw down, tear down (4 · 30 · 43) 248
גַּב		mound (7 · 13) 146
נתץ		to tear down (1 · 3 · 42) 683
רָמָה		high place (4 · 5) 928
הִפְשִׁיט		to strip (2 · 15 · 43) 833
הִנִּיחוּךְ		I will leave you (>50) 628 נוח *Hiph*. B. 2.
עֵירֹם		nakedness (6 · 10) 735
עֶרְיָה		nakedness (4 · 6) 789
רגם	40	to kill by stoning (2 · 15 · 15) 920
בִּתֵּק		to cut, cut down (1 · 1 · 1) 144
שֶׁפֶט	41	judgment (10 · 15) 1048
זוֹנָה		harlot (6 · 33) 275 זנה *Qal*. 3.
אֶתְנַן		hire [a harlot's earnings] (4 · 11) 1072
קִנְאָה	42	anger (10 · 43) 888
שׁקט		to be quiet, inactive (2 · 31 · 41) 1052

נְעוּרִים	43	youth (9 · 46) 655
רָגַז		to be excited, perturbed (1 · 30 · 41) 919
הָא		Lo! Behold! (1 · 2) 210
זִמָּה		wickedness (14 · 28) 273 I.
מָשַׁל	44	to use a proverb (6 · 7 · 15) 605 II.
גָּעַל	45	to abhor, loathe (2 · 8 · 10) 171
קָטֹן	46	small (3 · 47) 881
קַט	47	[dub.] only (1 · 1) 881
גָּאוֹן	49	exaltation, majesty, excellency (9 · 49) 144
שִׂבְעָה		satiety (3 · 7[?]) 960 שָׂבְעָה
שַׁלְוָה		ease, careless security (1 · 8) 1017
הִשְׁקִיט		to show quietness (1 · 10 · 41) 1052
גָּבַהּ	50	to be haughty (8 · 24 · 34) 146
צדק	51	to justify (2 · 5 · 41) 842
כְּלִמָּה	52	reproach, ignominy (13 · 30) 484
פלל		to mediate (1 · 4 · 5) 813
הִתְעִיב		to do abominably (1 · 4 · 21) 1073
צדק		to be justified (1 · 22 · 41) 842
צדק		to justify (2 · 5 · 41) 842
שְׁבִית	53	captivity (2 · 6) 986
שְׁבִית		captivity (5 · 26) 986
כְּלִמָּה	54	reproach, ignominy (13 · 30) 484
נכלם		to be humiliated, ashamed (6 · 26 · 38) 483
קַדְמָה	55	former state (4 · 6) 870
שְׁמוּעָה	56	mention (4 · 27) 1035
גָּאוֹן		exaltation, majesty, excellence (9 · 49) 144
בְּטֶרֶם	57	before (1 · 39) 382 טֶרֶם
שָׁאטוֹת		ptc. = one who despises (3 · 3 · 3) 1002 II. שׁוט
זִמַּת	58	wickedness (14 · 28) 273 I.
בָּזָה	59	to despise, regard with contempt (5 · 31 · 42) 102
אָלָה		oath (5 · 36) 46
הֵפֵר		to break, frustrate (5 · 41 · 44[?]) 830
נְעוּרִים	60	youth (9 · 46) 655

נכלם 61 to be humiliated, ashamed
(6 · 26 · 38) 483

קָטֹן small (3 · 47) 881

פִּתָּחוֹן 63 opening (2 · 2) 836

כְּלִמָּה reproach, ignominy (13 · 30) 484

Chapter 17

חוד 2 to propound a riddle (1 · 4 · 4) 295

חִידָה riddle (1 · 17) 295

משל to use a parable (6 · 7 · 15) 605 II.

מָשָׁל similitude, parable (8 · 39) 605 II.

נֶשֶׁר 3 vulture, eagle (4 · 26) 676

אָרֵךְ long (1 · 15) 74

אֵבֶר pinions (1 · 3) 7

נוֹצָה plumage (2 · 3) 663

רִקְמָה variegated work (8 · 12) 955

צַמֶּרֶת treetop (5 · 5) 856

יְנִיקָה 4 shoot, twig (1 · 1) 413

קָטַף to pluck off (2 · 4 · 5) 882

כְּנַעַן merchant[s] (2 · 4) 484 II.

רֹכֵל trader (11 · 17[?]) 940 רכל

צַפְצָפָה 5 [a kind of] willow (1 · 1) 861

צָמַח 6 to sprout, spring up (1 · 15 · 33) 855

סרח ptc. = overrunning, spreading
(1 · 3 · 4) 710

שָׁפָל low (6 · 18) 1050

קוֹמָה height (8 · 45) 879

דָּלִיּוֹת branches, boughs (7 · 8) 194

שֹׁרֶשׁ root (5 · 33) 1057

בַּד rods or shoots (2 · 41) 94 II. בַּד
3.(b)

פֹּארָה bough (6 · 6) 802

נֶשֶׁר 7 vulture, eagle (4 · 26) 676

נוֹצָה plumage (2 · 3) 663

כפן to stretch hungrily (1 · 1 · 1) 495

שֹׁרֶשׁ root (5 · 33) 1057

דָּלִיּוֹת branches, boughs (7 · 8) 194

עֲרוּגָה garden terrace, bed (2 · 4) 788

מַטָּע planting place; מ' עֲרֻגוֹת = beds

where it was planted (3 · 6) 642

שׁתל 8 to transplant (6 · 10 · 10) 1060

עָנָף branch[es], bough[s] (4 · 7) 778

אַדֶּרֶת glory, magnificence (1 · 12) 12

שֹׁרֶשׁ 9 root (5 · 33) 1057

נתק to tear out, up (2 · 11 · 27) 683

קוסס to strip off (1 · 1 · 1) 890

טָרָף fresh-plucked (1 · 2) 383

צֶמַח growth, sprout (3 · 12) 855

שׁתל 10 to transplant (6 · 10 · 10) 1060

עֲרוּגָה garden terrace or bed (2 · 4) 788

צֶמַח growth, sprout (3 · 12) 855

מְרִי 12 rebellion (15 · 22) 598

מְלוּכָה 13 royalty, kingship (2 · 24) 574

אָלָה oath (5 · 36) 46

אֵילֵי mighty (>50) 42 אל

שָׁפָל 14 low (6 · 18) 1050

מרד 15 to rebel, revolt (4 · 25 · 25) 597

הפר to break, frustrate (5 · 41 · 44) 830

בָּזָה 16 to despise, regard with contempt
(5 · 31 · 42) 102

אָלָה oath (5 · 36) 46

הֵפֵר to break, frustrate (5 · 41 · 44) 830

סֹלְלָה 17 mound (4 · 11) 700

דָּיֵק bulwark, siege wall (4 · 6) 189

בָּזָה 18 to despise, regard with contempt
(5 · 31 · 42) 102

אָלָה oath (5 · 36) 46

הֵפֵר to break, frustrate (5 · 41 · 44) 830

אָלָה 19 oath (5 · 36) 46

בָּזָה to despise, regard with contempt
(5 · 31 · 42) 102

הפיר to break, violate (1 · 3 · 3[?]) 830

רֶשֶׁת 20 net (4 · 22) 440

מְצוּדָה net (3 · 3) 845

מַעַל unfaithful, treacherous act (6 · 29)
591

מָעַל to act unfaithfully, treacherously
(7 · 35 · 35) 591

מִבְרָח 21 fugitive (1 · 1) 138

אֲגַף   bands, armies (7 · 7) 8

צַמֶּרֶת   22 treetop (5 · 5) 856

רָם   high (5 · 31[?]) 926 רום

יוֹנֶקֶת   shoot, twig (1 · 6) 413

רַךְ   tender, delicate, soft (1 · 16) 940

קטף   to pluck off (2 · 4 · 5) 882

שתל   to transplant (6 · 10 · 10) 1060

גָּבֹהַּ   high, exalted (6 · 41) 147

תָּלוּל   exalted, lofty (1 · 1) 1068

שתל   23 to transplant (6 · 10 · 10) 1060

עָנָף   branch[es], bough[s] (4 · 7) 778

אַדִּיר   majestic (2 · 27) 12

צִפּוֹר   bird [coll.] (3 · 40) 861

דָּלִיּוֹת   branches, boughs (7 · 8) 194

הִשְׁפִּיל   24 to lay low, humiliate (2 · 9 · 30) 1050

גָּבֹהַּ   high, exalted (6 · 41) 147

הגביה   to make high, exalt (2 · 10 · 34) 146

שָׁפָל   low (6 · 18) 1050

לַח   moist, fresh (2 · 6) 535

הפריח   to cause to bud, sprout (1 · 5 · 34) 827

יָבֵשׁ   dry (4 · 9) 386

Chapter 18

משל   2 to use a proverb (6 · 7 · 15) 605 II.

מָשָׁל   proverbial saying (8 · 39) 605 II.

בֹּסֶר   [coll.] unripe or sour grapes (1 · 5) 126

קהה   to be dull, blunt (1 · 3 · 4) 874

משל   3 to use a proverb (6 · 7 · 15) 605 II.

מָשָׁל   proverbial saying (8 · 39) 605 II.

גִּלּוּל   6 idol (39 · 48) 165

נִדָּה   impurity (5 · 30) 622

הוֹנָה   7 to oppress, maltreat (7 · 14 · 18) 413 ינה

חֲבֹלָה   pledge (5 · 6[?]) 287

חוֹב   debt (1 · 1) 295

גְּזֵלָה   plunder, spoil (4 · 6) 160

גָּזַל   to seize, plunder (5 · 29 · 30) 159

רָעֵב   hungry (2 · 19) 944

עֵירֹם   naked (6 · 10) 735

נֶשֶׁךְ   8 interest, usury (4 · 12) 675

תַּרְבִּית   increment, interest, usury (4 · 6) 916

עָוֶל   injustice, unrighteousness (10 · 21) 732

פָּרִיץ   10 violent one (2 · 6) 829

הוֹנָה   12 to oppress, maltreat (7 · 14 · 18) 413 ינה

גְּזֵלָה   plunder, spoil (4 · 6) 160

גָּזַל   to seize, plunder (5 · 29 · 30) 159

חֲבֹל   pledge (3 · 3) 287

גִּלּוּל   idol (39 · 48) 165

נֶשֶׁךְ   13 interest, usury (4 · 12) 675

תַּרְבִּית   increment, interest, usury (4 · 6) 916

גִּלּוּל   15 idol (39 · 48) 165

הוֹנָה   16 to oppress, maltreat (7 · 14 · 18) 413 ינה

חָבֹל   pledge (3 · 3) 287

חבל   to bind, pledge (2 · 13 · 14) 286

גְּזֵלָה   plunder, spoil (4 · 6) 160

גָּזַל   to seize, plunder (5 · 29 · 30) 159

רָעֵב   hungry (2 · 19) 944

עֵירֹם   naked (6 · 10) 735

נֶשֶׁךְ   17 interest, usury (4 · 12) 675

תַּרְבִּית   increment, interest, usury (4 · 6) 916

עָשַׁק   18 to practice extortion (3 · 36 · 37) 798

עֹשֶׁק   oppression, extortion (4 · 15) 799

גָּזַל   to seize, plunder (5 · 29 · 30) 159

גֵּזֶל   robbery; here as acc. cogn. = thing plundered, plunder (1 · 2) 160 גזל

עַם   kinsman (1 · 34) 769

מַדֻּעַ   19 defective for מדוע wherefore? 396

רִשְׁעָה   20 wickedness (5 · 15) 958

עָוֶל   24 injustice, unrighteousness (10 · 21) 732

מַעַל   unfaithful, treacherous act (6 · 29) 591

מָעַל   to act unfaithfully, treacherously (7 · 35 · 35) 591

נתכן 25 to be adjusted to standard
(9 · 10 · 18) 1067

עָוֶל 26 injustice, unrighteousness (10 · 21)
1067

רִשְׁעָה 27 wickedness (5 · 15) 958

נתכן 29 to be adjusted to standard
(9 · 10 · 18) 1067

מִכְשׁוֹל 30 stumbling block (8 · 14) 506

פָּשַׁע 31 to transgress (3 · 40 · 41) 833

Chapter 19

קִינָה 1 elegy, dirge (9 · 17) 884

לְבִיָּא 2 lioness (1 · 1) 522

אֲרִי lion (3 · 35) 71

רָבַץ to lie down, lie (3 · 24 · 30)
918

כְּפִיר young lion (7 · 31) 498

גּוּר whelp, young (3 · 7) 158 II.

גּוּר 3 whelp, young (3 · 7) 158 II.

כְּפִיר young lion (7 · 31) 498

טָרַף to tear, rend (4 · 19 · 24) 382

טֶרֶף prey (4 · 18) 383

שַׁחַת 4 pit (3 · 23) 1001

חָח hook, ring (4 · 7) 296

נוחל 5 to wait, tarry (1 · 2 · 42) 403

תִּקְוָה things hoped for, outcome (2 · 32)
876

גּוּר whelp, young (3 · 7) 158 II.

כְּפִיר young lion (7 · 31) 498

אֲרִי 6 lion (3 · 35) 71

כְּפִיר young lion (7 · 31) 498

טָרַף to tear, rend (4 · 19 · 24) 382

טֶרֶף prey (4 · 18) 383

הֶחֱרִיב 7 to lay waste, make desolate
(1 · 13 · 37) 351 II.

מְלֹא fullness (5 · 38) 571

שְׁאָגָה roaring (1 · 7) 980

מְדִינָה 8 province (1 · 44) 193

רֶשֶׁת net (4 · 22) 440

שַׁחַת pit (3 · 23) 1001

סוּגַר 9 prison, cage (1 · 1) 689

חָח hook, ring (4 · 7) 296

מְצוֹדָה net (1 · 3) 845

שָׁתַל 10 to transplant (6 · 10 · 10) 1060

פרה to be fruitful, bear fruit (2 · 22 · 29)
826

עָנֵף full of branches (1 · 1) 778

מֹשֵׁל 11 ruler (1 · 24) 605 III. מָשַׁל

גָּבַהּ to be high, lofty, tall (8 · 24 · 34)
146

קוֹמָה height (8 · 45) 879

עָבֹת interwoven foliage (6 · 24) 721

גֹּבַהּ height (6 · 17) 147

דָּלִיּוֹת branches, boughs (7 · 8) 194

התש 12 to be rooted up (1 · 1 · 21) 684

התפרק to be broken off (1 · 3 · 10) 830

שָׁתַל 13 to transplant (6 · 10 · 10) 1060

צִיָּה 13 drought (1 · 16) 851

צָמָא thirst (1 · 17) 854

בַּד 14 rods or shoots (2 · 41) 93 II. בַּד 3.
(b)

קִינָה elegy, dirge (9 · 17) 884

Chapter 20

עָשׂוֹר 1 tenth day (3 · 15) 797

תּוּר 6 to seek out, select (1 · 19 · 22) 1064

זוּב ptc. = flowing (2 · 29 · 29) 264

חָלָב milk (3 · 44) 316

צְבִי beauty, decoration (5 · 18) 840

שִׁקּוּץ 7 detested thing (8 · 28) 1055

גִּלּוּל idol (39 · 48) 165

המרה 8 to show disobedience, rebelliousness (4 · 22 · 43) 598

שִׁקּוּץ detested thing (8 · 28) 1055

גִּלּוּל idol (39 · 48) 165

המרה 13 to show disobedience, rebelliousness (4 · 22 · 43) 598

זוּב 15 ptc. = flowing (2 · 29 · 29) 264

חָלָב milk (3 · 44) 316

צְבִי beauty, decoration (5 · 18) 840

גִּלּוּל 16 idol (39 · 48) 165

חוּס 17 to pity, look upon with compassion (9 · 24 · 24) 299

כָּלָה complete destruction, annihilation (3 · 22) 478

גִּלּוּל 18 idol (39 · 48) 165

המרה 21 to show disobedience, rebellious-ness (4 · 22 · 43) 598

זרה 23 to scatter, disperse (10 · 25 · 38) 279

גִּלּוּל 24 idol (39 · 48) 165

מַתָּנָה 26 gift (5 · 17) 682

פֶּטֶר firstborn (1 · 11) 809

רֶחֶם womb (1 · 33) 933

גדף 27 to blaspheme (1 · 7 · 7) 154

מַעַל unfaithful, treacherous act (6 · 29) 591

מָעַל to act unfaithfully, treacherously (7 · 35 · 35) 591

רָם 28 high (5 · 31[?]) 926 רום

עָבוֹת leafy (2 · 4) 721

כַּעַס vexation, anger (1 · 25) 429

נִיחֹחַ a soothing, tranquilizing (4 · 43) 629

הִסִּיךְ to pour out libations (1 · 14 · 25) 650 I.

שִׁקּוּץ 30 detested thing (8 · 28) 1055

מַתָּנָה 31 gift (5 · 17) 682

גִּלּוּל idol (39 · 48) 165

מָסֹרֶת 37 bond (1 · 1) 64

ברר 38 to purge out, purify (1 · 7 · 15) 140

מרד to rebel, revolt (4 · 25 · 25) 597

פָּשַׁע to transgress (3 · 40 · 41) 833

מְגוּרִים sojourning (place) (1 · 11) 158 I.

מָגוֹר

מַתָּנָה 39 gift (5 · 17) 682

גִּלּוּל idol (39 · 48) 165

מַשְׂאֵת 40 offering, portion (1 · 16) 673

נִיחֹחַ 41 a soothing, tranquilizing (4 · 43) 629

עֲלִילָה 43 deed (8 · 24) 760

נקוט to feel loathing (3 · 4 · 7) 876

בִּפְנֵי against (4 · 17) 815 פָּנֶה II. 3.

עֲלִילָה 44 deed (8 · 24) 76

Chapter 21

תֵּימָן 2 south (4 · 24) 412

הטיף to discourse; to drip (2 · 9 · 18) 643

דָּרוֹם south (13 · 17) 204

הִצִּית 3 to kindle, set on fire (1 · 17 · 27) 428

לַח moist, fresh (2 · 6) 525

יָבֵשׁ dry (4 · 9) 386

כבה to be quenched, extinguished (2 · 14 · 24) 459

לֶהָבָה flame (1 · 19) 529

שַׁלְהֶבֶת flame (1 · 2[?]) 529

נצרב to be scorched (1 · 1 · 1) 863

כבה 4 to be quenched, extinguished (2 · 14 · 24) 459

אֲהָהּ 5 Alas! (4 · 15) 13

משׁל to make a parable (1 · 1 · 15) 605 II.

מָשָׁל similitude, parable (8 · 39) 605 II.

הטיף 7 to discourse, drip (2 · 9 · 18) 643

תַּעַר 8 sheath (5 · 13) 789

תַּעַר 9 sheath (5 · 13) 789

תַּעַר 10 sheath (5 · 13) 789

נאנח 11 to sigh (4 · 12 · 12) 58

שִׁבָּרוֹן breaking, crushing (1 · 2) 991

מָתְנַיִם loins (12 · 47) 608

מְרִירוּת bitterness (1 · 1) 601

נאנח 12 to sigh (4 · 12 · 12) 58

שְׁמוּעָה report (4 · 27) 1035

נָמֵס to faint, grow fearful (1 · 19 · 21) 587

רָפָה to lose heart (2 · 14 · 45) 951

כהה to grow faint (1 · 4 · 10) 462 I.

בֶּרֶךְ knee (3 · 25) 139

הוחד 14 to be sharpened (3 · 3 · 6) 292 חדד

מרט to polish, scour (4 · 7 · 14) 598

טבח 15 to slay, kill ruthlessly (1 · 11 · 11) 370

331

טֶבַח	slaughtering, slaughter (3 · 12) 370	קֶסֶם	divination (4 · 11) 890
הוחד	to be sharpened (3 · 3 · 6) 292 חדד	תְּרָפִים	idol (1 · 15) 1076
בָּרָק	lightning (4 · 21) 140	כָּבֵד	liver (1 · 14) 458
מרט	to be polished, scoured (2 · 5 · 14) 598	קֶסֶם 27	divination (4 · 11) 890
שָׂשׂ	to exult (1 · 26 · 26) 965	כַּר	battering ram (5 · 12) 305 III
מרט 16	to polish, scour (4 · 7 · 14) 598	רֶצַח	slaughter (1 · 2) 954
הוחד	to be sharpened (3 · 3 · 6) 292 חדד	תְּרוּעָה	alarm, war cry (1 · 36) 929
מרט	to be polished, scoured (2 · 5 · 14) 598	סֹלְלָה	mound (4 · 11) 700
הילל 17	to utter, make a howling, give a howl (2 · 30 · 30) 410	דָּיֵק	bulwark, siege wall (4 · 6) 189
מגר	ptc. pass. = thrown (1 · 1 · 2) 550	קסם 28	to practice divination (6 · 11 · 11) 890
ספק	to slap (1 · 6 · 6) 706	שְׁבֻעֵי	Qal pass. ptc. שבע 989
יָרֵךְ	thigh (2 · 34) 437	שְׁבוּעָה	oath, curse (1 · 30) 989
בֹּחַן 18	the trial has been made (1 · 1 · 29) 103 בֹּחַן Pual	עֲלִילָה 29	deed (8 · 24) 760
נכפל 19	[dub.] to be doubled (1 · 1 · 5) 495	מִצְנֶפֶת 31	turban (1 · 12) 857
חדר	to surround, enclose (1 · 1 · 1) 293	עֲטָרָה	crown (3 · 23) 742
מוג 20	to melt; inf. = faint (1 · 4 · 17) 556	שָׁפָל	low (6 · 18) 1050
מִכְשׁוֹל	a stumbling (8 · 14) 506	הַגְבִּיהַ	to make high, exalt (2 · 10 · 34) 146
אִבְחָה	slaughter (1 · 4) 5 Lis. טִבְחָה	גָּבֹהַּ	exalted, high (6 · 41) 147
אָח	Ah! Alas! (2 · 2) 25	הִשְׁפִּיל	to lay low, humiliate (2 · 9 · 30) 1050
בָּרָק	lightning (4 · 21) 140	עַוָּה 32	distortion, ruin (3 · 3) 730
מְעָטָה	read מְרֻטָה, ptc. pass. of מרט, to scour, polish (1 · 1) 598 מרט Qal 2.	טֶבַח 33	slaughtering (3 · 12) 370
טֶבַח	slaughtering, slaughter (3 · 12) 370	מרט	to polish, scour (4 · 7 · 14) 598
התאחד 21	to show oneself sharp; unite oneself (1 · 1 · 1[?]) 25 אחד	הכיל	to contain, hold, hold in, endure (2 · 12 · 38) 465
הימין	to go to the right (1 · 5 · 5) 412	בָּרָק	lightning (4 · 21) 140
השמיל	to go to the left (1 · 5 · 5) 970 שמאל	קסם 34	to practice divination (6 · 11 · 11) 890
אָנָה	whence? whither? (1 · 39) 33	כָּזָב	lie, falsehood (7 · 31) 469
מֻעָדוֹת	Hoph. ptc. = to be set (1 · 2 · 28) 416 יעד	צַוָּאר	neck, back of neck (1 · 41) 848
ברא 24	to cut down (3 · 5 · 5) 135 I. ברא Piel	תַּעַר 35	sheath (5 · 31) 789
בָּצוּר 25	cut off, made inaccessible (2 · 25) 130 בצר	נברא	to be created (3 · 10 · 48) 135 I.
קסם 26	to practice divination (6 · 11 · 11) 890	מְכוּרָה	origin (3 · 3) 468 מְכֹרָה
		זַעַם 36	indignation (3 · 22) 276
		עֶבְרָה	rage, fury (5 · 35) 720
		הפיח	to blow (1 · 12 · 14) 806
		בער	ptc. = inhuman, cruel, barbarous (1 · 3 · 7) 129 II.
		חָרָשׁ	graver, artificer (1 · 38) 360

מַשְׁחִית		destruction, ruin (4 · 19) 1008	
אָכְלָה	37	consuming, eating (10 · 18) 38	

Chapter 22

גִּלּוּל	3	idol (39 · 48) 165
אָשַׁם	4	to be [become] guilty (4 · 33 · 35) 79
גִּלּוּל		idol (39 · 48) 165
קַלָּסָה		derision (1 · 1) 887
הִתְקַלֵּס	5	to scoff, mock, deride (1 · 3 · 4) 887
מְהוּמָה		disturbance, turmoil (2 · 12) 223
עֹשֶׁק	7	oppression, extortion (4 · 15) 799
יָתוֹם		orphan (1 · 42) 450
הוֹנָה		to oppress, maltreat (7 · 14 · 18) 413
		ינה
בָּזָה	8	to despise, regard with contempt (5 · 31 · 42) 102
רָכִיל	9	slander (1 · 6) 940
זִמָּה		wickedness (14 · 28) 273 I.
נִדָּה	10	impurity (5 · 30) 622
כַּלָּה	11	daughter-in-law (1 · 34) 483
זִמָּה		wickedness (14 · 28) 273 I.
שֹׁחַד	12	bribe (1 · 23) 1005
נֶשֶׁךְ		interest, usury (4 · 12) 675
תַּרְבִּית		increment, interest, usury (4 · 6) 916
בָּצַע		to violently make gain of (1 · 6 · 16) 130
עֹשֶׁק		oppression, extortion (4 · 15) 799
בֶּצַע	13	unjust gain (3 · 23) 130
זרה	15	to scatter, disperse (10 · 25 · 38) 279
טֻמְאָה		uncleanness (8 · 37) 380
סוּג	18	dross (3 · 8) 691 סִיג
בְּדִיל		tin (3 · 5) 95
עֹפֶרֶת		lead [metal] (3 · 9) 780
כּוּר		smelting pot, furnace (3 · 9) 468
סְרַג	19	dross (3 · 8) 691 סִיג
קְבֻצָה	20	gathering (1 · 1) 868
עֹפֶרֶת		lead [metal] (3 · 9) 780
בְּדִיל		tin (3 · 5) 95
כּוּר		smelting pot, furnace (3 · 9) 468

לָפַחַת		inf. = to breathe, blow (3 · 9 · 12) 655 נפה
הַנְתִּיךְ		inf. cs. to melt (2 · 5 · 21) 677
הִתִּיךְ		to melt (2 · 5 · 21) 677 נתך
כָּנַס	21	to gather (2 · 3 · 11) 488
נפח		to breathe, blow; inf. = פַּחַת (3 · 9 · 12) 655
עֶבְרָה		rage, fury (5 · 34) 720
נִתַּךְ		to be poured forth (2 · 8 · 21) 677
הִתּוּךְ	22	a melting (1 · 1) 678
כּוּר		smelting pot, furnace (3 · 9) 468
הֻתַּךְ		to be melted (1 · 1 · 21) 677
גֶּשֶׁם	24	rain (1 · 1) 177
זַעַם		indignation (3 · 22) 276
קֶשֶׁר	25	conspiracy (1 · 16) 905
אֲרִי		lion (3 · 35) 71
שָׁאַג		to roar (1 · 20 · 20) 980
טָרַף		to tear, rend (4 · 19 · 24) 382
טֶרֶף		prey (4 · 18) 383
חֹסֶן		wealth, treasure (1 · 5) 340
יְקָר		precious things [coll.] (1 · 17) 430
חמס	26	to treat violently, wrong (1 · 7 · 7) 329
חֹל		profaneness, commonness (4 · 11) 320
הִבְדִּיל		to make a distinction, separate (3 · 32 · 42) 95
הֶעְלִים		to conceal, hide (1 · 11 · 29) 761
זְאֵב	27	wolf (1 · 8) 255
טָרַף		to tear, rend (4 · 19 · 24) 382
טֶרֶף		prey (4 · 18) 383
בֶּצַע		unjust gain (3 · 23) 130
בצע		to gain by violence or wrongfully (1 · 10 · 16) 130
טוּח	28	to coat, overlay (7 · 9 · 11) 376
תָּפֵל		whitewash (5 · 6[?]) 1074
קסם		to practice divination (6 · 11 · 11) 890
כָּזָב		lie, falsehood (7 · 31) 469
עָשַׁק	29	to practice extortion (3 · 36 · 37) 798

עֹשֶׁק		oppression, extortion (4 · 15) 799
גָּזַל		to seize, plunder (5 · 29 · 30) 159
גֵּזֶל		robbery; here as acc. cogn. = thing plundered, plunder (1 · 4) 160
הוֹנָה		to oppress, maltreat (7 · 14 · 18) ינה 413
בְּלֹא		without (1 · 30) 518 לֹא, 4.a.
גָּדַר	30	to wall up, shut off (2 · 7 · 7) 154
גָּדֵר		wall, fence (4 · 14) 154
פֶּרֶץ		breach (2 · 18) 829
זַעַם	31	indignation (3 · 22) 276
עֶבְרָה		rage, fury (5 · 34) 720

Chapter 23

נְעוּרִים	3	youth (9 · 46) 655
מָעַךְ		to press, squeeze (1 · 1 · 3) 590
שַׁד		breast (4 · 21) 994
עָשָׂה		to press, squeeze (2 · 2 · 3[?]) 796
דַּד		teat, nipple, breast (3 · 4) 186
בְּתוּלִים		virginity (2 · 10) 144
עָגַב	5	to lust (6 · 7 · 7) 721
מְאַהֵב		lover (6 · 16) 12 אָהֵב Piel
לָבוּשׁ	6	clothed with (9 · 16) 527 לבשׁ
תְּכֵלֶת		violet fabric (3 · 49) 1067
פֶּחָה		governor (3 · 28) 808
סָגָן		perfect (3 · 17) 688
בָּחוּר		young man (5 · 45) 104
חֶמֶד		desirable = fine, attractive (3 · 5) 326
תַּזְנוּת	7	fornication (20 · 20) 276
מִבְחָר		choicest, best (4 · 12) 104 I.
עָגַב		to lust (6 · 7 · 7) 721
גִּלּוּל		idol (39 · 48) 165
תַּזְנוּת	8	fornication (20 · 20) 276
נְעוּרִים		youth (9 · 46) 655
עָשָׂה		to press, squeeze (2 · 2 · 3[?]) 796
דַּד		teat, nipple, breast (3 · 4) 186
בְּתוּלִים		virginity (2 · 10) 144
מְאַהֵב	9	lover (6 · 16) 12 אָהֵב Piel

עָגַב		to lust (6 · 7 · 7) 721
שְׁפוֹט	10	judgment, act of judgment (1 · 2) 1048
עַגְבָה	11	lustfulness (1 · 1) 721
תַּזְנוּת		fornication (20 · 20) 276
זְנוּנִים		fornication (2 · 12) 276
עָגַב	12	to lust (6 · 7 · 7) 721
פֶּחָה		governor (3 · 28) 808
סָגָן		perfect (3 · 17) 688
לָבוּשׁ		clothed with (9 · 16) 527 לבשׁ
מִכְלוֹל		perfection (2 · 2) 483
בָּחוּר		young man (5 · 45) 104
חֶמֶד		desirable = fine, attractive (3 · 5) 326
לִשְׁתֵּיהֶן	13	הן + שְׁתַּיִם + לְ to both of them 1040 שְׁנַיִם 1.a.
תַּזְנוּת	14	fornication (20 · 20) 276
מְחֻקֶּה		Pual ptc. = carved (2 · 3 · 4) 348 חקה
צֶלֶם		image (3 · 17) 853
חָקַק		to engrave, inscribe (2 · 8 · 11) 349
שָׁשַׁר		red color, vermilion (1 · 2) 1059
חָגוֹר	15	girt, girded (1 · 1) 292
אֵזוֹר		waistcloth (1 · 14) 25
מָתְנַיִם		loins (12 · 47) 608
סָרוּחַ		overhung (1 · 3[?]) 710 סרח
טָבוּל		turban (1 · 1) 371
שָׁלִישׁ		adjutant, officer (2 · 16) 1026
דְּמוּת		likeness, similitude (16 · 25) 198
מוֹלֶדֶת		kindred (3 · 22) 409
עָגַב	16	to lust (6 · 7 · 7) 721
מִשְׁכָּב	17	lying down, couch (2 · 46) 1012
תַּזְנוּת		fornication (20 · 20) 276
יָקַע		to be torn away, alienated (2 · 4 · 8) 429
תַּזְנוּת	18	fornication (20 · 20) 276
נָקַע		to be estranged, alienated (3 · 3 · 3) 668
יָקַע		to be torn away, alienated (2 · 4 · 8) 429

תַּזְנוּת 19 fornication (20 · 20) 276

נְעוּרִים youth (9 · 46) 655

עגב 20 to lust (6 · 7 · 7) 271

פִּלֶגֶשׁ concubine (1 · 37) 811

זִרְמָה issue (2 · 2) 281

זִמָּה 21 wickedness (14 · 28) 273 I.

נְעוּרִים youth (9 · 46) 655

עשׂה to press, squeeze (1 · 1 · 3[?]) 796

דַּד teat, nipple, breast (3 · 4) 186

שַׁד breast (4 · 21) 994

מְאַהֵב 22 lover (6 · 16) 12 אהב Piel

נקע to be estranged, alienated (3 · 3 · 3) 668

בָּחוּר 23 young man (5 · 45) 104

חֶמֶד desirable, fine, attractive (3 · 5) 326

פֶּחָה governor (3 · 28) 808

סָגָן perfect (3 · 17) 688

שָׁלִישׁ adjutant, officer (2 · 16) 1026

הֹצֶן 24 [dub.] multitude; shoulder, arms (1 · 1) 246

גַּלְגַּל [coll.] wheel (5 · 11) 165

צִנָּה large shield (4 · 20) 857

קוֹבַע helmet (1 · 2) 875

קִנְאָה 25 anger (10 · 43) 888

הִפְשִׁיט 26 to strip (2 · 15 · 43) 844

זִמָּה 27 wickedness (14 · 28) 273 I.

זְנוּת fornication (3 · 9) 276

נקע 28 to be estranged, alienated (3 · 3 · 3) 668

שׂנְאָה 29 hating, hatred (2 · 17) 971

יָגִיעַ toil, product (1 · 16) 388

עֶירֹם nakedness (6 · 10) 735

עֶרְיָה nakedness (4 · 6) 789

זְנוּנִים fornication (2 · 12) 276

זִמָּה wickedness (14 · 28) 273 I.

תַּזְנוּת fornication (20 · 20) 276

גִּלּוּל 30 idol (39 · 48) 165

כּוֹס 31 cup (4 · 31) 468

כּוֹס 32 cup (4 · 31) 468

עָמֹק deep (1 · 17) 771

רָחָב wide, broad (1 · 21) 932

צְחֹק laughter (1 · 2) 850

לַעַג mocking, derision (2 · 7) 541

הכיל to contain, hold (2 · 12 · 38) 465

שִׁכָּרוֹן 33 drunkenness (2 · 3) 1016

יָגוֹן sorrow, grief (1 · 14) 387

כּוֹס cup (4 · 31) 468

שַׁמָּה waste (1 · 39) 1031

מצה 34 to drain, drain out (1 · 4 · 7) 594

חֶרֶשׂ sherd, a fragment of earthenware (1 · 17) 360

גרם to break bones, break (1 · 2 · 3) 175 II.

שַׁד breast (4 · 21) 994

נתק to tear out, away (2 · 11 · 27) 683

גַּו 35 back (1 · 3) 156

זִמָּה wickedness (14 · 28) 273 I.

תַּזְנוּת fornication (20 · 20) 276

נאף 37 to commit adultery (3 · 14 · 31) 610

גִּלּוּל idol (39 · 48) 165

אָכְלָה consuming, eating (10 · 18) 38

גִּלּוּל 39 idol (39 · 48) 165

מֶרְחָק 40 distance; ממ׳ = from afar (1 · 18) 935

לַאֲשֶׁר for whom (1 · 38) 81 אֲשֶׁר

כחל to paint (1 · 1 · 1) 471

עָדָה to ornament, deck oneself (3 · 8 · 8) 725

עֲדִי ornament (5 · 14) 725

מִטָּה 41 couch, bed (1 · 29) 641

כְּבוּדָּה glorious (1 · 3) 458 I. כבוד

שָׁלֵו 42 at ease, carefree (1 · 8) 1017

סוֹבָאִים drunkards (1 · 1) 685 סבא

צָמִיד bracelet (2 · 6) 855

עֲטָרָה crown (3 · 23) 742

בָּלֶה 43 worn out (1 · 5) 115

נאופים adulteries (1 · 2) 610 נאף

תַּזְנוּת fornication (20 · 20) 276

זוֹנָה 44 harlot (6 · 33) 275 זנה Qal 2.

זִמָּה wickedness (14 · 28) 273 I.

335

נָאַף 45 to commit adultery (3 · 17 · 31) 610

זַעֲוָה 46 terror, object of trembling (1 · 7) 266
זועה

בַּז spoiling, robbery (12 · 27) 103

רגם 47 to kill by stoning (2 · 15 · 15) 920

בָּרָא to cut down (3 · 5 · 5) 135 I. ברא
Piel

זִמָּה 48 wickedness (14 · 28) 273 I.

נִוַּסְרוּ [3 c.p.] to be disciplined, corrected
(1 · 1 · 41) 415 יסר *Niph.*

זִמָּה 49 wickedness (14 · 28) 273 I.

חֵטְא sin (1 · 33) 308

גִּלּוּל idol (39 · 48) 165

Chapter 24

עָשׂוֹר 1 tenth day (3 · 15) 797

סָמַךְ 2 to lean, rest (2 · 41 · 48) 701

משל 3 to use a proverb (6 · 7 · 15) 605 II.

מְרִי rebellion (15 · 22) 598

מָשָׁל similitude, parable (8 · 39) 605 II.

שְׁפֹת to set (2 · 5 · 5) 1046

סִיר pot (5 · 29) 696

נֵתַח 4 piece (3 · 12) 677

יָרֵךְ thigh, loin (2 · 34) 437

מִבְחָר choicest, best (4 · 12) 104 I.

מִבְחָר 5 choicest, best (4 · 12) 104 I.

דּוּר to heap up (1 · 2 · 2) 189

רֹתַח to cause to boil (1 · 1 · 3) 958

רֶתַח boiling (1 · 1) 958

בָּשַׁל to boil, cook (1 · 2 · 28) 143

אוֹי 6 Woe! Alas! (4 · 25) 17

סִיר pot (5 · 29) 696

חֶלְאָה rust (5 · 5) 316 I.

נֵתַח piece (3 · 12) 677

צְחִיחַ 7 shining, glaring surface (4 · 5) 850

נקם 8 to avenge, take vengeance
(2 · 13 · 35) 667

נָקָם vengeance (3 · 17) 667

צְחִיחַ shining, glaring surface (4 · 5) 850

אוֹי 9 Woe! Alas! (4 · 25) 17

מְדוּרָה pile (1 · 2) 190

הדליק 10 to kindle, inflame (1 · 2 · 9) 196

הרקיח to spice (1 · 1 · 8) 955

מֶרְקָחָה [dub.] spice seasoning (1 · 2) 955
רקח *Hiph.*

נָחוֹר to be scorched, charred (3 · 5 · 9)
359 I. חרר

גַּחֶלֶת 11 coal (3 · 18) 160

רֵיק empty (1 · 14) 938

חַם to be or grow warm (1 · 23 · 26)
328 חמם

חרר to be hot, scorched (1 · 3 · 9) 359 I.

נִתַּךְ to be poured forth (2 · 8 · 21) 677

טֻמְאָה uncleanness (8 · 37) 380

חֶלְאָה rust (5 · 5) 316 I.

תְּאֻנִים 12 toil (1 · 1) 20

הלאה to weary, make weary, exhaust
(1 · 6 · 19) 521

חֶלְאָה rust (5 · 5) 316 I.

זִמָּה 13 wickedness (14 · 28) 273 I.

טֻמְאָה uncleanness (8 · 37) 380

פָּרַע 14 to refrain (1 · 13 · 16) 828

חוס to pity, look upon with compassion
(9 · 24 · 24) 299

עֲלִילָה deed (8 · 24) 760

מַחְמָד 16 desire (3 · 13) 362

מַגֵּפָה blow; slaughter (1 · 26) 620

ספד to wail, lament (2 · 28 · 30) 704

דִּמְעָה [coll.] tears (1 · 23) 199

נאנק 17 to cry, groan (2 · 2 · 4) 60

דֹּם to be silent (1 · 23 · 30) 198 I. דמם

אֵבֶל mourning (1 · 24) 5

פְּאֵר headdress, turban (3 · 7) 802

חבש to bind, bind on; ptc. pass. =
bound, twisted (6 · 28 · 32) 289

נַעַל sandal, shoe (2 · 22) 653

עָטָה to wrap, envelope [oneself]
(2 · 11 · 14) 741

שָׂפָם moustache (2 · 5) 974

גָּאוֹן 21 pride, exaltation (9 · 49) 144
מַחְמָד desire (3 · 13) 326
מַחְמָל compassion (1 · 1) 328
שָׂפָם 22 moustache (2 · 5) 974
עָטָה to wrap, envelope [oneself] (2 · 11 · 14) 741
פְּאֵר 23 headdress, turban (3 · 7) 802
נַעַל sandal, shoe (2 · 22) 653
ספד to wail, lament (2 · 28 · 30) 704
נמוק to pine away (3 · 9 · 10) 596 מקק
נהם to groan, growl (1 · 5 · 5) 625
מוֹפֵת 24 sign, wonder (4 · 36) 68
מָעוֹז 25 fastness, place of safety (2 · 36) 731
מָשׂוֹשׂ exultation (1 · 17) 965
מַחְמָד desire (3 · 13) 326
מַשָּׂא lifting, uplifting (2 · 45) 672 II.
פָּלִיט 26 fugitive (7 · 19) 812
הַשְׁמָעוּת a causing to hear (1 · 1) 1036
פָּלִיט 27 fugitive (7 · 19) 812
נאלם to be dumb (3 · 8 · 9) 47
מוֹפֵת sign, wonder (4 · 36) 68

Chapter 25

הָאָח 3 Aha! (3 · 9) 210
גּוֹלָה exile (11 · 42) 163
מוֹרָשָׁה 4 a possession (7 · 9) 440
טִירָה encampment (2 · 7) 377
חָלָב milk (3 · 44) 316
נָוֶה 5 abode (3 · 45) 627
מַרְבֵּץ resting place, dwelling place (1 · 2) 918 מרבץ
מחא 6 to clap (1 · 3 · 3) 561
רקע to stomp down (2 · 6 · 11) 955
שָׁאט despite, contempt (3 · 3) 1002
בג 7 spoil, booty, plunder (12 · 27) 103 בַּז
צְבִי 9 beauty, decoration (5 · 18) 840
מוֹרָשָׁה 10 a possession (7 · 9) 440
שֶׁפֶט 11 judgment (10 · 16) 1048
נקם 12 to avenge, take vengeance

(2 · 13 · 35) 667
נָקָם vengeance (3 · 17) 667
אָשֵׁם to commit an offense, do a wrong; here w. inf. = to commit lasting [irreparable] wrong (4 · 33 · 35) 79
נקם to avenge oneself (2 · 12 · 35) 667
חָרְבָּה 13 waste, ruin (14 · 42) 352
נְקָמָה 14 vengeance (5 · 27) 668
נְקָמָה 15 vengeance (5 · 27) 668
נקם to avenge oneself (2 · 12 · 35) 667
נָקָם vengeance (3 · 17) 667
שָׁאט despite, contempt (3 · 3) 1002
מַשְׁחִית destruction, ruin (4 · 19) 1008
אֵיבָה enmity (2 · 5) 33
חוֹף 16 shore, coast (1 · 7) 342
נְקָמָה 17 vengeance (5 · 27) 668
תּוֹכַחַת correction, rebuke (2 · 24) 407

Chapter 26

הָאָח 2 Aha! (3 · 9) 210
החרב to be laid waste (2 · 3 · 7) 351 II. Hoph.
גַּל 3 wave, billow; heap (1 · 16) 164
הָרַס 4 to throw down, tear down (4 · 30 · 43) 248
מִגְדָּל tower (3 · 49) 153
סחה to scrape clean, scour (1 · 1 · 1) 695
צָחִיחַ shining, glaring surface (4 · 5) 850
מִשְׁטָח 5 spreading place (3 · 3) 1009
חֵרֶם net (4 · 9) 357 II.
בַּז spoil, booty, plunder (12 · 27) 103
דָּיֵק 8 bulwark, siege wall (4 · 6) 189
סֹלְלָה mound (4 · 11) 700
צִנָּה large shield (4 · 20) 857
מְחִי 9 stroke (1 · 1) 562
קָבָל attacking engine (1 · 1) 867
מִגְדָּל tower (3 · 49) 153
נָתַץ to pull down (2 · 31 · 42) 683
שִׁפְעָה 10 abundance, quantity (1 · 6) 1051

אָבָק	dust (1 · 6) 7
גַּלְגַּל	[coll.] wheel (5 · 11) 165
רַעַשׁ	to quake, shake (4 · 21 · 29) 950
מָבוֹא	entering (5 · 23) 99
פַּרְסָה	11 hoof (2 · 21) 828
רָמַס	to trample (2 · 17 · 18) 942
מַצֵּבָה	pillar (1 · 36) 663
שָׁלַל	12 to spoil, plunder (7 · 13 · 15) 1021
בָּזַז	to spoil, plunder (5 · 38 · 42) 102
רְכֻלָּה	merchandise (4 · 4) 940
הָרַס	to throw down, tear down (4 · 30 · 43) 248
חֶמְדָּה	desire (1 · 16) 326
נָתַץ	to pull down (2 · 31 · 42) 683
כִּנּוֹר	13 lyre (1 · 41) 490
צָחִיחַ	14 shining, glaring surface (4 · 5) 850
מִשְׁטָח	spreading place (3 · 3) 1009
חֵרֶם	net (4 · 9) 357 II.
מַפֶּלֶת	15 overthrow, ruin (6 · 8) 658
אנק	to cry, groan (1 · 2 · 4) 60
הֶרֶג	slaughter (1 · 5) 247
רַעַשׁ	to quake, shake (4 · 21 · 29) 950
אִי	coast, border, region (9 · 36) 15 I.
מְעִיל	16 robe (1 · 28) 591
רִקְמָה	variegated stuff (8 · 12) 955
פָּשַׁט	to strip off, put off (2 · 24 · 43) 833
חֲרָדָה	trembling, fear (1 · 9) 353
חָרַד	to tremble (3 · 23 · 39) 353
רֶגַע	moment (2 · 22) 921
קִינָה	17 elegy, dirge (9 · 17) 884
חִתִּית	terror (8 · 8) 369
חָרַד	18 to tremble, quake (3 · 23 · 39) 353
אִי	coast, border, region (9 · 36) 15 I.
מַפֶּלֶת	overthrow, ruin (6 · 8) 658
נבהל	to be disturbed, dismayed, terrified (2 · 24 · 39) 96
נחרב	19 ptc. = desolate (2 · 2 · 37) 351 II.
תְּהוֹם	deep, sea, abyss (3 · 36) 1062
תַּחְתִּי	20 lower, lowest (6 · 19) 1066
חָרְבָּה	waste, ruin (14 · 42) 352

צְבִי	honor (5 · 18) 840
בַּלָּהָה	21 calamity, destruction (3 · 10) 117

Chapter 27

קִינָה	2 elegy, dirge (9 · 17) 884
מָבוֹא	3 entrance (5 · 23) 99
רֹכֵל	trader (11 · 17[?]) 940 רכל
אִי	coasts, border, region (9 · 36) 15 I.
יָפִי	beauty (10 · 19) 421
כָּלִיל	entire, perfect, whole (3 · 15) 483
בֹּנַה	4 builder (1 · 9) 124 בָּנָה Qal 1.e.
כלל	to perfect (2 · 2 · 2) 480
יָפִי	beauty (10 · 19) 421
בְּרוֹשׁ	5 cypress or fir (2 · 20) 141
לוּחַ	planks, boards (1 · 43) 531
תֹּרֶן	mast (1 · 3) 1076
אַלּוֹן	6 oak (1 · 9) 47
מָשׁוֹט	oar (2 · 2) 1002
אֲשֻׁרִים	read בִּתְאַשֻּׁרִים = with boxwood אֲשֻׁרִים (1 · 3) 81
אִי	coast, border, region (9 · 36) 15 I.
שֵׁשׁ	7 linen (3 · 38) 1058
רִקְמָה	variegated work (8 · 12) 955
מִפְרָשׂ	spread [of canvas as sail] (1 · 2) 831
נֵס	ensign, signal (1 · 21) 651
תְּכֵלֶת	violet fabric (3 · 49) 1067
אַרְגָּמָן	purple thread (2 · 39) 71
אִי	coast, border, region (9 · 36) 15 I.
מְכַסֶּה	covering (1 · 4) 492
שׁוֹט	8 to go, rove about (2 · 7 · 13) 1001
חֹבֵל	sailor (4 · 5) 287
בֶּדֶק	9 fissure, rent, breach (2 · 10) 96
אֳנִיָּה	ship (3 · 31) 58
מַלָּח	mariner, sailor (3 · 4) 572
עָרַב	to exchange (2 · 15 · 17) 786
מַעֲרָב	[coll.] merchandise, articles of exchange (9 · 9) 786
כּוֹבַע	10 helmet (2 · 6) 464
תָּלָה	to hang up (2 · 2 · 27) 1067

338

הָדָר	splendor, honor (2 · 30) 214
מִגְדָּל 11	tower (3 · 49) 153
שֶׁלֶט	perh. shield (1 · 7) 1020
תָּלָה	to hang up (2 · 2 · 27) 1067
כָּלַל	to perfect (2 · 2 · 2) 480
יָפִי	beauty (10 · 19) 421
סֹחֵר 12	trafficker, trader (7 · 16) 695 סחר
הוֹן	wealth (4 · 26) 223
בְּדִיל	tin (3 · 5) 95
עֹפֶרֶת	lead [metal] (3 · 9) 780
עִזְּבוֹנִים	wares (7 · 7) 738 עִזָּבוֹן
רֹכֵל 13	trader (11 · 17[?]) 940 רכל
מַעֲרָב	[coll.] merchandise, articles of exchange (9 · 9) 786
פֶּרֶד 14	mule (1 · 14) 825
עִזְּבוֹנִים	wares (7 · 7) 738 עִזָּבוֹן
רֹכֵל 15	trader (11 · 17[?]) 940 רכל
אִי	coast, border, region (9 · 36) 15 I.
סְחֹרָה	merchandise (1 · 1) 695
הוֹבְנִים	ebony (1 · 1) 211 הָבְנִי
אֶשְׁכָּר	gift (1 · 2) 1016
סֹחֵר 16	trafficker, trader (7 · 16) 695 סחר
נֹפֶךְ	perh. ruby or carbuncle (2 · 4) 656
אַרְגָּמָן	purple thread (2 · 39) 71
רִקְמָה	variegated stuff (8 · 12) 955
בּוּץ	byssus [a fine white Egyptian linen] (1 · 8) 101
רָאמוֹת	corals (1 · 3) 910
כַּדְכֹּד	perh. ruby (1 · 2) 461
עִזְּבוֹנִים	wares (7 · 7) 738 עִזָּבוֹן
רֹכֵל 17	trader (11 · 17[?]) 940 רכל
חִטָּה	wheat (3 · 30) 334
פַּנַּג	some kind of food (1 · 1) 815
צְרִי	a kind of balsam (1 · 6) 863
מַעֲרָב	[coll.] merchandise, articles of exchange (9 · 9) 786
סֹחֵר 18	trafficker, trader (7 · 16) 695 סחר
הוֹן	wealth (4 · 26) 223
צֶמֶר	wool (3 · 16) 856
צַחַר	reddish grey, tawny (1 · 1) 850
אוּזָל 19	Uzal (1 · 1) 23
עִזְּבוֹנִים	wares (7 · 7) 738 עִזָּבוֹן
עָשׁוֹת	[dub.] smooth (1 · 1) 799
קִדָּה	cassia (1 · 2) 869
מַעֲרָב	[coll.] merchandise, articles of exchange (9 · 9) 786
רֹכֵל 20	trader (11 · 17[?]) 940 רכל
חֹפֶשׁ	[dub.] widespread (1 · 1) 344
רִכְבָּה	riding (1 · 1) 939
סֹחֵר 21	trafficker, trader (7 · 16) 695 סחר
כַּר	male lamb (5 · 12) 305 III.
עַתּוּד	male goat (3 · 29) 800
רֹכֵל 22	trader (11 · 17[?]) 940 רכל
בֹּשֶׂם	spice, perfume (1 · 30) 141
יָקָר	precious, rare (2 · 35) 429
עִזְּבוֹנִים	wares (7 · 7) 738 עִזָּבוֹן
רֹכֵל 23	trader (11 · 17[?]) 940 רכל
רֹכֵל 24	trader (11 · 17[?]) 940 רכל
מַכְלֻל	gorgeous garment (1 · 1) 483
גְּלוֹם	wrapping, garment (1 · 1) 166
תְּכֵלֶת	violet fabric (3 · 49) 1067
רִקְמָה	variegated stuff (8 · 12) 955
גְּנָזִים	chests (1 · 1) 170
בְּרֹמִים	variegated cloth (1 · 1) 140
חֶבֶל	cord, rope (2 · 49) 286
חבשׁ	to bind, bind on; here ptc. pass. [?] (6 · 28 · 32) 289
אָרוּז	firm, strong (1 · 1) 72
מַרְכֹּלֶת	market place (1 · 1) 940
אֳנִיָּה 25	ship (3 · 31) 58
שָׁרָה	perh. traveler (1 · 1[?]) 1003 I. שׁור
מַעֲרָב	[coll.] merchandise, articles of exchange (9 · 9) 786
שׁוּט 26	to go, rove about (2 · 7 · 13) 1001
הוֹן 27	wealth (4 · 26) 223
עִזְּבוֹנִים	wares (7 · 7) 738 עִזָּבוֹן
מַעֲרָב	[coll.] merchandise, articles of exchange (9 · 9) 786
מַלָּח	mariner, sailor (3 · 4) 572
חֹבֵל	sailor (4 · 5) 287

בֶּדֶק   fissure, rent, breach (2 · 10) 96

עָרַב   to exchange (2 · 15 · 17) 786

מַפֶּלֶת   overthrow, ruin (6 · 8) 658

זְעָקָה   28   cry, outcry (1 · 18) 277

חֹבֵל   sailor (4 · 5) 287

רעש   to quake, shake (4 · 21 · 29) 950

מִגְרָשׁוֹת   open land (1 · 1[?]) 177   מִגְרָשׁ

אֳנִיָּה   29   ship (3 · 31) 58

מָשׁוֹט   oar (2 · 2) 1002

מַלָּח   mariner, sailor (3 · 4) 572

חֹבֵל   sailor (4 · 5) 287

מַר   30   bitterly; bitter (3 · 38) 600 I.

אֵפֶר   ashes (2 · 22) 68

הִתְפַּלֵּשׁ   perh. to roll in (1 · 4 · 4) 814

הִקְרִיחַ   31   to make a baldness (1 · 1 · 5) 901

קָרְחָה   baldness, bald spot (2 · 11) 901

חגר   to gird on, bind on (3 · 44 · 44) 291

שַׂק   sackcloth (2 · 48) 974

מִסְפֵּד   wailing (1 · 16) 704

מַר   bitter; bitterness (3 · 38) 600 I.

בְּנִיהֶם   32   בְּ + נִי + suffix; נִי wailing (1 · 1) 624

קִינָה   elegy, dirge (9 · 17) 884

קוֹנֵן   to chant (4 · 8 · 8) 884

דֻּמָּה   one silenced, brought to silence; one destroyed [dub.] (1 · 1) 199

עִזְבוֹנִים   33   wares (7 · 7) 738   עִזָּבוֹן

הוֹן   wealth (4 · 26) 223

מַעֲרָב   wares, merchandise, articles of exchange (9 · 9) 786

הֶעֱשִׁיר   to make rich (1 · 14 · 17) 799

מַעֲמַקִּים   34   depths (1 · 5) 771

מַעֲרָב   [coll.] merchandise, articles of exchange (9 · 9) 786

אִי   35   coast, border, region (9 · 36) 15 I.

שָׂעַד   to bristle (2 · 3 · 3) 972

שַׂעַר   horror (2 · 3) 972

רעם   [dub.] to tremble (1 · 1 · 2) 947

סֹחֵר   36   trafficker, trader (7 · 16) 695   סחר

שָׁרַק   to hiss (1 · 12 · 12) 1056

בַּלָּהָה   calamity, destruction (3 · 10) 117

Chapter 28

נָגִיד   2   ruler, prince (1 · 44) 617

גָּבַהּ   to be haughty (8 · 24 · 34) 146

מוֹשָׁב   seat, dwelling (7 · 46) 444

סָתַם   3   ptc. pass. = secret (1 · 10 · 13) 711

עמם   to darken, dim (2 · 2 · 2[?]) 770

תְּבוּנָה   4   understanding (1 · 42) 108

רְכֻלָּה   5   traffic (4 · 4) 940

גָּבַהּ   to be haughty (8 · 24 · 34) 146

עָרִיץ   7   awe inspiring, terror striking (4 · 20) 792

הֵרִיק   to empty out (5 · 17 · 19) 937

יְפִי   beauty (10 · 19) 421

יִפְעָה   brightness, splendor (2 · 2) 422

שַׁחַת   8   pit (3 · 23) 1001

מָמוֹת   death (1 · 2) 560

מחלל   9   *Piel* ptc. = wounding ones (1 · 1 · 7) 319 חלל I.

עָרֵל   10   uncircumcised (16 · 35) 790

קִינָה   12   elegy, dirge (9 · 17) 884

חתם   to seal, seal up (1 · 23 · 27) 367

תָּכְנִית   measurement, proportion (2 · 2) 1067

כָּלִיל   entire, perfect, whole (3 · 15) 483

יֳפִי   beauty (10 · 19) 421

גַּן   13   garden (5 · 42) 171

יָקָר   precious, rare (2 · 35) 429

מְסֻכָּה   covering (1 · 1) 697

אֹדֶם   carnelian (1 · 3) 10

פִּטְדָה   topaz or chrysolite (1 · 4) 809

יַהֲלֹם   [dub.] jasper, onyx (1 · 3) 240

תַּרְשִׁישׁ   perh. yellow jasper (3 · 7) 1076

שֹׁהַם   gem [identity dub.] (1 · 11) 995

יָשְׁפֵה   jasper (1 · 3) 448

סַפִּיר   sapphire (3 · 11) 705

נֹפֶךְ   perh. ruby or carbuncle (2 · 4) 656

בָּרֶקֶת   emerald (1 · 3) 140

תֹּף   timbrel, tambourine (1 · 17) 1074

נֶקֶב grooves, sockets (1 · 1) 666 I.

נברא to be created (3 · 10 · 48) 135 I.

מִמְשָׁח 14 [dub.] expansion, covering (1 · 1) 603

סכך to screen, cover (2 · 12 · 18) 696 I.

נברא 15 to be created (3 · 10 · 48) 135 I.

עַוְלָה injustice (1 · 32) 732

רְכֻלָּה 16 traffic (4 · 4) 940

סכך to screen, cover (2 · 12 · 18) 696 I.

גָּבַהּ 17 to be haughty (8 · 24 · 34) 146

יֳפִי beauty (10 · 19) 421

יִפְעָה brightness, splendor (2 · 2) 421

עוֹל 18 injustice, unrighteousness (10 · 21) 732

רְכֻלָּה traffic (4 · 4) 940

אֵפֶר ashes (2 · 22) 68

בַּלָּהָה 19 calamity, destruction (3 · 10) 117

שֶׁפֶט 22 judgment (10 · 16) 1048

דֶּבֶר 23 plague, pestilence (12 · 46) 184

סִלּוֹן 24 brier (2 · 2) 699 סלון

מַמְאִיר *Hiph.* ptc. = prick, pain (1 · 4 · 4) 549

קוֹץ thorns (1 · 11) 881

הכאיב to pain, mar (2 · 4 · 8) 456

שָׁאטִים ptc. = one who despises (3 · 3 · 3) 1002 II. שוט

בֶּטַח 26 securely (11 · 43) 105

שֶׁפֶט judgment (10 · 16) 1048

שָׁאטִים ptc. = one who despises (3 · 3 · 3) 1002 II. שוט

Chapter 29

תַּנִּין 3 sea monster (2 · 15) 1072

רָבַץ to lie down, lie (3 · 24 · 30) 918

חַח 4 hook, ring (4 · 7) 296

לְחִי jaw, jawbone (2 · 21) 534

דָּגָה fish (6 · 15) 185

קַשְׂקֶשֶׂת scale [of fish] (2 · 8) 903

נָטַשׁ 5 to forsake, abandon (4 · 33 · 40) 643

דָּגָה fish (6 · 15) 185

אָכְלָה devouring, eating (10 · 18) 38

מִשְׁעֶנֶה 6 staff (1 · 12) 1044

נָרֹץ 7 to be crushed, broken (1 · 2 · 19) 954

נִשְׁעַן to lean, support oneself (1 · 22 · 22) 1043

מָתְנַיִם loins (12 · 47) 608

חָרְבָּה 9 waste, ruin (14 · 42) 352

חָרְבָה 10 waste, ruin (14 · 42) 352

חֹרֶב desolation (1 · 16) 351 II.

החרב 12 ptc. = laid waste (2 · 3 · 37) 351 II.

זרה to scatter, disperse (10 · 25 · 38) 279

שְׁבוּת 14 captivity (5 · 26) 986

מְכוּרָה origin (3 · 3) 468 מכרה

שָׁפָל low (6 · 18) 1050

שָׁפָל 15 low (6 · 18) 1050

המעיט to make small or few, diminish (1 · 13 · 22) 589

רדה to have dominion, rule, dominate (2 · 22 · 23) 921

מִבְטָח 16 confidence (1 · 15) 105

הקרח 18 to be made bald (1 · 1 · 5) 901

מרט to make bare, lay bare (4 · 7 · 14) 598

שָׂכָר hire, wages (2 · 29) 969

שָׁלַל 19 to spoil, plunder (7 · 13 · 15) 1021

בָּזַז to spoil, plunder (5 · 38 · 42) 102

בַּז spoil, booty, plunder (12 · 27) 103

שָׂכָר hire, wages (2 · 29) 969

פְּעֻלָּה 20 wages (1 · 14) 821

הִצְמִיחַ 21 to cause to grow (1 · 14 · 33) 855

פִּתְחוֹן opening (2 · 2) 836

Chapter 30

היליל 2 to utter, make a howling, give a howl (2 · 30 · 30) 410

הָהּ Alas! (1 · 1) 214

חַלְחָלָה 4 anguish (2 · 4) 298

נהרס to be thrown down, torn down (4 · 10 · 43) 248

341

יְסוֹד   foundation, base (2 · 19) 414

עֵרֶב   5 mixed company (1 · 5) 786

סָמַךְ   6 to uphold (2 · 41 · 48) 701

גָּאוֹן   pride, exaltation (9 · 49) 144

נחרב   7 *Niph.* ptc. desolate (2 · 2 · 37) 351
II.

עֹזֵר   8 help, helper (2 · 19[?]) 740 עזר

צִי   9 ship (1 · 4) 850

הֶחֱרִיד   to drive in terror, rout (3 · 13 · 39) 353

בֶּטַח   securely (11 · 43) 105

חַלְחָלָה   anguish (2 · 4) 298

עָרִיץ   11 awe inspiring, terror striking (4 · 20) 792

הריק   to empty out (5 · 17 · 19) 937

חָרְבָּה   12 dry ground (1 · 8) 351

מְלֹא   fullness (5 · 38) 571

גִּלּוּל   13 idol (39 · 48) 165

אֱלִיל   idolatrous worthlessness (1 · 20) 47

יִרְאָה   fear, terror (2 · 45) 432

שֶׁפֶט   14 judgment (10 · 16) 1048

מָעוֹז   15 fastness, place of safety (2 · 36) 731

חוּל   16 to be in severe pain, anguish (1 · 30 · 47) 296 I.

בָּחוּר   17 young man (5 · 45) 104

שְׁבִי   captivity (3 · 46) 985

חָשַׁךְ   18 to be grow, dark (1 · 26 · 28) 364
חשׁךְ

מוֹטָה   bar (2 · 11) 557

גָּאוֹן   pride, exaltation (9 · 49) 144

שְׁבִי   captivity (3 · 46) 985

שֶׁפֶט   19 judgment (10 · 16) 1048

חבֹשׁ   21 to be bound up (1 · 2 · 32) 289

רְפֻאָה   remedy, medicine (1 · 3) 951

חִתּוּל   bandage (1 · 1) 367

חבשׁ   to bind up (6 · 28 · 32) 289

זרה   23 to scatter, disperse (10 · 25 · 38) 279

נָאַק   24 to groan (1 · 2 · 2) 611

נְאָקָה   groaning (1 · 4) 611

זרה   26 to scatter, disperse (10 · 25 · 38) 279

Chapter 31

דָּמָה   2 to be like, resemble (4 · 13 · 27) 197

גֹּדֶל   magnificence (3 · 14) 152

יָפֶה   3 fair, beautiful (3 · 41) 421

עָנָף   branch[es], bough[s] (4 · 7) 778

חֹרֶשׁ   thicket, shade-giving wood (1 · 3) 361

מֵצַל   ptc. = a shadowing (1 · 1 · 2) 853

גָּבֹהַּ   high, exalted (6 · 41) 147

קוֹמָה   height (8 · 45) 879

עֲבֹת   interwoven foliage (6 · 24) 721

צַמֶּרֶת   treetop (5 · 5) 856

תְּהוֹם   4 deep, sea, abyss (3 · 36) 1062

מַטָּע   planting place (3 · 6) 642

תְּעָלָה   watercourse (1 · 9) 752

גָּבַה   5 to be high, lofty, tall (8 · 24 · 34) 146

קוֹמָה   height (8 · 45) 879

סַרְעַפָּה   bough (1 · 1) 703

ארךְ   to be long (2 · 3 · 34) 73

פֹּארָה   bough (6 · 6) 802

סְעַפָּת   6 bough, branch (2 · 2) 703

קנן   to make a nest (1 · 4 · 5) 890

פֹּארָה   bough (6 · 6) 802

יפה   7 to be beautiful (2 · 6 · 8) 421

גֹּדֶל   greatness, magnitude (3 · 14) 152

דָּלִיּוֹת   branches, boughs (7 · 8) 194

שֹׁרֶשׁ   root (5 · 33) 1057

עמם   8 [dub.] to eclipse, darken (2 · 2 · 2 [?]) 770

גַּן   garden (5 · 42) 171

בְּרוֹשׁ   cypress or fir (symbol of luxuriance) (1 · 20) 141

דָּמָה   to be like, resemble (4 · 13 · 27) 197

סְעַפָּת   bough, branch (2 · 2) 703

עַרְמוֹן   plane tree (1 · 2) 790

פֹּארָה   bough (6 · 6) 802

342

יְפִי	beauty (10 · 19) 421
יָפֶה	9 fair, beautiful (3 · 41) 421
דָּלִיּוֹת	branches, boughs (7 · 8) 194
קָנֵא	to be jealous of (2 · 30 · 34) 888
גַּן	garden (5 · 42) 171
גָּבַה	10 to be high, lofty, tall (8 · 24 · 34) 146
קוֹמָה	height (8 · 45) 879
גֹּבַה	height (6 · 17) 147
צַמֶּרֶת	treetop (5 · 5) 856
עָבֹת	interwoven foliage (6 · 24) 760
רָם	high (5 · 31[?]) 926 רום
אַיִל	11 mighty one (>50) 42 II. אֵל
רֶשַׁע	wickedness (4 · 30) 957
גרשׁ	to drive out, away (1 · 35 · 48) 176
עָרִיץ	12 awe inspiring, terror striking (4 · 20) 792
נָטַשׁ	to forsake, abandon (4 · 33 · 40) 643
גַּיְא	valley (10 · 47) 161
דָּלִיּוֹת	branches, boughs (7 · 8) 194
פֹּארָה	bough (6 · 6) 802
אָפִיק	channel (7 · 18) 67
מַפֶּלֶת	13 a ruin (6 · 8) 658
פֹּארָה	bough (6 · 6) 802
גָּבַה	14 to be high, lofty, tall (8 · 24 · 34) 146
קוֹמָה	height (8 · 45) 879
צַמֶּרֶת	treetop (5 · 5) 856
אַיִל	terebinth [a deciduous tree] (1 · 4) 18 IV.
גֹּבַה	height (6 · 17) 147
עָבֹת	interwoven foliage (6 · 24) 721
תַּחְתִּית	lower, lowest (6 · 19) 1066
הַאֲבִיל	15 to cause to mourn (1 · 1 · 1[?]) 5 I. *Hiph.*
תְּהוֹם	deep, sea, abyss (3 · 36) 1062
מָנַע	to withhold (1 · 25 · 29) 586
נכלא	to be restrained (1 · 3 · 17) 476
הקדיר	to cause to mourn (3 · 3 · 17) 871
עֻלְפֶּה	have fainted (1 · 1[?]) 763

מַפֶּלֶת	16 overthrow, ruin (6 · 8) 658
הרעישׁ	to cause to quake (1 · 7 · 29) 950
תַּחְתִּית	lower, lowest (6 · 19) 1066
מִבְחָר	choicest, best (4 · 12) 104 I.
דָּמָה	18 to be like, resemble (4 · 13 · 27) 197
כָּכָה	thus (2 · 34) 462
גֹּדֶל	magnificence (3 · 14) 152
תַּחְתִּית	lower, lowest (6 · 19) 1066
עָרֵל	uncircumcised (16 · 35) 790

Chapter 32

קִינָה	2 elegy, dirge (9 · 17) 884
כְּפִיר	young lion (7 · 31) 498
נִדְמָה	to be cut off, destroyed, ruined (1 · 13 · 17) 198
תַּנִּין	sea monster (2 · 15) 1072
הגיח	you thrust forth, burst forth, (1 · 2 · 5) 161 גיח
דלח	to stir up, trouble (3 · 3 · 3) 195
רָפַס	to stamp, tread (2 · 2 · 5) 952
רֶשֶׁת	3 net (4 · 22) 440
חֵרֶם	net (4 · 9) 357 II.
נָטַשׁ	4 to forsake, abandon (4 · 33 · 40) 643
הֵטִיל	to cast, cast out (1 · 9 · 14) 376
גַּיְא	5 valley (10 · 47) 161
רָמוּת	height, lofty stature (1 · 1) 928
צָפָה	6 outflow (1 · 1) 847
אָפִיק	channel (7 · 18) 67
כבה	7 to quench, extinguish (1 · 10 · 24) 459
הקדיר	to make dark (3 · 3 · 17) 871
הֵאִיר	to give light; to light up, cause to shine (2 · 34 · 40) 21
כּוֹכָב	star (1 · 37) 456
יָרֵחַ	moon (1 · 27) 437
מָאוֹר	8 light, luminary (1 · 19) 22
הקדיר	to make dark (3 · 3 · 17) 871
שֶׁבֶר	9 breaking, shattering (1 · 45) 991
שׂער	10 to bristle (2 · 3 · 3) 972

343

שַׂעַר	horror (2 · 3) 972
עוֹפֵף	to cause to fly about, to and fro (1 · 5 · 25) 733
חָרַד	to tremble (3 · 23 · 39) 353
רֶגַע	moment (2 · 22) 921
מַפֶּלֶת	overthrow, ruin (6 · 8) 658
עָרִיץ	12 awe inspiring, terror striking (4 · 20) 792
גָּאוֹן	exaltation, majesty, excellence (9 · 49) 144
דָּלַח	13 to stir up, trouble (3 · 3 · 3) 195
פַּרְסָה	hoof (2 · 21) 828
הִשְׁקִיעַ	14 to cause to sink (1 · 2 · 6) 1054
מָלֵא	15 fullness (5 · 38) 571
קִינָה	16 elegy, dirge (9 · 17) 884
קוֹנֵן	to chant (4 · 8 · 8) 884
נָהָה	18 to lament, wail (1 · 2 · 2[?]) 624
אַדִּיר	majesty (2 · 27) 12
תַּחְתִּי	lower, lowest (6 · 19) 1066
מִמִּי	19 from whom (1 · 2) 566 מִי b.
נעם	to be pleasant, delightful (1 · 8 · 8) 653
עָרֵל	uncircumcised (16 · 35) 790
מָשַׁךְ	20 to draw down (1 · 30 · 36) 604
אֵל	21 mighty (>50) 42 II.
עֵזֶר	help, helper (2 · 19[?]) 740
עָרֵל	uncircumcised (16 · 35) 790
יַרְכָּה	23 recess, innermost part (5 · 28) 438
קְבוּרָה	grave (2 · 14) 869
חִתִּית	terror (8 · 8) 369
קְבוּרָה	24 grave (2 · 14) 869
עָרֵל	uncircumcised (16 · 35) 790
תַּחְתִּי	lower, lowest (6 · 19) 1066
חִתִּית	terror (8 · 8) 369
כְּלִמָּה	reproach, ignominy (13 · 30) 484
מִשְׁכָּב	25 couch, bed (2 · 46) 1012
עָרֵל	uncircumcised (16 · 35) 790
חִתִּית	terror (8 · 8) 369
כְּלִמָּה	reproach, ignominy (13 · 30) 484
עָרֵל	26 uncircumcised (16 · 35) 790

מְחֻלָּל	Pual ptc. = pierced (1 · 1 · 7) 319 I. חלל
חִתִּית	terror (8 · 8) 369
עָרֵל	27 uncircumcised (16 · 35) 790
חִתִּית	terror (8 · 8) 369
עָרֵל	28 uncircumcised (16 · 35) 790
עָרֵל	29 uncircumcised (16 · 35) 790
נָסִיךְ	30 prince (1 · 6) 651
חִתִּית	terror (8 · 8) 369
עָרֵל	uncircumcised (16 · 35) 790
כְּלִמָּה	reproach, ignominy (13 · 30) 484
חִתִּית	32 terror (8 · 8) 369
עָרֵל	uncircumcised (16 · 35) 790

Chapter 33

צֹפֶה	2 watchman (5 · 19[?]) 859
הִזְהִיר	3 to warn, give a warning (10 · 13 · 21) 264 II.
נִזְהַר	4 to take warning (5 · 8 · 21) 264 II.
נִזְהַר	5 to take warning (5 · 8 · 21) 264 II.
צֹפֶה	6 watchman (5 · 19[?]) 859
נִזְהַר	to be warned, received warning (5 · 8 · 21) 264 II.
צֹפֶה	7 watchman (5 · 19[?]) 859
הִזְהִיר	to warn, give a warning (10 · 13 · 21) 264 II.
הִזְהִיר	8 to warn, give a warning (10 · 13 · 21) 264 II.
הִזְהִיר	9 to warn, give a warning (10 · 13 · 21) 264 II.
נָמוֹק	10 to pine away (3 · 9 · 10) 596 מקק
רִשְׁעָה	12 wickedness (5 · 15) 958
רֶשַׁע	wickedness (4 · 30) 957
עָוֶל	13 injustice, unrighteousness (10 · 21) 732
חֲבֹל	15 pledge (3 · 3) 287
גְּזֵלָה	plunder, spoil (4 · 6) 160
עָוֶל	injustice, unrighteousness (10 · 21) 732

344

נתכן 17 to be adjusted to standard; i.e., right, equitable (9 · 10 · 18) 1067

עָוֶל 18 injustice, unrighteousness (10 · 21) 732

רִשְׁעָה 19 wickedness (5 · 15) 958

נתכן 20 to be adjusted to standard; i.e., right, equitable (9 · 10 · 18) 1067

גָּלוּת 21 exile (3 · 15) 163

פָּלִיט fugitive (7 · 19) 812

פָּלִיט 22 fugitive (7 · 19) 812

נאלם to be dumb (3 · 8 · 9) 47

חָרְבָּה 24 waste, ruin (14 · 42) 352

מוֹרָשָׁה a possession (7 · 9) 440

גִּלּוּל 25 idol (39 · 48) 165

חָרְבָּה 27 waste, ruin (14 · 42) 352

מְצָד stronghold (1 · 11) 844

מְעָרָה cave (1 · 40) 792

דֶּבֶר plague, pestilence (12 · 46) 184

מְשַׁמָּה 28 devastation, waste (5 · 7) 1031

גָּאוֹן pride, exultation (9 · 49) 144

מֵאֵין without (2 · 48[?]) 34 II. אַיִן 6.d.

מְשַׁמָּה 29 devastation, waste (5 · 7) 1031

חַד 30 אֶחָד only here BDB 25

מָבוֹא 31 a coming in (5 · 23) 99

עֲגָבִים [sensuous] love (2 · 2) 721

בֶּצַע unjust gain (3 · 23) 130

עֲגָבִים 32 [sensuous] love (2 · 2) 721

יָפֶה fair, beautiful (3 · 41) 421

נָגֵן to play (1 · 13 · 14) 618

Chapter 34

צֶמֶר 3 wool (3 · 16) 856

בָּרִיא fat (2 · 14) 135

חבש 4 to bind up (6 · 28 · 32) 289

נדח ptc. = banished ones, outcasts (2 · 13 · 43) 623

חָזְקָה force, strength (1 · 6) 306

רדה to have dominion, rule, dominate (2 · 22 · 23) 921

פֶּרֶךְ harshness, severity (1 · 6) 827

מִבְּלִי 5 for lack of (2 · 25) 115

אָכְלָה devouring, eating (10 · 18) 38

שׁגה 6 to err, stray (2 · 17 · 21) 993

רָם high (5 · 31[?]) 926 רום

בַּז 8 spoil, booty, plunder (12 · 27) 103

אָכְלָה devouring, eating (10 · 18) 38

מֵאֵין from lack of (2 · 48[?]) 34

אָכְלָה 10 devouring, eating (10 · 18) 38

בקר 11 to seek (2 · 7 · 7) 133

בַּקָּרָה 12 a seeking (1 · 1) 134

עֵדֶר flock (1 · 39) 727

נפרש perh. to scatter (1 · 1 · 5) 831

בקר to seek (2 · 7 · 7) 133

עֲרָפֶל cloud, heavy cloud (1 · 15) 791

אָפִיק 13 channel (7 · 18) 67

מוֹשָׁב habitable places (7 · 46) 444

מִרְעֶה 14 pasture, pasturage (4 · 13) 945

נָוֶה abode (3 · 45) 627

רָבַץ to lie down, lie (3 · 24 · 30) 918

שָׁמֵן tertile (2 · 10) 1032

הרביץ 15 to cause to lie down (1 · 6 · 30) 918

נדח 16 ptc. = banished ones, outcasts (2 · 13 · 43) 623

חבש to bind up (6 · 28 · 32) 289

שָׁמֵן stout, robust (2 · 10) 1032

שֶׂה 17 sheep, goat (5 · 45) 961

עַתּוּד male goat (3 · 29) 800

מִרְעֶה 18 pasture, pasturage (4 · 13) 945

רָמַס to trample (2 · 17 · 18) 942

מִשְׁקָע clear (1 · 1) 1054

רפשׂ to stamp, tread (2 · 2 · 5) 952

מִרְמָס 19 trampling place (1 · 7) 942

מִרְפָּשׂ befouled (1 · 1) 952 מרפש

שֶׂה 20 sheep, goat (5 · 45) 961

בְּרִיָה fat (2 · 14) 135 בְּרִיא

רָזֶה lean (1 · 2) 931

צַד 21 side (6 · 32) 841

הדף to thrust, push (1 · 11 · 11) 213

נגח to push or thrust at (1 · 6 · 11) 618

בַּז 22 spoil, booty, plunder (12 · 27) 103

שֶׂה sheep, goat (5 · 45) 961

בֶּטַח 25 securely (11 · 43) 105 w. ל

יָשֵׁן to sleep, go to sleep (1 · 15 · 16) 445

גֶּשֶׁם 26 rain, shower (5 · 35) 177

יְבוּל 27 produce (1 · 13) 385

בֶּטַח securely (11 · 43) 105 w. ל

מוֹטָה bar (2 · 11) 557

עֹל yoke (1 · 40) 760

בַּז 28 spoil, booty, plunder (12 · 27) 103

בֶּטַח securely (11 · 43) 105 w. ל

הֶחֱרִיד to terrify (3 · 16 · 39) 353

מַטָּע 29 planting place (3 · 6) 642

כְּלִמָּה reproach, ignominy (12 · 30) 484

מַרְעִית 31 pasturing, shepherding (1 · 10) 945

Chapter 35

מְשַׁמָּה 3 devastation, waste (5 · 7) 1031

הָרְבָּה 4 waste, ruin (14 · 42) 352

אֵיבָה 5 enmity (2 · 5) 33

הִגִּיר to pour down, hurl down; impf. = יַגֵּר (1 · 5 · 10) 620

אֵיד calamity, distress (1 · 24) 15

שְׁמָמָה 7 devastation, waste (1 · 1) 1031

גַּיְא 8 valley (10 · 47) 161

אָפִיק channel (7 · 18) 67

קִנְאָה 11 anger (10 · 43) 888

שָׂנֵא hating, hatred (2 · 17) 971

נֶאָצָה 12 contempt, blasphemy (1 · 3) 611

אָכְלָה devouring, food (10 · 18) 38

הֶעְתִּיר 13 to multiply (1 · 1 · 2) 801

Chapter 36

מוֹרָשָׁה 2 a possession (7 · 9) 448

הֶאָח Aha! (3 · 9) 210

בְּיַעַן 3 by the cause (2 · 3) 774

שָׁאַף to trample on, crush (1 · 14 · 4) 983

מוֹרָשָׁה a possession (7 · 9) 440

דִּבָּה evil report (1 · 9) 179

אָפִיק 4 channel (7 · 18) 67

גַּיְא valley (10 · 47) 161

חָרְבָּה waste, ruin (14 · 42) 352

בַּז spoil, booty, plunder (12 · 27) 103

לַעַג mocking, derision (2 · 7) 541

קִנְאָה 5 anger (10 · 43) 888

מוֹרָשָׁה a possession (7 · 9) 440

שָׁאט despite, contempt (3 · 3) 1002

גרש to cast out, thrust out (2 · 8 · 48) 176

בַּז spoil, booty, plunder (12 · 27) 103

אָפִיק 6 channel (7 · 18) 67

גַּיְא valley (10 · 47) 161

קִנְאָה anger (10 · 43) 888

כְּלִמָּה reproach, ignominy (13 · 30) 484

כְּלִמָּה reproach, ignominy (13 · 30) 484

עָנָף 8 branch[es], bough[s] (4 · 7) 778

חָרְבָּה 10 waste, ruin (14 · 42) 352

פרה 11 to be fruitful, bear fruit (2 · 22 · 29) 82

קַדְמָה former state (4 · 6) 870

רֹאשָׁה beginning time, early time (1 · 1) 911

שִׁכֵּל 12 to make childless (5 · 18 · 24) 1013

אַתִּי 13 you [old form; fem.] (1 · 7) 61

שִׁכֵּל to make childless (5 · 18 · 24) 1013

שִׁכֵּל 14 to make childless (5 · 18 · 24) 1013

כְּלִמָּה 15 reproach, ignominy (13 · 30) 484

עֲלִילָה 17 deed (8 · 24) 760

טֻמְאָה uncleanness (8 · 37) 380

נִדָּה impurity (5 · 30) 622

גִּלּוּל 18 idol (39 · 48) 165

נזרה 19 to be scattered, dispersed (2 · 2 · 38) 279

עֲלִילָה deed (8 · 24) 760

חָמַל 21 to spare, have compassion (7 · 40 · 40) 328

זָרַק 25 to toss, throw (3 · 32 · 34) 284

טֻמְאָה uncleanness (8 · 37) 380

גִּלּוּל idol (39 · 48) 165

טֻמְאָה 29 uncleanness (8 · 37) 380

דָּגָן corn, grain (1 · 40) 186

תְּנוּבָה 30 fruit, produce (1 · 5) 626

מַעֲלָל 31 deed, practice (1 · 41) 760

נקוט to feel loathing (1 · 4 · 7) 876

בִּפְנֵי against (4 · 17) 816

נכלם 32 to be humiliated, ashamed (6 · 26 · 38) 483

חָרְבָּה 33 waste, ruin (14 · 42) 352

הַלֵּזוּ 35 this (1 · 3) 229 הַלָּזֶה

חָרֵב waste, desolate (2 · 10) 351 II.

גַּן garden (5 · 42) 171

נהרס to be thrown down, torn down (4 · 10 · 43) 248

בָּצוּר cut off, made inaccessible (2 · 25) 130 בצר

נהרס 36 to be thrown down, torn down (4 · 10 · 43) 248

חָרֵב waste, desolate (2 · 10) 351 II.

Chapter 37

בִּקְעָה 1 plain (5 · 19) 132

בִּקְעָה 2 plain (5 · 19) 132

יָבֵשׁ dry, dried (4 · 9) 386

יָבֵשׁ 4 dry, dried (4 · 9) 386

גִּיד 6 sinew (2 · 7) 161

קרם to spread (2 · 2 · 2) 901

רַעַשׁ 7 earthquake (5 · 17) 950

גִּיד 8 sinew (2 · 7) 161

קרם to spread (2 · 2 · 2) 901

מִלְמָעְלָה above (6 · 24) 751

נפח 9 to breathe, blow (3 · 9 · 12) 655

תִּקְוָה 11 things hoped for, outcome (2 · 32) 876

נִגְזַר to be cut off; i.e., destroyed (1 · 6 · 12) 160

חָבֵר 16 associate, fellow (3 · 12) 288

חָבֵר 19 associate, fellow (3 · 12) 288

מִבֵּין 21 from between (9 · 21) 107 בֵּין 2. d.

נחצה 22 to be divided (1 · 4 · 15) 345

גִּלּוּל 23 idol (39 · 48) 165

שִׁקּוּץ detested thing (8 · 28) 1055

מוֹשָׁב dwelling place (7 · 46) 444

Chapter 38

חָח 4 hook, ring (4 · 7) 296

לְחִי jaw, jawbone (2 · 21) 534

לָבוּשׁ clothed with (9 · 16) 527 לבש

מִכְלוֹל perfection (2 · 2) 483

צִנָּה large shield (4 · 20) 857

כּוֹבַע 5 helmet (2 · 6) 464

אֲגַף 6 bands, armies, hordes (7 · 7) 8

יַרְכָּה remote part (5 · 28) 438

נקהל 7 to assemble (1 · 19 · 39) 874

מִשְׁמָר [dub.] reserve, watch (1 · 22) 1038 Lis. "guard, prison"

חָרְבָּה 8 waste, ruin (14 · 42) 352

בֶּטַח securely (11 · 43) 105

שֹׁאָה 9 devastation, ruin (1 · 12) 996

אֲגַף bands, armies, hordes (7 · 7) 8

פְּרָזָה 11 open region, hamlet (1 · 3) 826

שָׁקַט to be quiet, undisturbed (2 · 31 · 41) 1052

בֶּטַח securely (11 · 43) 105

בְּאֵין without (1 · 10) 34 II. אֵין 6. a.

בְּרִיחַ bar (1 · 41) 138

שָׁלַל 12 to spoil, plunder (7 · 13 · 15) 1021

בָּזַז to spoil, plunder (5 · 38 · 42) 102

בַּז spoil, booty, plunder (12 · 27) 103

חָרְבָּה waste, ruin (14 · 42) 352

קִנְיָן acquisition (2 · 9) 889

טַבּוּר navel (1 · 2) 371

סֹחֵר 13 trafficker, trader (7 · 16) 695 סחר

כְּפִיר young lion (7 · 31) 498

שָׁלַל to spoil, plunder (7 · 13 · 15) 1021

בָּזַז to spoil, plunder (5 · 38 · 42) 102

בַּז spoil, booty, plunder (12 · 27) 103

הקהיל to summon an assembly (1 · 20 · 39) 875

קִנְיָן   acquisition (2 · 9) 889

בֶּטַח 14 securely (11 · 43) 105

יַרְכָּה 15 remote part (5 · 28) 432

קַדְמוֹנִי 17 former ancient (4 · 10) 870

קִנְאָה 19 anger (10 · 43) 888

עֶבְרָה rage, fury (5 · 34) 720

רַעַשׁ earthquake (5 · 17) 950

רָעַשׁ 20 to quake, shake (4 · 21 · 29) 950

דָּג fish (1 · 19) 185

רֶמֶשׂ creeping things (2 · 16) 943

רמשׂ to creep (1 · 16 · 16) 942

נהרס to be thrown down, torn down (4 · 10 · 43) 248

מַדְרֵגָה steep place, steep (1 · 2) 201

דֶּבֶר 22 plague, pestilence (12 · 46) 184

גֶּשֶׁם rain, shower (5 · 35) 177

שָׁטַף to overflow, rinse off, wash off (4 · 28 · 31) 1009

אֶלְגָּבִישׁ hail (3 · 3) 38

גָּפְרִית brimstone (1 · 7) 172

הִמְטִר to rain, send rain (1 · 16 · 17) 565

אַגַף bands, armies, hordes (7 · 7) 8

Chapter 39

שֵׁשֵׁא 2 to lead on (1 · 1 · 1) 1058

יַרְכָּה remote part (5 · 28) 438

אַגַף 4 bands, armies, hordes (7 · 7) 8

עַיִט bird[s] of prey (1 · 8) 743

צִפּוֹר bird, [coll.] (3 · 40) 861

אָכְלָה devouring, eating (10 · 18) 38

אִי 6 coast, border, region (9 · 36) 15 I.

בֶּטַח securely (11 · 43) 105

הִשִּׂיק 9 to make a fire, to burn (1 · 2 · 3) 969

נֶשֶׁק equipment, weapons (2 · 10) 676

צִנָּה large shield (4 · 20) 857

מַקֵּל stick, staff (1 · 18) 596

רֹמַח spear, lance (1 · 15) 942

חטב 10 to cut or gather (1 · 2 · 3) 310

נֶשֶׁק equipment, weapons (2 · 10) 676

שָׁלַל to spoil, plunder (7 · 13 · 15) 1021

בָּזַז to spoil, plunder (5 · 38 · 42) 102

גַּיְא 11 valley (10 · 47) 161

קִדְמָה on the east (1 · 4) 870

חֹסֶמֶת ptc. = stop (1 · 2 · 2) 340

הִבְדִּיל 14 to separate, set apart (3 · 32 · 42) 95

חקר to search [for] (1 · 22 · 27) 350

צִיּוּן 15 signpost, monument (1 · 3) 846

גַּיְא valley (10 · 47) 161

צִפּוֹר 17 bird [coll.] (3 · 40) 861

כַּר 18 male lamb (5 · 12) 503 III.

עַתּוּד male goat (3 · 29) 800

מְרִיא fatling (1 · 8) 597

שָׂבְעָה 19 satiety (3 · 7[?]) 960

שִׁכָּרוֹן drunkenness (2 · 3) 1016

הָלְאָה 22 onward (2 · 13) 229

מָעַל 23 to act unfaithfully, treacherously (7 · 35 · 35) 591

טֻמְאָה 24 uncleanness (8 · 37) 380

שְׁבִית 25 captivity (5 · 26) 986 שְׁבִית

רחם to have compassion (1 · 42 · 47) 933

קִנֵּא to be zealous (2 · 30 · 34) 888

כְּלִמָּה 26 reproach, ignominy (13 · 30) 484

מַעַל unfaithful, treacherous act (6 · 29) 591

מָעַל to act unfaithfully, treacherously (7 · 35 · 35) 591

בֶּטַח securely (11 · 43) 105

הֶחֱרִיד to terrify (3 · 13 · 39) 353

כנס 28 to gather (2 · 3 · 11) 488

Chapter 40

גָּלוּת 1 exile (3 · 15) 163

עָשׂוֹר tenth day (3 · 15) 797

מַרְאָה 2 vision (4 · 12) 909 I.

גָּבֹהַּ high, exalted (6 · 41) 147

מִבְנֶה structure (1 · 1) 125

פָּתִיל 3 cord, thread (1 · 11) 836

פֵּשֶׁת flax, linen (4 · 16) 833

הֵנָּה	4	hither (1·49) 244
טֹפַח	5	span, handbreadth (3·9) 381
בִּנְיָן		structure (7·7) 125
קוֹמָה		height (8·45) 879
מַעֲלָה	6	step, stair (9·47) 752
סַף		threshold, sill (7·25) 706 II.
תָּא	7	chamber (11·13) 1060
סַף		threshold, sill (7·25) 706 II.
מֵאֵצֶל		from beside (2·6) 69 I. אֵצֶל
אוּלָם		porch (32·49) 17 I.
אוּלָם	8	porch (32·49) 17 I.
אוּלָם	9	porch (32·49) 17 I.
אַיִל		pilaster, pillar (21·22) 18 II.
תָּא	10	chamber (11·13) 1060
מִפּוֹ מִפֹּה		repeated = on this side...on that side (33·33) 805 פֹה
אַיִל		pilaster, pillar (21·22) 18 II.
תָּא	12	chamber (11·13) 1060
מִפֹּה		on each side (33·33) 805 פֹה
מִפּוֹ		repeated = on this side...on that side (33·33) 805 פֹה
גָּג	13	roof (1·29) 150
תָּא		chamber (11·13) 1060
אַיִל	14	pilaster, pillar (21·22) 18 II.
אִיתוֹן	15	entrance (1·1) 87
אוּלָם		porch (32·49) 17 I.
פְּנִימִי		inner (24·33) 819
חַלּוֹן	16	window (12·30) 319
אֹטֻם		ptc. pass. = closed (3·8·8) 31
תָּא		chamber (11·13) 1060
אַיִל		pilaster, pillar (21·22) 18 II.
לִפְנִימָה		within (3·5) 819 פנימה
אֵילָם		porch (32·49) 19
תִּמֹרָה		palm figure (13·19) 1071
לִשְׁכָּה	17	room, cell (23·47) 545
חִיצוֹן		outer (18·25) 300
רִצְפָה		pavement (5·7) 954
רִצְפָה	18	pavement (5·7) 954
לְעֻמָּה		side by side with (15·31) 769 עמה
תַּחְתּוֹן		lower, lowest (6·13) 1066

תַּחְתּוֹן	19	lower, lowest (6·13) 1066
פְּנִימִי		inner (24·33) 819
חִיצוֹן	20	outer (18·25) 300
תָּא	21	chamber (11·13) 1060
מִפּוֹ		repeated = on this side...on that side (33·33) 805 פֹה
אַיִל		pilaster, pillar (21·22) 18 II.
אֵילָם		porch (32·49) 19
חַלּוֹן	22	window (12·30) 319
אֵילָם		porch (32·49) 19
תִּמֹרָה		palm figure (13·19) 1071
פְּנִימִי	23	inner (24·33) 819
דָּרוֹם	24	south (13·17) 204
אַיִל		pilaster, pillar (21·22) 18 II.
אֵילָם		porch (32·49) 19
חַלּוֹן	25	window (12·30) 319
אֵילָם		porch (32·49) 19
מַעֲלָה	26	step, stair (9·47) 752
אֵילָם		porch (32·49) 19
תִּמֹרָה		palm figure (13·19) 1071
מִפּוֹ		repeated = on this side...on that side (33·33) 805 פֹה
אַיִל		pilaster, pillar (21·22) 18 II.
פְּנִימִי	27	inner (24·33) 819
דָּרוֹם		south (13·17) 204
פְּנִימִי	28	inner (24·33) 819
דָּרוֹם		south (13·17) 204
תָּא	29	chamber (11·13) 1060
אַיִל		pilaster, pillar (21·22) 18 II.
אֵילָם		porch (32·49) 19
חַלּוֹן		window (12·30) 319
אוּלָם	30	porch (32·49) 17 I.
אוּלָם	31	porch (32·49) 17 I.
חִיצוֹן		outer (18·25) 300
תִּמֹרָה		palm figure (13·19) 1071
אַיִל		pilaster, pillar (21·22) 18 II.
מַעֲלָה		step, stair (9·47) 752
מַעֲלֶה		ascent (3·19) 751
פְּנִימִי	32	inner (24·33) 819
תָּא	33	chamber (11·13) 1060

אַיִל · pilaster, pillar (21 · 22) 18 II.

אֵילָם · porch (32 · 49) 19

חַלּוֹן · window (12 · 30) 319

אֵילָם 34 porch (32 · 49) 19

חִיצוֹן · outer (18 · 25) 300

תִּמֹרָה · palm figure (13 · 19) 1071

אַיִל · pilaster, pillar (21 · 22) 18 II.

מִפּוֹ · repeated = on this side...on that side (33 · 33) 805 פֹה

מַעֲלָה · step, stair (9 · 47) 752

מַעֲלֶה · ascent (3 · 19) 751

תָּא 36 chamber (11 · 13) 1060

אַיִל · pilaster, pillar (21 · 22) 18 II.

אֵילָם · porch (32 · 49) 19

חַלּוֹן · window (12 · 30) 319

אַיִל 37 pilaster, pillar (21 · 22) 18 II.

חִיצוֹן · outer (18 · 25) 300

תִּמֹרָה · palm figure (13 · 19) 1071

מִפּוֹ · repeated = on this side...on that side (33 · 33) 805 פֹה

מַעֲלָה · step, stair (9 · 47) 752

מַעֲלֶה · ascent (3 · 19) 751

לִשְׁכָּה 38 room, cell (23 · 47) 545

אַיִל · pilaster, pillar (21 · 22) 18 II.

הֵדִיחַ · *Hiph.* to rinse (1 · 4 · 4) 188 דוח

אוּלָם 39 porch (32 · 49) 17 I.

מִפּוֹ מִפֹה · repeated = on this side...on that side (33 · 33) 805 פֹה

אָשָׁם · trespass offering; offense, guilt (4 · 47) 79

אוּלָם 40 porch (32 · 49) 17 I.

מִפֹה 41 repeated = on this side...on that side (33 · 33) 805 פֹה

גָּזִית · a cutting, hewing; w/אבן hewn stones (1 · 11) 159

גֹּבַהּ · height (6 · 17) 147

שְׁפַתַּיִם 43 hooks, (1 · 2[?]) 1052

טֹפַח · span, handbreadth (3 · 9) 381

פְּנִימִי 44 inner (24 · 33) 819

לִשְׁכָּה · room, cell (23 · 47) 545

דָּרוֹם · south (13 · 17) 204

זֶה 45 this (1 · 11) 262

לִשְׁכָּה · room, cell (23 · 47) 545

דָּרוֹם · south (13 · 17) 204

לִשְׁכָּה 46 room, cell (23 · 47) 545

קָרֵב · approaching (2 · 11) 898

רבע 47 ptc. = square (2 · 3 · 12) 917

אוּלָם 48 porch (32 · 49) 17 I.

אַיִל · pilaster, pillar (21 · 22) 18 II.

מִפּוֹ מִפֹה · repeated = on this side...on that side (33 · 33) 805 פֹה

אוּלָם 49 porch (32 · 49) 17 I.

מַעֲלָה · step, stair (9 · 47) 752

אַיִל · pilaster, pillar (21 · 22) 18 II.

מִפֹה · repeated = on this side...on that side (33 · 33) 805 פֹה

Chapter 41

אַיִל 1 pilaster, pillar (21 · 22) 18 II.

מִפּוֹ · repeated = on this side...on that side (33 · 33) 805 פֹה

מִפּוֹ 2 repeated = on this side...on that side (33 · 33) 805 פֹה

לִפְנִימָה 3 toward the [in]side (3 · 5) 819 פְּנִימָה

אַיִל · pilaster, pillar (21 · 22) 18 II.

צֵלָע 5 side chamber (10 · 39) 854

צֵלָע 6 side chamber (10 · 39) 754

אָחוּז · ptc. pass. fastened, held (2 · 66) 28 אחז

רָחַב 7 to be or grow wide or large (1 · 3 · 25) 931

לְמַעְלָה · upward (8 · 24) 751 מעל 2. c.

צֵלָע · side chamber (10 · 39) 854

מוּסָב · encompassing, surrounding (1 · 1) 687

תַּחְתּוֹן · lower, lowest (6 · 13) 1066

תִּיכוֹן · middle (4 · 12) 1064

גֹּבַהּ 8 height (6 · 17) 147

מִיסָדָה · foundation (1 · 2) 414 מוּסָדָה

צֵלָע	side chamber (10 · 39) 854		beam, plank, threshold or projecting roof (2 · 3) 712
מְלֹא	fullness (5 · 38) 571	אוּלָם	porch (32 · 49) 17 I.
אַצִּיל	to the joining [obscure]; joining, joint (2 · 3) 69	חַלּוֹן	26 window (12 · 30) 319
צֵלָע	9 side chamber (10 · 39) 854	אָטַם	ptc. pass. = closed (3 · 8 · 8) 31
בֵּית	between (1 · 3) 108	תִּמֹרָה	palm figure (13 · 19) 1071
לִשְׁכָּה	10 room, cell (23 · 47) 545	מִפֹּו	repeated = on this side...on that side (33 · 33) 805 פֹּה
צֵלָע	11 side chamber (10 · 39) 854	אוּלָם	porch (32 · 49) 17 I.
דָרוֹם	south (13 · 17) 204	צֵלָע	side chamber (10 · 39) 854
בִּנְיָן	12 structure (7 · 7) 125	עָב	[dub.] structure of wood; perh.
גִּזְרָה	separation (7 · 8) 160		beam, plank, threshold or projecting roof (2 · 3) 712
גִּזְרָה	13 separation (7 · 8) 160		
בִּנְיָה	structure, building (1 · 1) 125		

Chapter 42

גִּזְרָה	14 separation (7 · 8) 160		
בִּנְיָן	15 structure (7 · 7) 125		
גִּזְרָה	separation (7 · 8) 160		
אַתּוּק	gallery, porch (5 · 5) 87 אַתִּיק	הִיצוֹן	1 outer (18 · 25) 300
מִפֹּו	repeated = on this side...on that side (33 · 33) 805 פֹּה	לִשְׁכָּה	room, cell (23 · 47) 545
		גִּזְרָה	separation (7 · 8) 160
פְּנִימִי	inner (24 · 33) 819	בִּנְיָן	structure (7 · 7) 125
אוּלָם	porch (32 · 49) 17 I.	פְּנִימִי	3 inner (24 · 33) 819
סַף	16 threshold, sill (7 · 25) 706 II.	רִצְפָּה	pavement (5 · 7) 954
חַלּוֹן	window (12 · 30) 319	חִיצוֹן	outer (18 · 25) 300
אָטַם	ptc. pass. = closed (3 · 8 · 8) 31	אַתִּיק	gallery, porch (5 · 5) 87
אַתִּיק	gallery, porch (5 · 5) 87	לִשְׁכָּה	4 room, cell (23 · 47) 545
שָׂחִיף	[dub.] paneled (1 · 1) 965	מַהֲלָךְ	walk (1 · 5) 237
פְּנִימִי	17 inner (24 · 33) 819	פְּנִימִי	inner (24 · 33) 819
חִיצוֹן	outer (18 · 25) 300	לִשְׁכָּה	5 room, cell (23 · 47) 545
תִּמֹרָה	18 palm figure (13 · 19) 1071	קָצוּר	short (1 · 1[?]) 894
תִּמֹרָה	19 palm figure (13 · 19) 1071	אַתִּיק	gallery, porch (5 · 5) 87
מִפֹּו	repeated = on this side...on that side (33 · 33) 805 פֹּה	תַּחְתּוֹן	lower, lowest (6 · 13) 1066
		תִּיכוֹן	middle (4 · 12) 1064
כְּפִיר	young lion (7 · 31) 498	בִּנְיָן	structure (7 · 7) 125
תִּמֹרָה	20 palm figure (13 · 19) 1071	שָׁלֹשׁ	6 ptc. = three-storied (1 · 5 · 9) 1026
מְזוּזָה	21 door post, gate post (7 · 20) 265	נֶאֱצַל	to be withdrawn; i.e., shortened or narrowed (1 · 1 · 5) 69
רבע	ptc. pass. = square (2 · 9 · 12) 917	תַּחְתּוֹן	lower, lowest (6 · 13) 1066
גָּבֹהַּ	22 high, exalted (6 · 41) 147	תִּיכוֹן	middle (4 · 12) 1064
מִקְצֹעַ	corner post (5 · 12) 893	גָּדֵר	7 wall, fence (3 · 14) 154
תִּמֹרָה	25 palm figure (13 · 19) 1071	לְעֻמָּה	side by side with (15 · 31) 769 עֻמָּה
עָב	[dub.] structure of wood; perh.		

לִשְׁכָּה room, cell (23 · 47) 545

חִיצוֹן outer (18 · 25) 300

לִשְׁכָּה 8 room, cell (23 · 47) 545

חִיצוֹן outer (18 · 25) 300

לִשְׁכָה 9 room, cell (23 · 47) 545

חִיצוֹן outer (18 · 25) 300

גָּדֵר 10 wall, fence (3 · 14) 154

גִּזְרָה separation (7 · 8) 160

בִּנְיָן structure (7 · 7) 125

לִשְׁכָה room, cell (23 · 47) 545

לִשְׁכָּה 11 room, cell (23 · 47) 545

מוֹצָא a going forth (4 · 27) 425 I.

לִשְׁכָה 12 room, cell (23 · 47) 545

דָּרוֹם south (13 · 17) 204

בִּפְנֵי in front of (4 · 17) 816 פָּנֶה II. 3.

גִּדֶרֶת wall (1 · 1[?]) 155 גְּדֵרָה

הַגִּין appropriate, suitable [dub.] (1 · 1) 212

לִשְׁכָה 13 room, cell (23 · 47) 545

דָּרוֹם south (13 · 17) 204

גִּזְרָה separation (7 · 8) 160

אָשָׁם trespass offering; offense, guilt (4 · 47) 79

חִיצוֹן 14 outer (18 · 25) 300

פְּנִימִי 15 inner (24 · 33) 819

דָּרוֹם 18 south (13 · 17) 204

הִבְדִּיל 20 to make a distinction, separate (3 · 32 · 42) 95

הֹל profaneness, commonness (4 · 7) 320

Chapter 43

הֵאִיר 2 to light up, cause to shine (2 · 34 · 40) 21

מַרְאָה 3 vision (4 · 12) 909

פְּנִימִי 5 inner (24 · 33) 819

זְנוּת 7 fornication (3 · 9) 276

פֶּגֶר corpse, carcass (3 · 22) 803

סַף 8 threshold, sill (7 · 25) 706 II.

מְזוּזָה doorpost, gatepost (7 · 20) 265

זְנוּת 9 fornication (3 · 9) 276

פֶּגֶר corpse, carcass (3 · 22) 803

נכלם 10 to be humiliated, ashamed (6 · 26 · 38) 483

תָּכְנִית measurement, proportion (2 · 2) 1067

נכלם 11 to be humiliated, ashamed (6 · 26 · 38) 483

צוּרָה form, fashion (4 · 5) 849

תְּכוּנָה arrangement, disposition (1 · 3) 467

מוֹצָא a going forth (4 · 27) 425 I.

מוֹבָא entrance (1 · 2) 100

טֹפַח 13 span, handbreadth (3 · 9) 381

חֵיק bosom [of hollow bottom of altar] (3 · 38) 300

זֶרֶת span [= ½ cubit] (1 · 7) 284

גַּב elevation (7 · 13) 146

חֵיק 14 bosom [of hollow bottom of altar] (3 · 38) 300

עֲזָרָה ledge surrounding (6 · 9) 741

תַּחְתּוֹן lower, lowest, (6 · 13) 1066

קָטָן small (3 · 47) 881

אֲרָאִיל 15 hearth, altar hearth (3 · 3) 72 II.

לְמַעְלָה upward (8 · 34) 751 מַעַל 2. c.

אֲרָאִיל 16 hearth, altar hearth (3 · 3) 72 II.

רבע ptc. pass. = square (2 · 9 · 12) 917

רֶבַע pl. = four sides (5 · 7) 917

עֲזָרָה 17 ledge surrounding (6 · 9) 741

רֶבַע pl. = four sides (5 · 7) 917

חֵיק bosom [of hollow bottom of altar] (3 · 38) 300

מַעֲלָה step, stair (9 · 47) 752

זָרַק 18 to toss, throw (3 · 32 · 34) 284

פִּנָּה 20 corner (2 · 30) 819

עֲזָרָה ledge surrounding (6 · 9) 741

מִפְקָד 21 appointed place (1 · 5) 824

חִטֵּא 22 to purify from sin (>50) 307

מֶלַח 24 salt (2 · 28) 571

הָלְאָה 27 onward (2 · 13) 229

352

Chapter 44

חִיצוֹן	1	outer (18 · 25) 300
אוּלָם	3	porch (32 · 49) 17 I.
מָבוֹא	5	entering (5 · 23) 99
מוֹצָא		a going forth (4 · 27) 425 I.
מְרִי	6	rebellion (15 · 22) 598
נֵכָר	7	foreignness; נ' בֶּן = foreigner (3 · 36) 648
עָרֵל		uncircumcised (16 · 35) 790
הֵפֵר		to break, frustrate (5 · 41 · 44) 830
נֵכָר	9	foreignness; נ' בֶּן = foreigner (3 · 36) 648
עָרֵל		uncircumcised (16 · 35) 790
תָּעָה	10	to err (7 · 26 · 50) 1073
גִּלּוּל		idol (39 · 48) 165
פְּקֻדָּה	11	overseer (2 · 32) 824
גִּלּוּל	12	idol (39 · 48) 165
מִכְשׁוֹל		stumbling block (8 · 14) 506
כִּהֵן	13	to act as priest (1 · 23 · 23) 464
כְּלִמָּה		reproach, ignominy (12 · 30) 484
תָּעָה	15	to err (7 · 27 · 50) 1073
פְּנִימִי	17	inner (24 · 33) 819
פֵּשֶׁת		flax, linen (4 · 16) 833
צֶמֶר		wool (3 · 16) 856
פְּאֵר	18	headdress, turban (3 · 7) 802
פֵּשֶׁת		flax, linen (4 · 16) 833
מִכְנָס		undergarments (1 · 5) 488
מָתְנַיִם		loins (12 · 47) 608
חגר		to gird oneself (3 · 44 · 44) 291
יֶזַע		sweat (1 · 1) 402
חִיצוֹן	19	outer (18 · 25) 300
פָּשַׁט		to strip off, put off (2 · 24 · 43) 833
לִשְׁכָּה		room, cell (23 : 47) 545
גִּלַּח	20	to shave, shave off (1 · 18 · 23) 164
פֶּרַע		long hair, locks (1 · 2) 828
כסם		to clip, shear (2 · 2 · 2) 493
פְּנִימִי	21	inner (24 · 33) 819
גרשׁ	22	to cast out, thrust out (2 · 8 · 48) 176
בְּתוּלָה		virgin (2 · 50) 143-144

הוֹרָה	23	to direct, instruct, teach (1 · 45 · 45 [?]) 434 ירה
חֹל		profaneness, commonness (4 · 7) 320
טָהֳרָה	26	cleansing, purification (1 · 13) 372
פְּנִימִי	27	inner (24 · 33) 819
אָשָׁם	29	trespass offering; offense, guilt (4 · 47) 79
חֵרֶם		devoted thing (1 · 29) 356 I.
בִּכּוּרִים	30	firstfruits (1 · 17) 114
עֲרִיסָה		[dub.] course meal (1 · 4) 791
נְבֵלָה	31	carcass, corpse (2 · 48) 615
טְרֵפָה		torn flesh (2 · 9) 383

Chapter 45

רבע	2	ptc. = square (3 · 3 · 12) 917
קָרֵב	4	approaching (2 · 11) 898
לִשְׁכָּה	5	room, cell (23 · 47) 545
לְעֻמָּה	6	side by side with (15 · 31) 769 עמה
מִזֶּה וּמִזֶּה	7	on one side...on the other [idiom] 262 זֶה 6.e.
קֶרֶם		eastward (3 · 26) 870
לְעֻמָּה		side by side with (15 · 31) 769 עמה
הוֹנָה	8	to oppress, maltreat (7 · 14 · 18) 413 ינה
שֹׁד	9	violence, havoc (1 · 25) 994
גְּרוּשָׁה		expulsion, violence (1 · 1) 177
מֹאזְנַיִם	10	balances, scales (2 · 15) 24 מאזן
אֵיפָה		ephah [grain measure] (17 · 39) 35
בַּת		bath [liquid measure] (7 · 13) 144 II.
אֵיפָה	11	ephah [grain measure] (17 · 39) 35
בַּת		bath [liquid measure] (7 · 13) 144 II.
תֹּכֶן		capacity (1 · 2) 1067
מַעֲשֵׂר		tenth part, tithe (2 · 33) 798
חֹמֶר		homer [dry measure] (7 · 13) 330 III.
מַתְכֹּנֶת		measurement, proportion (1 · 5) 1067
גֵּרָה	12	gerah [a weight, 20th part of shekel] (1 · 5) 176
מָנֶה		maneh, mina [measure of weight] (1 · 5) 584

חִטָּה 13 wheat (3 · 30) 334
אֵיפָה ephah [grain measure] (17 · 39) 35
שִׁשָּׁה to give a sixth part of (1 · 1 · 1) 995
חֹמֶר homer [dry measure] (7 · 13) 330 III.
שְׂעֹרָה barley (4 · 34) 972
בַּת 14 bath [liquid measure] (7 · 13) 144 II.
מַעֲשֵׂר tenth part, tithe (2 · 33) 798
כֹּר kor [dry measure] (1 · 8) 499
חֹמֶר homer [dry measure] (7 · 13) 330 III.
שֶׂה 15 sheep, goat (5 · 45) 961
מַשְׁקֶה well irrigated (2 · 19) 1052 II.
חָטָא 18 to purify (Piel) (>50) 307
מְזוּזָה 19 doorpost, gate post (7 · 20) 265
פִּנָּה corner (2 · 30) 819
עֲזָרָה ledge surrounding (6 · 9) 741
פְּנִימִי inner (24 · 33) 819
שָׁגָה 20 to commit sin of ignorance (2 · 17 · 21) 993
פֶּתִי simple (1 · 19) 834
פֶּסַח 21 passover (1 · 49) 820
שָׁבוּעַ period of seven, week (1 · 20) 988
אֵיפָה 24 ephah [grain measure] (17 · 39) 35
הִין hin [liquid measure] (6 · 22) 228

Chapter 46

פְּנִימִי 1 inner (24 · 33) 819
אוּלָם 2 porch (32 · 49) 17 I.
מְזוּזָה doorpost, gate post (7 · 20) 265
מִפְתָּן threshold (5 · 8) 837
אֵיפָה 5 ephah [grain measure] (17 · 39) 35
מַתַּת gift (2 · 6) 682
הִין hin [liquid measure] (6 · 22) 228
אֵיפָה 7 ephah [grain measure] (17 · 39) 35
הִין hin [liquid measure] (6 · 22) 228
אוּלָם 8 porch (32 · 49) 17 I.
נֹכַח 9 in front of (5 · 22) 647

אֵיפָה 11 ephah [grain measure] (17 · 39) 35
מַתַּת gift (2 · 6) 682
הִין hin [liquid measure] (6 · 22) 228
נְדָבָה 12 freewill [voluntary] offering (2 · 27) 621
אֵיפָה 14 ephah [grain measure] (17 · 39) 35
הִין hin [liquid measure] (6 · 22) 228
רסס to moisten (1 · 1 · 1) 944
מַתָּנָה 16 gift (5 · 17) 682
מַתָּנָה 17 gift (5 · 17) 682
דְּרוֹר liberty (1 · 7) 204 I.
הוֹנָה 18 to oppress, maltreat (7 · 14 · 18) 413 ינה
מָבוֹא 19 entrance (5 · 23) 99
לִשְׁכָּה room, cell (23 · 47) 545
יַרְכָה extreme, hinder part (5 · 28) 438
בשל 20 to boil (3 · 21 · 28) 143
אָשָׁם trespass offering; offense, guilt (4 · 47) 79
אָפָה to bake (1 · 10 · 13) 66
חִיצוֹן outer (18 · 25) 300
חִיצוֹן 21 outer (18 · 25) 300
מִקְצוֹעַ buttress place (5 · 12) 893
מִקְצוֹעַ 22 buttress place (5 · 12) 893
קטר Qal ptc. pass. = [dub.] enclosed (1 · 1 · 1) 883
מְהֻקְצָעוֹת Hoph. ptc. = cornered, set in corner (1 · 1 · 3[?]) 893
טוּר 23 course, row (1 · 27) 377
מְבַשְּׁלוֹת cooking places (1 · 1) 143
טִירָה row (2 · 7) 377
בשל 24 to boil (3 · 21 · 28) 143

Chapter 47

מִפְתָּן 1 threshold (5 · 8) 837
יְמָנִי right, right hand (3 · 33) 412
מִנֶּגֶד in front, opposite, at a distance (1 · 26) 2. c. נֶגֶד 617
פכה 2 to trickle (1 · 1 · 1) 810

יְמָנִי	right, right hand (3 · 33) 412
קַו	3 line (1 · 17) 876
אֲפָסַיִם	soles [of feet] or ankles (1 · 1) 67 אֶפֶס
מָתְנַיִם	4 loins (12 · 47) 608
בֶּרֶךְ	knee (3 · 25) 139
גָּאָה	5 to rise up (1 · 7 · 7) 144
שָׂחוּ	swimming (1 · 1) 965
מִזֶּה וּמִזֶּה	7 on the one side...on the other 262 זֶה 6. e.
גְּלִילָה	8 circuit, boundary, territory (1 · 6) 327
קַדְמוֹן	eastern (1 · 1) 870
שָׁרַץ	9 to swarm (1 · 14 · 14) 1056
דָּגָה	fish (6 · 15) 185
דַּוָּג	10 fisher, fisherman (1 · 1) 186
מִשְׁטוֹחַ	spreading place (3 · 3) 1009
חֵרֶם	net (4 · 9) 357 II.
מִין	kind, species (1 · 31) 568
דָּגָה	fish (6 · 15) 185
בִּצָּא	11 swamp (1 · 3) 130
גֶּבֶא	cistern, pool (1 · 2) 146
מֶלַח	salt (2 · 28) 571
מִזֶּה וּנְזֶה	12 on the one side...on the other 262 זֶה 6. e.
מַאֲכָל	food (3 · 30) 38
יִפּוֹל	impf. נָבֵל to droop, wither and fall, fade (1 · 19 · 23) 615

עָלֶה	leaf, leafage (2 · 17) 750
בכר	to bear early, new fruit (1 · 2 · 4) 114
תְּרוּפָה	healing (1 · 1) 930
חֵבֶל	13 measured portion, lot, part, region (2 · 49) 286
תִּיכוֹן	16 middle (4 · 12) 1064
מִבֵּין	18 from between (9 · 21) 107 בֵּין 2. d.
קַדְמוֹנִי	eastern (4 · 10) 870
תֵּימָן	19 south (4 · 24) 412
נֹכַח	20 in front of (5 · 22) 647
אֶזְרָח	22 [a] native (1 · 17) 280

Chapter 48

תָּעָה	11 to err (7 · 27 · 50) 1073
תְּרוּמִיָּה	12 allotment (1 · 1) 929
לְעֻמָּה	13 side by side with (15 · 31) 769 עֻמָּה
הֵמִיר	14 to exchange (1 · 13 · 14) 558 מור
חֹל	15 profaneness, commonness (4 · 7) 320
מוֹשָׁב	dwelling place (7 · 43) 444
לְעֻמָּה	18 side by side with (15 · 31) 769 עֻמָּה
תְּבוּאָה	product, yield (1 · 43) 100
לְעֻמָּה	21 side by side with (15 · 31) 769 עֻמָּה
תֵּימָן	28 south (4 · 24) 412
מַחֲלֹקֶת	29 division, part (1 · 35) 324
תּוֹצָאָה	30 outskirts (1 · 23) 426

HOSEA

Chapter 1

תְּחִלָּה 2 beginning; ת׳דבר יהוה = when Yhwh first spoke (1 · 22) 321

זְנוּנִים fornication (6 · 12) 276

הָרָה 3 to conceive, become pregnant (3 · 38 · 40) 247

מַמְלָכוּת 4 dominion, royal power, kingdom, reign (1 · 9) 575

הָרָה 6 to conceive, become pregnant (3 · 38 · 40) 247

רְחַם to have compassion, be compassionate (4 · 42 · 47) 933

רְחַם 7 to have compassion, be compassionate (4 · 42 · 47) 933

גָּמַל 8 to wean; to deal adequately with, deal out to; to ripen (1 · 34 · 37) 168

הָרָה to conceive, become pregnant (3 · 38 · 40) 247

Chapter 2

חוֹל 1 sand (1 · 22) 297

רחם 3 to be shown compassion (3 · 4 · 47) 933

זְנוּנִים 4 fornication (6 · 12) 276

נַאֲפוּף adultery (1 · 1) 610

שַׁד female breast (2 · 21) 994

מִבֵּין from between (1 · 21) בין w. preps. d. 107

הִפְשִׁיט 5 to strip, strip off (1 · 15 · 43) 832

עָרוֹם naked (1 · 16) 736

הִצִּיג to set, exhibit, place (1 · 15 · 16) 426

צִיָּה drought, dryness (1 · 16) 851

צָמָא thirst (1 · 17) 854

רחם 6 to have compassion, be compassionate (4 · 42 · 47) 933

זְנוּנִים fornication (6 · 12) 276

הָרָה 7 to conceive, become pregnant Lis. 435 has הרה "mother" (1 · 3) 247

מְאַהֵב ptc. = lover, friend (5 · 16) 12-13

צֶמֶר wool (2 · 16) 856

פֵּשֶׁת flax, linen (2 · 16) 833

שִׁקּוּי drink (1 · 3) 1052

שָׂךְ 8 שוך to hedge up, fence up (1 · 2 · 2) 962

סִיר thorn, hook (1 · 5) 696

גָּדַר to wall up or off, build a wall (1 · 7 · 7) 154

גָּדֵר wall, fence (1 · 14) 154

נְתִיבָה path, course of life (1 · 21) 677

מְאַהֵב 9 ptc. = lover, friend (5 · 16) 12-13

הִשִּׂיג to overtake, reach (2 · 49 · 49) 673

מֵעַתָּה from now, henceforth; but here comparative = "than now" עתה para. 2.e. BDB 774

דָּגָן 10 corn, grain of cereals (6 · 40) 186

תִּירוֹשׁ must, fresh or new wine (6 · 38) 440

יִצְהָר fresh oil (2 · 23) 844

דָּגָן 11 corn, grain of cereals (6 · 40) 186

תִּירוֹשׁ must, fresh or new wine (6 · 38) 440

צֶמֶר wool (2 · 16) 856

פֵּשֶׁת flax, linen (2 · 16) 833

נַבְלוּת 12 immodesty, shamelessness (1 · 1) 615

מְאַהֵב ptc. = lover, friend (5 · 16) 12-13

מָשׂוֹשׂ 13 exultation, rejoicing (1 · 17) 965

תְּאֵנָה 14 fig tree, fig (2 · 39) 1061

אֶתְנָה hire (1 · 1) 1071

מְאַהֵב ptc. = lover, friend (5 · 16) 12-13

עדה 15 to ornament, deck oneself (1 · 8 · 8) 725

נֶזֶם ring (1 · 17) 633

חֶלְיָה jewelry (1 · 1) 318

מְאַהֵב ptc. = lover, friend (5 · 16) 12-13

פתה 16 to persuade, entice, deceive (1 · 17 · 27) 834

תִּקְוָה 17 hope (1 · 32) 876

נְעוּרִים   youth, early life (1 · 46) 655

רֶמֶשׂ   20 [coll.] creeping things, moving things (1 · 16) 943

בֶּטַח   with לְ securely; quietness and security (1 · 43) 105

אָרַשׂ   21 to betroth (3 · 6 · 11) 77

רַחֲמִים   compassion (1 · 38) 933

אָרַשׂ   22 to betroth (3 · 6 · 11) 77

דָּגָן   24 corn, grain of cereals (6 · 40) 186

תִּירוֹשׁ   must, fresh or new wine (6 · 38) 440

יִצְהָר   fresh oil (2 · 23) 844

רָחַם   25 to have compassion, be compassionate (4 · 42 · 47) 933

רחם   to be shown compassion (3 · 4 · 47) 933

Chapter 3

נאף   1 to commit adultery (4 · 14 · 31) 610

אֲשִׁישָׁה   [pressed] raisin-cake (1 · 5) 84

עֵנָב   grape, grapes (2 · 19) 772

כרה   2 to get by trade, buy (1 · 4 · 4) 500

חֹמֶר   homer, dry measure (1 · 13) 330

שְׂעֹרָה   barley; pl. = barley grains (*1 · 33) 972 *occurs two times here; Lis. 1381 missed it.

לֵתֶךְ ,לֶתֶךְ   a barley measure (1 · 1) 547

מַצֵּבָה   4 pillar (3 · 36) 663

אֵפוֹד   ephod, means of consulting deity, priestly garment (1 · 49) 65

תְּרָפִים ,תרף   kind of idol, object of reverence and means of divination (1 · 15) 1076

פָּחַד   5 to be in dread, in awe (1 · 22 · 25) 808

טוּב   good things (2 · 32) 375

Chapter 4

אָלָה   2 to swear, take an oath, curse (2 · 3 · 6) 46

כָּחַשׁ   to deceive, act deceptively (2 · 19 · 22) 471

רָצַח   to murder, slay (1 · 35 · 41) 953

גנב   to steal, take by stealth (1 · 30 · 39) 170

נאף   to commit adultery (1 · 17 · 31) 610

פָּרַץ   to use violence, break through, into, out, etc. (2 · 46 · 49) 829

אָבַל   3 to mourn, lament (2 · 18 · 38) 5

אֻמְלַל   to be or grow feeble, to languish (1 · 15 · 15) 51

דָּג   fish (1 · 19) 185

דמה   5 to cause to cease, cut off (1 · 4 · 16) 198

נִדְמָה   6 to be cut off, destroyed, ruined (4 · 12 · 16) 198

מִבְּלִי   from want of, unawares (1 · 25) 115

כָּהֵן   to minister as a priest, be or become a priest (1 · 23 · 23) 464

רבב   7 [inf. constr.] to become many, much (3 · 23 · 24) 912

קָלוֹן   ignominy, shame (2 · 17) 885-886

הֵמִיר   to exchange, change (1 · 13 · 14) 558

מַעֲלָל   9 deed, practice, evil practice (5 · 41) 760

פָּרַץ   10 to break over [limits], increase; to break through, into, out, etc. (2 · 46 · 49) 829

זְנוּת   11 fornication (2 · 9) 276

תִּירוֹשׁ   must, fresh or new wine (6 · 38) 440

מַקֵּל   12 wand, staff, rod (1 · 18) 596

זְנוּנִים   fornication (5 · 11) 276

הִתְעָה   to cause to err, mislead, wander about (1 · 21 · 50) 1073

מִתַּחַת   from under, from beneath para. III.2.a. תחת 1066

357

אַלּוֹן 13 oak tree, oak (1 · 9) 47

לִבְנֶה poplar (1 · 2) 527

אֵלָה, אַלָּה terebinth, a deciduous tree with pinnate leaves and red berries (1 · 17) 18

כַּלָּה young wife, bride; daughter-in-law (2 · 34) 483

נאף to commit adultery (4 · 14 · 31) 610

כַּלָּה 14 young wife, bride; daughter-in-law (2 · 34) 483

נאף to commit adultery (4 · 14 · 31) 610

פרד to make a separation (1 · 1 · 26) 825

זוֹנָה ptc. = harlot (1 · 33) 275

קָדֵשׁ temple prostitute (1 · 11) 873

נלבט to be thrust down, away (1 · 3 · 3) 526

אָשַׁם 15 to be [become] guilty, be held guilty, do a wrong (5 · 33 · 35) 79

פָּרָה 16 heifer, cow (1 · 26) 831

סָרַר to be stubborn, rebellious (3 · 17 · 17) 710

מֶרְחָב broad or roomy place (1 · 6) 932

חבר 17 to unite, be joined, come as allies (1 · 11 · 28) 287

עָצָב idol (4 · 17) 781

סֹבֶא 18 drink, liquor (1 · 3) 685

הֵבוּ imper. of אהב pp 12-13; G.K.

קָלוֹן ignominy, shame (2 · 17) 885-886

מָגֵן shield (1 · 4); but Lis. 749 has sep. word = insolent. 171

הָ 19 all by itself [?] - text prob. no refs in G.K.; K and D; Davidson Grammar (Syntax)

Chapter 5

הַקְשִׁיב 1 to give attention (1 · 45 · 46) 904

הַאֲזִין to hear, give ear, listen (1 · 41 · 41) 24

פַּח bird trap (2 · 25) 809

רֶשֶׁת net (2 · 22) 440

שַׁחֲטָה 2 [mng. dub.] slaughtering (1 · 1) 1006

שֵׂט סֵט swerver, revolter; deeds that swerve (1 · 2) 962

הֶעְמִיק to make deep (2 · 8 · 9) 770

מוּסָר chastening, discipline (1 · 50) 416

נכחר 3 to be hidden (1 · 11 · 32) 470

מַעֲלָל 4 bad practice, deed, practice (5 · 41) 760

זְנוּנִים fornication (5 · 11) 276

גָּאוֹן 5 exaltation, majesty, excellence, pride (2 · 49) 144-145

בִּפְנֵי in the face of (2 · 17) para. II.3.a. פָּנֶה 816

חָלַץ 6 to withdraw; draw off or out (1 · 5 · 27) 322

בגד 7 to act or deal treacherously, faith-lessly, deceitfully (2 · 49 · 49) 93

חֲצֹצְרָה 8 clarion, wind instrument (1 · 29) 348

הֵרִיעַ to sound a signal for war or march, raise a shout, give a blast (1 · 40 · 44) 929

שַׁמָּה 9 appalling waste (1 · 39) 1031

תּוֹכֵחָה rebuke, correction (1 · 4) 407

הִסִּיג 10 to displace, move back, remove (1 · 7 · 25) 690

עֶבְרָה overflowing rage, fury; overflow (2 · 34) 720

עָשַׁק 11 to oppress, wrong; ptc. = op-pressed (2 · 36 · 37) 798-799

רצץ to crush, oppress (1 · 11 · 19) 954

הוֹאִיל to be determined, resolved; to ac-quiesce; to undertake (1 · 18 · 18) 383

צַו [mng. dub.] command, ordinance (1 · 9) 846

עָשׁ 12 moth (1 · 7) 799

רָקָב rottenness, decay (1 · 5) 799

חֳלִי 13 sickness (1 · 24) 318

יָרֵב let him contend (2 · 2) 937

מָזוֹר wound, injury (2 · 3) 267

גָּה to depart, be cured, healed
(1 · 1 · 1) 155

שַׁחַל 14 lion (2 · 7) 1006

כְּפִיר young lion (1 · 31) 498

טָרַף to tear, rend (2 · 19 · 24) 382

אָשַׁם,אָשָׁם 15 to be held guilty, bear punishment,
be guilty (5 · 33 · 35) 79

צַר straits, distress (0 · 20) 865 Lis.
1227 missed entry

שִׁחֵר to look early for, look diligently
for (1 · 12 · 13) 1007

גְּדוּד marauding band, troop (2 · 33) 151

חֶבֶר company, band, association, soci-
ety (1 · 7) 288

רָצַח to murder, assassinate (1 · 3 · 41) 953

זִמָּה wickedness, evil device; plan, purpose (1 · 28) 273

שַׁעֲרִירִיָּה 10 read שַׁעֲרוּרִיָּה, שַׁעֲרוּרִי horror, horrible
thing (1 · 2) 1045

זְנוּת fornication (2 · 9) 276

קָצִיר 11 what is harvested, harvesting, time
of harvest (1 · 49) 894

שְׁבוּת captivity (1 · 26) 986

Chapter 6

טָרַף 1 to tear, rend (2 · 19 · 24) 382

יַךְ Hiph. imperf. of נכה Lis. 929

חָבֵשׁ to bind up, bind, bind on
(1 · 28 · 32) 289

שַׁחַר 2 dawn (2 · 23) 1007

מוֹצָא a going forth; that which goes
forth; place of going forth (1 · 27)
425

גֶּשֶׁם rain, shower (1 · 35) 177

מַלְקוֹשׁ latter rain, spring rain (1 · 8) 545

יוֹרֶה early rain from last of Oct. to first
of Dec. (2 · 2 · 3); BDB lists as
noun (Lis. 639 as hiph. verb form
"to sprinkle") 435

טַל 4 dew, night mist (3 · 31) 378

חָצַב 5 to hew in pieces; hew, hew out
(1 · 14 · 17) 345

אֵמֶר utterance, word (1 · 48) 56

בָּגַד 7 to act or deal treacherously, faithlessly, deceitfully (2 · 49 · 49) 93

קִרְיָה 8 town, city (1 · 28) 900

עָקֹב foot-tracked; insidious, deceitful
(1 · 3) 784

חִכָּה 9 to wait, to tarry, to wait for
(1 · 13 · 14) 314

Chapter 7

גַּנָּב 1 thief (1 · 17) 170

פָּשַׁט to put off [one's shelter]; i.e., to
make a dash, to strip off
(1 · 24 · 43) 832-833

גְּדוּד marauding band, troop (2 · 33) 151

מַעֲלָל 2 practice, deed (5 · 41) 760

כַּחַשׁ 3 lying, untruthfulness (3 · 6) 471

נָאַף 4 to commit adultery (4 · 14 · 31) 610

תַּנּוּר portable stove, fire pot (3 · 15) 1072

אֹפֶה ptc. = baker (2 · 12) 66

לוּשׁ to knead (1 · 5 · 5) 534

בָּצֵק dough (1 · 5) 130

חָמֵץ to be leavened, soured (1 · 3 · 4) 329

מָשַׁךְ 5 BDB says text prob. corrupt; to
draw, drag, draw out; LXX, AV,
RV, to stretch out (2 · 30 · 36) 604

לוֹצֵץ Po 'lel ptc. מ dropped = scorner
(1 · 1 · 12) 539

תַּנּוּר 6 portable stove, fire pot (3 · 15)
1072

אֹרֵב ambush, intrigue (1 · 2) 70

יָשֵׁן asleep, sleeping (1 · 9) 653

אֹפֶה ptc. = baker (2 · 12) 66

לֶהָבָה flame (1 · 19) 529

חַם, חמם 7 to be [grow] warm (1 · 23 · 26) 328

תַּנּוּר portable stove, fire pot (3 · 15) 1072

הִתְבֹּלֵל 8 to mix oneself (1 · 1 · 43) 232

עֻגָה disc or cake of bread (1 · 7) 728

בְּלִי adv. of negation, not (3 · 23) 115

שֵׂיבָה 9 gray hair, hoary head, old age (1 · 20) 966

זָרַק to be profuse, toss or scatter abundantly (1 · 1 · 1) [note Lis. 458 has as sep. verb "to be white"] 248

גָּאוֹן 10 exaltation, majesty, excellence, pride (2 · 49) 144-145

בִּפְנֵי in the face of, against (2 · 17) para. II.3. פָּנֶה p. 816

יוֹנָה 11 dove (2 · 33) 401

פָּתָה to be open-minded, simple; to be enticed, deceived (1 · 5 · 27) 834

רֶשֶׁת 12 net (2 · 22) 440

הִיסִיר to chasten (1 · 1 · 38) 415

שֵׁמַע hearing, report (1 · 17) 1034

אוֹי 13 Woe! [an impassioned expression of grief and dispair] (2 · 25) 17

נדד to flee, depart, wander (2 · 20 · 24) 622

שֹׁד devastation, ruin, violence (4 · 25) 994

פָּשַׁע to transgress, rebel (3 · 40 · 41) 833

כָּזָב lie, falsehood, deceptive thing (2 · 31) 469

הֵילִיל 14 to howl, give a howl in distress (1 · 30 · 30) 410

מִשְׁכָּב couch, bed (1 · 46) 1012

דָּגָן corn, grain (6 · 40) 186

תִּירוֹשׁ must, fresh or new wine (6 · 38) 440

הִתְגּוֹרֵר Lis. has under גור; *Hithpol.* = to stay, loaf about as a client (1 · 3 · 83) Lis. 319; BDB lists as dub. under גור; to assemble themselves; and II גור to excite themselves [pp. 157-158] or even התגד to cut oneself [p. 151].

יָסַר 15 to discipline, correct (1 · 27 · 38) 416

עַל 16 height, upward (2 · 8 as subst.) 752

רְמִיָּה deceit, treachery (1 · 15) 941

זַעַם indignation (1 · 22) 276

זוּ this (1 · 2) 262

לַעַג mocking, derision (1 · 7) 541

Chapter 8

חֵךְ 1 palate, roof of mouth, gums (1 · 18) 335

נֶשֶׁר griffon-vulture, eagle (1 · 26) 676

פָּשַׁע to transgress, rebel (3 · 40 · 41) 833

זָנַח 3 to reject, spurn (2 · 16 · 19) 276

הִשִּׂיר 4 to make [i.e., appoint] princes (1 · 1 · 8) 979

עָצָב idol (4 · 17) 781

זָנַח 5 to reject, spurn (2 · 16 · 19) 276

עֵגֶל calf (3 · 35) 722

עַד־מָתַי how long[?] (1 ·) 607

נִקָּיוֹן freedom from punishment; innocency (1 · 5) 667

חָרָשׁ 6 graver, artificer (2 · 38) 360

שְׁבָבִים splinters (1 · 1) 985

עֵגֶל calf (3 · 35) 722

סוּפָה 7 storm wind (1 · 15) 693; see G.K. para. 90f. p. 250 for old accusative form ה.

קצר to reap, harvest (3 · 24 · 24) 894

קָמָה standing grain (1 · 10) 879

צֶמַח sprouting, growth (1 · 12) 855

בְּלִי adverb of negation, not (3 · 23) 115

קֶמַח flour, meal (1 · 14) 887

אוּלַי if perchance, peradventure (1 · 45) 19

בָּלַע to swallow up, engulf, swallow down (1 · 20 · 41) 118

נִבְלַע 8 to be swallowed (1 · 1 · 41) 118

חֵפֶץ delight, pleasure (1 · 39) 343

פֶּרֶא 9 wild ass (1 · 10) 825

בָּדַד to be separate, isolated (1 · 3 · 3) 94

הִתְנָה to hire [lovers] (1 · 1 · 3) 1071

אַהַב love, amour (1 · 2) 13

גַּם כִּי 10 yea though, yea when, even when [idiom] גַּם para. 6 169

תָנָה to hire; to hire [a lover] (1 · 2 · 3) 1071

מַשָּׂא load, burden; BDB says read משה w. LXX (1 · 45) 672

רִבּוֹ, רְבוֹא 12 ten thousand, myriad (1 · 11) 914

הַבְהָב 13 gift [dub.] (1 · 1) 396

רָצָה to accept, be pleased with (1 · 42 · 50) 953

עָשָׂה 14 ptc. = maker (1 · 24) 793

בָּצַר, בָּצוּר ptc. pass. = cut off, made inaccessible, fortified (1 · 25) 131

אַרְמוֹן citadel, castle, palace (1 · 33) 74

Chapter 9

גִּיל 1 rejoicing (1 · 8) 162

אֶתְנַן hire of harlot (1 · 11) 1072

גֹּרֶן threshing floor (3 · 34) 175

דָּגָן corn, grain (6 · 40) 186

גֹּרֶן 2 threshing floor (3 · 34) 175

יֶקֶב wine vat (1 · 16) 428

תִּירוֹשׁ must, fresh or new wine (6 · 38) 440

כָּחַשׁ to act deceptively, deceive (1 · 19 · 22) 471

נָסַךְ 4 to pour out libations, pour out, cast metal images (1 · 7 · 24) 650

ערב to be sweet, pleasing (1 · 8 · 8) 787

אֹנֶה, אָוֶן BDB אָוֶן trouble, sorrow, mourning; Lis. mourning (1[?] · 2[?]) 19-20

שֹׁד 6 violence, havoc, devastation, ruin; BDB read אשור (4 · 25) 994

מַחְמַד desirable thing, precious thing (2 · 13) 326

קִמּוֹשׂ [coll.] thistles or nettles (1 · 3) 888

חוֹחַ brier, bramble; hook, ring (1 · 11) 296

פְּקֻדָּה 7 visitation = punishment; oversight, charge; store (1 · 32) 824

שִׁלֵּם requital, retribution, reward (1 · 3) 1024

אֱוִיל foolish (1 · 26) 17

שֻׁגַּע to be mad; Pu. ptc. = maddened [Lis. 1404 "sad"] (1 · 5 · 7) 993

רָבַח to be or become much or many; BDB read רב (3 · 23 · 24) 912

מַשְׂטֵמָה animosity (2 · 2) 966

צפה 8 to look out, spy; ptc. = watchman (1 · 9 · 18) 859

פַּח bird trap (2 · 25) 809

יָקוּשׁ יָקוּשׁ bait layer, fowler (1 · 4) 430

מַשְׂטֵמָה animosity (2 · 2) 966

הֶעְמִיק 9 to make deep, to be in the depth of [sq. vb.] (2 · 8 · 9) 770

עֵנָב 10 grape[s] (2 · 19) 772

בִּכּוּרָה first ripe fig, early fig (1 · 4) 114

תְּאֵנָה fig tree, fig (2 · 39) 1061

נזר to devote or dedicate oneself, hold sacredly aloof from (1 · 4 · 10) 634

בֹּשֶׁת shameful thing, shame (1 · 30) 102

שִׁקּוּץ detested thing (1 · 28) 1055

אֹהַב love, loved object; amour [carnal] (1 · 2) 13

הִתְעוֹפֵף 11 to fly away (1 · 1 · 25) 733

לֵדָה [inf. cstr.] to bring forth, bringing forth (1 · 4) 408

הֵרָיוֹן conception, pregnancy (1 · 2) 248

שִׁכֵּל 12 to make childless, cause barrenness (1 · 18 · 23) 1013

כִּי־גַם for even [idiom] para. 6 גַּם 169

אוֹי Woe! [an impassioned expression of grief and dispair] (2 · 25) 17

שָׁתַל 13 to transplant [Lis. 1503 "plant"] (1 · 10 · 10) 1060

361

נָוֶה meadow, abode of shepherds; habitation (1 · 45) 627

רֶחֶם 14 womb (1 · 33) 933

הִשְׁכִּיל to miscarry; ptc. = miscarrying (1 · 2 · 23) 1013

שַׁד female breast (2 · 21) 994

צָמֵק to dry up, shrivel (1 · 1 · 1) 855

רֹעַ 15 evil, badness (1 · 19) 947-948

מַעֲלָל practice, deed, evil practice (5 · 41) 760

גָּרַשׁ to drive out, drive away (1 · 35 · 48) 176

סָרַר to be stubborn, rebellious (3 · 17 · 17) 710

שֹׁרֶשׁ 16 root (2 · 33) 1057

בְּלִי [בל] adv. of negation, not (3 · 23) 115

גַּם כִּי yea though, yea when, even when [idiom] גַּם para. 6. 169

מַחְמָד desirable thing, precious thing (2 · 13) 326

נדד 17 to wander, stray; retreat, flee, depart (2 · 20 · 24) 622

Chapter 10

בקק 1 to be luxuriant; II root = to lay waste (1 · 4 · 7) 132

שׁנה to make, produce [one time]; to set, place (1 · 5 · 5) 1001

רבב Lis. 1310 as inf. cstr. = to be [become] many, much; BDB רב (3 · 23 · 24) 1310

מַצֵּבָה pillar as a memorial, either personal or sacred (3 · 36) 663

חָלַק 2 to be smooth, slippery (1 · 2 · 9) 325

אָשַׁם to be held guilty, bear punishment, to be guilty (5 · 33 · 35) 79

ערף to break the neck [of an animal] (1 · 6 · 6) 791

מַצֵּבָה a pillar as a memorial, either personal or sacred (3 · 36) 663

אלה 4 to swear, take an oath (2 · 3 · 6) 46

פָּרַח to bud, sprout, send out shoots (3 · 28 · 33) 827

רוֹשׁ, רֹאשׁ a bitter and poisonous herb (1 · 12) 91

תֶּלֶם furrow (2 · 5) 1068

שָׂדַי field, land (2 · 13) 961

עֶגְלָה 5 heifer, young cow (2 · 12) 722

גוּר to be afraid, but BDB reads ינודו lament (1 · 10) 158

שָׁכֵן inhabitant, neighbor (1 · 20) 1015

אָבַל to mourn, lament (2 · 18 · 38) 5

כֹּמֶר idol-priest (1 · 3) 485

גִּיל to tremble, rejoice (1 · 45 · 45) 162

הוּבַל 6 to be borne along, carried; to be led, conducted (2 · 11 · 18) 384

יָרֵב let him contend (2 · 2) 937

בָּשְׁנָה shame (1 · 1) 292

נִדְמָה 7 to be cut off, destroyed, ruined (4 · 13 · 17) 198

קֶצֶף [prob.] splinter (1 · 1) 893

קוֹץ 8 thornbush, thorns (1 · 11) 881

דַּרְדַּר thistles [coll.] (1 · 2) 205

הִשִּׂיג 9 to overtake, reach (2 · 49 · 49) 673

עַלְוָה BH³ reads עולה Lis. 1070 "injustice" violent deed of injustice (1 · 1) 732

אַוָּה 10 desire, will (1 · 7) 16

יסר to discipline, chasten, admonish (1 · 4 · 38) 415

עוֹנָה BDB - no def. given; read עָוֹן iniquity, guilt; Lis. 1036 furrows [dub.] (1 · 1) 733,730

עֶגְלָה 11 heifer, young cow (2 · 12) 722

דּוֹשׁ דָּשׁ to thresh, tread on, trample on (1 · 13 · 16) 190

טוֹב	fairness, beauty, good things, goodness (2 · 32) 375	עֲבֹת	cord, rope (1 · 24) 721
צַוָּאר	neck, back of neck (1 · 41) 848	עֹל	yoke (1 · 40) 760
חרשׁ	to plow, cut in, engrave (2 · 23 · 26) 360	לְחִי	jaw, jawbone, cheek (1 · 21) 534
שׂדד	to harrow (1 · 3 · 3) 961	מֵאֵן	5 to refuse (1 · 46 · 46) 549
קצר	12 to reap, harvest (3 · 24 · 24) 894	חוּל	to whirl, whirl about, dance, writhe (1 · 6 · 9) 296-297 Lis. 468 2 roots
ניר	to break up, freshly till (1 · 2 · 2) 644	בַּד	gate bar, rod, pole (1 · 41) 94
ניר	untilled ground, tillable ground (1 · 3) 644	מוֹעֵצָה	counsel, plan, principle (1 · 7) 420
הוֹרה	to throw water, rain; to throw, shoot (2 · 2 · 3) Lis. sep. root "to sprinkle" 434	תלא	7 to hang; but Ho 117 prob. corrupt [hung to my backsliding = [?] (1 · 3 · 3) 1067
חרשׁ	13 to plow, cut in, engrave (2 · 23 · 26) 360	מְשׁוּבָה	turning back, apostasy (2 · 12) 1000
רֶשַׁע	wickedness (1 · 30) 957	עַל	subst. "height" as adv. upward w. אֶל (2 · 8) 752
עַוְלָה	injustice, unrighteousness, wrong (1 · 32) 732	יַחַד	all together, altogether (2 · 44) 403
קצר	to reap, harvest (3 · 24 · 24) 894	מָגֵן	8 to deliver up (1 · 3 · 3) 171
כַּחַשׁ	lying, falsehood; leanness (3 · 6) 471	יַחַד	all together, altogether (2 · 44) 403
שָׁאוֹן	14 din, crash, roar (1 · 18) 981	נכמר	to grow warm and tender, grow hot (1 · 4 · 4) 485
מִבְצָר	fortress, stronghold (1 · 37) 131	נחום,נחמים	compassion, comfort (1 · 3) 637
שׁד	devastation, ruin (4 · 25) 994; but BDB reads inf. to devastate	חָרוֹן	9 [burning of] anger (1 · 41) 354
רטשׁ	to be dashed in pieces (2 · 4 · 6) 936	עִיר	agitation (1 · 2) 735
כָּכָה	15 thus (1 · 34) 462	אַרְיֵה	10 lion (1 · 45) 71
שַׁחַר	dawn [obscure use] (2 · 23) 1007	שָׁאַג	to roar (2 · 20 · 20) 980
נדמה	to be cut off, destroyed, ruined (4 · 13 · 17) 198	חָרַד	to go or come trembling; to tremble, be anxiously careful (2 · 23 · 39) 353
		חָרַד	11 to go or come trembling; to tremble, be anxiously careful (2 · 23 · 39) 353
Chapter 11		צִפּוֹר	bird, birds (1 · 40) 861-862
פָּסִיל	2 idol, image (1 · 23) 820	יוֹנָה	dove (2 · 33) 401
תרגל	3 Tiph. verb form = to teach to walk (1 · 1 · 15) 920		
קחם	BDB p. 542 reads אכחם w. LXX, τ, etc. from vb. לקח	**Chapter 12**	
חֶבֶל	4 cord, band; humanely, kindly (1 · 49) 286	כַּחַשׁ	1 lying, falsehood; leanness (3 · 6) 471
מָשַׁךְ	to draw, lead [in love] (2 · 30 · 36) 604	מִרְמָה	deceit, treachery (2 · 39) 941
		רָד, רוד	to wander restlessly, roam; but BDB says crpt. (1 · 2 · 4) 923

363

כָּזָב 2 lie, falsehood, deceptive thing
(2 · 31) 469

שֹׁד violence, havoc, devastation, ruin
(4 · 25) 994

הוּבַל to be borne along, carried; to be
led, conducted (2 · 11 · 18) 384-385

מַעֲלָל 3 deed, practice, bad practice (5 · 41)
760

עָקַב 4 to attack at the heel, follow at the
heel; to overreach (1 · 3 · 3) 784
Lis. 1109 2 rts.

אוֹן vigor, strength, wealth (2 · 10) 20

שָׂרָה to persevere, persist, exert oneself
(1 · 2 · 2) 975

שָׂרָה,

שׂוּר 5 to persevere, persist, exert oneself
(1 · 1 · 1) 975

זֵכֶר 6 memorial, remembrance (2 · 23) 271

קַוֵּה 7 to wait or look eagerly for
(1 · 39 · 45) 875

כְּנַעַן 8 merchant; Canaan (1 · 4) 488

מֹאזֵן balances (1 · 15) 24-25

מִרְמָה deceit, treachery (2 · 39) 941

עָשַׁק to practice extortion, oppress,
wrong (2 · 36 · 37) 798

עָשַׁר 9 to be [become] rich (1 · 2 · 17) 799

אוֹן wealth; vigor; strength (2 · 10) 20

יְגִיעַ product, produce, acquired property
(1 · 16) 388

חֵטְא sin, guilt of sin, punishment for sin
(1 · 33) 307-308

חָזוֹן 11 divine communication in a vision,
oracle, prophecy; vision (1 · 35) 302-
303

דמה to use comparisons or similitudes;
to liken, compare, think
(*1 · 13 · 27) 197 *Lis. missed this
entry

גַּל 12 heap, wave, billow (1 · 20) 164

תֶּלֶם furrow (2 · 5) 1068

שָׂדַי field:land (2 · 13) 961

תַּמְרוּר 15 bitterness (1 · 3) 601

נָטַשׁ to leave, forsake, permit
(1 · 33 · 40) 643-644

Chapter 13

רְתֵת 1 trembling (1 · 1) 958

אָשַׁם to be [become] guilty, do wrong
(5 · 33 · 35) 79

מַסֵּכָה 2 molten metal or image; libation
(1 · 25) 651

תְּבוּנָה act of understanding, faculty of
understanding, object of knowledge
(1 · 42) 108

עָצָב idol (4 · 17) 781

חָרָשׁ graver, artificer, worker in metal
(2 · 38) 360

עֵגֶל calf, image of calf (3 · 35) 722

נָשַׁק to kiss (1 · 26 · 32) 676

טַל 3 dew, night mist (3 · 31) 378

מֹץ chaff (1 · 8) 558

סָעַר to be storm-driven (1 · 1 · 7) 704

גֹּרֶן threshing floor (3 · 34) 175

עָשָׁן smoke (1 · 25) 798

אֲרֻבָּה lattice, latticed opening, window,
sluice (1 · 9) 70

זוּלָה 4 except, besides (1 · 16) 265

מוֹשִׁיעַ ptc. = savior (1 · 27) 446

בִּלְתִּי after a preceding negation, not [=
except]; not (1 · 24) 116

תַּלְאֻבוֹת,

תַּלְאֵבָה 5 drought [Lis. 1519 fever] (1 · 1) 520

מַרְעִית 6 pasturage, pasturing (1 · 10) 945

שַׁחַל 7 lion (2 · 7) 1006

נָמֵר leopard (1 · 6) 649

שׁוּר to watch, lie in wait (2 · 16 · 16)
1003

פָּגַשׁ 8 to meet, encounter (1 · 10 · 14) 803

דֹּב bear (1 · 12) 179

שַׁכּוּל bereaved, robbed of offspring (1 · 6) 1014

סְגוֹר enclosure, encasement (1 · 2) 689

לָבִיא lion, lioness (1 · 11) 522

עֹזֵר 9 one who helps, help (1 · 21) 740

אֱהִי 10 where[?] (3 · 3) 13

אֵפוֹא enclitic part. = then (1 · 15) 66

עֶבְרָה 11 overflowing rage, fury; overflow (2 · 34) 720

צָפַן 12 to hide, lie hidden, lurk (1 · 24 · 29)

חֵבֶל 13 pains of travail, pain (1 · 7) 286

מַשְׁבֵּר,מִשְׁבָּר breach, mouth of womb (1 · 3) 991

אֱהִי 14 where[?] (3 · 3) 13

דֶּבֶר pestilence, plague (1 · 3) 184

קֹטֶב destruction (1 · 4) 881

נֹחַם sorrow, repentance (1 · 1) 637

הפרה, הפריא 15 to show fruitfulness, bear fruit (1 · 1 · 1) 826 Lis. sep. root פרא p.1183

מָקוֹר spring, fountain [= source of life and vigor] (1 · 18) 881

חרב to be dried up, be dry (1 · 17 · 37) 351

מַעְיָן spring (1 · 23) 745-746

שׁסה to spoil, plunder (1 · 4 · 5) 1042

חֶמְדָּה desire, delight (1 · 16) 326

Chapter 14

אָשַׁם 1 to be or become guilty (5 · 33 · 35) 79

מָרָה to be disobedient, rebellious (1 · 21 · 43) 598

עוֹלֵל,עוֹלָל child (1 · 11) 760

רטשׁ to be dashed in pieces (2 · 3 · 6) 936

הָרִיָה,הָרָה pregnant (1 · 15) 248

רחם 4 to be shown compassion (3 · 4 · 47) 933

יָתוֹם orphan (1 · 42) 450

מְשׁוּבָה 5 turning back, apostasy (2 · 12) 1000

נְדָבָה voluntariness (1 · 26) 621

טַל 6 dew, night mist (3 · 31) 378

פָּרַח to bud, sprout, send out shoots (3 · 28 · 33) 827

שׁוֹשַׁנָּה,שׁוּשַׁן lily, lilylike flower (1 · 17) 1004

שֹׁרֶשׁ root (2 · 33) 1057

יוֹנֶקֶת 7 young shoot, twig (1 · 6) 413

זַיִת olive tree, olives (1 · 38) 278

הוֹד splendor, majesty (1 · 24) 217

דָּגָן corn, cereal grain (6 · 40) 186

פָּרַח to bud, sprout, send out shoots (3 · 28 · 33) 827

זֵכֶר memorial, remembrance (2 · 23) 271

מַה־לּוֹ 9 [idiom] formula of repudiation or emphatic denial (XXXX) מה para. 1.d. (c) 553

עָצָב idol (4 · 17) 781

שׁוּר to regard, observe; to watch, lie in wait (2 · 16 · 16) 1003

בְּרוֹשׁ cypress, fir (1 · 20) 141

רַעֲנָן luxuriant, fresh (1 · 19) 947

נָבוֹן 10 ptc. = understanding, discerning (1 · 21) 106

פָּשַׁע to transgress, rebel, revolt (3 · 40 · 41) 833

JOEL

Chapter 1

הַאֲזִין 2 to hear, give ear, listen (1 · 41 · 41) 24

גָּזָם 4 [coll.] locusts (2 · 3) 160

אַרְבֶּה a kind of locust, locust swarm (3 · 24) 916

יֶלֶק a kind of locust (3 · 9) 410

חָסִיל a kind of locust (2 · 6) 340

הָקִיץ 5 to awake (1 · 22 · 23) 884

שִׁכּוֹר drunken; drunken one (1 · 13) 1016

הֵילִל to utter or make a howling, howl (3 · 30 · 30) 410

עָסִיס sweet wine (2 · 5) 779

עָצוּם 6 mighty, strong in numbers (4 · 31) 783

אַרְיֵה lion (1 · 45) 71

מְתַלְּעוֹת teeth, incisors (1 · 4) 1069

לָבִיא lion (1 · 11) 522

שַׁמָּה 7 appalling waste (1 · 39) 1031

תְּאֵנָה fig tree; fig (3 · 39) 1061

קְצָפָה a snapping or splintering (1 · 1) 893

חָשַׂף to strip, lay bear (2 · 10 · 10) 362

הִלְבִּין to show whiteness, grow white, make white (1 · 4 · 5) 526

שָׂרִיג tendril, twig (1 · 3) 974

אלה 8 to wail (1 · 1 · 1) 46

בְּתוּלָה virgin (1 · 50) 143

חגר to gird on, bind on (2 · 44 · 44) 291

שַׂק sackcloth, sack (2 · 48) 974

נְעוּרִים youth, early life (1 · 46) 655

אָבַל 9 to mourn, lament (2 · 18 · 38) 5

אָבַל 10 to mourn, lament (2 · 18 · 38) 5

דָּגָן corn, cereal grain (3 · 40) 186

תִּירוֹשׁ must, fresh or new wine (3 · 38) 440

אֻמְלַל to be or grow feeble, languish (2 · 15 · 15) 51

יִצְהָר fresh oil (3 · 23) 844

אִכָּר 11 plowman, husbandman (1 · 7) 38

הֵילִל to utter or make a howling, howl (3 · 30 · 30) 410

כֹּרֵם ptc. = vinedresser (1 · 5) 501

חִטָּה wheat (1 · 30) 334

שְׂעֹרָה barley (1 · 33) 972

קָצִיר what is harvested, crop; harvesting; time of harvest (2 · 49) 894

תְּאֵנָה 12 fig tree, fig (3 · 39) 1061

אֻמְלַל to be or grow feeble, languish (2 · 15 · 15) 51

רִמּוֹן pomegranate (1 · 32) 941

תָּמָר palm tree, date palm (1 · 12) 1071

תַּפּוּחַ apple tree, apple (1 · 6) 656

שָׂשׂוֹן exultation, joy (1 · 22) 965

חגר 13 to gird on, bind on (2 · 44 · 44) 291

ספד to wail, lament (1 · 28 · 30) 704

הֵילִל to utter or make a howling, howl (3 · 30 · 30) 410

שַׂק sackcloth, sack (2 · 48) 974

נִמְנַע to be withheld (1 · 4 · 29) 586

צוֹם 14 fast, fasting (3 · 26) 847

עֲצָרָה sacred assembly, assembly (2 · 11) 783

אֲהָהּ 15 [interj.] alas! (1 · 15) 13

שֹׁד devastation, ruin (1 · 25) 994

שַׁדַּי name of God = (1) self-sufficient, (2) almighty, or (3) my sovereign (1 · 48) 994-995

אֹכֶל 16 food (1 · 44) 38

גִּיל rejoicing (1 · 8) 162

עבש 17 to shrivel (1 · 1 · 1) 721

פְּרֻדָה grain of seed; Lis. 1184 "dried fig" (1 · 1) 825

מֶגְרָפָה shovel (1 · 1) 175

נהרס to be thrown down, torn down (1 · 10 · 43) 248

מַמְגֻרָה storehouse, granary (1 · 1) 158

דָּגָן corn, cereal grain (3 · 40) 186

נאנח 18 to sigh, groan (1 · 12 · 12) 58

נָבוֹךְ (בוך) to be confused, in confusion (1 · 3 · 3) 100

עֵדֶר flock, flocks and herds, herds (2 · 37) 727

מִרְעֶה pasturage, pasture (1 · 13) 945

נאשם to suffer punishment (1 · 1 · 35) 79

נָוֶה ,נָוָה 19 pasture, meadow (3 · 45) 627

לֶהָבָה flame (2 · 19) 529

לָהַט to set ablaze (2 · 9 · 11) 529

ערג 20 to long for (1 · 3 · 3) 788

אָפִיק channel, streambed, ravine (2 · 18) 67

נָוֶה ,נָוָה pasture, meadow (3 · 45) 627

Chapter 2

הריע 1 to sound a signal for war or march, to raise a shout (1 · 40 · 44) 929

רָגַז to quake, quiver, be excited, perturbed (2 · 30 · 41) 919

אֲפֵלָה 2 darkness (1 · 10) 66

עֲרָפֶל cloud, heavy cloud (1 · 15) 791

שַׁחַר dawn (1 · 23) 1007

עָצוּם mighty, strong in numbers (4 · 31) 783

דּוֹר וָדוֹר duration to come, future ages 189

לָהַט 3 to set ablaze (2 · 9 · 11) 529

גַּן garden, enclosure (1 · 41) 171

פְּלֵיטָה escaped remnant; escape, deliverance (2 · 28) 812

מֶרְכָּבָה 5 chariot (1 · 44) 939

רקד to dance, leap (1 · 5 · 9) 955

לַהַב flame; blade (1 · 12) 529

קַשׁ stubble, chaff (1 · 16) 905

עָצוּם mighty, strong in numbers (4 · 31) 783

חוּל ,חיל 6 to twist, writhe, dance (1 · 30 · 47) 297

פָּארוּר to gather a glow [dub.] (1 · 2) 802

עבט 7 lend on pledge [dub.], most read

עבט (1 · 1 · 1) Lis. 1018 "to change" 716

דחק 8 to thrust, crowd, oppress (1 · 1 · 1) 191

מְסִלָּה raised way, highway (1 · 27) 700

שֶׁלַח missile, weapon (1 · 8) 1019

בצע to cut off, break off (1 · 10 · 16) 130

שקק 9 to run, run about, rush (1 · 5 · 6) 1055

חַלּוֹן window (1 · 30) 319

גַּנָּב thief (1 · 30) 319

רָגַז 10 to quake, quiver, be excited, perturbed (2 · 30 · 41) 919

רעש to quake, shake (2 · 21 · 29) 950

יָרֵחַ moon (3-27) 437

קָדַר to be dark (2 · 13 · 17) 871

כּוֹכָב star (2 · 37) 456

נֹגַהּ brightness (2 · 19) 618

עָצוּם 11 mighty, strong in numbers (4 · 31) 783

נוֹרָא ptc. = awful, fearful (2 · 44) 431

הכיל to sustain, endure; to contain (1 · 12 · 38) 465 כיל ,כול

צוֹם 12 fast, fasting (3 · 26) 847

בְּכִי weeping (1 · 30) 113

מִסְפֵּד wailing (1 · 16) 704

חַנּוּן 13 gracious (1 · 13) 337

רַחוּם compassionate (1 · 13) 933

אָרֵךְ long (1 · 15) 74

צוֹם 15 fast, fasting (3 · 26) 847

עֲצָרָה sacred assembly, assembly (2 · 11) 783

עוֹלָל 16 child (1 · 9) 760

יוֹנֵק ptc. = suckling, babe (1 · 11) 413

שַׁד female breast (1 · 21) 994

חָתָן bridegroom; daughter's husband (1 · 20) 368

חֶדֶר chamber, room (1 · 37) 293

כַּלָּה bride; daughter-in-law (1 · 34) 483

חֻפָּה canopy, chamber (1 · 3) 342

אֵילָם,אוּלָם porch (1 · 49) 17

חוּס to pity, look upon with compassion (1 · 24 · 24) 299

אַיֵּה where? (1 · 44) 32

קָנָא 18 to be zealous, jealous, envious (1 · 18 · 32) 888

חָמַל to spare, have compassion (1 · 40 · 40) 328

דָּגָן 19 corn, cereal grain (3 · 40) 186

תִּירוֹשׁ must, fresh or new wine (3 · 38) 440

יִצְהָר fresh oil (3 · 23) 844

צְפוֹנִי 20 northern one, northerner (1 · 1) 861

הִדִּיחַ to thrust out, banish (1 · 27 · 43) 623

צִיָּה dryness, drought (1 · 16) 851

קַדְמֹנִי eastern; former, ancient (1 · 10) 870

סוֹף end, conclusion (1 · 5) 693

בָּאְשׁ stench (1 · 3) 93

צַחֲנָה stench (1 · 1) 850

גִּיל 21 to rejoice (2 · 45 · 45) 162

שָׂדַי 22 field, land (1 · 13) 961

דָּשָׁא to sprout, shoot, grow green (1 · 1 · 2) 205

נָוֶה ,נָוֶה pasture, meadow (3 · 45) 627

תְּאֵנָה fig tree, fig (3 · 39) 1061

גִּיל 23 to rejoice (2 · 45 · 45) 162

מוֹרֶה [early] rain (1 · 2) 435

גֶּשֶׁם rain, shower (1 · 35) 177

מַלְקוֹשׁ latter rain, spring rain, showers of Mar.-Apr. (1 · 8) 545

גֹּרֶן 24 threshing floor (1 · 34) 175

בַּר grain, corn (1 · 14) 141

הֵשִׁיק to overflow (2 · 2 · 3) 1003

יֶקֶב wine vat (2 · 16) 428

תִּירוֹשׁ must, fresh or new wine (3 · 38) 440

יִצְהָר fresh oil (3 · 23) 844

אַרְבֶּה 25 a kind of locust, locust swarm (3 · 24) 916

יֶלֶק a kind of locust (3 · 9) 410

חָסִיל a kind of locust (2 · 6) 340

גָּזָם [coll.] locusts (2 · 3) 160

הִפְלִיא 26 to do wonderfully, wondrously; to do a hard thing (1 · 10 · 24) 810

Chapter 3

אַחֲרֵי־כֵן 1 afterwards (1 · [?]) para. 3.a. כֵּן 486

חָלַם to dream (1 · 27 · 29) 321

בָּחוּר young man (1 · 45) 104

חִזָּיוֹן vision, divine communication in a vision (1 · 9) 303

מוֹפֵת 3 wonder, sign, portent

תִּימָרָה [palmlike] column (1 · 2) 1071

עָשָׁן smoke (1 · 25) 798

יָרֵחַ 4 moon (3 · 27) 437

נוֹרָא awful, fearful (2 · 44) 431

פְּלֵיטָה escaped remnant; escape, deliverance (2 · 28) 812

שָׂרִיד survivor (1 · 28) 975

Chapter 4

שְׁבוּת 1 captivity, captives (1 · 26) 986

פִּזַּר 2 to scatter (1 · 7 · 10) 808

יַדַּד 3 to cast (1 · 3 · 3) 391

זוֹנָה ptc. = harlot (1 · 33) 275

יַלְדָּה girl, damsel (1 · 3) 409

גְּלִילָה 4 circuit, boundary, territory (1 · 6) 165

גְּמוּל recompense, dealing (3 · 19) 168

גָּמַל to recompense, deal fully with; wean; ripen (1 · 34 · 37) 168

קַל swift, swiftly; light (1 · 13) 886

מְהֵרָה haste; hastily (1 · 20) 555

מַחְמַד 5 desirable, precious things; desire (1 · 13) 326

גְּמוּל 7 recompense, dealing (3 · 19) 168

כָּתַת 10 form = imv. masc. pl., to beat, hammer, crush (1 · 5 · 17) 510

אֵת a cutting instrument of iron, plowshare (1 · 5) 88

368

מַזְמֵרָה	pruning knife (1 · 4) 275
רֹמַח	spear, lance (1 · 15) 942
חַלָּשׁ	weak (1 · 1) 325
עוּשׁ 11	to lend aid, come to help [dub.] (1 · 1 · 1) 736
מִסָּבִיב	on every side, from round about (2 · 42) 687
הַנְחִית	to bring down; imv., on form sep. G.K. para. 64 h.3. (1 · 1 · 8) 639
מִסָּבִיב 12	on every side, from round about (2 · 42) 687
מַגָּל 13	sickle (1 · 2) 618
בָּשַׁל	to boil, cook (1 · 2 · 27) 143
קָצִיר	what is reaped, harvested; harvesting; time of harvest (2 · 49) 894
רדה	Lis. 1318 to tread; BDB ירד (1 · 22 · 22) 921.432
גַּת	winepress (1 · 5) 178
הֵשִׁיק	to overflow (2 · 2 · 3) 1003
יֶקֶב	wine vat (2 · 16) 428

חָרוּץ 14	strict decision (2 · 4) 358
יָרֵחַ 15	moon (3 · 27) 437
קָדַר	to be dark (2 · 13 · 17) 871
כּוֹכָב	star (2 · 37) 456
נֹגַהּ	brightness (2 · 19) 618
שָׁאַג 16	to roar (1 · 20 · 20) 980
רעשׁ	to quake, shake (2 · 21 · 29) 950
מַחֲסֶה	refuge, shelter (1 · 20) 340
מָעוֹז	refuge, place of safety (1 · 36) 731-732
נטף 18	to drip, drop (1 · 9 · 18) 642
עָסִיס	sweet wine (2 · 5) 779
חָלָב	milk (1 · 44) 316
אָפִיק	channel, streambed, ravine (2 · 18) 67
מַעְיָן	spring (1 · 23) 745
נָקִיא 19	innocent (1 · 43) 667
דּוֹר, נָדוֹר 20	duration to come; future ages 189
נקה 21	to leave unpunished (1 · 16 · 41) 667

AMOS

Chapter 1

נֹקֵד	1	sheep-raiser, -dealer, -tender (1 · 2) 667
רַעַשׁ		earthquake, quaking, shaking (1 · 17) 950
שָׁאַג	2	to roar (3 · 20 · 20) 980
אָבַל		to mourn, lament (3 · 18 · 20) 5
נָוֶה, נָוָה		pasture, meadow (1 · 45) 627
דּוּשׁ, דָּשׁ	3	to thresh, tread on (1 · 13 · 15) 190
חָרוּץ		sharp (1 · 4) 358
אַרְמוֹן	4	castle, palace (12 · 33) 74
בְּרִיחַ	5	bar, gate bar (1 · 41) 138
בִּקְעָה		plain, valley (0 · 19) 132
תָּמַךְ		to wield, grasp, lay hold of (2 · 20 · 21) 1069
קִיר		prop. noun
גָּלוּת	6	exiles, exile (2 · 15) 163
שָׁלֵם		full, complete; at peace (2 · 28) 1023
אַרְמוֹן	7	castle, palace (12 · 33) 74
תָּמַךְ	8	to wield, grasp, lay hold of (2 · 20 · 21) 1069
גָּלוּת	9	exiles, exile (2 · 15) 163
שָׁלֵם		full, complete; at peace (2 · 28) 1023
אַרְמוֹן	10	castle, palace (12 · 33) 74
רַחֲמִים	11	compassion (1 · 38) 933
טָרַף		to tear, rend (1 · 19 · 24) 383
עֶבְרָה		overflowing rage, fury; overflow, arrogance (1 · 34) 720
נֶצַח		everlastingness, ever (2 · 43) 664
אַרְמוֹן	12	castle, palace (12 · 33) 74
הָרָה, הָרֶה	13	pregnant woman, pregnant (1 · 15) 248
הִרְחִיב		to enlarge, make large (1 · 21 · 25) 931
הִצִּית	14	to kindle (1 · 17 · 27) 428
אַרְמוֹן		castle, palace (12 · 33) 74

תְּרוּעָה		war cry, shout or blast of war (2 · 36) 929-930
סַעַר		tempest (1 · 8) 704
סוּפָה		storm wind (1 · 15) 693
גּוֹלָה	15	exile, exiles (1 · 42) 163

Chapter 2

שִׂיד	1	lime, whitewash (1 · 4) 966
אַרְמוֹן		castle, palace (12 · 33) 74
שָׁאוֹן		roar, din (1 · 18) 980
תְּרוּעָה		war cry, shout or blast of war (2 · 36) 929-930
הִתְעָה	4	cause to err, mislead (1 · 21 · 50) 1073
כָּזָב		lie, falsehood (1 · 31) 469
אַרְמוֹן	5	castle, palace (12 · 33) 74
בַּעֲבוּר	6	for the sake of, on account of, in order that (2 · 45) 721
נַעַל		sandal, shoe (2 · 22) 653
שָׁאַף	7	to trample on, crush (2 · 14 · 14) 983
דַּל		reduced, weak, helpless (4 · 48) 195
עָנָו		poor and weak, needy (1 · 21) 776
חָבַל	8	to hold by a pledge (1 · 13 · 14) 286
עָנַשׁ		to punish; ptc. pass. = those fined (1 · 6 · 9)
גֹּבַהּ	9	height; exaltation, grandeur; haughtiness (2 · 9) 147
חָסֹן		strong (1 · 2) 340
אַלּוֹן		oak (1 · 9) 47
מִמַּעַל		above (1 · 29) 751 מַעַל para. 1.
שֹׁרֶשׁ		root (1 · 33) 1057
בָּחוּר	11	young man (3 · 45) 104
נָזִיר		devotee (2 · 16) 634
נָזִיר	12	devotee (2 · 16) 634
הֵעִיק	13	[dub.] read הֵפִיק to totter, cause to totter (2 · 2 · 2) 734
עֲגָלָה		cart (1 · 25) 722
עָמִיר		swath, row of fallen grain (1 · 4) 771

מָנוֹס 14 place of escape, refuge; flight (1·8) 631

קַל light, swift, fleet (2·13) 886-887

אָמֵץ to make firm, strengthen, assure, harden (1·19·41) 54-55

קַל 15 light, swift, fleet (2·13) 886-887

אַמִּיץ 16 mighty (1·6) 55

עָרוֹם naked (1·16) 736

Chapter 3

בִּלְתִּי אִם 3 save that, except (2·24) 116, 50

נוֹעַד to meet by appointment (1·18·28) 416

שָׁאַג 4 to roar (3·20·20) 980

אַרְיֵה lion (2·45) 71

טֶרֶף prey (1·17) 383

כְּפִיר young lion (1·31) 498

מְעֹנָה den, lair, refuge (1·9) 733

בִּלְתִּי אִם save that, except (2·24) 116, 50

צִפּוֹר 5 bird; [coll.] birds (1·40) 862

פַּח bird trap (2·25) 809

מוֹקֵשׁ bait, lure (1·27) 430

חָרַד 6 to be startled, tremble, be terrified (1·23·39) 353

סוֹד 7 secret counsel, counsel, council (1·21) 691

אַרְיֵה 8 lion (2·45) 71

שָׁאַג to roar (3·20·20) 980

אַרְמוֹן castle, palace (12·33) 74

מְהוּמָה tumult, confusion (1·12) 223

עֲשׁוּקִים oppression, extortion (1·3) 799

נָכֹחַ 10 straightforwardness, honesty; straight, right (1·8) 647

אָצַר to store up (1·3·5) 69

שֹׁד violence, havoc; ruin (3·25) 994

אַרְמוֹן castle, palace (12·33) 74

נבז 11 to be spoiled, plundered (1·3·41) 102-103

אַרְמוֹן castle, palace (12·33) 74

אֲרִי 12 lion (2·35) 71

כְּרָעַיִם, כֶּרַע leg, legs (1·9) 502

בָּדָל piece, severed piece (1·1) 95

מִטָּה couch, bed (2·29) 641

דְּמֶשֶׂק [meaning dub.] (1·1) 200

עֶרֶשׂ couch, divan (2·11) 793

הֵעִיד 13 to cause to testify, to take as witness, bear witness (1·38·43) 729-730

נִגְדַּע to be hewn off (1·7·22) 154

חֹרֶף 15 harvest time, autumn; w. בַּיִת = autumn house or palace (1·7) 358

קַיִץ summer, summer fruit (3·20) 884

סוּף to come to an end, cease (1·4·8) 692

Chapter 4

פָּרָה 1 heifer, cow (1·26) 831

עָשַׁק to oppress, wrong (1·36·37) 798

דַּל reduced, poor, weak (4·48) 195

רצץ to crush, oppress (1·11·19) 954

צִנָּה, צֵן 2 hook or barb (1·3) 856

סִיר hook, thorn (1·5) 696

דּוּגָה fishing, fishery (1·1) 186

פֶּרֶץ 3 breach, bursting forth, outburst (2·19) 829

הַרְמוֹן [meaning dub.] perh. a proper location (1·1) 248

פָּשַׁע 4 to transgress, rebel (2·40·41) 833

מַעֲשֵׂר tithe, payment of tenth part (1·33) 798

חָמֵץ 5 that which is leavened (1·11) 329

תּוֹדָה thank offering, thanksgiving (1·32) 392

נְדָבָה free will or voluntary offering, voluntariness (1·26) 621

נִקָּיוֹן 6 cleanness [though perh. קִהָיוֹן "bluntness"], innocency (1·5) 667

חֹסֶר want, lack (1·3) 341

מָנַע 7 to withhold, hold back (1 · 25 · 29) 586

גֶּשֶׁם rain, shower (1 · 35) 177

בְּעוֹד within yet (1 · 20) עוֹד 2.a. 729

קָצִיר harvesting; harvest; time of harvest (1 · 49) 894

הִמְטִיר to send rain; rain (3 · 16 · 17) 565

חֶלְקָה portion of ground (2 · 24) 324

נמטר to be rained on (1 · 1 · 17) 565

נוע 8 to totter, go tottering; to wave (2 · 22 · 38) 631

שִׁדָּפוֹן 9 smut [on crops] (1 · 5) 995

יֵרָקוֹן rust, mildew, paleness (1 · 6) 439

גַּנָּה garden, orchard (2 · 16) 171

תְּאֵנָה fig tree, fig (1 · 39) 1061

זַיִת olive tree, olive (1 · 38) 268

גָּזָם [coll.] locusts (1 · 3) 160

דֶּבֶר 10 plague, pestilence (1 · 46) 184

בָּחוּר young man (3 · 45) 104

שְׁבִי act of capture; captivity; captives (2 · 49) 985

בְּאֹשׁ stench (1 · 3) 93

מַהְפֵּכָה 11 overthrow (1 · 6) 246

אוּד brand, firebrand (1 · 3) 15

שְׂרֵפָה burning (1 · 13) 977

עֵקֶב 12 because, as a consequence of (1 · 15) 784

יָצַר 13 to form, fashion (2 · 41 · 44) 427

בָּרָא to shape, fashion, create (1 · 38 · 48) 135

שֵׂחַ thought (1 · 1) 967

עֹשֵׂה ptc. = maker (2 · 24) 793

שַׁחַר dawn (1 · 23) 1007

עֵיפָה darkness (1 · 2) 734

Chapter 5

קִינָה 1 elegy, dirge (2 · 17) 884

בְּתוּלָה 2 virgin (2 · 50) 143-144

נטשׁ to be forsaken (1 · 6 · 40) 643

כבה 6 to quench, extinguish (1 · 10 · 24) 459

לַעֲנָה 7 wormwood (2 · 8) 542

עֹשֶׂה 8 ptc. = maker (2 · 24) 793

כִּימָה Pleiades (1 · 3) 465

כְּסִיל Orion (1 · 4) 493

צַלְמָוֶת deep shadow, death shadow (1 · 18) 853

הֶחְשִׁיךְ to make dark, cause darkness (2 · 6 · 17) 364-365

הבליג 9 to cause to burst or flash; to smile, look cheerful (1 · 4 · 4) 114

שֹׁד devastation, ruin, violence, havoc (3 · 25) 994

עַז mighty one; mighty, strong (1 · 22) 738

מִבְצָר fortress, stronghold (1 · 37) 131

תעב 10 to regard as an abomination (1 · 15 · 22) 1073

בושׂס 11 to trample; [inf.] trampling (1 · 1 · 1) 143

דַּל reduced, poor, weak (4 · 48) 195

מַשְׂאָה, מַשְׂאֵת portion, present, offering; that which rises; utterance; burden (1 · 16) 673

בַּר grain, corn (3 · 14) 141

גָּזִית cutting, hewing (1 · 11) 159

חֶמֶד desire, delight (1 · 5) 326

עֲצוּם 12 numerous, countless (1 · 31) 783

צָרַר to show hostility toward, vex; ptc. = vexer, harasser (1 · 10 · 10) 865

כֹּפֶר the price of a life, ransom (1 · 13) 497

דמם 13 to be silent, be still (1 · 23 · 30) 198-199

כֵּן 14 emphasis of agreement כֵּן 2.d. or right, honest (1 · 24) 486, 487

הציג 15 to set up, establish; to place (1 · 15 · 16) 426

אוּלַי		peradventure, perhaps (1 · 45) 19
רְחוֹב, רְחֹב	16	broad open place, plaza (1 · 43) 932
מִסְפֵּד		wailing (3 · 16) 704
הוֹ		[interj.] Ah! (1 · 1) 214
אִכָּר		plowman, husbandman (1 · 7) 38
אֵבֶל		mourning (3 · 24) 5
נְהִי		mourning song, lamentation (1 · 7) 7
מִסְפֵּד	17	wailing (3 · 16) 704
הִתְאַוָּה	18	to desire, long for, lust after (1 · 16 · 27) 16
אֲרִי	19	lion (2 · 35) 71
פָּגַע		to meet, light upon, encounter (1 · 40 · 46) 803
דֹּב		bear (1 · 12) 179
סָמַךְ		to lean, lay, rest, support (1 · 41 · 48) 701
נָשַׁךְ		to bite (2 · 10 · 12) 675
נָחָשׁ		fleeing serpent, serpent (2 · 31) 638
אָפֵל	20	gloomy (1 · 1) 66
נֹגַהּ		brightness (1 · 19) 618
הֵרִיחַ	21	to smell or perceive odor; here metaph. = delight in (1 · 11 · 14) 926
עֲצָרָה		assembly, sacred assembly (1 · 11) 783
רָצָה	22	to accept favorably, be pleased with (1 · 42 · 50) 953
מְרִיא		fatling, fatlings (1 · 8) 597
זִמְרָה	23	melody, song (1 · 4) 274
נֶבֶל		harp, lute, guitar (2 · 27) 614
נָגוֹל	24	to roll, roll up, roll along (1 · 2 · 17) 164
אֵיתָן		ever-flowing, steady flow, permanent (1 · 14) 450
סִכּוּת	26	n. pr. div. Sakkut (1 · 1) 696
כִּיּוּן		n. pr. dei. Saturn (1 · 1) 475
צֶלֶם		image, likeness (1 · 17) 853
כּוֹכָב		star (1 · 37) 456
מֵהָלְאָה	27	out there, onward, further (1 · 3) 229
הָלְאָה		

Chapter 6

הוֹי	1	[interj.] Ah! (2 · 51) 222-223
שַׁאֲנָן		at ease, careless, wanton, arrogant; secure (1 · 11) 983
נָקוֹב		ptc. = noted, distinguished, to prick off, designate; pierce (1 · 13 · 19) 666
נדה	3	to thrust off, exclude, put away (1 · 2 · 2) 622
מִטָּה		couch, bed (2 · 29) 641
סרה		to go free, be unrestrained; to exceed, overhang (1 · 3 · 4) 710
שֶׁבֶת		seat, place of sitting (1 · 7) 443
עֶרֶשׂ	4	couch, divan (2 · 11) 793
כַּר		he-lamb (1 · 12) 503
עֵגֶל		calf (1 · 35) 722
מַרְבֵּק		stall, calves from stall = fattened calves (1 · 4) 918
פרט	5	[dub.] to chant, scatter, stammer (1 · 1 · 1) 827
נֶבֶל		harp, lute, guitar (2 · 27) 614
מִזְרָק	6	bowl, basin (1 · 32) 284
שֶׁבֶר		breaking, fracture (1 · 45) 991
מִרְזַח	7	cry, cry of mourning (1 · 2) 931
סָרוּחַ		ptc. pass. = sprawler (1 · 3) 710
תאב	8	to loathe (1 · 1 · 1) 1060
גָּאוֹן		exaltation, majesty, excellence, pride (2 · 49) 144-145
אַרְמוֹן		castle, palace (12 · 33) 74
מְלֹא		fullness, that which fills, entire contents (1 · 38) 571
סרף	10	ptc. = burner, one who burns something (1 · 1 · 1) 977
לַאֲשֶׁר		to him who, to that which, to those who (1 · 38) 82
יַרְכָה, יְרֵכָה		recess, innermost part; side, flank (1 · 28) 438
הַס		[interj.] Hush! Keep silent! (2 · 6) 245

רָסִיס 11 fragment (1 · 1) 944

בָּקִיעַ, בקע fissure, breach (1 · 2) 132

חרשׁ 12 to plow, cut in, engrave (2 · 23 · 26) 360

רוֹשׁ, רֹאשׁ a bitter and poisonous herb, venom (1 · 12) 912

לַעֲנָה wormwood (2 · 8) 542

שָׂמֵחַ 13 one showing joy; joyful, glad (1 · 21) 970

לְלֹא without (1 · 11) לֹא 4.e. 520

חֹזֶק strength (1 · 5) 305

לָחַץ 14 to oppress, squeeze, press (1 · 14 · 15) 537

Chapter 7

יָצַר 1 to form, fashion (2 · 41 · 44) 427-428

גֹּבַי [coll.] locusts (1 · 2) 146

תְּחִלָּה beginning (1 · 22) 321

לֶקֶשׁ aftergrowth, spring crop (2 · 2) 545

גֵּז shearing, mowing (1 · 4) 159

עֵשֶׂב 2 herb, herbage (1 · 33) 793

סלח to forgive, pardon (1 · 33 · 40) 699

תְּהוֹם 4 deep; deep sea, abyss (1 · 36) 1062

אֲנָךְ 7 plummet, plum bob (4 · 4) 59

אֲנָךְ 8 plummet, plum bob (4 · 4) 59

חרב 9 to be waste, desolate (1 · 9 · 37) 351

קָשַׁר 10 to league together, conspire, bind (1 · 35 · 43) 905

הכיל to sustain, endure; to contain, hold in (1 · 12 · 38) 465

חֹזֶה 12 seer (1 · 17) 302

בּוֹקֵר 14 herdsman (1 · 1) 133

בלס ptc. = gatherer of or gathering figs or sycamore fruit (1 · 1 · 1) 118

שִׁקְמָה sycamore tree (1 · 7) 1054

הטיף 16 to discourse; to drip (2 · 9 · 18) 642-643

חֶבֶל 17 measuring cord, line, band; measured portion, region (1 · 49) 28

Chapter 8

כְּלוּב 1 basket, cage (2 · 3) 477

קַיִץ summer fruit, summer (3 · 20) 884

כְּלוּב 2 basket, cage (2 · 3) 477

קַיִץ summer fruit, summer (3 · 20) 884

הֵילִיל 3 to become howlings, make a howling, howl (1 · 30 · 30) 410

שִׁירָה song (1 · 13) 1010

פֶּגֶר corpse, carcass (1 · 22) 803

הַס, הָס [inter.] Hush! Keep silent! (2 · 6) 245

שָׁאַף 4 to trample on, crush (2 · 14 · 14) 983

לשבית = ל = הָשׁבּית; see G.K. para. 53.q. 991

ענו poor, afflicted (1 · 21) 776

מָתַי 5 when[?] (1 · 42) 607

הַשׁבִּיר to sell grain (2 · 5 · 21) 991

שֶׁבֶר corn, grain (1 · 9) 991

בַּר grain, corn (3 · 14) 141

הקטין to make small (1 · 1 · 4) 881

אֵיפָה receptacle holding an ephah, ephah, a certain quantity (1 · 39) 35

עוה to make crooked, falsify, pervert (1 · 9 · 11) 736

מֹאזְנַיִם, מאזן balances, scales (1 · 15) 24-25

מִרְמָה deceit, treachery (1 · 39) 941

דַּל 6 reduced, poor, weak (4 · 48) 195

בַּעֲבוּר for the sake of, on account of, in order that (2 · 45) 721

נַעַל sandal, shoe (2 · 22) 653

מַפָּל fallings, refuse; hanging part (1 · 2) 658

בַּר grain, corn (3 · 14) 141

הַשׁבִּיר to sell grain (2 · 5 · 21) 991

גָּאוֹן 7 exaltation, majesty, excellence, pride (2 · 49) 144-145

נֶצַח everlastingness, ever, w. ל = forever (2 · 43) 664

רָגַז 8 to quake, be disquieted, perturbed, excited (1 · 30 · 41) 919

אָבַל to mourn, lament (3 · 18 · 20) 5

אֹר Nile

נִגְרַשׁ to be driven, tossed (1 · 3 · 48) 176

נִשְׁקָה Q נִשְׁקַע to sink (1 · 1 · 6) 1054

יְאוֹר Nile

צָהֳרַיִם 9 noon, midday (1 · 23) 843-844

הֶחְשִׁיךְ to cause darkness, make darkness (2 · 6 · 17) 364-365

אֵבֶל 10 mourning (3 · 24) 5

קִינָה elegy, dirge (2 · 17) 884

מָתְנַיִם loins (1 · 47) 608

שַׂק sackcloth, sack (1 · 48) 974

קָרְחָה bald spot, baldness (1 · 11) 901

יָחִיד only one, one (1 · 12) 402

מַר bitterness; bitter (1 · 38) 600

צָמָא 11 thirst (2 · 17) 854

נוּעַ 12 to totter, go tottering; to wave, quiver (2 · 22 · 38) 631

שׁוֹטֵט to go eagerly, quickly, to and fro (1 · 5 · 13) 1001-1002

הִתְעַלֵּף 13 to enwrap oneself, swoon away (1 · 3 · 5) 763

בְּתוּלָה virgin (2 · 50) 143-144

יָפֶה fair, beautiful (1 · 41) 421

בָּחוּר young man (3 · 45) 104

צָמָא thirst (2 · 17) 854

אַשְׁמָה becoming guilty, doing wrong (1 · 19) 80

Chapter 9

כַּפְתּוֹר 1 capital, knob, bulb (1 · 16) 499

רַעַשׁ to quake, shake (1 · 21 · 29) 950

סַף threshold, sill (1 · 25) 706

בָּצַע to cut off, break off (1 · 10 · 16) 130

פָּלִיט escaped one, fugitive (1 · 19) 812

חָתַר 2 to dig into; to row (1 · 8 · 8) 369

נֶחְבָּא 3 to hide oneself (1 · 16 · 34) 285

חִפֵּשׂ to search for, search through (1 · 8 · 23) 344

מִנֶּגֶד from before, in front of, opposite (1 · 26) 617

קַרְקַע floor (1 · 7) 903

נָחָשׁ serpent (2 · 31) 638

נָשַׁךְ to bite (2 · 10 · 12) 675

שְׁבִי 4 state of captivity, captives, act of capture (2 · 49) 985

מוּג 5 to melt, faint (1 · 4 · 17) 556

אָבַל to mourn, lament (3 · 18 · 20) 5

יְאֹר Nile

שָׁקַע to sink, sink down (1 · 3 · 6) 1054

מַעֲלָה 6 story, step, stair, ascent (1 · 47) 752

אֲגֻדָּה vault; band, bunch (1 · 4) 8

יָסַד to found, establish (1 · 20 · 41) 413-414

חַטָּא 7 sinful; sinner (2 · 19) 308

אֶפֶס כִּי 8 save that, yet (1 · 4) 67

הֵנִיעַ 9 to shake, cause to totter (1 · 14 · 38) 631

נָנוֹעַ to be tossed about (1 · 2 · 38) 631

כְּבָרָה sieve; netlike implement (1 · 1) 460

צְרוֹר bundle, parcel, pouch (1 · 2) 865

חַטָּא 10 sinner; sinful (2 · 19) 308

הִקְדִּים to come in front of (1 · 2 · 26) 869-870

סֻכָּה 11 booth, thicket (1 · 31) 697

גָּדַר to wall up, build a wall (1 · 7 · 7) 154

פֶּרֶץ breach, bursting forth, outburst (2 · 19) 829

הֲרִיסָה ruin (1 · 1) 249

חָרַשׁ 13 to plow; ptc. = plowman; to cut in, engrave (2 · 23 · 26) 360

קֹצֵר ptc. = reaper (1 · 10) 894

עֵנָב   grapes, grape (1 · 19) 772

מָשַׁךְ   to trail, draw along, draw, draw out, drag (1 · 30 · 36) 604

הִטִּיף   to drip; to discourse (2 · 9 · 18) 642-643

עָסִיס   sweet wine, pressed-out juice (1 · 5) 779

הִתְמוֹגֵג   to melt, flow (1 · 3 · 17) 556

שְׁבוּת   14 captivity, captives (1 · 26) 986

גַּנָּה   garden, orchard (2 · 16) 171

נָתַשׁ   15 to be rooted up, pulled up (1 · 4 · 21) 684

OBADIAH

Chapter 1

חָזוֹן 1 vision (1 · 35) 302-303

שְׁמוּעָה report (1 · 27) 1035

צִיר envoy, messenger (1 · 6) 851

בָּזָה 2 to despise; ptc. pass. = despised (1 · 31 · 42) 102

זָדוֹן 3 presumptuousness, presumption, insolence (1 · 10) 268

הִשִּׁיא to beguile (2 · 15 · 16) 674

חֲגוּ place of concealment, retreat (1 · 3) 291

הִגְבִּיהַ 4 to make high, exalt (1 · 10 · 34) 146-147

נֶשֶׁר griffon vulture, eagle (1 · 26) 676-677

כּוֹכָב star (1 · 37) 456-457

קֵן nest (1 · 13) 890

גַּנָּב 5 thief (1 · 17) 170

נִדְמָה to be cut off, destroyed, ruined (1 · 13 · 17) 198

גָּנַב to take by stealth, steal (1 · 30 · 39) 170

דַּי sufficient for + suffix (1 · 12) 191

בֹּצֵר to gather grapes; ptc. = grape gathering or gatherer (1 · 7 · 7) 130-131

עֹלֵלוֹת עֹלֵלוֹת gleaning (1 · 6) 760

נֶחְפַּשׂ 6 ptc. = searched out (1 · 1 · 23) 344

נִבְעָה to be searched out (1 · 2 · 4) 126

מַצְפֻּן hidden treasure, treasure (1 · 1) 861

הִשִּׁיא 7 to beguile (2 · 15 · 16) 674

מָזוֹר [dub.] net, fetter, stumbling block (1 · 1) 561

תְּבוּנָה act of understanding, faculty of understanding (2 · 42) 108

תְּבוּנָה 8 faculty of understanding, act of understanding (2 · 42) 108

קֶטֶל 9 slaughter (1 · 1) 881

בּוּשָׁה 10 shame (1 · 4) 102

מִנֶּגֶד 11 from or at a distance, in front of (1 · 26) נגד 2.c. 617

שָׁבָה to take captive (1 · 30 · 38) 985

נָכְרִי foreigner; foreign (1 · 45) 648

יָדַד to cast a lot (1 · 3 · 3) 391

נֵכֶר ,נֶכֶר 12 misfortune, calamity (1 · 2) 648

אֵיד 13 calamity, distress (3 · 24) 15

פֶּרֶק 14 parting of ways; plunder (1 · 2) 830

שָׂרִיט escaped one, fugitive (1 · 19) 812

שָׂרִיד survivor (2 · 28) 975

גְּמוּל 15 recompense; dealing; benefit (1 · 19) 168

לוּעַ ,לָעַע 16 to swallow, swallow down (1 · 1 · 1) 534

כְּלוֹא as though (1 · 1) לֹא 4.d. 520

פְּלֵיטָה 17 escaped remnant; escape (1 · 28) 812

מוֹרָשׁ possession (1 · 2) 440

לֶהָבָה 18 flame (1 · 19) 529

קַשׁ stubble, chaff (1 · 16) 905

דָּלַק to burn, hotly pursue (1 · 7 · 9) 196

שָׂרִיד survivor (2 · 28) 975

שְׁפֵלָה 19 lowland (1 · 20) 1050

גָּלֻת ,גָּלוּת 20 exiles, exile (2 · 15) 163

חֵל ,חֵיל fortress, rampart (1 · 9) 298

מוֹשִׁיעַ 21 ptc. = savior, deliverer (1 · 27) 446

מְלוּכָה kingship, kingly office, royalty (1 · 24) 574

JONAH

Chapter 1

אֳנִיָּה   3 ship, merchant ship (3 · 31) 58

שָׂכָר   passage money, fare, hire, wages (1 · 28) 969

הֵטִיל   4 to cast, cast out, hurl (4 · 9 · 14) 376

סַעַר   tempest (2 · 8) 704

אֳנִיָּה   ship, merchant ship (3 · 31) 58

מַלָּח   5 mariner, sailor (1 · 4) 572

הֵטִיל   to cast, cast out, hurl (4 · 9 · 14) 376

אֳנִיָּה   ship, merchant ship (3 · 31) 58

יַרְכָה   dual recess, extreme parts (1 · 28) 438

סְפִינָה   vessel, ship (1 · 1) 706

נִרְדָּם   to be or fall fast asleep (2 · 7 · 7) 922

חֹבֵל   6 sailor (1 · 5) 287

נִרְדָּם   to be or fall fast asleep (2 · 7 · 7) 922

אוּלַי   perhaps, peradventure (1 · 45) 19

הִתְעַשֵּׁת   to think, give a thought to (1 · 1 · 1) 799

בְּ שֶׁל מִי   7 on account of (1 · 1) שׁ para. 4.d. 980

בַּאֲשֶׁר לְמִי   8 [idiom] on account of me (1 · 1)

מִי (1 · 20) לְמִי (1 · 19) בַּאֲשֶׁר 85 בַּאֲשֶׁר b. 566

מֵאַיִן   so there is no, so there is not (1 · 48) אַיִן 6.d. 35

אֵי   where? אֵי־מִזֶּה whence? (1 · 39) 32

יַבָּשָׁה   9 dry land, dry ground (3 · 14) 387

יִרְאָה   10 fear, terror (2 · 45) 432

שָׁתַק   11 to be quiet (2 · 4 · 4) 1060

סָעַר   to storm, rage (2 · 3 · 7) 704

הֵטִיל   12 to cast, cast out, hurl (4 · 9 · 14) 376

שָׁתַק   to be quiet (2 · 4 · 4) 1060

בְּשֶׁל   on account of (1 · [?]) שׁ para. 4.d. 980

סָעַר   tempest (2 · 8) 704

חָתַר   13 to row, dig (1 · 8 · 8) 369

יַבָּשָׁה   dry land, dry ground (3 · 14) 387

סָעַר   to storm, rage (2 · 3 · 7) 704

אָנָּה   14 strong particle of entreaty, I [we] beseech (2 · 6) 58

נָקִיא, נָקִי   innocent (1 · 43) 667

הֵטִיל   15 to cast, cast out, hurl (4 · 9 · 14) 376

זַעַף   raging, storming; rage (1 · 7) 277

יִרְאָה   16 fear, terror (2 · 45) 432

נָדַר   to vow (2 · 31 · 31) 623

Chapter 2

מִנָּה   1 to appoint, ordain (4 · 9 · 28) 584

דָּג   fish (3 · 19) 185

בָּלַע   to swallow down, swallow up (1 · 20 · 41) 118

מֵעֶה   internal organ; here = stomach, belly (2 · 32) 588-589

מֵעֶה   2 internal organ; here = stomach, belly (2 · 32) 588-589

דָּגָה   fish (1 · 15) 185

שׁוּע   3 to cry for help (1 · 21 · 21) 1002

מְצוּלָה   4 deep, deep sea, depth (1 · 12) 846-847

מִשְׁבָּר   breaker of sea; i.e., big wave (1 · 5) 991

גַּל   wave, roller, billow, heap (1 · 16) 164

נִגְרַשׁ   5 to be driven, tossed (1 · 3 · 48) 176

מִגֶּגֶד   from before, in front of, opposite (1 · 26) 617

אָפַף   6 to encompass, surround (1 · 5 · 5) 67

תְּהוֹם   sea, deep sea; primeval (1 · 36) 1062-1063

סוּף   rushes, reeds (1 · 4) 693

חָבַשׁ   to bind, bind on or up; ptc. = bound (1 · 28 · 32) 289

קֶצֶב   7 extremity, bottom; shape, cut (1 · 3) 891

378

בְּרִיחַ   bar (1 · 41) 138

שַׁחַת   pit (1 · 23) 1001

הִתְעַטֵּף   8 to faint, faint away (1 · 6 · 11)

תּוֹדָה   10 thanksgiving in song, thanksgiving
(1 · 32) 392

נָדַר   to vow (2 · 31 · 31) 623

דָּג   11 fish (3 · 19) 185

הֵקִיא   to vomit up (1 · 7 · 9) 883

יַבָּשָׁה   dry land, dry ground (3 · 14) 387

Chapter 3

קְרִיאָה   2 proclamation (1 · 1) 896

מַהֲלָךְ   3 journey, walk (2 · 5) 237

מַהֲלָךְ   4 journey, walk (2 · 5) 237

צוֹם   5 fast, fasting (1 · 26) 847

שַׂק   sackcloth, sack (3 · 48) 974

קָטֹן   insignificant, small (1 · 47) 881-882

אַדֶּרֶת   6 mantle, cloak; glory (1 · 12) 12

שַׂק   sackcloth, sack (3 · 48) 974

אֵפֶר   ashes (1 · 22) 68

טַעַם   7 decision, decree; judgment, taste
(1 · 13) 381

טָעַם   to taste, perceive (1 · 11 · 11) 380-381

מְאוּמָה   anything (1 · 32) 548

שַׂק   8 sackcloth, sack (3 · 48) 974

חָזְקָה   severely, sharply; strength, force
(1 · 6) 306

חָרוֹן   9 anger, burning of anger (1 · 41) 354

Chapter 4

אָנָּה   2 strong particle of entreaty, I or we
beseech thee (2 · 6) 58

קֶדֶם   to be beforehand, go before, be in
front; to meet, confront (1 · 24 · 26)
869-870

חַנּוּן   gracious (1 · 13) 337

רַחוּם   compassionate (1 · 13) 938

אָרֵךְ   long, slow (1 · 15) 74

סֻכָּה   5 booth, temporary shelter (1 · 31) 697

מִנָּה   6 to appoint, ordain (4 · 9 · 28) 584

קִיקָיוֹן   plant, perh. bottle-gourd (5 · 5) 884

מִנָּה   7 to appoint, ordain (4 · 9 · 28) 584

תּוֹלַעַת   worm, grub, vine weevil (1 · 41)
1069

שַׁחַר   dawn (1 · 23) 1007

מָחֳרָת   the morrow, day following a past
day (1 · 32) 564

קִיקָיוֹן   plant, perh. bottle-gourd (5 · 5) 884

זָרַח   8 to rise, come forth, appear
(1 · 18 · 18) 280

מִנָּה   to appoint, ordain (4 · 9 · 28) 584

חֲרִישִׁי   [meaning dub.] silent, still, sultry
(1 · 1) 362   Lis. 531 "sharp, hot"

הִתְעַלֵּף   to swoon away; enwrap oneself
(1 · 3 · 5) 763

קִיקָיוֹן   9 plant, perh. bottle-gourd (5 · 5) 884

חוּס   10 to look upon with compassion
(2 · 24 · 24) 299

קִיקָיוֹן   plant, perh. bottle-gourd (5 · 5) 884

עָמָל   to labor, toil (1 · 11 · 11) 765

חוּס   11 to look upon with compassion
(2 · 24 · 24) 299

רִבּוֹ   ten thousand, myriad (1 · 11) 914

MICAH

Chapter 1

הַקְשִׁיב	2	to give attention (1 · 45 · 46) 904
מְלֹא		fullness, that which fills, entire contents (1 · 38) 571
נָמֵס	4	niph. מסס, to melt, dissolve (1 · 19 · 21) 587
דּוֹנַג		wax (1 · 4) 200
הֻגַּר		hoph. נגר to be poured out, melted (1 · 1 · 10) 620
מוֹרָד		descent, slope (1 · 5) 434
עִי	6	ruin, heap of ruins (2 · 5) 730
מַטָּע		planting place; act of planting (1 · 6) 642
הִגִּיר		to pour down, hurl down (1 · 5 · 10) 620
גַּיְא		valley (1 · 47) 161
יְסוֹד		foundation (1 · 19) 414
פָּסִיל	7	idol, image (2 · 23) 820-821
הֻכַּת		hoph. כתת to be crushed, beat in pieces (1 · 4 · 17) 510
אֶתְנַן		hire of harlot (3 · 11) 1072
עָצָב		idol (1 · 17) 781
זוֹנָה		ptc. = harlot (2 · 33) 275-276
ספד	8	to wail, lament (1 · 28 · 30) 704
הֵילִל		to utter or make a howling, give a howl (1 · 30 · 30) 410
שִׁילָל		Q שׁוֹלָל barefoot (1 · 3) 1021
עָרוֹם		naked (1 · 16) 736
מִסְפֵּד		wailing (2 · 16) 704
תַּן		jackal (1 · 14) 1072
אֵבֶל		mourning (1 · 24) 5
יַעֲנָה		[dub.] greed (1 · 8) 419 Lis. 617 ostrich
אָנוּשׁ	9	ptc. pass. = incurable (1 · 8) 60
מַכָּה		wound, beating, blow (1 · 48) 646
הִתְפַּלָּשׁ	10	to do an act of mourning; perh. roll in dust (1 · 4 · 4) 814
עֶרְיָה	11	nakedness (1 · 6) 789
בֹּשֶׁת		shame (1 · 30) 102
מִסְפֵּד		wailing (2 · 16) 704
עֶמְדָּה		standing ground (1 · 1) 765
חוּל, חִיל	12	to twist or writhe in anxious longing; to writhe, dance (1 · 3 · 5) 296-297 Lis. has sep. rt. 488
רתם	13	to bind, attach (1 · 1 · 1) 958
מֶרְכָּבָה		chariot (2 · 44) 939
רֶכֶשׁ		steeds, horses (1 · 3) 940
שִׁלּוּחִים	14	sending away, parting gift (1 · 3) 1019
אַכְזָב		deceptive, disappointing (1 · 2) 469
יוֹרֵשׁ	15	ptc. = heir, possessor, captor (1 · 5) 439
קרח	16	to make a baldness, make bald (1 · 2 · 5) 901
גזז		to shear, cut off (1 · 14 · 15) 159
תַּעֲנוּג		daintiness, luxury, exquisite delight (2 · 5) 772
הִרְחִיב		to make large, enlarge (1 · 21 · 25) 931
קָרְחָה		baldness, bald spot (1 · 11) 901
נֶשֶׁר		griffon vulture, eagle (1 · 26) 676-677

Chapter 2

מִשְׁכָּב	1	couch, bed; act of lying (1 · 46) 1012
אֵל		strength, power (1[?] · 5[?]) 7. אֵל 43
חָמַד	2	to desire, take pleasure in (1 · 16 · 21) 326
גָּזַל		to take violent possession of, to tear away, seize (2 · 29 · 30) 159
עָשַׁק		to oppress, wrong (1 · 36 · 37) 798
הֵמִישׁ		[Lis. Qal.] to remove, take away (2 · 20 · 20) 559
צַוָּאר		neck, back of neck (1 · 41) 848
רוֹמָה		haughtily (1 · 1) 928

380

מָשָׁל 4 prophetic figurative discourse, proverb, by-word, parable (1 · 39) 605

נָהָה to lament, wail (1 · 2 · 2) 624

נְהִי wailing, lamentation, mourning song (1 · 7) 624

הֵמִיר to change, alter, exchange (1 · 13 · 14) 558

הֵמִישׁ [Lis. *Qal.*] to remove, take away (2 · 20 · 20) 559

שׁוֹבֵב apostate, turning back (1 · 3) 1000

חֶבֶל 5 measuring cord, line, cord; measured portion (1 · 49) 286

הֵטִיף 6 to discourse; to drip (5 · 9 · 18) 642-643

נָסוֹג to turn oneself or itself away, hence = cease (1 · 14 · 25) 690-691

כְּלִמָּה insult, reproach, ignominy (1 · 30) 484

קָצַר 7 to be short, impatient (1 · 12 · 14) 894

מַעֲלָל deed, practice, act (3 · 41) 760

אֶתְמוּל 8 yesterday, w. מִן = already; formerly (1 · 8) 1069-1070

מִמּוּל from the front of, off the front of, in front of (1 · 9) 557

שַׂלְמָה wrapper, mantle; but BDB reads שׁלמה שׁלמה "him at peace with him" (1 · 16) 971

אֶדֶר mantle, cloak, glory, magnificence (1 · 2) 12

הִפְשִׁיט to strip off, strip, flay (2 · 15 · 43) 832-833

בֶּטַח securely; security (1 · 43) 105

גרשׁ piel., to drive out, drive away (1 · 35 · 48) 176-177

תַּעֲנוּג daintiness, luxury, exquisite delight (2 · 5) 772

עוֹלָל child (1 · 9) 760

הָדָר honor, glory, splendor, majesty, ornament (1 · 30) 214

מְנוּחָה 10 resting place, rest (1 · 21) 629

בַּעֲבוּר for the sake of, on account of, in order that (1 · 45) 721

טָמְאָה uncleanness (1 · 37) 380 Lis. puts w. טֻמְאָה

חבל to ruin, destroy (1 · 6 · 11) 287

חֶבֶל destruction (1 · 2) 287

נמרץ to be sick; ptc. = grievous (1 · 3 · 4) 599

לוּ 11 if, O that (1 · 19) 530

כָּזַב to lie, tell a lie (1 · 12 · 16) 469

הִטִּיף to discourse; to drip (5 · 9 · 18) 642-643

שֵׁכָר intoxicating drink, strong drink (1 · 22) 1016

יַחַד 12 together (1 · 44) 403

בָּצְרָה enclosure; i.e., [sheep]fold (1 · 1) 131

עֵדֶר flock, herd (3 · 37) 727

דֹּבֶר pasture (1 · 2) 184

הֵהִים to mutter, show disquietude (1 · 2 · 6) 223

פָּרַץ 13 to break through, break down, break out, burst out (2 · 46 · 49) 829

Chapter 3

קָצִין 1 ruler, man in authority, chief, dictator (2 · 11) 892

גָּזַל 2 to take violent possession of, to tear away, seize (2 · 29 · 30) 159

שְׁאֵר flesh (2 · 17) 984-985

שְׁאֵר 3 flesh (2 · 17) 984-985

הִפְשִׁיט to strip off, strip, flay (2 · 15 · 43) 832-833

פצח to break in pieces (1 · 1 · 1) 822 Lis. has sep. root 1178

סִיר pot, household utensil for boiling (1 · 29) 696

קְלָחַת caldron (1 · 2) 886

מַעֲלָל 4 practice, deed, act (3 · 41) 760

הִתְעָה 5 to cause to err, mislead; to be made to wander about (1 · 21 · 50) 1073

נָשַׁךְ to bite (1 · 10 · 12) 675

חָזוֹן 6 vision (1 · 35) 303

חָשַׁךְ to be [grow] dark (1 · 11 · 17) 364-365

קסם to practice divination (2 · 11 · 11) 890

קָדַר to be dark (1 · 13 · 17) 871

חֹזֶה 7 seer (1 · 17) 302

חפר to be abashed, ashamed (1 · 13 · 17) 344

קֹסֵם ptc. = diviner, practicing divination (1 · 9) 890

עָטָה to wrap, envelop oneself (1 · 11 · 14) 741

שָׂפָם moustache (1 · 5) 974

מַעֲנֶה answer, response (1 · 6) 775

אוּלָם 8 but, but indeed (1 · 19) 19

קָצִין 9 ruler, man in authority, chief, dictator (2 · 11) 892

תעב piel. to regard as an abomination, abhor (1 · 15 · 22) 1073

עקשׁ to twist (1 · 3 · 5) 786

עַוְלָה 10 violent deeds of injustice; unrighteousness, wrong (1 · 32) 732

שֹׁחַד 11 present, bribe (1 · 23) 1005

מְחִיר hire, price (1 · 15) 564

הורה to teach, instruct, direct (2 · 45 · 45) 435

קסם to practice divination (2 · 11 · 11) 890

נִשְׁעַן to lean, support oneself (1 · 22 · 22) 1043

בִּגְלַל 12 on account of, for the sake of (1 · 10) 164

נחרשׁ to be plowed (1 · 2 · 26) 360

עִי ruin, heap of ruins (2 · 5) 730

Chapter 4

נהר 1 to flow, stream (1 · 3 · 3) 625

הורה 2 to teach, instruct, direct (2 · 45 · 45) 435

עָצוּם 3 mighty, strong in numbers (2 · 31) 783

כִּתַּת to beat, hammer, crush (1 · 5 · 17) 510

אֵת a cutting instrument of iron, plowshare (1 · 5) 88

חֲנִית spear (1 · 47) 333

מַזְמֵרָה pruning knife (1 · 4) 275

תְּאֵנָה 4 fig tree, fig (1 · 39) 1061

הֶחֱרִיד to terrify, drive in terror, rout (1 · 16 · 39) 353

צלע 6 to limp (2 · 4 · 4) 854

נִדְחָה to be thrust out, banished; ptc. = banished one, outcast (1 · 13 · 43) 623

צלע 7 to limp (2 · 4 · 4) 854

נהלא ptc. removed far off (1 · 1 · 1) 229

עָצוּם mighty, strong in numbers (2 · 31) 783

מִגְדָּל 8 tower, מִ־עֵדֶר shepherd's watch-tower near Bethlehem (1 · 49) 153-154

עֵדֶר flock, herd (3 · 37) 727

עֹפֶל mound, hill (1 · 8) 779

אָתָה to come, come upon (1 · 19 · 21) 87

מֶמְשָׁלָה rule, dominion (1 · 17) 606

הֵרִיעַ 9 to cry out in distress, to shout a war cry, to shout in triumph (1 · 40 · 44) 929

רֵעַ shouting, roar (1 · 3) 929

יוֹעֵץ ptc. = counselor, adviser (1 · 22) 419

חִיל anguish, writhing (1 · 6) 297

חול, חִיל 10 to twist, writhe, dance, whirl (1 · 30 · 47) 296-297

382

גִּיחַ to thrust forth, bring forth, draw
forth, burst forth (1 · 3 · 5) 161

קִרְיָה town, city (1 · 30) 900

חָנֵף 11 to be polluted; to be profane
(1 · 7 · 11) 337-338

עָמִיר 12 swath, row of fallen grain (1 · 4)
771

גֹּרֶן threshing floor (1 · 34) 175

דָּשׁ, דּוּשׁ 13 to tread, thresh, trample
(1 · 13 · 16) 190

פַּרְסָה hoof (1 · 21) 828

נְחוּשָׁה bronze, copper (1 · 10) 639

הֵדַק to make dust of, pulverize
(1 · 8 · 13) 200

הֶחֱרִים to devote to [for sacred use]; to
devote to destruction, exterminate
(1 · 48 · 51) 355-356

בֶּצַע gain made by violence, unjust gain
(1 · 23) 130

הִתְגֹּדֵד 14 to gather in troops or bands; to cut
oneself (1 · 7 · 8) 151

גְּדוּד troops, marauding band; foray, raid
(1 · 33) 151

מָצוֹר siege, siege enclosure, siege works
(1 · 25) 848-849

לְחִי cheek, jaw, jawbone (1 · 21) 534

Chapter 5

צָעִיר 1 little, insignificant; young, younger
(1 · 22) 859

אֶלֶף family, thousand (1 · 12) 48-49 Lis.
102 has 2 rts

מֹשֵׁל ptc. = when one rules, ruler
(1 · 24) 605

מוֹצָאָה origin; place of going out to, privy
(1 · 2) 426

גָּאוֹן 3 exaltation, majesty, excellence,
pride (1 · 49) 144-145

אֶפֶס end, extremity (1 · 27) 67

אַרְמוֹן 4 citadel, castle, palace (1 · 33) 74

נָסִיךְ prince (1 · 6) 651 BDB has 2 roots
Lis. 932 has 1 root

טַל 6 dew, night mist (1 · 31) 378

רְבִיבִים copious showers (1 · 6) 914

עֵשֶׂב herb; herbage, incl. grass (1 · 33)
793

קוּה to lie in wait for, to wait for, look
eagerly for (1 · 39 · 45) 875

יחל Piel. to wait, tarry (1 · 25 · 42) 403-
404

אַרְיֵה 7 lion (1 · 45) 71

כְּפִיר young lion (1 · 31) 498

עֵדֶר flock, herd (3 · 37) 727

רָמַס to trample down, trample
(1 · 17 · 18) 942

טָרַף to tear, rend (1 · 19 · 24)
382

מֶרְכָּבָה 9 chariot (2 · 44) 939

הָרַס 10 to throw down, tear down, break
down (1 · 30 · 43) 248

מִבְצָר fortress, stronghold, fortication
(1 · 37) 131

כֶּשֶׁף 11 sorcery (1 · 6) 506

עוֹנֵן to practice soothsaying (1 · 10 · 11)
778

פָּסִיל 12 idol, image (2 · 23) 820-821

מַצֵּבָה sacred pillar, pillar used as personal or sacred memorial (1 · 36)
663

נָתַשׁ 13 to pull up, pluck up, root out
(1 · 16 · 21) 684

אֲשֵׁרָה sacred tree or pole representing Canaanite goddess (1 · 40) 81

נָקָם vengeance (1 · 17) 668

Chapter 6

אֵתָן, אֵיתָן 2 ever-enduring, permanent, ever-
flowing (1 · 14) 450-451

383

מוֹסָד foundation (1 · 13) 414

הלאה 3 to weary, make weary, exhaust (1 · 6 · 19) 521

בַּמָה 6 wherewith[?] by what[?] (1 · 29) מה 4.a. 552

קדם to come to meet; to confront; to go before (2 · 24 · 26) 869-870

נכף niph. to bow oneself (1 · 1 · 5) 496

עֵגֶל calf (1 · 35) 722

רָצָה 7 to accept, be pleased with, make acceptable (1 · 42 · 50) 953

רְבָבָה ten thousand, myriad, multitude (1 · 16) 914

הצניע 8 to make humble; w. הלך = to show a humble walk (1 · 1 · 1) 857

תּוּשִׁיָה 9 abiding success; sound and efficient wisdom (1 · 12) 444

יעד to appoint, assign (1 · 5 · 28) 416

רֶשַׁע 10 wickedness (2 · 30) 957

אֵיפָה ephah, grain measure (1 · 39) 35

רָזוֹן scantness, leanness; wasting (1 · 3) 931

זָעַם to denounce, curse; to be indignant (1 · 11 · 12) 276

זכה 11 to be clear, justified, regarded as just; to be clean, pure (1 · 4 · 8) 269

מאזנים balances, scales (1 · 15) 24

רֶשַׁע wickedness (2 · 30) 957

כִּיס bag, purse (1 · 5) 476

מִרְמָה deceit, treachery (1 · 39) 941

עָשִׁיר 12 the rich, rich (1 · 23) 799

רְמִיָה deceit, treachery (1 · 15) 941

יֵשַׁח 14 emptiness [dub.] (1 · 1) 445

הסיג to remove, carry away; to displace, move back (1 · 7 · 25) 690-691

הפליט to bring into security (1 · 2 · 27) 812

פלט to bring into security, cause to escape (1 · 24 · 27) 812

קצר 15 to reap, harvest (1 · 24 · 24) 894

זַיִת olive, olives, olive tree (1 · 38) 268

סוּךְ to anoint oneself, to anoint, to be poured (1 · 7 · 9) 691-692

תִּירוֹשׁ must, new wine (1 · 38) 440

מוֹעֵצָה 16 counsel, plan, principle, device (1 · 7) 760

שַׁמָּה horror, state of being appalled; a waste (1 · 39) 1031

שְׁרֵקָה [object of derisive] hissing (1 · 7) 1056-1057

Chapter 7

אֶלְלַי 1 Alas! Woe! (1 · 2) 47

אֹסֶף gathering (1 · 3) 63

קַיִץ summer fruit, summer (1 · 20) 884

עוֹלֵלוֹת gleaning (1 · 6) 760

בָּצִיר vintage (1 · 7) 131

אֶשְׁכּוֹל cluster (1 · 9) 79

בִּכּוּרָה first ripe fig, early fig (1 · 4) 114

אָוָה to desire (1 · 11 · 27) 16

חָסִיד 2 pious man, godly man; kind, pious (1 · 32) 339

אָרַב to lie in wait, ambush (1 · 20 · 23) 70

צוד to hunt (1 · 13 · 17) 844

חֵרֶם net (1 · 9) 357

שָׁלֵם, שָׁלוֹם reward, bribe, requital (1 · 3) 1024

הַוָּה desire; engulfing ruin, destruction (1 · 3) 217

עבת to wind, weave [dub.] (1 · 1 · 1) 721

חֵדֶק 4 brier (1 · 2) 293

מְסוּכָה hedge (1 · 1) 692

צפה to watch, look forth; ptc. = watchman (2 · 9 · 18) 859

פְּקֻדָּה visitation; oversight; mustering; store (1 · 32) 824

מְבוּכָה confusion, confounding (1 · 2) 100

אַלּוּף 5 friend, intimate; tame, docile (1 · 9) 48

חֵיק   bosom, fold of garment at breast (1 · 38) 300

נבל   6 to regard or treat as a fool (1 · 4 · 25) 614

כַּלָּה   daughter-in-law (1 · 34) 483

חָמוֹת   husband's mother (1 · 11) 327

צפה   7 to watch, look forth (2 · 9 · 18) 859

הוֹחִיל   to wait for, hope for (1 · 15 · 42) 403-404

יֵשַׁע   salvation, safety, welfare (1 · 36) 447

זַעַף   9 raging, rage, storming (1 · 7) 277

בּוּשָׁה   10 shame (1 · 4) 102

אַי   where? (1 · 39) 32

מִרְמָס   trampling, trampling place (1 · 7) 942

טִיט   mud, mire (1 · 13) 376

גָּדֵר   11 wall, fence (1 · 14) 154-155

לְמִן   12 from (2 · 14) מִן 9.b. 583

מַעֲלָל   13 practice, deed, act (3 · 41) 760

בָּדָד   14 isolation, separation (1 · 11) 94-95

כַּרְמֶל   garden land or n. pr. Carmel (1 · 14) 502

נִפְלָאוֹת   15 *Niph.* ptc. = wonderful acts (1 · 43) 810

חרש   16 to be silent (1 · 7 · 46) 361

לחך   17 to lick; w. עפר = sign of humiliation (1 · 5 · 6) 535

נָחָשׁ   serpent (1 · 31) 638

זחל   to crawl away, shrink back (1 · 3 · 3) 267

רָגַז   to come quivering, to quake, be excited, be perturbed (1 · 30 · 41) 919

מִסְגֶּרֶת   fastness, border, rim (1 · 17) 689

פָּחַד   to turn in dread, be in dread, be in awe (1 · 22 · 25) 808

רָחַם   19 to have compassion, be compassionate (1 · 42 · 47) 933

כבש   to subdue, dominate, tread down, bring into bondage (1 · 8 · 14) 461

מְצוּלָה   depth, deep (1 · 12) 846

NAHUM

Chapter 1

מַשָּׂא 1 utterance, prophetic utterance, oracle (1 · 21) 672

חָזוֹן vision, divine communication in a vision (1 · 35) 302-303

קַנּוֹא 2 jealous (1 · 2) 888

נקם to avenge, take vengeance (3 · 13 · 35) 667-668

בַּעַל חֵמָה [idiom] a possessor of fury = furious חמה para. 2.c. 404

נטר to keep, maintain; to keep, guard (1 · 5 · 5) 643 Lis. 924 "to be angry"

אָרֵךְ 3 long, אאפים = slow to anger (1 · 15) 74

נקה to leave unpunished; to hold innocent, acquit (2 · 16 · 41) 667

סוּפָה storm wind (1 · 15) 693

שְׂעָרָה storm (1 · 2) 973

אָבָק dust (1 · 6) 7

גָּעַר 4 to rebuke (1 · 14 · 14) 172

הֶחֱרִיב to dry up (1 · 13 · 37) 351

אֻמְלַל to be or grow weak, feeble, to languish (2 · 15 · 15) 51

פֶּרַח sprout, bud (1 · 17) 827

רעש 5 to quake, shake (1 · 21 · 29) 950

הִתְמוֹגָג to melt, flow (1 · 3 · 17) 556

תֵּבֵל world (1 · 35) 385

זַעַם 6 indignation (1 · 22) 276

חָרוֹן anger, [burning of] anger (1 · 41) 354

נִתַּךְ to be poured out, poured forth, poured (1 · 8 · 21) 677

נתץ to be pulled down, broken down (1 · 3 · 42) 683

מָעוֹז 7 refuge, place of safety or protection (2 · 36) 732

חָסָה to seek refuge (1 · 37 · 37) 340

שֶׁטֶף 8 flood (1 · 6) 1009

כָּלָה complete destruction, annihilation; completion (2 · 22) 478

כָּלָה 9 complete destruction, annihilation; completion (2 · 22) 478

סִיר 10 thorn, hook (1 · 5) 696

סבך to interweave, ptc. pass. = interwoven, entangled (1 · 1 · 2) 687

סֹבֶא liquor, drink (1 · 3) 685

סבא to imbibe, drink largely; ptc. act. = drunkard (1 · 2 · 2) 684-685

קַשׁ stubble, chaff (1 · 16) 905

יָבֵשׁ dry, dried (1 · 9) 386

יוֹעֵץ 11 ptc. = advising, counseling; counselor (1 · 22) 419

בְּלִיַּעַל ruin, destruction, worthlessness (2 · 27) 116

שָׁלֵם 12 full, perfect, complete; safe; peace (1 · 28) 1023-1024

נגז Niph. to be cut off (1 · 1 · 15) 159

מוֹט 13 bar of yoke, pole (1 · 4) 557

מוֹסֵר band, restraining band or bond (1 · 12) 64

נתק to tear apart, snap; to tear out or away (1 · 11 · 27) 683

פֶּסֶל 14 idol, image (1 · 31) 820

מַסֵּכָה molten metal or image; libation (1 · 25) 651

Chapter 2

מְבַשֵּׂר 1 heralding or herald of glad tidings; gladdening with good tidings (1 · 9) 142

חגג to keep a pilgrim feast; to behave as at a feast (1 · 16 · 16) 290

בְּלִיַּעַל man of ruin, destroyer; worthlessness (2 · 27) 116

הֵפִיץ,מֵפִיץ 2 to scatter; but BDB as noun scatter-er, disperser (1 · 36 · 65) 807

מְצוּרָה rampart, siege works (1 · 8) 849

צִפָּה to watch, look forth (1 · 9 · 18) 859

מָתְנַיִם loins (2 · 47) 608

אָמֵץ to make firm, strengthen, secure, harden (1 · 19 · 41) 54-55

גָּאוֹן 3 exaltation, majesty, excellence (2 · 49) 144-145

בָּקַק to empty, lay waste (2 · 5 · 8) 132

זְמוֹרָה twig, branch, shoot (1 · 5) 274

אָדַם 4 pu. ptc. reddened (1 · 7 · 10) 10

תֻּלָּע 4 to be clad in scarlet (1 · 1 · 1) 1069

פְּלָדָה iron, steel (1 · 1) 811

בְּרוֹשׁ cypress, fir; here fig. for spear shafts (1 · 20) 141

הָרְעַל to be made to quiver, to be made to shake (1 · 1 · 1) 947

הִתְהוֹלֵל 5 to act madly or like a madman (1 · 6 · 14) 237-239 Lis. 426 has 2 rts

הִשְׁתַּקְשֵׁק hitpalp. to rush to and fro (1 · 1 · 6) 1055

רְחוֹב broad open place, plaza (1 · 43) 932

לַפִּיד torch (1 · 13) 542

בָּרָק lightning, lightning flash (2 · 21) 140

אַדִּיר 6 majestic one; majestic (2 · 27) 12

הֲלִיכָה going, walking; traveling company (1 · 6) 237

סֹכֵךְ protector, a shielding structure (1 · 1) 697

נָמוֹג 7 to melt away; fig. for helplessness (1 · 8 · 17) 556 niph. מוג

נָהַג 8 to moan, lament (1 · 1 · 1) 624

יוֹנָה dove (1 · 33) 401

תּוֹפֵף ptc. = twittering (1 · 1 · 2) 1074

בְּרֵכָה 9 pool, pond (1 · 17) 140

בָּזַז 10 to spoil, take as spoil, plunder (2 · 38 · 42) 102

קֵצֶה end (3 · 5) 892

תְּכוּנָה preparation, things prepared, sup-ply; arrangement; fixed place (1 · 3) 467

חֶמְדָּה desire, thing desired, precious thing (1 · 16) 326

בּוּקָה 11 emptiness (1 · 1) 101

מְבוּקָה void, emptiness (1 · 1) 101

בָּלַק ptc. = devastated city (1 · 1 · 2) 118

נָמֵס niph. to melt = to faint, grow fearful; melt (1 · 19 · 21) 587

פִּק tottering, staggering (1 · 1) 807

בֶּרֶךְ knee (1 · 25) 139

חַלְחָלָה anguish (1 · 4) 298

מָתְנַיִם loins (2 · 47) 608

פָּארוּר [dub.] glow (1 · 2) 802

אַיֵּה 12 where? (1 · 44) 32

מָעוֹן lair, refuge, dwelling (1 · 18) 732

אֲרִי lion (1 · 35) 71

מִרְעֶה pasture, pasturage (1 · 13) 945

כְּפִיר young lion (2 · 31) 498

אַרְיֵה lion (3 · 45) 71

לָבִיא lion (1 · 11) 522

גּוֹר, גּוּר whelp (1 · 7) 158

הֶחֱרִיד to drive in terror; ptc. = one to terrify (1 · 16 · 39) 353

אַרְיֵה 13 lion (3 · 45) 71

טָרַף to tear, rend (1 · 19 · 24) 382

בְּדֵי for what suffices for, for the need of; in the abundance of; as often as (1 · 6) דַּי 2.a. 191

גּוֹר whelp (1 · 2) 158

חָנַק to strangle (1 · 1 · 2) 338

לְבָאָה, לְבִי lion (1 · 1) 522

טֶרֶף prey, food; leaf (3 · 17) 383

חֹר, חוֹר hole, hole as a den (1 · 7) 359

מְעֹנָה den, lair, refuge, habitation (1 · 9) 733

טְרֵפָה animal torn [by wild beasts] (1 · 9) 383

עָשָׁן 14 smoke (1 · 25) 798

כְּפִיר young lion (2 · 31) 498

טֶרֶף prey, food; leaf (3 · 17) 383

Chapter 3

כַּחַשׁ 1 lying; leanness (1 · 6) 471

פֶּרֶק plunder; parting of ways (1 · 2) 830

הֵמִישׁ ,מָשׁ to depart, leave its place; remove (1 · 20 · 20) 559

טֶרֶף prey, food; leaf (3 · 17) 383

שׁוֹט 2 whip, scourge (1 · 6) 1002

רַעַשׁ earthquake, shaking of earth; trembling, shaking, quivering (1 · 17) 950

אוֹפָן wheel (1 · 35) 66

דֹּהֵר to rush, dash (1 · 1 · 1) 187

מֶרְכָּבָה chariot (1 · 44) 939

רִקֵּד to dance, leap; here = jolting of chariot (1 · 5 · 9) 955

לַהַב 3 flashing point; blade; flame (1 · 12) 529

בָּרָק lightning, glitter (2 · 21) 140

חֲנִית spear (1 · 47) 333

כֹּבֶד mass, abundance; weight; vehemence (1 · 4) 458

פֶּגֶר corpse, carcass (1 · 22) 803

קֵצֶה end (3 · 5) 892

גְּוִיָּה dead body, corpse, body (2 · 13) 156

זְנוּנִים 4 fornication (2 · 12) 276

זוֹנָה ptc. = harlot (1 · 33) 275

בַּעֲלָה sorceress, mistress (1 · 4) 128

כֶּשֶׁף sorcery; fig. for seductive and corruptive influence (2 · 6) 506

שׁוּל 5 skirt of robe, train (1 · 11) 1002

מַעַר bare, naked place (1 · 2) 789

קָלוֹן ignominy, dishonor, disgrace (1 · 17) 885-886

שִׁקּוּץ ,שֶׁקֶץ 6 detested thing (1 · 28) 1055

נִבֵּל to treat as a fool (1 · 4 · 25) 614

רֳאִי sight, [warning] spectacle; appearance; seeing (1 · 4) 909

נדד 7 to retreat, flee; to depart, wander, stray (1 · 20 · 24) 622

נוד ,נָד to show grief, lament [by shaking the head]; to move to and fro, wander, flutter (1 · 20 · 27) 626

מֵאַיִן whence[?] (1 · 48[?]) אַיִן 32

חֵיל 8 rampart, little wall of outer fortification, fortress (1 · 9) 298

עֹצֶם 9 might; bones (1 · 4) 782   end (3 · 5) 892

עֶזְרָה help, one who helps (1 · 26) 740-741

גּוֹלָה 10 [coll.] exiles, exile (1 · 42) 163

שְׁבִי state of captivity; act of capture; [coll.] captives (1 · 49) 985

עוֹלָל child (1 · 9) 760

רֻטַּשׁ to be dashed in pieces (1 · 4 · 6) 936

ידד to cast a lot (1 · 3 · 3) 391

רֻתַּק to be bound (1 · 1 · 2) 958

זִקִּים ,זֵק fetters (1 · 4) 279

שׁכר 11 to become drunken, be drunk (1 · 9 · 18) 1016

נֶעְלָם to be obscured, concealed (1 · 11 · 29) 761

מָעוֹז place of safety, protection (2 · 36) 731-732

מִבְצָר 12 fortress, stronghold, fortification (2 · 37) 131

תְּאֵנָה fig tree, fig (1 · 39) 1061

בִּכּוּרִים firstfruits (1 · 17) 114

נָנוֹעַ niph. to be tossed about (1 · 2 · 38) 631

בְּרִיחַ 13 bar of city gate, bar (1 · 41) 138

מָצוֹר 14 siege, siege works (1 · 25) 848-849

שׁאב to draw [water] (1 · 14 · 14) 980

מִבְצָר fortress, stronghold, fortification (2 · 37) 131

טִיט   clay, mud (1 · 13) 376

רָמַס   to trample (1 · 17 · 18) 942

חֹמֶר   mortar, cement, clay, mire (1 · 17) 330

מַלְבֵּן   brick mold, quadrangle (1 · 3) 527

יֶלֶק   15 kind of locust (3 · 9) 410

אַרְבֶּה   kind of locust (2 · 24) 916

רֹכֵל   16 ptc. = trafficker, trader (1 · 18) 940

כּוֹכָב   star (1 · 37) 456-457

יֶלֶק   kind of locust (3 · 9) 410

פָּשַׁט   to strip off; make a dash (1 · 24 · 43) 832-833

עוּף   to fly away, fly (1 · 18 · 25) 733

מִנְּזָר, מִנְּזָרִים   17 consecrated ones, princes; Lis. 829 "guardsmen" (1 · 1) 634

אַרְבֶּה   kind of locust (2 · 24) 916

טִפְסָר   scribe, marshal (1 · 2) 381

גּוֹב   [coll.] locust (1 · 1) 146

גּוֹבַי   swarm of locusts; [coll.] locusts (1 · 1) 146

גְּדֵרָה   wall, hedge (1 · 8) 155

קָרָה   cold, coldness (1 · 5) 903

זָרַח   to rise, come forth (1 · 18 · 18) 280

נֹדַד   to be chased away (1 · 1 · 24) 622

אֵי   where? (1 · 39) 32

נוּם   18 to be drowsy, slumber (1 · 6 · 6) 630

אַדִּיר   majestic one; majestic (2 · 27) 12

נפוש   Niph. to be scattered (1 · 1 · 1) 807

כֵּהָה   19 lessening, alleviation (1 · 1) 462

שֶׁבֶר   breaking, shattering, crashing; breaking = solution (1 · 45) 991

נַחְלָה   Niph. ptc. = diseased, severe, sore (1 · 5) 317-318

מַכָּה   beating, scourging, blow, slaughter; defeat (1 · 48) 646-647

שֵׁמַע   report, hearing (1 · 17) 1034

HABAKKUK

Chapter 1

מַשָּׂא 1 revelation, utterance, oracle (1 · 21) 672

אָנָה 2 wither? עַד-אָנָה = how long? (1 · 39) 33

שׁוּע to cry out for help (1 · 21 · 21) 1002

שֹׁד 3 violence, havoc (2 · 25) 994

לְנֶגֶד in the sight of (1 · 32) נֶגֶד 2.b. 617

מָדוֹן strife, contention (1 · 12) 193

פוּג 4 to grow numb; w. תוֹרָה = to be ineffective (1 · 3 · 4) 806

נֶצַח everlastingness, ever; לָנֶצַח = forever (1 · 43) 664

הכתיר to throw out; to surround (1 · 3 · 6) 509

עקל to be bent out of shape, crooked (1 · 1 · 1) 785

התתמה 5 to astonish [your]selves, be astounded (1 · 1 · 9) 1069

תמה to be astounded (1 · 8 · 9) 1069

פֹּעַל deed, thing done (2 · 37) 821

מַר 6 fierce, bitter (1 · 38) 600

מֶרְחָב broad, roomy place; מ׳אֶרֶץ expanses of the earth (1 · 6) 932

אָיֹם 7 terrible, dreadful (1 · 3) 33

נוֹרָא Niph. ptc. = fearful, dreadful (1 · 44) 431

שְׂאֵת dignity, exaltation; swelling, uprising (1 · 7) 673

נָמֵר 8 leopard (1 · 6) 649

חדד to be sharp, keen (1 · 1 · 6) 292

זְאֵב wolf (1 · 8) 255

פוש to spring about [dub.] Lis. 115 "to paw" (1 · 3 · 3) 807

מֵרָחוֹק to a distance (1 · 34) רָחוֹק 2.(3) 935

עוף to fly (1 · 18 · 25) 733

נֶשֶׁר griffon vulture, eagle (1 · 26) 676

חָשׁ, חוּשׁ to make haste (1 · 15 · 21) 301

מְגַמָּה 9 uncertain meaning, Lis. 748 "striving" [dub.] (1 · 1) 169 poss. "assembling" of faces directed forward

חוֹל sand (1 · 22) 297

שְׁבִי captives, captivity (1 · 49) 985

התקלס 10 to mock, deride (1 · 3 · 4) 887

רֹזֵן ptc. = ruler (1 · 6) 931

מִשְׂחָק object of derision (1 · 1) 966

מִבְצָר fortress, stronghold (1 · 37) 131

שָׂחַק to laugh (1 · 19 · 36) 965

צבר to heap up (1 · 7 · 7) 840

חָלַף 11 to move or sweep on, pass on, pass through (1 · 14 · 26) 322

אָשֵׁם to be or become guilty (1 · 33 · 35) 79

זוּ this, which (1 · 15) 262

יָסַד 12 to found, establish (1 · 20 · 41) 413

בגד 13 to act treacherously (2 · 49 · 49) 93

הֶחֱרִישׁ to be silent (1 · 38 · 46) 361

בֶּלַע to swallow up, engulf, confuse, confound (1 · 20 · 41) 118

דָּג 14 fish (1 · 19) 185

רֶמֶשׂ creeping things (1 · 16) 943

מֹשֵׁל ptc. = ruler (1 · 24) 605

חַכָּה 15 fishhook (1 · 3) 335

גרר to drag away (1 · 3 · 4) 176

חֵרֶם net (3 · 9) 357

מִכְמֶרֶת net, fishing net (2 · 3[?]) 485

גיל to rejoice (2 · 45 · 45) 162

חֵרֶם 16 net (3 · 9) 357

מִכְמֶרֶת net, fishing net (2 · 3[?]) 485

שָׁמֵן fat, rich (1 · 10) 1032

מַאֲכָל food (1 · 30) 38

בָּרִיא fat (1 · 14) 135

הריק 17 to empty out (1 · 17 · 19) 937-938

חֵרֶם net (3 · 9) 357

חָמַל to spare, have compassion (1 · 40 · 40) 328

Chapter 2

הִתְיַצֵּב	1	to station oneself, take one's stand (1 · 48 · 48) 426
מָצוֹר		rampart, siege works (1 · 25) 848-849
צפה		to watch closely (1 · 9 · 18) 859
תּוֹכַחַת		argument, impeachment, reproof (1 · 24) 407
חָזוֹן	2	vision, divine communication in a vision (2 · 35) 302-303
בֵּאֵר		to make distinct, plain (1 · 3 · 3) 91
לוּחַ		tablet, board, plate (1 · 43) 531
חָזוֹן	3	vision, divine communication in a vision (2 · 35) 302-303
הפוח, הפיח		to pant, puff; here = to haste (1 · 12 · 13) 806
כָּזַב		to disappoint, fail; to lie (1 · 12 · 16) 469
התמהמה		Hithpael, to linger, tarry, wait (1 · 9 · 9) 554
חִכָּה		to wait for (1 · 13 · 14) 314
אָחַר		to delay (1 · 15 · 17) 29
עפל	4	to be swollen; but subst. needed (1 · 1 · 2) 779
יָשַׁר		to be upright, right (1 · 13 · 25) 448
אַף כִּי	5	furthermore, indeed, indeed that (1 · 20) 65
בגד		to act treacherously (2 · 49 · 49) 93
יָהִיר		proud, haughty (1 · 2) 397
נוה		to abide, dwell (1 · 1 · 1) 627
הִרְחִיב		to enlarge, make large (1 · 21 · 25) 931
מָשָׁל	6	proverb, parable (1 · 39) 605
מְלִיצָה		satire, mocking poem (1 · 2) 539
חִידָה		riddle, enigma (1 · 17) 295
מָתַי		when[?] עַד-מָתַי = until when[?] how long[?] (1 · 42) 607
עַבְטִיט		weight of pledges, heavy debts (1 · 1) 716

פֶּתַע	7	suddenness; suddenly (1 · 7) 837
נָשַׁךְ		to bite; to charge interest (1 · 10 · 12) 675
יקץ		to awake, become suddenly active (1 · 11 · 11) 429
זעזע		Pilp. to shake violently (1 · 1 · 3) 266
מְשִׁסָּה		plunder, spoil (1 · 6) 1042
שָׁלַל	8	to spoil, plunder (2 · 13 · 15) 1021
קִרְיָה		town, city (3 · 30) 900
בצע	9	to gain by violence, cut off (1 · 10 · 16) 130
בֶּצַע		unjust gain, gain made by violence (1 · 23) 130
קַן		nest (1 · 13) 890
בֹּשֶׁת	10	shame (1 · 30) 102
קצה		to cut off (1 · 1 · 5) 891
כָּפִיס	11	some beam in a house, perh. rafter or girder (1 · 1) 496
קִרְיָה	12	town, city (3 · 30) 900
עַוְלָה		violent deeds of injustice, injustice (1 · 32) 732
יגע	13	to toil or labor for (בְּ), grow weary (1 · 20 · 26) 388
בְּדֵי		what suffices for para. 2a דֵּי (2 · 6) 191
לְאֹם		people (1 · 35) 522
רִיק		emptiness, vanity (1 · 12) 938
יעף		to be or grow weary (1 · 8 · 9) 419
ספח	15	to join, attach to (1 · 1 · 5) 705
שכר		to make drunken (1 · 4 · 18) 1016
מָעוֹר		nakedness (1 · 1) 735
קָלוֹן	16	ignominy, dishonor (1 · 17) 885-886
נערל		to be counted uncircumcised (1 · 1 · 2) 790
כּוֹס		cup (1 · 31) 468
קִיקָלוֹן	17	disgrace (1 · 1) 887
שֹׁד		devastation, ruin (2 · 25) 994
קִרְיָה		town, city (3 · 30) 900
הוֹעִיל	18	to profit, benefit (1 · 23 · 23) 418

391

פֶּסֶל idol, image (1 · 31) 820

פָּסַל to hew, hew into shape (1 · 6 · 6) 820

יָצַר to form, fashion (2 · 41 · 44) 427

מַסֵּכָה molten metal, image (1 · 25) 651

הוֹרָה,מוֹרֶה to teach, instruct [ptc. = teacher (1[?] · 9[?])] (2[?] · 45[?] · 45[?]) 434

יֵצֶר form [of a graven image] (1 · 9) 428

אֱלִיל insufficiency, worthlessness; אלילים = worthless gods, idols (1 · 20) 47

אִלֵּם dumb (1 · 6) 48

הָקִיץ 19 to awake (1 · 22 · 23) 884

דוּמָם silence (1 · 3) 189

הוֹרָה to teach, instruct (2[?] · 45[?] · 45 [?]) 434

הַס 20 Hush! (1 · 6) 245

Chapter 3

שִׁגָּיוֹן 1 [meaning dub.] prob. a title (1 · 2) 993

שֵׁמַע 2 report (1 · 17) 1034

פֹּעַל deed, thing done (2 · 37) 821

רֹגֶז raging, wrath (1 · 7) 919

רִחַם to have compassion (1 · 42 · 47) 933

תֵּימָן 3 district of Edom, south country (1 · 24[?]) 412

הוֹד splendor, majesty (1 · 24) 217

נֹגַהּ 4 brightness (2 · 19) 618

חֶבְיוֹן hiding, hiding place, veil (1 · 1) 285

דֶּבֶר 5 plague, pestilence (1 · 46) 184

רֶשֶׁף fire-bolt, flame (1 · 7) 958

מוֹדֵד 6 Pol. to measure; Lis. מוד to shake up (1 · 1 · 1) מדד 556, 551

הִתִּיר to cause to spring or start up (1 · 5 · 7) 684

הִתְפָּצֵץ Hithpo. to be shattered (1 · 1 · 3) 822-823, 1126

עַד perpetuity (1 · 53) 723

שׁחה be bowed down, humbled (1 · 12 · 18) 1005

הֲלִיכָה going; of goings = doings, ways (1 · 6) 237

רָגַז 7 to quake (3 · 30 · 41) 919

עֶבְרָה 8 overflowing rage, fury (1 · 34) 720

מֶרְכָּבָה chariot (1 · 44) 939

עֶרְיָה 9 nakedness (1 · 6) 789

נֵעוֹר to be exposed, bare (1 · 1 · 1) 735

שְׁבוּעָה oath [dub. here] (1 · 30) 989-990

אֹמֶר ,אֵמֶר word, appointment [dub.] (1 · 6) 56-57

חוּל ,חִיל 10 to writhe, be in anguish (1 · 30 · 47) 296

זֶרֶם flood of rain, downpour (1 · 9) 281

תְּהוֹם deep, sea (1 · 36) 1062-1063

רוֹם adv. on high (1 · 1) 927

יָרֵחַ 11 moon (1 · 27) 437

זְבֻל height, lofty abode (1 · 5) 259

נֹגַהּ brightness, glitter (2 · 19) 618

בָּרָק lightning; fig. of flashing arrow-head (1 · 21) 140

חֲנִית spear, spearhead (1 · 47) 333-334

זַעַם 12 indignation (1 · 22) 276

צָעַד to step, march (1 · 7 · 8) 857

דוּשׁ ,דָּשׁ to trample on, thresh (1 · 13 · 16) 190

יֵשַׁע 13 deliverance, salvation (3 · 36) 447

מָשִׁיחַ anointed (1 · 39) 603

מָחַץ to smite through, shatter (1 · 14 · 14) 563

עָרָה to lay bare (1 · 9 · 15) 788

יְסוֹד foundation (1 · 19) 414

צַוָּאר neck, back of neck (1 · 41) 848

נָקַב 14 to pierce, bore (1 · 13 · 19) 666

פֶּרֶז warriors, leaders [dub.] (1 · 1) 826

סָעַר to storm (1 · 3 · 7) 704

עֲלִיצוּת exultation (1 · 1) 763

מִסְתָּר hiding place (1 · 10) 712

חָמַד 15 to ferment, foam up (1 · 1*) 330
    *Lis. 508 חֶמֶר "foaming waters"

רָגַז 16 to quake, come quivering
    (3 · 30 · 41) 919

צָלַל   to quiver, tingle (1 · 4 · 4) 852

רָקָב   rottenness, caries (1 · 5) 955

גוּד   to invade, attack (1 · 3 · 3) 156

תְּאֵנָה 17 fig tree (1 · 39) 1061

פָּרַח   to send out shoots, bud (1 · 28 · 33)
    827

יְבוּל   produce (1 · 13) 385

כָּחַשׁ   to disappoint, fail (1 · 19 · 22) 471

זַיִת   olive tree (1 · 38) 268

שְׁדֵמָה   field (1 · 6) 995

אֹכֶל   food (1 · 44) 38

גָּזַר   to cut off, destroy (1 · 6 · 12) 160

מִכְלָה   enclosure, fold (1 · 3) 476

רֶפֶת   stable, stall (1 · 1) 952

עָלַז 18 to exult, triumph (1 · 16 · 16) 759

גִּיל   to rejoice (2 · 45 · 45) 162

יֵשַׁע   deliverance, salvation (3 · 36) 447

אַיָּלָה 19 hind, doe (1 · 11) 19

נְגִינָה   music (1 · 14) 618

393

ZEPHANIAH

Chapter 1

הֵסִיף	2	to make an end of (3 · 4 · 8) 692
הֵסִיף	3	to make an end of (3 · 4 · 8) 692
דָּג		fish (2 · 19) 185
מַכְשֵׁלָה		stumbling block = idol [dub.] overthrown mass (1 · 2) 506
שְׁאָר	4	rest, residue, remainder (1 · 26) 984
כֹּמֶר		[idol-] priest (1 · 3) 485
גָּג	5	roof, top (1 · 29) 150
נָסוֹג	6	to turn oneself away, turn back = prove faithless (1 · 14 · 25) 690-691
הַס	7	[interj.] Hush! Keep silence! (1 · 6) 245
מַלְבּוּשׁ	8	raiment, attire (1 · 8) 528
נָכְרִי		foreign, alien (1 · 45) 648
דִּלֵּג	9	to leap; ptc. = one leaping (1 · 1 · 5) 194
מִפְתָּן		threshold (1 · 8) 837
מִרְמָה		treachery, deceit (1 · 39) 941
צְעָקָה	10	cry of distress, cry, outcry (1 · 21) 858
דָּג		fish (2 · 19) 185
יְלָלָה		howling (1 · 5) 410
מִשְׁנֶה		second quarter, second district; double, copy, second (1 · 36) 1041
שֶׁבֶר		crashing, breaking, fracture (1 · 45) 991
הֵילִל	11	to utter or make a howling (1 · 30 · 30) 410
מַכְתֵּשׁ		mortar, hollow resembling a mortar; here = a part of Jerusalem [not in Lis.] 509
נִדְמָה		to be cut off, destroyed, ruined (1 · 13 · 17) 198
כְּנַעַן		merchant, merchants (1 · 4) 448
נָטִיל		laden (1 · 1) 642
חִפֵּשׂ	12	to search through, search for (1 · 8 · 23) 344

נֵר		lamp (1 · 45) 632
קָפָא		to thicken, condense, congeal; here fig. of easygoing men (1 · 2 · 3) 891
שֶׁמֶר		pl. lees, dregs (1 · 5) 1038
מְשִׁסָּה	13	booty, plunder (1 · 6) 1042
מַר	14	bitter; bitterness (1 · 38) 600
צָרַח		to roar, cry (1 · 1 · 2) 863
עֶבְרָה	15	overflowing rage, fury; overflow (2 · 34) 720
מְצוּקָה		straits, stress (1 · 6) 848
שֹׁאָה		devastation, ruin (1 · 13) 996
מְשׁוֹאָה		desolation (1 · 3) 996
אֲפֵלָה		darkness, gloominess, calamity (1 · 10) 66
עֲרָפֶל		cloud, heavy cloud (1 · 15) 791
תְּרוּעָה	16	alarm of war, war-cry, blast for march, shout of joy (1 · 36) 929
בָּצוּר		ptc. pass. = cut off, made inaccessible, fortified (1 · 25) 130-131
פִּנָּה		corner (2 · 30) 819
גָּבֹהַּ		high, lofty, tall, exalted, haughty (1 · 41) 147
עִוֵּר	17	blind (1 · 26) 734
לְחוּם		intestines, bowels (1 · 2) 535-536
גָּלָל		dung (1 · 2) 165
עֶבְרָה	18	overflowing rage, fury; overflow (2 · 34) 720
קִנְאָה		ardor of anger, zeal, jealousy (2 · 43) 888
כָּלָה		complete destruction (1 · 22) 478
נִבְהַל		to be disturbed, dismayed, terrified; ptc. as adj. = "terrible" (1 · 24 · 39) 96

Chapter 2

הִתְקוֹשֵׁשׁ	1	to gather oneself together (1 · 1 · 8) 905
קוֹשׁ		to gather together (1 · 1 · 8) 905
נכסף		to long [for], turn pale [dub.] (1 · 4 · 6) 493-494

394

בְּטֶרֶם 2 before (3 · 39) 382

מֹץ chaff (1 · 8) 558

חָרוֹן [burning of] anger (1 · 41) 354

עָנָו 3 poor and weak, afflicted (1 · 21) 776

עֲנָוָה humility, meekness (1 · 4) 776

אוּלַי perhaps, peradventure (1 · 45) 19

צָהֳרַיִם 4 midday, noon (1 · 23) 843

גרש to drive out, drive away (1 · 35 · 48) 176-177

נעקר to pluck up, root up (1 · 1 · 7) 785

חֶבֶל 5 measured portion, lot; cord, rope (3 · 49) 286

מֵאֵין without, so that not (2 · 48[?]) para. 6. (d.) אֵין 35

חֶבֶל 6 measured portion, lot; cord, rope (3 · 49) 286

נָוֶה, נָוָה pasture, meadow (1 · 45) 627

כָּרָה cistern, well (1 · 1) 500

גְּדֵרָה wall, hedge (1 · 8) 155

חֶבֶל 7 measured portion, lot; cord, rope (3 · 49) 286

רָבַע to lie down, lie (3 · 24 · 30) 918

שְׁבוּת, שְׁבִית captivity, captives (1 · 6) 986

גִּדּוּף 8 pl. revilings, reviling words (1 · 3) 154

חֵרֵף to reproach, say sharp things about (2 · 34 · 38) 357

מִמְשָׁק 9 possession, place of possession, place possessed by (1 · 1) 606

חָרוּל a kind of weed, perh. chickpea (1 · 3) 355

מִכְרֵה pit [dub.] (1 · 1) 500

מֶלַח salt (1 · 28) 571

בָּזַז to plunder, dispoil, take as spoil (1 · 38 · 42) 102

גָּאוֹן 10 pride, exaltation (1 · 49) 144-145

חֵרֵף to reproach, say sharp things about (2 · 34 · 38) 357

נוֹרָא 11 Niph. ptc. = awe-inspiring, fearful (1 · 44) 431

רָזָה to be [grow] lean (1 · 1 · 2) 930

אִי coast, region; islands (1 · 36) 15-16

צִיָּה 13 drought, dryness (1 · 16) 851

רָבַץ 14 to lie down, lie (3 · 24 · 30) 918

עֵדֶר flock, herd (1 · 37) 727

קָאַת bird, usu. pelican but improb; Lis. 1231 owl [?] (1 · 5) 866

קִפֹּד porcupine (1 · 3) 891

כַּפְתּוֹר capital [of pillar]; knob, bulb (1 · 16) 499

חַלּוֹן window (1 · 30) 319

חֹרֶב desolation (1 · 16) 351

סַף threshold, sill (1 · 25) 706

אַרְזָה cedar panels, cedar work (1 · 1) 72

עֵרָה to lay bare (1 · 9 · 15) 788

עַלִּיז 15 exultant, jubilant (2 · 7) 759

בֶּטַח security; as adv. = securely (1 · 43) 105

אֶפֶס part. of negation, cessation; אֲנִי אִ׳עוֹד prob. = "I am and there is none besides" (1 · 27) 67

שַׁמָּה horror, an appalling thing (1 · 39) 1031

מַרְבֵּץ lying down, place of lying down (1 · 2) 918

שָׁרַק to hiss; perh. also whistle (1 · 12 · 12) 1056

הֵנִיעַ to shake, cause to totter, wag (1 · 14 · 38) 631

Chapter 3

מָרָה → מרא 1 ptc. f.s. = disobedient, rebelling (1 · 1 · 1) 598

נגאל to be defiled; ptc. = defiled, polluted one (1 · 3 · 11) 146

ינה to suppress; ptc. f. coll. = oppressors (1 · 4 · 18) 413

מוּסָר 2 discipline, correction (2 · 50) 416

אֲרִי 3 lion (1 · 35) 71

שָׁאַג roar (1 · 20 · 20) 980

זְאֵב wolf (1 · 8) 255

גרם to reserve [dub.], cut off (1 · 1 · 3) 175

פָּחַז 4 to be wanton, reckless (1 · 2 · 2) 808

בֹּגְדוֹת pl. abst. treachery (1 · 1) 93

חמס to treat violently, wrong (1 · 7 · 8) 329

עַוְלָה 5 violent deeds of injustice (2 · 21) 732

נֶעְדָּר to be lacking, to fail (1 · 5 · 6) 727

עַוָּל unjust, unrighteous one (1 · 5) 732

בֹּשֶׁת shame, shameful thing (2 · 30) 102

פִּנָּה 6 corner (2 · 30) 819

הֶחֱרִיב to lay waste, make desolate (1 · 13 · 37) 351

מִבְּלִי so that there is no; from want of (2 · 25) para 3.c. בְּלִי 115

נִצְדָה to be laid waste (1 · 1 · 1) 841

מֵאֵין so that not, without; from lack of (2 · 48[?]) para. 6.d. אַיִן 35

מוּסָר 7 discipline, correction (2 · 50) 416

מָעוֹן dwelling [but difficult in context] (1 · 18) 732-733

אָכֵן but in fact, but indeed; surely, truly (1 · 18) 38

עֲלִילָה evil deeds; deed, wantonness (2 · 24) 760

חִכָּה 8 to wait for, await, wait (1 · 13 · 14) 314

עַד booty, prey (1 · 3) 723

זַעַם indignation (1 · 22) 276

חָרוֹן [burning of] anger (1 · 41) 354

קִנְאָה ardor of anger; zeal, jealousy (2 · 43) 888

בָּרוּר 9 ptc. pass. = purified (1 · 2) 140

שְׁכֶם shoulder (1 · 22) 1014

עָתָר 10 suppliant, worshiper [dub.] (1 · 1) 801

הֵיבִיל to bear along, conduct, carry away (1 · 7 · 18) 384-385

עֲלִילָה 11 evil deeds, evil deed, wantonness (2 · 24) 760

פָּשַׁע to transgress, rebel (1 · 40 · 41) 838

עַלִּיז exultant, jubilant (2 · 7) 759

גַּאֲוָה pride, haughtiness, majesty (1 · 19) 144

גָּבַה to be lofty, [in bad sense] haughty; to be high, exalted (1 · 24 · 34) 146-147

דַּל 12 reduced, poor, weak, thin (1 · 48) 195

חָסָה to seek refuge (1 · 37 · 37) 340

עַוְלָה 13 violent deeds of injustice, unright-eousness (2 · 21) 732

כָּזָב lie, falsehood (1 · 31) 469

תַּרְמִית deceitfulness (1 · 5) 941

רָבַץ to lie down, lie (3 · 24 · 30) 918

הֶחֱרִיד to drive in terror, rout; ptc. = one who terrifies (1 · 16 · 39) 353

הֵרִיעַ 14 to shout in triumph, raise a shout or war-cry (1 · 40 · 44) 929

עלז to exult, triumph (1 · 16 · 16) 759

רפה 16 to sink down; [idiom] w. יָד = to lose heart or energy (1 · 14 · 44) 951

שִׂישׂ ,שׂוֹשׂ 17 to exult, display joy (1 · 27 · 27) 965

הֶחֱרִישׁ to be silent, make silent (1 · 38 · 46) 361

גִּיל to rejoice (1 · 45 · 45) 162

רִנָּה ringing cry in joy, proclamation, etc. (1 · 33) 943

נוגה 18 Niph. ptc. = grieved (1 · 2 · 8) 387

מַשְׂאֵת burden, portion carried; that which rises; oracle (1 · 16) 673

צלע 19 to limp (1 · 4 · 4) 854

נדח to be thrust out, banished (1 · 13 · 43) 623

בֹּשֶׁת shame, shameful thing (2 · 30) 102

שְׁבִית ,שְׁבוּת captivity, captives (1 · 6) 986

396

HAGGAI

Chapter 1

פֶּחָה	1	governor (4 · 27) 808
ספן	4	to cover; ptc. pass. = paneled (1 · 6 · 6) 706
חָרֵב		waste, desolate (2 · 10) 351
שָׂבְעָה,		
שָׂבְעָה	6	inf. abs. sated, satisfied (1 · 7) 959
שכר		to become drunken, be drunk (1 · 9 · 18) 1016
חמם, חַם		to be [grow] warm (1 · 23 · 26) 328
השׂתכר		to earn wages (2 · 2 · 20) 968
צְרוֹר		bundle, pouch (1 · 7) 865
נקב		to pierce (1 · 13 · 19) 666
רָצָה	8	to be pleased with, favorable to (1 · 42 · 50) 953
נפח	9	to breathe, blow (1 · 5 · 12) 655
חָרֵב		waste, desolate (2 · 10) 351
כלא	10	to withhold, restrain, shut up (2 · 14 · 17) 476
טַל		night mist, dew (1 · 31) 378
יְבוּל		produce (1 · 13) 385
חֹרֶב	11	drought, dryness, heat (1 · 16) 351
דָּגָן		corn, cereal grain (1 · 40) 186
תִּירוֹשׁ		must, fresh or new wine (1 · 38) 440
יִצְהָר		fresh oil (1 · 23) 844
יְגִיעַ		product, produce, acquired property (1 · 16) 388
מַלְאֲכוּת	13	message (1 · 1) 522
פֶּחָה	14	governor (4 · 27) 808

Chapter 2

פֶּחָה	2	governor (4 · 27) 808
כְּאַיִן	3	as nothing (1 · 7) 1. 34
הרעישׁ	6	to cause to quake (1 · 7 · 29) 950
חָרָבָה		dry ground (1 · 8) 351
הרעישׁ	7	to cause to quake (1 · 7 · 29) 950
חֶמְדָּה		desire, delight (1 · 16) 326
נָזִיד	12	thing sodden, or boiled, pottage (1 · 6) 268
מַאֲכָל		food (1 · 30) 38
מעלה	15	upward, onward (1 · 53) 751
מִטֶּרֶם		from before (1 · 1) 382
עֲרֵמָה	16	heap (1 · 11) 790
יֶקֶב		wine vay (1 · 16) 428
חָשַׂף		to take from the surface, skim, strip off (1 · 10 · 10) 362
פּוּרָה		wine press (1 · 2) 807
שִׁדָּפוֹן	17	smut (1 · 5) 995
יֵרָקוֹן		rust, mildew (1 · 6) 439
בָּרָד		hail (1 · 29) 135
לְמִן	18	from (1 · 14) מן 9.b. 577
יֻסַּד		to be founded, laid (1 · 6 · 41) 413
מְגוּרָה	19	storehouse, granary (1 · 2) 158
תְּאֵנָה		fig tree, fig (1 · 39) 1061
רִמּוֹן		pomegranate (1 · 32) 941
זַיִת		olive tree, olives (1 · 38) 268
פֶּחָה	21	governor (4 · 27) 808
הרעישׁ		to cause to quake (1 · 7 · 29) 950
חֹזֶק	22	strength (1 · 5) 305
מֶרְכָּבָה		chariot (1 · 44) 939
חוֹתָם	23	seal, signet ring (1 · 14) 368

ZECHARIAH

Chapter 1

קָצַף 2 to be angry (3 · 28 · 34) 893

קֶצֶף wrath (3 · 28) 893

מַעֲלָל 4 practice, deed (2 · 41) 760

הִקְשִׁיב to give attention (2 · 45 · 46) 904

אַיֵּה 5 where[?] (1 · 44) 32

הִשִּׂיג 6 to overtake, reach, attain to (1 · 49 · 49) 673

זָמַם to purpose, devise, consider (3 · 13 · 13) 273

מַעֲלָל practice, deed (2 · 41) 760

הֲדַס 8 myrtle [tree] (3 · 6) 213

מְצֻלָה basin, hollow [dub.] (2 · 12) 847

אָדֹם red (3 · 9) 10

שָׂרֹק sorrel [dub.], Lis. 1389 "bright red" (1 · 2) 977

לָבָן white (3 · 29) 526

הֲדַס 10 myrtle [tree] (3 · 6) 213

הֲדַס 11 myrtle [tree] (3 · 6) 213

שָׁקַט to be quiet, undisturbed (1 · 31 · 41) 1052-1053

עַד־מָתַי 12 until when? how long? (idiom) מָתַי (1 · 42) 607 607

רִחַם to have compassion, be compassionate (2 · 42 · 47) 933

זָעַם to be indignant, have indignation (1 · 11 · 12) 276

נִחֻמִים 13 comfort, compassion (1 · 3) 637

קִנֵּא 14 to be zealous, jealous (3 · 18 · 32) 888

קִנְאָה zeal, ardor of zeal, jealousy (2 · 43) 888

קֶצֶף 15 wrath (3 · 28) 893

קָצַף to be angry (3 · 28 · 34) 893

שַׁאֲנָן at ease; here with collateral qualities of carelessness, wantonness, and arrogance (1 · 11) 983

רַחֲמִים 16 compassion (2 · 38) 933

קָו, קַו קרה line, measuring line (1 · 25) 876

פּוּץ 17 to overflow (2 · 13 · 65*) 807
* BDB has sep. root

Chapter 2

זרה 2 to scatter, disperse (3 · 25 · 38) 279-280

חָרָשׁ 3 graver, artificer (1 · 38) 360

זרה 4 to scatter, disperse (3 · 25 · 38) 279-280

כְּפִי in such proportion that, according to, according to the mouth of (1 · 16) פה 6.b. 805

הֶחֱרִיד to drive in terror, rout (1 · 16 · 39) 353

ידה piel. = to cast down (1 · 2 · 3) 392

חֶבֶל 5 measuring cord, line, rope; territory (1 · 49) 286

אָנָה 6 where? whither? (2 · 39) 33

כַּמָּה, כַּמֶּה how much? how many? how often? (3 · 13) para. 4.c. מה 553

הַלָּז 8 synonym of זה this (1 · 7) 229

פְּרָזָה, פְּרָזוֹת open region, hamlet (1 · 3) 826

שָׁלַל 12 to spoil, plunder (1 · 13 · 15) 1021

בָּבָה [dub.] apple, opening, baby (1 · 1) 93

הֵנִיף 13 to shake, wave, brandish; shed abroad (1 · 32 · 34) 631-632

נִלְוָה 15 to join oneself, be joined (1 · 11 · 12) 530-531

הַס 17 Hush! Keep silence! (1 · 6) 245

מָעוֹן dwelling, refuge (1 · 18) 732

Chapter 3

שָׂטָן 1 adversary, Satan (3 · 26) 966

שׂטן to be [act as] adversary (1 · 6 · 6) 966

שָׂטָן 2 adversary, Satan (3 · 26) 966

גָּעַר to rebuke (2 · 14 · 14) 172

אוּד brand, firebrand (1 · 3) 15

לָבוּשׁ, לָבֵשׁ 3 ptc. pass. = clothed with (1 · 16) 527-528

צֹאִי filthy (2 · 2) 844

צֹאִי 4 filthy (2 · 2) 844

מַחֲלָצָה, מַחֲלָצוֹת robe of state (1 · 2) 323

צָנִיף 5 turban (2 · 5) 857

הֵעִיד to exhort solemnly, admonish, charge, warn, protest; to testify, cause to testify (1 · 38 · 43) 729-730

דָּן, דִּין 7 to govern, judge (1 · 23 · 24) 192

מַהֲלָךְ walk, journey, going (1 · 5) 237

מוֹפֵת 8 sign, token, wonder (1 · 36) 68-69

צֶמַח sprout, growth (2 · 12) 855

פִּתַּח 9 to engrave (1 · 8 · 9) 836

פִּתּוּחַ engraving (1 · 11) 836

מָשׁ, מוּשׁ to depart, remove (2 · 20 · 20) 559

תְּאֵנָה 10 fig tree, fig (1 · 39) 1061

Chapter 4

שֵׁנָה שׁנה 1 sleep (1 · 23) 446

מְנוֹרָה 2 lampstand (2 · 40) 633

גֻּלָּה bowl; here = oil receptacle of lamp (2 · 15) 165

נֵר lamp (2 · 45) 632

מוּצֶקֶת, מוּצָקָה pipe [through which oil is poured] (1 · 2) 427

זַיִת 3 olive tree, olives (5 · 38) 268

גֻּלָּה bowl; here = oil receptacle of lamp (2 · 15) 165

מִישׁוֹר 7 level country, tableland, plain; uprightness (1 · 23) 449

רֹאשָׁה top (1 · 1) 911

תְּשֻׁאָה noise (1 · 4) 996

יִסַּד 9 to found, establish (1 · 10 · 41) 413-414

בִּצַּע to cut off; here = to finish, complete (1 · 6 · 16) 130

בַּז, בּוּז 10 to despise (1 · 14 · 14) 100

קָטֹן small, unimportant, young (1 · 47) 881-882

בְּדִיל tin, alloy; הָאֶבֶן הַבּ׳ = plummet (1 · 5) 95

שׁוֹטֵט to go eagerly, quickly to an fro (1 · 5 · 13) 1001-1002

זַיִת 11 olive tree, olives (5 · 38) 268

מְנוֹרָה lampstand (2 · 40) 633

שִׁבֹּלֶת 12 ear of grain (1 · 20) 987

זַיִת olive tree, olives (5 · 38) 268

צַנְתְּרוֹת pipes (1 · 1) 857

רִיק to pour out (1 · 17 · 19) 938

יִצְהָר 14 fresh oil, anointing oil; בְּנֵי י׳ = anointed ones (1 · 23) 844

Chapter 5

מְגִלָּה 1 roll, writing, book (2 · 21) 166

עוּף to fly (2 · 18 · 25) 733

מְגִלָּה 2 roll, writing, book (2 · 21) 166

עוּף to fly (2 · 18 · 25) 733

אָלָה 3 curse, oath (1 · 36) 46

גנב to steal, take by stealth (1 · 30 · 39) 170

נִקָּה to be cleaned out, purged out (2 · 24 · 41) 667

גַּנָּב 4 thief (1 · 17) 170

אֵיפָה 6 receptacle holding an ephah; i.e., 40 liters (5 · 39) 35

עֹפֶרֶת 7 lead; כִּכַּר ע׳ a round wt. of lead (2 · 9) 780

אֵיפָה   receptacle holding an ephah; i.e.,
40 liters (5 · 39) 35

רִשְׁעָה   8 wickedness (1 · 15) 958

אֵיפָה   receptacle holding an ephah; i.e.,
40 liters (5 · 39) 35

עֹפֶרֶת   lead (2 · 9) 780

חֲסִידָה   9 stork (1 · 6) 339

אֵיפָה   receptacle holding an ephah; i.e.,
40 liters (5 · 39) 35

אָנָה   10 whither[?] (2 · 39) אן 33

אֵיפָה   receptacle holding an ephah; i.e.,
40 liters (5 · 39) 35

מְכוֹנָה   11 base or stand (1 · 25) 467

Chapter 6

מֶרְכָּבָה   1 chariot (5 · 44) 939

מִבֵּין   from between (2 · 21) 107

מֶרְכָּבָה   2 chariot (5 · 44) 939

אָדֹם   red (3 · 9) 10

שָׁחֹר   black (2 · 6) 1007

מֶרְכָּבָה   3 chariot (5 · 44) 939

לָבָן   white (3 · 29) 526

בָּרֹד   spotted, marked (2 · 4) 136

אָמֹץ   strong (2 · 2) 55

הִתְיַצֵּב   5 to set or station oneself; c. לפני =
present oneself before (1 · 48 · 48)
426

שָׁחֹר   6 black (2 · 6) 1007

לָבָן   white (3 · 29) 526

בָּרֹד   spotted, marked (2 · 4) 136

תֵּימָן   south, southern quarter (2 · 24) 412

אָמֹץ   7 strong (2 · 2) 55

גּוֹלָה   10 exile, exiles (2 · 42) 163

עֲטָרָה   11 crown, wreath (2 · 23) 742

צֶמַח   12 sprout, growth (2 · 12) 855

צָמַח   to sprout, spring up (1 · 15 · 33)
855

הוֹד   13 splendor, majesty (2 · 24) 217

עֲטָרָה   14 crown, wreath (2 · 23) 742

זִכָּרוֹן   memorial, reminder (1 · 24) 272

Chapter 7

נָזַר   3 Niph., to devote, dedicate oneself
(1 · 4 · 10) 634

כַּמָּה   how many? how much, how often
(3 · 13) para. 4.c. מה 553

צוֹם   5 to fast, abstain from food
(2 · 20 · 20) 847

סָפַד   to wail, lament (3 · 28 · 30)
704

שָׁלֵו   7 quiet, at ease, prosperous (1 · 8)
1017

שְׁפֵלָה   lowland, strip of land west of Ju-
dean mts. (1 · 20) 1050

רַחֲמִים   9 compassion (2 · 38) 933

יָתוֹם   10 orphan (1 · 42) 450

עָשַׁק   to oppress, wrong (1 · 36 · 37)
798

מֵאֵן   11 to refuse (1 · 46 · 46) 549

הִקְשִׁיב   to give attention (2 · 45 · 46) 904

סָרַר   to be stubborn, rebellious
(1 · 17 · 17) 710-711

שָׁמִיר   12 adamant, flint; thorn[s] (1 · 11) 1038-
1039

קֶצֶף   wrath (3 · 28) 893

סָעַר   14 Piel., to storm away, hurl by storm
wind (1 · 1 · 7) 704

חֶמְדָּה   desire, delight (1 · 16) 326

שַׁמָּה   appalling waste (1 · 39) 1031

Chapter 8

קָנָא   2 to be zealous, jealous (3 · 18 · 32)
888

קִנְאָה   zeal, ardor of zeal, jealousy (2 · 43)
888

רְחוֹב, רְחֹב   4 broad open place (3 · 43) 932

מִשְׁעֶנֶת, מַשְׁעֵנָה   staff, support (1 · 12) 1044

רְחֹב, רְחוֹב 5 broad open place (3 · 43) 932

יַלְדָּה girl, damsel (1 · 3) 409

שָׂחק to play, jest, make sport (1 · 16 · 36) 965-966

נפלא 6 to be beyond one's power, difficult to do; to be extraordinary (2 · 13 · 24) 810

מָבוֹא 7 entrance, entering; w. שֶׁמֶשׁ west (1 · 23) 99-100

יֻסַּד 9 to be founded, laid (1 · 6 · 41) 413-414

שָׂכָר 10 hire, wages (4 · 28) 969

יְבוּל 12 produce (1 · 13) 385

טַל night mist, dew (1 · 31) 378

קְלָלָה 13 curse (1 · 33) 887

זָמַם 14 to purpose, devise (3 · 13 · 13) 237

הקציף to provoke to wrath (1 · 5 · 34) 893

זָמַם 15 to purpose, devise (3 · 13 · 13) 273

שְׁבֻעָה, שֶׁבַע 16 oath (1 · 30) 989-990

צוֹם 19 fasting, fast (4 · 26) 847

שָׂשׂוֹן exultation, joy (1 · 22) 965

עָצוּם 22 mighty, strong in numbers (1 · 31) 783

Chapter 9

מַשָּׂא 1 utterance, oracle (2 · 21) 672-673

מְנוּחָה resting place (1 · 21) 629-630

גָּבַל 2 to bound, border (1 · 3 · 5) 148

חָכַם to be or become wise, act wisely (1 · 18 · 26) 314

מָצוֹר 3 rampart; siege works, siege (2 · 25) 848-849

צבר to heap up (1 · 7 · 7) 840

חָרוּץ gold (1 · 6) 359

טִיט mud, mire (2 · 13) 376

חֵיל 4 rampart (1 · 9) 298

חוּל, חִיל 5 to be in severe pain, twist, writhe (2 · 30 · 47) 296-297

מַבָּט expectation, object of hope or confidence (1 · 3) 613-614

מַמְזֵר 6 bastard, child of incest (1 · 2) 561

גָּאוֹן exaltation, majesty, excellence (3 · 49) 144-145

שִׁקּוּץ, שֶׁקֶץ 7 detested thing (1 · 28) 1055

מִבֵּין from between (2 · 21) 107

מֵעֹבֵר וּמִשָּׁב 8 [idiom] from those going to and fro para. 3. a. עבר p. 717

נֹגֵשׂ ptc. = exactor [of tribute], oppressor, tyrant (2 · 15) 620

גִּיל 9 to rejoice (2 · 45 · 45) 162

הריע to shout in triumph, raise a shout, sound a signal for war or march (1 · 40 · 44) 929

עַיִר male donkey [young and vigorous] (1 · 9) 747

אָתוֹן female donkey (1 · 33) 87

משל 10 dominion (1 · 2) 606

אֶפֶס end, extreme limit (1 · 27) 67

אָסִיר 11 bondman, prisoner, captive (2 · 17) 64

בִּצָּרוֹן 12 stronghold (1 · 1) 131

אָסִיר bondman, prisoner, captive (2 · 17) 64

תִּקְוָה hope (1 · 32) 876

מִשְׁנֶה double, double portion (1 · 36) 1041

בָּרָק 14 lightning (1 · 21) 140

סְעָרָה tempest, storm wind (1 · 16) 704

תֵּימָן south, southern quarter (2 · 24) 412

גנן, הגין to defend (2 · 8 · 8) 170-171

כבשׁ 15 to subdue, dominate, bring into bondage (1 · 8 · 14) 461

קֶלַע sling (1 · 6) 8

המה to be boisterous, turbulent; to murmur, growl, roar (1 · 33 · 33) 242

מִזְרָק bowl, basin (2 · 32) 284

זַיִת   corner (1 · 2) 265

גֵזֶר   16 crown, consecration (1 · 23) 643

התניסס   [dub.] to be raised, prominent (1 · 2 · 3) 651

טוּב   17 fairness, beauty, good things, goods (1 · 32) 375

יְפִי   beauty (1-19) 421

דָּגָן   corn, cereal grain (1 · 40) 186

בָּחוּר   young man (1 · 45) 104

תִּירוֹשׁ   must, fresh or new wine (1 · 38) 440

נובב   to make flourish (1 · 1 · 4) 626

בְּתוּלָה   virgin (1 · 50) 143-144

Chapter 10

מָטָר   1 rain (2 · 38) 564

מַלְקוֹשׁ   latter rain, spring rain (1 · 8) 545

חֲזִיז   thunderbolt, lightning flash (1 · 3) 304

גֶּשֶׁם   rain, shower (2 · 35) 177

עֵשֶׂב   herbage, herb (1 · 33) 793

תְּרָפִים   2 a kind of idol (1 · 15) 1076

קֹסֵם   ptc. = one who practices divination (1 · 9) 890

עַתּוּד   male goat (1 · 29) 800

עֵדֶר   flock (1 · 37) 727

הוֹד   majesty, splendor (2 · 24) 217

פִּנָּה   4 corner (2 · 30) 819

יָתֵד   tent pin; peg, pin (1 · 23) 450

נֹגֵשׂ   oppressor, tyrant (2 · 15) 620

בּוּס   5 to tread down, trample (1 · 7 · 12) 100

טִיט   mud, mire (2 · 13) 376

גבר   6 to make strong, strengthen (2 · 3 · 25) 149

רחם   to have compassion, be compassionate (2 · 42 · 47) 933

זָנַח   to reject, spurn (1 · 16 · 19) 276

גיל   7 to rejoice (2 · 45 · 45) 162

שָׁרַק   8 to hiss (1 · 12 · 12) 1056

מֶרְחָק   9 distant place, far country, distance (1 · 18) 935

גַּל   11 wave, roller; billow, heap (1 · 16) 164

מְצוּלָה   depth (2 · 12) 847

גָּאוֹן   exaltation, majesty, excellence (3 · 49) 144-145

גבר   to make strong, strengthen (2 · 3 · 25) 149

Chapter 11

הֵילִל   2 to utter or make a howling (2 · 30 · 30) 410

בְּרוֹשׁ   cypress or fir (1 · 20) 141

אַדִּיר   majestic one; majestic (1 · 27) 12

אַלּוֹן   oak (1 · 9) 47

בָּצִיר→בָּצוּר   vintage; but BDB reads kt. cut off, made inaccessible (1 · 1) 130, 131

יְלָלָה   3 howling (1 · 5) 410

אַדֶּרֶת   glory, magnificence; cloak (2 · 12) 12

שְׁאָגָה   roaring, cry (1 · 7) 980

כְּפִיר   young lion (1 · 31) 498

גָּאוֹן   majesty, exaltation, excellence (3 · 49) 144-145

חֲרֵגָה   slaughter (2 · 5) 247

קֹנֶה   5 ptc. = owner (1 · 7) 888-889

אָשֵׁם   to be held guilty, be guilty (1 · 33 · 35) 79

העשיר   to gain riches, make rich (1 · 14 · 17) 779

חָמַל   to spare, have compassion (2 · 40 · 40) 328

חָמַל   6 to spare, have compassion (2 · 40 · 40) 328

בָּתַת   to beat or crush fine, hammer (1 · 5 · 17) 510

הֲרֵגָה   7 slaughter (2 · 5) 247

מַקֵּל	rod, staff (3 · 18) 596	הָפִיר, הֵפֵר	to break, violate; to frustrate (2 · 42 · 45) 830
נֹעַם	delightfulness, pleasantness (2 · 7) 653	אַחֲוָה	brotherhood (1 · 1) 27
חֹבְלִים, חֶבֶל	to bind symbol of fraternity; to pledge (2 · 2) 286	אֱוִלִי	15 foolish (1 · 1) 17
הִכְחִיד	8 to efface, annihilate; hide (1 · 6 · 32) 470	נִכְחָד	16 to be effaced, destroyed; to be hidden (3 · 11 · 32) 470
יֶרַח	month (1 · 12) 437	נַעַר	shaking, scattering [dub. text] (1 · 1) 654
קָצַר	to be short, impatient (1 · 12 · 14) 894	כִּלְכֵּל	to sustain, support; to contain (1 · 24 · 38) 465
בָּחֹל	to feel loathing (1 · 1 · 1) 103	בְּרִיא	fat (1 · 14) 135
נִכְחַד	9 to be effaced, destroyed; to be hidden (3 · 11 · 32) 470	פַּרְסָה	hoof (1 · 21) 828
רְעוּת	fellow (1 · 6) 946	פרק	*Piel*, to tear off (1 · 3 · 10) 830
מַקֵּל	10 rod, staff (3 · 18) 596	אֱלִיל	17 worthlessness, insufficiency (1 · 20) 47
נֹעַם	delightfulness, pleasantness (2 · 7) 653	כהה	to grow dim, faint (2 · 6 · 10) 462
גָּדַע	to hew, cut in two (2 · 5 · 22) 154		
הֵפֵר, הָפִיר	to break, violate; to fustrate (2 · 42 · 45) 830		

Chapter 12

הֻפַר	11 *Hoph.*, to be broken; to be fustrated (1 · 3 · 45) 830	מַשָּׂא	1 utterance, oracle (2 · 21) 672-673
יהב	12 to give, set, ascribe (1 · 33 · 33) 396	יָסַר	to found, establish (1 · 20 · 41) 413
שָׂכָר	hire, wages (4 · 28) 969	יָצַר, יוֹצֵר	to form, fashion (1 · 41 · 44) 427
שָׁקַל	to weigh out, to weigh (1 · 19 · 22) 1053	סַף	2 goblet, basin (1 · 6) 706
יוֹצֵר	13 ptc. = potter (2 · 17) 427	רַעַל	reeling (1 · 1) 947
אֶדֶר	glory, magnificence; mantle, cloak (1 · 2) 12	מָצוֹר	siege, siege works (2 · 25) 848-849
יְקָר	price, preciousness; honor (1 · 17) 430	מַעֲמָסָה	3 load, burden (1 · 1) 770
יקר	to be appraised, valued; to be precious, highly valued, esteemed (1 · 9 · 11) 429	עמס	to carry a load, carry as a load; to load (1 · 7 · 9) 770
גָּדַע	14 to hew, cut in two (2 · 5 · 22) 154	שׂרט	to incise, scratch (1 · 2 · 3) 976
מַקֵּל	rod, staff (3 · 18) 596	נשׂרט	to be scratched (1 · 1 · 3) 976
חֶבֶל	to bind symbol of fraternity; to pledge (2 · 2) 286	תִּמָּהוֹן	4 bewilderment (1 · 2) 1069
		שִׁגָּעוֹן	madness (1 · 3) 993
		פָּקַח	to open eyes and [once] ears (1 · 17 · 20) 824
		עִוָּרוֹן	blindness (1 · 2) 734
		אַמְצָה	5 strength (1 · 1) 55
		כִּיּוֹר	6 pot, basin (1 · 23) 468
		לַפִּיד	torch (1 · 13) 542
		עָמִיר	swath, row of fallen grain (1 · 4) 771

תִּפְאָרָה 7 glory, honor, beauty (2 · 50) 802

גָּנַן, הגין 8 to defend (2 · 8 · 8) 170-171

תַּחֲנוּן 10 pl. abstr. = supplication for favor
(1 · 18) 337

דָּקַר to pierce, pierce through (2 · 7 · 11)
201

סָפַד to wail, lament (3 · 28 · 30) 704

מִסְפֵּד wailing (3 · 16) 704

יָחִיד only one, solitary (1 · 12) 402

הֵמַר *Hiph.*, to make bitter, show bitterness (2 · 5 · 16) 600

מִסְפֵּד 11 wailing (3 · 16) 704

בִּקְעָה valley (1 · 19) 132

סָפַד 12 to wail, lament (3 · 28 · 30) 704

Chapter 13

מָקוֹר 1 spring, fountain (1 · 18) 881

נִדָּה impure thing (1 · 30) 622

עָצָב 2 idol (1 · 30) 781

טֻמְאָה uncleanness (1 · 37) 380

דָּקַר 3 to pierce, pierce through (2 · 7 · 11)
201

חִזָּיוֹן 4 vision, divine communication in a
vision (1 · 9) 303

אַדֶּרֶת mantle, cloak; glory, magnificence
(2 · 12) 12

שֵׂעָר hair (1 · 27) 972

כָּחַשׁ to deceive, act deceptively
(1 · 19 · 22) 471

נְעוּרִים 5 youth, early life (1 · 46) 655

מַכָּה 6 beating, scourging; blow, stripe;
slaughter (1 · 48) 646-647

מְאַהֵב *Piel.* ptc. = friend (1 · 16) 12-13

עָמִית 7 fellow, associate, relation (1 · 12)
765

צָעַר to be [grow] insignificant (1 · 3 · 3)
858

פִּי 8 [idiom] portion para. 5. b. פֶּה 805

גָּוַע to expire, perish, die (1 · 23 · 23) 157

צָרַף 9 to smelt, refine, test (2 · 19 · 22)
864

בָּחַן to try, test, prove (2 · 25 · 29) 103

Chapter 14

נָשַׁס, נָשַׁסס 2 to be plundered, rifled (1 · 2 · 5)
1042

נִשְׁגַּל to be violated, ravished (1 · 2 · 4)
993

גּוֹלָה exile, exiles (2 · 42) 163

קְרָב 3 battle, war (1 · 8) 898

זַיִת 4 olives, olive tree (5 · 38) 268

מִקֶּדֶם eastward (1 · 26) 869

גַּיְא valley (3 · 47) 161

מָשׁ, מוּשׁ to depart; remove (2 · 20 · 20) 559

גַּיְא 5 valley (3 · 47) 161

רַעַשׁ earthquake, shaking (1 · 17) 950

יָקָר 6 precious, rare, splendid, weighty;
but BDB reads וקרות "cold"
(1 · 35) 429-430

קָפָא to be condensed, thickened; to con-
geal (0 · 2 · 3) 891

קִפָּאוֹן *Q.* congelation (1 · 1) 891

קַדְמֹנִי 8 eastern; former, ancient (1 · 10)
870

קַיִץ summer season, summer fruit
(1 · 20) 884

חֹרֶף harvest time, autumn (1 · 7) 358

רָאַם 10 to rise (1 · 1 · 1) 910

פִּנָּה corner (2 · 30) 819

מִגְדָּל tower (1 · 49) 153-154

יֶקֶב wine vat (1 · 16) 428

חֵרֶם 11 devotion, ban; devoted thing
(1 · 29) 356

בֶּטַח securely; security (1 · 43) 105

מַגֵּפָה 12 plague, pestilence, slaughter, blow
(4 · 26) 620

נָגַף to strike, smite (2 · 25 · 48) 619

צָבָא to wage war (1 · 12 · 14) 838

הֵמִיק   to cause to rot (1 · 1 · 10) 596

נמקק, נמק   to rot, rot away, pine away
(2 · 9 · 10) 596

חוֹר, חֹר   hole; w. עין = eye socket (1 · 7) 359

מְהוּמָה   13 tumult, confusion, turmoil (1 · 12)
223

מַגֵּפָה   15 plague, pestilence, slaughter, blow
(4 · 26) 620

פֶּרֶד   mule (1 · 14) 825

מִדֵּי   16 as often as (1 · 15) די 2.c. 191

שָׁנָה בְשָׁנָה   year by year (1 · [?]) 1040

חגג   to keep a pilgrim feast (3 · 16 · 16)
290

סֻכָּה   booth (3 · 31) 697

גֶּשֶׁם   17 rain, shower (2 · 35) 177

מַגֵּפָה   18 plague, pestilence, slaughter, blow
(4 · 26) 620

נָגַף   to strike, smite (2 · 25 · 48) 619

חגג   to keep a pilgrim feast (3 · 16 · 16)
290

סֻכָּה   booth (3 · 31) 697

חגג   19 to keep a pilgrim feast (3 · 16 · 16)
290

סֻכָּה   booth (3 · 31) 697

מְצִלָּה   20 bell (1 · 1) 853

סִיר   pot (2 · 29) 696

מִזְרָק   bowl, basin (2 · 32) 284

סִיר   21 pot (2 · 29) 696

בשל   to boil (1 · 21 · 28) 143

כְּנַעֲנִי   trader, merchant (1 · 4) 489

405

MALACHI

Chapter 1

מַשָּׂא 1 utterance, oracle (2 · 21) 672-673

בַּמָּה 2 whereby[?] by what means[?] מה
4.a. 553

תַּן 3 jackal (1 · 14) 1072

רשש 4 to be beaten down (1 · 1 · 2) 958

חָרְבָּה waste, ruin (1 · 42) 352

הָרַס to throw down, tear down; to break down, break through (1 · 30 · 43) 248

רִשְׁעָה wickedness (3 · 15) 958

זָעַם to be indignant, have indignation (1 · 11 · 12) 276

אַיֵּה 6 where? (3 · 44) 32

מוֹרָא reverence, object of reverence, fear (2 · 12) 432

בָּזָה to despise, regard with contempt (2 · 31 · 42) 102

בַּמָּה whereby[?] by what means[?] מה
4.a. 553

גאל ,מְגֹאָל 7 Pual, to be desecrated (2 · 4 · 11) 146

בַּמָּה whereby[?] by what means[?] מה
4.a. 553

גאל Piel, to pollute, desecrate (1 · 1 · 11) 146

נבזה to be despicable, contemptible, despised, vile (3 · 10 · 42) 102

עִוֵּר 8 blind (1 · 26) 734

פִּסֵּחַ lame (2 · 14) 820

פֶּחָה governor (1 · 27) 808

רָצָה to be pleased with, favorable to (3 · 42 · 50) 953

הֵאִיר 10 to light, give light, make shine (1 · 34 · 40) 21

חִנָּם for no purpose, in vain, gratis, for nothing (1 · 32) 336

חֵפֶץ delight, desire, good pleasure (2 · 39) 343

רָצָה to accept, be pleased with, favorable to (3 · 43 · 50) 953

מֻקְטָר 11 Lis. Ho. ptc.; but BDB incense (1 · 2 · 115) 883

מָבוֹא entrance, entering; w. שֶׁמֶשׁ = west (1 · 23) 99-100

גאל 12 Pual, to be desecrated (2 · 4 · 11) 146

נִיב fruit (1 · 2) 626

נבזה to be despicable, contemptible, despised, vile (3 · 10 · 42) 102

אֹכֶל food (1 · 44) 38

תְּלָאָה 13 weariness, hardship (1 · 5) 521

הפיח to sniff at [in contempt], cause to breathe out (1 · 2 · 12) 655-656

גָּזַל to tear away, rob, seize (1 · 29 · 30) 159

פִּסֵּחַ lame (2 · 14) 820

רָצָה to accept, be pleased with, favorable to (3 · 42 · 50) 953

נכל ,נוֹכֵל 14 to be crafty, deceitful, knavish; ptc. = knave (1 · 1 · 4) 647

עֵדֶר flock, herd (1 · 37) 727

נָדַר to row (1 · 31 · 31) 623

נוֹרָא inspiring reverence, awe; fearful (2 · 44) 431

Chapter 2

מְאֵרָה 2 curse (2 · 5) 76

גָּעַר 3 to rebuke (2 · 14 · 14) 172

זרה to scatter, disperse (1 · 25 · 38) 279-280

פֶּרֶשׁ offal; i.e., contents of stomach area (2 · 7) 831

מוֹרָא 5 object of reverence; reverence, fear (2 · 12) 432

עַוְלָה 6 injustice, unrighteousness, wrong (1 · 32) 732

מִישׁוֹר   uprightness; level place (1 · 23) 449

נבזה   9   to be despicable, contemptible, despised, vile (3 · 10 · 42) 102

שָׁפָל   humiliated, low (1 · 18) 1050

כְּפִי   according as (1 · 16) פֶּה 6.b. 805

בָּרָא   10   to shape, fashion, create (1 · 38 · 48) 135

בגד   to act or deal treacherously, faithlessly (5 · 49 · 49) 93

בגד   11   to act or deal treacherously, faithlessly (5 · 49 · 49) 93

בָּעַל   to marry, rule over (1 · 10 · 12) 127

נֵכָר   that which is foreign, foreignness (1 · 36) 648

דִּמְעָה   13   [coll.] tears (1 · 23) 199

בְּכִי   weeping (1 · 30) 113

אֲנָקָה   crying, groaning (1 · 4) 60

מֵאֵין   so that there is no (1 · 48) אַיִן 6.d. 35

הֵעִיד   14   to testify, bear witness, cause to testify, affirm solemnly, warn (1 · 38 · 43) 729

נְעוּרִים   youth, early life (2 · 46) 655

בגד   to act or deal treacherously, faithlessly (5 · 49 · 49) 93

חֲבֶרֶת   consort; i.e., wife (1 · 1) 289

שְׁאָר   15   remnant, rest, residue (1 · 26) 984

נְעוּרִים   youth, early life (2 · 46) 655

בגד   to act or deal treacherously, faithlessly (5 · 49 · 49) 93

לְבוּשׁ   16   garment, clothing (1 · 31) 528

בגד   to act or deal treacherously, faithlessly (5 · 49 · 49) 93

הוֹגִיעַ   17   to make to toil, make weary (2 · 4 · 26) 388

בַּמֶּה   whereby[?] by what means[?] מה 4.a. 553

Chapter 3

פִּתְאֹם   1   suddenly; suddenness (1 · 25) 837

חָפֵץ   delighting in, having pleasure in (1 · 12) 343

כִּלְכֵּל   2   to support, endure, to sustain; to contain (1 · 24 · 38) 465

צרף   *Piel* ptc. = a refiner (2 · 2 · 22) 864

בֹּרִית   lye, alkali, potash, soap (1 · 2) 141

צרף   3   *Piel* ptc. = a refiner (2 · 2 · 22) 864

זָקַק   to purify (1 · 1 · 7) 279

ערב   4   to be sweet, pleasing (1 · 8 · 8) 787

קַדְמֹנִי   former, ancient (1 · 10) 870

כִּשֵּׁף   5   to practice sorcery (1 · 6 · 6) 506

נאף   *Piel*, to commit adultery (1 · 14 · 31) 610

עָשַׁק   to oppress, wrong (1 · 36 · 37) 798

שָׂכָר   hire, wages (1 · 28) 969

שָׂכִיר   hired (1 · 18) 969

יָתוֹם   orphan (1 · 42) 450

שָׁנָה   6   to change (1 · 14 · 26) 1039

בַּמֶּה   7   whereby[?] by what means[?] מה 4.a. 553

קָבַע   8   to rob [dub.] (4 · 6 · 6) 867

בַּמֶּה   whereby[?] by what means[?] מה 4.a. 553

מַעֲשֵׂר   tithe, payment of tenth part, tenth part (2 · 33) 789

מְאֵרָה   9   curse (2 · 5) 76

קָבַע   to rob [dub.] (4 · 6 · 6) 867

מַעֲשֵׂר   10   tithe, payment of tenth part, tenth part (2 · 33) 798

טֶרֶף   food, prey (1 · 4) 383

בָּזֹאת   by or through this (1 · 4) זה 6. b. 261

בחן   to prove, test, try (2 · 25 · 29) 103

אֲרֻבָּה   lattice, latticed opening, window, sluice (1 · 9) 70

הריק   to pour out or down, to empty or draw out (1 · 17 · 19) 937-938

407

עַד־בְּלִי till there be no (1 · 2) para. d.
"with preps." d. בְּלִי 116 בְּלִי
(1 · 23) 115

דַּי sufficiency; w. idiom above = forever (1 · 12) דַּי 1. 191

גָּעַר 11 to rebuke (1 · 14 · 14) 172

שִׁכֵּל to show abortion, cause barrenness,
be made childless (1 · 18 · 23) 1013

אָשַׁר 12 to pronounce happy, call blessed;
to go straight on (2 · 7 · 9) 80

חֵפֶץ delight, pleasure (2 · 39) 343

בֶּצַע 14 profit, gain made by violence
(1 · 23) 130

קְדֹרַנִּית adv. as mourners (1 · 1) 871

אָשַׁר 15 to pronounce happy, call blessed;
to go straight on (2 · 7 · 9) 80

זֵד insolent, presumptuous (2 · 13) 267

רִשְׁעָה wickedness (3 · 15) 958

בָּחַן to prove, test, try (2 · 25 · 29) 103

הִקְשִׁיר 16 to give attention (1 · 45 · 46) 904

זִכָּרוֹן memorial, reminder (1 · 24) 272

יָרֵא vb. adj.; but BDB vb. = to fear,
reverence, honor (3 · 45) 431

סְגֻלָּה 17 valued property, peculiar treasure
(1 · 8) 688

חָמַל to spare, have compassion
(2 · 40 · 40) 328

תַּנּוּר 19 fire pot, portable stove (1 · 14) 1072

זֵד insolent, presumptuous (2 · 13) 267

רִשְׁעָה wickedness (3 · 15) 958

קַשׁ stubble, chaff (1 · 16) 905

לָהַט to set ablaze (1 · 9 · 11) 529

שֹׁרֶשׁ root (1 · 33) 1057

עָנָף branch[es], bough[es] (1 · 7) 778

זרח 20 to rise, come forth (1 · 18 · 18) 280

יָרֵא vb. adj.; but BDB vb. = to fear,
reverence, honor (3 · 45) 431

מַרְפֵּא health, healing, cure (1 · 13) 951

פּוּשׁ [apparently] to spring about
(1 · 3 · 3) 807

עֵגֶל calf (1 · 35) 722

מַרְבֵּק stall, place where calves are fattened (1 · 4) 918

עסס 21 to press, crush (1 · 1 · 1) 779

אֵפֶר ashes (1 · 22) 68

נוֹרָא 23 inspiring reverence, awe; fearful
(2 · 44) 431

חֵרֶם 24 devotion, ban, devoted thing
(1 · 29) 356

PSALMS

Psalm 1

אֶשֶׁר 1 happiness, blessedness (26 · 45[?]) 80

חַטָּא sinner (6 · 19) 308

מוֹשָׁב sitting, seat (6 · 46) 444

לֵץ scorner (1 · 16[?]) 539 לִיץ

חֵפֶץ 2 delight (3 · 39) 343

הָגָה to meditate, muse (10 · 23 · 25) 211 I

שָׁתַל 3 to transplant (2 · 10 · 10) 1060

פֶּלֶג channel, canal (4 · 10) 811

עָלֶה leaf, leafage (1 · 18) 750

נָבֵל to droop, wither and fall, fade (3 · 19 · 23) 615

מֹץ 4 chaff (2 · 8) 558

נָדַף to drive about (2 · 3 · 9) 623

חַטָּא sinner (6 · 19) 308

Psalm 2

רָגַשׁ 1 to be in tumult, commotion (1 · 1 · 1) 921

לְאֹם people (14 · 35) 522

הָגָה to imagine, devise (10 · 23 · 25) 211 I

רִיק emptiness, vanity (3 · 12) 938

הִתְיַצֵּב 2 to station oneself, take one's stand (4 · 48 · 48) 426

רֹזֵן ruler, potentate (1 · 6) 931

נוֹסַד to sit together, sit in conclave (2 · 2 · 2[?]) 413 יָסַד

יַחַד together, altogether (14 · 44) 403

מָשִׁיחַ anointed (10 · 39) 603

נָתַק 3 to tear apart, snap (2 · 11 · 27) 683

מוֹסֵר band, bond (3 · 12) 64

עֲבֹת cord, rope (3 · 24) 721

שָׂחַק 4 to laugh (4 · 18 · 36) 965

לָעַג to mock, deride (3 · 12 · 18) 541

חָרוֹן 5 [burning of] anger (6 · 41) 354

בָּהַל to dismay, terrify (2 · 10 · 39) 96

נָסַךְ 6 to install, set (1 · 7 · 25) 651 III

אֶפֶס 8 ends, extreme limits (6 · 27) 67

רָעַע 9 to break (1 · 3 · 5[?]) 949 II

יוֹצֵר potter (1 · 17[?]) 427 *Qal* 1.a

נָפַץ 10 to dash to pieces (2 · 15 · 21) 658 I

נוֹסַר to be corrected, admonished (1 · 5 · 41) 415 יָסַר

יִרְאָה 11 fear, terror (8 · 45) 432

גִּיל to rejoice (19 · 45 · 45) 162

רְעָדָה trembling (2 · 4) 944

נָשַׁק 12 to kiss (1 · 5) 676 II

בַּר son (1 · 2) 135 I

אָנַף to be angry (4 · 8 · 14) 60

אֶשֶׁר happiness, blessedness (19 · 45[?]) 80

חָסָה to seek refuge (25 · 37 · 37) 340

Psalm 3

רָבַב 2 to be, become, many (6 · 23 · 24) 912

יָשֵׁן 6 to sleep, go to sleep (5 · 15 · 16) 445

הֵקִיץ to awake (7 · 22 · 23) 884

סָמַךְ to support, uphold, sustain (10 · 41 · 48) 701

רְבָבָה 7 myriad, ten thousand (2 · 16) 914

לְחִי 8 cheek (1 · 21) 534

Psalm 4

נְגִינָה 1 music, song (9 · 14) 618

צַר 2 straits, distress (3 · 20) 865

הִרְחִיב to enlarge, make room (6 · 21 · 25) 931

כְּלִמָּה 3 ignominy, reproach (7 · 30) 484

רִיק emptiness, vanity (3 · 12) 938

כָּזָב lie, falsehood (6 · 31) 469

הַפְלֵה 4 to make separate, set apart (3 · 10 · 24[?]) 811

חָסִיד pious, godly (25 · 32) 339

רָגַז 5 to quake (5 · 30 · 41) 919

מִשְׁכָּב couch, bed (4 · 46) 1012

דמם to be silent (6 · 23 · 30) 198 I

נָסָה 7 for נָשָׂא, to lift up 669 *Qal* Imv.

דָּגָן 8 corn (3 · 40) 186

תִּירוֹשׁ fresh or new wine (1 · 38) 440

רבב to be, become, many (6 · 23 · 24) 912

יָשֵׁן 9 to sleep, go to sleep (5 · 15 · 16) 445

בָּדָד alone; isolation, separation (1 · 11) 94

בֶּטַח security; securely (3 · 43) 105

Psalm 5

נְחִילָה 1 musical term, perh. flute (1 · 1) 636

אֹמֶר 2 utterance, word (7 · 48) 56

הַאֲזִין to listen, give ear (15 · 41 · 41) 24

הָגִיג murmuring (2 · 2) 211

הִקְשִׁיב 3 to give attention (8 · 45 · 45) 904

שַׁוְעִי my cry for help (1 · 1[?]) 1002 שׁוֹע

צפה 4 to watch, look (1 · 9 · 18) 859 I

חָפֵץ 5 delighting in, taking pleasure in (6 · 12) 343

רֶשַׁע wickedness (6 · 30) 957

הִתְיַצֵּב 6 to hold one's ground (4 · 48 · 48) 426

הלל to be boastful (3 · 3 · 14[?]) 237 II

לְנֶגֶד before, in front of (13 · 32) 617 נֶגֶד 2.b

כָּזָב 7 lie, falsehood (6 · 31) 469

מִרְמָה deceit, treachery (14 · 39) 941

תעב to abhor, regard as an abomination (4 · 14 · 21) 1073

יִרְאָה 8 fear (8 · 45) 432

נחה 9 to lead, bring (6 · 14 · 40) 634

שׁוֹרֵר watcher (insidiously), foe (5 · 5) 1004

הוֹשֵׁר to make even (1 · 2 · 25) 448 יָשַׁר *Hiph.*

הַוָּה 10 destruction, chasm (8 · 13) 217

גָּרוֹן throat (4 · 8) 173

הֶחֱלִיק to make smooth (2 · 7 · 9) 325 II

הֶאְשִׁים 11 to declare guilty (1 · 31 · 33) 79

מוֹעֵצָה counsel, plan, device (2 · 7) 420

הִדִּיחַ to thrust out, banish (2 · 27 · 43) 623 נדה

מָרָה to be disobedient, rebellious (3 · 21 · 43) 598

חָסָה 12 to seek refuge (25 · 37 · 37) 340

הֵסִיךְ to screen, cover (2 · 5 · 18) 696 I סכך

עָלַץ to rejoice, exult (4 · 8 · 8) 763

אֹהֵב friend, lover (12 · 36) 12

צִנָּה 13 large shield (3 · 20) 857

עטר to surround (1 · 2 · 7) 742

Psalm 6

נְגִינָת 1 music, song (9 · 14) 618

יִסֵּר 2 to chasten, chastise (7 · 30 · 41) 415

אֻמְלַל 3 feeble (1 · 1) 51

נִבְהַל to be disturbed, dismayed, terrified (8 · 24 · 39) 96

נִבְהַל 4 to be disturbed, dismayed, terrified (8 · 24 · 39) 96

מָתַי when? (13 · 42) 607

חִלֵּץ 5 to rescue, deliver (10 · 14 · 27) 322 I

זֵכֶר 6 rememberance, memory (11 · 23) 271

יגע 7 to grow weary, be weary (2 · 20 · 26) 383

אֲנָחָה sighing, groaning (4 · 11) 58

הִשְׂחָה to cause to swim (1 · 1 · 3) 965

מִטָּה couch, bed (1 · 29) 641

דִּמְעָה tears (8 · 23) 199

עֶרֶשׂ couch, divan (3 · 10) 793

המסה to cause to melt, dissolve (3 · 4 · 4) 587

עָשֵׁשׁ 8 to waste away (3 · 3 · 3) 799

כַּעַס vexation, grief (4 · 25) 495

עָתֵק to advance; i.e., grow old (1 · 4 · 9) 801

צֹרֵר vexer, harasser (12 · 17) 865 III צרר

בְּכִי 9 weeping (3 · 32) 113

תְּחִנָּה 10 supplication for favor (3 · 25) 337

נִבְהַל 11 to be disturbed, dismayed, terrified (8 · 24 · 39) 96

רֶגַע in a moment, suddenly (3 · 22) 921

Psalm 7

שִׁגָּיוֹן 1 perh. a song with wild, passionate rhythm (1 · 1) 993

חָסָה 2 to seek refuge (25 · 37 · 37) 340

טָרַף 3 to tear, rend (4 · 19 · 24) 382

אַרְיֵה lion (5 · 45) 71

פָּרֵק to snatch, tear away (2 · 4 · 10) 830

עָוֶל 4 injustice, unrighteousness (3 · 21) 732

גָּמַל 5 to recompense, repay, requite (10 · 34 · 37) 168

חָלֵץ to rescue, deliver (10 · 14 · 27) 322 I

צֹרֵר vexer, harasser (12 · 17) 865 III צרר

רֵיקָם in vain, without effect (2 · 16) 938

הִשִּׂיג 6 to overtake (4 · 49 · 49) 673

רָמַס to trample (2 · 17 · 18) 942

עֶבְרָה 7 outburst of fury (5 · 34) 720

צֹרֵר vexer, harasser (12 · 17) 865 III צרר

לְאֹם 8 people (14 · 35) 522

דִּין 9 to judge, minister judgment (8 · 23 · 24) 192

תֹּם integrity, completeness (7 · 23) 1070

גָּמַר 10 to come to an end, be no more (5 · 5 · 5) 170

בָּחַן to prove, test, try (9 · 24 · 28) 103

כִּלְיָה kidney (5 · 31) 480

מוֹשִׁיעַ 11 savior (4 · 27) 446 ישע

זָעַם 12 to be indignant (1 · 10 · 11) 276

לָטַשׁ 13 to sharpen (1 · 4 · 5) 538

דָּרַךְ to tread; w. קֶשֶׁת = to bend the bow 201 דָּרַךְ Qal 4

דָּלַק 14 to burn; ptc. = burning ones (2 · 7 · 9) 196

חָבַל 15 to writhe, twist; i.e., travail (1 · 3 · 3[?]) 286 I

הָרָה to conceive, become pregnant (1 · 38 · 40) 247

כָּרָה 16 to dig (4 · 13 · 14) 500 I

חָפַר to dig (2 · 23 · 23) 343 I

שַׁחַת pit (9 · 23) 1001

קָדְקֹד 17 hairy crown, scalp (2 · 11) 869

זָמַר 18 to sing, make music (39 · 43 · 43) 274 I

Psalm 8

גִּתִּית 1 lyre, melody (3 · 3) 388

אַדִּיר 2 majestic (7 · 27) 12

תְּנָה to set (1 · 2 · 3[?]) 680 נתן Qal 2.b

הוֹד splendor, majesty (8 · 24) 217

עוֹלֵל 3 child (2 · 11) 760

יוֹנֵק suckling, babe (1 · 11[?]) 413 ינק

יָסַד to establish (1 · 10 · 41) 413

צֹרֵר vexer, harasser (12 · 17) 865 III צרר

הִתְנַקֵּם to avenge oneself (2 · 5 · 35) 667

אֶצְבַּע 4 finger (2 · 31) 840

יָרֵחַ moon (8 · 27) 437

כּוֹכָב star (4 · 37) 456

אֱנוֹשׁ 5 man, mankind (13 · 42) 60

חִסַּר 6 to cause to lack (1 · 2 · 23) 341

הָדָר splendor, majesty (13 · 30) 214

עָטַר to crown (3 · 4 · 7) 742

צֹנֶה 8 flocks (1 · 2) 856

אֶלֶף cattle (2 · 8) 48 I

שָׂדַי field, land (5 · 13) 961

צִפּוֹר 9 birds (coll.) (7 · 40) 861

דָּג fish (1 · 19) 185

אַדִּיר 10 majestic (7 · 27) 12

Psalm 9

עַלְמוּת 1 young woman (2 · 2[?]) 761 עַלְמָץ

נִפְלָאוֹת 2 wonderful acts (27 · 44) 810 פלא

עָלַץ 3 to rejoice, exult (4 · 8 · 8) 763

זמר to sing, make music (39 · 43 · 43) 247 I

אָחוֹר 4 backwards, behind (12 · 41) 30

דִּין 5 cause, plea (3 · 19) 192

גָּעַר 6 to rebuke (4 · 14 · 14) 172

מָחָה to blot out (3 · 22 · 34) 562 I

עַד ever (29 · 48) 723 I

חָרְבָּה 7 waste, ruin (3 · 42) 325

לָנֶצַח forever (18 · 42) 664 נצח 4

נָתַשׁ to pull or pluck up (1 · 16 · 21) 684

זֵכֶר remembrance, memory (11 · 23) 271

תֵּבֵל 9 world (15 · 35) 385

דין to judge, minister judgment (8 · 23 · 24) 192

לְאֹם people (14 · 35) 522

מֵישָׁר uprightness, equity (7 · 19) 449

מִשְׂגָּב 10 secure height, retreat (13 · 17) 960

דַּךְ oppressed, distressed (3 · 4) 194

בַּצָּרָה dearth, destitution (2 · 2) 131

זמר 12 to sing, make music (39 · 43 · 43) 274 I

עֲלִילָה deed (9 · 24) 760

צְעָקָה 13 cry of distress (1 · 21) 858

עָנָו poor, afflicted, meek (13 · 22) 776

עֳנִי 14 affliction (10 · 36) 777

שֹׂנֵא enemy (12 · 41[?]) 971 שָׂנֵא

גִּיל 15 to rejoice (19 · 45 · 45) 162

טָבַע 16 to sink (3 · 6 · 10) 371

שַׁחַת pit (9 · 23) 1001

רֶשֶׁת net (8 · 22) 440

זוּ which (9 · 14) 262

טָמַן to hide, conceal (7 · 28 · 31) 380

פֹּעַל 17 deed, thing done (11 · 37) 821

נקש to strike down (1 · 1 · 5) 669

הִגָּיוֹן resounding music (3 · 4) 212

שָׁכֵחַ 18 forgetting, forgetful (1 · 2) 1013

לָנֶצַח 19 forever (18 · 42) 664 נצח 4

תִּקְוָה hope (3 · 32) 876

עָנָו poor, afflicted, meek (13 · 22) 776

עַד = לְעַד forever (29 · 48) 723 I.2

עזז 20 to be strong, prevail (4 · 9 · 11) 738

אֱנוֹשׁ man, mankind (13 · 42) 60

מוֹרָה 21 terror (2 · 12[?]) 432 I

אֱנוֹשׁ man, mankind (13 · 42) 60

Psalm 10

הֶעֱלִים 1 to conceal, hide (1 · 11 · 29) 761

בַּצָּרָה dearth, destitution (2 · 2) 131

גַּאֲוָה 2 pride, haughtiness (7 · 19) 144

דלק to hotly pursue (2 · 7 · 9) 196

מְזִמָּה device (5 · 19) 273

זוּ which (9 · 14) 262

תַּאֲוָה 3 desire (8 · 21) 16

בצע ptc. = robber, greedy getter (1 · 10 · 16) 130

נָאֵץ to despise, spurn (4 · 15 · 24) 610

גֹּבַהּ 4 haughtiness (1 · 17) 147

מְזִמָּה thoughts (5 · 19) 273

חִיל 5 to be firm, strong (1 · 2 · 2) 298 II חול

מִנֶּגֶד at a distance from (2 · 26) 617 נגד

צָרַר vexer, harasser (12 · 17) 865 III צרר

הֵפִיחַ to puff, snort (2 · 12 · 14) 806

נמוט 6 to be shaken, moved, overthrown (16 · 22 · 39) 556

אָלָה 7 oath, curse (3 · 36) 46

מִרְמָה deceit, treachery (14 · 39) 941

תֹּךְ injury, oppression (3 · 4) 1067

מַאֲרָב 8 lurking place, ambush (1 · 5) 70

מִסְתָּר hiding place (4 · 10) 712

נָקִי free from guilt, clean, innocent (5 · 43) 667

חֵלְכָה hapless, unfortunate (3 · 3) 319

צָפַן to lurk, be hid (7 · 23 · 28) 860

אָרַב	9 to lie in wait (3 · 20 · 23) 70	
מִסְתָּר	hiding place (4 · 10) 712	
אַרְיֵה	lion (5 · 45) 71	
סֹךְ	covert, lair (3 · 4) 697	
חטף	to catch, seize (2 · 3 · 3) 310	
מָשַׁךְ	to draw, drag along (5 · 30 · 36) 604	
רֶשֶׁת	net (8 · 22) 440	
דכה	10 to be crushed or to crouch (1 · 1 · 5) 194	
שׁחח	to be bowed down, prostrated, humbled (4 · 12 · 18[?]) 1005	
עָצוּם	mighty, strong (3 · 31) 783	
חֵלְכָּאִים	hapless, unfortunate ones (3 · 3) 319 חֵלְכָה	
לָנֶצַח	11 forever (18 · 42) 664 נֶצַח	
עָנָו	12 poor, afflicted, meek (13 · 22) 776	
נִאֵץ	13 to despise, spurn (4 · 15 · 24) 610	
כַּעַס	14 vexation, grief (4 · 25) 495	
חֵלְכָה	hapless, unfortunate (3 · 3) 319	
יָתוֹם	orphan (8 · 42) 450	
עֹזֵר	help, helper (7 · 19) 740 עזר	
רֶשַׁע	15 wickedness (6 · 30) 957	
עַד	16 ever (29 · 48) 723 I	
תַּאֲוָה	17 desire (8 · 21) 16	
עָנָו	poor, afflicted, meek (13 · 22) 776	
הִקְשִׁיב	to give attention (8 · 45 · 46) 904	
יָתוֹם	18 orphan (8 · 42) 450	
דַּךְ	oppressed, distressed (3 · 4) 194	
ערץ	to cause to tremble (1 · 11 · 14) 791	
אֱנוֹשׁ	man, mankind (13 · 42) 60	

Psalm 11

חָסָה	1 to seek refuge (25 · 37 · 37) 340	
נוד	to flutter (2 · 19 · 26) 626	
צִפּוֹר	[coll.] birds (7 · 40) 861	
דרך	2 to tread; w. קֶשֶׁת = to bend the bow 201 דָּרַךְ Qal. 4	
יֶתֶר	cord, bowstring (1 · 6) 452	

יָרָה	to shoot, throw (2 · 13 · 25) 434	
בְּמוֹ	poetic for בְּ (1 · 10) 91	
אֹפֶל	darkness, gloom (2 · 9) 66	
שָׁת	3 foundation, stay (1 · 4) 1011	
נהרס	to be thrown down, torn down (1 · 10 · 43) 248	
עַפְעַף	4 eyelid (2 · 10) 733	
בחן	to examine, try (9 · 24 · 28) 103	
בחן	5 to examine, try (9 · 24 · 28) 103	
אֹהֵב	friend (12 · 36) 12 אהב	
הִמְטִיר	6 to send rain, rain (3 · 16 · 17) 565	
פַּח	bird trap, snare (9 · 25) 809	
גָּפְרִית	brimstone (1 · 7) 172	
זִלְעָפָה	raging heat (2 · 3) 273	
מְנָת	portion (3 · 9) 584	
כּוֹס	cup (5 · 31) 468	

Psalm 12

גָּמַר	2 to come to an end, be no more (5 · 5 · 5) 170	
חָסִיד	pious, godly (25 · 32) 339	
פסס	to disappear, vanish (1 · 1 · 1) 821 II	
אֱמוּנִים	faithful ones (2 · 3[?]) 52 אמן I.4.b	
חֶלְקַה	3 flattery (3 · 12) 325	
חֶלְקַה	4 flattery (3 · 12) 325	
הִגְבִּיר	5 to confirm a covenant, give strength, prevail (1 · 2 · 25) 149	
שֹׁד	6 violence, havoc (1 · 25) 994	
אֲנָקָה	crying, groaning (3 · 4) 60 I	
יֵשַׁע	safety, welfare, prosperity (20 · 60) 447	
הֵפִיחַ	to puff, pant (2 · 12 · 14) 806	
אִמְרָה	7 word, saying (26 · 36) 57	
צָרַף	to smelt, refine (7 · 18 · 21) 864	
עֲלִיל	furnace, crucible (1 · 1) 760	
זקק	to be refined (1 · 4 · 7) 279 I	
זוּ	8 this (9 · 14) 262	
זֻלָּת	9 worthlessness (1 · 1) 273	

Psalm 13

אָנָה 2 how long? (7 · 39) 33 אָן
נֶצַח   everlastingness, ever (18 · 42) 664
אָנָה 3 how long? (7 · 39) 33 אָן
יָגוֹן   sorrow, grief (4 · 14) 387
הָאִיר 4 to lighten (15 · 34 · 40) 21 אור
יָשֵׁן   to sleep, go to sleep (5 · 15 · 16) 445
גִּיל 5 to rejoice (19 · 45 · 45) 162
נָמוֹט   to be shaken, moved, overthrown
   (16 · 22 · 39) 556
גִּיל 6 to rejoice (19 · 45 · 45) 162
גָּמַל   to deal bountifully (10 · 34 · 37) 168

Psalm 14

נָבָל 1 senseless (5 · 18) 614 I
הִתְעִיב   to make abominable, do abomina-
   bly (2 · 4 · 21) 1073 תעב
עֲלִילָה   deed (9 · 24) 760
הִשְׁקִיף 2 to look down (3 · 12 · 22) 1054
נֶאֱלָח 3 to be corrupt (2 · 3 · 3) 47
פָּחַד 5 to be in dread (5 · 23 · 26) 808
פַּחַד   dread (9 · 49) 808
מַחְסֶה 6 refuge, shelter (12 · 20) 340
מִי 7 O that! (>50) 566 f.(a)
שְׁבוּת   captivity (2 · 26) 986
גִּיל   to rejoice (19 · 45 · 45) 162

Psalm 15

רָגַל 3 to slander (1 · 1 · 16) 920
קָרֹב   neighbor (>50) 898 2.c
נִבְזֶה 4 to be despised (2 · 10 · 42) 102
יָרֵא   afraid (27 · 46) 431
הֵמִיר   to change, alter (3 · 12 · 13) 558 מור
לְהָרַע   *Hiph.* inf. cstr. of רעע = to be
   evil, bad (>50) 949
נֶשֶׁךְ 5 interest, usury (1 · 12) 675
שֹׁחַד   bribe (2 · 23) 1005

נָקִי   free from guilt, clean, innocent
   (5 · 43) 667
נָמוֹט   to be shaken, moved, overthrown
   (16 · 22 · 39) 556

Psalm 16

מִכְתָּם 1 Mikhtam (6 · 6) 508
חָסָה   to seek refuge (25 · 37 · 37) 340
אַדִּיר 3 majestic (7 · 27) 12
חֵפֶץ   delight (3 · 39) 343
עַצְּבָה 4 hurt, injury, pain (2 · 5) 781
מָהַר   to obtain in exchange [dub.]
   (1 · 2 · 2) 555 III
הִסִּיךְ   to pour out libations (1 · 14 · 25)
   650 I
מְנָת 5 portion (3 · 9) 584
כּוֹס   cup (5 · 31) 468
תּוֹמִיךְ   *Qal* ptc. of תמך = to grasp, lay
   hold of, support (4 · 20 · 21) 1069
חֶבֶל 6 measuring cord, line (8 · 50) 286
נָעִים   delightful, pleasant (6 · 7) 653
שָׁפַר   to be beautiful, fair, comely
   (1 · 1 · 1) 1051
יִסַּר 7 to discipline, correct (7 · 30 · 41)
   415
כִּלְיָה   kidney (6 · 31) 480
שָׁוָה 8 to set, place (4 · 5 · 5) 1001 II
לְנֶגֶד   in front of, before (13 · 32) 617 נֶגֶד
   2.b
נָמוֹט   to be shaken, moved, overthrown
   (16 · 22 · 39) 556
גִּיל 9 to rejoice (19 · 45 · 45) 162
בֶּטַח   security; securely (3 · 43) 105
חָסִיד 10 pious, godly (25 · 32) 339
שַׁחַת   pit (9 · 23) 1001
שֹׂבַע 11 satisfying abundance (2 · 8) 959
נָעִים   pleasant, delightful (6 · 7) 653
נֶצַח   everlastingness, forever (18 · 42) 664

Psalm 17

הַקְשִׁיב	1 to give attention (8 · 45 · 46) 904	
רִנָּה	ringing cry (15 · 33) 943	
הֶאֱזִין	to listen, give ear (15 · 41 · 41) 24	
בְּלֹא	without (2 · 30) 518 לֹא 4.a	
מִרְמָה	deceit, treachery (14 · 39) 941	
מֵישָׁר	2 uprightness, equity (7 · 19) 449	
בחן	3 to prove, test, try (9 · 24 · 28) 103	
צָרַף	to test (7 · 18 · 21) 864	
זָמַם	to devise, purpose (3 · 13 · 13) 273	
פְּעֻלָּה	4 work, wages (3 · 14) 821	
פָּרִיץ	violent one (1 · 6) 829	
תמך	5 to hold, keep (4 · 20 · 21) 1069	
אֲשׁוּר	step, going (6 · 10) 81	
מַעְגָּל	track (4 · 13) 722	
נמוט	to be shaken, moved, overthrown (16 · 22 · 39) 556	
הַט	6 Hiph. of נטה, to incline (>50) 639	
אִמְרָה	utterance, speech (26 · 36) 57	
הִפְלָה	7 to make separate, make wonderful (3 · 13 · 24[?]) 811	
מוֹשִׁיעַ	savior (4 · 27) 446 ישׁע 15	
חָסָה	to seek refuge (25 · 37 · 37) 340	
אִישׁוֹן	8 pupil (1 · 4) 36	
זוּ	9 who (9 · 14) 262	
הִקִּיף	to surround, encompass (4 · 16 · 17) 668 II	
גֵּאוּת	10 pride (3 · 8) 145	
אַשֻּׁר	11 step, going (6 · 10) 81	
דִּמְיֹן	12 likeness (1 · 1) 198	
אַרְיֵה	lion (5 · 45) 71	
כסף	to long (1 · 2 · 6) 493	
טָרַף	to tear, rend (4 · 19 · 24) 382	
כְּפִיר	young lion (6 · 31) 498	
מִסְתָּר	hiding place (4 · 10) 712	
קדם	13 to meet, confront (12 · 24 · 26) 869	
הַכְרִיעַ	to cause to bow down (3 · 6 · 36) 502	
פלט	to deliver (19 · 24 · 27) 812	
מַת	14 male, man (3 · 22) 607	

חֶלֶד	duration of life (4 · 5) 317	
צָפִין	treasure; Q צָפוּן (1 · 3[?]) 860	
עוֹלֵל	child (2 · 11) 760	
הֵקִיץ	15 to awake (7 · 22 · 23) 884	
תְּמוּנָה	form, semblance (1 · 10) 568	

Psalm 18

שִׁירָה	1 song (1 · 13) 1010	
רחם	2 to love (1 · 1 · 47) 933	
חֵזֶק	strength (1 · 1) 305	
מְצוּדָה	3 fastness, stronghold (7 · 18) 845 II	
פלט	to deliver (19 · 24 · 27) 812	
חָסָה	to seek refuge (25 · 37 · 37) 340	
יֵשַׁע	salvation (20 · 36) 447	
מִשְׂגָּב	secure height, retreat (13 · 17) 960	
אפף	5 to surround, encompass (3 · 5 · 5) 67	
חֶבֶל	cord, rope (8 · 50) 286	
בְּלִיַּעַל	destruction, ruin (3 · 27) 116	
בעת	to assail (1 · 13 · 16) 129	
חֶבֶל	6 cord, rope (8 · 50) 286	
קדם	to meet, confront (12 · 24 · 26) 869	
מוֹקֵשׁ	lure, snare (6 · 27) 430	
שׁוע	7 to cry for help (9 · 21 · 21[?]) 1002	
שַׁוְעָה	cry for help (6 · 11) 1003	
געשׁ	8 to quake (1 · 2 · 10) 172	
רעשׁ	to shake, quake (4 · 21 · 29) 950	
מוֹסָד	foundation (3 · 13) 414	
רגז	to quake (5 · 30 · 41) 919	
התגעשׁ	to shake back and forth, toss or reel to and fro (1 · 5 · 10) 172	
עָשָׁן	9 smoke (4 · 25) 798	
גַּחֶלֶת	coal (5 · 18) 160	
עֲרָפֶל	10 cloud, heavy cloud (2 · 15) 791	
עוף	11 to fly (4 · 18 · 25) 733	
דאה	to fly swiftly, dart (1 · 4 · 4) 178	
סֵתֶר	12 covering, cover (10 · 35) 712	
סֻכָּה	booth (2 · 31) 697	
חַשְׁכָה	darkness (3 · 6) 365	

עָב — cloud mass, dark cloud (5·30) 728 II

שַׁחַק — cloud, sky (9·21) 1007

נֹגַהּ 13 — brightness (1·19) 618

עָב — dark cloud, cloud mass (5·30) 728 II

בָּרָד — hail (6·29) 135

גַּחֶלֶת — coal (5·18) 160

הִרְעִים 14 — to cause to thunder (2·8·11) 947

בָּרָד — hail (6·29) 135

גַּחֶלֶת — coal (5·18) 160

בָּרָק 15 — lightning (5·21) 140

הָמַם — to confuse, discomfit (2·13·13) 243

אָפִיק 16 — channel, stream bed, ravine (3·18) 67

מוֹסָד — foundation (3·13) 414

תֵּבֵל — world (15·36) 385

גְּעָרָה — rebuke (4·15) 172

נְשָׁמָה — breath (2·24) 675

הַמְשֵׁה 17 — to draw out (1·2·3) 602

עַז 18 — strong, mighty, fierce (2·22) 738

שֹׂנֵא — enemy (12·41[?]) 971

אָמֵץ — to be strong (2·16·41) 54

קִדֵּם 19 — to meet, confront (12·24·26) 869

אֵיד — distress, calamity (1·24) 15

מִשְׁעָן — support, staff (1·4) 1044

מֶרְחָב 20 — broad or roomy place (3·6) 932

חִלֵּץ — to rescue, deliver (10·14·27) 322

גָּמַל 21 — to deal bountifully, reward (10·34·37) 168

בֹּר — cleanness, pureness (2·7) 141 II

רֹשַׁע 22 — to be wicked, act wickedly (1·9·34) 957

לְנֶגֶד 23 — in front of, before (13·32) 617 נֶגֶד 2.bü

בֹּר 25 — cleanness, pureness (2·7) 141 II

לְנֶגֶד — in the sight of, in the presence of (13·32) 617 נֶגֶד 2.b

חָסִיד 26 — kind (25·32) 339

הִתְחַסֵּד — to show oneself kind (1·2·2) 338

נָבַר 27 Niph. ptc. = purified, pure (1·3·15) 140 ברר

הִתְבָּרֵר — to show oneself pure (1·3·15) 140

עִקֵּשׁ — twisted, perverted (2·11) 786

הִתְפַּתֵּל — to deal tortuously (1·2·5) 836

רָם 28 — high, lifted up, exalted (5·31[?]) 926 רום

הִשְׁפִּיל — to lay low, humiliate (4·19·30) 1050

הֵאִיר 29 — to light (15·34·40) 21 אור

נֵר — lamp (3·44) 632

הִגִּיהַּ — to enlighten (1·3·6) 618 נגה

גְּדוּד 30 — marauding band (1·33) 151 I

דָּלַג — to leap, leap over (1·4·5) 194

שׁוּר — wall (1·3) 1004

אִמְרָה 31 — word, saying (26·36) 57

צָרַף — to smelt, refine (7·18·21) 864

חָסָה — to seek refuge (25·37·37) 340

מִבַּלְעֲדֵי 32 — apart from, without (1·12) 116 בִּלְעֲדֵי b

זוּלָה — except, besides (1·16) 265

אָזַר 33 — to gird (3·6·16) 25

שִׁוָּה 34 — to set, place (2·5·16[?]) 1001 II

אַיָּלָה — hind, doe (3·11) 19

נִחַת 35 — to press down (2·3·8) 639

נְחוּשָׁה — copper, bronze (1·10) 639

יֵשַׁע 36 — salvation (20·36) 447

סָעַד — to support, sustain (6·12·12) 703

עֲנָוָה — condescension [dub.] (2·2[?]) 776

הִרְחִיב 37 — to enlarge (6·21·25) 931

צַעַד — step, pace (1·14) 857

מָעַד — to slip (3·5·7) 588

קַרְסֹל — ankle (1·2) 902

הִשִּׂיג 38 — to overtake (4·49·49) 673

מָחַץ 39 — to smite through (5·14·14) 563

אָזַר 40 — to gird (3·6·16) 25

הִכְרִיעַ — to cause to bow down (3·6·36) 502

קָם — adversary (5·12) 877 קום 2

עֹרֶף 41 — back of neck, neck (1·33) 791

הַצְמִית	to exterminate, annihilate (9 · 10 · 15) 856	תֵּבֵל	world (15 · 36) 385	

הַצְמִית to exterminate, annihilate
(9 · 10 · 15) 856

שַׁוַּע 42 to cry for help (9 · 21 · 21[?]) 1002

מוֹשִׁיעַ savior (4 · 27) 446 ישע

שָׁחַק 43 to rub away, beat fine, pulverize
(1 · 4 · 4) 1006

טִיט mud, mire (3 · 13) 376

הֵרִיק to empty out (2 · 17 · 19) 937

פָּלַט 44 to deliver (19 · 24 · 27) 812

שֵׁמַע 45 hearing, report (1 · 17) 1034

נֵכָר foreignness (6 · 36) 648

כָּחַשׁ to cringe = come cringing
(3 · 19 · 22) 471

נֵכָר 46 foreignness (6 · 36) 648

נָבֵל to sink, drop down (3 · 19 · 23) 615

חָרַג to quake (1 · 1 · 1) 353

מִסְגֶּרֶת fastness (1 · 17) 689 2

יֶשַׁע 47 salvation (20 · 36) 447

נְקָמָה 48 vengeance (5 · 27) 668

הַדְבִּיר to lead, put to flight (2 · 2 · 5[?])
דבר 180

פָּלַט 49 to deliver (19 · 24 · 27) 812

קָם adversary (5 · 12) 877 קום 2

זִמֵּר 50 to sing, make music (39 · 43 · 43)
274 I

מָשִׁיחַ 51 anointed (10 · 39) 603

Psalm 19

רָקִיעַ 2 firmament (2 · 17) 956

הִבִּיעַ 3 to pour forth, emit (6 · 10 · 11) 615
נבע

אֹמֶר utterance, word (4 · 6[?]) 56

חוה to declare, make known (1 · 6 · 6)
296 III

אֹמֶר 4 utterance, word (4 · 6[?]) 56

בְּלִי not (4 · 23) 115

קַו 5 chord (1 · 25[?]) 876 II

תֵּבֵל world (15 · 36) 385

מִלָּה word (2 · 38) 576

חָתָן 6 bridegroom (1 · 20) 368

חֻפָּה chamber (1 · 3) 342 I

שׂוֹשׂ to exult, rejoice (7 · 27) 965

מוֹצָא 7 a going forth; of sun = rising
(6 · 27) 425 I

תְּקוּפָה circuit (1 · 4) 880

קָצָה ends (1 · 7) 892

חַמָּה heat (1 · 6) 328

הֶחְכִּים 8 to make wise (1 · 1 · 26) 314

פֶּתִי simple (3 · 19) 834

פִּקּוּד 9 precept (24 · 24) 824

בַּר pure, clean (3 · 6) 141 I

הֵאִיר to lighten (15 · 34 · 40) 21 אור

יִרְאָה 10 fear (8 · 45) 432

עַד לָעַד = forever (29 · 48) 723 I

צָדַק to be just (3 · 22 · 41) 842

נֶחְמָד 11 to be desirable (1 · 4 · 21) 326

פַּז refined or pure gold (3 · 9) 808

מָתוֹק sweet (1 · 12) 608

נֹפֶת flowing honey, honey from the
combs (1 · 5) 661

צוּף honeycomb (1 · 2) 847 I

נִזְהָר 12 to be instructed, warned (1 · 8 · 21)
264 II

עֵקֶב gain, reward (5 · 15) 784

שְׁגִיאָה 13 error (1 · 1) 993

נקה to hold innocent, acquit (1 · 18 · 43)
667

זֵד 14 insolent, presumptuous (8 · 13)
267

חָשַׂךְ to keep, withhold (2 · 26 · 28)
362

נקה to be clean, free from guilt, innocent (1 · 24 · 43) 667

אֹמֶר 15 utterance, word (7 · 48) 56

הִגָּיוֹן meditation, musing (3 · 4) 212

גָּאַל redeemer, kinsman (2 · 44[?])
145 II

Psalm 20

שׂגב 2 to set on high (5 · 6 · 20) 960
עֵזֶר 3 help (11 · 21) 740
סעד to support, sustain (6 · 12 · 12) 703
דשׁן 4 to find fat; i.e., find acceptable (2 · 5 · 11) 206
דגל 6 to set up standard (1 · 2 · 4) 186 II
מִשְׁאָלָה request, petition (2 · 2) 982
מָשִׁיחַ 7 anointed (10 · 39) 603
יֵשַׁע salvation (20 · 36) 447
כָּרַע 9 to bow down (4 · 30 · 36) 502
התעודד to be restored (1 · 1 · 44) 728

Psalm 21

גִּיל 2 to rejoice (19 · 45 · 45) 162
תַּאֲוָה 3 desire (8 · 21) 16
אֲרֶשֶׁת desire, request (1 · 1) 77
מָנַע to withhold (2 · 25 · 29) 586
קדם 4 to come to meet (12 · 24 · 26) 869
עֲטָרָה crown, wreath (1 · 23) 742
פָּז refined or pure gold (3 · 9) 808
עַד 5 ever (29 · 48) 723 I
הוֹד 6 splendor, majesty (8 · 24) 217
הָדָר splendor, majesty (13 · 30) 214
שׁוה to set, place (4 · 5 · 5) 1001 II
עַד 7 לָעַד = forever (29 · 48) 723 I
חדה to make joyful (1 · 1 · 3) 292 II
נמוט 8 to be shaken, moved, overthrown (16 · 22 · 39) 556
שׂנא 9 enemy (12 · 41[?]) 971 שֹׂנֵא
תַּנּוּר 10 stove, fire pot (1 · 15) 1072
בָּלַע to swallow up; i.e., confuse, confound (2 · 20 · 41) 118
מְזִמָּה 12 device (5 · 19) 273
שְׁכֶם 13 back, shoulder (2 · 22) 1014 I
מֵיתָר cord, string (1 · 9) 452
זמר 14 to sing, make music (39 · 43 · 43) 274 I

Psalm 22

אַיֶּלָה 1 hind, doe (3 · 11) 19
שַׁחַר dawn (4 · 23) 1007
שְׁאָגָה 2 roaring (cry of distress) (2 · 7) 980
דּוּמִיָּה 3 repose (4 · 4) 189
פלט 5 to deliver (19 · 24 · 27) 812
תּוֹלֵעָה 7 worm, grub (1 · 41) 1069
בָּזָה to despise (6 · 31 · 42) 102
הלעיג 8 to mock, deride (1 · 5 · 18) 541
הפטיר to separate (1 · 1 · 9) 809
הניע to shake, wag (4 · 14 · 38) 631
גלל 9 to roll (2 · 10 · 17) 164 II
פלט to deliver (19 · 24 · 27) 812
גֹחִי 10 ptc. of גיח to draw forth (1 · 1[?]) 161
שַׁד breast (1 · 21) 994
רֶחֶם 11 womb (3 · 33) 933
עֹזֵר 12 help, helper (7 · 19) 740 עזר
אַבִּיר 13 mighty, valiant (5 · 17) 7
כתר to surround (1 · 3 · 6) 509
פצה 14 to part, open (5 · 15 · 15) 822
אַרְיֵה lion (5 · 45) 71
טָרַף to tear, rend (4 · 19 · 24) 382
שָׁאַג to roar (4 · 20 · 20) 980
התפרד 15 to be divided, separated, from each other (2 · 4 · 26) 825
דּוֹנַג wax (3 · 3) 200
נָמֵס to faint, grow fearful (4 · 19 · 21) 587 מסס
מֵעֶה inwards, inward part (3 · 31) 588
חֶרֶשׂ 16 earthen potsherds (1 · 16) 360
מַלְקוֹחַ jaw (1 · 1) 544
שׁפת to set (1 · 5 · 5) 1046
כֶּלֶב 17 dog (5 · 32) 476
מֵרַע evildoer (9 · 18) 949 רעע Hiph. 2
הקּיף to surround, encompass (4 · 16 · 17) 668 II
אֲרִי lion (1 · 36) 71
לְבוּשׁ 19 garment, clothing (6 · 30) 528

418

אֱיָלוּת 20 help (1 · 1) 33

עֶזְרָה help (14 · 26) 740 I

חוּשׁ to make haste (8 · 15 · 21) 301 I

כֶּלֶב 21 dog (5 · 32) 476

יָחִיד only one (4 · 21) 402

אַרְיֵה 22 lion (5 · 45) 71

רֵמִים wild oxen (3 · 9) 910 רְאֵם

יָרֵא 24 afraid (27 · 46) 431

גוּר to stand in awe (2 · 10 · 10) 158 III

בָּזָה 25 to despise (6 · 31 · 42) 102

שָׁקַץ to detest (1 · 6 · 6) 1055

עֱנוּת affliction (1 · 1) 776

שׁוֵּעַ to cry for help (9 · 21 · 21[?]) 1002

יָרֵא 26 afraid (27 · 46) 431

עָנָו 27 poor, afflicted, meek (13 · 22) 776

עַד לָעַד = forever (29 · 48) 723 I

אֶפֶס 28 ends, extreme limits (6 · 27) 67

מְלוּכָה 29 kingship, royalty (1 · 24) 574

דָּשֵׁן 30 subst. = vigorous, stalwart ones (2 · 3) 206

כָּרַע to bow (4 · 30 · 36) 502

Psalm 23

חָסֵר 1 to want, be in want (2 · 19 · 23) 341

נָאוֹת 2 pastures, meadows (5 · 45[?]) 627 II נָוֶה

דֶּשֶׁא grass (24B14) 206

הרביץ to cause to lie down (1 · 6 · 30) 918

מְנוּחָה rest, quietness (4 · 21) 629

נהל to lead (to a watering place and cause to rest there) (2 · 9 · 10) 624

הנחה 3 to lead, guide (12 · 26 · 40) 634

מַעְגָּל track (4 · 13) 722

גַּיְא 4 valley (2 · 48) 161

צַלְמָוֶת deep shadow, darkness (4 · 18) 853

מִשְׁעֶנֶת staff (1 · 12) 1044

צֹרֵר 5 vexer, harasser (12 · 17) 865 III צרר

דשׁן to make fat; i.e., anoint (2 · 5 · 11) 206

כּוֹס cup (5 · 31) 468

רְוָיָה saturation; i.e., well-filled (2 · 2) 924

Psalm 24

מְלֹא 1 fullness (5 · 38) 571

גֵּבֶל world (15 · 36) 385

יָסַד 2 to found, establish (7 · 20 · 41) 413

נָקִי 4 free from guilt, clean, innocent (5 · 43) 667

בַּר pure, clean (3 · 6) 141 II

מִרְמָה deceit, treachery (14 · 39) 941

יֶשַׁע 5 salvation (20 · 36) 447

עִזּוּז 8 mighty, powerful (1 · 2) 739

Psalm 25

עָלַץ 2 to rejoice, exult (4 · 8 · 8) 763

קוה 3 Qal, to wait (3 · 6 · 45) 875 I

בגד to act or deal treacherously, faithlessly, deceitfully (5 · 49 · 49) 93

רֵיקָם in vain, without effect (2 · 16)

יֶשַׁע 5 salvation (20 · 36) 447

קוה Piel, to wait for, look eagerly for (12 · 39 · 45) 875 I

רַחֲמִים 6 compassion (11 · 38) 933

נְעוּרִים 7 youth (8 · 46) 655

טוּב goodness (7 · 32) 375

הורה 8 to direct, teach, instruct (8 · 45 · 45) 434

חַטָּא sinner (6 · 19) 308

עָנָו 9 poor, afflicted, meek (13 · 22) 776

עֵדָה 10 testimony (25 · 32) 730

סלח 11 to forgive, pardon (2 · 33 · 46) 699

יָרֵא 12 afraid (27 · 46) 431

הורה to direct, teach, instruct (8 · 45 · 45) 434

סוֹד 14 secret counsel, intimacy (6 · 21) 691

יָרֵא afraid (27 · 46) 431

רֶשֶׁת 15 net (8 · 22) 440

יָחִיד 16 solitary (4 · 12) 402

הַרְחִיב 17 to enlarge (6 · 21 · 25) 931

מְצוּקָה straits, stress (5 · 7) 848

עֳנִי 18 affliction (10 · 36) 777

רבב 19 to be, become, many (6 · 23 · 24) 912 I

שִׂנְאָה hating, hatred (4 · 17) 971

חָסָה 20 to seek refuge (25 · 37 · 37) 340

תֹּם 21 integrity, completeness (7 · 23) 1070

יֹשֶׁר rightness, uprightness (2 · 14) 449

קוה *Piel*, to wait, look eagerly, for (12 · 39 · 45) 875 I

Psalm 26

תֹּם 1 integrity, completeness (7 · 23) 1070

מעד to slip (3 · 5 · 7) 588

בחן 2 to prove, test, try (9 · 24 · 28) 103

נִסָּה to try, test (6 · 36 · 36) 650

צָרַף to test (7 · 18 · 21) 864

כִּלְיָה kidney (5 · 31) 480

לְנֶגֶד 3 before, in front of (13 · 32) 617 נֶגֶד 2.b.

מַת 4 male, man (3 · 22) 607

נעלם to conceal oneself; i.e., one's thoughts (1 · 11 · 29) 761 I

מֵרַע 5 evildoer (9 · 18) 949 רעע *Hiph.* 2

נִקָּיוֹן 6 innocence, freedom from guilt (2 · 5) 667

תּוֹדָה 7 thanksgiving, praise (12 · 32) 392

נִפְלָאוֹת wonderful acts (27 · 44) 810 פלא

מָעוֹן 8 dwelling (5 · 18) 731

חַטָּא 9 sinner (6 · 19) 308

זִמָּה 10 evil device (2 · 28) 273

שֹׁחַד bribe (2 · 23) 1005

תֹּם 11 integrity, completeness (7 · 23) 1070

מִישׁוֹר 12 level place (5 · 23) 449

מַקְהֵל assembly (2 · 2) 879

Psalm 27

יֵשַׁע 1 salvation (20 · 36) 447

מִמִּי from whom? (2 · 3) 566 מִי

מָעוֹז refuge, protection (9 · 36) 731

פָּחַד to be in dread (5 · 23 · 26) 808

מֵרַע 2 evildoer (9 · 18) 949 רעע *Hiph.* 2

נֹעַם 4 delightfulness (2 · 7) 653

בקר to contemplate; seek, look for (1 · 7 · 7) 133

צָפַן 5 to hide (7 · 23 · 28) 860

סֹךְ covert, lair (3 · 4) 697

סֵתֶר hiding place, shelter (10 · 35) 712

תְּרוּעָה 6 shout of joy (5 · 36) 929

זמר to sing, make music (39 · 43 · 43) 274 I

עֶזְרָה 9 help (14 · 26) 740 I

נָטַשׁ to forsake, abandon (3 · 33 · 40) 643

יֵשַׁע salvation (20 · 36) 447

הוֹרָה 11 to direct, teach, instruct (8 · 45 · 45) 434

נחה to lead, bring (6 · 14 · 40) 634

מִישׁוֹר level place (5 · 23) 449

שׁוֹרֵר watcher (insidious) (5 · 5) 1004

יָפֵחַ 12 breathing or puffing out (1 · 1) 422

לוּלֵא 13 if not, unless (1 · 4) 530

טוּב good things (coll.) (7 · 32) 375

קוה 14 *Piel*. to wait, look eagerly, for (12 · 39 · 45) 875 I

הֶאֱמִיץ to be strong, exhibit strength (2 · 2 · 41) 54

Psalm 28

חרש 1 to be deaf (6 · 7 · 7) 361 I

חשׁה to be silent (2 · 7 · 16) 364

נִמְשַׁל to be like, similar (4 · 5 · 15) 605 I

תַּחֲנוּן 2 supplication for favor (8 · 18) 337

שׁוע to cry for help (9 · 21 · 21[?]) 1002

דְּבִיר hindmost chamber = Holy of Holies (1 · 16) 184

420

מָשַׁךְ 3 to lead, drag off (5 · 30 · 36) 604

פֹּעַל 4 deed, thing done (11 · 37) 821

רֹעַ evil, badness (1 · 19) 947

מַעֲלָל deed, practice (5 · 41) 760

גְּמוּל dealing, recompence (4 · 19) 168

פְּעֻלָּה 5 work, deed (3 · 14) 821

הָרַס to throw down, overthrow (2 · 30 · 43) 248

תַּחֲנוּן 6 supplication for favor (8 · 18) 337

עלז 7 to exult, triumph (7 · 16 · 16) 759

מָעוֹז 8 refuge, protection (9 · 36) 731

מָשִׁיחַ anointed (10 · 39) 603

Psalm 29

יהב 1 to ascribe (8 · 33 · 33) 396

יהב 2 to ascribe (8 · 33 · 33) 396

הֲדָרָה adornment (2 · 5) 214

הִרְעִים 3 to cause to thunder (2 · 8 · 11) 947

הָדָר 4 splendor, majesty (13 · 30) 214

הרקיד 6 to make to skip (1 · 1 · 9) 955

עֵגֶל calf (3 · 35) 722

רְאֵם wild ox (3 · 9) 910

חצב 7 to divide, cleave (1 · 14 · 17) 345

לֶהָבָה flame (4 · 19) 529

החיל 8 to cause to be in anguish (2 · 2 · 47) 296 חול I

חולל 9 to bear, bring forth (2 · 7 · 47) 296 חול I

אַיָּלָה hind, doe (3 · 11) 19

חָשַׂף to strip, lay bare (1 · 10 · 10) 362

מַבּוּל 10 flood (1 · 13) 550

Psalm 30

חֲנֻכָּה 1 dedication, consecration (1 · 8) 335

דלה 2 to draw up (1 · 1 · 5) 194

שׁוע 3 to cry for help (9 · 21 · 21[?]) 1002

זמר 5 to sing, make music (39 · 43 · 43) 274 I

חָסִיד pious, godly (25 · 32) 339

זֵכֶר remembrance, memory (11 · 23) 271

רֶגַע 6 moment (3 · 22) 921

בְּכִי weeping (3 · 32) 113

רִנָּה ringing cry (15 · 33) 943

שַׁלְוּ 7 ease, prosperity (1 · 1) 1017

נמוט to be shaken, moved, overthrown (16 · 22 · 39) 556

נבהל 8 to be disturbed, dismayed, terrified (8 · 24 · 39) 96

בֶּצַע 10 profit, unjust gain (2 · 23) 130

שַׁחַת pit (9 · 23) 1001

עֹזֵר 11 help, helper (7 · 19) 740 עזר

מִסְפֵּד 12 wailing (1 · 16) 704

מָחוֹל dance (3 · 6) 298

שַׂק sack cloth (3 · 48) 974

אזר to gird (3 · 6 · 16) 25

זמר 13 to sing, make music (39 · 43 · 43) 274 I

דמם to be silent (6 · 23 · 30) 198 I

Psalm 31

חָסָה 2 to seek refuge (25 · 37 · 37) 340

פלט to deliver (19 · 24 · 27) 812

מְהֵרָה 3 hastily, quickly (3 · 20) 555

מָעוֹז refuge (9 · 36) 731

מְצוּדָה fastness, stronghold (7 · 18) 845 II

מְצוּדָה 4 fastness, stronghold (7 · 18) 845 II

הנחה to lead, guide (12 · 26 · 40) 634

נהל to lead, guide (2 · 9 · 10) 624

רֶשֶׁת 5 net (8 · 22) 440

זוּ which (10 · 15) 262

טָמַן to hide, conceal (7 · 28 · 31) 380

מָעוֹז refuge (9 · 36) 731

גִּיל 8 to rejoice (19 · 45 · 45) 162

עֳנִי affliction (10 · 36) 777

מֶרְחָב 9 broad roomy place (3 · 6) 932

עשׁשׁ 10 to waste away (3 · 3 · 3) 799

כַּעַס vexation, grief (4 · 25) 495

יָגוֹן 11 sorrow, grief (4 · 14) 387

אֲנָחָה sighing, groaning (4 · 11) 58

עשׁשׁ to waste away (3 · 3 · 3) 799

צָרַר 12 vexer, harasser (12 · 17) 865 III צרר

שָׁכֵן neighbor (6 · 20) 1015

פַּחַד dread (9 · 49) 808

נדד to retreat, flee (4 · 21 · 25) 622 I

דִּבָּה 14 whispering (1 · 9) 179

מָגוֹר fear, terror (1 · 8) 159 II

נוסד to sit together, sit in conclave (2 · 2 · 2[?]) 413

יַחַד together, altogether (14 · 44) 403

זָמַם to purpose, devise (3 · 13 · 13) 273

הֵאִיר 17 to make shine (15 · 34 · 40) 21

דמם 18 to be still (6 · 23 · 30) 198 I

נאלם 19 to be made dumb (3 · 8 · 9) 47

עָתָק forward, arrogant (3 · 4) 801

גַּאֲוָה pride, haughtiness (7 · 19) 144

בּוּז contempt (5 · 11) 100 II

טוּב 20 goodness (7 · 32) 375

צָפַן to hide (7 · 23 · 28) 860

יָרֵא afraid (27 · 46) 431

חָסָה to seek refuge (25 · 37 · 37) 340

סֵתֶר 21 hiding place, shelter (10 · 35) 712

רֹכֶס [dub.] snare, band; league, conspiracy (1 · 1) 940

צָפַן to hide (7 · 23 · 28) 860

סֻכָּה booth (2 · 31) 697

הִפְלִיא 22 to do wondrously, to make wonderful (3 · 10 · 24) 810

מָצוֹר encolsure; עיר מ׳ = entrenched city (2 · 25) 848 I

חפז 23 inf. w ב = in my alarm (2 · 6 · 9) 342

נגרז to be cut off, cut off (1 · 1 · 1) 173

מִנֶּגֶד from before (2 · 26) 617 נֶגֶד 2.c

אָכֵן surely, truly (3 · 18) 38

תַּחֲנוּן supplication for favor (8 · 18) 337

שׁוּע to cry for help (9 · 21 · 21[?]) 1002

חָסִיד 24 pious, godly (25 · 32) 339

אֱמוּנִים faithful ones (2 · 3[?]) 52 I אמן Qal. 4.b

גַּאֲוָה pride, haughiness (7 · 19) 144

הֶאֱמִיץ 25 to be strong, exhibit strength (2 · 2 · 41) 54

יחל *Piel.* to wait for, hope for (14 · 25 · 42) 403

Psalm 32

מַשְׂכִּיל 1 contemplative poem (14 · 14) 968

אֶשֶׁר happiness, blessedness (19 · 45[?]) 80

חֲטָאָה sin (3 · 8) 308

אֶשֶׁר 2 happiness, blessedness (19 · 45[?]) 80

רְמִיָּה deceit, treachery (6 · 15) 941

הֶחֱרִשׁ 3 to be silent (2 · 38 · 46) 361 I

בלה to wear out (2 · 11 · 16) 115

שְׁאָגָה roaring (2 · 7) 980

לְשַׁד 4 juice (1 · 2) 545

חַרְבוֹן drought (1 · 1) 351

קַיִץ summer (2 · 20) 884

חָסִיד 6 pious, godly (25 · 32) 339

שֶׁטֶף flood (1 · 6) 1009

סֵתֶר 7 hiding place, shelter (10 · 35) 712

צַר straits, distress (3 · 20) 865 II

רֹן ringing cry (1 · 1) 943

פלט to deliver (19 · 24 · 27) 812

הורה 8 to direct, teach, instruct (8 · 45 · 45) 434

זוּ which (10 · 15) 262

פֶּרֶד 9 mule (1 · 14) 825

מֶתֶג bridle (1 · 5) 607

רֶסֶן halter (1 · 4) 943

עֲדִי trappings (2 · 14) 725

בלם to curb, hold in (1 · 1 · 1) 117

מַכְאוֹב 10 pain (3 · 16) 456

גִּיל 11 to rejoice (19 · 45 · 45) 162

Psalm 33

נָאוֶה 1 comely, seemly (2 · 9) 610

כִּנּוֹר 2 lyre (13 · 41) 490

נֵבֶל harp (8 · 27) 614 II

עָשׂוֹר a ten; עָשׂוֹר נֵבֶל = a ten-stringed harp
(3 · 15) 797

זמר to sing, make music (39 · 43 · 43)
274 I

נגן 3 to play (1 · 13 · 14) 618

תְּרוּעָה shout of joy (5 · 36) 929

כנס 7 to gather (1 · 7 · 11) 488

נֵד heap (2 · 6) 622

תְּהוֹם deep, sea, abyss (12 · 36) 1062

גור 8 to stand in awe (2 · 10 · 10) 158 III

תֵּבֵל world (15 · 36) 385

הֵפִיר 10 to frustrate, make ineffectual
(2 · 3 · 3[?]) 830 I פרר Hiph. 2.a

הֵנִיא to frustrate, hinder (2 · 8 · 8) 626 נוא

אֶשֶׁר 12 happiness, blessedness (19 · 45[?])
80

מָכוֹן 14 fixed place, place (4 · 17) 467

הִשְׁגִּיחַ to gaze (1 · 3 · 3) 993

יָצַר 15 to form, fashion (6 · 41 · 44)
427

יַחַד together, altogether (14 · 44)
403

תְּשׁוּעָה 17 deliverance (13 · 34) 448

יָרֵא 18 afraid (27 · 46) 431

יחל Piel, to wait for, hope for
(14 · 25 · 42) 403

חכה 20 to wait for, await (2 · 13 · 14)
314

עֵזֶר help (11 · 21) 740 I

יחל 22 Piel, to wait for, hope for
(14 · 25 · 42) 403

Psalm 34

שָׁנָה 1 to change, alter (2 · 9 · 26) 1039 I

טַעַם judgment, sense (2 · 13) 381

גרש Piel, to drive out, away (3 · 35 · 48)
176

עָנָו 3 poor, afflicted, meek (13 · 22) 776

מְגוֹרָה 5 fear, terror (1 · 3) 159

נהר 6 to beam, shine (1 · 3 · 3) 626 II

חפר to be abashed, ashamed (7 · 13 · 17)
344 II

יָרֵא 8 afraid (27 · 46) 431

חלץ to rescue, deliver (10 · 14 · 27) 322 I

טָעַם 9 to taste (1 · 11 · 11) 380

אֶשֶׁר happiness, blessedness (19 · 45[?])
80

חָסָה to seek refuge (25 · 37 · 37) 340

מַחְסוֹר 10 lack, want (1 · 13) 341

יָרֵא afraid (27 · 46) 431

כְּפִיר 11 young lion (6 · 31) 498

רוש to be in want, poor (1 · 2 · 3) 930

רָעֵב to be hungry (2 · 14 · 16) 944

חָסֵר to lack (2 · 19 · 23) 341

יִרְאָה 12 fear (8 · 45) 432

חָפֵץ 13 delighting in, taking pleasure in
(6 · 12) 343

מִרְמָה 14 deceit, treachery (14 · 39) 941

שַׁוְעָה 16 cry for help (6 · 11) 1003

זֵכֶר 17 remembrance, memory (11 · 23) 271

דַּכָּא 19 contrite (2 · 3) 194 I

אָשַׁם 22 to be held guilty, bear punishment
(2 · 31 · 33) 79

אָשַׁם 23 to be held guilty, bear punishment
(2 · 31 · 33) 79

חָסָה to seek refuge (25 · 37 · 37) 340

Psalm 35

יָרִיב 1 adversary (1 · 3) 937 I

צִנָּה 2 large shield (3 · 20) 857 III

423

עֶזְרָה help (14 · 26) 740 I

הֵרִיק 3 to empty out (2 · 17 · 19) 937

חֲנִית spear (3 · 47) 333

נכלם 4 to be put to shame, dishonored, confounded (5 · 26 · 38) 483

נָסוֹג to be turned back, repulsed (6 · 14 · 25) 690

אָחוֹר backwards, behind (12 · 41) 30

חפר to be abashed, ashamed (7 · 13 · 17) 344 II

מֹץ 5 chaff (2 · 8) 558

דחה to push (4 · 4 · 6) 190

חֲלַקְלַקּוֹת 6 slipperiness (1 · 4) 325

חִנָּם 7 gratuitously, without cause (6 · 32) 336

טָמַן to hide, conceal (7 · 28 · 31) 380

שַׁחַת pit (9 · 23) 1001

רֶשֶׁת net (8 · 22) 440

חָפַר to dig (2 · 23 · 23) 343 I

שׁוֹאָה 8 devastation, ruin (3 · 12) 996

רֶשֶׁת net (8 · 22) 440

טָמַן to hide, conceal (7 · 28 · 31) 380

גִּיל 9 to rejoice (19 · 45 · 45) 162

שׂוּשׂ to exult, rejoice (7 · 27) 965

גָּזַל 10 to seize, plunder (2 · 29 · 30) 159 I

שָׁכוּל 12 bereavement, loss of children (1 · 3) 1013

לְבוּשׁ 13 garment, clothing (6 · 30) 528

שַׂק sackcloth (3 · 48) 974

צוֹם fast, fasting (3 · 25) 847

חֵיק bosom (4 · 38) 300

אָבֵל 14 mourning (1 · 8) 5 I

קָדַר to be dark (4 · 13 · 17) 871

שׁחח to bow (4 · 12 · 18[?]) 1005

צֶלַע 15 limping, stumbling (2 · 4) 854

נֵכֶה smitten one, cripple (1 · 1) 646

דמם to be silent (6 · 23 · 30) 198 I

חָנֵף 16 profane, godless (1 · 13) 338

לָעֵג mocking, mocker (1 · 2) 541

מָעוֹג cake (1 · 2) 728

חָרַק to gnash, grind (3 · 5 · 5) 359

כַּמָּה 17 for how long? (3 · 13) 552 מָה 4.c

שׁוֹא ravage (1 · 1) 996

כְּפִיר young lion (6 · 31) 498

יָחִיד only one (4 · 12) 402

עָצוּם 18 numerous, (countless) (3 · 31) 783

שָׂנֵא 19 enemy (12 · 41[?]) 971

חִנָּם gratuitously, without cause (6 · 32) 336

קָרַץ to nip, pinch (1 · 4 · 5) 902

רָגַע 20 restful, quiet (1 · 1) 921

מִרְמָה deceit, treachery (14 · 39) 941

הִרְחִיב 21 to enlarge (6 · 21 · 25) 931

הֶאָח aha! (4 · 9) 210

חרשׁ 22 to be silent (6 · 7 · 47) 361 II

הֵקִיץ 23 to awake (7 · 22 · 23) 884 I

הֶאָח 25 aha! (4 · 9) 210

בִּלַּע to confuse, swallow up (2 · 20 · 41) 118

חפר 26 to be abashed, ashamed (7 · 13 · 17) 344 II

שָׂמֵחַ glad, joyful, merry (3 · 21) 970

בֹּשֶׁת shame (7 · 30) 102

כְּלִמָּה ignominy, reproach (7 · 30) 484

חָפֵץ 27 taking pleasure in, delighting in (6 · 12) 343

הגה 28 to utter (10 · 23 · 25) 211 I

Psalm 36

פַּחַד 2 dread (9 · 49) 808

לְנֶגֶד in the sight of, before (13 · 32) נֶגֶד 2.b 617

הֶחֱלִיק 3 to make smooth (2 · 7 · 9) 325 II

מִרְמָה 4 deceit, treachery (14 · 39) 941

מִשְׁכָּב 5 couch, bed (4 · 46) 1012

התיצב to station oneself, take one's stand (4 · 48 · 48) 426

שַׁחַק 6 cloud (9 · 21) 1007

תְּהוֹם 7 deep, sea, abyss (12 · 36) 1062

יָקָר 8 precious, prized (4 · 35) 429

חָסָה to seek refuge (25 · 37 · 37) 340

רוה 9 to be saturated, take one's fill (1 · 3 · 14) 924

דֶּשֶׁן fatness (3 · 15) 206

עֵדֶן delight (1 · 3) 726

מָקוֹר 10 spring (2 · 18) 881

מָשַׁךְ 11 to draw out, prolong (5 · 30 · 36) 604

גַּאֲוָה 12 pride, haughtiness (7 · 19) 144

הניד to cause to wander (1 · 3 · 26) 626 נוד

דחה 13 to be thrust down (1 · 1 · 6) 190

Psalm 37

מֵרַע 1 evildoer (9 · 18) 949 רעע Hiph. 2

קָנָא to be envious of (3 · 30 · 34) 888

עַוְלָה injustice, wrong (9 · 32) 732

חָצִיר 2 grass (6 · 18) 348 II

מְהֵרָה hastily, quickly (3 · 20) 555

מלל to wither, hang down (1 · 2 · 4) 576 III

יֶרֶק green, greenness (1 · 8) 438

דֶּשֶׁא grass (2 · 14) 206

נָבֵל to droop, wither and fall, fade (3 · 19 · 23) 615

התענג 4 to take exquisite delight in (2 · 9 · 10) 772

מִשְׁאָלָה request, petition (2 · 2) 982

גלל 5 to roll (2 · 10 · 17) 164 II

צָהֳרַיִם 6 midday, noon (3 · 23) 843 צֹהַר I

דמה 7 to be silent (6 · 23 · 30) 198 I

הִתְחוֹלֵל to wait longingly (1 · 1 · 5[?]) 296 חול

מִזְמָה wickedness (5 · 19) 273

הרפה 8 to refrain, let alone (3 · 21 · 45) 951

מֵרַע 9 evildoer (9 · 18) 949 רעע Hiph. 2

קיה to wait (3 · 6 · 45) 875 I

עָנָו 11 poor, afflicted, meek (13 · 22) 776

התענג to take exquisite delight in (2 · 9 · 10) 772

זָמַם 12 to purpose, devise (3 · 13 · 13) 273

חָרַק to gnash, grind (3 · 5 · 5) 359

שָׂחַק 13 to laugh (4 · 18 · 36) 965

טבח 14 to slay, kill ruthlessly (1 · 11 · 11) 370

סָמַךְ 17 to support, uphold, sustain (10 · 41 · 48) 701

רְעָבוֹן 19 hunger, famine (1 · 3) 944

יָקָר 20 precious, prized (4 · 35) 429

כַּר pasture (2 · 3) 499 II

עָשָׁן smoke (4 · 25) 798 I

לוה 21 to borrow (1 · 5 · 14) 531 II

מִצְעָד 23 step (1 · 3) 857

הטול 24 to be cast, hurled down (1 · 4 · 14) 376

סָמַךְ to support, uphold, sustain (10 · 41 · 48) 701

זָקֵן 25 to be or become old (1 · 25 · 27) 278

הלוה 26 to lend (2 · 9 · 14) 531

חָסִיד 28 pious, godly (25 · 32) 339

עַד 29 לְעַד = forever (29 · 48) 723 I

הגה 30 to utter (10 · 23 · 25) 211 I

מעד 31 to slip (3 · 5 · 7) 588

אָשׁוּר step, going (6 · 10) 81

צפה 32 to spy, keep watch (2 · 9 · 18) 859 I

הִרְשִׁיעַ 33 to condemn as guilty (3 · 25 · 34) 957 vb. demon.

קוה 34 Piel, to wait, look eagerly for (12 · 39 · 45) 875 I

עָרִיץ 35 ruthless, awe-inspiring (3 · 20) 792

התערה ptc = pouring oneself; i.e., pouring oneself out (1 · 2 · 15) 788

אֶזְרָח native (noun) (1 · 17) 280

רַעֲנָן luxuriant, fresh (4 · 19) 947

תָּם 37 complete, having integrity (2 · 15) 1070

פָּשַׁע 38 to transgress (2 · 40 · 41) 833

תְּשׁוּעָה 39 deliverance (13 · 34) 448

מָעוֹז refuge (9 · 36) 731

פלט 40 to deliver (19 · 24 · 27) 812

חָסָה   to seek refuge (25 · 37 · 37) 340

Psalm 38

קֶצֶף   2 wrath (2 · 28) 893

יָסַר   to chasten chastise (7 · 30 · 41) 415

נָחַת   3 to descend (1 · 3 · 8) 639

נָחַת   to penetrate (1 · 1 · 8) 639

מְתֹם   4 soundness (2 · 4) 1071

זַעַם   indignation (4 · 22) 276

מַשָּׂא   5 load, burden (1 · 45) 672

כָּבֵד   heavy (1 · 39) 458

הִבְאִישׁ   6 to become stinking (1 · 7 · 16) 92

נָמַק   to fester (1 · 9 · 10) 596 מקק

חַבּוּרָה   stripe, blow, stroke (1 · 7) 289

אִוֶּלֶת   folly (2 · 25) 17

נַעֲוָה   7 to be bent, bowed down, twisted (1 · 4 · 17[?]) 730 I

שָׁחַח   to bow (4 · 12 · 18[?]) 1005

קָדַר   to be dark (4 · 13 · 17) 871

כֶּסֶל   8 loins (1 · 7) 492

נִקְלֶה   *Niph.* ptc. = with burning (1 · 1 · 4) 885 I קלה

מְתֹם   soundness (2 · 4) 1071

נָפוּג   9 to be benumbed (1 · 1 · 4) 806

נִדְכָּה   to be crushed, broken (2 · 2 · 5) 194

שָׁאַג   to roar (4 · 20 · 20) 980

נְהָמָה   groaning (1 · 2) 625

תַּאֲוָה   10 desire (8 · 21) 16 I

אֲנָחָה   sighing, groaning (4 · 11) 58

סְחַרְחַר   11 to palpitate (1 · 1 · 5) 695 סחר

אֹהֵב   12 friend (12 · 36) 12

מִנֶּגֶד   at a distance from (3 · 26) 617 נגד 2.c

נָקַשׁ   13 to strike, take aim (2 · 2 · 5) 669

הַוָּה   chasm, ruin, destruction (8 · 13) 217

מִרְמָה   deceit, treachery (14 · 39) 941

הָגָה   to utter (10 · 23 · 25) 211 I

חֵרֵשׁ   14 deaf (2 · 9) 361

אִלֵּם   dumb (1 · 6) 48

אֱהִי   15 = אֶהְיֶה I am

תּוֹכַחַת   argument, impeachment (3 · 24) 407

הוֹחִיל   16 to wait for, hope for (5 · 15 · 42) 403

מוֹט   17 to totter, slip (8 · 15 · 39) 556

צֶלַע   18 limping, stumbling (2 · 4) 854

מַכְאוֹב   pain (3 · 16) 456

דָּאַג   19 to be anxious, concerned (1 · 7 · 7) 178

עָצַם   20 to be numerous, vast (5 · 16 · 18) 782

רָבַב   to be or become many (6 · 23 · 24) 912 I

שָׂנֵא   enemy (12 · 41[?]) 971 שָׂנֵא

שָׂטַן   21 to be, act, as adversary (5 · 6 · 6) 966

חוּשׁ   23 to make haste (8 · 15 · 21) 301 I

עֶזְרָה   help (14 · 26) 740 I

תְּשׁוּעָה   deliverance (13 · 34) 448

Psalm 39

מַחְסוֹם   2 muzzle (1 · 1) 340

בְּעוֹד   while, yet (3 · 20) 728 2.a

לְנֶגֶד   in the sight of, in the presence of (13 · 32) 617 נגד 2.b

נֶאֱלָם   3 to be dumb (3 · 8 · 9) 47

דּוּמִיָּה   silence (4 · 4) 189

הֶחֱשָׁה   to be silent, exhibit silence (1 · 9 · 16) 364

כְּאֵב   pain (1 · 6) 456

נֶעְכָּר   to be stirred up (1 · 2 · 14) 747

חַם   4 to be or grow warm (1 · 23 · 26[?]) 328 חמם

הָגִיג   musing (2 · 2) 211

חָדֵל   5 ceasing, transient (1 · 3) 293

טֶפַח   6 span, handbreadth (1 · 9) 381

חֶלֶד   duration of life (4 · 5) 317

כְּאַיִן   as nothing (2 · 7) 34 אין I

צֶלֶם   7 image (2 · 17) 853

הָמָה	to bustle about, be boisterous (11 · 33 · 33) 242
צבר	to heap up (1 · 7 · 7) 840
קוה	8 *Piel*, to wait, look eagerly, for (12 · 39 · 45) 875 I
תּוֹחֶלֶת	hope (1 · 6) 404
נָבָל	9 senseless (5 · 18) 614 I
נאלם	10 to be dumb (3 · 8 · 9) 47
תִּגְרָה	11 contention, strife, hostility (1 · 1) 173
תּוֹכַחַת	12 correction, rebuke (3 · 24) 407
יִסֵּר	to chasten, chastise (7 · 30 · 41) 415
המסה	to consume, cause to vanish (3 · 4 · 4) 587
עָשׁ	moth (1 · 7) 799 II
חָמַד	to desire, take pleasure in (2 · 16 · 21) 326
שַׁוְעָה	13 cry for help (6 · 11) 1003
הֶאֱזִין	to listen, give ear (15 · 41 · 41) 24
דִּמְעָה	tears (8 · 23) 199
חרש	to be silent (6 · 7 · 47) 361 II
תּוֹשָׁב	sojourner (1 · 14) 444
השעה	14 to cause to gaze (1 · 1 · 15) 1043
הבליג	to smile, look cheerful (1 · 4 · 4) 114
בְּטֶרֶם	before (3 · 39) 382 טֶרֶם 2

Psalm 40

קוה	2 *Piel*, to wait, look eagerly, for (12 · 39 · 45) 875 I
שַׁוְעָה	cry for help (6 · 11) 1003
שָׁאוֹן	3 roar, din, crash (4 · 18) 981
טִיט	mud, mire (3 · 13) 376
יָוֵן	mire (2 · 2) 401
אָשׁוּר	step, going (6 · 10) 81
אֶשֶׁר	5 happiness, blessedness (19 · 45[?]) 80
מִבְטָח	confidence (3 · 15) 105
רַהַב	storm, arrogance (3 · 7) 923
שׂוּט	to swerve, fall away (1 · 1) 962

כָּזָב	lie, falsehood (6 · 31) 469
נִפְלָאוֹת	6 wonderful acts (27 · 44) 810 פלא
עָצַם	to be numerous, vast (5 · 16 · 18) 782 I
כָּרָה	7 to dig (4 · 13 · 14) 500 I
חַטָּאָה	sin offering (3 · 8) 308
מְגִלָּה	8 roll (1 · 21) 166
מֵעֶה	9 inwards, inward part (3 · 31) 588
בִּשֵּׂר	10 to preach, herald as glad tidings (2 · 14 · 15) 142
כלא	to restrain (4 · 14 · 17) 476
תְּשׁוּעָה	11 deliverance (13 · 34) 448
כִּחֵד	to hide, conceal w ל = conceal from (2 · 15 · 32) 470
כלא	12 to withhold (4 · 14 · 17) 476
רַחֲמִים	compassion (11 · 38) 933
אפף	13 to surround, encompass (3 · 5 · 5) 67
הִשִּׂיג	to overtake (4 · 49 · 49) 673
עָצַם	to be numerous, vast (5 · 16 · 18) 782
שַׂעֲרָה	a hair (2 · 7) 972
עֶזְרָה	14 help (14 · 26) 740 I
חוּשׁ	to make haste (8 · 15 · 21) 301 I
חפר	15 to be abashed, ashamed (7 · 13 · 17) 344 II
יַחַד	together, altogether (14 · 44) 403
ספה	to snatch away (1 · 8 · 18) 705
נָסוֹג	to be turned back, repulsed (6 · 14 · 25) 690 I
אָחוֹר	backwards, behind (12 · 41) 30
נכלם	to be put to shame, dishonored, confounded (5 · 26 · 38) 483
חָפֵץ	delighting in, taking pleasure in (6 · 12) 343
עֵקֶב	16 in consequence of, for (5 · 15) 784
בֹּשֶׁת	shame (7 · 30) 102
הֶאָח	aha! (4 · 9) 210
שׂוּשׂ	17 to exult, rejoice (7 · 27) 965
אֹהֵב	friend (12 · 36) 12 אהב
תְּשׁוּעָה	deliverance (13 · 34) 448
עֶזְרָה	18 help (14 · 26) 740 I

פלט   to deliver (19 · 24 · 27) 812

אָחַר   to delay, tarry (3 · 15 · 17) 29

Psalm 41

אֶשֶׁר   2 happiness, blessedness (19 · 45[?]) 80

דַּל   low, weak, poor, thin (5 · 48) 195

אשר   3 to be make happy, blessed (1 · 2 · 9) 80

סעד   4 to support, sustain (6 · 12 · 12) 703

עֶרֶשׂ   couch, divan (3 · 10) 793

דְּוָי   illness (1 · 2) 188

מִשְׁכָּב   couch, bed (4 · 46) 1012

חֲלִי   sickness, disease (1 · 24) 318

מָתַי   6 when? (13 · 42) 607

יַחַד   8 together, altogether (14 · 44) 403

התלחש   to whisper together (1 · 2 · 3) 538

שֹׂנֵא   enemy (12 · 41[?]) 971 שׂנא

בְּלִיַּעַל   9 base, wicked (3 · 27) 116

עָקֵב   10 heel; footprint (5 · 14) 784 I

הריע   12 to shout in triumph (9 · 40 · 44) 929 רוע

תֹּם   13 integrity, completeness (7 · 23) 1070

תמך   to hold up, support (4 · 20 · 21) 1069

אָמֵן   14 verily, truly (4 · 30) 53

Psalm 42

מַשְׂכִּיל   1 contemplative poem (14 · 14) 968

אַיָּל   2 hart, stag (1 · 11) 19

ערג   to long for (2 · 3 · 3) 788

אָפִיק   channel, stream bed, ravine (3 · 18) 67

צמא   3 to be thirsty (2 · 10 · 10) 854

מָתַי   when? (13 · 42) 607

דִּמְעָה   4 tears (8 · 23) 199

אַיֵּה   where? (5 · 44) 32

סָךְ   5 throng (1 · 1) 697

דדה   to walk deliberately (1 · 2 · 2) 186

רִנָּה   ringing cry (15 · 33) 943 I

תּוֹדָה   thanksgiving, praise (12 · 32) 392

חגג   to keep festival (2 · 16 · 16) 290

השתוחח   6 to be cast down, despairing (4 · 4 · 6) 1005 שחח

המה   to murmur (11 · 33 · 33) 242

הוחיל   to wait for, hope for (5 · 15 · 42) 403

השתוחח   7 to be cast down, despairing (4 · 4 · 6) 1005 שחח

מִצְעָר   Mizar [mountain near Hermon] (1 · 6) 859 II

תְּהוֹם   8 deep, sea, abyss (12 · 36) 1062

צִנּוֹר   [dub.] pipe, spout, conduit (1 · 2) 857

מִשְׁבָּר   breaker (3 · 5) 991

גַּל   pl. = waves (5 · 16) 164

קדר   10 to be dark (4 · 13 · 17) 871

לַחַץ   oppression (3 · 10) 537

רֶצַח   11 shattering (1 · 2) 954

חֵרֵף   to reproach (9 · 34 · 38) 357 I

צֹרֵר   vexer, harasser (12 · 17) 865 III צרר

אַיֵּה   where? (5 · 44) 32

השתוחח   12 to be cast down, despairing (4 · 4 · 6) 1005 שחח

המה   to murmur (11 · 33 · 33) 242

הוחיל   to wait for, hope for (5 · 15 · 42) 403

Psalm 43

חָסִיד   1 pious, godly (25 · 32) 339

מִרְמָה   deceit, treachery (14 · 39) 941

עַוְלָה   injustice, wrong (9 · 32) 732

פלט   to deliver (19 · 24 · 27) 812

מָעוֹז   2 refuge (9 · 731) 731

זָנַח   to reject, spurn (10 · 16 · 19) 276 I

קדר   to be dark (4 · 13 · 17) 871

לַחַץ   oppression (3 · 10) 537

הנחה   3 to lead, guide (12 · 26 · 40) 634

גִּיל   4 rejoicing (3 · 8) 162 I

כִּנּוֹר   lyre (13 · 41) 490

הִשְׁתּוֹחֵחַ 5 to be cast down, despairing
(4 · 4 · 6) 1005 שׁחח

הָמָה to murmur (11 · 33 · 33) 242

הוֹחִיל to wait for, hope for (15 · 15 · 42)
403

Psalm 44

מַשְׂכִּיל 1 contemplative poem (14 · 14) 968

פֹּעַל 2 deed, thing done (11 · 37) 821

לְאֹם 3 people (14 · 35) 522

נָגַח 6 to push, gore (1 · 6 · 11) 618

בּוּס to tread down, trample (3 · 7 · 12)
100

קָם adversary (5 · 12) 877 קום 2

זָנַח 10 to reject, spurn (10 · 16 · 19) 276 I

הכלים to humiliate (1 · 10 · 38) 483

שָׁסָה to spoil, plunder (1 · 4 · 5) 1042

אָחוֹר 11 backwards, behind (12 · 41) 30

שָׁסָה to spoil, plunder (1 · 4 · 5) 1042

מַאֲכָל 12 food (3 · 30) 38

זרה *Piel*, to scatter, disperse
(2 · 25 · 38) 279

בְּלֹא 13 for no (2 · 30) 518 לא 4.a

הוֹן price, high value (3 · 26) 223

מְחִיר price, high (1 · 15) 564 I

שָׁכֵן 14 neighbor (6 · 20) 1015

לַעַג mocking, derision (3 · 7) 541

קֶלֶס derision (2 · 3) 887

מָשָׁל 15 byword (4 · 39) 605 II

מָנוֹד shaking, wagging (1 · 1) 627

לְאֹם people (14 · 35) 522

כְּלִמָּה 16 ignominy, reproach (7 · 30) 484

בֹּשֶׁת shame (7 · 30) 102

חֵרֵף 17 to reproach (9 · 34 · 38) 357

גדף to revile (1 · 7 · 7) 154

התנקם to avenge oneself (2 · 5 · 35) 667

שִׁקֵּר 18 to deal falsely (2 · 5 · 6) 1055

נָסוֹג 19 to be turned back, repulsed
(6 · 14 · 25) 690

אָחוֹר backwards, behind (12 · 41) 30

אָשׁוּר step, going (6 · 10) 81

זָכָה 20 to crush down (2 · 2 · 5) 194

תַּן jackel (1 · 14) 1072

צַלְמָוֶת deep shadow, death shadow (4 · 18)
853

חֵקֵר 22 to search out (3 · 22 · 27) 350

תַּעֲלֻמָה hidden thing, secret (1 · 3) 761

טִבְחָה 23 slaughter (1 · 4) 370

ישׁן 24 to sleep, go to sleep (5 · 15 · 16) 445

הֵקִיץ to awake (7 · 22 · 23) 884 I

זָנַח to reject, spurn (10 · 16 · 19) 276 I

לָנֶצַח forever (18 · 42) 664 נצח I.4

עֳנִי 25 affliction (10 · 36) 777

לַחַץ oppression (3 · 10) 537

שָׁחָה 26 to sink down pf. 3rd fem. sing.
(1 · 2 · 6) 1001 שוח

עֶזְרָה 27 help (14 · 26) 740 I

Psalm 45

שׁוֹשָׁן 1 lily (4 · 17) 1004 I

מַשְׂכִּיל contemplative poem (14 · 14) 968

יְדִידֹת love (1 · 1[?]) 391 ידיד 3

רָחַשׁ 2 to keep moving, stir (1 · 1 · 1) 935

עֵט stylus (1 · 4) 741

מָהִיר quick, prompt, ready, skilled (1 · 4)
555

יפה 3 to be beautiful (1 · 6 · 8) 421

חגר 4 to gird on, bind on (4 · 44 · 44) 291

יָרֵךְ thigh, loin (1 · 34) 437

הוֹד splendor, majesty (8 · 24) 217

הָדָר splendor, majesty (13 · 30) 214

הָדָר 5 splendor, majesty (13 · 30) 214

עַנְוָה humility, meekness [dub.] (2 · 2[?])
776

הורה to point out, show (8 · 45 · 45) 434

נוֹרָא awe-inspiring, awful (15 · 44) 431
ירא

שׁנן 6 to whet, sharpen (4 · 7 · 9) 1041

עַד 7 ever (29 · 48) 723 I

מִישׁוֹר uprightness (5 · 23) 449

רֶשַׁע 8 wickedness (6 · 30) 957

שָׂשׂוֹן exultation, joy (5 · 22) 965

חָבֵר associate, fellow (2 · 12) 288

מֹר 9 myrrh (1 · 12) 600

אֲהָלוֹת aloes (1 · 4) 14 III אחל

קְצִיעָה cassia (a powdered bark) (1 · 1) 893
I

מֵן string (2 · 2) 577 I

יָקָר 10 precious, prized (4 · 35) 429

שֵׁגָל consort (1 · 2) 993

כֶּתֶם gold (1 · 9) 508

הִתְאַוָּה 12 to desire, long for, lust after
(2 · 16 · 27) 16

עָשִׁיר 13 rich (2 · 23) 799

כְּבוּדָּה 14 glorious (1 · 3) 458 כָּבוֹד I

פְּנִימָה within (1 · 5) 819

מִשְׁבְּצוֹת checkered, plaited work (1 · 9) 990

לְבוּשׁ garment, clothing (6 · 30) 528

רִקְמָה 15 variegated stuff (1 · 12) 955

הוּבַל to be led, conducted (2 · 11 · 18) 384

בְּתוּלָה virgin (3 · 50) 143

רֵעָה companion, attendant (1 · 3) 946

הוּבַל 16 to be led, conducted (2 · 11 · 18) 384

גִּיל rejoicing (3 · 8) 162 I

עַד 18 ever (29 · 48) 723 I

Psalm 46

עַלְמָה 1 young woman (2 · 9) 761

מַחְסֶה 2 refuge, shelter (12 · 20) 340

עֶזְרָה help (14 · 26) 740 I

הֵמִיר 3 to change, alter (3 · 12 · 13) 558 מור

מוֹט to shake, totter, slip (8 · 15 · 39) 556

הָמָה 4 to roar (11 · 33 · 33) 242

חָמַר to ferment, boil or foam up
(2 · 3 · 5) 330 I

רעשׁ to quake, shake (4 · 21 · 29) 950

גַּאֲוָה rising up, swelling (7 · 19) 144

פֶּלֶג 5 channel, canal (4 · 10) 811 I

נמוט 6 to be shaken, moved, overthrown
(16 · 22 · 39) 556

הָמָה 7 to roar, be tumultuous (11 · 33 · 33)
242

מוֹט to shake, totter, slip (8 · 15 · 39) 556

מוּג to melt (1 · 4 · 17) 556

מִשְׂגָּב 8 secure height, retreat (13 · 17) 960 I

מִפְעָלָה 9 deed (2 · 3) 821

שַׁמָּה a waste (2 · 39) 1031 I

קָצַץ 10 to cut in two (2 · 9 · 14) 893

חֲנִית spear (3 · 47) 333

עֲגָלָה war chariot (1 · 25) 722

הִרְפָּה 11 to refrain, let alone (3 · 21 · 45) 951

מִשְׂגָּב 12 secure height, retreat (13 · 17) 960

Psalm 47

הֵרִיעַ 2 to shout (9 · 40 · 44) 929 רוע

רִנָּה ringing cry (15 · 33) 943 I

נוֹרָא 3 awe-inspiring, awful (15 · 44) 431
ירא

הִדְבִּיר 4 to lead; put to flight (2 · 2 · 5[?]) 180
דבר

לְאֹם people (14 · 3ˁ) 522

גָּאוֹן 5 exultation, majesty, excellence
(2 · 49) 144

תְּרוּעָה 6 shout of joy (5 · 36) 929

זמר 7 to sing, make music (39 · 43 · 43)
274 I

זמר 8 to sing, make music (39 · 43 · 43)
274 I

מַשְׂכִּיל contemplative poem (14 · 14) 968

נָדִיב 10 noble, princely (8 · 27) 622

מָגֵן shield, buckler (1 · 4[?]) 171

Psalm 48

יָפֶה 3 beautiful, fair (1 · 40) 421

נוֹף elevation, height (1 · 1) 632

430

מָשׂוֹשׂ	exultation (1 · 17) 965	עָקֵב 6	overreacher (5 · 14) 784 II
יַרְכָּה	extreme or remote parts (2 · 28) 438	עֹשֶׁר 7	riches (3 · 37) 799
קִרְיָה	town, city (1 · 30) 900	כֹּפֶר 8	ransom (1 · 13) 497 I
אַרְמוֹן 4	citadel, castle, palace (3 · 33) 74	יקר 9	to be costly (3 · 9 · 11) 429
מִשְׂגָּב	secure height, retreat (13 · 17) 960 I	פִּדְיוֹן	ransom (1 · 3) 804

מָשׂוֹשׂ exultation (1 · 17) 965

יַרְכָּה extreme or remote parts (2 · 28) 438

קִרְיָה town, city (1 · 30) 900

אַרְמוֹן 4 citadel, castle, palace (3 · 33) 74

מִשְׂגָּב secure height, retreat (13 · 17) 960 I

נוֹעַד 5 to gather, assemble (1 · 18 · 28) 416

תמה 6 to be astounded (1 · 8 · 9) 1069

נִבְהַל to be disturbed, dismayed, terrified (8 · 24 · 39) 96

נחפז to hurry (2 · 3 · 9) 342

רְעָדָה 7 trembling (2 · 4) 944

חִיל anguish (1 · 6) 297

אֳנִיָּה 8 ship (3 · 31) 58

דְּמָה 10 to think of (2 · 13 · 27) 197 I

קָצוּ 11 end, boundary (2 · 3) 892

גִּיל 12 to rejoice (19 · 45 · 45) 162

הִקִּיף 13 to surround, encompass (14 · 16 · 17) 668 II

מִגְדָּל tower (2 · 49) 153

חֵיל 14 rampart (2 · 9) 298 חל

פסג [dub.] to pass between (1 · 1 · 1) 819

אַרְמוֹן citadel, castle, palace (3 · 33) 74

עַד 15 ever (29 · 45) 723 I

נֵהַג to lead on, guide (3 · 10 · 30) 624 I

Psalm 49

הַאֲזִין 2 to listen, give ear (15 · 41 · 41) 24

חֶלֶד world, duration (4 · 5) 317

יַחַד 3 together, altogether (14 · 44) 403

עָשִׁיר rich (2 · 23) 799

חָכְמָה 4 wisdom (1 · 4[?]) 315 5.c

הָגוּת meditation, musing (1 · 1) 212

תְּבוּנָה understanding (4 · 42) 108

מָשָׁל 5 poem (4 · 39) 605 II

כִּנּוֹר lyre (13 · 41) 490

חִידָה riddle (2 · 17) 295

עָקֵב 6 overreacher (5 · 14) 784 II

עֹשֶׁר 7 riches (3 · 37) 799

כֹּפֶר 8 ransom (1 · 13) 497 I

יקר 9 to be costly (3 · 9 · 11) 429

פִּדְיוֹן ransom (1 · 3) 804

לָנֶצַח 10 forever (18 · 42) 664 נצח

שַׁחַת pit (9 · 23) 1001

יַחַד 11 together, altogether (14 · 44) 403

בַּעַר brutish (3 · 5) 129

יְקָר 13 honor (2 · 17) 430

נִמְשַׁל to be like, similar (4 · 5 · 15) 605 I

נִדְמָה to be cut off, destroyed, ruined (2 · 12 · 16) 198 II

כֵּסֶל 14 stupidity, folly (2 · 6) 492

שַׁתּוּ 15 to set, appoint (2 · 2 · 2) 1060

רדה to have dominion, rule, dominate (4 · 22 · 23) 921 I

צִיר form, image (1 · 5) 849 I cf. Q צורה 849

בלה to wear out (1 · 5 · 16) 115

זְבֻל lofty abode, height, elevation (1 · 5) 259 I

הֶעֱשִׁיר 17 to cause to be or become rich (2 · 14 · 17) 799

נֶצַח 20 everlastingness; עד-נ׳ = unto the end (18 · 42) 664

יְקָר 21 honor (2 · 17) 430

נִמְשַׁל to be like, similar (4 · 5 · 15) 605 I

דמה to be cut off, destroyed, ruined (2 · 12 · 16) 198 I

Psalm 50

מָבוֹא 1 entering; i.e., setting (3 · 23) 99

מִכְלָל 2 perfection (1 · 1) 483

הוֹפִיעַ to shine out, forth (3 · 8 · 8) 422

חרש 3 to be silent (6 · 7 · 47) 361 I

נִשְׂעַר to be tempestuous (1 · 1 · 4) 973 II

דין 4 to judge, minister judgment (8 · 23 · 24) 192

חָסִיד 5 pious, godly (25 · 32) 339

הֵעִיד 7 to exhort solemnly, admonish (2 · 39 · 44) 729 עוד

לְנֶגֶד 8 in the sight or presence of (13 · 32) 617 נֶגֶד 2.b

מִכְלָא 9 fold, enclosure (2 · 3) 476 נִכְלָה I

עַתּוּד male goat (3 · 29) 800

אֶלֶף 10 thousand (2 · 8[?]) 48 II

זִיז 11 [coll.] moving things (2 · 2) 265 I

שָׂדַי field, land (5 · 13) 961

רָעֵב 12 to be hungry (2 · 14 · 16) 944

תֵּבֵל world (15 · 36) 385

מְלֹא fullness (5 · 38) 571

אַבִּיר 13 mighty, valiant (5 · 17) 7

עַתּוּד male goat (3 · 29) 800

תּוֹדָה 14 sacrifice of thanksgiving, thank offering (12 · 32) 392

חָלַץ 15 to rescue, deliver (10 · 14 · 27) 322

מוּסָר 17 discipline, correction (1 · 50) 416

גַּנָּב 18 thief (1 · 17) 170

נאף Piel, to commit adultery (1 · 14 · 31) 610

הִצְמִיד 19 to combine; i.e., fit together, frame (1 · 1 · 5) 855

מִרְמָה deceit, treachery (14 · 39) 941

דֹּפִי 20 blemish, fault (1 · 1) 200

הֶחֱרַשׁ 21 to be silent (2 · 38 · 46) 361 II

דָּמָה to think that (2 · 13 · 27) 197 I

טָרַף 22 to rend, tear (4 · 19 · 24) 382

תּוֹדָה 23 sacrifice of thanksgiving, thank offering (12 · 32) 392

יֵשַׁע salvation (20 · 36) 447

Psalm 51

רַחֲמִים 3 compassion (11 · 38) 933

מָחָה to blot out (3 · 22 · 34) 562 I

צדק 6 to be just (3 · 22 · 41) 842

זכה to be clear, justified (1 · 4 · 8) 269

חוֹלֵל 7 to be brought forth (1 · 5 · 47) 296 חול

חֵטְא sin (3 · 33) 307

יחם to conceive (1 · 4 · 6) 404

טֻחוֹת 8 inward part (1 · 2) 376

סָתַם pass. ptc. = closed (1 · 10 · 13) 711

אֵזוֹב 9 hyssop (1 · 10) 23

שֶׁלֶג snow (3 · 20) 1017

הלבין to grow white, show whiteness (1 · 4 · 5) 526

שָׂשׂוֹן 10 exultation, joy (5 · 22) 965

גיל to rejoice (19 · 45 · 45) 162

דכה to crush to pieces (2 · 2 · 5) 194

חֵטְא 11 sin (3 · 33) 307

מָחָה to blot out (3 · 22 · 34) 562 I

בָּרָא 12 to create, fashion, shape (3 · 38 · 48) 135 I

חדשׁ to renew, make anew (2 · 9 · 10) 293

שָׂשׂוֹן 14 exultation, joy (5 · 22) 965

יֵשַׁע salvation (20 · 36) 447

נָדִיב willing (8 · 27) 622

סָמַךְ to support, uphold, sustain (10 · 41 · 48) 701

פָּשַׁע 15 to transgress (2 · 40 · 41) 833

חַטָּא sinner (6 · 19) 308

תְּשׁוּעָה 16 salvation (13 · 34) 448

נדכה 19 to be contrite (2 · 2 · 5) 194

בָּזָה to despise (6 · 31 · 42) 102

כָּלִיל 21 entire, whole, holocaust (1 · 15) 483

Psalm 52

מַשְׂכִּיל 1 contemplative poem (14 · 14) 968

הַוָּה 4 chasm, ruin, destruction (8 · 13) 217

תַּעַר razor (1 · 13) 789

לטשׁ to be sharpened (1 · 1 · 5) 538

רְמִיָּה deceit, treachery (6 · 15) 941

בֶּלַע 6 swallowing; דברי־ב׳ = devouring words (1 · 1) 118 I

מִרְמָה deceit, treachery (14 · 39) 941

432

נָתַץ	7	to pull down (2 · 31 · 42) 683
לָנֶצַח		forever (18 · 42) 664 נצח
חתה		to snatch away (1 · 1 · 1[?]) 367
נסח		to tear or pull away (1 · 3 · 4) 650
שָׁרַשׁ		to root up, out (1 · 2 · 8) 1057
שָׂחַק	8	to laugh (4 · 18 · 36) 965
מָעוֹז	9	refuge (9 · 36) 731
עֹשֶׁר		riches (3 · 37) 799
עזז		to be strong, prevail (4 · 9 · 11) 738
הַוָּה		desire (8 · 13) 217
זַיִת	10	olive tree, olive (2 · 38) 268
רַעֲנָן		luxuriant, fresh (4 · 19) 947
עַד		ever (29 · 48) 723 I
קוה	11	*Piel*, to wait for, look eagerly for (12 · 39 · 45) 875 I
חָסִיד		pious, godly (25 · 32) 339

Psalm 53

מָחֲלַת	1	[dub.] name of tune (2 · 2) 318 I
מַשְׂכִּיל		contemplative poem (14 · 14) 968
נָבָל	2	senseless (5 · 18) 614 I
התעיב		to make abominable, to do abominably (2 · 4 · 21) 1073 תעב
עָוֶל		injustice, unrighteousness (3 · 21) 732
הִשְׁקִיף	3	to look down (3 · 12 · 22) 1054 I
סוּג	4	to backslide (2 · 3 · 25) 690 I
נֶאֱלָח		to be corrupt (2 · 3 · 3) 47
פָּחַד	6	to be in dread (5 · 23 · 26) 808
פַּחַד		dread (9 · 49) 808 I
פזר		to scatter (4 · 7 · 10) 808
מִי	7	O that! (>50) 566 f
שְׁבוּת		captivity (2 · 26) 986
גיל		to rejoice (19 · 45 · 45) 162

Psalm 54

נְגִינָה	1	music, song (9 · 14) 618
מַשְׂכִּיל		contemplative poem (14 · 14) 968
דִּין	3	judge (8 · 23 · 24) 192
הַאֲזִין	4	to listen, give ear (15 · 41 · 41) 24
אֵמֶר		utterance, word (7 · 48) 56
עָרִיץ	5	awe-inspiring, terror striking (3 · 20) 792
לְנֶגֶד		over, for (13 · 32) 617 נֶגֶד 2.b
עֹזֵר	6	help, helper (7 · 19) 740 עזר I
סָמַךְ		to support, uphold, sustain (10 · 41 · 48) 701
שׁוֹרֵר	7	watcher (5 · 5) 1004
הצמית		to exterminate, annihilate (9 · 10 · 15) 856
נְדָבָה	8	voluntariness, freewill offering; בנדבה = voluntarily (4 · 27) 621

Psalm 55

נְגִינָה	1	music, song (9 · 4) 618
מַשְׂכִּיל		contemplative poem (14 · 14) 968
הַאֲזִין	2	to listen, give ear (15 · 41 · 41) 24
התעלם		to hide oneself (1 · 6 · 29) 761 I
תְּחִנָּה		supplication for favor (3 · 25) 337 I
הִקְשִׁיב	3	to give attention (8 · 45 · 46) 904
הָרִיד		to show restlessness (1 · 2 · 4) 923 רוד
שִׂיחַ		complaint (5 · 14) 967
הום		אָהִימָה = mpf. 1st sing., distracted or to show disquietude (1 · 2 · 6) 223
עָקָה	4	pressure (1 · 1) 734
המיט		to dislodge, let fall, drop (1 · 1 · 39) 556
שׂטם		to bear a grudge, cherish animosity, against (1 · 6 · 6) 966
חִיל	5	to twist, writhe, be in anguish (5 · 39 · 47) 296 חול I
אֵימָה		terror, dread (2 · 17) 33

יִרְאָה 6 fear, terror (8 · 45) 432

רַעַד trembling (1 · 2) 944

פַּלָּצוּת shuddering (1 · 4) 814

מִי 7 O that! (>50) 566 f

אֵבֶר pinions (1 · 3) 7

יוֹנָה dove (3 · 33) 401 I

עוּף to fly away (4 · 18 · 25) 733 I

נדד 8 to wander, stray (4 · 21 · 25) 622 I

הֵחִישׁ 9 to hasten (1 · 6 · 21) 301 I חושׁ

מִפְלָט escape, place of escape (1 · 1) 812

סֹעֶה ptc. = rushing (1 · 1 · 1) 703

סַעַר tempest (2 · 8) 704

בֶּלַע 10 to confuse, confound (1 · 3 · 6[?]) 118

פָּלַג to divide (1 · 2 · 4) 811

הַוָּה 12 chasm, ruin, destruction (8 · 13) 217

הֵמִישׁ to remove, take away (1 · 20 · 20 [?]) 559 I מושׁ

רְחוֹב broad open place, plaza (2 · 43) 932

תֹּךְ injury, oppression (3 · 4) 1067

מִרְמָה deceit, treachery (14 · 39) 941

חֵרֵף 13 to reproach (9 · 34 · 38) 357 I

אֱנוֹשׁ 14 man, mankind (13 · 42) 60

עֶרְךְ estimate, valuation (1 · 33) 789

אַלּוּף friend, intimate (2 · 9) 48 I.2

הִמְתִּיק 15 to make sweet (1 · 2 · 6) 608

סוֹד counsel (6 · 21) 691

רֶגֶשׁ throng (1 · 1) 921

יְשִׁימָה 16 desolation; Qere, deceitfully (1 · 1) 445

מָגוֹר dwelling place (1 · 2[?]) 158 I

צָהֳרַיִם 18 midday, noon (3 · 23) 843 I צֹהַר

שִׂיחַ to complain (13 · 18 · 20) 967

הָמָה to murmur (11 · 33 · 33) 242

חֲלִיפָה 20 changing, varying (1 · 12) 322

חָלַק 22 to be smooth, slippery (1 · 2 · 9) 325 II

מַחְמָאֹת curdlike words (1 · 1) 563

קְרָב battle, war (4 · 8) 898

רכך to be soft (1 · 6 · 8) 939

פְּתִיחָה drawn sword (1 · 1) 836

יְהָב 23 lot (1 · 1) 396

כִּלְכֵּל to sustain, support, nourish (2 · 24 · 38) 465

מוֹט to totter, slip (8 · 15 · 39) 556

בְּאֵר 24 well, pit (2 · 37) 91

שַׁחַת pit (9 · 23) 1001

מִרְמָה deceit, treachery (14 · 39) 941

חָצָה to divide, halve (1 · 11 · 15) 345

Psalm 56

יוֹנָה 1 dove (3 · 33) 401 I

אֵלֶם silence (2 · 2) 48

מִכְתָּם Mikhtam (6 · 6) 508

שָׁאַף 2 to trample upon, crush (4 · 14 · 14) 983

אֱנוֹשׁ man, mankind (13 · 42) 60

לָחַץ to oppress (2 · 14 · 15) 537

שָׁאַף 3 to trample upon, crush (4 · 14 · 14) 983

שׁוֹרֵר watcher (5 · 5) 1004

עצב 6 to vex (1 · 2 · 15) 780 I

גוּר 7 to stir up strife (3 · 4 · 4) 158 II

צָפַן to be hid, lurk (7 · 23 · 28) 860

עָקֵב footprint, heel (5 · 14) 784 I

קוה Piel, to lie in wait for (12 · 39 · 45) 875 I

פלט 8 to deliver (19 · 24 · 27) 812

נוֹד 9 wandering (1 · 1) 627 I

דִּמְעָה tears (8 · 23) 199

נֹאד skin (2 · 6) 609

סְפֹרָה book (1 · 1) 707

אָחוֹר 10 backwards, behind (12 · 41) 30

תּוֹדָה 13 sacrifice of thanksgiving, thank offering (12 · 32) 392

דְּחִי 14 stumbling (2 · 2) 191

Psalm 57

מִכְתָּם	1 Mikhtam (6 · 6) 508	
מְעָרָה	cave (2 · 40) 792	
חָסָה	2 to seek refuge (25 · 37 · 37) 340	
הַוָּה	chasm, ruin, destruction (8 · 13) 217	
גָּמַר	3 to bring to an end, complete (5 · 5 · 5) 170	
חָרַף	4 to reproach (1 · 1 · 1[?]) 357 I	
שָׁאַף	to trample upon, crush (4 · 14 · 14) 983	
לְבָאִם	5 pl. lions (1 · 1) 522 לְבִי	
להט	to flame, blaze up (2 · 2 · 11) 529	
חֲנִית	spear (3 · 47) 333	
חַד	sharp (1 · 4) 292 II	
רֶשֶׁת	7 net (8 · 22) 440	
כָּפַף	to be bowed down (3 · 4 · 5) 496	
כָּרָה	to dig (4 · 13 · 14) 500 I	
שִׁיחָה	pit (2 · 2) 1001	
זמר	8 to sing, make music (39 · 43 · 43) 274 I	
גֵּבֶל	9 harp (8 · 22) 614 I	
כִּנּוֹר	lyre (13 · 41) 490	
שָׁחַר	dawn (4 · 23) 1007	
זמר	10 to sing, make music (39 · 43 · 43) 274 I	
לְאֹם	people (14 · 35) 522	
שַׁחַק	11 cloud (9 · 21) 1007	

Psalm 58

מִכְתָּם	1 Mikhtam (6 · 6) 508	
אָמְנָם	2 verily, truly, indeed (1 · 5) 53	
אֵלֶם	silence (2 · 2) 48	
מֵישָׁר	uprightness, equity (7 · 19) 449	
עַוְלָה	3 injustice, wrong (9 · 23) 732	
פלס	to weigh out (2 · 6 · 6) 814	
זור	4 to become estranged (2 · 3 · 6) 266 I	
רֶחֶם	womb (3 · 33) 933	
תָּעָה	to wander about, err (5 · 27 · 50)	

1073

כָּזָב	lie, falsehood (6 · 31) 469	
דְּמוּת	5 כְּדֹ־ = in likeness of, like as (1 · 25) 198	
נָחָשׁ	serpent (2 · 31) 638 I	
פֶּתֶן	venomous serpent, perh. cobra (2 · 6) 837	
חֵרֵשׁ	deaf (2 · 9) 361	
אטם	to shut, stop (1 · 8 · 8) 31	
לחשׁ	6 to whisper, charm (1 · 1 · 3) 538	
חבר	to tie magic knots, charm (2 · 11 · 28) 287	
חֶבֶר	spell (1 · 7) 288 I	
חכם	Pual ptc. = made wise (1 · 2 · 26) 314	
חרס	7 to break down, break away (2 · 30 · 43) 248	
מַלְתָּעוֹת	teeth (1 · 4) 1069 מְתַלְּעוֹת	
כְּפִיר	young lion (6 · 31) 498	
נָתַץ	to break down, break off (2 · 31 · 42) 683	
נמאס	8 to run, flow (1 · 2 · 2) 549 II	
התמלל	to be cut off (1 · 1 · 4) 576 IV	
שַׁבְּלוּל	9 snail (1 · 1) 117	
תֶּמֶס	melting (1 · 1) 588	
נֵפֶל	miscarriage, abortion (1 · 3) 658	
בְּטֶרֶם	10 before (3 · 39) 382 טֶרֶם	
סִיר	pot (3 · 29) 696	
אָטָד	bramble, buck-thorn (1 · 4) 31	
חָרוֹן	burning anger (6 · 41) 354	
שׂער	to sweep away (1 · 1 · 4) 973 II	
נָקָם	11 vengeance (1 · 17) 668	

Psalm 59

מִכְתָּם	1 Mikhtam (6 · 6) 508	
שׂגב	2 to set on high (5 · 6 · 20) 960	
אָרַב	4 to lie in wait (3 · 20 · 23) 70	
גור	to stir up strife (3 · 4 · 4) 158 II	
עַז	strong, mighty, fierce (2 · 22) 738	

בְּלִי 5 without (4 · 23) 115

הֵקִיץ 6 to awake (7 · 22 · 23) 884 I

בגד to act or deal treacherously, faith-lessly, deceitfully (5 · 49 · 49) 93

הָמָה 7 to growl (11 · 33 · 33) 242

כֶּלֶב dog (5 · 32) 476

הִבִּיע 8 to pour forth, belch forth (6 · 10 · 11) 615 נבע

חֲרָבוֹת sword (1 · 1[?]) 352 חֶרֶב 1.k

שָׂחַק 9 to laugh (4 · 18 · 36) 965

לעג to mock, deride (3 · 12 · 18) 541

מִשְׂגָּב 10 secure height, retreat (13 · 17) 960

קדם 11 to come to meet (12 · 24 · 27) 869

שׁוֹרֵר watcher (5 · 5) 1004

הֵנִיע 12 to cause to wander (4 · 14 · 38) 631

גָּאוֹן 13 pride (2 · 49) 144

אָלָה oath, curse (2 · 36) 46

כַּחַשׁ lying (1 · 6) 471

אֶפֶס 14 ends, exreme limits (6 · 27) 67

הָמָה 15 to growl (11 · 33 · 33) 242

כֶּלֶב dog (5 · 32) 476

נוע 16 to totter, go tottering (4 · 14 · 38[?]) 631

מִשְׂגָּב 17 secure height, retreat (13 · 17) 960

מָנוֹס escape (2 · 8) 631

זמר 18 to sing, make music (39 · 43 · 43) 274 I

מִשְׂגָּב secure height, retreat (13 · 17) 960

Psalm 60

מִכְתָּם 1 Mikhtam (6 · 6) 508

שׁוּשַׁן lily (4 · 17) 1004 I

הצה 2 to engage in a struggle (1 · 3 · 8) 663 נצה II

גַּיְא valley (2 · 48) 161

מֶלַח salt (1 · 28) 571 II

זָנַח 3 to reject, spurn (10 · 16 · 19) 276 I

פָּרַץ to break out upon (4 · 46 · 49) 829 I

אָנַף to be angry (4 · 8 · 14) 60

הִרְעִישׁ 4 to cause to quake (1 · 7 · 29) 950

פצם to split open (1 · 1) 822

שֶׁבֶר breaking, shattering (1 · 45) 991 I

מוט to shake, totter, slip (8 · 15 · 39) 556

קָשֶׁה 5 severe, hard (1 · 36) 904

תַּרְעֵלָה reeling (1 · 3) 947

יָרֵא 6 afraid (27 · 46) 431

נֵס standard (1 · 21) 651

קֹשֶׁט bow (1 · 1) 905

נֶחֱלַץ 7 to be delivered (2 · 7 · 27) 322 I

יָדִיד beloved (4 · 8) 391

עָלַז 8 to exult, triumph (7 · 16 · 16) 759

מָעוֹז 9 protection (9 · 36) 731

מְחֹקֵק commander's staff (2 · 7[?]) 349 חקק

סִיר 10 pot (3 · 29) 696 I

רָחַץ wash (2 · 2) 934

נַעַל sandal, shoe (2 · 22) 653

התרועע to shout in triumph (3 · 3 · 44) 929

הוֹבִיל 11 to lead, conduct (4 · 7 · 18) 384

מָצוֹר enclosure; עִיר מ׳ = entrenched city (2 · 25) 848 I

נחה to lead, bring (6 · 14 · 40) 634

זָנַח 12 to reject, spurn (10 · 16 · 19) 276 I

יהב 13 to give (8 · 33 · 33) 396

עֶזְרָה help (14 · 26) 74 I

תְּשׁוּעָה deliverance (13 · 34) 448

בוס 14 to tread down, trample (3 · 7 · 12) 100

Psalm 61

נְגִינָה 1 music, song (9 · 14) 618

רִנָּה 2 ringing cry (15 · 33) 943 I

הִקְשִׁיב to give attention (8 · 45 · 46) 904

עטף 3 to be feeble, faint (2 · 3 · 11) 742 III

הנחה to lead, guide (12 · 26 · 40) 634

מַחְסֶה 4 refuge, shelter (12 · 20) 340

מִגְדָּל tower (2 · 49) 153

חָסָה 5 to seek refuge (25 · 37 · 37) 340

סֵתֶר hiding place, shelter (10 · 35) 712

יְרֵשָׁה 6 possession (1 · 14) 440

יָרֵא afraid (27 · 46) 431

מִנָּה 8 to appoint, ordain (1 · 9 · 28) 584

זמר 9 to sing, make music (39 · 43 · 43) 274 I

עַד לְעַד = forever (29 · 48) 723 I

Psalm 62

דּוּמִיָּה 2 still waiting, resignation (4 · 4) 189

מִשְׂגָּב 3 secure height, retreat (13 · 17) 960

נמוט to be shaken, moved, overthrown (16 · 22 · 39) 556

אָנָה 4 how long? (7 · 39) 33 אָן

הות to be frantic (1 · 1 · 1) 223

רצח to murder, assassinate (2 · 3 · 43) 953

גָּדֵר wall, fence (2 · 13) 154

דחה to push (4 · 4 · 6) 190

שְׂאֵת 5 dignity (1 · 7) 673

הִדִּיחַ to thrust out, banish (2 · 27 · 43) 623 נדח

כָּזָב lie, falsehood (6 · 31) 469

דמם 6 to be silent to; i.e., be resigned to (6 · 23 · 30) 198 I

תִּקְוָה hope, outcome (3 · 23) 876

מִשְׂגָּב 7 secure height, retreat (13 · 17) 960

נמוט to be shaken, moved, overthrown (16 · 22 · 39) 556

יֵשַׁע 8 salvation (20 · 36) 447

מַחְסֶה refuge, salvation (12 · 20) 340

מַחְסֶה 9 refuge, salvation (12 · 20) 340

כָּזָב 10 lie, falsehood (6 · 31) 469

מֹאזְנַיִם balances, scales (1 · 15) 24 מאזן

יַחַד together, altogether (14 · 44) 403

עֹשֶׁק 11 gain of extortion (3 · 15) 799

גָּזֵל robbery (1 · 4) 160

הבל to become vain (1 · 4 · 5) 211

נוב to bear fruit (2 · 3 · 4) 626

זוּ 12 these or which (9 · 14) 262

Psalm 63

שׁחר 2 to seek early, eagerly, for (2 · 12 · 13) 1007

צמא to be thirsty (2 · 10 · 10) 854

כָּמַהּ to faint (1 · 1 · 1) 484

צִיָּה drought, desert (4 · 16) 851

עָיֵף faint, weary (2 · 17) 746

בְּלִי without (4 · 23) 115

שׁבח 4 to laud, praise (4 · 6 · 8) 986 II

דֶּשֶׁן 6 fatness (3 · 15) 206

רְנָנָה ringing cry (2 · 4) 943

יָצוּעַ 7 couch, bed (2 · 5) 426

אַשְׁמוּרָה watch (div. of time) (3 · 7) 1038

הגה to meditate, muse (10 · 23 · 25) 211 I

עֶזְרָה 8 help (14 · 26) 740 I

תמך 9 to hold up, support (4 · 20 · 21) 1069

שׁוֹאָה 10 devastation, ruin (3 · 12) 996

תַּחְתִּי lower, lowest (4 · 19) 1066

הִגִּיר 11 to deliver over to (2 · 5 · 10) 620

מְנָת portion (3 · 9) 584

שׁוּעָל fox (1 · 7) 1043 I

נסכר 12 to be stopped, shut up (1 · 2 · 3) 698 I

Psalm 64

שִׂיחַ 2 complaint (5 · 14) 967

פַּחַד dread (9 · 49) 808

סוֹד 3 council, intimate circle (6 · 21) 691

מֵרַע *Hiph.* evildoer (9 · 18) רעע 949 2

רִגְשָׁה throng (1 · 1) 921

שׁנן 4 to whet, sharpen (4 · 7 · 9) 1041

מַר bitter (1 · 37) 600 I

יָרָה 5 to shoot, throw (2 · 13 · 25) 434

מִסְתָּר hiding place (4 · 10) 712

תָּם complete, having integrity (2 · 15) 1070

פִּתְאֹם suddenly (2 · 25) 837

437

הורה to shoot (2 · 11 · 25) 434

טָמַן 6 to hide, conceal (7 · 28 · 31) 380

מוֹקֵשׁ bait, lure (6 · 27) 430

חפשׂ 7 to think out, devise (1 · 4 · 23) 344

עַוְלָה injustice, wrong (9 · 32) 732

חֵפֶשׂ a (shrewd) device, plot (1 · 1) 344

חפשׂ to be searched for; חֵפֶשׂ מ׳ = a device well thought out (1 · 2 · 3) 344

עָמֹק unsearchable (1 · 17) 771

הורה 8 to shoot (2 · 11 · 25) 434

פִּתְאֹם suddenly (2 · 25) 837

מַכָּה blow, wound (1 · 48) 646

הִתְנוֹדֵד 9 to flee away (1 · 4 · 26[?]) 622 נדד I

פֹּעַל 10 deed, thing done (11 · 37) 821

חסה 11 to seek refuge (25 · 37 · 37) 340

Psalm 65

דּוּמִיָּה 2 still waiting, resignation (4 · 4) 189

גָּבַר 4 to be strong, mighty (3 · 17 · 25) 149

אֶשֶׁר 5 happiness, blessedness (19 · 45[?]) 80

טוֹב good things (coll.) (7 · 32) 375

נוֹרָא 6 awe inspiring, awful (15 · 44) 431 ירא

יֵשַׁע salvation (20 · 36) 447

מִבְטָח confidence (3 · 15) 105

קַצְוֵי end, boundary (2 · 3) 892

נֶאְזָר 7 to be girded (1 · 1 · 16) 25

הַשְׁבִּיחַ 8 ptc. = stilling (1 · 1 · 3) 986 I

שָׁאוֹן roar, din, crash (4 · 18) 981

גַּל pl. = waves (5 · 16) 164

לְאֹם people (14 · 35) 522

קָצֶת 9 end (1 · 9) 892

מוֹצָא east (6 · 27) 425 I

שׁוֹקֵק 10 to give abundance (1 · 1 · 3) 1003 II שׁוק

הֶעְשִׁיר to cause to be, become rich (2 · 14 · 17) 799

פֶּלֶג channel, canal (4 · 10) 811

דָּגָן corn (3 · 40) 186

תֶּלֶם 11 furrow (1 · 5) 1068

רוה to drench, water abundantly (1 · 6 · 14) 924

נחת Piel, to press down (2 · 3 · 8) 639

גְּדוּד furrow (1 · 1) 151 II

רְבִיבִים copious showers (2 · 6) 914

מוֹגֵג to soften, dissolve (1 · 2 · 17) 556

צֶמַח growth, sprout (1 · 12) 855

עטר 12 to crown (3 · 4 · 7) 742 vb. denom

מַעְגָּל track (4 · 13) 722

רעף to trickle, drip (2 · 4 · 5) 950

דֶּשֶׁן fatness (3 · 15) 206

רעף 13 to trickle, drip (2 · 4 · 5) 950

נְאוֹת cs.f נְוֵה pasture, meadow (5 · 45[?]) 627 II

גִּיל rejoicing (3 · 8) 162 II

חגר to gird oneself (4 · 44 · 44) 291

כַּר 14 pasture (2 · 3) 499 II

עטף to cover, envelope oneself (2 · 2 · 3) 742 II

בַּר grain, corn (2 · 14) 141 III

הִתְרוֹעֵעַ to shout for joy (3 · 3 · 44) 929

Psalm 66

הֵרִיעַ 1 to shout (9 · 40 · 44) 929 רוע

זמר 2 to sing, make music (39 · 43 · 43) 274 I

נוֹרָא 3 awe-inspiring, awful (15 · 44) 431 ירא

כחשׁ to cringe, come cringing (3 · 19 · 22) 471

זמר 4 to sing, make music (39 · 43 · 43) 274 I

מִפְעָלָה 5 deed (2 · 3) 821

נוֹרָא awe inspiring, awful (15 · 44) 431 ירא

עֲלִילָה deed (9 · 24) 760

יַבָּשָׁה 6 dry land (1 · 14) 387

438

צָפָה	7 to keep watch (2 · 9 · 18) 859 I	
סרר	ptc. = stubborn (4 · 18 · 18) 710	
מוט	9 to totter, slip (8 · 15 · 39) 556	
בחן	10 to prove, test, try (9 · 24 · 28) 103	
צָרַף	to test (7 · 18 · 21) 864	
מְצוּדָה	11 net (7 · 18[?]) 845 II	
מוּעָקָה	compression, distress (1 · 1) 734	
מָתְנַיִם	loins (2 · 50) 608	
אֱנוֹשׁ	12 man, mankind (13 · 42) 60	
רְוָיָה	saturation (2 · 2) 924	
פצה	14 to part, open (5 · 15 · 15) 822	
מֵחַ	15 fatling (1 · 2) 562	
עַתּוּד	male goat (3 · 29) 800	
יָרֵא	16 afraid (27 · 46) 431	
אָכֵן	19 surely, truly (3 · 18) 38	
הִקְשִׁיב	to give attention (8 · 45 · 46) 904	

Psalm 67

נְגִינָה	1 music, song (9 · 14) 618
הֵאִיר	2 to make shine (15 · 34 · 40) 21 אור
לְאֹם	5 people (14 · 35) 522
מִישׁוֹר	uprightness (3 · 23) 449
הנחה	to lead, guide (12 · 26 · 40) 634
יְבוּל	7 produce (3 · 13) 385
אֶפֶם	8 ends, extreme limits (6 · 27) 67

Psalm 68

נדף	3 to be driven about (1 · 6 · 9) 623
עָשָׁן	smoke (4 · 25) 798
נדף	to drive about (2 · 3 · 9) 623
נָמֵס	to melt (4 · 19 · 21) 587 מסס
דּוֹנַג	wax (3 · 3) 200
עָלַץ	4 to rejoice, exult (4 · 8 · 8) 763
שׂושׂ	to exult, rejoice (7 · 27) 965
זמר	5 to sing, make music (39 · 43 · 43) 274 I
סלל	to lift up (1 · 10 · 12) 699 I
עלז	to exult, triumph (7 · 16 · 16) 759

יָתוֹם	6 orphan (8 · 42) 450
דַּיָּן	judge (1 · 2) 193
מָעוֹן	dwelling (5 · 18) 732 I
יָחִיד	7 solitary (4 · 12) 402
אָסִיר	prisoner (5 · 17) 64
כּוֹשָׁרָה	prosperity (1 · 1) 507
סָרַר	ptc. = stubborn (4 · 18 · 18) 710
צְחִיחָה	scorched land (1 · 1) 850
צעד	8 to step, march (1 · 7 · 8) 857 I
יְשִׁימוֹן	waste, wilderness (4 · 13) 445
רעשׁ	9 quake, shake (4 · 21 · 29) 950
נטף	to drop, drip (1 · 9 · 18) 642
גֶּשֶׁם	10 rain, shower (2 · 35) 177 II
נְדָבָה	generous (4 · 27) 621
הֵנִיף	to shed abroad (1 · 1 · 2[?]) 631 I נוף Hiph. 5
נִלְאָה	to be weary; fig. of parched soil (1 · 10 · 19) 521
חַיָּה	11 community (1 · 3) 312 II, or creatures, living things 312 I
אֹמֶר	12 command (4 · 6[?]) 56 אָמַר 2
מְבַשֵּׂר	bearer of good tidings (1 · 9[?]) 142 בשׂר Piel 1
נדד	13 to retreat, flee (4 · 21 · 25) 622 I
נָוֶה	dwelling, abiding (1 · 2) 627 II
שְׁפַתַּיִם	14 [dub.] fire place, ash heap (1 · 2[?]) 1046
יוֹנָה	dove (3 · 33) 401
נחפה	to be covered (1 · 12) 341
אֶבְרָה	pinion (2 · 4) 7
יְרַקְרַק	greenish, pale green, green shimmering (1 · 3) 439
חָרוּץ	gold (1 · 6) 359 V
שַׁדַּי	15 name of God (2 · 48) 994
שלג	to snow (1 · 1 · 1) 1017
גַּבְנֹן	16 peak, rounded summit (2 · 2) 148
רצד	17 to watch stealthily (1 · 1 · 1) 952
גַּבְנֹן	peak, rounded summit (2 · 2) 148
חָמַד	to desire, take pleasure in (2 · 16 · 21) 326

לָנֶצַח	forever (18 · 42) 664 נצח	רַץ	piece, bar (1 · 1) 954
שִׁנְאָן	18 repetition (1 · 1) 1041	בזר	to scatter (1 · 1 · 2) 103
שָׁבָה	19 to take captive (1 · 30 · 38) 985	קְרָב	battle, war (4 · 18) 898
שְׁבִי	captivity, captive (2 · 49) 985	אָתָה	32 to come (1 · 19 · 21) 87
מַתָּנָה	gift (1 · 17) 682	חַשְׁמַנִּים	ambassadors, nobles [dub.] (1 · 1)
סָרַר	ptc. = stubborn (4 · 18 · 18) 710		חַשְׁמַן 365
עמס	20 to carry (1 · 7 · 9) 770	זמר	33 to sing, make music (39 · 43 · 43)
מוֹשָׁעָה	21 saving acts (1 · 1) 448		274 I
תּוֹצָאָה	escape (1 · 23) 426	גַּאֲוָה	35 majesty (7 · 19) 144
מָחַץ	22 to smite through (5 · 14 · 14) 563	שַׁחַק	cloud (9 · 21) 1007
קָדְקֹד	hairy crown, scalp (2 · 11) 869	נוֹרָא	36 awe inspiring, awful (15 · 44) 431
שֵׂעָר	hair (1 · 28) 972		ירא
אָשָׁם	offense, trespass, fault (1 · 46) 79	תַּעֲצֻמָה	might (1 · 1) 783
מְצוֹלָה	23 depth, deep (5 · 12) 846		
מָחַץ	24 to smite through (5 · 14 · 14) 563		
כֶּלֶב	dog (5 · 32) 476		**Psalm 69**
מֵן	part, portion (1 · 1 · 1) 585 II	שׁוֹשַׁנָּה	1 lily (4 · 17) 1004 שׁושׁן
הֲלִיכָה	25 going, walk; marching (2 · 6) 237	טָבַע	3 to sink (3 · 6 · 10) 371
קֶדֶם	26 to go before, in front (12 · 24 · 26)	יָוֵן	mire (2 · 2) 401
	869	מְצוֹלָה	depth, deep (5 · 12) 846
שָׁר	singer (2 · 9) 1010 שׁיר	מָעֳמָד	standing ground, foothold (1 · 1) 765
נגן	ptc. = player (1 · 1 · 14) 618	מַעֲמַקִּים	depths (3 · 5) 771
עַלְמָה	young woman (2 · 9) 761	שִׁבֹּלֶת	flowing stream (2 · 20) 987 I
תפף	to sound the timbrel, beat (1 · 1 · 2)	שָׁטַף	to overflow, rinse or wash off
	1074		(4 · 28 · 31) 1009
מַקְהֵל	27 assembly (2 · 2) 875	יגע	4 to grow or be weary (2 · 20 · 26) 388
מָקוֹר	spring (2 · 18) 881	נָחַר	to be parched (1 · 1 · 1[?]) 359 I חרר
צָעִיר	28 little, young (2 · 22) 859 I	גָּרוֹן	throat (4 · 8) 173
רדה	to have dominion, rule, dominate	יחל	to wait for, hope for (14 · 25 · 42)
	(4 · 22 · 23) 921		403
רִגְמָה	heap, crowd (1 · 1) 920	רבב	5 to be, become, many (6 · 23 · 24)
עזז	29 to be strong, prevail (4 · 9 · 11) 738		912 I
זוּ	who (9 · 14) 262	שַׂעֲרָה	a hair (2 · 7) 972
הוֹבִיל	30 to bear along (4 · 7 · 18) 384	חִנָּם	gratuitously, without cause (6 · 32)
שַׁי	gift (2 · 3) 1009		336
גער	31 to rebuke (4 · 14 · 14) 172	עָצַם	to be numerous, vast (5 · 16 · 18)
אַבִּיר	mighty, valiant (5 · 17) 7		782 I
עֵגֶל	calf (3 · 35) 722	הַצְמִית	to exterminate, annihilate
התרפס	ptc. = stamping, trampling		(9 · 10 · 15) 856
	(1 · 2 · 5) 952	גָּזַל	to seize, plunder (2 · 29 · 30) 159 I

אִוֶּלֶת 6 folly (2 · 25) 17

אַשְׁמָה doing wrong, committing a trespass or offense (1 · 19) 80

נִכְחַד to be hidden (2 · 11 · 32) 470

קוה 7 to wait (3 · 6 · 45) 875 I

נכלם to be put to shame, dishohored, confounded (5 · 26 · 38) 483

כְּלִמָּה 8 ignominy, reproach (7 · 30) 484

מוּזָר 9 Hoph. ptc. = estranged (1 · 1 · 6) 266 I זרר

נָכְרִי unknown, unfamiliar (1 · 45) 648

קִנְאָה 10 zeal (3 · 43) 888

חרף to reproach (2 · 4 · 38) 357 I

צוֹם 11 fast, fasting (3 · 25) 847

לְבוּשׁ 12 garment, clothing (5 · 30) 528

שַׂק sackcloth (3 · 48) 974

מָשָׁל byword (4 · 39) 605 II

שִׂיח 13 to talk, sing (13 · 18 · 20) 967

נְגִינָה music, song (9 · 14) 618

שֵׁכָר intoxicating drink, strong drink (1 · 23) 1016

יֵשַׁע 14 salvation (20 · 36) 447

טִיט 15 mud, mire (3 · 13) 376

טָבַע to sink (3 · 6 · 10) 371

שֹׂנֵא enemy (12 · 41[?]) 971 שׂנא

מַעֲמַקִּים depths (3 · 5) 771

שֶׁטֶף 16 to overflow, rinse or wash off (4 · 28 · 31) 1009

שִׁבֹּלֶת flowing stream (2 · 20) 987 I

בָּלַע to swallow up, engulf (3 · 20 · 41) 118

מְצוֹלָה depth, deep (5 · 12) 846

אטר to shut up, close (1 · 1 · 1) 32

בְּאֵר well, pit (2 · 37) 91

רַחֲמִים 17 compassion (11 · 38) 933

בֹּשֶׁת 20 shame (7 · 30) 102

כְּלִמָּה ignominy, reproach (7 · 30) 484

צֹרֵר vexer, harasser (12 · 17) 865 III צרר

נוּשׁ 21 to be sick (1 · 1 · 1) 633

קוה Piel, to wait, look eagerly, for (12 · 39 · 45) 875 I

נוד to condole, show sympathy (2 · 19 · 26) 626

בָּרוּת 22 food (1 · 2) 136

ראשׁ bitter and poisonous herb (1 · 12) 912 II

צָמָא thirst (2 · 17) 854

חֹמֶץ vinegar (1 · 5) 330

פַּח 23 bird trap (9 · 25) 809 I

מוֹקֵשׁ lure, snare (6 · 27) 430

חָשַׁךְ 24 to grow dim, dark (1 · 11 · 17) 364

מָתְנַיִם loins (2 · 50) 608

הַמְעַד to make to totter (1 · 1 · 7) 588

זַעַם 25 indignation (4 · 22) 276

חָרוֹן w/ אַף = fierceness of anger (6 · 41) 354, 60 I אַף 3

הִשִּׂיג to overtake (4 · 49 · 49) 673

טִירָה 26 encampment (1 · 7) 377

מַכְאוֹב 27 pain (3 · 16) 456

נמחה 29 to be wiped out (3 · 9 · 34) 562 I

כָּאַב 30 to be in pain (1 · 4 · 8) 456

שָׂגַב to set on high (5 · 6 · 20) 960

תּוֹדָה 31 thanksgiving, praise (12 · 32) 392

מַקְרִן 32 to display horns (1 · 1 · 4) 902 קרן

מַפְרִיס Hiph. ptc. = having hooves (1 · 12 · 14) 828 פרס

עָנָו 33 poor, afflicted, meek (13 · 22) 776

אָסִיר 34 prisoner (5 · 17) 64

בָּזָה to despise (6 · 31 · 42) 102

רָמַשׂ 35 to creep, move lightly, glide about (2 · 16 · 16) 942

אֹהֵב 37 friend (12 · 36) 12

Psalm 70

עֶזְרָה 2 help (14 · 26) 740 I

חוּשׁ to make haste (8 · 15 · 21) 301 I

חפר 3 to be abashed, ashamed (7 · 13 · 17) 344 II

נָסוֹג   to be turned back, repulsed (6 · 14 · 25) 690

אָחוֹר   backwards, behind (12 · 41) 30

נכלם   to be put to shame, dishonored, confounded (5 · 26 · 38) 483

חָפֵץ   delighting in, taking pleasure in (6 · 12) 343

עֵקֶב   4 in consequence of, for; על ע' according to the consequence of (5 · 15) 784

בֹּשֶׁת   shame (7 · 30) 102

הֶאָח   aha! (4 · 9) 210

שׂוֹשׂ   5 to exult, rejoice (7 · 27) 965

אֹהֵב   friend (12 · 36) 12

חוּשׁ   6 to make haste (8 · 15 · 21) 301 I

עֵזֶר   help (11 · 21) 740 I

פלט   to deliver (19 · 24 · 27) 812

אָחַר   to delay, tarry (3 · 15 · 17) 29

Psalm 71

חָסָה   1 to seek refuge (25 · 37 · 37) 340

פלט   2 to deliver (19 · 24 · 27) 812

מָעוֹן   3 dwelling, refuge (5 · 18) 732 I

מְצוּדָה   fastness, stronghold (7 · 18) 854 II

פלט   4 to deliver (19 · 24 · 27) 812

עוּל   to act wrongfully (1 · 2 · 2) 732 vb. denom.

חמץ   to be ruthless (1 · 1 · 1) 330 III

תִּקְוָה   5 hope, outcome (3 · 32) 876 II

מִבְטָח   confidence (3 · 15) 105

נְעוּרִים   youth (8 · 46) 655

נסמך   6 to support or brace yourself (1 · 6 · 48) 701

מֵעֶה   womb (3 · 31) 588

גזה   to cut (1 · 1 · 1) 159

מוֹפֵת   7 sign, wonder (5 · 36) 68

מַחְסֶה   refuge, shelter (12 · 20) 340

זִקְנָה   9 old age (2 · 6) 279

עֶזְרָה   12 help (14 · 26) 740 I

חוּשׁ   to make haste (8 · 15 · 21) 301 I

שׂטן   13 to be or act as adversary (5 · 6 · 6) 966

עָטָה   to wrap, envelop oneself (4 · 11 · 14) 741 I

כְּלִמָּה   ignominy, reproach (7 · 30) 484

יחל   14 to wait, hope (14 · 25 · 42) 403

תְּשׁוּעָה   15 deliverance (13 · 34) 448

סְפֹרָה   number (1 · 1) 708

נְעוּרִים   17 youth (8 · 46) 655

הֵנָּה   hither (1 · 49) 244 I

נִפְלָאוֹת   פלא 810 wonderful acts (27 · 44)

זִקְנָה   18 old age (2 · 6) 279

שֵׂיבָה   grey hair; old age (2 · 20) 966

תְּהוֹם   20 deep, sea, abyss (12 · 36) 1062

גְּדוּלָה   21 greatness (3 · 12) 153

נֵבֶל   22 harp (8 · 27) 614 II

זמר   to sing, make music (39 · 43 · 43) 274 I

כִּנּוֹר   lyre (13 · 41) 490

זמר   23 to sing, make music (39 · 43 · 43) 274 I

הגה   24 to utter (10 · 23 · 25) 211 I

חפר   to be abashed, ashamed (7 · 13 · 17) 344 II

Psalm 72

דין   2 to judge, minister judgment (8 · 23 · 24) 192

דָּכָא   4 to crush (4 · 11 · 18) 193

עָשַׁק   ptc. = oppressor, extortioner (6 · 36 · 37) 798

יָרֵחַ   5 moon (8 · 27) 437

מָטָר   6 rain (3 · 38) 564

גֵּז   mowing, shearing (1 · 4) 159

רְבִיבִים   copious showers (2 · 6) 914

זַרְזִיף   drop, dripping (1 · 1) 284

פָּרַח   7 to bud, sprout, shoot (3 · 29 · 34) 827 II

בְּלִי without (4 · 23) 115

יָרֵחַ moon (8 · 27) 437

רדה 8 to have dominion, rule, dominate (4 · 22 · 23) 921 I

אֶפֶס ends, extreme limits (6 · 27) 67

כָּרַע 9 to bow (4 · 30 · 36) 502

צִי desert dweller (here of people) (2 · 36) 850 II

לחך to lick (1 · 5 · 6) 535

אִי 10 coastlands, islands (2 · 36) 15 I

אֶשְׁכָּר gift (1 · 2) 1016

שׁוּע 12 to cry for help (9 · 21 · 21[?]) 1002

עֹזֵר help, helper (7 · 19) 740 עזר

חוס 13 to pity, have pity (1 · 24 · 24) 299

דַּל reduced, poor (5 · 48) 195

תֹּךְ 14 injury, oppression (3 · 4) 1067

יקר to be precious, prized (3 · 9 · 11) 429

פִּסָּה 16 [dub.] abundance, plenty (1 · 1) 821

בַּר grain, corn (2 · 14) 141 III

רעש to quake, shake (1 · 1 · 1[?]) 950

צוץ to blossom (5 · 7 · 8) 848 II

עֵשֶׂב herb, herbage (7 · 33) 793

נין 17 to increase (1 · 1 · 1) 630

אשר to pronouce happy, call blessed (1 · 7 · 9) 80

נִפְלָאוֹת 18 wonderful acts (27 · 44) 810 פלא

אָמֵן 19 verily, truly (4 · 30) 53

Psalm 73

בַּר 1 pure, clean (3 · 6) 141 II

כְּאַיִן 2 almost (2 · 7) 34 אִיס II.1

אָשׁוּר step, going (6 · 10) 81

קִנֵּא 3 to be envious of (3 · 4 · 4) 888

הלל to be boastful (3 · 3 · 14[?]) 237 II

חַרְצֻבָּה 4 pang (1 · 2) 359

בָּרִיא fat (1 · 14) 135

אוּל body, belly (1 · 1) 17 I

אֱנוֹשׁ 5 man, mankind (13 · 42) 60

ענק 6 to be a necklace for (1 · 1 · 3) 778

גַּאֲוָה pride, haughtiness (7 · 19) 144

עטף to put on for, envelop oneself (2 · 2 · 3) 742 II

שִׁית garment (1 · 2) 1011

מַשְׂכִּית 7 imagination, conceit (1 · 6) 967

המיק 8 to mock, deride (1 · 1 · 1) 558 מוק

עֹשֶׁק oppression, extortion (3 · 15) 799

שׁתת 9 to set, appoint (2 · 2 · 2) 1060

הֲלֹם 10 thither (1 · 11) 240

נמצה to be drained out (1 · 3 · 7) 594

אֵיכָה 11 in what manner? (1 · 18) 32

דֵּעָה knowledge (1 · 6) 395

שָׁלֵו 12 at ease, quiet (1 · 8) 1017

השׂגה to increase (1 · 1 · 4) 960

רִיק 13 emptiness, vanity (3 · 12) 938

זכה to make or keep clean, pure (2 · 3 · 8) 269

נִקָּיוֹן innocency, freedom from guilt (2 · 5) 667

תּוֹכַחַת 14 correction, rebuke (3 · 24) 407

בגד 15 to act or deal treacherously, faith-lessly, deceitfully (5 · 49 · 49) 93

חֶלְקָה 18 slippery place (3 · 12) 325 II

מַשּׁוּאוֹת deceptions, ruins (2 · 2) 674

שַׁמָּה 19 a waste (2 · 39) 1031 I

רֶגַע moment (3 · 22) 921

סרף to come to an end (1 · 4 · 10) 692

בַּלָּהָה calamity, destruction (1 · 10) 117

הֵקִיץ 20 to awake (7 · 22 · 23) 884 II

צֶלֶם image (2 · 17) 853

בָּזָה to despise (6 · 31 · 42) 102

התחמץ 21 to be soured, embittered (1 · 1 · 4) 329 I

כִּלְיָה kidney (5 · 31) 480

השתונן to be pierced (1 · 1 · 9) 1041 שנן

בַּעַר 22 brutish (3 · 5) 129

הנחה 24 to lead, guide (12 · 26 · 40) 634

שְׁאֵר 26 flesh (3 · 17) 984

רָחָק 27 removing, departing (1 · 1) 935

443

הַצְמִית   to exterminate, annihilate
(9 · 10 · 15) 935

קֵרְבָה   28 approach (1 · 2) 898

מַחְסֶה   refuge, shelter (12 · 20) 340

Psalm 74

מַשְׂכִּיל   1 contemplative poem (14 · 14) 968

זָנַח   to reject, spurn (10 · 16 · 19) 276 I

לָנֶצַח   forever (18 · 27) 664 נצח

עָשַׁן   to smoke (4 · 6 · 6) 798

מַרְעִית   pasturing, shepherding (4 · 10) 945

מַשּׁוּאוֹת   3 deceptions, ruins (2 · 2) 674

נֶצַח   everlastingness; משאות נ' = perpet-
ual desolations (18 · 42) 664

שָׁאַג   4 to roar (4 · 20 · 20) 980

צֹרֵר   vexer, harasser (12 · 17) 865 III צרר

יִוָּדַע   5 Niph., it is perceived, it appears
(>50) 393 ידע 3

לְמָעְלָה   upwards (1 · 34) 751 II מַעַל 2.c

סְבׇךְ   thicket (1 · 2) 687

קַרְדֹּם   axe (1 · 5) 899

פִּתּוּחַ   6 engraving (1 · 11) 836

יַחַד   together, altogether (14 · 44) 403

כַּשִּׁיל   axe (1 · 1) 506

כֵּילַפּוֹת   axe (1 · 1) 476

הלם   to smite down, strike off (2 · 8 · 8)
240

נִינָם   8 let us suppress them [dub.]
(1 · 4 [?]) 413 ינה

יַחַד   together, altogether (14 · 44) 403

מָתַי   10 when? (13 · 42) 607

חֵרֵף   to reproach (9 · 34 · 38) 357 I

נָאַץ   to contemn, spurn (4 · 15 · 24) 610

לָנֶצַח   forever (18 · 27) 664 נצח

חֵיק   11 bosom (4 · 38) 300

פּוֹרֵר   13 to divide (1 · 1 · 4[?]) 830 II

תַּנִּין   sea monster; dragon, serpent
(3 · 15) 1072

רצץ   14 to crush in pieces (1 · 3 · 19) 954

לִוְיָתָן   leviathan, serpent (2 · 5) 531

מַאֲכָל   food (3 · 30) 38

צִי   a wild beast, desert dweller (2 · 6)
850 II

מַעְיָן   15 spring (5 · 23) 745

אֵיתָן   steady flow, permanence (1 · 14)
450 I

מָאוֹר   16 light, luminary (2 · 17) 22

גְּבוּלָה   17 border, boundary (1 · 10) 148

קַיִץ   summer (2 · 20) 884

חֹרֶף   harvest time, autumn (1 · 7) 358

יָצַר   to form, fashion (6 · 41 · 44) 427

חֵרֵף   18 to reproach (9 · 34 · 38) 357 I

נָבָל   senseless (5 · 18) 614 I

נָאַץ   to contemn, spurn (4 · 15 · 24) 610

תּוֹר   19 turtle dove (1 · 14) 1076 II

חַיָּה   life (3 · 12[?]) 312 I.2

לָנֶצַח   forever (18 · 42) 664 נצח

מַחְשָׁךְ   20 dark place (4 · 7) 365

נָאוֹת   habitation (5 · 45[?]) 627 II נָוֶה 2

דַּךְ   21 oppressed, distressed (3 · 4) 194

נכלם   to be put to shame, dishonored,
confounded (5 · 26 · 38) 483

נָבָל   22 senseless (5 · 18) 614 I

צֹרֵר   23 vexer, harasser (12 · 17) 865 III צרר

שָׁאוֹן   roar, din, crash (4 · 18) 981

קָם   adversary (5 · 12) 877 קום 2

Psalm 75

נִפְלָאוֹת   2 wonderful acts (27 · 44) 810 פלא

מֵישָׁר   3 uprightness, equity (7 · 19) 449

נָמוֹג   4 to melt away (1 · 8 · 17) 556

תִּכֵּן   to regulate (1 · 4 · 18) 1067

הלל   5 to be boastful (3 · 3 · 14[?]) 237 II

צַוָּאר   6 neck, back of neck (1 · 41) 848

עָתָק   forward; arrogant (3 · 4) 801

מוֹצָא   7 east (6 · 27) 425 I.3.c

מַעֲרָב   west, setting place (3 · 14) 788 II

הִשְׁפִּיל   8 to lay low, humiliate (4 · 19 · 30) 1050

כּוֹס 9 cup (5 · 31) 468 I

חָמַר to ferment, boil or foam up
(2 · 3 · 5) 330 I

מֶסֶךְ mixture (1 · 1) 587

הִגִּיר to pour out (2 · 5 · 10) 620 נגר

שְׁמֶר pl. = lees, dregs (1 · 5) 1038 II

מצה to drain, drain out (1 · 4 · 7) 594

זמר 10 to sing, make music (39 · 43 · 43)
274 I

גָּדַע 11 to hew off, down, in two
(2 · 9 · 22) 154

Psalm 76

נְגִינָה 1 music, song (9 · 14) 618

סֹךְ 3 covert, lair (3 · 4) 697

מְעֹנָה den, lair (2 · 9) 733

רֶשֶׁף 4 flame (2 · 7) 958 I

נָאוֹר 5 light (1 · 1) 21 אור

אַדִּיר majestic (7 · 27) 12

טֶרֶף prey (3 · 18) 383

הִשְׁתּוֹלֵל 6 to be spoiled (1 · 2 · 15) 1021 שלל II

אַבִּיר mighty, valiant (5 · 17) 7

נום to slumber, be drowsy (3 · 6 · 6) 630

שֵׁנָה sleep (3 · 23) 446

גְּעָרָה 7 rebuke (4 · 15) 172

נִרְדָּם to be or fall fast asleep (1 · 7 · 7) 922

נוֹרָא 8 awe inspiring, awful (15 · 44) 431
ירא

מֵאָז from time of, since (2 · 18) 23

דִּין 9 judgment (3 · 19) 192

שָׁקַט to be quiet, undisturbed (2 · 31 · 41)
1052

עָנָו 10 poor, afflicted (13 · 22) 776

חגר 11 to gird oneself (4 · 44 · 44) 291

נָדַר 12 to make a vow (2 · 31 · 31) 623

הוֹבִיל to bear along (4 · 7 · 18) 384

שַׁי gift (2 · 3) 1009

מוֹרָא fear, object of reverence (2 · 12) 432

בצר 13 to cut off (1 · 1 · 1[?]) 130

נָגִיר leader, ruler, prince (1 · 44) 617

נוֹרָא awe inspiring, awful (15 · 44) 431
יָרֵא

Psalm 77

הַאֲזִין 2 to listen, give ear (15 · 41 · 41) 24

נגר 3 to be stretched out (1 · 4 · 10) 620

פוג to grow numb (1 · 3 · 4) 806

מאן to refuse (2 · 46 · 46) 549

המה 4 to murmur (11 · 33 · 33) 242

שׂיח to complain (13 · 18 · 20) 967

הִתְעַטֵּף to faint, faint away (4 · 6 · 11) 742
III

שְׁמֻרָה 5 eyelid (1 · 1) 1037

נפעם to be disturbed (1 · 3 · 5) 821

נְגִינָה 7 music, song (9 · 14) 618

שׂיח to muse, meditate, study
(13 · 18 · 20) 967

חפשׂ to search for (1 · 8 · 23) 344

זָנַח 8 to reject, spurn (10 · 16 · 19) 276 I

אָפֵס 9 to cease, fail, come to an end
(1 · 5 · 5) 67

לָנֶצַח forever (18 · 42) 664 נצח

גָּמַר to come to an end, be no more
(5 · 5 · 5) 170

אֹמֶר promise (4 · 6[?]) 56 אמר 2

קָפַץ 10 to draw together, shut (2 · 5 · 7) 891

רַחֲמִים compassion (11 · 38) 933

חָלַל 11 to pierce (2 · 2 · 7) 319 I

שָׁנָה to change (1 · 13 · 26) 1039 I

מַעֲלָל 12 deed, practice (5 · 41) 760

פֶּלֶא wonder (7 · 13) 810

הגה 13 to meditate, muse (10 · 23 · 25) 211
I

פֹּעַל deed, thing done (11 · 37) 821

עֲלִילָה deed (9 · 24) 760

שׂיח to muse, meditate, study
(13 · 18 · 20) 967

פֶּלֶא 15 wonder (7 · 13) 810

חִיל 17 to writhe, be in anguish (5 · 30 · 47) חול I 296

רָגַז to quake (5 · 30 · 41) 919

תְּהוֹם deep, sea, abyss (12 · 36) 1062

זֶרֶם 18 to pour forth, flood (1 · 1 · 2) 281

עָב dark cloud, cloud mass (5 · 30) 728 II

שַׁחַק cloud (9 · 21) 1007

רַעַם 19 thunder (3 · 6) 947

גַּלְגַּל wheel, whirlwing (2 · 11) 165

הֵאִיר to light up; cause to shine (15 · 34 · 40) אור 21

בָּרָק lightning (5 · 21) 140

תֵּבֵל world (15 · 36) 385

רָגַז to quake (5 · 30 · 41) 919

רעש to quake, shake (4 · 21 · 29) 950

שְׁבִיל 20 way, path (1 · 2) 987

עָקֵב footprint, heel (5 · 14) 784 I

נחה 21 to lead, bring (6 · 14 · 40) 634

Psalm 78

מַשְׂכִּיל 1 contemplative poem (14 · 14) 968

הַאֲזִין to listen, give ear (15 · 41 · 41) 24

אֹמֶר utterance, word (7 · 48) 56

מָשָׁל 2 poem (4 · 39) 605 II

הִבִּיעַ to pour forth, emit (6 · 10 · 11) 615 נבע

חִידָה riddle (2 · 17) 295

כָּחַד 4 to hide, conceal (2 · 15 · 32) 470

עֱזוּז strength, might, fierceness (2 · 3) 739

נִפְלָאוֹת wonderful acts (27 · 44) 810 פלא

כֶּסֶל 7 confidence (2 · 6) 492

מַעֲלָל deed, practice (5 · 41) 760

סרר 8 ptc. = stubborn (4 · 18 · 18) 710

מָרָה to be rebellious, disobedient (3 · 21 · 43) 598

נשק 9 to handle or be equipped (1 · 3 · 3) 676 II

רָמָה ptc. = bow shooter, bowman (1 · 4 · 4) 941 I

קְרָב battle, war (4 · 8) 898

מֵאֵן 10 to refuse (2 · 46 · 46) 898

עֲלִילָה 11 deed (9 · 24) 760

נִפְלָאוֹת wonderful act (27 · 44) 810 פלא

פֶּלֶא 12 wonder (7 · 13) 810

נֵד 13 heap (2 · 6) 622

הִנְחָה 14 to lead, bring (12 · 26 · 40) 634

תְּהוֹם 15 deep, sea, abyss (12 · 36) 1062

נָזַל 16 streams, floods (2 · 6) 633

הִמְרָה 17 to show disobedience, rebelliousness (7 · 22 · 43) 598

צִיָּה drought, desert (4 · 16) 851

נִסָּה 18 to test, try (6 · 36 · 36) 650

אֹכֶל food (6 · 44) 38

זוּב 20 to flow, gush (2 · 29 · 29) 264

שָׁטַף to flow, run (4 · 28 · 31) 1009

שְׁאֵר flesh (3 · 17) 984

הִתְעַבָּר 21 to become furious (4 · 8 · 8) 720

נִשְּׂקָה to be kindled (1 · 1 · 3) 969 שׂלק

שַׁחַק 23 cloud (9 · 21) 1007

מִמַּעַל above, on top of (1 · 29) 751 II.1.a

הִמְטִיר 24 to send rain, rain (2 · 16 · 17) 565

מָן manna (1 · 14) 577 I

דָּגָן corn (3 · 40) 186

אַבִּיר 25 mighty, valiant (5 · 17) 7

צֵידָה provision (1 · 9) 845

שֹׂבַע satiety (2 · 8) 959

נָהַג 26 to lead on, guide (3 · 10 · 30) 624 I

תֵּימָן south wind (1 · 24) 412 I

הִמְטִיר 27 to send rain, rain (3 · 16 · 17) 565

שְׁאֵר flesh (3 · 17) 984

חוֹל sand (2 · 22) 297

תַּאֲוָה 29 desire (8 · 22) 16 I

זוּר 30 to become estranged (2 · 3 · 6) 266 I

תַּאֲוָה desire (8 · 22) 16 I

אֹכֶל food (6 · 44) 38

מִשְׁמָן 31 stout or vigorous ones (1 · 4) 1032

בָּחוּר young man (3 · 45) 104

הִכְרִיעַ to cause to bow down (3 · 6 · 36) 502

נִפְלָאוֹת 32 wonderful acts (27 · 44) 810 פלא

בֶּהָלָה 33 dismay, sudden terror (1 · 2) 96

שִׁחֵר 34 to seek early, eagerly, for (2 · 12 · 13) 1007

גֹּאֵל 35 redeemer, kinsman (2 · 44[?]) 145 I גאל

פִּתָּה 36 to deceive; persuade (1 · 17 · 27) 834

כִּזֵּב to lie, tell a lie (2 · 12 · 16) 469

רַחוּם 38 compassionate (6 · 13) 933

כַּמָּה 40 how often? (3 · 13) 552 מָה 4.c

הִמְרָה to show disobedience, rebelliousness (7 · 22 · 43) 598

הֶעֱצִיב to cause pain (1 · 1 · 15) 780

יְשִׁימוֹן waste, wilderness (4 · 13) 445

נִסָּה 41 to test, try (6 · 36 · 36) 650

הִתְוָה to pain, wound (1 · 1 · 1) 1063 II

מוֹפֵת 43 sign, wonder (5 · 36) 68

נֹזֵל 44 streams, floods (2 · 6) 633

עָרֹב 45 swarm (2 · 9) 786

צְפַרְדֵּעַ [coll.] frogs (2 · 13) 862

חָסִיל 46 locust (1 · 6) 340

יְבוּל produce (3 · 13) 385

יְגִיעַ produce, product (3 · 16) 388

אַרְבֶּה locust (3 · 24) 916

בָּרָד 47 hail (6 · 29) 135

שִׁקְמָה sycamore tree (1 · 7) 1054

חֲנָמָל frost, devastating flood [dub.] (1 · 1) 335 חֲנָמֵל

בָּרָד 48 hail (6 · 29) 135

בְּעִיר [coll.] cattle, beasts (1 · 6) 129

רֶשֶׁף flame (2 · 7) 958 I

חָרוֹן 49 אַף w = fierceness of anger (6 · 41) 354, 60 אַף I.3

עֶבְרָה rage, fury (5 · 34) 720

זַעַם indignation (4 · 22) 276

מִשְׁלַחַת deputation, sending (1 · 2) 1020

פִּלֵּס 50 to make level (1 · 6 · 6) 814

נָתִיב path (2 · 5) 677

חָשַׂךְ to keep, withhold (2 · 26 · 28) 362

חַיָּה life (3 · 12[?]) 312 I.2

דֶּבֶר cattle-plague, murrain (1 · 46) 184

אוֹן 51 manly vigor (2 · 10) 20 I

נָהַג 52 to lead on, guide (3 · 10 · 30) 624 I

עֵדֶר flock (1 · 39) 727 I

הִנְחָה 53 to lead, guide (12 · 26 · 40) 634

בֶּטַח security; securely (3 · 43) 105 I

פָּחַד to be in dread (5 · 23 · 26) 808

גֵּרַשׁ 55 to drive out, away (3 · 35 · 48) 176

חֶבֶל measuring cord, line (8 · 50) 286 I

נִסָּה 56 to test, try (6 · 36 · 36) 650

הִמְרָה to show disobedience, rebelliousness (7 · 22 · 43) 598

עֵדָה testimony (25 · 32) 730 III

נָסוֹג 57 to be turned back, repulsed (6 · 14 · 25) 690 I

בָּגַד to act or deal treacherously, deceitfully (5 · 49 · 49) 93

רְמִיָּה deceit, treachery (6 · 15) 941

פָּסִיל 58 idol, image (1 · 23) 820

הִקְנִא to provoke to jealous anger (1 · 4 · 34) 888

הִתְעַבֵּר 59 to become furious (4 · 8 · 8) 720

נָטַשׁ 60 to forsake, abandon (3 · 33 · 40) 643

שְׁבִי 61 captivity, captive (2 · 49) 985

הִתְעַבֵּר 62 to become furious (4 · 8 · 8) 720

בָּחוּר 63 young man (3 · 45) 104

בְּתוּלָה virgin (3 · 50) 143

יָקַץ 65 to awake (1 · 11 · 11) 429

יָשֵׁן sleeping (1 · 9) 445 I

הִתְרוֹנֵן to be overcome (1 · 1 · 1) 929

אָחוֹר 66 backwards, behind (12 · 41) 30

רָם 69 heights; high, exalted (5 · 31[?]) 926 רום

יָסַד to found, establish (7 · 20 · 41) 413

מִכְלָא 70 fold, enclosure (2 · 3) 476 מִכְלָה I

עוּל 71 to give suck (1 · 5 · 5) 732 I

תֹּם 72 integrity, completeness (7 · 23) 1070

תְּבוּנָה understanding (4 · 42) 108

447

הנחה   to lead, guide (12 · 26 · 40) 634

Psalm 79

עִי   1 ruin, heap of ruins (1 · 5) 730

נְבֵלָה   2 carcass, corpse (1 · 48) 615

מַאֲכָל   food (3 · 30) 38

חָסִיד   pious, godly (25 · 32) 339

שָׁכֵן   4 neighbor (6 · 20) 1015

לַעַג   mocking, derision (3 · 7) 541

קֶלֶס   derision (2 · 3) 887

אנף   5 to be angry (4 · 8 · 14) 60

לָנֶצַח   forever (18 · 42) 664 נצח

קִנְאָה   anger (3 · 43) 888

נָוֶה   7 habitation (5 · 45[?]) 627 I

קדם   8 to come to meet (12 · 24 · 26) 869

רַחֲמִים   compassion (11 · 38) 933

דלל   to be low, brought low (3 · 8 · 8) 195

יֵשַׁע   9 salvation (20 · 36) 447

אַיֵּה   10 where? (5 · 44) 32

נְקָמָה   vengeance (5 · 27) 668

אֲנָקָה   11 crying, groaning (3 · 4) 60 I

אָסִיר   prisoner (5 · 17) 64

גֹּדֶל   greatness, magnitude (2 · 13) 152

תְּמוּתָה   death (2 · 2) 560

שָׁכֵן   12 neighbor (6 · 20) 1015

חֵיק   bosom (4 · 28) 300

חרף   to reproach (9 · 34 · 38) 357 I

מַרְעִית   13 pasturing, shepherding (4 · 10) 945

Psalm 80

שׁוֹשָׁן   1 lily (4 · 17) 1004 שׁוּשַׁן I

הַאֲזִין   2 to listen, give ear (15 · 41 · 41) 24

נהג   to drive (1 · 20 · 30) 624 I

הוֹפִיעַ   to shine out, forth (3 · 8 · 8) 422

הֵאִיר   4 to make shine (15 · 34 · 40) 21 אור

מָתַי   5 when? (13 · 42) 607

עשׁן   to fume, be wroth (4 · 6 · 6) 798

דִּמְעָה   6 tears (8 · 23) 199

שָׁלִישׁ   third (name of a measure) (1 · 2) 1026 I

מָדוֹן   7 object of contention (1 · 12) 193 I

שָׁכֵן   neighbor (6 · 20) 1015

לעג   to mock, deride (3 · 35 · 18) 541

הֵאִיר   8 to make shine (15 · 34 · 40) 21 אור

גרשׁ   9 to drive out, away (3 · 35 · 48) 176

הִשְׁרִישׁ   10 to take root (1 · 3 · 8) 1057

שֹׁרֶשׁ   root (1 · 33) 1057

עָנָף   11 branch, bough (1 · 7) 778

קָצִיר   12 bough, branch (1 · 5) 894 II

יוֹנֶקֶת   shoot, twig (1 · 6) 413

פָּרַץ   13 to break through, down (4 · 46 · 49) 829 I

גָּדֵר   wall, fence (2 · 13) 154

ארה   to pluck, gather (1 · 2 · 2) 71 I

כרסם   14 to tear off (1 · 1 · 1) 493

חֲזִיר   boar, swine (1 · 7) 360

זִיז   [coll.] moving things (2 · 2) 265 I

שָׂדַי   field, land (5 · 13) 961

כַּנָּה   16 root, stock (1 · 1) 488

אמץ   to assure, secure (3 · 19 · 41) 54

כסח   17 to cut off (1 · 2 · 2) 492

גְּעָרָה   rebuke (4 · 15) 172

אמץ   18 to assure, secure (3 · 19 · 41) 54

סוג   19 to backslide (2 · 3 · 25) 690 I

הֵאִיר   20 to make shine (15 · 34 · 40) 21 אור

Psalm 81

גִּתִּית   1 lyre, melody (3 · 3) 388

הֵרִיעַ   2 to shout (9 · 40 · 44) 929 רוע

זִמְרָה   3 melody, song (2 · 4) 274 I

תֹּף   timbrel, tamborine (3 · 17) 1074

כִּנּוֹר   lyre (13 · 41) 490

נָעִים   lovely, beautiful (6 · 7) 653 I

נֵבֶל   harp (8 · 27) 614 II

כֵּסֶא   4 full moon (1 · 2) 490

סֵבֶל   7 load, burden (1 · 3) 687

שְׁכֶם   shoulder, back (2 · 22) 1014 I

דּוּד — basket, pot (1 · 7) 188

חִלֵּץ — 8 to rescue, deliver (10 · 14 · 27) 322 I

סֵתֶר — covering, cover (10 · 35) 712

רַעַם — thunder (3 · 6) 947

בָּחַן — to prove, test, try (9 · 24 · 28) 103

הֵעִיד — 9 to exhort solemnly, admonish (2 · 39 · 44) 729 עוד

נֵכָר — 10 foreignness (6 · 36) 648

הִרְחִיב — 11 to enlarge (6 · 21 · 25) 931

שְׁרִירוּת — 13 stubbornness (1 · 10) 1057

מוֹעֵצָה — counsel, plan, principle, device (2 · 7) 420

לוּ — 14 oh that! if only! (1 · 19) 530

הִכְנִיעַ — 15 to subdue (2 · 11 · 36) 488

כָּחַשׁ — 16 to cringe = come cringing (3 · 19 · 22) 471

חִטָּה — 17 wheat (2 · 30) 334

Psalm 82

מָתַי — 2 when? (13 · 42) 607

עָוֶל — injustice, unrighteousness (3 · 21) 732

דַּל — 3 reduced, weak, helpless (5 · 48) 195

יָתוֹם — orphan (8 · 42) 450

רָשׁ — poor man (men) (1 · 21) 930 רוש

הִצְדִּיק — to do justice (1 · 12 · 41) 842

פִּלֵּט — 4 to deliver (19 · 24 · 27) 812

דָּל — reduced, poor (5 · 48) 195

חֲשֵׁכָה — 5 darkness (3 · 6) 365

נָמוֹט — to be shaken, moved, overthrown (16 · 22 · 39) 556

מוֹסָד — foundation (3 · 13) 414

אָכֵן — 7 surely, truly (3 · 18) 38

Psalm 83

דֳּמִי — 2 quiet (1 · 3) 198

חָרַשׁ — to be silent (6 · 7 · 47) 361 II

שָׁקַט — to be quiet, inactive (2 · 31 · 41) 1052

הָמָה — 3 to roar, be tumultuous (11 · 33 · 33) 242

הֶעֱרִים — 4 to make crafty (1 · 4 · 5) 791

סוֹד — counsel (6 · 21) 691

צָפַן — to hide (7 · 23 · 28) 860

הִכְחִיד — 5 to efface, annihilate (1 · 6 · 32) 470

נִלְוָה — 9 to join oneself, be joined (1 · 11 · 12) 530 I לוה

דֹּמֶן — 11 dung (1 · 6) 199

נָדִיב — 12 noble, princely (8 · 27) 622

נָסִיךְ — prince (1 · 6) 651 II

נָוֶה — 13 pasture, meadow (5 · 45[?]) 627 II

גַּלְגַּל — 14 whirl (2 · 11) 165

קַשׁ — stubble, chaff (1 · 16) 905

לֶהָבָה — 15 flame (4 · 19) 529

לָהַט — to set ablaze (3 · 9 · 11) 529

סַעַר — 16 tempest (2 · 8) 704

סוּפָה — storm wind (1 · 15) 693 I

בָּהַל — to dismay, terrify (2 · 10 · 39) 96

קָלוֹן — 17 dishonor, disgrace (1 · 17) 885

נִבְהַל — 18 to be disturbed, dismayed, terrified (8 · 24 · 39) 96

עֲדֵי — poetic for עד up to, until (6 · 12) 723 III עד

עַד — forever (29 · 48) 723 I

חָפֵר — to be abashed, ashamed (7 · 13 · 17) 344 II

Psalm 84

גִּתִּית — 1 lyre; melody (3 · 3) 388

יָדִיד — 2 lovely (4 · 8) 391

נִכְסַף — 3 to long for (1 · 4 · 6) 493

צִפּוֹר — 4 [coll.] birds 861 I

דְּרוֹר — swallow (1 · 2) 204 II

קֵן — nest (1 · 13) 890

אֶפְרֹחַ — pl. = young ones, young (of birds) (1 · 4) 827

אֶשֶׁר — 5 happiness, blessedness (19 · 45[?]) 80

449

אֶשֶׁר 6 happiness, blessedness (19 · 45[?]) 80

מְסִלָּה highway, raised way (1 · 27) 700

בָּכָא 7 balsam tree (1 · 5) 113

מַעְיָן spring (5 · 23) 745

העטה to wrap, envelop (2 · 3 · 14) 741 I

מוֹרֶה early rain (1 · 2) 435 I

הָאֱזִין 9 to listen, give ear (15 · 41 · 41) 24

מָשִׁיחַ 10 anointed (10 · 39) 603

הִסְתּוֹפֵף 11 *Hithpo.* inf = standing at the threshhold (1 · 1 · 1) 706 ספף

דוּר to dwell (1 · 2 · 2) 189

רֶשַׁע wickedness (6 · 30) 957

מָנַע 12 to withhold (2 · 25 · 29) 586

אֶשֶׁר 13 happiness, blessedness (19 · 45[?]) 80

Psalm 85

שְׁבִית 2 captivity, captives [coll.] (2 · 6) 986

עֶבְרָה 4 rage, fury (5 · 34) 720

חָרוֹן w אַף = fierceness of anger (6 · 41) 354, 60 אַף I.3

יֶשַׁע 5 salvation (20 · 36) 447

הֵפֵר to break, frustrate (2 · 41 · 44[?]) 830 פרר I

כַּעַס vexation, anger (4 · 25) 495

אנף 6 to be angry (4 · 8 · 14) 60

מָשַׁךְ to draw out, prolong (5 · 30 · 36) 604

יֶשַׁע 8 salvation (20 · 36) 447

חָסִיד 9 pious, godly (25 · 32) 339

כְּסִלָּה confidence; stupidity (1 · 2) 493

יָרֵא 10 afraid (27 · 46) 431

יֶשַׁע salvation (20 · 36) 447

נפגשׁ 11 to meet together, each other (1 · 3 · 14) 803

נָשַׁק to kiss (1 · 26 · 32) 676 I

צָמַח 12 to sprout, spring up (1 · 15 · 33) 855

נשׁקף to lean over, look down (1 · 10 · 22) 1054 I

יְבוּל 13 produce (3 · 13) 385

Psalm 86

חָסִיד 2 pious, godly (25 · 32) 339

סַלָּח 5 ready to forgive (1 · 1) 699

הָאֱזִין 6 to listen, give ear (15 · 41 · 41) 24 I

הִקְשִׁיב to give attention (8 · 45 · 46) 904

תַּחֲנוּן supplication for favor (8 · 18) 337

נִפְלָאוֹת 10 wonderful acts (27 · 44) 810 פלא

הוֹרָה 11 to direct, teach, instruct (8 · 45 · 45) 434 ירה

יַחֵד to unite (1 · 1 · 3) 402

תַּחְתִּי 13 lower. lowest (4 · 19) 1066

זֵד 14 insolent, presumptuous (8 · 13) 267

עָרִיץ awe inspiring, terror striking (3 · 20) 792

לְנֶגֶד over, for (13 · 32) 617 נֶגֶד 2.b

רַחוּם 15 compassionate (6 · 13) 933

חַנּוּן gracious (6 · 13) 337

אָרֵךְ long; א׳ אַפַּיִם = slow to anger (3 · 15) 74

שׂנֵא 17 enemy (12 · 41[?]) 971 שׂנֵא

Psalm 87

יְסוּדָה 1 foundation (1 · 1) 414

רַהַב 4 storm, arrogance; Rahab (3 · 7) 923

שָׁר 7 singer (2 · 9) 1010 שׁיר

חוֹלֵל to dance (1 · 2 · 9[?]) 296 I חול (cf. p.320 חלל II)

מַעְיָן spring (5 · 23) 745

Psalm 88

מַשְׂכִּיל 1 contemplative poem (14 · 14) 968

מָחֲלַת name of tune (2 · 2) 318 I

רִנָּה 3 ringing cry (15 · 33) 943 I

אֱיָל 5 help (1 · 1) 33

חָפְשִׁי 6 free (1 · 17) 344

נִגְזַר   to be cut off (1 · 6 · 12) 160

תַּחְתִּי   7 lower. lowest (4 · 19) 1066

מַחְשָׁךְ   dark place (4 · 7) 365

מְצוֹלָה   depth, deep (5 · 12) 846

סָמַךְ   8 to lean or lay (10 · 41 · 48) 701

מִשְׁבָּר   breaker (3 · 5) 991

כָּלָא   9 to shut up (4 · 14 · 17) 476

דָּאַב   10 to become faint, languish (1 · 3 · 3) 178

עֳנִי   affliction (10 · 36) 777

שׁטח   to spread out (1 · 1 · 5) 1008

פֶּלֶא   11 wonder (7 · 13) 810

רְפָאִים   shades, ghosts (1 · 8) 952 I

אֲבַדּוֹן   12 Abaddon; place of destruction (1 · 5) 2

פֶּלֶא   13 wonder (7 · 13) 810

נְשִׁיָּה   forgetfulness (1 · 1) 674

שׁוע   14 to cry for help (9 · 21 · 21[?]) 1002

קדם   to come to meet (12 · 24 · 26) 869

זנח   15 to reject, spurn (10 · 16 · 19) 276 I

גָּוַע   16 to perish, die (2 · 23 · 23) 157

נֹעַר   youth (1 · 4) 655

אֵימָה   terror, dread (2 · 17) 33

פוּן   to be numb, embarrassed (1 · 1 · 1) 806

חָרוֹן   17 pl. = bursts of burning anger (6 · 41) 354

בְּעוּתִים   terrors, alarms (1 · 2) 130

צמתת   to annihilate (2 · 2 · 15) 856

הִקִּיף   18 to surround, encompass (4 · 16 · 17) 668 II נקף

יַחַד   together, altogether (14 · 44) 403

אֹהֵב   19 lover; friend (12 · 36) 12

מַחְשָׁךְ   dark place (4 · 7) 365

Psalm 89

מַשְׂכִּיל   1 contemplative poem (14 · 14) 968

בָּחִיר   4 chosen, elect (5 · 13) 104

פֶּלֶא   6 wonder (7 · 13) 810

שַׁחַק   7 cloud (9 · 21) 1007

דָּמָה   to be like, resemble (3 · 13 · 27) 197 I

נערץ   8 ptc. = terrible (1 · 1 · 14) 791

סוֹד   assembly, company (6 · 21) 691

נוֹרָא   awe-inspiring, awful (15 · 44) 431 יָרֵא

חָסִין   9 strong, mighty (1 · 1) 340

גֵּאוּת   10 majesty; i.e., swelling (3 · 8) 145

גַּל   pl. = waves (5 · 16) 164

שׁבח   to still, soothe (1 · 2 · 3) 986 I

שׂוֹא   Qal inf. = rising (>50) 669 נשא

דִּכָּא   11 to crush (4 · 11 · 18) 193

רַהַב   storm, arrogance; Rahab (3 · 7) 923

פִּוַּר   to scatter (4 · 7 · 10) 808

תֵּבֵל   12 world (15 · 36) 385

מְלֹא   fullness (5 · 38) 571

יָסַד   to found, establish (7 · 20 · 41) 413

בָּרָא   13 to create, fashion, shape (3 · 38 · 48) 135 I

עזז   14 to be strong, prevail (4 · 9 · 11) 738

מָכוֹן   15 fixed place, place (4 · 17) 467

קדם   to come to meet (12 · 24 · 26) 869

אֶשֶׁר   16 happiness, blessedness (19 · 45[?]) 80

תְּרוּעָה   shout of joy (5 · 36) 929

גִּיל   17 to rejoice (19 · 45 · 45) 162

חָזוֹן   20 vision (1 · 35) 302

חָסִיד   pious, godly (25 · 32) 339

שׁוה   to set, place (4 · 5 · 5) 1001 II

עֵזֶר   help (11 · 21) 740 I

בָּחוּר   chosen (1 · 19) 103 בָּחַר Qal 7

אָמֵץ   22 to make firm, strengthen (3 · 19 · 41) 54

עַוְלָה   23 injustice, wrong (9 · 32) 732

הִשִּׁיא   to act as creditor, make exactions (2 · 15 · 16[?]) 673 I נשא

כָּתַת 24	to beat or crush fine (1 · 5 · 17) 510	
נָגַף	to strike, smite (2 · 25 · 49) 619	
עַד 30	עֲדֵי = forever (29 · 48) 723 I	
הֵפֵר 34	to frustrate, make ineffectual (2 · 3 · 3[?]) 830 I פרר Hiph 2.c	
שָׁקַר	to deal falsely (2 · 5 · 6) 1055	
מוֹצָא 35	utterance (6 · 27) 425 I	
שָׁנָה	to change, alter (2 · 9 · 26) 1039 I	
כָּזַב 36	to lie, tell a lie (2 · 12 · 16) 469	
יָרֵחַ 38	moon (8 · 27) 437	
שַׁחַק	cloud (9 · 21) 1007	
זָנַח 39	to reject, spurn (10 · 16 · 19) 276 I	
הִתְעַבֵּר	to become furious (4 · 8 · 8) 720	
מָשִׁיחַ	anointed (10 · 39) 603	
נֵאַר 40	to abhor, spurn (1 · 2 · 2) 611	
נֵזֶר	crown (2 · 25) 634	
פָּרַץ 41	to break through, down (4 · 46 · 49) 829 I	
גְּדֵרָה	wall, hedge (1 · 8) 155 I	
מִבְצָר	fortress, stronghold (2 · 37) 131	
מְחִתָּה	ruin (1 · 11) 369	
שָׁסַס 42	to plunder (1 · 3 · 5) 1042	
שָׁכֵן	neighbor (6 · 20) 1015	
צוּר 44	flint or edge (1 · 6) 866 צֹר il	
טֹהַר 45	luster [dub.] (1 · 1) 372	
מֵגֵר	to hurl (1 · 1 · 2) 550	
הִקְצִיר 46	to shorten (1 · 1 · 14) 894 I	
עֲלוּמִים	youth, youthful vigor (1 · 4) 761	
חעטה	to wrap, envelop (2 · 3 · 14) 741 I	
בּוּשָׁה	shame (1 · 4) 102	
לָנֶצַח 47	forever (18 · 42) 664 נצח	
חֶלֶד 48	duration of life (4 · 5) 317	
בָּרָא	to create, fashion, shape (3 · 38 · 48) 135 I	
אַיֵּה 50	where? (5 · 44) 32	
חֵיק 51	bosom (4 · 38) 300	
חֵרֵף 52	to reproach (9 · 34 · 38) 357 I	
מָשִׁיחַ	anointed (10 · 39) 603	
עָקֵב	footprint, heel (5 · 14) 784 I	
אָמֵן 53	verily, truly (4 · 30) 53	

Psalm 90

מָעוֹן 1	dwelling, refuge (5 · 18) 732 I	
בְּטֶרֶם 2	before (3 · 39) 382 טֶרֶם	
חוֹלֵל	to bear, bring forth (2 · 7 · 47) 297 חול I	
תֵּבֵל	world (15 · 36) 385	
אֱנוֹשׁ 3	man, mankind (13 · 42) 60	
דַּכָּא	dust (2 · 3) 194 II	
אֶתְמוֹל 4	yesterday (1 · 8) 1069 תְּמוֹל	
אַשְׁמוּרָה	watch (division of time) (3 · 7) 1038	
זָרַם 5	to flood, flood away (1 · 1 · 2) 281	
שֵׁנָה	sleep (3 · 23) 446	
חָצִיר	grass (6 · 18) 348 II	
חָלַף	to come on anew, sprout again (3 · 14 · 26) 322	
צוּץ 6	to blossom (5 · 7 · 8) 847 I	
חָלַף	to come on anew, sprout again (3 · 14 · 26) 322	
מוֹלֵל	to wither (1 · 1 · 4) 576 III	
נִבְהַל 7	to be disturbed, dismayed, terrified (8 · 24 · 39) 96	
לְנֶגֶד 8	over, for (13 · 32) 617 נֶגֶד 2.b	
עָלֻם	ptc. pass. = secret; i.e., hidden (1 · 1 · 29) 761 I	
מָאוֹר	light, luminary (2 · 17) 22	
עֶבְרָה 9	rage, fury (5 · 34) 720	
הֶגֶה	a sigh, moan (1 · 3) 211	
רֹהַב 10	pride (1 · 1) 923	
גּוּז	to pass away (1 · 2 · 2) 156 I	
חִישׁ	quickly (1 · 1) 301	
עוּף	to fly away (4 · 18 · 25) 733 I	
יִרְאָה 11	fear, reverence (8 · 45) 432	
עֶבְרָה	rage, fury (5 · 34) 720	
מָנָה 12	to count, number (2 · 12 · 28) 584	
מָתַי 13	when? (13 · 42) 607	
פֹּעַל 16	deed, thing done (11 · 37) 821	
הָדָר	splendor, dignity (13 · 30) 214	
נֹעַם 17	delightfulness, pleasantness (2 · 7) 653	

Psalm 91

סֵתֶר 1 hiding place, shelter (10 · 35) 712

שַׁדַּי name of God (2 · 48) 994

מַחְסֶה 2 refuge, shelter (12 · 20) 340

מְצוּדָה fastness, stronghold (7 · 18) 845 II

פַּח 3 bird trap (9 · 25) 809 I

יָקוּשׁ fowler, bait layer (1 · 4) 430

דֶּבֶר plague, pestilence (2 · 3[?]) 184

הַוָּה destruction (8 · 13) 217

אֶבְרָה 4 pinion (2 · 4) 7

הֵסִיךְ to screen, cover (2 · 5 · 18) 696 I
סכך

חָסָה to seek refuge (25 · 37 · 37) 340

צִנָּה large shield (3 · 20) 857 III

סֹחֵרָה buckler (1 · 1) 695

פַּחַד 5 dread (9 · 49) 808 I

עוּף to fly (4 · 18 · 25) 733 I

דֶּבֶר 6 plague, pestilence (2 · 3[?]) 184

אֹפֶל darkness (2 · 6) 66

קֶטֶב destruction (1 · 4) 881

צָהֳרַיִם midday, noon (3 · 23) 848 I צהר

צַד 7 side (1 · 32) 841

רְבָבָה myriad, ten thousand (2 · 16) 914

שִׁלֻּמָה 8 requital, retribution (1 · 1) 1024

מַחְסֶה 9 refuge, shelter (12 · 20) 340

מָעוֹן dwelling, refuge (5 · 18) 732 I

אֻנָּה 10 to be allowed to meet, be sent (1 · 2 · 6) 58 III

נָגַף 12 to strike, smite (2 · 25 · 49) 619

שַׁחַל 13 lion (1 · 7) 1006

פֶּתֶן venomous serpent, perh. cobra (2 · 6) 837

רָמַס to trample (2 · 17 · 18) 942

כְּפִיר young lion (6 · 31) 498

תַּנִּין serpent; sea monster, dragon (3 · 15) 1072

חָשַׁק 14 to be attached to; i.e., love (1 · 8 · 11) 365 I

פלט to deliver (19 · 24 · 27) 812

שׂגב to set on high (5 · 6 · 20) 960

חִלֵּץ 15 to rescue, deliver (10 · 14 · 27) 322 I

Psalm 92

זמר 2 to sing, make music (39 · 43 · 43) 274 I

עָשׂוֹר 4 a ten-stringed [instrument] (3 · 15) 797

נֵבֶל harp (8 · 27) 614 II

הִגָּיוֹן resounding music (3 · 4) 212

כִּנּוֹר lyre (13 · 41) 490

פֹּעַל 5 deed, thing done (11 · 37) 821

עמק 6 to be deep (1 · 1 · 9) 770

בַּעַר 7 brutish (3 · 5) 129

פָּרַח 8 to bud, sprout, shoot (3 · 29 · 34) 827 I

עֵשֶׂב herb, herbage (7 · 33) 793

צוּץ to blossom; i.e., to flourish (5 · 7 · 8) 847 I

עֲדֵי poetic for עַד up to, until (6 · 12) 723 III עַד

עַד forever (29 · 48) 723 I

הִתְפָּרֵד 10 to be divided, separated, from each other (2 · 4 · 26) 825 I

רְאֵם 11 wild ox (3 · 9) 910

בָּלַל to be anointed (1 · 42 · 43) 117 I

רַעֲנָן fresh, luxuriant (4 · 19) 947

שׁוּר 12 [dub.] watcher (1 · 1) 1004 I

קָם ptc. = adversary; קְ׳ עָלַי = those who rise up against me (5 · 12) 877 קום 2

מְרַע evildoer (9 · 18) 949 רעע Hiph. 2

תָּמָר 13 palm tree, date palm (1 · 12) 1071 I

פָּרַח to bud, sprout, shoot (3 · 29 · 34) 827 I

שׂגה to grow, increase (1 · 3 · 4) 960

שׁתל 14 to transplant (2 · 10 · 10) 1060

הִפְרִיחַ to flourish; to show buds, sprouts (1 · 5 · 34) 827 I

נוב 15 to bear fruit (2 · 3 · 4) 626

שֵׂיבָה old age; gray hair (2 · 20) 966

דָּשֵׁן fat (2 · 3) 206

רַעֲנָן fresh, flourishing (4 · 19) 947

עַוְלָה 16 injustice, wrong (9 · 32) 732

Psalm 93

גֵּאוּת 1 majesty (3 · 8) 145

הִתְאַזָּר to gird oneself (1 · 3 · 16) 25

תֵּבֵל world (15 · 36) 385

נמוט to be shaken, moved, overthrown (16 · 22 · 39) 556

מֵאָז 2 from time of, since (2 · 18) 23

דֳּכִי 3 pounding (waves)(1 · 1) 194

אַדִּיר 4 majestic (7 · 27) 12

מִשְׁבָּר breaker (3 · 5) 991

עֵדָה 5 testimony (25 · 32) 730 III

נאה to be comely (1 · 3 · 3) 610

Psalm 94

נְקָמָה 1 vengeance (5 · 27) 668

הוֹפִיעַ to shine out, forth (3 · 8 · 8) 422 יפע

גְּמוּל 2 dealing, recompense (4 · 19) 168

גֵּאֶה proud (2 · 8) 144

מָתַי 3 when? (13 · 42) 607

עלז to exult, triumph (7 · 16 · 16) 759

הביע 4 to pour forth, emit (6 · 10 · 11) 615 נבע

עָתָק forward, arrogant (3 · 4) 801

התאמר to act proudly, boast (1 · 1 · 1[?]) 55

דְּכָּא 5 to crush (4 · 11 · 18) 193

יָתוֹם 6 orphan (8 · 42) 450

רצח to murder, assassinate (2 · 3 · 43) 953

בער 8 ptc. = inhuman, cruel, barbarous (1 · 3 · 7) 129 II

מָתַי when? (13 · 42) 607

יָצַר 9 to form, fashion (6 · 41 · 44) 427

יסר 10 to discipline (1 · 4 · 41) 415

אֶשֶׁר 12 happiness, blessedness (19 · 45[?]) 80

יִסֵּר to discipline, correct (7 · 30 · 41) 415

הִשְׁקִיט 13 to cause quietness (1 · 10 · 41) 1052

נכרה to be dug (1 · 1 · 14) 500 II

שַׁחַת pit (9 · 23) 1001

נָטַשׁ 14 to forsake, abandon (3 · 33 · 40) 643

מֵרַע 16 evildoer (9 · 18) 949 רעע Hiph. 2

הִתְיַצֵּב to take a stand (4 · 48 · 48) 426

לוּלֵי 17 if not, unless (5 · 10) 530 לוּלֵא

עֶזְרָה help (14 · 26) 740 I

דּוּמָה silence (2 · 2) 189 I

מוט 18 to totter, slip (8 · 15 · 39) 556

סעד to support, sustain (6 · 12 · 12) 703

שַׂרְעַפִּים 19 disquieting thoughts (2 · 2) 972

תַּנְחוּם consolation (1 · 5) 637

שִׁרְעַשֵׁעַ to delight (2 · 3 · 6) 1044 II שׁעע

חֻבַּר 20 to be allied with (2 · 11 · 28) 287

הַוָּה destruction (8 · 13) 217

יָצַר to form, fashion (6 · 41 · 44) 427

גדד 21 to attack, penetrate (1 · 1 · 8) 151

נָקִי free from guilt, clean, innocent (5 · 43) 667

הִרְשִׁיעַ to condemn as guilty (3 · 25 · 34) 957 רשׁע Hiph. 1

מִשְׂגָּב 22 secure height, retreat (13 · 17) 960 I

מַחְסֶה refuge, shelter (12 · 20) 340

הִצְמִית 23 to exterminate, annihilate (9 · 10 · 15) 856

Psalm 95

הריע 1 to shout (9 · 40 · 44) 929 רוע

יֵשַׁע salvation (20 · 36) 447

קדם 2 to come to meet (12 · 24 · 27) 869

תּוֹדָה thanksgiving, praise (12 · 32) 392

זָמִיר song (2 · 6) 274 I

הריע to shout (9 · 40 · 44) 929 רוע

מֶחְקָר 4 range (1 · 1) 350

תּוֹעָפָה eminence (1 · 4) 419

454

יַבֶּשֶׁת 5 dry land (1 · 2) 387

יָצַר   to form, fashion (6 · 41 · 44) 427

כָּרַע 6 to bow (4 · 30 · 36) 502

ברך   to kneel (1 · 2 · 3[?]) 138

מַרְעִית 7 pasturing, shepherding (4 · 10) 945

הִקְשָׁה 8 to make stiff, stubborn (1 · 21 · 28) 904 I

נִסָּה 9 to test, try (6 · 36 · 36) 650

בחן   to prove, test, try (9 · 24 · 28) 103

פֹּעַל   deed, thing done (11 · 37) 821

קוּט 10 to feel a loathing at (1 · 1 · 7) 876

תָּעָה   to wander about, err (5 · 27 · 50) 1073

מְנוּחָה 11 resting place (4 · 21) 629

Psalm 96

בִּשַּׂר 2 to gladden with good tidings (2 · 14 · 15) 142

נִפְלָאוֹת 3 wonderful acts (27 · 44) 810 פלא

נוֹרָא 4 awe inspiring, awful (15 · 44) 431 ירא

אֱלִיל 5 dumb (2 · 20) 47

הוֹד 6 splendor, majesty (8 · 24) 217 I

הָדָר   splendor, majesty (13 · 30) 214

יהב 7 to ascribe (8 · 33 · 33) 396

יהב 8 to ascribe (8 · 33 · 33) 396

הֲדָרָה 9 adornment (2 · 5) 214

חיל   to dance (5 · 30 · 47) 296 חול I

תֵּבֵל 10 world (15 · 36) 385

נמוט   to be shaken, moved, overthrown (16 · 22 · 39) 556

דִין   to judge, minister judgment (8 · 23 · 24) 192

מֵישָׁר   uprightness, equity (7 · 19) 449

גִיל 11 to rejoice (19 · 45 · 45) 162

רעם   to thunder (2 · 3 · 11) 947

מְלֹא   fullness (5 · 38) 571

עלז 12 to exult, triumph (7 · 16 · 16) 759

שָׂדַי   land (5 · 13) 961

תֵּבֵל 13 world (15 · 36) 385

Psalm 97

גִיל 1 to rejoice (19 · 45 · 45) 162

אִי   coastlands, islands (2 · 36) 15 I

עֲרָפֶל 2 cloud, heavy cloud (2 · 15) 791

מָכוֹן   fixed place, place (4 · 17) 467

לִהַט 3 to set ablaze (3 · 9 · 11) 529

הֵאִיר 4 to light up, cause to shine (15 · 34 · 40) 21 אור

בָּרָק   lightning (5 · 21) 140

תֵּבֵל   world (15 · 36) 385

היל   to writhe, be in anguish (5 · 30 · 47) 296 חול I

דּוֹנַג 5 wax (3 · 3) 200

נָמֵס   to melt (4 · 19 · 21) 587 מסס

פֶּסֶל 7 idol, image (1 · 31) 820

אֱלִיל   vain, worthless (2 · 20) 47

גִיל 8 to rejoice (19 · 45 · 45) 162

אֹהֵב 10 friend (12 · 36) 12 אהב

חָסִיד   pious, godly (25 · 32) 339

זֵכֶר 12 remembrance, memorial (11 · 23) 271

Psalm 98

נִפְלָאוֹת 1 wonderful acts (27 · 44) 810 פלא

אֶפֶס 3 ends, extreme limits (6 · 27) 67

הֵרִיעַ 4 to shout (9 · 40 · 44) 929 רוע

זִמֵּר   to sing, make music (39 · 43 · 43) 274 I

זִמֵּר 5 to sing, make music (39 · 43 · 43) 274 I

כִּנּוֹר   lyre (13 · 41) 490

זִמְרָה   melody, song 274 I

חֲצֹצְרָה 6 clarion, trumpet (1 · 29) 348

הֵרִיעַ   to shout (9 · 40 · 44) 929 רוע

רעם 7 to thunder (2 · 3 · 11) 947

מְלֹא   fullness (5 · 38) 571

תֵּבֵל	world (15 · 36) 385	
מָחָא	8 to clap (1 · 3 · 3) 561	
יַחַד	together, altogether (14 · 44) 403	
תֵּבֵל	9 world (15 · 36) 385	
מֵישָׁר	uprightness, equity (7 · 19) 449	

Psalm 99

רָגַז	1 to quake (5 · 30 · 41) 919	
נוט	to shake (1 · 1 · 1) 630	
רָם	2 high, lifted up, exalted (5 · 31[?]) רום 926	
נוֹרָא	3 awe-inspiring, awful (15 · 44) 431 יָרֵא	
מֵישָׁר	4 uprightness, equity (7 · 19) 449	
הֲדֹם	5 stool, foot stool (3 · 6) 213	
עֵדָה	7 testimony (25 · 32) 730 III	
נקם	8 to avenge, take vengeance (1 · 13 · 35) 667	
עֲלִילָה	deed (9 · 24) 760	

Psalm 100

תּוֹדָה	1 sacrifice of thanksgiving, thank offering (12 · 32) 392	
הָרִיעַ	to shout (9 · 40 · 44) 929 רוע	
רְנָנָה	2 ringing cry (2 · 4) 943	
מַרְעִית	3 pasturing, shepherding (4 · 10) 945	
תּוֹדָה	4 thanksgiving, praise (12 · 32) 392	

Psalm 101

זמר	1 to sing, make music (39 · 43 · 43) 274 I	
תֹּם	2 integrity, completeness (7 · 23) 1070	
מָתַי	when? (13 · 42) 607	
לְנֶגֶד	3 over, for (13 · 32) 617 נֶגֶד 2.b	
בְּלִיַּעַל	base, wicked (3 · 27) 116	
סֵטִים	deeds that swerve (1 · 2) 962 שֵׂט	

עִקֵּשׁ	4 twisted, perverted (2 · 11) 786 I	
מְלָוֹשְׁנִי	5 *Poel* ptc. = slandering, to slander (1 · 1 · 2) 546 לשן	
סֵתֶר	secrecy; בַּסֵּ = secretly (10 · 35) 712	
הִצְמִית	to exterminate, annihilate (9 · 10 · 15) 856	
גְּבֹהַּ	haughty; high (3 · 41) 147	
רָחָב	exultant, arrogant (4 · 21) 932 I	
רְמִיָּה	7 deceit, treachery (6 · 15) 941	
לְנֶגֶד	before, in front of (13 · 32) 617 נֶגֶד 2.b	
הִצְמִית	8 to exterminate, annihilate (9 · 10 · 15) 856	

Psalm 102

עטף	1 to be feeble, faint (2 · 3 · 11) 742 III	
שִׂיחַ	complaint (5 · 14) 967 I	
שַׁוְעָה	2 cry for help (6 · 11) 1003	
עָשָׁן	4 smoke (4 · 25) 798 I	
מוֹקֵד	burning mass (1 · 3) 428	
נִחַר	to burn (1 · 5 · 9) 359 I חרר	
עֵשֶׂב	5 herb, herbage (7 · 33) 793	
אֲנָחָה	6 sighing, groaning (4 · 11) 58	
דָּמָה	7 to be like, resemble (3 · 13 · 27) 197 I	
קָאַת	bird, usually a pelican (1 · 5) 866	
כּוֹס	owl (1 · 3) 468 II	
חָרְבָּה	waste, ruin (3 · 42) 352	
שׁקד	8 to be wakeful, wake (1 · 1 · 1[?]) 1052	
צִפּוֹר	[coll.] birds (7 · 40) 861 I	
בדד	to be separate, isolated (1 · 3 · 3) 94 I	
גָּג	roof (2 · 29) 150	
חֵרֵף	9 to reproach (9 · 34 · 38) 357 I	
הוֹלֵל	*Poal* ptc. 1st sing. = those mad against me (1 · 4 · 14[?]) 237 II הלל	
אֵפֶר	10 ashes (2 · 22) 68	
שִׁקּוּי	drink (1 · 3) 1052	

בְּכִי weeping (3 · 32) 113

מָסַךְ to mix (1 · 5 · 5) 587

זַעַם 11 indignation (4 · 22) 276

קֶצֶף wrath (2 · 28) 893 I

עֵשֶׂב 12 herb, herbage (7 · 33) 793

זֵכֶר 13 remembrance, memory (11 · 23) 271

רָחַם 14 to have compassion (4 · 42 · 47) 933

עַרְעָר 18 stripped, destitute (1 · 2) 792

בָּזָה to despise (6 · 31 · 42) 102

נברא 19 to be created (3 · 10 · 48) 135 I

הִשְׁקִיף 20 to look down (3 · 12 · 22) 1054

אֲנָקָה 21 crying, groaning (3 · 4) 60 I

אָסִיר prisoner (5 · 17) 64

תְּמוּתָה death (2 · 2) 560

קִצַּר 24 to shorten (1 · 1 · 14) 894 I

יָסַד 26 to found, establish (7 · 20 · 41) 413

בלה 27 to wear out (2 · 11 · 16) 115

לְבוּשׁ garment, clothing (6 · 30) 528

הִשְׁלִיף to change (1 · 10 · 26) 322

חָלַף to pass away (3 · 14 · 26) 322

Psalm 103

גְּמוּל 2 benefit (4 · 19) 168

סלח 3 to pardon, forgive (2 · 33 · 46) 699

תַּחֲלֻאִים diseases (1 · 5) 316

שַׁחַת 4 pit (9 · 23) 1001

עטר to crown (3 · 4 · 7) 742

רַחֲמִים compassion (11 · 38) 933

עֲדִי 5 age, prime (2 · 14) 725

התחדש to renew oneself (1 · 1 · 10) 293

נֶשֶׁר eagle, vulture (1 · 26) 676

נְעוּרִים youth (8 · 46) 655

עָשַׁק 6 pass. ptc. = oppressed one (6 · 36 · 37) 798

עֲלִילָה 7 deed (9 · 24) 760

רַחוּם 8 compassionate (6 · 13) 933

חַנּוּן gracious (6 · 13) 337

אָרֵךְ long; א' אַפַּיִם = slow to anger (3 · 15) 74

נֶצַח 9 forever (18 · 42) 664 לָנֶצַח

נטר to keep, maintain (1 · 5) 643

חֵטְא 10 sin (3 · 33) 307

גָּמַל to recompense, repay, requite (10 · 34 · 37) 168

גָּבַהּ 11 to be high, lofty, tall (2 · 24 · 34) 146

גָּבַר to prevail (3 · 17 · 25) 149

יָרֵא afraid (27 · 46) 431

מַעֲרָב 12 west, setting place (3 · 14) 788 II

רְחַם 13 to have compassion (4 · 42 · 47) 933

יָרֵא afraid (27 · 46) 431

יֵצֶר 14 form, framing, purpose (1 · 9) 428 I

זָכוּר he remembers (1 · 1[?]) 269 זָכַר Qal II.3.c

אֱנוֹשׁ 15 man, mankind (13 · 42) 60

חָצִיר grass (6 · 18) 348 II

צִיץ blossom, flower (1 · 15) 847 I

צוּץ to blossom (5 · 7 · 8) 847 I

הִכִּיר 16 to be acquainted with (2 · 37 · 40) נכר 647 I

יָרֵא 17 afraid (27 · 46) 431

פִּקּוּד 18 precept (24 · 24) 824

מְשָׁרֵת 21 minister (2 · 20) שרת 1058

מֶמְשָׁלָה 22 rule, dominion (5 · 17) 606

Psalm 104

הוֹד 1 splendor, majesty (8 · 24) 217 I

הָדָר splendor, majesty (13 · 30) 214

עָטָה 2 to wrap, envelop oneself (4 · 11 · 14) 741 I

שַׂלְמָה garment, outer garment (1 · 16) 971 II

קרה 3 Piel to lay the beams of, to furnish with beam (1 · 5 · 28) 900

עֲלִיָּה roof chamber (2 · 20) 751

עָב dark cloud, cloud mass (5 · 30) 728 II

רְכוּב chariot (1 · 1) 939

457

מְשָׁרֵת 4 minister (2 · 20) 1058 שׁרת

לֹהֵט to flame, blaze up (2 · 2 · 11) 529

יָסַד 5 to found, establish (7 · 20 · 41) 413

מָכוֹן foundation (4 · 17) 467

נמוט to be shaken, moved, overthrown (16 · 22 · 39) 556

עַד ever (29 · 48) 723 I

תְּהוֹם 6 deep, sea, abyss (12 · 36) 1062

לְבוּשׁ garment, clothing (6 · 30) 528

גְּעָרָה 7 rebuke (4 · 15) 172

רַעַם thunder (3 · 6) 947

נחפז to hurry (2 · 3 · 9) 342

בִּקְעָה 8 valley (1 · 9) 132

יָסַד to found, establish (7 · 20 · 41) 413

מַעְיָן 10 spring (5 · 23) 745

שָׂדַי 11 field, land (5 · 13) 961

פֶּרֶא wild ass (1 · 10) 825

צָמָא thirst (2 · 17) 854

מִבֵּין 12 from among (1 · 21) 107

עֳפָאִים pl. = foliage (1 · 1) 779

עֲלִיָּה 13 roof chamber (2 · 20) 751

הַצְמִיחַ 14 to cause to grow (3 · 14 · 33) 855

חָצִיר grass (6 · 18) 348 II

עֵשֶׂב herb, herbage (7 · 33) 793

אֱנוֹשׁ 15 man, mankind (13 · 42) 60

הַצְהִיל to make shining (1 · 1 · 1) 843 II

סעד to support, sustain (6 · 12 · 12) 703

צִפּוֹר 17 [coll.] birds (7 · 40) 861 I

קנן to make a nest (1 · 4 · 5) 890

חֲסִידָה stork (1 · 6) 339

בְּרוֹשׁ cypress, fir (1 · 200 141

גָּבֹהַּ 18 high, lofty, tall (3 · 41) 147

יָעֵל mountain goat (1 · 3) d418 I

מַחְסֶה refuge, shelter (12 · 20) 340

שָׁפָן rock badger (1 · 4) 1050 I

יָרֵחַ 19 moon (8 · 27) 437

מָבוֹא entering; מ׳ הַשֶּׁמֶשׁ = sunset (3 · 23) 99

רמשׂ 20 to move about, prowl (2 · 16 · 16) 942

כְּפִיר 21 young lion (6 · 31) 498

שָׁאַג to roar (4 · 20 · 20) 980

טֶרֶף prey (3 · 18) 383

אֹכֶל food (6 · 44) 38

זָרַח 22 to rise (2 · 18 · 18) 280

מְעוֹנָה den, lair (2 · 9) 733

רָבַץ to lie down, lie (1 · 24 · 30) 918

פֹּעַל 23 deed, thing done (11 · 37) 821

עֲדֵי poetic for עַד up to, until (6 · 12) 723

עד III

רבב 24 to be, become, many (6 · 23 · 24) 912 I

קִנְיָן [coll.] creatures (1 · 1[?]) 889

רָחָב 25 wide, broad (4 · 21) 932 I

רֶמֶשׂ gliding things (2 · 16) 943

קָטָן small, insignificant (2 · 47) 881 I

אֳנִיָּה 26 ship (3 · 31) 58

לִוְיָתָן Leviathan, serpent (2 · 5) 531

יָצַר to form, fashion (6 · 41 · 44) 427

שׂחק to play (1 · 17 · 36) 965

שׂבר 27 to hope (3 · 6 · 8) 960 II

אֹכֶל food (6 · 44) 38

לקט 28 to pick up, gather (1 · 14 · 37) 544

נבהל 29 to be disturbed, dismayed, terrified (8 · 24 · 39) 96

גָּוַע to expire, perish, die (2 · 23 · 23) 157

נברא 30 to be created (3 · 10 · 48) 135 I

חדשׁ to renew, make anew (2 · 9 · 10) 293

רעד 32 to tremble, quake (1 · 1 · 3) 944

עָשַׁן to smoke (4 · 6 · 6) 798

זמר 33 to sing, make music (39 · 43 · 43) 274 I

בְּעוֹד so long as (3 · 20) 728 עוֹד 2.a

ערב 34 to be sweet, pleasing (1 · 8) 787 III

שִׂיחַ complaint (5 · 14) 967 I

חַטָּא 35 sinner (6 · 19) 308

458

Psalm 105

עֲלִילָה	1 deed (9 · 24) 760	
זמר	2 to sing, make music (39 · 43 · 43) 274 I	
שִׂיחַ	to talk, sing (13 · 18 · 20) 967	
נִפְלָאוֹת	wonderful acts (27 · 44) 810 פלא	
נִפְלָאוֹת	5 wonderful acts (27 · 44) 810 פלא	
מוֹפֵת	sign, wonder (5 · 36) 68	
בָּחִיר	6 chosen, elect (5 · 13) 104	
שְׁבוּעָה	9 oath, curse (1 · 30) 989	
חֵבֶל	11 portion, lot (8 · 50) 286 I.3	
מַת	12 male, man (3 · 22) 607	
עָשַׁק	14 to oppress, wrong (6 · 36 · 37) 798	
מָשִׁיחַ	15 anointed (10 · 39) 603	
כֶּבֶל	18 [coll.] fetters (2 · 2) 459	
אִמְרָה	19 word, saying (26 · 36) 57	
צָרַף	to test (7 · 18 · 21) 864	
הִתִּיר	20 to set free, unbind (2 · 5 · 7) 684 II נתר	
מֹשֵׁל	ruler (2 · 24) 605 III מָשַׁל	
מֹשֵׁל	21 ruler (2 · 24) 605 III מָשַׁל	
קִנְיָן	acquisition (1 · 9) 889	
חכם	22 to make wise, teach wisdom (2 · 3 · 26) 314	
הפרה	24 to cause to be fruitful, bear fruit (1 · 7 · 29) 826	
העצים	to make strong (1 · 1 · 18) 782 I	
הִתְנַכֵּל	25 to deal knavishly (1 · 2 · 4) 647	
מוֹפֵת	27 sign, wonder (5 · 36) 68	
הֶחְשִׁיךְ	28 to cause darkness (2 · 6 · 17) 364	
מָרָה	to be disobedient, rebellious (3 · 21 · 43) 598	
דָּגָה	29 fish (1 · 15) 185	
שָׁרַץ	30 to swarm, teem (1 · 14 · 14) 1056	
צְפַרְדֵּעַ	frogs (2 · 13) 682	
חֶדֶר	chamber, room (1 · 37) 293	
עָרֹב	31 swarm (2 · 9) 786	
כֵּן	gnat or lice [dub.] (1 · 5) 487 IV	
גֶּשֶׁם	32 rain, shower (2 · 35) 177 II	

בָּרָד	hail (6 · 29) 135	
לֶהָבָה	flame (4 · 19) 529	
תְּאֵנָה	33 fig, fig tree (1 · 39) 1061	
אַרְבֶּה	34 locust (3 · 24) 916	
יֶלֶק	locust (1 · 9) 410	
עֵשֶׂב	35 herb, herbage (7 · 33) 793	
אוֹן	36 manly vigor (2 · 10) 20 I	
פַּחַד	38 dread (9 · 49) 808	
מָסָךְ	39 screen (1 · 25) 697	
הֵאִיר	to give light (15 · 34 · 40) 21	
שְׂלָו	40 quail (1 · 4) 969	
זוּב	41 to flow, gush (2 · 29 · 29) 264	
צִיָּה	drought, desert (4 · 16) 851	
שָׂשׂוֹן	43 exultation, joy (5 · 22) 965	
רִנָּה	ringing cry (15 · 33) 943 I	
בָּחִיר	chosen, elect (5 · 13) 104	
לְאֹם	44 people (14 · 35) 522	
בַּעֲבוּר	45 in order that (3 · 45) 721 II עָבוּר	

Psalm 106

מִלֵּל	2 to utter, speak (1 · 4 · 5) 576 I	
אֶשֶׁר	3 happiness, blessedness (19 · 45[?]) 80	
בָּחִיר	5 chosen, elect (5 · 13) 104	
הֶעֱוָה	6 to commit iniquity (1 · 9 · 17[?]) 731	
הִרְשִׁיעַ	to act wickedly (3 · 25 · 34) 957	
נִפְלָאוֹת	7 wonderful acts (27 · 44) 810 פלא	
המרה	to show disobedience, rebellion (7 · 22 · 43) 598	
גָּעַר	9 to rebuke (4 · 14 · 14) 172	
חרב	to be dried up (1 · 17 · 37[?]) 351 I	
תְּהוֹם	deep, sea, abyss (12 · 36) 1062	
שָׂנֵא	10 enemy (12 · 41[?]) 971	
חכה	13 to wait for, await (2 · 13 · 14) 314	
התאוה	14 to desire, long for, lust after (2 · 16 · 27) 16 II	
תַּאֲוָה	desire (8 · 22) 16	
נִסָּה	to test, try (6 · 36 · 36) 650	
יְשִׁימוֹן	waste, wilderness (4 · 13) 445	

שְׁאֵלָה 15 petition, thing asked for (1 · 13) 982

רָזוֹן wasting (1 · 3) 931 I

קָנָא 16 to be envious of (3 · 30 · 34) 888

בָּלַע 17 to swallow up, engulf (3 · 20 · 41) 118

לֶהָבָה 18 flame (4 · 19) 529

לָהַט to set ablaze (3 · 9 · 11) 529

עֵגֶל 19 calf (3 · 35) 722

מַסֵּכָה molten metal or image (2 · 20) 651 I

הֵמִיר 20 to exchange (3 · 12 · 13) 558 מור

תַּבְנִית figure, image (2 · 20) 125

עֵשֶׂב herb, herbage (7 · 33) 793

מוֹשִׁיע 21 savior (4 · 27) 446 ישע

נִפְלָאוֹת 22 wonderful acts (27 · 44) 810 פלא

נוֹרָא awe-inspiring, awful (15 · 44) 431 ירא

לוּלֵי 23 if not, unless (5 · 10) 530 לוּלֵא

בָּחִיר chosen, elect (5 · 13) 104

פֶּרֶץ breach (2 · 19) 829 I

חֶמְדָּה 24 desire, delight (1 · 16) 326

נרגן 25 to murmur (1 · 2 · 3) 920

זרה 27 to scatter, disperse (2 · 25 · 38) 279

נצמד 28 to join, attach, oneself (1 · 3 · 5) 855

מַעֲלָל 29 deed, practice (5 · 41) 760

פָּרַץ to break out upon (4 · 46 · 49) 829 I

מַגֵּפָה plague, pestilence (2 · 26) 620

פלל 30 to interpose (1 · 4 · 5) 813

נעצר to restrain, retain (1 · 10 · 46) 783

מַגֵּפָה plague, pestilence (2 · 26) 620

הקציף 32 to provoke wrath (1 · 5 · 34) 893 I

בַּעֲבוּר for the sake of, on account of, because of (3 · 45) 721 II עָבוּר

המרה 33 to show disobedience, rebellion (7 · 22 · 43) 598

בטא to speak rashly, unadvisedly (1 · 3 · 4) 104 בטה

התערב 35 to have fellowship (1 · 5 · 5[?]) 786 II

עָצָב 36 idol (4 · 17) 781

מוֹקֵשׁ snare, lure (6 · 27) 430

שֵׁד 37 demon (1 · 2) 993

נָקִי 38 free from guilt, clean, innocent (5 · 43) 667

עָצָב idol (4 · 17) 781

חנף to be polluted (1 · 6 · 10) 337

מַעֲלָל 39 deed, practice (5 · 41) 760

תעב 40 to abhor, regard as an abomination (4 · 14 · 21) 1073

שׂנֵא 41 enemy (12 · 41[?]) 971 שׂנא

לָחַץ 42 to oppress (2 · 14 · 15) 537

נכנע to be humbled, subdued (1 · 25 · 33) 488

המרה 43 to show disobedience, rebellion (7 · 22 · 43) 598

מכך to be low, humiliated (1 · 1 · 3) 568

רִנָּה 44 ringing cry (15 · 33) 943 I

רַחֲמִים 46 compassion (11 · 38) 933

שֹׁבִים captives (2 · 9) 985 שָׁבָה

השתבח 47 to boast (1 · 2 · 8) 986 II שבח

אָמֵן 48 verily, truly (4 · 30) 53

Psalm 107

מַעֲרָב 3 west, setting place (3 · 14) 788 I

תָּעָה 4 to wander about (5 · 27 · 50) 1073

יְשִׁימוֹן waste, wilderness (4 · 13) 445

מוֹשָׁב dwelling place (6 · 46) 444

רָעֵב 5 hungry (4 · 19) 944

צָמֵא thirsty (1 · 9) 854

התעטף to faint, faint away (4 · 6 · 11) 742 III

מְצוּקָה 6 straits, stress (5 · 7) 848

מוֹשָׁב 7 dwelling place (6 · 46) 444

נִפְלָאוֹת 8 wonderful acts (27 · 44) 810 פלא

שקק 9 to long (1 · 5 · 6) 1055

רָעֵב hungry (4 · 19) 944

צַלְמָוֶת 10 deep shadow, darkness (4 · 18) 853

אָסִיר prisoner (5 · 17) 64

עָנִי affliction (10 · 36) 777

המרה 11 to rebel, disobey (7 · 22 · 43) 598

460

אֹמֶר utterance, word (7 · 48) 56
נָאַץ to contemn (1 · 8 · 24) 610
הִכְנִיעַ 12 to humble (2 · 11 · 36) 488
עֹזֵר help, helper (7 · 19) 740 עזר
מְצוּקָה 13 straits, stress (5 · 12) 848
צַלְמָוֶת 14 deep shadow, darkness (4 · 18) 853
מוֹסֵר band, bond (3 · 12) 64
נתק to tear apart, snap (2 · 11 · 27) 683
נִפְלָאוֹת 15 wonderful acts (27 · 44) 810 פלא
בְּרִיחַ 16 bar (2 · 41) 138
גָּדַע to hew off, down, in two (2 · 9 · 22) 154
אֱוִיל 17 foolish (1 · 26) 17
אֹכֶל 18 food (6 · 44) 38
תעב to abhor, regard as an abomination (4 · 14 · 21) 1073
מְצוּקָה 19 straits, stress (5 · 12) 848
שַׁחַת 20 pit (1 · 2) 1005
נִפְלָאוֹת 21 wonderful acts (27 · 44) 810 פלא
תּוֹדָה 22 thank offering, sacrifice of thanksgiving (12 · 32) 392
רִנָּה ringing cry (15 · 33) 943 I
אֳנִיָּה 23 ship (3 · 31) 58
נִפְלָאוֹת 24 wonderful acts (27 · 44) 810 פלא
מְצוֹלָה depth, deep (5 · 12) 846
סְעָרָה 25 tempest, storm wind (3 · 16) 704
גַּל pl. = waves (5 · 16) 164
תְּהוֹם 26 deep, sea, abyss (12 · 36) 1062
התמוגג to melt (1 · 3 · 17) 556
חגג 27 to reel (2 · 16 · 16) 290 3
נוע to stagger (2 · 22 · 38) 631
שִׁכּוֹר drunken one (1 · 13) 1016 שכר
התבלע to be swallowed up (1 · 1 · 6[?]) 118
מְצוּקָה 28 straits, stress (5 · 12) 848
סְעָרָה 29 tempest, storm wind (3 · 16) 704
דְּמָמָה whisper (1 · 3) 199
חשה to be silent, still (2 · 7 · 16) 364
גַּל pl. = waves (5 · 16) 164
שתק 30 to be quiet (1 · 4 · 4) 1060
הנחה to lead, guide (12 · 26 · 40) 634

מָחוֹז city (1 · 1) 562
חֵפֶץ desire, longing (3 · 39) 343
נִפְלָאוֹת 31 wonderful acts (27 · 44) 810 פלא
מוֹשָׁב 32 sitting (6 · 46) 444
מוֹצָא 33 source, spring
צִמָּאוֹן thirsty ground (1 · 3) 855
מְלֵחָה 34 saltness, barrenness (1 · 3) 572
אֲגַם 35 pool, pond (2 · 8) 8
צִיָּה drought (4 · 16) 851
מוֹצָא source, spring (6 · 27) 425 I
רָעֵב 36 hungry (4 · 19) 944
מוֹשָׁב dwelling place (6 · 46) 444
תְּבוּאָה 37 product, yield (1 · 43) 100
המעיט 38 to make small (1 · 13 · 22) 589
מעט 39 to be or become small (1 · 8 · 22) 589
שחח to be bowed down, prostrated, humbled (4 · 12 · 18[?]) 1005
עֹצֶר restraint, coercion (1 · 3) 783
יָגוֹן sorrow, grief (4 · 14) 387
בּוּז 40 contempt (5 · 11) 100 II
נָדִיב noble, princely (8 · 27) 622
הִתְעָה to cause to wander about (1 · 21 · 50) 1073
תֹּהוּ waste, formlessness (1 · 20) 1062
שׂגב 41 to set on high (5 · 6 · 20) 960
עֳנִי affliction (10 · 36) 777
עַוְלָה 42 injustice, wrong (9 · 32) 732
קָפַץ to draw together, shut (2 · 5 · 7) 891

Psalm 108

זמר 2 to sing, make music (39 · 43 · 43) 274 I
נֵבֶל 3 harp (8 · 27) 614 II
כִּנּוֹר lyre (13 · 41) 490
שַׁחַר dawn (4 · 23) 1007
זמר 4 to sing, make music (39 · 43 · 43) 274 I
לְאֹם people (14 · 35) 522

461

שַׁחַק 5 cloud (9 · 21) 1007

יָדִיד 7 beloved (4 · 8) 391

נֶחֱלַץ to be delivered (2 · 7 · 27) 322

עָלַז 8 to exult, triumph (7 · 16 · 16) 759

מָעוֹז 9 protection (9 · 36) 731

מְחֹקֵק commander's staff (2 · 7[?]) 349 חקק
Poel b

סִיר 10 pot (3 · 29) 696 I

רַחַץ washing (2 · 2) 934

נַעַל sandal, shoe (2 · 22) 653

התרועע to shout in triumph (3 · 3 · 44) 929
רוע

הוֹבִיל 11 to lead, conduct (4 · 7 · 18) 384 יבל

מִבְצָר fortification; w עיר = fortified city
(2 · 37) 131

נחה to lead, bring (6 · 14 · 40) 634

זָנַח 12 to reject, spurn (10 · 16 · 19) 276 I

יהב 13 to give (8 · 33 · 33) 396

עֶזְרָה help (14 · 26) 740 I

תְּשׁוּעָה deliverance (13 · 34) 448

בוס 14 to tread down, trample (3 · 7 · 12)
100

Psalm 109

חרש 1 to be silent (6 · 7 · 47) 361 II

מִרְמָה 2 deceit, treachery (14 · 39) 941

שִׂנְאָה 3 hating, hatred (4 · 17) 971

חִנָּם gratuitously, without cause (6 · 32)
336

שׂטן 4 to be or act as adversary (5 · 6 · 6)
966

שִׂנְאָה 5 hating, hatred (4 · 17) 971

שָׂטָן 6 adversary (1 · 27) 966

חֲטָאָה 7 sin (3 · 8) 308

פְּקֻדָּה 8 store; i.e., things laid up (1 · 32) 824

יָתוֹם 9 orphan (8 · 42) 450

נוע 10 to totter, go tottering (2 · 22 · 38)
631

חָרְבָּה waste, ruin (3 · 42) 352

נקש 11 to strike, take aim (2 · 2 · 5) 669

נוֹשֶׁה creditor, usurer (1 · 5) 674 I נָשָׁה

בָּזַז to spoil, plunder (1 · 37 · 41) 102

יְגִיעַ product, produce (3 · 16) 388

מָשַׁךְ 12 to draw out, prolong (5 · 30 · 36) 604

יָתוֹם orphan (8 · 42) 450

נמחה 13 to be blotted out (3 · 9 · 34) 562 I

נמחה 14 to be blotted out (3 · 9 · 34) 562 I

זֵכֶר 15 remembrance, memory (11 · 23) 271

נכְאָה 16 to be downhearted (1 · 2 · 3) 456

קְלָלָה 17 curse (2 · 33) 887

קְלָלָה 18 curse (2 · 33) 887

מַד garment (2 · 12) 551

עָטָה 19 to wrap, envelop oneself
(4 · 11 · 14) 741

מֵזַח girdle (1 · 1) 561

חגר to gird on, bind on (4 · 44 · 44) 291

פְּעֻלָּה 20 wages; work (3 · 14) 821

שׂטן to be or act as adversary (5 · 6 · 6)
966

חָלַל 22 to pierce (2 · 2 · 7) 319 I

ננער 23 to be shaken out (1 · 3 · 10) 654 II

אַרְבֶּה locust (3 · 24) 916

בֶּרֶךְ 24 knee (1 · 25) 139

צוֹם fast, fasting (3 · 25) 847

כָּחַשׁ to grow lean (1 · 1 · 22) 471

הניע 25 to shake, wag (4 · 14 · 38) 631 נוע

שׂטן 29 to be or act as adversary (5 · 6 · 6)
966

כְּלִמָּה ignominy, reproach (7 · 30) 484

עָטָה to wrap, envelop oneself
(4 · 11 · 14) 741

מְעִיל robe (1 · 28) 591

בֹּשֶׁת shame (7 · 30) 102

Psalm 110

הֲדֹם 1 stool, footstool (3 · 6) 213

רדה 2 to have dominion, rule, dominate
(4 · 22 · 23) 921

נְדָבָה 3 voluntariness, freewill offering (4 · 27) 621

הָדָר ornament (13 · 30) 214

רֶחֶם womb (3 · 33) 933

מִשְׁחָר dawn (1 · 1) 1007

טַל dew (2 · 31) 378

יַלְדוּת childhood, youth (1 · 3) 409

דִּבְרָה 4 order, manner (1 · 5) 184

מָחַץ 5 to smite through (5 · 14 · 14) 563

דִּין 6 to judge, vindicate (8 · 23 · 24) 192

גְּוִיָּה dead body, corpse, carcass (1 · 12) 156

מָחַץ to smite through (5 · 14 · 14) 563

Psalm 111

סוֹד 1 assembly, council (6 · 21) 691

חָפֵץ 2 delighting in, taking pleasure in (6 · 12) 343

הוֹד 3 splendor, majesty (8 · 24) 217 I

הָדָר splendor, majesty (13 · 30) 214

פֹּעַל deed, thing done (11 · 37) 821

עַד לָעַד = forever (29 · 48) 723 I

זֵכֶר 4 remembrance, memory (11 · 23) 271

נִפְלָאוֹת wonderful acts (27 · 44) 810 פלא

חַנּוּן gracious (6 · 13) 337

רַחוּם compassionate (6 · 13) 933

טֶרֶף 5 food (1 · 4) 383

יָרֵא afraid (27 · 46) 431

פִּקּוּד 7 precept (24 · 24) 824

סָמַךְ 8 to support, uphold, sustain (10 · 41 · 48) 701

עַד לָעַד = forever (29 · 48) 723 I

פְּדוּת 9 ransom (2 · 4) 804

נוֹרָא awe-inspiring, awful (15 · 44) 431 ירא

יִרְאָה 10 fear (8 · 45) 432

שֵׂכֶל insight, understanding (1 · 16) 968

עַד לָעַד = forever (29 · 48) 723 I

Psalm 112

אֶשֶׁר 1 happiness, blessedness (19 · 45[?]) 80

הוֹן 3 wealth (3 · 26) 223

עֹשֶׁר riches (3 · 37) 799

עַד לָעַד = forever (29 · 48) 723 I

זָרַח 4 to rise (2 · 18 · 18) 280

חַנּוּן gracious (6 · 13) 337

רַחוּם compassionate (6 · 13) 933

הלוה 5 to lend (2 · 9 · 14) 531 II

כִּלְכֵּל to support, endure (2 · 24 · 38) 465 כול

נמוט 6 to be shaken, moved, overthrown (16 · 22 · 39) 556

זֵכֶר remembrance, memory (11 · 23) 271

שְׁמוּעָה 7 report (1 · 27) 1035

בָּטוּחַ confident (1 · 2[?]) 105 I בטח

סָמַךְ 8 to support, uphold, sustain (10 · 41 · 48) 701

פִּזַּר 9 to scatter (4 · 7 · 10) 808

עַד לָעַד = forever (29 · 48) 723 I

חָרַק 10 to gnash, grind (3 · 5 · 5) 359

נָמֵס to melt (4 · 19 · 21) 587 מסס

תַּאֲוָה desire (8 · 21) 16 I

Psalm 113

מָבוֹא 3 entering: מ׳ הַשֶּׁמֶשׁ = sunset; i.e., west (3 · 23) 99

רָם 4 high, lifted, exalted (5 · 31[?]) 926 רום

הגביה 5 to make high, exalt (1 · 10 · 34) 146

השפיל 6 to make low, sit down (4 · 19 · 30) 1050

דַּל 7 reduced, poor (5 · 48) 195

אַשְׁפֹּת ash heap [dub.], refuse heap, dung hill (1 · 7) 1046

נָדִיב 8 noble, princely (8 · 27) 622

עָקָר 9 barren (1 · 11) 785

שָׂמֵחַ   glad, joyful, merry (3 · 21) 970

Psalm 114

לעז   1 to talk unintelligibly (1 · 1 · 1) 541

מֶמְשָׁלָה   2 rule, dominion (5 · 17) 606

אָחוֹר   3 backwards, behind (12 · 41) 30

רקד   4 to skip about (2 · 3 · 9) 955

אָחוֹר   5 backwards, behind (12 · 41) 30

רקד   6 to skip about (2 · 3 · 9) 955

חול   7 to writhe, be in anguish (5 · 30 · 47) 296 I

אֲגַם   8 pool, pond (2 · 8) 8

חַלָּמִישׁ   flint (1 · 5) 321

מַעְיָן   spring (5 · 23) 745

Psalm 115

אַיֵּה   2 where? (5 · 44) 32

עָצָב   4 idol (4 · 17) 781

הריח   6 to smell (1 · 11 · 14) 926

המיש   7 to feel (1 · 3 · 4) 559 II מוש

הָגָה   to speak (10 · 23 · 25) 211 I *Qal* 2

גָּרוֹן   throat (4 · 8) 173

עֹשֶׂה   8 maker, creator (10 · 24[?]) 793 I עשה

עֵזֶר   9 help (11 · 21) 740 I

עֵזֶר   10 help (11 · 21) 740 I

יָרֵא   11 afraid (27 · 46) 431

עֵזֶר   help (11 · 21) 740 I

יָרֵא   13 afraid (27 · 46) 431

קָטֹן   insignificant (2 · 47) 881 I

עֹשֶׂה   15 maker, creator (10 · 24[?]) 793 I עשה

דּוּמָה   17 silence (2 · 2) 189 I

Psalm 116

תַּחֲנוּן   1 supplication for favor (8 · 18) 337

אפף   3 to surround, encompass (3 · 5 · 5) 67

חֶבֶל   cord, rope (8 · 50) 286 I

מֵצַר   straits, distress (2 · 3) 865

יָגוֹן   sorrow, grief (4 · 14) 387

אָנָּה   4 ah, now! I (we) pray! (2 · 6) 58 אָנָּא

חַנּוּן   5 gracious (6 · 13) 337

רחם   to have compassion (4 · 42 · 47) 933

פֶּתִי   6 simple (3 · 19) 834

דלל   to be low, brought low (3 · 8 · 8) 195

מָנוֹחַ   7 rest, repose (1 · 7) 629 I

גָּמַל   to deal bountifully (10 · 34 · 37) 168

חלץ   8 to rescue, deliver (10 · 14 · 27) 322 I

דִּמְעָה   tears (8 · 23) 199

דְּחִי   stumbling (2 · 2) 191

חפז   11 inf. w בְּ = in my alarm (2 · 6 · 9) 342

כזב   to lie, be a liar (1 · 1 · 16) 469

תַּגְמוּל   12 benefit (1 · 1) 168

כּוֹס   13 cup (5 · 31) 468 I

יָקָר   15 precious, highly valued (4 · 35) 429

חָסִיר   pious, godly (25 · 32) 339

אָנָּה   16 ah, now! I (we) pray! (2 · 6) 58 אָנָּא

מוֹסֵר   band, bond (3 · 12) 64

תּוֹדָה   17 sacrifice of thanksgiving, thank offering (12 · 32) 392

Psalm 117

שׁבח   1 to laud, praise (4 · 6 · 8) 986 II

אֻמָּה   tribe, people (1 · 3) 52

גָּבַר   2 to prevail (3 · 17 · 25) 149

Psalm 118

יָרֵא   4 afraid (27 · 46) 431

מֵצַר   5 straits, distress (2 · 3) 865

מֶרְחָב   broad, roomy, place (3 · 6) 932

עֹזֵר   7 help, helper (7 · 19) 740 עזר

שֹׂנֵא   enemy (12 · 41[?]) 971 שׂנא

464

חָסָה 8 to seek refuge (25 · 37 · 37) 340

חָסָה 9 to seek refuge (25 · 37 · 37) 340

נָדִיב noble, princely (8 · 27) 622

הֵמִיל 10 to cause to be circumcised (3 · 3 · 3) 557 II מול

הֵמִיל 11 to cause to be circumcised (3 · 3 · 3) 557 II מול

דְּבוֹרָה 12 bee (1 · 4) 184 I

דָּעַךְ to be extinguished, quenched (1 · 1 · 9) 200

קוֹץ thornbush (1 · 11) 881 I

הֵמִיל to cause to be circumcised (3 · 3 · 3) 557 II מול

דחה 13 to push (4 · 4 · 6) 190

זִמְרָה 14 song, melody (1 · 4) 274 I

רָנָּה 15 ringing dry (15 · 33) 943 I

יסר 18 to discipline, correct (7 · 30 · 41) 415

בֹּנֶה 22 builder (2 · 8) 124 בנה Qal 1.e

פִּנָּה corner (1 · 30) 819

נפלא 23 to be extraordinary, wonderful (3 · 13 · 24) 810

גִּיל 24 to rejoice (19 · 45 · 45) 162

אָנָּא 25 ah, now! I (we) beseech thee! (2 · 7) 58

הֵאִיר 27 to give light, light up (15 · 34 · 40) 21 אור

עֲבֹת cord, rope (3 · 24) 721

Psalm 119

אֶשֶׁר 1 happiness, blessedness (19 · 45[?]) 80

אֶשֶׁר 2 happiness, blessedness (19 · 45[?]) 80

עֵדָה testimony (25 · 32) 730 III

עַוְלָה 3 injustice, wrong (9 · 32) 732

פִּקּוּד 4 precept (24 · 24) 824

אַחֲלַי 5 Oh that! (1 · 2) 25

יֹשֶׁר 7 rightness, uprightness (2 · 14) 449

בַּמֶּה 9 by what means (1 · 29) 552 מָה 4.a

זכה to make or keep clean, pure (2 · 3 · 8) 269

הִשְׁגָה 10 to lead astray (1 · 4 · 21) 993

צָפַן 11 to hide (7 · 23 · 28) 860

אִמְרָה word, saying (26 · 36) 57

עֵדָה 14 testimony (25 · 32) 730 III

שׂושׂ to exult, rejoice (7 · 27) 965

כְּעַל as concerning, as upon (1 · 5) 752 על IV.1

הוֹן wealth (3 · 26) 223

פִּקּוּד 15 precept (24 · 24) 824

שִׂיחַ to muse, meditate, study (13 · 18 · 20) 967

הִשְׁתַּעֲשַׁע 16 to delight oneself (2 · 2 · 6) 1044 שעע

גָּמַל 17 to deal bountifully (10 · 34 · 37) 168

נִפְלָאוֹת 18 wonderful acts (27 · 44) 810 פלא

גרס 20 to be crushed (1 · 1 · 2) 176

תַּאֲבָה longing (1 · 1) 1060

גָּעַר 21 to rebuke (4 · 14 · 14) 172

זֵד insolent, presumptuous (8 · 13) 267

שׁגה to go astray (2 · 17 · 21) 993

בּוּז 22 contempt (5 · 11) 100 II

עֵדָה testimony (25 · 32) 730 III

שִׂיחַ 23 to muse, meditate, study (13 · 18 · 20) 967

עֵדָה 24 testimony (25 · 32) 730 III

שַׁעֲשֻׁעִים delight (5 · 9) 1044

פִּקּוּד 27 precept (24 · 24) 824

שִׂיחַ to muse, meditate, study (13 · 18 · 20) 967

נִפְלָאוֹת wonderful acts (27 · 44) 810 פלא

דלף 28 to drop, drip (1 · 2 · 2) 196

תּוּגָה grief (1 · 4) 387

שִׁיָּה 30 to account suitable, meet (4 · 5 · 5) 1000 I (but cf. root II: to set, place 1001)

עֵדָה 31 testimony (25 · 32) 730 III

הִרְחִיב 32 to enlarge (6 · 21 · 25) 931

הוֹרָה 33 to direct, teach, instruct (8 · 45 · 45) 434 ירה

עֵקֶב	end (5 · 15) 784	חָבֵר 63	associate, fellow (2 · 12) 288
נָתִיב 35	path (2 · 5) 677	פִּקּוּד	precept (24 · 24) 824
עֵדָה 36	testimony (25 · 32) 730 III	טוּב 66	goodness (7 · 32) 375
בֶּצַע	unjust gain (2 · 23) 130	טַעַם	judgment, discretion, discernment (2 · 13) 381
אִמְרָה 38	word, saying (26 · 36) 57	טֶרֶם 67	ere, before that (1 · 16) 382
יִרְאָה	fear (8 · 45) 432	שָׁגַג	to sin, go astray (1 · 5 · 5) 992
יגר 39	to fear (1 · 5 · 5) 388	אִמְרָה	word, saying (26 · 36) 57
תאם 40	to long for (2 · 2 · 2) 1060 I	טפל 69	to plaster, smear (1 · 3 · 3) 381
פִּקּוּד	precept (24 · 24) 824	זֵד	insolent, presumptuous (8 · 13) 267
תְּשׁוּעָה 41	salvation (13 · 34) 448	פִּקּוּד	precept (24 · 24) 824
אִמְרָה	word, saying (26 · 36) 57	טָפַשׁ 70	to be gross (1 · 1 · 1) 382
חרף 42	to reproach (2 · 4 · 38) 357	שַׁעֲשַׁע	to take delight in (2 · 3 · 6) 1044 II שעע
יחל 43	to wait for, hope for (14 · 25 · 42) 403		
עַד 44	ever (29 · 48) 723 I	טוֹב 71	to be well with, good for (1 · 18 · 21) 373 I
רָחָב 45	wide, roomy, space (4 · 21) 932 I	יָרֵא 74	afraid (27 · 46) 431
פִּקּוּד	precept (24 · 24) 824	יחל	to wait for, hope for (14 · 25 · 42) 403
עֵדָה 46	testimony (25 · 32) 730 III		
השתעשע 47	to delight oneself (2 · 2 · 6) 1044 שעע	אִמְרָה 76	word, saying (26 · 36) 57
שִׂיח 48	to muse, meditate, study (13 · 18 · 20) 967	רַחֲמִים 77	compassion (11 · 38) 933
יחל 49	to make to hope (14 · 25 · 42) 403, 1124	שַׁעֲשֻׁעִים	delight (5 · 9) 1044
נֶחָמָה 50	comfort (1 · 2) 637	זֵד 78	insolent, presumptuous (8 · 13) 267
עֳנִי	affliction (10 · 36) 777	עות	to subvert, make crooked (2 · 9 · 11) 736
אִמְרָה	word, saying (26 · 36) 57	שִׂיח	to muse, meditate, study (13 · 18 · 20) 967
זֵד 51	insolent, presumptuous (8 · 13) 267	פִּקּוּד	precept (24 · 24) 824
הֵלִיץ	to deride (1 · 10 · 13) 539 ליץ	יָרֵא 79	afraid (27 · 46) 431
זַלְעָפָה 53	raging heat (2 · 3) 273	עֵדָה	testimony (25 · 32) 730 III
זָמִיר 54	song (2 · 6) 274 I	תְּשׁוּעָה 81	salvation (13 · 34) 448
מְגוּרִים	sojourning (1 · 11) 158 I מָגוֹר	יחל	to wait for, hope for (14 · 25 · 42) 403
פִּקּוּד 56	precept (24 · 24) 824		
אִמְרָה 58	word, saying (26 · 36) 57	אִמְרָה 82	word, saying (26 · 36) 57
עֵדָה 59	testimony (25 · 32) 730 III	מָתַי	when? (13 · 42) 607
חוּשׁ 60	to make haste (8 · 15 · 21) 301 I	נֹאד 83	skin (2 · 6) 609
התמהמה	to linger, tarry, wait (1 · 9 · 9) 554 מהה	קִיטוֹר	thick smoke (2 · 4) 882
חֶבֶל 61	cord, rope (8 · 50) 286 I	כַּמָּה 84	how much? how many? (3 · 13) 552
עוד	to surround (1 · 1 · 44) 728	מָה	4.c
חָצוֹת 62	division, middle (1 · 3) 345	מָתַי	when? (13 · 42) 607

כָּרָה 85 to dig (4 · 13 · 14) 500 I

זֵד insolent, presumptuous (8 · 13) 267

שִׁיחָה pit (2 · 2) 1001

פִּקּוּד 87 precept (24 · 24) 824

לוּלֵי 92 if not, unless (5 · 10) 530 לוּלֵא

שַׁעֲשֻׁעִים delight (5 · 9) 1044

עֳנִי affliction (10 · 36) 777

פִּקּוּד 93 precept (24 · 24) 824

פִּקּוּד 94 precept (24 · 24) 824

קוה Piel to lie in wait for (12 · 39 · 45) 875 I

עֵדָה testimony (25 · 32) 730 III

תִּכְלָה 96 completeness, perfection (1 · 1) 479

רָחָב wide, broad (4 · 21) 932 I

שִׂיחָה 97 complaint, musing (2 · 3) 967

חכם 98 to make wise, teach wisdom (2 · 3 · 26) 314

עֵדָה 99 testimony (25 · 32) 730 III

שִׂיחָה complaint, musing (2 · 3) 967

פִּקּוּד 100 precept (24 · 24) 824

כלא 101 to restrain (4 · 14 · 17) 476

הורה 102 to direct, teach, instruct (8 · 45 · 45) 434 ירה

נמלץ 103 to be smooth (1 · 1 · 1) 576

חֵךְ palate (2 · 18) 335

אִמְרָה word, saying (26 · 36) 57

פִּקּוּד 104 precept (24 · 24) 824

נֵר 105 lamp (3 · 44) 632 I

נְתִיבָה path (2 · 21) 677

נְדָבָה 108 freewill, voluntary, offering (4 · 27) 621

פַּח 110 bird trap, snare (9 · 25) 809 I

פִּקּוּד precept (24 · 24) 824

תָּעָה to wander about, err (5 · 27 · 50) 1073

עֵדָה 111 testimony (25 · 32) 730 III

שָׂשׂוֹן exultation, joy (5 · 22) 965

עֵקֶב 112 to the end (5 · 15) 784

סֵעֵף 113 half-hearted (1 · 1) 704 II

סֵתֶר 114 hiding place, shelter (10 · 35) 712

יחל to wait for, hope for (14 · 25 · 42) 403

מֵרַע 115 evildoer (9 · 18) 949 רעע Hiph. 2

סָמַךְ 116 to support, uphold, sustain (10 · 41 · 48) 701

אִמְרָה word, saying (26 · 36) 57

שֵׂבֶר hope (2 · 2) 960

סָעַד 117 to support, sustain (6 · 12 · 12) 703

שָׁעָה to gaze, regard (1 · 12 · 15) 1043

סלה 118 to make light of (1 · 1 · 2) 699 I

שגה to go astray (2 · 17 · 21) 993

תַּרְמִית deceitfulness (1 · 5) 941

סִיג 119 dross, silver (1 · 8) 691

עֵדָה testimony (25 · 32) 730 III

סָמַר 120 to bristle up (1 · 1 · 2) 702

פַּחַד dread (9 · 49) 808 I

עָשַׁק 121 ptc. = oppressor, extortioner (6 · 36 · 37) 798

עָרַב 122 to take a pledge, go surety (1 · 15 · 17) 786 II

עָשַׁק to oppress, wrong (6 · 36 · 37) 798

זֵד insolent, presumptuous (8 · 13) 267

אִמְרָה 123 word, saying (26 · 36) 57

עֵדָה 125 testimony (25 · 32) 730 III

הֵפֵר 126 to break, frustrate (2 · 41 · 44[?]) 830 פרר I

פַּז 127 refined or pure gold (3 · 9) 808

פִּקּוּד 128 precept (24 · 24) 824

ישר to esteem right, approve (1 · 9 · 25) 448

פֶּלֶא 129 wonder, wonderful (7 · 13) 810

עֵדָה testimony (25 · 32) 730 III

פֵּתַח 130 opening, unfolding (1 · 1) 836

הֵאִיר to give light (15 · 34 · 40) 21 אור

פֶּתִי simple (3 · 19) 834

פָּעַר 131 to open wide (1 · 4 · 4) 822

שָׁאַף to gasp, pant (4 · 14 · 14) 983 I

יאב to long (1 · 1 · 1) 383

אֹהֵב 132 friend (12 · 36) 12 אָהֵב

אִמְרָה 133 word, saying (26 · 36) 57

467

הַשְׁלִיט   to get mastery of $(1 \cdot 3 \cdot 8)$ 1020 I

עֹשֶׁק 134 oppression, extortion $(3 \cdot 15)$ 799

פִּקּוּד   precept $(24 \cdot 24)$ 824

הֵאִיר 135 to make shine $(15 \cdot 34 \cdot 40)$ 21 אור 21

פֶּלֶג 136 channel, canal $(4 \cdot 10)$ 811 I

עֵדָה 138 testimony $(25 \cdot 32)$ 730 III

צמת 139 to put an end to, annihilate $(2 \cdot 2 \cdot 15)$ 856

קִנְאָה   ardor, zeal $(3 \cdot 43)$ 888

צָרַף 140 to smelt, refine $(7 \cdot 18 \cdot 21)$ 864

אִמְרָה   word, saying $(26 \cdot 36)$ 57

צָעִיר 141 insignificant, little $(2 \cdot 22)$ 859 I

נבזה   to be despised $(2 \cdot 10 \cdot 42)$ 102

פִּקּוּד   precept $(24 \cdot 24)$ 824

צַר 143 straits, distress $(3 \cdot 20)$ 865 II

מָצוֹק   straits, distress $(1 \cdot 6)$ 848

שַׁעֲשֻׁעִים   delight $(5 \cdot 9)$ 1044

עֵדָה 144 testimony $(25 \cdot 32)$ 730 III

עֵדָה 146 testimony $(25 \cdot 32)$ 730 III

קִדֵּם 147 to be beforehand, anticipate $(12 \cdot 24 \cdot 27)$ 869

נֶשֶׁף   morning twilight $(1 \cdot 12)$ 676

שׁוע   to cry for help $(9 \cdot 21 \cdot 21[?])$ 1002

יחל   to wait for, hope for $(14 \cdot 25 \cdot 42)$ 403

קִדֵּם 148 to anticipate, forestall $(12 \cdot 24 \cdot 27)$ 869

אַשְׁמוּרָה   watch (division of time) $(3 \cdot 7)$ 1038

שִׂיחַ   to muse, meditate, study $(13 \cdot 18 \cdot 20)$ 967

אִמְרָה   word, saying $(26 \cdot 36)$ 57

זִמָּה 150 evil device $(2 \cdot 28)$ 273 I

עֵדָה 152 testimony $(25 \cdot 32)$ 730 III

יָסַד   to found, establish $(7 \cdot 20 \cdot 41)$ 413

עֳנִי 153 affliction $(10 \cdot 36)$ 777

חלץ   to rescue, deliver $(10 \cdot 14 \cdot 27)$ 322 I

אִמְרָה 154 word, saying $(26 \cdot 36)$ 57

רַחֲמִים 156 compassion $(11 \cdot 38)$ 933

בגד 158 to act or deal treacherously, deceitfully $(5 \cdot 49 \cdot 49)$ 93

הִתְקוֹטֵט   to feel a loathing $(2 \cdot 2 \cdot 7)$ 876 קוט

אִמְרָה   word, saying $(26 \cdot 36)$ 57

פִּקּוּד 159 precept $(24 \cdot 24)$ 824

חִנָּם 161 gratuitously, without cause $(6 \cdot 32)$ 336

פָּחַד   to be in dread $(5 \cdot 23 \cdot 26)$ 808

שׂושׂ 162 to exult, rejoice $(7 \cdot 27)$ 965

אִמְרָה   word, saying $(26 \cdot 36)$ 57

תעב 163 to abhor, regard as an abomination $(4 \cdot 14 \cdot 21)$ 1073

אֹהֵב 165 friend $(12 \cdot 36)$ 12 אהב

מִכְשׁוֹל   stumbling block $(1 \cdot 14)$ 506

שׂבר 166 to hope $(3 \cdot 6 \cdot 8)$ 960 II

עֵדָה 167 testimony $(25 \cdot 32)$ 730 III

פִּקּוּד 168 precept $(24 \cdot 24)$ 824

עֵדָה   testimony $(25 \cdot 32)$ 730 III

רִנָּה 169 ringing cry $(15 \cdot 33)$ 943 I

תְּחִנָּה 170 supplication for favor $(3 \cdot 25)$ 337 I

אִמְרָה   word, saying $(26 \cdot 36)$ 57

הִבִּיע 171 to pour forth, emit $(6 \cdot 10 \cdot 11)$ נבע 615

אִמְרָה 172 word, saying $(26 \cdot 36)$ 57

פִּקּוּד 173 precept $(24 \cdot 24)$ 824

תאב 174 to long for $(2 \cdot 2 \cdot 2)$ 1060 I

שַׁעֲשֻׁעִים   delight $(5 \cdot 9)$ 1044

תָּעָה 176 to wander about $(5 \cdot 27 \cdot 50)$ 1073

שֶׂה   sheep, goat $(1 \cdot 45)$ 961

Psalm 120

מַעֲלָה 1 ascent $(15 \cdot 47)$ 752 II

רְמִיָּה 2 deceit, treachery $(6 \cdot 15)$ 941

רְמִיָּה 3 deceit, treachery $(6 \cdot 15)$ 941

שׁנן 4 to whet, sharpen $(4 \cdot 7 \cdot 9)$ 1041

גַּחֶלֶת   coal $(5 \cdot 18)$ 160

רֹתֶם   broom plant $(1 \cdot 4)$ 958

אוֹיָה 5 woe! alas! $(1 \cdot 25)$ 17

Psalm 121

מַעֲלָה 1 ascent (15 · 47) 752 II

מֵאַיִן whence? (1 · 48[?]) 32 I אַיִן

עֵזֶר help (11 · 21) 740 I

עֵזֶר 2 help (11 · 21) 740 I

עֹשֶׂה maker, creator (10 · 24[?]) 793 I עשׂה

מוֹט 3 to totter, slip (8 · 15 · 39) 556 (cf. מוֹט a shaking, p.557)

נוּם to slumber, be drowsy (3 · 6 · 6) 630

נוּם 4 to slumber, be drowsy (3 · 6 · 6) 630

יָשֵׁן to sleep, go to sleep (5 · 15 · 16) 445

יָרֵחַ 6 moon (8 · 27) 437

Psalm 122

מַעֲלָה 1 ascent (15 · 47) 752 II

שֶׁחֻבְּרָה 3 שֶׁ + חָבְרָה to be joined together (1 · 4 · 28) 287

שָׁשָּׁם 4 where (1 · 1) 1027 שָׁם 2

שׁלה 6 to be at ease, prosper (1 · 5 · 7) 1017 I

אֹהֵב friend (12 · 36) 12 אָהֵב

חֵיל 7 rampart (2 · 9) 298 חֵל

שַׁלְוָה quietness, peace (1 · 8) 1017

אַרְמוֹן citadel, castle, palace (3 · 33) 74

Psalm 123

מַעֲלָה 1 ascent (15 · 47) 752 II

גְּבֶרֶת 2 mistress (1 · 15) 150

שֶׁיְּחָנֵּנוּ שֶׁ + חָנַן, to be gracious 979 שֶׁ, 335 I חָנַן

בּוּז 3 contempt (5 · 11) 100 II

לַעַג 4 mocking, derision (3 · 7) 541

שַׁאֲנָן at ease; i.e., careless, wanton, arrogant (1 · 11) 983

בּוּז contempt (5 · 11) 100 II

גַּאֲיוֹן proud (1 · 1) 145

Psalm 124

מַעֲלָה 1 ascent (15 · 47) 752 II

לוּלֵי except that (5 · 10) 530 לוּלֵא

שֶׁהָיָה שֶׁ + הָיָה to be 979 שֶׁ, 224 היה

לוּלֵי 2 except that (5 · 10) 530 לוּלֵא

אֲזַי 3 then, in that case (3 · 3) 23

בָּלַע to swallow up, engulf (3 · 20 · 41) 118

אֲזַי 4 then, in that case (3 · 3) 23

שָׁטַף to overflow, rinse or wash off (4 · 28 · 31) 1009

אֲזַי 5 then, in that case (3 · 3) 23

זֵידוֹן insolent, raging (1 · 1) 268

שֶׁלֹּא 6 who has not שֶׁ + לֹא (2 · 4) 518, 979

טֶרֶף prey (3 · 18) 383

צִפּוֹר 7 [coll.] birds (7 · 40) 861 I

פַּח bird trap (9 · 25) 809 I

יקשׁ to lay snares, bait (2 · 3 · 8) 430

עֵזֶר 8 help (11 · 21) 740 I

עֹשֶׂה maker, creator (10 · 24[?]) 793 I עשׂה

Psalm 125

מַעֲלָה 1 ascent (15 · 47) 752 II

נמוט to be shaken, moved, overthrown (16 · 23 · 39) 556

רֶשַׁע 3 wickedness (6 · 30) 957

עַוְלָה injustice, wrong (9 · 32) 732

עֲקַלְקַל 5 crooked (1 · 2) 785

Psalm 126

מַעֲלָה 1 ascent (15 · 47) 752 II

שִׁיבָה restoration (1 · 1) 1000 II

חלם to dream (1 · 26 · 28) 321 II

שְׂחוֹק 2 laughter (1 · 15) 966 שׂחק

רִנָּה ringing cry (15 · 33) 943 I

שָׂמֵחַ 3 glad, joyful, merry (3 · 21) 970

469

שְׁבִית‎ 4 [coll.] captivity, captives (2 · 6) 986

אָפִיק‎ channel (3 · 18) 67

דִּמְעָה‎ 5 tears (8 · 23) 199

רִנָּה‎ ringing cry (15 · 33) 943 I

קצר‎ to reap, harvest (1 · 24 · 24) 894 II

מֶשֶׁךְ‎ 6 trail (1 · 2) 604 I

רִנָּה‎ ringing cry (15 · 33) 943 I

אֲלֻמָּה‎ sheaf (1 · 5) 48

Psalm 127

מַעֲלָה‎ 1 ascent (15 · 47) 752 II

עָמַל‎ to labor (1 · 11 · 11) 765

שָׁקַד‎ to keep watch, be wakeful (1 · 11 · 17[?]) 1052

אָחַר‎ 2 to delay, tarry (3 · 15 · 17) 29

עֶצֶב‎ toil; pain (1 · 6) 780 I

יָדִיד‎ beloved (4 · 8) 391

שֵׁנָא‎ sleep (1 · 1) 446 שֵׁנָה‎

שָׂכָר‎ 3 hire, wages (1 · 29) 969 I

נְעוּרִים‎ 4 youth (8 · 46) 655

אֶשֶׁר‎ 5 happiness, blessedness (19 · 45[?]) 80

אַשְׁפָּה‎ quiver (1 · 6) 80

Psalm 128

מַעֲלָה‎ 1 ascent (15 · 47) 752 II

אֶשֶׁר‎ happiness, blessedness (19 · 45[?]) 80

יָרֵא‎ afraid (27 · 46) 431

יְגִיעַ‎ 2 product, produce (3 · 16) 388

אֶשֶׁר‎ happiness, blessedness (19 · 45[?]) 80

פרה‎ 3 to be fruitful, bear fruit (1 · 22 · 29) 826

יַרְכָה‎ recesses, innermost part (2 · 28) 438

שָׁתִיל‎ transplanted shoot, slip (1 · 1) 1060

זַיִת‎ olive tree, olive (2 · 38) 268

יָרֵא‎ 4 afraid (27 · 46) 431

טוּב‎ 5 prosperity (7 · 32) 375

Psalm 129

מַעֲלָה‎ 1 ascent (15 · 47) 752 I

צרר‎ to vex, harass (2 · 10 · 10) 865 III

נְעוּרִים‎ youth (8 · 46) 655

צרר‎ 2 to vex, harass (2 · 10 · 10) 865 III

נְעוּרִים‎ youth (8 · 46) 655

גַּב‎ 3 back (1 · 13) 146

חרשׁ‎ to plough (1 · 23 · 26) 360 I

הֶאֱרִיךְ‎ to make long, prolong (1 · 31 · 34) 73

מַעֲנָה‎ ploughing ground (1 · 2) 776

קִצֵּץ‎ 4 to cut in two (2 · 9 · 14) 893

עֲבֹת‎ cord, rope (3 · 24) 721

נָסוֹג‎ 5 to be turned back, repulsed (6 · 14 · 25) 690 I

אָחוֹר‎ backwards, behind (12 · 41) 30

שֹׂנֵא‎ enemy (12 · 41[?]) 971 שָׂנֵא‎

חָצִיר‎ 6 grass (6 · 18) 348 II

גָּג‎ roof (2 · 29) 150

שֶׁקַּדְמַת‎ שֶׁ‎ + קַדְמָה‎ = before (1 · 6) 979 שֶׁ‎, 870 קַדְמָה‎

שָׁלַף‎ to shoot up (1 · 25) 1025

שֶׁלֹּא‎ 7 that which not שֶׁ‎ + לֹא‎ (2 · 4) 979, 518

קֹצֵר‎ reaper (1 · 10[?]) 894 קצר‎

חֹצֶן‎ bosom (1 · 3) 346

עמר‎ to bind sheaves (1 · 1 · 1) 771

Psalm 130

מַעֲלָה‎ 1 ascent (15 · 47) 752 II

מַעֲמַקִּים‎ depths (3 · 5) 771

קַשֵּׁב‎ 2 attentive (1 · 3) 904

תַּחֲנוּן‎ supplication for favor (8 · 18) 337

סְלִיחָה‎ 4 forgiveness (1 · 3) 699

קוה‎ 5 *Piel*, to wait, look eagerly, for (12 · 39 · 45) 875 I

470

הוֹחִיל	to wait for, hope for (14 · 25 · 42) יחל 403	
יָחֵל	7 to wait for, hope for (14 · 25 · 42) 403	
פְּדוּת	ransom (2 · 4) 804	

Psalm 131

מַעֲלָה	1 ascent (15 · 47) 752 II
גָּבַהּ	to be haughty (2 · 24 · 34) 146
נִפְלָאוֹת	wonderful acts (27 · 44) 810 פלא
שָׁוָה	2 to smooth; i.e., compose (2 · 5 · 16 [?]) 1000 I
דוֹמֵם	to quiet (1 · 1 · 30) 198 I
גָּמֻל	pass. ptc. = weaned child (10 · 34 · 37) 168
יָחֵל	3 to wait for, hope for (14 · 25 · 42) 403

Psalm 132

מַעֲלָה	1 ascent (15 · 47) 752 II
נָדַר	2 to make a vow (2 · 31 · 31) 623
אָבִיר	strong; the strong (2 · 6) 7
עֶרֶשׂ	3 couch, divan (3 · 10) 793
יָצוּעַ	couch, bed (2 · 5) 426
שְׁנָת	4 sleep (3 · 23) 446 שֵׁנָה
עַפְעַף	eyelid (2 · 10) 733
תְּנוּמָה	slumber (1 · 5) 630
אָבִיר	5 strong; the strong (2 · 6) 7
הֲדֹם	7 stool, footstool (3 · 6) 213
מְנוּחָה	8 resting place (4 · 21) 629
חָסִיד	9 pious, godly (25 · 32) 339
בַּעֲבוּר	10 for the sake of, on account of, because of (3 · 45) 721 II עֲבוּר
מָשִׁיחַ	anointed (10 · 39) 603
זוֹ	12 which (1 · 2) 262
עֲדֵי	poetic for עַד up to, until (6 · 12) 723 עַד III
עַד	forever (29 · 48) 723 I

אַוָּה	13 to desire (2 · 11 · 27) 16 I
מוֹשָׁב	dwelling place (6 · 46) 444
מְנוּחָה	14 resting place (4 · 21) 629
עֲדֵי	poetic for עַד up to, until (6 · 12) עַד III 723
עַד	forever (29 · 48) 723 I
פֹּה	here, hither (1 · 44) 805
אַוָּה	to desire (2 · 11 · 27) 16 I
צַיִד	15 food, food supply (1 · 5) 845 I
יֵשַׁע	16 salvation (20 · 36) 447
חָסִיד	pious, godly (25 · 32) 339
הַצְמִיחַ	17 to cause to grow (3 · 14 · 33) 855
נֵר	lamp (3 · 44) 632 I
מָשִׁיחַ	anointed (10 · 39) 603
בֹּשֶׁת	18 shame (7 · 30) 102
צוּץ	to shine, gleam (5 · 7 · 8) 847 I
נֵזֶר	crown (2 · 25) 634

Psalm 133

מַעֲלָה	1 ascent (15 · 47) 752 II
נָעִים	delightful, pleasant (6 · 7) 653 I
יַחַד	together, altogether (14 · 44) 403
זָקָן	2 beard (2 · 19) 278
שֶׁיֹּרֵד	שֶׁ + ירד to go down 979 שֶׁ, 432 ירד
מִדָּה	garment (2 · 21) 551 I
טַל	3 dew (2 · 31) 378

Psalm 134

מַעֲלָה	1 ascent (15 · 47) 752 II
עֹשֶׂה	3 maker, creator (10 · 24[?]) 793 I עשה

Psalm 135

זמר	3 to sing, make music (39 · 43 · 43) 274 I
נָעִים	delightful, pleasant (6 · 7) 653 I

471

סְגֻלָּה	4	possession, peculiar treasure (1 · 8) 688
תְּהוֹם	6	deep, sea, abyss (12 · 36) 1062
נָשִׂיא	7	vapor, mist (1 · 4) 672 II
בָּרָק		lightning (5 · 21) 140
מָטָר		rain (3 · 38) 564
מוֹפֵת	9	sign, wonder (5 · 63) 68
עָצוּם	10	mighty (3 · 31) 783
זֵכֶר	13	memorial (11 · 23) 271
דִּין	14	to judge, minister judgment (8 · 23 · 24) 192
עֶצֶב	15	idol (4 · 17) 781
הֶאֱזִין	17	to listen, give ear (15 · 41 · 41) 24
עֹשֶׂה	18	maker, creator (10 · 24[?]) 793 I עשה
יָרֵא	20	afraid (27 · 46) 431

Psalm 136

עֹשֶׂה	4	maker, creator (10 · 24[?]) 793 I עשה
נִפְלָאוֹת		wonderful acts (27 · 44) 810 פלא
עֹשֶׂה	5	maker, creator (10 · 24[?]) 793 I עשה
תְּבוּנָה		understanding (4 · 42) 108
רקע	6	to spread out (1 · 6 · 11) 955
עֹשֶׂה	7	maker, creator (10 · 24[?]) 793 I עשה
מֶמְשָׁלָה	8	rule, dominion (5 · 17) 606
יָרֵחַ	9	moon (8 · 27) 437
כּוֹכָב		star (4 · 37) 456
מֶמְשָׁלָה		rule, dominion (5 · 17) 606
גָּזַר	13	to divide (1 · 6 · 12) 160
גֶּזֶר		part (1 · 2) 160 I
נָעַר	15	to shake off (1 · 3 · 10) 654 I
אַדִּיר	18	majestic (7 · 27) 12
שֵׁפֶל	23	low estate, condition (1 · 2) 1050

פרק	24	to snatch, tear away (2 · 4 · 10) 830

Psalm 137

עֲרָבָה	2	poplar (1 · 5) 788 II
תָּלָה		to hang up (1 · 23 · 27) 1067
כִּנּוֹר		lyre (13 · 41) 490
שֹׁבֶה	3	captive (2 · 9) 985 שָׁבָה
תּוֹלָל		[dub.] oppressor (1 · 1) 1064
נֵכָר	4	foreignness (6 · 36) 648
חֵךְ	6	palate (2 · 18) 335
עֵרָה	7	to lay bare (3 · 9 · 15) 788
יְסוֹד		foundation, base (1 · 19) 414
אֶשֶׁר	8	happiness, blessedness (19 · 45[?]) 80
גְּמוּל		dealing, recompense (4 · 19) 168
גָּמַל		to recompense, repay, requite (10 · 34 · 37) 168
אֶשֶׁר	9	happiness, blessedness (19 · 45[?]) 80
נָפֵץ		to dash to pieces (2 · 15 · 21) 658 I
עוֹלָל		child (1 · 9) 760

Psalm 138

זמר	1	to sing, make music (39 · 43 · 43) 274 I
אִמְרָה	2	word, saying (26 · 36) 57
הרהיב	3	to make proud, bold (1 · 2 · 4) 923
אֵמֶר	4	utterance, word (7 · 48) 56
רָם	6	high, lifted, exalted (5 · 31[?]) 926 רום
שָׁפָל		lowly (1 · 18) 1050
גָּבֹהַּ		haughty; high (3 · 41) 147
מֶרְחָק		distant place, far (1 · 18) 935
גָּמַר	8	to bring to an end, complete (5 · 5 · 5) 170
הרפה		to refrain, let alone (3 · 21 · 45) 951

Psalm 139

חָקַר 1 to search (3 · 22 · 27) 350

רֵעַ 2 purpose, aim (2 · 2) 946 III

רבע 3 to lie down (1 · 3 · 4) 918 II

זרה to winnow, sift (1 · 1 · 1[?]) 279

הִסְכִּין to be familiar with, know intimately (1 · 4 · 11) 698 I

מִלָּה 4 word (2 · 38) 576

אָחוֹר 5 behind, backwards (12 · 41) 30

צוּר to shut up, enclose (1 · 31 · 31) 848 II

פְּלִאי 6 wonderful, incomprehensible (1 · 2) 811

נִשְׂגָּב to be high, exalted (2 · 10 · 20) 960

אָנָה 7 where? whither? (7 · 39) 33 אָן

אֶסַּק 8 I ascend (1 · 1 · 1) 701 סלק

הַצִּיעַ to spread out (1 · 2 · 4) 426 יצע

שַׁחַר 9 dawn (4 · 23) 1007

הנחה 10 to lead, guide (12 · 26 · 40) 634

שׁוּף 11 perh. to cover, screen (1 · 3 · 3) 1003

הַחְשִׁיךְ 12 to hide, conceal (2 · 6 · 17) 364

הֵאִיר to shine, cause to shine (15 · 34 · 40) 21 אור

חֲשֵׁכָה darkness (3 · 6) 365

אוֹרָה light (1 · 2) 21 I

קָנָה 13 to get, acquire (1 · 5 · 5) 888 I

כִּלְיָה kidney (5 · 31) 480

סכך to weave together (2 · 12 · 18[?]) 697 II

נוֹרָא 14 awe-inspiring, awful (15 · 44) 431 יָרֵא

נפלא to be extraordinary, wonderful (3 · 13 · 24) 810

נֻכְחַד 15 to be hidden (2 · 11 · 32) 470

עֹצֶם bones (1 · 4) 782

סֵתֶר secret place (10 · 35) 712

רקם to be skillfully wrought (1 · 9) 955

תַּחְתִּי lower, lowest (4 · 19) 1066

גֹּלֶם 16 embryo (1 · 1) 166

יצר to be preordained (1 · 1 · 44) 427

יָקַר 17 to be precious, highly esteemed (3 · 9 · 11) 429

רֵעַ purpose, aim (2 · 2) 946 III

עָצַם to be numerous, vast (5 · 16 · 18) 782

חוֹל 18 sand (2 · 22) 297

הֱקִיץ to awake (7 · 22 · 23) 884 I

קטל 19 to slay (1 · 3 · 3) 881

לִמְזִמָּה 20 wickedly (5 · 19) 273 מְזִמָּה

עָר [dub.] adversary (1 · 2) 786 II

בְּתִקוֹמְמֶיךָ 21 one rising up against you (1 · 1[?]) 877 קום Hithpol.

הִתְקוֹטֵט to feel a loathing (2 · 2 · 7) 876 קוט

תַּכְלִית 22 completeness; end (1 · 5) 479

שִׂנְאָה hating, hatred (4 · 17) 971

חָקַר 23 to search (3 · 22 · 27) 350

בחן to examine, try (9 · 24 · 28) 103

שַׂרְעַפִּים disquieting thoughts (2 · 2) 972

עֹצֶב 24 hurt, pain (1 · 3) 780 I

נחה to lead, bring (6 · 14 · 40) 634

Psalm 140

חִלֵּץ 2 to rescue, deliver (10 · 14 · 27) 322

גוּר 3 to stir up strife (3 · 4 · 4) 158 II

שׁנן 4 to whet, sharpen (4 · 7 · 9) 1041

נָחָשׁ serpent (2 · 31) 638 I

עַכְשׁוּב asp, viper; perh. = spider (1 · 1) 747

דחה 5 to push (4 · 4 · 6) 190

טָמַן 6 to hide, conceal (7 · 28 · 31) 380

גֵּאֶה proud (2 · 8) 144

פַּח bird trap (9 · 25) 809 II

חֶבֶל cord, rope (8 · 50) 286 II

רֶשֶׁת net (8 · 22) 440

מַעְגָּל track (4 · 13) 722

מוֹקֵשׁ bait, lure (6 · 27) 430

הַאֲזִין 7 to listen, give ear (15 · 41 · 41) 24

תַּחֲנוּן supplication for favor (8 · 18) 337

סְכָךְ 8 to screen, cover (2 · 12 · 18) 696 I

נֶשֶׁק equipment, weapons (1 · 10) 676

מַאֲוַי 9 desire (1 · 1) 273

זָמָם plan, device (1 · 1) 273

הֵפִיק to promote (2 · 8 · 9) 807 II פיק

מֵסַב 10 encompassing, surrounding (1 · 5 [?]) 685 סָבַב *Hiph.* 2.c

נָמוֹט 11 to be shaken, moved, overthrown (16 · 22 · 39) 556

גַּחֶלֶת coal (5 · 18) 160

מַהֲמֹרָה flood (1 · 1) 243

צוּד 12 to hunt (1 · 12 · 16) 844 I

מַדְחֵפָה thrust (1 · 1) 191

דִּין 13 cause, plea (3 · 19) 192

Psalm 141

חוּשׁ 1 to make haste (8 · 15 · 21) 301 I

הַאֲזִין to listen, give ear (15 · 41 · 41) 24

מַשְׂאַת 2 uplifting, lifting up (1 · 16) 673

שָׁמְרָה 3 guard, watch (1 · 1) 1037

דָּל door (1 · 1) 194

הִתְעוֹלֵל 4 to practice (1 · 1 · 17) 759 I

עֲלִילָה deed (9 · 24) 760

רֶשַׁע wickedness (6 · 30) 957

לחם to eat (1 · 6 · 6) 536 II

מַנְעַמִּים delicacies, dainties (1 · 1) 654

הלם 5 to smite (2 · 8 · 8) 240

הֵנִיא to refuse, restrain (2 · 8 · 8) 626 נוא

נשׁמט 6 to be thrown down (1 · 1 · 9) 1030

אֹמֶר utterance, word (7 · 48) 56

נעם to be pleasant, lovely (1 · 8 · 8) 653 I

פלח 7 to cleave (1 · 1 · 5) 812

נפזר to be scattered (1 · 1 · 10) 808

בְּכָה 8 בְּ + suffix 2nd m. sing. 88

חָסָה to seek refuge (25 · 37 · 37) 340

עֵרָה to pour out (3 · 9 · 15) 788

פַּח 9 bird trap (9 · 25) 809 I

יקשׁ to lay snares, bait (2 · 3 · 8) 430

מוֹקֵשׁ bait, lure (6 · 27) 430

מִכְמָר 10 net, snare (1 · 2) 485

יַחַד together, altogether (14 · 44) 403

Psalm 142

מַשְׂכִּיל 1 contemplative poem (14 · 14) 968

מְעָרָה cave (2 · 40) 792

שִׂיחַ 3 complaint (5 · 14) 967 I

הִתְעַטֵּף 4 to faint, faint away (4 · 6 · 11) 742 III

נְתִיבָה path (2 · 21) 677

זוּ which (9 · 14) 262

טָמַן to hide, conceal (7 · 28 · 31) 380

פַּח bird trap (9 · 25) 809 I

הִכִּיד 5 to acknowledge (2 · 37 · 40) 647 I נכר

מָנוֹס escape (2 · 8) 631

מַחְסֶה 6 refuge, shelter (12 · 20) 340

הִקְשִׁיב 7 to give attention (8 · 45 · 46) 904

רִנָּה ringing cry (15 · 33) 943 I

דלל to be low, brought low, (3 · 8 · 8) 195

אמץ to be strong (2 · 16 · 41) 54

מַסְגֵּר 8 dungeon (1 · 7) 689

הִכְתִּיר [dub.] to throw out crowns; i.e., appear with crowns (1 · 3 · 6) 509

גָּמַל to deal bountifully (10 · 34 · 37) 168

Psalm 143

הַאֲזִין 1 to listen, give ear (15 · 41 · 41) 24

תַּחֲנוּן supplication for favor (8 · 18) 337

צדק 2 to be justified (3 · 22 · 41) 842

דִּכָּא 3 to crush (4 · 11 · 18) 193

חַיָּה life (3 · 12[?]) 312 I

מַחְשָׁךְ dark place (4 · 7) 365

הִתְעַטֵּף 4 to faint, faint away (4 · 6 · 11) 742 III

הָגָה 5 to meditate, muse (10 · 23 · 25) 211
I

פֹּעַל deed, thing done (11 · 37) 821

שׂוֹחֵחַ to meditate, consider (1 · 2 · 20) 967
שׂיח vb. denom.

עָיֵף 6 faint, weary (2 · 17) 746

נִמְשָׁל 7 to be like, similar (4 · 5 · 15) 605 I

זוּ 8 which (9 · 14) 262

הִנְחָה 10 to lead, bring (12 · 26 · 40) 634

מִישׁוֹר level place (5 · 23) 449

הִצְמִית 12 to exterminate, annihilate
(9 · 10 · 15) 856

צֹרֵר vexer, harasser (12 · 17) 865 III צרר

Psalm 144

קְרָב 1 battle, war (898

אֶצְבַּע finger (2 · 31) 840

מְצוּדָה 2 fastness, stronghold (7 · 18) 845 II

מִשְׂגָּב secure height, retreat (13 · 17) 960 I

פלט to deliver (19 · 24 · 27) 812

חָסָה to seek refuge (25 · 37 · 37) 340

רדד to beat down (1 · 2 · 3) 921

אֱנוֹשׁ 3 man, mankind (13 · 42) 60

דָּמָה 4 tb be like, resemble (3 · 13 · 27) 197

עָשַׁן 5 to smoke (4 · 6 · 6) 798

ברק 6 to flash (1 · 1 · 1) 140

בָּרָק lightning (5 · 21) 140

הָמַם to confuse, discomfit (2 · 13 · 13)
243

פָּצָה 7 to snatch away, set free (5 · 15 · 15)
822

נֵכָר foreignness (6 · 36) 648

נֵבֶל 9 harp (8 · 27) 614 II

עָשׂוֹר a ten-stringed harp (3 · 15) 797

זמר to sing, make music (39 · 43 · 43)
274 I

תְּשׁוּעָה 10 deliverance (13 · 34) 448

פָּצָה to snatch away, set free (5 · 15 · 15)
822

פָּצָה 11 to snatch away, set free (5 · 15 · 15)
822

נֵכָר foreignness (6 · 36) 648

נָטִיעַ 12 plant (1 · 1) 642

נְעוּרִים youth (8 · 46) 655

זָוִית corner (1 · 2) 265

חטב pass. ptc. = hewn (1 · 1 · 3)
310 I

תַּבְנִית construction, structure (2 · 20) 125

מָזוּ 13 garner (1 · 1) 265

הֵפִיק to produce, furnish (2 · 8 · 9) 807 II
פוק

זַן kind, sort (1 · 2) 275

מַאֲלִיפוֹת Hiph. ptc. = producing thousands
(1 · 1 · 1) 1120:49a

מְרֻבָּבוֹת Pual ptc. = multiplied ten thou-
sand-fold (1 · 1 · 24[?]) 1126:914b

אַלּוּף 14 tame; here = cattle (2 · 9) 48 I

סָבָל ptc. = laden (1 · 1 · 9) 687

פֶּרֶץ breach (2 · 19) 829 I

יוֹצֵאת going forth (1 · 1[?]) 422 יָצָא Qal 2.a

צְוָחָה outcry (1 · 4) 486

רְחוֹב broad open place, plaza (2 · 43)
932 I

אֶשֶׁר 15 happiness, blessedness (19 · 45[?])
80

שֶׁכָּכָה thus (1 · 2) 462

Psalm 145

עַד 1 ever (29 · 48) 723 I

עַד 2 ever (29 · 48) 723 I

גְּדוּלָה 3 greatness (3 · 12) 153

חֵקֶר searchable, searching (1 · 11)
350

שׁבח 4 to laud, praise (4 · 6 · 8) 986 II

הָדָר 5 splendor, majesty (13 · 30) 214

הוֹד splendor, majesty (8 · 24) 217 I

נִפְלָאוֹת wonderful acts (27 · 44) 810 פלא

שִׂיחַ to muse, meditate, study (13 · 18 · 20) 967

עֱזוּז 6 strength, might, fierceness (2 · 3) 739

נוֹרָא awe inspiring, awful (15 · 44) 431
יָרֵא

גְּדוּלָּה greatness (3 · 12) 153

זֵכֶר 7 remembrance, memory (11 · 23) 375

טוֹב goodness (7 · 23) 375

הִבִּיעַ to pour forth, emit (6 · 10 · 11) 615
נבע

חַנּוּן 8 gracious (6 · 13) 337

רַחוּם compassionate (6 · 13) 933

אֶרֶךְ long; אַפַּיִם א׳ slow to anger (3 · 15) 74

רַחֲמִים 9 compassion (11 · 38) 933

חָסִיד 10 pious, godly (25 · 32) 339

הָדָר 12 splendor, majesty (13 · 30) 214

מֶמְשָׁלָה 13 rule, dominion (5 · 17) 606

סָמַךְ 14 to support, uphold, sustain (10 · 41 · 48) 701

זָקַף to raise up (2 · 2 · 2) 279

כָּפַף pass. ptc. = those bowed down (3 · 4 · 4) 496

שָׂבַר 15 to hope (3 · 6 · 8) 960 II

אֹכֶל food (6 · 44) 38

חָסִיד 17 kind (25 · 32) 339

יָרֵא 19 afraid (27 · 46) 431

שַׁוְעָה cry for help (6 · 11) 1003

אֹהֵב 20 friend (12 · 36) 12 אָהֵב

עַד 21 ever (29 · 48) 723 I

Psalm 146

זָמַר 2 to sing, make music (39 · 43 · 43) 274 I

בְּעוֹד so long as (3 · 20) 728

נָדִיב 3 noble, princely (8 · 27) 622

שֶׁאֵין whom there is no (1 · 1) 34 II אֵין שֶׁ 979

תְּשׁוּעָה deliverance (13 · 34) 448

עֶשְׁתֹּן 4 thought (1 · 1) 799

אֶשֶׁר 5 happiness, blessedness (19 · 45[?]) 80

עֵזֶר help (11 · 21) 740 I

שֵׂבֶר hope (2 · 2) 960

עָשַׁק 7 pass. ptc. = oppressed one (6 · 36 · 37) 798

רָעֵב hungry (4 · 19) 944

הִתִּיר to set free, unbind (2 · 5 · 7) 684 II נתר

עִוֵּר 8 blind (1 · 26) 734

זָקַף to raise up (2 · 2 · 2) 279

כָּפַף pass. ptc. = those bowed down (3 · 4 · 5) 496

יָתוֹם 9 orphan (8 · 42) 450

עוֹדֵד to restore, relieve (2 · 2 · 44) 728

עִוֵּת to make crooked, pervert (2 · 9 · 11) 736

Psalm 147

זָמַר 1 to sing, make music (39 · 43 · 43) 274 I

נָעִים delightful, beautiful (6 · 7) 653 I

נָאוֶה comely, seemly (2 · 9) 610

בֹּנֶה 2 ptc. = builder (2 · 8) 124 בָּנָה Qal 1.e

נִדָּח outcasts, banished ones (1 · 11) 623 נדח Niph. 2

כִּנֵּס to gather together (1 · 3 · 11) 488

מְחַבֵּשׁ 3 Piel ptc. = to bind up (1 · 2 · 32) 289 חבשׁ

עַצֶּבֶת hurt, injury, pain (2 · 5) 781

כּוֹכָב star (4 · 37) 456

מָנָה 4 to count, number (2 · 12 · 28) 584

כּוֹכָב star (4 · 37) 456

תְּבוּנָה 5 understanding (4 · 42) 108

עוֹדֵד 6 to restore, relieve (2 · 2 · 44) 728

עָנָו poor, afflicted, meek (13 · 22) 776

הִשְׁפִּיל	to lay low, humiliate (4 · 19 · 30) 1050	
עֲדֵי	poetic for עַד up to, until (6 · 12) 723 III עַד	
תּוֹדָה	7 thanksgiving, praise (12 · 32) 392	
זמר	to sing, make music (39 · 43 · 43) 274 I	
כִּנּוֹר	lyre (13 · 41) 490	
עָב	8 dark cloud, cloud mass (5 · 30) 728 II	
מָטָר	rain (3 · 38) 564	
הצמיח	to cause to grow (3 · 14 · 33) 855	
חָצִיר	grass (6 · 18) 348 II	
עֹרֵב	9 raven (1 · 12) 788	
שׁוֹק	10 leg (1 · 19) 1003	
יָרֵא	11 afraid (27 · 46) 431	
יחל	to wait for, hope for (14 · 25 · 42) 403, 1124	
שׁבח	12 to laud, praise (4 · 6 · 8) 986 II	
בְּרִיחַ	13 bar (2 · 41) 138	
חִטָּה	14 wheat (2 · 30) 334	
אִמְרָה	15 word, saying (26 · 36) 57	
מְהֵרָה	hastily, quickly (3 · 20) 555	
שֶׁלֶג	16 snow (3 · 20) 1017	
צֶמֶר	wool (1 · 16) 856	
כְּפוֹר	hoar frost (1 · 3) 499 II	
אֵפֶר	ashes (2 · 22) 68	
פזר	to scatter (4 · 7 · 10) 808	
קֶרַח	17 ice (1 · 7) 901	
פַּת	fragment, bit, morsel (1 · 14) 837	
קָרָה	cold (1 · 5) 903	
המסה	18 to cause to dissolve, melt (3 · 4 · 4) 587	
הִשִּׁיב	to cause to blow (1 · 2 · 3) 674 נשׁב	
נזל	to flow (1 · 8 · 9[?]) 633	

Psalm 148

יָרֵחַ	3 moon (8 · 27) 437	

כּוֹכָב	star (4 · 37) 456	
נברא	5 to be created (3 · 10 · 48) 135 I	
עַד	6 לְעַד = forever (29 · 48) 723 I	
תַּנִּין	7 sea monster; serpent, dragon (3 · 15) 1072	
תְּהוֹם	deep, sea, abyss (12 · 36) 1062	
בָּרָד	8 hail (6 · 29) 135	
שֶׁלֶג	snow (3 · 20) 1017	
קִיטוֹר	thick smoke (2 · 4) 882	
סְעָרָה	tempest, storm wind (3 · 16) 704	
רֶמֶשׂ	10 creeping things (2 · 16) 943	
צִפּוֹר	[coll.] birds (7 · 40) 861 I	
לְאֹם	11 people (14 · 35) 522	
בָּחוּר	12 young man (3 · 45) 104	
בְּתוּלָה	virgin (3 · 50) 143	
נשׂגב	13 to be exalted; be high (2 · 10 · 20) 960	
הוֹד	splendor, majesty (8 · 24) 217 I	
חָסִיד	14 pious, godly (25 · 32) 339	

Psalm 149

חָסִיד	1 pious, godly (25 · 32) 339	
עֹשֶׂה	2 maker, creator (10 · 24[?]) 793 I עשה	
גיל	to rejoice (19 · 45 · 45) 162	
מָחוֹל	3 dance (3 · 6) 298 I	
תֹּף	timbrel, tambourine (3 · 17) 1074	
כִּנּוֹר	lyre (13 · 41) 490	
זמר	to sing, make music (39 · 43 · 43) 274 I	
פאר	4 to beautify, glorify (1 · 6 · 13) 802 I	
עָנָו	poor, afflicted, meek (13 · 22) 776	
עלז	5 to exult, triumph (7 · 16 · 16) 759	
חָסִיד	pious, godly (25 · 32) 339	
מִשְׁכָּב	couch, bed (4 · 46) 1012	
רוֹמֵם	6 praise, extolling (1 · 1) 928	
גָּרוֹן	throat (4 · 8) 173	
פִּיפִיּוֹת	edges (1 · 2) 804 פֶּה 3	

נְקָמָה 7 vengeance (5 · 27) 668

תּוֹכֵחָה rebuke, correction (1 · 4) 407

לְאֹם people (14 · 35) 522

זִקִּים 8 fetters (1 · 4) 279 II זֵק

כֶּבֶל fetter (2 · 2) 459

הָדָר 9 honor, glory (13 · 30) 214

חָסִיד pious, godly (25 · 32) 339

Psalm 150

רָקִיעַ 1 firmament (2 · 17) 956, 1126: 956a

גֹּדֶל 2 magnificence (2 · 13) 152

תֵּקַע 3 blast (1 · 1) 1075

נֵבֶל harp (8 · 27) 614 II

כִּנּוֹר lyre (13 · 41) 490

תֹּף 4 timbrel, tambourine (3 · 17) 1074

מָחוֹל dance (3 · 6) 298 II

מֵן string (2 · 2) 577 I

עוּגָב pipe or flute (1 · 4) 721

צֶלְצְלִים 5 cymbals (2 · 3) 852

שֵׁמַע sound (1 · 1) 1034 I

תְּרוּעָה blast (5 · 36) 929

נְשָׁמָה 6 breath (2 · 24) 675

JOB

Chapter 1

תָּם 1 complete, morally innocent, having integrity (7 · 15) 1070 תמם

יָרֵא ptc. = fearing, reverencing (3 · 45) 431

צֶמֶד 3 couple, pair (2 · 15) 855

אָתוֹן female ass (3 · 33) 87

עֲבֻדָּה service (1 · 2) 715

מִשְׁתֶּה 4 feast, banquet, occasion for drinking (2 · 46) 1059

הִקִּיף 5 to complete the circuit; to surround, enclose (2 · 16 · 17) 668

מִשְׁתֶּה feast, banquet, occasion for drinking (2 · 46) 1059

אוּלַי peradventure, perhaps (1 · 45) 19 II

בֵּרַךְ idiom: to curse, to overdo a blessing (4 · 7) 138 5

כָּכָה thus (1 · 35) 462

הִתְיַצֵּב 6 w. לִפְנֵי to present oneself before; to station oneself (6 · 48 · 48) 426

שָׂטָן Satan, adversary (14 · 26) 966

שָׂטָן 7 Satan, adversary (14 · 26) 966

מֵאַיִן whence? (3[?] · 19) 32 אַיִן I

שׁוּט to go or rove about (2 · 7 · 13) 1001 I

שָׂטָן Satan, adversary (14 · 26) 966

תָּם complete, morally innocent, having integrity (7 · 15) 1070

יָרֵא ptc. = fearing, reverencing (3 · 45) 431

שָׂטָן 9 Satan, adversary (14 · 26) 966

חִנָּם gratis, for nothing (4 · 32) 336

שׂוּךְ 10 to hedge or fence up, about (1 · 2 · 2) 962

מִסָּבִיב from round about, from every side (1 · 42) 687 סָבִיב d

פָּרַץ to break over [limits], increase; break through (3 · 46 · 49) 829

אוּלָם 11 but, but indeed (10 · 19) 19 III

בֵּרַךְ idiom: to curse, to overdo a blessing (4 · 7) 158 5

שָׂטָן 12 Satan, adversary (14 · 26) 966

חרשׁ 14 to plough; to engrave, cut in (2 · 23 · 26) 360

אָתוֹן female ass (3 · 33) 87

פָּשַׁט 17 to put off, w. עַל against [of a marauding foray]; to strip off (1 · 24 · 43) 832

מֵעֵבֶר 19 from the other side of (1 · 30) 719 עֵבֶר I

פִּנָּה corner (2 · 30) 819

מְעִיל 20 robe (3 · 28) 591

גזז to shear (1 · 14 · 15) 159

עָרוֹם 21 naked (6 · 16) 736

תִּפְלָה 22 unsavoriness, unseemliness (2 · 3) 1074

Chapter 2

הִתְיַצֵּב 1 w. לִפְנֵי to present oneself before; to station oneself (6 · 48 · 48) 426

שָׂטָן Satan, adversary (14 · 26) 966

שָׂטָן 2 Satan, adversary (14 · 26) 966

אֵי מִזֶּה whence? (1 · 9) 32 אֵי 2.b

שׁוּט to go or rove about (2 · 7 · 13) 1001

שָׂטָן 3 Satan, adversary (14 · 26) 966

תָּם complete, morally innocent, having integrity (7 · 15) 1070

יָרֵא ptc. = fearing, reverencing (3 · 45) 431

תֻּמָּה integrity (4 · 5) 1070

הֵסִית to instigate + בְּ against, to incite, allure (3 · 18 · 18) 694 סות

בִּלַּע to swallow up, engulf (3 · 20 · 41) 118

חִנָּם without cause, undeservedly; gratis (4 · 32) 336

שָׂטָן 4 Satan, adversary (14 · 26) 966

אוּלָם 5 but, but indeed (10 · 19) 19 III

בֵּרַךְ idiom: to curse, to overdo a
blessing (4 · 7) 138 5

שָׂטָן 6 Satan, adversary (14 · 26) 966

שָׂטָן 7 Satan, adversary (14 · 26) 966

שְׁחִין boil, [coll.] eruption (1 · 13) 1006

קָדְקֹד head, crown of head (1 · 11) 869

חֶרֶשׂ 8 fragment of earthenware, sherd;
earthenware (2 · 17) 360

הִתְגָּרֵד to scrape oneself (1 · 1 · 1) 173

אֵפֶר ashes (4 · 22) 68

תֻּמָּה 9 integrity (4 · 5) 1070

בֵּרַךְ idiom: to curse, to overdo a
blessing (4 · 7) 138 5

נָבָל 10 fool, senseless one (2 · 18) 614 I

קִבֵּל to accept, receive; take (2 · 11 · 13)
867

נוֹעַד 11 to meet by appointment; meet at
appointed place (1 · 18 · 28) 416 יעד

נָד to show grief or lament by shaking
the head; to move to and fro
(2 · 20 · 27) 626 נוד

מֵרָחוֹק 12 from a distance (5 · 34) 935 רָחוֹק 2.a

הִכִּיר to recognize; regard, pay attention
(6 · 38 · 41) 647 נכר

מְעִיל robe (3 · 28) 591

זָרַק to toss, throw, scatter abundantly;
be profuse (1 · 32 · 34) 284

כְּאֵב 13 pain (2 · 6) 456

Chapter 3

אַחֲרֵי־כֵן 1 afterwards (1 · 46) 29 אַחַר pl.2.b

הֹרָה 3 *Pual*, to be conceived (1 · 1 · 40)
247

מִמַּעַל 4 above (4 · 29) 751 II מַעַל 1.c

הוֹפִיעַ to shine out, forth; display beams
(4 · 8 · 8) 422 יפע

נְהָרָה light, daylight (1 · 1) 626

גָּאַל 5 [unus. mng.] claim as a kinsman;

act as kinsman, redeem (1 · 46 · 54)
145

צַלְמָוֶת deep shadow, darkness; death shadow (10 · 18) 853

עֲנָנָה cloud (1 · 1) 778

בעת *Piel*, to overwhelm, fall upon; terrify (8 · 13 · 16) 129

מְרִירִים bitter; or, darkness, gloominess
(1 · 1[?]) 601, 485

אֹפֶל 6 darkness, gloom (6 · 9) 66

חדה to rejoice (1 · 2 · 3) 292 II

יֶרַח a calendar month, month (4 · 12)
437 I

גַּלְמוּד 7 barren, hard (3 · 4) 166

רְנָנָה ringing cry of joy (2 · 4) 943

קבב 8 to curse (2 · 14 · 14) 866

עָתִיד ready = skilled (2 · 5) 800

לִוְיָתָן dragon, serpent, leviathan (2 · 6) 531

חָשַׁךְ 9 to be dark, grow dark (2 · 11 · 17)
364

כּוֹכָב star (5 · 37) 456

נֶשֶׁף twilight, evening twilight (3 · 12)
676

קוה *Piel*, to wait or look eagerly for; to
lie in wait for (5 · 39 · 45) 875

עַפְעַף eyelid (3 · 10) 733

שַׁחַר dawn (3 · 23) 1007

רֶחֶם 11 womb (5 · 33) 933

גָּוַע to expire, perish, die (8 · 23 · 23) 157

קדם 12 to meet, receive; meet, confront;
go before (2 · 24 · 26) 869

בֶּרֶךְ knee (2 · 25) 139

שַׁד female breast (1 · 21) 994

ינק to suck (2 · 8 · 18) 413

שָׁקַט 13 to be quiet, undisturbed (2 · 31 · 41)
1052

ישׁן to sleep, go to sleep, be asleep
(1 · 15 · 16) 445

יוֹעֵץ 14 ptc. = counselor, king's adviser
(2 · 22) 419 יעץ

חָרְבָּה ruin, waste (1 · 42) 352

נֵפֶל 16 miscarriage, abortion (1 · 3) 658

טָמַן to hide, conceal; *Qal* pass. ptc. = hidden (6 · 28 · 31) 380

עוֹלֵל child (1 · 11) 760

רֹגֶז 17 raging; disquiet, turmoil; excitement (5 · 7) 919

יְגִיעַ weary (1 · 1) 388

יַחַד 18 all together, together (13 · 45) 403

אָסִיר prisoner (1 · 17) 64

שַׁאֲנַן *Pa'l*, to be at ease, secure (1 · 5 · 5) 983

נֹגֵשׂ ptc. = driver, taskmaster (2 · 15) 620

חָפְשִׁי 19 free (2 · 17) 344

עָמֵל 20 sufferer (2 · 9) 766 I

מַר bitter, bitterness (4 · 38) 600 I

חָכָה 21 to wait for, await; wait (2 · 13 · 14) 314

חָפַר to dig; search for (4 · 23 · 23) 343

מַטְמוֹן hidden treasure, treasure (1 · 5) 380

שָׂמֵחַ 22 joyful one, glad, joyful (1 · 21) 970

אֱלֵי poetic for אֶל 39

גִּיל rejoicing, שָׂמֵחַ אֱלֵי גִּיל glad unto rejoicing (1 · 8) 162 I

שׂוּשׂ to exult, display joy (2 · 27 · 27) 965 שׂוּשׂ, שִׂישׂ

סוּךְ 23 to shut in, hedge or fence about (2 · 2 · 4[?]) 692

אֲנָחָה 24 sighing, groaning (2 · 11) 58

נתךְ to pour forth (1 · 7 · 21) 677

שְׁאָגָה roaring (2 · 7) 980

פַּחַד 25 object of dread; dread (10 · 49) 808 I

פָּחַד to be in dread; be in awe (2 · 22 · 25) 808

אָתָה to come (4 · 19 · 21) 87

יגר to fear, be afraid (2 · 5 · 5) 388

שָׁלוּ,שׁלה 26 to be quiet; be at ease, prosper (2 · 5 · 7) 107

שָׁקַט to be quiet, undisturbed (2 · 31 · 41) 1052

רֹגֶז disquiet, turmoil; raging; excitement (5 · 7) 919

Chapter 4

נָסָה 2 to try, test, here w. מִלָּה = venture a word (1 · 36 · 36) 650

לאה to be weary, impatient (2 · 3 · 19) 521

עָצַר to rule over, restrain; retain (3 · 36 · 46) 783

מִלָּה word, speech, utterance (34 · 38) 576

יָסַר 3 to discipline, correct; chastize (1 · 27 · 38) 415

רָפֶה slack, weak (1 · 4) 952

מִלָּה 4 word, speech, utterance (34 · 38) 576

בֶּרֶךְ knee (2 · 25) 139

כָּרַע to bow down; ptc. w. בֶּרֶךְ = feeble knees (3 · 30 · 36) 502

אָמֵץ to make firm, strengthen (2 · 19 · 41) 54

לאה 5 to be weary, impatient (2 · 3 · 19) 521

נִבְהַל to be disturbed, dismayed, terrified; be in haste (3 · 24 · 39) 96

יִרְאָה 6 fear of God, reverence, piety; fear, terror (5 · 45) 432

כִּסְלָה confidence; source of confidence (1 · 2) 493

תִּקְוָה ground of hope; hope; things hoped for (13 · 32) 876 II

תֹּם integrity; completeness; innocence (2 · 23) 1070

נָקִי 7 free from guilt, clean, innocent (6 · 43) 667

אֵיפֹה where? (7 · 25) 33 אֵי + פֹּה

נִכְחַד to be effaced, destroyed (3 · 11 · 32) 470

481

חָרַשׁ 8 to plough; cut in, engrave
(2 · 23 · 26) 360

קָצַר to reap, harvest (2 · 24 · 24) 894 II

נְשָׁמָה 9 breath (7 · 24) 675

שְׁאָגָה 10 roaring (2 · 7) 980

אַרְיֵה lion (1 · 45) 71

שַׁחַל lion (3 · 7) 1006

כְּפִיר young lion (2 · 31) 498

נתע *Niph.* to be broken down or out
(1 · 1 · 1) 683

לַיִשׁ 11 lion (1 · 3) 539 I

מִבְּלִי without, from want of (7 · 25) 115
בְּלִי [para. w. preps. c.]

טֶרֶף prey, food (3[?] · 17[?]) 383

לָבִיא lion, lioness (2 · 11) 522

התפרד to be divided, separated from each
other (2 · 4 · 26) 825

גֻּנַּב 12 to be brought by stealth; be stolen
away (1 · 4 · 39) 170

שֵׁמֶץ whisper (2 · 2) 1036

שְׂעִפִּים 13 disquietings, excited thoughts
(2 · 2) 972

חֶזְיוֹן vision (4 · 9) 303

תַּרְדֵּמָה deep sleep (2 · 7) 922

פַּחַד 14 dread; object of dread (10 · 49) 808 I

רְעָדָה trembling (1 · 4) 944

הִפְחִיד to fill with dread (1 · 1 · 25) 808

חָלַף 15 to pass on quickly, to move or
sweep on (4 · 14 · 26[?]) 322

סמר to bristle up (1 · 1 · 2) 702

שַׂעֲרָה hair (1 · 7) 972

הִכִּיר 16 to distinguish, understand; regard,
recognize (6 · 38 · 41) 647

תְּמוּנָה likeness, form (1 · 10) 568

לְנֶגֶד in front of, before (1 · 32) 617 נֶגֶד 2.b

דְּמָמָה whisper (1 · 3) 199

אֱנוֹשׁ 17 man, mankind; a man; men
(18 · 42) 60

צדק to be justified; have a just cause
(14 · 22 · 41) 842

עֹשֶׂה ptc. – Maker, maker (2 · 24) 794
עשׂה para. II.1

תָּהֳלָה 18 error (1 · 1) 1062 [or rd. תִּפְלָה unsavoriness, unseemliness 1074] תהל

חֹמֶר 19 clay; mortar, cement (7 · 17) 330

יְסוֹד foundation; base (2 · 19) 414

דִּכָּא to crush (3 · 11 · 18) 193

עָשׁ moth (3 · 7) 799

הוּכַת 20 *Hoph.*, to be crushed (1 · 4 · 17) 510
כתת

מִבְּלִי without, from want of מִבְּלִי מְשִׂים =
without heeding (7 · 25) 115 בְּלִי
[para. w. preps. c.]

מֵשִׂים *Hiph.* ptc. masc. 964

נֶצַח everlastingness, לָנֶצַח forever (6 · 43)
664 I

יֶתֶר 21 cord, tent-cord (2 · 6) 452 II

Chapter 5

אֱוִיל 2 fool, foolish (2 · 26) 17

כַּעַשׂ vexation, anger (4 · 25) 495 כַּעַס

פתה to be open-minded, simple; be deceived (2 · 5 · 27) 834

קִנְאָה ardor of anger; zeal; jealousy
(1 · 43) 888

אֱוִיל 3 fool, foolish (2 · 26) 17

הִשְׁרִישׁ to take root (1 · 3 · 8) 1057

קבב to utter a curse against (2 · 14 · 14)
866 II

נָוֶה habitation; abode of a shepherd or
flocks (3 · 45) 627 I

פִּתְאֹם suddenly; suddeness (3 · 25) 837

יֵשַׁע 4 safety, welfare, prosperity; salvation (2 · 36) 447

הֻדְכָּא *Hiph.* to be crushed, to let oneself
be crushed (2 · 2 · 18) 193

קָצִיר 5 what is harvested, crop; harvesting;
harvest time (1 · 49) 894 I

רָעֵב hungry (4 · 19) 944

צֵן thorn, barb [dub.] (1 · 3[?]) 856

שָׁאַף to pant after, be eager; gasp
(3 · 14 · 14) 983 I

צַמִּים [dub.] usu. snare, trap (2 · 2) 855

צָמַח 6 to sprout, spring up (2 · 15 · 33) 855

רֶשֶׁף 7 flame, firebolt, בְּנֵי ר = sparks
(1 · 7) 958 I

הִגְבִּיהַ to make high; exalt (2 · 10 · 34) 146
גבה

עוּף to fly (2 · 18 · 25) 733 עוּף

אוּלָם 8 but, but indeed (10 · 19) 19 III

דִּבְרָה cause, suit; reason, manner (1 · 5)
דבר 184

חֵקֶר 9 thing to be searched out, searching;
אֵין ח׳ = it is unsearchable (7 · 12)
350

נִפְלָאוֹת Hiph., ptc. = wonderful acts
(5 · 44) 810 פלא 4

מָטָר 10 rain (7 · 38) 564

שָׁפָל 11 low (1 · 18) 1050

קָדַר to be dark (3 · 13 · 17) 871

שָׂגַב to be high (1 · 2 · 20) 960

יֵשַׁע safety, welfare, prosperity; salvation (2 · 36) 447

הֵפֵר 12 Hiph., to frustrate, make ineffectual (3 · 42 · 45) 830 פרר I

עָרוּם crafty, shrewd, sensible (2 · 11) 791

תּוּשִׁיָּה sound, efficient wisdom (6 · 12)
444

עֹדֶם 13 craftiness (1 · 4 · 5[?]) 791

נפתל to be twisted, tortuous; עֲצַת-נ׳ the
plan of the tortuous (1 · 3 · 5) 836

פָּגַשׁ 14 Piel, to keep encountering
(1 · 1 · 14) 803

מִשֵּׁשׁ Piel, to grope, feel over or through
(2 · 6 · 8) 606

צָהֳרַיִם noon (2 · 23) 843 I צהר

דַּל 16 poor, reduced (6 · 48) 195

תִּקְוָה hope, ground of hope; things hoped
for (13 · 32) 876 II

עַוְלָה injustice, unrighteousness, wrong
(10 · 32) 732

קָפַץ to shut, draw together (1 · 5 · 7) 891

אֶשֶׁר 17 blessedness, happiness (1 · 45) 80

אֱנוֹשׁ individual man; mankind, men
(18 · 42) 60

מוּסָר chastening, chastisement; discipline, correction (4 · 50) 416

שַׁדַּי name of God perh. (1) sufficient
one, (2) almighty one, or (3) my
sovereign (31 · 48) 994

הִכְאִיב 18 to pain, mar (1 · 4 · 8) 456

חבשׁ to bind up [a wound]; to bind
(3 · 28 · 32) 289

מָחַץ to smite through, scatter
(2 · 14 · 14) 563

שׁוֹט 21 scourge, whip (1 · 6[?]) 1002

נֶחְבָּא to be hidden; hide oneself
(3 · 16 · 34) 285

שֹׁד devastation, ruin (2 · 25) 994

שֹׁד 22 devastation, ruin (2 · 25) 994

כָּפָן hunger, famine (2 · 2) 495

שָׂחַק to laugh; sport (7 · 19 · 36) 965

נָוֶה 24 habitation; abode of shepherd or
flocks (3 · 45) 627

חָטָא to miss something [unus. use]; to
sin 306

צֶאֱצָא 25 offspring; produce (4 · 11) 425

עֵשֶׂב herb, herbage (1 · 33) 793

כֶּלַח 26 firm or rugged strength (2 · 2) 480 I

אֱלֵי poetic for אֶל 39

גָּדִישׁ heap, stack [i.e., of grain] (2 · 4[?])
155

חָקַר 27 to search through, explore; search
(6 · 22 · 27) 350

Chapter 6

לוּ 2 if only...! O that! if (2 · 19) 530

שָׁקַל to weigh (2 · 19 · 22) 1053

נִשְׁקַל   to be weighed $(2 \cdot 3 \cdot 22)$ 1053

כַּעַשׂ   vexation, grief $(4 \cdot 25)$ 495 כַּעַס

הַוָּה   destruction; engulfing ruin; desire $(3 \cdot 13[?])$ 217

מֹאזְנָיִם   balances $(2 \cdot 15)$ 24

יַחַד   together $(13 \cdot 45)$ 403

חוֹל   3 sand $(1 \cdot 22[?])$ 297

לוּע   to talk wildly $(1 \cdot 2 \cdot 2)$ 534

שַׁדַּי   4 name of God $(31 \cdot 48)$ 994 see 5:17

עִמָּדִי   = עִם + 1st sing. suff. [same as עִמִּי] 767

בִּעוּתִים   terrors, alarms $(1 \cdot 2)$ 130

נָהַק   5 to bray, cry $(2 \cdot 2 \cdot 2)$ 625

פֶּרֶא   wild ass $(4 \cdot 10)$ 825

דֶּשֶׁא   grass $(2 \cdot 14)$ 206

גָּעָה   to low $(1 \cdot 2 \cdot 2)$ 171

בְּלִיל   fodder $(2 \cdot 3)$ 117

תָּפֵל   6 tasteless, unseasoned $(1 \cdot 1[?])$ 1074

מִבְּלִי   without; from want of $(7 \cdot 25)$ 115 בְּלִי (para. w. preps c)

מֶלַח   salt $(1 \cdot 28)$ 571

טַעַם   taste $(2 \cdot 13)$ 381

רִיר   slimy juice $(1 \cdot 2)$ 938

חַלָּמוּת   name of a plant w. thick slimy juice, purslain $(1 \cdot 1)$ 321

מֵאֵן   7 to refuse $(1 \cdot 46 \cdot 46)$ 549

דְּוַי   illness $(1 \cdot 2)$ 188

מִי־יִתֵּן   8 idiom: who will give or grant = O that! $(9 \cdot 24)$ 678 נתן

שְׁאֵלָה   thing asked for; request $(1 \cdot 13)$ 982

תִּקְוָה   things hoped for; ground of hope, hope $(13 \cdot 32)$ 876

הוֹאִיל   9 to be pleased; to be willing, show willingness, acquiesce $(2 \cdot 18 \cdot 18)$ 383

דָּכָא   to crush $(3 \cdot 11 \cdot 18)$ 193

הִתִּיר   to set free, unbind $(1 \cdot 5 \cdot 7)$ 684

בִּצַּע   to cut off, dissever $(1 \cdot 6 \cdot 16)$ 130

נֶחָמָה   10 comfort $(1 \cdot 2)$ 637

סָלַד   [dub.] to spring $(1 \cdot 1 \cdot 1)$ 698

חִילָה   anguish $(1 \cdot 1)$ 297

חָמַל   to spare, have compassion $(4 \cdot 40 \cdot 40)$ 328

כִּחֵד   to conceal from, disown $(3 \cdot 15 \cdot 32)$ 470

אֵמֶר   utterance, word $(11 \cdot 48)$ 56

יִחֵל   11 *Piel*, to wait; tarry for $(6 \cdot 25 \cdot 42)$ 403

הֶאֱרִיךְ   to prolong, postpone $(1 \cdot 31 \cdot 34)$ 73

נָחוּשׁ   12 of bronze $(1 \cdot 1)$ 639

עֶזְרָה   13 help, succour, assistance $(2 \cdot 26)$ 740 עזר I

תּוּשִׁיָּה   abiding success; sound, efficient wisdom $(6 \cdot 12)$ 444

נדח   *Hiph.*, to be thrust out, banished, here = nonexistent $(1 \cdot 13 \cdot 43)$ 623

מָס   14 despairing $(1 \cdot 1)$ 588

יִרְאָה   fear of God, reverence, piety; fear, terror $(5 \cdot 45)$ 432

שַׁדַּי   name for God $(31 \cdot 48)$ 994 see 5:17

בָּגַד   15 to act or deal faithlessly, deceitfully; to act treacherously $(1 \cdot 49 \cdot 49)$ 93

אָפִיק   channel = streambed $(3 \cdot 18[?])$ 67

קָדַר   16 to be dark $(3 \cdot 13 \cdot 17)$ 871

קֶרַח   frost, ice $(3 \cdot 7)$ 901

עָלֵימוֹ   poetic for 3rd m. pl. עֲלֵיהֶם $(8 \cdot 12)$ 752

הִתְעַלֵּם   to hide oneself $(1 \cdot 6 \cdot 29)$ 761 I

שֶׁלֶג   snow $(5 \cdot 20)$ 1017

זֹרַב   17 to be burnt, scorched [dub.] $(1 \cdot 1 \cdot 1)$ 279

נִצְמַת   to be ended, annihilated $(1 \cdot 2 \cdot 15)$ 856

חַם   to be or grow warm $(1 \cdot 23 \cdot 26)$ 328 חמם

נִדְעַךְ   to be made extinct, dried up $(1 \cdot 1 \cdot 9)$ 200

נִלְפַּת   18 to turn aside, twist, twist oneself $(1 \cdot 2 \cdot 3)$ 542

תֹּהוּ   nothingness, empty space, waste; formlessness (3 · 20) 1062

אֹרְחָה 19   traveler, pl. = caravan (1 · 3[?]) 73   ארח 4

הֲלִיכָה   traveling company, caravan; going, walk (1 · 6) 237 הלך

קוה   to wait, or look eagerly for (5 · 39 · 45) 875 I

חפר 20   to be put to shame; be ashamed, abashed (1 · 13 · 17) 344 II

חֲתַת 21   terror (1 · 1) 369 I

יהב 22   to give (1 · 33 · 33) 396

שחד   to give a bribe or present (1 · 2 · 2) 1005

עָרִיץ 23   awe-inspiring, terror-striking (3 · 20) 792

הורה 24   to point out, show; direct, teach; throw or shoot (6 · 45 · 45) 434 ירה

הֶחֱרִישׁ   to be silent (9 · 38 · 46) 361 II

שגה   to go astray, err (2 · 17 · 21) 993

נמרץ 25   to be sore, grievous, but here [dub.] perh. be strong 599 [or נמלץ, be sweet (1 · 3 · 4) 576]

אֵמֶר   utterance, word (11 · 48) 56

יֹשֶׁר   rightness, uprightness; straightness (3 · 14) 449

מִלָּה 26   word, speech, utterance; byword (34 · 38) 576

אֵמֶר   utterance, word (11 · 48) 56

נוֹאָשׁ   to despair, ptc. = despairing, desperate (1 · 5 · 6) 384 יאש

יָתוֹם 27   orphan (7 · 42) 450

כרה   to trade in, make trade of; get by trade (2 · 4 · 4) 500 II

הוֹאִיל 28   to show willingness, be willing, acquiesce; be pleased (2 · 18 · 18) 383 II

כֶּזֶב   to lie, tell a lie (2 · 12 · 16) 469

עַוְלָה 29   injustice, wrong, violent deeds of injustice (10 · 32) 732

עַוְלָה 30   injustice, wrong, violent deeds of injustice (10 · 32) 732

חֵךְ   palate, roof of mouth (7 · 18) 335

הַוָּה   destruction; engulfing ruin; desire (3 · 13 [?]) 217

Chapter 7

צָבָא 1   service, hard service [rare meaning] 839 3.b

אֱנוֹשׁ   man, mankind (18 · 42) 60

עֲלֵי   poetic for עַל 752

שָׂכִיר   hired, hired laborer (3 · 18) 969

שָׁאַף 2   to gasp or pant, be eager for (3 · 14 · 14) 983 I

שָׂכִיר   hired, hired laborer (3 · 18) 969

קוה   *Piel*, to wait, look eagerly for; lie in wait for (5 · 39 · 45) 875 I

פֹּעַל   wages of work; work; thing done (5 · 37) 821

יֶרַח 3   month; calendar month (4 · 12) 437 I

מִנָּה   to appoint, ordain (1 · 9 · 28) 584

מָתַי 4   when? (1 · 42[?]) 607

נְדֻדִים   tossings (1 · 1) 622

עֲדֵי   poetic for עַד (2 · 12) 723

נֶשֶׁף   morning twilight (3 · 12) 676

רִמָּה 5   worm (5 · 7) 942

גּוּשׁ   clod, lump (1 · 1) 159

רָגַע   to harden [Lis. to come to rest] (2 · 4 · 13[?]) 921

נמאס   to flow, run (1 · 1 · 2[?]) 549

מִנִּי 6   poetic for מִן (19 · 30) 577

אָרֶג   loom (1 · 2) 71

בְּאֶפֶס   without (1 · 4[?]) 67 אֶפֶס 2.b

תִּקְוָה   hope; ground of hope; things hoped for (13 · 32) 876

שׁוּר 8   to behold; regard; watch (10 · 16 · 16) 1003

הִכִּיר 10 to be acquainted with; recognize; distinguish (6 · 38 · 41) 647

חָשַׂךְ 11 to hold in check; withhold, keep back; restrain (5 · 26 · 28) 362

צַר distress, straits (6 · 20) 865

שִׂיחַ to complain; muse (2 · 18 · 20) 967

מַר bitterness, bitter (4 · 38) 600

תַּנִּין 12 sea [or river] monster (1 · 15) 1072

מִשְׁמָר guard, watch; prison (1 · 22) 1038

עֶרֶשׂ 13 couch, divan (1 · 11) 793

שִׂיחַ complaint; musing, anxiety (5 · 14) 967

מִשְׁכָּב place of lying, couch; act of lying (3 · 46) 1012

חֶזְיוֹן 14 vision (4 · 9) 303

בעת Piel, to terrify; fall upon, overwhelm (8 · 13 · 16) 129

מַחֲנַק 15 strangling, suffocation (1 · 1) 338

עֶצֶם bone; here = substance, self 782 I.3 [but BDB prefers reading עָצְבָה, hurt, injury, pain 781 cf. also Lis. p 1108, עַצְמָה pain, evil deed) (1 · 3)] עצם I 782 עצב 781

אֱנוֹשׁ 17 man, mankind (18 · 42) 60

רֶגַע 18 moment; in a moment (4 · 22) 921

בחן to examine, scrutinize; try (4 · 5 · 29) 103

כַּמָּה 19 for how long? how much? how many? (3 · 13) 553 מָה 4.c

שָׁעָה to gaze at, regard (2 · 12 · 15) 1043

הרפה to refrain, let (one) alone; let go, drop (2 · 21 · 44) 951

בָּלַע to swallow, swallow up (3 · 20 · 41 [?]) 118

רֹק spittle (2 · 3) 956

מִפְגָּע 20 thing hit, mark (1 · 1) 803

מַשָּׂא load, burden (1 · 45) 672

שׁחר 21 Piel, to seek, seek eagerly (3 · 21 · 13) 1007

Chapter 8

עַד־אָן 2 to what point in time? how long? (1 · 1) 33 אָן

מלל to speak, utter, say (2 · 4 · 5) 576

כַּבִּיר mighty, great (7 · 10) 460

אֹמֶר utterance, word, speech (11 · 48) 56

עות 3 Piel, make crooked, falsify, pervert; bend (4 · 9 · 11) 736

שַׁדַּי name of God (31 · 48) 994 see 5:17

שׁחר 5 Piel, to seek, seek eagerly (3 · 12 · 13) 1007

שַׁדַּי name of God (31 · 48) 994 see 5:17

זַךְ 6 pure, clean, righteous (4 · 11) 269

נָוֶה habitation, abode (1 · 1[?]) 627

מִצְעָר 7 small thing (1 · 6) 859

שׂגה to grow, increase (2 · 3 · 4) 960

חֵקֶר 8 thing to be searched out; searching (7 · 12) 350

תְּמוֹל 9 yesterday, recently (1 · 23) 1069

הורה 10 Hiph., to direct, teach, instruct; point out; shoot, throw (6 · 45 · 45 [?]) 434 ירה

מִלָּה word, speech, utterance; byword (34 · 38) 576

גָּאָה 11 to grow up; rise up; be lifted up (2 · 7 · 7) 144

גֹּמֶא rush, paper-reed (1 · 4) 167

בְּלֹא without; of time = outside of, before (3 · 31) 520 לֹא 4.a

בִּצָּה swamp (2 · 3) 130

שׂגה to grow, increase (2 · 3 · 4) 960

אָחוּ [coll.] reeds, rushes (1 · 3) 28

בְּלִי adv. of negation, not; w. subst. = without (10 · 23) 115

אֵב 12 freshness, fresh green, green shoot (1 · 2) 1

נקטף to be plucked off (1 · 1 · 5) 882

חָצִיר green grass, herbage [Lis. p.520 reed] (1 · 3) 348 II

תִּקְוָה 13 things hoped for; hope; ground of hope (13 · 32) 876 II

חָנֵף godless man; godless, profane (8 · 13) 338

קוֹט, יָקוֹט 14 to break, snap [or, noun, fragile thing, see Lis. p.631] (1 · 1) 876 קוט

כֶּסֶל confidence; stupidity; loins (2 · 6 [?]) 492

עַכָּבִישׁ spider (1 · 2) 747

מִבְטָח object of confidence, confidence (3 · 15) 105

נִשְׁעַן 15 to lean, support oneself (2 · 22 · 22) 1043

רָטֹב 16 moist, juicy, fresh (1 · 1) 936

גַּנָּה garden (1 · 16) 171

יוֹנֶקֶת young shoot, twig (3 · 6) 413

גַּל 17 heap; wave, billow (2[?] · 20[?]) 164

שֹׁרֶשׁ root (9 · 33) 1057

סֻבָּךְ Pual, to be interwoven (1 · 1 · 2) 687

בָּלַע 18 to swallow up, engulf = destroy; confuse; swallow (3 · 20 · 41[?]) 118

כָּחַשׁ to act deceptively against (בְּ), deceive (2 · 19 · 22) 471

מָשׂוֹשׂ 19 exultation, rejoicing (1 · 17) 965

צָמַח to sprout, spring up (2 · 15 · 33) 855

תָּם 20 morally innocent, having integrity; complete (7 · 15) 1070

מֵרַע Hiph. ptc. = evildoer (1 · 18) 949

יְמַלֶּה 21 to fill; Piel impf. for מְלֵא 569

שְׂחוֹק laughter; derision (3 · 15) 966 שחק

תְּרוּעָה shout of joy; alarm of war; blast for march (3 · 36) 929

שֹׂנֵא 22 ptc. = enemy, foe (2 · 41) 971

בֹּשֶׁת shame; shameful thing (1 · 30) 102

Chapter 9

אָמְנָם 2 verily, truly (6 · 9) 53

צָדֵק to be justified; be just, righteous (14 · 22 · 41) 842

אֱנוֹשׁ man, mankind (18 · 42) 60

אַמִּיץ 4 mighty (2 · 6) 55

הִקְשָׁה to show stubbornness, make hard; make difficult; make severe (1 · 21 · 28) 904

הֶעְתִּיק 5 to remove; move forward, away; transcribe (1 · 5 · 9) 801

הִרְגִּיז 6 to shake, cause to quake; disquiet (2 · 7 · 41) 919

הִתְפַּלֵּץ to shudder (1 · 1 · 1) 814

חֶרֶס 7 sun (1 · 2) 357

זָרַח to rise, come forth (1 · 18 · 18) 280

כּוֹכָב star (5 · 37) 456

חָתַם to put a seal on, seal up (4 · 23 · 27) 367

עָשׁ 9 BDB rd. עַיִשׁ constellation. perh. Great Bear (2 · 2) 747

כְּסִיל Orion (2 · 4) 493

כִּימָה Pleiades (2 · 30) 465

חֶדֶר chamber, room (2 · 37) 293

תֵּימָן south, southern quarter; south wind (2 · 24) 412

חֵקֶר 10 searching, אֵין ח׳ = it is unsearchable (7 · 21) 350

נִפְלָאוֹת Niph. ptc. = wonderful acts (5 · 44) 810 פלא 4

חָלַף 11 to pass on quickly, move or sweep on; pass through (4 · 14 · 26) 322

חָתַף 12 to seize, snatch away (1 · 1 · 1) 368

שָׁחַח 13 to be bowed down, prostrated, humbled; to bow, crouch (2 · 12 · 18) 1005

עֹזֵר ptc. = helper, helping (3 · 19) 740

רַהַב storm, arrogance, name of mythical sea monster; symbolic name of Egypt (2 · 7) 923

אַף־כִּי 14 'tis indeed that, how much more..., indeed (4 · 26) 65

צָדֵק 15 to have a just cause; be justified, be just (14 · 22 · 41) 842

הַאֲזִין 16 to hear, give ear, listen (6·41·41) 24

שְׂעָרָה 17 storm (1·2) 973

שׁוּף to bruise (1·3·3) 1003

פֶּצַע bruise, wound (1·8) 822

חִנָּם without cause, for no purpose, gratis (4·32) 336

הֵשִׁיב רוּחַ 18 idiom: to draw in breath 999 שׁוב (*Hiph.* 1.c)

מַמְרוֹר bitter thing (1·1) 601

אַמִּיץ 19 mighty (2·6) 55

הוֹעִיד to summon, arraign; make to meet at an appointed place (1·3·28) 416

צדק 20 to have a just cause, be in the right; be justified; be just (14·22·41) 842

הִרְשִׁיעַ to condemn as guilty; act wickedly (8·25·34) 957

תָּם morally innocent, having integrity; complete (7·15) 1070

חעקיש to declare (one) crooked (1·1·5) 786

תָּם 21 morally innocent, having integrity; complete (7·15) 1070

תָּם 22 morally innocent, having integrity; complete (7·15) 1070

שׁוֹט 23 scourge, whip (1·3[?]) 1002

פִּתְאֹם suddenness, suddenly (3·25) 837

מַסָּה despair (1·1) 588

נָקִי free from guilt, clean innocent (6·43) 667

לעג to mock, deride, have in derision (3·12·18) 541

אֵפוֹא 24 then...? אִם-לֹא אֵפוֹא מִי-הוּא = if not, then who is it? (7·25) 66

מִנִּי 25 poetic for מִן (19·30) 577

רָץ ptc. = runner (1·25) 930 רוץ

חָלַף 26 to pass on quickly, move or sweep on; pass through (4·14·26) 322

אֳנִיָּה ship, א׳ אֵבֶה = swift ships (1·31) 58

אֵבֶה reed, papyrus (1·1) 3

נֶשֶׁר griffon vulture, eagle (2·26) 676

טוּשׂ to rush, dart (1·1·1) 377

אֹכֶל food (6·44) 38

שִׂיחַ 27 complaint; musing; anxiety (5·14) 967

הבליג to show a smile, look cheerful; cause to flash (2·4·4) 114

יגר 28 to be afraid (2·5·5) 388

עַצֶּבֶת hurt, pain injury (1·5) 781

נקה *Piel*, to hold innocent, acquit (2·16·41) 667

רשע 29 to be wicked, act wickedly (3·9·34) 957

יגע to toil, labor; grow weary (1·20·26) 388

שֶׁלֶג 30 snow (5·20) 1017

הזכיך to cleanse (1·1·4) 269

בֹּר lye, potash (2·7[?]) 141

שַׁחַת 31 pit (7·23) 1001

טָבַל to dip (1·15·16) 371

תעב *Piel*, to cause to be an abomination, regard as an abomination (3·15·22) 1073

שַׂלְמָה wrapper, mantle, outer garment (1·16) 971

אֵימָה 34 terror, dread (6·17) 33

בעת *Piel*, to fall upon, overwhelm; terrify (8·13·16) 129

אָנֹכִי עֹסְמָדִי idiom: I with myself 786 עם 4.b

Chapter 10

נקוט 1 *Niph.*, to feel a loathing (1·4·7) 876 קיט

שִׂיחַ complaint; musing, anxiety (5·14) 967

מַר bitterness, bitter (4·38) 600

הִרְשִׁיעַ 2 to condemn as guilty; act wickedly (8·25·34) 957

488

עָשַׁק 3 to deal tryannically, oppress,
wrong (2 · 36 · 37) 798

יְגִיעַ product, produce; toil (316) 388

הוֹפִיעַ to shine out, forth, display beams
(4 · 8 · 8) 422 יפע

אֱנוֹשׁ 4 man, mankind (18 · 42) 60

אֱנוֹשׁ 5 man, mankind (18 · 42) 60

רָשַׁע 7 to be wicked, act wickedly
(3 · 8 · 34) 957

עָצַב 8 to shape, fashion (1 · 1 · 2) 781 II

יַחַד together, altogether (13 · 45) 403

בָּלַע to swallow up, engulf; swallow,
confuse (3 · 20 · 41[?]) 118

חֹמֶר 9 clay; mortar, cement (7 · 17) 330

חָלָב 10 milk (2 · 44) 316

הִתִּיךְ to pour out (1 · 5 · 21) 677 נתך

גְּבִנָּה curd, cheese (1 · 1) 148 גבינה

הִקְפִּיא to curdle (1 · 1 · 3) 891

גִּיד 11 sinew (2 · 7) 161

סוֹכֵךְ *Poel*, to weave together (1 · 1 · 18)
697 II

פְּקֻדָּה 12 visitation; oversight; store (1 · 32)
824

צָפַן 13 to hide; treasure up; lie hid
(4 · 24 · 39) 860

נקה 14 *Piel*., to hold innocent, acquit
(2 · 16 · 41) 667

רָשַׁע 15 to be wicked, act wickedly
(3 · 9 · 34) 957

אַלְלַי alas! woe! (1 · 2) 47

צדק to be just, righteous; be justified;
have a just cause (14 · 22 · 41) 842

שָׂבֵעַ sated, satisfied (3 · 10) 960

קָלוֹן dishonor, disgrace (1 · 17) 885

רָאֶה seeing [dub.] (1 · 1) 909

עֳנִי affliction, poverty (6 · 36) 777

גָּאָה 16 to be lifted up, exalted (2 · 7 · 7)
144

שַׁחַל lion (3 · 7) 1006

צוּד to hunt (2 · 13 · 17) 844 I

הִתְפַּלָּא to show oneself marvelous
(1 · 1 · 24[?]) 810

חִדֵּשׁ 17 to renew, make anew (1 · 9 · 10) 293

כַּעַשׂ anger, vexation (4 · 25) 495 כַּעַס

חֲלִיפָה to relay, change; varying (2 · 12) 322

רֶחֶם 18 womb (5 · 33) 933

גָּוַע to expire, perish, die (8 · 23 · 23)
157

הוּבַל 19 to be borne, borne along
(1 · 11 · 18) 384 יבל

הִבְלִיג 20 to show a smile, look cheerful;
cause to flash (2 · 4 · 4) 114

בְּטֶרֶם 21 before that, ere, not yet (1 · 39) 382

צַלְמָוֶת death-shadow, deep shadow
(10 · 18) 853

עֵיפָה 22 darkness (1 · 2) 734

אֹפֶל darkness, gloom (6 · 9) 66

צַלְמָוֶת death-shadow, deep shadow
(10 · 18) 853

סֵדֶר arrangement, order לֹא ס׳ = disor-
der (1 · 1) 690

הוֹפִיעַ to shine out, forth, display beams
(4 · 8 · 8) 422 יפע

Chapter 11

צדק 2 to be justified; be just; have a just
cause (14 · 22 · 41) 842

בַּד 3 empty talk, idle talk (2 · 6) 95 III

מַת man, male (6 · 21) 607

הֶחֱרִישׁ to make silent; be silent; be deaf
(9 · 38 · 46) 361 II

לָעַג to mock, deride, have in derision
(3 · 12 · 18) 541

הִכְלִים to put to shame, insult, humiliate;
exhibit shame (2 · 10 · 38) 483

זַךְ 4 pure, clean, righteous (4 · 11) 269

לֶקַח teaching, instruction (1 · 9) 544

בַּר pure, clean (1 · 6) 141

אוּלָם 5 but indeed (10 · 19) 19 III

489

מִי יִתֵּן idiom: who will give or grant = O that (9 · 24) 678 1.f

תַּעֲלֻמָה 6 hidden thing, secret (2 · 3) 761

כֶּפֶל double (2 · 3) 495

תּוּשִׁיָּה sound, efficient wisdom (6 · 12) 444

הִשָּׁה to allow to be forgotten, to cause to forget (2 · 2 · 5) 674 II

חֵקֶר 7 searching, ח׳ אֱלוֹהַּ = what is to be explored in God (7 · 12) 350

תַּכְלִית end, completeness (3 · 5) 479

שַׁדַּי name of God (31 · 48) 994

גֹּבַהּ 8 height; exaltation, grandeur; haughtiness (3 · 17) 147

עָמֹק deep; unsearchable (2 · 17) 771

אָרֹךְ 9 long (1 · 3) 74

רָחָב wide, broad (2 · 21) 932 I

מִנִּי poetic form מִן (19 · 30) 577

חָלַף 10 to pass on quickly, move or sweep on; pass through (4 · 14 · 26) 322

הִקְהִיל to summon an assembly (1 · 20 · 39) 874

מַת 11 man, male (6 · 21) 607

נבב 12 to hollow out, pass. ptc. = hollow, hollowed (1 · 4 · 4) 612

נלוב Niph., to have or get a mind (1 · 1 · 3) 525 לבב

עַיִר male ass (1 · 9) 747

פֶּרֶא wild ass (4 · 10) 825

עַוְלָה 14 injustice, unrighteousness, wrong (10 · 32) 732

נָשָׂא פָנִים 15 idiom: to lift up face or countenance = to show good conscience; show favor, grant request etc. 670 נשא 1.b (3)

מוּם blemish, defect (2 · 21[?]) 548

צָהֳרַיִם 17 noon (2 · 23) 843

חֶלֶד duration; world (1 · 5) 317

עוּף to be dark (1 · 1 · 1) 734 II

תִּקְוָה 18 hope; ground of hope; things hoped for (13 · 32) 876 II

חָפַר to search, search out, explore; dig (4 · 23 · 23) 343

בֶּטַח security, w. לְ = securely (2 · 43) 105 I

רָבַץ 19 to make a lair, to lie down (1 · 24 · 30) 918

הֶחֱרִיד to terrify; drive in terror (1 · 16 · 39) 353

מָנוֹס 20 escape, place of escape; מָנוֹס אָבַד מִן = there was no escape for (1 · 8) 631

תִּקְוָה hope; ground of hope; things hoped for (13 · 32) 876

מַפַּח breathing out (1 · 1) 656

Chapter 12

אָמְנָם 2 verily, truly (6 · 9) 53

נָפַל מִן 3 idiom: to be inferior to (2 · 2) 657 Qal 6

כְּמוֹ אֵלֶּה idiom; the like of these things 455 1.a

שְׂחֹק 4 [object of] derision, laughter (3 · 15) 966

פִּיד 5 ruin, disaster (3 · 4) 810

בּוּז contempt (3 · 11) 100

עַשְׁתּוּת thought (1 · 1) 799 עשת II

שַׁאֲנָן one at ease; at ease (2 · 11[?]) 983

נָכוֹן blow [dub.] (1 · 1) 646

מעד to slip, slide, totter (1 · 5 · 7) 588

שָׁלוּ, שָׁלָה 6 to be at ease, prosper (2 · 5 · 7) 1017

בַּתֻּחֹת security, safety (1 · 1) 105

הִרְגִּיז to shake, cause to quake; disquiet (2 · 7 · 41) 919

לַאֲשֶׁר to him who, to that which, etc. (1 · 36) 82 אֲשֶׁר 1

אוּלָם 7 but indeed (10 · 19) 19 III

הוֹרָה Hiph., to direct, teach, instruct; point out; shoot, throw (6 · 45 · 45 [?]) 434 ירה

שִׂיחַ 8 to speak [w. לְ] to; complain, muse
(2 · 18 · 20) 967

הורה *Hiph.*, to direct, teach, instruct;
point out; shoot, throw (6 · 45 · 45
[?]) 434 ירה

דָּג fish (2 · 19) 185

מִלָּה 11 word, speech, utterance; byword
(34 · 38) 576

בחן to prove, test, try; examine
(4 · 25 · 29) 103

חֵךְ palate, roof of mouth (7 · 18) 335

אֹכֶל food (6 · 44) 38

טָעַם to taste, experience (2 · 11 · 11) 380

יָשִׁישׁ 12 aged (4 · 4) 450

תְּבוּנָה faculty of understanding, understanding (4 · 42) 108

תְּבוּנָה 13 faculty of understanding, understanding (4 · 42) 108

הָרַס 14 to throw down, break down
(1 · 30 · 43) 248

עָצַר 15 to restrain, shut up, keep away,
retain (3 · 36 · 46) 783

תּוּשִׁיָּה 16 sound, efficient wisdom (6 · 12) 444

שׁגג to err, go astray; sin (1 · 5 · 5) 992

השׁגה to lead astray, mislead (1 · 4 · 21) 993

יוֹעֵץ 17 ptc. = counselor, king's advisor
(2 · 22) 419 יעץ

שׁוֹלָל barefoot (2 · 3) 1021

הולל *Po'el*, to make into a fool; make
fool of ([?] · 4 · 14) 237

מוּסָר 18 restraining, band; bond; [but Lis.
מוּסָר chastening, discipline] (4 · 50)
64 אסר, 416 יסר

אֵזוֹר waistcloth (1 · 14) 25

מָתְנַיִם loins (2 · 47) 608

שׁוֹלָל 19 barefoot (2 · 3) 1021

אֵתָן permanent, firmly seated, ever-
flowing (2 · 14) 450

סלף to subvert, turn upside down, ruin;
pervert (1 · 7 · 7) 701

טַעַם 20 judgment, discretion, discernment;
taste (2 · 13) 381

בּוּז 21 contempt (3 · 11) 100

נָדִיב noble, princely; inclined (3 · 37) 622

מְזִיחַ girdle (1 · 1) 561

אָפִיק channel [dub.] [Lis. strong] (1 · 1
[?]) 67

רִפָּה to let drop, fig. for weaken
(1 · 4 · 44) 951

עָמֹק 22 unsearchable, deep (2 · 17) 771

מִנִּי poetic for מִן (19 · 30) 577

צַלְמָוֶת deep shadow, darkness; death
shadow (10 · 18) 853

השׂגיא 23 to make great, magnify (1 · 2 · 2)
960

שׁטח to expand, spread, spread abroad
(1 · 4 · 5) 1008

הנחה to guide, lead (3 · 26 · 40) 634

התעה 24 to cause to wander about; cause to
err (2 · 21 · 50) 1073

תֹּהוּ formlessness, empty space, track-
less waste (3 · 20) 1062

משׁשׁ 25 to grope; feel over or through
(2 · 6 · 8) 606

התעה to cause to wander about; cause to
err (2 · 21 · 50) 1073

שִׁכּוֹר drunkard, drunken (1 · 13) 1016

Chapter 13

נָפַל מִן 2 idiom: to be inferior to (2 · 2) 657
נפל *Qal* 6

אוּלָם 3 but indeed (10 · 19) 19 III

שַׁדַּי name of God (31 · 48) 994 see 5:17

אוּלָם 4 but indeed (10 · 19) 19 III

טפל to plaster, glue (2 · 3 · 3) 381

אֱלִיל worthlessness, insufficiency (1 · 20
47

מִי יִתֵּן 5 idiom: who will give or grant = O
that! (9 · 24) 698 נתן 1.f

491

הֶחֱרִישׁ   to be silent; make silent; be deaf (9 · 38 · 46) 361

תּוֹכַחַת   6 argument, impeachment; reproof (2 · 24) 407

הִקְשִׁיב   to give attention (2 · 45 · 46) 904

עַוְלָה   7 injustice, unrighteousness, wrong (10 · 32) 732

רְמִיָּה   deceit, treachery (2 · 15) 941

נָשָׂא פָנִים   8 to lift up face or countenance = grant a request, show favor, show partiality 670 נשׂא Qal 1.b.(3)

חָקַר   9 to search through, explore (6 · 22 · 27) 350

הֵתֵל   Hiph., to mock, trifle with; (2 · 8 · 9) 1068

אֱנוֹשׁ   man, mankind (18 · 42) 60

סֵתֶר   10 secrecy; hiding place; covering (5 · 35) 712

נָשָׂא פָנִים   to lift up face or countenance = grant a request, show favor, show partiality 670 נשׂא Qal 1.b.(3)

שְׂאֵת   11 dignity, exaltation; swelling; uprising (3 · 7) 673

בִּעֵת   Piel, to overwhelm, fall upon, terrify (8 · 13 · 16) 129

פַּחַד   dread, object of dread (10 · 49) 808 I

זִכָּרוֹן   12 memorial, reminder; remembrance (1 · 24) 272

מָשָׁל   sentence of ethical wisdom; parable; proverbial saying (3 · 39) 605

אֵפֶר   ashes (4 · 22) 68

גַּב   breastworks, bulwarks; mound; shield protection; back (3 · 13) 146

חֹמֶר   clay; mortar (7 · 17) 330 I

הֶחֱרִישׁ   13 to be silent; make silent; be deaf (9 · 38 · 46) 361

עַל־מָה   14 upon what? on what ground? wherefore? (3 · 14[?]) 552 מה 4.f

קָטַל   15 to slay (2 · 3 · 3) 881

יָחַל   Piel, to wait, tarry for; hope for (6 · 25 · 42) 403

חָנֵף   16 godless man; godless, profane (8 · 13) 338

מִלָּה   17 utterance, speech; word, byword (34 · 38) 576

אַחְוָה   declaration (1 · 1) 296

צָדֵק   18 to have a just cause; be justified, be just (14 · 22 · 41) 842

הֶחֱרִישׁ   19 to be silent; make silent; be deaf (9 · 38 · 46) 361

גָּוַע   to expire, perish, die (8 · 23 · 23) 157

אֵימָה   21 terror, dread (6 · 17) 33

בִּעֵת   Piel, to overwhelm, fall upon, terrify (8 · 13 · 16) 129

כַּמָּה   23 how much? how many? how often? (3 · 13) 554 מה 4.c

עָלֶה   25 leaf, leafage (1 · 18) 750

נִדָּף   to be driven, driven about (1 · 6 · 9) 623

עָרַץ   to cause to tremble, strike with awe (2 · 11 · 14) 791

קַשׁ   stubble, chaff (3 · 16) 905

יָבֵשׁ   dry, dried (1 · 9) 386

מְרֹרָה   26 bitter thing, poison; gall (1 · 5[?]) 601

נְעוּרִים   youth, early life (2 · 46) 655

סַד   27 stocks [for confining feet] (2 · 2) 690

שֹׁרֶשׁ   root (9 · 33) 1057

הִתְחַקָּה   to make an engraving, mark a line (1 · 1 · 4) 348

רָקָב   28 rottenness, decay (1 · 5) 955

בָּלָה   to wear out (1 · 11 · 16) 115

עָשׁ   moth (3 · 7) 799

Chapter 14

קָצֵר   1 short (1 · 5) 894

שָׂבֵעַ   sated, satisfied (3 · 10) 960

רֹגֶז · disquiet, turmoil (5 · 7) 919

צִיץ · 2 blossom, flower; shining thing (1 · 15) 847

מלל · to hang down, wither (2 · 3 · 4[?]) [Lis. p. 824 as *Niph.* נמול to be cut off] 576 III

אַף־עַל־זֶה · 3 = upon one such as this 261 זה 3

פָּקַח · to open eyes; open ears (2 · 17 · 20) 824

מִי־יִתֵּן · 4 idiom: who will give or grant = O that! (9 · 24) 678 נתן 1.f

חָרַץ · 5 to decide, determine, ptc. = determined, fixed; cut (1 · 5 · 10) 358 I

שָׁעָה · 6 to gaze at, regard (2 · 12 · 15) 1043

רָצָה · to be pleased with, favorable to; accept (3 · 42 · 50) 953

שָׂכִיר · hireling, hired laborer (3 · 18) 969

תִּקְוָה · 7 hope; ground of hope; things hoped for (13 · 32) 876

הֶחֱלִיף · to show newness, change (2 · 10 · 26) 322

יוֹנֶקֶת · shoot, twig (3 · 6) 413

הִזְקִין · 8 to show age, grow old (1 · 2 · 27) 278

שֹׁרֶשׁ · root (9 · 33) 1057

גֶּזַע · stock, stem (1 · 3) 160

הִפְרִיחַ · 9 to cause to bud or sprout (1 · 5 · 33) 827 I

קָצִיר · boughs, branches (3 · 5) 894 II

נֶטַע · plant; planting; plantation (1 · 1) 642

חלשׁ · 10 to be prostrate, be weak; to disable (1 · 3 · 3) 325

גָּוַע · to expire, perish, die (8 · 23 · 23) 157

אַי · where? (8 · 40) 32

אָזַל · 11 to go; go away, be gone (1 · 5 · 5) 23

מִנִּי · poetic for מִן (19 · 30) 577

חרב · to be dried up; be dry (2 · 17 · 37) 351 I

עַד־בִּלְתִּי · 12 till there be no… (1 · 7) 117 בֶּלֶת 4.c

הֵקִיץ · to awake (1 · 22 · 23[?]) 884 I

שֵׁנָה · sleep (1 · 23) 446 ישׁן

מִי־יִתֵּן · 13 idiom; who will give or grant = O that! (9 · 24) 678 נתן 1.f

הִצְפִּין · to hide (1 · 2 · 29) 860

צָבָא · 14 service, hard service [rare mng.] 838 3.b

יחל · to wait, tarry [for לְ]; hope [for לְ] (6 · 25 · 42) 403

חֲלִיפָה · revival, relief; change; changing (2 · 12) 322

כסף · 15 to long [for לְ] (1 · 2 · 6) 493

צַעַד · 16 step, steps; pace (5 · 14) 857

חתם · 17 to seal up, fasten up by sealing; affix one's seal (4 · 23 · 27) 367

צְרוֹר · 17 bundle, pouch (1 · 7) 865 I

טפל · to glue, plaster (2 · 3 · 3) 381

אוּלָם · 18 but indeed (10 · 19) 19 III

נָבֵל · to sink or drop down; droop, wither and fall (1 · 21 · 25) 615

עתק · to move, proceed, advance (3 · 4 · 9) 801

שׁחק · 19 to rub away (1 · 4 · 4) 1006

שָׁטַף · to rinse or wash off; overflow; flow (1 · 28 · 31) 1009

סָפִיחַ · outpouring (1 · 1) 705

תִּקְוָה · hope; ground of hope; things hoped for (13 · 32) 876

אֱנוֹשׁ · man, mankind, men (18 · 42) 60

תקף · 20 to overpower, prevail over (2 · 3 · 4) 1075

נֶצַח · everlastingness, ever, לָנֶצַח forever (6 · 43) 664

שָׁנָה · to change, alter (1 · 9 · 26) 1039

צער · 21 to be or grow insignificant (1 · 3 · 3) 858

כאב · 22 to be in pain (1 · 4 · 8) 456

אָבַל · to mourn, lament (1 · 18 · 38) 5 I

Chapter 15

סָכַן 3 to benefit, profit; be of use or service (5 · 5 · 10) 698 I

מִלָּה word, speech, utterance; byword (34 · 38) 576

הוֹעִיל to profit, avail, benefit (4 · 23 · 23) 418 I

הֵפֵר 4 to annul, make ineffectual; frustrate; break, violate (3 · 42 · 45) 830
פרר I

יִרְאָה fear of God, reverence, piety; fear, terror (5 · 45) 432

גָּרַע to restrain; diminish; withdraw (3 · 14 · 22) 175

שִׂיחָה complaint, musing (1 · 3) 967

אַלֵּף 5 to teach (3 · 3 · 4) 48

עָרוּם crafty; shrewd, sensible (2 · 11) 791

הִרְשִׁיעַ 6 to condemn as guilty; act wickedly (8 · 25 · 34) 957

הוֹלֵל 7 Polal., to be brought forth; be mad, writhe (2 · 5 · 47[?]) 296 I

סוֹד 8 council, intimate circle; counsel (3 · 21) 691

גָּרַע to restrain; diminish; withdraw (3 · 14 · 22) 175

שָׂיב 10 to be hoary, old (1 · 2 · 2) 966

יָשִׁישׁ aged (4 · 4) 450

כַּבִּיר mighty, great (7 · 10) 460

תַּנְחוּם 11 pl. = consolation (2 · 5) 637

אַט with לְ = gently, softly; gentleness (1 · 5) 31

רָזַם 12 to flash, wink (1 · 1 · 1) 931

מִלָּה 13 word, speech, utterance; byword (34 · 38) 576

אֱנוֹשׁ 14 man, mankind, men (18 · 42) 60

זכה to be clean, pure (2 · 4 · 8) 269

צדק to be just; be justified; have a just cause (14 · 22 · 41) 842

זָכַךְ 15 to be clean, pure (2 · 2 · 4) 269

אַף כִּי 16 'tis indeed that, how much more…, indeed (4 · 26) 65 אַף 3

נִתְעָב to be abhorred (1 · 3 · 22) 1073

נֶאֱלָח to be corrupt (1 · 3 · 3) 47

עַוְלָה injustice, unrighteousness, wrong (10 · 32) 732

חוה 17 Piel, to tell, declare, show that… (5 · 6 · 6) 296 III

כָּחַד 18 to conceal (לְ = from) (3 · 15 · 32) 470

הִתְחוֹלֵל 20 ptc., = writhing, suffering torture; whirling (1 · 1 · 47[?]) 296 I חול

נִצְפַּן to be stored up, be hidden (2 · 3 · 29) 860

עָרִיץ ruthless, terror striking; awe inspiring (3 · 20) 792

פַּחַד 21 object of dread, קוֹל פ׳ = sound of terror; dread (10 · 49) 808 I

מְנִי 22 poetic for מִן (19 · 30) 577

צפה to look out, spy, pass. ptc. = spied out (1 · 9 · 18) 859

אֱלֵי poetic for אֶל (4 · 4) 39

נדד 23 to wander, stray; flee (1 · 20 · 24) 622 I

אַיֵּה where? (5 · 44) 32

בעת 24 Piel., to overwhelm, fall upon, terrify (8 · 13 · 16) 129

צַר straits, distress (6 · 20) 865

מְצוּקָה straitness, straits, stress (1 · 6) 848

תָּקַף to overpower, prevail over (2 · 3 · 4) 1075

עָתִיד ready, prepared (2 · 5) 800

כִּידוֹר onset (1 · 1) 461

שַׁדַּי 25 name of God (31 · 48) 994

הִתְגַּבֵּר to behave proudly; show oneself mighty (2 · 3 · 25) 149

צַוָּאר 26 neck, back of neck (3 · 41) 848

עֲבִי thickness (1 · 5) 716

494

גַּב   convex projection of shield, boss; back; mound; anything convex (3 · 13) 146

פִּימָה 27 superabundance (1 · 1) 810

כֶּסֶל   loins; stupidity; confidence (1 · 5 [?]) 492

נִכְחַד 28 to be effaced, destroyed; be hidden (3 · 11 · 32) 470

הִתְעַתַּד   to be prepared for (1 · 1 · 2) 800

גַּל   heap; wave, billow (2 · 20[?]) 164

עָשַׁר 29 to be rich; gain riches (1 · 2 · 17) 799

מִנְלֶה   gain, acquisition [dub.] (1 · 1) 649

מִנִּי 30 poetic for מִן (19 · 30) 577

יוֹנֶקֶת   shoot, twig (3 · 6) 413

שַׁלְהֶבֶת   flame (1 · 2[?]) 529

נִתְעָה 31 to be led astray; be made to wander about (1 · 2 · 50) 1073

תְּמוּרָה   recompense, exchange (3 · 6) 558

כִּפָּה 32 branch, frond (1 · 4) 497

רַעֲנָן   *Palel*, to be or grow luxuriant, fresh, green (1 · 1 · 1) 947

חָמַס 33 to do violence, wrong, treat violently (2 · 7 · 8) 329

בֹּסֶר   [coll.] unripe or sour grapes (1 · 5) 126

זַיִת   olive tree; olive[s] (1 · 38) 268

נִצָּה   blossom (1 · 4) 665

חָנֵף 34 godless man; godless, profane (8 · 13) 338

גַּלְמוּד   hard, barren, unproductive (3 · 4) 166

שֹׁחַד   present, bribe (1 · 23) 1005

הָרָה 35 to conceive, become pregnant (1 · 38 · 40) 247 I

מִרְמָה   deceit, treachery (2 · 39) 941

Chapter 16

הֵמְרִיץ 3 to sicken, i.e., vex, disturb (1 · 1 · 4) 599

לוּ 4 if; though; if only, O that! (2 · 19) 530

הֶחְבִּיר   to make a joining, to join [מִלִּים words] together (1 · 1 · 1[?]) 287

מִלָּה   word, speech, utterance; byword (34 · 38) 576

הֵנִיעַ   to shake or wag (e.g., head), cause to totter; toss about; disturb; cause to wander (1 · 14 · 38) 631 נוע

בְּמוֹ   poetic for בְּ (4 · 10) 91

אָמֵץ 5 to make firm, strengthen (2 · 19 · 41) 54

בְּמוֹ   poetic for בְּ (4 · 10) 91

נִיד   quivering motion [Lis. 925 condolence] (1 · 1) 627 נוד

חָשַׂךְ   to restrain, check; refrain; withhold; hold on check (5 · 26 · 28) 362

נֵחָשֵׂךְ 6 to be assuaged; spared (2 · 2 · 28) 362

כְּאֵב   pain (2 · 6) 456

מִנִּי   poetic for מִן (19 · 30) 577

הֶלְאָה 7 to weary, make weary, exhaust (1 · 6 · 19) 521

קָמַט 8 to seize (1 · 1 · 2) 888

כַּחַשׁ   leanness; lying (1 · 6) 471

בְּפָנַי   against, in the face of; in front of (1 · 17) 816 פָּנֶה para. II 3

טָרַף 9 to tear, rend; pluck (2 · 19 · 24) 382

שָׂטַם   to bear a grudge; cherish animosity against (2 · 6 · 6) 966

חָרַק   to gnash or grind (1 · 5 · 5) 359

לָטַשׁ   to sharpen, whet; to hammer (1 · 4 · 5) 538

פָּעַר 10 to open wide (2 · 4 · 4) 822

לְחִי   cheek; jaw, jawbone (2 · 21) 534

יַחַד   all together; altogether; together (13 · 45) 403

עֲוִיל 11 young boy (3 · 3[?]) [but BDB עַוָּל unjust, unrighteous one] 732

רטה	to wring out [dub.] (1 · 1 · 1) 936
שָׁלֵו 12	at ease, quiet (3 · 8) 1017
פרפר	*Pilp.*, to scatter [Lis. 1191 to shake] (1 · 1 · 4[?]) 830 I
עֹרֶף	back of neck (1 · 33) 791
פצפץ	to dash in pieces (1 · 1 · 3) 822 פצץ
מַטָּרָה	target, mark (1 · 16) 643
רַב 13	archer [Lis. 1309 arrow] (1 · 2) 914
פלח	to cleave open; cause to cleave open (2 · 4 · 5) 812
כִּלְיָה	pl., kidneys (2 · 31) 480
חָמַל	to spare, have compassion (4 · 40 · 40) 328
מְרֵרָה	gall (1 · 1) 601
פָּרַץ 14	to break out upon; break through, down, into, out, up (3 · 46 · 49) 829 I
פֶּרֶץ	outburst, bursting forth; breach (3 · 19) 829 I
שַׂק 15	sackcloth, sack (1 · 48) 974
תפר	to sew together (1 · 3 · 4) 1074
גֶּלֶד	skin (1 · 1) 162
עולל	*Poel*, to insert, thrust in (1 · 1 · 1) 760 III
חמרמר 16	*Pealal* to be reddened (1 · 1 · 1) 331 IV
מְנִי	poetic for מִן (19 · 30) 577
בְּכִי	weeping (2 · 30) 113
עַפְעַף	eyelid (3 · 10) 733
צַלְמָוֶת	deep shadow, darkness; death-shadow (10 · 18) 853
זַךְ 17	pure, clean, righteous (4 · 11) 269
זְעָקָה 18	cry of distress, cry, outcry (1 · 18) 277
שָׂהֵד 19	witness (1 · 1) 962
הליץ 20	to deride; ptc., = interpreter (2 · 9 · 12) 539
דלף	to drop, drip (1 · 2 · 2) 196

אָתָה 22	to come (4 · 19 · 21) 87

Chapter 17

חָבַל 1	to be ruined, broken (1 · 2 · 11) 287 II
נזעך	to be extinguished (1 · 1 · 1) 276
הֲתֻלִים 2	mockery (1 · 1) 251
המרה	to show disobedience, rebelliousness (1 · 22 · 43) 598
עָרַב 3	to take on pledge; go surety for (1 · 15 · 17) 786 II
צָפַן 4	to treasure up, [מִן] from = keep it from; treasure up, hide (4 · 24 · 29) 860
שֵׂכֶל	insight, understanding; prudence (1 · 16) 968
חֵלֶק 5	BDB says use here is dubious, "a share" [of feast or booty?] (>50) 324 5
הִצִּיג 6	to set, place [so all may see + לְ] (1 · 15 · 16) 426 יצג
מְשֹׁל	[but Lis. 874 to say mock verses] (1 · 7 · 15) 605
תֹּפֶת	act of spitting, spitting (1 · 1) 1064
כהה 7	to grow dim, faint (1 · 6 · 10) 462 I
כַּעַשׂ	vexation; anger of vexation (4 · 25) 495 כַּעַס
יְצֻרִים	forms, members (1 · 1) 428
עַל־זֹאת 8	idiom: on this account 262 זה 6.f
נָקִי	clean, free from guilt, innocent; free from punishment, obligation (6 · 43) 667
חָנֵף	godless man; profane, godless (8 · 13) 338
אֹמֶץ 9	strength (1 · 1) 55
אוּלָם 10	but in very deed, but, but indeed (10 · 19) 19
זִמָּה 11	plan, purpose (1 · 1[?]) 273

נָתַק to be torn apart, in two; be separated; be drawn away from (2 · 10 · 27) 683

מוֹרָשׁ possession [Lis. ארשׁ, desire] (1 · 1 [?]) 440

קָוָה 13 *Piel.*, to wait, look eagerly for [לְ]; lie in wait for (5 · 39 · 45) 875 I

רפד to spread out (1 · 2 · 3) 951

יָצוּעַ couch, bed (1 · 5) 426

שַׁחַת 14 pit; sheol (7 · 23) 1001

רִמָּה worm (5 · 7) 942

אַיֵּה 15 where? (5 · 44) 32

אֵפוֹ then (7 · 25) 66

תִּקְוָה hope, thing hoped for; ground of hope (13 · 32) 876

שׁוּר to behold; regard; watch, lie in wait (10 · 16 · 16) 1003

בַּד 16 pole, stave, bar (1 · 41) 94 3

יַחַד together; all together, altogether (13 · 45) 403

נַחַת rest; quietness (2 · 7) 629 I נוח

Chapter 18

עַד־אָנָה 2 how long? (2 · 13) 33 אָן d

קֶנֶץ snare, net (1 · 1) 890

מִלָּה word, speech, utterance, byword (34 · 38) 576

נטמה 3 to be stopped up, stupid [dub.] (1 · 1 · 1) 380

טָרַף 4 to tear, rend; pluck (2 · 19 · 24) 382

עתק to move, advance (3 · 4 · 9) 801

דָּעֵךְ 5 to go out, be extinguished (3 · 7 · 9) 200

נָגַהּ to shine (2 · 3 · 6) 618

שָׁבִיב flame (1 · 1) 985

חָשֵׁךְ 6 to be or grow dark (2 · 11 · 17) 364

נֵר lamp (3 · 45) 632

דָּעֵךְ to go out, be extinguished (3 · 7 · 9) 200

צַעַד 7 step (5 · 14) 857

אוֹן strength, vigor; wealth [but Lis. 34 אָוֶן mischief, evil (2 · 10[?])] (15 · 80) 20 19

רֶשֶׁת 8 net (1 · 22) 440

שְׂבָכָה network [for catching animals], net ornament, lattice (1 · 17) 959

עָקֵב 9 heel; footprint; hinder part (1 · 14) 784 I

פַּח birdtrap (2 · 25) 809

צַמִּים [dub.] snare, trap (2 · 2) 855

טמן 10 to hide, conceal [a snare]; hide (6 · 28 · 31) 380

חֶבֶל cord, rope; measuring cord; measured portion (3 · 49) 286 I

מַלְכֹּדֶת a catching instrument, snare, trap (1 · 1) 540

נָתִיב path, pathway (3 · 5) 677

בעת 11 *Piel*, to fall upon, overwhelm (8 · 13 · 16) 129

בַּלָּהָה terror, calamity (5 · 10) 117

רָעֵב 12 hungry (4 · 19) 944

אוֹן strength, vigor; wealth [but Lis. 34 אָוֶן mischief, evil (2 · 10[?])] (15 · 80) 20 19

אֵיד distress, calamity (6 · 24) 15

צֶלַע stumbling, limping (1 · 4) 854

בַּד 13 member, limb (2 · 3) 94

נָתַק 14 to be torn apart, in two; be separated; be drawn away from (2 · 10 · 27) 683

מִבְטָח confidence, object of confidence, act of confiding (3 · 5) 105

הצעיד to make [one] march, cause to march (1 · 1 · 8) 857 I

בַּלָּהָה terror, calamity (5 · 10) 117

מִבְּלִי 15 without (7 · 25) 115 בְּלִי (para. w. preps. c)

זרה *Pual*, to be scattered (1 · 2 · 38) 279

נָוֶה	habitation; abode of shepherd or flocks (3 · 45) 627 I
גָּפְרִית	brimstone (1 · 7) 172
שֹׁרֶשׁ 16	root (9 · 33) 1057
מִמַּעַל	above (4 · 29) 751 II מַעַל 1
מלל	to hang down, wither (1 · 2 · 4[?]) 576 III
קָצִיר	[coll.] boughs, branches (3 · 5) 894 II
זֵכֶר 17	remembrance, memory (1 · 23) 271
מִנִּי	poetic for מִן (19 · 30) 577
הדף 18	to thrust out, drive out [מִן] from; thrust, push (1 · 11 · 11) 213
תֵּבֵל	world, earth (3 · 35) 385
נדד	Hiph., to chase away (1 · 1 · 24) 622 I
נִין 19	offspring, posterity (1 · 4[?]) 630
נֶכֶד	progeny, posterity (1 · 3) 645
שָׂרִיד	survivor (4 · 28) 975 I
מָגוּר	sojourning place, dwelling place, sojourning (1 · 11) 158 I
קַדְמֹנִי 20	eastern, m. pl. = those of the East; former (1 · 10) 870
שַׂעַר	horror (1 · 3) 972
עַוָּל 21	unjust, unrighteous one (4 · 5) 732

Chapter 19

עַד־אָנָה 2	how long? (2 · 13) 33 אָן d
הוֹגָה	to cause grief or sorrow (1 · 5 · 8) 387
דכא	to crush (3 · 11 · 18) 193
מִלָּה	word, speech, utterance (34 · 38) 576
הכלים 3	to put to shame, insult, humiliate; exhibit shame (2 · 10 · 38) 483
הכר	Qal or Hiphil, to cause to wonder, deal hardly with [dub] (1 · 1 · 1) 229
אָמְנָם 4	verily, truly (6 · 9) 53
שָׁגָה	to go astray [morally]; to stray; to swerve, reel; commit sin of ignorance (2 · 17 · 21) 993

מְשׁוּגָה	error (1 · 1) 1000
אָמְנָם 5	verily, truly (6 · 9) 53
אֵפוֹ 6	then (7 · 25) 66
עות	Piel, to make crooked, pervert (4 · 9 · 11) 736
מָצוֹד	hunting implement, net (1 · 4) 844 II
הִקִּיף	to surround, encompass, enclose; complete the circuit; make round (2 · 16 · 17) 668 II
שׁוע 7	Piel, to cry for help (8 · 21 · 21) 1002
גדר 8	to wall up, shut off (1 · 7 · 7) 154
נְתִיבָה	path, pathway, = course of life (4 · 21) 677
הִפְשִׁיט 9	to strip off, strip (2 · 15 · 43) 834
עֲטָרָה	crown, wreath (2 · 23) 742
נָתַץ	to pull down, break down (1 · 31 · 42) 683
תִּקְוָה	hope, ground of hope, thing hoped for (13 · 32) 876
יַחַד 12	all together, altogether; together (13 · 45) 403
גְּדוּד	marauding band; troop; foray (3 · 33) 151
סלל	to cast up a way; to lift up (2 · 10 · 12) 699 I
זָר 13	to become estranged; ptc. as adj. = strange (1 · 3 · 6[?]) 266
נָכְרִי 15	foreign, unfamiliar, unknown; foreigner (1 · 45) 648
בְּמוֹ 16	poetic for בְּ (4 · 10) 91
זור 17	to be loathsome (1 · 1 · 1) 266 II
חנן	to be loathsome (1 · 1 · 1) 337 II
עֲוִיל 18	young boy (3 · 3) 732
תעב 19	Piel, to regard as an abomination; abhor; cause to be an abomination (3 · 15 · 22) 1073
מַת	man, male (6 · 21) 607
סוֹד	council, intimate circle; counsel (3 · 21) 691

הִתְמַלֵּט 20 to escape, slip forth (1 · 1 · 1[?])
[Lis. sep. = to be bald, be hairless] 572

מִי–יִתֵּן 23 idiom: who will give or grant = O
that! (9 · 24) 678 נתן 1.f

אֵפוֹ then (7 · 25) 66

מִלָּה word, speech, utterance; byword
(34 · 38) 576

הוּחָק Hoph., to be inscribed (1 · 1 · 11)
349 חקק

עֵט 24 stylus (1 · 4) 741

עֹפֶרֶת lead (1 · 9) 780

נֶחְצַב to be cut, hewn, graven (1 · 1 · 17)
345

גֹּאֵל 25 ptc. = redeemer, kinsman redeemer (1 · 44) 145 I

נִקַּף 26 Piel, to strike off (1 · 2 · 2[?]) 668
I

כִּלְיָה 27 pl. kidneys (2 · 31) 480

חֵיק bosom; בְּחֵקִי = within me; as fold
of garment (1 · 38) 300

שֹׁרֶשׁ 28 root (9 · 33) 1057

גּוּר 29 to be afraid; stand in awe
(2 · 10 · 10) 158

שַׁדִּין = דִּין = שַׁ [but dub.] judgment
(4 · 19) [note: perhaps שַׁדַּי freq.
name for God in Job] 192

שַׁדּוּן 29 Qere for previous entry 192

Chapter 20

שְׂעִיפִּים 2 disquietings = disquieting or exciting thoughts (2 · 2) 972

בַּעֲבוּר for the sake of, on account of, in
order that (1 · 45) 721

חָשׁ to make haste (1 · 15 · 21) 301

מוּסָר 3 correction, discipline; chastening
(4 · 50) 416

כְּלִמָּה insult, reproach; ignominy (1 · 30)
484

בִּינָה faculty of understanding, understanding, act of understanding, object of knowledge (8 · 37) 108

מִנִּי 4 poetic for מִן (19 · 30) 577

רְנָנָה 5 ringing cry; exultation (2 · 4) 943

חָנֵף godless man; profane, godless
(8 · 13) 338

עֲדֵי poetic for עַד (2 · 12) 723

רֶגַע moment, עֲדֵי–רְ' while a moment
lasts; for one moment (4 · 22) 921

שִׂיא 6 loftiness, fig. of pride (1 · 1) 673

עָב dark cloud, cloud mass; thicket
(8 · 30) 728

גֵּל 7 dung (1 · 3) 165

נֶצַח everlastingness, ever; לָנֶצַח = forever; endurance in time, life; eminence (6 · 43) 664 4

אֵי where? אַיּוֹ = where is he? (8 · 40) 32

עוּף 8 to fly away, fly (2 · 18 · 25) 733

הֻדַּד Hoph., to be chased away
(1 · 2 · 24) 622 נדד

חִזָּיוֹן vision; divine communication in a
vision (4 · 9) 303

שָׁזַף 9 to catch sight of, look on (2 · 3 · 3)
1004

שׁוּר to behold; regard; watch, lie in
wait (10 · 16 · 16) 1003 II

רצה 10 to seek the favor of (1 · 1 · 50) 953

דַּל reduced, poor; low, weak (6 · 48)
195

אוֹן wealth; strength, vigor (2 · 10[?]) 20

עֲלוּמִים 11 youth, youth vigor (2 · 4) 761

הַמְתִּיק 12 to give a sweet taste (1 · 2 · 6) 608

הִכְחִיד to hide; efface, annihilate
(1 · 6 · 32) 470

חָמַל 13 to spare, have compassion
(4 · 40 · 40) 328

מָנַע to withold (3 · 25 · 29) 586

חֵךְ palate, roof of mouth, gums
(7 · 18) 335

מֵעֶה 14 internal organs, inward parts, here = stomach, belly (2 · 32) 588

מְרֹרָה poison; gall, gall bladder; bitter thing; bitterness (2 · 2[?]) 601

פֶּתֶן venomous serpent, perh. cobra (2 · 6) 837

בָּלַע 15 to swallow up, engulf; swallow down (3 · 20 · 41) 118

הֵקִיא to vomit up (1 · 7 · 9) 883

רֹאשׁ 16 venom; poisonous herb (1 · 12) 912 II

פֶּתֶן venomous serpent, perh. cobra (2 · 6) 837

ינק to suck (2 · 8 · 18) 413

אֶפְעֶה a kind of viper (1 · 3) 821

פְּלַגָּה 17 stream; division (1 · 3) 811

חֶמְאָה curd, curdled milk (2 · 10) 326 חמא

יָגַע 18 toil (1 · 1) 388

בָּלַע to swallow up, engulf; swallow down (3 · 20 · 41) 118

תְּמוּרָה exchange, recompense (3 · 6) 558

עלס to rejoice (1 · 1 · 3) 763

רצץ 19 to crush in pieces, fig. = grievously oppress (1 · 3 · 19) 954

דַּל reduced, poor; low, weak (6 · 48) 195

גָּזַל to take violent possession of, tear away, rob (4 · 29 · 30) 159 I

שָׁלֵו 20 to be quiet, at ease (3 · 8) 1017 I

חָמַד to take pleasure, delight in, desire, pass. ptc. = desired things (1 · 16 · 21) 326

שָׂרִיד 21 an escaped thing, survivor (4 · 28) 975 I

אֹכֶל food (6 · 44) 38

חול to be firm (1 · 2 · 2) 298 II

טוּב fairness, beauty; good things, goods (2 · 32) 375

שֶׂפֶק 22 sufficiency, plenty (1 · 1) 974

עָמֵל sufferer; laborer (2 · 9) 766 I

חָרוֹן 23 anger, burning of anger (1 · 41) 354

הַמְתִּיר to send rain, rain (2 · 16 · 17) 565

עָלֵימוֹ poetic for עַל = 3rd m. pl. suff. 305 note 2 or 3rd m. sing. suff. 752

לְחוּם perh. = intestines, bowels (1 · 2) 535

נֶשֶׁק 24 equipment, weapons; armory (2 · 10) 676

חָלַף to pass through, pierce; pass on, or away (1 · 2 · 2[?]) 322

נְחוּשָׁה copper, bronze (4 · 10) 639

שָׁלַף 25 to draw out; draw off (1 · 24 · 24) 1025

גֵּוָה back (1 · 1) 156 II

בָּרָק flashing, lightning (2 · 21) 140

מְרֹרָה gall bladder; poison; bitter thing; bitterness (2 · 2[?]) 601

אֵימָה terror, dread (6 · 17) 33

טָמַן 26 to hide, conceal; pass. ptc. = darkness (6 · 28 · 31) 380

צָפוּן pass. ptc. = treasured place or thing, treasure (1 · 3) 860

נֻפַּח to be blown (1 · 1 · 12) 655

שָׂרִיד survivor (4 · 28) 975 I

יְבוּל 28 produce (1 · 13) 385

נגר Niph., to be poured, split, fig. for vanish (1 · 4 · 10) 620

אֹמֶר 29 promise, appointment; utterance, word (11 · 48) 56

Chapter 21

מִלָּה 2 speech, utterance, word (34 · 38) 576

תַּנְחוּם consolation (2 · 5) 637

הִלְעִיג 3 to mock, deride (1 · 5 · 18) 541

שִׂיחַ 4 complaint; musing; anxiety (5 · 14) 967

קָצַר to be short, w. נֶפֶשׁ = to be impatient (1 · 12 · 14) 894 I

נִבְהַל 6 to be disturbed, terrified, dismayed; as adj. terrible; to be in haste (3 · 24 · 39) 96

פַּלָּצוּת shuttering (1 · 4) 814 פלץ

עתק 7 to move, advance (3 · 4 · 9) 801

גָּבַר to be strong, mighty; prevail (1 · 17 · 25) 149

צֶאֱצָא 8 pl. only, offspring; produce (4 · 11) 425

פַּחַד 9 dread; obj. of dread (10 · 49) 808 I

עִבַּר 10 idiom: "to impregnate"; i.e., make semen pass over (1 · 2 · >50) 718

הִגְעִיל to cause or allow to reject as loathsome (1 · 1 · 10) 171

פלט to cause to escape; bring into security (2 · 24 · 27) 812

פָּרָה heifer, cow (1 · 26) 831

שכל to show barrenness, abort; make childless (1 · 18 · 23) 1013

עֲוִיל 11 young boy (3 · 3) 732

רקד to dance, leap (1 · 5 · 9) 955

תֹף 12 timbrel, tambourine (1 · 17) 1074

כִּנּוֹר lyre, stringed instrument (2 · 41) 490

עוּגָב musical instrument, perh. reed-pipe (2 · 4) 721

בָּלָה 13 to wear out [trans.], consume away (1 · 5 · 16) 115

רֶגַע moment, for a moment; בְּרֶגַע = in a moment (4 · 22) 921

שַׁדַּי 15 name of God (31 · 48) 994 see 5:17

הוֹעִיל to profit, avail, benefit (4 · 23 · 23) 418

פָּגַע to encounter, meet, reach (1 · 40 · 46) 803

טוּב 16 fairness, beauty; good things, goods, goodness (2 · 32) 375

מֶנִּי = מִמֶּנִּי (3 · 6) 577 מִן

כַּמָּה 17 how often? [here = how seldom!] (3 · 13) 552 מָה 4.c.a

נֵר lamp (3 · 45) 632

דָּעֵךְ to go out, be extinguished (3 · 7 · 9) 200

עָלֵימוֹ poetic for עַל + 3rd. m. sing. suff. or 3rd. m. pl. suff. 752

אֵיד distress, calamity (6 · 24) 15

חֶבֶל pain; birth pain 286 [re. Lis. destruction (1 · 2) cf. BDB 287 II]

תֶּבֶן 18 straw (2 · 17) 1061

מֹץ chaff (1 · 8) 558

גנב to take by stealth, steal (2 · 30 · 39) 170

סוּפָה storm-wind (3 · 15) 693

צָפַן 19 to treasure up, hide (4 · 24 · 29) 860

כִּיד 20 mng. unknown [Lis. p. 676 = decay, BDB = פִּיד misfortune as 12:5] (1 · 1) 475

שַׁדַּי name of God (31 · 48) 994 see 5:17

חֵפֶץ 21 delight, pleasure, desire (3 · 39) 343

חצץ Pual, to be cut in two, fig. for curtailed (1 · 1 · 3) 346 I

רָם 22 Qal ptc. as adjective = high, uplifted (2 · 31) 926 רום

תֹם 23 completeness, fullness; integrity (2 · 23) 1070

שַׁלְאֲנָן scribal error for שַׁאֲנָן, at ease, secure (2 · 11) 1016, 983

שָׁלֵו at ease, quiet (3 · 8) 1017 I

עֲטִין 24 prob. pail, bucket; [Lis. p. 1044 bowels] (1 · 1) 742

חָלָב milk (2 · 44) 316

מֹחַ marrow, fig. of prosperity (1 · 1) 562

מַר 25 bitter, bitterness (4 · 38) 600 I

יַחַד 26 together = alike; altogether; all together (13 · 45) 403

רִמָּה worm (5 · 7) 942

מְזִמָּה 27 thought, evil thought; purpose, discretion (2 · 19) 273

חמס to treat violently, wrong (2 · 7 · 8) 329

אַיֵּה 28 where? (5 · 44) 32

501

נָדִיב noble, princely; inclined, willing (3 · 27) 622

נִכַּר 29 to recognize, regard; [but Lis. to mistake, reject] (1 · 4 · 8[?]) 647

אֵיד 30 distress, calamity (6 · 24) 15

נחשׁךְ to be spared; assuaged (2 · 2 · 28) 362

עֶבְרָה overflowing rage, fury; overflow; arrogance (2 · 34) 720

חוּבל to be led, conducted; be borne along (3 · 11 · 18) 384

חוּבל 32 to be led, conducted; be borne along (3 · 11 · 18) 384

גָּדִישׁ tomb (1 · 4) 155

שָׁקַד to keep guard עַל over; keep watch; be wakeful (1 · 11 · 16) 1052

מתק 33 to be pleasant, sweet; suck (2 · 4 · 6) 608

רֶגֶב clod [of earth] (2 · 2) 918

מָשַׁךְ to proceed, march; draw, drag; draw out; trail (3 · 30 · 36) 604

תְּשׁוּבָה 34 answer; return (2 · 8) 1000

מַעַל faithlessness; unfaithful, treacherous act (1 · 29) 591 I

Chapter 22

סכן 2 to benefit, profit; be of use or service (5 · 5 · 10) 698 I

עָלֵימוֹ poetic for עַל + 3rd. m. sing. suff. or 3rd. m. pl. suff. 752

חֵפֶץ 3 delight, pleasure, desire (3 · 39) 343

שַׁדַּי name of God (31 · 48) 994 see 5:17

צדק 3 to be just; be justified; have a just cause (14 · 22 · 41) 842

בֶּצַע profit; gain made by violence (1 · 23) 130

יִרְאָה 4 fear, reverence, piety; terror; object of terror (5 · 45) 432

חבל 6 to hold by a pledge; bind (3 · 13 · 14) 286 I

חִנָּם gratuitously, without cause; gratis, for nothing (4 · 33) 432

עָרוֹם naked (6 · 16) 736

הִפְשִׁיט to strip off, strip (2 · 15 · 43) 832

עָיֵף 7 faint, weary (1 · 17) 746

רָעֵב hungry (4 · 19) 944

מָנַע to withdraw (3 · 25 · 29) 586

נְשָׂא פָנִים 8 idiom: to lift up face or countenance = grant request, show favor or partiality, as subst. honorable, eminent one 670 1.b.(3)

רֵיקָם 9 in empty condition (1 · 16) 938

יָתוֹם orphan (7 · 42) 450

דכא *Pual*, to be crushed (1 · 4 · 18) 193

פַּח 10 birdtrap (2 · 25) 809

בהל *Piel*. to dismay, terrify; to hasten (1 · 10 · 39) 96

פַּחַד dread; object of dread (10 · 49) 808 I

פִּתְאֹם suddenness, suddenly (3 · 25) 837

שִׁפְעָה 11 abundance, multitude (2 · 6) 1051

גֹּבַהּ 12 height (3 · 17) 147

כּוֹכָב star (5 · 37) 456

עֲרָפֶל 13 cloud, heavy cloud (2 · 15) 791

עָב 14 dark cloud; cloud mass; thicket (8 · 30) 728

סֵתֶר covering; hiding place; secrecy (5 · 35) 712

חוּג vault, horizon (1 · 3) 295

מַת 15 man, male (6 · 21) 607

קמט 16 *Pual*, to be snatched (1 · 1 · 2) 888

יְסוֹד foundation; base (2 · 19) 414

שַׁדַּי 17 name of God (31 · 48) 994 see 5:17

נָקִי 19 free from guilt, clean, innocent; free from punishment, obligations (6 · 43) 667

לעג to mock, deride, have in derision (3 · 12 · 18) 541

נִכְחַד 20 to be effaced, destroyed; be hidden (3 · 11 · 32) 470

קִים adversary (1 · 1) 879

502

הַסְכֶּן 21 to be familiar with, know intimately, show harmony with [עִם]; to
show habit (1 · 4 · 10) 698

תְּבוּאָה product, income [Lis.] but BDB as
vb. to come, come in, go, go in
(2 · 43) 100, 97

אֹמֶר 22 utterance, word; promise, decree
(11 · 48) 56

שַׁדַּי 23 name of God (31 · 48) 994 see 5:17

עַוְלָה injustice, unrighteousness, wrong
(10 · 32) 732

בֶּצֶר 24 precious ore, ingot, ring-gold (2 · 2)
131

צוּר rock; rocky wall [Lis. p. 1228, צר
= flint] (1 · 6) 866

אוֹפִיר fine gold [named after place by that
name] (1 · 1[?]) 20

שַׁדַּי 25 name of God (31 · 48) 994 see 5:17

בֶּצֶר precious ore, ingot, ring-gold (2 · 2)
131

תּוֹעָפָה eminence (1 · 4) 419

שַׁדַּי 26 name of God (31 · 48) 994 see 5:17

הִתְעַנֵּג to take exquisite delight; be of
dainty habit (2 · 9 · 10) 772

הֶעְתִּיר 27 to make supplication (1 · 7 · 20) 801 I

גָּזַר 28 to decree [Lis. p.322 decide] divide, cut in two; cut down, off
(1 · 6 · 12) 160

אֹמֶר, אָמַר promise, decree; utterance, word
(11 · 48[?]) 56 אֹמֶר

נָגַהּ to shine (2 · 3 · 6) 618

הִשְׁפִּיל 29 to make low, sit down; set in a
lower; lay low (2 · 19 · 30) 1050

גֵּוָה lifting up; pride (2 · 3) 145

שַׁח low, lowly (1 · 1) 1006

אִי 30 not; אִי-נָקִי = the noninnocent
(1 · 1) 33 IV

נָקִי free from guilt, clean, innocent;
free from punishment, obligations
(6 · 43) 667

בֹּר cleanness, pureness (2 · 7[?]) 141

Chapter 23

מְרִי 2 rebellion (1 · 22) 598

שִׂיחַ complaint; musing; anxiety (5 · 14)
967

אֲנָחָה sighing, groaning (1 · 11) 58

מִי-יִתֵּן 3 idiom: who will give or grant? =
O that!, here w.יָדַעְתִּי = O that I
knew! 678 נתן 1.f

תְּבוּנָה fixed place; preparation; arrangement (1 · 3) 467

תּוֹכַחַת 4 argument, impeachment; reproof;
correction (2 · 24) 407

מִלָּה 5 speech, utterance, word; byword
(34 · 38) 576

עִמָּדִי 6 = עִם + 1st. pers. sing. suff. 767

פִלֵּט 7 Piel, to be delivered; to cause to
escape; bring into security
(2 · 24 · 27) 812

נֶצַח everlastingness, ever; לָנֶצַח = forever; endurance in time, life; eminence (6 · 43) 664

אָחוֹר 8 behind, backwards; back part
(1 · 41) 30

עטף 9 to turn aside (1 · 3 · 3[?]) 742 I

עִמָּדִי 10 = עִם + 1st. sing. suff. 767

בחן to prove, test, try; examine, scrutinize (4 · 25 · 29) 103

אָשׁוּר 11 step, going (2 · 10[?]) 81

אָט = Hiph. imperf. 1st. sing. נטה; to
turn aside 639

מָשׁ הֵמִישׁ 12 [Lis. Qal, BDB Hiph.] to depart,
recede (1 · 20 · 20[?]) 559 I מוש

צָפַן to treasure up, hide (4 · 24 · 29)
860

אֹמֶר utterance, word; promise, decree
(11 · 48) 56

אָוָה 13 to desire (1 · 11 · 27) 16 I

נִבְהַל 15 to be disturbed, terrified, dismayed; be in haste (3 · 24 · 39) 96

פָּחַד to be in dread, to dread; be in awe (2 · 22 · 25) 808

הֵרַךְ 16 to make tender, weak, timid, fearful, soft (1 · 1 · 8) 939-940 רכך

שַׁדַּי name of God (31 · 48) 994 see 5:17

הבהיל to dismay; hasten (1 · 3 · 39) 96

נצמת 17 to be ended, annihilated (2 · 2 · 15) 856

אֹפֶל darkness, gloom, fig. of calamity (6 · 9) 66

Chapter 24

שַׁדַּי 1 name of God (31 · 48) 994 see 5:17

נצפן to be stored up (2 · 3 · 29) 860

גְּבוּלָה 2 border, boundary (1 · 10) 148

הִשִּׂיג to displace, move back; remove (1 · 7 · 25) 690

עֵדֶר flock, herd (1 · 37) 727

גָּזַל to tear away, rob (4 · 29 · 30) 159 I

יָתוֹם 3 orphan (7 · 42) 450

נָהַג to drive, conduct, lead (1 · 20 · 30) 624 I

חבל to hold by pledge; bind (3 · 13 · 14) 286 I

יַחַד 4 together = alike; all together; altogether (13 · 45) 403

חבא Pual, to be hidden (1 · 1 · 34) 285

פֶּרֶא 5 wild ass (4 · 10) 825

פֹּעַל deed, thing done; work, thing made; wages of work; acquisition (5 · 37) 821

שׁחר Piel, to seek early (3 · 12 · 13) 1007

טֶרֶף food, prey (1 · 4[?]) 383

בְּלִיל 6 fodder (2 · 3) 117

קָצַר to reap, harvest (2 · 24 · 24) 894 II

לקש to take the aftermath; i.e., take everything (1 · 1 · 1) 545

עָרוֹם 7 naked (6 · 16) 736

מִבְּלִי without (7 · 25) 115 בְּלִי c. w. preps.

לְבוּשׁ garment, clothing (7 · 31) 528

כְּסוּת covering, clothing (3 · 8) 492

קָרָה coldness (2 · 5) 903

זֶרֶם 8 flood of rain, rainstorm, downpour (1 · 9) 281

רטב to be moist (1 · 1 · 1) 936

מִבְּלִי without (7 · 25) 115 בְּלִי c. w. preps.

מַחְסֶה shelter, refuge (1 · 20) 340

חבק to embrace (1 · 10 · 13) 287

גָּזַל 9 to tear away, rob (4 · 29 · 30) 159 I

שׁד female breast (1 · 3) 994

יָתוֹם orphan (7 · 42) 450

חבל to hold by pledge; bind (3 · 13 · 14) 286 I

עָרוֹם 10 naked (6 · 16) 736

בְּלִי adv. used to negate an adjective, noun, etc. = without (10 · 23) 115

לְבוּשׁ garment, clothing (7 · 31) 528

רָעֵב hungry (4 · 19) 944

עֹמֶר sheaf (1 · 8) 771 I

שׁוּר 11 wall, row (1 · 2[?]) 1004 II

הצהיר to press out oil (1 · 1 · 1) 844

יֶקֶב winepress, usually = wine vat (1 · 16) 428

צמא to be thirsty (1 · 10 · 10) 854

מַת 12 man, male (6 · 21) 607

נָאַק to groan (1 · 2 · 2) 611

שׁוּע Piel, to cry for help (8 · 21 · 21) 1002

תִּפְלָה unsavoriness, unseemliness (2 · 3) 1074

מָרַד 13 to rebel, revolt (1 · 25 · 25) 597

הִכִּיר to be acquainted with; recognize, distinguish; regard, observe (6 · 38 · 41) 647 I

נְתִיבָה path, pathway (4 · 21) 677

רָצַח 14 to murder, slay; ptc. = slayer, murderer (1 · 35 · 41) 953

קטל to slay (2 · 3 · 3) 881

504

גַּנָּב   thief (2 · 17) 170

נאף 15 to commit adultery (1 · 17 · 31) 610

נֶשֶׁף   evening twilight; morning twilight (3 · 12) 676

שׁוּר   to behold; to regard; watch, lie in wait (10 · 16 · 16) 1003 II

סֵתֶר   covering, cover; hiding place; secrecy (5 · 35) 712

חָתַר 16 to dig into, dig; row (1 · 1 · 8) 369

חתם   *Piel*, to seal up (1 · 1 · 27) 367

צַלְמָוֶת 17 deep shadow, darkness; death shadow (10 · 18) 853

הִכִּיר   to be acquainted with; recognize; distinguish; regard, observe (6 · 38 · 41) 647 I נכר

בַּלָּהָה   terror, calamity (5 · 10) 117

קַל 18 swift, light (1 · 13) 886

חֶלְקָה   field, portion of ground (1 · 24) 324 I

צִיָּה 19 drought, dryness (2 · 16) 851

חֹם   heat (1 · 4) 328

גָּזַל   to tear away, rob (4 · 29 · 30) 159 I

שֶׁלֶג   snow (5 · 20) 1017

רֶחֶם 20 womb (5 · 33) 933

מתק   to suck, be pleasant; be or become sweet (2 · 4 · 6) 608

רִמָּה   worm (5 · 7) 942

עַוְלָה   injustice, unrighteousness, wrong (10 · 32) 732

רָעָה 21 re Lis., p. 1346, to have dealings with, to associate with [not in BDB] (1 · 5 · 7) 945

עָקָר   barren (1 · 11) 785

מָשַׁךְ 22 to draw out, prolong; draw; proceed, march; trail (3 · 30 · 36) 604

אַבִּיר   mighty (2 · 17) 7

בֶּטַח   security לטח = securely (2 · 43) 105 I

נִשְׁעַן   to lean, support oneself, fig. of trust (2 · 22 · 22) 1043

רמם 24 perh. pass. form to be exalted (1 · 1 · 5) 942

הוּמַךְ   to be brought low (1 · 1 · 3) 568 מכך

נקפץ   to draw oneself together (1 · 1 · 7) 891

שִׁבֹּלֶת   ear of grain (1 · 20) 987

מלל   to hang down, wither (2 · 3 · 4[?]) 576 III

אֵפוֹ 25 then (7 · 25) 66

הכזיב   to make or prove to be a liar (1 · 1 · 16) 469

לְאַל   to make worthless (1 · 1) 39 II אל c

מִלָּה   speech, utterance, word (34 · 38) 576

Chapter 25

פַּחַד 2 dread, obj. of dread (10 · 49) 808 I

גְּדוּד 3 marauding band; troop; foray, raid (3 · 33) 151

צדק 4 to be justified; be just; have a just cause (14 · 22 · 41) 842

אֱנוֹשׁ   man, mankind; [coll.] men; indiv. man (18 · 42) 60

זכה   to be clean, pure (2 · 4 · 8) 269

יָרֵחַ 5 moon (2 · 27) 437

האהיל   to be clear, shine (1 · 1 · 1) 14 II

כּוֹכָב   star (5 · 37) 456

זכך   to be clean, pure (2 · 3 · 4) 269

אַף־כִּי 6 'tis indeed that, how much more, indeed, furthermore (4 · 25) 65 אף 3

אֱנוֹשׁ   man, mankind; [coll.] men; indiv. man (18 · 42) 60

רִמָּה   worm (5 · 7) 942

תּוֹלֵעָה   worm, grub; coccus ilicis yielding scarlet (1 · 41) 1069

Chapter 26

לְלוֹא 2 without, in the condition of no..., (3 · 10) 520 לא 4.e

לְלֹא 3 without, in the condition of no..., (3 · 10) 520 לֹא 4.e

תּוּשִׁיָּה sound, efficient wisdom; abiding success (6 · 12) 444

מִלָּה 4 word, speech, utterance; byword (34 · 38) 576

נְשָׁמָה spirit; breath (7 · 24) 675

רְפָאִים 5 shades, ghosts (1 · 8) 952

חוֹלֵל *Polal*, to be made to writhe; be brought forth (2 · 5 · 47) 296

עֵרוֹם 6 naked (6 · 16) 736

כְּסוּת covering; clothing (3 · 8) 492

אֲבַדּוֹן place of destruction, ruin, Abaddon (3 · 5) 2

תֹּהוּ 7 nothingness, empty space, formlessness, confusion (3 · 20) 1062

תָּלָה to hang up; put to death by hanging (1 · 23 · 27) 1067

בְּלִימָה nothingness (1 · 1) 116

עָב 8 dark cloud, cloud mass; thicket (8 · 30) 728

פרשׁז, כרשׁז 9 *Piel* inf. abs. = spreading (1 · 1 · 1) 831

חָג 10 to draw a circle (1 · 1 · 1) 952

הַכְלִית end, completeness (3 · 5) 479

רוֹפֵף 11 to shake, rock (1 · 1 · 1) 952

תמה to be astounded (1 · 8 · 9) 1069

גְּעָרָה rebuke (1 · 15) 172

רָגַע 12 to disturb (1 · 4 · 13) 920 I

תְּבוּנָה understanding, act of understanding; faculty of understanding; obj. of knowledge (4 · 42) 108

מָחַץ to smite through, wound severely (2 · 14 · 14) 563

רַהַב storm, arrogance, name of mythical sea monster (2 · 7) 923

שִׁפְרָה 13 fairness, clearness (1 · 1) 1051

חוֹלֵל *Poel*, to pierce (1 · 3 · 7) 319 I

נָחָשׁ serpent (1 · 31) 638 I

בָּרִיחַ fleeing (1 · 3) 138

קָצֶה 14 end (2 · 28) 892

שֵׁמֶץ whisper (2 · 2) 1036

רַעַם thunder (2 · 6) 947

Chapter 27

מָשָׁל 1 sentence of ethical wisdom; proverb; byword, parable, etc. (3 · 39) 605

שַׁדַּי 2 name of God (31 · 48) 994 see 5:17

הֵמַר to make bitter, show bitterness (1 · 5 · 16) 600 I מרר

נְשָׁמָה 3 breath (7 · 24) 675

עַוְלָה 4 injustice, unrighteousness, wrong (10 · 32) 732

הגה to utter; growl, muse (1 · 23 · 25) 211 I

רְמִיָּה treachery, deceit (2 · 15) 941

חָלִילָה 5 far be it (from me, you, etc.) (2 · 21) 321

הצדיק to declare righteous, justify; do justice (1 · 12 · 41) 842

גָּוַע expire, perish, die (8 · 23) 157

תֻּמָּה integrity of (4 · 5) 1070

הרפה 6 to let go; let drop; refrain (2 · 21 · 44) 951

חרף to reproach (1 · 4 · 38) 357 I

עַוָּל 7 unjust, unrighteous one (4 · 5) 732

תִּקְוָה 8 things hoped for, outcome; hope, ground of hope (13 · 32) 876

חָנֵף godless man; profane, godless (8 · 13) 338

בצע to cut off, break off; gain by violence (1 · 10 · 16) 130

שׁלו, שׁלה from I שׁלה to be at ease; or from II שׁלה to draw out (1 · 1 · 1[?]) 1017

צְעָקָה 9 cry of distress, outcry (3 · 21) 858

שַׁדַּי 10 name of God (31 · 48) 994 see 5:17

הִתְעַנֵּג to take exquisite delight; be of
dainty habit (2 · 9 · 10) 772

הוֹרָה 11 to direct, teach, instruct; point out;
show; shoot (6 · 45 · 45[?]) 434 ירה

שַׁדַּי name of God (31 · 48) 994 see 5:17

כָּחַד to hide, conceal from (3 · 15 · 32)
470

הָבַל 12 to act emptily, become vain
(1 · 4 · 5) 211

עָרִיץ 13 awe-inspiring, terror-striking
(3 · 20) 792

שַׁדַּי name of God (31 · 48) 994 see 5:17

לְמוֹ 14 poetic for לְ (4 · 4) 518

צֶאֱצָא pl. = offspring; produce (4 · 11)
425

שָׂרִיד 15 survivor (4 · 28) 975

צָבַר 16 to heap up (1 · 7 · 7) 840

חֹמֶר mire, clay; mortar, cement (7 · 17)
330 I

מַלְבּוּשׁ raiment, attire (1 · 8) 528

נָקִי 17 free from guilt, clean, innocent;
free from punishment, obligations
(6 · 43) 667

עָשׁ 18 moth (3 · 7) 799 II

סֻכָּה booth; thicket (3 · 31) 697

עָשִׁיר 19 rich (1 · 23) 799

פָּקַח to open eyes and (once) ears
(2 · 17 · 20) 824

הִשִּׂיג 20 to overtake; reach, attain
(2 · 49 · 49) 673 נשׂג

בַּלָּהָה terror, calamity (5 · 10) 117

גָּנַב to take by stealth, to steal
(2 · 30 · 39) 170

סוּפָה storm-wind (3 · 15) 693

שָׂעַר 21 Piel, to whirl away (1 · 1 · 4)
973 II

חָמַל 22 to spare, have compassion
(4 · 40 · 40) 328

שָׂפַק 23 to slap, clap (1 · 1 · 2[?]) 706 ספק

עָלֵימוֹ poetic for עַל + 3rd m. sing. suff.
or 3rd m. pl. suff.; see 21:17 752

שָׁרַק to hiss, whistle (1 · 12 · 12) 1056

Chapter 28

מוֹצָא 1 place of going forth, here = mine;
act of going forth; issue, spring,
source (2 · 27) 425

זָקַק to refine, purify (2 · 2 · 7) 279 I

צוּק 2 to melt, pour out (2 · 3 · 3) 848 II

נְחוּשָׁה copper, bronze (2 · 10) 639

תַּכְלִית 3 end, completeness (3 · 5) 479

חָקַר to search through, explore; search
for (6 · 22 · 27) 350

אֹפֶל darkness, gloom (6 · 9) 66

צַלְמָוֶת deep shadow, darkness; death-shadow (10 · 18) 853

פָּרַץ 4 to break open; break out, through,
into, up, over, down (3 · 46 · 49)
829 I

מִנִּי poetic for מִן (19 · 30) 577

דָּלַל to hang, depend; be low; languish
(1 · 8 · 8) 195

אֱנוֹשׁ man, mankind; [coll.] men; indiv.
man (18 · 42) 60

נָע to swing to and fro; to wave; totter
(1 · 22 · 38) 631 נוע

סַפִּיר 6 sapphire, perh. also lapis lazuli
(2 · 11) 705

נָתִיב 7 path, pathway (3 · 5) 677

עַיִט bird(s) of prey (1 · 8) 743

שָׁזַף to catch sight of, look on (2 · 3 · 3)
1004

אַיָּה hawk, falcon, kite (1 · 3) 17

שַׁחַץ 8 dignity, pride (2 · 2) 1006

עָדָה to advance, pass on (1 · 1 · 2)
723 I

שַׁחַל lion (3 · 7) 1006

חַלָּמִישׁ 9 flint (1 · 5) 321

507

שֹׁרֶשׁ   root (9 · 33) 1057

יְאֹר   10 generally stream, canal, stream of Nile, but here pl. = shafts made in mining (1 · 64) 384

יְקָר   preciousness = precious things price; honor (1 · 17) 430

בְּכִי   11 here, weeping = trickling, weeping (2 · 30) 113

חִבֵּשׁ   to bind, restrain (1 · 2 · 32) 289

תַּעֲלֻמָה   what is hidden, hidden thing, secret (2 · 3) 761

מֵאַיִן   12 whence? from where? (3 · 19) 32 I אַיִן

אֵי זֶה   idiom: which (of two or more)? (5 · 15) 32 אֵי 2.a

בִּינָה   object of knowledge; understanding; act or faculty of understanding (8 · 37) 108

אֱנוֹשׁ   13 man, mankind; [coll.] men; indiv. man (18 · 42) 60

עֵרֶךְ   row, order, estimate (2 · 33) 789

תְּהוֹם   14 deep, sea, abyss (4 · 36) 1062

עִמָּדִי   = עִם + 1st sing. suff. 767

סְגוֹר   15 enclosure, encasement; but here = fine gold (1 · 2) 689

נִשְׁקָל   to be weighed out (2 · 3 · 22) 1053

מְחִיר   price; hire (1 · 15) 564

סֻלָּה   16 *Pual*, to be weighed (2 · 2 · 2) 699

כֶּתֶם   gold (3 · 9) 508

אוֹפִיר   name of location assoc. w. fine gold (1 · 1[?]) 20

שֹׁהַם   a gem, perh. onyx, chrysoprasus, beryl or malachite (1 · 11) 995 I

יָקָר   precious, valuable, costly; glorious (2 · 35) 429

סַפִּיר   sapphire, lapis lazuli (2 · 11) 705

זְכוֹכִית   17 glass (1 · 1) 269

תְּמוּרָה   exchange, thing acquired by exchange; recompense (3 · 6) 558

פָּז   refined, pure gold (1 · 9) 808

רָאמוֹת   18 corals (1 · 3) 910 I

גָּבִישׁ   crystal (1 · 1) 150

מֶשֶׁךְ   drawing up, drawing (1 · 2) 604 I

פְּנִינִים   corals (1 · 6) 819

פִּטְדָה   19 topaz or chrysolite (1 · 4) 809

כֶּתֶם   gold (3 · 9) 508

סֻלָּה   *Pual*, to be weighed (2 · 2 · 2) 699 II

מֵאַיִן   20 whence? from where? (3 · 19) 32 I אַיִן

אֵי זֶה   idiom: which (of two or more)? (5 · 15) 32 אֵי 2.a

בִּינָה   understanding as object of knowledge; act or faculty of understanding (8 · 37) 108

נֶעְלָם   21 to be concealed; to conceal oneself (1 · 11 · 29) 761

אֲבַדּוֹן   22 place of destruction, ruin; Abaddon (3 · 5) 2

שֵׁמַע   report, hearing (2 · 17) 1034

קָצֶה   24 end (2 · 28) 892

מִשְׁקָל   25 heaviness, weight (1 · 49) 1054

תִּבֵּן   to mete out (1 · 4 · 18) 1067

מָטָר   26 rain (7 · 38) 564

חֲזִיז   thunderbolt, lightning flash (2 · 3) 304

חָקַר   27 to search through, explore; search for (6 · 27 · 27) 350

יִרְאָה   28 fear, reverence, piety; terror, object of terror (5 · 45) 432

בִּינָה   understanding as object of knowledge; act or faculty of understanding (8 · 37) 108

Chapter 29

מָשָׁל   1 sentence of ethical wisdom; proverb; by-word, parable, etc. (3 · 39) 605

מִי־יִתֵּן   2 idiom: who will give or grant = O that! (9 · 24) 678 נתן 1.f

יֶרַח — month (4 · 12) 437 I

הלל 3 — to shine [Lis. *Hiph*] (3 · 4 · 4) 237 I

נֵר — lamp (3 · 45) 632

חֹרֶף 4 — harvest time, autumn (1 · 7) 358

סוֹד — intimacy, counsel; intimate circle, council (3 · 21) 691

בְּעוֹד 5 — in the continuance of, while yet (1 · 20) 729 עוֹד 2.a

שַׁדַּי — name of God (31 · 48) 994 see 5:17

עִמָּדִי — poetic for עִמִּי 767

הָלִיךְ 6 — step (1 · 1) 237

חֵמָה — curd, curdled milk (2 · 10) 326

צוק — to pour out, melt (2 · 3 · 3) 848 II

עִמָּדִי — poetic for עִמִּי 767

פֶּלֶג — channel, canal (1 · 10) 811 I

קֶרֶת 7 — town, city (1 · 5) 900

רְחוֹב — broad open place (1 · 43) 932

מוֹשָׁב — seat, sitting; dwelling place; dwelling; dwellers (1 · 44) 444

נֶחְבָּא 8 — to hide oneself (3 · 16 · 34) 285

יָשִׁישׁ — aged (4 · 4) 450

עָצַר 9 — to restrain, retain (3 · 36 · 46) 783

מִלָּה — word (34 · 48) 576

כַּף שִׂים לְפֶה — idiom of spreading hand in prayer or silence (1 · 1) 496 כַּף 1.d (4), (5)

נָגִיד 10 — ruler, prince, leader (2 · 44) 617

נֶחְבָּא — to hide oneself (3 · 16 · 34) 285

חֵךְ — gums, palate, roof of mouth (7 · 18) 335

אשר 11 — *Piel*, to pronounce happy, call blessed; go straight, lead straight; set right (1 · 7 · 9) 80

הֵעִיד — to testify, bear witness; cause to testify, take as witness (1 · 38 · 43) 729

שׁוּע 12 — *Piel*, to cry for help (8 · 21 · 21) 1002

יָתוֹם — orphan (7 · 42) 450

עֹזֵר — ptc. = helper, helping (3 · 19) 740

מְעִיל 14 — robe (3 · 28) 591

צָנִיף — turban (1 · 5) 857

עִוֵּר 15 — blind (1 · 26) 734

פִּסֵּחַ — lame (1 · 14) 820

חקר 16 — to search through, explore, examine; search for (6 · 22 · 27) 350

מְתַלְּעוֹת 17 — teeth, incisors (1 · 4) 1069

עַוָּל — unjust, unrighteous one (4 · 5) 732

טֶרֶף — prey; food; leaf (3 · 17) 383

קֵן 18 — nest, nestlike cell or room (2 · 13) 890

גָּוַע — to expire, perish, die (8 · 23 · 23) 157

חוֹל — sand (1 · 22[?]) 297

שֹׁרֶשׁ 19 — root (9 · 33) 1057

אֱלֵי — poetic for אֶל 39

טַל — night mist, dew (2 · 31) 378

קָצִיר — [coll.] boughs, branches (3 · 5) 894

עִמָּדִי 20 — poetic for עִמִּי 767

הֶחֱלִיף — to show newness, change (2 · 10 · 26) 322

יחל 21 — *Piel*, to wait for [לְ] = hope for; wait (6 · 25 · 42) 403

דמם — to be still, silent (3 · 23 · 30) 198

לָמוֹ — poetic for לְ (4 · 4) 518

שָׁנָה 22 — to repeat, do again (1 · 14 · 26[?]) 1040 III

עָלֵימוֹ — poetic for עַל + 3rd m. pl. suff.; see 21:17

נטף — to drop, drip (1 · 9 · 18) 642

מִלָּה — speech, utterance, word; byword (34 · 38) 576

יחל 23 — *Piel*, to wait for [לְ] = hope for; wait (6 · 25 · 42) 403

מָטָר — rain (7 · 38) 564

פָּעַר — to open wide (2 · 4 · 4) 822

מַלְקוֹשׁ — latter rain, spring rain (1 · 8) 545

שָׂחַק 24 — to laugh; sport, play (7 · 19 · 36) 965

גְּדוּד 25 — troop; marauding band; foray, raid (3 · 33) 151

אָבֵל   adj. mourning (1 · 8) 5 I

Chapter 30

שָׂחַק   1 to laugh; sport, play (7 · 19 · 36) 965

צָעִיר   young; little, insignificant (2 · 22) 859

כֶּלֶב   dog, כַּלְבֵי צֹאן = sheep dog (1 · 32) 476

עָלֵימוֹ   2 poetic for עַל + 3rd m. pl. suff. (8 · 12) see 21:17 752

כֶּלַח   vigor, firm or rugged strength (2 · 2) 480 I

חֶסֶר   3 want, poverty (1 · 2) 341

כָּפָן   hunger, famine (2 · 2) 495

גַּלְמוּד   hard, barren, unproductive (3 · 4) 166

ערק   to gnaw; ptc. = one who gnaws (2 · 2 · 2) 792

צִיָּה   land of drought, drought, dryness (2 · 16) 851

אֶמֶשׁ   yesterday; א' שׁוֹאָה is difficult and uncertain, perh. darkness, gloom of wasteness (1 · 5) 57

שׁוֹאָה   ruin, waste; devastation (4 · 13) 996

מְשׁוֹאָה   noise [of devastation or storm], but see previous entry (2 · 3) 996

קָטַף   4 to pluck out or off (1 · 4 · 5) 882

מַלּוּחַ   mallow, plant growing in salt marsh (1 · 1) 572

שִׂיחַ   bush, shrub, plant (2 · 4) 967 II

שֹׁרֶשׁ   root (9 · 33) 1057

רֹתֶם   broom plant, retem (1 · 4) 958

גֵּו   5 midst [Lis. 314 community] (1 · 1) 156

גרשׁ   Pual, to be cast out, driven out (1 · 2 · 48) 176

הריע   to sound a signal for war or march; raise a shout; give a blast [w. horn] (2 · 40 · 44) 929 רוע

עָלֵימוֹ   poetic for עַל + 3rd pl. m. suff. (8 · 12) 752

גַּנָּב   thief (2 · 17) 170

עָרוּץ   6 dreadful (1 · 1) 792

חֹר   hole (1 · 7) 359 III

כֵּף   rock (1 · 1) 495

שִׂיחַ   7 bush, shrub, plant (2 · 4) 967 II

נהק   to bray, cry (2 · 2 · 2) 625

חָרוּל   weed, perh. chickpea (1 · 3) 355

ספח   *Pual*, to be joined together, hold together (1 · 1 · 5) 705 I

נָבָל   senseless, foolish (2 · 18) 614 II

בְּלִי   8 adv. used to negate an adj., noun, etc. = without (10 · 23) 115

נכא   *Niph.*, to be scourged (1 · 1 · 1) 644

נְגִינָה   9 song, music (1 · 14) 618

מִלָּה   word, byword; speech, utterance (34 · 38) 576

תעב   10 *Piel*, to regard as an abomination, abhor; cause to be an abomination (3 · 15 · 22) 1073

מִנִּי   = מִמֶּנִּי (3 · 6) 577

חָשַׂךְ   to withhold; refrain; keep from; to restrain (5 · 26 · 28) 362

רֹק   spittle (2 · 3) 956

יֶתֶר   11 cord (2 · 6) 452 II

רֶסֶן   halter (fig. of restraint) (2 · 4) 943 I

פִּרְחָה   12 [coll.] brood (1 · 1) 827

סלל   to cast up a way, highway; to lift up (2 · 10 · 12) 699 I

אֵיד   distress, calamity (6 · 24) 15

נתס   13 to tear or break down (1 · 1 · 1) 683

נְתִיבָה   path, pathway = course of life (4 · 21) 677

הַוָּה   engulfing ruin, destruction, chasm; desire (3 · 13[?]) 217

הוֹעִיל   to profit, avail, benefit (4 · 23 · 23) 418 יעל I

עֹזֵר   ptc. = helper, helping (3 · 19) 740 I

פֶּרֶץ   14 breach; bursting forth (2 · 19) 829 I

רָחָב	wide, broad (2 · 21) 932 I
אָתָה	to come (4 · 19 · 21) 87
שׁוֹאָה	ruin, waste; devastation (4 · 13) 996
הִתְגַּלְגֵּל	to roll away (1 · 1 · 17) 164 II גלל
בַּלָּהָה	15 terror, calamity (5 · 10) 117
נְדִיבָה	nobility, nobleness, honor (1 · 3) 622
עָב	dark cloud, cloud mass; thicket (8 · 30) 728
עֳנִי	16 affliction, poverty (6 · 36) 777
נָקַר	17 to bore, pick, dig (1 · 3 · 6) 669
ערק	to gnaw; ptc. here = gnawing [pain] (2 · 2 · 2) 792
הִתְחַפֵּשׂ	18 to disguise oneself (1 · 8 · 23) 344
לְבוּשׁ	garment, clothing (7 · 31) 528
כֻּתֹּנֶת	tunic פי כ׳ mouth of tunic = collar (1 · 29) 509
אזר	to gird, gird on (3 · 6 · 16) 25
הוֹרָה	19 to throw, cast (2 · 11 · 25[?]) 434 ירה
חֹמֶר	mire, clay; cement, mortar (7 · 17) 330
הִתְמַשֵּׁל	to become like [כְּ] (1 · 1 · 15) 605 I
אֵפֶר	ashes (4 · 22) 68
שִׁוַּע	20 Piel. to cry for help (8 · 21 · 21) 1002
אַכְזָר	21 cruel one, cruel (2 · 4) 470
עֹצֶם	might; bones (1 · 4) 782
שׂטם	to bear a grudge, cherish animosity against (2 · 6 · 6) 966
מוֹגֵג	22 Po'l, to soften, dissolve (1 · 2 · 17) 556 מוג
תֻּשִׁיָּה	rd. תּוּשִׁיָּה sound, efficient wisdom; abiding success (6 · 12) 444 or rd. K. as תְּשֻׁאָה = roar, noise 996
עִי	24 ruin, heap of ruins (1 · 5) 730
פִּיד	ruin, disaster (3 · 4) 810
שׁוּעַ	cry for help (2 · 2) 1002 III
קָשֶׁה	25 severe, hard, קְשֵׁה־יוֹם hard life (1 · 36) 904
עגם	to be grieved (1 · 1 · 1) 723
קוּה	26 Piel, to wait or look eagerly for

	[לְ]; to lie in wait (5 · 39 · 45) 875 I
יהל	Piel, to wait for [לְ] = hope for; to wait (6 · 25 · 42) 403
אֹפֶל	darkness, gloom, fig. of calamity (6 · 9) 66
מֵעֶה	27 pl. only, internal organs, inward parts, here fig. for seat of emotions (2 · 32) 588
רתח	Pual, to be made to boil (1 · 1 · 3) 958
דמם	to be still, be silent (3 · 23 · 30) 198 I
קדם	to meet, confront; come to meet (2 · 24 · 26) 869
עֳנִי	affliction; poverty (6 · 36) 777
קָדַר	28 to be dark (3 · 13 · 17) 871
בְּלֹא	without; of time = outside of, before (3 · 31) 520 לא 4.a
חַמָּה	sun, heat (1 · 6) 328
שִׁוַּע	Piel, to cry for help (8 · 21 · 21) 1002
תַּן	29 jackal (1 · 14) 1072
יַעֲנָה	ostrich; greed [dub.] (1 · 8) 419
שָׁחַר	30 to be black (1 · 1 · 1) 1007 I
חרר	to burn; be hot (1 · 3 · 9) 359 I
מִנִּי	poetic for מִן (19 · 30) 577
חֹרֶב	parching heat [of fever]; dryness, drought (1 · 16) 351 I
אֵבֶל	31 mourning (1 · 24) 5
כִּנּוֹר	lyre, stringed instrument (2 · 41) 490
עוּגָב	musical instrument, perh. reed pipe (2 · 4) 721

Chapter 31

בְּתוּלָה	1 virgin (1 · 50) 143
מִמַּעַל	2 above (4 · 29) 751 II מַעַל 1.a עלה
שַׁדַּי	name of God (31 · 48) 994 see 5:17
אֵיד	3 distress, calamity (6 · 24) 15
עַוָּל	unjust, unrighteous one (4 · 5) 732

גֶּכֶּר   misfortune, calamity (1 · 2) 648

צַעַד 4 step, steps (5 · 14) 857

חָשׁ הֵחִישׁ 5 to make haste, [Lis., *Hiph.*] (1 · 6 · 21) 301 חושׁ

מִרְמָה   deceit, treachery (2 · 39) 941

שָׁקַל 6 to weigh (2 · 19 · 22) 1053

מֹאזְנַיִם   balances, scales (2 · 15) 24 מאזן

תֻּמָּה   integrity (4 · 5) 1070

אַשֻּׁר 7 step, going (2 · 10[?]) 81

מִנִּי   poetic for מִן (19 · 30) 577

מְאוּם   blemish, defect (2 · 21) 548

צֶאֱצָא 8 pl. offspring; produce (4 · 11) 425

שָׁרַשׁ   *Pual*, to be rooted up (1 · 1 · 8) 1057

נִפְתָּה 9 to be deceived, enticed to [עַל] (1 · 2 · 27) 834

אָרַב   to lie in wait [usually w. hostile purpose] (1 · 20 · 23) 70

טָחַן 10 to grind (1 · 7 · 7) 377

כָּרַע   to bow down over [עַל]; to bow, bow down (3 · 30 · 36) 502

אֲחֵרִין   pl. of אַחֵר 29

זִמָּה 11 evil device, plan; wickedness (1 · 28[?]) 273

פָּלִיל   judge (1 · 3) 813

אֲבַדּוֹן 12 place of destruction, ruin; Abaddon (3 · 5) 2

תְּבוּאָה   income, revenue; product, yield (2 · 43) 100 בוא

שָׁרַשׁ   *Piel*, to deal with the roots, root [בְּ] at; root up (1 · 2 · 8) 1057

עִמָּדִי 13 = עִמִּי 767

רֶחֶם 15 womb (5 · 33) 933

מָנַע 16 to withhold (3 · 25) 586

חֵפֶץ   desire, delight, pleasure (3 · 39) 343

דַּל   reduced, weak, helpless; poor, thin (6 · 48) 195

פַּת 17 fragment, bit, morsel (1 · 14) 837

יָתוֹם   orphan (7 · 42) 450

נְעוּרִים 18 youth; early life (2 · 46) 655

הִנְחָה   *Hiph.*, to guide [here = treat kindly], lead (3 · 26 · 40) 634

מִבְּלִי 19 without (7 · 25) 115 בְּלִי c. w. preps.

לְבוּשׁ   garment, clothing (7 · 31) 528

כְּסוּת   covering, clothing (3 · 8) 492

חָלָץ 20 dual only = loins (3 · 10) 323

גֵּז   shearing = thing sheared off, wool, fleece; mowing (1 · 4) 159

הִתְחַמֵּם   to warm oneself (1 · 1 · 26) 328

הֵנִיף 21 to shake or brandish against [עַל]; to wield; swing; wave (1 · 32 · 34) 631

יָתוֹם   orphan (7 · 42) 450

עֶזְרָה   help, one who helps; assistance (2 · 26) 740

שְׁכֶם 22 back; shoulder (2 · 22) 1014 I

אֶזְרוֹעַ   arm (1 · 2) 284

קָנֶה   idiom for a shoulder-joint; usually stalk, reed (1 · 60) 889

פַּחַד 23 object of dread, terror; dread (10 · 49) 808 I

אֵיד   distress, calamity (6 · 24) 15

שְׂאֵת   dignity, loftiness; swelling; uprising [= getting up] (3 · 7) 673 נשׂא

כֶּסֶל 24 confidence; loins; stupidity (2 · 6 [?]) 492

כֶּתֶם   gold (3 · 9) 508

מִבְטָח   confidence, object of confidence, act of confiding (3 · 15) 105

כַּבִּיר 25 mighty, much, great (7 · 10) 460

הֵהֵל 26 *Hiph.*, to flash forth light (3 · 4 · 4 [?]) 237

יָרֵחַ   moon (2 · 27) 437

יָקָר   glorious, splendid; precious, costly, valuable (2 · 35) 429

פתה 27 to be enticed, deceived; be openminded, simple, foolish (2 · 5 · 27) 834

סֵתֶר   secrecy; covering; hiding place (5 · 35) 712

נָשַׁק   to kiss (1 · 26 · 32) 676 I

פְּלִילִי 28 adj., for a judge, calling for a judge (1 · 1) 813

כָּחַשׁ to deceive; act deceptively against; cringe; disappoint, fail (2 · 19 · 22) 471

מִמַּעַל above (4 · 29) 751 II מַעַל 1.a עלה

פִּיד 29 ruin, disaster (3 · 4) 810

חֵךְ 30 palate, roof of mouth; gums (7 · 18) 335

אָלָה curse; oath (1 · 36) 46

מַת 31 man, male (6 · 21) 607

מִי־יִתֵּן idiom: who will give or grant? = O that! (9 · 24) 678 נתן 1.f

טָמַן 33 to hide, conceal (6 · 28 · 31) 380

חֹב bosom [Lis. p. 459 "shirt-pocket"] (1 · 11) 285

עָרַץ 34 to tremble; cause to tremble (2 · 11 · 14) 791

בּוּז contempt (3 · 11) 100 II

דמם to be still, silent (3 · 23 · 30) 198 I

מִי־יִתֵּן 35 idiom: who will give or grant? = O that! (9 · 24) 678 נתן 1.f

תָּו mark (1 · 1) 1063

שַׁדַּי name of God (31 · 48) 994

שֶׁכֶם 36 back; shoulder (2 · 22) 1014 I

ענד to bind around, upon (1 · 2 · 2) 772

עֲטָרָה crown, wreath (2 · 23) 742

צַעַד 37 step, steps (5 · 14) 857

נָגִיד ruler, prince, leader (2 · 44) 617

יַחַד 38 all together, altogether; in union, together (13 · 45) 403

תֶּלֶם furrow (2 · 5) 1068

כֹּחַ 39 strength, of soil = produce [idiom] 470

בְּלִי adv. used to negate an adj., noun, etc. = without (10 · 23) 115

הִפִּיחַ to cause to breathe out; to sniff (1 · 2 · 12) 655 נפח

חִטָּה 40 wheat (1 · 30) 334

חוֹחַ brier, bramble; hook, ring (2 · 11) 296

שְׂעֹרָה barley (1 · 33) 972

בָּאְשָׁה stinking or noxious weeds (1 · 1) 93

Chapter 32

צדק 2 Piel, to justify (2 · 5 · 41) 842

מַעֲנֶה 3 answer, reply, refutation (2 · 6) 775

הִרְשִׁיעַ to condemn as guilty; to act wickedly (8 · 25 · 34) 957

חכה to wait, tarry (2 · 13 · 14) 314

מַעֲנֶה 5 answer, reply, refutation (2 · 6) 775

צָעִיר 6 young; little, insignificant (2 · 22) 859

יָשִׁישׁ aged (4 · 4) 450

זחל to fear, be afraid [Lis. to hide] (1 · 3 · 3) 267 II

חוה Piel, to declare, tell (5 · 6 · 6) 296 III

דֵּעַ opinion, judgment; knowledge (5 · 5) 395

אָכֵן 8 but indeed, but in fact; surely, truly (1 · 18) 38

אֱנוֹשׁ man, mankind; [coll.] men; indiv. man (18 · 42) 60

נְשָׁמָה breath (7 · 24) 675

שַׁדַּי name of God (31 · 48) 994 see 5:17

חָכַם 9 to be or become wise, act wisely (1 · 18 · 26) 314

חוה 10 Piel, to declare, tell (5 · 6 · 6) 296

דֵּעַ opinion, judgment; knowledge (5 · 5) 395

הוֹחִיל 11 to wait for [לְ], hope for; wait (2 · 15 · 42) 403 יחל

הֶאֱזִין to hear, give ear, listen (6 · 41 · 41) 24

תְּבוּנָה obj. of knowledge, understanding, act of understanding; faculty of understanding (4 · 42) 108

חקר to search, search for, search through, examine (6 · 22 · 27) 350

מִלָּה   word, speech, utterance (34 · 38) 576

אָמַר 12 utterance, word; promise, decree
(11 · 48) 56

נָדַף 13 to drive about, drive asunder
(1 · 3 · 9) 623

מִלָּה 14 word, speech, utterance (34 · 38) 576

אֵמֶר   utterance, word; promise, decree
(11 · 48) 56

הֶעְתִּיק 15 to move forward; remove; transcribe (2 · 5 · 9) 801

מִלָּה   word, speech, utterance (34 · 38) 576

הוֹחִיל 16 to wait, wait for [לְ], hope for;
(2 · 15 · 42) 403 יחל

חָוָה 17 *Piel*, to declare, tell (5 · 6 · 6) 296
III

דֵּעַ   opinion, judgment; knowledge
(5 · 5) 395

מִלָּה 18 word, speech, utterance (34 · 38) 576

הֵצִיק   to bring into straits, constrain
(1 · 11 · 11) 847 I

אוֹב 19 skin bottle; necromancer (1 · 1[?])
15

רָוַח 20 to be wide, spacious; here = to be
relief [לְ] for (1 · 2 · 14) 926

נָשָׂא פָּנִי 21 to lift up one's face, countenance
= show favor or even partiality 670
1.b (3)

כִּנָּה   *Piel*, to give a title to; perh. *Pual*
here = to give a flattering title
(2 · 4 · 4) 487

כִּנָּה 22 *Piel*, to give a title to; perh. *Pual*
here = to give a flattering title
(2 · 4 · 4) 487

Chapter 33

אוּלָם 1 but in very deed, but indeed, but
(10 · 19) 19 III

מִלָּה   word, speech, utterance; byword
(34 · 38) 576

הֶאֱזִין   to hear, give ear, listen (6 · 41 · 41)
24

חֵךְ 2 palate, roof of mouth, gums
(7 · 18) 335

יֹשֶׁר 3 rightness, uprightness; straightness
(3 · 14) 449

אֵמֶר   utterance, word; promise, decree
(11 · 48) 56

בָּרוּר   pass. ptc. = pure, sincere (1 · 2)
140

מָלַל   to say, utter (2 · 4 · 5) 576 I

נְשָׁמָה 4 breath (7 · 24) 675

שַׁדַּי   name of God (31 · 48) 994 see 5:17

הִתְיַצֵּב 5 to station oneself, take one's stand
(6 · 48 · 48) 426

כְּפִי 6 in proportion of or to; according as
(2 · 16) 805 פֶּה 6.b

חֹמֶר   clay, mire; mortar, cement (7 · 17)
330

קֹרַץ   *Pual*, to be nipped off (1 · 1 · 5) 902

אֵימָה 7 terror, dread (6 · 17) 33

בָּעַת   *Piel*, to fall upon, overwhelm
(8 · 13 · 16) 129

אֶכֶף   pressure (1 · 1) 38

מִלָּה 8 word, speech, utterance (34 · 38) 576

זַךְ 9 pure, clean, righteous (4 · 11) 269

בְּלִי   adv. used to negate an adj., noun,
etc. = without (10 · 23) 115

חַף   clean (1 · 1) 342

תְּנוּאָה 10 opposition (1 · 2) 626

סַד 11 stocks [for confining the feet]
(2 · 2) 690

הֵן 12 = הֵן (10 · 12) 243

צדק   to have a just cause, be in the
right; to be justified; be just
(14 · 22 · 41) 842

אֱנוֹשׁ   man, mankind; [coll.] men; indiv.
man (18 · 42) 60

שׁוּר 14 to regard, observe; watch, lie in
wait; behold (10 · 16 · 16) 1003 II

הַזָּיוֹן 15 vision; divine communication in a vision (4 · 9) 303

תַּרְדֵּמָה deep sleep (2 · 7) 922

תְּנוּמָה slumber (1 · 5) 630

מִשְׁכָּב bed, couch (3 · 46) 1012

מוּסָר 16 discipline, correction; chastisement (4 · 50[?]) 416 [but Lis. מוּסֵר fm. אסר = band, bond (2 · 12) 64]

חתם to seal, affix one's seal; seal up (4 · 23 · 27) 367

גֵּוָה 17 pride; lifting up (2 · 3) 145 I גאה

חָשַׂךְ 18 to keep מִן from; to withhold, keep back, hold in check; restrain (3 · 26 · 28) 362

מִנִּי poetic for מִן (19 · 30) 577

שַׁחַת pit, Sheol (7 · 23) 1001

חַיָּה life; living thing, animal (6 · 12[?]) 312 I

שֶׁלַח missile, weapon; sprout, shoot (2 · 8) 1019 I

מַכְאוֹב 19 pain (1 · 16) 456

מִשְׁכָּב bed, couch (3 · 46) 1012

אֵתָן constant, enduring, permanent; ever-flowing (2 · 14) 450

זהם 20 Piel, to make loathsome, foul (1 · 1 · 1) 263

חַיָּה life; living thing, animal (6 · 12[?]) 312 I

מַאֲכָל food (1 · 30) 38

תַּאֲוָה desire, wish (1 · 21) 16 I

רֳאִי 21 appearance; sight, looking, seeing (1 · 4) 909

שְׁפִי bareness; bare place, height (1 · 10) 1046 I

שפה Q Pual, to be laid bare (1 · 1 · 2) 1045 I

שַׁחַת 22 pit, Sheol (7 · 23) 1001

חַיָּה life; living thing, animal (6 · 12[?]) 312 I

לַמְמִתִים ל + Hiph. ptc. pl. מות 559

מֵלִיץ 23 Hiph. ptc. = interpreter; to deride (2 · 9 · 12) 539 ליץ

מִנִּי poetic for מִן (19 · 30) 577

יֹשֶׁר rightness, uprightness; straightness (3 · 14) 449

פדע 24 [dub.] impv.m. sing. suff. = deliver him (1 · 1 · 1) 804

שַׁחַת pit, Sheol (7 · 23) 1001

כֹּפֶר a price for ransom of a life (2 · 13) 497

רֳטֲפַשׁ 25 pass., to grow fresh (1 · 1 · 1) 936

נֹעַר youth, early life (2 · 4) 655

עֲלוּמִים youth, youthful vigor (2 · 4) 761

עתר 26 to pray, supplicate (1 · 5 · 20) 801 I

רָצָה to be pleased with, favorable to; accept; make acceptable (3 · 42 · 50) 953

תְּרוּעָה shout of joy, shout or blast of war, or alarm (3 · 36) 929

אֱנוֹשׁ man, mankind; [coll.] men; indiv. man (18 · 42) 60

שׁוּר 27 to behold, regard, watch, lie in wait (10 · 16 · 16[?]) [BDB, שׁיר to sing 1010] 1003 II

העוה to pervert (1 · 9 · 17) 730 I

שָׁוָה to be equal to [לְ], be like, resemble, agree with (1 · 8 · 16) 1000 I

שַׁחַת 28 pit, Sheol (7 · 23) 1001

חַיָּה life; living thing, animal (6 · 12 · [?]) 312 I

הֵן 29 = הֵן (10 · 12) 243

מִנִּי 30 poetic for מִן (19 · 30) 577

שַׁחַת pit, Sheol (7 · 23) 1001

נאור Niph., to be or become lighted up (1 · 1 · 40[?]) 21

הִקְשִׁיב 31 to give attention (2 · 45 · 46) 904

הֶחֱרִישׁ to be silent; make silent; be deaf (9 · 38 · 46) 361

מִלָּה 32 word, speech, utterance; byword (34 · 38) 576

צדק Piel, to justify (2 · 5 · 41) 842

515

הַחֲרֵישׁ 33 to be silent; make silent; be deaf
(9 · 38 · 46) 361

אלף   *Piel*, to teach (3 · 3 · 4) 48 I

Chapter 34

מִלָּה 2 word, speech, utterance (34 · 38) 576

הַאֲזִין   to hear, give ear, listen (6 · 41 · 41)
24 I

מִלָּה 3 word, speech, utterance; byword
(34 · 38) 576

בָּחַן   to prove, test, try; examine
(4 · 25 · 29) 103

חֵךְ   palate, roof of mouth, gums
(7 · 18) 335

טָעַם   to taste (2 · 11 · 11) 380

צדק 5 to have a just cause, be in the
right; to be justified; be just
(14 · 22 · 41) 842

כָּזַב 6 to lie, tell a lie; disappoint, fail
(2 · 12 · 16) 469

אָנוּשׁ   pass. ptc. = adj. incurable (1 · 8)
60 I

חֵץ   here idiom for "wound"; elsewhere arrow (>50) 346

בְּלִי   adv. used to negate an adj., noun,
etc. = without (10 · 25) 115

לַעַג 7 mocking, derision, nearly; here =
blasphemy (1 · 7) 541

אָרַח 8 to journey, go (1 · 2 · 2[?]) 72

חֶבְרָה   company, association (1 · 1) 288

רֶשַׁע   wickedness (3 · 30) 957

סכן 9 to benefit, profit; be of use or service to (5 · 5 · 10) 698 I

רָצָה   to be pleased with, favorable to;
accept; make acceptable (3 · 43 · 50)
953

חָלִילָה 10 far be it (from me, you, etc.)
(2 · 21) 321

רֶשַׁע   wickedness (3 · 30) 957

שַׁדַּי   name of God (31 · 48) 994 see 5:17

עָוֶל   injustice, unrighteousness (2 · 21)
732

פֹּעַל 11 deed, thing done; work, thing
made; wages; acquisition (5 · 37) 821

אָמְנָם 12 verily, truly (6 · 9) 53

הִרְשִׁיעַ   to act wickedly; condemn as guilty
(8 · 25 · 34) 957

שַׁדַּי   name of God (31 · 48) 994 see 5:17

עוּת   *Piel*, to make crooked, pervert
(4 · 9 · 11) 736

תֵּבֵל 13 world, earth (3 · 35) 385

נְשָׁמָה 14 breath (7 · 24) 675

גָּוַע 15 to expire, perish, die (8 · 23 · 23)
157

יַחַד   all together, altogether; together
(13 · 45) 403

בִּינָה 16 understanding, understanding as
obj. of knowledge (8 · 37) 108, 106

הַאֲזִין   to hear, give ear, listen (6 · 41 · 41)
24 I

מִלָּה   word, speech, utterance (34 · 38) 576

שֹׂנֵא 17 ptc. = enemy, foe (2 · 41) 971

חבש   to restrain, control; to bind
(3 · 28 · 32) 289

כַּבִּיר   mighty, here = aged; great, much
(7 · 10) 460

הִרְשִׁיעַ   to condemn as guilty; to act
wickedly (8 · 25 · 34) 957

בְּלִיַּעַל 18 worthlessness; ruin, destruction
(1 · 27) 116

נָדִיב   noble, princely; inclined, willing
(3 · 27) 622

נָשָׂא פָנִים 19 to lift up one's face, countenance
= show favor or even partiality 670
1.b (3)

נִכַּר   *Piel*, to regard (1 · 1 · 41) 647 I

שׁוֹעַ   independent, noble (1 · 2) 447

דַּל   reduced, weak, helpless; poor, thin
(6 · 48) 195

רֶגַע 20 in a moment, suddenly; moment; for a moment (4 · 22) 921

חָצוֹת division, middle (1 · 3) 345

גָּעַשׁ *Pual*, to be shaken up, convulsed (1 · 1 · 10) 172

אַבִּיר mighty [here = violent], valiant (2 · 17) 7

צַעַד 21 step, steps (5 · 14) 857

צַלְמָוֶת 22 deep shadow, darkness; death shadow (10 · 18) 853

שִׂים 23 idiom; pay attention to, שִׂים *Qal* 2.b 963

רָעַע 24 to break; be broken (1 · 3 · 5) 949 II

כַּבִּיר mighty, here = aged; great, much (7 · 10) 460

חֵקֶר searching, thing to be searched out; לֹא חֵקֶר = it is unsearchable (7 · 12) 350

הִכִּיר 25 to regard, observe; recognize; be acquainted with; distinguish (6 · 38 · 41) 647

מַעְבָּד work (1 · 1) 716

הִדַּכָּא *Hithpael*, to be crushed, let oneself be crushed (2 · 2 · 18) 193

סָפַק 26 to slap, chastise; clap (2 · 6 · 6) 706

צְעָקָה 28 cry of distress, outcry (3 · 21) 858

דַּל reduced, weak, helpless; poor, thin (6 · 48) 195

הִשְׁקִיט 29 to cause quietness, show quietness (2 · 10 · 41) 1052

הִרְשִׁיעַ to condemn as guilty; to act wickedly (8 · 25 · 34) 957

שׁוּר to regard, observe; watch, lie in wait; behold (10 · 16 · 16) 1003 II

יַחַד all together, altogether; together (13 · 45) 403

חָנֵף 30 profane, godless; godless man (8 · 13) 338

מוֹקֵשׁ snare, bait or lure (2 · 27) 430

חָבַל 31 to act corruptly [לְ] against (1 · 3 · 11) 287 II

בִּלְעֲדֵי 32 except, apart from (1 · 5) 116

הוֹרָה to direct, teach, instruct; to point out; to throw (6 · 45 · 45[?]) 434 ירה

עָוֶל injustice, unrighteousness (2 · 21) 732

בִּי 36 to entreat אָבִי [1st imperf.] entreat that = would that (1 · 1 · 1) 106 ביי

נִבְחַן to be tried, proved (1 · 3 · 29) 103

נֶצַח endurance in time; עַד-נֶצַח = unto the end; enduring of time, life (6 · 43) 664 I

תְּשׁוּבָה answer; return (2 · 8) 1000

סָפַק 37 to slap, clap (2 · 6 · 6) 706

אֹמֶר utterance, word; promise, decree (11 · 48) 56

Chapter 35

סָכַן 3 to benefit, profit; be of use or service to (5 · 5 · 10) 698 I

הוֹעִיל to benefit, profit; be of use or service to (4 · 23 · 23) 418 I יעל

מִלָּה 4 word, byword; speech, utterance (34 · 38) 576

שׁוּר 5 to regard, observe; watch, lie in wait; behold (10 · 16 · 16) 1003 II

שַׁחַק cloud, fine dust (5 · 21) 1007

גָּבַה to be high, lofty, tall; be exalted (2 · 24 · 34) 146

רָבַב 6 to be [become] many; become great (1 · 23 · 24) 912 I

צָדַק 7 to be just; be justified; have a just cause (14 · 22 · 41) 842

רֶשַׁע 8 wickedness (3 · 30) 957

עֲשׁוּקִים 9 oppression, extortion (1 · 4) 799

שׁוַּע *Piel*, to cry for help (8 · 21 · 21) 1002

אַיֵּה 10 where? (5 · 44) 32

עֹשֶׂה ptc. = maker (2 · 24) 794 II 1.b

517

זָמִיר   song (1 · 6) 274   I

אלף   11 *Piel* ptc. = to teach (3 · 3 · 4) 48   I
אלף

חכם   to make wise, teach wisdom
(1 · 3 · 26) 314

גָּאוֹן   12 pride; exaltation, majesty, excellence (4 · 49) 144

שַׁדַּי   13 name of God (31 · 48) 994 see 5:17

שׁוּר   to regard, observe; watch, lie in
wait; behold (10 · 16 · 16) 1003   II

אַף־כִּי   14 normally = how much more, but
here is simply yea, when... (4 · 26)
65 אף 3

שׁוּר   to behold; regard, watch; lie in
wait (10 · 16 · 16) 1003   II

דִּין   cause, plea; judgment (4 · 19) 192

חוֹלל   *Polel* [Lis. pil.] to wait anxiously;
to writhe (1 · 1 · 5[?]) 296   I

פַּשׁ   15 folly (1 · 1) 832

פצה   16 to open; w. פֶּה = utter (1 · 15 · 15)
822

בִּבְלִי   without (2 · 5) 115 בלה

מִלָּה   word, byword; speech, utterance
(34 · 38) 576

הכביר   to make many, in abundance
(2 · 2 · 2) 460

Chapter 36

כתר   2 to surround, but here wait, I pray
(1 · 3 · 6) 509

זְעֵיר   a little (1 · 4) 277

חוה   *Piel*, to declare, tell (5 · 6 · 6) 296
III

מִלָּה   word, byword; speech, utterance
(34 · 38) 576

דֵּעַ   3 opinion, judgment; knowledge
(5 · 5) 395

לְמֵרָחוֹק   from a distance (2 · 8) 935 רחוק   2.a
(5)

אָמְנָם   4 verily, truly (6 · 9) 53

מִלָּה   word, byword; speech, utterance
(34 · 38) 576

דֵּעָה   knowledge (1 · 6) 395

הֵן   5 = הִנֵּה (10 · 12) 243

כַּבִּיר   mighty, much, great (7 · 10) 460

גרע   7 to withdraw; restrain; diminish
(3 · 14 · 22) 175

נֶצַח   endurance in time; לָנֶצַח = forever
(6 · 43) 664   I

גָּבַהּ   to be exalted; be high, lofty
(2 · 24 · 34) 146

זֵק   8 fetter (1 · 4) 279   II

חֶבֶל   cord, rope; measuring cord; measured portion (3 · 49) 286   I

עֳנִי   affliction, poverty (6 · 36) 777

פֹּעַל   9 deed, thing done; work, thing
made; wages; acquisition (5 · 37) 821

התגבר   to behave proudly; to show oneself
mighty (2 · 3 · 25) 149

מוּסָר   10 correction, discipline; chastening
(4 · 50) 416

נָעִים   11 as subst. = delight; delightful;
lovely, beautiful (1 · 13) 653   I

שֶׁלַח   12 missile, weapon; sprout, shoot
(2 · 8) 1019

גָּוַע   to expire, perish, die (8 · 23 · 23)
157

בִּבְלִי   without (2 · 5) 115 בלה

חָנֵף   13 godless man; profane, godless
(8 · 13) 338

שׁוּע   *Piel*, to cry for help (8 · 21 · 21)
1002

נֹעַר   14 youth, early life (2 · 4) 655

חַיָּה   life; living thing, animal (6 · 12[?])
312   I

קָדֵשׁ   temple prostitute (1 · 11) 873   I

חָלַץ   15 to rescue, deliver; pull out, tear out
(1 · 14 · 27) 322

עֳנִי   affliction, poverty (6 · 36) 777

518

לַחַץ		oppression, distress (1 · 12) 537
הסית	16	to allure, incite; instigate (3 · 18 · 18) 694 סות
צַר		straights, distress (6 · 20) 865
רַחַב		broad expanse, breadth (2 · 2) 931
מוּצָק		distress, constraint (2 · 3) 848 צוק
נַחַת		quietness, quiet attitude; rest (2 · 7) 629
דֶּשֶׁן		fatness; fat ashes (1 · 15) 206
דִּין	17	judgment, condemnation; cause, plea (4 · 19) 192
תמך		to grasp, lay hold of; hold up, support; hold, keep (1 · 20 · 21) 1069
הסית	18	to allure, incite; instigate (3 · 18 · 18) 694 סות
סֶפֶק		[dub.] handclapping; i.e., mockery (1 · 1) 706 שֶׁפֶק
כֹּפֶר		a price for ransom of a life (2 · 13) 497
שׁוּעַ	19	cry for help (2 · 2) 1002
צַר		straights, distress (6 · 20) 865
מַאֲמָץ		power, strength, force (1 · 1) 55
שָׁאַף	20	to gasp, pant, be eager for (3 · 14 · 14) 983
עֲנִי	21	affliction, poverty (6 · 36) 777
הֵן	22	= הֵן (10 · 12) 243
הַשְׂגִּיב		to act exaltedly (1 · 1 · 20) 960
מוֹרֶה		teacher (1 · 9) 435 II ירה
עַוְלָה	23	injustice, unrighteousness, wrong (10 · 32) 732
הַשְׂגִּיא	24	to magnify; make great (2 · 2 · 2[?]) 960
פֹּעַל		deed, thing done; work, thing made; wages; acquisition (5 · 37) 821
אֱנוֹשׁ	25	man, mankind; [coll.] men; indiv. man (18 · 42) 60
מֵרָחוֹק		from a distance (3 · 24) 935 רָחוֹק 2.a (1)
הֵן	26	= הֵן (10 · 12) 243
שַׂגִּיא		great (2 · 2) 960 שגא

חֵקֶר		searching, thing to be searched out; לֹא חֵקֶר = it is unsearchable (7 · 12) 350
גרע	27	Piel, to withdraw = draw up (1 · 1 · 22) 175
נָטָף		drop (1 · 1) 643
זקק		to refine, purify (2 · 2 · 7) 279 I
מָטָר		rain (7 · 38) 564
אֵד		mist (1 · 2) 15
נזל	28	to flow, trickle, drop; distil (1 · 8 · 9) 633
שַׁחַק		cloud, fine dust (5 · 21) 1007
רעף		to trickle, drip (1 · 4 · 5) 950
מִפְרָשׂ	29	spreading out, thing spread out (1 · 2) 831
עָב		dark cloud mass; thicket (8 · 30) 728
תְּשֻׁאָה		noise (2 · 4) 996
סֻכָּה		booth; thicket (3 · 31) 697
שֹׁרֶשׁ	30	root (9 · 33) 1057
דָּן	31	to execute judgment; act as a judge; plead the cause; govern (1 · 23 · 24) 192 דין
אֹכֶל		food (6 · 44) 38
הכביר		to make in abundance, make many (2 · 2 · 2) 460
הִפְגִּיעַ	32	unus. mng.: to make attack; to make entreaty (1 · 6 · 46) 803
רֵעַ	33	shouting, roar [dub] (1 · 3) 929
עוֹלָה		Lis p. 1065 Qal ptc. but BDB עַוְלָה injustice, unrighteousness, wrong (10 · 32) 732 (cf. 749 Qal 10)

Chapter 37

חָרַד	1	to tremble at [לְ], quake, be terrified (1 · 23 · 29) 353
נתר		to start up, spring up (1 · 1 · 7) 684 I
רֹגֶז	2	raging, wrath; agitation; excitement (5 · 7) 919

הֶגֶה   a rumbling, growling sound; a moaning; sigh (1 · 3) 211

שָׁרָה   3 to let loose (1 · 1 · 2) 1056 I

שָׁאַג   4 to roar (1 · 20 · 20) 980

הרעים   to thunder, cause to thunder (3 · 8 · 11) 947

גָּאוֹן   exaltation, majesty, excellence; pride (4 · 49) 144

עקב   to attack at the heel [dub.] [Lis. p.1109 to hold back] (1 · 1 · 1) 784

הרעים   5 to thunder, cause to thunder (3 · 8 · 11) 947

נִפְלָאוֹת   *Niph.* ptc. = wonderful acts (5 · 44) 810 פלא 3.b

שֶׁלֶג   6 snow (5 · 20) 1017

הוא   to fall (1 · 1 · 1) 216

גֶּשֶׁם   rain, shower (2 · 35) 177 II

מָטָר   rain (7 · 38) 564

חתם   7 to seal, affix one's seal; seal up (4 · 23 · 27) 367

בְּמוֹ   8 poetic for בְּ (4 · 10) 91

אֶרֶב   covert, lair; a lying in wait (2 · 2) 70

מְעוֹנָה   den, lair; habitation (2 · 9) 733

חֶדֶר   9 chamber (2 · 37) 293

סוּפָה   storm-wind (3 · 15) 693

מְזָרִים   *Piel* ptc. pl. = scatterers (1 · 1) 279

קָרָה   coldness (2 · 5) 903

נְשָׁמָה   10 breath (7 · 24) 675

קֶרַח   ice, frost (3 · 7) 901

מוּצָק   constraint, distress (2 · 3) 848 צוק

רִי   11 moisture (1 · 1) 924

הטריח   to burden (1 · 1 · 1) 382

עָב   dark cloud, cloud mass; thicket (8 · 30) 728

מֵסַב   12 that which surrounds or is round = on all sides, in all directions (1 · 5) 687

תַּחְבֻּלָה   direction, guidance, counsel (1 · 6) 287

תֵּבֵל   world, earth (3 · 35) 385

הַאֲזִין   14 to hear, give ear, listen (6 · 41 · 41) 24

נִפְלָאוֹת   *Niph.* ptc. = wonderful acts (5 · 44) 810 פלא 3.b

הוֹפִיעַ   15 to cause to shine; shine out (4 · 8 · 8) 422 יפע

מִפְלָשׂ   16 swaying, poising (1 · 1) 814

עָב   dark cloud, cloud mass; thicket (8 · 30) 728

מִפְלָאָה   wondrous work (1 · 1) 811

דֵּעַ   knowledge; opinion, judgment (5 · 5) 395

חַם   17 hot (1 · 2) 328

הִשְׁקִיט   to show quietness; cause quietness (2 · 10 · 41) 1052

דָּרוֹם   south (1 · 17) 204

הִרְקִיעַ   18 to make a spreading (1 · 1 · 11) 955

שַׁחַק   cloud, fine dust (5 · 21) 1007

רְאִי   mirror (1 · 1) 909

בלע   20 *Pual*, to be swallowed up (1 · 2 · 2 [?]) 118

בָּהִיר   21 bright, brilliant (1 · 1) 97

שַׁחַק   cloud, fine dust (5 · 21) 1007

אָתָה   22 to come (4 · 19 · 21) 87

נוֹרָא   *Niph.* ptc = awe-inspiring, dreadful (1 · 44) 431 ירא

הוֹד   splendor, majesty (3 · 24) 217 I

שַׁדַּי   23 name of God (31 · 48) 994 see 5:17

שַׂגִּיא   great (2 · 2) 960

Chapter 38

סְעָרָה   1 tempest, storm-wind (2 · 16) 704

הֶחְשִׁיךְ   2 to obscure, confuse; make dark; to hide, conceal (1 · 6 · 17) 364

מִלָּה   word, byword; speech, utterance (34 · 38) 576

בְּלִי   adv. used to negate an adj., noun, etc. = without (10 · 23) 115 בלה

אזר   3 to gird, gird on (3 · 6 · 16) 25

520

חָלָץ	dual only, loins (3 · 10) 323	הִתְיַצֵּב	to station oneself, take one's stand (6 · 48 · 48) 426
אֵיפֹה 4	where? (7 · 25) 33	לְבוּשׁ	garment, clothing (7 · 31) 528
יָסַד	to found, establish; appoint (1 · 20 · 41) 413	נִמְנַע 15	to be withheld (1 · 4 · 29) 586
בִּינָה	understanding as object of knowledge; act or faculty of understanding (8 · 37) 108	רָם	Qal ptc. as adj. (2 · 31) 926 רום
		גֶּבֶךְ 16	spring (1 · 1) 614
מֵמַד 5	measurement (1 · 1) 551	חֵקֶר	searching, thing to be searched out; לֹא חֵקֶר = it is unsearchable (7 · 12) 350
קָו	line, measuring line (1 · 25) 876		
עַל־מָה 6	upon what? (3[?]-) 552 מָה 4.f	תְּהוֹם	deep sea, abyss (4 · 36) 1062
הָטְבַּע	to be sunk, settled, planted (1 · 3 · 10) 371	צַלְמָוֶת 17	deep shadow, darkness; death shadow (10 · 18) 853
יָרָה	to cast [= lay, set]; throw; shoot; teach (1 · 13 · 25) 434	רַחַב 18	breadth, broad expanse (2 · 2) 931
פִּנָּה	corner (2 · 30) 819	אֵי־זֶה 19	idiom; which [of two or more]? (5 · 15) 32 אֵי 2a
יַחַד 7	all together, altogether; in union, together (13 · 45) 403	נְתִיבָה 20	path, pathway (4 · 21) 677
		שֶׁלֶג 22	snow (5 · 20) 1017
כּוֹכָב	star (5 · 37) 456	בָּרָד	hail (1 · 29) 135
הֵרִיעַ	to shout in applause; raise a shout in triumph, for march, etc,; to give a blast [w. horn] (2 · 40 · 44) 929 רוע	חָשַׂךְ 23	to reserve [לְ] for; = withhold; keep back (5 · 26 · 28) 362
		צַר	straights, distress (6 · 20) 865
הֵסִיךְ 8	to shut in (2 · 2 · 4) 692 II סוּךְ	קְרָב	battle, war (1 · 8) 898
גִיחַ	to burst forth; draw forth (2 · 3 · 5) 161	אֵי־זֶה 24	idiom; which [of two or more]? (5 · 15) 32 אֵי 2a
רֶחֶם	womb (5 · 33) 933	פָּלַג 25	to cleave; split, divide (1 · 2 · 4) 811
לְבוּשׁ 9	garment, clothing (7 · 31) 528	שֶׁטֶף	flood (1 · 6) 1009
עֲרָפֶל	cloud, heavy cloud (2 · 15) 791	תְּעָלָה	watercourse, conduit, trench (1 · 9) 752
חֲתֻלָּה	swaddling band (1 · 1) 367		
בְּרִיחַ 10	bar (1 · 41) 138	חֲזִיז	thunderbolt, lightning flash (2 · 3) 304
עַד־פֹּה 11	until here (1 · 1) 805 פֹּה 1.b	הִמְטִיר 26	to send rain, to rain (2 · 6 · 17) 565
פֹּא	here, hither (2 · 45) 805 פֹּה	שֹׁאָה 27	ruin, waste; devastation (4 · 13) 996
גָּאוֹן	exaltation, majesty, excellence; pride (4 · 49) 144	מְשׁוֹאָה	noise [of devastation or storm], but see previous entry (2 · 3) 996
גַּל	wave, roller; heap (1 · 16) 164	הִצְמִיחַ	to cause to grow, cause to sprout (1 · 14 · 33) 855
שַׁחַר 12	dawn (3 · 23) 1007		
נִנְעַר 13	Niph., to be shaken (1 · 3 · 11) 654 II	מוֹצָא	place of going forth, here = mine; act of going forth; issue, export; source, spring (2 · 27) 425
חֹמֶר 14	[entry not in BDB] cement, mortar, clay (7 · 17) 330	דֶּשֶׁא	grass (2 · 14) 206
חוֹתָם	seal, signet ring (2 · 14) 368	מָטָר 28	rain (7 · 38) 564

אֵגֶל drop [dub.] (1 · 1) 8

טַל night mist, dew (2 · 31) 378

קֶרַח 29 ice; frost (3 · 7) 901

כְּפוֹר hoar frost (1 · 3) 499 IV

הִתְחַבָּא 30 to draw together, thicken, harden; draw back; hide oneself (1 · 10 · 34) 285

תְּהוֹם deep sea, abyss (4 · 36) 1062

קָשַׁר 31 to bind fast; bind on (1 · 2 · 43) 905

מַעֲדַנּוֹת bonds, bands (1 · 2) 772

כִּימָה Pleiades (2 · 3) 465

מֹשֶׁכֶת cord (1 · 1) 604

כְּסִיל Orion (2 · 4) 493

מַזָּרוֹת 32 a particular star or constellation [dub.] (1 · 1) 561

עַיִשׁ a constellation, perh. Great Bear (2 · 2) 747

הנחה Hiph., to guide, lead (3 · 26 · 40) 634

מִשְׁטָר 33 rule, authority [Lis. p.871 writing] (1 · 1) 1009

עָב 34 dark cloud, cloud mass; thicket (8 · 30) 728

שִׁפְעָה multitude, abundance (2 · 6) 1051

בָּרָק 35 lightning, lightning flashes (2 · 21) 140

טֻחוֹת 36 inward parts (1 · 2) 376

שֶׂכְוִי perh. a celestial appearance, phenomenon [Lis. p.1373 cock] (1 · 1) 967

בִּינָה understanding as object of knowledge; act or faculty of understanding (8 · 37) 108

שַׁחַק 37 cloud, fine dust (5 · 21) 1007

נֵבֶל skin bottle, skin; jar, pitcher (1 · 11) 614

מוּצָק 38 a casting (1 · 2) 427

רֶגֶב clod [of earth] (2 · 2) 918

צוד 39 to hunt (2 · 13 · 17) 844 I

לָבִיא lion, lioness (2 · 11) 522

טֶרֶף prey; food; leaf (3 · 17) 383

חַיָּה appetite [here only]; life; living thing, animal (6 · 12[?]) 312

כְּפִיר young lion (2 · 31) 498

שׁחח 40 to crouch, be bowed down, bow (2 · 12 · 28) 1005

מְעוֹנָה den, lair; habitation (2 · 9) 733

סֻכָּה thicket; booth (3 · 31) 697

לְמוֹ poetic for לְ (4 · 4) 518

אֶרֶב a lying in wait; covert, lair (2 · 2) 70

עֹרֵב 41 raven (1 · 12) 788

צַיִד provision, food (1 · 5) 845

שׁוע Piel, to cry for help (8 · 21 · 21) 1002

תָּעָה to wander about, err (1 · 27 · 50) 1073

לִבְלִי regardless of, without (2 · 3) 115 בְּלִי w. preps. b.

אֹכֶל food (6 · 44) 38

Chapter 39

יָעֵל 1 mountain goat (1 · 3) 418

חולל Polel [Lis. pil.] to writhe with, bear, bring forth (1 · 7 · 47) 296

אַיָּלָה hind, doe (1 · 11) 19

יֶרַח 2 month (4 · 12) 437 I

כָּרַע 3 to bow down, bow (3 · 30 · 36) 502

פלח to cause to cleave open, cleave open (2 · 4 · 5) 812

חֵבֶל pains of travail (1 · 8) 286 [Lis. fetus (1 · 1) p.460]

חָלַם 4 to be healthy, strong (1 · 27 · 29) 321 I

בַּר field, open field (1 · 1) 141

פֶּרֶא wild ass (4 · 10) 825

חָפְשִׁי free (2 · 17) [spec. entry not in BDB] 344

מוֹסֵר band, bond (2 · 12) 64

עָרוֹד wild ass (1 · 1) 789

מְלֵחָה 6 saltness, barrenness (1 · 3) 572
שָׂחַק 7 to laugh; sport, play (7 · 19 · 36) 965
קִרְיָה town, city (1 · 30) 900
תְּשֻׁאָה noise (2 · 4) 996
נֹגֵשׂ ptc. = driver, taskmaster (2 · 15) 620
יְתוּר 8 a searching (1 · 1) 1064
מִרְעֶה pasturage, pasture (1 · 13) 945
יָרוֹק green thing (1 · 1) 438
רְאֵם wild ox (2 · 9) 910
אֵבוּס crib, feeding-trough (1 · 3) 7
קָשַׁר 10 to bind, confine; league together (2 · 35 · 43) 905
רְאֵם wild ox (2 · 9) 910
תֶּלֶם furrow (2 · 5) 1068
עֲבֹת cord, rope (1 · 24) 721
שָׂדַד to harrow (1 · 3 · 3) 961
יְגִיעַ 11 toil; result of toil, product, produce (3 · 16) 388
גֹּרֶן 12 threshing floor (1 · 34) 175
רְנָנִים 13 [bird of] piercing cries [i.e., ostrich] (1 · 1) 943
נֶעֱלָס to be joyous, here = flap joyously (1 · 1 · 3) 763
אֶבְרָה pinion (1 · 4) 7
חֲסִיד kind [Lis. p.514 stork] (1 · 6) 339
נוֹצָה plumage (1 · 3) 663
בֵּיצָה 14 egg (1 · 6) 101
חָמַם to keep warm (1 · 1 · 26) 328
זוּר 15 to press, wring out (1 · 3 · 3) 266 III
דָּשׁ to tread on, trample on; thresh (1 · 13 · 16) 190 דושׁ
הִקְשִׁיחַ 16 to treat harshly, roughly; make hard (1 · 2 · 2) 905
לְלוֹא without, in the condition of no...(3 · 10) 520 לא 4.e
רִיק emptiness, vanity; לְרִיק = in vain (1 · 12) 938
יְגִיעַ toil, result of toil, product, produce (3 · 16) 388

בְּלִי adv. used to negate an adj., noun, etc. = without (10 · 23) 115
פַּחַד dread, object of dread (10 · 49) 808 I
הִשָּׁה 17 to cause to forget; allow to be forgotten (2 · 2 · 5) 674 II נשׁה
בִּינָה understanding as object of knowledge; act or faculty of understanding (8 · 37) 108
המריא 18 [dub.] to flap away (1 · 1 · 1) 597 I
שָׂחַק to laugh; sport, play (7 · 19 · 36) 965
צַוָּאר 19 neck, back of neck (3 · 41) 848
רַעְמָה vibration, quivering [dub.] (1 · 1) 947
הרעישׁ 20 to cause to spring, leap; cause to quake (1 · 7 · 29) 950
אַרְבֶּה a kind of locust (1 · 24) 916
הוֹד majesty, majestic force; splendor (3 · 24) 217
נַחַר a snorting (1 · 1) 637
אֵימָה terror, dread (6 · 17) 33
חָפַר 21 to dig; search, search out (4 · 23 · 23) 343 I
שָׂשׂ to exult, display joy (2 · 27 · 27) 965 שׂושׂ
נֶשֶׁק equipment, weapons; armory (2 · 10) 676
שָׂחַק 22 to laugh; sport, play (7 · 19 · 36) 965
פַּחַד dread, object of dread (10 · 49) 808 I
רנה 23 to rattle (1 · 1 · 1) 943
אַשְׁפָּה quiver for arrows (1 · 6) 80
לַהַב flashing point, blade; flame (2 · 12) 529
חֲנִית spear; shaft of spear (2 · 47) 333
כִּידוֹן dart, javelin (2 · 9) 475
רַעַשׁ 24 earthquake, quaking; shaking (2 · 17) 950
רֹגֶז excitement; agitation; (5 · 7) 919
גמא to swallow (1 · 1 · 2) 167

בְּדֵי 25 as often as, what suffices for, in the abundance of (1 · 6) 191 דֵּי 2.a

הֶאָח Aha! (1 · 9) 210

מֵרָחוֹק from a distance (3 · 24) 935 רָחוֹק 2.a (1)-(4)

הֵרִיחַ to smell, perceive odor (1 · 11 · 14) 929

רַעַם thunder (2 · 6) 947

תְּרוּעָה shout or blast of war; or of alarm or joy (3 · 36) 929

בִּינָה 26 understanding as object of knowledge; act or faculty of understanding (8 · 37) 108

הַאֲבֶר to fly (1 · 1 · 1) 7

נֵץ a bird of prey, generic name incl. hawk and falcon (1 · 3) 665

תֵּימָן south, southern quarter; southwind (2 · 24) 412

הַגְבִּיהַ 27 to make high, exalt (2 · 10 · 34) 146

נֶשֶׁר griffon, vulture, eagle (2 · 26) 676

קֵן nest; nestlike cell or room (2 · 13) 890

הִתְלוֹנֵן 28 Hithpoel, to dwell, abide 533 לוּן

מְצוּדָה fastness, stronghold (1 · 18) 845

חָפַר 29 to dig; search, search out (4 · 23 · 23) 343 I

אֹכֶל food (6 · 44) 38

לְמֵרָחוֹק from a distance (2 · 8) 935 רחוק 2.a (5)

אֶפְרֹחַ 30 young one (1 · 4) 827 פרח I

עָלַע Piel [dub.] to drink (1 · 1 · 1) 763

בַּאֲשֶׁר in [the place] where; in [that] which; conj., in that, inasmuch as (1 · 19) 84

Chapter 40

שַׁדַּי name of God (31 · 48) 994 see 5:17

יִסּוֹר one who reproves, faultfinder (1 · 1) 416

לָמוֹ 4 poetic for לְ (4 · 4) 518

מִנִּי 6 poetic for מִן (19 · 30) 577

סְעָרָה tempest, storm wind (2 · 16) 704

אָזַר 7 to gird, gird on (3 · 16 · 16) 25

חָלָץ dual only, loins (3 · 10) 323

הֵפֵר 8 Hiph., to frustrate, make ineffectual (3 · 42 · 45) 830 פרר I

הִרְשִׁיעַ to condemn as guilty; act wickedly (8 · 25 · 34) 957

צָדַק to be justified; be just; have a just cause (14 · 22 · 41) 842

הַרְעֵים 9 to thunder; cause to thunder (3 · 8 · 11) 947

עָדָה 10 to deck oneself, ornament (1 · 8 · 8) 725 II

גָּאוֹן exaltation, majesty, excellence; pride (4 · 49) 144

גֹּבַהּ height (3 · 17) 147

הוֹד splendor, majesty (3 · 24) 217 I

הָדָר splendor, majesty; ornament (1 · 3) 214

עֶבְרָה 11 overflow, outburst; overflowing rage; arrogance (2 · 34) 720

גֵּאֶה proud (2 · 8) 144

הִשְׁפִּיל to lay low, humiliate; to set in a lower place; make low (2 · 19 · 30) 1050

גֵּאֶה 12 proud (2 · 8) 144

הַכְנִיעַ to humble; subdue (1 · 11 · 35) 488

הֲדֹךְ to cast or tread down (1 · 1 · 1) 213

טָמַן 13 to hide, conceal; טָמוּן = that which is darkened; darkness (6 · 28 · 31) 380

יַחַד altogether, all together; in union, together (13 · 45) 403

חָבַשׁ to bind, bind on, here in the sense of veil; bind up (3 · 28 · 32) 289

בְּהֵמוֹת 15 behemoth; i.e., hippopotamus (1 · 1) 97

חָצִיר green grass, herbage (1 · 18) 348

מָתְנַיִם 16 loins (2 · 47) 608

אוֹן strength; vigor; wealth (2 · 10[?]) 20 I

שָׁרִיר sinew, muscle (1 · 1) 1057

חפץ 17 to bend down (1 · 1 · 1) 343 II

זָנָב tail; end, stump (1 · 11) 275

גִּיד sinew (2 · 7) 161

פַּחַד thigh (1 · 1) 808 II

שׂרג Pual. to be intertwined (1 · 1 · 2) 974

אָפִיק 18 channel (3 · 18) 67

נְחוּשָׁה copper, bronze (4 · 10) 639

גֶּרֶם bone; strength; self (1 · 5) 175

מְטִיל wrought-metal rod (1 · 1) 564

בּוּל 20 produce, outgrowth (1 · 2) 385

שׂחק Piel, to sport, play (2 · 16 · 36) 965

צֶאֱלִים 21 a kind of lotus (2 · 2) 838

סֵתֶר hiding place; secrecy; covering (5 · 35) 712

בִּצָּה swamp (2 · 3) 130

סכך 22 to screen, cover, overshadow (1 · 12 · 18) 696 I

צֶאֱלִים a kind of lotus (2 · 2) 838

צְלָלוֹ from צֵל shadow 853

עֲרָבָה poplar (1 · 5) 788 II

עָשַׁק 23 to oppress, here [dub.] rush violently upon (2 · 36 · 37) 798

חפז to be alarmed; be in a hurry or alarm (1 · 6 · 9) 342

גיח to burst forth; draw forth (2 · 3 · 5) 161

מוֹקֵשׁ 24 snare, bait or lure (2 · 27) 430

נקב to pierce, bore; prick off, designate (2 · 13 · 19) 666 I

מָשַׁךְ 25 to draw, drag; proceed, march; draw out; trail (3 · 30 · 36) 604

לִוְיָתָן sea monster [= crocodile]; serpent, dragon, leviathan (2 · 6) 531

חַכָּה hook fastened in jaw, fishhook (1 · 3) 335

חֶבֶל cord, rope; measuring cord; mea-

sured portion (3 · 49) 286 I

הֵשְׁקִיעַ to make sink (1 · 2 · 6) 1054

אַגְמוֹן 26 rush, bulrush (2 · 5) 8

חוֹחַ hook, ring; brier, bramble (2 · 11) 296

נקב to pierce, bore; prick off, designate (2 · 13 · 19) 666 I

לְחִי jaw, jawbone; cheek (2 · 21) 534

תַּחֲנוּן 27 supplication for favor (1 · 18) 337

רַךְ soft; tender, delicate; weak (1 · 16) 940

שׂחק 29 Piel, to sport, play (2 · 16 · 36) 965

צִפּוֹר bird; birds (1 · 40) 861

קָשַׁר to bind, confine; league together (2 · 35 · 43) 905

כרה 30 to get by trade, make trade of (2 · 4 · 4) 500 II

חַבָּר partner, associate (1 · 1) 289

חָצָה to divide; halve (1 · 11 · 15) 345

כְּנַעֲנִי trader, merchant (1 · 4) 489, 1124

שֻׂכָּה 31 barb, spear (1 · 1) 968 IV

צִלְצָל spear (1 · 1) 852

דָּג fish (2 · 19) 185

Chapter 41

תּוֹחֶלֶת 1 hope (1 · 6) 404

נכזב to be made deceptive, be shown deceptive; be proved a liar (1 · 2 · 16) 469

הוּטַל Hoph., to be overwhelmed; to be hurled, hurled down (1 · 4 · 14) 376 טול

אַכְזָר 2 fierce, cruel; cruel one (2 · 4) 470

הִתְיַצֵּב to station oneself, take one's stand (6 · 48 · 48) 426

הִקְדִּים 3 to anticipate, come in front (1 · 2 · 26) 869

הֶחֱרִישׁ 4 to be silent; make silent; be deaf (9 · 38 · 46) 361

בַּדִּים parts, limbs; sing. = separation, part (2 · 6) 94

חִין grace [dub.] (1 · 1) 336

עֵרֶךְ order, row, here = symmetry; estimate (2 · 33) 789

לְבוּשׁ garment, clothing (7 · 31) 528

כֶּפֶל 5 double (2 · 3) 495

רֶסֶן jaw; halter (2 · 4) 943 I

אֵימָה 6 terror, dread (6 · 17) 33

גַּאֲוָה majesty, pride (1 · 19) 144

אָפִיק 7 channel (3 · 18) 67

מָגֵן from מָגֵן shield 171

חוֹתָם seal, signet ring (2 · 14) 368 I חתם 171

צַר tight, narrow, distress (6 · 20) 865 II

הִתְפָּרֵד 9 to be divided, separated from each other (2 · 4 · 26) 825 I

עֲטִישָׁה 10 sneezing (1 · 1) 743

ההל Hiph., to flash forth light (3 · 4 · 4 [?]) 237

עַפְעַף eyelid (3 · 10) 733

שַׁחַר dawn (3 · 23) 1007

לַפִּיד 11 torch (1 · 13) 542

כִּידוֹד spark (1 · 1) 461

נָחִיר 12 nostril (1 · 1) 638

עָשָׁן smoke (1 · 25) 798 I

דּוּד pot, kettle (1 · 7) 188

נפח to breathe, blow; דּוּד נ׳ a blown or heated pot (1 · 5 · 12) 655

אַגְמוֹן rush, bulrush (2 · 5) 8

גַּחֶלֶת 13 coal (1 · 18) 160

להט Piel, to set ablaze (1 · 9 · 11) 529

לַהַב flame; flashing point (2 · 12) 529

צַוָּאר 14 neck, back of neck (3 · 41) 848

דוץ to dance, spring, leap (1 · 1 · 1) 189

דְּאָבָה faintness, failure (1 · 1) 178

מַפָּל 15 hanging parts; refuse (1 · 2) 658

נמוט to be shaken, moved, overthrown (1 · 22 · 39) 556

פֶּלַח 16 millstone; cleavage, split, slice (1 · 6) 812

תַּחְתִּי lower; lowest (1 · 19) 1066

שְׂאֵת 17 uprising, getting up; dignity; swelling (3 · 7) 673

גור to be afraid; stand in awe (2 · 10 · 10) 158

שֶׁבֶר breaking, shattering; מִשְׁבָּרִים = from terror (1 · 45) 991 I

התחטא idiom: to miss oneself, be beside oneself (1 · >50) 307

הִשִּׂיג 18 to reach, attain to; overtake (2 · 29 · 49) 673 נשׂג

בְּלִי adv. used to negate an adj., noun, etc. = without (10 · 23) 115

חֲנִית spear; shaft of spear (2 · 47) 333

מַסָּע missile, dart (1 · 1) 652 II

שִׁרְיָה a weapon, perh. = lance, javelin (1 · 1) 1056

תֶּבֶן 19 straw (2 · 17) 1061

רִקָּבוֹן rottenness (1 · 1) 955

נְחוּשָׁה copper, bronze (4 · 10) 639

בֶּן־קֶשֶׁת 20 idiom: son of a bow = arrow 119 בֶּן 6

קַשׁ stubble, chaff (3 · 16) 905

קֶלַע sling (1 · 6) 887

קַשׁ 21 stubble, chaff (3 · 16) 905

תּוֹתָח name of a weapon, perh. club, mace (1 · 1) 450

שָׂחַק to laugh; sport, play (7 · 19 · 36) 965

רַעַשׁ shaking, quivering; (2 · 17) 950

כִּידוֹן dart, javelin (2 · 9) 475

חַדּוּד 22 sharpened, sharp, pointed (1 · 1) 292

חֶרֶשׂ fragment of earthenware, sherd; earthenware (1 · 17) 360

רפד to spread (1 · 1 · 3) 951

חָרוּץ sharp; diligent (1 · 4) 358

טִיט mire, mud (1 · 13) 376

הרתיח 23 to make to boil (1 · 1 · 3) 958

סִיר pot (1 · 29) 696 I

מְצוּלָה   deep, deep sea; depth (1 · 12) 846

מֶרְקָחָה   ointment pot, spice seasoning
(1 · 1) 955

הֵאִיר 24 to shine; cause to shine; give light
(1 · 34 · 40) 21 אור

נָתִיב   path, pathway (3 · 5) 677

תְּהוֹם   deep sea, abyss (4 · 36) 1062

שֵׂיבָה   grey hair, old age (1 · 20) 966

מָשָׁל 25 likeness, one like (1 · 1) 605 I

לִבְלִי   regardless of, without (2 · 3) 115 בְּלִי
w. preps. b

חַת   terror, fear (1 · 4) 369

גָּבֹהַּ 26 high, lofty, tall; exalted; haughty
(1 · 41) 147

שַׁחַץ   dignity, pride (2 · 2) 1006

Chapter 42

נבצר 2 to be withheld (1 · 2 · 4) 130

מְזִמָּה   purpose, discretion, device (2 · 19)
273

מִי זֶה 3 idiom: Who is this? 261 זֶה 4.b

הַעְלִים   to hide, conceal (1 · 11 · 29) 761 I

בְּלִי   adv. used to negate an adj., noun,
etc. = without (10 · 23) 115

נִפְלָאוֹת   *Niph*. ptc. = wonderful acts
(5 · 44) 810 פלא 4

שֵׁמַע 5 report, hearing (2 · 17) 1034

אֵפֶר 6 ashes (4 · 22) 68

נָשָׂא פָנִים 8 idiom: to lift up one's face, countenance = grant request or show fa-
vor [even partiality] 670 1.b.(3)

נְבָלָה   disgrace, disgraceful folly (1 · 13)
615

נָשָׂא פָנִים   idiom: to lift up one's face, countenance = grant request or show fa-
vor [even partiality] 670 1.b.(3)

שְׁבִית 10 in phrases w. שׁוּב or הֵשִׁיב = to restore the captivity or fortunes of
(1 · 26) 986

מִשְׁנֶה   double portion, double copy, second (1 · 36) 1041

נָד 11 to condole, show sympathy, show
grief; move to and fro, wander
aimlessly (2 · 20 · 27) 626 נוד

קְשִׂיטָה   a unit of unknown value, perh.
weight (1 · 3) 903

נֶזֶם   ring, earring, nose-ring (1 · 17)
633

צֶמֶד 12 couple, pair; span (2 · 15) 855

אָתוֹן   female ass (3 · 33) 87

שִׁבְעָנָה 13 rd. שִׁבְעָה seven 987 I שֶׁבַע 1.b

יָפֶה 15 fair, beautiful (1 · 41) 421

שָׂבֵעַ 17 satisfied, sated (3 · 10) 960

PROVERBS

Chapter 1

מָשָׁל 1 sentence of ethical wisdom; proverb; parable (6 · 39) 605 II

מוּסָר 2 discipline, correction; chastisement (30 · 50) 416

אֵמֶר utterance, word (22 · 48) 56

בִּינָה understanding (14 · 37) 108

מוּסָר 3 discipline, correction; chastisement (30 · 50) 416

מֵישָׁר uprightness, equity; evenness (5 · 19) 449

פֶּתִי 4 simple, open-minded (15 · 18) 834

עָרְמָה prudence; craftiness (3 · 5) 791

מְזִמָּה power of devising, discretion; purpose; evil thought, device (8 · 19) 273

לֶקַח 5 instruction; thing taught, teaching (6 · 9) 544

נָבוֹן *Niph*.ptc. = understanding or intelligent (one) (9 · 21) 106 בין

תַּחְבֻּלוֹת pl. only, counsels, direction, counsel (5 · 6) 287

מָשָׁל 6 sentence of ethical wisdom; proverb; parable (6 · 39) 605 II

מְלִיצָה satire, mocking poem (1 · 2) 539

חִידָה riddle, perplexing saying or question (1 · 17) 295

יִרְאָה 7 fear of God, reverence, piety; terror (14 · 45) 432

מוּסָר discipline, correction; chastisement (30 · 50) 416

אֱוִיל fool; foolish (19 · 26) 17

בַּז to despise (8 · 14 · 14) 100 I בוז

מוּסָר 8 discipline, correction; chastisement (30 · 50) 416

נָטַשׁ to forsake, abandon; leave; permit (3 · 33 · 40) 643

לִוְיָה 9 wreath (2 · 2) 531

עֲנָק necklace, neck pendant (1 · 3) 778 II

גַּרְגְּרוֹת neck (4 · 4) 176

פָּתָה 10 to entice, persuade, seduce; deceive (3 · 17 · 27) 834

חַטָּא sinner (3 · 19) 308

אָרַב 11 to lie in wait [with hostile purpose] (6 · 20 · 23) 70

צָפַן to lie hid, lurk; hide, treasure up (9 · 24 · 29) 860

נָקִי innocent [person], free from guilt, clean; exempt (2 · 43) 667

חִנָּם without cause; for no purpose; gratis (6 · 32) 336 חנן

בָּלַע 12 to swallow up, engulf; swallow down (1 · 20 · 41) 118

הוֹן 13 wealth; high value, price; sufficiency (18 · 26) 223

יָקָר precious, costly; glorious; weighty (6 · 35) 429

כִּיס 14 purse, bag (2 · 5) 476

מָנַע 15 to withhold, hold back (5 · 25 · 29) 586

נְתִיבָה path, course [of life] (6[?] · 21) 677

חִנָּם 17 without cause; for no purpose; gratis (6 · 32) 336 חנן

זרה *Pual*, to be scattered (1 · 2 · 38) 279

רֶשֶׁת net (2 · 22) 440

אָרַב 18 to lie in wait [with hostile purpose] (6 · 20 · 23) 70

צָפַן to lie hid, lurk; hide, treasure up (9 · 24 · 29) 860

בצע 19 to gain by violence; cut off, break off (2 · 10 · 16) 130

בֶּצַע unjust gain, gain by violence (3 · 23) 130

חָכְמוֹת 20 wisdom (3 · 4[?]) 315

רְחוֹב broad open place in city (5 · 43) 932

המה 21 ptc. fem. pl. = bustling streets; to murmur, growl, roar; (4 · 33 · 33) 242

אֹמֶר utterance, word (22 · 48) 56

עַד־מָתַי 22 until when? how long? (2 · 29) 607
מתי

פֶּתִי simple, open-minded (15 · 18) 834

פֶּתִי simplicity, lack of wisdom (1 · 1)
834

לֵץ ptc. = scorner (14 · 16) 539 ליץ

לָצוֹן scorning (2 · 3) 539

חָמַד to delight, take pleasure in, desire
(3 · 16 · 21) 326

תּוֹכַחַת 23 reproof, chiding; argument (16 · 24)
407

הַבִּיע to pour out; cause to bubble, ferment; to pour forth, belch
(3 · 10 · 11) 615 נבע

מֵאֵן 24 to refuse (3 · 46 · 46) 549

הִקְשִׁיב to give attention (8 · 45 · 46) 904

פָּרַע 25 to let alone = neglect; to let go,
let loose (5 · 13 · 16) 828

תּוֹכַחַת reproof, chiding; argument (16 · 24)
407

אֵיד 26 distress, calamity (6 · 24) 15

שָׂחַק to laugh; sport, play (3 · 19 · 36) 965

לַעַג to mock, deride (3 · 12 · 18) 541

פַּחַד dread; object of dread (4 · 49) 808 I

שָׁאֲוָה 27 to be read שׁוֹאָה = devastating
storm (1 · 1) 996 (cf. שָׁאֲוָה p.981) שׁוֹא

פַּחַד dread; object of dread (4 · 49) 808 I

אֵיד distress, calamity (6 · 24) 15 אוד

סוּפָה storm wind (2 · 15) 693 I

אָתָה to come (1 · 19 · 21) 87

צוּקָה pressure, distress (1 · 3) 848

שִׁחֵר 28 Piel, to seek early (4 · 12 · 13)
1007

יִרְאָה 29 fear of God, reverence, piety; fear,
terror (14 · 45) 432

נָאַץ 30 to contemn, spurn (3 · 8 · 24) 610

תּוֹכַחַת reproof, chiding; argument (16 · 24)
407

מוֹעֵצָה 31 counsel, plan, principle (2 · 7) 420

מְשׁוּבָה 32 apostate one; apostate, turning back
(1 · 12) 1000

פֶּתִי simple, open-minded (15 · 18) 834

שַׁלְוָה ease, careless security; quietness
(2 · 8) 1017

בֶּטַח 33 securely, security (4 · 43) 105 I

שַׁאֲנַן vb. Pa'l (Lis. Pil.) to be at ease,
secure (1 · 5 · 5) 983 שׁאן

פַּחַד dread; object of dread (4 · 49) 808 I

Chapter 2

אֹמֶר 1 word, utterance (22 · 48) 56

צָפַן to treasure up; lie hid, lurk; hide
(9 · 24 · 29) 860

הִקְשִׁיב 2 to give attention, here apparently
= cause to attend (8 · 45 · 46) 904

תְּבוּנָה understanding (19 · 42) 108

בִּינָה 3 understanding (14 · 37) 108

תְּבוּנָה understanding (19 · 42) 108

מַטְמוֹן 4 hidden treasure, treasure (1 · 5) 380

חפשׂ to search for, search; think out;
search = test (2 · 4 · 23) 344

יִרְאָה 5 fear of God, reverence, piety; fear,
terror (14 · 45) 432

תְּבוּנָה 6 understanding (19 · 42) 108

צָפַן 7 to treasure up, reserve; lie hid,
lurk; hide (9 · 24 · 29) 860

תּוּשִׁיָּה abiding success; sound efficient
wisdom (4 · 12) 444

תֹּם integrity; completeness; innocence
(7 · 23) 1070

חָסִיד 8 pious one, godly one[s]; kind,
pious (1 · 32) 339

מֵישָׁר 9 pl., uprightness, equity; evenness
(5 · 19) 449

מַעְגָּל track = course of life; entrenchment (7 · 13) 722

נעם 10 to be pleasant, delightful, lovely
(3 · 8 · 8) 653

529

מְזִמָּה 11 power of devising, descretion; purpose; evil thought, evil device (8 · 19) 273

תְּבוּנָה understanding (19 · 42) 108

תַּהְפֻּכָה 12 perverse thing, perversity (9 · 10) 246

יֹשֶׁר 13 straightness, evenness; uprightness; what is due, right (5 · 14) 449

שָׂמֵחַ 14 glad, joyful, merry, here = subst., joy (4 · 21) 970

גִּיל to rejoice (5 · 54 · 54) 163

תַּהְפֻּכָה perverse thing, perversity (9 · 10) 246

עִקֵּשׁ 15 twisted, perverted (7 · 11) 786

נָלוֹז to be devious, crooked (3 · 4 · 6) 531

מַעְגָּל track = course of life; entrenchment (7 · 13) 722

נָכְרִי 16 fem. = foreign woman, harlot; foreign (9 · 45) 648

אֵמֶר utterance, word (22 · 48) 56

הֶחֱלִיק to make smooth, w. tongue = to flatter (4 · 7 · 9) 325

אַלּוּף 17 friend, intimate; tame (3 · 9) 48 I

נְעוּרִים youth, early life (2 · 46) 655

שׁוּחַ 18 to sink down (1 · 1 · 1[?]) 1001

רְפָאִים shades, ghosts (3 · 8) 952 I

מַעְגָּל track = course of life; entrenchment (7 · 13) 722

הִשִּׂיג 19 to reach, attain to; overtake (1 · 49 · 49) 673 נשׂג

בָּגַד 22 to act or deal treacherously, faithlessly, deceitfully (9 · 49 · 49) 93

נסח to tear away, pull away (2 · 3 · 4) 650

Chapter 3

קָשַׁר 3 to bind, confine; league together (4 · 35 · 43) 905

גַּרְגְּרוֹת neck (4 · 4) 176

לוּחַ tablet, tablet of stone, wood or metal (2 · 43) 531

שֵׂכֶל 4 insight, understanding; prudence, good sense (6 · 16) 968

בִּינָה 5 understanding, here = faculty of understanding (14 · 37) 108

נִשְׁעַן to lean, support oneself (1 · 22 · 22) 1043

יָשַׁר 6 to make smooth, straight; lead straight along; esteem right (4 · 9 · 25) 448

רְפֻאוֹת 8 healing (1 · 1) 951

שֹׁר umbilical cord (1 · 3) 1057

שִׁקּוּי drink (1 · 3) 1052

הוֹן 9 wealth; high value, price; sufficiency (18 · 26) 223

תְּבוּאָה product, yield; income, revenue, gain (8 · 43) 100

אָסָם 10 storehouse (1 · 2) 62

שָׂבָע plenty, satiety (1 · 8) 960

תִּירוֹשׁ must, fresh or new wine (1 · 38) 440

יֶקֶב wine-vat (1 · 16) 428

פָּרַץ to burst open; to break out, through, down, up, open, over (2 · 46 · 49) 829 I

מוּסָר 11 discipline, correction; chastisement (30 · 50) 416

קִיע to feel loathing, abhor (1 · 8 · 8[?]) 880

תּוֹכַחַת reproof, chiding; argument (16 · 24) 407

רָצָה 12 to be pleased with, favorable to; accept favorably (3 · 42 · 50) 953

אֶשֶׁר 13 pl. cstr. = happiness, blessedness of (8 · 45) 80

הֵפִיק to bring out, elicit, obtain; produce; promote (4 · 8 · 9) פוק

תְּבוּנָה understanding (19 · 42) 108

סַחַר 14 gain from commerce; commerce (3 · 7) 695

תָּרוּץ gold (4 · 6) 359 V

תְּבוּאָה product, yield; income, revenue, gain (8 · 43) 100

יָקָר 15 precious, highly valued; glorious; weighty (6 · 35) 429

פְּנִיִּים 15 Qere = פְּנִינִים corals (4 · 6) 819

חֵפֶץ desire, longing; delight; pleasure (3 · 39) 343

שָׁוָה to be like; comparable; resemble, agree with (3 · 8 · 16) 1000

עֹשֶׁר 16 riches (9 · 37) 799

נֹעַם 17 pleasantness; delightfulness (3 · 7) 653

נְתִיבָה path, course [of life] (6 · 21[?]) 677

תָּמַךְ 18 to grasp, lay hold of; hold up; keep (8 · 20 · 21) 1069

אֻשָּׁר Pual, to be made happy, blessed (1 · 2 · 9[?]) 80

יָסַד 19 to found, establish, fix (1 · 21 · 41) 413

תְּבוּנָה understanding (19 · 42) 108

תְּהוֹם 20 deep; deep sea; primeval ocean; depth, abyss (4 · 36) 1062

שַׁחַק cloud; fine dust (2 · 21) 1007

רָעַף to trickle, drip (1 · 4 · 5) 950

טַל night mist, dew (2 · 31) 378

לוּז 21 to turn aside, depart (1 · 1 · 6) 531

תּוּשִׁיָּה abiding success; sound efficient wisdom (4 · 12) 444

מְזִמָּה power of devising; discretion; evil thought, device (8 · 19) 273

גַּרְגְּרוֹת 22 neck (4 · 4) 176

בֶּטַח 23 securely; security (4 · 43) 105 I

נָגַף to strike, smite (1 · 25 · 48) 619

פָּחַד 24 to be in dread; be in awe (1 · 22 · 25) 808

עָרַב to be sweet, pleasing (2 · 8 · 8) 787 II

שֵׁנָה sleep (7 · 23) 446

פַּחַד 25 object of dread; dread (4 · 49) 808

פִּתְאֹם suddenly, suddenness (4 · 25) 837

שׁוֹאָה devastation, ruin (2 · 13) 996

כֶּסֶל 26 confidence; stupidity, folly (1 · 6 [?]) 492

לֶכֶד capture, a taking (1 · 1) 540

מָנַע 27 to withhold, hold back (5 · 25 · 29) 586

אֵל strength, power (1 · 5) 43 II אֵל 7

חָרַשׁ 29 to devise; plough; engrave (7 · 23 · 26) 360

בֶּטַח securely; security (4 · 43) 105 I

חִנָּם 30 without cause; for no purpose; gratis (6 · 32) 336 חנן

גָּמַל to deal out to, do to; wean; ripen (3 · 34 · 37) 168

קִנֵּא 31 to be envious of; be jealous of; be zealous for (4 · 18 · 32) 888

נָלוֹז 32 to be devious, crooked (3 · 4 · 6) 531

סוֹד secret counsel, counsel; council; assembly (5 · 21) 691

מְאֵרָה 33 a curse (2 · 5) 76

נָוֶה [country] habitation; abode of shepherd or flocks (3 · 45) 627

לֵץ 34 ptc. = scorner (14 · 16) 539 ליץ

לִיץ to scorn [but Lis. Hiph. "to deride" p. 727] (14 · 16[?]) 539

עָנִי 34 Qere = humble, lowly, meek; poor (3 · 21) 776

קָלוֹן 35 dishonor, disgrace; ignominy (8 · 17) 885

Chapter 4

מוּסָר 1 discipline, correction; chastisement (30 · 50) 416

הַקְשִׁיב to give attention (8 · 45 · 46) 904

בִּינָה understanding (14 · 37) 108

לֶקַח 2 teaching, thing taught; instruction (6 · 9) 544

רַךְ 3 tender, delicate; weak; soft (3 · 16) 940 רכך

531

יָחִיד   only one (1 · 12) 402

הוֹרָה   to direct, teach, instruct; point out; throw, shoot (3 · 45 · 45[?]) 434 ירה

תָּמַךְ   to hold, keep; grasp, lay hold; hold up, support (8 · 20 · 21) 1069

בִּינָה   5 understanding (14 · 37) 108

אֵמֶר   utterance, work (22 · 48) 56

קִנְיָן   7 thing acquired, got, acquisition (1 · 9) 889

בִּינָה   understanding (14 · 37) 108

סִלְסֵל   8 *Pilp.*, to exalt, esteem highly, prize (1 · 1 · 12) 699 סלל

חִבֵּק   to embrace (2 · 10 · 13) 287

לִוְיָה   9 wreath (2 · 2) 531

עֲטָרָה   crown, wreath (5 · 23) 742 I

תִּפְאֶרֶת   glory; honor; beauty (6 · 50) 802

מִגֵּן   to deliver up, deliver (1 · 3 · 3) 171

אֵמֶר 10 utterance, word (22 · 48) 56

הוֹרָה 11 to direct, teach, instruct; point out; throw, shoot (3 · 45 · 45[?]) 434 ירה

מַעְגָּל   track = course of life; entrench-ment (7 · 13) 722

יֹשֶׁר   straightness, evenness; rightness; what is due, right (5 · 14) 449

צַעַד 12 step, steps; pace (4 · 14) 857

מוּסָר 13 discipline, correction; chastisement (30 · 50) 416

הִרְפָּה   to let go; let drop; relax; refrain (1 · 21 · 44) 951

אִשֵּׁר 14 to go straight on, advance; lead on, set right; pronounce happy (2 · 5 · 7 [?]) 80

פָּרַע 15 to let alone = avoid; let go, let loose (5 · 13 · 16) 828

שָׂטָה   to turn aside (2 · 6 · 6) 966

יָשֵׁן 16 to sleep, go to sleep, be asleep (1 · 15 · 16) 445

נִגְזַל   to be seized, torn away, robbed (1 · 1 · 30) 159

שֵׁנָה   sleep (7 · 23) 446

לֶחֶם 17 to eat (4 · 6 · 6) 536 II

רֶשַׁע   wickedness (5 · 30) 957

נֹגַהּ 18 brightness (1 · 19) 618 I

אוֹר   to be or become light (1 · 5 · 40) 21

אֲפֵלָה 19 darkness; gloominess, calamity (2 · 10) 66

בַּמֶּה   wherein? whereby? wherewith? by what means? for what? at what? (1 · 29) 553 מָה 4.a

הִקְשִׁיב 20 to give attention (8 · 45 · 46) 904

אֵמֶר   utterance, word (22 · 48) 56

הֵלִיז 21 to let or make depart (1 · 1 · 6) 531 לוז

מַרְפֵּא 22 health, profit; healing, cure (6 · 13) 951

מִשְׁמָר 23 act of guarding, guard, prison (1 · 22) 1038

תּוֹצָאָה   sources; outgoing, extremity, es-cape, source [sing.] (1 · 23) 426

עִקְּשׁוּת 24 crookedness (2 · 2) 786

לָזוּת   deviation, crookedness (1 · 1) 531 לוז

לְנֹכַח 25 to the front, right on (1 · 3) 647 נכח 2.b

עַפְעַף   eyelid (4 · 10) 733

הֵישִׁיר   to make straight, here w. eyes = look straight (1 · 2 · 25) 448

פִּלֵּס 26 to make level, smooth; weigh out (3 · 6 · 6) 814

מַעְגָּל   track = course of life; entrench-ment (7 · 13) 722

Chapter 5

הִקְשִׁיב 1 to give attention (8 · 45 · 46) 904

תְּבוּנָה   understanding (19 · 42) 108

הַט   *Hiph.* נטה to stretch out 639

מְזִמָּה 2 power of devising, discretion; pur-pose; evil thought, device (8 · 19) 273

נֹפֶת 3 flowing honey, honey from the comb (3 · 5) 661

532

נטף — to drop, drip (1 · 9 · 18) 642

חָלָק — smooth; as subst. = flattery (2 · 12) 325

חֵךְ — palate, roof of mouth; gums (3 · 18) 335

מַר — 4 bitter; bitterness (3 · 38) 600

לַעֲנָה — wormwood (1 · 8) 542

חַד — sharp (1 · 4) 292

חֶרֶב־פִּיּוֹת — idiom: sword with edges 805 פֶּה 3

צַעַד — 5 step, steps; pace (4 · 14) 857

תָּמַךְ — to lay hold of, grasp; hold up, support; hold, keep (8 · 20 · 21) 1069

פלס — 6 to make level, smooth; weigh out (3 · 6 · 6) 814

נוע — to wave, quiver, be unstable; totter (1 · 22 · 38) 631

מַעְגָּל — track = course of life; entrenchment (7 · 13) 722

אֹמֶר — 7 utterance, word (22 · 48) 56

הוֹד — 9 splendor; here = vigor, majesty (1 · 24) 217 I

אַכְזָרִי — cruel one, cruel (4 · 8) 470

עֶצֶב — 10 toil; hurt, pain (4 · 6) 780 I

נָכְרִי — alien, foreign; fem. = foreign woman, harlot (9 · 45) 648 נכר

נהם — 11 to groan, growl (2 · 5 · 5) 625

שְׁאֵר — flesh; flesh (= blood) relation; self (2 · 17) 984

מוּסָר — 12 discipline, correction; chastisement (30 · 50) 416

תּוֹכַחַת — reproof, chiding; argument (16 · 24) 407

נָאַץ — to despise, spurn (3 · 8 · 24) 610

מוֹרֶה — 13 teacher (1 · 9) 435 II

נֹזֵל — 15 ptc. = streams, floods (1 · 6) 633

בְּאֵר — well, pit (2 · 38) 91

מַעְיָן — 16 spring (3 · 23) 745

רְחוֹב — broad open place in city (5 · 43) 932

פֶּלֶג — channel, canal (2 · 10) 811 I

מָקוֹר — 18 spring, source (7 · 18) 881

נְעוּרִים — youth, early life (2 · 46) 655

אַיָּלָה — 19 hind, doe (1 · 11) 19

אָהַב — loves; here = loving (1 · 2) 13

יַעֲלָה — female mountain goat, fig. of wife (1 · 1) 418 I

דַּד — breast, teat, nipple (1 · 4) 186

רוה — Piel, to sate, saturate, drench; be intoxicated (1 · 6 · 14) 924

שגה — to swerve = be intoxicated, reel; stray, err (5 · 17 · 21) 993

שגה — 20 to swerve = be intoxicated, reel; stray, err (5 · 17 · 21) 993

חבק — to embrace (2 · 10 · 13) 287

חֵיק — bosom; fold of garment at breast (5 · 38) 300 חוק

נָכְרִי — alien, foreign; fem. = foreign woman, harlot (9 · 45) 648 נכר

נֹכַח — 21 in front of, opposite to (1 · 22) 647

מַעְגָּל — track = course of life; entrenchment (7 · 13) 722

פלס — to make level, smooth; weigh out (3 · 6 · 6) 814

חֶבֶל — 22 rope, cord; territory; band (1 · 49) 286 I

נתמך — to be seized, grasped (1 · 1 · 21) 1069

בְּאֵין — 23 for want of, without, for lack of; of time = when there was [were] not (8 · 10) 35 II אַיִן 6.a

מוּסָר — discipline, correction; chastisement (30 · 50) 416

אִוֶּלֶת — folly (23 · 25) 17

שגה — to swerve = be intoxicated, reel; stray, err (5 · 17 · 21) 993

Chapter 6

עָרַב — 1 to go surety to, for, take on pledge; give in pledge (6 · 15 · 17) 786

533

נוקש	2 to be caught by a bait, ensnared (1 · 4 · 8) 430 יקש	אִישׁ מָגֵן	idiom: armed man (2 · 2) [but Lis. p. 749 (2 · 4) insolent] 171
אֹמֶר	utterance, word (22 · 48) 56	בְּלִיַּעַל	12 worthlessness, good-for-nothing (3 · 27) 116
אֵפוֹא	3 then; enclitic particle with demonstr. force (1 · 15) 66	עִקְּשׁוּת	crookedness (2 · 2) 786
הִתְרַפֵּס	to humble oneself [stamp oneself down] (1 · 2 · 5) 952	קָרַץ	13 to pinch, nip, w. eye = wink (3 · 4 · 5) 902
רהב	to storm against, act stormily, importune (1 · 2 · 4) 923	מלל	to rub, scrape [scrape w. feet = making signs](1 · 1 · 5[?]) 576
שֵׁנָה	4 sleep (7 · 23) 446	הורה	to point out; direct, teach, instruct; throw, shoot (3 · 45 · 45[?]) 434 ירה
תְּנוּמָה	slumber (3 · 5) 630	אֶצְבַּע	finger (2 · 31) 840
עַפְעַף	eyelid (4 · 10) 733	תַּהְפֻּכָה	14 perverse thing, perversity (9 · 10) 246
צְבִי	5 gazelle (1 · 11) 840 II צבה	חרשׁ	to devise; plough; engrave (7 · 23 · 26) 360
צִפּוֹר	bird; birds (4 · 40) 861 I	מָדוֹן	strife, contention (10 · 10[?]) 193 I דין
יָקוּשׁ	fowler, bait-layer(1 · 4) 430	פִּתְאֹם	15 suddenly, suddenness (4 · 25) 837
נְמָלָה	6 ant (2 · 2) 649	אֵיד	distress, calamity (6 · 24) 15
עָצֵל	sluggard; sluggish, lazy (14 · 15) 782	פֶּתַע	suddenly; suddenness (2 · 7) 837
חָכַם	to be or become wise, act wisely (12 · 19 · 27) 314	מַרְפֵּא	health, profit; healing, cure (6 · 13) 951
קָצִין	7 ruler, dictator, chief, commander (2 · 11) 892	רָם	17 ptc. = high, lifted up (1 · 31) 926 רום
שֹׁטֵר	official, officer (1 · 25) 1009	נָקִי	innocent, free from guilt, clean; exempt (2 · 43) 667
מֹשֵׁל	ptc. = ruler, one who rules (5 · 24) 605	חרשׁ	18 to devise; to plough; engrave (7 · 23 · 26) 360
קַיִץ	8 summer; summer-fruit (4 · 20) 884	הֵפִיחַ	19 to breathe out, utter; blow (7 · 12 · 13) 806 פוח
אגר	to gather (2 · 3 · 3) 8	כָּזָב	lie, falsehood, deceptive thing (9 · 31) 469
קָצִיר	time of harvest; what is harvested; harvesting (5 · 49) 894 I קצר	מָדוֹן	strife, contention (10 · 10[?]) 193
מַאֲכָל	food (1 · 30) 38	נָטַשׁ	20 to forsake, abandon; leave; permit (3 · 33 · 40) 643
עַד־מָתַי	9 until when? how long? (2 · 29) 607 c מָתַי	קָשַׁר	21 to bind, confine; league together (4 · 35 · 43) 905
עָצֵל	sluggard; sluggish, lazy (14 · 15) 782	ענד	to bind around, upon (1 · 2 · 2) 772
מָתַי	when? (2 · 42) 607	גַּרְגְּרוֹת	neck (4 · 4) 176
שֵׁנָה	sleep (7 · 23) 446		
שֵׁנָה	10 sleep (7 · 23) 446		
תְּנוּמָה	slumber (3 · 5) 630		
חִבֻּק	a clasping or folding (2 · 2) 287		
רֵאשׁ	11 poverty (7 · 7) 930 ריש		
מַחְסוֹר	need, poverty; thing needed (8 · 13) 341		

הִנְחָה 22	to lead, guide (3·26·40) 634
הֵקִיץ	to show signs of waking, awake (2·22·23) 884 I
שִׂיחַ	to talk; muse; complain (1·18·20) 967
נֵר 23	lamp (6·45) 632 נור I
תּוֹכַחַת	reproof, chiding; argument (16·24) 407
מוּסָר	discipline, correction; chastisement (30·50) 416
חֶלְקָה 24	smoothness = flattery; smooth part (1·2) 325 II
נָכְרִי	fem. = foreign woman, harlot; foreign, alien (9·45) 648 נכר
חָמַד 25	to desire, take pleasure in (3·16·21) 326
יְפִי	beauty (2·19) 421
עַפְעַף	eyelid (4·10) 733 עוף
זוֹנָה 26	ptc. fem. = harlot (4·33) 275
יָקָר	precious, highly valued; glorious; weighty (6·35) 429
צוּד	to hunt (1·13·17) 844
חָתָה 27	to snatch up (2·3·3) 367
חֵיק	fold of garment at breast; bosom (5·38) 300
גַּחֶלֶת 28	coal (3·18) 160
נכוה	Niph., to be scorched, burned, branded (1·2·2) 464
נָקָה 29	to be free, exempt from punishment (7·24·41) 667
בַּז 30	to despise (8·14·14) 100 I בוז
גַּנָּב	thief (2·7) 170
גנב	to take by stealth, to steal (3·30·39) 170
רָעֵב	to be hungry (3·12·14) 944
שִׁבְעָתַיִם 31	sevenfold, seven times (1·6) 988
הוֹן	wealth; high value, price; sufficiency (18·26) 223
נאף 32	to commit adultery (1·17·31) 610

חָסֵר	needy, lacking; idiom חֲסַר-לֵב = lacking understanding, sense [(11·11)], (13·17) 341
קָלוֹן 33	dishonor, disgrace; ignominy (8·17) 885
נמחה	to be blotted out; wiped out; exterminated (1·9·34) 562
קִנְאָה 34	ardor of jealousy, of zeal, of anger (3·43) 888 קנא
חָמַל	to spare (1·40·40) 328
נָקָם	vengeance (1·17) 668
כֹּפֶר 35	a price for ransom of life, ransom (3·13) 497 I
שֹׁחַד	bribe, present (4·23) 1005

Chapter 7

אֵמֶר 1	utterance, word (22·48) 56
צָפַן	to lie hid, lurk; hide, treasure up (9·24·29) 860
אִישׁוֹן 2	pupil of eye (2·4) 36
קָשַׁר 3	to bind, confine; league together (4·35·43) 905
אֶצְבַּע	finger (2·31) 840
לוּחַ	tablet, tablet of stone, wood, or metal (4·35·43) 531
מוֹדָע 4	kinsman (1·2) [Lis. "together"] ידע 396
בִּינָה	understanding (14·37) 108
נָכְרִי 5	fem. = foreign woman, harlot; foreign, alien (9·45) 648 נכר
אֵמֶר	utterance, word (22·48) 56
הֶחֱלִיק	to make smooth, w. tongue = flatter (4·7·9) 325
חַלּוֹן 6	window (1·30) 319
אֶשְׁנָב	window lattice (1·2) 1039
נשקף	to lean over and look down, w. בְּעַד to look through (1·10·22) 1054
פֶּתִי 7	simple, open-minded (15·18) 834

חָסֵר   needy, lacking; idiom: חֲסַר־לֵב =
lacking understanding, sense
[(11 · 11)](13 · 17) 341

שׁוּק   8   street (1 · 4) 1003

פִּנָּה   corner (4 · 30) 819

צָעַד   to step, march (1 · 7 · 8) 857

נֶשֶׁף   9   evening twilight, morning twilight
(1 · 12) 676

אִישׁוֹן   pupil of eye; בְּאִישׁוֹן לַיְלָה = middle of
night (2 · 4) 36

אֲפֵלָה   darkness; gloominess, calamity
(2 · 10) 66

שִׁית   10   garment (1 · 2) 1011

זוֹנָה   ptc. fem. = harlot (4 · 33) 275

הָמָה   11   to be boisterous, turbulent; growl,
murmur, roar (4 · 33 · 33) 242

סָרַר   to be stubborn, rebellious
(1 · 17 · 17) 710

רְחוֹב   12   broad open place [in city] (5 · 43)
932

פִּנָּה   corner (4 · 30) 819

אָרַב   to lie in wait [with hostile pur-
pose](6 · 20 · 23) 70

נָשַׁק   13   to kiss (2 · 26 · 32) 676 I

הֵעֵז   to make firm; w. face = show
boldness (2 · 2 · 11) 738 עזז

שָׁחַר   15   *Piel*, to seek early (4 · 12 · 13) 1007

מַרְבָד   16   spread, coverlet (2 · 2) 915

רָבַד   to be spread, deck (1 · 1 · 1) 914

עֶרֶשׂ   couch, divan, bed (1 · 11) 793

חֲטֻבוֹת   dark-hued yarn of Egypt [Lis. psv.
ptc. = many-colored] (1 · 1 · 1)
310

אֵטוּן   thread, yarn (1 · 1) 32

נוּף   17   to sprinkle (1 · 1 · 2[?]) 631

מִשְׁכָּב   couch, bed, act of lying (2 · 46)
1012

מֹר   myrrh, gum from Arabian tree bark
(1 · 12) 600 מרר

אֲהָלִים   aloes; odorif. trees (1 · 4) 14 III אהל

קִנָּמוֹן   cinnamon (1 · 3) 890

רָוָה   18   to be saturated, drink one's fill
(1 · 3 · 14) 924

הִתְעַלֵּס   *Hithp.*, to delight oneself (1 · 1 · 3)
763

אֹהַב   loved object, amour [carnal sense]
(1 · 2) 13

מֵרָחוֹק   19   to a distance, at a distance (1 · 34)
934 רחוק 2.a. (2)

צְרוֹר   20   pouch [purse], bundle (1 · 7) 865 I

כֵּסֶא   full moon (1 · 2) 490

הִטַּתּוּ   21   *Hiph.*, נטה to stretch out
639 .

לֶקַח   teaching, power of teaching = persuasiveness; instruction (6 · 9) 544

חֵלֶק   seductiveness (1 · 1) 325 III

הִדִּיחַ   to compel, force; thrust, move, impel; thrust out, banish (1 · 27 · 43)
623 נדח

פִּתְאֹם   22   suddenly, suddenness (4 · 25) 837

טֶבַח   slaughtering, slaughter (2 · 12) 370 I

עֶכֶס   anklet (1 · 2) 747

מוּסָר   discipline, correction; chastisement
(30 · 50) 416

אֱוִיל   fool; foolish (19 · 26) 17

פִּלַּח   23   to cleave open, pierce, cut up,
open (1 · 4 · 5) 812

כָּבֵד   liver (1 · 14) 458

צִפּוֹר   bird; birds (4 · 40) 861 I צפר

פַּח   bird trap (2 · 25) 809 I פחח

הִקְשִׁיב   24   to give attention (8 · 45 · 46) 904

אֵמֶר   utterance, word (22 · 48) 56

שָׂטָה   25   to turn aside (2 · 6 · 6) 966

תָּעָה   to wander about; err (3 · 27 · 50)
1073

נְתִיבָה   path, course [of life](6 · 21[?]) 677

עָצוּם   26   numerous, countless, subst. =
many; mighty (3 · 31) 783

חֶדֶר   27   room, chamber [usually private]
(6 · 37) 293

Chapter 8

תְּבוּנָה 1 understanding (19 · 42) 108

עֲלֵי 2 poetic for על 752

נְתִיבָה path, course [of life] (6 · 21[?]) 677

לְיַד 3 by the side of 391 יָד 5.f

קֶרֶת town, city (4 · 5) 900

מָבוֹא 3 entrance, entering, a coming in (1 · 23) 99

פֶּתִי 5 simple, open-minded (15 · 18) 834

עָרְמָה prudence; craftiness (3 · 5) 791

נָגִיד 6 ruler, prince (2 ·. 44) 617

מִפְתָּה opening, utterance (1 · 1) 836

מֵישָׁר 6 pl., uprightness, equity (5 · 19) 449

הָגָה 7 to utter; growl; meditate, muse (3 · 23 · 25) 211

חֵךְ palate, roof of mouth; gums (3 · 18) 335

רֶשַׁע wickedness (5 · 30) 957

אֹמֶר 8 utterance, word (22 · 48) 56

נִפְתָּל to be twisted, tortuous (1 · 3 · 5) 836

עִקֵּשׁ perverted, twisted (7 · 11) 786 I

נְכֹחִים 9 right, straight, true (2 · 8) 647 נָכֹחַ

מוּסָר 10 discipline, correction; chastisement (30 · 50) 416

חָרוּץ gold (4 · 6) 359 V חרץ

פְּנִינִים 11 corals (4 · 6) 819

חֵפֶץ desire, longing (3 · 39) 343

שָׁוָה to be like, comparable; resemble, agree with (3 · 8 · 16) 1000

עָרְמָה 12 prudence; craftiness (3 · 5) 791

מְזִמָּה power of devising, discretion; purpose, evil thought, device (8 · 19) 273

יִרְאָה 13 fear of God, reverence, piety; fear, terror (14 · 45) 432

גֵּאָה pride (1 · 1) 144

גָּאוֹן pride; exaltation; majesty (2 · 49) 144

תַּהְפֻּכָה perverse thing, perversity (9 · 10) 246

תּוּשִׁיָּה 14 sound, efficient wisdom; abiding success (4 · 12) 444

בִּינָה understanding (14 · 37) 108

רֹזֵן 15 ptc. = ruler, potentate (2 · 6) 931

חוֹקֵק Poel, to inscribe, enact (1 · 1 · 11) חקק 349

שׂרר 16 to be or act as prince, to rule (1 · 5 · 8) 979

נָדִיב adj. and noun, noble, princely, generous (5 · 27) 622 נדב

אֹהֵב 17 ptc. = lover, friend (6 · 36) 12

אָהֵב Qal imperf. אֱהַב

שִׁחֵר to seek early (3 · 12 · 13) 1007

עֹשֶׁר 18 riches (9 · 37) 799

הוֹן wealth; high value, price; sufficiency (18 · 26) 223

עָתֵק eminent, valuable, surpassing (1 · 1) 801

חָרוּץ 19 gold (4 · 6) 359 V חרץ

פָּז refined, pure gold (1 · 9) 808

תְּבוּאָה gain, product, income; yield (8 · 43) 100

נְתִיבָה 20 path, course [of life] (6 · 21[?]) 677

אֹהֵב 21 ptc. = lover, friend (6 · 36) 12

יֵשׁ [only here] substance; elsewhere = existence 441 I

קָנָה 22 to get, acquire; here as originating, creating (1 · 5 · 5[?]) 888 I

מִפְעָל work, thing made (1 · 3[?]) 821

מֵאָז in time past, of old; since; from that time (1 · 17) 23

נֹסַךְ 23 Niph., to be installed (1 · 1 · 25[?]) 651 III

מִקֶּדֶם from the beginning, from of old (1 · 26) 869 קֶדֶם 2.c and e

בְּאֵין 24 for want of, without, for lack of, of time = when there was [were] not (8 · 10) 35 אַיִן 6.a

537

תְּהוֹם   deep; deep sea; primeval ocean;
depth; abyss (4 · 36) 1062

חוֹלָל   *Polal*, to be brought forth; to be
made to writhe (2 · 5 · 47) 296

חול

מַעְיָן   spring (3 · 23) 745 עין

בְּטֶרֶם 25 before (3 · 38) 382 טֶרֶם 2

הָטְבַּע   *Hoph.*, to be settled, planted; be
sunk (1 · 3 · 10) 371

חוֹלָל   *Polal*, to be brought forth; to be
made to writhe (2 · 5 · 47) 296

תֵּבֵל 26 world (2 · 35) 385

חָקַק 27 to cut in, engrave, inscribe
(2 · 8 · 11) 349

חוּג   vault, horizon (1 · 3) 295

תְּהוֹם   deep; deep sea; primeval ocean;
depth; abyss (4 · 36) 1062

אָמֵץ 28 to make firm, strengthen; assure;
harden (3 · 19 · 41) 54

שַׁחַק   cloud; fine dust (2 · 21) 1007

מִמַּעַל   above; on the top of [לְ] (1 · 29) 751
II מַעַל 1.a

עזז   to grow strong, be strong, prevail
(1 · 9 · 11) 738

תְּהוֹם   deep; deep sea; primeval ocean;
depth; abyss (4 · 36) 1062

חָקַק 29 to cut in, engrave, inscribe
(2 · 8 · 11) 349

מוֹסָד   foundation (1 · 13) 414

אָמוֹן 30 architect, master workman (1 · 2)
54 II אמן

שַׁעֲשֻׁעִים   delight (2 · 9) 1044

שׂחק   *Piel*, to make sport; jest; play
(3 · 16 · 36) 965

שׂחק   *Piel*, to make sport; jest; play
(3 · 16 · 36) 965

תֵּבֵל   world (2 · 35) 385

שַׁעֲשֻׁעִים   delight (2 · 9) 1044

אֶשֶׁר 32 pl. cstr. = happiness, blessedness
of (8 · 45) 80

מוּסָר 33 discipline, correction; chastisement
(30 · 50) 416

חָכַם   to be or become wise, act wisely
(12 · 19 · 27) 314

פָּרַע   to let alone = neglect; let go, let
loose (5 · 13 · 16) 828

אֶשֶׁר 34 pl. cstr. = happiness, blessedness
of (8 · 45) 80

שָׁקַד   to keep watch of, be wakeful over;
wake (1 · 11 · 16) 1052

מְזוּזָה   doorpost, gatepost (1 · 20) 265 זוז

הֵפִיק 35 to bring out, elicit, obtain; produce;
promote (4 · 8 · 9) 807 פוק

חמס 36 to treat violently, wrong (1 · 7 · 8)
329

Chapter 9

חָכְמוֹת 1 wisdom (3 · 4[?]) 315

חָצֵב   to hew, hew out, cleave
(1 · 14 · 17) 345

טֶבַח 2 slaughtering, slaughter (2 · 12) 370 I

טבח   to slaughter, butcher, kill
(1 · 11 · 11) 370

מָסַךְ   to mix; pour, produce by mixing
(2 · 5 · 5) 587

גַּף 3 height, elevation; body, self [Lis.
back](1 · 1) 172

קֶרֶת   town, city (4 · 5) 900

פֶּתִי 4 simple, open-minded (15 · 18) 834

הֵנָּה   hither, here (3 · 48) 244 I

חָסֵר   needy, lacking; idiom חֲסַר־לֵב =
lacking understanding, sense
[11 · 11] (13 · 17) 341

לחם 5 to eat (4 · 6 · 6) 536

מָסַךְ   to mix; pour, produce by mixing
(2 · 5 · 5) 587

פֶּתִי 6 simple, open-minded (15 · 18) 834

אשר   to go straight on, advance (1 · 1 · 7)
80

בִּינָה understanding (14 · 37) 108

יסר 7 to admonish; discipline; chasten (1 · 4 · 38) 415

לֵץ ptc. = scorner (14 · 16) 539 ליץ

קָלוֹן dishonor, disgrace; ignominy (8 · 17) 885

מוּם blemish, defect (1 · 21) 548

לֵץ 8 ptc. = scorner (14 · 16) 539 ליץ

חָכַם 9 to be or become wise, act wisely (12 · 19 · 27) 314

לֶקַח instruction; teaching, thing taught; persuasiveness (6 · 9) 544

תְּחִלָּה 10 beginning, first principle (1 · 22) 321

יִרְאָה fear of God, reverence, piety; fear, terror (14 · 45) 432

בִּינָה understanding (14 · 37) 108

חָכַם 12 to be or become wise, act wisely (12 · 19 · 27) 314

ליץ to scorn (1 · 1 · 12) 539

כְּסִילוּת 13 stupidity (1 · 1) 493

המה to be boisterous, turbulent; to murmur, growl, roar (4 · 33 · 33) 242

פְּתַיּוּת simplicity; i.e., lack of wisdom (1 · 1) 834

קֶרֶת 14 town, city (4 · 5) 900

ישר 15 to make smooth, straight; to lead straight along; esteem right (4 · 9 · 25) 448

פֶּתִי 16 simple, open-minded (15 · 18) 834

הֵנָּה hither, here (3 · 48) 244 I

חָסֵר needy, lacking; idiom: חֲסַר־לֵב = lacking understanding, sense [11 · 11] (13 · 17) 341

גנב 17 to steal, take by stealth (3 · 30 · 39) 170

מתק to become sweet, be sweet, pleasant (1 · 4 · 6) 608

סֵתֶר secrecy; 'להם = bread gained secretly, by stealth; hiding place, covering (3 · 35) 712

נעם to be pleasant, delightful, lovely (3 · 8 · 8) 653

רְפָאִים 18 shades, ghosts (3 · 8) 952 II

עֵמֶק depth (2 · 2) 771

Chapter 10

מָשָׁל 1 sentence of ethical wisdom; proverb; parable (6 · 39) 605 II

תּוּגָה grief (3 · 4) 387

הוֹעִיל 2 to profit, avail, benefit (2 · 23 · 23) 418 יעל

רֶשַׁע wickedness (5 · 30) 957

הִרְעִיב 3 to allow one to hunger (1 · 2 · 14) 944

הַוָּה desire; engulfing ruin, destruction (2 · 3[?]) 217

הדף to push away = reject, thrust out, drive out (1 · 11 · 11) 213

רָשׁ 4 to be poor; ptc. = poor man [men] (1 · 3 · 4) 930 רוש

רְמִיָּה slack [negligent, idle], slackness, laxness (4 · 15) 941 II רמה

חָרוּץ diligent (5 · 5[?]) 358 I חרץ

הֶעֱשִׁיר to gain riches, make rich (5 · 14 · 17) 799

אגר 5 to gather; ptc. = one who gathers (2 · 3 · 3) 8

קַיִץ summer; summer fruit (4 · 20) 884

נִרְדָּם to be or fall fast asleep (1 · 7 · 7) 922

קָצִיר time of harvest; what is harvested; harvesting (5 · 49) 894 I קצר

זֵכֶר 7 memorial; remembrance (1 · 23) 271

רקב to rot (1 · 2 · 2) 955

אֱוִיל 8 fool; foolish (19 · 26) 17

נלבט to be thrust down, away (1 · 3 · 3) 526

תֹּם 9 integrity; completeness; innocence (7 · 23) 1070

בֶּטַח securely; security (4 · 43) 105 I

עָקַשׁ *Piel*, to twist, make crooked
(1 · 3 · 5) 786

קָרַץ 10 to pinch, nip (3 · 4 · 5) 902

עַצֶּבֶת hurt, pain, injury (2 · 5) 781 עצב

אֱוִיל fool; foolish (19 · 26) 17 I

נִלְבָּט to be thrust down, away (1 · 3 · 3) 526

מָקוֹר 11 spring, source (7 · 18) 881

שִׂנְאָה 12 hatred, hating (4 · 17) 971

מָדוֹן 13 strife, contention (9 · 12) 193 I דִּין

נָבוֹן *Niph.* ptc. = understanding or intelligent [one] (9 · 21) 106

גֵּו back (3 · 6) 156 I גוה

חָסֵר needy, lacking; idiom: חֲסַר־לֵב =
lacking understanding, sense
[11 · 11] (13 · 17) 341

צָפַן 14 to treasure up; lie hid, lurk; hide
(9 · 24 · 29) 860

אֱוִיל fool; foolish (19 · 26) 17

מְחִתָּה ruin; terror (7 · 11) 369

הוֹן 15 wealth; high value, price; sufficiency (18 · 26) 223

עָשִׁיר the rich; rich (9 · 23) 799

קִרְיָה city, town (5 · 30) 900

מְחִתָּה ruin; terror (7 · 11) 369

דַּל poor, reduced, low, thin (15 · 48)
195

רֵישׁ poverty (7 · 7) 930

פְּעֻלָּה 16 wages from work; work (2 · 14) 821
פעל

תְּבוּאָה income, revenue; gain, product,
yield (8 · 43) 100

מוּסָר 17 discipline, correction; chastisement
(30 · 50) 416

תּוֹכַחַת reproof, chiding; argument (16 · 24)
407

הִתְעָה to cause to wander about, cause to
err (2 · 21 · 50) 1073

שִׂנְאָה 18 hatred, hating (4 · 17) 971 שנא

דִּבָּה defamation; evil report; whispering
(2 · 9) 179

חָשַׂךְ 19 to hold in check; withhold, keep
back, refrain; restrain (6 · 26 · 28)
362

אֱוִיל 21 fool; foolish (19 · 26) 17

חָסֵר needy, lacking; idiom: חֲסַר־לֵב =
lacking understanding, sense
[11 · 11](13 · 17) 341

הֶעֱשִׁיר 22 to make rich, enrich; gain riches
(5 · 14 · 17) 799

עֶצֶב pain, hurt, toil (4 · 6) 780 I

שְׂחוֹק 23 sport; laughter; derision (2 · 15)
966

זִמָּה evil device; purpose, plan (3 · 28)
273 I

תְּבוּנָה understanding (19 · 42) 108

מְגוֹרָה 24 fear, terror (1 · 3) 159

תַּאֲוָה thing desired; desire, wish; lust
(8 · 21) 16 I אוה

סוּפָה 25 storm wind (2 · 15) 693 I סוף

יְסוֹד foundation; base, bottom (1 · 19)
414

חֹמֶץ 26 vinegar (2 · 5) 330

עָשָׁן smoke (1 · 25) 798 I

עָצֵל sluggard; sluggish, lazy (14 · 15) 782

יִרְאָה 27 fear of God, reverence, piety; fear,
terror (14 · 45) 432

קָצַר to be short (1 · 12 · 14) 894

תּוֹחֶלֶת 28 hope (3 · 6) 404 יחל

תִּקְוָה things hoped for, outcome; hope
(8 · 32) 876 II קוה

מָעוֹז 29 place or means of safety, protection
(1 · 36) 731

תֹּם integrity; completeness; innocence
(7 · 23) 1070

מְחִתָּה ruin; terror (7 · 11) 369 חתת

נִמּוֹט 30 to be shaken, moved, overthrown
(2 · 22 · 39) 556

נוּב 31 to bear fruit (1 · 3 · 4) 626

תַּהְפֻּכָה perverse thing, perversity (9 · 10)
246 הפך

תַּהְפֻּכָה 32 perverse thing, perversity (9 · 10)
הפך 246

Chapter 11

מֹאזְנַיִם 1 balances, scales (3 · 15) 24

מִרְמָה treachery, deceit (8 · 39) 941 I רמה

שָׁלֵם full, perfect, complete; safe, at
peace (1 · 28) 1023 I

זָדוֹן 2 insolence, presumptuousness
(3 · 10) 268

קָלוֹן dishonor, disgrace; ignominy
(8 · 17) 885

צָנוּעַ modest (1 · 1) 857

תֻּמָּה 3 integrity (1 · 5) 1070

הנחה to lead, guide (3 · 26 · 40) 634

סֶלֶף crookedness, crooked dealing (2 · 2)
701

בגד to act or deal treacherously, faithlessly, deceitfully (9 · 49 · 49) 93

הוֹעִיל 4 to profit, avail, benefit (2 · 23 · 23)
יעל 418

הוֹן wealth; high value, price; sufficiency (18 · 26) 223

עֶבְרָה overflowing rage, fury; arrogance;
overflow (5 · 34) 720

ישר 5 Piel, to make smooth, straight; to
lead straight along; esteem right
(4 · 9 · 25) 448

רִשְׁעָה wickedness (2 · 15) 958

הַוָּה 6 desire; engulfing ruin, destruction
(2 · 3[?]) 217

בגד to act or deal treacherously, faithlessly, deceitfully (9 · 49 · 49) 93

תִּקְוָה 7 things hoped for, outcome; hope
(8 · 32) 876 II

תּוֹחֶלֶת hope (3 · 6) 404 יחל

נֶחֱלָץ 8 to be delivered (2 · 7 · 27) 322 I

חָנֵף 9 godless man, godless, profane, ir-
religious (1 · 13) 338

נֶחֱלָץ to be delivered (2 · 7 · 27) 322 I

טוּב 10 prosperity, fairness, beauty, goodness; goods; good (1 · 32) 375

עָלַץ to rejoice, exult (2 · 8 · 8) 763

קִרְיָה city, town (5 · 30) 900

רִנָּה ringing cry [in joy], of entreaty, or
proclamation (1 · 33) 943 I

קֶרֶת 11 town, city (4 · 5) 900

נהרס to be thrown or torn down
(2 · 10 · 43) 248

בָּז 12 to despise (8 · 14) 100 בוז

חָסֵר needy, lacking; idiom: חֲסַר־לֵב =
lacking understanding, sense
[11 · 11] (13 · 17) 341

תְּבוּנָה understanding (19 · 42) 108

הֶחֱרִישׁ to be silent; make silent, be deaf
(2 · 38 · 46) 361

רָכִיל 13 slander, talebearer, informer (2 · 6) 940

סוֹד secret counsel, counsel; council,
assembly (5 · 21) 691

בְּאֵין 14 for want of, without, for lack of;
of time = when there was [were]
not (8 · 10) 35 II אֵין 6.a

תַּחְבֻּלָה pl. only, counsel, direction, guidance (5 · 6) 287

תְּשׁוּעָה deliverance; salvation (3 · 34) 448

יוֹעֵץ ptc. = counselor, adviser (3 · 22)
419

יֵרוֹעַ 15 Niph., רעע = to suffer (>50) 949

עָרַב take on pledge, to go surety to,
for; give in pledge (6 · 15 · 17) 786 II

תֹּקְעִים ptc. pl. = striking or clapping [of
hands כַּף = ratifying a bargain]
(1 · 1) 1075

תמך 16 to lay hold of, attain, grasp; hold
up, support; hold, keep (8 · 20 · 21)
1069

עָרִיץ one who strikes terror; awe-inspiring, terror-striking (1 · 20) 792

עֹשֶׁר riches (9 · 37) 799

גָּמַל 17 to deal out to, do to; wean; ripen (3 · 34 · 37) 168

עָכַר to disturb, trouble, stir up (3 · 13 · 15) 747

שְׁאֵר self; flesh; flesh [= blood-] relation (2 · 17) 984

אַכְזָרִי cruel one, cruel (4 · 8) 470

פְּעֻלָּה 18 work; wages earned by work (2 · 14) 821

שֶׂכֶר hire, wages (1 · 2) 969

כֵּן 19 veritable, true; right; honest (2 · 24) 467 II

עִקֵּשׁ 20 twisted, perverted (7 · 11) 786 I

יָד לְיָד 21 idiom: hand to hand, surely (1 · [?]) 391 יד 5.f

נָקָה to be free, exempt from punishment; exempt from guilt, from obligation; be cleaned out (7 · 24 · 41) 667

נֶזֶם 22 ring (2 · 17) 633

חֲזִיר swine; wild boar (1 · 7) 306

יָפֶה fair, beautiful (1 · 41) 421

טַעַם taste, fig. for judgment, discretion, discernment; taste; decision (2 · 13) 381

תַּאֲוָה 23 desire, wish; lust; thing desired (8 · 21) 16 I

תִּקְוָה things hoped for, outcome; hope (8 · 32) 876 II קוה

עֶבְרָה overflowing rage, fury; arrogance; overflow (5 · 34) 720

פָּזַר 24 to scatter (1 · 7 · 10) 808

חָשַׂךְ to withhold, keep back; hold in check; refrain; restrain (6 · 26 · 28) 362

יֹשֶׁר what is due, right; straightness, evenness; rightness (5 · 14) 449

מַחְסוֹר need, poverty; thing needed (8 · 13) 341

דֻּשַׁן 25 Pual, to be made fat (3 · 4 · 11) 206

הִרְוָה to saturate, water, cause to drink (1 · 5 · 14) 924

יוֹרָא Hoph., to be saturated 924 (cf. יָרָא p. 432) ([?] · [?] · 14) 924 רוה

מָנַע 26 to withhold, hold back (5 · 25 · 29) 586

בַּר grain, corn (2 · 14) 141

קָבַב to curse (2 · 14 · 14) 866 II

לְאוֹם people (4 · 35) 522

הִשְׁבִּיר to sell grain (1 · 5 · 21) 991

שָׁחַר 27 to look eagerly, diligently for (1 · 1 · 13) 1007

עֹשֶׁר 28 riches (9 · 37) 799

עָלֶה leaf, leafage (1 · 18) 750

פָּרַח to bud, sprout, send out shoots (1 · 28 · 33) 827 II

עָכַר 29 to disturb, trouble, stir up (3 · 13 · 15) 747

אֱוִיל fool; foolish (19 · 26) 17

אַף־כִּי how much more! furthermore, tis indeed that; yea when (6 · 26) 65

Chapter 12

מוּסָר 1 discipline, correction; chastisement (30 · 50) 416

תּוֹכַחַת reproof, chiding; argument (16 · 24) 407

בַּעַר brutishness (2 · 5) 129

הֵפִיק 2 to bring out, elicit, obtain; produce; promote (4 · 8 · 9) 807 פוק

מְזִמָּה evil thought, device; purpose; power of devising, discretion (8 · 19) 273

הִרְשִׁיעַ to condemn as guilty; act wickedly (2 · 25 · 34) 957

רֶשַׁע 3 wickedness (5 · 30) 957

שֹׁרֶשׁ root (2 · 33) 1057

נָמוֹט Niph., to be shaken, moved, overthrown (2 · 22 · 39) 556

עֲטָרָה 4 crown, wreath (5 · 23) 742 I

רָקָב rottenness, decay (2 · 5) 955

תַחְבֻּלָה 5 pl. only, counsels, direction, guidance (5 · 6) 287

מִרְמָה treachery, deceit (8 · 39) 941 I

אָרַב 6 to lie in wait [with hostile purpose] (6 · 20 · 23) 70

שֵׂכֶל 8 insight, understanding; prudence, good sense (6 · 16) 968

נַעֲוֵה to be bent, bowed down, twisted, נ׳לֵב = perverted of mind (1 · 4 · 17) 730 I

בּוּז contempt (2 · 11) 100 II

נִקְלָה 9 to be lightly esteemed, dishonored (1 · 5 · 6) 885

חָסֵר needy, lacking (13 · 17) 341

רַחֲמִים 10 pl. intens., compassion (1 · 38) 933

אַכְזָרִי cruel, cruel one (4 · 8) 470

רֵיק 11 empty, idle, worthless (2 · 14) 938

חֲסַר needy, lacking; idiom: = חֲסַר לֵב lacking understanding, sense [11 · 11] (13 · 17) 341

חָמַד 12 to desire, take pleasure in (3 · 16 · 21) 326

מָצוֹד hunting net (1 · 4) 844 II צוד

שֹׁרֶשׁ root (2 · 33) 1057

מוֹקֵשׁ 13 lure, bait, snare (8 · 27) 430

גְּמוּל 14 dealing; recompense; benefit (2 · 19) 168

אֱוִיל 15 fool; foolish (19 · 26) 17

כַּעַס 16 vexation, anger, grief (4 · 25) 495

קָלוֹן dishonor, disgrace; ignominy (8 · 17) 885

עָרוּם shrewd, sensible; crafty (8 · 11) 791

הֵפִיחַ 17 to breathe out, utter; blow (7 · 12 · 13) 806 פוח

מִרְמָה treachery, deceit (8 · 39) 941 I

בֹטֶה 18 to speak rashly, thoughtlessly; ptc. = babbler (1 · 1 · 4) 104

מַדְקָרָה thrust, piercing stab (1 · 1) 201

מַרְפֵּא health, profit; healing, cure (6 · 13) 951

עַד 19 perpetuity, continuous existence, forever (2 · 48) 723 I

הַרְגִּיעַ to twinkle = do something in a moment (1 · 8 · 13[?]) 920 I

מִרְמָה 20 treachery, deceit (8 · 39) 941 I

חרשׁ to devise; plough; engrave (7 · 23 · 26) 360

אנה 21 *Pual*, to be allowed to meet, to be sent (1 · 2 · 4) 58

עָרוּם 23 shrewd, sensible; crafty (8 · 11) 791

אִוֶּלֶת folly (23 · 25) 17

חָרוּץ 24 diligent (5 · 5[?]) 358 I חרץ

רְמִיָּה slackness, laxness (4 · 15) 941 II רמה

מַס slaving labor band; body of forced laborers, task work (1 · 23) 586 I

דְּאָגָה 25 anxiety, anxious care (1 · 6) 178 דאג

הֵתִיר 26 to search out, make reconnaissance [mng. dub. here] (1 · 3 · 22) 1064 תור

הִתְעָה to cause to wander about; cause to err (2 · 21 · 50) 1073

חָרַךְ 27 to start, set in motion (1 · 1 · 1) 355 I

רְמִיָּה slackness, laxness (4 · 15) 941 II

צַיִד game [hunted and taken]; hunting (1 · 14) 844 I צוד

הוֹן wealth; high value, price; sufficiency (18 · 26) 223

יָקָר precious, costly, highly valued; glorious; weighty (6 · 35) 429

חָרוּץ diligent (5 · 5[?]) 358 I

נְתִיבָה 28 path or course [of life][BDB נתיב path, pathway] (6 · 21[?]) 677

אַל unusual use w. a subst. = no 39 אל II.b

Chapter 13

מוּסָר 1 discipline, correction; chastisement (30 · 50) 416

לֵץ   ptc. = scorner (14 · 16) 539
לִיץ

גְּעָרָה   rebuke (3 · 15) 172

בָּגַד   2 to act or deal treacherously, faithlessly, deceitfully (9 · 49 · 49) 93

פָּשַׂק   3 to part, open wide (1 · 1 · 2) 832

מְחִתָּה   ruin; terror (7 · 11) 369

הִתְאַוָּה   4 to desire, long for, lust after
(5 · 16 · 27) 16

עָצֵל   sluggard; sluggish, lazy (14 · 15)
782

חָרוּץ   diligent (5 · 5[?]) 358 I

דָּשֵׁן   Pual, to be made fat (3 · 4 · 11)
206

הִבְאִישׁ   5 to cause to stink; emit a stinking
odor (1 · 7 · 16) 92

הֶחְפִּיר   to cause shame; display shame
(2 · 4 · 17) 344 II

תֹּם   6 integrity; completeness; innocence
(7 · 23) 1070

רִשְׁעָה   wickedness (2 · 15) 958

סִלֵּף   to subvert, turn upside down, ruin;
pervert (4 · 7 · 7) 701

הִתְעַשֵּׁר   7 to enrich oneself (1 · 1 · 17) 799

הִתְרוֹשֵׁשׁ   Hithpo'lel, to impoverish oneself
(1 · 1 · 3) 930 רושׁ

הוֹן   wealth; high value, price; sufficiency (18 · 26) 223

כֹּפֶר   8 the price of a life, ransom (3 · 13)
497 I

עֹשֶׁר   riches (9 · 37) 799

רָשׁ   ptc. = poor, poor man [men]
(14 · 21) 930 רושׁ

גְּעָרָה   rebuke (3 · 15) 172

נֵר   9 lamp (6 · 45) 632

דָּעַךְ   to go out, be extinguished (3 · 7 · 9)
200

זָדוֹן   10 insolence, presumptuousness
(3 · 10) 268

מַצָּה   strife, contention (2 · 3) 663

הוֹן   11 wealth; high value, price; sufficiency (18 · 26) 223

מָעַט   to be or become small, few, diminished (1 · 8 · 22) 589

תּוֹחֶלֶת   12 hope (3 · 6) 404

מֻשָּׁךְ   Pual, to be postponed, deferred,
drawn out (1 · 3 · 36) 604

תַּאֲוָה   desire, wish; lust; thing desired
(8 · 21) 16

בַּז   13 to despise (8 · 14) 100 בזז

נֶחְבַּל   to become pledged (1 · 1 · 14) 286
I

יָרֵא   ptc. = fearing, reverencing, honoring (3 · 45) 431

מָקוֹר   14 spring, source (7 · 18) 881

מוֹקֵשׁ   lure, bait, snare (8 · 27) 430

שֵׂכֶל   15 insight, understanding; prudence,
good sense (6 · 16) 968

בָּגַד   to act or deal treacherously, faithlessly, deceitfuly (9 · 49 · 49) 93

אֵיתָן   ever-flowing, permanent; but mng.
here dub., perhaps firm, hard,
rugged (1 · 14) 450 I יתן

עָרוּם   16 shrewd, sensible; crafty (8 · 11) 791

אִוֶּלֶת   folly (23 · 25) 17

צִיר   17 messenger, envoy (2 · 6) 851 II

מַרְפֵּא   health, profit; healing, cure (6 · 13)
951

רֵישׁ   18 poverty (7 · 7) 930 רישׁ

קָלוֹן   dishonor, disgrace; ignominy
(8 · 17) 885

פָּרַע   to let alone = neglect; to let go,
let loose (5 · 13 · 16) 828

מוּסָר   discipline, correction; chastisement
(30 · 50) 416

תּוֹכַחַת   reproof, chiding; argument (16 · 24)
407

תַּאֲוָה   19 desire, wish; lust; thing desired
(8 · 21) 16 I אוה

עָרֵב   to be sweet, pleasing (2 · 8 · 8) 787

חָכַם 20 to be or become wise, act wisely (12 · 19 · 27) 314

רעה to associate with (3 · 4 · 6) 945 II

יֵרוֹעַ Niph., רעע = to suffer (>50) 949

חַטָּא 21 sinner (3 · 19) 308

צָפַן 22 to lie hid, lurk; hide, treasure up (9 · 24 · 29) 860

אֹכֶל 23 food (1 · 44) 38

נִיר fallow ground, untilled ground (1 · 3) 644 II

רָאשׁ for יוֹרָשׁ = poor, poor man [men] (14 · 21) 930 רושׁ

נִסְפָּה to be swept away, destroyed (1 · 9 · 18) 705

בְּלֹא without; ב' מִשְׁפָּט = through injustice (3 · 31) 520 לֹא 4.a.(c)

חָשַׂךְ 24 to hold in check; withhold, keep back, refrain; restrain (6 · 26 · 28) 362

שִׁחֵר Piel, to seek early (3 · 12 · 13) 1007

מוּסָע discipline, correction; chastisement (30 · 50) 416

שֹׂבַע 25 fill, satiety, abundance (1 · 8) 959

חָסֵר to lack; be lacking (2 · 19 · 23) 341

Chapter 14

אִוֶּלֶת 1 folly (23 · 25) 17

הָרַס to tear down, throw down; break down or through (2 · 30 · 43) 248

יֹשֶׁר 2 rightness, uprightness; straightness, evenness; what is due, right (5 · 14) 449

יָרֵא ptc. = fearing, reverencing, honoring (3 · 45) 431

נָלוֹז to be devious, crooked (3 · 4 · 6) 531

בָּזָה to despise, regard with contempt (3 · 31 · 42) 102

אֱוִיל 3 fool; foolish (19 · 26) 17

חֹטֶר rod, branch, twig (1 · 2) 310

גַּאֲוָה pride, haughtiness; majesty, rising up (2 · 19) 144

תִּשְׁמוּרֵם prob. rd. תִּשְׁמְרוּס; שָׁמַר to protect 1036

בְּאֵין 4 for want of, without, for lack of; of time = when there was [were] not (8 · 10) 35 II אַיִן 6.a

אֶלֶף pl. only, cattle (1 · 8) 48 I

אֵבוּס crib, feeding trough (1 · 3) 7

בַּר clean; pure, clear (2 · 14[?]) 141

תְּבוּאָה gain, product, income; yield (8 · 43) 100

כָּזַב 5 to lie, tell a lie (1 · 12 · 16) 469

הֵפִיחַ to breathe out, utter; blow (7 · 12 · 13) 806 פוח

כָּזָב lie, falsehood, deceptive thing (9 · 31) 469

לֵץ 6 ptc. = scorner (14 · 16) 539 ליץ

נָבוֹן Niph. ptc. = understanding or intelligent [one] (9 · 21) 106 בין

נָקַל Niph., קלל = to be easy 886

מִנֶּגֶד 7 from before; in front of; from the front of; opposite (1 · 26) 617 2.c.(b)(γ)

עָרוּם 8 shrewd, sensible; crafty (8 · 11) 791

אִוֶּלֶת folly (23 · 25) 17

מִרְמָה treachery, deceit (8 · 39) 941 I

אֱוִיל 9 fool; foolish (19 · 26) 17

לִיץ to scorn [Lis. 727 Hiph., to deride] (3 · 9 · 12) 539

אָשָׁם guilt; offence, trespass; compensation, satisfaction; trespass-offering (1 · 46) 79

מָרָה 10 bitterness (1 · 2[?]) 601

הִתְעָרֵב to share in [ב]; to have fellowship; exchange pledges (3 · 5 · 5[?]) 786 II

הִפְרִיחַ 11 to show buds, sprouts; cause to bud, sprout (1 · 5 · 33) 827

שְׂחֹק 13 laughter; derision; sport (2 · 15) 966

כָּאַב to be in pain (1 · 4 · 8) 456

תּוּגָה grief (3 · 4) 387

סָג 14 to backslide; ptc. = backslider
(1 · 3 · 25) 690 סוג

פֶּתִי 15 simple, open-minded (15 · 18) 834

עָרוּם prudent man, shrewd, sensible;
crafty (8 · 11) 791

אָשׁוּר step, going (1 · 10) 81 אשר

הִתְעַבֵּר 16 to be arrogant; put oneself in a
fury; incite to fury against oneself
(3 · 8 · 8) 720

קָצֵר 17 short; אַפַּיִם ק׳ = impatient (2 · 5)
894

אִוֶּלֶת folly (23 · 25) 17

מְזִמָּה power of devising, discretion; purpose; evil thought, device (8 · 19)
273

פֶּתִי 18 simple, open-minded (15 · 18) 834

אִוֶּלֶת folly (23 · 25) 17

עָרוּם prudent man, shrewd, sensible;
crafty (8 · 11) 791

הכתיר to throw out as a crown [dub.],
perh. encompass (1 · 3 · 6) 509

שַׁח 19 to bow; be bowed down, prostrated, humbled; crouch (1 · 12 · 18)
1005 שחח

רָשׁ 20 ptc. = poor, poor man [men]
(14 · 21) 930 רוש

אֹהֵב ptc. = lover, friend (6 · 36) 12

עָשִׁיר rich (9 · 23) 799

בַּז 21 to despise (8 · 14) 100 בוז

עָנָו 21 Qere = poor, needy; humble,
lowly, meek (3 · 21) 776

אֶשֶׁר pl. cstr. = happiness, blessedness
of (8 · 45) 80

תָּעָה 22 to err, go astray, wander about
(3 · 27 · 50) 1073

חרשׁ to devise; plough; engrave
(7 · 23 · 26) 360

עֶצֶב 23 toil, hurt, pain (4 · 6) 780 I

מוֹתָר abundance, plenty; superiority
(2 · 3) 452

מַחְסוֹר need, poverty; thing needed (8 · 13)
341

עֲטָרָה 24 crown, wreath (5 · 23) 742 I

עֹשֶׁר riches (9 · 37) 799

אִוֶּלֶת folly (23 · 25) 17

הפיח 25 to breath out, utter; blow
(7 · 12 · 13) 806 פוח

כָּזָב lie, falsehood, deceptive thing
(9 · 31) 469

מִרְמָה treachery, deceit (8 · 39) 941 I

יִרְאָה 26 fear of God, reverence, piety; fear,
terror (14 · 45) 432

מִבְטָח security, confidence (4 · 15) 105

מַחְסֶה refuge, shelter (1 · 20) 340

יִרְאָה 27 fear of God, reverence, piety; fear,
terror (14 · 45) 432

מָקוֹר spring, source (7 · 18) 881 קור

מוֹקֵשׁ lure, bait, snare (8 · 27) 430

הֲדָרָה 28 glory, adornment (1 · 5) 214

בְּאֶפֶס without (1 · 3) 67 אֶפֶס 2.b

לְאֹם people = population (4 · 35) 522

מְחִתָּה ruin; terror (7 · 11) 369

רָזוֹן potentate (1 · 1) 931 II

אֶרֶךְ 29 long; אַפַּיִם א׳ = slow to anger
(3 · 15) 74

תְּבוּנָה understanding (19 · 42) 108

קָצֵר short; רוּחַ ק׳ = impatient (2 · 5) 894

אִוֶּלֶת folly (23 · 25) 17

מַרְפֵּא 30 health, profit; healing, cure (2 · 3
[?]) 951 Lis. calmness

רָקָב rottenness, decay (2 · 5) 955

קִנְאָה ardor of anger, of zeal, of jealousy
(3 · 43) 888

עָשַׁק 31 to oppress, wrong; extort
(4 · 36 · 37) 798

דַּל poor, reduced, low; thin (15 · 48)
195

חֵרֵף to reproach, say sharp things
against (2 · 34 · 38) 357

עֹשֵׂה ptc. = maker (2 · 24) 793 עשה 1.b

נִדְחֶה 32 to be thrust or cast down
(1 · 1 · 4 [?]) 190

חָסָה to seek refuge (2 · 37 · 37) 340

נָבוֹן 33 *Niph.* ptc. = understanding or intelligent [-one] (9 · 21) 106 בין

חֶסֶד 34 reproach, shame (1 · 2) 340 II

לְאֹם people (4 · 35) 522

עֶבְרָה 35 overflowing rage, fury; arrogance;
overflow (5 · 34) 720

Chapter 15

מַעֲנֶה 1 answer, response (3 · 6) 775

רַךְ soft = gentle; weak; tender, delicate (3 · 16) 940

עֶצֶב hurt, pain, toil (4 · 6) 780 I

הַבִּיעַ 2 to pour forth, belch forth; to pour
out; to cause to bubble, ferment
(3 · 10 · 11) 615 נבע

אִוֶּלֶת folly (23 · 25) 17

צָפָה 3 to keep watch, look out, spy
(2 · 9 · 18) 859

מַרְפֵּא 4 health, profit; healing, cure (2 · 3
[?]) 951 Lis. calmness

סֶלֶף crookedness, crooked dealing (2 · 2)
701

שֶׁבֶר breaking, shattering; crashing; solving (4 · 45) 991 I

אֱוִיל 5 fool; foolish (19 · 26) 17 אול

נָאַץ to contemn, spurn (3 · 8 · 24) 610

מוּסָר chastisement; discipline, correction
(30 · 50) 416

תּוֹכַחַת reproof, chiding; argument (16 · 24)
407

הֶעְרִים to be or become shrewd [Lis. 1116
Qal w. similar meaning] (2 · 4 · 5)
791

חֹסֶן 6 wealth, treasure (2 · 5) 340

תְּבוּאָה income revenue, gain; product,
yield (8 · 43) 100

נֶעְכָּר to be stirred up; ptc. fem. = disturbance, calamity (1 · 2 · 15) 747

זָרָה 7 *Piel,* to disperse, scatter; winnow,
sift (3 · 25 · 38) 279

כֵּן right, לֹא־כֵן = [is] not right (2 · 24) 467

מוּסָר 10 chastisement; discipline, correction
(30 · 50) 416

תּוֹכַחַת reproof, chiding; argument (16 · 24)
407

אֲבַדּוֹן 11 destruction, ruin, place of ruin in
Sheol (1 · 5) 2

אַף־כִּי 'tis indeed that, how much more!
furthermore; yea, when (6 · 26) 65

לֵץ 12 ptc. = scorner (14 · 16) 539 ליץ

שָׂמֵחַ 13 joyful, glad, merry (4 · 21) 970

עַצֶּבֶת hurt, pain, injury (2 · 5) 781

נָכֵא stricken (3 · 3) 644

נָבוֹן 14 *Niph.* ptc. = understanding or intelligent [one] (9 · 21) 106 בין

אִוֶּלֶת folly (23 · 25) 17

מִשְׁתֶּה 15 feast, banquet (1 · 46) 1059

יִרְאָה 16 fear of God, reverence, piety; fear,
terror (14 · 45) 432

מְהוּמָה disquietude, confusion, tumult; discomfiture (1 · 12) 223

אֲרֻחָה 17 meal, allowance (1 · 7) 73

יָרָק herbs, herbage = green, greens
(1 · 3) 438

אָבַס pass. ptc. = fattened (1 · 2 · 2) 7

שִׂנְאָה hatred, hating (4 · 17) 971 שׂנא

גָּרָה 18 *Piel,* to excite or stir up [strife]
(3 · 3 · 14) 173

מָדוֹן strife, contention (9 · 12[?]) 193 I דין

אָרֵךְ long; אַ אַפַּיִם = slow to anger
(3 · 15) 74

הִשְׁקִיט to pacify, allay, cause quietness;
show quietness (1 · 10 · 41) 1052

עָצֵל 19 sluggard; sluggish, lazy (14 · 15) 782

מְשֻׂכָה hedge (1 · 1) 962

חֵדֶק brier (1 · 2) 293

סָלַל   to cast up, lift up (1 · 10 · 12) 699

בָּזָה 20   to despise, regard with contempt (3 · 31 · 42) 102

אִוֶּלֶת 21   folly (23 · 25) 17

חָסֵר   needy, lacking; idiom = חֲסַר־לֵב lacking understanding, sense [11 · 11] (13 · 17) 341

תְּבוּנָה   understanding (19 · 42) 108

יָשַׁר   Piel, to make smooth, straight; to lead straight along; esteem right (4 · 9 · 25) 448

הֵפֵר 22   to frustrate, make ineffectual; break, violate (1 · 42 · 45) 830 פרר

בְּאֵין   for want of, without, for lack of; of time = when there was [were] not (8 · 10) 35 II אַיִן 6.a

סוֹד   secret counsel; counsel; council, assembly (5 · 21) 691

יוֹעֵץ   ptc. = counselor, adviser (3 · 22) 419

מַעֲנֶה 23   answer, response (3 · 6) 775

לְמַעְלָה 24   upward; exceedingly (1 · 34) 751 II מכעל 2.c

מַטָּה   downwards (1 · 3) 641

גֵּאֶה 25   proud (2 · 8) 144

נסח   to tear down, away, pull away (2 · 3 · 4) 650

אֵמֶר 26   utterance, word (22 · 48) 56

נֹעַם   pleasantness; delightfulness (3 · 7) 653

עָכַר 27   to disturb, trouble, stir up (3 · 13 · 15) 747

בצע   to gain by violence, cut off, break off (2 · 10 · 16) 130

בֶּצַע   unjust gain, gain made by violence (3 · 23) 130

מַתָּנָה   gift = bribe (1 · 17) 682 I נתן

הָגָה 28   to imagine, devise, meditate; growl, moan; utter (3 · 23 · 25) 211 I

הִבִּיעַ   to pour forth, belch forth; pour out;

---

cause to bubble forth, ferment (3 · 10 · 11) 615 בע

מָאוֹר 30   luminary, lamp; מ׳ עֵינַיִם = the eyes as a lamp (1 · 19) 22

שְׁמוּעָה   report = news; mention (2 · 27) 1035

דשׁן   Piel, to make fat; clear away fat ashes (1 · 5 · 11) 206

תּוֹכַחַת 31   reproof, chiding; argument (16 · 24) 407

פָּרַע 32   to let alone, = neglect; to let go, let loose (5 · 13 · 16) 828 III

מוּסָר   discipline, correction; chastisement (30 · 50) 416

תּוֹכַחַת   reproof, chiding; argument (16 · 24) 407

יִרְאָה 33   fear of God, reverence, piety; fear, terror (14 · 45) 432

מוּסָר   discipline, correction; chastisement (30 · 50) 416

עֲנָוָה   humility, meekness; condescension (3 · 4) 776

Chapter 16

מַעֲרָךְ 1   arrangement (1 · 1) 790

מַעֲנֶה   answer, response (3 · 6) 775

זַךְ 2   pure, clean, righteous (3 · 11) 269

תכן   to estimate; ptc. = an estimate (3 · 3 · 18) 1067

גלל 3   to roll, roll away (2 · 10 · 17) 164 II

מַעֲנֶה 4   answer, response; here w. ל + suffix = for its purpose (1 · 1[?]) 775

גְּבֹהַּ 5   haughty; exalted; high, tall; loftiness (1 · 41) 147

יָד לְיָד   idiom: hand to hand, surely 391 יָד 5.f

נָקָה   to be free, exempt from punishment; exempt from guilt, from obligation; be cleaned out (7 · 24 · 41) 667

יִרְאָה 6 fear of God, reverence, piety; fear, terror (14 · 45) 432

רָצָה 7 to be pleased with, favorable to; accept favorably (3 · 42 · 50) 953

תְּבוּאָה 8 income, revenue, gain; product, yield (8 · 43) 100

בְּלֹא without; בְּ׳ מִשְׁפָּט = through injustice, without justice (3 · 31) 520 לֹא 4.a.(c)

צַעַד 9 step, steps; pace (4 · 14) 857

קֶסֶם 10 divination, oracle (1 · 11) 890

מָעַל to act unfaithfully, treacherously (1 · 35 · 35) 591

פֶּלֶס 11 balance, scale (1 · 2) 813

מֹאזְנַיִם balances, scales (3 · 15) 24

כִּיס bag, purse (2 · 5) 476

רֶשַׁע 12 wickedness (5 · 30) 957

עָב 15 dark cloud, cloud mass, thicket (1 · 30) 728

מַלְקוֹשׁ spring rain, later rain (1 · 8) 545

חָרוּץ 16 gold (4 · 6) 359

בִּינָה understanding; here = faculty of understanding (14 · 37) 108

מְסִלָּה 17 highway, public road [not in city] (1 · 27) 700

שֶׁבֶר 18 breaking, shattering; crashing; solving (4 · 45) 991 I

גָּאוֹן pride; exaltation; majesty (2 · 49) 144

כִּשָּׁלוֹן a stumbling; fig. = calamity (1 · 1) 506

גֹּבַהּ haughtiness; exaltation, grandeur; height (1 · 17) 147

שָׁפָל 19 const. of adj. שָׁפָל low [Lis.], or infin. const. of שָׁפֵל "to be low" (2 · 18[?]) 1050

עָנָו Qere = humble, lowly, meek; poor (3 · 21) 776

גֵּאֶה proud (2 · 8) 144

אֶשֶׁר 20 pl. cstr. = happiness, blessedness of (8 · 45) 80

נָבוֹן 21 Niph. ptc. = understanding or intelligent [one] (9 · 21) 106 גין

מֶתֶק sweetness (2 · 2) 608

לֶקַח teaching power, persuasiveness; thing taught; instruction (6 · 9) 544

מָקוֹר 22 spring, source (7 · 18) 881

שֵׂכֶל insight, understanding; prudence, good sense (6 · 16) 968

מוּסָר discipline, correction; chastisement (30 · 50) 416

אֱוִיל fool; foolish (19 · 26) 17

אִוֶּלֶת folly (23 · 25) 17

לֶקַח 23 teaching power, persuasiveness; thing taught; instruction (6 · 9) 544

צוּף 24 [honey]comb (1 · 2) 847 I

אֹמֶר utterance, word (22 · 48) 56

נֹעַם pleasantness, delightfulness (3 · 7) 653

מָתוֹק sweet, sweetness (3 · 12) 608

מַרְפֵּא health, profit; healing, cure (6 · 13) 951

עָמֵל 26 laborer; sufferer (1 · 9) 766 I

עָמַל to labor (1 · 11 · 11) 765

אָכַף to press, urge (1 · 1 · 1) 38

בְּלִיַּעַל 27 worthless, good-for-nothing, base; worthlessness (3 · 27) 116 בְּלִי + יַעַל

כָּרָה to dig (2 · 13 · 14) 500

צָרֶבֶת burning, scorching (1 · 1) 863

תַּהְפֻּכָה 28 perverse thing, perversity (9 · 10) 246

מָדוֹן strife, contention (9 · 12[?]) 193 I

נִרְגָּן Niph. ptc. = backbiter (4 · 4) 920

הִפְרִיד to divide, separate; make a division (3 · 7 · 26) 825

אַלּוּף friend, intimate; tame (3 · 9) 48 I אלף

פָּתָה 29 to entice, persuade, seduce; deceive (3 · 17 · 27) 834

549

עצה 30 to shut (1 · 1 · 1) 781 I

תַהְפֻּכָה perverse thing, perversity (9 · 10) 246

קרץ to pinch, nip (3 · 4 · 5) 902

עֲטָרָה 31 crown, wreath (5 · 23) 742 I

תִּפְאָרֶת glory; honor; beauty (6 · 50) 802

שֵׂיבָה gray hair; old age (2 · 20) 966 שׁיב

אָרֵךְ 32 long; אֶרֶךְ אַפַּיִם = slow to anger (3 · 15) 74

חֵיק 33 fold of garment at breast; bosom (5 · 38) 300

הוטל *Hoph.*, to be cast, thrown; be hurled (1 · 4 · 14) 376 טול

Chapter 17

פַּת 1 morsel, fragment, bit (3 · 14) 837

חָרֵב dry (1 · 10[?]) 351

שַׁלְוָה quietness, peace; ease, careless security (2 · 8) 1017

מַצְרֵף 3 crucible (2 · 2) 864 צרף

כּוּר smelting pot, furnace (2 · 9) 468

בחן to prove, test; examine, scrutinize (1 · 25 · 29) 103

מֵרַע 4 *Hiph.* ptc. = evildoer (2 · 18) 949 רעע

הִקְשִׁיב to give attention (8 · 45 · 46) 904

הֶאֱזִין to give ear, listen, hear (1 · 41 · 41) 24

הַוָּה engulfing ruin, destruction; desire (2 · 13[?]) 217

לעג 5 to mock, deride (3 · 12 · 18) 541

רָשׁ ptc. = poor, poor man [men] (14 · 21) 930 רושׁ

חֵרֵף to reproach, say sharp things against (2 · 34 · 38) 357 I

עֹשֵׂה ptc. = maker (2 · 24) 794 עשׂה I 1.b

שָׂמֵחַ glad, joyful, merry, here = subst. (4 · 21) 970

אֵיד distress, calamity (6 · 24) 15

נקה to be free, exempt from punishment; exempt from guilt, from obligation; be cleaned out (7 · 24 · 41) 667

עֲטָרָה 6 crown, wreath (5 · 23) 742 I

תִּפְאֶרֶת honor, glorying, boasting; beauty; glory (6 · 50) 802

נָאוֶה 7 seemly, comely, beautiful (3 · 9) 610

נָבָל fool, foolish (3 · 18) 614 I

יֶתֶר idiom: here w. שׂפה = lip of excess = arrogant speech 451 I 2.a

אַף־כִּי 'tis indeed that, how much more! furthermore; yea, when (6-26) 65

נָדִיב adj. or noun m. noble, princely, generous (5 · 27) 622

שֹׁחַד 8 bribe, present (4 · 23) 1005

שָׁנָה 9 to repeat, do again (3 · 14 · 26) 1040 III

הִפְרִיד to divide, separate; make a division (3 · 7 · 26) 825 I

אַלּוּף friend, intimate; tame (3 · 9) 48 I

נחת 10 to go down, descend (1 · 3 · 8) 639

גְּעָרָה rebuke (3 · 15) 172

מְרִי 11 rebellion (1 · 22) 598

אַכְזָרִי cruel, cruel one (4 · 8) 470

פגשׁ 12 to meet, encounter (1 · 10 · 14) 803

דֹּב bear (2 · 12) 179

שַׁכּוּל bereaved, robbed of offspring (1 · 6) 1014

אִוֶּלֶת folly (23 · 25) 17

הֵמִישׁ 13 to depart (*Qal*) or, to remove, take away (*Hiph.*) (1 · 20 · 20) 559 מושׁ

פָּטַר 14 to set free, let out; remove oneself (1 · 8 · 9) 809

מָדוֹן strife, contention (9 · 12[?]) 193 I

הִתְגַּלַּע to disclose oneself, break or burst out (3 · 3 · 3) 166

נָטַשׁ to forsake, abandon; leave; permit (3 · 33 · 40) 643

הִצְדִּיק 15 to declare righteous, justify; do justice; vindicate cause of, save; turn to righteousness (1 · 12 · 41) 842

הִרְשִׁיעַ to condemn as guilty; act wickedly
(2 · 25 · 34) 957

מְחִיר 16 price; hire (2 · 15) 564 I מחר

חָסֵר 18 needy, lacking; idiom: חֲסַר־לֵב =
lacking understanding, sense
[11 · 11] (13 · 17) 341

תָּקַע כַּף to strike hands, gesture ratifying a
bargain pledging oneself for surety
(3 · 3) 1075 תקע 3

עָרַב to give in pledge; take on pledge,
go surety for (6 · 15 · 17) 786

עֲרֻבָּה pledge, token; thing exchanged
(1 · 2) 786

מַצָּה 19 strife, contention (2 · 3) 663 II

הגבה Hiph., to make high, exalt
(1 · 10 · 34) 146

שֶׁבֶר breaking, shattering; crashing; solving (4 · 45) 991 I

עִקֵּשׁ 20 twisted, perverted (7 · 11) 786 I

תּוּגָה 21 grief (3 · 4) 387

נָבָל fool; foolish (3 · 18) 614 I

שָׂמֵחַ 22 joyful, glad, merry (4 · 21) 970

גֵּהָה healing, cure (1 · 1) 155

נָכֵא stricken (3 · 3) 644

גֶּרֶם bone; strength; self (2 · 5) 175

שֹׁחַד 23 bribe, present (4 · 23) 1005

חֵיק fold of garment at breast; bosom
(5 · 38) 300

כַּעַס 25 vexation, anger; grief (4 · 25) 495

מֶמֶר bitterness (1 · 1) 601

ענש 26 to fine, punish (2 · 6 · 9) 778

נָדִיב noble, princely, generous (5 · 27)
622

יֹשֶׁר rightness, uprightness; straightness,
evenness; what is due, right (5 · 14)
449

חָשַׂךְ 27 to restrain; hold in check; keep
back (6 · 26 · 28) 362

אֵמֶר utterance, word (22 · 48)
56

קַר cool; קַר־רוּחַ = calm, self-possessed
(2 · 43) 903 [Qere = יָקָר, weighty,
precious, influential (6 · 35) 429]

תְּבוּנָה understanding (19 · 42) 108

אֱוִיל 28 fool; foolish (19 · 26) 17

הֶחֱרִישׁ to be silent; make silent; be deaf
(2 · 38 · 46) 361 II

אטם to shut, stop (2 · 8 · 8) 31

נָבוֹן Niph. ptc. = understanding or intelligent [one] (9 · 21) 106 בין

Chapter 18

תַּאֲוָה 1 thing desired; desire, wish; lust
(8 · 21) 16 I

נפרד to divide, separate (2 · 12 · 26) 825

תּוּשִׁיָּה abiding success; sound, efficient
wisdom (4 · 12) 444

הִתְגַּלַּע to disclose oneself, break or burst
out (3 · 3 · 3) 166

תְּבוּנָה 2 understanding (19 · 42) 108

בּוּז 3 contempt (2 · 11) 100

קָלוֹן dishonor, disgrace; ignominy
(8 · 17) 885

עָמֹק 4 deep = insearchable (4 · 17) 771

נבע to flow; ptc. = flowing (1 · 1 · 11)
615

מָקוֹר spring, source (7 · 18) 881 קור

מַהֲלֻמּוֹת 6 strokes, blows (2 · 2) 240 הלם

מְחִתָּה 7 ruin; terror (7 · 11) 369

מוֹקֵשׁ lure, bait, snare (8 · 27) 430

נִרְגָּן 8 Niph. ptc. = backbiter (4 · 4) 920

התלהם to swallow greedily; ptc. = bits
greedily swallowed, dainty
(2 · 2 · 2) 529

חֶדֶר room, chamber [usually private]
(6 · 37) 293

הִתְרַפָּה 9 to show oneself slack (2 · 3 · 44) 951

מַשְׁחִית Hiph. ptc. destroyer (2 · 19) 1008

מִגְדָּל 10 tower; elevated stage (1 · 49) 153 גדל

551

נִשְׂגָּב to be set on high, be high; be exalted (2 · 10 · 20) 960

הוֹן wealth; high value, price; sufficiency (18 · 26) 223

עָשִׁיר the rich; rich (9 · 23) 799

קִרְיָה city, town (5 · 30) 900

נִשְׂגָּב to be high, be set on high; be exalted (2 · 10 · 20) 960

מַשְׂכִּית imagination, conceit; showpiece, carved figure (2 · 6) 967

שֶׁבֶר 12 breaking, shattering; crashing; solving (4 · 45) 991 I

גבה to be haughty; be encouraged [= be lofty]; be high, tall; be exalted (1 · 24 · 34) 146

עֲנָוָה humility, meekness; condescension (3 · 4) 776 ענה

בְּטֶרֶם 13 before (3 · 38) 382 טרם 2

אִוֶּלֶת folly (23 · 25) 17

כְּלִמָּה reproach, ignominy; insult (1 · 30) 484

כִּלְכֵּל 14 Pilp., to support, endure; sustain, support; contain (1 · 24 · 38) 465 כול

מַחֲלָה sickness, disease (1 · 2) 318

נָכֵא stricken (3 · 3) 644

נָבוֹן 15 Niph. ptc. = understanding or intelligent [one] (9 · 21) 106 בין

מַתָּן 16 gifts (3 · 5) 682 I נתן

הִרְחִיב to make room for [= gain access for], enlarge; make large (1 · 21 · 25) 931

הנחה to lead, guide (3 · 26 · 40) 634

חקר 17 to examine thoroughly, search (4 · 22 · 27) 350

מִדְיָן 18 strife, contention (10 · 10[?]) 193 I דין

עָצוּם mighty, strong in numbers (3 · 31) 783

הִפְרִיד to make a division; to divide, separate (3 · 7 · 26) 825

נִפְשַׁע 19 to be offended; ptc. = offended [dub.] (1 · 1 · 41) 833

קִרְיָה city, town (5 · 30) 900

מָדוֹן strife, contention (10 · 10[?]) 193 I דין

בְּרִיחַ bar (1 · 41) 138

אַרְמוֹן citadel, castle (1 · 33) 74

תְּבוּאָה 20 gain, product, income; yield (8 · 43) 100

אֹהֵב 21 ptc. = lover, friend (6 · 36) 12

הֵפִיק 22 to bring out, elicit, obtain; produce; promote (4 · 8 · 9) 807 II פוק

תַּחֲנוּן only pl., supplication for favor (1 · 18) 337

רָשׁ 23 ptc. = poor, poor man [men] (14 · 21) 930 רוש

עָשִׁיר the rich, rich (9 · 23) 799

עַז fierce; here pl. = fiercely; strong, mighty (3 · 22) 738

הִתְרֹעֵעַ 24 Hithp., to be broken in pieces [BDB sugg. rd. התרעה "to be companions" rt. רעה p. 945] (1 · 2 · 5 [?]) 949

אֹהֵב ptc. = lover, friend (6 · 36) 12

דָּבֵק clinging, cleaving (1 · 3) 180

Chapter 19

רָשׁ 1 ptc. = poor, poor man [men] (14 · 21) 930 רוש

תֹּם integrity; completeness; innocence (7 · 23) 1070

עִקֵּשׁ twisted, perverted (7 · 11) 786 I

בְּלֹא 2 without (3 · 31) לֹא 4.a

אץ to hasten, make haste; press; be pressed (4 · 8 · 10) 21 אוץ

אִוֶּלֶת 3 folly (23 · 25) 17 I

סלף to subvert, turn upside down, ruin; pervert (4 · 7 · 7) 701

זָעַף to be out of humor, dejected, fret; be enraged (1 · 4 · 4) 277

הוֹן 4 wealth; high value, price; sufficiency (18 · 26) 223

דַּל poor, reduced, weak, helpless, low; thin (15 · 48) 195

נִפְרָד to divide, separate (2 · 12 · 26) 825 I

נָקָה 5 to be free, exempt from punishment; exempt from guilt, from obligation; be cleaned out (7 · 24 · 41) 667

הֵפִיחַ to breathe out, utter; blow פוח (7 · 12 · 13) 806

כָּזָב lie, falsehood, deceptive thing (9 · 31) 469

נָדִיב 6 noble, princely, generous (5 · 27) 622

מַתָּן [coll.] gifts; אישמ׳ = a giver of gifts (3 · 5) 682 I נתן

רָשׁ 7 ptc. = poor, poor man [men] רוש (14 · 21) 930

אַף־כִּי 'tis indeed that, how much more! furthermore; yea, when (6 · 26) 65

מֵרֵעַ companion, confidential friend, friend (1 · 7) 946

אֹמֶר utterance, word (22 · 48) 56

תְּבוּנָה 8 understanding (19 · 42) 108

נָקָה 9 to be free, exempt from punishment; exempt from guilt, from obligation; be cleaned out (7 · 24 · 41) 667

הֵפִיחַ to breathe out, utter; blow פוח (7 · 12 · 13) 806

כָּזָב lie, falsehood, deceptive thing (9 · 31) 469

נָאוֶה 10 seemly, comely, beautiful (3 · 9) 610

תַּעֲנוּג luxury; daintiness; delight (1 · 5) 772

אַף־כִּי 'tis indeed that, how much more! furthermore; yea, when (6 · 26) 65

שֵׂכֶל 11 insight, understanding; prudence, good sense (6 · 16) 968

הֶאֱרִיד to prolong; grow long, continue long (3 · 31 · 34) 73

תִּפְאֶרֶת honor, glorying, boasting; beauty; glory (6 · 50) 802

נַהַם 12 growling (2 · 2) 625

כְּפִיר young lion (3 · 31) 498

זַעַף rage, raging; storming (1 · 7) 277

טַל night mist, dew (2 · 31) 378 I

עֵשֶׂב herb, herbage (2 · 33) 793

הַוָּה 13 engulfing ruin, destruction; desire [Lis. sep. rt] (2 · 13) 217

דֶּלֶף a dropping [of rain] (2 · 2) 196

טָרַד to be continuous; to persue, chase (2 · 2 · 2) 382

מִדְיָן strife, contention (10 · 10[?]) 193 I דין

הוֹן 14 wealth; high value, price; sufficiency (18 · 26) 223

עַצְלָה 15 sluggishness (1 · 1) 782

תַּרְדֵּמָה deep sleep (1 · 7) 922

רְמִיָּה slackness, laxness (4 · 15) 941 II רמה

רָעֵב to be hungry (3 · 12 · 14) 944

בָּזָה 16 to despise, regard with contempt (3 · 31 · 42) 102

הִלְוָה 17 Hiph. to lend; ptc. = lender (2 · 9 · 14) 531 II

דַּל poor, reduced, weak, helpless, low; thin (15 · 48) 195

גְּמוּל recompense; dealing; benefit (2 · 19) 168

יִסַּר 18 to discipline, correct; chasten (3 · 27 · 38) 415

תִּקְוָה hope; things hoped for, outcome (8 · 32) 876 II קוה

גְּרָל 19 Qere = גְּדָל 175

עֹנֶשׁ indemnity, fine (1 · 2) 778

קַבֵּל 20 to accept; take, receive (1 · 11 · 13) 867

מוּסָר discipline, correction; chastisement (30 · 50) 416

חָכַם to be or become wise, act wisely (12 · 19 · 27) 314

תַּאֲוָה 22 thing desired; desire, wish; lust (8 · 21) 16 I

רָשׁ ptc. = poor, poor man [men] (14 · 21) 930 רושׁ

כָּזָב lie, falsehood, deceptive thing (9 · 31) 469

יִרְאָה 23 fear of God, reverence, piety; fear, terror (14 · 45) 432

שָׂבֵעַ sated, satisfied; surfeited (2 · 10) 960

טָמַן 24 to hide, bury; conceal (2 · 28 · 31) 380

עָצֵל sluggard; sluggish, lazy (14 · 15) 782

צַלַּחַת dish (2 · 4) 852

לֵץ 25 ptc. = scorner (14 · 16) 539 ליץ

פֶּתִי simple, open-minded (15 · 18) 834

הֶעְרִים to be or become shrewd [Lis. p. 1116, Qal w. similar meaning] (2 · 4 · 5) 791

נָבוֹן Niph. ptc. = understanding or intelligent [one] (9 · 21) 106 בין

הֶחְפִּיר 26 to cause shame; display shame (2 · 4 · 17) 344 II

מוּסָר 27 discipline, correction; chastisement (30 · 50) 416

שׁגה to go astray; commit sin of ignorance; err; swerve, meander (5 · 17 · 21) 993

אֵמֶר utterance, word (22 · 48) 56

בְּלִיַּעַל 28 worthlessness, good-for-nothing (3 · 27) 116 בְּלִי + יַעַל

לִיץ to scorn [Lis. Hiph. to deride] (3 · 9 · 12) 539

בָּלַע to swallow up, engulf = destroy; swallow (2 · 20 · 41) 118

לֵץ 29 ptc. = scorner (14 · 16) 539 ליץ

שְׁפֶט judgment (1 · 16) 1048

מַהֲלֻמוֹת strokes, blows (2 · 2) 240

גֵּו back (3 · 6) 156 I בוה

Chapter 20

לֵץ 1 ptc. = scorner (14 · 16) 539 ליץ

המה to be boisterous, turbulent; to murmur, growl, roar (4 · 33 · 33) 242

שֵׁכָר intoxicating drink, strong drink (3 · 22) 1016

שׁגה to swerve, meander = be intoxicated (5 · 17 · 21) 993

חָכַם to be or become wise, act wisely (12 · 19 · 27) 314

נַהַם 2 growling (2 · 2) 625

כְּפִיר young lion (3 · 31) 498

אֵימָה terror, dread (1 · 17) 33

הִתְעַבֵּר to incite [one to] fury for oneself (3 · 8 · 8) 720

שֶׁבֶת 3 Qal. inf. = sitting [Lis. = sitting quietly] (1 · 7) 442 ישׁב I

אֱוִיל fool; foolish (19 · 26) 17

הִתְגַּלַּע to disclose oneself, break out, burst out (3 · 3 · 3) 166

חֹרֶף 4 harvest time, autumn (1 · 7) 358

עָצֵל sluggard; sluggish, lazy (14 · 15) 782

חרשׁ to plough; engrave; devise (7 · 23 · 26) 360 I

קָצִיר time of harvest; what is harvested; harvesting (5 · 49) 894 I קצר

עָמֹק 5 deep; unsearchable (4 · 17) 771

תְּבוּנָה understanding (19 · 42) 108

דלה to draw (2 · 5 · 6) 194

תֹּם 7 integrity; completeness; innocence (7 · 23) 1070

אֶשֶׁר pl. cstr. = happiness, blessedness of (8 · 45) 80

דִּין 8 judgment; cause, plea (5 · 19) 192

זרה Piel, to scatter, disperse; winnow, sift (3 · 25 · 38) 279

554

זכה 9 *Piel*, to make or keep clean, pure (1 · 4 · 8) 269

אֶבֶן וָאֶבֶן 10 idiom: = different [dishonest] weights (2 · 3[?]) 6 5

אֵיפָה ephah, dry measure = appr. 1 bath [appr. 40 liters] liquid measure (1 · 38) 35 בת 144

מַעֲלָל 11 acts [pl.], deed, practice (1 · 41) 760

הִתְנַכֵּר to make oneself known (1 · 1 · 41) 647 I

זַךְ pure, clean, righteous (3 · 11) 269

פֹּעַל deed, thing done; work, thing made; wages; acquisition (5 · 37) 821

שֵׁנָה 13 sleep (7 · 23) 446

פָּקַח to open [eyes or ears] (1 · 17 · 20) 824

אָזַל 14 to go away, go about (1 · 5 · 5) 23

פְּנִינִים 15 corals (4 · 6) 819

יָקָר preciousness; price; honor (1 · 17) 430

עָרַב 16 to take in pledge, go surety for; give in pledge (6 · 15 · 16) 786 II

נָכְרִי foreign, alien; fem. = foreign woman, harlot (9 · 45) 648

חבל to bind, hold in pledge (2 · 13 · 14) 286 I

עָרֵב 17 sweet, pleasant (1 · 2) 787

חָצָץ gravel (1 · 2) 346 I

תַּחְבֻּלָה pl. only, counsels, direction, guidance (5 · 6) 287

סוֹד 19 secret counsel, counsel; council, assembly (5 · 21) 691

רָכִיל slanderer, talebearer, informer (2 · 6) 940

פתה to be open-minded, simple (1 · 5 · 27) 834

הִתְעָרֵב to have fellowship; exchange pledges (3 · 5 · 5[?]) 786 II

דָּעַךְ 20 to go out, be extinguished (3 · 7 · 9) 200

נֵר lamp (6 · 45) 632 I

אִישׁוּן from אִישׁוֹן, pupil; בְּאִישׁוֹן חֹשֶׁךְ = in deep darkness [Lis. p. 170, time] (1 · 1) 36

בהל 21 *Pual*, to be hastened, ptc. = hastily gained (1 · 2 · 30) 96

קוה 22 *Piel*, to wait or look eagerly for (1 · 39 · 45) 875 I

אֶבֶן וָאֶבֶן 23 idiom: different [dishonest] weights (2 · 3[?]) 6 5

מֹאזְנַיִם balances, scales (3 · 15) 24

מִרְמָה treachery, deceit (8 · 39) 941 I

מִצְעָד 24 step (1 · 3) 857

מוֹקֵשׁ 25 lure, bait, snare (8 · 27) 430

לע to talk wildly, cry rashly (1 · 2 · 2) 534 I

בקר to consider, reflect; seek, inquire (1 · 7 · 7) 133

זרה 26 *Piel*, to disperse, scatter; winnow, sift (3 · 25 · 38) 279

אוֹפָן wheel (1 · 35) 66 אפן

נֵר 27 lamp (6 · 45) 632 I נון

נְשָׁמָה spirit, breath (1 · 24) 675 נשם

חפשׂ to search = test; think out (2 · 4 · 23) 344

חֶדֶר chamber, room [usually private] (6 · 37) 293

סָעַד 28 to support, uphold; sustain (1 · 12 · 12) 703

תִּפְאֶרֶת 29 honor, glorying, boasting; beauty; glory (6 · 50) 802

בָּחוּר young man (1 · 45) 104

הָדָר ornament; splendor, majesty; honor, glory (2 · 30) 214

שֵׂיבָה gray hair, old age (2 · 20) 966

חַבּוּרָה 30 stripe, blow (1 · 7) 289

פֶּצַע bruise, wound (3 · 8) 822

הַמְרִיק to cleanse away (1 · 1 · 4) 599 [Qere = תַּמְרוּק, a scraping, rubbing (1 · 4) 600]

מַכָּה   blow, stripe (1 · 48) 646

חֶדֶר   chamber, room [usually private] (6 · 37) 293

Chapter 21

פֶּלֶג   1 channel, canal (2 · 10) 811 I

תֹּכֵן   2 to estimate; ptc. = estimate (3 · 3 · 18) 1067

רוּם   4 haughtiness, height, loftiness (2 · 6) 927

רָחָב   wide, broad ר׳ לֵב = exultant, arrogant (2 · 21) 932 I

נִיר   lamp (1 · 5) 633 I נוּר

חָרוּץ   5 diligent; sharp (5 · 5) 358 I

מוֹתָר   abundance, plenty; superiority (2 · 3) 452

אָץ   to hasten, make haste; press; be pressed (4 · 8 · 10) 21 אוץ

מַחְסוֹר   need, poverty; thing needed (8 · 13) 341

פֹּעַל   6 acquisition (here only); deed, thing made; wages (5 · 37) 821

נִדָּף   to be driven, driven about (1 · 6 · 9) 623

שֹׁד   7 violence, havoc; devastation, ruin (2 · 25) 994 I

גָּרַר   to drag away (1 · 3 · 4) 176

מֵאֵן   to refuse (3 · 46 · 46) 549

הֲפַכְפַּךְ   8 crooked (1 · 1) 246

וָזָר   guilty, criminal [dub.] (1 · 1) 255

זַךְ   pure, clean, righteous (3 · 11) 269

פֹּעַל   deed, thing done; work, thing made; wages; acquisition (5 · 37) 821

פִּנָּה   9 corner (4 · 30) 819

גָּג   roof; top (2 · 29) 150

מִדְיָן   strife, contention (10 · 10[?]) 193 I דין

חָבֵר   association, בֵּית ח׳ = house in common; company; spell (2 · 7) 288 I

אִוָּה   10 to desire (1 · 11 · 27) 16 I

עָנַשׁ   11 to fine, punish (2 · 6 · 9) 778

לֵץ   ptc. = scorner (14 · 16) 539 ליץ

חָכַם   to be or become wise, act wisely (12 · 19 · 27) 314

פֶּתִי   simple, open-minded (15 · 18) 834

סִלֵּף   12 to subvert, turn upside down, ruin; pervert (4 · 7 · 7) 701

אָטַם   13 to shut, stop (2 · 8 · 8) 31

זְעָקָה   cry, outcry (1 · 18) 277 זעק

דַּל   reduced, weak, helpless, poor, low; thin (15 · 48) 195

מַתָּן   14 gifts (3 · 5) 682 I

סֵתֶר   secrecy; hiding place; covering (3 · 35) 712

כָּפָה   to subdue [prob.] (1 · 1 · 1) 495

שֹׁחַד   bribe, present (4 · 23) 1005

חֵיק   fold of garment at breast, bosom (5 · 38) 300

עַז   fierce, formidable; mighty, strong (3 · 22) 738

מְחִתָּה   15 dismay; ruin; terror (7 · 11) 369

תָּעָה   16 to err, go astray; wander about (3 · 27 · 50) 1073

רְפָאִים   shades, ghosts (3 · 8) 952

מַחְסוֹר   17 poverty, need; thing needed (8 · 13) 341

הֶעֱשִׁיר   to gain riches; make rich, enrich (5 · 14 · 17) 799

כֹּפֶר   18 the price of a life, ransom (3 · 13) 497 I

בָּגַד   to act or deal treacherously, faithlessly, deceitfully (9 · 49 · 49) 93

מָדוֹן   19 strife, contention (10 · 10[?]) 193 I דין

כַּעַס   vexation, anger; grief (4 · 25) 495

נֶחְמָד   20 to be desirable (1 · 4 · 21) 326

נָוֶה   [country-]habitation; abode of shepherd or flocks (3 · 45) 627 I

בִּלַּע   to swallow up, engulf = destroy; swallow (2 · 20 · 41) 118

מִבְטָח 22 act of confiding, security, confidence (4 · 15) 105 בטח

זֵד 24 insolent, presumptuous (1 · 13) 267

יָהִיר proud, haughty (1 · 2) 397

לֵץ ptc. = scorner (14 · 16) 539 ליץ

עֶבְרָה overflow, excess, outburst; overflowing rage, fury; arrogance (5 · 34) 720 עבר

זָדוֹן insolence, presumptuousness (3 · 10) 268

תַּאֲוָה 25 lust, appetite; desire, wish (8 · 21) 16 I אוה

עָצֵל sluggard; sluggish, lazy (14 · 15) 782

מֵאֵן to refuse (3 · 46 · 46) 549

הִתְאַוָּה 26 to desire, long for, lust after (5 · 16 · 27) 16

תַּאֲוָה lust, appetite; desire, wish (8 · 21) 16 I אוה

חָשַׂךְ to withhold, keep back; hold in check; restrain (6 · 26 · 28) 362

אַף־כִּי 27 ' tis indeed that, how much more! furthermore; yea, when (6 · 26) 65

זִמָּה evil device; plan, purpose (3 · 28) 273 I

כָּזָב 28 lie, falsehood, deceptive thing (9 · 31) 469

נֶצַח endurance in time, here w. ל = continually, everlastingness, ever; imminence (1 · 43) 664 I

הֵעֵז 29 Hiph., to make firm, w. face = show boldness (2 · 2 · 11) 738 עזז

בִּפְנֵי in the face of, in front of (1 · 17) 816 פָּנֶה II.3

תְּבוּנָה 30 understanding (19 · 42) 108

לְנֶגֶד in front of, before; in the sight of; over; for (1 · 32) 617 נֶגֶד 2.b

מוּכָן 31 = Hoph. ptc. 465 כון 2

תְּשׁוּעָה deliverance; salvation (3 · 34) 448

Chapter 22

עֹשֶׁר 1 riches (9 · 37) 799

עָשִׁיר 2 the rich; rich (9 · 23) 799 עשר

רָשׁ ptc. = poor, poor man [men] (14 · 21) 930 רוש

נִפְגָּשׁ to meet together, meet each other (2 · 3 · 14) 803

עָרוּם 3 prudent man, shrewd, sensible; crafty (8 · 11) 791

פֶּתִי simple, open-minded (15 · 18) 834

נֶעֱנָשׁ to be fined, punished (2 · 3 · 9) 778

עֵקֶב 4 consequence = gain, reward; end; (1 · 3) 784

עֲנָוָה humility, meekness; condescension (3 · 4) 776

יִרְאָה fear of God, reverence, piety; fear, terror (14 · 45) 432

עֹשֶׁר riches (9 · 37) 799

צֵן 5 thorn, barb (1 · 3) 856

פַּח bird trap (2 · 25) 809 I

עִקֵּשׁ twisted, perverted (7 · 11) 786 I

חָנַךְ 6 to train, train up; dedicate (1 · 5 · 5) 335 II

הִזְקִין to show age, grow old (1 · 2 · 27) 278

עָשִׁיר 7 the rich; rich (9 · 23) 799

רָשׁ ptc. = poor, poor man [men] (14 · 21) 930 רוש

לֹוֶה to borrow; ptc. = borrower (1 · 5 · 14) 531 II

הִלְוָה Hiph., to lend; ptc. = lender (2 · 9 · 14) 531 II

עַוְלָה 8 injustice, unrighteousness, wrong (1 · 32) 732

קָצַר to reap (1 · 24 · 24) 894 II

עֶבְרָה overflowing rage, fury; arrogance, overflow (5 · 34) 720

טוֹב־עַיִן 9 = bountiful 744 I עַיִן 3.b

דַּל   poor, reduced, weak, low, helpless; thin (15 · 48) 195

גרש   10   *Piel*, to drive out, away (1 · 35 · 48) 176

לֵץ   ptc. = scorner (14 · 16) 539   ליץ

מָדוֹן   strife, contention (9 · 12[?]) 193

דִּין   strife; judgment; cause, plea (5 · 19) 192

קָלוֹן   dishonor, disgrace; ignominy (8 · 17) 885

סלף   12   to subvert, turn upside down, ruin; pervert (4 · 7 · 7 ·) 701

בגד   to act or deal treacherously, faithlessly, deceitfully (9 · 49 · 49) 93

עָצֵל   13   sluggard; sluggish, lazy (14 · 15) 782

אֲרִי   lion (3 · 35) 71

רְחוֹב   broad open place in city (5 · 43) 932

נרצח   to be slain, be murdered (1 · 2 · 41) 953

שׁוּחָה   14   pit (2 · 5) 1001

עָמֹק   deep = unsearchable (4 · 17) 771

זָעַם   to be indignant; to express indignation in words, denounce, curse (2 · 11 · 12) 276

אִוֶּלֶת   15   folly (23 · 25) 17

קָשַׁר   to bind, confine; to league together (4 · 35 · 43) 905

מוּסָר   chastisement; discipline, correction (30 · 50) 416

עָשַׁק   16   to oppress, wrong; extort (4 · 36 · 37) 798

דַּל   poor, reduced, weak, low, helpless; thin (15 · 48) 195

עָשִׁיר   the rich; rich (9 · 23) 799

מַחְסוֹר   need, poverty; thing needed (8 · 13) 341

נָעִים   18   delightful; lovely (3 · 13) 653   I

מִבְטָח   19   act of confiding, confidence; security (4 · 15) 105

שִׁלְשׁם   20   three days ago, previously (1 · 25) 1026   Qere = שָׁלִישׁ, adjutant, officer [dub.] (1 · 16)   1026

מוֹעֵצָה   counsel, plan, principle (2 · 7) 420

קֹשְׁטְ   21   truth (1 · 1) 905

אֹמֶר   utterance, word (22 · 48) 56

גָּזַל   22   to tear away, rob, plunder, seize (2 · 29 · 30) 159

דַּל   reduced, weak, helpless, poor, low; thin (15 · 48) 195

דִּכָּא   to crush (1 · 11 · 18) 193

קָבַע   23   [dub.] to rob (2 · 6 · 6) 867

הִתְרָעָה   24   *Hithp.*, to make companionship with (1 · 1 · 6) 945

בַּעַל־אַף   = given to anger 60   I   אַף   3

אלף   25   to learn (1 · 1 · 4) 48   I

מוֹקֵשׁ   lure, bait, snare (8 · 27) 430

תָּקַע־כַּף   idiom: to strike hands, gesture ratifying a bargain, pledging oneself for surety (3 · 3) 1075   תָּקַע   3

עָרַב   to go surety for or (ל) take in pledge; give in pledge (6 · 15 · 17) 786   II

מַשָּׁאָה   loan (1 · 2) 673

מִשְׁכָּב   27   couch, bed; act of lying (2 · 46) 1012

הסיג   28   to displace, move back; remove (2 · 7 · 25) 690   I

מָהִיר   29   quick, prompt, ready, skilled (1 · 4) 555   מהר   I

התיצב   to present oneself, station oneself, take one's stand (2 · 48 · 48) 426

חָשֹׁךְ   obscure, low (1 · 1) 365

Chapter 23

לחם   1   to eat (4 · 6 · 6) 536   II

מֹשֵׁל   ptc. = ruler, one who rules (5 · 24) 605

שַׂכִּין   2   knife (1 · 1) 967

לֹעַ   throat [prob.] (1 · 1) 534

בַּעַל נֶפֶשׁ	idiom: one given to appetite בעל 127 para.I. 5.a
הִתְאַוָּה 3	to desire, long for, lust after (5 · 16 · 27) 16
מַטְעָם	pl. only, tasty or savory food, dainties (2 · 7) 381
כָּזָב	lie, falsehood, deceptive thing; w. לֶחֶם = deceptive or disappointing bread (9 · 31) 469
יָגַע 4	to toil, labor; grow or be weary (1 · 20 · 26) 388
הֶעְשִׁיר	to gain riches; make rich, enrich (5 · 14 · 17) 799
בִּינָה	understanding; here = faculty of understanding (14 · 37) 108
הֵעִיף 5	Q. to cause to fly or light upon (1 · 1 · 25) 733 עוף I
נֶשֶׁר	griffon vulture, eagle (3 · 26) 676
לָחַם 6	to eat (4 · 6 · 6) 536 II
רַע עַיִן	idiom: stingy (2 · 2) 744 I עַיִן 3.b
הִתְאַוָּה	to desire, long for, lust after (5 · 16 · 27) 16
מַטְעָם	pl. only, tasty or savory food, dainties (2 · 7) 381
שָׁעַר 7	to calculate, reckon (1 · 1 · 1) 1045 II
פַּת 8	fragment, bit, morsel (3 · 14) 837
קִיא	to vomit up, spew out, disgorge [Hiph., also poss.] (2 · 7 · 9) 883
נָעִים	delightful; lovely (3 · 13) 653 I
בַּז 9	to despise (8 · 14 · 14) 100 בוז
שֵׂכֶל	insight, understanding; prudence, good sense (6 · 16) 968
מִלָּה	word; words, speech, utterance (1 · 38) 576
הִסִּיג 10	to displace, move back; remove (2 · 7 · 25) 690 סוג I
יָתוֹם	orphan (1 · 42) 450
גָּאַל 11	ptc. = kinsman, kinsman redeemer, kinsman avenger (1 · 44) 145 I
מוּסָר 12	discipline, correction; chastisement (30 · 50) 416 יסר
אֵמֶר	utterance, word (22 · 48) 56
מָנַע 13	to withhold, hold back, (5 · 25 · 29) 5
מוּסָר	chastiscment; discipline, correction (30 · 50) 416
חָכַם 15	to be or become wise, act wisely (12 · 19 · 27) 314
עָלַז 16	to exult (1 · 16 · 16) 759
כִּלְיָה	pl. only, kidneys, fig. as seat of emotions (1 · 31) 480 כלה
מֵישָׁר	pl., uprightness, equity; evenness (5 · 19) 449
קִנֵּא 17	to be envious of; be jealous; be zealous for (4 · 18 · 32) 888
חַטָּא	sinner (3 · 19) 308
יִרְאָה	fear of God, reverence, piety; fear, terror (14 · 45) 432
תִּקְוָה 18	things hoped for, outcome; hope (8 · 32) 876 II
חָכַם 19	to be or become wise, act wisely (12 · 19 · 27) 314
אִשֵּׁר	to lead on; advance; set right; pronounce blessed or happy (2 · 5 · 7 [?]) 80
סָבָא 20	to imbibe, drink; ptc. = drunkard (2 · 3) 684
זוֹלֵל	to make light of = be lavish with, squander [but Lis. adj., lavish, low] (3 · 6) 272
סֹבֵא 21	to imbibe, drink heavily, ptc. = drunkard (2 · 3) 684 II
זוֹלֵל, זָלַל	to make light of = be lavish with, squander [but Lis. adj., lavish, low] (3 · 6) 272 II
קֶרַע	torn piece of garment, rag (1 · 4) 902
נוּמָה	somnolence; i.e., slumber, fig. for indolence (1 · 1) 630
בַּז 22	to despise (8 · 14 · 14) 100 בוז
זָקֵן	to be or become old (1 · 25 · 27) 278

מוּסָר 23 discipline, correction; chastisement (30 · 50) 416

בִּינָה understanding (14 · 37) 108

גִּיל 24 to rejoice (5 · 54 · 54) 162

גִּיל 25 to rejoice (5 · 54 · 54) 162

רָצָה 26 to be pleased with, favorable; accept favorably (3 · 42 · 50) 953

שׁוּחָה 27 pit (2 · 5) 1001

עָמֹק deep = unsearchable (4 · 17) 771

זוֹנָה ptc. fem. = harlot (4 · 33) 275

בְּאֵר pit, well (2 · 38) 91

צַר narrow, tight (2 · 20) 865 I

נָכְרִי fem. = foreign woman, harlot; foreign, alien (9 · 45) 648

חֶתֶף 28 prey (1 · 1) 369

אָרַב to lie in wait [with hostile purpose] (6 · 20 · 23) 70

בגד to act or deal treacherously, faithlessly, deceitfully (9 · 49 · 49) 93

לְמִי 29 to whom[?] whose[?] (6 · 20) 566 מִי b

אוֹי woe! (1 · 24) 17

אֲבוֹי exclam. of pain, Oh! (1 · 1) 5

מָדוֹן strife, contention (10 · 10[?]) 193 I

שִׂיחַ complaint, musing; anxiety (1 · 14) 967 I

פֶּצַע bruise, wound (3 · 8) 822

חִנָּם without cause; for no purpose; gratis (6 · 32) 336 חנן

חַכְלִילוּת dullness (1 · 1) 314 חכל

אָחַר 30 to delay, tarry (1 · 15 · 17) 29

חקר to search for, search through, examine thoroughly (4 · 22 · 27) 350

מִמְסָךְ mixed drink (1 · 2) 587

הִתְאַדַּם 31 to redden, grow or look red (1 · 1 · 10) 10

כִּיס Qere = כוס cup (1 · 31) 468 I

נָתַן עֵינוֹ idiom: sparkle, gleam 745 עַיִן 4.c

מֵישָׁר pl., evenness, hence smoothness; uprightness, equity (5 · 19) 449

נָחָשׁ 32 serpent (2 · 31) 638 I

נָשַׁךְ to bite (1 · 10 · 12) 675

צִפְעוֹנִי a poisonous serpent (1 · 5) 861

הִפְרִישׁ to pierce, sting [dub] (1 · 1 · 5[?]) 831 II

תַּהְפֻּכָה 33 perverse thing, perversity (9 · 10) 246

חֵבֶל 34 mast [prob.], here fig. of man in lookout basket of mast (1 · 1) 287

הלם 35 to smite, hammer, strike down (1 · 8 · 8) 240

מָתַי when[?] (2 · 42) 607

הֵקִיץ to show signs of awaking, to awake (2 · 22 · 23) 884 I

Chapter 24

קִנֵּא 1 to be envious of; be jealous of; be zealous for (4 · 18 · 32) 888

הִתְאַוָּה to desire, long for, lust after (5 · 16 · 27) 16

שֹׁד 2 violence, havoc; devastation, ruin (2 · 25) 994 I

הָגָה to imagine, devise, meditate; growl, moan; utter (3 · 23 · 25) 211 I

תְּבוּנָה 3 understanding (19 · 42) 108

חֶדֶר 4 storeroom, room, chamber [usually private] (6 · 37) 293

הוֹן wealth; high value, price; sufficiency (18 · 26) 223

יָקָר precious, costly; glorious; weighty (6 · 35) 429

נָעִים delightful, lovely (3 · 13) 653 I

אָמֵץ 5 to make firm, strengthen; assure; harden (3 · 19 · 41) 54

תַּחְבֻּלָה 6 pl. only, counsels, direction, guidance (5 · 6) 287

תְּשׁוּעָה deliverance; salvation (3 · 34) 448

יוֹעֵץ ptc. = counselor, adviser (3 · 22) 419

רָאמוֹת 7 corals (1 · 3) 910 I

אֱוִיל fool; foolish (19 · 26) 17

חָכְמוֹת wisdom (3 · 4[?]) 315

בַּעַל־מְזִמּוֹת 8 idiom: mischievous person 127 I בַּעַל 5.a

מְזִמָּה evil thought, device; power of devising, discretion; purpose (8 · 19) 273

זִמָּה 9 evil device, plan, purpose (3 · 28) 273 I

אִוֶּלֶת folly (23 · 25) 17

לֵץ ptc. = scorner (14 · 16) 539 ליץ

הִתְרַפָּה 10 to show oneself slack (2 · 3 · 44) 951

צַר narrow, tight (2 · 20) 865 I

מוֹט 11 to totter, slip (2 · 15 · 39) 556

הֶרֶג slaughter (1 · 5) 247

חָשַׂךְ to withhold, hold back; hold in check; restrain (6 · 26 · 28) 362

תֹּכֵן 12 to estimate; ptc. = estimate (3 · 3 · 11) 1067

פֹּעַל deed, thing done; work, thing made; wages; acquisition (5 · 37) 821

נֹפֶת 13 flowing honey, honey from the comb (3 · 5) 661

מָתוֹק sweet, sweetness (3 · 12) 608

חֵךְ palate, roof of mouth, gums (3 · 18) 335 חנך

דְּעֵה 14 Qal impv. ידע 393

תִּקְוָה things hoped for, outcome; hope (8 · 32) 876 II

אָרַב 15 to lie in wait [with hostile purpose] (6 · 20 · 23) 70

נָוֶה [country-]habitation; abode of shepherd or flocks (3 · 45) 627 I

רֵבֶץ [place of] lying down, resting or dwellingplace (1 · 4) 918

גִיל 17 to rejoice (5 · 54 · 54) 162

מֵרַע 19 Appar. Hiph. ptc. = evildoer (2 · 18) 949 רעע

קָנָא to be envious of; be jealous of; be zealous for (3 · 34 · 37) 888

נֵר 20 lamp (6 · 45) 632 I נור

דָּעַךְ to go out, be extinguished (3 · 7 · 9) 200

שָׁנָה 21 to change, differ (3 · 14 · 26[?]) 1039 I

הִתְעָרֵב to have fellowship; exchange pledges (3 · 5 · 5) 786 II

פִּתְאֹם 22 suddenly, suddenness (4 · 25) 837

אֵיד distress, calamity (6 · 24) 15

פִּיד ruin, disaster (1 · 4) 810

הַכִּיר 23 to regard, observe; recognize; be acquainted; distinguish (2 · 38 · 41) 647 I

קָבַב 24 to curse (2 · 14 · 14) 866 II

זָעַם to express indignation in speech, denounce, curse; be indignant (2 · 11 · 12) 276

לְאֹם people (4 · 35) 522

נָעֵם 25 to be pleasant, delightful, lovely (3 · 8 · 8) 653 I

נָשַׁק 26 to kiss (2 · 26 · 32) 676 I

נָכֹחַ right, correct, straight (2 · 8) 647

עָתַד 27 to make ready (1 · 1 · 2) 800

חִנָּם 28 without cause; for no purpose; gratis (6 · 32) 336 חנן I

פָּתָה to deceive, entice, persuade [or poss. sep. rt. Hiph., ''make wide with''] (3 · 17 · 27) 834

פֹּעַל 29 deed, thing done; work, thing made; wages, acquisition (5 · 37) 821

עָצֵל 30 sluggish, lazy; sluggard (14 · 15) 782

חָסֵר needy, lacking; idiom: חֲסַר־לֵב = lacking understanding or sense [11 · 11] (13 · 17) 341

קִמּוֹשׂ 31 [coll.] thistles or nettles (1 · 3) 888

חָרוּל a kind of weed, perh. = chickpea (1 · 3) 355

גְּדֵר   wall, fence (1 · 14) 154

נהרס   to be thrown or torn down (2 · 10 · 43) 248

מוּסָר 32 discipline, correction; chastisement (30 · 50) 416

שֵׁנָה 33 sleep (7 · 23) 446

תְּנוּמָה   slumber (3 · 5) 630

חִבֻּק   a clasping or folding (2 · 2) 287

רֵישׁ 34 poverty (7 · 7) 930

מַחְסוֹר   need, poverty; thing needed (8 · 13) חסר 341

אִישׁ מָגֵן   idiom: armed man (2 · 2) [but Lis. (2 · 4) insolent 749] 171

Chapter 25

מָשָׁל 1 sentence of ethical wisdom, proverb; parable (6 · 39) 605 II

העתיק   to transcribe; move forward (1 · 5 · 9) 801

חקר 2 to search out, through, for; examine thoroughly (4 · 22 · 27) 350

רוּם 3 height, loftiness; haughtiness (2 · 6) 927

עֹמֶק   depth (2 · 2) 771

חֵקֶר   searching, w. אֵין = it is unsearchable (2 · 12) 350

הָגָה 4 to remove (2 · 3 · 3) 212 II

סִיג   dross; a moving back or away (2 · 8) 691

צָרַף   ptc. = smelter, refiner, goldsmith (1 · 10) 864

הָגָה 5 to remove (2 · 3 · 3) 212 II

התהדר 6 to honor oneself, claim honor (1 · 1 · 6) 213

הֵנָּה 7 hither, here (3 · 48) 244 I

השפיל   to set in a lower place; make low; lay low (2 · 19 · 30) 1050

נָדִיב   noble, princely, generous (5 · 27) 622

מַהֵר 8 *Piel*. inf. abs. as adv. = quickly, speedily (1 · 18) 555

הכלים   to put to shame = insult, humiliate; cause shame to; exhibit shame (2 · 10 · 38) 483

סוֹד 9 secret counsel, counsel; council, assembly (5 · 21) 691

חסד 10 to reproach, expose to shame (1 · 1 · 1) 340 II

דִּבָּה   evil report; defamation; whispering (2 · 9) 179

תַּפּוּחַ 11 apple, apple tree (1 · 6) 656

מַשְׂכִּית   showpiece, carved figure; imagination, conceit (2 · 6) 967

אֹפֶן   circumstance, condition (1 · 1) 67

נֶזֶם 12 ring (2 · 17) 633

חֲלִי   ornament (1 · 2) 318 I

כֶּתֶם   gold (1 · 9) 508

צִנָּה 13 coolness (1 · 1) 856 II

שֶׁלֶג   snow (3 · 20) 1017

קָצִיר   time of harvest; what is harvested; harvesting (5 · 49) 894 I

צִיר   messenger, envoy (2 · 6) 851 II

נָשִׂיא 14 rising mist, vapor (1 · 4) 672

גֶּשֶׁם   rain, shower (2 · 35) 177 II

מַתָּת   gift (1 · 6) 682

פֻּתָּה 15 *Pual*, to be persuaded; be deceived (1 · 3 · 27) 834

קָצִין   ruler, dictator, chief, commander (2 · 11) 892

רַךְ   soft = gentle; weak; tender, delicate (3 · 16) 940

גֶּרֶם   bone; strength; self (2 · 5) 175

דַּי 16 what is sufficient, sufficiency, enough (2 · 12) [total freq. 35] 191

קִיא   to vomit up, spew out, disgorge [*Hiph*., poss.] (2 · 7 · 9) 883

הוקיר 17 to make rare = withhold; make rare = precious (1 · 2 · 11) 429 יקר

מֵפִיץ 18 scatterer, disperser (1 · 1) 807 פוץ

שָׁנַן	to whet, sharpen (1 · 7 · 9) 1041
מָעַד	19 *Pual* ptc. = shaken, tottered, slidden, slipped (1 · 1 · 7) 588
מִבְטָח	act of confiding, confidence; security (4 · 15) 105
בָּגַד	to act or deal treacherously, faithlessly, deceitfully (9 · 49 · 49) 93
הֶעְדָה	20 *Hiph.* ptc. = removing (1 · 1 · 2) 723 I
קָרָה	cold (1 · 5) 903
חֹמֶץ	vinegar (2 · 5) 330
נֶתֶר	natron, carbonate of soda [perh. used for washing hands] (1 · 2) 684
רָעֵב	21 hungry; to be hungry (3 · 12 · 14) 944
שֹׂנֵא	ptc. = enemy (3 · 41) 971
צָמֵא	thirsty, thirsty one (1 · 9) 854
גַּחֶלֶת	22 coal (3 · 18) 160 גחל
חתה	to snatch up (2 · 3 · 3) 367
חולל	23 *Polel*, to writhe in travail with, bear, bring forth; dance (2 · 7 · 47) 296 I חול
גֶּשֶׁם	rain, shower (2 · 35) 177 II
נזעם	*Niph.* ptc. = stirred with indignation (1 · 1 · 12) 276
סֵתֶר	secrecy; לְשׁוֹן ס׳ = tongue of secrecy; i.e., slanderous; hiding place, covering (3 · 35) 712
פִּנָּה	24 corner (4 · 30) 819
גָּג	roof (2 · 29) 150
מָדוֹן, מִדְיָן	strife, contention (10 · 10[?]) 193 I דין
חָבֵר	association; בֵּית־ח׳ = house in common (2 · 7) 288 I
קַר	25 cool (2 · 3) 903
עָיֵף	faint, weary (1 · 17) 746
שְׁמוּעָה	report = news; mention (2 · 27) 1035
מֶרְחָק	distant place, far country; distance (2 · 18) 935

מַעְיָן	26 spring (3 · 23) 745
נרפש	to be fouled [by stamping, treading], ptc. = befouled (1 · 1 · 5) 952 רפס
מָקוֹר	spring, source (7 · 18) 881
מוט	to totter, slip (2 · 15 · 39) 556
חֵקֶר	27 searching, thing to be searched out (2 · 12) 350
פֶּרֶץ	28 to make a breach, to break through, out, down, up, into, over (2 · 46 · 49) 829 I
מַעְצָר	restraint, control (1 · 1) 784

Chapter 26

שֶׁלֶג	1 snow (3 · 20) 1017
קַיִץ	summer, summer fruit (4 · 20) 884
מָטָר	rain (2 · 38) 564
קָצִיר	time of harvest; what is harvested; harvesting (5 · 49) 894 I
נָאוֶה	seemly, comely, beautiful (3 · 9) 610
צִפּוֹר	2 bird; birds (4 · 40) 861 II
נָד	to flutter, move to and fro, waver, shake; show grief (3 · 20 · 27) 626
דְּרוֹר	swallow (1 · 2) 204 II
עוּף	to fly; fly away (2 · 18 · 25) 733 I
קְלָלָה	curse (2 · 33) 887
חִנָּם	without cause; for no purpose; gratis (6 · 32) 336 חנן
שׁוֹט	3 whip; scourge (1 · 6) 1002
מֶתֶג	bridle (1 · 5) 607
גֵּו	back (3 · 6) 156 גוה
אִוֶּלֶת	4 folly (23 · 25) 17
שָׁוָה	to be like, comparable to; resemble, agree with (3 · 8 · 16) 1000 I
אִוֶּלֶת	5 folly (23 · 25) 17
קצה	6 to cut off (1 · 2 · 5) 891 I
דלה	7 to draw [dub.]; perh. דָּלְיוּ 3rd m. pl., hang down [helpless] (2 · 5 · 6) 194

563

שׁוֹק   leg (1 · 19) 1003

פִּסֵּחַ   lame (1 · 14) 820

מָשָׁל   sentence of ethical wisdom; proverb; parable (6 · 39) 605

מַרְגֵּמָה   8   sling (1 · 1) 920

חוֹחַ   9   brier, bramble; hook (1 · 11) 296

שִׁכּוֹר   drunken one, drunkard (1 · 13)
1016

מָשָׁל   sentence of ethical wisdom; wisdom; proverb; parable (6 · 39) 605

חוֹלֵל   10   *Polel*, to writhe in travail with,
bear, bring forth; dance (2 · 7 · 47)
296 I

שָׂכַר   to hire (2 · 17 · 20) 968

כֶּלֶב   11   dog (2 · 32) 476

קֵא   vomit (1 · 1) 883

שָׁנָה   to repeat, do again (3 · 14 · 26) 1040
III

אִוֶּלֶת   folly (23 · 25) 17

תִּקְוָה   12   hope, things hoped for, outcome
(8 · 32) II

עָצֵל   13   sluggard; sluggish, lazy (14 · 15) 782

שַׁחַל   lion (1 · 7) 1006

אֲרִי   lion (3 · 35) 71

רְחוֹב   broad open place [in city] (5 · 43)
932

צִיר   14   pivot, hinge (1 · 1) 852 III

עָצֵל   sluggard; sluggish, lazy (14 · 15) 782

מִטָּה   couch, bed (1 · 29) 641

טָמַן   15   to hide, bury; conceal (2 · 28 · 31)
380

עָצֵל   sluggard; sluggish, lazy (14 · 15) 782

צַלַּחַת   dish (2 · 4) 852

נִלְאָה   to make oneself weary, be weary;
be impatient (1 · 10 · 19) 521

עָצֵל   16   sluggard; sluggish, lazy (14 · 15) 782

טַעַם   taste, fig. for judgment, discretion,
discernment; taste; decision (2 · 13)
381

כֶּלֶב   17   dog (2 · 32) 476

הִתְעַבֵּר   to put oneself in a fury, become
furious; be arrogant (3 · 8 · 8) 720

הִתְלַהְלֵהַּ   18   *Hithpalp.* ptc., as subst. = madman (1 · 1 · 2) 529 להלה

יָרָה   to shoot, cast, throw; rain
(1 · 13 · 25[?]) 434

זֵק   spark, brand; missile (1 · 1[?]) 278

רִמָּה   19   to beguile, deceive, mislead
(1 · 8 · 8) 941 II

שָׂחַק   *Piel*, to jest; play; make sport
(3 · 16 · 36) 965

בְּאֶפֶס   20   without (2 · 5) 67 אֶפֶס 2.b

כָּבָה   to be quenched, extinguished, go
out (2 · 14 · 24) 459

בְּאֵין   without, for lack of, for want of
(8 · 10) II 35 אַיִן 6.a

נִרְגָּן   *Niph.* ptc. = backbiter (4 · 4) 920

שָׁתַק   to be quiet (1 · 4 · 4) 1060

מָדוֹן   strife, contention (9 · 12[?]) 193 I

פֶּחָם   21   coal, charcoal (1 · 3) 809

גַּחֶלֶת   coal (3 · 18) 160 גחל

מָדוֹן   strife, contention (10 · 10[?]) 193

חַרְחַר   *Pilp.* to kindle (1 · 1 · 9) 359 חרר I

נִרְגָּן   22   *Niph.* ptc. = backbiter (4 · 4) 920

הִתְלַהֵם   to swallow greedily; ptc. = bit
greedily swallowed, dainty
(2 · 2 · 2) 529

חֶדֶר   chamber, room [usually private]
(6 · 37) 293

סִיג   23   dross; a moving back or away
(2 · 8) 691 סוג

צֻפָּה   *Pual*, to be overlaid; ptc. = overlaid (1 · 2 · 46) 860 II

חֶרֶשׂ   earthenware (1 · 17) 360

דָּלַק   to burn; hotly pursue (1 · 7 · 9) 196

נִכַּר   24   *Niph.*, to disguise oneself, misconstrue; act or treat as foreign,
strange (1 · 1 · 8) 649

שֹׂנֵא   ptc. = enemy (3 · 41) 971

מִרְמָה   treachery, deceit (8 · 39) 941

שִׂנְאָה 26 hatred, hating (4 · 17) 971 שנא
מַשָּׁאוֹן hypocrisy, guile (1 · 1) 674
כָּרָה 27 to dig (2 · 13 · 14) 500 I
שַׁחַת pit (1 · 23) 1001
גלל to roll, roll away (2 · 10 · 17) 164 II
דַּךְ 28 crushed, oppressed (1 · 4) 194
חָלָק smooth; as subst. = flattery (2 · 12) 325
מִדְחֶה means or occasion of stumbling (1 · 1) 191

Chapter 27

נָכְרִי 2 foreign, alien; fem. = foreign woman, harlot (9 · 45) 648
כֹּבֶד 3 heaviness, weight; mass; vehemence (1 · 4) 458
נֵטֶל burden, weight (1 · 1) 642
חוֹל sand (1 · 22) 297
כַּעַס vexation, anger; grief (4 · 25) 495
אֱוִיל fool; foolish (19 · 26) 17
כָּבֵד heavy (1 · 40) 458
אַכְזְרִיּוּת 4 cruelty, fierceness (1 · 1) 470
שֶׁטֶף flood (1 · 6) 1009
קִנְאָה ardor of jealousy, of zeal, of anger (3 · 43) 888
תּוֹכַחַת 5 reproof, chiding; argument (16 · 24) 407
פֶּצַע 6 bruise, wound (3 · 8) 822
אֹהֵב friend, lover (6 · 36) 12
נעתר to be abundant (1 · 1 · 2) 801 II
נְשִׁיקָה kiss (1 · 2) 676
שָׂנֵא ptc. = enemy (3 · 41) 971
שָׂבֵעַ 7 sated, satisfied; surfeited (2 · 10) 960
בוס to tread down, trample; fig., to reject, loathe (1 · 7 · 12) 100
נֹפֶת flowing honey, honey from the comb (3 · 5) 661
רָעֵב hungry (1 · 19) 944
מַר bitter; bitterness (3 · 38) 600 I

מָתוֹק sweet, sweetness (3 · 12) 608
צִפּוֹר 8 bird; birds (4 · 40) 861 I
נדד to wander, stray; retreat, flee (3 · 20 · 27) 622
קֵן nest (1 · 13) 890
מֶתֶק 9 sweetness (2 · 2) 608
רֵעֶה 10 friend (1 · 5) 946
אֵיד distress, calamity (6 · 24) 15
שָׁכֵן neighbor; inhabitant (1 · 20) 1015
חָכַם 11 to be or become wise, act wisely (12 · 19 · 27) 314
חרף to reproach (1 · 4 · 38) 357 I
עָרוּם 12 prudent man, shrewd, sensible; crafty (8 · 11) 791
פֶּתִי simple, open-minded (15 · 18) 834
נענש to be fined, punished (2 · 3 · 9) 778
עָרַב 13 to take on pledge, go surety for; to give in pledge (6 · 15 · 17) 786 II
נָכְרִי fem. = foreign woman, harlot; foreign, alien (9 · 45) 648
חבל to bind, hold by pledge (2 · 13 · 14) 286 I
קְלָלָה 14 curse (2 · 33) 887
דֶּלֶף 15 a dropping [of rain] (2 · 2) 196
טרד to pursue, chase; to be continuous (2 · 2 · 2) 382
סַגְרִיר steady, persistent rain (1 · 1) 690
מָדוֹן strife, contention (10 · 10[?]) 193 I דין
נשתוה Nithp., to be alike, or Niph. נשוה same mng. (1 · 1 · 16) 1000 שוה I
צָפַן 16 to hide, treasure; lie hid, lurk (9 · 24 · 29) 860
חדה 17 to grow sharp (2 · 2 · 6[?]) 292 I
החדה to sharpen (2 · 2 · 6[?]) 292 I
תְּאֵנָה 18 fig tree; fig (1 · 39) 1061
אֲבַדֹּה 20 = אֲבַדּוֹן destruction, place of ruin in Sheol (1 · 1) 2
מַצְרֵף 21 crucible (2 · 2) 864
כּוּר smelting pot, furnace (2 · 9) 468 I

מַהֲלָל   praise (1 · 1) 239

כָּתַשׁ 22   to pound, pound fine (1 · 1 · 1) 509

אֱוִיל   fool; foolish (19 · 26) 17

מַכְתֵּשׁ   mortar, place of pounding (1 · 2) 509

רִיפָה   grain or fruit (1 · 2) 937

עֱלִי   pestle (1 · 1) 750

אִוֶּלֶת   folly (23 · 25) 17

עֵדֶר 23   flock; flocks and herds, flocks (1 · 37) 727 I

חֹסֶן 24   wealth, treasure (2 · 5) 340

נֵזֶר   crown; consecration; state of being a Nazirite (1 · 23) 634

חָצִיר 25   grass, green grass, herbage (1 · 18) 348

דֶּשֶׁא   grass (1 · 24) 206

עֵשֶׂב   herb, herbage (2 · 33) 793

לְבוּשׁ 26   garment, clothing, raiment (3 · 31) 528

מְחִיר   price; hire (2 · 15) 564 I מחר

עַתּוּד   male goat (1 · 29) 800

דַּי 27   sufficiency, what is sufficient, enough (2 · 12) [total freq. 35] 191

חָלָב   milk (2 · 44) 316

Chapter 28

כְּפִיר 1   young lion (3 · 31) 498

הַאֲרִיךְ 2   to last long; be long, grow long; prolong (3 · 31 · 34) 73

רָשׁ 3   ptc. = poor, poor man [men] (14 · 21) 930 רוש

עָשַׁק   to oppress, wrong; extort (4 · 36 · 37) 798

דַּל   reduced, weak, helpless, poor, low; thin (15 · 48) 195

מָטָר   rain (2 · 38) 564

סחף   to prostrate (1 · 1 · 2) 695

הִתְגָּרָה 4   to engage in strife, excite oneself (1 · 11 · 14) 173

רָשׁ 6   ptc. = poor, poor man [men] (14 · 21) 930 רוש

תֹּם   integrity; completeness; innocence (7 · 23) 1070

עִקֵּשׁ   twisted, perverted (7 · 11) 786 I

עָשִׁיר   rich (9 · 23) 799

רעה 7   to associate with (3 · 4 · 6) 945 II

זוֹלֵל   ptc. = lavishing with, squandering, making light of (3 · 6) 272

הכלים   to cause shame to; to put to shame = insult, humiliate; exhibit shame (2 · 10 · 38) 483

הוֹן 8   wealth; high value, price; sufficiency (18 · 26) 223

נֶשֶׁךְ   usury, interest (1 · 12) 675

תַּרְבִּית   increment, interest, usury (1 · 6) 916

דַּל   reduced, weak, helpless, poor, low; thin (15 · 48) 195

הִשְׁגָּה 10   to lead astray (1 · 4 · 21) 993

שְׁחוּת   pit (1 · 1) 1005

עָשִׁיר 11   the rich; rich (9 · 23) 799

דַּל   poor, reduced, weak, helpless, low; thin (15 · 48) 195

חקר   to examine thoroughly, search (4 · 22 · 27) 350

עָלַץ 12   to rejoice, exult (2 · 8 · 8) 763

תִּפְאֶרֶת   honor, glorying, boasting; beauty; glory (6 · 50) 802

חפשׂ   Pual, to be searched for = be hidden (1 · 2 · 23) 344

רחם 13   Pual, to be shown compassion (1 · 4 · 47) 933

אֶשֶׁר 14   pl. cstr. = happiness, blessedness (8 · 45) 80

פחר   Piel, to be in great dread (1 · 2 · 25) 808

הִקְשָׁה   to make hard, stiff, stubborn; make difficult; make severe (2 · 21 · 28) 904 I

אֲרִי 15   lion (3 · 35) 71

נהם   to growl, groan (2·5·5) 625

דֹּב   bear (2·12) 179

שָׁקַק   to rove, range, run, run about (1·5·6) 1055

מֹשֵׁל   ptc. = ruler; one who rules (5·24) 605 III

דַּל   poor, reduced, weak, helpless, low; thin (15·48) 195

נָגִיד   16 ruler, prince, leader (2·44) 617

חָסֵר   lacking, needy, in want of (13·17) 341

תְּבוּנָה   understanding (19·42) 108

מַעֲשַׁקָּה   extortionate act, extortion (1·2) 799

בֶּצַע   unjust gain, gain made by violence (3·23) 130

הֶאֱרִיךְ   to last long; be long, grow long; prolong (3·31·34) 73

עָשַׁק   17 to oppress, wrong; extort; ptc. psv. = oppressed (4·36·37) 798

תָּמַךְ   to lay hold of, grasp; hold up, support; hold, keep (8·20·21) 1069

נעקש   18 to be twisted (1·1·5) 786

רֵיק   19 empty, idle, worthless, here = unprofitable things (2·14) 938

רִישׁ   poverty (7·7) 930

אָץ   20 to hasten, make haste; press; be pressed (4·8·10) 21 אוץ

העשיר   to gain riches; make rich, enrich (5·14·17) 799

נִקָּה   to be free, exempt from punishment; exempt from guilt; exempt from obligation; be cleaned out (7·24·41) 667

הִכִּיר   21 to regard, recognize; be acquainted with; distinguish (2·38·41) 647 I

פַּת   fragment, bit, morsel (3·14) 837

פָּשַׁע   to transgress [against]; rebel, revolt (1·40·41) 833

נִבְהַל   22 to be in haste, hasty; be disturbed, dismayed, terrified (1·24·39) 96

הוֹן   wealth, high value, price; sufficiency (18·26) 223

רַע עַיִן   idiom: stingy (2·2) 744 I עַיִן 3.b

חֶסֶר   want, poverty (1·2) 341

הֶחֱלִיק   23 to make smooth; w. tongue = flatter (4·7·9) 325 II

גָּזַל   24 to tear away, rob, plunder, seize (2·29·30) 159 I

חָבֵר   associate, companion; united (1·12) 288

מַשְׁחִית   Hiph. ptc. = destroyer (2·19) 1008 2

רָחָב   25 wide, broad; רְחַב־נֶפֶשׁ = greedy (2·21) 932 I

גרה   Piel, to excite or stir up [strife] (3·3·14) 173

מָדוֹן   strife, contention (9·12[?]) 193 I דין

דֹּשַׁן   Pual, to be made fat (3·4·11) 206

רָשׁ   27 ptc. = poor, poor man [men] (14·21) 930 רוש

מַחְסוֹר   need, poverty; thing wanted (8·13) 341

הֶעְלִים   to conceal, hide, of eyes = disregard (1·11·29) 761 I

מְאֵרָה   a curse (2·5) 76

Chapter 29

תּוֹכַחַת   1 reproof, chiding; argument (16·24) 407

הִקְשָׁה   to make hard, stiff, stubborn; make difficult; make severe (2·21·28) 904 I

עֹרֶף   neck, back of neck; w. הקשה = be or become obstinate (1·33) 791 I

פֶּתַע   suddenly; suddenness (2·7) 837

מַרְפֵּא   health, profit; healing, cure (6·13) 951

נֶאֱנַח   2 to sigh, groan (1·12·12) 58

רעה   3 to associate with (3·4·6) 945 II

זוֹנָה   ptc. = harlot (4·33) 275

הוֹן	wealth; high value, price; sufficiency (18·26) 223
הָרַס	4 to throw down, tear down; break down, break through (2·30·43) 248
הֶחֱלִיק	5 to make smooth; w. tongue = flatter (4·7·9) 325 II
רֶשֶׁת	net (2·22) 440 ירשׁ
מוֹקֵשׁ	6 lure, bait, snare (8·27) 430
יָרוֹן	Qal רנן 943
דִּין	7 cause, plea; judgment; strife (5·19) 192
דַּל	reduced, weak, helpless, poor, low; thin (15·48) 195
לָצוֹן	8 scorning (2·3) 539
הפיח	to excite, inflame; to breathe; blow (7·12·13) 806 פוח
קִרְיָה	city, town (5·30) 900
אֱוִיל	9 foolish; fool (19·26) 17
רָגַז	to be excited, perturbed, agitated; quake (2·30·41) 919
שָׂחַק	to laugh; sport, play (3·19·36) 965
נַחַת	quietness, quiet attitude; rest (1·7) 629 I
תָּם	10 morally innocent, having integrity; complete; wholesome (1·15) 1070
אָחוֹר	11 back side, back part; בְּאָחוֹר = backwards (1·41) 30
שׁבח	Piel, to still, soothe; w. רוּחַ = still one's temper (1·2·3) 986 I
מֹשֵׁל	12 ptc. = one who rules, ruler (5·24) 605 III
הִקְשִׁיב	to give attention (8·45·46) 904
מְשָׁרֵת	Piel ptc. = officer, minister; ministering, serving (1·20) 1058
רָשׁ	13 ptc. = poor, poor man [men] (14·21) 930 רושׁ
תֹּךְ	injury, oppression (1·4) 1067 תכך
נפגשׁ	to meet together, meet each other (2·3·14) 803

הֵאִיר	to lighten; give light; light up, cause to shine; light (1·34·40) 21 אור
דַּל	14 reduced, weak, helpless, poor, low; thin (15·48) 195
עַד	w. ל = forever; perpetuity, continuous existence (2·48) 723 I
תּוֹכַחַת	15 correction, rebuke; reproof, chiding; argument (16·24) 407
מַפֶּלֶת	16 overthrow; ruin; carcass (1·8) 658
יִסֵּר	17 to discipline, correct; chasten (3·27·38) 415
מַעֲדָן	delight; dainty [food] (1·3) 726
בְּאֵין	18 for want of, without (8·10) 35 II אַיִן 6.a
חָזוֹן	divine communication in a vision, oracle, prophecy; vision (1·35) 302
נפרע	to be let loose = lack restraint (1·1·16) 828 III
אֶשֶׁר	pl. cstr. = happiness, blessedness of (8·45) 80
נוסר	19 to let oneself be corrected, admonished, chastened (1·5·38) 415
אָץ	20 to hasten, make haste; press; be pressed (4·8·10) 21 אוץ
תִּקְוָה	hope; things hoped for, outcome (8·32) 876 II
פנק	21 to indulge, pamper; ptc. = one pampering (1·1·1) 819
נַעַר	youth, early life (1·4) 655
מָנוֹן	[dub.] thankless one [Lis. despiser] (1·1) 584
גרה	22 Piel, to excite, stir up [strife] (3·3·14) 173
מָדוֹן	strife, contention (9·12[?]) 193 I דין
בַּעַל חֵמָה	idiom: wrathful (1·2) 127 I בַּעַל 5.a
גַּאֲוָה	23 pride, haughtiness; majesty; rising up (2·19) 144
הִשְׁפִּיל	to set in a lower place; make low; lay low (2·19·30) 1050

שָׁפָל   lowly, lowliness; low; humiliated (2 · 18) 1050

תָּמַךְ   to hold up, support; grasp, lay hold of; hold, keep (8 · 20 · 21) 1069

גַּנָּב 24 thief (2 · 17) 170

אָלָה   oath, curse (1 · 36) 46

חֲרָדָה 25 trembling, quaking, anxious care, fear (1 · 9) 353 I

מוֹקֵשׁ   lure, bait, snare (8 · 27) 430

שָׂגַב   *Pual*, to be set [securely] on high (1 · 1 · 20) 960

מֹשֵׁל 26 ptc. = ruler, one who rules (5 · 24) 605 III

עָוֶל 27 injustice, unrighteousness (1 · 21) 732

Chapter 30

מַשָּׂא 1 utterance, oracle (2 · 21) 672 III

בַּעַר 2 brutishness (2 · 5) 129

בִּינָה   understanding, here = faculty of understanding (14 · 37) 108

חֹפֶן 4 hollow of hand (1 · 6) 342

שִׂמְלָה   wrapper, mantle, outer garment (1 · 29) 971

אֶפֶס   end, extremity, extreme limit (1 · 27) 67

אִמְרָה 5 saying, word; utterance, speech (1 · 37) 57

צָרַף   to smelt, refine; test (1 · 19 · 22) 864

חָסָה   to seek refuge (2 · 37 · 37) 340

נכזב 6 to be proved a liar; be made deceptive (1 · 2 · 16) 469

מָנַע 7 to withhold, hold back (5 · 25 · 29) 586

בְּטֶרֶם   before (3 · 39) 382   טֶרֶם 2

כָּזָב 8 lie, falsehood, deceptive thing (9 · 31) 469

רָאשׁ   poverty (7 · 7) 930   רִישׁ

עֹשֶׁר   riches (9 · 37) 799

הַטְרִיף   to let devour (1 · 1 · 24) 382

כָּחַשׁ 9 to act deceptively against; deceive; cringe; disappoint, fail (1 · 19 · 22) 471

גָּנַב   to take by stealth, to steal (3 · 30 · 39) 170

הִלְשִׁין 10 to use the tongue, slander (1 · 1 · 2) 546

אָשַׁם   to be held guilty, bear punishment; to be or become guilty; to commit an offense, trespass, injury (1 · 33 · 35) 79

צֹאָה 12 filth (1 · 5) 844

עַפְעַף 13 eyelid (4 · 10) 733

מַאֲכֶלֶת 14 knife (1 · 4) 38

מְתַלְּעוֹת   teeth, incisors (1 · 4) [Lis. jaw bones] 1069

עֲלוּקָה 15 leech (1 · 1) 763

הַב   imp. of יהב, to give; set; w. ל = provide; come now (2 · 33 · 33) 396

הוֹן   sufficiency; enough! wealth; high value, price (18 · 26) 223

עֹצֶר 16 restraint, coercion w. womb = barrenness (1 · 3) 783

רֶחֶם   womb (1 · 33) 933

הוֹן   sufficiency; enough! wealth; high value, price (18 · 26) 223

לָעַג 17 to mock, deride (3 · 12 · 18) 541

בּוּז   to despise (8 · 14 · 14) 100 I

יְקָהָה   obedience (1 · 2) 429

נָקַר   to bore, pick out, dig (1 · 2 · 6) 669

עֹרֵב   raven (1 · 12) 788

נֶשֶׁר   griffon vulture, eagle (3 · 26) 676

נִפְלָא 18 to be difficult, be too difficult, beyond one's power (1 · 13 · 24) 810

נֶשֶׁר 19 griffon vulture, eagle (3 · 26) 676

נָחָשׁ   serpent (2 · 31) 638

עֲלֵי   poetic for עַל 752

אֳנִיָּה   ship (2 · 31) 58

עַלְמָה   young woman (1 · 9) 761 עלם

נאף 20 to commit adultery (1 · 14 · 31) 610

מָחָה to wipe, blot out; exterminate (1 · 22 · 34) 562 I

רָגַז 21 to quake; be excited, agitated, perturbed (2 · 30 · 41) 919

נָבָל 22 fool; foolish (3 · 18) 614 I

נבעל 23 to be married (1 · 2 · 12) 127

גְּבֶרֶת mistress [of servants]; lady, queen (1 · 15) 150

קָטָן 24 young, small, insignificant (1 · 47) 881 I

חכם *Pual*, to be made wise, ptc. = made wise (1 · 2 · 27) 314

נְמָלָה 25 ant (2 · 2) 649

עַז strong, mighty; fierce, formidable (3 · 22) 738

קַיִץ summer; summer fruit (4 · 20) 884

שָׁפָן 26 rock badger (1 · 4) 1050 I

עָצוּם mighty, strong in numbers (3 · 31) 783

אַרְבֶּה 27 a kind of lucust (1 · 24) 916

חצץ to divide (1 · 1 · 3) 346 I

שְׂמָמִית 28 a kind of lizard (1 · 1) 971

צַעַד 29 step, pace; steps (4 · 14) 857

לַיִשׁ 30 lion (1 · 3) 539 I

זַרְזִיר 31 girded, girt, that which is girt (1 · 1) 267

מָתְנַיִם loins; זַרְזִיר מ׳ = that which is girt in the loins; perh. = greyhound, warhorse, charger (2 · 47) 608 1.d

תַּיִשׁ male goat (1 · 4) 1066

אַלְקוּם band of soldiers (1 · 1) 39

נבל 32 to be foolish (1 · 21 · 25[?]) 614 II

זָמַם to purpose, devise; consider (2 · 13 · 13) 273

מִיץ 33 squeezing, pressing, wringing (3 · 3) 568

חָלָב milk (2 · 44) 316

חֶמְאָה curd, curdled milk (1 · 10) 326

Chapter 31

מַשָּׂא 1 utterance, oracle (2 · 21) 672 III

יסר to discipline, correct; chasten (3 · 27 · 38) 415

בַּר 2 son (3 · 4) 135 I

המחה 3 to blot out (1 · 3 · 34) 562 I

רֹזֵן 4 ptc. = ruler, potentate (2 · 6) 931

אוֹ from אוּ, desire; Qere = אֵי, where (1 · 1) 16

שֵׁכָר intoxicating drink, strong drink (3 · 22) 1016

חקק 5 *Pual* ptc. = that which is decreed (1 · 1 · 11) 349

שָׁנָה to pervert, change (1 · 9 · 26) 1039

דִּין cause, plea; judgment; strife (5 · 19) 192

עָנִי affliction, poverty (1 · 36) 777

שֵׁכָע 6 intoxicating drink, strong drink (3 · 22) 1016

מַר bitter; bitterness (3 · 38) 600 I

רִישׁ 7 poverty (7 · 7) 930

אִלֵּם 8 dumb, unable to speak (1 · 6) 48

דִּין cause, plea; judgment; strife (5 · 19) 192

חֲלוֹף a passing away, vanishing (1 · 1) 322

דִּין 9 to plead the cause; act as judge; execute judgment; govern (1 · 23 · 24) 192

פְּנִינִים 10 corals (4 · 6) 819

מֶכֶר value, price of; merchandise (1 · 3) 569

חָסֵר 11 to lack; be lacking (2 · 19 · 23) 341

גָּמַל 12 to deal out to, do to; wean; ripen (3 · 34 · 37) 168

צֶמֶר 13 wool (1 · 16) 856

פֵּשֶׁת flax, linen (1 · 16) 833

חֵפֶץ that in which one takes delight, business; delight; desire; good pleasure (3 · 39) 343

אֳנִיָּה 14 ship (2 · 31) 58

סֹחֵר ptc. = trafficker, trader (1 · 16) 695

מֶרְחָק distant place, far country; distance (2 · 18) 935

בְּעוֹד 15 while yet, so long as; within yet (1 · 20) 728 עוֹד 2.a

טֶרֶף food; prey; leaf (1 · 4[?]) 383

זָמַם 16 to consider, fix thought on; purpose, devise (2 · 13 · 13) 273

חגר 17 to gird; gird on, bind on; gird oneself (1 · 44 · 44) 291

מָתְנַיִם loins (2 · 47) 608

אָמַץ to make firm, strengthen; assure; harden (3 · 19 · 41) 54

טָעַם 18 to taste; here = experience (1 · 11 · 11) 380

סַחַר gain from traffic; traffic (3 · 7) 695

כבה to be quenched, be extinguished, go out (2 · 14 · 24) 459

נֵר lamp (6 · 45) 632 I נוּר

כִּישׁוֹר 19 distaff (1 · 1) 507

תָּמַךְ to grasp, lay hold of; hold up, support; hold, keep (8 · 20 · 21) 1069

פֶּלֶךְ whirl of spindle; district (1 · 9) 813

שֶׁלֶג 21 snow (3 · 20) 1017

לָבוּשׁ pass. ptc. = clothed with (1 · 16) 527

שָׁנִי scarlet (1 · 42) 1040

מַרְבָד 22 spread, coverlet (2 · 2) 915

שֵׁשׁ byssus, fine Egyptian linen [both thread or cloth woven from it] (1 · 38) 1058 III

אַרְגָּמָן purple cloth; purple thread; purple (1 · 39) 71

לְבוּשׁ garment, clothing, raiment (3 · 31) 528

סָדִין 24 linen wrapper (1 · 4) 690

חֲגוֹר belt, girdle (1 · 3) 292

כְּנַעֲנִי trader, merchant (1 · 4) 489 II

הָדָר 25 splendor, majesty; honor, glory; ornament (2 · 30) 214

לְבוּשׁ garment, clothing, raiment (3 · 31) 528

שָׂחַק to laugh; sport, play (3 · 19 · 36) 965

צפה 27 to keep watch, look out, spy (2 · 9 · 18) 859 I

הֲלִיכָה going, walking, here pl. = doings; traveling company (1 · 6) 237

עַצְלוּת sluggishness (1 · 1) 782

אשר 28 to pronounce happy, call blessed; to advance; lead on; set right (1 · 7 · 9[?]) 80

יֳפִי 30 beauty (2 · 19) 421

יָרֵא ptc. = fearing, revering, honoring (3 · 45) 431

RUTH

Chapter 1

מֹאֲבִיּוֹת 4 fem. pl. of מוֹאֲבִיָּה, Moabitish (4 · 18) 555

כַּלָּה 6 daughter-in-law; bride (7 · 34) 483

כַּלָּה 7 daughter-in-law; bride (7 · 34) 483

כַּלָּה 8 daughter-in-law; bride (7 · 34) 483

לֵכְנָה Qal impv. fem. pl. הלך 229

שֹׁבְנָה Qal impv. fem. pl. שוב 996

עִמָּדִי עם + 1st sing suff. 767

מְצֶאןָ 9 Qal impv. fem. pl. מצא 592

מְנוּחָה rest, quietness; resting place (1 · 21) 629

נָשַׁק to kiss (2 · 26 · 32) 676 I

כִּי 10 here = No! (cf. Koehler-Baumgartner כִּי I.7)

שֹׁבְנָה 11 Qal impv. fem. pl. שוב 996

מֵעֶה source of procreation; internal organs, inward parts (1 · 32) 588

שֹׁבְנָה 12 Qal impv. fem. pl. שוב 996

לֵכְןָ Qal impv. fem. pl. הלך 229

זָקֵן to be or become old (1 · 25 · 27) 278

תִּקְוָה hope (1 · 32) 876 II

לָהֵן 13 on this account, therefore (2 · 2) 530

שׂבר to wait, hope (1 · 6 · 8) 960 II

נעגן to shut oneself in or off (1 · 1 · 1) 723

מַר to be bitter (1 · 6 · 16) 600 I

נָשַׁק 14 to kiss (2 · 26 · 32) 676 I

חָמוֹת husband's mother (10 · 11) 327

יְבֶמֶת 15 sister-in-law, husband's brother's wife (2 · 5) 386

פָּגַע 16 to encounter [with request] = entreat (2 · 20 · 46) 803

אֶל־אֲשֶׁר to [the place] 82 אֲשֶׁר 4.b.γ

בַּאֲשֶׁר in the place where; in which where (2 · 19) 84

עַם people (3 · 34) 766 I

בַּאֲשֶׁר 17 in the place where, in which (2 · 19) 84

כֹּה יַעֲשֶׂה 17 imprecation formula = may the
יהוה לִי LORD do thus to me

וְכֹה יוֹסִיף and more also if . . . 415 Hiph.

כִּי I רימף

הִפְרִיד to make a division, separation (1 · 7 · 26) 825 I

הִתְאַמֵּץ 18 to confirm oneself, be determined (1 · 4 · 41) 54

בֹּאֲנָה 19 Qal inf. + fem. pl. suff. בוא 97

נהום to be in a stir (1 · 3 · 6) 223

מָרָא 20 bitter (Lis. prop. name) 600

הֵמַר to embitter, make bitter, show bitterness (1 · 5 · 16) 600 I

שַׁדַּי name for God: (1) Almighty, (2) Sovereign, or (3) Self-sufficient One (2 · 48) 994

רֵיקָם 21 in empty condition, empty (2 · 16) 938

שַׁדַּי name for God (see 1:20) (2 · 48) 994

מוֹאֲבִיָּה 22 Moabite (9 · 18) 555

כַּלָּה daughter-in-law; bride (7 · 34) 483

תְּחִלָּה beginning (1 · 22) 321

קָצִיר time of harvest (4 · 49) 894 I

שְׂעֹרָה barley (6 · 33) 972

Chapter 2

מוֹדַע 1 kinsman (1 · 2) 396

מוֹאֲבִיָּה 2 Moabite (9 · 18) 555

לקט to glean (11 · 21 · 37) 544

שִׁבֹּלֶת ear of grain (1 · 20) 987 II

לקט 3 to glean (11 · 21 · 37) 544

קֹצֵר ptc. = reaper (6 · 10) 894 II

קרה to light upon, meet, encounter (1 · 13 · 28) 899

מִקְרֶה accident, chance (1 · 10) 899

חֶלְקָה field, portion of ground (2 · 24) 324 I

קֹצֵר	4 ptc. = reaper (6 · 10) 894 II
קֹצֵר	5 ptc. = reaper (6 · 10) 894 II
לְמִי	to whom? whose? (1 · 20) 566 מי b
קֹצֵר	6 ptc. = reaper (6 · 10) 894 II
מוֹאֲבִיָּה	Moabite (9 · 18) 555
לקט	7 to glean (11 · 21 · 37) 544
עֹמֶר	sheaf (2 · 8) 771 I
קֹצֵר	ptc. = reaper (6 · 10) 894 II
מֵאָז	from time of, from that time, since (1 · 17) 23
שֶׁבֶת	Qal inf. sitting, staying (1 · 17) 442 ישב
לקט	8 to glean (1 · 14 · 37) 544
קצר	9 to reap, harvest (1 · 24 · 24) 894
צמא	to be thirsty (1 · 10 · 10) 854
מֵאֲשֶׁר	from [the place] where; from that (1 · 17) 84
שאב	to draw [water] (1 · 14 · 14) 980
הכיר	10 to pay attention, regard, observe (3 · 38 · 41) 647 I נכר
נָכְרִי	foreigner (1 · 45) 648
חָמוֹת	11 husband's mother (10 · 11) 327
מוֹלֶדֶת	kindred (1 · 22) 409
תְּמוֹל	yesterday, lately, w. שלשום = formerly (1 · 23) 1069
שִׁלְשׁוֹם	three days ago, day before yesterday (1 · 25) 1026
פֹּעַל	12 deed, thing done (1 · 37) 821
מַשְׂכֹּרֶת	wages (1 · 4) 969
שָׁלֵם	full (1 · 28) 1023
חָסָה	to seek refuge (1 · 37 · 37) 340
דִּבֶּר עַל לֵב	13 idiom: to speak to the heart = kindly (1 · 8) 524 לֵב 9.a לבב
אֹכֶל	14 food, לְעֵת הָאֹכֶל = mealtime (1 · 44) 38
גְּשִׁי	2nd fem. sing. impv. נגש 620
הֲלֹם	adv. of place, here (1 · 11) 240
טָבַל	to dip (1 · 15 · 16) 371 I
פַּת	fragment, bit, morsel of bread (1 · 14) 837

חֹמֶץ	vinegar (1 · 5) 330
צַד	side, מִצַּד = at the side of; on this side of (1 · 31) 841
קֹצֵר	ptc. = reaper (6 · 10) 894 II
צבט	to reach, hold out (1 · 1 · 1) 840
קָלִי	parched grain (1 · 5) 885
לקט	15 to glean (11 · 21 · 37) 544
עֹמֶר	sheaf (2 · 8) 771 I
הכלים	to put to shame = insult, humiliate (1 · 10 · 38) 483
שׁלל	16 to draw out; here impf. and inf. abs. (2 · 13 · 15[?]) 1021
צֶבֶת	pl. only, bundles [of grain] (1 · 1) 841
לקט	to glean (11 · 21 · 37) 544
גָּעַר	to rebuke (1 · 14 · 14) 172
לקט	17 to glean (11 · 21 · 37) 544
חבט	to beat out; beat off (1 · 4 · 5) 286
אֵיפָה	ephah, a grain measure (1 · 39) 35
שְׂעֹרָה	barley (6 · 33) 972
חָמוֹת	18 husband's mother (10 · 11) 327
לקט	to glean (11 · 21 · 37) 544
שֹׂבַע	satiety, abundancc, fill (1 · 8) 959
חָמוֹת	19 husband's mother (10 · 11) 327
אֵיפֹה	where? (1 · 10) 33
לקט	to glean (11 · 21 · 37) 554
אָן	where? whither? [with ה locale] (1 · 37) 33
הכיר	to pay attention, regard, observe (3 · 38 · 41) 647
כַּלָּה	20 daughter-in-law; bride (7 · 34) 483
גאל	ptc. = one who does the part of the next of kin, redeemer (9 · 44) 145 I
מוֹאֲבִיָּה	21 Moabite (9 · 18) 555
קָצִיר	time of harvest (4 · 49) 894 I
כַּלָּה	22 daughter-in-law; bride (7 · 34) 483
פָּגַע	to encounter [with hostility] = fall upon (2 · 20 · 46) 803

לקט 23 to glean (11 · 21 · 37) 544

קָצִיר   time of harvest (4 · 49) 894 I

שְׂעֹרָה   barley (6 · 33) 972

חִטָּה   wheat (1 · 30) 334

חָמוֹת   husband's mother (10 · 11) 327

Chapter 3

חָמוֹת 1 husband's mother (10 · 11) 327

מָנוֹחַ   rest, repose (1 · 7) 629 I

מֹדַעַת 2 kindred, kinship (1 · 1) 396

זרה   to winnow, fan, scatter (1 · 9 · 38) 279

גֹּרֶן   threshing floor (4 · 34) 175

שְׂעֹרָה   barley (6 · 33) 972

סוּךְ 3 to anoint oneself (1 · 7 · 9) 691 I

שִׂמְלָה   wrapper, mantle, garment (1 · 29) 971

גֹּרֶן   threshing floor (4 · 34) 175

מַרְגְּלוֹת 4 place of the feet, feet (4 · 5) 920

גֹּרֶן 6 threshing floor (4 · 34) 175

חָמוֹת   husband's mother (10 · 11) 327

עֲרֵמָה 7 heap (1 · 11) 790

לָט   secretly (1 · 7) 532

מַרְגְּלוֹת   place of the feet, feet (4 · 5) 920

חָרַד 8 to start, start up [out of a sleep]; tremble, quake (1 · 23 · 39) 353

נלפת   to twist oneself (1 · 2 · 3) 542

מַרְגְּלוֹת   place of the feet, feet (4 · 5) 920

גָּאַל 9 ptc. = one who does the part of the next of kin, redeemer (9 · 44) 145 I

בָּחוּר 10 young man (1 · 45) 104

דַּל   poor (1 · 48) 195

עָשִׁיר   rich; the rich (1 · 23) 799

עַם 11 people (3 · 34) 766 I

אָמְנָם 12 verily, truly (1 · 9) 53 אמן I

גָּאַל   ptc. = one who does the part of the next of kin, redeemer (9 · 44) 145 I

מַרְגְּלוֹת 14 place of the feet, feet (4 · 5) 920

בְּטֶרֶם   before (1 · 39) 382 טֶרֶם 2

הכיר   to recognize (3 · 38 · 41) 647

גֹּרֶן   threshing floor (4 · 34) 175

יהב 15 to give (1 · 33 · 33) 396

מִטְפַּחַת   cloak (1 · 2) 381

שְׂעֹרָה   barley (6 · 33) 972

חָמוֹת 16 husband's mother (10 · 11) 327

שְׂעֹרָה 17 barley (6 · 33) 972

רֵיקָם   in empty condition, empty (2 · 16) 938

חָמוֹת   husband's mother (10 · 11) 327

שָׁקַט 18 to be quiet, inactive (1 · 31 · 41) 1052

Chapter 4

גָּאַל 1 ptc. = one who does the part of the next of kin, redeemer (9 · 44) 145

פֹּה   here (2 · 44) 805

פְּלֹנִי   a certain one [always joined with אַלְמֹנִי] (1 · 6) 811

אַלְמֹנִי   someone, a certain person [name unspoken] (1 · 3) 48

פֹּה   here (2 · 44) 805

חֶלְקָה 3 field, portion of ground (2 · 24) 324

זוּלָה 4 except, besides (1 · 16) 265

מוֹאֲבִיָּה 5 Moabite (9 · 18) 555

גָּאַל 6 ptc. = one who does the part of the next of kin, redeemer (9 · 44) 145 I

גְּאֻלָּה   right of redemption (2 · 14) 145

גְּאֻלָּה 7 right of redemption (2 · 14) 145

תְּמוּרָה   exchanging, exchange (1 · 6) 558

לְקַיֵּם   = לְ + Piel inf. cstr. קום 877

שָׁלַף   to draw off (2 · 24 · 24) 1025

נַעַל   sandal, shoe (2 · 22) 653

תְּעוּדָה   attestation; testimony (1 · 3) 730

גָּאַל 8 ptc. = one who does the part of

574

the next of kin, redeemer (9 · 44) 145 I

שָׁלַף to draw off (2 · 24 · 24) 1025

נַעַל sandal, shoe (2 · 22) 653

מוֹאֲבִיָּה 10 Moabite (9 · 18) 555

הֵרָיוֹן 13 conception, pregnancy (1 · 2) 248

גָּאַל 14 ptc. = one who does the part of the next of kin, redeemer (9 · 44) 145 I

כִּלְכֵּל 15 *Pilp*. to sustain, support, nourish (1 · 24 · 38) 465 כול

שֵׂיבָה old age (1 · 20) 966

כַּלָּה daughter-in-law; bride (7 · 34) 483

יְלָדַתּוּ *Qal* 3rd fem. sing. + 3rd m. sing. suff. 408

חֵיק 16 bosom; fold of garment at breast (1 · 38) 300

אֹמֶנֶת ptc. fem, = foster mother (1 · 7[?]) 52 I

שָׁכֵן 17 neighbor (1 · 20) 1015

תּוֹלְדוֹת 18 account of men and their descendants (1 · 39) 410

SONG OF SONGS

Chapter 1

נָשַׁק	2 to kiss (2 · 26 · 32) 676 I	
נְשִׁיקָה	kiss (1 · 2) 676	
הוּרַק	3 to be emptied out (1 · 2 · 19) 937 רִיק	
עַלְמָה	young woman (2 · 9) 761	
מָשַׁךְ	4 to draw, drag (1 · 30 · 36) 604	
חֶדֶר	room, chamber (2 · 37) 293	
גִּיל	to rejoice (1 · 45 · 45) 162	
מֵישָׁר	rightly (2 · 19) 449	
שָׁחֹר	5 black (2 · 6) 1007	
נָאוֶה	comely, seemly (4 · 9) 610	
שֶׁאֲנִי	6 because I 979 שֶׁ 3.b	
שְׁחַרְחֹר	blackish (1 · 1) 1007	
שָׁזַף	to look on (1 · 3 · 3) 1004	
נטר	to keep, guard (4 · 4 · 4[?]) 643	
שֶׁלִּי	my; שֶׁל (mark of genitive) + 1st sing. suff. 979 שֶׁ 4.d	
אֵיכָה	7 where? (2 · 18) 32	
הרביץ	to cause to lie down (1 · 6 · 30) 918	
צָהֳרַיִם	midday, noon (1 · 23) 843 I	
שַׁלָּמָה	lest (1 · 1) 979 שֶׁ׳ 3.b	
עָטָה	to wrap oneself, enwrap (1 · 11 · 14) 741 I	
עֵדֶר	flock, herd (5 · 37) 727 I	
חָבֵר	associate, fellow (2 · 12) 288	
יָפֶה	8 beautiful, fair (11 · 40) 421	
עָקֵב	footprint (1 · 14) 784 I	
גְּדִיָּה	kid (1 · 1) 152	
סוּסָה	9 mare (1 · 1) 692	
דָּמָה	to liken, compare (1 · 13 · 27) 197 I	
רַעְיָה	companion (8 · 8) 946	
נאה	10 to be fitting (1 · 3 · 3) 610	
לְחִי	cheek (2 · 21) 534 I	
תּוֹר	plaits, circlets (2 · 5) 1064 I	
צַוָּאר	neck, back of neck (3 · 41) 848	
חָרוּז	string of beads (1 · 1) 354	
תּוֹר	11 plaits, circlets (2 · 5) 1064 I	

נְקֻדָּה	point or drop (1 · 1) 667	
מֵסַב	12 [dub.] round table, cushion, divan (1 · 5) 687	
גֵרְדְּ	nard (3 · 3) 669	
צְרוֹר	13 bundle, pouch (1 · 7) 865 I	
מֹר	myrrh (8 · 12) 600	
שַׁד	breast (8 · 21) 994	
אֶשְׁכּוֹל	14 cluster (3 · 9) 79	
כֹּפֶר	henna, a shrub or low tree (3 · 3) 499 III	
יָפֶה	15 beautiful, fair (11 · 40) 421	
רַעְיָה	companion (8 · 8) 946	
יוֹנָה	dove (6 · 33) 401 I	
יָפֶה	16 beautiful, fair (11 · 40) 421	
נָעִים	pleasant (1 · 13) 653 I	
עֶרֶשׂ	couch, divan (1 · 10) 793	
רַעֲנָן	luxuriant, fresh (1 · 19) 947	
קוֹרָה	17 rafter, beam (1 · 5) 900	
רָהִיט	[coll.] perh. rafters, boards (1 · 1) 923	
בְּרוֹת	cypress or fir (1 · 1) 141	

Chapter 2

חֲבַצֶּלֶת	1 crocus (1 · 2) 287	
שׁוֹשַׁנָּה	lily (8 · 17) 1004 I שׁוּשַׁן	
שׁוֹשַׁנָּה	2 lily (8 · 17) 1004 I שׁוּשַׁן	
חוֹחַ	brier, bramble (1 · 11) 296	
רַעְיָה	companion (8 · 8) 946	
תַּפּוּחַ	3 apple tree, apple (4 · 6) 656 I	
חמד	to delight greatly (1 · 1 · 21) 326	
מָתוֹק	sweet (1 · 12) 608	
חֵךְ	palate (3 · 18) 335	
דֶּגֶל	4 standard, banner (1 · 14) 186	
סמך	5 to sustain (1 · 1 · 48) 701	
אֲשִׁישָׁה	raisin cake (1 · 5) 84	
רפד	to support (1 · 2 · 3) 951	
תַּפּוּחַ	apple, apple tree (4 · 6) 656	
חבק	6 to embrace (2 · 10 · 13) 287	
צְבָאָה	7 gazelle (2 · 2[?]) 840 II עְבִי	

אַיָּלָה   hind, doe (1 · 11) 19

דָּלַג   8 to leap, leap over (1 · 4 · 5) 194

מְקַפֵּץ   *Piel* ptc. = springing (1 · 1 · 7) 891 קפץ

דָּמָה   9 to be like, resemble (4 · 13 · 27) 197 I

צְבִי   gazelle (3 · 11[?]) 840

עֹפֶר   young hart, stag (5 · 5) 780

אַיָּל   hart, stag (3 · 11) 19

כֹּתֶל   wall (1 · 1) 508

הִשְׁגִּיחַ   to gaze (1 · 3 · 3) 993

חַלּוֹן   window (1 · 30) 319

הֵצִיץ   to gaze, peep (1 · 1 · 1) 847 II צוץ

חֲרַכִּים   lattice (1 · 1) 355

רַעְיָה   10 companion (8 · 8) 946

יָפֶה   beautiful, fair (11 · 40) 421

סְתָו   11 winter (1 · 1) 711

גֶּשֶׁם   rain, showerr (1 · 35) 177 II

חָלַף   to pass away (1 · 14 · 26) 322

נִצָּנִים   12 blossoms (1 · 4) 665 נִצָּה

זָמִיר   trimming, pruning (1 · 1) 274 II

תּוֹר   turtle dove (1 · 14) 1076 II

תְּאֵנָה   13 fig tree, fig (1 · 38) 1061

חנט   to spice, make spicy (1 · 4 · 4) 334

פַּגָּה   early fig (1 · 1) 803

סְמָדַר   blossom (3 · 3) 701

רַעְיָה   companion (8 · 8) 946

יָפֶה   beautiful, fair (11 · 40) 421

יוֹנָה   14 dove (6 · 33) 401 I

חֲגָוִים   places of concealment, retreats, (1 · 3) 291

סֵתֶר   hiding place (1 · 35) 712

מַדְרֵגָה   steep place, steep (1 · 2) 201

עָרֵב   sweet, pleasant (1 · 2) 787

נָאוֶה   comely, seemly (4 · 9) 610

שׁוּעָל   15 fox (2 · 7) 1043 I

קָטָן   small, young (2 · 47) 881 I

חבל   to ruin, destroy (1 · 6 · 10) 287 II

סְמָדַר   blossom (3 · 3) 701

שׁוֹשַׁנָּה   16 lily (8 · 17) 1004 I שׁוֹשָׁן

פּוּחַ   17 to breathe, blow (2 · 2 · 14) 806

דָּמָה   to be like, resemble (4 · 13 · 27) 197 I

צְבִי   gazelle (3 · 11[?]) 840

עֹפֶר   young hart, stag (5 · 5) 780

אַיָּל   hart, stag (3 · 11) 19

בֶּתֶר   cutting, separation (1 · 1) 144

Chapter 3

מִשְׁכָּב   1 couch, bed (1 · 46) 1012

שׁוּק   2 street (1 · 4) 1003

רְחוֹב   broad, open place (1 · 43) 932 I

הִרְפָּה   4 to let go (1 · 21 · 44) 951

חֶדֶר   room, chamber (2 · 37) 293

הָרָה   one who conceives; i.e., mother (1 · 3) 247 I הרה *Qal* I

צְבָאָה   5 gazelle (2 · 2[?]) 840 II צְבִי

תִּימָרָה   6 column (1 · 2) 1071

עָשָׁן   smoke (1 · 25) 798 I

מְקֻטֶּרֶת   fumigated; *Pual* ptc. of קטר 882

מֹר   myrrh (8 · 12) 600

לְבֹנָה   frankincense (3 · 21) 526 I

אֲבָקָה   powder (1 · 1) 7

רֹכֵל   trader (1 · 17) 940 רכל

מִטָּה   7 couch, bed (1 · 29) 641

אָחַז   8 holding (1 · 1[?]) 28 אָחֻז

יָרֵךְ   thigh (2 · 34) 437

פַּחַד   dread (1 · 49) 808 I

אַפִּרְיוֹן   9 sedan, litter (1 · 1) 68

רְפִידָה   10 support (1 · 1) 951

מֶרְכָּב   seat (1 · 3) 939

אַרְגָּמָן   purple, red purple (2 · 39) 71

רָצוּף   pass. ptc. = fitted out with (1 · 1 · 1) 954 I רצף

עֲטָרָה   11 crown, wreath (1 · 23) 742 I

עטר   to crown (1 · 4 · 7[?]) 742

חֲתֻנָּה   marriage, wedding (1 · 1) 368

577

Chapter 4

יָפֶה	1	beautiful, fair (11 · 40) 421
רַעְיָה		companion (8 · 8) 946
יוֹנָה		dove (6 · 33) 401 I
מִבַּעַד		from behind (3 · 3) 126 בַּעַד
צַמָּה		veil (3 · 4) 855
שֵׂעָר		hair (2 · 28) 972
עֵדֶר		flock, herd (5 · 37) 727 I
גלשׁ		to sit, sit up, or recline (2 · 2 · 2) 167
עֵדֶר	2	flock, herd (5 · 37) 727 I
קצב		to cut off, shear (1 · 2 · 2) 891
רַחְצָה		washing (2 · 2) 934
שֶׁכֻּל		all of which, each of which (4 · 4) 481 שֶׁ 979; כֹּל 481
הִתְאִים		to bear twins (2 · 2 · 2) 1060
שַׁכּוּל		bereaved, robbed of offspring (2 · 6) 1014
חוּט	3	thread, cord (1 · 7) 296
שָׁנִי		scarlet (1 · 42) 1040
מִדְבָּר		mouth (1 · 1) 184 I
נָאוֶה		comely, seemly (4 · 9) 610
פֶּלַח		cleavage, split (2 · 6) 812
רִמּוֹן		pomegranate (6 · 32) 941
רַקָּה		temple [of the head] (2 · 5) 956
מִבַּעַד		from behind (3 · 3) 126 בַּעַד
צַמָּה		veil (3 · 4) 855
מִגְדָּל	4	tower (5 · 49) 153
צַוָּאר		neck, back of neck (3 · 41) 848
תַּלְפִּיּוֹת		weapons (1 · 1) 1069
תָּלָה		to hang, hang up (1 · 23 · 27) 1067
שֶׁלֶט		shield, arms, equipment (1 · 7) 1020
שַׁד	5	breast (8 · 21) 994
עֹפֶר		young hart, stag (5 · 5) 780
תּוֹאָם		twin (2 · 6) 1060
צְבִיָּה		gazelle (2 · 2) 840 I
שׁוֹשַׁנָּה		lily (8 · 17) 1004 I שׁוֹשָׁן
פוּחַ	6	to breathe, blow (2 · 2 · 14) 806
מֹר		myrrh (8 · 12) 600

לְבֹנָה		frankincense (3 · 21) 526
יָפֶה	7	beautiful, fair (11 · 40) 421
רַעְיָה		companion (8 · 8) 946
מוּם		blemish, defect (1 · 21) 548
כַּלָּה	8	bride (6 · 34) 483
שׁוּר		to look, gaze (1 · 16 · 16) 1003 II
מְעֹנָה		den, lair (1 · 9) 733
אֲרִי		lion (1 · 36) 71
נָמֵר		leopard (1 · 6) 649
לבב	9	to encourage (1 · 1 · 2) 525 I
כַּלָּה		bride (6 · 34) 483
עֲנָק		necklace, neck pendant (1 · 3) 778 II
צַוָּרוֹן		necklace (1 · 1) 848
יפה	10	to be beautiful (3 · 6 · 8) 421
כַּלָּה		bride (6 · 34) 483
טוֹב		to be pleasant, delightful (1 · 18 · 21) 373
בֹּשֶׂם		spice, balsam juice (7 · 30) 141
נֹפֶת	11	flowing honey, honey from the comb (1 · 5) 661
נטף		to drip, drop (3 · 9 · 18) 642
כַּלָּה		bride (6 · 34) 483
חָלָב		milk (3 · 44) 316
שַׂלְמָה		clothes (1 · 16) 971 II
גַּן	12	garden (8 · 41) 171
נָעַל		to bar, bolt, lock (1 · 6 · 7) 653
כַּלָּה		bride (6 · 34) 483
גַּל		spring (1 · 16) 164
מַעְיָן		spring (2 · 23) 745
חתם		to seal, seal up (1 · 23 · 27) 367
שֶׁלַח	13	sprout, shoot (1 · 8) 1019 I
פַּרְדֵּס		preserve, park (1 · 3) 825
רִמּוֹן		pomegranate (6 · 32) (6 · 32) 941 I
מֶגֶד		excellence (3 · 8) 550
כֹּפֶר		henna, a shrub or low tree (3 · 3) 499 III
נֵרְדְּ		nard (3 · 3) 669
נֵרְדְּ	14	nard (3 · 3) 669
כַּרְכֹּם		saffron (1 · 1) 501

קָנֶה calamus 889 3

קִנָּמוֹן cinnamon (1 · 3) 890

לְבֹנָה frankincense (3 · 21) 526 I

מֹר myrrh (8 · 12) 600

אֲהָלוֹת aloes (1 · 4) 14 III אהל 2

בֹּשֶׂם spice, balsam juice (7 · 30) 141

מַעְיָן 15 spring (2 · 23) 745

גַּן garden (8 · 41) 171

בְּאֵר well, pit (1 · 38) 91

נֹזֵל stream, flood (1 · 6) 633 נצל

תֵּימָן 16 south wind (1 · 24) 412 I

הֵפִיחַ to cause to exhale (1 · 12 · 14) 806 פוח

גַּן garden (8 · 41) 171

נזל to flow (1 · 8 · 9) 633

בֹּשֶׂם balsam juice, spice (7 · 30) 141

מֶגֶז excellence (3 · 5) 550

Chapter 5

גַּן 1 garden (8 · 41) 171

כַּלָּה bride (6 · 34) 483

ארה to pluck, gather (1 · 2 · 2) 71 I

מֹר myrrh (8 · 12) 600

בֹּשֶׂם spice, balsam juice (7 · 30) 141

יַעַר honeycomb (1 · 3) 421 II

חָלָב milk (3 · 44) 316

שׁכר to become drunken (1 · 9 · 20) 1016 I

יָשֵׁן 2 asleep, sleeping (2 · 9) 445 I

דפק to beat, knock (1 · 2 · 3) 200

רַעְיָה companion (8 · 8) 946

יוֹנָה dove (6 · 33) 401 I

תָּם complete, perfect (2 · 15) 1070

טַל dew (1 · 31) 378

קְוֻצּוֹת locks (of hair) (2 · 2) 881

רָסִיס drop (1 · 1) 944 I

פָּשַׁט 3 to strip off, put off (1 · 24 · 43) 832

כֻּתֹּנֶת tunic (1 · 29) 509

אֵיכָכָה how? (2 · 4) 32

טנף to soil (1 · 1) 380

חֹר 4 hole (1 · 7) 359 III

מֵעֶה inward part, belly (2 · 31) 588

המה to murmur, growl (1 · 33 · 33) 242

נטף 5 to drip, drop (3 · 9 · 18) 642

מֹר myrrh (8 · 12) 600

אֶצְבַּע finger (1 · 31) 840

מַנְעוּל bolt (1 · 6) 653

חמק 6 to turn away (1 · 1 · 2) 330

דָּבַר to turn away (2 · 2 · 5) 180 דבר

פצע 7 to bruise (1 · 3 · 3) 822

רְדִיד large veil, large wrapper (1 · 2) 921

יָפֶה 9 beautiful, fair (11 · 40) 421

שֶׁכָּכָה thus (1 · 2) 462 ככה

צַח 10 dazzling, glowing (1 · 4) 850

אָדֹם ruddy, red (1 · 9) 10

דָּגוּל pass. ptc. = conspicuous (1 · 2 · 4) דגל 186 I

רְבָבָה myriad (1 · 16) 914

כֶּתֶם 11 gold (1 · 9) 508

כֵּז refined, pure gold (2 · 9) 808

קְוֻצּוֹת locks [of hair] (2 · 2) 881

תַּלְתַּלִּים [dub.] envelopes, heaps, piles (1 · 1) 1068

שָׁחֹר black (2 · 6) 1007

עֹרֵב raven (1 · 12) 788

יוֹנָה 12 dove (6 · 33) 401 I

אָפִיק channel (1 · 18) 67

חָלָב milk (3 · 44) 316

מִלֵּאת [dub.] setting, border, rim (1 · 1) 571

לְחִי 13 cheek (2 · 21) 534 I

עֲרוּגָה bed, garden terrace (2 · 4) 788

בֹּשֶׂם balsam, spice (7 · 30) 141

מִגְדָּל tower (5 · 49) 153

מֶרְקָח spice, perfume (1 · 1) 955

שׁוֹשַׁנָּה lily (8 · 17) 1004 I שׁושׁן

נטף to drip, drop (3 · 9 · 18) 642

מֹר myrrh (8 · 12) 600

גָּלִיל 14 cylinder, rod (1 · 4) 165 II

תַּרְשִׁישׁ a precious stone, perh. yellow jasper (1 · 7) 1076 I

מֵעֶה belly (2 · 31) 588

עֶשֶׁת plate (1 · 1) 799

עֶלֶף to be covered, encrusted (1 · 2 · 5) 763

סַפִּיר sapphire (1 · 11) 705

שׁוֹק 15 leg (1 · 19) 1003

שֵׁשׁ alabaster (1 · 3) 1010 II

יָסַד to be founded, be laid (1 · 6 · 41) 413

פָּז refined, pure gold (2 · 9) 808

בָּחוּר chosen (1 · 19[?]) 103 בחר Qal 7

חֵךְ 16 palate (3 · 18) 335

מַמְתַקִּים sweet things (1 · 2) 609

מַחְמַד desire, desirable thing (1 · 13) 326

Chapter 6

אָנָה 1 whither? where? (2 · 39) 33 אָן

יָפֶה beautiful, fair (11 · 40) 421

גַּן 2 garden (8 · 41) 171

עֲרוּגָה bed, garden terrace (2 · 4) 788

בֹּשֶׂם balsam, spice (7 · 30) 141

לקט to gather, pick up (1 · 14 · 37) 544

שׁוֹשַׁנָּה lily (8 · 17) 1004 I שׁוּשַׁן

שׁוֹשַׁנָּה 3 lily (8 · 17) 1004 I שׁוּשַׁן

יָפֶה 4 beautiful, fair (11 · 40) 421

רַעְיָה companion (8 · 8) 946

נָאוֶה comely, seemly (4 · 9) 610

אָיֹם awe-inspiring (2 · 3) 33

נִדְגָּלוֹת *Niph.* ptc = bannered hosts (2 · 2 · 4) 186 II דגל

מִנֶּגֶד 5 away from (1 · 26) 617 נגד 2.c

הִרְהִיב [dub.] to alarm, awe, confuse, disturb (1 · 2 · 4) 923

שֵׂעָר hair (2 · 28) 972

עֵדֶר flock, herd (5 · 37) 727 I

גלשׁ to sit, sit up or recline (2 · 2 · 2) 167

עֵדֶר 6 flock, herd (5 · 37) 727 I

רָחֵל ewe (1 · 4) 932 I

רַחְצָה washing (2 · 2) 934

שֶׁכֻּל all of which, each of which (4 · 4) שֶׁ׳, 979 כֹּל 481

הִתְאִם to bear twins (2 · 2 · 2) 1060

שַׁכּוּל bereaved, robbed of offspring (2 · 6) 1014

פֶּלַח 7 cleavage, split (2 · 6) 812

רִמּוֹן pomegranate (6 · 32) 941 I

רַקָּה temple [of the head] (2 · 5) 956

מִבַּעַד from behind (3 · 3) 126 בַּעַד

צַמָּה veil (3 · 4) 855

מַלְכָּה 8 queen (2 · 35) 573

פִּלֶגֶשׁ concubine (2 · 37) 811

עַלְמָה young woman (2 · 9) 761

יוֹנָה 9 dove (6 · 33) 401 I

תָּם complete, perfect (2 · 15) 1070

בַּר clean, pure (2 · 6) 141 II

אָשַׁר to pronounce happy, call blessed (1 · 7 · 9) 80

מַלְכָּה queen (2 · 35) 573

פִּלֶגֶשׁ concubine (2 · 37) 811

נִשְׁקָף 10 to look down, look forth (1 · 10 · 22) 1054 I

שַׁחַר dawn (1 · 23) 1007

יָפֶה beautiful, fair (11 · 40) 421

לְבָנָה moon (1 · 3) 526 I

בַּר clean, pure (2 · 6) 141 II

חַמָּה sun, heat (1 · 6) 328

אָיֹם awe-inspiring (2 · 3) 33

נִדְגָּלוֹת *Niph.* ptc. = bannered hosts (2 · 2 · 4) 186 II דגל

גִּנָּה 11 garden (1 · 16) 171

אֱגוֹז nuts (1 · 1) 8

אֵב pl. = green shoots (1 · 2) 1

פָּרַח to bud, sprout, send out shoots (2 · 27 · 32) 827 I

הֵנֵץ to bloom, blossom (2 · 3 · 4) 665 נצץ

רִמּוֹן pomegranate (6 · 32) 941 I

מֶרְכָּבָה 12 chariot (1 · 44) 939

נָדִיב noble, princely (2 · 27) 622

Chapter 7

מְחוֹלָה 1 dancing (1 · 8) 298
יפה 2 to be beautiful (3 · 6 · 8) 421
נַעַל sandal, shoe (1 · 22) 653
נָדִיב noble, princely (2 · 27) 622
חַמּוּק curving, curve (1 · 1) 330
יָרֵךְ thigh (2 · 34) 437
חֲלִי ornament (1 · 2) 318
אָמָּן artist, master workman (1 · 1) 53
שֹׁר 3 umbilical cord, navel (1 · 3) 1057
אַגָּן bowl (1 · 3) 8
סַהַר roundness (1 · 1) 690
חָסֵר to be lacking (1 · 19 · 23) 341
מֶזֶג mixture (1 · 1) 561
עֲרֵמָה heap (1 · 10) 790
חִטָּה wheat (1 · 30) 334
סוּג to fence about (1 · 1 · 1) 691 II
שׁוֹשַׁנָּה lily (8 · 17) 1004 I שׁוֹשַׁן
שַׁד 4 breast (8 · 21) 994
עֹפֶר young hart, stag (5 · 5) 780
תּוֹאָם twin (2 · 6) 1060
צְבִיָּה gazelle (2 · 2) 840
צַוָּאר 5 neck, back of neck (3 · 41) 848
מִגְדָּל tower (5 · 49) 153
בְּרֵכָה pool, pond (1 · 17) 140
צפה to look, keep watch (1 · 9 · 18) 859 I
דַּלָּה 6 hair (1 · 2) 195 I
אַרְגָּמָן purple, red purple (2 · 39) 71
רַהַט lock [of hair] (1 · 4[?]) 923 II
יפה 7 to be beautiful (3 · 6 · 8) 421
נעם to be lovely, delightful (1 · 8 · 8) 653 I
תַּעֲנוּג delight (1 · 5) 772
קוֹמָה 8 stature, height (1 · 45) 879
דָּמָה to be like, resemble (4 · 13 · 27) 197 I
תָּמָר date palm (2 · 12) 1071 I
שַׁד breast (8 · 21) 994
אֶשְׁכּוֹל cluster (3 · 9) 79

תָּמָר 9 date palm (2 · 12) 1071 I
סַנְסִנִּים fruit stalks (1 · 1) 703
שַׁד breast (8 · 21) 994
אֶשְׁכּוֹל cluster (3 · 9) 79
תַּפּוּחַ apple, apple tree (4 · 6) 656 I
חֵךְ 10 palate (3 · 18) 335
טוֹב best sort (1 · 3) 373 II.1.b
מֵישָׁר smoothness, evenness, level (2 · 19) 449
דבב to glide, move gently (1 · 1 · 1) 179
יָשֵׁן asleep, sleeping (2 · 9) 445 I
תְּשׁוּקָה 11 longing (1 · 3) 1003
כָּפָר 12 village (3 · 3[?]) 499
פָּרַח 13 to bud, sprout, send out shoots (2 · 27 · 32) 827 I
סְמָדַר blossom (3 · 3) 701
הנץ to bloom, blossom (2 · 3 · 4) 665 נצץ
רִמּוֹן pomegranate (6 · 32) 941 I
דּוּדָאִים 14 mandrakes (1 · 8) 188 דודי
מֶגֶד excellence (3 · 5) 550
יָשָׁן old (1 · 8) 445
צָפַן to hide, treasure up (1 · 23 · 28) 861

Chapter 8

ינק 1 to suck (1 · 8 · 18) 413
שַׁד breast (8 · 21) 994
נָשַׁק to kiss (2 · 26 · 32) 676 I
בֵּז to despise (2 · 13 · 13) 100 I בוז
נָהַג 2 to lead on, drive (8 · 20 · 30) 624 I
רֶקַח spice (1 · 1) 955
עָסִיס sweet wine (1 · 5) 779
רִמּוֹן pomegranate (6 · 32) 941 I
חבק 3 to embrace (2 · 10 · 13) 287
התרפק 5 to support oneself, lean (1 · 1 · 1) 952
תַּפּוּחַ apple tree, apple (4 · 6) 656 I
חבל to writhe, twist (2 · 3 · 3[?]) 286 I
חוֹתָם 6 seal, signet ring (1 · 14) 368 I
עַז strong, mighty, fierce (1 · 22) 738

קָשֶׁה fierce, intense, vehement (1 · 36) 904

קִנְאָה jealousy, ardent love (1 · 43) 888

רֶשֶׁף flame (2 · 7) 958 I

שַׁלְהֶבֶתְיָה Yahweh flame (1 · 1) 529 שַׁלְהֶבֶת

כבה 7 to quench, extinguish (1 · 10 · 24) 459

שָׁטַף to overflow (1 · 28 · 31) 1009

הוֹן wealth sufficiency (1 · 26) 223

בַּז to despise (2 · 13 · 13) 100 I בוז

קָטָן 8 small, young (2 · 47) 881 I

שַׁד breast (8 · 21) 994

טִירָה 9 battlement (1 · 7) 377

צוּר to shut in, besiege (1 · 31 · 21) 848 II

לוּחַ boards, planks (1 · 43) 531

שַׁד 10 breast (8 · 21) 994

מִגְדָּל tower (5 · 49) 153

נטר 11 to keep, guard (4 · 4 · 4[?]) 643

נטר 12 to keep, guard (4 · 4 · 4[?]) 643

גַּן 13 garden (8 · 41) 171

חָבֵר associate, fellow (2 · 12) 288

הִקְשִׁיב to give attention (1 · 45 · 46) 904

דָּמָה 14 to be like, resemble (4 · 13 · 27) 197 I

צְבִי gazelle (3 · 11[?]) 840

עֹפֶר young hart, stag (5 · 5) 780

אַיָּל hart, stag (3 · 11) 19

בֹּשֶׂם balsam, spice (7 · 30) 141

582

ECCLESIASTES

Chapter 1

קֹהֶלֶת 1 collector of sentences, preacher, speaker in assembly (7 · 7) 875

קֹהֶלֶת 2 collector of sentences, preacher, speaker in assembly (7 · 7) 875

יִתְרוֹן 3 advantage, profit (10 · 10) 452

עָמַל to labor, toil (8 · 11 · 11) 765

זָרַח 5 to rise (2 · 18 · 18) 280

שָׁאַף to pant, gasp (1 · 14 · 14) 983 I

דָּרוֹם 6 south (2 · 17) 204

יָגֵעַ 8 wearisome, weary (1 · 3) 388

כְּבָר 10 already (9 · 9) 460 I

זִכָּרוֹן 11 remembrance, reminder (3 · 24) 272

קֹהֶלֶת 12 collector of sentences, preacher, speaker in assembly (7 · 7) 875

תּוּר 13 to explore (3 · 19 · 22) 1064

עִנְיָן task, occupation (8 · 8) 775

ענה to be occupied with, busy with (2 · 2 · 3) 775

רְעוּת 14 longing, striving (7 · 7) 946 II

עוּת 15 *Pual*, to be bent; ptc. = what is bent (1 · 1 · 11) 736

תקן to become straight (1 · 1 · 3) 1075

חֶסְרוֹן thing lacking, deficiency (1 · 1) 341

נִמְנָה to be counted, numbered (1 · 12 · 28) 584

הוֹלֵלוֹת 17 madness (5 · 5[?]) 239 הלל

שִׂכְלוּת = סִכְלוּת folly (7 · 7) 698

שֶׁגַּם־זֶה = שֶׁ + גַּם + זֶה this also (3 · 3) 168

רַעְיוֹן striving, longing (3 · 3) 946

כַּעַס 18 vexation, grief, anger (5 · 25) 495

מַכְאוֹב mental pain, pain (2 · 16) 456

Chapter 2

נִסָּה 1 to test; attempt (2 · 36 · 36) 650

שְׂחוֹק 2 laughter (4 · 15) 966

מְהוֹלָל *Poal* ptc. = mad [Lis. noun = folly (1 · 1)] (1[?] · 4[?] · 14[?]) 239 II הלל

זֶה this (6 · 11) 262

תּוּר 3 to find out how, to seek out, explore (3 · 19 · 22) 1064

מָשַׁךְ to cheer; [here only] to draw, drag or lead on or off (1 · 30 · 36) 604

נָהַג [here only] to behave oneself [itself] (1 · 20 · 30) 624

סִכְלוּת folly (7 · 7) 698

אֵי־זֶה which? (2 · 15) [אֵי where? (2 · 40)] 32

גַּנָּה 5 garden, orchard (1 · 16) 171

פַּרְדֵּס preserve, park (2 · 3) 825

בְּרֵכָה 6 pool, pond (1 · 17) 140 ברך

צָמַח to sprout, spring up (1 · 15 · 33) 855

כנס 8 to gather, collect (3 · 7 · 11) 488

סְגֻלָּה treasure (1 · 8) 688

שָׁר ptc. = singer (2 · 11) 1010 שיר

תַּעֲנוּג luxury, delight (1 · 5) 772

שִׁדָּה mng. unknown; LXX = having to do with pouring out wine, cupbearer [Lis. 1406 lady, Hol. 361 lady (concubine)] (2 · 2) 994

אצל 10 to withhold, reserve, lay aside (1 · 4 · 5) 69

מָנַע to withhold, hold back (1 · 25 · 29) 586

שָׂמֵחַ showing joy, joyful, merry; joy (1 · 21) 970

עָמַל 11 to labor, toil (8 · 11 · 11) 765

רְעוּת longing, striving (7 · 7) 946 II

יִתְרוֹן advantage, profit (10 · 10) 452

הוֹלֵלוֹת 12 madness (5 · 5[?]) 239

סִכְלוּת folly (7 · 7) 698

כְּבָר already (9 · 9) 460 I

שֶׁיֵּשׁ 13 = שֶׁ [conj. that] + יֵשׁ [there is, et al.] (1 · 1) 979, 441

יִתְרוֹן advantage, profit (10 · 10) 452

סִכְלוּת folly (7 · 7) 698

מִקְרֶה 14 fortune, fate (7 · 10) 899

קרה to befall; encounter, meet (3 · 13 · 28) 899

מִקְרֶה 15 fortune, fate; accident, chance (7 · 10) 899

קרה to befall, meet (3 · 13 · 28) 899

חָכַם to be or become wise, act wisely (3 · 19 · 27) 314

יוֹתֵר as adv. to excess, overmuch; superiority, advantage (7 · 9) 452

שֶׁגַּם־זֶה = שֶׁ + גַּם + זֶה (3 · 3) this also 979

זִכָּרוֹן 16 remembrance (3 · 24) 272

כְּבָר already (9 · 9) [שׁ + כּבר (2 · 2)] 460 I

רְעוּת 17 longing, striving (7 · 7) 946 II

עָמֵל 18 toiling (5 · 9) 766

סָכָל 19 fool (5 · 7) 698

שָׁלַט to domineer, (2 · 5 · 8) 1020 I

עָמַל to labor, toil (8 · 11 · 11) 765

חָכַם to be or become wise, act wisely (3 · 19 · 27) 314

יאשׁ 20 *Piel*, to make to despair (1 · 1 · 6) 384

עָמָל to labor, toil (8 · 11 · 11) 765

כִּשָׁרוֹן 21 skill (3 · 3) 507

שֶׁלֹּא = שֶׁ + לוֹא who has not (2 · 4) 979, 518

עָמָל to labor, toil (8 · 11 · 11) 765

הוה 22 to become (2 · 5 · 5) 217

רַעְיוֹן striving, longing (3 · 3) 946

עָמֵל toiling (5 · 9[?]) 766 II

מַכְאוֹב 23 mental pain, pain (2 · 16) 456

כַּעַס vexation, grief; anger (5 · 25) 495

עִנְיָן task, occupation (8 · 8) 775

זֶה 24 this (6 · 11) 262

חוּשׁ 25 to feel, enjoy pleasure (1 · 1 · 1) 301

עִנְיָן 26 task, occupation (8 · 8) 775

כנס to amass, gather (3 · 7 · 11) 488

רְעוּת longing, striving (7 · 7) 946 II

Chapter 3

זְמָן 1 appointed time, time (1 · 4) 273

חֵפֶץ that in which one takes delight = business, matter, delight (7 · 39) 343

לָלֶדֶת 2 inf. cstr. of יָלַד + ל 408

לָטַעַת inf. cstr. of נָטַע + ל 642

עקר to pluck up, root up (1 · 1 · 7[?]) 785

פָּרַץ 3 to break down, through (2 · 46 · 49) 829 I

שָׂחַק 4 to laugh [friendly, more often in derision] (1 · 19 · 36) 965

ספר to wail, lament (2 · 28 · 30) 704

רקד to skip about [gaily] (1 · 3 · 9) 955

כנס 5 to collect, gather, amass (3 · 7 · 11) 488

חֹבק to embrace (2 · 3 · 13) 287

חבק *Piel*, to embrace (1 · 10 · 13) 287

תפר 7 to sew together (1 · 3 · 4) 1074

חשה to be silent, inactive, still (1 · 7 · 16) 364

יִתְרוֹן 9 advantage, profit (10 · 10) 452

בַּאֲשֶׁר in which; in [the place] where (3 · 19) 84

עָמֵל toiling (5 · 9[?]) 766 II

עִנְיָן 10 occupation, task (8 · 8) 775

ענה to be occupied, busied with (בּ) (2 · 2 · 3) 775 II

יָפֶה 11 fair, beautiful (2 · 41) 421

מִבְּלִי with אֲשֶׁר לֹא = so that not, without (1 · 25) 115 בְּלִי [with preps.] c

סוֹף end (3 · 5) 693

מַתָּת 13 gift (2 · 6) 682

גרע 14 to diminish (1 · 14 · 22) 175

כְּבָר 15 already (9 · 9) 460 I

רֶשַׁע 16 wickedness (4 · 30) 957

חֵפֶץ 17 that in which one takes delight = business, matter (7 · 39) 343

דִּבְרָה 18 cause, reason, manner; עַל דברה

= because of, for the sake of (3 · 5) 184
בְּרַר to test, prove (2 · 7 · 15) 140
מִקְרֶה 19 fortune, fate (7 · 10) 899
מוֹתָר preeminence, superiority (1 · 3) 452
לְמַעְלָה 21 upwards; exceedingly (1 · 34) 751 II
2.c עלה מַעַל
לְמַטָּה downwards (1 · 10) 641 נטה 2 מַטָּה
מֵאֲשֶׁר 22 than that (1 · 17) 84 אֲשֶׁר

Chapter 4

עֲשׁוּקִים 1 pl., oppression, extortion (2 · 4) 799
עָשַׁק to oppress, wrong; ptc. = oppressor (2 · 36 · 37) 798
דִּמְעָה [coll.] tears (1 · 23) 199
שָׁבַח 2 to commend, congratulate (2 · 6 · 8) 986 II
כְּבָר already (9 · 9) [שׁ + כבר (2 · 2)] 460 I
עֲדֶנָה contracted from הֵנָּה + עַד hitherto, still (1 · 1) 725
עֲדֶן 3 contracted from הֵן + עַד hitherto, still (1 · 1) 725
כִּשְׁרוֹן 4 skill (3 · 3) 507
קִנְאָה jealousy; zeal (2 · 43) 888
רְעוּת longing, striving (7 · 7) 946 II
חָבַק 5 to embrace [of hands = fold hands] (2 · 3 · 13) 287
מְלֹא 6 fullness (2 · 38) 571
נַחַת quietness, rest (3 · 7) 629 I נוח
חֹפֶן hollow of hand; מְלֹא ח׳ = handful (1 · 6) 342
רְעוּת longing, striving (7 · 7) 946 II
עֹשֶׁר 8 riches (6 · 37) 799
לְמִי to whom? whose? (1 · 20) 566 b מִי
עָמֵל toiling (5 · 9[?]) 766 II
חסר to deprive, cause to lack (1 · 2 · 23) 341
עִנְיָן task, occupation (8 · 8) 775
שָׂכָר 9 reward, wages; fare (2 · 28) 969 I

חָבֵר 10 companion (1 · 12) 288
אִי alas! [אִילוֹ = alas for him] (2 · 2) 33
III
חַם 11 to be or grow warm (2 · 23 · 26) 328
חמם
תָּקַף 12 to overpower (1 · 3 · 4) 1075
חוּט cord, thread, line (1 · 7) 296
שָׁלֻשׁ Pual in ptc. form only = threefold (1 · 5 · 8) 1026 I
מְהֵרָה haste, speed; with בְּ = in haste, quickly; hastily (2 · 20) 555
נִתַּק to be torn in two or apart (1 · 10 · 27) 683
מִסְכֵּן 13 poor (4 · 4) 587
נִזְהַר to be warned, admonished, instructed (2 · 8 · 21) 264 II
הַסּוּרִים 14 Qal pass. ptc. pl. of אסר + ה־ 63
כִּי גַם idiom: although 168 גַּם 6
רָשׁ ptc. = poor (2 · 21) 930 רושׁ
כִּי גַם 16 idiom: although 168 גַּם 6
רַעְיוֹן longing, striving (3 · 3) 946
מִתֵּת 17 Qal inf. נתן + מִן 678

Chapter 5

בהל 1 Piel, to hasten, make haste, act hastily (2 · 10 · 39) 96
עִנְיָן 2 task, occupation (8 · 8) 775
נָדַר 3 to vow (4 · 31 · 31) 623
אִחֵר to delay, cause one to delay (1 · 15 · 17) 29
חֵפֶץ delight (7 · 39) 343
נָדַר 4 to vow (4 · 31 · 31) 623
לַחֲטִיא 5 Hiph. inf. חטא with elided ה + prep. ל.
שְׁגָגָה error, sin of error, inadvertence (2 · 19) 993
קָצַף to be angry (1 · 28 · 34) 893 I
חִבֵּל to ruin, destroy (1 · 6 · 11) 287 II
עֹשֶׁק 7 oppression, extortion (2 · 15) 799

רָשׁ ptc. = poor man, poor (2 · 21) 930
רושׁ

גֵּזֶל thing plundered; robbery (1 · 2) 160

תמה to be astounded, dumbfounded (1 · 8 · 9) 1069

חֵפֶץ here = matter (7 · 39) 343

גָּבֹהַ exalted in station, high, גָּבֹהַ מֵעַל גָּבֹהַ = high one above high one; tall; haughty (5 · 41) 147

יִתְרוֹן 8 advantage, profit (10 · 10) 452

תְּבוּאָה 9 income, gain (1 · 43) 100

רבב 10 to be or become many (1 · 23 · 24) 912

כִּשְׁרוֹן profit, success; skill (3 · 3) 507

רְאוּת Qere = a look (1 · 1) 909

מָתוֹק 11 sweet = pleasant (2 · 12) 608

שֵׁנָה sleep (2 · 23) 446

שָׂבָע satiety, plenty (1 · 8) 960

עָשִׁיר the rich, rich (3 · 23) 799

ישׁן to sleep, go to sleep, be asleep (1 · 15 · 16) 445

עֹשֶׁר 12 riches (6 · 37) 799

עֹשֶׁר 13 riches (6 · 37) 799

עִנְיָן business, task, occupation (8 · 8) 775

מְאוּמָה anything (4 · 32) 548

עָרוֹם 14 naked; here = without possessions (1 · 16) 736

כְּשֶׁבָּא = כְּ+שֶׁ+בּוֹא, even as he came

מְאוּמָה anything (4 · 32) 548

שֶׁיֵּלֵךְ = שֶׁ+הוֹלִיךְ [Hiph. of הלך] 229

זה 15 this (6 · 11) 262

עֻמָּה juxtaposition, but used always w. force of prep. = parallel to = exactly as, agreeing with, corresponding to, close by, side by side with (1 · 1) with לְ (2 · 32) 769 I

שֶׁבָּא = שֶׁ+בּוֹא, as he comes

יִתְרוֹן advantage, profit (10 · 10) 452

עָמָל to labor, toil (8 · 11 · 11) 765

חֳלִי 16 sickness, disease (2 · 24) 318

קֶצֶף wrath (1 · 28) 893 I

יָפֶה 17 fair, beautiful (2 · 41) 421

עָמָל to labor, toil (8 · 11 · 11) 765

עֹשֶׁר 18 riches (6 · 37) 799

נֶכֶס pl. only, riches, treasures (2 · 5) 647

הִשְׁלִיט to get power of; get mastery of (2 · 3 · 8) 1020 I

לָשֵׂאת לְ + Qal inf. cstr. נשא 669

זה this (6 · 11) 262

מַתַּת gift (2 · 6) 682

הענה 19 [dub.] to cause to respond (1 · 1 · 3 [?]) 772 I

Chapter 6

עֹשֶׁר 2 riches (6 · 37) 799

נֶכֶס pl. only, riches, treasures (2 · 5) 647

חָסֵר lacking, needy, in want of (1 · 17) 341

הִתְאַוָּה to desire, long for, lust after (1 · 16 · 27) 16 I

הִשְׁלִיט to get power of, get mastery of (2 · 3 · 8) 1020 I

נָכְרִי foreigner (1 · 45) 648

חֳלִי sickness, disease (2 · 24) 318

קְבוּרָה 3 burial (1 · 14) 869

נֵפֶל miscarriage, abortion (1 · 3) 658

נַחַת 5 rest, quietness (3 · 7) 629 I

לָזֶה מִזֶּה = זֶה+מִן and זֶה+לְ phrase = it has more [rest] than he

אִלּוּ 6 if, though (1 · 2) 47

יוֹתֵר 8 advantage, superiority, excess (7 · 9) 452

רְעוּת 9 longing, striving (7 · 7) 946 II

כְּבָר 10 already (9 · 9) 460 I

דָּן to contend; judge, decide (1 · 23 · 24) 192 דין

שֶׁהַתַּקִּיף שֶׁ + Hithp. תקף [to overpower, p. 1075]; Qere = שׁתקיף, שֶׁ+תַּקִּיף mighty (1 · 1) 1076

יוֹתֵר 11 more, superiority, excess, advantage (7 · 9) 452

Chapter 7

לָלֶכֶת 2 inf. cstr. of הלך + ל 229

אֵבֶל mourning (2 · 24) 5

מִשְׁתֶּה feast, banquet (1 · 46) 1059

בַּאֲשֶׁר in that, inasmuch as (3 · 19) 84 אשר

סוֹף end (3 · 5) 693

כַּעַס 3 vexation, grief, anger (5 · 25) 495

שְׂחוֹק laughter (4 · 15) 966

רֹע sadness (1 · 19) 947

אֵבֶל 4 mourning (2 · 24) 5

גְּעָרָה 5 rebuke (1 · 15) 172

סִיר 6 thorn (1 · 5) 696 II

סִיר pot (1 · 29) 696 I

שְׂחוֹק laughter (4 · 15) 966

עֹשֶׁק 7 oppression, extortion (2 · 15) 799

הוֹלֵל *Poel*, to make into a fool, make fool of (1 · 4 · 14[?]) 237

מַתָּנָה bribe, gift (1 · 17) 682

אָרֵךְ 8 long; here = patient (1 · 15) 74

גְּבַהּ haughty; lofty, tall; exalted in station (5 · 41) 147

בהל 9 *Piel*, to hasten, make haste, act hastily (2 · 10 · 39) 96

כַּעַס vexation, grief; anger (5 · 25) 495

חֵיק bosom, fold of the garment at breast (1 · 38) 300

עַל־זֶה 10 on this account; concerning this 260 זֶה 6.5

יוֹתֵר 11 more, superiority, excess, advantage (7 · 9) 452

יִתְרוֹן 12 advantage, profit (10 · 10) 452

תָּקֵן 13 to make straight, put straight, arrange in order (2 · 2 · 3) 1075

עות *Piel*, to bend, make crooked = falsify (1 · 9 · 11) 736

לְעֻמָּה 14 as well as; corresponding to (2 · 32) 769

דִּבְרָה cause, reason, manner, עַל דִּ׳ = because of, for the sake of (3 · 5) 184

שֶׁלֹּא עַל דִּבְרַת שֶׁלֹּא = שֶׁ + לֹוא to the intent that not (2 · 4) 979 שֶׁ 3.2 (a)

מְאוּמָה anything (4 · 32) 548

הַאֲרִיךְ 15 to prolong, postpone (3 · 31 · 34) 73

התחכם 16 to make or show oneself wise (1 · 2 · 27) 314

יוֹתֵר as adv. = to excess, overmuch (7 · 9) 452

רשע 17 to be wicked, act wickedly (1 · 9 · 34) 957

סָכָל fool (5 · 7) 698

בְּלֹא here = before (2 · 31) 520 לֹא 4.a.(b)

יָרֵא 18 ptc. = fearing, one who fears (2 · 45) 431

עזז 19 to be strong, prevail (1 · 9 · 11) 738

שַׁלִּיט ruler (3 · 4) 1020

זֶה 23 this (6 · 11) 262

נִסָּה to test (2 · 36 · 36) 650

חָכַם to be or become wise, act wisely (3 · 19 · 27) 314

עָמֹק 24 deep; here = unsearchable (2 · 17) 771

תּוּר 25 to explore mentally (3 · 19 · 22) 1064

חֶשְׁבּוֹן reckoning, account (3 · 3) 363 I

רֶשַׁע wickedness (4 · 30) 957

כֶּסֶל stupidity, folly (1 · 6[?]) 492

סִכְלוּת folly (7 · 7) 698

הוֹלֵלוֹת madness (5 · 5[?]) 239

מַר 26 bitter, bitterness (1 · 38) 600 I

מָצוֹד hunting implement (2 · 4) 844 II

חֵרֶם hunting net, fishing net (1 · 9) 357 II

אֵסוּר band, bond [fetter] (1 · 3) 64

קֹהֶלֶת 27 collector [of sentences], preacher (7 · 7) 875

חֶשְׁבּוֹן reckoning, account (3 · 3) 363 I

חִשָּׁבוֹן 29 device, invention (1 · 2) 364

Chapter 8

פֵּשֶׁר 1 solution, interpretation (1 · 1) 833

הָאִיר to make light, lighten (1 · 34 · 40) 21
אור

שֻׁנָּה *Pual*, to be changed, here = mollified (1 · 1 · 26) 1039 I

דִּבְרָה 2 cause, reason, manner, עַל דִּ = because of, for the sake of (3 · 5) 184

שְׁבוּעָה oath (2 · 30) 989

נבהל 3 to be in haste, be in a hurry; be disturbed (1 · 24 · 39) 96

בַּאֲשֶׁר 4 in that, inasmuch as (3 · 19) 84

שִׁלְטוֹן mastery (2 · 2) 1020

חֵפֶץ 6 that in which one takes delight = business, matter; or delight (7 · 39) 343

שַׁלִּיט 8 having mastery (3 · 4) 1020

כלא to restrain (1 · 14 · 17) 476

שִׁלְטוֹן mastery (2 · 2) 1020

מִשְׁלַחַת discharge (1 · 2) 1020

רֶשַׁע wickedness (4 · 30) 957

שָׁלַט 9 to domineer, lord it over [עַל] (2 · 5 · 8) 1020 I

בְּכֵן 10 in such circumstances; i.e., thereupon, then (1 · 2) 486 כֵּן 3.b

פִּתְגָם 11 edict, decree (1 · 2) 834

מְהֵרָה haste, speed; usually as adv. = hastily, speedily (2 · 20) 555

הֶאֱרִיךְ 12 to prolong, postpone (3 · 31 · 34) 73

כִּי גַם idiom: even though, although 169 גַּם 6

יָרֵא *Qal* ptc. = fearing, one who fears (2 · 45) 431

הֶאֱרִיךְ 13 to prolong, postpone (3 · 31 · 34) 73

שֶׁגַּם־זֶה 14 = שֶׁ + גַּם + זֶה this also (3 · 3) 168

שבח 15 to commend, congratulate (2 · 6 · 8) 986 II

לוה to be joined to, attend (1 · 1 · 12) 530 I

עִנְיָן 16 occupation, task (8 · 8) 775

שֵׁנָה sleep (2 · 23) 446

בְּשֶׁל 17 on account of (1 · 3) 980 שֶׁ 4.d

עָמַל to labor, toil (8 · 11 · 11) 765

Chapter 9

בָּרַד 1 to test, prove, purify (2 · 7 · 15) 140
but BDB reads בּוּר to explain (1 · 1) 101

עֶבֶד 1 work (1 · 1) 714

שִׂנְאָה hatred, hating (2 · 17) 971

מִקְרֶה 2 fortune, fate (7 · 10) 899

לַאֲשֶׁר to him who, that which, those who (1 · 36) 82 אֲשֶׁר 1 & 2

שְׁבוּעָה oath (2 · 30) 989

מִקְרֶה 3 fortune, fate (7 · 10) 899

הוֹלֵלוֹת madness (5 · 5[?]) 239

חֻבַּר 4 to be united to, be joined together (1 · 4 · 28) 287

בִּטָּחוֹן trust (1 · 3) 105

כֶּלֶב dog (1 · 32) 476

אַרְיֵה lion (1 · 45) 71

מְאוּמָה 5 anything (4 · 32) 548

שָׂכָר wages, here = reward (2 · 28) 969 I

זֵכֶר memorial, remembrance (1 · 23) 271

שִׂנְאָה 6 hatred, hating (2 · 17) 971

קִנְאָה rivalry, jealousy, zeal (2 · 43) 888

כְּבָר already (9 · 9) 460 I

כְּבָר 7 already (9 · 9) 460 I

רָצָה to be pleased with, favorable to (1 · 42 · 50) 953

לָבָן 8 white (1 · 29) 526 I

חָסֵר to be lacking (2 · 19 · 23) 341

עָמֵל 9 toiling (5 · 9) 766 II

חֶשְׁבּוֹן 10 reckoning, account (3 · 3) 363 I

קַל 11 swift, fleet (1 · 13) 886

מֵרוֹץ running, race (1 · 1) 930

נָבוֹן *Niph*. ptc. as subst = the intelligent,

discerning, understanding (1 · 21) בִּין 106

עֹשֶׁר riches (6 · 37) 799

פֶּגַע chance, occurrence (1 · 2) 803

קרה to befall (3 · 13 · 28) 899

דָּג 12 fish (1 · 19) 185

מְצוֹדָה net (1 · 3) 845 I

צִפּוֹר bird, birds (2 · 40) 861 I

פַּח bird trap (1 · 25) 809

יקשׁ *Pual*, to be entrapped (1 · 1 · 8) 430

פִּתְאֹם suddenly (1 · 25) 837

זֹה 13 this (6 · 11) 262

קָטֹן 14 small, insignificant (1 · 47) 881 I

מָצוֹד pl. siegeworks [dub.] (2 · 4) 844 I

מִסְכֵּן 15 poor, poor man (4 · 4) 587

מִסְכֵּן 16 poor man, poor (4 · 4) 587

בָּזָה to despise, regard with contempt; pass. ptc. = despised (1 · 31 · 42) 102

נַחַת 17 quietness, quiet attitude (3 · 7) 629 I

זְעָקָה outcry, cry (1 · 1 · 18) 277 זעק

מֹשֵׁל ptc. = ruler (2 · 24) 605 III

קְרָב 18 war, battle (1 · 8) 898

Chapter 10

זְבוּב 1 fly [insect] (1 · 6) 256

הבאישׁ to cause to stink (1 · 7 · 16) 92

הביע to cause to bubble, ferment (1 · 10 · 11) 615 נבע

רקח to mix or compound oil or ointment; ptc. = mixer, perfumer (1 · 6 · 8) 955

יָקָר weighty, influential (1 · 35) 429

סִכְלוּת folly (7 · 7) 698

סָכָל 3 fool (5 · 7) 698

חָסֵר to be lacking (2 · 19 · 23) 341

מֹשֵׁל 4 ptc. = ruler (2 · 24) 605 III

מַרְפֵּא here = composure; health, healing, cure (1 · 3[?]) 951

חֵטְא sin (1 · 33) 307

שְׁגָגָה 5 error; sin of error or inadvertence (2 · 19) 993

שַׁלִּיט ruler (3 · 4) 1020

סֶכֶל 6 folly (1 · 1) 698

עָשִׁיר the rich, rich (3 · 23) 799

שֵׁפֶל low estate, condition (1 · 2) 1050

חָפַר 8 to dig (1 · 23 · 23) 343 I

גּוּמָץ pit (1 · 1) 170

פָּרַץ to break through, break down (2 · 46 · 49) 829 I

גָּדֵר wall, fence (1 · 14) 154

נָשַׁךְ to bite (2 · 10 · 12) 675

נָחָשׁ serpent (2 · 31) 638 I

נֶעְצַב 9 to be hurt, be pained, be grieved (1 · 7 · 15) 780 I

נסכן to endanger oneself (1 · 1 · 10[?]) 698

קֵהָה 10 *Piel*, to be blunt (1 · 1 · 4) 874

קִלְקַל *Pilp.*, to whet, sharpen (1 · 2 · 82) 886 קלל

גבר to make strong, strengthen (1 · 3 · 25) 149

יִתְרוֹן advantage, profit (10 · 10) 452

הכשׁיר to give success (1 · 1 · 3) 506

נָשַׁךְ 11 to bite (2 · 10 · 12) 675

נָחָשׁ serpent (2 · 31) 638 I

בְּלוֹא here = before (2 · 31) 520 לא 4.a.(b)

לַחַשׁ serpent-charming; amulet, whisper of prayer (1 · 5) 538

יִתְרוֹן advantage, profit (10 · 10) 452

בַּעַל הַלָּשׁוֹן idiom: charmer (1 · 1) 127 I בַּעַל 5.a

בֶּלַע 12 to swallow up, here = annihilate, engulf, destroy (1 · 20 · 41) 118

תְּחִלָּה 13 beginning (1 · 22) 321

סִכְלוּת folly (7 · 7) 698

הוֹלֵלוֹת madness (5 · 5[?]) 239

סָכָל 14 fool (5 · 7) 698

יגע 15 to weary, make weary (1 · 2 · 26) 388

לָלֶכֶת inf. cstr. of הלך + ל 229

אִי 16 alas! (2 · 2) 33 III

אֶשֶׁר 17 happiness, blessedness (1 · 45) 80

חֹר noble (1 · 13) 359 II

שְׁתִי drinking, drinking bout (1 · 1) 1059 I

עַצְלָה 18 sluggishness [dual form = double or great sluggishness] (1 · 15) 782

נִמַּךְ *Niph.* to sink (1 · 1 · 3) 568 מכך

מְקָרֶה beam work (1 · 1) 900

שִׁפְלוּת sinking [of hands = negligence] (1 · 1) 1050

דֶּלֶף to drip; i.e., leak (1 · 1 · 1[?]) 196

שְׂחוֹק 19 laughter (4 · 15) 966

מַדָּע 20 mind, thought (1 · 6) 396

חֶדֶר room, chamber (1 · 37) 293

מִשְׁכָּב couch, bed (1 · 46) 1012

עָשִׁיר the rich, rich (3 · 23) 799

בַּעַל כְּנָפַיִם idiom: winged thing, a bird (1 · 2) 127 I בַּעַל 5.a

Chapter 11

עָב 3 cloud, dark cloud, cloud mass (3 · 30) 728 II

גֶּשֶׁם rain, shower (2 · 35) 177 II

הֵרִיק to pour out or down, to empty, empty out (1 · 17 · 19) 937

דָּרוֹם south (2 · 17) 204

הָוָה to be, become (2 · 5 · 5) 217

עָב 4 cloud, dark cloud, cloud mass (3 · 30) 728 II

קָצַר to reap, harvest (1 · 24 · 24) 894 II

כָּכָה 5 thus (1 · 33) 462

אֵי־זֶה 6 which? (2 · 15) [אֵי where? (2 · 40)] 32

כָּשֵׁר to succeed, be advantageous, proper, suitable (1 · 2 · 3) 506

מָתוֹק 7 sweet = pleasant; sweetness (2 · 12) 608

בָּחוּר 9 young man, young men (1 · 45) 104

יַלְדוּת youth, childhood (2 · 3) 409

בְּחוּרִים youth (2 · 3) 104

כַּעַס 10 vexation, grief, anger (5 · 25) 495

יַלְדוּת youth, childhood (2 · 3) 409

שַׁחֲרוּת blackness; viz., of hair [i.e., prime of life; usu. dawn of youth] (1 · 1) 1007

Chapter 12

בָּרָא 1 to shape, fashion, create (1 · 38 · 48 [?]) 135 I

בְּחוּרִים youth (2 · 3) 104

חֵפֶץ delight (7 · 39) 343 I

חָשַׁךְ 2 to be or grow dark (2 · 11 · 17) 364

יָרֵחַ moon (1 · 27) 437

כּוֹכָב star (1 · 37) 456

עָב cloud, dark cloud, cloud mass (3 · 30) 728 II

גֶּשֶׁם rain, shower (2 · 35) 177 II

זָע 3 to tremble, quake (1 · 2 · 3) 266 זוע

הִתְעַוֵּת to bend oneself (1 · 1 · 11) 736

בָּטַל to cease (1 · 1 · 1) 105

טָחֲנוֹת ptc. fem. pl. = teeth (1 · 1) 377

מָעַט *Piel,* to grow few (1 · 1 · 22) 589

חָשַׁךְ to grow dim (2 · 11 · 17) 364

אֲרֻבָּה lattice, window (1 · 9) 70

שׁוּק 4 street (2 · 4) 1003

שָׁפֵל to be or become low (1 · 11 · 30) 1050

טַחֲנָה mill (1 · 1) 377

צִפּוֹר bird, birds (2 · 40) 861 I

נָשַׁח to be reduced, weakened, prostrated, humbled (1 · 4 · 18) 1005 שחח

גָּבֹהַּ 5 high, lofty, tall (5 · 41) 147

חַתְחַת pl. only, terrors (1 · 1) 369

הֵנִיץ to wear blossoms, put forth blossoms (1 · 3 · 4) 665 נצץ

שָׁקֵד almond tree, almond (1 · 4) 1052

הסתבל   *Hiph.*, to stuff itself, grow fat (1 · 1 · 9) 687 סבל

חָגָב   grasshopper (1 · 5) 290 I

הֵפִיר   to make ineffectual, frustrate [but use here dub.] (1 · 42 · 45) 830 I

אֲבִיּוֹנָה   caperberry [as stimulating desire] (1 · 1) 2

שׁוּק   street (2 · 4) 1003

ספד   to wail, lament; ptc. = wailer (1 · 28 · 30) 704

נרתק   6 to be snapped, broken (1 · 1 · 2), fm. "to bind" 958; BDB sugg. ינתק to be torn apart or in two (1 · 10 · 27) 683

חֶבֶל   cord, rope (1 · 49) 286 I

רצץ   to be crushed (1 · 11 · 19) 954

גֻּלָּה   bowl, basin (1 · 15) 165 גלל

כַּד   jar (1 · 18) 461

מַבּוּעַ   spring of water (1 · 3) 616

נרץ   to be crushed, broken (1 · 2 · 19) 954 רצץ

גַּלְגַּל   wheel (1 · 11) 165

קֹהֶלֶת   8 collector of sentences, preacher (7 · 7) 875

יוֹתֵר   9 excess, superiority; here in idiom יֹתֵר שֶׁהָיָה = besides that (7 · 9) 452

קֹהֶלֶת   collector of sentences, preacher (7 · 7) 875

אָזַן   to weigh, test, prove (1 · 1 · 1) 24 II

חִקֵּר   to search for, seek out (1 · 1 · 27) 350

תִּקֵּן   to make straight, put straight, arrange in order (2 · 2 · 3) 1075

מָשָׁל   proverb, parable, poem (1 · 39) 605 II

קֹהֶלֶת   10 collector of sentences, preacher (7 · 7) 875

חֵפֶץ   delight (7 · 39) 343

יֹשֶׁר   rightness, uprightness (1 · 14) 449

דָּרְבֹנָה   11 goad (1 · 2) 201

מַסְמֵר   nail (1 · 5) 702

בַּעֲלֵי אֲסֻפּוֹת   idiom: members of assemblies, or well-grouped sayings (1 · 1) 127 I בַּעַל 5.b

אֲסֻפָּה   collection (1 · 1) 63

יוֹתֵר   12 more [מִן] than (7 · 9) 452

נִזְהַר   to be instructed, admonished, warned (2 · 8 · 21) 264 II

לַהַג   study, devotion (1 · 1) 529

יְגִעָה   wearying (1 · 1) 388

סוֹף   13 end (3 · 5) 693

נֶעְלָם   14 to be concealed, obscured (1 · 11 · 29) 761 I

591

LAMENTATIONS

Chapter 1

אֵיכָה 1 how! (4 · 18) 32

בָּדָד alone (2 · 11) 94

שָׂרָה princess, noble lady (1 · 5) 979 I

מְדִינָה province (1 · 44) 193

מַס labor bands, slave gangs (1 · 2 · 3) 586 I

דִּמְעָה 2 tears (3 · 23) 199

לְחִי cheek (2 · 21) 534 I

אֹהֵב lover, friend (1 · 36) 12 אהב

בגד to act or deal treacherously (1 · 49 · 49) 93

מָנוֹחַ 3 resting place (1 · 7) 629 I

הִשִּׂיג to overtake (1 · 49 · 49) 673 נשׂג

מֵצַר distress, straits (1 · 3) 865

אָבֵל 4 mourning (1 · 8) 5 I

מִבְּלִי for lack of (1 · 25) 115 בְּלִי c

נאנח to sigh (4 · 12 · 12) 58

בְּתוּלָה virgin (7 · 50) 143

נוגה to be grieved (1 · 2 · 8) 387 I יגה

מַר to be bitter (1 · 6 · 15) 600 I מרר

שלה 5 to be at ease, prosper (1 · 5 · 7) 1017 I

הוֹגָה to cause grief, sorrow (3 · 5 · 8) 387 יגה I

עוֹלָל child (3 · 9) 760 עוֹלָל

שְׁבִי captive, captivity (2 · 46) 985

הָדָר 6 splendor, majesty (1 · 30) 214

אַיָּל hart, stag (1 · 11) 19

מִרְעֶה pasture, pasturage (1 · 13) 945

בְּלֹא without (2 · 30) 518 ליגא 4.a

מָרוּד 7 restlessness, straying (2 · 3) 924

מַחְמֹד desirable, precious thing (1 · 1) 327

עֹזֵר helper (1 · 19[?]) 740 I עזר

שָׂחַק to laugh (1 · 18 · 36) 965

מִשְׁבָּת cessation, annihilation (1 · 1) 992

חֵטְא 8 sin (2 · 33) 307

נִדָּה impurity, impure thing (2 · 30) 622

מְכַבֵּד one who honors (1 · 2[?]) 457 Piel

הזל to despise, make light of (1 · 1 · 4) 272 זלל II

נאנח to sigh (4 · 12 · 12) 58

אָחוֹר backwards, behind (3 · 41) 30

טֻמְאָה 9 uncleanness (1 · 37) 380

שׁוּל skirt (1 · 11) 1002

פֶּלֶא wonder (1 · 13) 810

מַחְמַד 10 desirable, precious things (3 · 13) 326

נאנח 11 to sigh (4 · 12 · 12) 58

מַחְמַד desirable, precious things (3 · 13) 326

אֹכֶל food (2 · 44) 38

זוֹלֵל worthless, insignificant (1 · 6) 272 II זלל

מַכְאוֹב 12 pain (3 · 16) 456

עוֹלַל to deal out severely (1 · 1 · 17) 759 I

הוֹגָה to cause grief, sorrow (3 · 5 · 8) 387 יגה I

חָרוֹן burning (2 · 41) 354

רדה 13 to prevail (1 · 22 · 23) 921

רֶשֶׁת net (1 · 22) 440

אָחוֹר backwards, behind (3 · 41) 30

דָּוֶה faint (2 · 5) 188

נִשְׂקַד 14 [dub.] to be bound (1 · 1 · 1) 974

עֹל yoke (2 · 40) 760

הִשְׂתָּרֵג to intertwine oneself (1 · 1 · 2) 974 שׂרג

צַוָּאר neck, back of neck (2 · 41) 848

סלה 15 to flout, toss aside (1 · 1 · 2) 699 I

אַבִּיר mighty (1 · 17) 7

בָּחוּר young man (5 · 45) 104

גַּת winepress (1 · 5) 387 I

בְּתוּלָה virgin (7 · 50) 143

גבר 16 to prevail (1 · 17 · 25) 149

נִדָּה 17 impurity, impure thing (2 · 30) 622

מרה 18 to be rebellious, disobedient (3 · 21 · 43) 598

מַכְאוֹב   pain (3 · 16) 456

בְּתוּלָה   virgin (7 · 50) 143

בָּחוּר   young man (5 · 45) 104

שְׁבִי   captivity (2 · 46) 985

מְאַהֵב   19 lover (1 · 16[?]) 12 אָהֵב *Piel*

רָמָה   to beguile, deceive, mislead (1 · 8 · 8) 941 II

גָּוַע   to expire, perish, die (1 · 23 · 23) 157

אֹכֶל   food (2 · 44) 38

מֵעֶה   20 internal organs, bowels; fig. for seat of emotions (2 · 31) 588 5

חמרמר   to be in a ferment (2 · 2 · 5) 330 I חמר

מָרָה   to be rebellious, disobedient (3 · 21 · 43) 598

שכל   to make childless (1 · 18 · 23) 1013

נאנח   21 to sigh (4 · 12 · 12) 58

שָׂשׂ   to exult, rejoice (2 · 26 · 26) 965 שוש

עולל   22 to act severely (4 · 8 · 17) 759 I

אֲנָחָה   sighing, groaning (1 · 11) 58

דַּוָּי   faint (1 · 3) 188

Chapter 2

אֵיכָה   1 how! (4 · 18) 32

העיב   to becloud (1 · 1 · 1) 728 עוב

הֲדֹם   footstool (1 · 6) 213

בִּלַּע   2 to swallow up, engulf (5 · 20 · 41) 118

חָמַל   to spare (4 · 40 · 40) 328

נָאוֹת   pasture, meadow (1 · 45[?]) 627 II נוה

הָרַס   to throw down, tear down (2 · 30 · 43) 248

עֶבְרָה   overflowing rage, fury (2 · 34) 720

מִבְצָר   fortress, stronghold (2 · 37) 131

גָּדַע   3 to hew off (1 · 5 · 22) 154

חֲרִי   burning (1 · 6) 354

אָחוֹר   backwards, behind (3 · 41) 30

לֶהָבָה   flame (1 · 19) 529

מַחְמַד   4 desirable, precious things (3 · 13) 326

בִּלַּע   5 to swallow up, engulf (5 · 20 · 41) 118

אַרְמוֹן   castle, palace (2 · 33) 74

מִבְצָר   fortress, stronghold (2 · 37) 131

תַּאֲנִיָּה   mourning (1 · 2) 58

אֲנִיָּה   mourning (1 · 2) 58

חמס   6 to do violence to (1 · 7 · 8) 329

גַּן   garden (1 · 41) 171

שֹׂךְ   booth, pavilion (1 · 1) 968

נָאַץ   to spurn, contemn (1 · 8 · 24) 610

זַעַם   indignation (2 · 22) 276

זָנַח   7 to reject (3 · 16 · 19) 276 I

נאר   to abhor, spurn (1 · 2 · 2) 611

אַרְמוֹן   castle, palace (2 · 33) 74

קָו   8 line (1 · 17) 876 II

בִּלַּע   to swallow up, engulf (5 · 20 · 41) 118

האביל   to cause to mourn (1 · 1 · 38) 5 I

חֵל   rampart, fortress (1 · 9) 298

אָמְלַל   to be or grow feeble, languish (1 · 15 · 15[?]) 51

טָבַע   9 to sink (1 · 6 · 10) 371

בְּרִיחַ   bar (1 · 41) 138

חָזוֹן   vision (1 · 35) 302

דמם   10 to be silent, still (3 · 23 · 30) 198

חגר   to gird, gird on (1 · 44 · 44) 291

שַׂק   sackcloth (1 · 48) 974

בְּתוּלָה   virgin (7 · 50) 143

דִּמְעָה   11 tears (3 · 23) 199

חמרמר   to be in a ferment (2 · 2 · 5) 330 I חמר

מֵעֶה   internal organs, bowels; fig. for seat of emotions (2 · 31) 588 5

כָּבֵד   liver (1 · 14) 458

שֶׁבֶר   breaking, fracture (5 · 44) 991 I

נעטף   to faint (1 · 1 · 11) 742 III

עוֹלֵל   child (2 · 11) 760

יוֹנֵק suckling babe (2 · 11[?]) 413 ינק

רְחוֹב broad open place (3 · 43) 932 I

קִרְיָה town, city (1 · 30) 900

אַיֵּה 12 where? (1 · 44) 32

דָּגָן corn (1 · 40) 186

הִתְעַטֵּף to faint, faint away (1 · 6 · 11) 742 III

רְחוֹב broad open place (3 · 43) 932 I

חֵיק bosom (1 · 38) 300

הֵעִיד 13 to testify, bear witness (1 · 40 · 45 [?]) 729 עוד

דָּמָּה to liken, compare (1 · 13 · 27) 197 I

הִשְׁוָה to make like (1 · 2 · 16) 1000 I

בְּתוּלָה virgin (7 · 50) 143

שֶׁבֶר breaking, fracture (5 · 44) 991 I

תָּפֵל 14 tasteless, unseasoned (1 · 6[?]) 1074 I

שְׁבוּת captivity, captives (1 · 26) 986 שְׁבִית

מַשְׂאֵת utterance, oracle (1 · 21[?]) 673

מַדּוּחַ enticing (1 · 1) 623

סָפַק 15 to clap (1 · 6 · 6) 706

שָׁרַק to hiss (2 · 12 · 12) 1056

הֵנִיעַ to shake, wag (1 · 14 · 38) 631 נוע

כָּלִיל entire, perfect (1 · 15) 483

יֹפִי beauty (1 · 19) 421

מָשׂוֹשׂ exultation (2 · 17) 965

פָּצָה 16 to open (2 · 15 · 15) 822

שָׁרַק to hiss (2 · 12 · 12) 1056

חָרַק to gnash, grind (1 · 5 · 5) 359

בָּלַע to swallow up, engulf (5 · 20 · 41) 118

קָוָה to wait for, look eagerly for (1 · 39 · 45) 875 I Piel

זָמַם 17 to purpose, devise (1 · 13 · 13) 273

בִּצַּע to accomplish (1 · 6 · 16) 130

הָרַס to throw down, overthrow (2 · 20 · 43) 248

חָמַל to spare (4 · 40 · 40) 328

דִּמְעָה 18 tears (3 · 23) 199

פּוּגַת cessation, benumbing (1 · 1) 806

דָּמַם to be still, silent (3 · 23 · 30) 198 I

אַשְׁמוּרָה 19 watch [a division of time] (1 · 7) 1038

נֹכַח before (1 · 22) 647

עוֹלָל child (3 · 9) 760 עוֹלֵל

עָטוּף feeble (2 · 2[?]) 742 III

לְמִי 20 to whom? whose? (1 · 20) 566 מִי b

עוֹלֵל to act severely (4 · 8 · 17) 759 I

עוֹלֵל child (2 · 11) 760

טִפֻּחִים dandling (1 · 1[?]) 381

בְּתוּלָה 21 virgin (7 · 50) 143

בָּחוּר young man (5 · 45) 104

טבח to slay, kill ruthlessly (1 · 11 · 11) 370

חָמַל to spare (4 · 40 · 40) 328

מָגוֹר 22 fear, terror (1 · 9) 159 II

פָּלִיט fugitive, escaped one (1 · 19) 812

שָׂרִיד survivor (1 · 28) 975 I

טפח to carry on the palms, dandle (1 · 1 [?]) 381

Chapter 3

עֶבְרָה 1 overflowing rage, fury (2 · 34) 720

נָהַג 2 to lead on, drive (1 · 20 · 30) 624 I

בלה 4 to wear out (1 · 5 · 16) 115

הִקִּיף 5 to surround, enclose (1 · 16 · 17) 668 נקף II

רֹאשׁ a bitter and poisonous herb (2 · 12) 912 II

תְּלָאָה weariness, hardship (1 · 5) 521

מַחְשָׁךְ 6 dark place (1 · 7) 365

גָּדַר 7 to wall up, shut off (2 · 7 · 7) 154

שִׁוַּע 8 to cry for help (1 · 21 · 21) 1002

שָׂתַם to shut out, stop up (1 · 1 · 1) 979

גָּדַר 9 to wall up, shut off (2 · 7 · 7) 154

גָּזִית hewn stones (1 · 11) 159

נְתִיבָה path (1 · 21) 677

עִוָּה to twist (1 · 2 · 17[?]) 730 I

דֹּב 10 bear (1 · 12) 179

אֹרֵב to lie in wait (2·20·23) 70

אֲרִי lion (1·36) 71

מִסְתָּר hiding place (1·10) 712

פָּשַׁח 11 to tear in pieces (1·1·1) 832

מַטָּרָא 12 target, mark (1·16) 643 מַטָּרָה

כִּלְיָה 13 kidney (1·31) 480

אַשְׁפָּה quiver [for arrows] (1·6) 80

שְׂחֹק 14 derision, laughter (1·15) 966

נְגִינָה music, song (2·14) 618

מְרֹר 15 bitter herb (1·5) 601

הִרְוָה to cause to drink (1·5·14) 924

לַעֲנָה wormwood (2·8) 542

הַגְרִיס 16 to crush (1·1·2) 176

חָצָץ gravel (1·2) 346

הִכְפִּישׁ to make to cower (1·1·1) 499

אֵפֶר ashes (1·22) 68

זָנַח 17 to reject (3·16·19) 276 I

נשה to forget (1·1·5) 674 II

נֵצַח 18 endurance (2·42) 664 I

תּוֹחֶלֶת hope (1·6) 404

מָרוּד 19 straying, restlessness, (2·3) 924

לַעֲנָה wormwood (2·8) 542

רֹאשׁ a bitter and poisonous herb (2·12) 912 II

שׁוּחַ 20 to sink down (1·12·18[?]) 1001

הוֹחִל 21 to wait, tarry (2·15·42) 403 יחל

רַחֲמִים 22 compassion (1·38) 933

הוֹחִל 24 to wait, tarry (2·15·42) 403 יחל

קֹוה 25 to wait for (1·6·45) 875 I

יָחִיל 26 waiting (1·1) 404

דּוּמָם silently (1·3) 189

תְּשׁוּעָה deliverance (1·34) 448

עֹל 27 yoke (2·40) 760

נְעוּרִים youth (1·46) 655

בָּדָד 28 alone (2·11) 94

דמם to be silent, still (3·23·30) 198 I

נטל to lift and lay upon (1·3·4) 642

אוּלַי 29 perhaps (1·45) 19

תִּקְוָה hope (1·32) 876 II

לְחִי 30 cheek (2·21) 534 I

זָנַח 31 to reject (3·16·19) 276 I

הוֹגָה 32 to cause grief, sorrow (3·5·8) 387 I יגה

רִחַם to have compassion (1·41·46) 933

יגה 33 to grieve (1·1·8) 387 I

דִּכָּא 34 to crush (1·11·18) 193

אָסִיר prisoner (1·18) 64

עות 36 to subvert (1·9·11) 736

הִתְאוֹנֵן 39 to complain, murmur (1·2·2) 59

חֵטְא sin (2·33) 307

חפש 40 to search; i.e., test (1·4·23) 344

חקר to search, examine thoroughly (1·22·27) 350

פָּשַׁע 42 to transgress (1·40·41) 833

מָרָה to be rebellious, disobedient (3·21·43) 598

סלח to forgive, pardon (1·33·46) 699

סָכַךְ 43 to cover oneself (2·12·18) 696 I

חָמַל to spare (4·40·40) 328

סָכַךְ 44 to screen, cover (2·12·18) 696 I

סְחִי 45 offscouring (1·1) 695

מָאוֹס refuse (1·1) 549

פצה 46 to open (2·15·15) 822

פַּחַד 47 dread (1·49) 808 I

פַּחַת pit (1·10) 809

שְׁאֵת perh. = devastation, desolation (1·1) 981

שֶׁבֶר breaking, fracture (5·44) 991 I

פֶּלֶג 48 channel (1·10) 811 I

שֶׁבֶר breaking, fracture (5·44) 991 I

נגר 49 to pour oneself, flow, trickle (1·4·10) 620

דמה to cease (1·4·16) 198 II

מֵאֵין without (1·48[?]) 34 I אֵין 6.d

הֲפוּגָה cessation, benumbing (1·1) 806

הִשְׁקִיף 50 to look down (1·12·22) 1054 I

עוֹלֵל 51 to deal severely (4·8·17) 759 I

צוֹד 52 to hunt (2·12·16) 844 I

צִפּוֹר bird (1·40) 861 I

חִנָּם without cause (1·32) 336

צָמַת 53	to put an end to, exterminate (1·1·15) 856	
יָדָה	to cast, throw (1·2·3) 392	
צוּף 54	to flow, overflow (1·1·3) 847	
נִגְזַר	to be cut off, destroyed (1·6·12) 160	
תַּחְתִּי 55	lower, lowest (1·19) 1066	
הֶעֱלִים 56	to hide (1·11·29) 761 I	
רְוָחָה	respite, relief (1·2) 926	
שַׁוְעָה	cry for help (1·11) 1003	
עַוָּתָה 59	subversion (1·1) 736	
נְקָמָה 60	vengeance (1·27) 668	
קָם 62	adversary (1·12[?]) 877 קום 2	
הִגָּיוֹן	imagining, plotting (1·4) 212	
קִימָה 63	rising up (1·1) 879	
מַנְגִּינָה	mocking song (1·1) 618	
גְּמוּל 64	dealing, recompense (1·19) 168	
מְגִנָּה 65	covering מ׳לֵב = obstinacy (1·1) 171	
תַּאֲלָה	curse (1·1) 46	

Chapter 4

אֵיכָה 1	how! (4·18) 32	
הוּעַם	to be darkened, dimmed (1·1·1) עמם II 770	
שָׁנָה	to change (1·13·25) 1039 I	
כֶּתֶם	gold (1·9) 508	
יָקָר 2	precious, costly (1·35) 429	
סֻלָּא	to be weighed (1·1·1) 698	
פָּז	refined, pure gold (1·9) 808	
אֵיכָה	how! (4·18) 32	
נֵבֶל	jar, pitcher (1·11) 614 I	
חֶרֶשׂ	earthen vessel (1·16) 360	
יוֹצֵר	potter (1·17) 427 יצר	
תַּן 3	jackal (1·14) 1072	
חָלַץ	to draw out, present (1·5·27) 322 I	
שַׁד	breast (1·21) 994	
הֵינִיק	to nurse (1·10·18) 413 ינק	
גּוּר	whelp, young (1·7) 158 II	
אַכְזָר	cruel, fierce (1·4) 470	

כְּיְעֵנִים	like ostriches (1·1) 419 יְעֵן	
יוֹנֵק 4	suckling babe (2·11[?]) 413 ינק	
חֵךְ	palate (1·18) 335	
צָמָא	thirst (1·17) 854	
עוֹלָל	child (3·9) 760 עוֹלֵל	
מַעֲדָן 5	daintily (1·3) 726	
הָאֱמֻנִים	those brought up (1·1[?]) 52 I אמן Qal 4.a	
תּוֹלָע	scarlet stuff (1·2) 1068 I	
חִבֵּק	to embrace (1·10·13) 287	
אַשְׁפֹּת	ash heap, dung hill (1·7) 1046	
רֶגַע 6	moment (1·22) 921	
חוּל	to twist, writhe (1·6·9[?]) 296 I	
זָכַךְ 7	to be bright, shining (1·3·4) 269	
נָזִיר	prince (1·15) 634	
שֶׁלֶג	snow (1·20) 1017	
צַחח	to be dazzling (1·1·1) 850	
חָלָב	milk (1·44) 316	
אדם	to be red (1·1·10) 10	
פְּנִינִים	corals (1·6) 819	
סַפִּיר	sapphire (1·11) 705	
גִּזְרָה	cutting, form (1·8) 160	
חָשַׁךְ 8	to be dark (2·11·17) 364	
שְׁחוֹר	blackness (1·1) 1007	
תֹּאַר	form, outline (1·15) 1061	
נכר	to be recognized (1·1·40) 647 I	
צָפַד	to contract, shrivel (1·1·1) 859	
זוֹב 9	to pine away (1·29·29) 264	
מְדֻקָּרִים	Pual. ptc. = pierced, riddled (1·3·11) 201 דקר	
תְּנוּבָה	fruit, produce (1·5) 626	
שָׂדַי	field (1·13) 961	
רַחֲמָנִי 10	compassionate (1·1) 933	
בִּשֵּׁל	to boil, cook (1·20·27) 143	
בָּרוֹת	= for devouring (1·2) 136 I בָּרָה	
שֶׁבֶר	breaking, fracture (5·44) 991 I	
חָרוֹן 11	burning (2·41) 354	
הִצִּית	to kindle, set on fire (1·17·27) 428 יצת	
יְסוֹד	foundation, base (1·19) 414	

תֵּבֵל 12 world (1 · 36) 385

נוע 14 to totter, go tottering (2 · 22 · 38) 631

עִוֵּר blind (1 · 25) 734

נגאל to be defiled (1 · 3 · 11) 146 II

בְּלֹא without (2 · 30) 518 לא 4.a

לְבוּשׁ garment, clothing (1 · 30) 528

נצה 15 to fly, depart (1 · 1 · 1) 663 I

נוע to totter, go tottering (2 · 22 · 38) 631

עֶזְרָה 17 help, succor (1 · 26) 740 I

צְפִיָּה outlook (1 · 1) 859

צפה to watch (1 · 9 · 18) 859 I

צוד 18 to hunt (2 · 12 · 16) 844 I

צַעַד step, pace (1 · 14) 857

רְחוֹב broad open place (3 · 43) 932 I

קַל 19 swift, fleet (1 · 13) 886

נֶשֶׁר eagle, vulture (1 · 26) 676

דלק to hotly pursue (1 · 7 · 9) 196

אָרַב to lie in wait (2 · 20 · 23) 70

מָשִׁיחַ 20 anointed (1 · 39) 603

שְׁחִית pit (1 · 2) 1005

שָׂשׂ 21 to exult, rejoice (2 · 26 · 26) 965 שוש

כּוֹס cup (1 · 31) 468 I

שכר to become drunken (1 · 9 · 20) 1016 I

התערה to make oneself naked (1 · 2 · 14) 788

Chapter 5

נָכְרִי 2 foreigner (1 · 45) 648

יָתוֹם 3 orphan (1 · 42) 450

מְחִיר 4 price, hire (1 · 15) 564 I

צַוָּאר 5 neck, back of neck (2 · 41) 848

יגע to be weary (1 · 20 · 26) 388

סבל 7 to bear (1 · 7 · 9) 687

פרק 8 to tear away, tear apart (1 · 4 · 10) 830

תַּנּוּר 10 fire pot (1 · 15) 1072

נכמר to be or grow hot (1 · 4 · 4) 485 I

זַלְעָפָה raging heat (1 · 3) 273

בְּתוּלָה 11 virgin (7 · 50) 143

נתלה 12 to be hanged (1 · 2 · 27) 1067

נהדר to be honored (1 · 1 · 6) 213

בָּחוּר 13 young man (5 · 45) 104

טְחוֹן hand mill (1 · 1) 377

בָּחוּר 14 young man (5 · 45) 104

נְגִינָה music, song (2 · 14) 618

מָשׂוֹשׂ 15 exultation (2 · 17) 965

אֵבֶל mourning (1 · 24) 5

מָחוֹל dance (1 · 6) 298 I

עֲטָרָה 16 crown, wreath (1 · 23) 742 I

אוֹי woe! alas! (1 · 25) 17

דָּוֶה 17 faint (2 · 5) 188

חָשַׁךְ to grow dim (2 · 11 · 17) 364

שָׁמֵם 18 devastated (1 · 3[?]) 1030 שמם Qal 1 [cf. שָׁמֵם 1031]

שׁוּעָל fox (1 · 7) 1043 I

לָנֶצַח 20 forever (2 · 42) 664 I נצח 4

חדש 21 to renew (1 · 9 · 10) 293

קצף 22 to be angry (1 · 28 · 34) 893 I

ESTHER

Chapter 1

מְדִינָה 1 province (30 · 44) 193

בִּירָה 2 citadel, castle (10 · 18) 108

מִשְׁתֶּה 3 feast (20 · 45) 1059

פַּרְתְּמִים nobles (2 · 3) 832

מְדִינָה province (30 · 44) 193

עֹשֶׁר 4 riches (2 · 37) 799

יְקָר honor (10 · 17) 430

גְּדוּלָה greatness (3 · 12) 153

בִּירָה 5 citadel, castle (10 · 18) 108

קָטָן small, insignificant (2 · 47) 881 I

מִשְׁתֶּה feast (20 · 45) 1059

גַּנָּה garden (3 · 16) 171

בִּיתָן house, palace (3 · 3) 113

חוּר 6 white material (2 · 2) 301 I

כַּרְפַּס cotton or fine linen (1 · 1) 502

תְּכֵלֶת violet, violet thread (2 · 49) 1067

חֶבֶל cord, rope (1 · 50) 286 I

בּוּץ byssus (2 · 8) 101

אַרְגָּמָן purple, red purple (2 · 39) 71

גָּלִיל cylinder, rod (1 · 4) 165 II

שֵׁשׁ alabaster (2 · 3) 1010 II

מִטָּה couch, bed (2 · 29) 641

רִצְפָה pavement (1 · 7) 954

בַּהַט costly stone, perh. porphyry (1 · 1) 96

דַּר perh. pearl, mother of pearl (1 · 1) 204

סֹחָרֶת a stone used in paving (1 · 1) 695

שׁוֹנִים 7 ptc. = differing, different (2 · 13 · 25) 1039 I שׁנה

שְׁתִיָּה 8 drinking (1 · 1) 1059

דָּת decree, law (20 · 22) 206

אנס to compel, constrain (1 · 1 · 1) 60

יָבֵז to appoint, ordain (1 · 10 · 41) 413

מַלְכָּה 9 queen (25 · 35) 573

מִשְׁתֶּה feast (20 · 45) 1059

טוֹב 10 to be glad, joyful (1 · 18 · 21) 373 I

סָרִיס eunuch (12 · 45) 710

מַלְכָּה 11 queen (25 · 35) 573

כֶּתֶר crown (3 · 3) 509

יְפִי beauty (1 · 19) 421

מאן 12 to refuse (1 · 46 · 46) 549

מַלְכָּה queen (25 · 35) 573

סָרִיס eunuch (12 · 45) 710

קָצַף to be angry (2 · 28 · 34) 893 I

דָּת 13 decree, law (20 · 22) 206

דִּין government, judgment (1 · 19) 192

דָּת 15 decree, law (20 · 22) 206

מַלְכָּה queen (25 · 35) 573

מַאֲמָר word, command (3 · 3) 57

סָרִיס eunuch (12 · 45) 710

עוה 16 to do wrong (1 · 2 · 17[?]) 731

מַלְכָּה queen (25 · 35) 573

מְדִינָה province (30 · 44) 193

מַלְכָּה 17 queen (25 · 35) 573

הבזה to cause to despise (1 · 1 · 42) 102

שָׂרָה 18 princess, noble lady (1 · 5) 979 I

מַלְכָּה queen (25 · 35) 573

כְּדַי as much as (1 · 5) 191 דַּי 2.b

בִּזָּיוֹן contempt (1 · 1) 102

קֶצֶף wrath (1 · 29) 893 I

דָּת 19 decree, law (20 · 22) 206

רְעוּת fellow [woman] (1 · 6) 946 I

פִּתְגָם 20 edict, decree (1 · 2) 834

יְקָר honor (10 · 17) 430

קָטָן small, insignificant (2 · 47) 881 I

מְדִינָה 22 province (30 · 44) 193

כְּתָב writing, language (9 · 17) 508

שׂרר to rule, act as prince (1 · 5 · 7) 979

Chapter 2

שׁכך 1 to decrease, abate (2 · 4 · 5) 1013

נִגְזַר to be decreed (1 · 6 · 12) 160

מְשָׁרֵת 2 minister (2 · 20) 1058 שׁרת

בְּתוּלָה virgin (4 · 50) 143

פָּקִיד 3	commissioner, overseer (1 · 13) 824
מְדִינָה	province (30 · 44) 193
בְּתוּלָה	virgin (4 · 50) 143
בִּירָה	citadel, castle (10 · 18) 108
סָרִיס	eunuch (12 · 45) 710
תַּמְרוּק	rubbing, a scraping (3 · 4) 600
בִּירָה 5	citadel, castle (10 · 18) 108
גּוֹלָה 6	exiles, exile (1 · 42) 163
אֹמֵן 7	to support, nourish (1 · 7[?]) 52 I אמן Qal 1
יָפֶה	beautiful, fair (1 · 40) 421
תֹּאַר	form, outline (1 · 15) 1061
דָּת 8	decree, law (20 · 22) 206
בִּירָה	citadel, castle (10 · 18) 108
בהל 9	to make haste (1 · 10 · 39) 96
תַּמְרוּק	rubbing, a scraping (3 · 4) 600
מָנָה	part, portion (3 · 12) 584
רְאֻיוֹת	pass. ptc. = suitable 906 רָאָה Qal 6.g
שָׁנָה	to change (1 · 9 · 25) 1039 I
מוֹלֶדֶת 10	kindred (3 · 22) 409
תּוֹר 12	turn (2 · 5) 1064 I
דָּת	decree, law (20 · 22) 206
מָרוּק	rubbing, a scraping (1 · 1) 599
מֹר	myrrh (1 · 12) 600
בֹּשֶׂם	spice, perfume (1 · 30) 141
תַּמְרוּק	rubbing, a scraping (3 · 4) 600
סָרִיס 14	eunuch (12 · 45) 710
פִּלֶגֶשׁ	concubine (1 · 37) 811
תּוֹר 15	turn (2 · 5) 1064 I
סָרִיס	eunuch (12 · 45) 710
בְּתוּלָה 17	virgin (4 · 50) 143
כֶּתֶר	crown (3 · 3) 509
מִשְׁתֶּה 18	feast (20 · 45) 1059
הֲנָחָה	a giving of rest, perh. holiday-making (1 · 1) 629
מְדִינָה	province (30 · 44) 193
מַשְׂאֵת	present, largess (1 · 16) 673
בְּתוּלָה 19	virgin (4 · 50) 143
מוֹלֶדֶת 20	kindred (3 · 22) 409

מַאֲמָר	word, command (3 · 3) 57
אָמְנָה	bringing up, nourishment (1 · 3[?]) 53 I
קָצַף 21	to be wroth (2 · 28 · 34) 893 I
סָרִיס	eunuch (12 · 45) 710
סַף	threshold, sill (2 · 25) 706 II
מַלְכָּה 22	queen (25 · 35) 573
נתלה 23	to be hanged (1 · 2 · 27) 1067

Chapter 3

כָּרַע 2	to bow (3 · 30 · 36) 502
כָּרַע 5	to bow (3 · 30 · 36) 502
בָּזָה 6	to despise (1 · 31 · 42) 102
פּוּר 7	lot (8 · 8) 807
יֶשְׁנוֹ 8	שֶׁ +נ+ 3rd. m. sing. suff. 441
מְפֻזָּר	Pual ptc. = scattered (1 · 1 · 10) 808 פזר
מְפֹרָד	Pual ptc. = divided (1 · 1 · 26) 825 I פרד
מְדִינָה	province (30 · 44) 193
דָּת	decree, law (20 · 22) 206
שֹׁנוֹת	ptc. = differing, different (2 · 13 · 25) 1039 I שנה
שָׁוָה	to be suitable (3 · 8 · 16) 1000 I
שָׁקַל 9	to weigh out (2 · 19 · 22) 1053
גְּנָזִים	treasury (2 · 2) 170
טַבַּעַת 10	signet ring (6 · 49) 371
צֹרֵר	ptc. = vexer, harasser (1 · 10 · 10) 865 III צרר
אֲחַשְׁדַּרְפְּנִים 12	satraps (3 · 4) 31
פֶּחָה	governor (3 · 28) 808
מְדִינָה	province (30 · 44) 193
כְּתָב	writing (9 · 17) 508
נֶחְתָּם	to be sealed (2 · 2 · 27) 367
טַבַּעַת	signet ring (6 · 49) 371
רָץ 13	runner (4 · 25[?]) 930 רוץ
מְדִינָה	province (30 · 44) 193
טַף	[coll.] children, little ones (2 · 42) 381

בָּזַז	to spoil, plunder (2 · 37 · 41) 102
פַּתְשֶׁגֶן 14	copy (3 · 3) 837
כְּתָב	writing (9 · 17) 508
דָּת	decree, law (20 · 22) 206
מְדִינָה	province (30 · 44) 193
עָתִיד	ready, prepared (2 · 5) 800
רָץ 15	runner (4 · 25[?]) 930 רוּץ
דחף	to drive, hasten (2 · 2 · 4) 191
דָּת	decree, law (20 · 22) 206
בִּירָה	citadel, castle (10 · 18) 108
נבוך	to be confused, in confusion (1 · 3 · 3) 100

Chapter 4

שַׂק 1	sackcloth (4 · 48) 974
אֵפֶר	ashes (2 · 22) 68
זְעָקָה	cry (2 · 18) 277
מַר	bitter (1 · 37) 600 I
לְבוּשׁ 2	garment, clothing (6 · 30) 528
שַׂק	sackcloth (4 · 48) 974
מְדִינָה 3	province (30 · 44) 193
דָּת	decree, law (20 · 22) 206
אֵבֶל	mourning (2 · 24) 5
צוֹם	fast, fasting (2 · 25) 847
בְּכִי	weeping (1 · 30) 113
מִסְפֵּד	wailing, mourning (1 · 16) 704
שַׂק	sackcloth (4 · 48) 974
אֵפֶר	ashes (2 · 22) 68
הוצע	to be laid, spread (1 · 2 · 4) 426 יצע
סָרִיס 4	eunuch (12 · 45) 710
התחלחל	to writhe (1 · 1 · 47) 296 I חול
מַלְכָּה	queen (25 · 35) 573
שַׂק	sackcloth (4 · 48) 974
קִבֵּל	to accept (3 · 11 · 13) 867
סָרִיס 5	eunuch (12 · 45) 710
רְחוֹב 6	broad open place (3 · 43) 932 I
קרה 7	to befall (2 · 13 · 27) 899
פָּרָשָׁה	exact statement (2 · 2) 831
שָׁקַל	to weigh out (2 · 19 · 22) 1053

גְּנָזִים	treasury (2 · 2) 170
פַּתְשֶׁגֶן 8	copy (3 · 3) 837
כְּתָב	writing (9 · 17) 508
דָּת	decree, law (20 · 22) 206
מְדִינָה 11	province (30 · 44) 193
פְּנִימִי	inner (2 · 33) 819
דָּת	decree, law (20 · 22) 206
מֵאֲשֶׁר	from that; לְבַד מֵאֲשֶׁר here = unless בַּד (1 · 17) 84, 94
הוֹשִׁיט	to extend, hold out (3 · 3 · 3) 445 ישׁט
שַׁרְבִיט	sceptre (4 · 4) 987
דָּמָה 13	to think, imagine (1 · 13 · 27) 197
הֶחֱרֵשׁ 14	to be silent (3 · 39 · 47) 361 I
הַצָּלָה	deliverance (1 · 1) 665
כנס 16	to gather (1 · 7 · 11) 488
צוּם	to fast (2 · 20 · 20) 847
בְּכֵן	thereupon, then (1 · 2) 485 I כֵּן 3.b
דָּת	decree, law (20 · 22) 206

Chapter 5

פְּנִימִי 1	inner (2 · 33) 819
נֹכַח	in front of (2 · 22) 647
מַלְכָּה 2	queen (25 · 35) 573
הוֹשִׁיט	to extend, hold out (3 · 3 · 3) 445 ישׁט
שַׁרְבִיט	sceptre (4 · 4) 987
מַלְכָּה 3	queen (25 · 35) 573
בַּקָּשָׁה	request, entreaty (7 · 8) 135
מִשְׁתֶּה 4	feast (20 · 45) 1059
מִשְׁתֶּה 5	feast (20 · 45) 1059
מִשְׁתֶּה 6	feast (20 · 45) 1059
שְׁאֵלָה	request, petition (6 · 13) 982
בַּקָּשָׁה	request, entreaty (7 · 8) 135
שְׁאֵלָה 7	request, petition (6 · 13) 982
בַּקָּשָׁה	request, entreaty (7 · 8) 135
שְׁאֵלָה 8	request, petition (6 · 13) 982
בַּקָּשָׁה	request, entreaty (7 · 8) 135
מִשְׁתֶּה	feast (20 · 45) 1059

שָׂמֵחַ 9 joyful, glad (2 · 21) 970

זָע to tremble, quake (1 · 2 · 3) 266 זוע

התאפק 10 to restrain oneself, refrain (1 · 7 · 7) 67

אֹהֵב friend (3 · 36) 12 אָהֵב

עֹשֶׁר 11 riches (2 · 37) 799

מַלְכָּה 12 queen (25 · 35) 573

מִשְׁתֶּה feast (20 · 45) 1059

שָׁוָה 13 to be adequate (3 · 8 · 16) 1000 I

אֹהֵב 14 friend (3 · 36) 12 אָהֵב

גָּבֹהַּ high, exalted (2 · 41) 147

תָּלָה to hang, hang up (8 · 23 · 27) 1067

מִשְׁתֶּה feast (20 · 45) 1059

שָׂמֵחַ joyful, glad (2 · 21) 970

Chapter 6

נדד 1 to flee, depart (1 · 21 · 25) 622 I

שֵׁנָה sleep (1 · 23) 446

זִכָּרוֹן memorial, remembrance (1 · 24) 272

סָרִיס 2 eunuch (12 · 45) 710

סַף threshold, sill (2 · 25) 706 II

יְקָר 3 honor (10 · 17) 430

גְּדוּלָה greatness (3 · 12) 153

מְשָׁרֵת minister (2 · 20) 1058 שרת 2.b

חִיצוֹן 4 outer, external (1 · 25) 300

תָּלָה to hang, hang up (8 · 23 · 27) 1067

יְקָר 6 honor (10 · 17) 430

לְמִי to whom? whose? (1 · 20) 566 מִי b

יוֹתֵר more, excess (1 · 9) 452

יְקָר 7 honor (10 · 17) 430

לְבוּשׁ 8 garment, clothing (6 · 30) 528

כֶּתֶר crown (3 · 3) 509

לְבוּשׁ 9 garment, clothing (6 · 30) 528

פַּרְתְּמִים nobles (2 · 3) 832

יְקָר honor (10 · 17) 430

רְחוֹב broad open place (3 · 43) 932 I

כָּכָה thus (3 · 34) 462

לְבוּשׁ 10 garment, clothing (6 · 30) 528

לְבוּשׁ 11 garment, clothing (6 · 30) 528

רְחוֹב broad open place (3 · 43) 932 I

כָּכָה thus (3 · 34) 462

יְקָר honor (10 · 17) 430

נדחף 12 to hurry, hasten (1 · 2 · 4) 191

אָבֵל mourning (1 · 8) 5 I

חפה to cover (2 · 6 · 12) 341

אֹהֵב 13 friend (3 · 36) 12 אָהֵב

קרה to befall (2 · 13 · 27) 899

סָרִיס 14 eunuch (12 · 45) 710

הבהיל to make haste (1 · 3 · 39) 96

מִשְׁתֶּה feast (20 · 45) 1059

Chapter 7

מַלְכָּה 1 queen (25 · 35) 573

מִשְׁתֶּה 2 feast (20 · 45) 1059

שְׁאֵלָה request, petition (6 · 13) 982

מַלְכָּה queen (25 · 35) 573

בַּקָּשָׁה request, entreaty (7 · 8) 135

מַלְכָּה 3 queen (25 · 35) 573

שְׁאֵלָה request, petition (6 · 13) 982

בַּקָּשָׁה request, entreaty (7 · 8) 135

אִלּוּ 4 if, though (1 · 2) 47

הֶחֱרַשׁ to be silent (3 · 39 · 47) 361 I

צַר adversary, foe (1 · 20[?]) 865 III

שָׁוָה to be equivalent; אֵין שׁ׳ בְּנֵזֶק הַמֶּלֶךְ = is not an equivalent for the price of injury to the king (3 · 8 · 16) 1000 I

נֵזֶק injury, damage (1 · 1) 634

מַלְכָּה 5 queen (25 · 35) 573

אֵי where? (1 · 39) 32 אי 1.b

נִבְעַת 6 to be terrified (1 · 3 · 16) 129

מַלְכָּה queen (25 · 35) 573

מִשְׁתֶּה 7 feast (20 · 45) 1059

גַּנָּה garden (3 · 16) 171

בִּיתָן house, palace (3 · 3) 113

מַלְכָּה queen (25 · 35) 573

גַּנָּה 8 garden (3 · 16) 171

בִּיתָן house, palace (3 · 3) 113

מִשְׁתֶּה feast (20 · 45) 1059

מִטָּה   couch, bed (2 · 29) 641

כבשׁ   to subdue, force (1 · 8 · 14) 461

מַלְכָּה   queen (25 · 35) 573

חפה   to cover (2 · 6 · 12) 341

סָרִיס   9 eunuch (12 · 45) 710

גָּבֹהַּ   high, exalted (2 · 41) 147

תָּלָה   to hang, hang up (8 · 23 · 27) 1067

תָּלָה   10 to hang, hang up (8 · 23 · 27) 1067

שׁכך   to decrease, abate (2 · 4 · 5) 1013

Chapter 8

מַלְכָּה   1 queen (25 · 35) 573

צֹרֵר   vexer, harasser (3 · 17[?]) 865 III   צרר

טַבַּעַת   2 signet ring (6 · 49) 371

הוֹשִׁיט   4 to extend, hold out (3 · 3 · 3) 445   ישׁט

שַׁרְבִיט   sceptre (4 · 4) 987

כָּשֵׁר   5 to be proper, suitable (1 · 2 · 3) 506

מְדִינָה   province (30 · 44) 193

אֵיכָכָה   6 how? (2 · 4) 32

אַבְדָן   destruction (2 · 2) 2

מוֹלֶדֶת   kindred (3 · 22) 409

מַלְכָּה   7 queen (25 · 35) 573

תָּלָה   to hang, hang up (8 · 23 · 27) 1067

חתם   8 to seal, seal up (2 · 23 · 27) 367

טַבַּעַת   signet ring (6 · 49) 371

כְּתָב   writing (9 · 17) 508

נֶחְתָּם   to be sealed (2 · 2 · 27) 367

אֲחַשְׁדַּרְפְּנִים   9 satraps (3 · 4) 31

פֶּחָה   governor (3 · 28) 808

מְדִינָה   province (30 · 44) 193

כְּתָב   writing, language (9 · 17) 509

חתם   10 to seal, seal up (2 · 23 · 27) 367

טַבַּעַת   signet ring (6 · 49) 371

רָץ   runner (4 · 25[?]) 930 רוץ Qal 2.a

רֶכֶשׁ   [coll.] steeds (2 · 4) 940

אֲחַשְׁתְּרָן   royal (2 · 2) 31

רַמָּךְ   [dub.] mares (1 · 1) 942

נקהל   11 to assemble (5 · 19 · 39) 874

מְדִינָה   province (30 · 44) 193

צור   to show hostility to (1 · 5 · 5) 849 III

טַף   [coll.] children, little ones (2 · 42) 381

בָּזַז   to spoil, plunder (2 · 37 · 41) 102

מְדִינָה   12 province (30 · 44) 193

פַּתְשֶׁגֶן   13 copy (3 · 3) 837

כְּתָב   letter, writing (9 · 17) 508

דָּת   decree, law (20 · 22) 206

מְדִינָה   province (30 · 44) 193

עָתוּד   ready, prepared (2 · 5) 800 עָתִיד

נקם   to avenge oneself (1 · 12 · 35) 667 Niph.

רָץ   14 runner (4 · 25[?]) 930 רוץ Qal 2.a

רֶכֶשׁ   [coll.] steeds (2 · 4) 940

אֲחַשְׁתְּרָן   royal (2 · 2) 31

מְבֹהָלִים   *Pual* ptc. = hastened (1 · 2 · 39) 96   בהל

דחף   to drive, hasten (2 · 2 · 4) 191

דָּת   decree, law (20 · 22) 206

בִּירָה   citadel, castle (10 · 18) 108

לְבוּשׁ   15 garment, clothing (6 · 30) 528

תְּכֵלֶת   violet, violet thread (2 · 49) 1066

חוּר   white material (2 · 2) 301 I

עֲטָרָה   crown, wreath (1 · 23) 742 I

תַּכְרִיךְ   robe (1 · 1) 501

בּוּץ   byssus (2 · 8) 101

אַרְגָּמָן   purple, red purple (2 · 39) 71

צהל   to cry shrilly (1 · 7 · 8) 843 I

אוֹרָה   16 light (1 · 2) 21 I

שָׂשׂוֹן   exultation, joy (2 · 22) 965

יְקָר   honor (10 · 17) 430

מְדִינָה   17 province (30 · 44) 193

דָּת   decree, law (20 · 22) 206

שָׂשׂוֹן   exultation, joy (2 · 22) 965

מִשְׁתֶּה   feast (20 · 45) 1059

הִתְיַהֵד   to become a Jew (1 · 1 · 1) 397

פַּחַד   dread (3 · 49) 808 I

Chapter 9

דָּת	1	decree, law (20 · 22) 206
שָׂבַּר		to hope, wait (1 · 6 · 8) 960 II
שָׁלַט		to become master of (2 · 5 · 8) 1020 I
שֹׂנֵא		enemy (3 · 41[?]) 971 שָׂנֵא
נקהל	2	to assemble (5 · 19 · 39) 874
מְדִינָה		province (30 · 44) 193
פַּחַד		dread (3 · 49) 808 I
מְדִינָה	3	province (30 · 44) 193
אֲחַשְׁדַּרְפְּנִים		satraps (3 · 4) 31
פֶּחָה		governor (3 · 28) 808
פַּחַד		dread (3 · 49) 808 I
שֹׁמַע	4	report (1 · 4) 1035
מְדִינָה		province (30 · 44) 193
מַכָּה	5	blow, stripe (1 · 48) 646
הֶרֶג		slaughter (1 · 5) 247
אַבְדָן		destruction (2 · 2) 2
שֹׂנֵא		enemy (3 · 41[?]) 971 שָׂנֵא
בִּירָה	6	citadel, castle (10 · 18) 108
בֹּשֶׁת	7	shame (1 · 30) 102
צֹרֵר	10	vexer, harasser (3 · 17[?]) 865 III צרר
בִּזָּה		spoil, booty (3 · 10) 103
בִּירָה	11	citadel, castle (10 · 18) 108
מַלְכָּה	12	queen (25 · 35 ·) 573
בִּירָה		citadel, castle (10 · 18) 108
שְׁאָר		rest, remnant, remainder (2 · 26) 984
מְדִינָה		province (30 · 44) 193
שְׁאֵלָה		request, petition (6 · 13) 982
בַּקָּשָׁה		request, entreaty (7 · 8) 135
דָּת	13	decree, law (20 · 22) 206
תָּלָה		to hang, hang up (8 · 23 · 27) 1067
דָּת	14	decree, law (20 · 22) 206
תָּלָה		to hang, hang up (8 · 23 · 27) 1067
נקהל	15	to assemble (5 · 19 · 39) 874
בִּזָּה		spoil, booty (3 · 10) 103
שְׁאָר	16	rest, remnant, remainder (2 · 26) 984
מְדִינָה		province (30 · 44) 193

נקהל		to assemble (5 · 19 · 39) 874
נוּחַ		inf. w. מִן = to have rest from 628 נוּחַ
שֹׂנֵא		enemy (3 · 41[?]) 971 שָׂנֵא
בִּזָּה		spoil, booty (3 · 10) 103
נוֹחַ	17	rest (2 · 3[?]) 628 נוּחַ
מִשְׁתֶּה		feast (20 · 45) 1059
נקהל	18	to assemble (5 · 19 · 39) 874
נוֹחַ		rest (2 · 3[?]) 628 נוּחַ
מִשְׁתֶּה		feast (20 · 45) 1059
פְּרָזִים	19	hamlet dwellers (1 · 3) 826 פְּרָזִי
פְּרָזוֹת		open regions, hamlets (1 · 3) 826 פְּרָזָה
מִשְׁתֶּה		feast (20 · 45) 1059
מִשְׁלוֹחַ		sending (2 · 3) 1020
מָנָה		part, portion (3 · 12) 584
מְדִינָה	20	province (30 · 44) 193
יָגוֹן	22	sorrow, grief (1 · 14) 387
אֵבֶל		mourning (2 · 24) 5
מִשְׁתֶּה		feast (20 · 45) 1059
מִשְׁלוֹחַ		sending (2 · 3) 1020
מָנָה		part, portion (3 · 12) 584
מַתָּנָה		gift (1 · 17) 682 I
קִבֵּל	23	to accept, assume (3 · 11 · 13) 867
צֹרֵר	24	vexer, harasser (4 · 17[?]) 865 III צרר
פוּר		lot (8 · 8) 807
הָמַם		to discomfit, vex (1 · 13 · 13) 243
תָּלָה	25	to hang, hang up (8 · 23 · 27) 1067
פוּר	26	lot (8 · 8) 807
אִגֶּרֶת		letter (2 · 10) 8
כָּכָה		thus (3 · 34) 462
קִבֵּל	27	to accept, assume (3 · 11 · 13) 867
נִלְוָה		to join oneself or be joined to (1 · 11 · 12) 530 I
כְּתָב		writing (9 · 17) 508
זְמָן		appointed time (2 · 4) 273
מְדִינָה	28	province (30 · 44) 193
פוּר		lot (8 · 8) 807
זֵכֶר		remembrance, memory (1 · 23) 271

סוֹף to come to an end (1 · 4 · 10) 692

מַלְכָּה 29 queen (25 · 35) 573

תֹּקֶף power, strength (2 · 3) 1076

אִגֶּרֶת letter (2 · 10) 8

פּוּר lot (8 · 8) 807

מְדִינָה 30 province (30 · 44) 193

פּוּר 31 lot (8 · 8) 807

זְמָן time, appointed time (2 · 4) 273

מַלְכָּה queen (25 · 35) 573

צוֹם fast, fasting (2 · 25) 847

זְעָקָה cry (2 · 18) 277

מַאֲמָר 32 word, command (3 · 3) 57

פּוּר lot (8 · 8) 807

Chapter 10

מַס 1 tribute, enforced payment (1 · 23) 586 I

אִי coasts, regions; אִ׳ הַיָּם = coast lands, islands (1 · 36) 15 I

תֹּקֶף 2 power, strength (2 · 3) 1076

פָּרָשָׁה exact statement (2 · 2) 831

גְּדוּלָה greatness (3 · 12) 153

מִשְׁנֶה 3 second (1 · 35) 1041

DANIEL

Chapter 1

צוּר 1 to shut in, besiege (1·31·31) 848 II

מִקְצָת 2 some of (4·9) 892 קְצָת 2

סָרִיס 3 eunuch (7·45) 710

מְלוּכָה kingship, royalty (1·24) 574

פַּרְתְּמִים nobles (1·3) 832

מאוּם 4 blemish, defect (1·21[?]) 548

מַדָּע knowledge, thought (2·6) 396

מָנָה 5 to appoint, ordain (3·9·28) 584

דָּבָר portion 182 IV.1

פַּת־בָּג delicacies (6·6) 834

מִשְׁתֶּה drink (4·45) 1059

מִקְצָת at the end of (4·9) 892 קְצָת 3

סָרִיס 7 eunuch (7·45) 710

הִתְגָּאֵל 8 to defile oneself (2·2·11) 146 II

פַּת־בָּג delicacies (6·6) 834

מִשְׁתֶּה drink (4·45) 1059

סָרִיס eunuch (7·45) 710

רַחֲמִים 9 compassion (3·38) 933

סָרִיס eunuch (7·45) 710

סָרִיס 10 eunuch (7·45) 710

מָנָה to appoint, ordain (3·9·28) 584

מַאֲכָל food (1·30) 38

מִשְׁתֶּה drink (4·45) 1059

זעף to be dejected (1·4·4) 277

גִּיל circle, age (1·1) 162 II

תוב to inculpate, incriminate (1·1·1) 295

מֶלְצַר 11 [dub.] guardian (2·2) 576

מָנָה to appoint, ordain (3·9·28) 584

סָרִיס eunuch (7·45) 710

נִסָּה 12 to test, try (2·36·36) 650

זֵרְעַ vegetable (1·1) 283

פַּת־בָּג 13 delicacies (6·6) 834

נִסָּה 14 to test, try (2·36·36) 650

מִקְצָת 15 at the end of (4·9) 892 קְצָת 3

בָּרִיא fat (1·14) 135

פַּת־בָּג delicacies (6·6) 834

מֶלְצַר 16 [dub.] guardian (2·2) 576

פַּת־בָּג delicacies (6·6) 834

מִשְׁתֶּה drink (4·45) 1059

זֵרְעוֹ vegetable (1·1) 283

מַדָּע 17 knowledge, thought (2·6) 193

חָזוֹן vision (12·35) 302

מִקְצָת 18 at the end of (4·9) 892 קְצָת 3

סָרִיס eunuch (7·45) 710

בִּינָה 20 understanding (4·37) 108

יָדוֹת times, repetitions 388 יָד 4.c

תַרְטֹם magician (2·11) 355

אַשָּׁף conjurer, necromancer (2·2) 80

Chapter 2

תָּלַם 1 to dream (2·26·28) 321 II

הִתְפָּעֵם to be disturbed (1·1·5) 821

שֵׁנָה sleep (1·23) 446

תַרְטֹם 2 magician (2·11) 355

אַשָּׁף conjurer, necromancer (2·2) 80

כִּשֵּׁף to practice sorcery (1·6) 506

כַּשְׂדִּים Chaldeans (2·2) 505

תָּלַם 3 to dream (2·26·28) 321 II

נפעם to be disturbed, impelled (1·3·5) 821

כַּשְׂדִּים 4a Chaldeans (2·2) 505

אֲרָמִית Aramaic (1·5) 74

Aramaic Section (2:4b-7:28) (See pages 271-275 for Aramaic Appendix containing words occurring over nine times in biblical Aramaic.)

חיא 4b to live (5·5·6) 1092

עֲבַד slave, servant (5·7) 1105

תוא = חוה to declare 1092

כַּשְׂדִּי 5 Chaldean, astrologer (6·6) 1098

אַזְדָּא sure, assured (2 · 2) 1079

הַדָּם member, limb (2 · 2) 1089

נְוָלִי refuse heap (2 · 3) 1102

מַתְּנָא 6 gift (3 · 3) 1103

נְבִזְבָּה reward (2 · 2) 1102

יְקָר honor (7 · 7) 1096

קַבֵּל to receive (3 · 3 · 3) 1110

לָהֵן therefore (3 · 3) 1099 I

תִּנְיָנוּת 7 a second time (1 · 1) 1118

עֲבַד slave, servant (5 · 7) 1105

יַצִּיב 8 certain, true; מִן־יַצִּ׳ = of a surety (5 · 5) 1096

אַנְתּוּן you [pl.] (1 · 1) 1082

זְבַן to buy (1 · 1) 1091

אַזְדָּא sure, assured (2 · 2) 1079

כְּדַב 9 false (1 · 1) 1096

שְׁחִיתָה corrupt (3 · 3) 1115 שחת

הִזְמִן to agree together (1 · 1 · 1) 1091

לָהֵן therefore (3 · 3) 1098 I

אִנְדַּע Peal impf. 1st sing. of ידע, to know 1095

כַּשְׂדָּי 10 Chaldean, astrologer (6 · 6) 1098

יַבֶּשֶׁת earth (1 · 1) 1094

כִּדְנָה like this, thus (2 · 4) 1088 דְּנָה c

חַרְטֹם magician (5 · 5) 1093

אָשַׁף conjurer, enchanter (6 · 6) 1083

יַקִּיר 11 difficult (1 · 2) 1096

לָהֵן except (6 · 7) 1099 II

מְדָר dwelling place (1 · 1) 1087

בְּשַׂר flesh (3 · 3) 1085

קְבֵל 12 to be angry (1 · 1 · 1) 1084

קְצַף to be wroth (1 · 1 · 1) 1111

הוֹבֵד to destroy (5 · 5 · 7) 1078 אבד

מִתְקַטְּלִין 13 ptc. = to be killed (2 · 2 · 7) 1111 קטל

חֲבַר fellow, comrade (3 · 3) 1092

הִתְקַטָלָה inf. = to be killed (2 · 2 · 7) 1111 קטל

הֲתִיב 14 to return (2 · 5 · 8) 1117 תוב

עֵטָא counsel (1 · 1) 1096

טְעֵם here = judgment, discretion 1094

רַב here = captain, chief 1112

טַבָּח guardsman (1 · 1) 1094

קְטַל to kill (2 · 2 · 7) 1111

עַל־מָה 15 wherefore 1099 מה 3.c

מְהַחְצְפָה ptc. = harsh (2 · 2 · 2) 1093 חצף

אֲזַל 17 to go, go off (4 · 7 · 7) 1079

חַבַר fellow, comrade (3 · 3) 1092

רַחֲמִין 18 compassion (1 · 1) 1113

רָז secret (9 · 9) 1112

הוּבַד to be destroyed (5 · 5 · 7) 1078 אבד

חַבַר fellow, comrade (3 · 3) 1092

לֵילְא 19 night (5 · 5) 1099

רָז secret (9 · 9) 1112

גְּלִי to be revealed (7 · 7 · 9) 1086 גלא

בָּרֵךְ to bless, praise (3 · 3 · 5) 1085

בָּרֵךְ 20 Pael ptc. = blessed (3 · 3 · 4) 1085

גְּבוּרָה might (2 · 2) 1086

דִּי לֵהּ = his 1098 ל 4.b

הֶעְדָּה 21 to remove, dispose (4 · 4 · 9) 1105 עדא

מַנְדַּע knowledge, power of knowing (4 · 4) 1095

בִּינָה understanding (1 · 1) 1084

גְּלָא 22 to reveal (7 · 7 · 9) 1086

עֲמִיק deep (1 · 1) 1107

מְסַתְּרָתָא ptc. = hidden things (1 · 1 · 1) 1104 סתר I

חֲשׁוֹךְ darkness (1 · 1) 1094

נְהִיר light (1 · 1) 1102

שְׁרֵא to abide (3 · 3 · 6) 1117

אַב 23 father, ancestor (7 · 9) 1078

מְהוֹדֵא ptc. = praising (2 · 2 · 2) 1095 ידא

שַׁבַּח to laud, praise (5 · 5 · 5) 1114

גְּבוּרָה might (2 · 2) 1086

מנה 24 to appoint (3 · 4 · 5) 1101

הוֹבֵד to destroy (5 · 5 · 7) 1078 אבד

אֲזַל to go, go off (4 · 7 · 7) 1079

אַל do not, let not (3 · 3) 1080

הִתְבְּהָלָה 25 haste (3 · 3[?]) 1084 בהל

הַנְעֵל	*Haph.* prf. 3rd m. sing. of עלל to bring in 1106	שָׁק 33	leg (1 · 1) 1114
גָּלוּ	exile (3 · 4) 1086	רְגַל	foot (7 · 7) 1112
כְּהֵל 26	to be able (4 · 4 · 4) 1096	מִנְּהוֹן	מִנְּהוֹן ... מִנְּהוֹן = some of them ... others of them 1100 מִן 3
רָז 27	secret (9 · 9) 1112	חֲסַף	clay (9 · 9) 1093
אָשַׁף	conjurer, enchanter (6 · 6) 1083	הִתְגְּזֶרֶת 34	to be cut out (2 · 2 · 6) 1086
חַרְטֹם	magician (5 · 5) 1093	מְחָא	to smite (2 · 2 · 4) 1099
גָּזְרִין	ptc. = astrologers (4 · 4 · 6) 1086 גזר	רְגַל	foot (7 · 7) 1112
בְּרַם 28	only, nevertheless (4 · 5) 1085	חֲסַף	clay (9 · 9) 1093
גְּלָא	to reveal (7 · 7 · 9) 1086	חֲסַף 35	clay (9 · 9) 1093
רָז	secret (9 · 9) 1112	נְחָשׁ	copper, bronze (9 · 9) 1102
אַחֲרִית	end [cstr. form] (1 · 1) 1079	עוּר	chaff (1 · 1) 1105
מִשְׁכַּב	couch, bed (6 · 6) 1115	אִדַּר	threshing floor (1 · 1) 1078
רַעְיוֹן 29	thought (6 · 6) 1113	קַיִט	summer (1 · 1) 1111
מִשְׁכַּב	couch, bed (6 · 6) 1115	נְשָׂא	to lift, take, carry (1 · 2 · 3) 1103
סְלִק	to come up (4 · 5 · 8) 1104	אֲתַר	place (1 · 5) 1083
אַחֲרֵי	after (3 · 3) 1079 אחר	מְחָא	to smite (2 · 2 · 4) 1099
גְּלָא	to reveal (7 · 7 · 9) 1086	טוּר	mountain (2 · 2) 1094
רָז	secret (9 · 9) 1112	מְלָא	to fill (1 · 1 · 2) 1100
רָז 30	secret (9 · 9) 1112	חֲסֵן 37	power (2 · ?) 1093
גֱּלִי	to be revealed (7 · 7 · 9) 1086 גלא	תְּקֹף	might (1 · 1) 1118
לָהֵן	but (6 · 7) 1099 II	יְקָר	honor (7 · 7) 1096
דִּבְרָה	cause, reason (2 · 2) 1087	בְּכָל־דִּי 38	wherever 1097 כֹּל 2
רַעְיוֹן	thought (6 · 6) 1113	דּוּר	to dwell (7 · 7 · 7) 1087
לְבַב	heart (7 · 7) 1098	בַּר	field (8 · 8) 1085 II
תִנְדַּע	*Peal* impf. 2nd m. sing. of יְדַע to know 1095	עוֹף	fowl (2 · 2) 1105
		הַשְׁלֵט	to make ruler (2 · 2 · 7) 1115
אֲלוּ 31	lo! (4 · 4) 1080	בָּתְרָךְ 39	after you (3 · 3) 1083 אֲתַר
דִּכֵּן	this, that (3 · 3) 1088	אָחֳרִי	fem. of אָחֳרָן another, other 1079
זִיו	splendor, brightness (6 · 6) 1091	אֲרַע	here = downward, inferior 1079
יַתִּיר	preeminent, surpassing (8 · 8) 1096	נְחָשׁ	copper, bronze (9 · 9) 1102
לְקָבֵל	before (5 · 7) 1110	שְׁלֵשׁ	to have power, rule (5 · 5 · 7) 1115
רֵו	appearance (2 · 2) 1112	תַּקִּיף 40	strong, mighty (4 · 5) 1118
דְּחִיל	terrible (3 · 3[?]) 1087 דחל	חֲשַׁל	to shatter (1 · 1 · 1) 1094
טָב 32	good (1 · 2) 1094	רְעַע	to crush, shatter (1 · 1 · 2) 1113
חֲדִי	breast (1 · 1) 1092	אִלֵּין	these (5 · 5) 1080
דְּרָע	arm (1 · 1) 1089	רַע	to crush, shatter (1 · 1 · 2) 1113 רעע
מְעָא	belly (1 · 1) 1101	רְגַל 41	foot (7 · 7) 1112
יַרְכָה	thigh, loin (1 · 1) 1096	אֶצְבַּע	finger, toe (3 · 3) 1109
נְחָשׁ	copper, bronze (9 · 9) 1102	מִנְּהוֹן	מִנְּהוֹן ... מִנְּהוֹן = some of them ...

3 מִן 1100	others of them	
חֲסַף	clay (9 · 9) 1093	
פֶּחָר	potter (1 · 1) 1108	
פְּלִיגָה	ptc. = divided (1 · 1 · 1) 1108	
נִצְבָּה	firmness (1 · 1) 1103	
מְעָרַב	pass. ptc. = mixed (2 · 2 · 4) 1107	
טִין	clay (2 · 2) 1094	
אֶצְבַּע	42 finger, toe (3 · 3) 1109	
רְגַל	foot (7 · 7) 1112	
מִנְּהוֹן	מִנְּהוֹן ... מִנְּהוֹן = some of them ... others of them 1100 מִן 3	
חֲסַף	clay (9 · 9) 1093	
קְצָת	end; 'מִן־ק = part of (3 · 3) 1111	
תַּקִּיף	strong, mighty (4 · 5) 1118	
תְּבִירָה	pass. ptc. = broken in pieces (1 · 1 · 1) 1117	
מְעָרַב	43 pass. ptc. = mixed (2 · 2 · 4) 1107	
חֲסַף	clay (9 · 9) 1093	
טִין	clay (2 · 2) 1094	
מִתְעָרַב	pass. ptc. = mixed (2 · 2 · 4) 1107	
זְרַע	seed (1 · 1) 1091	
דבק	to cling (1 · 1 · 1) 1087	
הָא	like (1 · 1) 1089	
אִנּוּן	44 they, those (3 · 4) 1081	
התחבל	to be destroyed (3 · 3 · 6) 1091	
השתבק	to be left (1 · 1 · 5) 1114 שבק	
תְּסִיף	to put an end to (1 · 1 · 2) 1104 סוף	
אִלֵּין	these (5 · 5) 1080	
טוּר	45 mountain (2 · 2) 1094	
התגזר	to be cut out (2 · 2 · 6) 1086	
נְחָשׁ	copper, bronze (9 · 9) 1102	
חֲסַף	clay (9 · 9) 1093	
אַחֲרֵי	after (3 · 3) 1079	
יַצִּיב	certain, sure (5 · 5) 1096 אחר	
מְהֵימַן	pass. ptc. = trustworthy (3 · 3 · 3) 1081 אמן	
אֲנַף	46 face (2 · 2) 1081	
מִנְחָה	gift, offering (1 · 2) 1101	
נִיחֹחַ	soothing, tranquilizing (1 · 2) 1102	
נסך	to pour out (1 · 1 · 1) 1103	

קְשֹׁט	47 truth; 'מִן־ק = of a truth (2 · 2) 1112	
מָרֵא	lord (4 · 4) 1101	
גלה	to reveal (7 · 7 · 9) 1086	
רָז	secret (9 · 9) 1112	
רַבִּי	48 Pael of רבה to make great 1112	
מַתְּנָא	gift (3 · 3) 1103	
השלט	to make ruler (2 · 2 · 7) 1115	
רַב	here = chief, captain 1112	
סְגַן	prefect (5 · 5) 1104	
מנה	49 to appoint (3 · 4 · 5) 1101	
עֲבִידָה	administration (2 · 6) 1105	
תְּרַע	gate; here = court, palace (2 · 2) 1118	

Chapter 3

רום	1 height (4 · 5) 1112	
אַמָּה	cubit (2 · 4) 1081	
פְּתָי	breadth (1 · 2) 1109	
בִּקְעָא	plain (1 · 1) 1085	
כנש	2 to, gather (1 · 1 · 3) 1097	
אֲ־חַשְׁדַּרְפְּנִין	satraps (9 · 9) 1080	
סְגַן	prefect (5 · 5) 1104	
אֲדַרְגָּזַר	counselor (2 · 2) 1078	
גְּדָבְרַיָּא	[dub.] treasurers, ministers (2 · 2) 1086	
דְּתָבָר	judge (2 · 2) 1089	
תִּפְתָּיֵא	an official, perh. judge (2 · 2) 1118	
שִׁלְטוֹן	governor (2 · 2) 1127; cf. שַׁלְטָן 1115	
לְמֵתֵא	Peal inf. of אתה to come 1083	
חֲנֻכָּה	dedication (2 · 4) 1093	
מִתְכַּנְּשִׁין	3 ptc. = assembled (2 · 2 · 3) 1097 כנש	
אֲ־חַשְׁדַּרְפְּנִין	satraps (9 · 9) 1080	
סְגַן	prefect (5 · 5) 1104	
אֲדַרְגָּזַר	counselor (2 · 2) 1078	
גְּדָבְרַיָּא	[dub.] treasurers, ministers (2 · 2) 1086	
דְּתָבָר	judge (2 · 2) 1089	
תִּפְתָּיֵא	an official, perh. judge (2 · 2) 1118	
שִׁלְטוֹן	governor (2 · 2) 1127; cf. שַׁלְטָן 1115	

חֲנֻכָּה	dedication (2 · 4) 1093	
לָקֳבֵל	before (5 · 7) 1110	
כָּרוֹז	4 herald (1 · 1) 1097	
קָרֵא בְחָיִל	called loudly 1093 חָיִל	
אֻמָּה	nation (7 · 8) 1081	
לְשָׁן	tongue (7 · 7) 1099	
קָל	5 voice (7 · 7) 1110	
מַשְׁרוֹקִי	pipe, flute (4 · 4) 1117	
קִיתָרוֹס	harp, lyre (4 · 4) 1111	
סַבְּכָא	trigon (4 · 4) 1113 שַׂבְּכָא	
פְּסַנְתֵּרִין	psaltery (4 · 4) 1108 פְּסַנְטֵרִין	
סוּמְפֹּנְיָה	bagpipe (3 · 3) 1104	
זַן	sort, kind (4 · 4) 1091	
זְמָר	music (4 · 4) 1091	
שָׁעָה	6 moment (5 · 5) 1116	
יקד	to burn (8 · 8 · 8) 1096	
כְּדִי	7 when, as soon as 1087 דִּי	
	4.a	
קָל	voice (7 · 7) 1110	
מַשְׁרוֹקִי	pipe, flute (4 · 4) 1117	
קִיתָרֹס	harp, lyre (4 · 4) 1111	
שַׂבְּכָא	trigon (4 · 4) 1113	
פְּסַנְטֵרִין	psaltery (4 · 4) 1091	
זַן	sort, king (4 · 4) 1091	
זְמָר	music (4 · 4) 1091	
אֻמָּה	nation (7 · 8) 1081	
לְשָׁן	tongue (7 · 7) 1099	
קְרַץ	8 אֲכַלוּ ק' = to accuse maliciously (2 · 2) 1111	
חיא	9 to live (5 · 5 · 6) 1092	
קָל	10 voice (7 · 7) 1110	
מַשְׁרוֹקִי	pipe, flute (4 · 4) 1117	
קִיתָרֹס	harp, lyre (4 · 4) 1111	
שַׂבְּכָא	trigon (4 · 4) 1113	
פְּסַנְתֵּרִין	psaltery (4 · 4) 1108 פְּסַנְטֵרִין	
סִיפֹּנְיָה	bagpipe (3 · 3) 1104 סוּמְפֹּנְיָה	
זַן	sort, kind (4 · 4) 1091	
זְמָר	music (4 · 4) 1091	
יקד	11 to burn (8 · 8 · 8) 1096	
מנה	12 to appoint (3 · 4 · 5) 1101	

יָתְהוֹן	mark of accus. + 3rd pl. pron. suff. 1096 יָת	
עֲבִידָה	administration (2 · 6) 1105	
טְעֵם	here = deference, discretion 1094	
רְגַז	13 rage, anger (1 · 1) 1112	
חֱמָה	rage, anger (2 · 2) 1095 חֲמָא	
צְדָא	14 true (1 · 1) 1109	
עֲתִיד	15 ready (1 · 1) 1108	
קָל	voice (7 · 7) 1110	
מַשְׁרוֹקִי	pipe, flute (4 · 4) 1117	
קִיתָרֹס	harp, lyre (4 · 4) 1111	
שַׂבְּכָא	trigon (4 · 4) 1113	
פְּסַנְתֵּרִין	psaltery (4 · 4) 1108 פְּסַנְטֵרִין	
סוּמְפֹּנְיָה	bagpipe (3 · 3) 1104	
זַן	sort, kind (4 · 4) 1091	
זְמָר	music (4 · 4) 1091	
שָׁעָה	moment (5 · 5) 1116	
יקד	to burn (8 · 8 · 8) 1096	
שֵׁיזִב	to deliver (9 · 9 · 9) 1115	
חשׁח	16 to need (1 · 1 · 1) 1093	
אֲנַחְנָא	we (2 · 4) 1081	
עַל־דְּנָה	on account of this 1088 דְּנָה d	
פִּתְגָם	thing, affair (2 · 6) 1109	
הֲתִיב	to return (2 · 5 · 8) 1117 תוב	
אֲנַחְנָא	17 we (2 · 4) 1081	
שֵׁיזִב	to deliver (9 · 9 · 9) 1115	
יקד	to burn (8 · 8 · 8) 1096	
הִתְמְלָא	19 to be filled (1 · 1 · 2) 1100	
חֲמָא	rage, anger (2 · 2) 1095	
אֲנַף	face (2 · 2) 1081	
מֵזֵא	to heat, inf. of אזא (3 · 3 · 3) 1079	
חַד שִׁבְעָה	= seven times 1114, 1079	
חֲזֵה	customary, proper (1 · 1[?]) 1092	
גֻּבַּר	20 mighty one (1 · 1) 1086	
כפת	to bind (3 · 3 · 4) 1097	
יקד	to burn (8 · 8 · 8) 1096	
כפת	21 to be bound (1 · 1 · 4) 1097	
סַרְבָּל	mantle (2 · 2) 1104	
פְּטַשׁ	[dub.] garment (1 · 1) 1108	
כַּרְבְּלָה	cap, helmet (1 · 1) 1097	

לְבוּשׁ	garment (2 · 2) 1098
יקד	to burn (8 · 8 · 8) 1096
מַחְצְפָה 22	ptc. = overbearing (2 · 2 · 2) 1093
אזא	to make hot (3 · 3 · 3) 1079
יַתִּיר	exceedingly (8 · 8) 1096
הַסִּקוּ	*Haph.* pf. of סלק to take up, lift (2 · 2 · 8) 1104
קַטֵל	to kill (2 · 2 · 7) 1111
שְׁבִיב	flame (2 · 2) 1114
יקד 23	to burn (8 · 8 · 8) 1096
כפח	to bind (3 · 3 · 4) 1097
תְּוַה 24	to be startled, alarmed (1 · 1 · 1) 1117
הִתְבְּהָלָה	haste (3 · 3[?]) 1084 בהל
הַדָּבַר	counselor, minister (4 · 4) 1089
כפח	to bind (3 · 3 · 4) 1097
יַצִּיב	undoubtedly! (5 · 5) 1096
הָא 25	lo! behold! (1 · 1) 1089
שְׁרַיִן	pass. ptc. = loosed (4 · 4 · 6) 1117 שרא
הלך	to walk about (2 · 2 · 7) 1090
חֲבָל	hurt, injury (2 · 3) 1092
רֵו	appearance (2 · 2) 1112
דמה	to be like (2 · 2 · 2) 1088
תְּרַע 26	gate, door (2 · 2) 1118
יקד	to burn (8 · 8 · 8) 1096
עֲבֵד	slave, servant (5 · 7) 1105
מִתְכַּנְּשִׁין	ptc. = assembled (2 · 2 · 3) 1097 כנשׁ
אֲ־חַשְׁדַּרְפְּנִין	satraps (9 · 9) 1080
סְגַן	prefect (5 · 5) 1104
הַדָּבַר	counselor, minister (4 · 4) 1089
שְׁלֵט	to have power, rule (5 · 5 · 7) 1115
גְּשֵׁם	body (5 · 5) 1086
שְׂעַר	hair (3 · 3) 1114
הִתְחָרַךְ	to be singed (1 · 1 · 1) 1093
סַרְבָּל	mantle (2 · 2) 1104
רֵיחַ	smell (1 · 1) 1112
עדא	to pass on, over (5 · 5 · 9) 1105
ברך 28	to bless (2 · 2 · 5) 1085
מַלְאַךְ	angel (2 · 2) 1098

שֵׁיזִב	to deliver (9 · 9 · 9) 1115
עֲבַד	slave, servant (5 · 7) 1105
הִתְרְחִץ	to set one's trust (1 · 1 · 1) 1113
שׁנה	to frustrate 1116
גְּשֵׁם	body (5 · 5) 1086
לָהֵן	except (6 · 7) 1099 II
אֻמָּה 29	nation (7 · 8) 1081
לִשָּׁן	tongue (7 · 7) 1099
שָׁלָה	neglect, error (2 · 4) 1115 שָׁלוּ
הַדָּם	member, limb (2 · 2) 1089
נְוָלוּ	refuse heap (2 · 3) 1102
הֻשְׁתְּוָה	to be set, made (1 · 1 · 1) 1114 II שׁוה
הַצֵּל	to deliver (3 · 3 · 3) 1103 נצל
כִּדְנָה	like this, thus (2 · 4) 1088 דְּנָה c
הַצְלַח 30	to cause to prosper (2 · 4 · 4) 1109
אֻמָּה 31	nation (7 · 8) 1081
לִשָּׁן	tongue (7 · 7) 1099
דור	to dwell (7 · 7 · 7) 1087
שְׁלָם	welfare, prosperity (2 · 4) 1116
שׂגא	to grow great (2 · 3 · 3) 1113
אָת 32	sign (3 · 3) 1079
תְּמַהּ	wonder (3 · 3) 1118
שְׁפַר	to be fair, seemly (3 · 3 · 3) 1117
אָת 33	sign (3 · 3) 1079
כְּמָה	how! 1099 מה
תְּמַהּ	wonder (3 · 3) 1118
תַּקִּיף	strong, mighty (4 · 5) 1118
דָּר	generation (4 · 4) 1087

Chapter 4

שְׁלֵה 1	at ease, quiet (1 · 1) 1115
רַעֲנַן	flourishing (1 · 1) 1113
דחל 2	to make afraid (1 · 1 · 6) 1087
הַרְהֹר	fancy, imagining (1 · 1) 1090
מִשְׁכַּב	couch, bed (6 · 6) 1115
בהל	to alarm, dismay (7 · 7 · 8) 1084
חַרְטֹם 4	magician (5 · 5) 1093
אָשַׁף	conjurer, enchanter (6 · 6) 1083

כַּשְׂדָּי	Chaldean, astrologer (6 · 6) 1098	נוד	to flee (1 · 1 · 1) 1102
גָּזְרִין	ptc. = astrologers (4 · 4 · 6) 1086 גזר	תְּחוֹת	under (4 · 5) 1117
עַד אָחֲרֵין	5 = at last (1 · 1) 1079 אחרין	צְפַּר	bird (4 · 4) 1110
רַב	6 here = captain, chief 1112	בְּרַם	12 only, nevertheless (4 · 5) 1085
חַרְטֹם	magician (5 · 5) 1093	עִקַּר	root, stock (3 · 3) 1107
רָז	secret (9 · 9) 1112	שֹׁרֶשׁ	root (3 · 3) 1117
אנס	to oppress (1 · 1) 1081	שבק	to leave, let alone (3 · 4 · 5) 1114
מִשְׁכַּב	7 couch, bed (6 · 6) 1115	אֱסוּר	band, bond (2 · 3) 1082
אֲלוּ	lo! (4 · 4) 1080	נְחָשׁ	copper, bronze (9 · 9) 1102
אִילָן	tree (6 · 6) 1079	דְּתֵא	grass (2 · 2) 1089
רוּם	height (4 · 5) 1112	בַּר	field (8 · 8) 1085 II
אִילָן	8 tree (6 · 6) 1079	טַל	dew (5 · 5) 1094
תקף	to grow strong (4 · 4 · 5) 1118	הצטבע	to be wet (4 · 4 · 5) 1109 I צבע
רוּם	height (4 · 5) 1112	חֲלָק	portion, possession (2 · 3) 1093
מְטָא	to reach, extend (8 · 8 · 8) 1100	עֲשַׂב	herbage, grass (5 · 5) 1108
חֲזוֹת	sight, visibility (2 · 2) 1092	לְבַב	13 heart (7 · 7) 1098
סוֹף	end (5 · 5) 1104	חלף	to pass (4 · 4 · 4) 1093
עֳפִי	9 leafage, foliage (3 · 3) 1107	גְּזֵרָה	14 decree (2 · 2) 1086
שַׁפִּיר	fair, beautiful (2 · 2) 1117	עִיר	angel (3 · 3) 1105
אִנְבֵּהּ	its fruit (3 · 3) 1078 אב	פִּתְגָם	thing, affair (2 · 6) 1109
מָזוֹן	food (2 · 2) 1091	מֵאמַר	word (1 · 2) 1081
תְּחוֹת	under (4 · 5) 1117	שְׁאֵלָה	affair (1 · 1) 1114
הטלל	to have shade (1 · 1 · 1) 1094	דִּבְרָה	cause, reason עַל־דִּבְרַת דִּי = for the
בַּר	field (8 · 8) 1085 II		cause that (2 · 2) 1087
עֲנַף	bough (4 · 4) 1107	יִנְדְּעוּן	*Peal* impf. 3rd m. pl. of ידע to
דור	to dwell (7 · 7 · 7) 1087		know 1095
צְפַּר	bird (4 · 4) 1110	שְׁפַל	low (1 · 1) 1117
התזין	to be fed (1 · 1 · 1) 1091 זון	כהל	15 to be able (4 · 4 · 4) 1096
בְּשַׂר	flesh (3 · 3) 1085	אֶשְׁתּוֹמַם	16 to be appalled (1 · 1 · 1) 1116 שמם
מִשְׁכַּב	10 couch, bed (6 · 6) 1115	שָׁעָה	moment (5 · 5) 1116
אֲלוּ	lo! (4 · 4) 1080	רַעְיוֹן	thought (6 · 6) 1113
עִיר	angel (3 · 3) 1105	בהל	to alarm, dismay (7 · 7 · 8) 1084
גדד	11 to hew down (2 · 2 · 2) 1086	אַל	do not, let not (3 · 3) 1080
אִילָן	tree (6 · 6) 1079	מָרֵא	lord (4 · 4) 1101
קצץ	to cut off (1 · 1 · 1) 1127	שָׂנֵא	enemy, foe (1 · 1) 1114
עֲנַף	bough (4 · 4) 1107	עָר	foe (1 · 1) 1108
נתר	to strip off (1 · 1 · 1) 1103	אִילָן	17 tree (6 · 6) 1079
עֳפִי	leafage, foliage (3 · 3) 1107	תקף	to grow strong (4 · 4 · 5) 1118
בדר	to scatter (1 · 1 · 1) 1084	רוּם	height (4 · 5) 1112
אִנְבֵּהּ	its fruit (3 · 3) 1078 אב	מְטָא	to reach, extend (8 · 8 · 8) 1100

חֲזוֹת   sight, visibility (2 · 2) 1092

עֳפִי   18 leafage, foliage (3 · 3) 1107

שַׁפִּיר   fair, beautiful (2 · 2) 1117

אִנְבֵּה   its fruit (3 · 3) 1078 אב

מָזוֹן   food (2 · 2) 1091

תְּחוֹת   under (4 · 5) 1117

דּוּר   to dwell (7 · 7 · 7) 1087

בַּר   field (8 · 8) 1085 II

עֲנַף   bough (4 · 4) 1107

שְׁכַן   to dwell (1 · 1 · 2) 1115

צִפַּר   bird (4 · 4) 1110

תְּקֵף   19 to grow strong (4 · 4 · 5) 1118

רְבוּ   greatness (5 · 5) 1112

מְטָא   to reach, extend (8 · 8 · 8) 1100

סוֹף   end (5 · 5) 1104

עִיר   20 angel (3 · 3) 1105

נחת   to descend (2 · 2 · 6) 1102

גדד   to hew down (2 · 2 · 2) 1086

אִילָן   tree (6 · 6) 1079

חבל   to destroy, hurt (2 · 3 · 6) 1091

בְּרַם   only, nevertheless (4 · 5) 1085

עִקַּר   root, stock (3 · 3) 1107

שֹׁרֶשׁ   root (3 · 3) 1117

שְׁבַק   to leave, let alone (3 · 4 · 5) 1114

אֱסוּר   band, bond (2 · 3) 1082

נְחָשׁ   copper, bronze (9 · 9) 1102

דִּתְאָא   grass (2 · 2) 1089

בַּר   field (8 · 8) 1085 II

טַל   dew (5 · 5) 1094

הצטבע   to be wet (4 · 4 · 5) 1109 I צבע

חֲלָק   portion, possession (2 · 3) 1093

חלף   to pass (4 · 4 · 4) 1093

גְּזֵרָה   21 decree (2 · 2) 1086

מְטָא   to come upon, befall (8 · 8 · 8) 1100

מָרֵא   lord (4 · 4) 1101

טרד   22 to chase away (2 · 2 · 4) 1094

בַּר   field (8 · 8) 1085 II

מְדוֹר   dwelling place (3 · 3) 1087

עֲשַׂב   herbage, grass (5 · 5) 1108

תּוֹר   bullock (4 · 7) 1117

טעם   to feed (3 · 3 · 3) 1094

טַל   dew (5 · 5) 1094

צבע   to dip, wet (1 · 1 · 5) 1109 I צבע

חלף   to pass (4 · 4 · 4) 1093

תִּנְדַּע   Peal impf. 2nd m. sing. of ידע, to know 1095

שׁבק   23 to leave, let alone (3 · 4 · 5) 1114

עִקַּר   root, stock (3 · 3) 1107

שֹׁרֶשׁ   root (3 · 3) 1117

אִילָן   tree (6 · 6) 1079

קַיָּם   enduring (2 · 2) 1111

תִּנְדַּע   Peal impf. 2nd m. pl. of ידע, to know 1095

לָהֵן   24 therefore (3 · 3) 1099 I

מְלַךְ   counsel, advise (1 · 1) 1100

שְׁפַר   to be fair, seemly (3 · 3 · 3) 1117

חֲטָי   sin (1 · 1) 1092

צִדְקָה   righteousness (1 · 1) 1109

פרק   to tear away, break off (1 · 1 · 1) 1108

עֲוָיָה   iniquity (1 · 1) 1105

חכן   to show mercy, favor (1 · 1 · 2) 1093

עֲנִי   poor, needy (1 · 1) 1107

אַרְכָה   a lengthening, prolonging (2 · 2) 1082

שְׁלֵוָה   ease, prosperity (1 · 1) 1115

מְטָא   25 to come upon, befall (8 · 8 · 8) 1100

קְצָת   26 end; לק׳ = at the end of (3 · 3) 1111

יְרַח   month (1 · 2) 1096

הלך   to walk (1 · 1 · 7) 1090

דָּא   27 this (6 · 6) 1086

תְּקַף   might (1 · 1) 1118

חֲסֵן   power (2 · 2) 1093

יְקָר   honor (7 · 7) 1096

הֲדַר   honor, majesty (3 · 3) 1089

עוֹד   28 still, yet (1 · 1) 1105

פֻּם   mouth (6 · 6) 1108

קָל   voice (7 · 7) 1110

עדא   to pass away (5 · 5 · 9) 1105

טרד   29 to chase away (4 · 4 · 4) 1094

612

בַּר field (8 · 8) 1085 II

מְדוֹר dwelling place (3 · 3) 1087

עֲשַׂב herbage, grass (5 · 5) 1108

תּוֹר bullock (4 · 7) 1117

טעם to feed (3 · 3 · 3) 1094

חלף to pass (4 · 4 · 4) 1093

תִּנְדַּע *Peal* impf. 2nd m. sing. of ידע, to know 1095

שָׁעָה 30 moment (5 · 5) 1116

סְפַת to be fulfilled (1 · 1 · 2) 1104 סוף

טְרִיד to chase away (4 · 4 · 4) 1094

עֲשַׂב herbage, grass (5 · 5) 1108

תּוֹר bullock (4 · 7) 1117

טַל dew (5 · 5) 1094

גְּשֶׁם body (5 · 5) 1086

הצטבע to be wet (4 · 4 · 5) 1109 I צבע

שְׂעַר hair (3 · 3) 1114

נְשַׁר eagle, vulture (2 · 2) 1103

טְפַר nail, claw (2 · 2) 1094

צְפַר bird (4 · 4) 1110

קְצָת 31 end; לְקְ = at the end of (3 · 3) 1111

עַיִן eye (4 · 5) 1105

נטל to lift (1 · 1 · 2) 1102

מַנְדַּע knowledge, power of knowing (4 · 4) 1095

תוב to return (3 · 3 · 8) 1117

בָּרֵךְ to bless, praise (3 · 3 · 5) 1085

שׁבח to laud, praise (5 · 5 · 5) 1114

הדר to glorify (3 · 3 · 3) 1089

דָּר generation (4 · 4) 1087

דור 32 to dwell (7 · 7 · 7) 1087

כְּלָה = כְּ+לָה[for לָא, not] כלה = as nothing 1098 לָא

חֲשִׁיבִין pass. ptc. = accounted for (1 · 1 · 1) 1093 חשב

מחא to smite (1 · 1 · 4) 1099

מַנְדַּע 33 knowledge, power of knowing (4 · 4) 1095

תוב to return (3 · 3 · 8) 1117

יְקָר honor (7 · 7) 1096

הֲדַר honor, majesty (3 · 3) 1089

זִיו brightness, splendor (6 · 6) 1091

הַדָּבַר counselor, minister (4 · 4) 1089

רַבְרְבָן lord, noble (8 · 8) 1112

בְּעָא here = to resort [to] (1 · 1 · 11) 1085

התקן to be established (1 · 1 · 1) 1118

רְבוּ greatness (5 · 5) 1112

יַתִּיר preeminent, surpassing (8 · 8) 1096

הוֹסַף to be added (1 · 1 · 1) 1095 יסף

שׁבח 34 to laud, praise (5 · 5 · 5) 1114

רומם to extol (1 · 1 · 4) 1112

הדר to glorify (3 · 3 · 3) 1089

מַעֲבַד work (1 · 1) 1105

קְשֹׁט truth (2 · 2) 1112

אֹרַח way (2 · 2) 1082

דִּין judgment, justice (4 · 5) 1088

הלך to walk about (2 · 2 · 7) 1090

גֵּוָה pride (1 · 1) 1085

הַשְׁפֵּל to bring low, humble (4 · 4 · 4) 1117

Chapter 5

לְחֶם 1 feast (1 · 1) 1099

רַבְרְבָן lord, noble (8 · 8) 1112

אֲלַף one thousand (4 · 4) 1081

לָקֳבֵל before (5 · 7) 1110

חֲמַר wine (4 · 6) 1093

שׁתה to drink (5 · 5 · 5) 1117

טְעֵם 2 here = taste 1094

חֲמַר wine (4 · 6) 1093

מָאן vessel, utensil (3 · 7) 1099

אב father (7 · 9) 1078

שׁתה to drink (5 · 5 · 5) 1117

רַבְרְבָן lord, noble (8 · 8) 1112

שֵׁגָל consort (3 · 3) 1114

לְחֵנָה concubine (3 · 3) 1099

מָאן 3 vessel, utensil (3 · 7) 1099

שׁתה to drink (5 · 5 · 5) 1117

רַבְרְבָן lord, noble (8 · 8) 1112

שֵׁגָל consort (3 · 3) 1114

613

לְחֵנָה	concubine (3 · 3) 1099
שתה	4 to drink (5 · 5 · 5) 1117
חֲמַר	wine (4 · 6) 1093
שבח	to laud, praise (5 · 5 · 5) 1114
נְחָשׁ	copper, bronze (9 · 9) 1102
אָע	wood (2 · 5) 1082
שָׁעָה	5 moment (5 · 5) 1116
אֶצְבַּע	finger, toe (3 · 3) 1109
לְקָבֵל	before (5 · 7) 1110
נֶבְרַשְׁתָּא	the candlestick (1 · 1) 1102
גִּיר	chalk, plaster (1 · 1) 1086
כְּתַל	wall (1 · 2) 1098
פַּס	palm [of hand] (2 · 2) 1108
זִיו	6 brightness, splendor (6 · 6) 1091
רַעְיוֹן	thought (6 · 6) 1113
בהל	to alarm, dismay (7 · 7 · 8) 1084
קְטַר	joint, know (3 · 3) 1111
חֲרַץ	loin (1 · 1) 1093
השתרא	to be loosened (1 · 1 · 6) 1117 שרא
אַרְכֻּבָּה	knee (1 · 1) 1085
דָּא	this; דָּא לְדָא = one to another (6 · 6) 1086
נקשׁ	to knock (1 · 1 · 1) 1103
אָשַׁף	7 conjurer, enchanter (6 · 6) 1083
כַּשְׂדָּי	Chaldean, astrologer (6 · 6) 1098
גָּזְרִין	ptc. = astrologers (4 · 4 · 6) 1086 גזר
אַרְגְּוָן	purple, reddish purple (3 · 3) 1082
לבשׁ	to be clothed (2 · 2 · 3) 1098
הַמְוּנְכָא	chain, necklace (3 · 3) 1090 הַמְנִיכָא
צַוַּאר	neck (3 · 3) 1109
תְּלָת	a third part (3 · 3) 1118
שְׁלֵט	to have power, rule (5 · 5 · 7) 1115
כהל	8 to be able (4 · 4 · 4) 1096
מִתְבְּהַל	9 ptc. = alarmed (1 · 1 · 8) 1084 בהל
זִיו	brightness, splendor (6 · 6) 1091
רַבְרְבָן	lord, noble (8 · 8) 1112
השתבשׁ	to be perplexed (1 · 1 · 1) 1114 שבשׁ
מַלְכָּה	10 queen (2 · 2) 1100
לְקָבֵל	in view of, by reason of (5 · 7) 1110
רַבְרְבָן	lord, noble (8 · 8) 1112

מִשְׁתֵּי	feast (1 · 1) 1117
חיא	to live (5 · 5 · 6) 1092
אַל	let not (3 · 3) 1080
בהל	to alarm, dismay (7 · 7 · 8) 1084
רַעְיוֹן	thought (6 · 6) 1113
זִיו	brightness, splendor (6 · 6) 1091
אַב	11 father (7 · 9) 1078
נַהִירוּ	illumination, insight (2 · 2) 1102
שָׂכְלְתָנוּ	insight (3 · 3) 1114
רַב	here = captain, chief 1112
חַרְטֹם	magician (5 · 5) 1093
אָשַׁף	conjurer, enchanter (6 · 6) 1083
כַּשְׂדָּי	Chaldean, astrologer (6 · 6) 1098
גָּזְרִין	ptc. = astrologers (4 · 4 · 6) 1086 גזר
יַתִּיר	12 preeminent, surpassing (8 · 8) 1096
מַנְדַּע	knowledge, power of knowing (4 · 4) 1095
שָׂכְלְתָנוּ	insight (3 · 3) 1114
פְּשַׁר	to interpret (1 · 1 · 2) 1109
אַחֲוָיָה	a declaring, interpretation (1 · 1) 1092
אֲחִידָה	riddle (1 · 1) 1092
שרא	to loosen, solve (4 · 4 · 6) 1117
קְטַר	joint, knot (3 · 3) 1111
התקרי	to be summoned 1111
גָּלוּ	13 exile (3 · 4) 1086
אַב	father (7 · 9) 1078
נַהִירוּ	14 illumination, insight (2 · 2) 1102
שָׂכְלְתָנוּ	insight (3 · 3) 1114
יַתִּיר	preeminent, surpassing (8 · 8) 1096
אָשַׁף	15 conjurer, enchanter (6 · 6) 1083
כהל	to be able (4 · 4 · 4) 1096
פְּשַׁר	16 to interpret (1 · 1 · 2) 1109
קְטַר	joint, knot (3 · 3) 1111
שרא	to loosen, solve (3 · 3 · 6) 1117
אַרְגְּוָן	purple, reddish purple (3 · 3) 1082
לבשׁ	to be clothed (2 · 2 · 3) 1098
הַמְוּנְכָא	chain, necklace (3 · 3) 1090 הַמְנִיכָא
צַוַּאר	neck (3 · 3) 1109
תְּלָת	a third part (3 · 3) 1118

שְׁלֵט	to have power, rule (5 · 5 · 7) 1115
מַתְּנָא 17	gift (3 · 3) 1103
נְבִזְבָּה	reward (2 · 2) 1102
בְּרַם	nevertheless, only (4 · 5) 1085
רְבוּ 18	greatness (5 · 5) 1112
יְקָר	honor (7 · 7) 1096
הֲדַר	honor, majesty (3 · 3) 1089
אַב	father (7 · 9) 1078
רְבוּ 19	greatness (5 · 5) 1112
אֻמָּה	nation (7 · 8) 1081
לִשָּׁן	tongue (7 · 7) 1099
זָאְעִין	ptc. = trembling (2 · 2 · 2) 1091 זוע
דחל	to fear (2 · 2 · 3) 1087
קטל	to slay (3 · 3 · 7) 1111
מַחֵא	ptc. = letting live (1 · 1 · 6) 1092 חיא
מָרִים	ptc. = exalted (1 · 1 · 4) 1112 רום
השפל	to bring low, humble (4 · 4 · 4) 1117
כְּדִי 20	as soon as 1087 דִּי 4.a
רם	to be lifted up (1 · 1 · 4) 1112 רום
לְבַב	heart (7 · 7) 1098
תקף	to grow arrogant (4 · 4 · 5) 1118
הֲזֵדָה	to act presumptuously, inf. of זוד (1 · 1 · 1) 1091
חָנְחַת	to be deposed (1 · 1 · 6) 1102
כָּרְסֵא	throne (3 · 3) 1097
יְקָר	honor (7 · 7) 1096
העדא	to take away (4 · 4 · 9) 1105
טְרִיד 21	to be chased away (4 · 4 · 4) 1094
לְבַב	heart (7 · 7) 1098
שׁוה	to become like (1 · 1 · 1) 1114 I
עֲרָד	wild ass (1 · 1) 1107
מְדוֹר	dwelling place (3 · 3) 1087
עֲשַׂב	herbage, grass (5 · 5) 1108
תּוֹר	bullock (4 · 7) 1117
טעם	to feed (3 · 3 · 3) 1094
טַל	dew (5 · 5) 1094
גְּשֶׁם	body (5 · 5) 1086
הצטבע	to be wet (4 · 4 · 5) 1109 I צבע
השפל 22	to bring low, humble (4 · 4 · 4) 1117
לְבַב	heart (7 · 7) 1098
מָרֵא 23	lord (4 · 4) 1101
התרומנ	to lift oneself up (1 · 1 · 4) 1112
מָאן	vessel, utensil (3 · 7) 1099
רַבְרְבָן	lord, noble (8 · 8) 1112
שֵׁגָל	consort (3 · 3) 1114
לְחֵנָה	concubine (3 · 3) 1099
חֲמַר	wine (4 · 6) 1093
שׁתה	to drink (5 · 5 · 5) 1117
נְחָשׁ	copper, bronze (9 · 9) 1102
אָע	wood (2 · 5) 1082
שבח	to laud, praise (5 · 5 · 5) 1114
נִשְׁמָה	breath (1 · 1) 1103
אֹרַח	way (2 · 2) 1082
הדר	to glorify (3 · 3 · 3) 1089
פַּס 24	palm [of hand] (2 · 2) 1108
רְשִׁים	to be inscribed, written (7 · 7 · 7[?]) 1113
רְשִׁים 25	to be written, inscribed (7 · 7 · 7[?]) 1113
מְנֵא	manch, mina (3 · 3) 1101
תְּקֵל	shekel (2 · 2) 1118
פְּרֵס	half mina (2 · 2) 1108
מְנֵא 26	maneh, mina (3 · 3) 1101
מְנָה	to number, reckon (1 · 1 · 5) 1101
השלם	to finish (1 · 2 · 3) 1115
תְּקֵל 27	shekel (2 · 2) 1118
תקיל	to be weighed (1 · 1 · 1) 1118
מֹאזַנְיָא	scale, balance (1 · 1) 1079
חַסִּר	deficient, wanting (1 · 1) 1093
פְּרֵס 28	half mina (2 · 2) 1108
פריס	to be broken in two (1 · 1 · 1) 1108
הלבש 29	to clothe (1 · 1 · 3) 1098
אַרְגְּוָן	purple, reddish purple (3 · 3) 1082
הַמְונְכָא	chain, necklace (3 · 3) 1090 הַמְנִיכָא
צַוַּאר	neck (3 · 3) 1109
הכרז	to make proclamation (1 · 1 · 1) 1097
תְּלָת	a third part (3 · 3) 1118
לֵילְא 30	night (5 · 5) 1099
קְטִיל	to be killed (3 · 3 · 7) 1111

Chapter 6

קַבֵּל 1 to receive (3 · 3 · 3) 1110

שְׁנָה year (2 · 7) 1116 I

שְׁפַר 2 to be fair, seemly (3 · 3 · 3) 1117

אֲחַשְׁדַּרְפְּנִין satraps (9 · 9) 1080

עֵלָּא 3 above (1 · 1) 1106

סָרֵךְ chief, overseer (5 · 5) 1104

אֲחַשְׁדַּרְפְּנִין satraps (9 · 9) 1080

אִלֵּין these (5 · 5) 1080

טְעֵם here = report 1094

נְזַק to suffer injury (1 · 1 · 3) 1102

הִתְנַצַּח 4 to distinguish oneself (1 · 1 · 1) 1103

סָרֵךְ chief, overseer (5 · 5) 1104

אֲחַשְׁדַּרְפְּנִין satraps (9 · 9) 1080

יַתִּיר preeminent, surpassing (8 · 8) 1096

עֲשֵׁת to think plan (1 · 1 · 1) 1108

סָרֵךְ 5 chief, overseer (5 · 5) 1104

אֲחַשְׁדַּרְפְּנִין satraps (9 · 9) 1080

עִלָּה matter, affair, occasion (3 · 3) 1106

צַד side; מצ׳ = arising from, touching (2 · 2) 1109

שְׁחִיתָה fault (3 · 3) 1115 שחת

מְהֵימַן pass. ptc. = trusty, trustworthy (3 · 3 · 3) 1081 אמן

שָׁלוּ neglect, error (2 · 4) 1115

עִלָּה 6 matter, affair, occasion (3 · 3) 1106

לָהֵן except (6 · 7) 1099 II

סָרֵךְ 7 chief, overseer (5 · 5) 1104

אֲחַשְׁדַּרְפְּנִין satraps (9 · 9) 1080

אֵלֶּן these (5 · 5) 1080 אֵלֶּין

הרגש to come thronging (4 · 4 · 4) 1112

חְיָא to live (5 · 5 · 6) 1092

אתיעט 8 to take counsel together (1 · 1 · 1) 1095 יעט

סָרֵךְ chief, overseer (5 · 5) 1104

סְגַן prefect (5 · 5) 1104

אֲחַשְׁדַּרְפְּנִין satraps (9 · 9) 1080

הַדָּבַר counselor, minister (4 · 4) 1089

קַיָּמָה Pael inf. = to establish, set up 1110 קום

קְיָם statute (2 · 2) 1111

תקף to make strong, stringent (1 · 1 · 5) 1118

אֱסָר interdict (7 · 7) 1082

בָּעוּ petition (2 · 2) 1085

לָהֵן except (6 · 7) 1099 II

אֱסָר 9 interdict (7 · 7) 1082

רְשַׁם to inscribe, sign (7 · 7 · 7[?]) 1113

עדא to pass away (5 · 5 · 9) 1105

רְשַׁם 10 to inscribe, sign (7 · 7 · 7[?]) 1113

אֱסָר interdict (7 · 7) 1082

כְּדִי 11 when 1087 דִּי 4 a

רְשִׁים to be inscribed, signed (7 · 7 · 7[?]) 1113

כַּוָּה window (1 · 1) 1096

פְּתִיחַ to be opened (2 · 2 · 2) 1109

עִלִּי roof chamber (1 · 1) 1106

נֶגֶד in front of, facing (1 · 1) 1102

בְּרַךְ to kneel (2 · 2 · 5) 1085

בְּרַךְ knee (1 · 1) 1085

מְצַלֵּא ptc. = praying (1 · 2 · 2) 1109 צלא

מוֹדֵא ptc. = praising (2 · 2 · 2) 1095 ידא

קַדְמָה former time (1 · 2) 1110

הרגש 12 to throng (4 · 4 · 4) 1112

הִתְחַנַּן to implore favor (1 · 1 · 2) 1093

אֱסָר 13 interdict (7 · 7) 1082

רְשַׁם to inscribe, sign (7 · 7 · 7[?]) 1113

לָהֵן except (6 · 7) 1099 II

יַצִּיב true (5 · 5) 1096

עדא to pass away (5 · 5 · 9) 1105

גָּלוּ 14 exile (3 · 4) 1086

טְעֵם here = deference, discretion 1094

אֱסָר interdict (7 · 7) 1082

רְשַׁם to inscribe, sign (7 · 7 · 7[?]) 1113

בָּעוּ petition (2 · 2) 1085

כְּדִי 15 when 1087 דִּי 4.a

בְּאֵשׁ to be evil, bad; ב׳ עֲלוֹהִי = it was

בְּאֵשׁ לֵהּ evil [displeasing] to him (1 · 1 · 1) 1084

בָּל mind (1 · 1) 1084

שֵׁיזִב to deliver (9 · 9 · 9) 1115

מֶעָל going in; i.e., setting (1 · 1) 1106

שֶׁמֶשׁ sun (1 · 1) 1116

הִשְׁתַּדַּר to struggle, strive (1 · 1 · 1) 1114

הַצָּל to deliver (3 · 3 · 3) 1103 נצל

הַרְגִּשׁ 16 to throng (4 · 4 · 4) 1114

אֱסָר interdict (7 · 7) 1082

קְיָם statute (2 · 2) 1111

תְּדִירָא 17 continuance (2 · 2) 1087

שֵׁיזִב to deliver (9 · 9 · 9) 1115

פֻּם 18 mouth (6 · 6) 1108

חֲתַם to seal (1 · 1 · 1) 1094

עִזְקָה signet ring (1 · 1) 1105

רַבְרְבָן lord, noble (8 · 8) 1112

צְבוּ thing, anything (1 · 1) 1109

אֲזַל 19 to go, go off (4 · 7 · 7) 1079

בָּת to pass the night (1 · 1 · 1) 1084 בית

טְוָת in fasting, hungrily (1 · 1) 1094

דַּחֲוָה [dub.] instrument of music, concubines, dancing girls (1 · 1) 1087

שְׁנָה sleep (1 · 1) 1096

נְדַד to flee (1 · 1 · 1) 1102

שְׁפַרְפָּר 20 dawn (1 · 1) 1117

נְגַהּ brightness, light (1 · 1) 1102

הִתְבְּהָלָה haste (3 · 3[?]) 1084 בהל

אֲזַל to go, go off (4 · 7 · 7) 1079

קָל 21 voice (7 · 7) 1110

עֲצִיב pained (1 · 1) 1107 עצב

זְעִק to cry, call (1 · 1 · 1) 1091

עֲבֵד slave, servant (5 · 7) 1105

תְּדִירָא continuance (2 · 2) 1087

שֵׁיזִב to deliver (9 · 9 · 9) 1115

מַלִּל 22 to speak (5 · 5 · 5) 1100

חַיָּא to live (5 · 5 · 6) 1092

מַלְאַךְ 23 angel (2 · 2) 1098

סְגַר to shut (1 · 1 · 1) 1104

פֻּם mouth (6 · 6) 1108

חֲבַל to destroy, hurt (2 · 3 · 6) 1091

זָכוּ purity, innocence (1 · 1) 1091

אַף also (1 · 4) 1082

חֲבוּלָה crime (1 · 1) 1092 חבולא

טְאֵב 24 to be good; ט' עֲלוֹהִי = it was good to him (1 · 1 · 1) 1094

הַנְסָקָה Haph. inf., to lift up, take up (2 · 2 · 8) 1104 סלק

הֻסַּק to be taken up (1 · 1 · 8) 1104 סלק

חֲבָל hurt, injury (2 · 3) 1092

הֵימִן to trust (3 · 3 · 3) 1081 אמן

קְרַץ 25 piece; אכל ק' = to accuse maliciously (2 · 2) 1111; cf. 1080 אכל

אִנּוּן they, those (3 · 4) 1081

נְשִׁין wives (1 · 1) 1081

מְטָא to reach, come to (8 · 8 · 8) 1100

אַרְעִי bottom (1 · 1) 1083

שְׁלֵט to fall upon, assault (5 · 5 · 7) 1115

גְּרַם bone (1 · 1) 1086

אֻמָּה 26 nation (7 · 8) 1081

לִשָּׁן tongue (7 · 7) 1099

דּוּר to dwell (7 · 7 · 7) 1087

שְׁלָם welfare, prosperity (2 · 4) 1116

שְׂגָא to grow great (2 · 3 · 3) 1113

זוּעַ 27 to tremble (2 · 2 · 2) 1091

דְּחַל to fear (5 · 5 · 6) 1087

קַיָּם enduring (2 · 2) 1111

הִתְחַבַּל to be destroyed (3 · 3 · 6) 1091

סוֹף end (5 · 5) 1104

שֵׁיזִב 28 to deliver (9 · 9 · 9) 1115

הַצָּל to rescue, deliver (3 · 3 · 3) 1103 נצל

אָת sign (3 · 3) 1079

תְּמַהּ wonder (3 · 3) 1118

הַצְלַח 29 to be prosperous (2 · 4 · 4) 1109

Chapter 7

שְׁנָה 1 year (2 · 7) 1116 I

רֵאשׁ here = beginning 1112

מִשְׁכַּב couch, bed (6 · 6) 1115
עִם 2 during 1107
לֵילְא night (5 · 5) 1099
אֲרוּ lo! (5 · 5) 1082
מְגִיחָן ptc. = breaking forth (1 · 1 · 1) 1127 גוח
יַם sea (2 · 2) 1095
סלק 3 to come up (4 · 5 · 8) 1104
יַם sea (2 · 2) 1095
דָא this; דָא מִן־דָא = one from another (6 · 6) 1086
קַדְמָי 4 first (3 · 3) 1110
גַּף wing (3 · 3) 1086
נְשַׁר eagle, vulture (2 · 2) 1103
מריט to be plucked (1 · 1 · 1) 1101
נטיל to be lifted (1 · 1 · 2) 1102
רְגַל foot (7 · 7) 1112
לְבַב heart (7 · 7) 1098
אֲרוּ 5 lo! (5 · 5) 1082
דמה to be like (2 · 2 · 2) 1088
דֹּב bear (1 · 1) 1087
שְׂטַר side (1 · 1) 1113
עֲלַע rib (1 · 1) 1106
פֻּם mouth (6 · 6) 1108
בֵּין between (2 · 2) 1084
שֵׁן tooth (3 · 3) 1116
בְּשַׂר flesh (3 · 3) 1085
בָּאתַר 6 after (3 · 3) 1083 אתר
אֲרוּ lo! (5 · 5) 1082
נְמַר leopard (1 · 1) 1103
גַּף wing (3 · 3) 1086
עוֹף fowl (2 · 2) 1105
גַּב back or side (1 · 1) 1085
בָּאתַר 7 after (3 · 3) 1083 אתר
לֵילְא night (5 · 5) 1099
אֲרוּ lo! (5 · 5) 1082
דְּחִיל dreadful, terrible (3 · 3) 1087
אֵימְתָן terrible (1 · 1) 1080
תַּקִּיף strong, mighty (4 · 5) 1118
יַתִּיר exceedingly (8 · 8) 1096
שֵׁן tooth (3 · 3) 1116

רְגַל foot (7 · 7) 1112
רפס to tread, trample (2 · 2 · 2) 1113
מְשַׁנְּיָה pass. ptc. = different 1116 שנא
מִשְׂתַּכַּל 8 ptc. = contemplating, considering (1 · 1 · 1) 1114 שכל
אֲלוּ lo! (4 · 4) 1080
זְעֵיר little, small (1 · 1) 1091
סלק to come up (4 · 5 · 8) 1104
בֵּין between (2 · 2) 1084
קַדְמָי first (3 · 3) 1110
אתעקרו to be rooted up (1 · 1 · 1) 1107 עקר
עַיִן eye (4 · 5) 1105
דָא this (6 · 6) 1086
פֻּם mouth (6 · 6) 1108
מלל to speak (5 · 5 · 5) 1100
כָּרְסֵא 9 throne (3 · 3) 1097
עַתִּיק advanced, aged (3 · 3) 1108
יְתֵב to sit, be seated (3 · 4 · 5) 1096
לְבוּשׁ garment (6 · 6) 1098
תְּלַג snow (1 · 1) 1117
חִוָּר white (1 · 1) 1092
שְׂעַר hair (3 · 3) 1114
עֲמַר wool (1 · 1) 1107
נְקֵא clean, pure (1 · 1) 1103
שְׁבִיב flame (2 · 2) 1114
גַּלְגַּל wheel (1 · 1) 1086
דלק to burn (1 · 1 · 1) 1088
נגד 10 to stream, flow (1 · 1 · 1) 1102
אֲלַף thousand (4 · 4) 1081
שמש to minister (1 · 1 · 1) 1116 II
רִבּוֹ myriad (2 · 2) 1112
דִּין judges, court (4 · 5) 1088
יְתֵב to sit, be seated (3 · 4 · 5) 1096
סְפַר book (1 · 5) 1104
פתיח to be opened (2 · 2 · 2) 1109
קָל 11 voice (7 · 7) 1110
מלל to speak (5 · 5 · 5) 1100
קְטִיל to be killed (3 · 3 · 7) 1111
הוּבַד to be destroyed (1 · 1 · 7) 1078 אבד
גְּשֵׁם body (5 · 5) 1086

יְקֵדָה burning (1 · 1) 1096

אֶשָּׁא fire (1 · 1) 1083

הֶעְדָּא 12 to take away (4 · 4 · 9) 1105

אַרְכָה a lengthening, prolonging (2 · 2) 1082

לֵילָא 13 night (5 · 5) 1099

אֲרוּ lo! (5 · 5) 1082

עֲנָן cloud (1 · 1) 1107

עַתִּיק advanced, aged (3 · 3) 1108

מְטָא to reach, come to (8 · 8 · 8) 1100

הקרב here = to bring near 1111

יְקָר 14 honor (7 · 7) 1096

אֻמָּה nation (7 · 8) 1081

לְשָׁן tongue (7 · 7) 1099

עדה to pass away (5 · 5 · 9) 1105 עדא

התחבל to be destroyed (3 · 3 · 6) 1091

אתכרא 15 to be distressed (1 · 1 · 1) 1097

נִדְנֶה sheath (1 · 1) 1102

בהל to alarm, dismay (7 · 7 · 8) 1084

יַצִּיבָא 16 the truth (5 · 5) 1096 יַצִּיב

אִלֵּין 17 these (5 · 5) 1080

אִנּוּן they, those (3 · 4) 1081

קַבֵּל 18 to receive (3 · 3 · 3) 1110

עֶלְיוֹן Most High (4 · 4) 1106

החסן to take possession of, possess (2 · 2 · 2) 1093

צבה 19 here = to desire 1109

יצב to make certain (1 · 1 · 1) 1096

דְּחִיל terrible (3 · 3) 1087 דחל

יַתִּיר exceedingly (8 · 8) 1096

שֵׁן tooth (3 · 3) 1116

טְפַר nail, claw (2 · 2) 1094

נְחָשׁ copper, bronze (9 · 9) 1102

רְגַל foot (7 · 7) 1112

רפס to tread, trample (2 · 2 · 2) 1113

סלק 20 to come up (4 · 5 · 8) 1104

דְּכֵן this, that (3 · 3) 1088

עַיִן eye (4 · 5) 1105

פֻּם mouth (6 · 6) 1108

מלל to speak (5 · 5 · 5) 1100

חַבְרָה fellow (1 · 1) 1092

דְּכֵן 21 this, that (3 · 3) 1088

קְרָב war (1 · 1) 1111

יְכֵל here = to prevail against w/ לְ 1095

עַתִּיק 22 advanced, aged (3 · 3) 1108

דִּין judges, court (4 · 5) 1088

עֶלְיוֹן Most High (4 · 4) 1106

מְטָא to arrive (8 · 8 · 8) 1100

החסן to take possession of, possess (2 · 2 · 2) 1093

דושׁ 23 to tread down (1 · 1 · 1) 1087

אַחֲרִי 24 after (3 · 3) 1079 אחר

קַדְמָי first (3 · 3) 1110

השפל to bring low, humble (4 · 4 · 4) 1117

צַד 25 side (2 · 2) 1109

מלל to speak (5 · 5 · 5) 1100

עֶלְיוֹן Most High (4 · 4) 1106

בלא to wear away, out (1 · 1 · 1) 1084

סבר to think, intend (1 · 1 · 1) 1104

פְּלַג half (1 · 1) 1108

דִּין 26 judges, court (4 · 5) 1088

יְתֵב to sit, be seated (3 · 4 · 5) 1096

הֶעְדָּא to take away (4 · 4 · 9) 1105

השמד to destroy (1 · 1 · 1) 1116

הובד to destroy (5 · 5 · 7) 1078 אבד

סוֹף end (5 · 5) 1104

רְבוּ 27 greatness (5 · 5) 1112

תְּחוֹת under (4 · 5) 1117

עֶלְיוֹן Most High (4 · 4) 1106

כָּה 28 here (1 · 1) 1096

סוֹף end (5 · 5) 1104

רַעְיוֹן thought (6 · 6) 1113

בהל to alarm, dismay (7 · 7 · 8) 1084

זִיו brightness, splendor (6 · 6) 1091

לֵב heart (2 · 2[?]) 1098

נטר to keep (1 · 1 · 1) 1102

End of Aramaic Section

Chapter 8

חָזוֹן	1	vision (12 · 35) 302
תְּחִלָּה		beginning (3 · 22) 321
חָזוֹן	2	vision (12 · 35) 302
בִּירָה		citadel, castle (1 · 18) 108
מְדִינָה		province (2 · 44) 193
אוּבָל		river, stream (3 · 3) 385
אוּבָל	3	river, stream (3 · 3) 385
גָּבֹהַּ		high, exalted (2 · 41) 147
נגח	4	to push, thrust (1 · 6 · 11) 618
צָפִיר	5	male goat; צ׳־הָעִזִּים = male goat, ram (4 · 6) 862
מַעֲרָב		west (1 · 14) 788 II
חָזוּת		conspicuous (2 · 5) 303
אוּבָל	6	river, stream (3 · 3) 385
הִתְמַרְמַר	7	to be enraged (2 · 2 · 15) 600 I מרר
רָמַס		to trample down (2 · 17 · 18) 942
צָפִיר	8	male goat; צ׳־הָעִזִּים = male goat, ram (4 · 6) 862
עָצַם		to be mighty (3 · 16 · 18) 782 I
חָזוּת		conspicuous (2 · 5) 303
צָעִיר	9	little, insignificant (1 · 2[?]) 859 I
יֶתֶר		exceedingly 451 I.2.b
צְבִי		beauty (4 · 18) 840 I
כּוֹכָב	10	star (2 · 37) 456
רָמַס		to trample down (2 · 17 · 18) 942
תָּמִיר	11	daily burnt offering 556 2.c
מָכוֹן		place (1 · 17) 467
תָּמִיר	12	daily burnt offering 556 2.c
פַּלְמוֹנִי	13	a certain one (1 · 1) 811 I פְּלֹנִי
מָתַי		when? (2 · 42) 607
חָזוֹן		vision (12 · 35) 302
תָּמִיד		daily burnt offering 556 2.c
מִרְמָס		trampling (1 · 7) 942
נִצְדַּק	14	to be put right (1 · 1 · 41) 842
חָזוֹן	15	vision (12 · 35) 302
בִּינָה		understanding (4 · 37) 108
לְנֶגֶד		in front of, before (3 · 32) 617 נֶגֶד 2.b
הַלָּז		this (1 · 7) 229
עֹמֶר	17	standing place (3 · 9) 765

נִבְעַת		to be terrified (1 · 3 · 16) 129
חָזוֹן		vision (12 · 35) 302
נִרְדַּם	18	to be or fall fast asleep (2 · 7 · 7) 922
עֹמֶר		standing place (3 · 9) 765
זַעַם	19	indignation (2 · 22) 276
צָפִיר	21	male goat (4 · 6) 862
פָּשַׁע	23	to transgress (1 · 40 · 41) 833
עַז		strong, mighty, fierce (1 · 22) 738
חִידָה		double dealing (1 · 17) 295
עָצַם	24	to be mighty (3 · 16 · 18) 782 I
נִפְלָאוֹת		wonderful acts (2 · 44) 810 פלא 4
עָצוּם		mighty, numerous (2 · 31) 783
שֵׂכֶל	25	cunning, craft (1 · 16) 968
מִרְמָה		deceit, treachery (2 · 39) 941
שַׁלְוָה		quietness, ease, בְּשׁ׳ = unawares (3 · 8) 1017
אֶפֶס		without (1 · 27) 67
סָתַם	26	to shut up, keep close (3 · 10 · 13) 711
חָזוֹן		vision (12 · 35) 302

Chapter 9

חָרְבָּה	2	waste, ruin (1 · 42) 352
תַּחֲנוּן	3	supplication (4 · 18) 337
צוֹם		fast, fasting (1 · 25) 847
שַׂק		sackcloth (1 · 48) 974
אֵפֶר		ashes (1 · 22) 68
אָנָּא	4	ah, now! (1 · 7) 58
נוֹרָא		awe-inspiring, awful (1 · 44) 431 יָרֵא Niph.
אֹהֵב		loving (1 · 36[?]) 12 אָהֵב
עוה	5	to commit iniquity (1 · 2 · 17[?]) 731
הִרְשִׁיעַ		to act wickedly (3 · 25 · 34) 957
מרד		to rebel, revolt (2 · 25 · 25) 597
בֹּשֶׁת	7	shame (2 · 30) 102
הִדִּיחַ		to thrust out, banish (1 · 27 · 43) 623 נדח
מַעַל		unfaithful act (1 · 29) 591 I

מָעַל	to act unfaithfully, treacherously (1 · 35 · 35) 591	
בֹּשֶׁת	8 shame (2 · 30) 102	
רַחֲמִים	9 compassion (3 · 38) 933	
סְלִיחָה	forgiveness (1 · 3) 699	
מרד	to rebel, revolt (2 · 25 · 25) 597	
נתך	11 to pour forth (2 · 7 · 21) 677	
אָלָה	oath, curse (1 · 36) 46	
שְׁבוּעָה	oath, curse (1 · 30) 989	
שָׁקַד	14 to keep watch, be wakeful (1 · 12 · 17) 1052	
רשע	15 to be wicked, act wickedly (1 · 9 · 34) 957	
חֵטְא	16 sin (1 · 33) 307	
תַּחֲנוּן	17 supplication (4 · 18) 337	
הָאִיר	to make shine (1 · 34 · 40) 21 אור	
שָׁמֵם	devastated (1 · 3) 1031	
פָּקַח	18 to open (1 · 17 · 20) 824	
תַּחֲנוּן	supplication (4 · 18) 337	
רַחֲמִים	compassion (3 · 38) 933	
סלח	19 to forgive, pardon (1 · 33 · 46) 699	
הִקְשִׁיב	to give attention (1 · 45 · 46) 904	
אָחַר	to delay, tarry (1 · 15 · 17) 29	
תְּחִנָּה	20 supplication (1 · 25) 337 I	
חָזוֹן	21 vision (12 · 35) 302	
תְּחִלָּה	beginning (3 · 22) 321	
מֻעָף	*Hoph*. ptc. = wearied (1 · 1 · 9) 419 I יעף	
יָעֵף	weariness, faintness; מֻעָף בִּי׳ = utterly weary (1 · 1) 419	
בִּינָה	22 understanding (4 · 37) 108	
תְּחִלָּה	23 beginning (3 · 22) 321	
תַּחֲנוּן	supplication (4 · 18) 337	
חֲמוּדָה	precious, preciousness (6 · 9) 326	
שָׁבוּעַ	24 week (8 · 20) 988	
נֶחְתַּךְ	to be determined (1 · 1 · 1) 367	
חתם	to seal, seal up (4 · 23 · 27) 367	
חָזוֹן	vision (12 · 35) 302	
מוֹצָא	25 going forth (1 · 27) 425 I	
מָשִׁיחַ	anointed (2 · 39) 603	

נָגִיד	leader, ruler, prince (3 · 44) 617	
שָׁבוּעַ	week (8 · 20) 988	
רְחוֹב	broad open place (1 · 43) 932 I	
חָרוּץ	trench, moat (1 · 4[?]) 358 III	
צוֹק	constraint, distress (1 · 1) 848	
שָׁבוּעַ	26 week (8 · 20) 988	
מָשִׁיחַ	anointed (2 · 39) 603	
נָגִיד	leader, ruler, prince (3 · 44) 617	
שֶׁטֶף	flood (2 · 6) 1009	
נחרץ	to determine, decide (3 · 5 · 10) 358 I	
הִגְבִּיר	27 to confirm (1 · 2 · 25) 149	
שָׁבוּעַ	week (8 · 20) 988	
שִׁקּוּץ	detested thing, abomination (3 · 28) 1055	
כָּלָה	destruction, annihilation (2 · 22) 478	
נחרץ	to determine, decide (3 · 5 · 10) 358 I	
נתך	to pour forth (2 · 7 · 21) 677	

Chapter 10

בִּינָה	1 understanding (4 · 37) 108	
הִתְאַבֵּל	2 to mourn (1 · 19 · 38) 5 I	
שָׁבוּעַ	week (8 · 20) 988	
חֲמוּדָה	3 precious things (6 · 9) 326	
סוּךְ	to anoint oneself (2 · 8 · 10) 691	
שָׁבוּעַ	week (8 · 20) 988	
לָבוּשׁ	5 clothed with (3 · 16) 527 לבש	
בַּד	linen (3 · 23) 94 I	
מָתְנַיִם	loins (1 · 50) 608	
הגר	to gird, gird on (1 · 44 · 44) 291	
כֶּתֶם	gold (1 · 9) 508	
גְּוִיָּה	6 body, corpse (1 · 12) 156	
תַּרְשִׁישׁ	precious stone, perh. yellow jasper (1 · 7) 1076 I	
בָּרָק	lightning (1 · 21) 140	
לַפִּיד	torch (1 · 13) 542	
מַרְגְּלוֹת	feet (1 · 5) 920	
קָלָל	burnished (1 · 2) 887	

621

מַרְאָה 7 vision (4 · 12) 909 I
אֲבָל howbeit, but (2 · 11) 6
חֲרָדָה trembling, quaking (1 · 9) 353 I
נֶחְבָּא to hide oneself (1 · 16 · 34) 285
מַרְאָה 8 vision (4 · 12) 909 I
הוֹד vigor, splendor (2 · 24) 217 I
מַשְׁחִית ruin, destruction (1 · 19) 1008
עָצַר to retain (3 · 36 · 46) 783
נִרְדָּם 9 to be or fall fast asleep (2 · 7 · 7) 922
הֵנִיע 10 to shake, cause to totter (1 · 14 · 38) נוע 631
בֶּרֶךְ knee (1 · 25) 139
חֲמוּדָה 11 precious, preciousness (6 · 9) 326
עֹמֶר standing place (3 · 9) 765
מַרְעִיד Hiph. ptc. = trembling (1 · 2 · 3) 944
לְנֶגֶד 13 in front of, before (3 · 32) 617 נגר 2.b
קרה 14 to befall (1 · 13 · 27) 899
חָזוֹן vision (12 · 35) 302
נֶאֱלַם 15 to be silent (1 · 8 · 9) 47
דְּמוּת 16 likeness, similitude (1 · 25) 198
לְנֶגֶד in front of, before (3 · 32) 617 נגר 2.b
מַרְאָה vision (4 · 12) 909 I
צִיר pang (1 · 5) 852 IV
עָצַר to retain (3 · 36 · 46) 783
הֵיךְ 17 how? (1 · 2) 228
זֶה as adj. = such a, such as 260 3
נְשָׁמָה breath (1 · 24) 675
חֲמוּדָה 19 precious things, preciousness (6 · 9) 326
אֲבָל 21 howbeit, but (2 · 11) 6
רָשׁוּם pass. ptc. = inscribed (1 · 1 · 1) 957
כְּתָב writing (1 · 17) 508

Chapter 11

מָעוֹז 1 protection, refuge (7 · 36) 731

הַעְשִׁיר 2 to gain riches (1 · 14 · 17) 799
עֹשֶׁר riches (2 · 37) 799
חֶזְקָה strength, force (1 · 4) 305
מִמְשָׁל 3 dominion (2 · 3) 606
נֶחֱצָה 4 to be divided (1 · 4 · 15) 345
מֹשֶׁל dominion (1 · 2) 606 I
נָתַשׁ to be rooted up (1 · 4 · 21) 684
מִלְּבַד besides (1 · 33) 94 II בַּד 1.e
מִמְשָׁל 5 dominion (2 · 3) 606
מֶמְשָׁלָה dominion, rule (1 · 17) 606
הִתְחַבֵּר 6 to league together (2 · 4 · 28) 287
מֵישָׁר uprightness, equity (1 · 19) 449
עָצַר to retain (3 · 36 · 46) 783
נֵצֶר 7 sprout, shoot (1 · 4) 666
שֹׁרֶשׁ root (1 · 33) 1057
כֵּן place, office (4 · 17) 487 III
מָעוֹז fastness, place of safety (7 · 36) 731
נָסִיךְ 8 molten image (1 · 6) 651 I
חֶמְדָּה desire, delight (2 · 16) 326
שְׁבִי captivity (2 · 46) 985
הִתְגָּרָה 10 to wage war (3 · 11 · 14) 173
שָׁטַף to overflow (3 · 28 · 31) 1009
מָעוֹז fastness, place of safety (7 · 36) 731
הִתְמַרְמַר 11 to embitter oneself; i.e., be enraged (2 · 2 · 15) 600 I מרר
רִבּוֹא 12 ten thousand, myriad (1 · 11) 914 רבּוֹ
עזז to prevail, be strong (1 · 9 · 11) 738
רְכוּשׁ 13 property, goods (3 · 28) 940
פָּרִיץ 14 violent one (1 · 6) 829
חָזוֹן vision (12 · 35) 302
סֹלְלָה 15 mound (1 · 11) 700
מִבְצָר fortification (3 · 37) 131
צְבִי 16 beauty (4 · 18) 840 I
כָּלָה destruction, annihilation (2 · 22) 478
תֹּקֶף 17 power, strength (1 · 3) 1076
אִי 18 pl. = coastlands (1 · 36) 15 I
קָצִין chief, commander (1 · 12) 892
בִּלְתִּי besides that, certainly (1 · 24) 116 בְּלַת 3
מָעוֹז 19 fastness, place of safety (7 · 36) 731

כֵּן 20 place, office (4 · 17) 487 III

נֹגֵשׂ driver, taskmaster (1 · 15[?]) 620 נלש Qal 3

הֶדֶר splendor (1 · 1) 214

כֵּן 21 place, office (4 · 17) 487 III

נִבְזֶה ptc. = despicable, contemptible (1 · 10 · 42) 102

הוֹד splendor, majesty (2 · 24) 217 I

שַׁלְוָה quietness, ease, 'בְּשׁ = unawares (3 · 8) 1017

חֲלַקְלַקּוֹת fine promises (2 · 4) 325

שֶׁטֶף 22 flood (2 · 6) 1009

נשטף to be swept away (1 · 2 · 31) 1009

נָגִיד leader, ruler, prince (3 · 44) 617

התחבר 23 to make an alliance (2 · 4 · 28) 287

מִרְמָה deceit, treachery (2 · 39) 941

עָצַם to be mighty (3 · 16 · 18) 782 I

שַׁלְוָה quietness, ease, 'בְּשׁ = unawares (3 · 8) 1017

מִשְׁמָן fertile spots (1 · 4) 1032

מְדִינָה province (2 · 44) 193

בִּזָּה spoil, booty (2 · 10) 103

רְכוּשׁ property, goods (3 · 28) 940

בזר to scatter (1 · 1 · 2) 103

מִבְצָר fortress, stronghold (3 · 37) 131

התגרה 25 to wage war (3 · 11 · 14) 173

עָצוּם mighty, numerous (2 · 31) 783

פַּת־בָּג 26 delicacies (6 · 6) 834

שָׁטַף to overflow (3 · 28 · 31) 1009

מֶרַע 27 mischief (1 · 1[?]) 949 רעע Hiph.1

כָּזָב lie, falsehood (1 · 31) 469

רְכוּשׁ 28 property, goods (3 · 28) 940

צִי 30 ship (1 · 4) 850 I

נכאה to be cowed, disheartened (1 · 2 · 3) 456

זָעַם to be indignant (1 · 10 · 11) 276

מָעוֹז 31 fastness, place of safety (7 · 36) 731

תָּמִיד daily burnt offering 556 2.c

שִׁקּוּץ detested thing, abomination (3 · 28) 1055

הִרְשִׁיעַ 32 to act wickedly (3 · 25 · 34) 957

הֶחֱנִיף to make profane, godless (1 · 4 · 10) 337

חָלָק smooth (1 · 12) 325

לֶהָבָה 33 flame (1 · 19) 529

שְׁבִי captivity (2 · 46) 985

בִּזָּה spoil, booty (2 · 10) 103

עֵזֶר 34 help, succor (1 · 21) 740 I

נִלְוָה to join oneself to or be joined (1 · 'ל · 12) 530

חֲלַקְלַקּוֹת fine promises (2 · 4) 325

צָרַף 35 to smelt, refine (1 · 18 · 21) 864

ברר to purify (1 · 1 · 15) 140

הלבין to make white (1 · 4 · 5) 526

נִפְלָאוֹת 36 wonderful acts (2 · 44) 810 פלא Niph. 4

זַעַם indignation (2 · 22) 276

נֶחֱרָצָה Niph ptc. = strict decision (3 · 5 · 10) 358 I חיע

חֶמְדָּה 37 desire, delight (2 · 16) 326

מָעוֹז 38 refuge (7 · 36) 731

כֵּן place, office (4 · 17) 487 III

יָקָר precious, costly (1 · 35) 429

חֲמוּדָה precious, choice things (6 · 9) 326

מִבְצָר 39 fortress, stronghold (3 · 37) 131

מָעוֹז fastness, place of safety (7 · 36) 731

נֵכָר foreignness (1 · 36) 648

הִכִּיר to regard, observe (1 · 37 · 40) 647 I נכר

מְחִיר price, hire (1 · 15) 564 I

התנגח 40 to wage war with (1 · 1 · 11) 618

השתער to storm against (1 · 1 · 4) 973 II

אֳנִיָּה ship (1 · 31) 58

שָׁטַף to overflow (3 · 28 · 31) 1009

צְבִי 41 beauty (4 · 18) 840 I

פְּלֵיטָה 42 escaped remnant (1 · 28) 812

מִכְמָן 43 hidden stores (1 · 1) 485

חֲמוּדָה precious, choice things (6 · 9) 326

מִצְעָד step (1 · 3) 857

שְׁמוּעָה 44 report (1 · 27) 1035

בָּהַל — to dismay, terrify (1 · 10 · 39) 96

חֵמָא — rage חֵמָה 404

הֶחֱרִים — to destroy, exterminate (1 · 46 · 49) 355 I

אַפֶּדֶן — 45 palace (1 · 1) 66

צְבִי — beauty (4 · 18) 840 I

עֹזֵר — helper (1 · 19[?]) עזר 740 I

Chapter 12

יָשֵׁן — 2 asleep, sleeping (1 · 9) 445 I

הֵקִיץ — to awake (1 · 22 · 23) 884 I

דְּרָאוֹן — aversion, abhorrence (1 · 2) 201

הִזְהִיר — 3 to shine (1 · 1 · 1) 263 I

זֹהַר — shining, brightness (1 · 2) 264

רָקִיעַ — expanse, firmament (1 · 17) 956

הִצְדִּיק — to make righteous (1 · 12 · 41) 842

כּוֹכָב — star (2 · 37) 456

וָעֶד — and ever (1 · 48) 723 I עד

סָתַם — 4 to shut up, keep close (3 · 10 · 13) 711

חָתַם — to seal, seal up (4 · 23 · 27) 367

שׁוֹטֵט — to go eagerly, quickly, to and fro (1 · 5 · 13) 1001

חֵנָּה — 5 hither (2 · 49) 244 II

לָבוּשׁ — 6 clothed with (3 · 16) לבש 527

בַּד — linen (3 · 23) 94 I

מִמַּעַל — above, on top of (2 · 29) 751 II מַעַל 1

מָתַי — when? (2 · 42) 607

פֶּלֶא — wonder (1 · 13) 810

לָבוּשׁ — 7 clothed with (3 · 16) לבש 527

בַּד — linen (3 · 23) 94 I

מִמַּעַל — above, on top of (2 · 29) 751 II מַעַל 1

נַפֵּץ — to dash to pieces (1 · 15 · 21) 658 I

סָתַם — 9 to shut up, keep closed (3 · 10 · 13) 711

חָתַם — to seal, seal up (4 · 23 · 27) 367

הִתְבָּרֵר — 10 to purify oneself (1 · 3 · 15) 140

הִתְלַבֵּן — to be purified (1 · 1 · 5) 526

נִצְרַף — to be refined (1 · 1 · 21) 864

הִרְשִׁיעַ — to act wickedly (3 · 25 · 34) 957

תָּמִיד — 11 daily burnt offering 556 2.c

שִׁקּוּץ — detested thing, abomination (3 · 28) 1055

אֶשֶׁר — 12 blessedness, happiness (1 · 45[?]) 80

חִכָּה — to wait for (1 · 13 · 14) 314

EZRA

Chapter 1

מִכְתָּב 1 writing (1 · 9) 508

רְכוּשׁ 4 property, goods (4 · 28) 940

נְדָבָה freewill offering (3 · 27) 621

רְכוּשׁ 6 property, goods (4 · 28) 940

מִגְדָּנָה choice or excellent thing (1 · 4) 550

הִתְנַדֵּב to offer freewill offerings (3 · 14 · 17) 621

גִּזְבָּר 8 treasurer (1 · 1) 159

אֲגַרְטָל 9 basin, basket (2 · 2) 173

מַחֲלָף perh., knife (1 · 1) 322

כְּפוֹר 10 bowl (3 · 7) 499 I

מִשְׁנֶה second, double (1 · 35) 1041

גּוֹלָה 11 exiles, exile (12 · 42) 163

Chapter 2

גּוֹלָה 1 exiles, exile (12 · 42) 163

מְדִינָה province (1 · 44) 193

שְׁבִי captivity (4 · 46) 985

שֹׁעֵר 42 porter (4 · 37) 1045

נְתִינִים 43 servants (7 · 17) 682

נְתִינִים 58 servants (7 · 17) 682

כְּתָב 62 register, enrollment (2 · 17) 508

הִתְיַחֵשׂ to be enrolled by genealogy (3 · 20 · 20) 405

גָּאַל to be desecrated; i.e., deposed (1 · 4 · 11) 146 II

כְּהֻנָּה priesthood (1 · 13) 464

תִּרְשָׁתָא 63 title of Persian governor (4 · 5) 1077

אוּרִים Urim (1 · 7) 22

תֻּמִּים [dub.] Thummim (1 · 5) 1070 תם 4

רִבּוֹא 64 ten thousand, myriad (2 · 11) 914

מִלְּבַד 65 besides (1 · 33) 94 II בַּד 1.e

פֶּרֶד 66 mule (1 · 14) 825

הִתְנַדֵּב 68 to offer freewill offerings (3 · 14 · 17) 621

מָכוֹן place site (1 · 17) 467

דַּרְכְּמוֹן 69 daric, drachma (1 · 4) 204

רִבּוֹא ten thousand, myriad (2 · 11) 914

מָנֶה mina, maneh (1 · 5) 584

כֻּתֹּנֶת tunic (1 · 29) 509

שֹׁעֵר 70 porter (4 · 37) 1045

נְתִינִים servants (7 · 17) 682

Chapter 3

מְכוֹנָה 3 base, stand (1 · 25) 467

אֵימָה terror, dread (1 · 17) 33

סֻכָּה 4 booth (1 · 31) 697

הִתְנַדֵּב 5 to offer freewill offerings (3 · 14 · 17) 621

נְדָבָה freewill offering (3 · 27) 621

יֻסַּד 6 to be founded (1 · 6 · 41) 413

חֹצֵב 7 hewer, stone mason (1 · 8[?]) 345 חצב

חָרָשׁ craftsman (1 · 38) 360

מַאֲכָל food (1 · 30) 38

מִשְׁתֶּה drink (1 · 45) 1059

רִשְׁיוֹן permission (1 · 1) 957

שְׁאָר 8 rest, remnant, remainder (3 · 26) 984

שְׁבִי captivity (4 · 46) 985

נִצַּח to act as overseer, director (2 · 7 · 8) 663 I

נִצַּח 9 to act as overseer, director (2 · 7 · 8) 663 I

בֹּנֶה 10 builder (1 · 8[?]) 124 בנה Qal 1.e

יִסַּד to found (1 · 10 · 41) 413

חֲצֹצְרָה clarion (1 · 29) 348

מְצִלְתַּיִם cymbals (1 · 13) 853

עָנָה 11 to sing (1 · 13 · 16) 777 IV

הֵרִיעַ to shout (2 · 40 · 44) 929 רוע

תְּרוּעָה shout of joy (4 · 36) 929

הוּסַד to be founded (1 · 3 · 41) 413 יסד

יִסַּד 12 to found, establish (1 · 20 · 41) 413

תְּרוּעָה shout of joy (4 · 36) 929

הִכִּיר 13 to distinguish, understand (1 · 37 · 40) 647 I נכר

תְּרוּעָה	shout of joy (4·36) 929
בְּכִי	weeping (1·30) 113
הֵרִיע	to shout (2·40·44) 929 רוע

Chapter 4

גּוֹלָה	1 exiles, exile (12·42) 163
פֹּה	2 here, hither (1·44) 805
שְׁאָר	3 rest, remnant, remainder (3·26) 984
יַחַד	together, altogether (1·44) 403
רָפָה	4 to let drop (1·4·44) 951
בלה	to trouble (1·1·1) 117; בהל Q to dismay, terrify (1·10·39) 96
סכר	5 to hire (1·1·1) 698 II
יוֹעֵץ	counselor, adviser (3·22) 419 יעץ
הֵפֵר	to frustrate, make ineffectual (2·41·44) 830 I פרר
תְּחִלָּה	6 beginning (1·22) 321
שִׂטְנָה	accusation (1·1) 966 I
שְׁאָר	7 rest, remnant, remainder (3·26) 984
כְּנָת	associate, colleague (1·1) 490
כְּתָב	writing (2·17) 508
נִשְׁתְּוָן	letter (2·2) 677
אֲרָמִית	in Aramaic (2·5) 74
מְתַרְגָּם	translated (1·1·1) 1076 תרגם

First Aramaic Section in Ezra (4:8-6:18) (See pp. 000-000 for Aramaic Appendix containing words occurring over nine times in biblical Aramaic.)

בְּעֵל	8 owner, lord (3·3) 1085
טְעֵם	בְּעֵל ט׳ = commander 1094
סְפַר	secretary, scribe (6·6) 1104
אִגְּרָה	letter (3·3) 1078
כְּנֵמָא	accordingly, thus (5·5) 1097
בְּעֵל	9 owner, lord (3·3) 1085
טְעֵם	גְּעֵל ט׳ = commander, government of-
טְעֵם	גְּעֵל ט׳ = commander 1094

סְפַר	secretary, scribe (6·6) 1104
כְּנָת	associate (7·7) 1097
דִּינָיֵא	judges (1·1) 1088 דִּין
אֲפַרְסַתְכָיֵא	Persian, lesser governors, generals (1·1) 1082
אֲפַרְסֵיֵא	secretaries (1·1) 1082
דְּהוּא	that is (but see BDB) 1087
אֻמָּה	10 nation (1·8) 1081
הַגְלִי	to take into exile (2·2·9) 1086 גלא
יַקִּיר	honorable (1·2) 1096
הוֹתֵב	to cause to dwell (1·1·5) 1096 יתב
קִרְיָה	city, town (9·9) 1111
כְּעֶנֶת	now (4·4) 1107
פַּרְשֶׁגֶן	11 copy (4·4) 1109
אִגְּרָה	letter (3·3) 1078
עֲבַד	slave, servant (2·7) 1105
כְּעֶנֶת	now (4·4) 1107
סְלִק	12 to come up (1·5·8) 1104
לְוָת	beside, to, at (1·1) 1099
קִרְיָה	city, town (9·9) 1111
מָרָד	rebellious (2·2) 1101
בְּאִישׁ	bad (1·1) 1084
שׁוּר	wall (3·3) 1114
שַׁכְלֵל	to complete, finish (5·5·7) 1097 כלל
אֹשׁ	foundation (3·3) 1083
הַחִיט	to repair (1·1·1) 1092 חוט
קִרְיָה	13 city, town (9·9) 1111
שׁוּר	wall (3·3) 1114
יִשְׁתַּכְלְלוּן	they are completed (2·2·7) 1097 כלל
מִנְדָּה	tribute (4·4) 1101
בְּלוֹ	tribute, tax (3·3) 1084
הֲלָךְ	toll (3·3) 1090
אַפְּתֹם	treasuries (1·1) 1082
הנזק	to injure (2·2·3) 1102
מְלַח	14 salt (3·3) 1100
מלח	to eat [salt] (1·1·1) 1100
עַרְוָה	dishonor (1·1) 1107

אֲרִיךְ   fitting, proper (1 · 1) 1082

עַל־דְּנָה   therefore 1088 דְּנָה d

בקר 15   to inquire, seek (4 · 4 · 5) 1085

סְפַר   book (4 · 5) 1105

דָּכְרָן   memorandum, record (2 · 2) 1088

אַב   father (7 · 9) 1078

תִּנְדַּע   *Peal* impf. 2nd. m. sing. of ידע, to know 1095

קִרְיָה   city, town (9 · 9) 1111

מָרָד   rebellious (2 · 2) 1101

הנזק   to injure (2 · 2 · 3) 1102

אֶשְׁתַּדּוּר   revolt (2 · 2) 1114

עָלַם   here = antiquity 1106

עַל־דְּנָה   therefore 1088 דְּנָה d

החרב   to be laid waste (1 · 1 · 1) 1093

אֲנַחְנָה 16   we (2 · 4) 1081

קִרְיָה   city, town (9 · 9) 1111

שׁוּר   wall (3 · 3) 1114

יִשְׁתַּכְלְלוּן   they are completed (2 · 2 · 7) 1097 כלל

לָקֳבֵל   in view of, by reason of (2 · 7) 1110

חֲלָק   possession, portion (1 · 3) 1093

פִּתְגָם 17   command, word (4 · 6) 1109

בְּעֵל   owner, lord (3 · 3) 1085

טְעֵם   בְּעֵל ט׳ = commander 1094

סָפַר   secretary, scribe (6 · 6) 1104

כְּנָת   associate (7 · 7) 1097

יְתֵב   to dwell (1 · 4 · 5) 1096

שְׁלָם   welfare, prosperity (2 · 4) 1116

כְּעֶת   now (4 · 4) 1107 כְּעֶנֶת

נִשְׁתְּוָן 18   letter (3 · 3) 1103

מְפָרַשׁ   pass. ptc. = made distinct; i.e., translated (1 · 1 · 1) 1109 פרשׁ

בקר 19   to inquire, seek (4 · 4 · 5) 1085

קִרְיָה   city, town (9 · 9) 1111

עָלַם   here = antiquity 1106

מִתְנַשְּׂאָה   to make a rising, an insurrection (1 · 1 · 3) 1103

מְרַד   rebellion (1 · 1) 1101

אֶשְׁתַּדּוּר   revolt (2 · 2) 1114

תַּקִּיף 20   strong, mighty (1 · 5) 1118

מִדָּה   tribute (4 · 4) 1101 מִנְדָּה

בְּלוֹ   tribute, tax (3 · 3) 1084

הֲלָךְ   toll (3 · 3) 1090

התיהב   here = to be paid 1095

בטל 21   to make to cease, stop (4 · 4 · 6) 1084

קִרְיָה   city, town (9 · 9) 1111

זהר 22   to warn (1 · 1 · 1) 1091

שָׁלוּ   neglect, error (2 · 4) 1115

עַל־דְּנָה   on account of this 1088 דְּנָה d

לְמָה   why? 1099 מָה 3.b

שׂגא   to grow great (1 · 3 · 3) 1113

חֲבָל   hurt, injury (1 · 3) 1092

הַנְזָקַת   damage, injury (1 · 1) 1102 נזק

פַּרְשֶׁגֶן 23   copy (4 · 4) 1109

נִשְׁתְּוָן   letter (3 · 3) 1103

סָפַר   secretary, scribe (6 · 6) 1104

כְּנָת   associate (7 · 7) 1097

אֲזַל   to go, go off (3 · 7 · 7) 1079

בְּהִילוּ   haste (1 · 1) 1084

בטל   to make to cease, stop (4 · 4 · 6) 1084

אֶדְרָע   force (1 · 1) 1089

בטל 24   to cease (2 · 2 · 6) 1084

עֲבִידָה   work (4 · 6) 1105

שְׁנָה   year (5 · 7) 1116 I

Chapter 5

הִתְנַבִּי 1   to prophesy (1 · 1 · 1) 1127

נְבִיא   prophet (4 · 4) 1101

שׁרא 2   to begin (1 · 2 · 6) 1117

נְבִיא   prophet (4 · 4) 1101

סעד   to support, sustain (1 · 1 · 1) 1104

כְּנָת 3   associate (7 · 7) 1097

אֻשַּׁרְנָא   [dub.] wall, sanctuary (2 · 2) 1083

שׁכלל   to complete, finish (5 · 5 · 7) 1097 כלל

כְּנֵמָא 4   as follows, thus (5 · 5) 1097

אִנּוּן   they, those (1 · 4) 1081

בִּנְיָן   building (1 · 1) 1084

627

עֵיִן 5 eye (1 · 5) 1105

שָׂב elder (5 · 5) 1114   שׂיב

בטל to make to cease, stop (4 · 4 · 6) 1084

טְעֵם here = report 1094

יְהָךְ *Peal* impf. of הלך, to go (4 · 4 · 7) 1090

הֲתִיב to return (3 · 5 · 8) 1117   תוב

נִשְׁתְּוָן letter (3 · 3) 1103

עַל־דְּנָה on account of this 1088   דְּנָה d

פַּרְשֶׁגֶן 6 copy (4 · 4) 1109

אִגְּרָה letter (3 · 3) 1078

כְּנָת associate (7 · 7) 1097

אֲפַרְסְכָיֵא Persians, generals, lesser rulers (2 · 2) 1082

פִּתְגָם 7 command, word (4 · 6) 1109

כְּדְנָה like this, thus (1 · 4) 1088   דְּנָה c

שְׁלָם welfare, prosperity (2 · 4) 1116

אֲזַל 8 to go, go off (3 · 7 · 7) 1079

גְּלָל rolling (2 · 2) 1086

אָע timber, wood (3 · 5) 1082

כְּתַל wall (1 · 2) 1098

עֲבִידָה work (4 · 6) 1105

אָסְפַּרְנָא thoroughly (7 · 7) 1082

מַצְלַח ptc., having success (2 · 4 · 4) 1109   צלח

שָׂב 9 elder (5 · 5) 1114   שׂיב

כְּנֵמָא as follows, thus (5 · 5) 1097

אֻשַּׁרְנָא [dub.] wall, sanctuary (2 · 2) 1083

שׁכלל to complete, finish (5 · 5 · 7) 1097   כלל

אַף 10 also (3 · 4) 1082

כְּנֵמָא 11 as follows, thus (5 · 5) 1097

פִּתְגָם command, word (4 · 6) 1109

הֲתִיב to return (3 · 5 · 8) 1117   תוב

לְמֵמַר *Peal* inf. = saying 1081   אֲמַר

אֲנַחְנָא we (2 · 4) 1081

עֲבַד slave, servant (2 · 7) 1105

קַדְמָה former time (1 · 2) 1110

שְׁנָה year (5 · 7) 1116   I

שׁכלל to complete, finish (5 · 5 · 7) 1097   כלל

לָהֵן 12 however, but (1 · 7) 1099   II

הַרְגִז to enrage (1 · 1 · 1) 1112

אַב father (7 · 9) 1078

סְתַר to destroy (1 · 1 · 1) 1104   II

הַגְלִי to take into exile (2 · 2 · 9) 1086

בְּרַם 13 only, nevertheless (1 · 5) 1085

שְׁנָה year (5 · 7) 1116   I

אַף 14 also (3 · 4) 1082

מָאן vessel, utensil (4 · 7) 1099

הֵיבֵל to bear along, carry (3 · 3 · 3) 1094

אֵל 15 these (1 · 1) 1080

מָאן vessel, utensil (4 · 7) 1099

נְשָׂא to take, lift (1 · 2 · 3) 1103

אֲזַל to go, go off (3 · 7 · 7) 1079

אֲחֵת *Haph.* imv. of נחת, to deposit (3 · 3 · 6) 1102

אֲתַר place (4 · 5) 1083

יְהַב 16 here = to place, lay 1095

אֻשׁ foundation (3 · 3) 1083

מִן־אֱדַיִן from that time 1078   אֱדַיִן

שְׁלַם to be complete (1 · 1 · 3) 1115

טָב 17 good (1 · 2) 1094

הִתְבַּקַּר to be searched (1 · 1 · 5) 1085

גְּנַז treasure (3 · 3) 1086

תַּמָּה there (4 · 4) 1118

רְעוּ good pleasure, will (2 · 2) 1113

עַל־דְּנָה on account of this 1088   דְּנָה d

Chapter 6

בְּקַר 1 to inquire, seek (4 · 4 · 5) 1085

סְפַר book (4 · 5) 1104

גְּנַז treasure (3 · 3) 1086

מְהַחֲתִין pass. ptc. = deposited (3 · 3 · 6) 1102   נחת

תַּמָּה there (4 · 4) 1118

בִּירְתָא 2 castle (1 · 1) 1084

מְגִלָּה roll, scroll (1 · 1) 1086

דִּכְרוֹן memorandum, record (1 · 1) 1088

שְׁנָה 3 year (5 · 7) 1116   I

אֲתַר	place (4·8) 1083	בְּטֵל	to make to cease, stop (4·4·6) 1084
דבח	to sacrifice (1·1·1) 1087	חַשְׁחָה 9	thing needed (1·1) 1093
דְּבַח	sacrifice (1·1) 1087	תּוֹר	bullock (3·7) 1117
אֹשׁ	foundation (3·3) 1083	דְּכַר	ram (3·3) 1088
מְסוֹבְלִין	pass. ptc. = to be raised [dub.] (1·1·1) 1103 סבל	אִמַּר	lamb (3·3) 1081
רוּם	height (1·5) 1112	עֲלָת	burnt offering (1·1) 1106
אַמָּה	cubit (2·4) 1081	חִנְטָה	wheat (2·2) 1093
פְּתָי	breadth (1·2) 1109	מְלַח	salt (3·3) 1100
נִדְבָּךְ 4	row, layer, course (2·2) 1102	חֲמַר	wine (2·6) 1093
גְּלָל	rolling (2·2) 1086	מְשַׁח	oil (2·2) 1101
אָע	timber, wood (3·5) 1082	מֵאמַר	word (1·2) 1081
חֲדַת	new (1·1) 1092	כָּהֵן	priest (8·8) 1096
נִפְקָה	outlay, expense (2·2) 1103	דִּי־לָא	without 1087 דִּי 1.a
הִתְיְהִב	here = to be paid 1095	שָׁלוּ	neglect, error (2·4) 1115
אַף 5	also (3·4) 1082	נִיחוֹחַ 10	soothing, tranquilizing (1·2) 1102
מָאן	vessel, utensil (4·7) 1099	מְצַלַּיִן	praying (1·2·2) 1109 צלא
הֵיבֵל	to bear along, carry (3·3·3) 1094	הַשְׁנָא 11	here = to frustrate 1116
הֲתֵיב	to restore (3·5·8) 1117 תוב	פִּתְגָם	command, word (4·6) 1109
יְהָךְ	Peal impf. of הלך to go (4·4·7) 1090	הִתְנְטַח	to be pulled away (1·1·1) 1103
אֲתַר	place (4·8) 1083	אָע	beam, wood (3·5) 1082
תַּחֵת	impf. 2nd m. sing of נחת to deposit (3·3·6) 1102	זְקַף	to raise, lift up (1·1·1) 1091
		הִתְמְחָא	to be impaled (1·1·4) 1099
כְּנָת 6	associate (7·7) 1097	נְוָלוּ	refuse heap (1·3) 1102
אֲפַרְסְכָיֵא	Persians, generals, lesser rulers (2·2) 1082	עַל־דְּנָה	on account of this 1088 דְּנָה d
רְחִיק	far (1·1) 1113	שְׂכַן 12	to cause to swell (1·1·2) 1115
תַּמָּה	there (4·4) 1118	תַּמָּה	there (4·4) 1118
שְׁבַק 7	to leave, let alone (1·4·5) 1114	מְגַר	to overthrow (1·1·1) 1099
עֲבִידָה	work (4·6) 1105	חֲבַל	to destroy, hurt (1·3·6) 1091
שָׂב	elder (5·5) 1114 שיב	אָסְפַּרְנָא	thoroughly (7·7) 1082
אֲתַר	place (4·5) 1083	כְּנָת 13	associate (7·7) 1097
מָא 8	= מָה, what? 1099	לָקֳבֵל	with דִּי = because that (2·7) 1110
שָׂב	elder (5·5) 1114 שיב	כְּנֵמָא	as follows, thus (5·5) 1097
נִכְסִין	riches, property (2·2) 1103	אָסְפַּרְנָא	thoroughly (7·7) 1082
מִדָּה	tribute (4·4) 1101 מנדה	שָׂב 14	elder (5·5) 1114 שיב
אָסְפַּרְנָא	thoroughly (7·7) 1082	מַצְלְחִין	being successful (2·4·4) 1109 צלח
נִפְקָה	outlay, expense (2·2) 1103	נְבוּאָה	prophesying (1·1) 1102
חֲתִיהֵב	here = to be paid 1095	נְבִיא	prophet (4·4) 1101
		שַׁכְלִל	to complete, finish (5·5·7) 1097 כלל

שֵׁיצִיא	15	to finish (1 · 1 · 1) 1115
יְרַח		month (1 · 2) 1096
שְׁנָה		year (5 · 7) 1116 I
כָּהֵן	16	priest (8 · 8) 1096
גָּלוּ		exile (1 · 4) 1086
חֲנֻכָּה		dedication (2 · 4) 1093
חֶדְוָה		joy (1 · 1) 1092
חֲנֻכָּה	17	dedication (2 · 4) 1093
תּוֹר		bullock (3 · 7) 1117
דְּכַר		ram (3 · 3) 1088
אִמַּר		lamb (3 · 3) 1081
צְפִיר		male goat (1 · 1) 1110
עֵז		goat (1 · 1) 1107
חַטָּיָה		sin-offering (1 · 1) 1092
מִנְיָן		number (1 · 1) 1101
שֵׁבֶט		tribe (1 · 1) 1114
כָּהֵן	18	priest (8 · 8) 1096
פְּלֻגָּה		division (1 · 1) 1108
מַחְלְקָה		class, division (1 · 1) 1093
עֲבִידָה		ritual, service (4 · 6) 1105
כְּתָב		here = written requirement 1098
סְפַר		book (4 · 5) 1104

End of First Aramaic Section

גּוֹלָה	19	exiles, exile (12 · 42) 163
פֶּסַח		passover (2 · 49) 820
פֶּסַח	20	passover (2 · 49) 820
גּוֹלָה		exiles, exile (12 · 42) 163
גּוֹלָה	21	exiles, exile (12 · 42) 163
נבדל		to separate oneself (5 · 10 · 42) 95
טֻמְאָה		uncleanness (2 · 37) 380

Chapter 7

מָהִיר	6	skilled, quick, ready (1 · 4) 555
בַּקָּשָׁה		request, entreaty (1 · 8) 135
שֹׁעֵר	7	porter (4 · 37) 1045
נְתִינִים		servants (7 · 17) 682

יְסַד	9	beginning, foundation (1 · 1) 414
מַעֲלָה		ascent (1 · 47) 752 II 4
פַּרְשֶׁגֶן	11	copy (4 · 4) 1109
נִשְׁתְּוָן		letter (2 · 2) 677

Second Aramaic Section (7:12-26) (See pp. 271-275 for Aramaic Appendix containing words occurring over nine times in biblical Aramaic.)

כָּהֵן	12	priest (8 · 8) 1096
סָפַר		secretary, scribe (6 · 6) 1104
גְּמִיר		pass. ptc. = perfect (1 · 1 · 1) 1086 גמר
כְּעֶנֶת		now (4 · 4) 1107
התנדב	13	to volunteer (3 · 3 · 3) 1102
כָּהֵן		priest (8 · 8) 1096
מְהָךְ		Peal inf. of הלך to go (4 · 4 · 7) 1090
יְהָךְ		Peal impf. of הלך to go (4 · 4 · 7) 1090
יָעֵט	14	counselor (2 · 2) 1096
בקר		to inquire, seek (4 · 4 · 5) 1085
הֵיבֵל	15	to bear along, carry (3 · 3 · 3) 1094 יבל
יָעֵט		counselor (2 · 2) 1096
התנדב		to give, offer freely (3 · 3 · 3) 1102
מִשְׁכַּן		abode (1 · 1) 1115
הִתְנַדָּבוּת	16	freewill gift (1 · 1[?]) 1102 נדב
כָּהֵן		priest (8 · 8) 1096
התנדב		to offer freely, volunteer (3 · 3 · 3) 1102
אָסְפַּרְנָא	17	thoroughly (7 · 7) 1082
קְנָא		to buy, acquire (1 · 1 · 1) 1111
תּוֹר		bullock (3 · 7) 1117
דְּכַר		ram (3 · 3) 1088
אִמַּר		lamb (3 · 3) 1081

אִמַּר lamb (3 · 3) 1081

מִנְחָה meal offerings (1 · 2) 1101

נְסַךְ drink offering (1 · 1) 1103

מַדְבַּח altar (1 · 1) 1087

אָח 18 brother (1 · 1) 1079

יטב to be pleasing (1 · 1 · 1) 1095

רְעוּ good pleasure, will (2 · 2) 1113

מָאן 19 vessel, utensil (4 · 7) 1099

פָּלְחָן service, worship (1 · 1) 1108

השלם to render in full (1 · 2 · 3) 1115

חַשְׁחוּ 20 (coll.) things needed, requirement (1 · 1) 1093

יִפֶּל־לָךְ it shall fall to you (i.e., you shall need) 1103 נְפַל

גְּנַז treasure (3 · 3) 1086

גִּזְבָּר 21 treasurer (1 · 1) 1086

כָּהֵן priest (8 · 8) 1096

סָפַר secretary, scribe (6 · 6) 1104

אָסְפַּרְנָא thoroughly (7 · 7) 1082

כְּכַר 22 talent (1 · 1) 1098

חִנְטָה wheat (2 · 2) 1093 חִנְטָה

כּוֹר kor, a measure of wheat (1 · 1) 1096

חֲמַר wine (2 · 6) 1093

בַּת bath, a liquid measure (2 · 2) 1085

מְשַׁח oil (2 · 2) 1101

מְלַח salt (3 · 3) 1100

דִּי לָא without 1087 דִּי 1.a

כְּתָב here = written requirement 1098

אַדְרַזְדָּא 23 correctly, exactly (1 · 1) 1079

דִּי לְמָה for why? 1099 מָה 3.b

קְצַף wrath (1 · 1) 1111

כָּהֵן 24 priest (8 · 8) 1096

זַמָּר singer (1 · 1) 1091

תָּרָע porter, doorkeeper (1 · 1) 1118

נְתִינִין servants (1 · 1) 1103

פלח Peal ptc. pl. = servants 1108

מִנְדָּה tribute (4 · 4) 1101

בְּלוֹ tribute, tax (3 · 3) 1084

הֲלָךְ toll (3 · 3) 1090

שַׁלִּיט here = it is authorized 1115

מנה 25 to appoint (1 · 4 · 5) 1101

שָׁפֵט judge (1 · 1) 1117 שפט

דַּיָּן judge (1 · 1) 1088

דין to judge (1 · 1 · 1) 1088

אָסְפַּרְנָא 26 thoroughly (7 · 7) 1082

דִּין judgment (1 · 5) 1088

מוֹת death (1 · 1) 1099

שְׁרֹשׁוּ uprooting; fig., banishment (1 · 1) 1117

עֲנָשׁ confiscation (1 · 1) 1107

נִכְסִין riches, property (2 · 2) 1103 נְכַס

אֱסוּר band, bond (1 · 3) 1082

(End of Second Aramaic Section)

פאר 27 to beautify, glorify (1 · 6 · 13) 802 I

יוֹעֵץ 28 counselor, adviser (3 · 22) 419 יָעַץ

Chapter 8

התיחש 1 to be enrolled by genealogy (3 · 20 · 20) 405

התיחש 3 to be enrolled by genealogy (3 · 20 · 20) 405

נְתִינִים 17 servants (7 · 17) 682

מְשָׁרֵת minister (1 · 20) 1058 שרת

שֵׂכֶל 18 insight, understanding (1 · 16) 968

נְתִינִים 20 servants (7 · 17) 682

נקב to be designated (1 · 6 · 19[?]) 666 I

צוֹם 21 fast, fasting (1 · 25) 847

טַף [coll.] children, little ones (1 · 42) 381

רְכוּשׁ property, goods (4 · 28) 940

צום 23 to fast (1 · 20 · 20) 847

נֵעָתֵר to be entreated, supplicated (1 · 8 · 20) 801 I

הִבְדִּיל 24 to separate, set apart (1 · 32 · 42) 95

שָׁקַל 25 to weigh (3 · 19 · 22) 1053

הַהֵרִימוּ art. as relative w. Hiph. of רום 206 ה' 3

יוֹעֵץ counselor, advisor (3 · 22) 419 יָעַץ

שָׁקַל 26 to weigh (3 · 19 · 22) 1053

כְּפוֹר 27 bowl (3 · 7) 499 I

אֲדַרְכּוֹן drachma, daric (1 · 2) 204 דַּרְכְּמוֹן

מְצֻהָב gleaming ware [ptc. of צהב] (1 · 1 · 1) 843

חֲמוּדָה precious, choice things (1 · 9) 326

נְדָבָה 28 freewill offering (3 · 27) 621

שָׁקַד 29 to keep a guard over, watch (1 · 12 · 17) 1052

שָׁקַל to weigh (3 · 19 · 22) 1053

לִשְׁכָּה room, chamber (2 · 47) 545

קִבֵּל 30 to take (1 · 11 · 13) 867

מִשְׁקָל weight (3 · 49) 1054

אוֹרֵב 31 ambush (1 · 18) 70 אָרַב

נִשְׁקַל 33 to be weighed (1 · 3 · 22) 1053

מִשְׁקָל 34 weight (3 · 49) 1054

שְׁבִי 35 captivity (4 · 46) 985

גּוֹלָה exiles, exile (12 · 42) 163

צָפִיר male goat (1 · 6) 862

דָּת 36 decree, edict (1 · 22) 206

אֲחַשְׁדַּרְפְּנִים satraps (1 · 4) 31

פֶּחָה governor (1 · 28) 808

Chapter 9

נִבְדַּל 1 to separate oneself (5 · 10 · 42) 95

הִתְעָרֵב 2 to have fellowship, share (1 · 5 · 5 [?]) 786 II

סָגָן official (1 · 17) 688

מַעַל unfaithful act (3 · 29) 591 I

מְעִיל 3 robe (2 · 28) 591

מָרַט to make bare (1 · 7 · 14) 598

שֵׂעָר hair (1 · 28) 972

זָקָן beard (1 · 19) 278

חָרֵד 4 trembling (2 · 6) 353

מַעַל unfaithful act (3 · 29) 591 I

גּוֹלָה exiles, exile (12 · 42) 163

תַּעֲנִית 5 humiliation (1 · 1) 777

מְעִיל robe (2 · 28) 591

כָּרַע to bow (1 · 30 · 36) 502

בֶּרֶךְ knee (1 · 25) 139

נכלם 6 to be humiliated, ashamed (1 · 26 · 38) 483

לְמַעְלָה upwards (1 · 34) 751 II מַעַל 2.c

אַשְׁמָה wrongdoing, guiltiness (6 · 19) 80

אַשְׁמָה 7 wrongdoing, guiltiness (6 · 19) 80

שְׁבִי captivity (4 · 46) 985

בִּזָּה spoil, booty (1 · 10) 103

רֶגַע 8 moment (1 · 22) 921

תְּחִנָּה favor (1 · 25) 337 I

פְּלֵיטָה escaped remnant (4 · 28) 812

יָתֵד peg, tent pin (1 · 24) 450

הֵאִיר to lighten (1 · 34 · 40) 21 אור

מִחְיָה reviving (2 · 8) 313

עַבְדוּת servitude, bondage (2 · 3) 715

עַבְדוּת 9 servitude, bondage (2 · 3) 715

מִחְיָה reviving (2 · 8) 313

חָרְבָּה waste, ruin (1 · 42) 352

גָּדֵר wall, fence (1 · 13) 154

נִדָּה 11 impurity, impure thing (2 · 30) 622

טֻמְאָה uncleaness (2 · 37) 380

טוֹב 12 good things (1 · 32) 375

אַשְׁמָה 13 wrongdoing, guiltiness (6 · 19) 80

חָשַׂךְ to withhold; חֹ׳ לְמַטָּה מֵעֲוֹנֵנוּ = you have kept part of our iniquity (1 · 26 · 28) 362

לְמַטָּה downward, below (1 · 10) 641 מַטָּה

פְּלֵיטָה escaped remnant (4 · 28) 812

הֵפֵר 14 to break, violate (2 · 41 · 44) 830 I פרר

הִתְחַתֵּן to form a marriage alliance with (1 · 11 · 11) 368 II

אָנַף to be angry (1 · 8 · 14) 60

לְאֵין so that there was no (1 · 9) 34 II אין 6.c

פְּלֵיטָה escaped remnant (4 · 28) 812

פְּלֵיטָה 15 escaped remnant (4 · 28) 812

אַשְׁמָה wrongdoing, guiltiness (6 · 19) 80

Chapter 10

בֶּכֶה 1 weeping (1 · 1) 113

מָעַל 2 to act unfaithfully, treacherously (2 · 35 · 35) 591

נָכְרִי foreign (7 · 45) 648

מִקְוֶה hope (1 · 5) 876 I

חָרֵד 3 trembling (2 · 6) 353

לִשְׁכָּה 6 room, chamber (2 · 47) 545

הִתְאַבֵּל to mourn (1 · 19 · 38) 5 I

מַעַל unfaithful act (3 · 29) 591 I

גּוֹלָה exiles, exile (12 · 42) 163

גּוֹלָה 7 exiles, exile (12 · 42) 163

הֶחֳרִים 8 to be devoted, forfeited (1 · 3 · 49) 355

רְכוּשׁ property, goods (4 · 28) 940

נבדל to separate oneself (5 · 10 · 42) 95

גּוֹלָה exiles, exile (12 · 42) 163

רְחוֹב 9 broad open place (1 · 43) 932 I

מַרְגִּיד ptc. = trembling (1 · 2 · 3) 944 רגז

גֶּשֶׁם rain, shower (2 · 35) 177 II

מָעַל 10 to act unfaithfully, treacherously (2 · 35 · 35) 591

נָכְרִי foreign (7 · 45) 648

אַשְׁמָה wrongdoing, guiltiness (6 · 19) 80

תּוֹדָה 11 thanksgiving, praise (1 · 32) 392

נבדל to separate oneself (5 · 10 · 42) 95

נָכְרִי foreign (7 · 45) 648

אֲבָל 13 howbeit, but (1 · 11) 6

גֶּשֶׁם rain, shower (2 · 35) 177 II

פֶּשַׁע to transgress (1 · 40 · 41) 833

נָכְרִי 14 foreign (7 · 45) 648

זמן to be fixed, appointed (1 · 3 · 3) 273

חָרוֹן ח׳ אַף = burning anger, fierce anger (1 · 41) 354

גּוֹלָה 16 exiles, exile (12 · 42) 163

נבדל to be set apart, separate oneself (5 · 10 · 42) 95

נָכְרִי 17 foreign (7 · 45) 648

נָכְרִי 18 foreign (7 · 45) 648

אַשְׁמָה 19 wrongdoing, guiltiness (6 · 19) 80

אָשֵׁם guilty; or perh. = offense, trespass offering (1 · 3) 79

שֹׁעֵר 24 porter (4 · 37) 1045

נָכְרִי 44 foreign (7 · 45) 648

633

NEHEMIAH

Chapter 1

בִּירָה	1 citadel, castle (3 · 18) 108
פְּלֵיטָה	2 escaped remnant (1 · 28) 812
שְׁבִי	captivity (5 · 46) 985
שְׁבִי	3 captivity (5 · 46) 985
מְדִינָה	province (3 · 44) 193
מְפֹרָצֶת	*Pual* ptc. = broken down (1 · 1 · 49) 829 I פרץ
נִצְּתָה	to be burned (2 · 6 · 27) 428 יצת
הִתְאַבֵּל	4 to mourn (2 · 19 · 38) 5 I
צוּם	to fast (1 · 20 · 20) 847
אָנָּא	5 ah, now! (2 · 7) 58
נוֹרָא	awe-inspiring, awful (3 · 44) 431 יָרֵא *Niph.*
אֹהֵב	loving, friend (1 · 36) 12 אָהֵב
קַשָּׁב	6 attentive (2 · 2) 904
חבל	7 to act corruptly (1 · 2 · 10) 287 II
מָעַל	8 to act unfaithfully, treacherously (2 · 35 · 35) 591
נִדָּח	9 outcasts, banished ones (1 · 11[?]) 623 *Niph.* 2
אָנָּא	11 ah, now! (2 · 7) 58
קַשָּׁב	attentive (2 · 2) 904
חָפֵץ	delighting in, having pleasure in (1 · 12) 343
רַחֲמִים	compassion (5 · 38) 933
מַשְׁקֶה	cup-bearer (1 · 19[?]) 1052 I

Chapter 2

רַע	2 sadness (1 · 19) 947
חָרֵב	3 waste, desolate (2 · 10) 351 II
שֵׁגָל	6 consort (1 · 2) 993
מָתַי	when? (2 · 42) 607
מַהֲלָךְ	journey (1 · 5) 237
זְמָן	time, appointed time (1 · 4) 273
אִגֶּרֶת	7 letter (6 · 10) 8

פֶּחָה	governor (8 · 28) 808
אִגֶּרֶת	8 letter (6 · 10) 8
פַּרְדֵּס	preserve, park (1 · 3) 825
קרה	to lay beams (3 · 5 · 27[?]) 900
בִּירָה	citadel, castle (3 · 18) 108
פֶּחָה	9 governor (8 · 28) 808
אִגֶּרֶת	letter (6 · 10) 8
גַּיְא	13 valley (5 · 49) 161
תַּנִּין	dragon (1 · 15) 1072
אַשְׁפֹּת	ash heap, dunghill (4 · 7) 1046
שׁבר	to examine, inspect (2 · 2 · 8[?]) 960 I
פָּרַץ	to break through, break down (3 · 46 · 49) 829 I
בְּרֵכָה	14 pool, pond (3 · 17) 140
שׁבר	15 to examine, inspect (2 · 2 · 8[?]) 960 I
גַּיְא	valley (5 · 49) 161
סָגָן	16 official (9 · 17) 688
אָנָה	where? (1 · 39) 33 אָן
חֹר	noble (7 · 13) 359 II
חָרֵב	17 waste, desolate (2 · 10) 351 II
נִצְּתָה	to be burned (2 · 6 · 27) 428 יצת
הלעיג	19 to mock, deride (2 · 5 · 18) 541
בָּזָה	to despise (1 · 31 · 42) 102
מרד	to rebel, revolt (3 · 25 · 25) 597
זִכָּרוֹן	20 memorial, remembrance (1 · 24) 272

Chapter 3

מִגְדָּל	1 tower (9 · 49) 153
דָּג	3 fish (3 · 19) 185
קרה	to lay beams (3 · 5 · 27[?]) 900
מַנְעוּל	bolt (5 · 6) 653
בְּרִיחַ	bar (5 · 41) 138
אַדִּיר	5 majestic (2 · 27) 12
צַוָּאר	neck, back of neck (3 · 41) 848
יָשָׁן	6 old (2 · 8) 445
קרה	to lay beams (3 · 5 · 27[?]) 900
מַנְעוּל	bolt (5 · 6) 653

634

בְּרִיחַ	bar (5 · 41) 138	מַטָּרָה	guard, ward, prison (2 · 16) 643
פֶּחָה	7 governor (8 · 28) 808	נְתִינִים	26 servants (9 · 17) 682
צֹרֵף	8 goldsmith (2 · 10[?]) 864 צרף	עֹפֶל	mound, hill (3 · 8) 779 I
רַקָּח	perfumer (1 · 2) 955	מִגְדָּל	tower (9 · 49) 153
עזב	to restore, repair (2 · 2 · 2) 738 II	מִנֶּגֶד	27 opposite to (3 · 26) 617 נגד 2.c
רָחָב	wide, broad (5 · 21) 932 I	מִגְדָּל	tower (9 · 49) 153
פֶּלֶךְ	9 district (8 · 10) 813	עֹפֶל	mound, hill (3 · 8) 779 I
מִגְדָּל	11 tower (9 · 49) 153	לְנֶגֶד	28 in front of, before (5 · 32) 617 נגד 2.b
תַּנּוּר	fire pot (2 · 15) 1072	נִשְׁכָּה	30 chamber (3 · 3) 675
פֶּלֶךְ	12 district (8 · 10) 813	צֹרְפִי	31 [coll.] goldsmiths (1 · 1) 864
גַּיְא	13 valley (5 · 49) 161	נְתִינִים	servants (9 · 17) 682
מַנְעוּל	bolt (5 · 6) 653	רֹכֵל	trader (3 · 17) 940
בְּרִיחַ	bar (5 · 41) 138	מִפְקָד	muster, appointment (1 · 5) 824
אַשְׁפֹּת	ash heap, dunghill (4 · 7) 1046	עֲלִיָּה	roof chamber (2 · 20) 751
אַשְׁפֹּת	14 ash heap, dunghill (4 · 7) 1046	פִּנָּה	corner (3 · 30) 819
פֶּלֶךְ	district (8 · 10) 813	עֲלִיָּה	32 roof chamber (2 · 20) 751
מַנְעוּל	bolt (5 · 6) 653	פִּנָּה	corner (3 · 30) 819
בְּרִיחַ	bar (5 · 41) 138	צֹרֵף	goldsmith (2 · 10[?]) 864
פֶּלֶךְ	15 district (8 · 10) 813	רֹכֵל	trader (3 · 17) 940
טלל	to cover over (1 · 1 · 1) 378 II	הלעיג	33 to mock, deride (2 · 5 · 18) 541
מַנְעוּל	bolt (5 · 6) 653	אֻמְלָל	34 feeble (1 · 1) 51
בְּרִיחַ	bar (5 · 41) 138	עזב	to restore, repair 738 II (736 I.1.h)
בְּרֵכָה	pool, pond (3 · 17) 140	עֲרֵמָה	heap (2 · 10) 790
גַּן	garden (1 · 41) 171	שׁוּעָל	35 fox (1 · 7) 1043 I
מַעֲלָה	step, stair (2 · 47) 752 II.1	פָּרַץ	to break through, break down
פֶּלֶךְ	16 district (8 · 10) 813		(3 · 46 · 49) 829 I
בְּרֵכָה	pool, pond (3 · 17) 140	בּוּזָה	36 contempt (1 · 1) 100
פֶּלֶךְ	17 district (8 · 10) 813	בִּזָּה	spoil, booty (1 · 10) 103
פֶּלֶךְ	18 district (8 · 10) 813	שִׁבְיָה	captivity (1 · 9) 986
מִנֶּגֶד	19 opposite to (3 · 26) 617 נגד 2.c	נמחה	37 to be blotted out (1 · 9 · 34) 562 I
נֶשֶׁק	armory (1 · 10) 676	לְנֶגֶד	in the sight, presence, of (5 · 32)
מִקְצֹעַ	buttress (4 · 12) 893		617 נגד 2.b
החרה	20 to burn with zeal 354	נקשר	38 to be joined together (1 · 2 · 44) 905
מִקְצֹעַ	buttress (4 · 12) 893		
תַּכְלִית	21 end (1 · 5) 479		
מִקְצֹעַ	24 buttress (4 · 12) 893		**Chapter 4**
פִּנָּה	corner (3 · 30) 819	אֲרוּכָה	1 healing (1 · 6) 74
מִנֶּגֶד	25 opposite to (3 · 26) 617 נגד 2.c	פָּרַץ	to break through, break down
מִקְצֹעַ	buttress (4 · 12) 893		(3 · 46 · 49) 829 I
מִגְדָּל	tower (9 · 49) 153	נסתם	to be stopped up (1 · 1 · 13) 711

קָשַׁר 2 to league together, conspire
(1 · 35 · 44) 905

תּוֹעָה confusion, disturbance (1 · 2) 1073

מִשְׁמָר 3 guard (7 · 20) 1038

סַבָּל 4 burden-bearer (1 · 5) 688

תַּחְתִּי 7 below, lower (1 · 19) 1066

צְחִיחַ glaring or bare places (1 · 5) 850

רֹמַח spear, lance (3 · 15) 942

חֹר 8 noble (7 · 13) 359 II

סָגָן official (9 · 17) 688

נוֹרָא ptc. = awe-inspiring, awful (3 · 44)
431 יָרֵא Niph.

הֵפֵר 9 to frustrate, make ineffectual
(1 · 41 · 44) 830 I פרר

רֹמַח 10 spear, lance (3 · 15) 942

שִׁרְיוֹן body armor (1 · 8) 1056

סֵבֶל 11 load, burden (1 · 3) 687

עמשׁ to load (2 · 7 · 9) 770 עמס

שֶׁלַח weapon, missile (2 · 8) 1019 I

מָתְנַיִם 12 loins (1 · 50) 608

חֹר 13 noble (7 · 13) 359 II

סָגָן official (9 · 17) 688

רָחָב wide, broad (5 · 21) 932 I

נפרד to be divided, separated (1 · 12 · 26)
825 I

רֹמַח 15 spear, lance (3 · 15) 942

שַׁחַר dawn (1 · 23) 1007

כּוֹכָב star (2 · 37) 456

מִשְׁמָר 16 guard (7 · 20) 1038

מִשְׁמָר 17 guard (7 · 20) 1038

פָּשַׁט to strip off, put off (1 · 24 · 43) 832

שֶׁלַח weapon, missile (2 · 8) 1019 I

Chapter 5

צְעָקָה 1 cry (1 · 21) 858

נִקְחָה 2 let us procure 542 לקח 4.b

דָּגָן corn (7 · 40) 186

עָרַב 3 to give in pledge (1 · 15 · 17) 786 II

דָּגָן corn (7 · 40) 186

לוה 4 to borrow (1 · 5 · 14) 531 II

מִדָּה tribute (1 · 1) 551 II

כבשׁ 5 to bring into bondage (1 · 8 · 14) 461

נכבשׁ to be subdued (1 · 5 · 14) 461

אֵל strength, power (1 · 5) 42 II.7

זְעָקָה 6 cry (2 · 18) 277

נמלך 7 to consider (1 · 1 · 1) 576 III

חֹר noble (7 · 13) 359 II

סָגָן official (9 · 17) 688

מַשָּׁא usury (3 · 3) 673

נשׁא to lend on interest, be a creditor
(3 · 12 · 14) 673 I (or 674 I נָשָׁה)

קְהִלָּה assembly, congregation (1 · 2) 875

כְּדִי 8 as much as (1 · 5) 191 דַּי 2.b

הֶחֱרִישׁ to be silent (1 · 39 · 44) 361

יִרְאָה 9 fear, reverence, piety (2 · 45) 432

נָשָׁה 10 to lend, become a creditor
(3 · 12 · 14) 674 I

דָּגָן corn (7 · 40) 186

מַשָּׁא usury (3 · 3) 673

זַיִת 11 olive tree, olive (3 · 38) 268

דָּגָן corn (7 · 40) 186

תִּירוֹשׁ new wine (5 · 38) 440

יִצְהָר fresh oil (5 · 23) 844 I

נָשָׁה to lend, become a creditor
(3 · 12 · 14) 674 I

חֹצֶן 13 bosom (1 · 3) 346

נער to shake out (2 · 4 · 11) 654 II

כָּכָה thus (2 · 34) 462

נער Piel, to shake out utterly (1 · 3 · 11)
654 II

יְגִיעַ product, produce, property (1 · 16)
388

רֵיק empty (1 · 14) 938

אָמֵן verily, truly (3 · 30) 53

פֶּחָה 14 governor (8 · 28) 808

פֶּחָה 15 governor (8 · 28) 808

שָׁלַט to domineer (1 · 5 · 8) 1020 I

יִרְאָה fear, reverence, piety (2 · 45) 432

סָגָן 17 official (9 · 17) 688

ברר 18 to choose, select (1 · 7 · 15) 140

צִפּוֹר bird (1 · 40) 861 I

פֶּחָה governor (8 · 28) 808

Chapter 6

פֶּרֶץ 1 breach (1 · 18) 829 I

נועד 2 to meet by appointment (2 · 18 · 28) יָעַד 416

בִּקְעָה valley, plain (1 · 19) 132

הרפה 3 to abandon, forsake (1 · 21 · 44) 951

אִגֶּרֶת 5 letter (6 · 10) 8

מרד 6 to rebel, revolt (3 · 25 · 25) 597

הוה to become (1 · 5 · 5) 217

בָּדָא 8 to invent, devise (1 · 2 · 2) 94

רפה 9 to drop, sink (1 · 14 · 44) 951

עָצוּר 10 pass. ptc. = shut up, hindered (1 · 36 · 46) 783

נועד to meet by appointment (2 · 18 · 28) יָעַד 416

הִכִּיר 12 to perceive (2 · 37 · 40) 647 I נכר

נְבוּאָה prophecy (1 · 3) 612

שָׂכַר to hire (3 · 16 · 18) 968

שָׂכַר 13 to hire (3 · 16 · 18) 968

חֵרֵף to reproach, taunt (1 · 34 · 38) 357 I

נְבִיאָה 14 prophetess (1 · 6) 612

חֹר 17 noble (7 · 13) 359 II

אִגֶּרֶת letter (6 · 10) 8

שְׁבוּעָה 18 oath, curse (2 · 30) 989; בַּעֲלֵי שׁ' = conspirators 127 I בַּעַל 5.b

חָתָן son-in-law (2 · 20) 368

אִגֶּרֶת 19 letter (6 · 10) 8

Chapter 7

שֹׁעֵר 1 porter (10 · 37) 1045

בִּירָה 2 citadel, castle (3 · 18) 108

חַם 3 to be warm, grow warm (1 · 23 · 26 [?]) 328 חמם

הגיף to shut, close (1 · 1 · 1) 157 גוף

מִשְׁמָר guard (7 · 20) 1038

רָחָב 4 wide, broad (5 · 21) 932 I

חֹר 5 noble (7 · 13) 359 II

סָגָן official (9 · 17) 688

התיחש to be enrolled by genealogy (2 · 20 · 20) 405

יַחַשׂ genealogy (1 · 1) 405

מְדִינָה 6 province (3 · 44) 193

שְׁבִי captivity (5 · 46) 985

גּוֹלָה exiles, exile (1 · 42) 163

שֹׁעֵר 45 porter (10 · 37) 1045

נְתִינִים 46 servants (9 · 17) 682

נְתִינִים 60 servants (9 · 17) 682

כְּתָב 64 register, enrollment (1 · 17) 508

התיחש to be enrolled by genealogy (2 · 20 · 20) 405

גאל to be desecrated; i.e., deposed (1 · 4 · 11) 146 II

כְּהֻנָּה priesthood (2 · 13) 464

תִּרְשָׁתָא 65 title of Persian governor (4 · 5) 1077

אוּרִים Urim (1 · 7) 22

תֻּמִּים [dub.] Thummim (1 · 5) 1070 תם 4

רִבּוֹא 66 ten thousand, myriad (3 · 11) 914

מִלְּבַד 67 besides (1 · 33) 94 II בַּד 1.e

קְצָת 69 end (1 · 9) 892

תִּרְשָׁתָא title of Persian governor (4 · 5) 1077

דַּרְכְּמוֹן daric, drachma (3 · 4) 204

מִזְרָק bowl, basin (1 · 32) 284

כֻּתֹּנֶת tunic (2 · 29) 509

דַּרְכְּמוֹן 70 daric, drachma (3 · 4) 204

רִבּוֹ ten thousand, myriad (3 · 11) 914

מָנֶה mina, maneh (2 · 5) 584

דַּרְכְּמוֹן 71 daric, drachma (3 · 4) 204

רִבּוֹא ten thousand, myriad (3 · 11) 914

מָנֶה mina, maneh (2 · 5) 584

כֻּתֹּנֶת tunic (2 · 29) 509

שֹׁעֵר 72 porter (10 · 37) 1045

נְתִינִים servants (9 · 17) 682

Chapter 8

רְחוֹב	1	broad open place (4 · 43) 932 I
רְחוֹב	3	broad open place (4 · 43) 932 I
מַחֲצִית		middle (1 · 16) 345
מִגְדָּל	4	tower (9 · 49) 153
אָמֵן	6	verily, truly (3 · 30) 53
מֹעַל		lifting (1 · 1) 751
קדד		to bow down (1 · 15 · 15) 869 I
עֹמֶד	7	standing place (3 · 9) 765
פֹּרַשׁ	8	to be distinctly declared (1 · 2 · 5) 831 I
שֶׂכֶל		insight, understanding (1 · 16) 968
מִקְרָא		reading (1 · 23) 896
תִּרְשָׁתָא	9	title of Persian governor (4 · 5) 1077
הִתְאַבֵּל		to mourn (2 · 19 · 38) I
מַשְׁמָן	10	fat piece, tidbit (1 · 1) 1032
מַמְתַקִּים		sweet things (1 · 2) 609
מָנָה		part, portion (2 · 12) 584
לְאֵין		without, not having (1 · 9) 34 II אֵין 6.c
נֶעֱצַב		to be grieved (2 · 7 · 15) 780 I
חֶדְוָה		joy (1 · 2) 292
מָעוֹז		refuge (1 · 36) 731
הַחְשׁוּ	11	to make still, quiet (1 · 9 · 16) 364
הַס		hush! keep silence (1 · 7) 245
נֶעֱצַב		to be grieved (2 · 7 · 15) 781 I
מָנָה	12	part, portion (2 · 12) 584
סֻכָּה	14	booth (5 · 31) 697
עָלֶה	15	leaf, leafage (5 · 18) 750
זַיִת		olive tree, olive (3 · 38) 268
הֲדַס		myrtle (1 · 6) 213
תָּמָר		date palm (1 · 12) 1071 I
עָבוֹת		leafy (1 · 4) 721
סֻכָּה		booth (5 · 31) 697
סֻכָּה	16	booth (5 · 31) 697
גָּג		roof (1 · 29) 150
רְחוֹב		broad open place (4 · 43) 932 I
שְׁבִי	17	captivity (5 · 46) 985
סֻכָּה		booth (5 · 31) 697

עֲצָרָה	18	assembly (1 · 11) 783

Chapter 9

צוֹם	1	fast, fasting (1 · 25) 847
שַׂק		sackcloth (1 · 48) 974
נִבְדַּל	2	to separate oneself (2 · 10 · 42) 95
נֵכָר		foreignness (2 · 36) 648
עֹמֶד	3	standing place (3 · 9) 765
מַעֲלֶה	4	ascent (2 · 19) 751
אַתָּ	6	you (m. sing.) 61 אַתָּה
זְעָקָה	9	cry (2 · 18) 277
מוֹפֵת	10	sign, wonder (1 · 36) 68
הֵזִיד		to act presumptuously, insolently (3 · 8 · 10) 267
יַבָּשָׁה	11	dry land (1 · 14) 387
מְצוֹלָה		depth, deep (1 · 12) 846
עַז		strong, mighty, fierce (1 · 22) 738
הִנְחָה	12	to lead, guide (1 · 26 · 40) 634
הֵאִיר	21	to give light (2 · 34 · 40) אור
צָמָא	15	thirst (2 · 17) 854
הֵזִיד	16	to act presumptuously, insolently (3 · 8 · 10) 267
הִקְשָׁה		to stiffen, harden (3 · 21 · 28) 904 I
עֹרֶף		neck (3 · 33) 791
מֵאֵן	17	to refuse (1 · 46 · 46) 549
נִפְלָאוֹת		wonderful acts (1 · 44) 810 פלא Niph. 4
הִקְשָׁה		to stiffen, harden (3 · 21 · 28) 904 I
עֹרֶף		neck (3 · 33) 791
עֲבֹדוּת		servitude, bondage (1 · 3) 715
מְרִי		rebellion (1 · 22) 598
סְלִיחָה		forgiveness (1 · 3) 699
חַנּוּן		gracious (2 · 13) 337
רַחוּם		compassionate (2 · 13) 933
אֶרֶךְ		long (1 · 15) 74
עֵגֶל	18	calf (1 · 35) 722
מַסֵּכָה		molten metal or image (1 · 25) 651 I
נֶאָצָה		contempt, blasphemy (2 · 3) 611
רַחֲמִים	19	compassion (5 · 38) 933

נחה	to lead, bring (1 · 14 · 40) 634	
הֵאִיר	to give light (2 · 34 · 40) 21 אור	
מָן	20 manna (1 · 14) 577 I	
מָנַע	to withhold (1 · 25 · 29) 586	
צָמָא	thirst (2 · 17) 854	
כִּלְכֵּל	21 to sustain, nourish (1 · 24 · 38) 465	
	כול	
חָסֵר	to be in want, to want (1 · 19 · 23) 341	
שַׂלְמָה	clothes (1 · 16) 971 II	
בלה	to wear out (1 · 11 · 16) 115	
בָּצֵק	to swell (1 · 2 · 2) 130	
כּוֹכָב	23 star (2 · 37) 456	
הִכְנִיעַ	24 to subdue (1 · 11 · 36) 488	
בָּצוּר	25 inaccessible, cut off (1 · 25[?]) 130	
	בצר	
שָׁמֵן	fat, rich (2 · 10) 1032	
טוּב	goods, property, goodness (4 · 32) 375	
חצב	to hew out (1 · 14 · 17) 345	
זַיִת	olive tree, olive (3 · 38) 268	
מַאֲכָל	food (1 · 30) 38	
השמין	to show fatness (1 · 2 · 5) 1031 I	
התעדן	to luxuriate (1 · 1 · 1) 726	
המרה	26 to be disobedient, rebellious (1 · 22 · 43) 598	
מרד	to rebel, revolt (3 · 25 · 25) 597	
גַּו	back (1 · 2) 156	
הֵעִיד	to warn, protest (6 · 40 · 45) 729 עוד	
נְאָצָה	blasphemy, contempt (2 · 3) 611	
רַחֲמִים	27 compassion (5 · 38) 933	
מוֹשִׁיעַ	savior (1 · 27[?]) 446 ישע	
רדה	28 to have dominion, rule (1 · 22 · 23) 921 I	
רַחֲמִים	compassion (5 · 38) 933	
הֵעִיד	29 to exhort solemnly, admonish (6 · 40 · 45) 729 עוד	
הֵזִיד	to act presumptuously, insolently (3 · 8 · 10) 267	

סוֹרֶרֶת	ptc. = stubborn (1 · 18 · 18) 710 סרר	
עֹרֶף	neck (3 · 33) 791	
הִקְשָׁה	to stiffen, harden (3 · 21 · 28) 904 I	
מָשַׁךְ	30 to prolong, continue (1 · 30 · 36) 604	
הֵעִיד	to exhort solemnly, admonish (6 · 40 · 45) 729 עוד	
הֶאֱזִין	to listen, give ear (1 · 41 · 41) 24 I	
רַחֲמִים	31 compassion (5 · 38) 933	
כָּלָה	destruction, annihilation (1 · 22) 478	
חַנּוּן	gracious (2 · 13) 337	
רַחוּם	compassionate (2 · 13) 933	
נוֹרָא	32 awe-inspiring, awful (3 · 44) 431 ירא	
מעט	to become small, diminished, few (1 · 8 · 22) 589	
תְּלָאָה	hardship, weariness (1 · 5) 521	
הִרְשִׁיעַ	33 to act wickedly (1 · 25 · 34) 957	
הִקְשִׁיב	34 to give attention (1 · 45 · 46) 904	
הֵעִיד	to enjoin solemnly (6 · 40 · 45) 729 עוד	
טוּב	35 good things (4 · 32) 375	
רָחָב	wide, broad (5 · 21) 932 I	
שָׁמֵן	fat, rich (2 · 10) 1032	
מַעֲלָל	deed, practice (1 · 41) 760	
טוּב	36 good things (4 · 32) 375	
תְּבוּאָה	37 product, yield (1 · 43) 100	
גְּוִיָּה	body (1 · 12) 156	

Chapter 10

אֲמָנָה	1 faith, support (2 · 2) 53 I	
חתם	to seal, seal up (2 · 23 · 27) 367	
חתם	2 to seal, seal up (2 · 23 · 27) 367	
תִּרְשָׁתָא	title of Persian governor (4 · 5) 1077	
שְׁאָר	29 rest, remnant, remainder (3 · 26) 984	
שֹׁעֵר	porter (10 · 37) 1045	
נְתִינִים	servants (9 · 17) 682	
נבדל	to separate oneself (2 · 10 · 42) 95	
אַדִּיר	30 majestic one (2 · 27) 12	
אָלָה	oath, curse (1 · 36) 46	

שְׁבוּעָה	oath, curse (2 · 30) 989
מַקָּחָה 32	wares (1 · 1) 544
שֶׁבֶר	grain (1 · 9) 991 I
נָטַשׁ	to leave, let alone (1 · 33 · 40) 643
מַשָּׁא	usury (3 · 3) 673
מַעֲרֶכֶת 34	row, line (1 · 9) 790
קָרְבָּן 35	offering (2 · 2) 898
זְמָן	to be fixed, appointed (2 · 2 · 3) 273
בִּכּוּרִים 36	first fruits (2 · 16) 114
עֲרִיסָה 38	[dub.] coarse meal (1 · 4) 791
תִּירוֹשׁ	new wine, must (5 · 38) 440
יִצְהָר	fresh oil (5 · 23) 844 I
לִשְׁכָּה	room, chamber (7 · 47) 545
מַעֲשֵׂר	tithe, tenth part (6 · 31) 798
מְעַשְּׂרִים	ptc. = taking the tenth (1 · 5 · 9) 797
עשר	
בַּעֲשֵׂר 39	inf. + בְּ = when receiving tithes (1 · 2 · 9) 797 עשר
מַעֲשֵׂר	tithe, tenth part (6 · 31) 798
לִשְׁכָּה	room, chamber (7 · 47) 545
לִשְׁכָּה 40	room, chamber (7 · 47) 545
דָּגָן	corn (7 · 40) 186
תִּירוֹשׁ	new wine, must (5 · 38) 440
יִצְהָר	fresh oil (5 · 23) 844 I
שֹׁעֵר	porter (10 · 37) 1045

Chapter 11

שְׁאָר 1	rest, remnant, remainder (3 · 26) 984
הִתְנַדֵּב 2	to volunteer (1 · 14 · 17) 621
מְדִינָה 3	province (3 · 44) 193
נְתִינִים	servants (9 · 17) 682
פָּקִיד 9	overseer, commissioner (4 · 13) 824
מִשְׁנֶה	second quarter (2 · 35) 1041
נָגִיד 11	leader, ruler, prince (1 · 44) 617
פָּקִיד 14	overseer, commissioner (4 · 13) 824
חִיצוֹן 16	outer, external (1 · 25) 300
תְּחִלָּה 17	Beginning (1 · 22) 321
מִשְׁנֶה	second (2 · 35) 1041
שֹׁעֵר 19	porter (10 · 37) 1045

שְׁאָר 20	rest, remnant, remainder (3 · 26) 984
נְתִינִים 21	servants (9 · 17) 682
עֹפֶל	mound, hill (3 · 8) 779 I
פָּקִיד 22	overseer, commissioner (4 · 13) 824
לְנֶגֶד	over, for (5 · 32) 617 נֶגֶד 2.b
אֲמָנָה 23	fixed provision, support (2 · 2) 53 I
גַּיְא 30	valley (5 · 49) 161
גַּיְא 35	valley (5 · 49) 161
חָרָשׁ	graver, artificer (1 · 38) 360
מַחֲלֹקֶת 36	division, course (1 · 44) 324

Chapter 12

הֵידוֹת 8	songs of praise (1 · 1) 392
לְנֶגֶד 9	opposite to (5 · 32) 617 נֶגֶד 2.b
לְנֶגֶד 24	opposite to (5 · 32) 617 נֶגֶד 2.b
מִשְׁמָר	guard (7 · 20) 1038
לְעֻמָּה	agreeing with, corresponding to (1 · 31) 769 I עֻמָּה
שֹׁעֵר 25	porter (10 · 37) 1045
מִשְׁמָר	guard (7 · 20) 1038
אָסֹף	store (1 · 3) 63
פֶּחָה 26	governor (8 · 28) 808
חֲנֻכָּה 27	dedication, consecration (2 · 8) 335
תּוֹדָה	songs of thanksgiving (4 · 32) 392
מְצִלְתַּיִם	cymbals (1 · 13) 853
נֵבֶל	harp (1 · 27) 614 II
כִּנּוֹר	lyre (1 · 41) 490
תּוֹדָה 31	thanksgiving choir (4 · 32) 392
תַּהֲלוּכָה	procession (1 · 1) 237
אַשְׁפֹּת	ash heap, dung hill (4 · 7) 1046
חֲצֹצְרָה 35	clarion (2 · 29) 348
מַעֲלָה 37	step, stair (2 · 47) 752 II.1
מַעֲלֶה	ascent (2 · 19) 751
תּוֹדָא 38	thanksgiving choir (4 · 32) 392
לְמוֹאל	in the opposite direction (1 · 1) 557 I מוּל
מִגְדָּל	tower (9 · 49) 153
תַּנּוּר	firepot (2 · 15) 1072
רָחָב	wide, broad (5 · 21) 932 I

יָשָׁן 39 old (2 · 8) 445

דָּג fish (3 · 19) 185

מִגְדָּל tower (9 · 49) 153

מַטָּרָה guard, ward, prison (2 · 16) 643

תּוֹדָה 40 thanksgiving choir (4 · 32) 392

סָגָן official (9 · 17) 688

חֲצֹצְרָה 41 clarion (2 · 29) 348

פָּקִיד 42 overseer, commissioner (4 · 13) 824

נִשְׁכָּה 44 chamber (3 · 3) 675

מַעֲשֵׂר tithe, tenth part (6 · 31) 798

כנס to gather, collect (1 · 7 · 11) 488

מְנָת portion (3 · 9) 584

טָהֳרָה 45 purification, cleansing (1 · 13) 372

שֹׁעֵר porter (10 · 37) 1045

מְנָת 47 portion (3 · 9) 584

שֹׁעֵר porter (10 · 37) 1045

Chapter 13

קדם 2 to come to meet (1 · 24 · 26) 869

שָׂכַר to hire (3 · 16 · 18) 968

קְלָלָה curse (1 · 33) 887

הִבְדִּיל 3 to separate, set apart (1 · 32 · 42) 95

עֵרֶב mixture, mixed company (1 · 5) 786 I

לִשְׁכָּה 4 room, chamber (7 · 47) 545

לִשְׁכָּה 5 room, chamber (7 · 47) 545

לְבֹנָה frankincense (2 · 21) 526 I

מַעֲשֵׂר tithe, tenth part (6 · 31) 798

דָּגָן corn (7 · 40) 186

תִּירוֹשׁ new wine (5 · 38) 440

יִצְהָר fresh oil (5 · 23) 844 I

שֹׁעֵר porter (10 · 37) 1045

נִשְׁכָּה 7 chamber (3 · 3) 675

לִשְׁכָּה 8 room, chamber (7 · 47) 545

לִשְׁכָּה 9 room, chamber (7 · 47) 545

לְבֹנָה frankincense (2 · 21) 526 I

מְנָת 10 portion (3 · 9) 584

סָגָן 11 official (9 · 17) 688

עֹמֶד standing place (3 · 9) 765

מַעֲשֵׂר 12 tithe, tenth part (6 · 31) 798

דָּגָן corn (7 · 40) 186

תִּירוֹשׁ new wine (5 · 38) 440

יִצְהָר fresh oil (5 · 23) 844 I

אוֹצְרָה 13 I appointed as treasurer (1 · 1 · 5) אצר 69

הִמְחָה 14 to blot out (1 · 3 · 34) 562 I

מִשְׁמָר observance (7 · 20) 1038

גַּת 15 winepress (1 · 5) 387 I

עֲרֵמָה heap (2 · 10) 790

עמס to load (2 · 7 · 9) 770

עֵנָב grapes (1 · 19) 772

תְּאֵנָה fig, fig tree (1 · 38) 1061

מַשָּׂא load, burden (2 · 45) 672 I

הֵעִיד to protest, affirm solemnly, warn (6 · 40 · 45) עוד 729

צַיִד provision, food (1 · 5) 845 II

דָּאג 16 fish (3 · 19) 185 דָּג

מֶכֶר merchandise (1 · 3) 569

חֹר 17 noble (7 · 13) 359 II

חָרוֹן 18 anger (1 · 41) 354

צלל 19 to be or grow dark (1 · 1 · 2) 853 III

מַשָּׂא load, burden (2 · 45) 672 I

רֹכֵל 20 trader (3 · 17) 940 רכל

מִמְכָּר ware, sale (1 · 10) 569

הֵעִיד 21 to protest, affirm solemnly, warn (6 · 40 · 45) עוד 729

שָׁנָה to do again, repeat (1 · 13 · 25[?]) 1040 III

חוס 22 to pity, look upon with compassion (1 · 24 · 24) 299

אַשְׁדּוֹדִית 24 in the language of Ashdod (1 · 1) 78

הִכִּיר to understand, distinguish (2 · 37 · 40) 647 I נכר

יְהוּדִית in Hebrew (1 · 6) 397 I

מרט 25 to make bare (1 · 7 · 14) 598

נָכְרִי 26 foreign (2 · 45) 648

מעל 27 to act unfaithfully, treacherously (2 · 35 · 35) 591

נָכְרִי foreign (2 · 45) 648

חָתָן 28 bridegroom, son-in-law (2 · 20) 368

גָּאֵל 29 defiling, defilement (1 · 1) 146

כְּהֻנָּה priesthood (2 · 13) 464

נֵכָר 30 foreignness (2 · 36) 648

קָרְבָּן 31 offering (2 · 2) 898

זְמַן to be fixed, appointed (2 · 2 · 3) 273

בַּכּוּרִים firstfruits (2 · 16) 114

1 CHRONICLES

Chapter 1

נִפְלַג 19 to be divided (1 · 2 · 4) 811

תּוֹלְדוֹת 29 account of people and their descendents, successive generations,
genealogical divisions (9 · 39) 410

פִּלֶגֶשׁ 32 concubine (5 · 37) 811

Chapter 2

כַּלָּה 4 daughter-in-law; bride or young
wife (1 · 34) 483

עָכַר 7 to disturb, trouble, stir up
(2 · 13 · 15) 747

מָעַל to act unfaithfully (3 · 35 · 35) 591

חֵרֶם thing devoted [to sacred use or de-
struction], devotion (1 · 29) 356 I

חַוָּה 23 tent village (1 · 7) 295 II

פִּלֶגֶשׁ 46 concubine (5 · 37) 811

פִּלֶגֶשׁ 48 concubine (5 · 37) 811

Chapter 3

מִלְּבַד 9 besides (1 · 34) 94 II בַּד 1.e

פִּלֶגֶשׁ concubine (5 · 37) 811

אַסִּיר 17 the captive [Lis. 1587 takes as
prop. name (1 · 1)] (1 · 3) 64 I

Chapter 4

אֲבִי 3 text uncertain, perh. rd בְּנֵי w. LXX
& Vulg.

עֹצֶב 9 pain (1 · 3) 780 I

עצב 10 to pain, hurt, grieve (1 · 3 · 15) 780 I

גַּיְא 14 valley (3 · 47) 161

חָרָשׁ graver, artificer (6 · 38) 360

הָרָה 17 to conceive, become pregnant
(2 · 38 · 40) 247 I

בּוּץ 21 byssus, fine white Egyptian linen
and cloth (2 · 8) 101

בָּעַל 22 to rule over (1 · 10 · 12) 127

עַתִּיק old, ancient, removed (1 · 2) 801

יוֹצֵר 23 ptc. = potter (1 · 17) 427

מוֹשָׁב 33 dwelling place; seat; location; etc.
(3 · 44) 444

הִתְיַחֵשׂ to be registered by genealogy, here
inf. = genealogical enrollment
(10 · 20 · 20) 405

פָּרַץ 38 to break over [limits], increase,
break out (5 · 46 · 49) 829 I

מָבוֹא 39 entrance (2 · 23) 99

גַּיְא valley (3 · 47) 161

מִרְעֶה pasturage, pasture (3 · 13) 945

מִרְעֶה 40 pasturage, pasture (3 · 13) 945

שָׁמֵן fat, rich; stout, robust (1 · 10) 1032

רָחָב wide, broad (1 · 21) 932 I

יָדַיִם idiom: both hands = both directions
יָד 3.d 388

שָׁקַט to be quiet, undisturbed, at peace
(1 · 31 · 41) 1052

שָׁלֵו quiet, at ease (1 · 8) 1017

הֶחֱרִים 41 to ban or devote, most often by destruction, hence = to exterminate,
destroy (1 · 46 · 49) 355 I

מִרְעֶה pasturage, pasture (3 · 13) 945

פְּלֵיטָה 43 escaped remnant; escape, deliverance (1 · 28) 812

Chapter 5

יָצוּעַ 1 bed, couch (1 · 5) 426

בְּכֹרָה right of firstborn (3 · 10) 114 בכר

הִתְיַחֵשׂ to be registered by genealogy
(10 · 20 · 20) 405

גָּבַר 2 to be strong, mighty, prevail
(1 · 17 · 25) 149

נָגִיד leader, ruler, prince (12 · 44) 617

בְּכֹרָה right of firstborn (3 · 10) 114

הִתְיַחֵשׂ 7 to be registered by genealogy
(10 · 20 · 20) 405

תּוֹלְדוֹת account of people and their descendents, successive generations,
genealogical divisions (9 · 39) 410

לְמִן 9 from (1 · 14) 583 מִן 9.b

לְנֶגֶד 11 here = parallel to [?], opposite to;
(1 · 32) 617 נֶגֶד 2.b

מִשְׁנֶה 12 second in age or rank; double; copy
(3 · 36) 1041

תּוֹצָאָה 16 outskirts, extremity (1 · 23) 426

הִתְיַחֵשׂ 17 to be registered by genealogy
(10 · 20 · 20) 405

שֶׁעָם 20 = שֶׁ + עָם (1 · 1) 979, 767

נֶעְתַּר to be suplicated, entreated
(1 · 8 · 20) 801 I

שָׁבָה 21 to take captive (1 · 30 · 38) 985

גּוֹלָה 22 exile, exiles (1 · 42) 163

מָעַל 25 to act unfaithfully, treacherously
(3 · 35 · 35) 591

כִּהֵן 36 to minister as a priest (2 · 23 · 23)
464

Chapter 6

מָנוֹחַ 16 resting place, rest; here w. force of
inf. = coming to rest (1 · 7) 629 I

מוֹשָׁב 39 dwelling place; seat; location
(3 · 44) 444

טִירָה encampment = habitation, settlement (1 · 7) 377

מִקְלָט 42 refuge, asylum (2 · 20) 886

מַחֲצִית 46 half, middle (2 · 16) 345

מִקְלָט 52 refuge, asylum (2 · 20) 886

מֵעֵבֶר 63 beyond, across [the river] = E. Jordan (4 · 40) 719 I 1.a

Chapter 7

תּוֹלְדוֹת 2 account of people and their descendents, successive generations,
genealogical divisions (9 · 39) 410
ילד

תּוֹלְדוֹת 4 account of people and their descendents, successive generations,
genealogical divisions (9 · 39) 410

גְּדוּד troop, marauding band (3 · 33) 151 I

הִתְיַחֵשׂ 5 to be registered by genealogy
(10 · 20 · 20) 405

הִתְיַחֵשׂ 7 to be registered by genealogy
(10 · 20 · 20) 405

הִתְיַחֵשׂ 9 to be registered by genealogy
(10 · 20 · 20) 405

תּוֹלְדוֹת account of people and their descendents, successive generations,
genealogical divisions (9 · 39) 410

פִּלֶגֶשׁ 14 concubine (5 · 37) 811

הִתְאַבֵּל 22 to mourn (1 · 19 · 38) 5 I

הָרָה 23 to conceive, become pregnant
(2 · 38 · 40) 247 I

תַּחְתּוֹן 24 lower, lowest (1 · 13) 1066

מוֹשָׁב 28 dwelling place; seat; location
(3 · 44) 444

מַעֲרָב west (5 · 14) 788 II

ברר 40 to choose, select; pass. ptc. = chos-
en (3 · 7 · 15) 140

הִתְיַחֵשׂ to be registered by genealogy
(10 · 20 · 20) 405

Chapter 8

תּוֹלְדוֹת 28 account of people and their descendants, successive generations,
genealogical divisions (9 · 39) 410

Chapter 9

הִתְיַחֵשׂ 1 to be registered by genealogy
(10 · 20 · 20) 405

מַעַל unfaithful, treacherous act (2 · 29)
591 I

נְתִינִים 2 those given to the service at the
sanctuary (1 · 17) 682

תּוֹלֵדוֹת 9 account of people and their descendants, successive generations,
genealogical divisions (9 · 39) 410

נָגִיד 11 leader, ruler, prince (12 · 44) 617

שֹׁעֵר 17 gatekeeper, porter (14 · 37) 1045

עַד־הֵנָּה 18 of time = hitherto, until now (2 · 13)
244 I.b

שֹׁעֵר gatekeeper, porter (14 · 37) 1045

סַף 19 threshold; שֹׁמֵר הַסַּף doorkeeper [an
important temple official] (2 · 25)
706

מָבוֹא entrance (2 · 23) 99

נָגִיד 20 leader, ruler, prince (12 · 44) 617

שֹׁעֵר 21 gatekeeper, porter (14 · 37) 1045

בּרר 22 to choose, select; pass. ptc. = chos-
en (3 · 7 · 15) 140

שֹׁעֵר gatekeeper, porter (14 · 37) 1045

סַף threshold; שֹׁמֵר הַסַּף doorkeeper [an
important temple official] (2 · 25)
706 II

הִתְיַחֵשׂ to be registered by genealogy
(10 · 20 · 20) 405

יָסַד to establish (1 · 10 · 41) 413

רֹאֶה seer (3 · 12) 909 I

שֹׁעֵר 24 gatekeeper, porter (14 · 37) 1045

שֹׁעֵר 26 gatekeeper, porter (14 · 37) 1045

לִשְׁכָּה room, chamber, hall, cell (4 · 47)
545

מַפְתֵּחַ 27 key (1 · 3) 836

לַבֹּקֶר לַבֹּקֶר morning by morning, every morning (idiom 1 · 1) 133   1.f

מנה 29 *Pual* ptc. = appointed (1 · 1 · 28) 584

לְבֹנָה frankincense (1 · 21) 526

בֹּשֶׂם spice, perfume, sweet odor (2 · 30)
141

רקח 30 to compound, mix; ptc. = com-
pounder (1 · 6 · 8) 955

מִרְקַחַת ointment mixture (1 · 3) 955

בֹּשֶׂם spice, perfume, sweet odor (2 · 30)
141

חֲבִתִּים 31 some kind of flat cakes or bread
wafers (1 · 1) 290

מַעֲרֶכֶת 32 row, line [used only of lines of the
bread of the Presence] (3 · 10) 790

לִשְׁכָּה 33 room, chamber, hall, cell (4 · 47)
545

פטר to set free, here w. pass. sense = be
freed from, exempt [presumably
from other service obligation]
(1 · 8 · 9) 809

תּוֹלֵדוֹת 34 account of people and their descendants, successive generations,
genealogical divisions (9 · 39) 410

Chapter 10

מוֹרֶה 3 *Hiph.* ptc. = archer (1 · 4[?]) 434   ירה

חול to be in severe anguish; writhe,
dance (2 · 30 · 47) 296

יוֹרֶה *Qal* ptc. = archer (1 · 2[?])

שָׁלַף 4 to draw out (4 · 24 · 24) 1025

דקר to pierce, run through (1 · 7 · 11) 201

עָרֵל uncircumcised, having foreskin
(1 · 35) 790

הִתְעַלֵּל to deal wantonly, ruthlessly
(1 · 7 · 18) 759 I

יָרֵא *Qal* ptc. = fearing (1 · 45[?]) 431

מָחֳרָת 8 the next day, w. מִן = on the next
day (2 · 32) 564

פשט *Piel*, to strip (1 · 3 · 43) 832

הִפְשִׁיט 9 to strip, strip off (1 · 15 · 43) 832

בִּשֵּׂר to gladden with good tidings (2 · 14 · 15) 142

עָצָב idol (1 · 17) 781

גֻּלְגֹּלֶת 10 skull, head (3 · 12) 166

גּוּפָה 12 corpse (2 · 2) 157

אֵלָה a deciduous tree with pinnate leaves and red berries and growing to a great age (1 · 17) 18 I

צוֹם to fast, abstain from food (1 · 20 · 20) 847

מַעַל 13 unfaithful, treacherous act (2 · 29) 591 I

מָעַל to act unfaithfully, treacherously (3 · 35 · 35) 591

אוֹב necromancy (1 · 16) 15

מְלוּכָה 14 kingship, kingly office, royalty (1 · 24) 574

Chapter 11

תְּמוֹל 2 yesterday, recently; usually in comb. w. שִׁלְשׁוֹם = before, in the past, formerly (1 · 23) 1069

שִׁלְשׁוֹם three days ago (1 · 25) 1026

נָגִיד leader, ruler, prince (12 · 44) 617

הֵנָּה 5 hither, here (3 · 48) 244 I

מְצוּדָה stronghold, fastness (2 · 18) 845

מְצָד 7 stronghold, fastness (3 · 11) 844

מִסָּבִיב 8 on every side (3 · 42) 687 סָבִיב 1.d

שְׁאָר rest, residue, remainder (2 · 26) 984

שָׁלוֹשׁ 11 Qere = שָׁלִישׁ adjutant, officer (2 · 16) 1026 III

חֲנִית spear (7 · 47) 333

חֶלְקָה 13 portion [of ground], w. שָׂדֶה = clearly divided field (2 · 24) 324

שְׂעֹרָה barley (1 · 33) 972

הִתְיַצֵּב 14 to station oneself, take one's stand, stand (1 · 48 · 48) 426

חֶלְקָה portion [of ground], w. שָׂדֶה = clearly divided field (2 · 24) 324 I

תְּשׁוּעָה deliverance; here = victory (2 · 34) 448

מְעָרָה 15 cave (1 · 40) 792

מְצוּדָה 16 stronghold, fastness (2 · 18) 845

נְצִיב pillar [garrison?]; prefect, deputy (2 · 11) 662 I

הִתְאַוָּה 17 to desire, long for, lust after (1 · 16 · 27) 16 I

שָׁאַב 18 to draw [water] (1 · 14 · 14) 980

נָסַךְ Piel, to pour out as libation (1 · 1 · 25) 650 I

חָלִילָה 19 far be it [from me] (1 · 21) 321

חֲנִית 20 spear (7 · 47) 333

פֹּעַל 22 deed, thing done; here pl. = achievements (1 · 37) 821

אֲרִי lion (1 · 35) 71

שֶׁלֶג snow (1 · 20) 1017

חֲנִית 23 spear (7 · 47) 333

מָנוֹר weaver's beam (2 · 4) 644

אָרַג ptc. = weaver (2 · 10) 70

גָּזַל to tear away, rob, plunder, sieze (1 · 29 · 30) 159

מִשְׁמַעַת 25 bodyguard, obedient band, body of subjects (1 · 4) 1036

פְּלֹנִי 27 a certain one; BDB rds. הַפַּלְטִי as 2 Sam. 23:26; (3 · 6) 813 פלל I

פְּלֹנִי 36 a certain one; BDB rds. הַגִּלֹנִי as 2 Sam. 23:34 (3 · 6) 813 I

Chapter 12

עָצַר 1 to restrain; here pass. ptc. = kept away (2 · 36 · 46) 783

עֹזֵר Qal ptc. = helper (2 · 19) 740 I

נשׁק 2 [exact mng. uncert.] prob. = to handle or be equipped with (1 · 3 · 3) 676 II

הֵימִינוּ to use the right hand (1 · 5 · 5) 412 ימן II

הַשְׂמֵאל to use the left hand (1 · 5 · 5) 970

נִבְדַּל 9 to separate oneself to (אֶל)
(2 · 10 · 42) 95

מְצָד fastness, stronghold (3 · 11) 844

צִנָּה large shield (3 · 20) 857

רֹמַח spear, lance (2 · 15) 942

אַרְיֵה lion (1 · 45) 71

צְבִי gazelle (1 · 1) 840 II

קָטָן 15 insignificant, small; young (2 · 47)
881 I

גָּדָה 16 bank of river (1 · 4) 152

מַעֲרָב west (5 · 14) 788

מְצָד 17 fastness, stronghold (3 · 11) 844

יַחַד 18 w. לְ = for unitedness [ready to
become one]; elsewhere as adverb:
together, altogether (1 · 44) 403

רִמָּה to deal treacherously with, betray
(1 · 8 · 8) 941 II

בְּלֹא without (2 · 31) 520 לֹא 4.a

שָׁלוֹשׁ 19 Qere = שָׁלִישׁ adjutant, officer (2 · 16)
1026 III

עֹזֵר Qal ptc. = helper (2 · 19) 740 I

קִבֵּל to receive, take = choose
(2 · 11 · 13) 867

גְּדוּד marauding band, troop (3 · 33)
151 I

גְּדוּד 22 marauding band, troop (3 · 33) 151 I

חָלוּץ 24 pass. ptc. = equipped, or equipped
ones (2 · 2 · 17) 323 II

כְּפִי according to the command of; according to (1 · 16) 804 פֶּה 6.b

צִנָּה 25 large shield (3 · 20) 857

רֹמַח spear, lance (2 · 15) 942

חָלוּץ pass. ptc. = equipped, equipped
ones (2 · 2 · 17) 323 II

נָגִיד 28 leader, ruler, prince (12 · 44) 617

עַד־הֵנָּה 30 of time = hitherto, until now (2 · 13)
244 I.b

מַרְבִּית greater part, great number (1 · 5) 916

נקב 32 Niph., to be pricked off, designated
(2 · 6 · 19) 666 I

בִּינָה 33 understanding (2 · 37) 108

עדר 34 [prob.] to help (2 · 2 · 2) 727 I

בְּלֹא without (2 · 31) 520 לֹא 4.a

צִנָּה 35 large shield (3 · 20) 857

חֲנִית spear (7 · 47) 333

מֵעֵבֶר 38 beyond, across [the river] = E. Jordan (4 · 40) I.1A & B

עדר 39 [prob.] to help (2 · 2 · 2) 727 I

מַעֲרָכָה battle line; row (1 · 19) 790

שָׁלֵם complete, perfect, full (4 · 28) 1023

פֶּרֶד 41 mule (1 · 14) 825

מַאֲכָל food (1 · 30) 38

קֶמַח flour, meal (1 · 14) 887

דְּבֵלָה lump, pressed cake (1 · 5) 179

צִמּוּק bunch of raisins, dried grapes
(1 · 4) 856

Chapter 13

נָגִיד 1 leader, ruler, prince (12 · 44) 617

פָּרַץ 2 to spread [dub.] (5 · 46 · 49) 829 I

יָשַׁר 4 to be pleasing, agreeable, right
(1 · 13 · 25) 448

הִקְהִיל 5 to summon an assembly (3 · 20 · 39)
874

שִׁיחוֹר prob. E. branch of the Nile; the
Nile (1 · 4) 1009

עֲגָלָה 7 cart (2 · 25) 722

נָהַג to drive, conduct (2 · 20 · 30) 624 I

שׂחק 8 Piel, to play (2 · 16 · 36) 965

כִּנּוֹר lyre, stringed instrument (8 · 41) 490

נֶבֶל portable harp, or lute, guitar
(7 · 27) 614

תֹּף timbrel, tambourine (1 · 17) 1074

מְצִלְתַּיִם cymbals (8 · 13) 853

חֲצֹצְרָה clarion (5 · 29) 348

גֹּרֶן 9 threshing floor (6 · 34) 175

שמט to let drop, fall [dub. here]
(1 · 7 · 9) 1030

פָּרַץ 11 to break out [violently] upon; break

over (5 · 46 · 49) 829 I

פֶּרֶץ outburst, bursting forth; breach (2 · 19) 829 I

הֵיךְ 12 how[?] (1 · 2) 228

Chapter 14

חָרָשׁ 1 graver, artificer (6 · 38) 360

לְמַעְלָה 2 upwards; here = exceedingly (6 · 34) 751 II מַעַל 2.c.(b)

בַּעֲבוּר for the sake of, because of (3 · 45) 721

פָּשַׁט 9 to make a dash against (2 · 24 · 43) 832

פָּרַץ 11 to break out [violently] upon; break over (5 · 46 · 49) 829 I

פֶּרֶץ outburst, bursting forth; breach (2 · 19) 829 I

פָּשַׁט 13 to make a dash against; strip off (2 · 24 · 43) 832

מִמּוּל 14 in front of (1 · 9) 557 I מוּל 2.b

בָּכָא balsam tree (2 · 5) 113

צְעָדָה 15 marching (1 · 3) 857 I

בָּכָא balsam tree (2 · 5) 113

פַּחַד 17 dread (1 · 49) 808 I

Chapter 15

הִקְהִיל 3 to summon an assembly (3 · 20 · 39) 874

פָּרַץ 13 to break out [violently] upon; break over (5 · 46 · 49) 829 I

גֶּבֶל 16 portable harp or lute, guitar (7 · 27) 614 II

כִּנּוֹר lyre, stringed instrument (8 · 41) 490

מְצִלְתַּיִם cymbals (8 · 13) 853

מִשְׁנֶה 18 second in age or rank; double, copy (3 · 36) 1041

שֹׁעֵר gatekeeper, porter (14 · 37) 1045

מְצִלְתַּיִם 19 cymbals (8 · 13) 853

גֶּבֶל 20 portable harp or lute, guitar (7 · 27) 614 II

עַלְמָה young woman; w. עַל = [w.pl.] to [the voice of] young women [either lit., or of soprano or falsetto of boys] (1 · 9) 761

כִּנּוֹר 21 lyre, stringed instrument (8 · 41) 490

נצח to act as overseer, director, super-intendent (2 · 7 · 8) 663 I

מַשָּׂא 22 bearing, carrying (3 · 45) 672

יסר to instruct (1[?] · 4 · 38) 415

שֹׁעֵר 23 gatekeeper, porter (14 · 37) 1045

החצצר 24 Hiph. to sound with clarions (1 · 5 · 6) 348

חֲצֹצְרָה clarion (5 · 29) 348

שֹׁעֵר gatekeeper, porter (14 · 37) 1045

כרבל 27 to clothe, bind around (1 · 1 · 1) 499

מְעִיל robe (1 · 28) 591

בּוּץ byssus, fine white Egyptian linen and cloth (2 · 8) 101

מַשָּׂא bearing, carrying (3 · 45) 672 נשא

אֵפוֹד ephod, priestly garment, shoulder cape or mantle (1 · 49) 65

בַּד white linen (1 · 23) 94 I

תְּרוּעָה 28 shout of joy; war cry; blast for march (1 · 36) 929 רוע

חֲצֹצְרָה clarion (5 · 29) 348

מְצִלְתַּיִם cymbals (8 · 13) 853

גֶּבֶל portable harp or lute, guitar (7 · 27) 614

כִּנּוֹר lyre, stringed instrument (8 · 41) 490

נשקף 29 to lean over [and look], look down; w. בעד = look through (1 · 10 · 22) 1054 I

חַלּוֹן window (1 · 30) 319

רקד to dance, leap (1 · 5 · 9) 955

שׂחק Piel, to play (2 · 16 · 36) 965

בָּזָה to despise, regard with contempt (1 · 31 · 42) 102

648

Chapter 16

הַצִּיג 1 to set, place (1 · 15 · 16) 426 יצג

אֶשְׁפָּר 3 mng. unknown, Aq. Symm "cake" or "roll" (1 · 2) 80

אֲשִׁישָׁה raisin-cake (1 · 5) 84

מְשָׁרֵת 4 *Piel* ptc. = minister (1 · 20) 1058

מִשְׁנֶה 5 second in age or rank; double; copy (3 · 36) 1041

נֵבֶל portable harp or lute, guitar (7 · 27) 614

כִּנּוֹר lyre, stringed instrument (8 · 41) 490

מְצִלְתַּיִם cymbals (8 · 13) 853

חֲצֹצְרָה 6 clarion (5 · 29) 348

עֲלִילָה 8 deed (1 · 24) 760

זמר 9 to make music (1 · 45 · 45) 274 I

שִׂיח talk about, sing of, about (1 · 18 · 20) 967

נִפְלָאוֹת *Niph.* ptc. pl. = wonderful acts (3 · 44) 810 פלא 4

נִפְלָאוֹת 12 *Niph.* ptc. pl. = wonderful acts (3 · 44) 810 פלא 4

מוֹפֵת wonder, sign, portent (1 · 36) 68

בָּחִיר 13 chosen (1 · 13) 104

שְׁבוּעָה 16 oath (1 · 30) 989

חֶבֶל 18 measured lot, portion, region, w. נַחֲלָה = inherited portion (1 · 49) 286

מַת 19 man, מְתֵי מִסְפָּר = men of number [numerable; i.e., a few] (1 · 21) 607

עָשַׁק 21 to oppress, wrong (1 · 36 · 37) 798

מָשִׁיחַ 22 anointed (1 · 39) 603

בִּשֵּׂר 23 to herald as glad tidings (2 · 14 · 15) 142

נִפְלָאוֹת 24 *Niph.* ptc. pl. = wonderful acts (3 · 44) 810 פלא 4

נוֹרָא 25 *Niph.* ptc. = awful, inspiring reverence (2 · 44) 431 ירא

אֱלִיל 26 pl. = worthless gods, idols; worthlessness (1 · 20) 47

הוֹד 27 splendor, majesty; honor, glory

(3 · 24) 217 I

הָדָר majesty, splendor (1 · 30) 214

חֶדְוָה joy (1 · 2) 292

יהב 28 to ascribe (3 · 33 · 33) 396

יהב 29 to ascribe (3 · 33 · 33) 396

הַדְרָה adornment, glory (1 · 5) 214

חול 30 to be in severe anguish (2 · 30 · 47) 296 I

תֵּבֵל world (1 · 35) 385

נמוט to be shaken, moved, overthrown (1 · 22 · 39) 556

גיל 31 to rejoice (1 · 45 · 45) 162

רעם 32 to thunder (1 · 3 · 11) 947

מְלֹא fullness, that which fills (1 · 38) 571

עָלַץ to rejoice, exult (1 · 8 · 8) 763

יֵשַׁע 35 salvation (1 · 36) 447

הִשְׁתַּבֵּחַ *Hithp.*, to boast (1 · 2 · 8) 986 II שבח

אָמֵן 36 verily, truly (1 · 30) 53

בְּיוֹמוֹ

דְּבַר־יוֹם 37 idiom: each day's affair in its day, each day's requirements (1 · 14) 400 בְּיוֹמוֹ 7.e.(3) יוֹם

שֹׁעֵר 38 gatekeeper, porter (14 · 37) 1045

שְׁאָר 41 rest, residue, remainder (2 · 26) 984

ברר to choose, select; pass. ptc. = chosen (3 · 7 · 15) 140

נקב *Niph.*, to be pricked off, designated (2 · 6 · 19) 666 I

חֲצֹצְרָה 42 clarion (5 · 29) 348

מְצִלְתַּיִם cymbals (8 · 13) 853

Chapter 17

נָוֶה 7 abode of sheep, flocks, or shepherd (1 · 45) 627

נָגִיד leader, ruler, prince (12 · 44) 617

רָגַז 9 to be disquieted, excited, perturbed, quake (1 · 30 · 41) 919

עַוְלָה violent deeds of injustice (1 · 32) 732

הִכְנִיעַ 10 to subdue (2 · 11 · 35) 488

מֵאֲשֶׁר 13 from him who; from the place where; since (1·17) 84

חָזוֹן 15 divine communication, vision (1·35) 302

הֲלֹם 16 w. עַד = hitherto, thus far; hither (1·11) 240

קָטֹן 17 to be insignificant, small (1·3·4) 881

לְמֵרָחוֹק from afar 935 רָחֹק 2.b

תּוּר [dub.] turn, plait (1·5) 1064 I

מַעֲלָה ascent (1·47) 752 II.5

בַּעֲבוּר 19 for the sake of, because of; in order that (3·45) 721

גְּדוּלָה greatness (4·12) 153

זוּלָה 20 except, with the exception of, only (1·16) 265

גְּדוּלָה 21 greatness (4·12) 153

נוֹרָא Niph. ptc. = awful, inspiring reverence (2·44) 431 ירא

גרשׁ Piel, to drive out, away (1·35·48) 176

הוֹאִיל 27 to be pleased (1·18·18) 383 יאל II

Chapter 18

הִכְנִיעַ 1 to subdue (2·11·35) 488

רַגְלִי 4 on foot, אִישׁ רַגְלִי = footmen, footsoldiers (2·12) 920

עִקֵּר to hamstring (1·5·7) 785

שֶׁלֶט 7 shield, arms, equipment (1·7) 1020

גַּיְא 12 valley (3·47) 161

מֶלַח salt (1·28) 571 II

נְצִיב 13 pillar [garrison[?]]; deputy (2·11) 662

מַזְכִּיר 15 Hiph. ptc. = recorder (1·9) 271 זכר

Chapter 19

אַחֲרֵי־כֵן 1 afterward (2·?) 29 אַחַר pl. 2.b

בַּעֲבוּר 3 in order to; for ——'s sake; be-

cause of (3·45) 721

חקר to search through, explore (1·22·27) 350

רגל to go about as explorer, spy (1·13·15) 920

גִּלַּח 4 to shave, shave off (1·18·23) 164

מָדוּ, מִזְוֶה garment (1·2) 551

מִפְשָׂעָה hip or buttock (1·1) 832

נכלם 5 to be humiliated, ashamed, be put to shame (1·26·38) 483

צָמַח to grow abundantly [always of hair] (1·4·33) 855

זָקָן beard (1·19) 278

התבאשׁ 6 to make oneself odious (1·1·16) 92

שָׂכַר to hire (2·17·20) 968

שָׂכַר 7 to hire (2·17·20) 968

אָחוֹר 10 behind (1·41) 30

בָּחוּר pass. ptc. = chosen [but also see following entry "young man"] (1·19) 104

תְּשׁוּעָה 12 deliverance, victory; salvation (2·34) 448

נִגַּף 16 Niph., to be smitten (2·22·48) 619

מֵעֵבֶר beyond, across [the river] = E. Jordan (4·40) 719 I.1.A & B

רַגְלִי 18 on foot, אִישׁ רַגְלִי = footmen, footsoldiers (2·12) 920

נִגַּף 19 Niph., to be smitten (2·22·48) 619

Chapter 20

תְּשׁוּבָה 1 return [w. year = spring] (1·8) 1000 שׁוב

נָהַג to lead out, drive; drive away (2·20·30) 624 I

צוּר to shut in, besiege (1·31·31) 848

הָרַס to throw down, tear down (1·30·43) 248

עֲטָרָה 2 crown, wreath (1·23) 742 I

מִשְׁקָל weight (13 · 49) 1054

יָקָר precious, costly, valued; w. sto- nes = gems, jewels (2 · 35) 429

שׂוּר 3 to saw (1 · 1 · 1) 965

מְגֵרָה saw (2 · 4) 176

חָרִיץ sharp instrument (1 · 2) 358

אַחֲרֵי־כֵן 4 afterward (2 · ?) 29 אַחַר pl. 2.b

יָלִיד born; subst. pl. = children (1 · 13) 409

נִכְנַע to be subdued (1 · 24 · 35) 488

חֲנִית 5 spear (7 · 47) 333

מָנוֹר weaver's beam (2 · 4) 644

אֹרֵג ptc. = weaver (2 · 10) 70

אֶצְבַּע 6 finger, toe (1 · 31) 840

חֵרֵף 7 to reproach, taunt (1 · 34 · 38) 357 I

אֵל 8 these [variation of אֵלֶּה] (1 · 10) 41 I

Chapter 21

שָׂטָן 1 Satan; adversary (1 · 26) 966

הֵסִית instigate; incite (1 · 18 · 18) 695 סוּת

מָנָה to count, number (3 · 12 · 28) 584

אַשְׁמָה 3 becoming guilty; doing wrong; bringing a trespass offering (1 · 19) 80

מִפְקָד 5 muster of people; appointment; ap- pointed place (1 · 5) 824

שָׁלַף to draw out (4 · 24 · 24) 1025

נִתְעָב 6 to be abhorred (1 · 3 · 22) 1073

נִסְכַּל 8 to act or do foolishly (1 · 4 · 8) 698

חֹזֶה 9 seer (3 · 17) 302

קִבֵּל 11 to take, here = choose, receive (2 · 11 · 13) 867

נִסְפָּה 12 to be swept away, destroyed (1 · 9 · 18) 705

הִשִּׂיג to overtake (1 · 49 · 49) 673 נשׂג

דֶּבֶר plague, pestilence (2 · 46) 184

רַחֲמִים 13 compassion (1 · 38) 933

דֶּבֶר 14 plague, pestilence (2 · 46) 184

הִרְפָּה 15 to let drop (2 · 21 · 44) 951

גֹּרֶן threshing floor (6 · 34) 175

שָׁלַף 16 to draw out (4 · 24 · 24) 1025

שַׂק sackcloth, sack (1 · 48) 974

מָנָה 17 to count, number (3 · 12 · 28) 584

מַגֵּפָה plague (2 · 26) 620

גֹּרֶן 18 threshing floor (6 · 34) 175

הִתְחַבֵּא 20 to draw back, hide oneself (1 · 10 · 34) 285

דָּשׁ to thresh; tread on, trample (1 · 13 · 16) 190 דּוּשׁ

חִטָּה wheat (2 · 30) 334

גֹּרֶן 21 threshing floor (6 · 34) 175

גֹּרֶן 22 threshing floor (6 · 34) 175

נֶעְצַר to be restrained, stayed (1 · 10 · 46) 783

מַגֵּפָה plague (2 · 26) 620

מוֹרַג 23 threshing sledge (1 · 3) 558

חִטָּה wheat (2 · 30) 334

חִנָּם 24 for nothing = at no cost (1 · 33) 336

מִשְׁקָל 25 weight (13 · 49) 1054

נָדָן 27 sheath (1 · 1) 623 II

גֹּרֶן 28 threshing floor (6 · 34) 175

נִבְעַת 30 to be terrified (1 · 3 · 16) 129

Chapter 22

כָּנַס 2 to gather, collect (1 · 7 · 11) 488

חֹצֵב ptc. = hewer [of stone] (2 · 8) 345

חָצַב to hew out (1 · 14 · 17) 345

גָּזִית a cutting, hewing, אַבְנֵי ג׳ = hewn stones [building stones] (1 · 11) 159

מַסְמֵר 3 nail (1 · 5) 702

מְחַבְּרָה binder, clamp, joint; only pl. = clamps (1 · 2) 289

מִשְׁקָל weight (13 · 49) 1054

לְאֵין 4 without, w. "number" = innu- merable (1 · 9) 34 II אַיִן

רַךְ 5 tender, inexperienced; delicate; soft (2 · 16) 939

651

לְמַעְלָה   upwardsl here = exceedingly (6 · 34) 751 II מַעַל 2.c.(b)

תִּפְאָרָה   glory; honor; beauty, finery (3 · 50) 802

מְנוּחָה   9 rest, quietness (2 · 21) 629

מִסָּבִיב   on every side (3 · 42) 686   סָבִיב 1.d

שֶׁקֶט   quietness (1 · 1) 1053

שֵׂכֶל   12 insight, understanding (2 · 16) 968

בִּינָה   understanding (2 · 37) 108

אמץ   13 to be bold, strong (2 · 16 · 41) 54

עֳנִי   14 affliction, poverty (1 · 36) 777

מִשְׁקָל   weight (13 · 49) 1054

חֹצֵב   15 ptc. = hewer [of stone] (2 · 8) 345

חָרָשׁ   graver, artificer (6 · 38) 360

מִסָּבִיב   18 on every side (3 · 42) 686   סָבִיב 1.d

נכבשׁ   to be brought into bondage; be dominated (1 · 5 · 14) 461

Chapter 23

זָקֵן   1 to be or become old (1 · 25 · 27) 278

מַעְלָה   3 upward [here of age] (2 · 43) 751 II מַעַל 2.b

גֻּלְגֹּלֶה   head or poll [in counting, taxing, etc.]; skull (3 · 12) 166

נצח   4 *Piel*, to act as overseer, director, superintendent (2 · 7 · 8) 663

שֹׁטֵר   official, officer (3 · 25) 1009

שֹׁעֵר   5 gatekeeper, porter (14 · 37) 1045

מַחֲלֹקֶת   6 division, course (26 · 42) 324

פְּקֻדָּה   11 class of officers; charge; mustering (4 · 32) 824

נבדל   13 to be set apart (2 · 10 · 42) 95

לְמַעְלָה   17 upwards; here = exceedingly (6 · 34) 751 II מַעַל 2.c.(b)

גֻּלְגֹּלֶת   24 head or poll [in counting, taxing, etc.]; skull (3 · 12) 166

מַעְלָה   upwards [here of age] (2 · 42) 751 II מַעַל 2.b

לְמַעְלָה   27 upwards; herc = cxcccdingly (6 · 34) 751 II מַעַל 2.c.(b)

מַעֲמָד   28 office, function; station; service (1 · 5) 765

לִשְׁכָּה   room, chamber, hall, cell (4 · 47) 545

טָהֳרָה   cleansing, purification (1 · 13) 372

מַעֲרֶכֶת   29 row, line [used only of lines of the bread of the Presence] (3 · 10) 790

רָקִיק   a thin cake (1 · 8) 956

מַחֲבַת   flat plate, pan or griddle for baking (1 · 5) 290

הרבך   *Ho*. ptc. = well-mixed (1 · 3 · 3) 916

מְשׂוּרָה   measure (1 · 4) 601

בַּבֹּקֶר בַּבֹּקֶר   30 morning by morning; idiom: every morning 133   1.f

Chapter 24

מַחֲלֹקֶת   1 division, course (26 · 42) 324

כֹּהֵן   2 to minister as priest (2 · 23 · 23) 464

פְּקֻדָּה   3 class of officers; charge; mustering (4 · 32) 824

פְּקֻדָּה   19 class of officers; charge; mustering (4 · 32) 824

לְעֻמָּה   31 corresponding to, agreeing with (4 · 31) 769 I עֻמָּה b

קָטָן   small, young; here w. art. = youngest (2 · 47) 881 I

Chapter 25

הִבְדִּיל   1 to separate, set apart; divide (1 · 32 · 42) 95

כִּנּוֹר   lyre, stringed instrument (8 · 41) 490

נֵבֶל   portable harp or lute, guitar (7 · 27) 614

מְצִלְתַּיִם   cymbals (8 · 13) 853

עַל־יָד   2 idiom: at the guidance of, at the direction of 391   יָד 5.h

עַל־יָד 3 idiom: at the guidance of, at the direction of 391 יָד 5.h

כִּנּוֹר lyre, stringed instrument (8·41) 490

חֹזֶה 5 seer (3·17) 302

עַל־יָד 6 idiom: at the guidance of, at the direction of 391 יָד 5.h

מְצִלְתַּיִם cymbals (8·13) 853

נֵבֶל portable harp or lute, guitar (7·27) 614

כִּנּוֹר lyre, stringed instrument (8·41) 490

לְעֻמָּה 8 corresponding to, agreeing with (4·31) 769 I עֻמָּה b

תַּלְמִיד scholar (1·1) 541

Chapter 26

מַחֲלֹקֶת 1 division, course (26·42) 324

שׁוֹעֵר gatekeeper, porter (14·37) 1045

מִמְשָׁל 6 rulers (1·3) 606

מַחֲלֹקֶת 12 division, course (26·42) 324

שׁוֹעֵר gatekeeper, porter (14·37) 1045

לְעֻמָּה corresponding to, agreeing with (4·31) 769 I עֻמָּה b

יוֹעֵץ 14 ptc. = counselor, advisor (3·22) 419

שֶׂכֶל insight, understanding (2·16) 968

אָסֹף 15 store; pl. + בית = storehouse (2·3) 63

מַעֲרָב 16 west (5·14) 788

מְסִלָּה raised way, highway, public road (2·27) 700

מִשְׁמָר band of guards (2·22) 1038

לְעֻמָּה agreeing with, corresponding to (4·31) 769 I עֻמָּה b

אָסֹף 17 store, pl. + בות = storehouse (2·3) 63

פַּרְבָּר 18 structure, colonnade[?] perh. court (2·3) 826

מַעֲרָב west (5·14) 788

מְסִלָּה raised way, highway, public road (2·27) 700

מַחֲלֹקֶת 19 division, course (26·42) 324

שֹׁעֵר gatekeeper, porter (14·37) 1045

נָגִיד 24 leader, ruler, prince (12·44) 617

רֹאֶה 28 seer (3·12) 909 I

עַל־יָד idiom: at the guidance of, at the direction of 388 יָד 5.h

חִיצוֹן 29 outward, external (1·25) 300

שֹׁטֵר official, officer (3·25) 1009

פְּקֻדָּה 30 class of officers; charge; visitation (4·32) 824

מֵעֵבֶר beyond, across [the river] = E. Jordan (4·40) 719 I.1.a

מַעֲרָב west (5·14) 788

תּוֹלְדוֹת 31 account of people and their descendents, successive generations, genealogical divisions (9·39) 410

Chapter 27

שֹׁטֵר 1 official, officer (3·25) 1009

מַחֲלֹקֶת division, course (26·42) 324

מַחֲלֹקֶת 2 division, course (26·42) 324

מַחֲלֹקֶת 4 division, course (26·42) 324

נָגִיד leader, ruler, prince (12·44) 617

מַחֲלֹקֶת 5 division, course (26·42) 324

מַחֲלֹקֶת 6 division, course (26·42) 324

מַחֲלֹקֶת 7 division, course (26·42) 324

מַחֲלֹקֶת 8 division, course (26·42) 324

מַחֲלֹקֶת 9 division, course (26·42) 324

פְּלֹנִי 10 a certain one; BDB rds הַפַּלְטִי as 2 Sam. 23:26 (3·6) 813 II; 811 I

מַחֲלֹקֶת division, course (26·42) 324

מַחֲלֹקֶת 11 division, course (26·42) 324

מַחֲלֹקֶת 12 division, course (26·42) 324

מַחֲלֹקֶת 13 division, course (26·42) 324

מַחֲלֹקֶת 14 division, course (26·42) 324

מַחֲלֹקֶת 15 division, course (26·42) 324

נָגִיד 16 leader, ruler, prince (12·44) 617

וּלְמַטָּה 23 of age = younger; and under (1·10) 641

כּוֹכָב star (1·37) 456

מָנָה 24 to count, number (3 · 12 · 28) 584

בְּזֹאת for this cause (1 · 4) 261 זֶה 6.b.(d)

קֶצֶף wrath (1 · 28) 893 I

כָּפָר 25 village (1 · 1) 499

מִגְדָּל tower (1 · 49) 153

זַיִת 28 olive tree; olives (1 · 38) 268

שִׁקְמָה sycamore tree (1 · 7) 1054

שְׁפֵלָה lowland, strip of land west of Ju-
daean mountains, [the] Shephelah
(1 · 20) 1050

אָתוֹן 30 female ass (1 · 33) 87

רְכוּשׁ 31 property, goods (2 · 28) 940

יוֹעֵץ 32 ptc. = counselor, advisor (3 · 22) 419

יוֹעֵץ 33 ptc. = counselor, advisor (3 · 22) 419

Chapter 28

הִקְהִיל 1 to summon an assembly (3 · 20 · 39)
874

מַחֲלֹקֶת division, course (26 · 42) 324

רְכוּשׁ property, goods (2 · 28) 940

סָרִיס eunuch (1 · 45) 710

מְנוּחָה 2 resting place (2 · 21) 629

הֲדֹם stool, footstool (1 · 6) 213

נָגִיד 4 leader, ruler, prince (12 · 44) 617

רָצָה to be pleased (3 · 42 · 50) 953

שָׁלֵם 9 complete, perfect (4 · 28) 1023 I

חֵפֶץ delighting in, having pleasure in;
w. נֶפֶשׁ = a willing (1 · 12) 343

יֵצֶר imagination, device, purpose (2 · 9)
428

הִזְנִיחַ to reject (1 · 3 · 16) 276 I

עַד forever (1 · 48) 723

תַּבְנִית 11 pattern (4 · 20) 125

אוּלָם porch (1 · 49) 17 I

גַּנְזַךְ treasury (1 · 1) 170

עֲלִיָּה roof-chamber (1 · 20) 751

חֶדֶר room, chamber [usually private]
(1 · 37) 293

פְּנִימִי inner (1 · 33) 819

כַּפֹּרֶת propitiatory (1 · 27) 498

תַּבְנִית 12 pattern (4 · 20) 125

לִשְׁכָּה room, chamber, hall, cell (4 · 47)
545

מַחֲלֹקֶת 13 division, course (26 · 42) 324

מִשְׁקָל 14 weight (13 · 49) 1054

מִשְׁקָל 15 weight (13 · 49) 1054

מְנֹרָה lampstand (5 · 40) 633

נֵר lamp (2 · 45) 632

מִשְׁקָל 16 weight (13 · 49) 1054

מַעֲרֶכֶת row, line [used only of lines of
bread of the Presence] (3 · 10) 790

מִזְלָגָה 17 three-pronged fork used with sacrifices (1 · 5) 272

מִזְרָק basin, bowl (1 · 32) 284

קַשְׂוָה jug, jar (1 · 4) 903

כְּפוֹר bowl (5 · 8) 499 I

מִשְׁקָל weight (13 · 49) 1054

זָקַק 18 Pual ptc. = refined (2 · 4 · 7) 279 I

מִשְׁקָל weight (13 · 49) 1054

תַּבְנִית pattern (4 · 20) 125

מֶרְכָּבָה chariot (1 · 44) 939

סָכַךְ to screen, cover (1 · 12 · 18) 696

כְּתָב 19 writing (1 · 17) 508

תַּבְנִית pattern (4 · 20) 125

אָמֵץ 20 to be bold, strong (2 · 16 · 41) 54

הרפה Hiph. to abandon, forsake
(2 · 21 · 44) 951

מַחֲלֹקֶת 21 division, course (26 · 42) 324

נָדִיב incited, inclined, willing (1 · 27) 622

Chapter 29

רַךְ 1 tender, inexperienced (2 · 16) 940

בִּירָה castle, palace (2 · 18) 108

שֹׁהַם 2 precious stone, perh. onyx (1 · 11)
995

מִלֻּא setting; אַבְנֵי מ׳ = stones of briliant
settings (1 · 15) 571

פוּךְ	antimony, w. אַבְנֵי = stones of brilliant antimony hue (1·4) 806
רִקְמָה	variegated material (1·12) 955
יָקָר	precious, costly, valued; w. stones = gems, jewels (2·35) 429
שַׁיִשׁ	alabaster (1·1) 1010
רָצָה 3	to be pleased with, favorable to; accept (3·42·50) 953
סְגֻלָּה	treasure (1·8) 688
לְמַעְלָה	upwards; here = exceedingly (6·34) 751 II מַעַל 2.c.(b)
זקק 4	Pual ptc. = refined (2·4·7) 279 I
טָח	to overlay, coat (1·9·11) 376 טוח
חָרָשׁ 5	graver, artificer (6·38) 360
התנדב	to offer free-will offerings (7·14·17) 621
התנדב 6	to offer free-will offerings (7·14·17) 621
אֲדַרְכּוֹן 7	drachma, daric (1·2) 204
רִבּוֹ	ten thousand, myriad (2·11) 914
התנדב 9	to offer free-will offerings (7·14·17) 621
שָׁלֵם	complete; at peace; full (4·28) 1023
גְּדוּלָה 11	greatness (4·12) 153
תִּפְאָרָה	glory; honor; beauty, finery (3·50) 802
נֵצַח	eminence (1·43) 664
הוֹד	splendor, majesty (3·24) 217
עֹשֶׁר 12	riches (2·37) 799
תִּפְאָרָה 13	glory; honor; beauty, finery (3·50) 802
עָצַר 14	to retain; here with inf. = be able to (2·36·46) 783

התנדב	to offer free-will offerings (7·14·17) 621
כָּזֹאת	in like manner, thus (1·28) 262 זֶה 6.d
תּוֹשָׁב 15	sojourner (1·14) 444
מִקְוֶה	hope (1·5) 876
בחן 17	to test, try, examine (1·24·29) 103
מֵישָׁר	equity, uprightness (1·19) 449
רָצָה	to be pleased with (3·42·50) 953
יֹשֶׁר	rightness, uprightness (1·14) 449
התנדב	to offer free-will offerings (7·14·17) 621
פֹּה	here (1·45) 805
יֵצֶר 18	imagination, device, purpose (2·9) 428 I
שָׁלֵם 19	complete, perfect (4·28) 1023 I
עֵדָה	testimony (1·32) 730 BDB עדות
בִּירָה	castle, palace (2·18) 108
קדד 20	to bow down (1·15·15) 869 I
מָחֳרָת 21	the next day, w. ל = on the next day (2·32) 564
נָגִיד 22	leader, ruler, prince (12·44) 617 II מַעַל 2.c.(b)
לָתֵת יָד תַּחַת 24	idiom: to submit 389 יָד 1.d
לְמַעְלָה 25	upwards; here = exceedingly (6·34) 751 II מַעַל 2.c
הוֹד	splendor, majesty, vigor (3·24) 217 I
שֵׂיבָה 28	old age (1·20) 966
שָׂבֵעַ	sated, satisfied (1·10) 960
עֹשֶׁר	riches (2·37) 799
רֹאֶה 29	seer (3·12) 909 I
חֹזֶה	seer (3·17) 302

2 CHRONICLES

Chapter 1

לְמַעְלָה 1 exceedingly; sq. מִן = over and above (8 · 34) 751 II מֵעַל 2.c

אֲבָל 4 howbeit, but (3 · 11) 6

מַדָּע 10 knowledge (3 · 6) 396

יַעַן אֲשֶׁר 11 because, since (2 · 32) 774 יַעַן 2

עֹשֶׁר riches (6 · 37) 799

נֶכֶס pl. = riches, treasures (2 · 5) 647

שֹׂנֵא ptc. = enemy (2 · 41) 971

מַדָּע knowledge (3 · 6) 396

מַדָּע 12 knowledge (3 · 6) 396

עֹשֶׁר riches (6 · 37) 799

נֶכֶס pl. = riches, treasures (2 · 5) 647

שִׁקְמָה 15 sycamore tree (2 · 7) 1054

שְׁפֵלָה lowland, foothills, [the] Shephelah (4 · 20) 1050

מוֹצָא 16 that which goes forth, here = export (2 · 27) 425 I

מִקְוֵה collection (2 · 7) 876 II

סֹחֵר ptc. = trader (2 · 16) 695

מְחִיר price (1 · 15) 564

מֶרְכָּבָה 17 chariot (6 · 44) 939

Chapter 2

סַבָּל 1 burden-bearer (3 · 5) 688

חֹצֵב ptc. = stone cutter, stone mason (3 · 8) 345

נצח to act as overseer (3 · 7 · 8) 663 I

סַם 3 spice, incense (2 · 16) 702

מַעֲרֶכֶת row, line (3 · 10) 790

עָצַר 5 to retain, w. inf. = be able to; to restrain (6 · 36 · 46) 783

כִּלְכֵּל Pilp., to contain, hold in (2 · 24 · 38) 465 כול

אַרְגָּוָן 6 purple, purple thread (3 · 39[?]) 71

כַּרְמִיל crimson, carmine; i.e., crimson cloth (3 · 3) 502

תְּכֵלֶת violet; i.e., violet thread or cloth (3 · 49) 1067

פָּתַח to engrave (2 · 8 · 9) 836 II

פִּתּוּחַ engraving (2 · 11) 836

בְּרוֹשׁ 7 cypress or fir (2 · 20) 141

אַלְגּוּמִּים tree [kind unknown] (3 · 6) 38

הִפְלִיא 8 to do [or make] marvelously, wondrously to do a hard or difficult thing (2 · 10 · 24) 810

חֹטֵב 9 ptc. = cutter or gatherer of wood (1 · 6) 310 I

חִטָּה wheat (3 · 30) 334

מַכָּה blow, wound, slaughter [BDB rd. מַכֹּלֶת food, from 1 Kings 5:25] (4 · 48) 646 נכה

כֹּר kor [dry measure] (3 · 8) 499

שְׂעֹרָה barley (3 · 33) 972

בַּת bath [liquid measure] = 40 liters (3 · 13) 144

כְּתָב 10 letter; writing (2 · 17) 508

שֵׂכֶל 11 insight, understanding (2 · 16) 968

בִּינָה understanding (2 · 37) 108

בִּינָה 12 understanding (2 · 37) 108

אַרְגָּמָן 13 purple, purple thread (3 · 39[?]) 71

תְּכֵלֶת violet; i.e., violet thread or cloth (3 · 49) 1067

בּוּץ byssus, a fine white Egyptian linen (3 · 8) 101

כַּרְמִיל crimson, carmine; i.e., crimson cloth (3 · 3) 502

פָּתַח to engrave (2 · 8 · 9) 836 II

פִּתּוּחַ engraving (2 · 11) 836

חִטָּה 14 wheat (3 · 30) 334

שְׂעֹרָה barley (3 · 33) 972

צֹרֶךְ 15 need (1 · 1) 863

רַפְסֹדָה raft (1 · 1) 952

סְפָר 16 enumeration, census (1 · 1) 708 I

סַבָּל 17 burden-bearer (3 · 5) 688

חֹצֵב ptc. = stone cutter, stone mason (3 · 8) 345

נצח to act as overseer (3 · 7 · 8) 663 I

Chapter 3

גֹּרֶן 1 threshing floor (2 · 34) 175

הוּסַד 3 *Hoph.*, to be founded; inf. = founding (1 · 3 · 41) 413 יסד

אוּלָם 4 porch (5 · 49) 17 I

גֹּבַהּ height (2 · 17) 147

צִפָּה to overlay (5 · 44 · 46) 860 II

מִפְּנִימָה within (1 · 3) 819 פְּנִימָה 2

חִפָּה 5 to overlay (5 · 5 · 12) 341

בְּרוֹשׁ cypress or fir (2 · 20) 141

תִּמֹרָה palm [tree] figure (1 · 19) 1071

שַׁרְשְׁרָה chain (3 · 8) 1057

צִפָּה 6 to overlay (5 · 44 · 46) 860 II

יָקָר precious, w. אֶבֶן gem = costly, rare (5 · 35) 429

תִּפְאָרָה beauty, finery (1 · 50) 802

חִפָּה 7 to overlay (5 · 5 · 12) 341

קוֹרָה rafter, beam (1 · 5) 900

סַף threshold, sill (3 · 25) 706

פִּתַּח to engrave (2 · 8 · 9) 836 II

חִפָּה 8 to overlay (5 · 5 · 12) 341

מִשְׁקָל 9 weight (3 · 49) 1054

מַסְמֵר nail (1 · 5) 702

עֲלִיָּה roof chamber (2 · 20) 751

חִפָּה to overlay (5 · 5 · 12) 341

צַעֲצֻעִים things formed [sculptured] (1 · 1) 847

צִפָּה 10 to overlay (5 · 44 · 46) 860 II

דָּבֵק 12 clinging; cleaving [to] (1 · 3) 180

פָּרֹכֶת 14 curtain (1 · 25) 827

תְּכֵלֶת violet; i.e., violet thread or cloth (3 · 49) 1067

אַרְגָּמָן purple, purple thread (3 · 39) 71

כַּרְמִיל crimson, carmine; i.e., crimson stuff, cloth (3 · 3) 502

בּוּץ byssus, a fine white Egyptian linen (3 · 8) 101

צֶפֶת 15 capital [of pillar] (1 · 1) 860

שַׁרְשְׁרָה 16 chain (3 · 8) 1057

דְּבִיר inner sanctuary (4 · 16) 184

רִמּוֹן ornament shaped like a pomegranate (3 · 32) 941 I

יְמִינִי 17 Qere = יְמָנִי right, on the right (3 · 33) 412

שְׂמָאלִי left, on the left (2 · 9) 970

Chapter 4

קוֹמָה 1 height (3 · 45) 879

עָגוֹל 2 round (1 · 5) 722

קוֹמָה height (3 · 45) 879

קַו line, measuring line (1 · 25) 876

דְּמוּת 3 likeness, image (1 · 25) 198

הִקִּיף to surround, encompass, enclose (2 · 16 · 17) 668 II

טוּר row, course (2 · 27) 377

מוּצֶקֶת a casting, pipe (1 · 2) 427

מִלְמַעְלָה 4 above (2 · 26) 752 II מַעַל עלה 2.d

אָחוֹר back, behind; פָּנִים וא׳ = in front and behind; (2 · 41) 30

עֳבִי 5 thickness (2 · 5) 716

טֶפַח a span, handbreadth (1 · 9) 381

כּוֹס cup (1 · 31) 468 I

פֶּרַח bud, sprout; here of bud-shaped ornament (2 · 21) 827

שׁוּשַׁן lily- or flower-shaped capital of a pillar (1 · 17) 1004 I

בַּת bath [liquid measure] = 40 liters (3 · 13) 144

הֵכִיל to contain, hold; sustain (2 · 12 · 38) 465 כול

כִּיּוֹר 6 basin; pot (3 · 23) 468

הֵדִיחַ to rinse, cleanse (1 · 4 · 4) 188

מְנוֹרָה 7 lampstand (3 · 40) 633

מִזְרָק 8 bowl, basin (3 · 32) 284

עֲזָרָה 9 court, enclosure (3 · 9) 741

צִפָּה to overlay (5 · 44 · 46) 860 II

יְמָנִי 10 right, on the right (3 · 33) 412

קֶדֶם eastward, toward the East (1 · 26) 870

657

מִמּוּל from the front of, off the front of (1 · 9) 557

סִיר 11 pot (3 · 29) 696 I

יָע shovel (2 · 9) 418

מִזְרָק bowl, basin (3 · 32) 284

גֻּלָּה 12 bowl, basin (3 · 15) 165

כֹּתֶרֶת capital of pillar (3 · 24) 509

שְׂבָכָה lattice-work, network, net ornament [on pillar] (3 · 17) 959

רִמּוֹן 13 ornament shaped like a pomegranate (3 · 32) 941 I

שְׂבָכָה lattice-work, network, net ornament (3 · 17) 959

טוּר row, course (2 · 27) 377

גֻּלָּה bowl, basin (3 · 15) 165

כֹּתֶרֶת capital of pillar (3 · 24) 509

מְכוֹנָה 14 base, stand (2 · 25) 467

כִּיּוֹר basin, pot (3 · 23) 468

סִיר 16 pot (3 · 29) 696 I

יָע shovel (2 · 9) 418

מִזְלָגָה three-pronged fork (1 · 5) 272

מרק polish; pass. ptc. = polished (1 · 2 · 4) 599 I

עֳבִי 17 thickness (2 · 5) 716

נֶחְקַר 18 to be searched out, found out, ascertained (1 · 4 · 27) 350

מִשְׁקָל weight (3 · 49) 1054

מְנוֹרָה 20 lampstand (3 · 40) 633

נֵר lamp (4 · 45) 632 I

דְּבִיר inner sanctuary (4 · 16) 184

סָגוּר pass. ptc. = closed up, closely joined (3 · 8) 688 I.4

פֶּרַח 21 bud, sprout; here of bud-shaped ornament (2 · 21) 827

נֵר lamp (4 · 45) 632

מֶלְקָחַיִם [dual] snuffers; tongs (1 · 6) 544

מִכְלָה pl. completeness, perfection (1 · 1) 479 II

מְזַמֶּרֶת 22 pl., snuffers (1 · 5) 275

מִזְרָק bowl, basin (3 · 32) 284

מַחְתָּה fire pan, fire holder (1 · 22) 367

סָגוּר pass. ptc. = closed up, closely joined (3 · 8) 688 I.4 [Holladay = pure, p. 253]

פְּנִימִי inner (2 · 33) 819

Chapter 5

הִקְהִיל 2 to summon an assembly (2 · 20 · 39) 874

נִקְהַל 3 to assemble (2 · 19 · 39) 874

נוֹעַד 6 to gather or assemble by appointment (1 · 18 · 28) 416

נִמְנָה to be counted, numbered (1 · 6 · 28) 584

דְּבִיר 7 inner sanctuary (4 · 16) 184

בַּד 8 poles, staves (3 · 41) 94 II

מִלְמַעְלָה above (2 · 26) 751 II מַעַל 2.d

הָאֱרִיךְ 9 to be long (1 · 31 · 34) 73

בַּד poles, staves (3 · 41) 94 II

דְּבִיר inner sanctuary (4 · 16) 184

לוּחַ 10 tablet, board, plank, plate (1 · 43) 531

מַחֲלֹקֶת 11 division, course (11 · 42) 324

בּוּץ 12 byssus, a fine white Egyptian linen (3 · 8) 101

מְצִלְתַּיִם cymbals (3 · 13) 853

נֵבֶל harp, lute, guitar (4 · 27) 614

כִּנּוֹר lyre (4 · 41) 490

הַחְצֹצְרִם Hiph., to sound with clarions (4 · 5 · 6) 348

חֲצֹצְרָה clarion (11 · 29) 348

חצצר 13 Piel ptc. = clarion player (1 · 1 · 6) 348

וּכְהָרִים = ו+כ+Hiph. of רום

חֲצֹצְרָה clarion (11 · 29) 348

מְצִלְתַּיִם cymbals (3 · 13) 853

Chapter 6

עֲרָפֶל 1 cloud, heavy cloud (1 · 15) 791

זְבֻל 2 elevation, height, lofty abode (1 · 5) 259

מָכוֹן fixed place, place (4 · 17) 467

נָגִיד 5 leader, ruler (9 · 44) 617

יַעַן אֲשֶׁר 8 because, since (2 · 32) 774   2 יַעַן

הֵטִיב to do well, act right (1 · 3 · 21) 373 I טוב

חָלָץ 9 [dual] loins (1 · 10) 323

כִּיּוֹר 13 platform or stage (3 · 23) 468

עֲזָרָה court, enclosure (3 · 9) 741

קוֹמָה height (3 · 45) 879

בֵּרֵךְ to kneel (1 · 2 · 3[?]) 138

בֶּרֶךְ knee [dual = knees] (1 · 25) 139

אָמְנָם 18 verily, truly, indeed (1 · 5) 53

כִּלְכֵּל Pilp. to contain, hold in; sustain (2 · 24 · 38) 465   כול

אַף כִּי how much less [or more]; indeed (2 · 26) 65

תְּחִנָּה 19 supplication for favor (5 · 25) 337

רִנָּה ringing cry (2 · 33) 943

תַּחֲנוּן 21 supplication for favor (1 · 18) 337

סלח to forgive, pardon (6 · 33 · 46) 699

נשא 22 to lend (1 · 11 · 12) 673 I but BDB reads נשא, to lift 669 1.b(5)

אָלָה oath (3 · 36) 46

הֶאֱלָה to adjure, put under oath (1 · 3 · 6) 46 II

הִצְדִּיק 23 to declare righteous, justify (1 · 12 · 14) 842

נִגַּף 24 to be smitten (3 · 22 · 48) 619

סלח 25 to forgive, pardon (6 · 33 · 46) 699

נֶעְצַר 26 to be shut up, be restrained, stayed (1 · 10 · 46) 783

מָטָר rain (3 · 38) 564

סלח 27 to forgive, pardon (6 · 33 · 46) 699

הוֹרָה to direct, teach, instruct (2 · 45 · 45 [?]) 434   ירה

מָטָר rain (3 · 38) 564

דֶּבֶר 28 plague, pestilence (3 · 46) 184

שִׁדָּפוֹן smut [on crops] (1 · 5) 995

יֵרָקוֹן rust, mildew (1 · 6) 439

אַרְבֶּה locust (1 · 24) 916

חָסִיל locust (1 · 6) 340

מַחֲלָה sickness, disease (1 · 4) 318

תְּחִנָּה 29 supplication for favor (5 · 25) 337 I

מַכְאוֹב pain (1 · 16) 456

מָכוֹן 30 fixed place, place (4 · 17) 467

סלח to forgive, pardon (6 · 33 · 46) 699

נָכְרִי 32 foreigner (2 · 45) 648

מָכוֹן 33 fixed place, place (4 · 17) 467

נָכְרִי foreigner; foreign (2 · 45) 648

תְּחִנָּה 35 supplication for favor (5 · 25) 337 I

אָנַף 36 to be angry (1 · 8 · 14) 60

שָׁבָה to take captive (9 · 30 · 38) 985

שֹׁבִים ptc. = captives (2 · 10) 985

נִשְׁבָּה 37 to be taken captive (1 · 8 · 38) 985

שְׁבִי state of captivity; captives (4 · 49) 985

הֶעֱוָה to commit iniquity (1 · 9 · 17) 731

רשע to be wicked, act wickedly (1 · 9 · 34) 957

שְׁבִי 38 state of captivity; captives (4 · 49) 985

שָׁבָה to take captive (9 · 30 · 38) 985

מָכוֹן 39 fixed place, place, site (4 · 17) 467

תְּחִנָּה supplication for favor (5 · 25) 337 I

סלח to forgive, pardon (6 · 33 · 46) 699

קַשֻּׁב 40 attentive (2 · 3) 904

נוּחַ 41 inf. abs. = resting place (1 · 1) 629

תְּשׁוּעָה salvation; deliverance, victory (1 · 34) 448

חָסִיד pious man, the godly (1 · 32) 339

מָשִׁיחַ 42 anointed one (1 · 39) 603

Chapter 7

כָּרַע 3 to bow, bow down (1 · 30 · 36) 502

רִצְפָה pavement (1 · 7) 954

חָנַךְ 5 to dedicate, consecrate (1 · 5 · 5) 335 II

הַחְצֵר 6 *Hiph.*, to sound with clarions
(4 · 5 · 6) 348

הֵכִיל 7 to contain, hold; sustain (2 · 12 · 38)
465 כּוּל

עֲצֶרֶת 9 assembly, company (1 · 11) 783

חֲנֻכָּה dedication, consecration (1 · 8) 335

שָׂמֵחַ 10 glad, joyful, merry (2 · 21) 970

עָצַר 13 to restrain, stop (6 · 36 · 46) 783

מָטָר rain (3 · 38) 564

חָגָב locust, grasshopper (1 · 5) 290 I

דֶּבֶר plague, pestilence (3 · 46) 184

נִכְנַע 14 to humble oneself; be humbled
(15 · 24 · 35) 488

סָלַח to forgive, pardon (6 · 33 · 46) 699

קַשֵּׁב 15 attentive (2 · 3) 904

מֹשֵׁל 18 ptc. ruler, when one rules (2 · 24)
605

נָתַשׁ 20 to pull or pluck up, root out
(1 · 16 · 21) 684

מָשָׁל byword (1 · 39) 605 II

שְׁנִינָה sharp word, taunt (1 · 4) 1042

בַּמֶּה 21 for what? why? (2 · 29) 553 מָה 4.a

כָּכָה thus, in this way (3 · 33) 462

עַל אֲשֶׁר 22 because that 758 עַל III.a

Chapter 8

מִסְכְּנוֹת 4 supply, storage (5 · 7) 698

תַּחְתּוּן 5 lower, lowest (1 · 13) 1066

מָצוֹר enclosure, siege-works; עִיר מ' = entrenched or fortified city (3 · 25) 848 I

בְּרִיחַ bar (2 · 41) 138 ברח

מִסְכְּנוֹת 6 supply, storage (5 · 7) 698 I

חֵשֶׁק desire = thing desired (1 · 4) 366

חָשַׁק to be attached to = love (1 · 8 · 11)
365 I

מֶמְשָׁלָה rule, dominion (2 · 17) 606

מַס 8 labor band or gang, forced service
(2 · 23) 586 I

שָׁלִישׁ 9 adjutant or officer (1 · 16) 1026

נִצָּב 10 *Niph.* ptc. = deputy, prefect (1 · 7)
662

נָצִיב pillar [or garrison?] (1 · 11) 662 I

רָדָה to have dominion, rule over, dominate (1 · 22 · 28) 921 I

אוּלָם 12 porch (5 · 49) 17 I

שָׁבוּעַ 13 week, period of seven [days]
(1 · 20) 988

סֻכָּה booth [made of boughs] (1 · 31) 697

מַחֲלֹקֶת 14 division, course (11 · 42) 324

דְּבַר יוֹם

בְּיוֹמוֹ idiom: each day's affair in its day,
each day's requirement (2 · 14) 400
יוֹם 7.e.(3)

שֹׁעֵר porter, gatekeeper (6 · 37) 1045

מוּסָד 16 foundation laying; foundation (1 · 2) 414

שָׁלֵם finished, complete (5 · 28) 1023 I

אֳנִיָּה 18 ship (6 · 31) 58

Chapter 9

מַלְכָּה 1 queen (4 · 35) 573

שֵׁמַע report, hearing (1 · 17) 1034

נִסָּה to test, try (2 · 36 · 36) 650

חִידָה perplexing question, riddle, enigma
(1 · 17) 295

כָּבֵד very numerous (3 · 40) 458

בֹּשֶׂם spice, perfume (6 · 30) 141

יָקָר preciouous; w. אֶבֶן = gem; costly;
rare; glorious (5 · 35) 429

נֶעְלָם 2 to be concealed (1 · 11 · 29) 761 I

מַלְכָּה 3 queen (4 · 35) 573

מַאֲכָל 4 food (2 · 30) 38

מוֹשָׁב sitting = those sitting; seat; dwelling
(1 · 44) 444

מַעֲמָד service (2 · 5) 765

מְשָׁרֵת *Piel* ptc. = minister (2 · 20) 1058

מַלְבּוּשׁ garment, rainment (2 · 20) 528

מַשְׁקֶה butler, cup bearer (2 · 19[?]) 1052 I

עֲלִיָּה roof-chamber (2 · 20) 751 עלה [but BDB rd. עֲלִיתָו fm. II עֹלָה, burnt offering, p.750]

מַרְבִּית 6 greatness (2 · 5) 916

שְׁמוּעָה report (1 · 27) 1035

אֹשֶׁר 7 happiness, blessedness (1 · 45) 80

בֹּשֶׂם 9 spice, perfume (6 · 30) 141

יָקָר precious; w. אֶבֶן (gem) = costly, rare (5 · 35) 429

מַלְכָּה queen (4 · 35) 573

אַלְגּוּמִּים 10 tree [kind unknown] (3 · 6) 38

יָקָר precious, w. אֶבֶן (gem) = costly, rare (5 · 35) 429

אַלְגּוּמִּים 11 tree [kind unknown] (3 · 6) 38

מְסִלָּה highway (1 · 27) 700 [but BDB rd. מִסְעָד w. 1 Kings 10:12 = support (1 · 2) 703]

כִּנּוֹר lyre (4 · 41) 490

נֶבֶל harp, lute, guitar (4 · 27) 614

מַלְכָּה 12 queen (4 · 35) 573

חֵפֶץ desire, longing (1 · 39) 343

מִלְּבַד besides (3 · 33) בַּד 94 1.e

מִשְׁקָל 13 weight (3 · 49) 1054

תָּרִים 14 Qal ptc. pl. = merchants (1 · 2) 1064 תּוּר 3

סֹחֵר ptc. = trader (2 · 16) 695

פֶּחָה governor (1 · 27) 808

צִנָּה 15 large shield (5 · 20) 857 III

שָׁחֵט pass. ptc. = beaten, hammered (3 · 6 · 6) 1006

שָׁחֵט 16 pass. ptc. = beaten hammered (3 · 6 · 6) 1006

צִפָּה 17 to overlay (5 · 44 · 46) 860 II

מַעֲלָה 18 step, stair (2 · 47) 752 II

כֶּבֶשׁ footstool (1 · 1) 461

מִזֶּה וּמִזֶּה on one side . . . on the other (2 · 12) 262 זֶה 6.e

אֲרִי lion (2 · 35) 71

אֲרִי 19 lion (2 · 35) 71

מַעֲלָה step, stair (2 · 47) 752 II.1

מִזֶּה וּמִזֶּה on one side . . . on the other (2 · 12) 262 זֶה 6.e

מַשְׁקֶה 20 drink, w. כְּלִי = butlership (2 · 20[?]) 1052 II

סָגוּר pass. ptc. = closed up, closely joined (3 · 8) 688 4

מְאוּמָה anything (1 · 32) 548

אֳנִיָּה 21 ship (6 · 31) 58

שֶׁנְהַבִּים ivory (1 · 2) 1042

קוֹף ape (1 · 2) 880

תֻּכִּיִּים peacocks (1 · 2) 1067

עֹשֶׁר 22 riches (6 · 37) 799

שַׂלְמָה 24 wrapper, mantle (1 · 16) 971 II

נֶשֶׁק equipment, weapons (1 · 10) 676

בֹּשֶׂם spice, perfume (6 · 30) 141

פֶּרֶד mule (1 · 14) 825

שָׁנָה בְּשָׁנָה idiom: year by year, annually 1040

אֻרְיָה 25 crib, manger [= stall, stable] (2 · 3) 71

מֶרְכָּבָה chariot (6 · 44) 939

מֹשֵׁל 26 ptc. = when one rules; ruler (2 · 24) 605

שִׁקְמָה 27 sycamore tree (2 · 7) 1054

שְׁפֵלָה lowland, foothills, [the] Shephelah (4 · 20) 1050

שְׁאָר 29 rest, residue, remnant (2 · 26) 984

נְבוּאָה prophetic writing (2 · 3) 612

חָזוֹת vision (1 · 1) 303

חֹזֶה seer (7 · 17) 302

Chapter 10

הִקְשָׁה 4 to make severe, burdensome; make hard (3 · 21 · 28) 904 I

עֹל yoke (7 · 40) 760

קָשֶׁה severe, hard (2 · 36) 904

כָּבֵד oppressive, grievous, burdensome (3 · 40) 458

רָצָה 7 to be pleased with, favorable to (1 · 42 · 50[?]) 953

עֹל 9 yoke (7 · 40) 760

עֹל 10 yoke (7 · 40) 760

קֹטֶן little [finger] (1 · 2) 882

עָבָה to be thick (1 · 3 · 3) 716

מָתְנַיִם loins (1 · 47) 608

הֶעְמִיס 11 to load (1 · 2 · 9) 1126 [770b]

עֹל yoke (7 · 40) 760

כָּבֵד oppressive, grievous, burdensome (3 · 40) 458

יִסַּר to chasten, chastise (2 · 27 · 38) 415

שׁוֹט scourge (2 · 8) 1002

עַקְרָב scorpion (2 · 8) 785

קָשֶׁה 13 severe, hard (2 · 36) 904

עֹל 14 yoke (7 · 40) 760

יִסַּר to chasten, chastise (2 · 27 · 38) 415

שׁוֹט scourge (2 · 8) 1002

עַקְרָב scorpion (2 · 8) 785

נְסִבָּה 15 turn [of affairs] (1 · 1) 687

מַס 18 labor band or gang; forced service (2 · 23) 586

רגם to stone, kill by stoning (2 · 16 · 16) 920

הִתְאַמֵּץ make oneself alert, strengthen oneself (2 · 4 · 41) 54

מֶרְכָּבָה chariot (6 · 44) 939

פָּשַׁע 19 to rebel, revolt (4 · 40 · 41) 833

Chapter 11

הִקְהִיל 1 to summon an assembly (2 · 20 · 39) 874

בָּחוּר pass. ptc. = chosen (5 · 19) 103

מָצוֹר 5 enclosure, siege-works; עִיר מ' = entrenched or fortified city (3 · 25) 848 I

מְצוּרָה 10 rampart; עָרֵי מ' = fortified cities (6 · 8) 849

מְצוּרָה 11 rampart; עָרֵי מ' = fortified cities (6 · 8) 849

נָגִיד leader, ruler (9 · 44) 617

מַאֲכָל food (2 · 30) 38

צִנָּה 12 large shield (5 · 20) 857 III

רֹמַח spear, lance (4 · 15) 942

הִתְיַצֵּב 13 to station oneself, take one's stand (3 · 48 · 48) 426

הִזְנִיחַ 14 to reject, spurn (2 · 3 · 19) 276 I

כֹּהֵן to minister as a priest (1 · 23 · 23) 464

שָׂעִיר 15 satyr, demon (1 · 4) 972 III

עֵגֶל image of calf (2 · 35) 722

אִמֵּץ 17 to make firm, strengthen (3 · 19 · 41) 54

פִּילֶגֶשׁ 21 concubine (2 · 37) 811

נָגִיד 22 leader, ruler (9 · 44) 617

פָּרַץ 23 to distribute [dub.] (7 · 46 · 49) 829 I

מְצוּרָה rampart; עָרֵי מ' = fortified cities (6 · 8) 849

מָזוֹן food, sustenance (1 · 2) 266 זון

Chapter 12

חֶזְקָה 1 strength, force (2 · 4) 305

מָעַל 2 to act unfaithfully, treacherously (8 · 35 · 35) 591

מְצוּרָה 4 rampart; עָרֵי מ' = fortified cities (6 · 8) 849

נִכְנַע 6 to humble oneself; be humbled (15 · 24 · 35) 488

נִכְנַע 7 to humble oneself; be humbled (15 · 24 · 35) 488

פְּלֵיטָה escaped remnant; escape (3 · 28) 812

נתך to pour forth (2 · 7 · 21) 677

רָץ 10 ptc. = runner (6 · 25) 930 רוץ

מִדֵּי 11 as often as, whenever (2 · 15) 191 דַּי 2.c

רָץ ptc. = runner (6 · 25) 930 רוץ

תָּא chamber (1 · 13) 1060

נִכְנַע 12 to humble oneself (15 · 24 · 35) 488

כָּלָה annihilation, complete destruction (1 · 22) 478

חֹזֶה 15 seer (7 · 17) 302

הִתְיַחֵשׂ to be enrolled by genealogy (5 · 20 · 20) 405

Chapter 13

בָּחוּר 3 pass. ptc. = chosen (5 · 19) 103

מֶלַח 5 salt (2 · 28) 571 II

מָרַד 6 to rebel, revolt (2 · 25 · 25) 597

רֵיק 7 worthless (1 · 14) 938

בְּלִיַּעַל worthlessness; 'אִישׁ בּ = worthless fellow, good-for- nothing (1 · 27) 116

הִתְאַמֵּץ to strengthen oneself, be strong (2 · 4 · 41) 54

רַךְ weak; רַךְ לֵבָב = timid; tender (1 · 16) 940

הִתְחַזֵּק לִפְנֵי idiom: to withstand (2 · 2) 305

הִתְחַזֵּק לִפְנֵי 8 idiom: to withstand (2 · 2) 305

עֵגֶל image of calf (2 · 35) 722

הִדִּיחַ 9 to thrust out, banish (2 · 27 · 43) 623 נדח

לְלֹא without (3 · 10) 520 לֹא 4.e

בַּבֹּקֶר בַּבֹּקֶר 11 morning by morning, every morning (1 · 13) 133 בֹּקֶר 1.f

בָּעֶרֶב בָּעֶרֶב evening by evening, every evening 787 1.a

סַם spice, incense (2 · 16) 702

מַעֲרֶכֶת row, line (3 · 10) 790

מְנוֹרָה lampstand (3 · 40) 633

נֵר lamp (4 · 45) 632

חֲצֹצְרָה 12 clarion (11 · 29) 348

תְּרוּעָה blast of horn (2 · 36) 929

הֵרִיעַ to sound a signal for war or march (3 · 40 · 44) 929 רוע

מַאֲרָב 13 men waiting in ambush (2 · 5) 70

אָחוֹר 14 behind back; פָּנִים וָא' = in front and behind; hind (2 · 41) 30

הַחֲצֵר Hiph., to sound with clarions (4 · 5 · 6) 348

חֲצֹצְרָה clarion (11 · 29) 348

הֵרִיעַ 15 to shout a war-cry, or alarm of battle (3 · 40 · 44) 929 רוע

נָגַף to strike, smite (5 · 25 · 48) 619

מַכָּה 17 slaughter; beating; plague (4 · 48) 646

בָּחוּר pass. ptc. = chosen (5 · 19) 103

נִכְנַע 18 to be humbled (15 · 24 · 35) 488

אמץ to be strong (2 · 16 · 41) 54

נִשְׁעַן trust (5 · 22 · 22) 1043

עָצַר 20 to retain; inf. = be able to—; restrain (6 · 36 · 46) 783

נָגַף to strike, smite (5 · 25 · 48) 619

מִדְרָשׁ 22 commentary, exposition, midrash (2 · 2) 205

שָׁקַט 23 to be at peace; be quiet (5 · 31 · 41) 1052

Chapter 14

נֵכָר 2 that which is foreign (2 · 36) 648

מַצֵּבָה pillar [as a monument or memorial] (2 · 36) 663

גִּדַּע to cut down (4 · 9 · 22) 154

אֲשֵׁרָה sacred tree or pole representing a Canaanite goddess of fortune and happiness (11 · 40) 81

חַמָּן 4 sun-pillar idolatrous worship (3 · 8) 329

שָׁקַט to be at peace; be quiet (5 · 31 · 41) 1052

מְצוּרָה 5 rampart; עָרֵי מ' = fortified cities (6 · 8) 849

שָׁקַט to be at peace; be quiet (5 · 31 · 41) 1052

מִגְדָּל 6 tower (6 · 49) 153

בְּרִיחַ bar (2 · 41) 138

מִסָּבִיב from every side (4 · 42) 687 סָבִיב 1.d

663

צִנָּה 7 large shield (5 · 20) 857 III

רֹמַח spear, lance (4 · 15) 942

מֶרְכָּבָה 8 chariot (6 · 44) 939

גַּיְא 9 valley (3 · 47) 161

לְאֵין 10 without (5 · 9) 35 II אֵין 6.c

נִשְׁעָן to lean, here = trust (5 · 22 · 22) 1043

עָצַר to retain + inf. = be able to; to restrain (6 · 36 · 46) 783

אֱנוֹשׁ man, mankind (1 · 42) 60

נָגַף 11 to strike, smite (5 · 25 · 48) 619

לְאֵין 12 without; so that not (5 · 9) 35 II אֵין
6.c

מִחְיָה preservation of life; (1 · 8) 313

פַּחַד 13 dread; object of dread (4 · 49) 808 I

בָּזַז to spoil, plunder (5 · 38 · 42) 102

בִּזָּה spoil, prey (3 · 10) 103

שָׁבָה 14 to take captive (9 · 30 · 38) 985

Chapter 15

לְלֹא 3 without (3 · 10) 520 לֹא 4.e

הוֹרָה to direct, teach, instruct (2 · 45 · 45
[?]) 434 ירה

מְהוּמָה 5 turmoil, disturbance, confusion
(1 · 12) 223

כָּתַת 6 to be beaten in pieces, be crushed
(1 · 1 · 17) 510

הָמַם to discomfit, vex, confuse
(1 · 13 · 13) 243

רָפָה 7 to sink, drop; fig. = to lose heart
(1 · 14 · 44) 951

שָׂכָר wages = reward (1 · 28) 969 I

פְּעֻלָּה work (1 · 14) 821

נְבוּאָה 8 prophecy (2 · 3) 612

שִׁקּוּץ detested thing (1 · 28) 1055

חִדֵּשׁ to repair; renew (3 · 9 · 10) 293

אוּלָם porch (5 · 49) 17

לְמִן 13 from (1 · 14) 583 מִן 9.b

תְּרוּעָה 14 shout of joy; blast of horn or voice
for war (2 · 36) 929

חֲצֹצְרָה clarion (11 · 29) 348 IV

שְׁבוּעָה 15 oath (1 · 30) 989

מִסָּבִיב from every side (4 · 42) 687 סָבִיב
1.d

גְּבִירָה 16 queen mother (1 · 15) 150

אֲשֵׁרָה sacred tree or pole representing a
Canaanite goddess of fortune and
happiness (11 · 40) 81

מִפְלֶצֶת horrid thing (2 · 4) 814

הָדַק to make dust of, pulverize
(3 · 8 · 13) 200 דקק

שָׁלֵם 17 complete, full (5 · 28) 1023

Chapter 16

הֵפֵר 3 to break, violate (1 · 42 · 45) 830 I

מִסְכְּנוֹת 4 supply, storage (5 · 7) 698

רֹאֶה 7 seer (2 · 12) 909 I

נִשְׁעָן to trust; lean, support oneself
(5 · 22 · 22) 1043

נִשְׁעָן 8 to trust; lean, support oneself
(5 · 22 · 22) 1043

שׁוֹטֵט 9 *Poel*, to go quickly to and fro
(1 · 5 · 13) 1001 I

שָׁלֵם complete, full (5 · 28) 1024

נִסְכַּל to act or do foolishly (1 · 4 · 8) 698

רֹאֶה 10 seer (2 · 12) 909 I

מַהְפֶּכֶת stocks [or similar instrument of
punishment] (1 · 4) 246

זַעַף raging, rage (3 · 3) 277

רִצֵּץ *Piel*, to crush in pieces, here
fig. = oppress (1 · 3 · 19) 954

חָלָא 12 to be sick, diseased (1 · 1 · 2) 316 I

לְמַעְלָה exceedingly (8 · 34) 751 II מַעַל 2.c

חֳלִי sickness, disease (6 · 24) 318

רֹפֵא ptc. = healer, physician (1 · 5) 950

כָּרָה 14 to dig (1 · 13 · 14) 500 I

מִשְׁכָּב couch, bed (1 · 46) 1012

בֹּשֶׂם spice, perfume (6 · 30) 141

זַן sort, kind (1 · 2) 275

רקח *Pual*, ptc. = mixed (1 · 1 · 8) 955
מֶרְקַחַת ointment pot or ointment mixture (1 · 3) 955
שְׂרֵפָה burning (3 · 13) 977

Chapter 17

בָּצוּר 2 pass. ptc. = cut off, made inaccessible [fortified] (4 · 25) 130
נָצִיב deputy [or garrison[?]]; pillar (1 · 11) 662
עֹשֶׁר 5 riches (6 · 37) 799
גָּבַהּ 6 to be lofty [here w. heart = to be encouraged] (3 · 24 · 34) 146
אֲשֵׁרָה sacred tree or pole representing a Canaanite goddess of fortune and happiness (11 · 40) 81
פַּחַד 10 dread; object of dread (4 · 49) 808 I
מַשָּׂא 11 what is brought here = tribute; carrying; load (3 · 45) 672
תַּיִשׁ male goat (1 · 4) 1066
גָּדֵל 12 becoming great, growing up (1 · 4) 152
לְמַעְלָה exceedingly (8 · 34) 751 II מַעַל 2.c
בִּירָנִית fortress, fortified place (2 · 18) 108
מִסְכְּנוֹת supply, storage (5 · 7) 698
פְּקֻדָּה 14 mustering; oversight (4 · 32) 824
התנדב 16 to volunteer; over freewill offerings (1 · 14 · 17) 621
נשק 17 to handle, be equipped with [exact mng. uncert.] (1 · 3 · 3) 676 II
חָלוּץ 18 pass. ptc. = equipped, armed (3 · 17) 323 II
מִלְבַד 19 besides (3 · 33) 94 II בַּד 1.e בדד
מִבְצָר fortification (1 · 37) 131

Chapter 18

עֹשֶׁר 1 riches (6 · 37) 799
התחתן to become son-in-law of (1 · 11 · 11) 368 II

הסית 2 to instigate, allure (4 · 18 · 18) 694 סות
פֹּה 6 here, hither (1 · 45) 805
סָרִיס 8 eunuch (1 · 45) 710
גֹּרֶן 9 threshing floor (2 · 34) 175
נגח 10 *Piel*, to push or thrust (1 · 6 · 11) 618
כַּמָּה 15 how much[?] how many[?] (1 · 13) 553 מָה 4.c
פִּתָּה 19 to deceive (3 · 17 · 27) 834
כָּכָה thus; כ׳ ... כ׳ = in this way ... in that way (3 · 33) 462
פִּתָּה 20 to deceive (3 · 17 · 27) 834
בַּמָּה by what means? (2 · 29) מָה 4.a
פִּתָּה 21 to deceive (3 · 17 · 27) 834
לְחִי 23 cheek (1 · 21) 534
אֵי זֶה where then? אֵי הַדֶּרֶךְ = where is the way [that]? (1 · 15) 32 אֵי 1.b
חֶדֶר 24 room, chamber (2 · 37) 293
נֶחְבָּא to hide oneself (1 · 16 · 24) 285
כֶּלֶא 26 confinement, restraint, imprisonment (1 · 10) 476
לַחַץ oppression, distress (2 · 12) 537
הִתְחַפֵּשׂ 29 to disguise oneself (3 · 8 · 23) 344
הסית 31 to allure (4 · 18 · 18) 694 סות
מָשַׁךְ 33 to draw; draw and lift out; proceed (1 · 30 · 36) 604
תֹּם innocence, simplicity [= without definite aim]; integrity, completeness (1 · 23) 1070
דֶּבֶק appendage, attachment, joint (1 · 3) 180
שִׁרְיָן body armor (2 · 8) 1056
רַכָּב charioteer (1 · 3) 939
מֶרְכָּבָה 34 chariot (6 · 44) 939
נֹכַח in front of (1 · 22) 647

Chapter 19

חֹזֶה 2 seer (7 · 17) 302
שֹׂנֵא ptc. = enemy (2 · 41) 971

בְּזֹאת for this cause (2·4)261 זֶה 6.b.(d)

קֶצֶף wrath (6·28)893

אֲבָל 3 howbeit, but truly (3·11)6

בָּעַר to consume, burn (1·26·28) *Piel* 3

אֲשֵׁרָה sacred tree or pole representing a Canaanite goddess of fortune and happiness (11·40)81

בָּצוּר 5 pass. ptc. = cut off, made inaccessible [= fortified] (4·25)130

פַּחַד 7 dread; object of dread (4·49)808 I

עַוְלָה injustice (1·31)732

מַשָּׂא lifting up; מ׳ פָּנִים = regarding of persons = partiality (1·1)673 נשא

מִקָּח a taking, receiving (1·1)544

שֹׁחַד bribe, present (1·23)1005

יִרְאָה 9 fear (1·45)432

שָׁלֵם in covenant of peace; safe; complete, full (5·28)1023

הִזְהִיר 10 to instruct, teach, warn (1·13·21)264 II

אָשֵׁם to commit an offense, be or become guilty (2·33·35)79

קֶצֶף wrath (6·28)893 I

נָגִיד 11 leader, ruler (9·44)617

שֹׁטֵר officer, official (3·25)1009

Chapter 20

אַחֲרֵיכֵן 1 afterwards (4·46)29 אַחַר pl. 2.b

מֵעֵבֶר 2 from the other side of (1·30)719 I עֵבֶר 1

צוֹם 3 fasting, fast (1·26)847

הִתְיַצֵּב 6 to station oneself, take one's stand (3·48·48)426

אֹהֵב 7 ptc. = friend (2·36)12

שְׁפוֹט 9 judgment, act of judgment (1·2)1048

דֶּבֶר plague, pestilence (3·46)184

גָּמַל 11 repay, requite, wean (1·34·37)168

גֵּרֵשׁ *Piel*, to drive out, away (1·35·48)176

יְרֻשָּׁה possession, inheritance (1·14)440

טַף 13 children (2·42)381

הִקְשִׁיב 15 to give attention (2·45·46)904

מַעֲלֵה 16 ascent (2·19)751

סוֹף end (1·5)693

בְּזֹאת 17 in this matter (2·4)261 זֶה 6.b.(d)

הִתְיַצֵּב to station oneself, take one's stand (3·48·48)426

קָדַד 18 to bow down (2·15·15)869 I

לְמַעְלָה 19 exceedingly (8·34)751 II מַעַל 2.c

הֲדָרָה 21 adornment (1·5)214

חָלוּץ pass. ptc. = equipped, armed [man] (3·17)323 II

רִנָּה 22 ringing cry (2·33)943

אָרַב *Piel*, ptc., ambusher (1·2·23)70

נִגַּף to be smitten (3·22·48)619

הֶחֱרִים 23 to destroy, exterminate (2·46·49)355 I

מִצְפֶּה 24 outlook point; watchtower (1·2)859 I

פֶּגֶר corpse, carcass (2·22)803

פְּלֵיטָה escaped remnant (3·28)812

בָּזַז 25 to spoil, plunder (5·38·42)102

רְכוּשׁ property, goods (6·28)940

פֶּגֶר corpse, carcass (2·22)803

חֲמוּדָה pl., desirable, precious things (1·9)326

לְאַיִן so that not without, no (5·9)35 II אַיִן 6.c

מַשָּׂא bearing, carrying; load (3·45)672

נִקְהַל 26 to assemble (2·19·39)874

נֵבֶל 28 harp, lute, guitar (4·27)614 II

כִּנּוֹר lyre (4·41)490

חֲצֹצְרָה clarion (11·29)348

פַּחַד 29 dread; object of dread (4·49)808 I

שָׁקַט 30 to be undisturbed, at peace (5·31·41)1052

מִסָּבִיב every side (4 · 42) 686 סָבִיב 1.d

אַחֲרֵ־כֵן 35 afterward (4 · 46) 29 אַחַר pl. 2.b

אתחבר [unusual verb form] to join oneself to, make an alliance [עִם with] (2 · 4 · 28) 287

הִרְשִׁיעַ to act wickedly; condemn as guilty (2 · 25 · 34) 957

חִבַּר 36 to make an ally of (1 · 9 · 28) 287

אֳנִיָּה ship (6 · 31) 58

הִתְחַבֵּר 37 to join oneself to, make an alliance [עִם with] (2 · 4 · 28) 287

פָּרַץ to break up or in pieces; break through, over, etc. (7 · 46 · 49) 829 5

אֳנִיָּה ship (6 · 31) 58

עָצַר to retain, + inf. = be able to; restrain, hinder (6 · 36 · 46) 783

שָׁבָה 17 to take captive, lead captive (9 · 30 · 38) 985

רְכוּשׁ property, goods (6 · 28) 940 רכשׁ

נָגַף 18 to strike, smite (5 · 25 · 48) 619

מֵעֶה bowels; internal organs (5 · 32) 588

חֳלִי sickness, disease (6 · 24) 318

לְאֵין without, no; here לְ מַרְפֵּא = incurable (5 · 9) 35 II אַיִן 6.c(b)

מַרְפֵּא healing, cure, health (2 · 13) 951

לְיָמִים מִיָּמִים 19 idiom: in the course of time (1 · 1) יוֹם 398 7.i

מֵעֶה bowels; internal organs (5 · 32) 588

חֳלִי sickness, disease (6 · 24) 318

תַּחֲלֻאִים diseases (1 · 5) 316

שְׂרֵפָה burning (3 · 13) 977

בְּלֹא 20 without (2 · 31) 518 לֹא 4.a

חֶמְדָּה desire, delight (3 · 16) 326

Chapter 21

מַתָּנָה 3 gift (1 · 17) 682 I

מִגְדָּנוֹת choice or excellent things (2 · 4) 550

מְצוּרָה rampart; עָרֵי מ׳ = fortified cities (6 · 8) 849

נִיר 7 lamp (1 · 5) 633 I

פָּשַׁע 8 to rebel, revolt (4 · 40 · 41) 833

פָּשַׁע 10 to rebel, revolt (4 · 40 · 41) 833

הִדִּיחַ 11 to thrust away, thrust aside (2 · 27 · 43) 623 נדח

מִכְתָּב 12 writing (3 · 9) 508

תַּחַת אֲשֶׁר in return for that, because that; instead of (2 · 13) 1066 תחת para. II 3.a.(b)

נָגַף 14 to strike, smite (5 · 25 · 48) 619

מַגֵּפָה plague, pestilence; slaughter, blow (1 · 26) 620

רְכוּשׁ property, goods (6 · 28) 940

חֳלִי 15 sickness, disease (6 · 24) 318

מַחֲלֶה sickness, disease (1 · 2) 318

Chapter 22

גְּדוּד 1 marauding band, troop (5 · 33) 151

יוֹעֵץ 3 ptc. = counselor (3 · 22) 419

הִרְשִׁיעַ to act wickedly; condemn as guilty (2 · 25 · 34) 957

יוֹעֵץ 4 ptc. = counselor (3 · 22) 419

מַכָּה 6 blow, beating; slaughter (4 · 48) 646

תְּבוּסָה 7 ruin, downfall (1 · 1) 101

הִתְחַבֵּא 9 to draw back, hide oneself (2 · 10 · 34) 285

עָצַר to retain, + inf. = be able to; restrain (6 · 36 · 46) 783

דִּבֶּר 10 to speak 180 [but see special note p. 181 6: note read אַבֵּד, to destroy, w. 2 Kings 11:1]

גנב 11 to take by stealth, steal (1 · 30 · 39) 170

הַמּוּמָתִים Hoph. ptc. מות 559

מֵינֶקֶת Hiph. ptc. fem. = nurse (1 · 5) 413 ינק

חֶדֶר room, chamber ח׳ הַמִּטּוֹת = bedroom (2 · 37) 293

מִטָּה couch, bed (2 · 29) 641

הִתְחַבֵּא 12 to draw back, hide oneself (2 · 10 · 34) 285

Chapter 23

שֹׁעֵר 4 porter, gatekeeper (6 · 37) 1045

סַף threshold, sill (3 · 25) 706

יְסוֹד 5 foundation (1 · 19) 414

מְשָׁרֵת 6 *Piel* ptc. = minister (2 · 20) 1058

הִקִּיף 7 to surround, encompass, enclose (2 · 16 · 17) 668 II נקף

פָּטַר 8 to set free, release (1 · 8 · 9) 809

מַחְלֹקֶת division, course (11 · 42) 324

חֲנִית 9 spear (1 · 47) 333

שֶׁלֶט shield (1 · 7) 1020

שֶׁלַח 10 missile, weapon (2 · 8) 1019

יְמָנִי right (3 · 33) 412

שְׂמָאלִי left, on the left (2 · 9) 970

נֵזֶר 11 crown (1 · 23) 634

רָץ 12 ptc. = runner (6 · 25) 930 רוץ

מָבוֹא 13 entrance (2 · 23) 99

חֲצֹצְרָה clarion (11 · 29) 348

שָׂמֵחַ glad, joyful, merry (2 · 21) 970

קֶשֶׁר conspiracy (3 · 16) 905

שְׂדֵרָה 14 row, rank (1 · 4) 690

מָבוֹא 15 entrance (2 · 23) 99

נָתַץ 17 to pull down, break down (1 · 31 · 42) 683

צֶלֶם image (1 · 17) 853

פְּקֻדָּה 18 oversight, charge; here = office (4 · 32) 824

שֹׁעֵר 19 porter, gatekeeper (6 · 37) 1045

אַדִּיר 20 majestic one (1 · 27) 12

שָׁקַט 21 to be quiet, undisturbed (5 · 31 · 41) 1052

Chapter 24

אַחַר־כֵּן 4 afterward (4 · 46) 30 אַחַר "Plur." 2.b

חִדֵּשׁ to repair (3 · 9 · 10) 293

בְּשָׁנָה

מִדֵּי שָׁנָה 5 idiom: = yearly, annually (1 · 3) 191 דַּי 2.c 1040

מַשְׂאֵת 6 contribution, tax (2 · 16) 673

מִרְשַׁעַת 7 wickedness (1 · 1) 958

פָּרַץ to break into (7 · 46 · 49) 829

מַשְׂאֵת 9 contribution, tax; burden; oracle (2 · 16) 673

פְּקֻדָּה 11 overseer; oversight, visitation (4 · 32) 824

פָּקִיד commissioner, deputy (2 · 13) 824

עֵרָה *Piel*, to lay bare, empty; pour out (1 · 9 · 15) 788

לְיוֹם בְּיוֹם idiom: day by day (1 · 1) 400 יוֹם 7.e.(1)

שָׂכַר 12 to hire (2 · 17 · 20) 968

חֹצֵב ptc. = stonecutter, stone mason (3 · 8) 345

חָרָשׁ craftsman (3 · 38) 360

חִדֵּשׁ to repair (3 · 9 · 10) 293

אֲרוּכָה 13 restoration (1 · 6) 74

מַתְכֹּנֶת measurement, proportion (1 · 5) 1067

אָמֵץ to make firm, strengthen; assure (3 · 19 · 41) 54

שְׁאָר 14 rest, residue, remnant (2 · 26) 984

שָׁרֵת ministry [religious] (1 · 2) 1058

זָקֵן 15 to be or become old (1 · 25 · 27) 278

אֲשֵׁרָה 18 sacred tree or pole representing a Canaanite goddess of fortune and happiness (11 · 40) 81

עָצָב idol (1 · 17) 781

קֶצֶף wrath (6 · 28) 893 I

אַשְׁמָה doing wrong (6 · 19) 80

הֵעִיד 19 to affirm solemnly, warn, testify (1 · 38 · 43) 729 עוד

הֶאֱזִין to listen = be obedient (1 · 41 · 41) 24

668

קָשַׁר 21 to league together, conspire (4 · 35 · 43) 905

רגם to stone, kill by stoning (2 · 16 · 16) 920

תְּקוּפָה 23 coming around, circuit (1 · 4) 880

מִצְעָר 24 small thing (1 · 6) 859

שֶׁפֶט judgment (1 · 16) 1048

מַחֲלוּי 25 sickness, suffering (1 · 1) 318

הִתְקַשֵּׁר to conspire (2 · 3 · 43) 905

מִטָּה couch, bed (2 · 29) 641

הִתְקַשֵּׁר 26 to conspire (2 · 3 · 43) 905

מַשָּׂא 27 utterance, oracle (1 · 21) 672

יָסַד to found, establish (2 · 20 · 41) 413

מִדְרָשׁ study, exposition, midrash (2 · 2) 205

Chapter 25

שָׁלֵם 2 in covenant of peace with; complete, full (5 · 28) 1023

חֵטְא 4 guilt of sin, sin (1 · 33) 307

לְמִבֶּן 5 בֶּן + מִן + לְ =

בָּחוּר pass. ptc. = chosen (5 · 19) 103

רֹמַח spear, lance (4 · 5) 942

צִנָּה large shield (5 · 20) 857

שָׂכַר 6 to hire (2 · 17 · 20) 968

גְּדוּד 9 troop (5 · 33) 151

הִבְדִּיל 10 to separate, set apart (1 · 32 · 42) 95

גְּדוּד troop (5 · 33) 151

חֲרִי burning (1 · 6) 354

נָהַג 11 to lead out (1 · 20 · 30) 624 I

גַּיְא valley (3 · 47) 161

מֶלַח salt (2 · 28) 571 II

שָׁבָה 12 to take captive (9 · 30 · 38) 985

גְּדוּד 13 troop (5 · 33) 151

פָּשַׁט to make a dash, raid (2 · 24 · 43) 832

בָּזַז to spoil, plunder (5 · 38 · 42) 102

בִּזָּה spoil, prey (3 · 10) 103

יוֹעֵץ 16 ptc. = counselor (3 · 22) 419

חוֹחַ 18 brier, bramble (3 · 11) 296

רָמַס to trample down, trample (1 · 17 · 18) 942

הִתְגָּרָה 19 to engage in strife with (1 · 11 · 14) 173

נָגַף 22 to be smitten (3 · 22 · 48) 619

פָּרַץ 23 to break through, out, over, etc. (7 · 46 · 49) 829

פּוֹנֶה = פִּנָּה corner (3 · 30) 819

תַּעֲרֻבָה 24 pledge; בְּנֵי תּ' = hostages (1 · 2) 787

קָשַׁר 27 to league together, conspire (4 · 35 · 43) 905

קֶשֶׁר conspiracy (3 · 16) 905

Chapter 26

פָּרַץ 6 to break through, down [= make a breach]; break out, over, etc. (7 · 46 · 49) 829 I

לְמַעְלָה 8 exceedingly (8 · 34) 751 II מַעַל 2.c

מִגְדָּל 9 tower (6 · 49) 153

פִּנָּה corner (3 · 30) 819

גַּיְא valley 3 · 47) 161

מִקְצוֹעַ corner buttress (1 · 12) 893

מִגְדָּל 10 tower (6 · 49) 153

חָצַב to hew out, dig (1 · 14 · 17) 345

שְׁפֵלָה lowland, foothills, [the] Shephelah (4 · 20) 1050

מִישׁוֹר level country, tableland, plain (1 · 23) 449

אִכָּר ploughman, husbandman (1 · 7) 38

כֹּרֵם ptc. = vinedresser (1 · 5) 501

כַּרְמֶל garden land (1 · 14) 502

אֹהֵב ptc., friend, lover

גְּדוּד 11 troop (5 · 33) 151

פְּקֻדָּה mustering (4 · 32) 824

שֹׁטֵר official, officer (3 · 25) 1009

רֹמַח 14 spear, lance (4 · 15) 942

כּוֹבַע helmet (1 · 6) 464

שִׁרְיוֹן body armor (2 · 8) 1056

קֶלַע sling (1 · 6) 887

669

חֶשְׁבּוֹן 15 device, invention (1 · 2) 364

חֹשֵׁב ptc. = inventive workman (1 · 12) 362

מִגְדָּל tower (6 · 49) 153

פִּנָּה corner (3 · 30) 819

ירא to shoot Lis ירה (1 · 13 · 25) 432

לְמֵרָחוֹק w. עַד = to a distance (1 · 8) 935 רָחֹק 2.a.(7).7

הִפְלִיא to do [or make] marvelously, wondrously (2 · 10 · 24) 810

חֶזְקָה 16 strength, force (2 · 4) 305

גָּבַהּ to be lofty [here w. heart = to be haughty] (3 · 24 · 34) 146

מָעַל to act unfaithfully, treacherously (8 · 35 · 35) 591

מָעַל 18 to act unfaithfully, treacherously (8 · 35 · 35) 591

זָעַף 19 to be enraged (2 · 5 · 5) 277

מִקְטֶרֶת censer (1 · 2) 883

זַעַף raging, rage (3 · 7) 277 [but see verb above]

צָרַעַת leprosy (1 · 35) 863

זָרַח to come out, appear (1 · 18 · 18) 280

מֵצַח brow, forehead (2 · 13) 594

מְצֹרָע 20 Pual ptc. = leper, leprous (4 · 15) 863

מֵצַח brow, forehead (2 · 13) 594

הִבְהִיל to hasten hurry (1 · 3 · 39) 96

נִדְחַף hurry (1 · 2 · 4) 191

מְצֹרָע 21 Pual ptc. = leper, leprous (4 · 15) 863

חָפְשִׁית freedom, separation, w. בֵּית = a separate house (1 · 2) 345

נִגְזַר to be cut off = be separated מִן from (1 · 6 · 12) 160

קְבוּרָה 23 grave, burial (1 · 14) 869

מְצֹרָע Pual ptc. = leper, leprous (4 · 15) 863

Chapter 27

עֹפֶל 3 mound, hill (2 · 8) 779

חֹרֶשׁ 4 wooded height, wood (1 · 3) 361

בִּירָנִית fortress, fortified place (2 · 18) 108

מִגְדָּל tower (6 · 49) 153 גדל

כֹּר 5 kor [dry measure] (3 · 8) 499

חִטָּה wheat (3 · 30) 334

שְׂעֹרָה barley (3 · 33) 972

Chapter 28

מַסֵּכָה 2 molten image (3 · 25) 651

גַּיְא 3 valley (3 · 47) 161

רַעֲנָן 4 luxuriant, fresh, flourishing (1 · 19) 947

שָׁבָה 5 to take captive (9 · 30 · 38) 985

שִׁבְיָה captives (5 · 9) 986

מַכָּה defeat; slaughter, plague (4 · 48) 646

נָגִיד 7 leader, ruler (9 · 44) 617

מִשְׁנֶה second rank; double, copy (4 · 36) 1041

שָׁבָה 8 to take captive (9 · 30 · 38) 985

בָּזַז to spoil, plunder (5 · 38 · 42) 102

זַעַף 9 raging, rage (3 · 7) 277

כבש 10 to bring into bondage (1 · 8 · 14) 461

אַשְׁמָה doing wrong, becoming guilty; trespass offering (6 · 19) 80

שִׁבְיָה 11 captives (5 · 9) 986

שָׁבָה to take captive, lead captive (9 · 30 · 38) 985

חָרוֹן anger (4 · 41) 354

שִׁבְיָה 13 captives (5 · 9) 986

הֵנָּה here, hither (1 · 49) 244 I

אַשְׁמָה doing wrong, becoming guilty; trespass offering (6 · 19) 80

חָרוֹן anger (4 · 41) 354

חָלוּץ 14 pass. ptc. = equipped, armed (3 · 17) 323

שִׁבְיָה captives (5 · 9) 986

בִּזָּה spoil, prey (3 · 10) 103

נקב 15 Niph., to be pricked off, designated (2 · 6 · 19) 666

שִׁבְיָה captives (5 · 9) 986

מַעֲרֹם naked thing; pl. = nakedness (1 · 1) 736

הִנְעִיל to give sandals (1 · 1 · 8) 653

סוּךְ to anoint (1 · 7 · 9) 691 I

נָהַל *Piel*, to lead to a station or goal; conduct; give rest to (2 · 9 · 10) 624

תָּמָר palm tree, date palm (1 · 12) 1071 I

שָׁבָה 17 to take captive (9 · 30 · 38) 985

שְׁבִי captives (4 · 49) 985

פָּשַׁט 18 to make a dash (2 · 24 · 43) 832

שְׁפֵלָה lowland, foothills, [the] Shephelah (4 · 20) 1050

הִכְנִיעַ 19 to humble (1 · 11 · 35) 488

בַּעֲבוּר because of, in order to (1 · 45) 721 II עָבוּר

הִפְרִיעַ to show lack of restraint (1 · 2 · 16) 828 III

מָעַל to act unfaithfully, treacherously (8 · 35 · 35) 591

מַעַל unfaithful, treacherous act (2 · 29) 591 I

עֶזְרָה 21 help, support (1 · 26) 740 I

מָעַל 22 to act unfaithfully, treacherously (8 · 35 · 35) 591

קִצֵּץ 24 to cut in pieces (1 · 9 · 14) 893

פִּנָּה corner (3 · 30) 819

Chapter 29

רְחוֹב 4 broad open place, plaza (2 · 43) 932 I

נִדָּה 5 inpurity (1 · 30) 622

מָעַל 6 to act unfaithfully, treacherously (8 · 35 · 35) 591

עֹרֶף back of neck, neck (3 · 33) 791

אוּלָם 7 porch (5 · 49) 17

כָּבָה to quench, extinguish (1 · 10 · 24) 459

נֵר lamp (4 · 45) 632 I

קֶצֶף 8 wrath (6 · 28) 893 I

זַעֲוָה object of terror, fright (1 · 7) 266 זוע

שַׁמָּה horror (2 · 39) 1031

שְׁרֵקָה hissing, scorn (1 · 7) 1056

שְׁבִי 9 captivity (4 · 49) 985

חָרוֹן 10 anger (4 · 41) 354

נִשְׁלָה 11 to be negligent, easygoing (1 · 1 · 7) 1017 I

לִפְנִימָה 16 toward the [in]side (1 · 5) 819 1 פְּנִימָה

טֻמְאָה uncleanness (1 · 37) 380

קִבֵּל to take, receive (2 · 11 · 13) 867

אוּלָם 17 porch (5 · 49) 17

פְּנִימָה 18 toward the [in]side (1 · 5) 819 or פְּנִימִי

מַעֲרֶכֶת row, line (3 · 10) 790

הִזְנִיחַ 19 to reject, spurn (2 · 3 · 19) 276 I

מַעַל unfaithful, treacherous act (2 · 29) 591 I

חֵכִנוּ *Hiph.*, כּוּן, to arrange 465

צָפִיר 21 male goat (1 · 6) 862 V

קִבֵּל 22 to take, receive; accept (2 · 11 · 13) 867

זָרַק to toss or throw, to sprinkle (6 · 32 · 34) 284

סָמַךְ 23 to lay; lean, support (1 · 41 · 48) 701

מְצִלְתַּיִם 25 cymbals (3 · 13) 853

נֵבֶל harp, lute, guitar (4 · 27) 614

כִּנּוֹר lyre (4 · 41) 490

חֹזֶה seer (7 · 17) 302

חֲצֹצְרָה 26 clarion (11 · 29) 348

חֲצֹצְרָה 27 clarion (11 · 29) 348

חֲצֹצְרָה 28 clarion (11 · 29) 348 or Qere החצצר

כָּרַע 29 to bow, bow down (1 · 30 · 36) 502

חֹזֶה 30 seer (7 · 17) 302

קָדַד to bow down (2 · 15 · 15) 869 I

תּוֹדָה 31 thank offering, thanksgiving (3 · 32) 392

נָדִיב incited, inclined, willing; noble (1 · 27) 622

הִפְשִׁיט 34 to flay; skin, strip off (2 · 15 · 43) 832

פִּתְאֹם 36 suddenly, suddenness (1 · 25) 837

Chapter 30

אִגֶּרֶת 1 letter (2 · 10) 8
פֶּסַח   Passover (19 · 49) 820

פֶּסַח 2 Passover (19 · 49) 820

לְמַדַּי 3 i.e., דַּי + מַה + לְ = to what is suf-ficient = enough, in sufficient num-bers (1 · 1) 553 מַה 1.c; 191 דַּי 1

יָשַׁר 4 to be pleasing, right (1 · 13 · 25) 448

פֶּסַח 5 Passover (19 · 49) 820

רָץ 6 ptc. = runner (6 · 25) 930 רוּץ
אִגֶּרֶת   letter (2 · 10) 8
פְּלֵיטָה   escaped remnant (3 · 28) 812

מָעַל 7 to act unfaithfully, treacherously (8 · 35 · 35) 591
שַׁמָּה   horror (2 · 39) 1031

הִקְשָׁה 8 to make hard, stiff, stubborn (3 · 21 · 28) 904 I
עֹרֶף   back of neck, neck (3 · 33) 791
חָרוֹן   anger (4 · 41) 354

רַחֲמִים 9 compassion (1 · 38) 933
שֹׁבֶה   ptc. captive (2 · 10) 985
חַנּוּן   gracious (1 · 13) 337
רַחוּם   compassionate (1 · 13) 933

רָץ 10 ptc. = runner (6 · 25) 930 רוּץ
הִשְׂחִיק   to mock (1 · 1 · 36) 965
הִלְעִיג   to mock, deride (1 · 5 · 18) 541

נִכְנַע 11 to humble oneself (15 · 24 · 35) 488

מְקַטְרָה 14 incense altar (1 · 1) 883

פֶּסַח 15 animal victim of Passover; Pass-over (19 · 49) 820
נכלם   to be humiliated, ashamed (1 · 26 · 38) 483

זָרַק 16 to toss or throw (6 · 32 · 34) 284

שְׁחִיטָה 17 slaying (1 · 1) 1006

פֶּסַח   animal victim of Passover; Pass-over (19 · 49) 820

מַרְבִּית 18 great number, increase (2 · 5) 916
פֶּסַח   animal victim of Passover; Pass-over (19 · 49) 820
בְּלֹא   without (2 · 31) 518 לֹא 4.a

טָהֳרָה 19 cleansing, purification (1 · 13) 372

שֵׂכֶל 22 insight, understanding (2 · 16) 968

כָּזֹאת 26 the like of this, things such as these (4 · 28) 262 זֶה 6.d

מָעוֹן 27 dwelling; lair, refuge (2 · 18) 732

Chapter 31

מַצֵּבָה 1 pillar [as a monument or memorial] (2 · 36) 663
גִּדַּע   to cut down, in two (4 · 9 · 22) 154
אֲשֵׁרָה   sacred tree or pole representing a Canaanite goddess of fortune and happiness (11 · 40) 81
נִתַּץ   to tear down (5 · 6 · 42) 683

מַחְלֹקֶת 2 division, course (11 · 42) 324
כְּפִי   according to, in proportion to (1 · 16) 805 פֶּה

מְנָת 3 portion (2 · 9) 584
רְכוּשׁ   property, goods (6 · 28) 940

מְנָת 4 portion (2 · 9) 584

פָּרַץ 5 to spread; break through, down, out, etc. (7 · 46 · 49) 829 I
דָּגָן   corn, grain (2 · 40) 186
תִּירוֹשׁ   new wine (2 · 38) 440
יִצְהָר   fresh oil (2 · 23) 844
תְּבוּאָה   product, yield (2 · 43) 100
מַעֲשֵׂר   tithe, payment of tenth part (4 · 33) 798

מַעֲשֵׂר 6 tithe, payment of tenth part (4 · 33) 798
עֲרֵמָה   heap (5 · 11) 790

עֲרֵמָה 7 heap (5 · 11) 790

יָסַד here = to begin, establish (2 · 20 · 41) 413

עֲרֵמָה 8 heap (5 · 11) 790

עֲרֵמָה 9 heap (5 · 11) 790

לְבִיא 10 ל + *Hiph.* inf. בוא

לִשְׁכָּה 11 storeroom (1 · 47) 545

מַעֲשֵׂר 12 tithe, payment of tenth part (4 · 33) 798

נָגִיד leader, ruler (9 · 44) 617

מִשְׁנֶה second rank; double, copy (4 · 36) 1041

פָּקִיד 13 commissioner, deputy (2 · 13) 824

מִפְקָד appointment; appointed place (1 · 5) 824

נָגִיד leader, ruler (9 · 44) 617

שֹׁעֵר 14 porter, gatekeeper (6 · 37) 1045

נְדָבָה freewill, voluntary, offering (2 · 26) 621

מַחֲלֹקֶת 15 division, course (11 · 42) 324

קָטֹן small, young (3 · 47) 881 I

מִלְּבַד 16 besides (3 · 33) 94 II בדד 1.e

הִתְיַחֵשׂ to be enrolled by genealogy (5 · 20 · 20) 405

לְמַעְלָה upwards, over, above (8 · 34) 751 II מעל 2.b

דְּבַר־יוֹם בְּיוֹמוֹ idiom: each day's affair in its day, each day's requirement (2 · 14) 398 יוֹם 7.e.(3)

מַחֲלֹקֶת division, course (11 · 42) 324

הִתְיַחֵשׂ 17 to be enrolled by genealogy (5 · 20 · 20) 405

לְמַעְלָה upwards, over, above (8 · 34) 751 II מעל 2.c

מַחֲלֹקֶת division, course (11 · 42) 324

הִתְיַחֵשׂ 18 to be enrolled by genealogy (5 · 20 · 20) 405

טַף children (2 · 42) 381

נקב 19 to be pricked off, designated (2 · 6 · 19) 666 I

מָנָה part, portion (1 · 11) 584

הִתְיַחֵשׂ to be enrolled by genealogy (5 · 20 · 20) 405

כָּזֹאת 20 thus (4 · 28) 262 זה 6.d

Chapter 32

בָּצוּר 1 pass. ptc. = cut off, made inaccessible [fortified] (4 · 25) 130

סָתַם 3 to stop up, shut up (3 · 10 · 13) 711

סָתַם 4 to stop up, shut up (3 · 10 · 13) 711

מַעְיָן spring (1 · 23) 745

שָׁטַף to flow, run (1 · 28 · 30) 1009

פָּרַץ 5 to break through, down; over, etc. (7 · 46 · 49) 829 I

מִגְדָּל tower (6 · 49) 153

מִלּוֹא citadel in Jerusalem (1 · 10) 571

שֶׁלַח missile, weapon (2 · 8) 1019

רְחוֹב 6 broad open place (2 · 43) 932 I

אמץ 7 to be bold, be strong (2 · 16 · 41) 54

נסמך 8 to support or brace oneself (1 · 6 · 48) 701

מֶמְשָׁלָה 9 rule, dominion (2 · 17) 606

מָצוֹר 10 enclosure, siege-works; עיר מ׳ = entrenched or fortified city (3 · 25) 848

הֵסִית 11 to instigate (4 · 18 · 18) 694 סות

צָמָא thirst (1 · 17) 854

הֶחֱרִים 15 to destroy, exterminate; devote for sacred use (2 · 46 · 49) 355

הִשִּׁיא 16 to beguile, deceive (1 · 15 · 16) 674 II

הֵסִית to instigate, allure, incite (4 · 18 · 18) 694 סות

כָּזֹאת thus (4 · 28) 262 זה 6.d

אַף כִּי how much less (2 · 26) 65

חֵרֵף 17 to reproach, say sharp things against, taunt (1 · 34 · 38) 357 I

יְהוּדִית 18 Jewish = Jewish language (1 · 6) 397 I

בהל *Piel*, to dismay, terrify; hasten (2 · 10 · 39) 96

כְּעַל 19 as concerning, as upon (1 · 5) 758 עַל IV.1.a

הִכְחִיד 21 to efface, annihilate (1 · 6 · 32) 470

נָגִיד leader, ruler (9 · 44) 617

בֹּשֶׁת shame (1 · 30) 102

יָצִיא coming forth (1 · 1) 425

מֵעֶה bowels (5 · 32) 588

נהל 22 *Piel*, to give rest to (2 · 9 · 10) 624

מִסָּבִיב from every side (4 · 42) 687 סָבִיב 1.d

מִגְדָּנוֹת 23 choice or excellent things (2 · 4) 550

מֵאַחֲרֵי־כֵן = from then on, thereafter (1 · 3) 30 אַחַר pl. 4.a

מוֹפֵת 24 sign or token (2 · 36) 68

גְּמוּל 25 benefit (1 · 19) 168

גָּבַהּ to be lofty [here w. heart = be haughty] (3 · 24 · 34) 146

קֶצֶף wrath (6 · 28) 893

נִכְנַע 26 to humble oneself (15 · 24 · 35) 488

גֹּבַהּ haughtiness (2 · 17) 147

קֶצֶף wrath (6 · 28) 893 I

עֹשֶׁר 27 riches (6 · 37) 799

יָקָר precious; w. אֶבֶן = (of gem) rare, costly (5 · 35) 429

בֹּשֶׂם spice, perfume (6 · 30) 141

חֶמְדָּה desire, delight (3 · 16) 326

מִסְכְּנוֹת 28 storage places (5 · 7) 698

תְּבוּאָה product, yield (2 · 43) 100

דָּגָן corn, grain (2 · 40) 186

תִּירוֹשׁ new wine (2 · 38) 440

יִצְהָר fresh oil (2 · 23) 844

אֻרְיָה crib, manger (2 · 3) 71

עֵדֶר flock, herds (1 · 37) 727

אֲוֵרוֹת BDB incl. as pl. אריה this verse: cribs (1 · 1) 71, 1120

רְכוּשׁ 29 property, goods (6 · 28) 940

סָתַם 30 to stop up, shut up (3 · 10 · 13) 711

מוֹצָא place of going forth; outlet, source, spring (2 · 27) 425

יֹשֶׁר to direct, make smooth; esteem right (1 · 9 · 25) 448

לְמַטָּה downward (1 · 10) 641 מַטָּה 2.a

מַעֲרָב west (2 · 14) 788 II

הֵלִיץ 31 here, ptc. = ambassador; to interpret; deride (1 · 9 · 12) 539

מוֹפֵת sign or token (2 · 36) 68

נִסָּה to test, prove (2 · 36 · 36) 650

חָזוֹן 32 vision (1 · 35) 302

מַעֲלֶה 33 ascent (2 · 19) 751

Chapter 33

נָתַץ 3 to tear down (5 · 6 · 42) 683

אֲשֵׁרָה sacred tree or pole representing a Canaanite goddess of fortune and happiness (11 · 40) 81

עונן 6 *Poel*, to practice soothsaying (1 · 10 · 11[?]) 778 II

נַחֵשׁ to practice divination (1 · 9 · 9) 638 II

כִּשֵּׁף to practice sorcery (1 · 6 · 6) 506

אוֹב necromancer (1 · 16) 15

יִדְּעֹנִי familiar spirit (1 · 11) 396

פֶּסֶל 7 idol, image (1 · 31) 820

סֶמֶל image, statue; פֶּסֶל הַס' = idol-image (2 · 5) 702

הִתְעָה 9 to cause to err, cause to wander about; mislead (1 · 21 · 50) 1073

הִקְשִׁיב 10 to give attention (2 · 45 · 46) 904

חוֹחַ 11 here = hook, ring, brier (3 · 11) 296

נִכְנַע 12 to humble oneself (15 · 24 · 35) 488

נֶעְתַּר 13 to be supplicated, entreated (2 · 8 · 20) 801 I

תְּחִנָּה supplication for favor (5 · 25) 337

אַחֲרֵי־כֵן 14 afterward; (4 · 46) 29 אַחַר pl. 2.b

חִיצוֹן outer (1 · 25) 300

מַעֲרָב west (2 · 14) 788 II

דָּג fish (1 · 19) 185

עֹפֶל mound, hill (2 · 8) 779 I

הַגְבִּיהַ — to make high, exalt (1·10·34) 146
בָּצוּר — pass. ptc. = cut off, made inaccessible [fortified] (4·25) 130
נָכְרִי 15 foreigner, foreign (2·45) 648
סֶמֶל — image, statue (2·5) 702 see 33:7
תּוֹדָה 16 thank offering, thanksgiving (3·32) 392
אֲבָל 17 howbeit, but truly (3·11) 6
חֹזֶה 18 seer (7·17) 302
נֶעְתַּר 19 to be supplicated, entreated (2·8·20) 801 I
מַעַל — unfaithful, treacherous act (2·29) 591 I
אֲשֵׁרָה — sacred tree·or pole representing a Canaanite goddess of fortune and happiness (11·40) 81
פָּסִיל — idol, image (5·23) 820
נִכְנַע — to humble oneself (15·24·35) 488
פָּסִיל 22 idol, image (5·23) 820
נִכְנַע 23 to humble oneself (15·24·35) 488
אַשְׁמָה — doing wrong, becoming guilty (6·19) 80
קָשַׁר 24 to league together, conspire (4·35·43) 905
קָשַׁר 25 to league together, conspire (4·35·43) 905

Chapter 34

אֲשֵׁרָה 3 sacred tree or pole representing a Canaanite goddess of fortune and happiness (11·40) 81
פָּסִיל — idol, image (5·23) 820
מַסֵּכָה — molten image (3·25) 651
נִתַּץ 4 to tear down (5·6·42) 683
חַמָּן — sun-pillar [for idolatrous worship] (3·8) 329
לְמַעְלָה — above, over (8·34) 751 II מַעַל 2.c
גָּדַע — to cut down or in two (4·9·22) 154
אֲשֵׁרָה — sacred tree or pole representing a

Canaanite goddess of fortune and happiness (11·40) 81
פָּסִיל — idol, image (5·23) 820
מַסֵּכָה — molten image (3·25) 651
הֵדַק — to make dust of, pulverize (3·8·13) 200 דקק
זָרַק — to toss or throw, sprinkle (6·32·34) 284
בחר 6 Rd.K. בחר 3rd. m. sing. of to choose
בָּתֵּיהֶם — Rd. K. בית their houses
נִתַּץ 7 to tear down (5·6·42) 683
אֲשֵׁרָה — sacred tree or pole representing a Canaanite goddess of fortune and happiness (11·40) 81
פָּסִיל — idol, image (5·23) 820
כִּתֵּת — to beat or crush (1·5·17) 510
הֵדַק — to make dust of, pulverize (3·8·13) 200 דקק
חַמָּן — sun-pillar [for idolatrous worship] (3·8) 329
גָּדַע — to cut down or in two (4·9·22) 154
מַזְכִּיר 8 ptc. = recorder (1·9) 271 *Hiph.* 4 זכר
סַף 9 threshold, sill (3·25) 706
בדק 10 to mend, repair (1·1·1) 96
חָרָשׁ 11 craftsman (3·38) 360
מַחְצֵב — hewing; always מ׳ אַבְנֵי = hewn stones (1·3) 345
מְחַבְּרָה — pl. = binder, coupling (1·2) 289
קרה — *Piel*, to lay the beams of (1·5·28 [?]) 900
נצח 12 to act as overseer (3·7·8) 663 I
סַבָּל 13 burden-bearer (3·5) 688
שֹׁטֵר — official, officer (3·25) 1009
שֹׁעֵר — porter, gatekeeper (6·37) 1045
הִתִּיךְ 17 to pour out (1·5·21) 677 נתך
נִתַּךְ 21 to be poured out, forth (1·8·21) 677

עַל אֲשֶׁר idiom: because that 758 עַל III.a

נְבִיאָה 22 prophetess (1 · 6) 612

מִשְׁנֶה second district; double, copy
(4 · 36) 1041

כָּזֹאת accordingly to that effect, thus
(4 · 28) 262 זֶה 6.d

אָלָה 24 curse, oath (3 · 36) 46

תַּחַת אֲשֶׁר 25 in return for that; instead of (2 · 13)
1066 תַּחַת II. 3.a.(b)

נתך to pour forth (2 · 7 · 21) 677

כבה to be quenched, extinguished
(1 · 14 · 24) 459

רַךְ 27 to be softened, penitent (1 · 6 · 8)
939 רכך

נִכְנַע to humble oneself (15 · 24 · 35) 488

קָטָן 30 small, young (3 · 47) 881 I

עֹמֶד 31 standing-place (3 · 9) 765

עֵדָה testimonies, solemn charges (1 · 32)
730

Chapter 35

פֶּסַח 1 Passover (19 · 49) 820

מַשָּׂא 3 bearing, carrying; load, burden
(3 · 45) 672 II

מַחֲלֹקֶת 4 division, course (11 · 42) 324

כְּתָב edict, letter, writing (2 · 17) 508

מִכְתָּב edict, writing (3 · 9) 508

פְּלַגָּה 5 division (1 · 1) 811

חֲלֻקָּה part, portion (1 · 1) 324

פֶּסַח 6 animal victim of Passover; Passover (19 · 49) 820

פֶּסַח 7 animal victim of Passover; Passover (19 · 49) 820

רְכוּשׁ property, goods (6 · 28) 940

נְדָבָה 8 freewill offering, voluntary, offering (2 · 26) 621

נָגִיד leader, ruler (9 · 44) 617

פֶּסַח animal victim of Passover; Passover (19 · 49) 820

פֶּסַח 9 animal victim of Passover; Passover (19 · 49) 820

עֹמֶד 10 standing place (3 · 9) 765

מַחֲלֹקֶת division, course (11 · 42) 324

פֶּסַח 11 animal victim of Passover; Passover (19 · 49) 820

זָרַק to toss or throw, sprinkle
(6 · 32 · 34) 284

הִפְשִׁיט to flay, skin; strip (2 · 15 · 43)
832

מִפְלַגָּה 12 division (1 · 1) 811

בִּשֵּׁל 13 to boil, cook (2 · 21 · 28) 143

פֶּסַח animal victim of Passover; Passover (19 · 49) 820

סִיר pot (3 · 29) 696 I

דּוּד pot, jar (1 · 7) 188

צַלַּחַת pot for cooking (1 · 4) 852

מַעֲמָד 15 station, post (2 · 5) 765

חֹזֶה seer (7 · 17) 302

שֹׁעֵר porter, gatekeeper (6 · 37) 1045

פֶּסַח 16 Passover; see 35:1 (19 · 49) 820

פֶּסַח 17 Passover; see 35:1 (19 · 49) 820

פֶּסַח 18 Passover; see 35:1 (19 · 49) 820

פֶּסַח 19 Passover; see 35:1 (19 · 49) 820

בהל 21 Piel, to hurry (2 · 10 · 39) 96

הִתְחַפֵּשׂ 22 to disguise oneself (3 · 8 · 23) 344

בִּקְעָה valley, plain (1 · 19) 132

הוֹרָה 23 to shoot (2 · 45 · 45[?]) 434 ירה

יוֹרֶה ptc. = archer (1 · 2) 435 Qal 3

מֶרְכָּבָה 24 chariot (6 · 44) 939

מִשְׁנֶה second rank; second, double, copy
(4 · 36) 1041

הִתְאַבֵּל to mourn (1 · 19 · 38) 5 I

קוֹנֵן 25 Poel, to chant a dirge (1 · 8 · 8) 884

שָׁר ptc. = singer (3 · 11) 1010 שׁיר

קִינָה elegy, dirge (2 · 17) 884

Chapter 36

ענשׁ 3 to fine, punish (1 · 6 · 9) 778

676

תְּשׁוּבָה 10 return + שָׁנָה = at the return of the year; i.e., spring (1 · 8) 1000

חֶמְדָּה desire, delight (3 · 16) 326

נִכְנַע 12 to humble oneself (15 · 24 · 35) 488

מָרַד 13 to rebel, revolt (2 · 25 · 25) 597

הִקְשָׁה to make hard, stiff, stubborn (3 · 21 · 28) 904 I

עֹרֶף back of neck, neck (3 · 33) 791

אָמֵץ to harden, make obstinate (3 · 19 · 41) 54

מָעַל 14 to act unfaithfully, treacherously (8 · 35 · 35) 591

מַעַל unfaithful, treacherous act (2 · 29) 591 I

חָמַל 15 to spare, have compassion (2 · 40 · 40) 328

מָעוֹן dwelling place; lair (2 · 18) 732

הִלְעִיב 16 to be making jest at (1 · 1 · 1) 541

בָּזָה to despise, regard with contempt (1 · 31 · 42) 102

הִתְעַתֵּעַ to mock (1 · 1 · 2) 1073 תעע

לְאֵין without, עַד לְ; i.e., until there was no מַרְפֵּא [remedy] (5 · 9) 35 II אֵין 6.c.(γ)

מַרְפֵּא healing, cure, health (2 · 13) 951

בָּחוּר 17 young man (2 · 45) 104

חָמַל to spare, have compassion on (2 · 40 · 40) 328

בְּתוּלָה virgin (1 · 50) 143

יָשֵׁשׁ aged, decrepit (1 · 1) 450

קָטָן 18 small = young, weak, etc. (3 · 47) 881 I

נָתַץ 19 to tear down (5 · 6 · 42) 683

אַרְמוֹן palace, castle, citadel (1 · 33) 74

מַחְמָד desirable thing; desire (1 · 13) 326

רָצָה 21 to make acceptable (1 · 42 · 50[?]) 953

הָשַׁמָּה *Hoph.* inf. abs. שׁמם, being desolate 1031

מִכְתָּב 22 writing (3 · 9) 508

ARAMAIC APPENDIX

words occurring ten or more times

ARAMAIC APPENDIX

1. This Aramaic appendix includes all Aramaic words (excluding proper nouns) occurring ten or more times in the Aramaic portions of the Old Testament, as well as a few that correspond to their Hebrew cognates.
2. The number at the end of the definition is the page number in BDB where the word occurs.
3. The forms in parentheses are alternate forms of that word (usually involving the interchange of the letters ה and א).
4. Unidentified meanings for verbs are understood to be the *peal* meaning. Significant meanings of other stems are noted where necessary.
5. A list of Aramaic numerical notations used in Daniel and Ezra appears at the end of this appendix.
6. For a brief survey of the Aramaic language, see the article by William S. LaSor in the revised *International Standard Bible Encyclopedia* (Grand Rapids: Eerdmans, 1979), 1:229–33 Franz Rosenthal's *Grammar of Biblical Aramaic* (Porta Linguarum Orientalium, n.s.; Wiesbaden: Otto Harrassowitz, 1983 [5th printing]) vol. 5, is a much more detailed account of biblical Aramaic.

אֶבֶן   stone 1078

אֱדַיִן   then; same meaning with בְּ 1078

אָחֳרָן   another 1079

אִיתַי   there exists, there is/are (predicates existence) 1080

אֲכַל   to eat, devour 1080

אֱלָה   god, God 1080

אִלֵּךְ   these 1080

אֲמַר   to say, tell, command 1081

אֲנָה   I 1081

אֱנָשׁ   mankind, people, a man 1081

אנתה   Qere = אַנְתְּ, you (m. sing.) 1082

אַרְיֵה   lion 1082

אֲרַע   (the) earth 1083

(אָתָא) אֲתָה   to come 1083 Haph., to bring

אַתּוּן   furnace 1083

בְּ   in, into, through, by (means of), for 1083

בַּיִת   house 1084

(בְּנָא) בנה   to build 1084 Hithpe., to be built

(בְּעָא) בְּעָה   to request, ask, seek 1085

בַּר   son; בְּנִי pl. constr. 1085 I

גֹּב   pit, den (of lions) 1085

גְּבַר   man 1086

גַּו   middle, midst גוֹא constr. 1086

דְּהַב   gold 1087

דִּי   particle of relation 1087

1. relative pronoun: who, which, that

2. mark of the genitive

3. conjunction: that, because

4. מָה דִּי = whoever, whichever, whatever, what

דָּךְ   (fem.)　} this 1088

דֵּךְ   (m.)

דְּנָה   this 1088

דְּקַק   to be shattered, fall to pieces 1089 Haph., to break in pieces

דָּת   decree, law 1089

הוּא   he; also used as copula 1090

(הֲוָא) הֲוָה   to be, become, exist 1089

הִיא   she; also used as copula 1090

הֵיכַל   palace, temple 1090

הִמּוֹ   (Ezra) they, them 1090

הִמּוֹן   (Dan.) they, them 1090

הֵן   if, whether; repeated = whether . . . or 1090

וְ, וּ   and 1090

זְמָן   time, occurrence 1091

חֲדָה   (fem.)　} one, a (indefinite article)

חַד   (m.)　} 1079

חֲוָה   to declare 1092

חֲזָה   to see, behold 1092

חֵזוּ   vision, appearance 1092

חַי   living; as abstr. n. = life 1092

(חֵיוָא) חֵיוָה   beast, animal 1092

חַיִל   power, strength, army 1093

חַכִּים   wise man 1093

חָכְמָה   wisdom 1093

חֵלֶם   dream 1093

טְעֵם   command 1094

יַד   1. hand, 2. power 1094

יְדַע   to know 1095 Haph., to cause to know, inform

יְהַב   to give 1095 Hithpe., to be given

יוֹם   day 1095

יְכִל   to be able 1095

כְּ   like, as, about, according to 1096

כֹּל, כָּל־   all, (the) whole; every, any (with sing. nouns) 1097 כֹּלָּא = all, all things; כָּל־דִּי = whoever, whatever

כֵּן   thus, as follows 1097

כְּסַף   silver 1097

כְּעַן   now 1107

כְּתַב   to write 1098

כְּתָב   writing, inscription, document 1098

לְ   to, into, toward, at, for, according to, in regard to, in order to; mark of the accusative 1098

לָא	not 1098
מְדִינָה	province, district 1088
מָה	what? what, whatever 1099
מִלָּה	word, thing, matter 1100
מֶלֶךְ	king 1100
מַלְכוּ	royalty, kingdom, realm, reign 1100
מַן	who? whoever; מַן־דִּי = whosoever 1100
מִן	1. of place and time: from, out of 1100
	2. of source: from, by, at, according to
	3. partitively: some
	4. comparison: from, more than
נְהַר	river 1102
נוּר	fire 1102
נְפַל	to fall 1103
נְפַק	to go out, come forth, appear 1103 Haph., to bring forth
נתן	to give, pay 1103
סְגִד	to pay homage 1104
עֲבַד	to make, do 1104 Hithpe., to be made into, be done, be performed
עֲבַר	region across, beyond 1105
עַד	up to, until, to, during 1105
עִדָּן	time, year 1105
עַל	on, upon, over, against, toward, concerning, above 1106
עִלָּי	highest 1106
עלל	to go in, come in 1106 Haph., to bring in
עָלַם	forever 1106
עַם	people; עַמְמַיָּא pl. emph. 1107
עִם	with 1107
ענה	to answer, respond 1107 I
פֶּחָה	governor 1108
פלח	to serve, pay reverence to 1108
פַּרְזֶל	iron 1108
פְּשַׁר	interpretation 1109
(צבא) צבו	to be pleased, will 1109
צְלֵם	image, statue 1109

קֳבֵל	in front of, before, because of 1110
	לְ־קֳבֵל דְּנָה = because כָּל־קֳבֵל דִּי ,
	כּ = because of this, therefore
קְבֵל	in front of, before, because of 1110
	כָּל־קֳבֵל דְּנָה = because כָּל־קֳבֵל דִּי = because of this, therefore, accordingly
קַדִּישׁ	holy 1110
קֳדָם	before 1110
קוּם	to arise, stand up 1110 Haph., to set up, establish, appoint
קְרָא	to call, proclaim, read 1111
קְרֵב	to approach 1111 Pael = Haph., to offer
קֶרֶן	horn (of animal, musical instrument) 1111
רֵאשׁ	head 1112
רַב	great (four times = captain, chief) רַבְרְבִין = m. pl.1112; רַבְרְבָן = fem. pl
רְבָה	to grow great, increase 1112
רוּחַ	wind, spirit 1112
(רמא) רמה	to throw, place 1113
שַׂגִּיא	great, much, many, exceedingly 1113
(שׂוֹם) שִׂים	to make, appoint, set 1113 Peil = to be made; Hithpe = to be made
שְׁאֵל	to ask, inquire, request 1114
שְׁאָר	rest, remainder 1114
שכח	Haph., to find 1115 Hithpe., to be found
שְׁלַח	to send 1115
שָׁלְטָן	dominion, sovereignty 1115
שַׁלִּיט	having mastery; ruler, captain 1115
שֻׁם	name 1116
שְׁמַיִן	heavens, sky 1116
שְׁמַע	to hear 1116 Hithpe. to show oneself obedient
(שׂנא) שׁנה	(intrans.) to change, be changed 1116 Ithpa., to be changed; Haph., (trans.) to change

The following Aramaic numerical notations are used in Daniel and Ezra.

	Masc.		Fem.
one	חַד		חֲדָה
two	תְּרֵי (cs.)		תַּרְתֵּין
three	תְּלָתָה		תְּלָת
four	אַרְבְּעָה		אַרְבַּע
six			שֵׁת (שֶׁת)
seven	שִׁבְעָה		
ten	עֲשָׂרָה		עֲשַׂר
twenty		עֶשְׂרִין	
thirty		תְּלָתִין	
sixty		שִׁתִּין	
one hundred		מְאָה	
two hundred		מָאתַיִן	
one thousand		אֲלַף	
second			תִּנְיָנָה
third			תְּלִיתָיָה
fourth			רְבִיעָיָה

HEBREW APPENDIX

Words occurring more than fifty times

HEBREW APPENDIX

1. This list includes all words occurring over fifty times in the Old Testament, excluding proper nouns and numerals.

2. The number with the definition is the page number in BDB where the word occurs. E.g., "בְּאֵר well (24·38) 91" indicates that בְּאֵר can be found on page 91 of BDB.

3. The first definition listed for verbs is always the Qal meaning. E.g., אָבַד means "to perish" in the Qal stem.

4. Meanings for stems other than Qal are listed normally only if they differ from the following:

Niph.	=	passive of *Qal*
Piel	=	intensive of *Qal*
Pual	=	passive of *Piel*
Hiph.	=	causative of *Qal*
Hoph.	=	passive of *Hiph.*
Hithp.	=	reflexive of *Qal*

5. The occurrence of the stem with the meaning shown in item 4 above is indicated by an asterisk (*).

אָב   father 3

אָבַד   to perish 1

Pi. to cause to perish

Hiph. to destroy, put to death

אָבָה   to be willing, consent 2

אֶבְיוֹן   in want, needy, poor 2

אֶבֶן   stone 6

אָדוֹן   lord (see BDB for explanation of

(אֲדֹנָי, אֲדֹנִי, אֲדֹנִי) 10

אָדָם   man, mankind 9

אֲדָמָה   ground, land 9

אֶדֶן   base, pedestal 10

אָהֵב   to love 12

Niph. ptc. =lovely, lovable 2 S 1:23

Pi. ptc.=friends Zech. 13:6; lovers

אַהֲבָה   love 13

אֹהֶל   tent 13

אוֹ   or 14

אָוֶן   trouble, sorrow, wickedness 19

אוֹצָר   treasure, store, treasury, storehouse 69

אוֹר   light, lightning Job 36:32; 37:3, 11,15 (p.) 21

אוֹת   sign 16

אָז   at that time, then 23

אֹזֶן   ear 23

אָח   brother 26

אָחוֹת   sister 27

אָחַז   to grasp, take hold, take possession 28

Pi. to enclose, overlay Job 26:9

Hoph. to be fastened to 2 Chron. 9:18

אֲחֻזָּה   possession 28

אַחַר   behind, after 29

אַחֵר   another 29

אַחֲרוֹן   coming after, behind 30

אַחֲרִית   after-part, end 31

אֹיֵם   (ptc. of איב) enemy 33

אֵיךְ   how? how! 32

אַיִל   ram 17

אַיִן   subst., nothing, naught 34

part of negation, is not, are not

אִישׁ   man 35

אַךְ   surely, howbeit 36

אָכַל   to eat 37

אַל   Adv. of negation 39

אֵל   god, God; power (5t) 42

אֶל   to, towards 39

אֱלוֹהַּ   god, God 43

אַלּוּף   chief 49

אַלְמָנָה   widow 48

אֶלֶף   thousand 48

אִם   hypoth. part., interrog. part. 49

אֵם   mother 51

אָמָה   maid, hand maid 51

אַמָּה   cubit 52

אֱמוּנָה   firmness, steadfastness, fidelity 53

אמן   to confirm, support 52

Hiph. to stand firm, to trust, believe

אָמַר   to utter, say 55

Niph. to be called

Hiph. to avow Deut. 26:17, 18

Hithp. to act proudly, boast Ps. 94:4, Isa. 61:6

אֱמֶת   firmness, faithfulness, truth 54

אֲנַחְנוּ   we 59

אֲנִי   I 58

אָנֹכִי   I 59

אָסַף   to gather, remove 62

Pi. ptc. as subst.=rearguard, rearward

אסר   to tie, bind, imprison, to harness 63

Pu. to be taken prisoner Isa. 22:3

אַף   nose, nostril, face, anger 60

אַף   also, yea 64

אֵצֶל   in proximity to, beside 69

אָרוֹן   chest, ark 75

אֶרֶז   cedar 72

אֹרַח   way, path 73

אֹרֶךְ   length 73

אֶרֶץ   earth, land 75

ארר   to curse 76

Hoph. to be cursed Num. 22:6

אֵשׁ   fire 77

אִשָּׁה   pl. בָשִׁים woman, wife, female 61

אִשֶּׁה   an offering made by fire 77

אֲשֶׁר   part. of relation 81

אֵת   mark of the accusative 84

אֵת   with 85

אַתְּ   you (sing. fem.) 61

אַתָּה you (sing. masc.) 61

אַתֶּם you (pl. masc.) 61

בְּ in, at, by, with 88

בֶּגֶד garment, covering 93

בְּהֵמָה beast, animal, cattle 96

בּוֹא to come in, come, go in, go 97

בּוֹר pit, cistern, well 92

בּוֹשׁ to be ashamed 101

Po'lel to delay Exod. 32:1 Judg. 5:28

Hithpo'l to be ashamed before one another Gen. 2:25

בָּחַר to choose 103

Pu. to be chosen, selected Eccl. 9:4

בֶּטֶן belly, body, womb 105

בָּטַח to trust 105

בִּין to discern, understand 106

Niph. to be intelligent, discerning, have understanding

Po'l. to attentively consider Deut. 32:10

*Hiph. to understand

Hithpo'l. to show oneself attentive, consider diligently

to get understanding Jer. 23:20; Job 26:14; Ps. 119:104

to show oneself to have understanding Ps. 119:100

בַּיִן in the interval of, between 107

בַּיִת house, מִבַּיִת = on the inside, מִבַּיִת = within 108

בָּכָה to weep, bewail 113

Pi. to lament Jer. 31:25

to bewail Ezek. 8:14

בְּכֹר, בְּכוֹר first born 114

בַּל Adv., not 115

בָּמָה high place 119

בֵּן son 119

בָּנָה to build 124

בַּעַד away from, behind, about, on behalf of 126

בַּעַל owner, lord, husband, citizens 127

בער to burn, consume 128

*Pi. to kindle, light

Pu. to burn Jer. 36:22

בָּקַע to cleave, break open or through 131

Pu. to be ripped open Josh. 9:4 Ezek.

26:10 Hos. 14:1

Hoph. to be broken into Jer. 39:2

Hithp. to burst (themselves) open Josh. 9:13

to cleave asunder Mic. 1:4

בָּקָר cattle, herd, ox 133

בֹּקֶר morning 133

בקש Pi. to seek 134

Pu. to be sought Jer. 50:20 Esth. 2:23 Ezek. 26:21

בַּרְזֶל iron 137

בָּרַח to go through, flee 137

*Hiph. to pass through Ex. 26:28

בְּרִית covenant 136

ברך to kneel, bless 138

Niph. to bless oneself Gen. 12:3, 18:18, 28:14

Pi. to bless; to salute, greet

Pu. to be prospered

to have prosperity invoked Num. 22:6

Hiph. to cause to kneel Gen. 24:11

בְּרָכָה blessing 139

בָּשָׂר flesh 142

בַּת daughter 123

בְּתוֹךְ in the midst of 1063 תָּוֶךְ

גָּאַל to redeem, act as kinsman 145

*Niph. to redeem oneself Lev. 25:49

גְּבוּל border, boundary, territory 147

גִּבּוֹר strong, mighty 150

גְּבוּרָה strength, might 150

גִּבְעָה hill 148

גֶּבֶר man 149

גָּדוֹל great 152

גָּדַל to grow up, become great 152

Pi. to cause to grow

to make great, powerful

to magnify

Pu. to be brought up Ps. 144:12

Hiph. to make great

to magnify

to do great things

Hithp. to magnify oneself Isa. 10:15 Ezek. 38:23 Dan. 11:36

גּוֹי nation, people 156

גּוּר to sojourn 157

Hithpoʻl. to seek hospitality with
1 Kings 17:20 (Hos. 7:14 dub.)

גּוֹרָל lot 174

גָּלָה to uncover, remove 162

Niph. to uncover oneself

Pi. to disclose, lay bare
to make known, reveal

Hiph. to carry away into exile,
take into exile

Hithp. to be uncovered Gen. 9:21
to reveal oneself Prov. 18:2

גַּם also, moreover, yea 168

גָּמָל camel 168

גֶּפֶן vine 172

גֵּר sojourner 158

דָּבֵק to cling, cleave, keep 179

Pu. to be joined together Job 38:38,
41:9

Hiph. to pursue closely
to overtake

Hoph. to be made to cleave Ps. 22:16

דִּבֵּר to speak 180

Niph. to speak with one another
Hiph. to lead, or put to flight Ps. 18:48,
47:4

Hithp. to speak

דָּבָר speech, word; saying, utterance;
matter, affair 182

דְּבַשׁ honey 185

דּוֹד beloved, love, uncle 187

דּוֹר period, generation;
dwelling Isa. 38:12 Ps. 49:20 189

דֶּלֶת door 195

דָּם blood 196

דַּעַת knowledge 395

תָּרַד to tread, march 201

Hiph. to tread, tread down 202

דֶּרֶךְ way, road, distance, journey, manner 201

דָּרַשׁ to resort to, seek 205

Niph. to let oneself be inquired of
to be required Gen. 42:22
to be sought out 1 Chron. 26:31

הַ, הָ, הֵ (def. art.) the 206

הֲ, הַ, הָ interrog. part. 209

הֶבֶל vapor, breath; fig. of vanity 210

הוּא (3rd pers. sing. pron.) he, she (in
Pent.), it; with art. = that 214–216

הוֹי ah, alas, ha 222

הִיא (3rd pers. sing. pron.) she, it; with
art. = that 214–216

הָיָה to be, become, come to pass, fall out
224

הֵיכָל palace, temple 228

הָלַךְ to go, come, walk 229

Niph. to be gone Ps. 109:23

Hithp. to walk, walk about, move to
and fro

הלל to be boastful 237

Pi. to praise

Hithpa. to make one's boast Ps. 10:3
44:9

Hithpa. to glory, boast, make one's
boast

Poʻel. to make fool of Isa. 44:25 Job
12:17 Eccl. 7:7

Poʻal. to be mad Ps. 102:9, Eccl. 2:2

Hithpo. to act madly, like a madman

הֵם, הֵמָּה (3rd pers. pl. masc. pron.; as neuter,
rarely) they; with art=those (not
defined in BDB) 241

הָמוֹן sound, murmur, roar, crowd,
abundance 242

הֵן lo! behold! 243

הֵנָּה fem. of הֵמָּה (see above) 241

הִנֵּה lo! behold! 243

הָפַךְ to turn, overturn 245

Niph. to turn oneself, turn, turn
back

Hithp. to turn this way and that Gen.
3:24 Judg. 7:13 Job 37:12
to transform oneself Job 38:14

Hoph. to be turned (upon) Job 30:15

הַר mountain, hill, hill country 249

הָרַג to kill, slay 246

Pu. to be slain Is. 27:7

וָ, וּ, וְ (adv., conj.) so, then, and, and also,
but, both . . . and (וְ . . . וְ), consecutive
verb formations, (cohort.) so that
(introduces apodosis after כִּ, אִם) then
251–255

זֹאת   fem, of זֶה (see below)

זָבַח   to slaughter for sacrifice 256
Pi. to sacrifice

זֶבַח   sacrifice 257

זֶה   (demonstr. sing. masc. pron. |fem., זֹאת] and adv.) this, here; also used idiomatically with prepositions 260–262

זָהָב   gold 262

זָכַר   to remember 269

זָכָר   male 271

זָנָה   to commit fornication, to be a harlot 275
Pu. Ezek. 16:34 לֹא ז׳=fornication was not done
Hiph. to cause to commit fornication
to commit fornication

זעק   to cry, cry out, call 277
Niph. to be called together.
to assemble
to join
Hiph. to call, call out, or together
to make a crying Job 35:9 (וַי ז׳ וַיֹּאמֶר)
to have proclamation made Jonah 3:7
to call out to, or at Zech. 6:8

זָקֵן   old 278

זר   strange (adj.), stranger (noun) BDB under זור 266

זְרוֹעַ   arm, shoulder, strength 283

זָרַע   to sow, scatter seed 281
Niph. to be made pregnant Num. 5:28
Pu. to be sown Isa. 40:24
Hiph. to produce seed Gen. 1:11, 12
to bear a child Lev. 12:2

זֶרַע   sowing, seed, offspring 282

חַג   festive-gathering, feast 290

חָדַל   to cease 292
Hoph. to be made to leave Judg. 9:9, 11, 13

חָדָשׁ   new 294

חֹדֶשׁ   new moon, month 294

חוֹמָה   wall 327

חוּץ   the outside, a street 299

חָזָה   to see, behold 302

חָזַק   to be or grow firm, strong, strengthen 304
Pi. to make strong, firm, hard
to strengthen
Hiph. to prevail
to take or keep hold, seize, grasp
Hithp. to strengthen oneself
to put forth strength
to withstand 2 Chron. 13:7, 8
to hold strongly with

חָזָק   strong, stout, mighty 305

חָטָא   to miss, go wrong, sin 306
Pi. to make a sin offering
Hiph. to miss the mark Judg. 20:16
to bring into guilt, condemnation
Hithp. to miss or lose oneself Job 41:17
to purify oneself

חַטָּאת   sin, sin offering 308

חַי   alive, living 311

חָיָה   to live 310
Pi. to preserve alive, let live
to give life Job 33:4
to quicken, revive, refresh
Hiph. to preserve alive, let live
to quicken, revive

חַיָּה   living thing, animal; life (some poetry); appetite Job 38:39; revival, renewal Isa. 57:10, 312

חַיִּים   life 313

חַיִל   strength, efficiency, wealth, army 298

חָכָם   wise 314

חָכְמָה   wisdom 315

חֵלֶב   fat 316

חָלָה   to be weak, sick 317
Niph. to make oneself sick Jer. 12:13
to be made sick Dan. 8:27 Amos 6:6; Ptc.=diseased
Pi. to make sick Deut. 29:21 Ps. 77:11, w. פְּנֵי to appease, entreat the favor of
Pu. to be made weak Isa. 14:10
Hithp. to make oneself sick 2 Sam. 13:2, 5, 6
Hiph. to become sick Hos. 7:5

חֲלוֹם dream 321

חלל Niph. to pollute, defile oneself Lev. 21:4, 9, 320

to be polluted, defiled

Pi. to defile, pollute

to dishonor

to violate

to treat as common

Pu. to be profaned Ezek. 36:23

Hiph. to allow to be profaned Ezek. 39:7, 20:9

to begin

Hoph. to be begun Gen. 4:26

חָלָל pierced 319

חָלַק to divide, share 323

*Niph. to divide oneself Gen. 14:15

to assign, distribute 1 Chron. 23:6, 24:3 (see Pi.)

*Pi. to assign, distribute 1 Chron. 23:6, 24:3 (see Niph.)

to scatter Gen. 49:7 Lam. 4:16

Pu. to be divided Isa. 33:23 Amos 7:17 Zech. 14:1

Hiph. to receive a portion Jer. 37:12

Hithp. to divide among themselves Josh. 18:5

חֵלֶק portion, tract, territory 324

חֵמָה heat, rage, venom 404

חֲמוֹר he-ass, male donkey 331

חָמָס violence, wrong 329

חֵן favor, grace 336

חָנָה to decline, bend down, encamp 333

חָנַן to show favor, be gracious 335

Niph. to be pitied Jer. 22:23

Pi. to make gracious Jer. 26:25

Po'el to direct favor to Ps. 102:15 Prov. 14:21

Hoph. to be shown favor Isa. 26:10 Prov. 21:10

Hithp. to seek or implore favor

חֶסֶד goodness, kindness 338

חָפֵץ to delight in 342

חֵץ arrow 346

חֲצִי half 345

חָצֵר enclosure, court, settlement, village 346, 347

חֹק something prescribed, a statute, decree, ordinance 349

חֻקָּה something prescribed, enactment, statute 349

חֶרֶב sword 352

חָרָה to burn, be kindled (of anger) 354

Niph. to be angry Isa. 41:11, 45:24 Song of Sol. 1:6

Hiph. to cause to be kindled Job 19:11

Hithp. to heat oneself in vexation Ps. 37:1, 7, 8, Prov. 24:19

to hotly contend (dub.) Jer. 12:5

to strive eagerly (dub.) Jer. 22:15

הֶרְפָּה reproach 357

חָשַׁב to think, account, reckon 362

Hithp. to reckon oneself Num. 23:9

חֹשֶׁךְ darkness, obscurity 365

חתת to be shattered, dismayed 369

Niph. to be put in awe Mal. 2:5

Pi. to dismay, scare Job 7:14

to be shattered (?) Jer. 51:56

טָהוֹר clean, pure 373

טָהֵר to be clean, pure 372

Pi. to cleanse, purify

to pronounce clean Pu. to be cleansed 1 Sam. 20:26 Ezek. 22:24

Hithp. to purify oneself

to present oneself for purification

טוֹב pleasant, agreeable, good 373

טָמֵא to be, become unclean 379

Niph. to defile oneself, be defiled

to be regarded as unclean Job 18:3

Pi. to defile

to pronounce unclean

Hithp. to defile oneself

Hothp. to be defiled Deut. 24:4

טָמֵא unclean 379

יְאֹר stream, canal; stream of Nile 384

יָבֵשׁ to be dry, dried up, withered 386

Pi. to make dry, dry up

*Hiph. to exhibit dryness

יָד   hand 388

יָדה   to shoot Jer. 50:14, 392
Pi. to cast Lam. 3:53 Zech. 2:4
Hiph. to give thanks, laud, praise
to confess
Hithp. to confess
to give thanks 2 Chron. 30:22

יָדַע   to know 393
Niph. to make oneself known
to be perceived Gen. 41:21 Ps. 74:5
to be instructed Jer. 31:19
Pi. to cause to know Job 38:12 Ps.
104:19(?)
Po. to cause to know 1 Sam. 21:3
Pu. ptc: known Isa. 12:5 as subst.=ac-
quaintance (remaining Pu.)
Hithp. to make oneself known Gen.
45:1 Num. 12:6

יוֹם   day 398

יוֹמָם   daytime, by day 401

יַחְדָּו   together 403

יטב   to be good, well, glad, pleasing 405

יַיִן   wine 406

יכח   *Hiph.* to decide, adjudge, prove,
chide, rebuke 406
Hoph. to be chastened Job. 33:19
Niph. to reason together Isa. 1:18
to reason Job 23:7
to be set right, justified Gen. 20:16
Hithp. to argue Mic. 6:2

יָכֹל   to be able, have power, prevail,
endure 407

יָלַד   to bear, bring forth, beget 408
Pi. to cause (or help) to bring forth
Exod. 1:16
Ptc. as subst. = midwife
Pu. to be born
Hiph. to beget
Hithp. to declare pedigree Num. 1:18

יֶלֶד   child, son, boy, youth 409
descendants Isa. 29:23

יָם   sea, freq. indicates western point of
compass, west 410

יָמִין   right hand 411

יָסַף   to add 414
Niph. to join oneself to Exod. 1:10

יַעַן   on account of, because 774

יָעַץ   to advise, counsel 419
Niph. to consult together. exchange
counsel
Hithp. to conspire Ps. 83:4

יַעַר   wood, forest, thicket 420

יָצָא   to go or come out 422

יָצַק   to pour, cast. flow 427
Hiph. to pour out
Hoph. ptc.=cast, molten firmly es-
tablished Job 11:15

יָרֵא   to fear 431
Pi. to make afraid, terrify

יָרַד   to come or go down, descend 432

יְרִיעָה   curtain 438

יָרַשׁ   take possession of, inherit. dispossess
439
Niph. to be impoverished
Pi. to take possession of, devour Deut.
28:42
Hiph. to take possession of Num.
14:24

יֵשׁ   is, are 441

יָשַׁב   to sit, remain. dwell 442
Pi. to set Ezek. 25:4
Hiph. to cause to be inhabited Ezek.
36:33 Isa. 54:3
to marry (only Ezra and Nehemiah)
Hoph. to be made to dwell Isa. 5:8
to be inhabited Isa. 44:26

יֹשֵׁב   inhabitant 442 יָשַׁב *Qal* 3

יְשׁוּעָה   salvation; victory 447

ישע   *Hiph.* to deliver 446
Niph. to be liberated. saved

יָשָׁר   straight, right 449

יתר   *Qal* ptc. = remainder 1 Sam. 15:15. 451
Niph. to be left over, remain over
Hiph. to leave over. leave
to excel, show preeminence Gen. 49:4
to show excess=have more than enough
Exod. 36:7
to make abundant Deut. 28:11; 30:9

יֶתֶר remainder, excess, preeminence 451

כְּ the like of, like, as 453

כַּאֲשֶׁר according as, as, when 455

כָּבֵד to be heavy, weighty, burdensome, honored 457

Niph. to be made heavy Prov. 8:24

to be honored, enjoy honor

to get oneself glory

Pi. to make heavy, insensible 1 Sam. 6:66

to make honorable

to honor, glorify

Pu. to be made honorable, honored Isa. 58:13 Pr. 13:18, 27:18

*Hiph. to display honor

Hithp. to make oneself heavy Nah. 3:15

to honor oneself Prov. 12:9

כָּבוֹד abundance, honor, glory 458

כבס to wash, ptc. only = fuller, washer 460

Pu. to be washed Lev. 13:58, 15:17

Hothp. to be washed out Lev. 13:55, 56

כֶּבֶשׂ lamb 461

כֹּה thus, here 462

כֹּהֵן priest 463

כּוּן *Niph.* to be set up, established, fixed 465

to be directed aright

to be prepared, ready

Hiph. to establish, set up

to fix, make ready

to direct

to arrange, order 2 Chron. 29:19, 35:20

Po'lel to set up, establish

to constitute, make

to fix

to direct Job 8:8

Po'lal to be established Ps. 37:23

to be prepared Ezek. 28:13

Hithpo'l to be established

כֹּחַ strength, power 470

כִּי that, for, when, because, since 471

כִּי אִם except, but, only 474

כִּכָּר a round; hence

1. a round district

2. a round loaf

3. a round weight, talent 503

כֹּל whole, all 481

כָּלָה to be complete, at an end, finished, accomplished, spent 477

Pi. to complete, bring to an end, finish accomplish

to cause to cease Num. 17:25, Ps. 78:33

to exhaust, use up

to consume Lev. 26:16

to destroy

Pu. to be finished, ended Ps. 72:20

to be complete Gen. 2:1

כְּלִי article, utensil, vessel 479

כְּמוֹ like, as, when 455

כֵּן so, thus 485

כָּנָף wing, extremity; skirt, corner 489

כִּסֵּא (כִּסֶּה) seat of honor, throne 490

כסה to conceal, cover, ptc. only: Act.=to conceal Prov. 12:16, 23 491

Pass.="covered" Ps. 32:1

Niph. to be covered Jer. 51:42 Ezek. 24:8

*Pual to be clothed 1 Chron. 21:16 Eccl. 6:4

כְּסִיל stupid fellow, fool 493

כֶּסֶף silver, money 494

כָּעַס to be vexed, angry 494

Pi. to be angered 1 Sam. 1:6 Deut. 32:21

כַּף hollow, flat of hand, palm, sole, pan 496

כְּפִי according to the command of, according to the mouth of, in proportion to (of, that) 805

כָּפַר *Pi.* to cover over, pacify, make propitiation, atone 497

Hithp. to be covered 1 Sam. 3:14

Nithp. to be covered Deut. 21:8

כְּרוּב cherub 500

כֶּרֶם vineyard 501

כָּרַח to cut off, cut down, cut 503

*Niph. to be chewed Num. 11:33

Pual to be cut off Ezek. 16:4
to be cut down Judg. 6:28
Hiph. to cut off, to take away 1 Sam. 20:15; to permit to perish 1 Kings 18:5

כָּשַׁל to stumble, stagger, totter 505
Niph. (= Qal)
to be tottering. feeble Isa. 40:30, 1 Sam. 2:4. Zech. 12:8
Pi. Ezek. 36:14 only (but see BDB)
*Hiph. to make feeble, weak Lam. 1:14
Hoph. ptc. only=the ones who have stumbled Jer. 18:23 Ezek. 21:20(?)

כָּתַב to write 507
Pi. to write Isa. 10:1

כָּתֵף shoulder, shoulder-blade; side; support 1 Kings 7:30, 34 509

לְ to, for, in regard to 510
לֹא, לוֹא Adv., not 518
לֵב inner man, mind, will, heart 524
לֵבָב inner man, mind, will, heart 523
לְבַד in a state of separation, alone, by itself 94
לְבַד מִן besides, apart from 94
לְבִלְתִּי so as not, in order not (to) 116
לָבַשׁ to put on, wear, clothe, be clothed 527
Pu. ptc. only=arrayed

לחם to fight, do battle Ps. 35:1, 56:2, 3 535
Niph. to engage in battle, wage war
לֶחֶם bread, food 536
לַיִל, לַיְלָה night 538
לוּן, לִין to lodge, pass the night 533
Hiph. to cause to rest, lodge 2 Sam. 17:8
Hithpo'l to dwell, abide Job 39:28 Ps. 91:1

לָכַד to capture, seize, take 539
Hithp. to grasp each other Job 41:9
to compact Job 38:30
לָכֵן therefore 485 כֵּן 3.d
לָמַד to exercise in, learn 540

Pi. to teach
לָמָה, לָמָה why? 552 מָה 4.d
לְמַעַן for the sake of, on account of, to the intent that, in order that 775
לְפִי according to (as) 805
לִפְנֵי at the face of or front of, in the presence of, before 816
לָקַח to take 542
Pu. to be taken Gen. 2:23 3:19, 23 Jer. 29:22
to be stolen Judg. 17:2
to be taken captive Jer. 48:46
to be taken away, removed 2 Kings 2:10 Isa. 53:8
Hoph. to be taken, brought
Hithp. to take hold of oneself Exod. 9:24 Ezek. 1:4
לָשׁוֹן tongue 546
מְאֹד muchness, force, abundance, exceedingly 547
מֵאַחַר from after 29
מָאַס to reject, refuse, despise 549
מֵאֵת from 85 II אֵת 4
מָגֵן shield 171
מִגְרָשׁ common, common land, open land 177
מִדְבָּר wilderness 184
מָדַד to measure 551
Pi. to extend, continue Job 7:4
to measure, measure off 2 Sam. 8:2 Ps. 60:8, 108:8
Po. to be measured Hab. 3:6
Hithpo. to measure himself 1 Kings 17:21
מִדָּה measure, measurement 551
garment Ps. 133:2
size Jer. 22:14
stature 1 Chron. 11:23, 20:6
מַדּוּעַ wherefore? on what account? 396
מְדִינָה province 193
מֶה, מָה what? how? aught? 552
מהר *Niph.* to be hurried, hasty 554
Pi. to hasten, make haste
Inf. Abs. מַהֵר quickly, speedily

מָהַר   quickly, speedily 555

מוֹעֵד   appointed time, place, meeting 417

מוּת   to die 559

Po'lel to kill, put to death

*Hoph. to die prematurely Prov 19:16

מָוֶת   death 560

מִזְבֵּחַ   altar 258

מִזְמוֹר   melody 274

מִזְרָח   place of sunrise, east 280

מַחֲנֶה   encampment, camp 334

מָחָר   tomorrow, in time to come 563

מַחֲשָׁבָה   thought, device 364

מַטֶּה   staff, rod, shaft; tribe, branch
Ezek. 19:11, 12, 14 641

מִי   who? 566

מַיִם   (pl. of מֵי) pl. only; water, waters 565

מָכַר   to sell 569

*Niph. to sell oneself

מָלֵא   to be full, fill 569

*Niph. to be accomplished, ended Exod.
7:25 Job 15:32

*Pi. to confirm 1 Kings 1:14

Pu. ptc.=set Song of Sol. 5:14

Hithp. to mass oneself Job 16:10

מָלֵא   full 570

מַלְאָךְ   messenger 521

מְלָאכָה   occupation, work; workmanship;
property; service, use; public business
521

מִלְחָמָה   battle, war 536

מלט   *Niph.* to slip away 1 Sam. 20:29 2
Sam. 4:6 572

to escape

to be delivered

Pi. to lay (eggs) Isa. 34:15

to let escape 2 Kings 23:18

to deliver

Hiph. to give birth to Isa. 66:7

to deliver Isa. 31:5

Hithp. to slip forth, escape Job 41:11

to escape Job 19:20

מָלַךְ   to be, become, king or queen, to
reign 573

Hoph. to be made king Dan. 9:1

מֶלֶךְ   king 572

מַלְכוּת   royalty, royal power, reign, kingdom
574

מִלִּפְנֵי   from before, because 817

מַמְלָכָה   kingdom, sovereignty, dominion,
reign 575

מִן   out of, from, on account of, off, on
the side of, since, above, than, so that
not 577

מִנְחָה   gift, tribute, offering 585

מְנַצֵּחַ   *Pi.* ptc. of נצח; in Psalms=perh.
musical director, choir master;
elsewhere=director 663

מִסְפָּר   number; recounting Judg. 7:15 708

מְעַט   a little, fewness, a few 589

מַעַל   above, upwards 751

מֵעַל   from upon, from over, from by
(beside) 752 עַל IV.2

מַעְלָה   upwards 751

מֵעִם   from with or beside; away from,
from 768

מַעֲשֶׂה   deed, work 795

מִפְּנֵי   from the face or presence of, from
before, because 815 פָּנֶה II.6

מָצָא   to attain to, find 592

to learn, devise Eccl. 7:27, 27, 29

to experience Ps. 116:3 Eccl. 7:14

to find out

to come upon, light upon

to hit Deut. 19:5 1 Sam. 31:3 1 Chron.
10:3

*Niph. to be gained; secured Ho. 14:9

to be left

to be present

to prove to be 1 Chron. 24:4 2 Chron.
2:16

to be sufficient Josh. 17:16

*Hiph. to cause to encounter 2 Sam.
3:8 Zech. 11:6

to present Lev. 9:12, 13, 18

מַצָּה   unleavened bread or cake(s) 595

מִצְוָה   commandment 846

מִקְדָּשׁ   sacred place, sanctuary 874

מָקוֹם   standing place, place 879

מִקְנֶה   cattle 889

מַרְאֶה   sight, appearance, vision 909

מָרוֹם   height 928

מָשַׁח   to smear, anoint 602

מִשְׁכָּן   dwelling place, 'tabernacle' 1015

מָשַׁל   to rule, have dominion, reign 605

Hiph. to cause to rule Ps. 8:7 Dan. 11:39

to exercise dominion Job 25:2

מִשְׁמֶרֶת   guard, watch; charge, function 1038

מִשְׁפָּחָה   clan 1046

מִשְׁפָּט   judgment, justice, right manner, fitting 1 Kings 5:8; fitness Isa. 28:26; 40:14 1048

מֵת   dead one, corpse 559 (מוּת)

מִתַּחַת   from under, from beneath, from 1065 תַּחַת III.2

נָא   part. of entreaty of exhortation, I pray, now 609

נְאֻם   utterance, declaration 610

נבא   *Niph.* to prophesy 612

Hithp. to prophesy

נבט   *Pi.* to look Isa. 5:30 613

Hiph. to look

to regard, show regard

נָבִיא   spokesman, speaker, prophet 611

נֶגֶב   south country, Negeb, south 616

נגד   *Hiph.* to declare, tell 616

to avow, acknowledge, confess Isa. 3:9 Ps. 38:19

Hoph. to be told, announced, reported

נֶגֶד   in front of, in sight of, opposite to 617

נָגַע   to touch, reach, strike 619

Niph. to be stricken, defeated Josh. 8:15

Pi. to strike Gen. 12:17 2 Kings 15:5 2 Chron. 26:20

Pu. to be stricken Ps. 73:5

Hiph. to reach, extend

to approach

to befall

נֶגַע   stroke, plague, mark 619

נגש   to draw near, approach 620

Niph. (as Qal)

Hoph. to be brought near 2 Sam. 3:34 Mal. 1:11

Hithp. to draw near Isa. 45:20

נֶדֶר   vow 623

נָהָר   stream, river 625

נוּחַ   to rest 628

Hiph. to leave, set down, place

to abandon Jer. 14:9 Ps. 119:121

to permit

Hoph. to be caused to rest La. 5:5 Zech. 5:11

ptc. as subst=space left, open space Ezek. 41:9, 11

נוּס   to flee, escape 630

Po'lel to cause to flee, to drive Isa. 59:19

Hithpo'l to take flight Ps. 60:6

Hiph. to put to flight Deut. 32:30

to drive hastily Exod. 9:20

to cause to disappear, hide Judg. 6:11

נָחַל   to get or take as a possession 635

Pi. to divide for a possession

נַחַל   torrent, torrent valley, wady 636

נַחֲלָה   possession, property, inheritance 635

נחם   *Niph.* to be sorry 636

to comfort oneself

Pi. to comfort, console

Pual to be relieved, consoled Isa. 54:11, 66:13

Hithp. to be sorry, have compassion Deut. 32:36 Ps. 135:14

to rue Num. 23:19

to comfort oneself, be relieved Gen. 37:35 Ps. 119:52

to ease oneself Ezek. 5:13 Gen. 27:42

נְחֹשֶׁת   copper, bronze, (dual) fetter of copper or bronze 638

נָטָה   to stretch out, spread out, extend, incline, bend 639

Niph. to be stretched out Num. 24:6 Zech. 1:16

to stretch themselves out Jer. 6:4

Hiph. to stretch out Isa. 31:3 Jer. 6:12, 15:6

to spread out 2 Sam. 16:22, 21:10 Isa. 54:2

to turn, incline

נטע   to plant 642

Niph. to be planted Isa. 40:24

נכה   *Niph.* to be smitten 2 Sam. 11:15 645

Pu. to be smitten Exod. 9:31, 32

Hiph. to smite, strike

נֶסֶךְ   drink-offering; molten images 651

נָסַע   to pull out or up, set out, journey 652

Niph. to be pulled up Isa. 38:12 Job 4:21

נַעַר   boy, lad, youth; servant 654

נַעֲרָה   girl, damsel 655

נָפַל   to fall, lie 656

Pi'lel Ezek. 28:23 But BDB="rd. "וְנָפַל

נֶפֶשׁ   soul, living being, life, self, person, desire, appetite, emotion, passion 659

נצב   *Niph.* to take one's stand, stand 662

Hiph. to station, set, set up

Hoph. to be fixed, determined Gen. 28:12 Judg. 9:6 Nah. 2:8

נצל   *Niph.* to deliver oneself, be delivered 664

Pi. to strip off, spoil 2 Chron. 20:25 Exod. 3:22, 12:36

to deliver Ezek. 14:14

Hiph. to snatch away, deliver

Hoph. to be plucked out Amos. 4:11 Zech. 3:2

Hithp. to strip oneself Exod. 33:6

נצר   to watch, guard, keep 665

נָשָׂא   to lift, carry, take 669

נָשִׂיא   a chief, prince 672

נָתַן   to give, put, set 678

Hoph. (as *Niph.*)

סָבַב   to turn about, go around, surround 685

Niph. to turn oneself

to be turned over Jer. 6:12

Pi. to change 2 Sam. 14:20

Po. to encompass, surround

סָבִיב   circuit, round about 686

סָגַר   to shut, close 688

Pi. to deliver up

Pu. to be shut up

Hiph. to deliver up

to shut up

סוּס   horse 692

סוֹפֵר   secretary, muster officer, scribe 708

סוּר   to turn aside 693

Po'lel to turn aside Lam. 3:11

**Hiph.* to put aside

סֶלָה   (a benediction[?]) see BDB 699

סֶלַע   crag, cliff 700

סֹלֶת   fine flour 701

סָפַר   to count 707

Pi. to recount, rehearse, declare

סֵפֶר   document, writing, book 706

סתר   *Niph.* to hide oneself 711

to be hid, concealed

Pi. to carefully hide Isa. 16:3

Pu. to be carefully concealed Prov. 27:5

Hithp. to hide oneself

Hiph. to conceal, hide

עָבַד   to work, serve 712

Niph. to be tilled Deut. 21:4 Ezek. 36:9, 34

ptc.=cultivated Eccl. 5:8 (dub.)

Pu. to be worked Deut. 21:3 Isa. 14:3

עֶבֶד   servant, slave, subject 713

עֲבֹדָה   labor, service 715

עָבַר   to pass over, through, by, on 716

Niph. to be forded Ezek. 47:5

Pi. to impregnate Job 21:10

to cause to pass across 1 Kings 6:21

עֵבֶר   region across or beyond, side 719

עַד   as far as, even to, up to, until, while 723

עֵד   witness 729

עֵדָה   congregation 417

עֵדוּת   testimony 730

עוֹד   still, yet, again, besides 728

עוֹלָם   forever, always, everlasting; ancient, old; age 761

עָוֹן   iniquity, guilt; punishment of iniquity 730

עוֹף   coll. birds, fowl; flying insects 733

עוּר   to rouse oneself, awake 734
Po'l to rouse, incite
Pilp. to rouse, (raise?) Isa. 15:5
Hithpo'l to be excited Job 31:29, 17:8
to rouse oneself Isa. 64:6
Hiph. to rouse
to act aroused Ps. 35:23, 73:20

עוֹר   skin, hide 736

עֵז   she-goat; pl. subst.=goat's hair 777

עֹז   strength, might 738

עָזַב   to leave, forsake, loose 736
Pu. to be deserted Isa. 32:14 Jer. 49:25

עָזַר   to help 740
Hiph. (dub.) as Qal 2 Sam. 18:3 2
Chron. 28:23

עַיִן   eye; surface Exod. 10:5, 15 Num.
22:5, 11
appearance Lev. 13:5, 37, 55 Num.
11:7 1 Sam. 16:7(?), gleam, sparkle
Ezek. 1 (5t), 8:2, 10:9 Dan. 10:6 Prov.
23:31 744

עִיר   city, town; fortress 746

עַל   poetic: עֲלֵי ; on, on the ground of,
according to, on account of, on behalf
of, concerning, besides, in addition
to, together with, beyond, above,
over, by, onto, toward, to, against
752–759

עַל־כֵּן   therefore 485 כֵּן 3.f

עַל־פְּנֵי   in front of, in the presence of, in
preference to, on the face of, over the
face of; w. verbs: over, toward 815
II.7

עָלָה   to go up, ascend, climb 748
Niph. to take oneself away 2 Sam.
2:27
to be exalted Ps. 47:10, 97:9
Hiph. to take away Ps. 102:25 Job
36:20
Hoph. to be carried away Nah. 2:8
to be taken up 2 Chron. 20:34
to be offered Judg. 6:23
Hithp. to lift oneself Jer. 51:3

עֹלָה   whole burnt offering 750

עֶלְיוֹן   upper, high, highest 751

עַם, עָם   people, nation 766

עִם   with 767

עָמַד   to take one's stand, stand; to arise,
appear
to be appointed Ezek. 10:14
to grow flat, insipid Jer. 48:11 763
Hiph. to station, set
to have a fixed look ע׳ אֶת־פָּנָיו 2 Kings
8:11
to restore Ezra 9.9
to raise Dan. 11:11, 13

עַמּוּד   pillar, column 765

עָמָל   trouble, mischief, toil 765

עֵמֶק   valley, lowland 770

עָנָה   to answer, respond 772
Niph. to make answer Ezra 14:4, 7
Hiph. ptc. Eccl. 5:19 (dub.) See BDB

ענה   to be put down or become low Isa.
25:5 776
to be depressed, down cast Isa. 31:4
to be afflicted Ps. 116:10, 119:67 Zech.
10:2
Niph. to humble oneself Exod. 10:3
to be afflicted Isa. 53:7, 58:10 Ps.
119:107
Pi. to humble, afflict
Pu. to be afflicted Ps. 119:71, 132:1
Isa. 53:4
to be humbled Lev. 23:29
Hiph. to afflict 1 Kings 8:35 2 Chon.
6:26
Hithp. to humble oneself Gen. 16:9
Ezek. 8:21 Dan. 10:12
to be afflicted 1 Kings 2:26 Ps. 107:17

עָנִי   poor, afflicted, humble 776

עָנָן   cloudmass, cloud 777

עָפָר   dry earth, dust; ore Job 28:2 779

עֵץ   tree, trees, wood 781

עֵצָה   counsel, advice 420

עֶצֶם   bone, substance; self (same) 782

עֶרֶב   evening; night Job 7:4 787

עֲרָבָה   desert plain, steppe 787

עֶרְוָה nakedness, pudenda 788

עָרַךְ to arrange, set in order

to compare Isa. 40:18 Ps. 40:6

to be comparable Ps. 89:7 Job 28:17, 19 789

Hiph. to value, tax

עָשָׂה to do, work

to make

to acquire

to use 1 Sam. 8:16 Exod. 38:24

to spend, pass. Eccl. 6:12 793

Pu. to be made Ps. 139:15

עֵת time; experiences, fortunes Isa. 33:6 Ps. 31:16 1 Chron. 29:30 773

עַתָּה now 773

פֵּאָה corner, side 802

פָּדָה to ransom 804

פֶּה mouth; end 2 Kings 10:21, 21:16 Ezra. 9:11

portion Deut. 21:17 2 Kings 2:9 Zech. 13:8 804

פוּץ to be dispersed, scattered 806

Niph. (as Qal)

פלל *Pi.* to mediate, arbitrate, interpose 813

Hithp. to pray, intercede

פֶּן lest 814

פָּנָה to turn, turn and look, look 815

Pi. to turn away, put out of the way

Hiph. to turn Judg. 15:4 1 Sam. 10:9 Jer. 48:39

to make a turn

Hoph. to be turned Jer. 49:8 Ezek. 9:2

פָּנֶה face 815

פָּעַל to do, make 821

פַּעַם once, time, step, now; anvil 821

פָּקַד to attend to, visit, muster, appoint 823

Niph. to be missed, lacking

Pi. to muster Isa. 13:4

Pu. to be passed in review Exod. 38:21

to be caused to miss Isa. 38:10

Hithp. to be mustered Judg. 20:15, 17, 21:9

Hothp. (as Hithp.)

Hiph. to set, make overseer

to commit, entrust

to deposit

Hoph. to be visited Jer. 6:6

to be deposited Lev. 5:23

to be made overseer

פַּר young bull, steer 830

פְּרִי fruit 826

פַּרְעֹה Pharaoh 829

פָּרַשׂ to spread out, spread 831

Niph. to be scattered Ezek. 17:21, 34:12

פָּרָשׁ horseman; horse 832

פֶּשַׁע transgression; guilt of transgression; punishment for transgression; Dan. 8:12, 13, 9:24; offering for transgression Mic. 6:7 833

פתח to open 834

פֶּתַח doorway, opening, entrance 835

צֹאן (coll.) small cattle, sheep and goats, flock, flocks 838

צָבָא army, host; war, warfare, service 838

צַדִּיק just, righteous 843

צֶדֶק rightness, righteousness 841

צְדָקָה righteousness 842

צוה *Pi.* to lay charge (upon), give charge (to), charge, command, order 845

צוּר rock, cliff 849

צֵל shadow, shade 853

צלח to rush

to be successful, prosper 852

Hiph. to show experience, prosperity

צָעַק to cry, cry out 858

Niph. to be summoned

Hiph. to call together 1 Sam. 10:17

Pi. to cry aloud 2 Kings 2:12

צָפוֹן north 860

צַר adversary, foe 865

צָרָה straits, distress 865

צרר to bind, tie up

to be scant, cramped 864

Pu. to be tied up Josh. 9:4

Hiph. to make narrow, press hard, cause distress

קָבַץ to gather, collect, assemble 867

Niph. (as Qal)

Hithp. to gather together, be gathered together

קָבַר to bury 868

קֶבֶר grave, tomb 868

קָדוֹשׁ sacred, holy 872

קָדִים East, east wind 870

קֶדֶם front, east; ancient, of old; beginning Prov. 8:22, 23 869

קָדַשׁ to be set apart, consecrated 872

Niph. to show oneself sacred, majestic

to be honored

to be consecrated Exod. 29:43

Pi. to consecrate, dedicate;

to keep sacred

to honor as sacred, hallow

Hiph. (as Pi.)

Hithp. to be observed as holy Isa. 30:29

to consecrate oneself

קֹדֶשׁ apartness, sacredness 871

קָהָל assembly, company, congregation 874

קוֹל sound, voice 876

קוּם to arise, stand up, stand

to be fulfilled 877

Pi. to fulfil Ezek. 13:6 Ps. 119:106

to confirm, ratify Ruth 4:7

to establish Ps. 119:28

to impose Esth. 9 (7 times)

Po'l. to raise up

Hithpo'l to rise up

*Hiph. to raise, set up

קָטֹן small, insignificant 882

קטר *Pi.* to make sacrifices smoke 882

Pu. to be fumigated Song of Sol. 3:6

Hiph. to make (sacrifices) smoke

Hoph. to be made to smoke Lev. 6:15 Mal. 1:11

קְטֹרֶת incense, sweet smoke of sacrifice 1 Sam. 2:28 (?) Isa. 1:13 Ps. 66: 15, 141:2 882

קִיר wall 885

קָלַל to be slight, swift, trifling 886

Niph. to show oneself swift Isa. 30:16

to be, appear trifling

to be lightly esteemed 2 Sam. 6:22

Pi. to curse

Hiph. to make light, lighten

to treat with contempt

Pilp. to shake Ezek. 21:26

to whet Eccl. 10:10

Hithpalp. to shake oneself Jer. 4:24

קָנָה to get, acquire; buy 888

קָנֶה stalk, reed; shoulder joint Job 31:22 889

קֵץ end 893

קָצֶה end; border, outskirts 892

קָרָא to call, proclaim, read 894

*Niph. to call oneself Isa. 48:2

קרא to encounter, befall, often

with ל (לִקְרַאת) = toward, against

Niph. to meet unexpectedly Exod. 5:3 Deut. 22:6 2 Sam. 18:9, 20:1

Hiph. to cause to befall Jer. 32:23

קָרַב to approach, come near 897

Niph. to be brought Exod. 22:7 Josh. 7:14

Pi. to cause to approach, bring near

קֶרֶב inward part, midst 899

קָרְבָּן offering, oblation 898

קָרוֹב near 898

קֶרֶן horn; hill Isa. 5:1; rays Hab. 3:4 901

קָרַע to tear 902

קֶרֶשׁ board, coll. boards Ezek. 27:6 903

קֶשֶׁת bow 905

רָאָה to see 906

to select 2 Kings 10:3 1 Sam. 16:1

to provide, furnish Deut. 33:21 Gen. 22:8, 14

to consider, reflect Eccl. 7:14

*Niph. to appear

Pu. to be seen, detected Job 33:21

*Hiph. to cause to experience Hab. 1:3 Ps. 60:5 71:20 85:8

Hithp.=reciprocal

ראש   head, top; beginning, first; chief; sum 910

רִאשׁוֹן   former, first, chief; before, formerly 911

רֵאשִׁית   beginning, first, chief 912

רַב   much, many, great, chief 912

רֹב   multitiude, abundance 913

רבה   to be, become, much, many, great 915

Pi. to increase, enlarge Judg. 9:29 Ps. 44:13

to bring up, rear Lam. 2:22 Ezek. 19:2

Hiph. הַרְבֵּה greatly, exceedingly

רֶגֶל   foot 919

רָדַף   to pursue, chase, persecute 922

Hiph. to chase Judg. 20:43

רוּחַ   breath, wind, spirit; quarter, side Ezek. 42:16, 17, 18, 19, 20 1 Chron. 9:24 Jer. 52:23 924

רוּם   to be high, exalted, rise 926

Po'lel to cause to rise

to erect, raise, exalt

Hoph. to be taken off Lev. 4:10

be abolished Dan. 8:11

Hithpo'l to exalt oneself Isa. 33:10 Dan. 11:36

רוּץ   to run 930

Po'lel to run swiftly, dart Nah. 2:5

רֹחַב   breadth, width 931

רָחוֹק   distant, far; distance 935

רָחַץ   to wash 934

Pu. to be washed Prov. 30:12 Ezek. 16:4

Hithp. to wash oneself Job 9:30

רָחַק   to be or become far, distant 934

Pi. to send far away

רִיב   to strive, contend 936

Hiph. ptc.=displaying contention 1 Sam. 2:10 Hos. 4:4

רִיב   strife, dispute 936

רֵיחַ   scent, odor 926

רָכַב   to ride, mount and ride 938

רֶכֶב   chariots; upper millstone Deut. 24:6 Judg. 9:53 2 Sam. 11:21 riders, troop 2

Kings 7:14 Isa. 21:7, 9, 22:6 939

רנן   to give ringing cry 943

Pu. "no ringing cry shall be given" Isa. 16:10

רַע   bad, evil; distress, misery, injury, calamity 948

רֵעַ   friend, companion, fellow 945

רָעָב   famine, hunger 944

רָעָה   to pasture, tend, graze 944

רָעָה   evil, misery, distress, injury 949

רֹעֶה   shepherd, herdsman 945 (רָעָה)

רעע   to be evil, bad 949

Niph. to suffer hurt Prov. 11:15, 13:20

Hiph. to do an injury, hurt to do evil, wickedly

רָפָא   to heal 950

Hithp. Inf. cstr. to get healed 2 Kings 8:29, 9:15 2 Chron. 22:6

רצה   to be pleased with, to accept 953

to be pleased Ps. 40:14 1 Chron. 28:4

to make acceptable

Niph. to be accepted

Pi. to seek favor Job 20:10

Hiph. to pay off Lev. 25:34

Hithp. to make oneself acceptable 1 Sam. 29:4

רָצוֹן   goodwill, favor, acceptance, will 953

רַק   only, altogether, surely 956

רָשָׁע   wicked, criminal; guilty 957

שָׂבַע   to be sated, satisfied, surfeited 959

Niph. ptc. sated Job 31:31

Pi. to satisfy Ezek. 7:19 Ps. 90:14

שָׂדֶה   field, land 961 שָׂדֶה

שִׂים, שׂוּם   to put, place, set 962

Hiph. (see BDB) Ezek. 14:8, 21:21 Job 4:20

Hoph. to be set Gen. 24:33

שָׂכַל   to be prudent 1 Sam. 18:30 968

Hiph. to look at Gen. 3:6

to consider, ponder

to have insight

to cause to consider

to give insight

to act prudently
to prosper
to cause to prosper Deut. 29:8 1 Kings 2:3

שְׂמֹאל the left 969
שָׂמַח to rejoice, be glad 970
Pi. to cause to rejoice
Hiph. (= *Pi.*) Ps. 89:43
שִׂמְחָה joy, gladness, mirth 970
שָׂנֵא to hate 971
Niph. to be hated Prov. 14:17, 20
Pi. ptc. only, enemy
שָׂעִיר he-goat, buck 972
שָׂפָה lip, speech. edge 973
שַׂר chief, ruler, official, captain, prince 978
שָׂרַף to burn 976
Pi. ptc. one burning Amos 6:10
Pu. to be burnt up Lev. 10:16
שֶׁ, שַׁ, שָׁ who, which, that 979
שְׁאוֹל sheol, hades 982
שָׁאַל to ask, inquire 981
Niph. to ask for oneself 1 Sam. 20:6, 28 Neh. 13:6
Pi. to inquire carefully 2 Sam. 20:18 to beg Ps. 109:10
Hiph. to grant, make over to 1 Sam. 1:28, 2:20(?) Exod. 12:36
שָׁאַר to remain, be left over 1 Sam. 16:11 983
Niph. (as Qal)
שְׁאֵרִית rest, residue, remnant, remainder 984
שֵׁבֶט rod, staff, club, sceptre; tribe 986
שבע *Qal* ptc. pass. those sworn Ezek. 21:28 989
Niph. to swear
Hiph. to cause to swear
to adjure
שָׁבַר to break, break in pieces 990
Hiph. to cause to break out Isa. 66:9
Hoph. to be broken, shattered Jer. 8:21
שָׁבַת to cease, desist, rest 991

Niph. to cease
**Hiph.* to cause to fail Lev. 2:13 Jer. 48:35 Ruth 4:14
שַׁבָּת Sabbath 992
שדד to deal violently with, despoil, devastate, ruin 994
Niph. to be utterly ruined Mic. 2:4
Pi. to assault Prov. 24:15, 19:26
Pu. to be devastated
Po'el to violently destroy Hos. 10:2
Hoph. to be devastated Hos. 10:14 Isa. 33:1
שָׁוְא emptiness, vanity 996
שׁוּב to turn back, return 996
Po'l. to bring back
to restore Ps. 23:3 Isa. 58:12
to lead away Ezek. 38:4, 39:2 Isa. 47:10
to apostatize Jer. 8:5
Pu. to be restored Ezek. 38:8
שׁוֹפָר horn 1051
שׁוֹר a head of cattle (without reference to sex); bullock, ox 1004
שׁחה to bow down Isa. 51:23 1005
Hiph. to depress Prov. 12:25
Hithpa'lel to bow down, prostrate oneself
שָׁחַט to slaughter, beat 1006
Niph. to be slaughtered Num. 11:22 Lev. 6:18
שחת *Niph.* to be marred, spoiled Jer. 13:7, 18:4 1007
to be injured Exod. 8:20
to be corrupted, corrupt Gen. 6:11, 12 Ezek. 20:44
Pi. to spoil, ruin
to pervert, corrupt
Hiph. (= *Pi.*)
Hoph. ptc. spoiled, ruined Prov. 25:26 Mal. 1:14
שִׁיר to sing 1010
Po'l. to sing
Hoph. to be sung Isa. 26:1
שִׁיר song 1010

702

שִׁית to put, set
to make 1011
Hoph. to be imposed Exod. 21:30
שָׁכַב to lie down 1011
שָׁכַח to forget 1013
Pi. to cause to forget Lam. 2:6
Hiph. (=*Pi.*) Jer. 23:27
Hithp. to be forgotten Eccl. 8:10
שׁכם *Hiph.* to start early, rise early 1014
שָׁכֵן to settle down, abide, dwell 1014
Pi. to make settle down, establish
to make to dwell Num. 14:30 Jer. 7:3, 7
Hiph. to lay Ps. 7:6
to place, set, establish Gen. 3:24 Josh. 18:1
to cause to settle Ezek. 32:4
to cause to dwell Ps. 78:55
שָׁלוֹם peace, completeness, soundness, welfare 1022
שָׁלַח to send, stretch out
to let loose Ps. 50:19 1018
Pi. to send away
to let go, set free
to shoot forth
to let down Jer. 38:6, 11
to shoot 1 Sam. 20:20
Hiph. to send
שֻׁלְחָן table 1020
שׁלך *Hiph.* to throw, fling, cast 1020
שָׁלָל prey, spoil, plunder, booty 1021
שׁלם to be complete, sound Job 9:4 1022
Pi. to complete, finish 1 Kings 9:25
to make whole
to make safe Job 8:6
to make good
to reward, recompense
Pu. to be performed Ps. 65:2
to be repaid, requited Jer. 18:20 Prov. 11:31, 13:13
Hiph. to make and end of Isa. 38:12, 13
to complete, perform Job 23:14 Isa. 44:26, 28
שֶׁלֶם peace offering; sacrifice for alliance

or friend 1023
שָׁם there, thither 1027
שֵׁם name 1027
שׁמד *Niph.* to be exterminated, destroyed 1029
Hiph. to annihilate, exterminate to destroy
שָׁמַיִם heavens, sky 1029
שׁמם to be desolated, appalled 1030
Niph. (as Qal)
Po'. to be appalled Ezra 9:3, 4
to be appalling, causing horror
Hithpo. to be appalled
to cause oneself desolation, ruin Eccl. 7:16
שְׁמָמָה devastation, waste 1031
שֶׁמֶן fat, oil 1032
שָׁמַע to hear 1033
*Niph. to grant hearing 2 Chron. 30:27
Pi. to cause to hear 1 Sam. 15:4, 23:8
שָׁמַר to keep, watch, preserve 1036
Niph. to be on one's guard
to keep oneself, refrain 1 Sam. 21:5
to be kept, guarded Hos. 12:14 Ps. 37:28
Pi. to pay regard Jonah 2:9
Hithp. to keep oneself from Ps. 18:24 2 Sam. 22:24 Mic. 6:16
שֹׁמֵר watchman 1036 (שָׁמַר)
שֶׁמֶשׁ sun; pinnacle, battlement 1039
שֵׁן tooth, ivory 1042
שָׁנָה year 1040
שַׁעַר gate 1044
שִׁפְחָה maid, maid-servant 1046
שָׁפַט to judge, govern 1047
Niph. to enter into controversy, plead
to be judged Ps. 9:20, 37:33, 109:7
Po'el ptc. opponent-at-law Job 9:15 Zeph. 3:15 Ps. 109:31
שֹׁפֵט judge 1047 (שָׁפַט)
שָׁפַךְ to pour out, pour 1049
Pu. to be poured out, shed Zeph. 1:17 Num. 35:33
to be caused to slip Ps. 73:2

Hithp. to pour oneself out Job 30:16
Lam. 4:1, 2:12

שקה   *Hiph.* to cause to drink, give to
drink 1052
Pu. to be watered Job 21:24

שֶׁקֶל   shekel 1053

שֶׁקֶר   deception, falsehood 1055

שרת   *Pi.* to minister, serve 1058

שָׁתָה   to drink 1059
Niph. to be drunk Lev. 11:34

תְּהִלָּה   praise, song of praise; renown, fame
239

תָּוֶךְ   midst 1063

תּוֹעֵבָה   abomination 1072

תּוֹרָה   direction, instruction, law; custom,

manner 2 Sam. 7:19 435

תַּחַת   underneath, below, instead of 1065

תָּמִיד   continually, continuity 556

תָּמִים   complete, whole, sound, healthful,
wholesome, innocent 1071

תמם   to be complete, finished 1070

תִּפְאָרָה   beauty, glory 802

תְּפִלָּה   prayer 813

תָּפַשׂ   to lay hold of, seize, grasp 1074
Pi. to grasp Prov. 30:28

תָּקַע   to thrust, clap, give a blow 1075
Niph. to be blown Amos. 3:6 Isa. 27:13
to strike oneself into (pledge oneself)
Job 17:3

תְּרוּמָה   contribution, offering 929